CRITICAL SURVEY OF

Long Fiction

Fourth Edition

CRITICAL SURVEY OF

Long Fiction

Fourth Edition

Volume 6

Mary McCarthy—Ann Patchett

Editor

Carl Rollyson

Baruch College, City University of New York

SALEM PRESS

Pasadena, California   Hackensack, New Jersey

Editor in Chief: Dawn P. Dawson

Editorial Director: Christina J. Moose
Development Editor: Tracy Irons-Georges
Project Editor: Judy Selhorst
Manuscript Editor: Desiree Dreeuws
Acquisitions Editor: Mark Rehn
Editorial Assistant: Brett S. Weisberg
Research Supervisor: Jeffry Jensen
Research Assistant: Keli Trousdale
Production Editor: Joyce I. Buchea
Design and Graphics: James Hutson
Layout: William Zimmerman
Photo Editor: Cynthia Breslin Beres

Cover photo: Alberto Moravia (©Ulf Andersen/Getty Images)

Some of the essays in this work, which have been updated, originally appeared in the following Salem Press publications: *Critical Survey of Long Fiction, English Language Series* (1983), *Critical Survey of Long Fiction, Foreign Language Series* (1984), *Critical Survey of Long Fiction, Supplement* (1987), *Critical Survey of Long Fiction, English Language Series, Revised Edition* (1991; preceding volumes edited by Frank N. Magill), *Critical Survey of Long Fiction, Second Revised Edition* (2000; edited by Carl Rollyson).

∞ The paper used in these volumes conforms to the American National Standard for Permanence of Paper for Printed Library Materials, Z39.48-1992 (R1997).

Library of Congress Cataloging-in-Publication Data

Critical survey of long fiction / editor, Carl Rollyson. — 4th ed.
p. cm.
Includes bibliographical references and index.
ISBN 978-1-58765-535-7 (set : alk. paper) — ISBN 978-1-58765-536-4 (vol. 1 : alk. paper) — ISBN 978-1-58765-537-1 (vol. 2 : alk. paper) — ISBN 978-1-58765-538-8 (vol. 3 : alk. paper) — ISBN 978-1-58765-539-5 (vol. 4 : alk. paper) — ISBN 978-1-58765-540-1 (vol. 5 : alk. paper) — ISBN 978-1-58765-541-8 (vol. 6 : alk. paper) — ISBN 978-1-58765-542-5 (vol. 7 : alk. paper) — ISBN 978-1-58765-543-2 (vol. 8 : alk. paper) — ISBN 978-1-58765-544-9 (vol. 9 : alk. paper) — ISBN 978-1-58765-545-6 (vol. 10 : alk. paper)
1. Fiction—History and criticism. 2. Fiction—Bio-bibliography—Dictionaries. 3. Authors—Biography—Dictionaries. I. Rollyson, Carl E. (Carl Edmund)
PN3451.C75 2010
809.3—dc22

2009044410

First Printing

PRINTED IN CANADA

CONTENTS

COMPLETE LIST OF CONTENTS

Volume 1

Volume 2

Volume 3

Volume 4

Volume 5

Volume 6

Volume 7

Volume 8

Volume 9

Volume 10

PRONUNCIATION KEY

Foreign and unusual or ambiguous English-language names of profiled authors may be unfamiliar to some users of the *Critical Survey of Long Fiction*. To help readers pronounce such names correctly, phonetic spellings using the character symbols listed below appear in parentheses immediately after the first mention of the author's name in the narrative text. Stressed syllables are indicated in capital letters, and syllables are separated by hyphens.

VOWEL SOUNDS

Symbol	*Spelled (Pronounced)*
a	answer (AN-suhr), laugh (laf), sample (SAM-puhl), that (that)
ah	father (FAH-thur), hospital (HAHS-pih-tuhl)
aw	awful (AW-fuhl), caught (kawt)
ay	blaze (blayz), fade (fayd), waiter (WAYT-ur), weigh (way)
eh	bed (behd), head (hehd), said (sehd)
ee	believe (bee-LEEV), cedar (SEE-dur), leader (LEED-ur), liter (LEE-tur)
ew	boot (bewt), lose (lewz)
i	buy (bi), height (hit), lie (li), surprise (sur-PRIZ)
ih	bitter (BIH-tur), pill (pihl)
o	cotton (KO-tuhn), hot (hot)
oh	below (bee-LOH), coat (koht), note (noht), wholesome (HOHL-suhm)
oo	good (good), look (look)
ow	couch (kowch), how (how)
oy	boy (boy), coin (koyn)
uh	about (uh-BOWT), butter (BUH-tuhr), enough (ee-NUHF), other (UH-thur)

CONSONANT SOUNDS

Symbol	*Spelled (Pronounced)*
ch	beach (beech), chimp (chihmp)
g	beg (behg), disguise (dihs-GIZ), get (geht)
j	digit (DIH-juht), edge (ehj), jet (jeht)
k	cat (kat), kitten (KIH-tuhn), hex (hehks)
s	cellar (SEHL-ur), save (sayv), scent (sehnt)
sh	champagne (sham-PAYN), issue (IH-shew), shop (shop)
ur	birth (burth), disturb (dihs-TURB), earth (urth), letter (LEH-tur)
y	useful (YEWS-fuhl), young (yuhng)
z	business (BIHZ-nehs), zest (zehst)
zh	vision (VIH-zhuhn)

CRITICAL SURVEY OF

Long Fiction

Fourth Edition

MARY McCARTHY

Born: Seattle, Washington; June 21, 1912
Died: New York, New York; October 25, 1989
Also known as: Mary Therese McCarthy

Principal long fiction

The Oasis, 1949
The Groves of Academe, 1952
A Charmed Life, 1955
The Group, 1963
Birds of America, 1971
Cannibals and Missionaries, 1979

Other literary forms

First known as a book reviewer, drama critic, and essayist, Mary McCarthy also wrote short stories, collected in *The Company She Keeps* (1942), *Cast a Cold Eye* (1950), and *The Hounds of Summer, and Other Stories* (1981). Her drama criticism is collected in *Sights and Spectacles, 1937-1956* (1956) and in *Mary McCarthy's Theatre Chronicles, 1937-1962* (1963). *Venice Observed* (1956) and *The Stones of Florence* (1959) are books of travel and art history. *The Writing on the Wall, and Other Literary Essays* (1970) and *Ideas and the Novel* (1980) are literary essays and lectures. *On the Contrary: Articles of Belief* (1961) contains autobiographical essays and literary criticism. *Memories of a Catholic Girlhood* (1957) and *How I Grew* (1987) are memoirs of her childhood and youth. Her books *Vietnam* (1967) and *Hanoi* (1968) oppose U.S. involvement in the Vietnam War, an interest that she continued in *Medina* (1972) and in *The Seventeenth Degree* (1974). *The Mask of State* (1974) presents impressions of the Watergate affair hearings.

Achievements

From the appearance of her first book reviews, when she was just out of college, to the time of her death, Mary McCarthy was one of the leading figures of the American literary scene. In her novels as much as in her essays and reviews, she was above all a critic, a sharp observer of contemporary society. For students of twentieth century American culture, her work is indispensable.

Biography

Mary Therese McCarthy was born into an affluent family of mixed Irish and Jewish heritage on June 21, 1912, in Seattle, Washington, and had a segmented childhood. After six years of what she called a "fairy-tale" existence of happiness, both parents died of influenza in 1918 during a move to Minneapolis. McCarthy and her three younger brothers, placed with their grand-aunt and uncle, then entered a bleak phase of intense, strict Catholicism, which McCarthy described in *Memories of a Catholic Girlhood.*

In 1923, McCarthy's grandparents moved her to a convent school in Seattle for the seventh and eighth grades; she spent her ninth grade year in a public school and then her remaining high school years at the Annie Wright Seminary in Tacoma, Washington, from which she graduated in 1929 at the top of her class. In the same year of her graduation as a Phi Beta Kappa from Vassar College in 1933, she married Harold Johnsrud, a marriage that lasted three years. She reviewed novels and biographies for *The New Republic* and *The Nation*, worked for the left-wing publishing company Covici Friede, and, in 1937, participated in Trotskyite politics. In 1937, she also became drama editor for *Partisan Review.*

The next year, McCarthy married Edmund Wilson and gave birth to a son, Reuel Wilson; also, at Wilson's urging, McCarthy wrote her first work of fiction, a short story. Thereafter, the stories she wrote for *Southern Review*, *Partisan Review*, and *Harper's Bazaar* were collected in 1942 in *The Company She Keeps*. She separated from Wilson in 1945, the same year that she was teaching literature at Bard College. In 1946, she married Bowden Broadwater, and in 1948, she taught one semester at Sarah Lawrence College. In 1949, she was a Guggenheim Fellow (a fellowship she received again in 1959) and also received the *Horizon* literary prize from the publishers of her novel *The Oasis*. In 1961, she was divorced from Broadwater, married James Raymond West—a U.S. State Department official assigned to Paris—and lived with him in France.

Two events dominated the 1960's for McCarthy. The first was the enormous popular success of her novel *The*

Group, which became a best seller. The second was the Vietnam War; she was an outspoken critic of U.S. policy in Vietnam. In the 1970's, she published two novels with social and political themes: *Birds of America* in 1971 and *Cannibals and Missionaries* in 1979; the latter, she said, would be her last novel.

In 1980, an offhand remark on *The Dick Cavett Show* embroiled McCarthy in a prolonged legal battle that became a cause célèbre in the literary community. McCarthy said of dramatist Lillian Hellman that "every word she writes is a lie, including [the words] 'and' and 'the.'" Hellman responded by suing McCarthy. The resulting legal maneuvering was costly for McCarthy (in contrast, the wealthy Hellman did not count the cost), ending only in 1984, when, after Hellman's death, the suit was dropped before going to trial. Meanwhile, legal issues aside, the controversy brought several of Hellman's autobiographical works under close scrutiny, and the consensus was that McCarthy's judgment, clearly stated in hyperbolic terms, was vindicated.

In 1987, McCarthy published *How I Grew*, the first installment in what was projected to be a multivolume intellectual autobiography. In general, critics found it inferior to *Memoirs of a Catholic Girlhood*, which had covered some of the same territory from a different perspective. McCarthy died in New York City on October 25, 1989.

Analysis

Mary McCarthy's novels often feature herself, with an assumed name, as protagonist; she also exploited her husbands and other people close to her for fictional purposes. Her characters generally have a superior education or intellect, or both, so that citations and quotations from learned sources—mainly classical or artistic—spring into their conversations. This heightened discourse promotes compact paragraphs of dialogue, in which several persons speak to the same topic, in contrast with the usual fictional technique of a separate paragraph for each speaker. Yet, in the close conceptual unity of McCarthy's novels, lengthy paragraphs of extensive character analyses frequently fill several pages without interruption. As a result, the technique of several speakers in one paragraph seems to support the general schema. It supports, also, the paradigm of the group.

Structurally, the three novels preceding *The Group* develop around separate chapters, each presenting the viewpoints and the consciousness of the different characters; their point of unity is the common awareness of the social group. A protagonist, often a reflection of the author, generally emerges from among these peripheral persons, but the effect of each chapter remains that of the portrait or sketch.

Several factors of McCarthy's work can be inferred from this structure. As an orphan and a Catholic among Protestants, she no doubt had an early sensitivity to the significance of the group and the outsider. Furthermore, the intensely autobiographical nature of her work blurs the lines of genre, so that her essays read like short stories and her short stories like essays. Genre distinction, then, becomes a problem in any analysis of her work. An example is *The Company She Keeps*, short stories that are pulled into book form and revolve around a central theme—the quest—and parallel the structure of her novels. Also, McCarthy did not term *The Oasis* a "novel" but called it a *conte philosophique*, and several chapters of her novels were published individually as short stories before being incorporated in the novels. The effect of this technique raises the question of whether she pushed the boundaries of the traditional novel outward or merely retreated to its earliest phases of development. She lamented the loss of a "sense of character" in modern novels, saying it began to fade with D. H. Lawrence. She admired Leo Tolstoy, Gustave Flaubert, George Eliot, Charles Dickens, and "all the Elizabethans."

The dominant quality of McCarthy's work is satire, and much of it is achieved by exaggeration and generalization. The dominant organization is the pairing of a separate character with each chapter, infused with an occasional chorus of viewpoints. McCarthy compared the technique to ventriloquism: The author throws her voice into various characters who speak for her. The long paragraphs of explication or character analysis tend to minimize plot; the concentration is on the psychological effects of what are frequently trivial incidents—as in *The Oasis*, when a couple illegally picking berries on the group's farm destroys the group.

The themes of McCarthy's novels generally concern the social failures of a group—of utopian communities in *The Oasis*, of progressive education in *The Groves of*

Mary McCarthy. (© Jerry Bauer)

Academe, or of cultural progress in *The Group*. The interest in group attitudes can be best observed in the political content of McCarthy's novels, many of which feature a person who had some affiliation with the Communist Party and defected or failed to become a member. Her work also shows a persistent aversion to the efforts of Senator Joseph McCarthy to eradicate communists in the United States.

The Oasis

McCarthy's first novel, *The Oasis*, was published serially in *Horizon* magazine as *A Source of Embarrassment*. The work puts into practice the theories of Arthur Koestler about "oases," small libertarian groups that would try, as McCarthy said, "to change the world on a small scale." Set at Pawlet, Vermont, at an abandoned hotel on an isolated mountain in 1946 or 1947, the novel brings together a group of about fifty people of varying backgrounds and motives. The characters seek to revive the concept of utopian communities and welcome defectors from Europe. Their efforts, however, remain confined to the daily problems of food gathering and management and fall short of the larger goals.

First, the group fails to agree on its purpose. The purists aspire to a millennium but the realists seek only a vacation or a retreat from atomic warfare. They disagree, also, about who should be permitted to join the group, and some oppose the admission of businessman Joe Lockman. Next, they find that intellect, good intentions, and the simple life without electricity do not bring about moral reform: Personal relationships and property ownership intrude. Lockman leaves oil in the kitchen stove that singes the eyebrows of Katy Norell, and then, as a prank, he frightens Will Taub by pointing a gun at him. Later, when intruders pick their wild strawberries (the stolen fruit in their Eden), Katy is highly offended at the theft of her property, and Joe is indignant about the other colonists' attempts to drive away the berry pickers until he realizes that it was his property, the gun, they used in the assault.

The first to defect from the community is Taub, in whom many readers recognized Philip Rahv, and Katy, who resembles McCarthy, dreams of the dissolution of the community at the book's end. With Lockman cast in the role of the outsider, with little plot and with incident minimized, and with much explication of philosophical theory and discussion of ideals and goals, the book sets the style for McCarthy's other novels.

The Groves of Academe

Suspense is greatly improved in McCarthy's next novel, *The Groves of Academe*, set in a small Pennsylvania college called Jocelyn and resembling Bard College. Directing its satire at progressive education, this novel pits the progressive against the classical, satirizes the small college in general, and exposes the evils of McCarthyism, focusing on Joseph McCarthy's House Committee on Un-American Activities. The group here is the English Department faculty, from which Professor Henry Mulcahy finds himself dismissed. He rallies the faculty to his support, although he is a poor academician and deserves dismissal, and gains it through an appeal for sympathy for his wife and children. McCarthyism brought him to the position—the president hired him because he had been unjustly accused of being a Communist sympathizer—and, finally, it accounts for his retention. Mulcahy loses his chief faculty supporter when she discovers that he lied about his wife's illness, but he gains another weapon through a visiting poet who recognizes him from Communist Party meetings.

At the climax of the novel, the Joseph McCarthy scare is shown at its most evil: Protecting the college, the well-meaning president conducts an interview into Mulcahy's past, which results in his being charged with libel. The unstable Mulcahy triumphs and secures his position at Jocelyn—certain to continue bullying students and colleagues alike—and the president resigns.

A Charmed Life

In *A Charmed Life*, Martha Sinnott returns to a group of artistic people at New Leeds, a small New England village based on Wellfleet, Cape Cod, where she had lived with her former husband (much like McCarthy had lived at Wellfleet and returned with a second husband). Martha returns determined to be different from and independent of the New Leedsians who live a charmed life of many accidents, none of which kills them. Here, time, which signifies the mortal, is askew and awry, as indicated by the many problems with clocks and calendars. Part of Martha's anxiety about her return to New Leeds is the possibility of meeting her former husband (based on McCarthy's former husband, Edmund Wilson) with his new wife and child and the fear that he will reestablish domination over her. When he seduces her and she later finds herself pregnant, she cannot remember the date well enough to determine whether her former or present husband is the father. Her moral decision to have an abortion because she cannot live a lie results in her death; returning from borrowing money for the abortion, she drives on the right side of the road, contrary to New Leeds custom, and meets another car head-on. The charmed life of New Leeds goes on, but Martha lives and dies an outsider.

McCarthy called this novel a fairy tale. Loosely analogous to "Sleeping Beauty," Sinnott pricks her hand at the beginning of the novel, lives in self-doubt on the fringes of the immortality of New Leeds (the timelessness of a century of sleep), and is awakened to the new existence of pregnancy and decision. The prince who wakens her with a kiss (the seduction), however, is an evil prince.

The Group

With a theme of the failure of modern progress, *The Group* was published in November, 1963. At that time, Betty Friedan's *The Feminine Mystique* (1963) and other feminist writings had focused on the problems of women, and the public was responsive to works focused on the problems of the emancipated woman. Although *The Group* is set in the seven years from 1933 to 1940, the progressiveness of the eight-cum-nine young Vassar women seemed to be the progress that was engulfing women of the 1960's. Like gleanings from an alumnae bulletin, the random appearances, different voices, and loose ends are not expected to be resolved. The undistinguished occupations of the group, also, confirm the alumnae magazine reports of most women graduates, but somehow more is expected of Vassar women. Not only the money but also increased competition for admission meant that, by 1963, most women could not get into Vassar. For the general public, there is some comfort in the failure of the culturally advantaged.

The novel begins with the wedding of Kay Strong in 1933 and ends with her death seven years later at the age of twenty-nine. Of the eight members of the group who had lived in the same dormitory, plus one outsider, Kay seemed to be most forward-looking and progressive. Like McCarthy, she comes from the West and, immediately upon graduation, she marries her lover of some time, a mostly unemployed playwright named Harald Petersen who resembles Harold Johnsrud. Part of McCarthy's personality is dispersed among the other characters, especially Libby MacAusland, a woman of formidable intellect who writes book reviews and becomes a literary agent.

The elegant, beautiful, and wealthy Elinor Eastlake disappears into Europe and reemerges as a lesbian prior to Kay's death. Polly Andrews becomes attached to a married man who is obviously well adjusted except that he pays twenty-five dollars a week for psychiatric counseling. Working in a hospital, Polly becomes engaged to another man, a psychiatrist who has defected from the profession and thus augments the satiric attack on psychiatry. Helena Davison, in Cleveland, remains the stable rich girl, highly intelligent and analytic. Priss Hartshorn marries a pediatrician, and, attempting to breast-feed her son and train him by modern theories, provides the satire on this aspect of progressivism. Pokey Prothero, from a household organized and represented by an invaluable butler, plans to become a veterinarian.

Kay, during a fight with Harald, gets a black eye and finds herself committed to a mental hospital. Despite Harald's admission that she does not belong there, she decides to stay for a rest and then disappears from the story until she reemerges after a divorce and a year in the West. Back East, ready to start a career again, she falls to her death while spotting planes from her window and becomes the first casualty of the war.

Representing a culmination of the group philosophy and the disjointed voices of the earlier novels, *The Group*, with its timely feminist content, earned for McCarthy a great deal of money and many appearances on talk shows and in magazines. Some Vassar alumnae were recognizable in the book, and the film version did not name the college. This novel established McCarthy as a popular writer, but she did not attempt to capitalize on it with a follow-up novel. Instead, eight years later, she brought out a novel of a different sort altogether.

Birds of America

Departing from the group structure, McCarthy's next novel, *Birds of America*, begins in 1964 with Peter Levi's return at age nineteen to Rocky Port, Maine, after an absence of five years. During his absence, his favorite horned owl died. With his divorced and remarried mother Rosamund, he searches for a waterfall that they cannot find—the victim of a highway project. In their respective ways, the village and the mother cling to fashions of the past but rapidly succumb to modern times.

Peter goes to the Sorbonne for his junior year in college but finds his ideals of French culture in conflict with the realities. His friends are American; he has a painful Thanksgiving dinner at an American general's home discussing vegetarianism and the war in Vietnam; he runs afoul of the French police while watching a demonstration; and he spends Christmas vacation in Rome where the masses of tourists interfere with his appreciation of the Sistine Chapel. Returned to Paris, he attempts in his Kantian way—"Behave as if thy maxim could be a universal law"—to help the street drunkards. Everywhere he goes, he tangles with human refuse, which is best revealed in a long letter home about the filth of Parisian toilets. Clinging to his preferences for nature, however, he grows vegetables and other plants in his apartment and joins a bird study group. At a zoo at the close of the novel, he is attacked by a swan while attempting to feed it from his hand. He wakens, later, in a hospital recovering from a reaction to a penicillin shot. At this point, Kant speaks to him, saying that "nature is dead, my child."

Peter (obviously modeled on Reuel Wilson) calls his father babbo, is familiar with Italy, speaks both French and Italian, and is an intellectual like his mother. This novel, much different from the other seven, is the only one with a clear and unmistakable protagonist. The group Peter satirizes are tourists as a group; but the group does not make up the novel's characters.

Cannibals and Missionaries

The group of *Cannibals and Missionaries*, originally formed as a committee of six to fly by Air France to Iran to investigate reports of the shah's torturing of prisoners, expands, by the time the plane is hijacked to Holland, to twenty-four hostages and eight terrorists. Set during the administration of U.S. president Gerald R. Ford, the novel takes its title from the puzzle in which three cannibals and three missionaries must cross a river in a boat that will hold only two people, and if the cannibals outnumber the missionaries, they might eat the missionaries. In the novel, however, there is no clear indication as to which group represents the cannibals and which the missionaries.

In one passage of explication, McCarthy points out that the terrorists' demands accomplish nothing but the reabsorption into the dominant society of whatever they demanded; prisoners released, for example, are eventually returned to prison. Confined in a Dutch farmhouse, hostages learn of their terrorists' demands from television: $1.25 million, Holland's withdrawal from the North Atlantic Treaty Organization (NATO), the breaking of relations with Israel, and the release of "class war" prisoners from Dutch jails. Like the other groups in McCarthy's fiction, the members of this group are pulled together in a common cause; even though divided between hostages and terrorists, the hostages willingly aid the terrorists in some efforts and feel triumphant in the successful completion of a task, such as hiding the helicopter that brought them to the farmhouse. At the novel's conclusion, however, all but four are killed, one of whom claims that she has not been changed by the experience.

The European settings of the last two novels reflect McCarthy's travel experiences and utilize her interest in art. In *Cannibals and Missionaries*, McCarthy returned to her early interest in communism and to the group structure with separate narrative voices.

While *The Groves of Academe* is still highly esteemed as an example of the academic novel, and *The Group* is read by students of popular fiction and women's studies, McCarthy's novels considered by themselves do not make up a lasting body of work. Rather, they derive their lasting significance from their place in the life and work of an exemplary woman of letters.

Grace Eckley

Other major works

SHORT FICTION: *The Company She Keeps*, 1942; *Cast a Cold Eye*, 1950; *The Hounds of Summer, and Other Stories*, 1981.

NONFICTION: *Sights and Spectacles, 1937-1956*, 1956; *Venice Observed*, 1956; *Memories of a Catholic Girlhood*, 1957; *The Stones of Florence*, 1959; *On the Contrary: Articles of Belief*, 1961; *Mary McCarthy's Theatre Chronicles, 1937-1962*, 1963; *Vietnam*, 1967; *Hanoi*, 1968; *The Writing on the Wall, and Other Literary Essays*, 1970; *Medina*, 1972; *The Mask of State*, 1974; *The Seventeenth Degree*, 1974; *Ideas and the Novel*, 1980; *Occasional Prose*, 1985; *How I Grew*, 1987; *Intellectual Memoirs: New York, 1936-1938*, 1992; *Between Friends: The Correspondence of Hannah Arendt and Mary McCarthy, 1949-1975*, 1995 (Carol Brightman, editor); *A Bolt from the Blue, and Other Essays*, 2002 (A. O. Scott, editor).

Bibliography

Abrams, Sabrina Fuchs. *Mary McCarthy: Gender, Politics, and the Postwar Intellectual*. New York: Peter Lang, 2004. Abrams examines McCarthy the fiction writer and McCarthy the cultural critic, discussing how her marginalized identity as a Catholic woman among the Jewish, male-dominated New York intelligentsia influenced her view of post-World War II American culture.

Brightman, Carol. *Writing Dangerously: Mary McCarthy and Her World*. New York: Clarkson Potter, 1992. Supplements but does not supersede Carol W. Gelderman's earlier biography. Like Gelderman, Brightman was able to interview her subject, and her book reflects not only inside knowledge but also, as its subtitle suggests, a strong grasp of the period in which McCarthy published. Includes a biographical glossary and notes.

Ebest, Sally Barr. "Mary McCarthy: Too Smart to Be Sentimental." In *Too Smart to Be Sentimental: Contemporary Irish American Women Writers*, edited by Ebest and Kathleen McInerney. Notre Dame, Ind.: University of Notre Dame Press, 2008. This collection of essays on twelve writers begins with Ebest's discussion of McCarthy. Ebest says it is "fitting" that her essay comes first in the collection because McCarthy "single-handedly reformulated the Irish American literary tradition characterizing her female predecessors," and she describes how McCarthy updated the traditional depiction of women characters.

Epstein, Joseph. "Mary McCarthy in Retrospect." *Commentary* 95 (May, 1993): 41-47. Provides a summary of McCarthy's work. Comments on her role in intellectual life in America, and discusses the relationship of her life to her fiction.

Freeman, Kimberly A. "Mary McCarthy's *A Charmed Life*: Divorcing Fiction from Fact." In *Love American Style: Divorce and the American Novel, 1881-1976*. New York: Routledge, 2003. Freeman analyzes McCarthy's book as well as novels by William Dean Howells, Edith Wharton, and John Updike to examine these authors' treatment of divorce and how that depiction reflects conflicting ideas about American identity. Includes notes, a bibliography, and an index.

Gelderman, Carol W. *Mary McCarthy: A Life*. New York: St. Martin's Press, 1988. Gelderman offers an objective biography of McCarthy. Although much of the narrative is familiar, the book is well written and amply documented. The photographs provide important perspective on McCarthy's childhood and a satisfying glimpse into her adult life. This biography is appropriate for general readers as well as students studying McCarthy.

Kiernan, Frances. *Seeing Mary Plain: A Life of Mary McCarthy*. New York: W. W. Norton, 2000. A comprehensive biography full of vivid details and anecdotes but marred by a lack of focus on certain essential aspects of McCarthy's life and work.

Kufrin, Joan. *Uncommon Women*. Piscataway, N.J.: New Century, 1981. In a book that examines women who have succeeded within several different fields, McCarthy is "The Novelist" in the chapter so named. The portrayal of the writer is friendly and informal, largely the transcription of an interview in McCarthy's home in Maine. McCarthy comments on her writing process of extensive revision. The two photographs capture a sense of fun and humor in McCarthy.

McKenzie, Barbara. *Mary McCarthy*. New York: Twayne, 1966. McKenzie offers a one-page chronology of McCarthy's life as well as an opening chapter titled "The Fact in Biography." She analyzes McCarthy's novels and short stories and assesses McCarthy's overall contribution to literature. McKenzie's book, with notes, a bibliography, and an index, would benefit serious students of McCarthy's work.

Pierpont, Claudia Roth. *Passionate Minds: Women Rewriting the World*. New York: Alfred A. Knopf, 2000. Evocative, interpretive essays on the life paths and works of twelve women, including McCarthy, connecting the circumstances of their lives with the shapes, styles, subjects, and situations of their art.

Stwertka, Eve, and Margo Viscusi, eds. *Twenty-Four Ways of Looking at Mary McCarthy: The Writer and Her Work*. Westport, Conn.: Greenwood Press, 1996. Based on papers originally presented at a conference in 1993, this book includes discussions of McCarthy's position as a public intellectual, Edmund Wilson's role in McCarthy's career, political dilemma in *The Groves of Academe*, and other aspects of her work and career.

CARSON McCULLERS

Born: Columbus, Georgia; February 19, 1917
Died: Nyack, New York; September 29, 1967
Also known as: Lula Carson Smith

Principal long fiction

The Heart Is a Lonely Hunter, 1940
Reflections in a Golden Eye, 1941
The Ballad of the Sad Café, 1943 (serial), 1951 (book)
The Member of the Wedding, 1946
Clock Without Hands, 1961

Other literary forms

Carson McCullers published a number of short stories, some of which are included in the volume containing *The Ballad of the Sad Café* and some in a collection of short works, *The Mortgaged Heart* (1971), edited by her sister, Margarita G. Smith. The latter also contains some magazine articles and notes of McCullers's writing. McCullers adapted *The Member of the Wedding* for the stage in 1950 (a film version appeared in 1952). She wrote two plays, including *The Square Root of Wonderful* (pr. 1957). McCullers's poetry is published in *The Mortgaged Heart* and in a children's book, *Sweet as a Pickle and Clean as a Pig* (1964).

Achievements

Like William Faulkner, McCullers has literary kinship with those older, midnight-haunted writers—Edgar Allan Poe, Nathaniel Hawthorne, and Herman Melville among them—who projected in fable and with symbol the story of America's unquiet mind. Against her southern background, she created a world of symbolic violence and tragic reality, indirectly lighted by the cool Flaubertian purity of her style. Of the writers of her generation, none was more consistent or thorough in achieving a sustained body of work.

Several of McCullers's works received critical acclaim. "A Tree, a Rock, a Cloud," a short story sometimes compared in theme to Samuel Taylor Coleridge's

"The Rime of the Ancient Mariner" (1798), was chosen for the O. Henry Memorial Prize in 1942. The dramatic version of *The Member of the Wedding* was extremely successful, running on Broadway continuously for nearly fifteen months, and it was named for both the Donaldson Award and the New York Drama Critics Circle Award in 1950. In addition, McCullers was a Guggenheim Fellow in 1942 and 1946, and she received an award from the American Academy of Arts and Letters in 1943.

Biography

Carson McCullers was born Lula Carson Smith on February 19, 1917, in Columbus, Georgia. Marguarite Smith, McCullers's mother, was very early convinced that her daughter was an artistic genius and sacrificed herself and, to some extent, McCullers's father, brother, and sister, to the welfare of her gifted child. McCullers grew up, therefore, with a peculiar kind of shyness and emotional dependence on her mother, combined with supreme self-confidence about her abilities. McCullers announced early in life that she was going to be a concert pianist, and she indeed displayed a precocious talent in that direction. Smith placed her daughter under the tutelage of Mary Tucker, a concert musician, who agreed that McCullers was talented.

McCullers came to love Tucker and her family with an all-consuming passion, a pattern she was to follow with a number of other close friends during her life. Mary Mercer, a psychiatrist friend of McCullers during her later years, suggested that the emotional devastation of the adolescent girl in *The Member of the Wedding*, when she was not allowed to accompany her beloved brother and his bride on their honeymoon, was an expression of McCullers's despair when the Tuckers moved away from her hometown. She seemed to experience every break in human contact as personal betrayal or tragedy.

Writing was also an early enthusiasm of McCullers. As a child, she created shows to be acted by herself and her siblings in the sitting room. Her mother would gather in neighbors or relatives for an appreciative audience. In the article "How I Began to Write" (*Mademoiselle*, September, 1948), McCullers said that these shows, which she described as anything from "hashed-over movies to Shakespeare," stopped when she discovered Eugene O'Neill. She was soon writing a three-act play "about revenge and incest" calling for a cast of a "blind man, several idiots and a mean old woman of one hundred years." Her next opus was a play in rhymed verse called "The Fire of Life," starring Jesus Christ and Friedrich Nietzsche. Soon after, she became enthralled by the great Russian writers Fyodor Dostoevski, Anton Chekhov, and Leo Tolstoy—a fascination she never outgrew. Years later, she was to suggest, with considerable cogency, that modern southern writing is most indebted to the Russian realists.

The Smith household, while never wealthy, was not so financially hard-pressed as McCullers sometimes later pretended. Lamar Smith, her father, was a respected jeweler in Columbus, Georgia, and a skilled repairer of clocks and watches. There was enough money, at least, to send the seventeen-year-old McCullers to New York City to attend the famous Juilliard School to study music. There was not enough, however, to replace the tuition money she had lost in the subway. Perhaps she was too mortified to ask for help, foreseeing that her father would simply send her a ticket to return home.

Whether through carelessness or naïveté, McCullers found herself almost penniless in New York. Having already paid her tuition for night classes at Columbia University, however, she intended to survive as best she could with whatever odd jobs she could find. Her inexperience and ineptness led to her being fired repeatedly from the jobs she found. One way or another, McCullers managed to support herself through the school term. By the time she came home in the summer, she had begun to write in earnest, and the dream of being a concert pianist was entirely displaced by the vision of becoming a great writer. She had launched her publishing career by selling two short stories to *Story* magazine: "Wunderkind" and "Like That." Her first novel, *The Heart Is a Lonely Hunter*, was in its formative stages.

Back home, McCullers met a handsome young soldier, Reeves McCullers, who shared both her ambitions of living in New York and of becoming a writer. In 1936, Reeves left the Army and traveled to New York to attend Columbia, as McCullers was doing. His college career lasted only a few weeks, however, before he withdrew entirely to escort McCullers back home to Georgia to recover from one of her many serious illnesses.

In 1937, Carson and Reeves were married, although Reeves was financially in no condition to support her. Though idyllically happy at first, their marriage became increasingly troubled. While McCullers's first novel, published when she was twenty-two years old, brought her immediate recognition in the literary world of New York, her husband met with continual frustration in his own ambitions.

Their problems did not derive simply from the professional dominance and success of McCullers. Both she and her husband were sexually ambivalent. The homosexuality and odd love triangles that are so characteristic of McCullers's fiction had some correlation to real-life situations. McCullers had a tendency to fall in love with both men and women, and to suffer inordinately when such attentions were repulsed. As her fiction suggests, she believed that one of the central problems of living was to love and be loved in equal measure.

McCullers often left Reeves to his own devices when professional opportunities or invitations came her way. She was offered a fellowship, for example, in the prestigious Bread Loaf Writers' Conference, where she consorted with such persons as Robert Frost, Louis Untermeyer, John Marquand, and Wallace Stegner. That same summer, she also met Erika and Klaus Mann, Thomas Mann's children, and Annemarie Clarac-Schwartzenbach, a prominent Swiss journalist and travel writer. McCullers fell deeply in love with the stunning Clarac-Schwartzenbach. When Clarac-Schwartzenbach left the country, it was another terrible "desertion" for McCullers. *Reflections in a Golden Eye*, McCullers's second novel, was dedicated to Clarac-Schwartzenbach.

In 1940, McCullers and her husband separated, and McCullers moved into a two-room apartment in a large Victorian house in Brooklyn Heights, owned by George Davis, editor of *Harper's Bazaar*. The old house became the temporary home for a stimulating group of artists, including poets W. H. Auden and Louis MacNeice; the composer Benjamin Britten; Peter Pears, tenor; Gypsy Rose Lee, fan dancer and writer; and novelist Richard Wright. These were only the earlier residents. A group of musicians and composers, including Aaron Copland, Leonard Bernstein, and David Diamond, joined the ranks at one time or another. Diamond was to become another of those fateful friends who was emotionally involved with both McCullers and Reeves. Also temporarily in residence were Salvador Dali and his wife, Gala, as well as other prominent Surrealist painters.

A new and terrifying illness drove McCullers back to the South to her mother's care. She was afraid this time that she was going blind. Years later, doctors declared that this episode, when she was barely twenty-four years old, was her first cerebral stroke. There was no paralysis, but her recovery was slow.

McCullers and Reeves tried again to live together in New York and for a time took comfort in a new intimacy with their friend, Diamond. McCullers was invited to Yaddo, a retreat for resident artists situated a few miles from Saratoga Springs, New York. The motherly overseer of the colony, Elizabeth Ames, became almost a second mother to McCullers, who returned again and again to this peaceful setting and considered it the place most conducive to writing.

McCullers eventually divorced Reeves; he went back into the service, became a much-decorated war hero, was wounded several times in action, and finally returned as a beloved officer. McCullers was so admiring

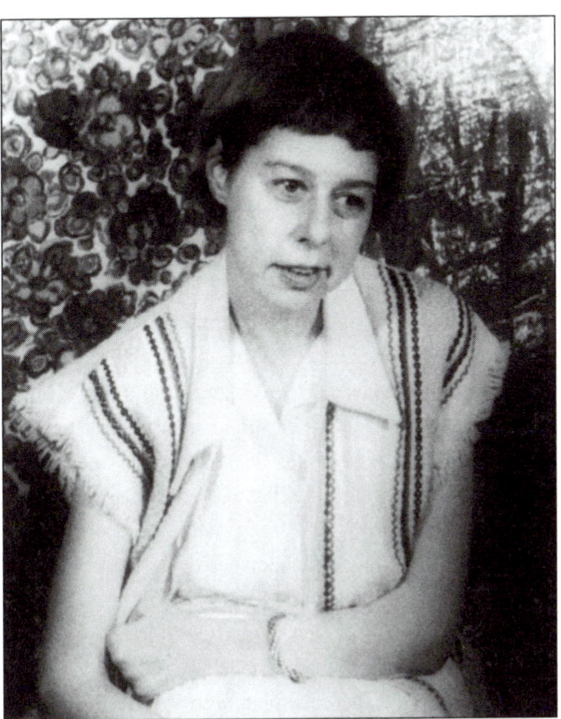

Carson McCullers. (Library of Congress)

of his new role that they were remarried. As a civilian husband, however, Reeves could not maintain the independence and pride he had so hardily won as a soldier. He turned increasingly to alcohol and eventually expressed the desire to commit suicide. When, in Europe, he seemed determined that they should both hang themselves, McCullers responded by fleeing from him in terror and returning home alone. Shortly thereafter, Reeves was found dead in a Paris hotel.

After McCullers finished *The Member of the Wedding*, which proved immensely popular, her friendship with dramatist Tennessee Williams encouraged her to attempt a stage adaptation of the work. After many trials in deciding on an agreeable version for the stage, the play finally was produced, starring Ethel Waters and Julie Harris. McCullers wrote one other play, *The Square Root of Wonderful*, which was not nearly as successful. *The Member of the Wedding* was eventually adapted into a motion picture (released in 1952) with the original cast. John Huston produced a film version of another of McCullers's works, *Reflections in a Golden Eye* (released in 1967), shortly before her death on September 29.

McCullers's last years were a nightmare of pain, though she continued to maintain a fairly cheerful social life while partially paralyzed and often bedridden. She had two strokes; underwent several operations on her paralyzed left arm, leg, and hand; had a cancerous breast removed; broke her hip and elbow in a fall; and died after another massive stroke. She was fifty years old.

Analysis

Carson McCullers's fiction has a childlike directness, a disconcerting exposure of unconscious impulses in conjunction with realistic detail. She is like the candid child who announces that the emperor in his new clothes is really naked. She sees the truth, or a partial truth, of the human psyche, then inflates or distorts that truth into a somewhat grotesque fable that is sometimes funny but always sad.

Such a tragicomic effect derives, apparently, from an unusual openness to subconscious direction, combined with conscious cultivation of a style that best exploits such material, weaving into it just enough objectively observed reality to achieve plausibility. McCullers herself explained the technique by which she achieved the fusion of objective reality with symbolic, psychic experience. In "The Russian Realists and Southern Literature," first published in *Decision*, July, 1941 (also in *The Mortgaged Heart*), she speaks of the charge of cruelty that was brought against both Russian writers (particularly Dostoevski) and southern writers such as Faulkner and herself, although she does not refer to her own works:

> No single instance of "cruelty" in Russian or Southern writing could not be matched or outdone by the Greeks, the Elizabethans, or, for that matter, the creators of the Old Testament. Therefore it is not the specific "cruelty" itself that is shocking, but the manner in which it is presented. And it is in this approach to life and suffering that the southerners are so indebted to the Russians. The technique briefly is this: a bold and outwardly callous juxtaposition of the tragic with the humorous, the immense with the trivial, the sacred with the bawdy, the whole soul of a man with a materialistic detail.

What is peculiar to the Russians and the southerners is not the inclusion of farce and tragedy in the same work, but the fusion of the two so that they are experienced simultaneously. McCullers uses Faulkner's *As I Lay Dying* (1930) as an example of this technique. She could as effectively have demonstrated it with her own *Ballad of the Sad Café*, which is a masterpiece of tragicomedy. The relative lack of success of the earlier *Reflections in a Golden Eye* results partly, perhaps, from her inability to balance the sadomasochistic elements with elements of satire or farce. She reportedly claimed that incidents such as the rejected wife cutting off her nipples with garden shears were "hilariously funny." This may demonstrate an oddly warped sense of humor, a failure of craft, or simply ignorance about her own creative processes, or it may simply be a way of shunting off rational explanations of a work of art, a red herring to confuse critics. As a novelist, McCullers operates like a poet or perhaps like a Surrealist painter, who tells the truth but "tells it slant."

The thematic content of McCullers's works is consistent: All her stories deal with the metaphysical isolation of individuals and their desperate need to transcend this isolation through love. Love is the key to a magnificent transformation of leaden existence into gold, but the exalted state is doomed because love is so seldom reciprocated. Though this feeling (and it is more feeling than thought) may stem from McCullers's early fears and dependence on her mother, it strikes a universal chord. That McCullers projects this terrible sense of unrequited love into all kinds of human relationships except that between mother and daughter may be suggestive in itself. In an interview with Virginia Spencer Carr, Lamar Smith, Jr., said that his sister did not depict a meaningful mother-daughter relationship in her fiction because she did not want to strip herself bare and show the utter dependence that she felt for her mother.

The Heart Is a Lonely Hunter

Nevertheless, McCullers successfully universalizes the state of metaphysical isolation as a perennial human condition, not merely a neurotic regression to childhood. Her first novel, *The Heart Is a Lonely Hunter*, has Mick Kelly as its child character, who clings to John Singer, the deaf-mute, who, she fancies, understands and sympathizes with her problems. McCullers's own definition of the character in "Author's Outline of 'The Mute'" (in *The Mortgaged Heart*) reveals an almost transparent self-dramatization: "Her story is that of the violent struggle of a gifted child to get what she needs from an unyielding environment." Only metaphorically is Mick's struggle "violent," but even when McCullers presents physical violence in fiction it often seems to function as the objective correlative to mental anguish.

McCullers casts Jake Blount, the ineffectual social agitator, as a would-be Marxist revolutionary, but he may seem more like an overgrown frustrated child. Her outline says,

> His deepest motive is to do all that he can to change the predatory, unnatural social conditions existing today. . . . He is fettered by abstractions and conflicting ideas. . . . His attitude vacillates between hate and the most unselfish love.

Dr. Benedict Copeland is the more believable character, representing the peculiar plight of the educated African American in the South, who has internalized the white person's condemnation of black cultural traits. His daughter's black dialect and careless posture embarrass him, and he frowns on what he considers the irresponsible fecundity and emotionality of the black youth. What McCullers calls his "passionate asceticism" has driven away even his own family.

Biff Brannon, the proprietor of the local restaurant, is the dispassionate observer of people, sympathetic, in a distant way, with all human oddities. Like Mick, he seems almost a part of McCullers, a grown-up version of the child who sat silently in the corners of stores watching people, who loved to listen to the voices of African Americans, and who paid her dimes repeatedly to see the freaks in the side shows. Brannon is also sexually impotent, with homosexual feelings. He is cold and withdrawn with his wife and has a repressed attraction for Mick in her tomboyish prepuberty—an impulse that fades as soon as she shows sexual development.

All of these characters pivot around the deaf-mute, John Singer, who is the central symbol of the metaphysical isolation of humanity. They take his silence as wisdom and pour out their hearts to his patient but unreceptive ears. He does lip-read, so he knows what they are saying, but he has no way to communicate with them in reply. Moreover, the experiences they confide to him seem so alien to his own that he does not really understand. Mick talks about music, which he has never heard; Jake Blount rants about the downtrodden working classes; Dr. Copeland speaks of his frustrations as a racial leader without any followers; and Biff Brannon simply looks on with no project of his own.

Singer, though, shares their universal need to love and communicate with a kindred soul. The object of his adoration is another mute, a sloppy, mentally disabled Greek named Antonopoulus, who loves nothing but the childish pleasure of a full stomach. When Antonopoulus dies in an institution, Singer commits suicide. The whole pyramid of illusion collapses.

This bleak tale suggests that the beloved is created in the lover's mind out of the extremity of his need and projected upon whomever is available. Singer drew the love of these desperate souls on account of his polite tolerance of their advances coupled with an essential blankness. They looked into his eyes and saw their own dreams reflected there, just as Singer himself read a secret sympathy and understanding in the blank round face of Antonopoulus, who was actually incapable of such sentiments.

The haunting quality of this story may derive partly

from the impression of getting an inside look at a multiple personality. McCullers displays a curious ability to divide her ambivalent psyche to create new, somewhat lopsided beings. McCullers had never seen a deaf-mute, for example, and when Reeves wanted to take her to a convention of deaf-mutes, she declined, saying she already knew Singer. Marxist political agitators may have been just as foreign to her actual experience, but she could create one from the jumble of liberal sentiment she acquired through educated friends and through reading. If the issues were not clear in her own mind, it did not really matter, because Jake was a confused and drunken loser. McCullers has been praised by black writers for her sensitive portrayal of African Americans, yet the peculiar warmth of the relationship between Dr. Copeland's daughter, Portia, and her husband and brother suggests the triangular love affairs McCullers sometimes acted out in her own life and dramatized several times in other fiction.

Reflections in a Golden Eye

McCullers wrote *Reflections in a Golden Eye* in a short period of time, "for fun," she said, after the long session with *The Heart Is a Lonely Hunter*. The idea for the story germinated when, as an adolescent, she first went to Fort Benning, but she also drew on her experience of Fayetteville, where she and Reeves lived for a while, and nearby Fort Bragg. The story caused considerable shock in conservative southern communities. Americans generally were not prepared for a fictional treatment of homosexuality. A perceptive reader might suspect the homosexuality in Biff Brannon, but there is no doubt about Captain Penderton's sexual desires. Moreover, the sadomasochism, the weird voyeurism, and the Freudian implications of horses and guns are unmistakable. If *The Heart Is a Lonely Hunter* is about love, *Reflections in a Golden Eye* is about sex and its various distortions. These characters are lonely, isolated people, driven by subconscious impulses. The story concerns two Army couples, a houseboy, and a rather primitive young man, all of them somewhat abnormal, as well as a horse. One suspects the horse is akin to a dream symbol for the ungovernable libido.

Penderton is impotent with his beautiful wife, Leonora, but is drawn to her lover, Major Langdon. The major's wife is sickly and painfully aware of her husband's affair with Leonora. Mrs. Langdon is solicitously attended by a Filipino houseboy, who is also maladjusted. The other character is Private Williams, an inarticulate young man who seems to be a fugitive from somebody's unconscious (probably Penderton's). He has a mystical affinity for nature, and he is the only person who can handle Leonora's high-spirited stallion, Firebird. Penderton is afraid of the horse, and he both loves and hates Williams.

D. H. Lawrence's *The Prussian Officer* (1914) may have provided a model for Penderton's relationship to Williams, since McCullers was an admirer of Lawrence. Williams is quite different, however, from the perfectly normal, healthy orderly who is the innocent victim of the Prussian officer's obsession. The silent Williams enacts a psychodrama that repeats, in different terms, the sexual impotence of Penderton. Having seen Leonora naked through an open door, he creeps into the Penderton house each night to crouch silently by her bedside, watching her sleep. When Penderton discovers him there, he shoots him. The scene in the dark bedroom beside the sleeping woman is loaded with psychological overtones. Not a word is spoken by either man. In one sense, the phallic gun expresses the captain's love-hate attraction to the private; in another sense, Penderton is killing his impotent shadow self.

Technically speaking, *Reflections in a Golden Eye* is superior to McCullers's first novel; at least, it has an admirable artistic unity. Its four-part structure has the precision of a tightly constructed musical composition. In content, the story line seems as gothic as Poe's "The Fall of the House of Usher" (1839), yet the style is objective and nonjudgmental—like the impersonal eye of nature in which it is reflected. McCullers was perfecting the kind of perception and style she spoke of in her essay on the Russian realists, presenting human action starkly without editorial comment.

The Ballad of the Sad Café

McCullers's next work, *The Ballad of the Sad Café*, was a more successful treatment of archetypal myth, with its psychodramatic overtones tempered this time by humor. Like the true folk ballad, it is a melancholy tale of love. The setting is an isolated southern village—little more than a trading post with a few dreary, unpainted buildings. The most prominent citizen is known as Miss

Emelia, a strong, mannish, cross-eyed woman with a sharp business sense. She runs the general store and operates a still that produces the best corn liquor for miles around. There is nothing to do for entertainment in town except drink her brew, follow the odd career of this sexless female, and listen to the melancholy singing of the chain gang, which suggests a universal entrapment in the dreary reality of one's life.

The story concerns a temporary hiatus from boredom when Miss Emelia and the observing townspeople become a real community. Love provides the means for a temporary transcendence of Miss Emelia's metaphysical isolation and, through her, sheds a reflected radiance on all. Like John Singer, Miss Emelia chooses an odd person to love, a homeless dwarf who straggles into town, claiming to be her cousin and hoping for a handout. Although Miss Emelia had thrown out her husband, the only man who had ever loved her, because he expected sexual favors when they were married, she unaccountably falls in love with this pathetic wanderer. She takes Cousin Lymon in and, because he likes company, begins a restaurant, which becomes the social center of the entire community. All goes well until the despised husband, Marvin Macy, is released from the penitentiary and returns to his hometown, bent on revenge for the monstrous humiliation Miss Emelia had visited upon him.

Another unusual threesome develops when Cousin Lymon becomes infatuated with Marvin Macy. The competition between Macy and Miss Emelia for the attention of Cousin Lymon comes to a tragicomic climax in a fistfight between the rivals. Miss Emelia, who has been working out with a punching bag, is actually winning when the treacherous Cousin Lymon leaps on her back, and the two men give her a terrible drubbing. Macy and Cousin Lymon flee after they vandalize Miss Emelia's store and her still in the woods. Miss Emelia is left in a more desolate isolation than she has ever known and becomes a solitary recluse thereafter. The coda at the end recalls again the mournful song of the chain gang.

There is no more somber image of spiritual isolation than the glimpse of the reclusive Miss Emelia at the window of her boarded-up café:

> It is a face like the terrible, dim faces known in dreams—sexless and white, with two gray crossed eyes which are turned inward so sharply that they seem to be exchanging with each other one long and secret gaze of grief.

This story, written in a style that precludes sentimentality, is surely McCullers's most successful treatment of unrequited love and betrayal. The fight scene is a satire of all traditionally masculine brawls for the love of a woman, witnessed by the entire community as a battle larger than life, for a prize both morally and physically smaller than life. In addition to the satire on all crude American substitutes for the duel of honor, this story may also call to mind Faulkner's famous gothic tale, "A Rose for Emily," about the genteel aristocratic lady who murdered her lover to keep him in her bed. Miss Emelia is certainly the absolute opposite to all conventions about the beautiful but fragile southern lady, who is entirely useless.

The Member of the Wedding

The Member of the Wedding is possibly the most popular of McCullers's novels, partly because it was converted into a successful Broadway play—in defiance of one critic's judgment that the novel is entirely static, totally lacking in drama. In fact, the story has a quality somewhat akin to closet drama, such as George Bernard Shaw's "Don Juan in Hell," which is performed by readers with no attempt at action. The endless conversation occurs in one spot, the kitchen of a lower-middle-class home in the South. There are occasional forays into the outer world, but always the principals return to the kitchen, where real experience and visionary ideals blend in an endless consideration of human possibilities.

The protagonist, a motherless adolescent girl named Frankie Addams, is the central quester for human happiness, foredoomed to disappointment. She is similar to Mick in *The Heart Is a Lonely Hunter*. It is no accident that both their names reflect the genderless state of prepuberty; moreover, neither has been indoctrinated into the attitudes and conventional expectations of little girls. In the isolation and boredom of Frankie's life, the only exciting event is the upcoming marriage of her older brother. Frankie conceives of the dream that will sustain her in the empty weeks of the long, hot summer: She will become a member of the wedding and join her brother and his bride on their honeymoon and new idyllic life of love and communion.

This impossible dream is the central issue of those long conversations in the kitchen where the girl is flanked by a younger cousin, John Henry, who represents the childhood from which Frankie is emerging, and the black maid, Berenice, who tries to reason with Frankie without stripping her of all solace. Ignorant as she is of the dynamics of sexual love, what Frankie aspires to is not a love so self-seeking as eros, nor quite so all-encompassing as agape. She envisions an ideal love that establishes a permanent and free-flowing communication among the members of a small, select group. This imagined communion seems to express an unvoiced dream of many, sometimes situated in a visionary future or an equally visionary past. Berenice, for all her gentle earthiness, shows that her vision of a golden age is in the past, when she was married to her first husband. She admits that after that man died, her other two marriages were vain attempts to recapture the rapport she had known with her first husband.

A curious irony of the story is that Frankie, with her persistent goal of escaping her isolated personal identity in what she calls the "we of me," actually comes closest to that ideal in the course of these endless conversations with the child and the motherly black woman. This real communion also passes away, as surely as the imagined communion with the wedded pair never materializes. John Henry dies before the end of the story, symbolic perhaps of the passing of Frankie's childhood. Reality and banality seem to have conquered in a world unsuited to the dreams of sensitive human beings.

Clock Without Hands

McCullers's last novel, *Clock Without Hands*, written during a period of suffering and ill health, moves beyond the not quite adult problems of adolescence at the cost of much of her lyricism. Perhaps the novel is a somewhat feeble attempt to emulate the moral power of Tolstoy's *The Death of Ivan Ilyich* (1886). It concerns a very ordinary man who faces death from leukemia and suspects that he has never lived on his own terms. The theme is still loneliness and spiritual isolation, but it has taken on existential overtones. The protagonist, J. T. Malone, like Tolstoy's Ivan, discovers too late that moral dignity requires some kind of commitment to action. In his new and painful awareness of his own moral vacuity, there are few decisions left to make. He does make one small gesture, however, to redeem an otherwise meaningless life. He refuses to accept the community's order to bomb the home of an African American who had dared to move into a white neighborhood. McCullers's description of Judge Clane, Malone's aging friend, reveals with precision the peculiar combination of sentimentality and cruelty that characterizes conventional white racism of the old southern variety.

Although McCullers will probably endure as a writer with a very special talent for describing the in-between world before a child becomes an adult, the no-man's-land of closeted homosexuality, and the irrational demands of love in the absence of any suitable recipient of love, the range of her fiction is quite limited. Somehow, the "child genius" never quite achieved maturity. Nevertheless, all people are immature or maimed in some secret way; in that sense, every reader must admit kinship to McCullers's warped and melancholy characters.

Katherine Snipes

Other major works

SHORT FICTION: *The Ballad of the Sad Café: The Novels and Stories of Carson McCullers*, 1951; *The Ballad of the Sad Café and Collected Short Stories*, 1952, 1955; *The Shorter Novels and Stories of Carson McCullers*, 1972.

PLAYS: *The Member of the Wedding*, pr. 1950 (adaptation of her novel); *The Square Root of Wonderful*, pr. 1957.

NONFICTION: *Illumination and Night Glare: The Unfinished Autobiography of Carson McCullers*, 1999 (Carlos L. Dews, editor).

CHILDREN'S LITERATURE: *Sweet as a Pickle and Clean as a Pig*, 1964.

MISCELLANEOUS: *The Mortgaged Heart*, 1971 (short fiction, poetry, and essays; Margarita G. Smith, editor).

Bibliography

Carr, Virginia Spencer. *The Lonely Hunter: A Biography of Carson McCullers*. 1975. New ed. Athens: University of Georgia Press, 2003. This definitive biography, with an updated preface by Carr, provides significant biographical elements that are related to

McCullers's works. The complexity, pain, and loneliness of McCullers's characters are matched by those of their creator. Includes a foreword by Tennessee Williams, an extensive chronology of McCullers's life, a primary bibliography, and endnotes.

_______. *Understanding Carson McCullers*. Columbia: University of South Carolina Press, 2005. A thoughtful guide to McCullers's works, with separate chapters analyzing the novels *The Heart Is a Lonely Hunter*, *The Member of the Wedding*, *Reflections in a Golden Eye*, and *The Ballad of the Sad Café*. This new edition of the book originally published in 1990 includes updated scholarship about McCullers.

Clark, Beverly Lyon, and Melvin J. Friedman, eds. *Critical Essays on Carson McCullers*. New York: G. K. Hall, 1996. A collection of essays ranging from reviews of McCullers's major works, to tributes by such writers as Tennessee Williams and Kay Boyle, and to critical analyses from a variety of perspectives.

Cook, Richard M. *Carson McCullers*. New York: Frederick Ungar, 1975. A good general introduction to McCullers's novels, short stories, and plays. Cook's analysis of *The Ballad of the Sad Café* is especially good, though the book includes chapters on each of the novels, McCullers's life, and her achievements as well. Cook, while admiring McCullers, recognizes her limitations but nevertheless praises her success with portraying human suffering and isolation and enabling readers to relate to the most grotesque of characters.

Gleeson-White, Sarah. *Strange Bodies: Gender and Identity in the Novels of Carson McCullers*. Tuscaloosa: University of Alabama Press, 2003. Gleeson-White analyzes McCullers's major novels, describing how their "grotesque" depiction of gender roles and sexuality provides the possibility of freedom and redemption for her characters.

James, Judith Giblin. *Wunderkind: The Reputation of Carson McCullers, 1940-1990*. Columbia, S.C.: Camden House, 1995. Examines McCullers's critical reception during a fifty-year period that begins with the publication of her first novel, *The Heart Is a Lonely Hunter*. James describes how critics' interpretations have changed over the years to reflect changes in cultural preoccupations.

Jenkins, McKay. *The South in Black and White: Race, Sex, and Literature in the 1940's*. Chapel Hill: University of North Carolina Press, 1999. Covers McCullers along with several other writers in a consideration of the role of race and sex in Southern literature.

McDowell, Margaret B. *Carson McCullers*. Boston: Twayne, 1980. A good general introduction to McCullers's fiction, with a chapter on each of the novels. Stressing McCullers's versatility, McDowell emphasizes the lyricism, the musicality, and the rich symbolism of McCullers's fiction as well as McCullers's sympathy for lonely individuals. Includes a chronology, endnotes, and a select bibliography.

Rich, Nancy B. *The Flowering Dream: The Historical Saga of Carson McCullers*. Chapel Hill, N.C.: Chapel Hill Press, 1999. An examination of four of McCullers's novels and a play, analyzing their unifying elements and stylistic techniques and how each builds upon the others to create an overall saga of the human struggle for freedom.

Savigneau, Josyane. *Carson McCullers: A Life*. Translated by Joan E. Howard. Boston: Houghton Mifflin, 2001. The McCullers estate granted Savigneau access to McCullers's unpublished papers, enabling her to obtain details of the author's life that were previously unavailable to biographers.

Westling, Louise. *Sacred Groves and Ravaged Gardens: The Fiction of Eudora Welty, Carson McCullers, and Flannery O'Connor*. Athens: University of Georgia Press, 1985. In this study, important comparisons are made between these three major southern writers. While Westling is not the first to use a feminist approach with McCullers, the book offers useful insight concerning the portrayal of the female characters and the issue of androgyny in McCullers's fiction. Her analysis of *The Ballad of the Sad Café* is particularly good. Supplemented by useful endnotes and a bibliography of secondary material.

Whitt, Jan, ed. *Reflections in a Critical Eye: Essays on Carson McCullers*. Lanham, Md.: University Press of America, 2008. A collection of critical essays on McCullers's work, including a feminist interpretation of *The Heart Is a Lonely Hunter* and *The Ballad of the Sad Café* and discussions of lesbian desire in her novels. Includes the chapter "Carson McCullers, Eleanor Roosevelt, and Surrealist History."

ALICE McDERMOTT

Born: Brooklyn, New York; June 27, 1953

Principal long fiction

A Bigamist's Daughter, 1982
That Night, 1987
At Weddings and Wakes, 1992
Charming Billy, 1998
Child of My Heart, 2002
After This, 2006

Other literary forms

Although she had written some short stories while she was working in New York after graduating from college, Alice McDermott did not attempt to publish them. However, when she was a graduate student at the University of New Hampshire, her teacher Mark Smith, who was himself a writer, was so impressed by her stories that he persuaded her to begin submitting them to magazines. The first publication to accept one of McDermott's stories was *Ms.* magazine. Before long, her short fiction had also appeared in *Redbook*, *Mademoiselle*, and *Seventeen.*

Achievements

Alice McDermott is lauded by critics both for her lyrical prose and for her insight into the inner lives of the Irish Catholic families about whom she writes. Her second book, *That Night*, won the 1987 Whiting Writers Award and was nominated both for a National Book Award in 1987 and for a PEN/Faulkner Award in 1998. She received a National Book Award in 1998 and an American Book Award, Before Columbus Foundation, in 1999, both for *Charming Billy*. In 2007, McDermott was a finalist for the Pulitzer Prize for fiction for *After This*. In 2008, she was the recipient of the Corrington Award for Literary Excellence.

Biography

Alice McDermott was born in Brooklyn, New York, the third child and only daughter of William J. McDermott, a Consolidated Edison representative, and Mildred Lynch McDermott, a secretary and homemaker. Her parents were first-generation Irish Americans and devout Roman Catholics. Early in her childhood, her family moved to suburban Elmont, New York, on Long Island. McDermott attended Catholic schools, first Saint Boniface School in Elmont and then Sacred Heart Academy in Hempstead. After graduating from Sacred Heart, she enrolled in the State University of New York at Oswego. Though she admits to taking college writing courses merely because she believed that they would be easy, a chance comment by one of her teachers made her begin to think seriously about a writing career. However, her parents convinced her that the idea was impractical, and after she graduated in 1975, McDermott went to work as a typist at Vantage Press, a vanity press in New York.

Nevertheless, McDermott felt that she should at least try to fulfill her dream of becoming a writer. If in two years she had made no progress, she decided, she would find another line of work. As soon as she had secured a teaching assistantship at the University of New Hampshire, which would enable her to support herself while she studied creative writing, McDermott quit her job in New York, moved to New Hampshire, and began work on a master's degree. She received her M.A. in 1978, then remained at the university for one more year, teaching English. When *Ms.* magazine accepted one of McDermott's stories, the author and her friends went to New York to celebrate, and it was then that McDermott met David M. Armstrong, who was studying to be a neuroscientist. The couple was married on June 16, 1979, and McDermott moved to Manhattan, where she worked as a fiction reader for *Redbook* and *Esquire* while Armstrong completed medical school.

Meanwhile, McDermott had begun her first novel, *A Bigamist's Daughter*. After seeing the first segment of the book, Mark Smith had McDermott contact his agent, Harriet Wasserman, who was also impressed by McDermott's writing. Within a few weeks, Wasserman had sold the unfinished novel to Houghton Mifflin. After publication, the book received favorable reviews, and McDermott's career as a novelist was launched.

McDermott and Armstrong moved to La Jolla, California; McDermott taught at the University of California at San Diego and completed her second novel. In 1985, she gave birth to her first child, Willie. The family then moved back to the East Coast and made their permanent home in Bethesda, Maryland. In 1989, McDermott had a daughter, Eames. Another son, Patrick, was born in 1993. McDermott taught writing at American University and in both 1995 and 1997 was a writer-in-residence at Virginia Center for the Creative Arts. Later she was named Johns Hopkins University's Richard A. Macksey Professor of the Humanities.

Analysis

Alice McDermott sets her novels in the places and among the people she knows best, the Irish Catholic families who had put down their roots in Brooklyn, New York, and those who, like her own parents, had moved out to suburban Long Island in the hope of offering their children greater opportunities. As it turned out, while the new environment did give the young more freedom, they lost the sense of stability that they would have had in the tight-knit community in which their parents had been reared.

Indeed, McDermott's novels are pervaded by the theme of loss. Not only do her young people lose their innocence, but they also do not replace it with the mature faith that had sustained previous generations. Their loneliness drives them into marriage, but they soon find that they still feel as isolated as they had before. With the births of their children comes new hope: Surely family life will prove to be the antidote to loneliness. The harmonious existence of which they had dreamed turns out to be another illusion, however. The children squabble with each other and rebel against their parents. Eventually they desert their parents, who, despite all that they have shared, are still strangers to each other and thus quite alone.

McDermott's novels are not essentially pessimistic, however. If loss is a fact of life, so also is the power of the imagination to transcend grim reality. This gift is reflected in the flights of fancy in which many of her characters indulge. It is also evident in McDermott's use of language. Her lyrical style transforms the ordinary into the extraordinary, a beach or a backyard into a place of great beauty and magical possibilities. The hope McDermott offers her characters and her readers, however, is based on more than aesthetics. Her vision of human existence is in keeping with her Catholic faith: Although we are fallen creatures living in a fallen world, we can obtain redemption through divine grace.

That Night

That Night is the story of two teenage lovers who are separated by fate and circumstances. It is set in the early 1960's in a Long Island suburb. The narrator, now a grown woman, was a ten-year-old girl when the events took place that would change her community forever. Before that summer night, everyone felt secure. Each morning the men went off to work, and at the day's end they came home; meanwhile, their wives stayed home and kept house, periodically gathering to gossip a bit. Their children had the run of the neighborhood.

Sheryl, who is the Juliet of the novel, differs from the other sixteen-year-old girls in the neighborhood in two ways: She was the first of them to reach puberty, and she was the first to lose a parent. Everyone remembers how shattered she was when her father died. Otherwise,

Alice McDermott. (Eames Armstrong/Library of Congress)

Sheryl is rather ordinary. She is not especially pretty, nor does she look any different from other girls her age, or at least from those who associate with the hot-rodding toughs at the local high school. Sheryl's boyfriend, Rick, is one of them. The neighbors agree that if her father had been alive, Sheryl would never have been permitted to date someone with Rick's bad reputation and abysmal prospects.

In the first chapter of the novel, the narrator describes the events that led up to a confrontation between Rick's friends and the neighborhood fathers. After days of trying to reach Sheryl by telephone, Rick has led his friends to her house. The neighborhood watches while he stands on the front lawn, bellowing her name; they see him push her mother down when she insists that Sheryl is no longer there; and when the other boys drive their cars onto the lawn and emerge from them carrying chains, the neighborhood men seize snow shovels and baseball bats and rush into battle. Soon the police arrive, and the boys flee. No one is seriously injured. The safe little neighborhood has been threatened by violent outsiders, however; those who live there will never again have the same sense of security.

Ironically, the battle was unnecessary. Sheryl's mother was telling the truth—Sheryl was no longer at home. After her mother discovered that Sheryl was pregnant, she took her to relatives in Ohio, who watched over her until her baby was born and taken away to be adopted. Sheryl's mother sold her home and moved away. Later, both Rick and Sheryl married other people.

After that dramatic opening, the narrator provides details from the period before the confrontation in order to explain how the love affair came about; for example, she suggests that Sheryl thought her love for Rick would somehow fill the emptiness left by her father's death. She also fills in her description of the neighborhood families, not only showing them as they were that important summer but also commenting on their later lives. At times the narrator takes on the role of an omniscient author, revealing the unexpressed thoughts of her characters, but McDermott's story is so compelling that one tends to overlook this technical flaw. *That Night* is a memorable story about an ancient theme: the power of grace, which alone makes it possible for human beings to survive the loss of innocence.

Charming Billy

Like *That Night*, McDermott's award-winning novel *Charming Billy* has a nameless narrator who is more an observer than a participant in the action. By moving away, she has broken free from the close-knit Irish Catholic community in Queens where she was reared and where the title character spent his entire life. She has returned only to join the friends and relatives of Billy Lynch who have gathered to bury him. Billy's death at the age of sixty was the direct result of his alcoholism. Although he was a chronic drunk, Billy was so witty and charming that he is mourned by everyone who knew him. During the three days when they are together, the mourners recall the major events in Billy's life and reflect on the lie that made him an alcoholic and established him as a romantic hero.

The crucial event in Billy's life occurred when he was still a young man. Billy and his cousin and close friend Dennis Lynch had just returned from fighting in World War II, and before going back to their jobs, they decided to go to the beach in East Hampton on Long Island. There Billy spotted a young girl who was helping her sister, a nanny for a wealthy New York couple, take care of the children in her charge. Billy fell in love with Eva, who was visiting from Ireland, and though she insisted on going home to say good-bye to her family, she agreed to return and marry him. It took Billy a year to accumulate the money, but finally he sent Eva a ring and five hundred dollars for her passage. He never heard from her again.

When Dennis found out that Eva had married someone else and that she had used Billy's money to buy a gas station, he did not have the heart to tell Billy. Instead, Dennis informed him that Eva had died of pneumonia. Although Billy eventually married, he spent the rest of his life grieving for his lost love and drinking to dull the pain. To those around him, Billy became a romantic hero, someone who had the courage to live and die for love; in a sense, he was also an exemplification of faith. His will to believe inspired those who knew him to believe in what reason told them was unlikely or impossible.

Child of My Heart

Child of My Heart is much simpler than McDermott's previous works, which are crowded with characters. This time, the first-person narrator is also the central character in the novel. In the 1960's, when she was fifteen, Theresa spent her summer babysitting and minding dogs for the wealthy people who had homes on the North Shore of Long Island; her Irish American parents had moved to that area so that their daughter could make the contacts that would enable her to move into upper-class society.

Although Theresa is aware of what is going on in the lives of the adults she encounters, she feels that her mission is to protect the vulnerable. One of her charges, Flora, a toddler, has been abandoned by her mother and is largely ignored by her father, a famous painter. Another is Theresa's cousin Daisy, who is spending the summer with her. Emotionally and physically neglected at home, Daisy clings to Theresa as her only security. Theresa also feels responsible for the Moran children, who wander about the neighborhood unwashed, ragged, hungry, and desperate for attention. Theresa cannot remedy the abysmal family situations of any of these children, but she can use her own imagination to create for them an illusory world filled with angels to keep them safe and lollipop trees to keep them happy.

Perhaps her love for the world of the imagination is the reason that Theresa chooses to lose her virginity to the seventy-year-old painter rather than to one of the other men who are eyeing her. In any case, in this episode, as in her dealings with dogs and children, she is in total control. What she cannot control is the fact of human cruelty and the threat of death, which stalks and then takes one of her charges. *Child of My Heart* was written as a response to the terrorist attacks on New York City of September 11, 2001. In Theresa, the author creates a heroine who uses her imagination to remake a world she cannot change. McDermott thus once again states her faith in the human spirit, empowered by grace, to transform human existence.

Rosemary M. Canfield Reisman

Bibliography

Carden, Mary Paniccia. "Making Love, Making History: (Anti)Romance in Alice McDermott's *At Weddings and Wakes* and *Charming Billy*." In *Double Plots: Romance and History*, edited by Susan Strehle and Mary Paniccia Carden. Jackson: University Press of Mississippi, 2003. Explains that romantic love is both a source of cultural identity and a cherished ideal for McDermott's characters, despite the fact that it repeatedly proves to be a shaky foundation for happiness.

Ebest, Sally Barr. "'Reluctant Catholics': Contemporary Irish-American Women Writers." In *The Catholic Church and Unruly Women Writers: Critical Essays*, edited by Jeana DelRosso, Leigh Eicke, and Ana Kothe. New York: Palgrave Macmillan, 2007. McDermott is among the authors discussed in this chapter within a larger work that focuses on the struggles of Western women writers within the Roman Catholic Church.

Jacobson, Beatrice. "Alice McDermott's Narrators." In *Too Smart to Be Sentimental: Contemporary Irish American Women Writers*, edited by Sally Barr Ebest and Kathleen McInerney. Notre Dame, Ind.: University of Notre Dame Press, 2008. Argues that McDermott's women narrators are particularly effective because they live on the margins between past and present, between Irish Catholic culture and the secular world, and between traditional views of gender roles and feminists' insistence on equality and independence.

McDermott, Alice. "Confessions of a Reluctant Catholic." *Commonweal* 127, no. 3 (February 11, 2000): 12-16. In a moving essay, the author describes her religious upbringing, her later rejection of her childhood faith, her belief that she could find the truth through her fiction, and her discovery that only in the Catholic Church could she find answers to the questions that were raised in her fiction.

Richards, Rand. "Charming Alice: A Unique Voice in American Fiction." *Commonweal* 125, no. 6 (March 27, 1998): 10-13. Provides an insightful overview of McDermott's works. Comments on her development over the course of her career, points out major themes, and discusses at length the tension between her narrative patterns and issues of identity.

ROSS MACDONALD

Kenneth Millar

Born: Los Gatos, California; December 13, 1915
Died: Santa Barbara, California; July 11, 1983
Also known as: Kenneth Millar; John Macdonald; John Ross Macdonald

Principal long fiction

The Dark Tunnel, 1944 (as Kenneth Millar; also known as *I Die Slowly*, 1955)
Trouble Follows Me, 1946 (as Millar; also known as *Night Train*, 1955)
Blue City, 1947 (as John Macdonald; reissued as *Harper*, 1966)
The Drowning Pool, 1950
The Ivory Grin, 1952 (reissued as *Marked for Murder*, 1953)
Meet Me at the Morgue, 1953 (as John Ross Macdonald; also known as *Experience with Evil*, 1954)
The Barbarous Coast, 1956
The Doomsters, 1958
The Galton Case, 1959
The Ferguson Affair, 1960
The Wycherly Woman, 1961
The Zebra-Striped Hearse, 1962
The Chill, 1964
The Far Side of the Dollar, 1965
Black Money, 1966
The Instant Enemy, 1968
The Goodbye Look, 1969
The Underground Man, 1971
Sleeping Beauty, 1973
The Blue Hammer, 1976

Other literary forms

Ross Macdonald's reputation is based primarily on his twenty-four published novels, particularly on the eighteen that feature private detective Lew Archer. He also published a collection of short stories, *Lew Archer, Private Investigator* (1977), which includes all the stories from an earlier collection, *The Name Is Archer* (1955). *Self-Portrait: Ceaselessly into the Past* (1981) gathers a selection of his essays, interviews, and lectures about his own work and about other writers, including two essays first published in his *On Crime Writing* (1973). *The Archer Files: The Complete Short Stories of Lew Archer, Private Investigator* (2007) collects all the brief Archer fiction, including never-before-published pieces that remained unfinished by Macdonald. Macdonald also wrote dozens of book reviews and several articles on conservation and politics.

Achievements

Ross Macdonald was recognized early in his career as the successor to Dashiell Hammett and Raymond Chandler in the field of realistic crime fiction, and his detective, Lew Archer, was recognized as the successor to Sam Spade and Philip Marlowe. Macdonald's advance over his predecessors was in the greater emphasis he placed on psychology and character, creating a more humane and complex detective and more intricate plotting. He is generally credited with raising the detective novel to the level of serious literature. The Mystery Writers of America awarded him Edgar Allan Poe scrolls in 1962 and 1963. In 1964, *The Chill* was awarded the Silver Dagger by the Crime Writers' Association of Great Britain. The same organization gave his next novel, *The Far Side of the Dollar*, the Golden Dagger as the best crime novel of the year.

Macdonald served as president of the Mystery Writers of America in 1965 and was made a Grand Master of that organization in 1974. In a review of *The Goodbye Look* in *The New York Times Book Review*, William Goldman called the Lew Archer books "the finest series of detective novels ever written by an American." His work has gained popular as well as critical acclaim: *The Goodbye Look*, *The Underground Man*, *Sleeping Beauty*, and *The Blue Hammer* were all national best sellers. Three of his books have been made into successful motion pictures, two starring Paul Newman as Lew Archer: *The Moving Target*, which was made into the film *Harper* (1966), and the film version of *The Drowning Pool*, which was released in 1975. *The Three Roads* was adapted into the film *Double Negative* (1980).

BIOGRAPHY

Ross Macdonald, whose given name is Kenneth Millar, was born in Los Gatos, California, on December 13, 1915. He published his early novels as Millar or John Macdonald or John Ross Macdonald, but settled on the pseudonym Ross Macdonald by the time he wrote *The Barbarous Coast*, in order to avoid being confused with two other famous mystery writers: his wife, Margaret Millar, whom he had married in 1938, and John D. Macdonald.

Ross Macdonald's family moved to Vancouver, British Columbia, soon after he was born, and he was reared and educated in Canada. After he graduated with honors from the University of Western Ontario in 1938, he taught English and history at a high school in Toronto and began graduate work at the University of Michigan in Ann Arbor during the summers. He returned to the United States permanently in 1941, when he began full-time graduate studies at Ann Arbor, receiving his master's degree in English in 1943. During World War II, he served as a communications officer aboard an escort carrier in the Pacific and participated in the battle for Okinawa. In 1951, he was awarded a doctorate in English from the University of Michigan, writing his dissertation on the psychological criticism of Samuel Taylor Coleridge. Macdonald belonged to the American Civil Liberties Union and, as a dedicated conservationist, was a member of the Sierra Club and helped found the Santa Barbara, California, chapter of the National Audubon Society. He lived in Santa Barbara from 1946 until his death from complications of Alzheimer's disease on July 11, 1983.

ANALYSIS

Ross Macdonald's twenty-four novels fall fairly neatly into three groups: Those in which Lew Archer does not appear form a distinct group, and the Archer series itself may be separated into two periods. His first four books, *The Dark Tunnel*, *Trouble Follows Me*, *Blue City*, and *The Three Roads*, together with two later works, *Meet Me at the Morgue* and *The Ferguson Affair*, do not feature Lew Archer. These six novels, especially the first three, are typical treatments of wartime espionage or political corruption and are primarily of interest to the extent that they prefigure the concerns of later works: *The Three Roads*, for example, contains Macdonald's first explicit use of the Oedipus myth as a plot structure and of California as a setting.

The first six Archer books—*The Moving Target*, *The Drowning Pool*, *The Way Some People Die*, *The Ivory Grin*, *Find a Victim*, and *The Barbarous Coast*—introduce and refine the character of Archer, build the society and geography of California into important thematic elements, and feature increasingly complex plots, with multiple murders and plot lines. Archer still shows traces of the influence of the hard-boiled detectives of Hammett and Chandler (he is named for Miles Archer, Sam Spade's partner in Hammett's *The Maltese Falcon*, 1930, but is closely patterned on Philip Marlowe), but he also shows marks of the sensitivity and patience, the reliance on un-

Ross Macdonald. (Hal Boucher)

derstanding and analysis, that separate him from his models. Even in these early books, Archer is more often a questioner than a doer.

The Doomsters

The next twelve Archer novels constitute Macdonald's major achievement. Crimes in these books are not usually committed by professional criminals but rather by middle-class people going through emotional crises. They followed a period of personal crisis in Macdonald's own life, during which he underwent psychotherapy. All these novels deal more or less explicitly with psychological issues. *The Doomsters*, although begun before Macdonald's psychoanalysis, presents his first extended treatment of the plot of intrafamilial relations that dominates all the later books.

Carl Hallman, a psychologically disturbed young man, appears at Archer's door after escaping from the state mental hospital. He has been confined there as a murder suspect in the mysterious death of his father. Although he knows himself to be legally innocent, he feels guilty for having quarreled violently with his father on the night of his death. This Oedipal tension between father and son, following the pattern of Sigmund Freud's famous interpretation, often serves as the mainspring of the plot in Macdonald's later novels. After hiring Archer to investigate the death, Carl panics and escapes again as Archer is returning him to the hospital. Carl's brother, Jerry, and sister-in-law, Zinnie, are subsequently murdered under circumstances that appear to incriminate Carl.

As it turns out, the case really began three years earlier, with the apparently accidental drowning of Carl's mother, Alicia. She had forced Carl's wife, Mildred, to undergo an abortion at gunpoint at the hands of Dr. Grantland. Mildred hit Alicia over the head with a bottle when she came out of anesthesia and assumed that she had killed her. Dr. Grantland actually killed Alicia and made it look like a drowning, but he conceals this fact and uses his power over Mildred, who is becoming psychologically unstable, to persuade her to kill Carl's father. He has designs on the family's money, and Mildred is greedy herself. She is also influenced, however, by her hatred of her own father, who deserted her mother, and by her desire to possess Carl entirely, to gain his love for herself by eliminating conflicting familial claims to it. She murders his brother and sister-in-law, his only remaining family, as she increasingly loses touch with sanity.

Women are frequently the murderers in Macdonald's books, and he analyzed the reasons behind this in an interview. He considered that people who have been victims tend to victimize others in turn, and he regarded American society as one that systematically victimizes women. Mildred's difficult childhood and gunpoint abortion provide a clear illustration of this theme.

The Galton Case

While the focus on family psychology constituted a clean break with the Hammett and Chandler school as well as with most of Macdonald's own early work, the next Archer novel, *The Galton Case*, was of even greater importance for Macdonald's career. In *The Doomsters*, the case is rooted in a crime committed three years earlier; in *The Galton Case*, as in most of the novels to follow, the present crime is rooted deeper in the past, in the preceding generation. This gives Macdonald the means to show the long-term effects of the influence of the family on each of its members. The elderly Maria Galton hires Archer to trace her son, Anthony, who had stolen money from his father after a quarrel (reminiscent of that between Carl Hallman and his father) and run off to the San Francisco area with his pregnant wife, Teddy, twenty-three years before. Archer discovers that Anthony, calling himself John Brown, was murdered not long after his disappearance. He also finds a young man calling himself John Brown, Jr., who claims to be searching for his long-lost father. Events lead Archer to Canada, where he learns that the young man is Theo Fredericks, the son of Nelson Fredericks and his wife. Maria Galton's lawyer, Gordon Sable, has planned Theo's masquerade as her grandson to acquire her money when she dies. Yet a further plot twist reveals that Theo really is Anthony Galton's son. Fred Nelson had murdered Anthony twenty-three years before for the money he had stolen from his father and had taken Anthony's wife and son as his own under the name Fredericks.

This summary does not reflect the true complexity of the novel, which ties together a number of other elements, but does bring out the major theme of the son searching for his father, a theme that will recur in later works such as *The Far Side of the Dollar*, *The Instant*

Enemy, *The Goodbye Look*, *The Underground Man*, and *The Blue Hammer*. As Macdonald explains in his essay "Writing *The Galton Case*" (1973), this plot is roughly shaped on his own life. His own father left him and his mother when he was three years old. Like Macdonald, John Brown, Jr., was born in California, grew up in Canada, and attended the University of Michigan before returning to California. It is interesting that each man assumed his lost father's name: Macdonald was Kenneth Millar's father's middle name. This transformation of personal family history into fiction seems to have facilitated the breakthrough that led Macdonald to write the rest of his novels about varying permutations of the relations between parents and children.

THE ZEBRA-STRIPED HEARSE

The exploration of the relations between three generations of fathers and sons in *The Galton Case* was followed by examinations of father and daughter relationships in *The Wycherly Woman* and *The Zebra-Striped Hearse*. Macdonald always counted the latter among his favorites for its intensity and range. In *The Zebra-Striped Hearse*, Archer is hired by Mark Blackwell to investigate his daughter Harriet's fiancé, Burke Damis, with a view to preventing their marriage. The implication is made that Mark sees Damis as a rival for his daughter's love. Archer discovers that Damis is really Bruce Campion and is suspected of having murdered his wife, Dolly, and another man, Quincy Ralph Simpson. Suspicion shifts to Mark when it is revealed that he is the father of Dolly's baby and then to Mark's wife, Isobel, who knew Dolly as a child. Harriet disappears and Mark confesses to murdering her, Dolly, and Simpson before committing suicide. Yet Archer believes that Harriet is still alive and tracks her down in Mexico. She had killed Dolly to clear the way for her marriage to Bruce and had also killed Simpson when he discovered her crime. Underlying her motive for Dolly's murder, however, is another Freudian pattern. The child of Mark and Dolly is Harriet's half brother, making Dolly a sort of mother figure and, by extension, making her husband, Bruce, a sort of father figure. Harriet thus symbolically kills her mother and marries her father.

THE CHILL

The Chill features one of Macdonald's most complex plots, but at its center is another basic family relationship, this time between a mother and son. Archer is brought into the case by Alex Kincaid, who hires him to find his wife, Dolly, who has disappeared the day after their wedding after a visit from an unknown man. The visitor turns out to have been her father, Thomas McGee, who has just been released from prison after serving a ten-year sentence for the murder of his wife and Dolly's mother, Constance. Later, it is revealed that he had convinced her of his innocence and told her that Constance was having an affair with Roy Bradshaw.

To learn more about Roy, Dolly has left Alex to go to work for Roy's mother, Mrs. Bradshaw, as a driver and companion. Shortly thereafter, she is found, hysterical, at the Bradshaws', talking about the murder of her college counselor, Helen Haggerty. Helen is soon discovered murdered and the weapon used is found under Dolly's mattress, though under circumstances that suggest that it may have been planted there. Archer learns from Helen's mother that she had been deeply affected by a death that occurred twenty years before. Luke Deloney had been killed in a shooting that was ruled accidental on the basis of an investigation that was conducted by Helen's father, but Helen was convinced that the facts had been covered up. Luke's widow admits to Archer that there had been a cover-up, that her husband committed suicide. Archer later discovers another connection between the recent death and those of ten and twenty years ago: Roy Bradshaw was the elevator boy at the building in which Luke died.

Investigation of Roy reveals that he has been secretly married to Laura Sutherland, having recently obtained a divorce from a woman named Letitia Macready. Archer confronts Mrs. Bradshaw with the latter fact (though not the former), and after an initial denial she confirms that twenty years ago Roy had briefly been married to a much older woman. Letitia turns out to have been the sister of Luke's wife, and it was rumored that she was having an affair with her sister's husband. Letitia apparently died in Europe during World War II, shortly after Luke's death. Archer eventually draws a fuller story out of Roy: Luke, who was indeed Letitia's lover, found her in bed with Roy. There had been a violent struggle, during which Letitia accidentally shot and killed Luke. Roy married her and took her to Europe, later returning with her to America. He had been leading a secret double life ever since, concealing Letitia, now quite old and sick, from all of his friends as well as from the police and, especially, from his possessive mother. During this confession, Archer answers a telephone call and hears Laura, who believes that she is speaking to Roy, tell him that "she" has discovered their secret marriage. Roy attacks Archer at this news and escapes in his car to attempt to intercept the other woman, who had vowed to kill Laura. Roy is killed when Mrs. Bradshaw's car crashes into his. Archer knows by now that Mrs. Bradshaw is not Roy's mother, but his first wife: She is Letitia Macready.

Roy has acted out the Oedipal drama of the death of a father figure, Letitia's lover Luke, and the marriage to a mother figure, the older woman who posed as his real mother. (Macdonald develops the obverse of this plot in *Black Money*, which pairs a young woman with a much older man.) Letitia murdered Constance McGee because Roy had been having an affair with her and murdered Helen Haggerty in the belief that it was she rather than Laura Sutherland whom Roy was currently seeing.

This unraveling of the plot has come a long way from Alex Kincaid's request that Archer find his wife, but one of the characteristics of Macdonald's later novels is the way in which seemingly unrelated events and characters come together. The deeper Archer goes into a set of circumstances involving people who know one another, the more connectedness he finds. These novels all have large casts of characters and a series of crimes, often occurring decades apart. Once the proper connections are made, however, there is usually only one murderer and one fundamental relationship at the center of the plot. All the disparate elements, past and present, hang together in one piece.

While Freudian themes continued to dominate Macdonald's work, he often combined them with elements adapted from other stories from classical mythology or the Bible. *The Far Side of the Dollar* has been seen as a modern, inverted version of the story of Ulysses and Penelope. Jasper Blevins, the fratricidal murderer of *The Instant Enemy*, explicitly draws the analogy between his story and that of Cain and Abel. He has also murdered one of his stepfathers, adding the Oedipal master plot to the biblical plot, and murdered his own wife in one of the series' most violent books, perhaps reflecting the violence of the Vietnam War period, during which the book was written. The complex events of *The Goodbye Look* are catalyzed by the search for a gold box that is specifically compared to Pandora's box. Again the myth is combined with the primal story of the parricide, this time committed by a child. All three of these books also repeat the quintessential Macdonald plot of a young man's search for his missing father.

THE UNDERGROUND MAN

The search for the absent father also sets in motion the events of *The Underground Man*, probably the most admired of Macdonald's works. This novel, together with his next, *Sleeping Beauty*, also reflects its author's abiding concern with conservation. Each novel examines an ecological crime as well as a series of crimes committed against individuals. In *Sleeping Beauty*, Macdonald uses an offshore oil spill, inspired by the 1967 spill near his home in Santa Barbara, as a symbol of the moral life of the society responsible for it, in particular that of the Lennox family, which runs the oil corporation and is also the locus of the series of murders in the book. In *The Underground Man*, the disaster of a human-made brush fire serves similar ends.

The story begins unexceptionally: Archer is taking a day off at home, feeding the birds in his yard. He strikes up an acquaintance with young Ronny Broadhurst and Ronny's mother, Jean, who are staying at the home of Archer's neighbors. The boy's father, Stanley, disrupts the meeting when he drives up with a young girl, later identified as Sue Crandall, and takes his son to visit Stanley's mother, Elizabeth Broadhurst. They never pay the planned visit, and when Jean hears that a fire has broken out in that area, she enlists Archer to help her look for them. On the way there, Jean explains that her husband has gradually become obsessed by his search for his father, Leo, who apparently ran away with Ellen Kilpatrick, the wife of a neighbor, Brian, some fifteen years ago. It turns out that Stanley, accompanied by Ronny and Sue, obtained a key from Elizabeth's gardener, Fritz Snow, and had gone up to her cabin on a mountain nearby. There, Archer finds Stanley, murdered and half-buried. The fire originated from a cigarillo Stanley dropped when he was killed, creating a causal as well as symbolic link between the personal and ecological disasters.

After an investigation that is complex even by Macdonald's standards, Archer is able to reconstruct the past events that explain those of the present. The seeds of the present crimes are found in the previous generation. Eighteen years ago, Leo Broadhurst got Martha Nickerson, an underage girl, pregnant. She ran away with Fritz Snow and Al Sweetner in a car they stole from Lester Crandall. The incident was planned by Leo and Martha to provide a scapegoat to assume the paternity of her coming child. When they were tracked down, Al went to jail for three years, Fritz was sentenced to work in a forestry camp for six months, and Martha married Lester Crandall.

Three years later, Leo was having an affair with Ellen Kilpatrick. She went to Reno to obtain a divorce from her husband, Brian, and waited there for Leo to join her. While she was gone, however, Leo went up to the cabin with Martha and their child, Sue. Brian, who knew about his wife's affair with Leo and wanted revenge, discovered the renewal of this earlier affair and informed Leo's wife, Elizabeth. She went up to the mountain cabin and shot her husband, believing that she killed him. Stanley, who had followed his mother that night, was an aural witness to the shooting of his father, as was Susan, also Leo's child. Yet Leo had not been killed by the bullet. He was stabbed to death, as he lay unconscious, by Edna Snow, Fritz's mother, in revenge for the trouble that Leo and Martha's affair had caused her son and also as a self-appointed agent of judgment on Leo's adulteries. She forced Fritz and Al to bury Leo near the cabin. Fifteen years later, on almost the same spot, she murders Stanley, who is on the verge of discovering his father's body and Edna's crime. Life moves in a circle as Ronny witnesses Stanley's death in the same place that Stanley witnessed Leo's shooting. The connection is reinforced by Sue's presence at both events.

THE BLUE HAMMER

The last novel Macdonald wrote is *The Blue Hammer*, and whether he consciously intended it to be the last, it provides in certain ways an appropriate conclusion to the series. It is the first time, apart from a brief interlude in *The Goodbye Look*, that Archer has a romantic interest. The effects of a lack of love preoccupy all the Archer novels, and Archer recognizes in this book that the same lack has had its effects on him. He has been single since his divorce from his wife, Sue, which took place before the first book begins. In the last book, he meets and soon falls in love with Betty Jo Siddon, a young newspaper reporter. Yet Macdonald knew that Raymond Chandler was unable to continue the Philip Marlowe novels after marrying off his detective, and perhaps he intended to end his own series similarly. It seems that the genre requires a detective who is himself without personal ties, who is able to and perhaps driven to move freely into and then out of the lives of others. Indeed, the involvement of Betty in the case does create a tension between Archer's personal and professional interests.

Another suggestion that *The Blue Hammer* may have been intended to be the last of the Archer novels lies in its symmetry with the first, *The Moving Target*. In the earlier book, Archer kills a man in a struggle in the ocean, the only such occurrence in the eighteen books and an indication of the extent to which the compassionate Archer differs from his more violent predecessors. In the last book, he finds himself in a similar struggle, but this time manages to save his adversary. Archer specifically parallels the two events and feels that he has balanced out his earlier sin, somehow completing a pattern.

The plot of *The Blue Hammer* is built around the Dostoevskian theme of the double, a theme that Macdonald treated before in *The Wycherly Woman*, in which Phoebe Wycherly assumes the identity of her murdered mother, and in *The Instant Enemy*, in which Jasper Blevins takes on the role of his murdered half brother. The motif is developed here in its most elaborate form and combined with the familiar themes of the crimes of the past shaping those of the present and of the son's search for his true father, forming an appropriate summation of the major themes of MacDonald's entire Archer series.

Thirty-two years ago, Richard Chantry stole the paintings of his supposed half brother, William Mead, then serving in the Army, and married William's girlfriend Francine. William murdered Richard when he returned and assumed his identity as Francine's husband, though he had already married a woman named Sarah and had a son with her named Fred. Seven years later, Gerard Johnson, a friend of William from the Army, appears at William's door with Sarah and Fred, threatening to blackmail him. William kills Gerard and then takes his name, in a doubling of the theme of doubleness. He returns to live with Sarah and Fred and remains a recluse for twenty-five years to hide his crimes.

The case begins for Archer when he is called in to locate a painting that has been stolen from Jack Biemeyer. He learns that it was taken by Fred Johnson, who wanted to study it to determine whether it was a recent work by the famous artist Richard Chantry, who had mysteriously vanished twenty-five years before. If genuine, it would establish that the painter was still alive. Fred had seen similar pictures in the Johnson home and had formed the idea that Chantry might be his real father. William steals the painting, which is one of his own works, in a doubling of his earlier theft of his own paintings from Richard. The painting had been sold by Sarah to an art dealer, and William is forced to kill again to prevent the discovery of his true identity and his earlier murders. By the book's guardedly positive resolution, three generations of men—Fred Johnson; his father, William Mead; and Jack Biemeyer, who turns out to be William's father—have all come to the admission or recognition of their previously concealed identities and have come to a kind of redemption through their suffering.

Macdonald's work, in terms of quantity as well as quality, constitutes an unparalleled achievement in the detective genre. The twenty-four novels, particularly the eighteen that feature Lew Archer, form a remarkably coherent body of work both stylistically and thematically. The last twelve Archer books have received especially high critical as well as popular acclaim and have secured Macdonald's standing as the author of the finest series of detective novels ever written, perhaps the only such series to have bridged the gap between popular and serious literature.

William Nelles

Other major works

SHORT FICTION: *The Name Is Archer*, 1955; *Lew Archer, Private Investigator*, 1977; *Strangers in Town: Three Newly Discovered Mysteries*, 2001 (Tom Nolan, editor); *The Archer Files: The Complete Short Stories of Lew Archer, Private Investigator*, 2007 (Nolan, editor).

NONFICTION: *On Crime Writing*, 1973; *Self-Portrait: Ceaselessly into the Past*, 1981 (Ralph B. Sipper, editor).

Bibliography

Bruccoli, Matthew J. *Ross Macdonald*. San Diego, Calif.: Harcourt Brace Jovanovich, 1984. Describes the development of Macdonald's popular reputation as a prolific author of detective fiction and his critical reputation as a writer of literary merit. Includes illustrations, an appendix with an abstract of his doctoral thesis, notes, a bibliography, and an index.

Bruccoli, Matthew J., and Richard Layman, eds. *Hardboiled Mystery Writers: Raymond Chandler, Dashiell Hammett, Ross Macdonald*. New York: Carroll & Graf, 2002. A study of the lives and works of Macdonald, Dashiell Hammett, and Raymond Chandler. Includes photographs, reproductions of manuscript pages, interviews, articles, excerpts from earlier studies, letters, and contemporary reviews.

Gale, Robert. *A Ross Macdonald Companion*. Westport, Conn.: Greenwood Press, 2002. A Macdonald reference work with alphabetically arranged entries on his novels, fictional characters, family members, and professional acquaintances. The entries about the novels offer plot summaries, lists of characters, and brief critical commentaries. Includes a select bibliography and a chronology.

Kreyling, Michael. *The Novels of Ross Macdonald*. Columbia: University of South Carolina Press, 2005. An examination of eighteen detective novels by Macdonald. Kreyling compares Macdonald's work to that of Dashiell Hammett and Raymond Chandler, and he argues that Macdonald's books in particular deserve a more serious reading by critics of detective fiction.

Mahan, Jeffrey H. *A Long Way from Solving That One: Psycho/Social and Ethical Implications of Ross Macdonald's Lew Archer Tales*. Lanham, Md.: University Press of America, 1990. Mahan explores the Lew Archer stories and their importance in the detective fiction canon from a variety of perspectives, applying social, ethical, and Freudian theories to Macdonald's fiction. Includes a bibliography.

Nolan, Tom. *Ross Macdonald: A Biography*. New York: Scribner, 1999. The first full-length biography of Macdonald, providing many previously unknown details of his life. Nolan also discusses the origins of Macdonald's novels and critical responses they have received.

Schopen, Bernard A. *Ross Macdonald*. Boston: Twayne, 1990. A sound introductory study that examines Macdonald's development of the Lew Archer character, his mastery of the form of the detective novel, and the maturation of his art culminating in *The Underground Man*. Includes detailed notes and an annotated bibliography.

Sipper, Ralph B., ed. *Ross Macdonald: Inward Journey*. Santa Barbara, Calif.: Cordelia Editions, 1984. This collection of twenty-seven articles includes two by Macdonald—one a transcription of a speech about mystery fiction and the other a letter to a publisher that discusses Raymond Chandler's work in relation to his own.

Skinner, Robert E. *The Hard-Boiled Explicator: A Guide to the Study of Dashiell Hammett, Raymond Chandler, and Ross Macdonald*. Metuchen, N.J.: Scarecrow Press, 1985. An indispensable volume for readers interested in finding unpublished dissertations as well as mainstream criticism on the three writers. Includes brief introductions to each author, followed by annotated bibliographies of books, articles, and reviews.

Speir, Jerry. *Ross Macdonald*. New York: Frederick Ungar, 1978. A good introduction to Macdonald's work, with a brief biography and a discussion of his novels. Includes chapters on his character Lew Archer, on alienation and other themes, on Macdonald's writing style, and on scholarly criticism. Contains a bibliography, notes, and an index.

JOSEPH McELROY

Born: Brooklyn, New York; August 21, 1930
Also known as: Joseph Prince McElroy

Principal long fiction

A Smuggler's Bible, 1966
Hind's Kidnap: A Pastoral on Familiar Airs, 1969
Ancient History: A Paraphrase, 1971
Lookout Cartridge, 1974
Plus, 1977
Women and Men, 1987
The Letter Left to Me, 1988
Actress in the House, 2003

Other literary forms

Joseph McElroy's literary reputation stands on his achievements as a novelist. A number of excerpts from his massive novel *Women and Men* first appeared in short-story form; the excellence of three of these pieces ("The Future," "The Message for What It Was Worth," and "Daughter of the Revolution") was acknowledged by their selection for the anthologies *O. Henry Prize Stories* and *The Best American Short Stories*. In addition, McElroy has published a number of uncollected essays on topics as various as the Apollo 17 launch, the influence on his generation of Vladimir Nabokov's fiction, and autobiographical aspects of his own work. Between 1971 and 1976 he was also a regular reviewer for *The New York Times Book Review*. In 2003, McElroy collected some of his most distinguished journalistic pieces—a representative selection of book reviews but also essays on science and technology (an abiding interest in his fiction) as well as his probing analysis of the terrorist attacks on the United States of September 11, 2001—in a volume titled *Exponential*, released through an Italian publisher.

Achievements

From the start, Joseph McElroy was received as one of the generation of American novelists that includes Robert Coover, Thomas Pynchon, and William Gaddis—writers of long and technically demanding fictions. Among them, McElroy remains the dark star, outshone by their well-publicized brilliance while being acknowledged among his peers as a writer's writer, one who is committed to giving fictional order to a complex "information society" by optimistically recognizing its possibilities for narrative art and human growth. In 1977, McElroy's writing was acclaimed by an Award in Literature from the American Academy of Arts and Letters. Still, the regard of critics was slow in coming, and reviewers have long argued that the complexity of internal reference and detail in McElroy's work is too demanding of the reader. In a 1979 interview, McElroy countered that he continued to "hope . . . for readers who would be willing to commit themselves to a strenuous, adventurous fiction." As the critical community has begun to explicate the intricate achievement of McElroy's fictions, and as the author's place within his generation of audacious postmodern experimenters becomes clear, readers have begun to appreciate how McElroy's fictions upend the traditional expectations of the reader's function and in turn open the reader toward an ascendant vision that expresses a stubborn faith in the connectedness of experience, an affirmation that places McElroy in clear contrast to the often bleak vision of his far more noted contemporaries.

Biography

Joseph Prince McElroy was born in Brooklyn, New York, on August 21, 1930, and has lived near there for most of his life. He received a baccalaureate degree from Williams College in 1951 and a master of arts degree from Columbia University in 1952. After two years with the U.S. Coast Guard (1952-1954), he returned to graduate studies at Columbia, completing his Ph.D. in 1962 with a dissertation on seventeenth century poet Henry King. From 1956 to 1961, he held positions as instructor and assistant professor of English at the University of New Hampshire. Beginning in 1964, he was a full professor of English at Queens College, City University of New York, until his retirement in 1995 (although he maintained his residence in Manhattan). McElroy has been a visiting professor or a writer-in-residence at a number of major universities, has received a wide range of fellowships and awards, and has served editorial terms on several prestigious literary magazines.

Analysis

Joseph McElroy's novels unfold in the topographies of mind. He has called them "neural neighborhoods." Within those imaginary spaces, McElroy's fictions grow from a profound desire for order, for a meaningful landscape of human intentions and actions. Also, they grow from a profound recognition that such orders may be unobtainable amid the fragmenting stresses of advanced machine culture. The point, as his novels illustrate, is not to kick against this crux but to set the mind in motion within it, thus to create form and meaning. This precept is the source of both difficulty and great achievement in McElroy's writing.

Not that McElroy's neural landscapes stand apart from ordinary surroundings—quite the opposite: His novels are saturated with the stuff of contemporary society, with references to and metaphors from urban culture, and from such wide-ranging pursuits as cinematography, information processing, linguistics, and the space program. Richly detailed and technically specific, these familiar endeavors illustrate the fragmentary nature of human knowledge. At the same time, they point out unsuspected possibilities for human growth. McElroy's narrator-protagonists are imbued with an almost claustrophobic variety of concise memories and everyday desires, yet within these mental topographies they are driven to discover order, or "plot," for novels are also "plotted," and it is of the essence of McElroy's novels that the action, the narrators' attempted discoveries, be seen as contemporary variations on the detective plot. They solve no significant enigmas. Not "representations" of events that have been rarefied by memory, McElroy's fictions are instead "demonstrations" of the complexities involved in reconstructing any past event. Inevitably the characters' memories involve their own categories of feeling and linguistic mapping, which themselves become objects of scrutiny. The best one can do, suggests McElroy, is to "smuggle" or "kidnap" a perception or idea over the received boundary of some other. By thus learning to manipulate the inadequacies and paradoxes of human knowledge, one surmounts them.

This brief sketch of McElroy's principal concerns will suggest the interests he shares with many modern and contemporary writers. With modernists such as Marcel Proust and André Gide, he is concerned to show both the complexity and the potential illicitness of narratively reconstructed events, which are "counterfeit" creations precisely to the degree that they recognize themselves as ordered rememberings of life's dismembered orderings. With contemporaries such as Michel Butor, William Gaddis, Nicholas Moseley, and Thomas Pynchon, McElroy reflects on the linguistic nature of this narrative activity. Like them, he sees the ability to manipulate hypothetical, alternative structures—for example, the worlds of "stories"—as a condition of social existence, and he reflects on how we also hastily suppose that continuity and causality are absolute requirements of that structuring work.

A Smuggler's Bible

A Smuggler's Bible is McElroy's brilliant first articulation of these themes. By the author's own account, this novel was not his first, but it developed after several aborted attempts at a rather conventionally sequential, causal type of long narrative. Its title describes the book's main emblem: A "smuggler's Bible" is a hollowed-out volume designed for carrying contraband over borders. Similarly, McElroy's narrative develops by making illicit leaps. Even though its eight parts are essentially disconnected, the reader still "smuggles" bits of information across their boundaries to reconstruct a "story" about its narrator-protagonist, David Brooke. In fact, readers are encouraged in this by another, omniscient narrative voice, which appears in short interchapters. This voice advertises itself as David's "creator" and comments on his task, itself also the reader's, which is to "analyze, synthesize, [and] assimilate" details gleaned by "projecting" oneself into others' experience. This is the task framed by a conventional, "realistic" novel. Yet a smuggler's Bible is also a clever deception: an illegal, profane business tucked inside an authorized, holy cover. In similar ways, David's eightfold story, a kind of experimental writing, can be read as trying, and failing, to disguise itself as an artistically conventional novel replete with causal plot.

The essentials of that inner narrative are as follows. David and his wife, Ellen, are passengers aboard a ship, the *Arkadia*, bound for London. There David must deliver to a mysterious "Old Man" the manuscript of a book he has written, each of its eight parts the story of an event or of characters with special significance in his own life. The ship's passage takes eight days. During that time, at the rate of a story per day, David struggles to give the manuscript continuity. He provides narrative transitions and "smuggles" characters from one narrative into another. He even attempts to structure each story according to some mythic subtext, such as those of Oedipus, Midas, or the Golden Ass. This technique of highly self-conscious parody—what poet T. S. Eliot called the "mythic method" in reference to James Joyce's *Ulysses* (1922)—is revealed as yet another mode of smuggling, which has lost that sacred magic it once promised to modernist writers. Thus, while David may think of himself as "an epistemological reuniac" attempting an integral, totalizing reconstruction of the past, *A Smuggler's Bible*, especially in its interchapters, tends contrariwise toward disjunction and incompleteness. McElroy has said that it "was designed to fracture."

Throughout this long, stylistically brilliant performance, the image one gets (not a "picture" but an immanence or field theory) is of women and men existing in a grand relational network. Yet only David's acts of memory hold that web in balance. This field of charged particles did exist, and had "reality," but only when a single mind was composing it, and that mind is, in the best sense of the term, *trivial*: It finds pattern and meaning in the accidental minutiae of ordinary lives. A few examples: In the fourth of his "principal parts," David recounts the story of his acquaintance, at the University of New Hampshire, with an intellectual con artist named Duke Amerchrome. An immensely popular historian and theorist of American culture, Duke engineered his fame on forged sources and blustering rhetoric. He is an exemplar of the literati who smuggle themselves into positions of "authority." Tony Tanner has asserted that the character is patterned on Norman Mailer, yet almost any other (such as Marshall McLuhan) would do, and one could also point to the autobiographical aspects and note that McElroy may have been exorcising personal as well as professional demons. In any event, much of Duke's story is transmitted to David through his son Michael, who discloses the man's use of counterfeited trivia about the Battle of Ticonderoga. Michael, however, has selfish motives for these disclosures, such as coveting his father's nubile young wife (Duke's third).

This Oedipal motif broadens; the idea of "shadowing" a (supposed) father, tracking him and absorbing the minutiae of his days until one knows enough to expose and supplant him, recurs in other chapters. The first memory concerns a bored rare-book dealer named Peter St. John who is being followed by a boy who thinks that the man resembles his father. In the second, David's association with a group of eccentric fellow boarders eventually centers on a rare-coin dealer named Pennitt, who may be a counterfeiter; whether he is or not is never certain, because the old man brushes David off before disclosing any conclusive evidence. In the final part, David's father spins through his last, trivial thoughts while dying of angina and rectal cancer. David *inhabits* these memories, seeking safe harbor between antinomies: the imploding heart of humanity, symbolizing powers of empathy and connection, versus the exploding rectum, David's symbol of dispersal and "apartness." The book ends there, with the mind shuttling in between, never resolving that antinomy but finding art in the act of composing.

Hind's Kidnap

Hind's Kidnap, McElroy's next novel, takes these ideas a step further. Once again the concern is with detection, with the mind moving inside a labyrinthine network of information that points equally to integral order and to zeros of disorder. This novel, however, falls short of its ambition. Critics have aptly noted that the book succeeds better in its idea than in its stylistic performance, which often becomes tiresome.

The reasons are several. One is that the narrator's attention to matters of trivial but feasibly significant detail achieves a still closer focus than in *A Smuggler's Bible*, but this attention must be borne by units of narrative (sentences on up to chapters) that strain from sheer length, and hence from the span of attention demanded of readers. Another reason, and doubtless an attempt to explain (that is, to naturalize) the first, is that in *Hind's Kidnap* the narrator-protagonist is virtually obsessed with the dialectic of detection.

The story is related by Jack Hind, a six-foot, seven-inch lookout tower of a man who, for years, has been intermittently tracking his way back and forth through the same case. A four-year-old boy, Hershey Laurel, was kidnapped from his rural home, and for seven years there has been no trace of the boy. Desperate to solve the enigma, Hind tells and retells the known facts to everyone he knows; in time, his auditors become so knowledgeable as to seem implicated in the original crime. Hind's recollections thus become a labyrinth without boundaries, as if all were "suspicioned" into the plot, often on the slightest of linguistic associations, such as a name. Midway through the narrative, with the book's reader now equally knowledgeable of the main "facts," it becomes necessary for Hind to "de-kidnap" everyone, to extricate them from the paranoid plottings of his own mind. Thus, Hind also becomes implicated. In the novel's second part, he turns his detective skills onto his own past: the early deaths of both parents, his childhood with a guardian (a linguist, as it happens), and the question of his own paternity (the guardian appears to have been his actual father). These matters explain his obsession. Hind's quest for the boy is a means of asserting his own guardianship, and so of questing into the self, of separating illusion from reality and discovering how he was misled by language. As the novel's subtitle—*A Pastoral on Familiar Airs*—implies, Hind thereby seeks to become a truer shepherd of both memories and the discourses used to shape them.

Ancient History

The intimidating density of *Ancient History* comes from McElroy's ongoing philosophical interrogation of language itself as a dynamic field within which meaning—and for that matter plot and character—is recovered only at great risk to the intricacy of the larger construction. Language cannot be relied on to "translate" experience into conventional linear narratives, those aesthetic structures that privilege the trajectory of character growth toward inevitable insight. Rather, McElroy conceives of language as a paraphrase of experience, a reinterpretation of experience in which the original text, or experience within the temporal world, is reconceived within a dynamic field that draws less on the artificial structures of narrative theory and more from mathematics (particularly Kurt Gödel), quantum physics, and, supremely, chaos theory. Indeed, in the novel, McElroy applies the liberating dynamic of paraphrase to the assumed realities of experience, a premise that anatomizes the complexities and viability of memory itself, the flimsy construction of responsibility, and ultimately the enterprise of friendship (all of which are, after all, exercises in paraphrasing experience into convenient terms). Language, for McElroy, is our only technology for clarifying the rush of experience into the consolation of design—yet those constructions, we find, are themselves fluid.

Here McElroy investigates that most stubborn of mysteries—suicide—and subjects its ambiguities to investigation by a resilient narrator who struggles to comprehend the logic of a friend's suicide, complicated because that friend did not leave a note. The narrator is named Cyrus, a name that recalls the greatest empire ruler of the pre-Christian era and suggests his daunting role as builder of a history, a designer of experience into clarity. Reeling from the suicide of his friend, identified as Dom, who was apparently a disenchanted activist unable to adjust to life after the counterculture movement of the 1960's, Cyrus writes ostensibly the narrative of a relationship between two men—Al, who hails from rural roots, and Bob, from the city—that comes, the reader realizes, to stand as his paraphrase of his own relationship with the dead Dom and thus represents Cyrus's searching history (his-story) using language to conceive the reassurance of explanation; indeed, the narrative acts as a kind of surrogate suicide note, the explanation Dom did not leave behind.

McElroy resists the expectations of such a premise—the friend's investigations will not yield comprehension. Indeed, Cyrus does not record experience but rather recovers telling moments in a fluid kind of associational logic (mystifying to a first-time reader), a free-flow field of consciousness that sorts through a childhood on the streets of Brooklyn (drawing on McElroy's own life), an assortment of love affairs, and ultimately Cyrus's relationship with his own shattered family. McElroy sets into play a resonating field of narrative premises that in turn reveals the delicate links that create a kind of community of human experience among four characters who remain stubbornly apart (anthropology figures as the novel's scientific motif). Structuring the forbidding density of the narrator's investigation into the past are two suggestive metaphors, diving (specifically a childhood experience diving into a Massachusetts quarry reservoir) and throwing a boomerang (tossed, apparently, off the Brooklyn Bridge when Cy was a child, out toward the Statue of Liberty), both suggesting the liberating (and terrifying) freedom of investigation, the scrutiny of experience that celebrates scrutiny itself.

Lookout Cartridge

Lookout Cartridge is arguably McElroy's best work. The plot crackles with action, and the style surges ahead in a declarative mode while never weakening the complex power of the novel's main idea. A further "demonstration" of the dynamics and the essential incompleteness of memory in an information society, *Lookout Cartridge* asks to be read as a mystery-thriller.

The narrator-protagonist, Cartwright, a filmmaker who has been collaborating with a director named Dagger DiGorro on a politically radical documentary project, is literally pushed into his detective research. The narrative opens with the momentary fall (as a result of mechanical failure) of a helicopter hovering over a terrorist explosion in New York, itself partly explained at the novel's end. This recollection spins Cartwright into another beginning: an unseen hand that pushed him violently down an escalator, a fall he transforms by half-coordinated steps into a self-preserving forward stagger. In the narrative order, Cartwright's second "fall" thus redeems the mindless near accident of his first. It also eventually emblematizes the detective activity as a type of half-random, half-volitional motion. For a novel preoccupied with kinds of drive (physical and cinematic, social and narrational, epistemological and historical), this paradox is crucial.

Persons unknown, for reasons that are never fully explained, want Cartwright and Dagger's film destroyed, along with Cartwright's shooting diary, Cartwright himself, and perhaps even members of Cartwright's family who have knowledge of the film at second hand. All of this is apparently necessary because the film may have inadvertently recorded minute details of "an international power struggle." It may have, but without replaying or at least mentally reconstructing the footage, Cartwright can never know for certain. Therefore he sets to work. Like McElroy's previous detectives, he takes up the fragmentary evidence: the remaining chunks of the diary, recollections (often prompted) of friends and associates, material objects—whatever comes to hand during his headlong plunge through England, where much of the footage was shot, and New York City.

This urgency of self-survival gives *Lookout Cartridge* a sense of immediate purpose missing from the more abstract plots of *Hind's Kidnap* and *Ancient His-*

tory and is something McElroy would capitalize on again in *Plus*. As Cartwright shuttles back and forth between London and New York, and between pieces of contrary evidence, his in-betweenness becomes the basis for an uncannily creative power. Though he imagines himself as a "lookout cartridge" of film inserted "in someone else's system," still Cartwright discovers how, "between blind coghood" (the camera as simple recording instrument) and "that sinister hint of godhead" (in the conspiracies of unknown others), he himself has the power—even by using purest accident—of pushing events toward disclosure. Indeed, Cartwright finally nails both his assailants and their banal secrets. This resolution is the result, equally, of his power to manipulate details of story and his power simply to act by lunging forward, by reacting. Through it all, readers "have" only this Cartwright-Cartridge: the mind as recording machine, the machine as uncanny intercessor for the mind. What the lens records will depend entirely on where one is, what one wants to see, how long one rolls the film, and, later, how it is spliced. The camera thus becomes, like the remembering human subject, part of a relational system or associational grid whose power is greater than that of its parts.

This idea underwrites the lexicons of cinematography and information processing evident on the novel's every page. There is much, much more. Cartwright's narrative also includes speculations on Mayan calendars, on Mercator maps, and on Stonehenge or the standing stones of Callanish as ancient data-processing systems; details about the topographies of Corsica, London, and New York; and countless oblique references to the conspiracy-racked politics of the 1960's and 1970's. Involving readers in this labyrinth of events, representation techniques, and forms of knowledge, *Lookout Cartridge* surpasses the excesses and the feigned completion of other contemporary encyclopedic novels, such as Pynchon's *Gravity's Rainbow* (1973) or Coover's *The Public Burning* (1977). By comparison to these, *Lookout Cartridge* makes far more demands on the reader.

As the title suggests, the reader is also inserted into this survival experience and discovers that what matters is not a final why, but how one might manipulate the journey. Many of the novel's critics, however, were so taken by its profusion of reference and detail that they missed commenting on one of its completed enigmas, a palpable bit of political absurdity worthy of Joseph Conrad's *The Secret Agent* (1907). That explosion in Chapter 1 was set off by a faction of Cartwright's assailants, who were terrorizing the city for towing their illegally parked car. This detail points to a wry, detached satire of a contemporary society in which politics is managed as sequences of media events.

Plus

At first glance, that potential for satire would also seem to be the motive force of McElroy's fifth novel, *Plus*, one of his most accessible works of fiction. Given the novel's premise, the chances for targeting the absurdities of contemporary "information society" were numerous. Its story concerns a disembodied brain inserted, cartridgelike, in an orbiting space platform called Imp, the computer for which he—or it—was programmed to be. The engineers dubbed the combination "Imp Plus." Relaying technical data, controlling Imp's self-sustaining internal environment, with its glucose-producing algae—these are its simple programmed functions. As a relational network, an ecosystem, however, Imp Plus is more than a mere machine. It has the power of self-induced growth. In sum, once more the narration unfolds in the topography, now absolute, of mind, and the primary action again involves the composition of self from fragments of memory.

In a reconstruction of its past and present states (made difficult by its linguistic limitations), Imp Plus forms a new identity. Looking backward from this perspective, its story is simple. Exposed to lethal doses of radiation, a space scientist donates his brain, and Imp Plus is launched as an experiment in photosynthesis and symbiosis—the algae providing necessary glucose for the brain, the brain respiring carbon dioxide necessary for the algae, the brain and its mechanical platform interpreting and relaying data. Then, however, the brain begins re-forming itself. Imp Plus expands inwardly by recovering discrete sensual memories and thereby reconstructing language. (In an elegantly structured argument, Christine Brooke-Rose has shown how this develops from a hypothetically "nonsensical" sentence by linguist Noam Chomsky: "Colorless green ideas sleep furiously.") Imp Plus also expands outward by linking the neural sites of previous sensory activity, such as vision, to the platform's circuitry. It thereby realizes the practical and virtual reciprocity of mind and matter, a discovery tantamount to the age-old philosopher's stone. It also begins disregarding and disobeying signals from Earth, and when Ground Control threatens fiery destruction, Imp Plus carries out a ploy that will carom the platform off Earth's atmosphere and into deep space. There Imp Plus envisions further growth—leaving matter behind to become pure light, the wholly disembodied "Plus" of McElroy's title.

Plus can be read as a recapitulation of the principal themes of McElroy's previous books—a work of summary and consolidation. With *Plus*, he had published five challenging novels in just over a decade; his sixth novel, *Women and Men*, was itself ten years in the writing.

Women and Men

Everything about *Women and Men* proclaims its enormous ambition. Its title has the immodest sweep of Fyodor Dostoevski's *Prestupleniye i nakazaniye* (1866; *Crime and Punishment*, 1886) or Leo Tolstoy's *Voyna i mir* (1865-1869; *War and Peace*, 1886). In sheer bulk, nearly twelve hundred pages, it easily outweighs any of McElroy's earlier books. In the complexity of its structure, the density of information it conveys, it is even more daunting than *Lookout Cartridge*. Reviewing the novel in *The Washington Post Book World*, Tom LeClair suggested that "*Women and Men* is the single book—fiction or nonfiction—that best manifests what human beings can know and be and imagine now and, just as importantly, in the future." Whether such claims will stand up is a matter for time to tell.

A first reading of *Women and Men* is essentially a reconnaissance mission. The action of the novel is set primarily in the mid-1970's. The two central characters—James Mayn, a journalist specializing in science and technology and economic issues, and Grace Kimball, a radical feminist guru—live in the same apartment building in New York. They do not know each other, but they have mutual acquaintances, and they are connected in more subtle ways as well. This pattern of coincidence is a model for the novel as a whole, which traces a multitude of unexpected connections both in the private lives and family histories of the characters and in the life of the planet.

While the intertwining stories of Mayn and Kimball constitute a loose narrative line, many chapters are self-contained vignettes that illuminate, from diverse perspectives, the relation between women and men at a time of significant change: change in assumptions concerning sexual roles, but also more broadly change in the assumptions by which we organize our experience. "The ways in which we embrace the world and embrace other people," McElroy has said, "can be more precise and clear than we sometimes think." Weather patterns, body chemistry, economic cycles—these are not merely esoteric academic subjects but rather the stuff of everyday life. All that is required is attentiveness to available knowledge.

Much of the knowledge that informs *Women and Men* is scientific, but this is complemented by a strong emphasis on what has been called New Age spirituality. Native American lore plays an important role in the book; Grace Kimball frequently invokes the Goddess (the primeval Earth Mother who, many feminists contend, was universally worshiped by humankind before the onset of patriarchy); and there are hints of reincarnation throughout the novel. Indeed, several long sections, set in the future, are given to a chorus of disembodied spirits who comment on the action and the characters of the main narrative. Here McElroy seems to suggest a collective consciousness in which individual identity is subsumed. It is not clear how literally this vision is to be taken; even readers who find it unpersuasive will be left with a vivid sense of intricate order within the dizzying multiplicity of things.

The Letter Left to Me

Though McElroy's *The Letter Left to Me* is his shortest novel, in several respects it is also his most complicated. On its surface, the story is simple enough. A mother delivers to her son a letter from his recently deceased father, which was written three years before the father's death. Soon, the boy's mother and stepgrandfather, impressed with the letter's contents, decide to distribute copies of it to friends and relatives. Eventually, a copy even ends up in the hands of a dean at the small New England college the boy attends. The dean, in turn, disseminates copies to the entire freshman class for analysis, believing that the letter contains lessons in survival.

As narrator, the son draws a parallel between the range of reactions to the letter and the pattern of events in his life. The letter itself is simple in style and replete with paternal platitudes, the most important of which is the father's admonition to his son to make something of himself, as the father had failed to do while at college. For McElroy the letter serves as a starting point to explore the intricate connections between the past and the present. By the time the letter leaves home, it has taken on a life of its own. No longer is it merely an inanimate object; it has become instead a mysterious metaphor.

As an object of interpretation, the letter represents the intrinsic distinction that McElroy sees between the spoken word and the written word. The writing process, he intimates, requires a degree of detachment from the body as words are transformed into the graphic form. As a consequence, the product (letter) and interpreter (reader) are distanced from the agent (writer). On the other hand, the words engaged in conversation are part of a collaborative effort between speaker and listener. The written word in effect moves beyond the author's control, where it easily can be appropriated and re-created by successive subjective explications. Ownership thus becomes an issue, as it does in *The Letter Left to Me* when the original letter evolves into something akin to a communal piece of property for all to claim through a process of interpretation. In the end the letter becomes a metaphor for the culture, with all its diversities and complexities.

There is no mistaking the autobiographical nature of many elements in *The Letter Left to Me*. Like the boy narrator, McElroy grew up in the 1940's in Brooklyn and attended a small New England college; like the narrator's father, McElroy's went to Harvard University. As critics have noted, the novel embraces nearly all of the major themes McElroy addresses in his earlier works. Among them are how the interdependence between people, and particularly family members, can be at once suffocating and comforting, how the continuities of life are connected, and how the reliance on the written word causes the culture to become a prisoner of vocabulary and of the convolutions of syntax. As a leading practitioner of postmodern fiction, McElroy aims to identify the forces shaping society and connect them in ways consistent with the truth.

Actress in the House

Given the intensely protected nature of McElroy's personal life—despite copious interviews, he studiously avoids conflating biography with the argument of his fiction, preferring his novels to find their way to their own integrity—it is a matter of conjecture how or why, in the fifteen-year hiatus that separates the cerebral anatomy of language that is *The Letter Left to Me* from the compassionate assertion of community that is *Actress in the House*, McElroy, himself approaching seventy, reclaimed recovery as an option, the unshakable conviction that need and isolation not be the last argument in contemporary fiction. The premise of *Actress in the House* is deceptively simple: a 1990's love affair between a middle-aged Manhattan attorney (Bill Daley), tormented by memories of his involvement with atrocities in a war more than twenty years earlier and of the death of his first wife from cystic fibrosis, and an Off-Off-Broadway actor nearly half his age (Becca Lang), a chameleon presence herself haunted by a lifetime of emotionally abusive love. The affair carries with it psychological complexities that recall not Pynchon or Don DeLillo so much as the authors of towering works of subtle psychological realism from nearly a century earlier, particularly Henry James.

What begins as a professional relationship (Becca hires Daley to represent her) quickly escalates as Daley struggles to understand the implications of his fascination with the mysterious actor—her presence sends a shock wave through his tidy life (indeed, earthquakes form a motif in the novel, as does McElroy's juxtaposition of the controlled parameters of jurisprudence with the improvisations of jazz). That fascination is heightened when, as he watches her during a performance, she takes a slap across the face from another actor, a shocking act of violence that, Daley is convinced eight rows from the stage, was genuine (her nose is bloodied). That shock convinces him to pursue what becomes an incendiary affair that—during the week the novel tracks—becomes as well a joint enterprise of two lonely isolates who, under the tonic implosion of strong feeling, are compelled to explore their separate histories and in the process recover (for the reader) a fragile, fractal design. Becca and Daley cannot hope for exorcism of their considerable ghosts (that is the stuff of sentimental fiction); rather, they recover the depth of their experience, recovering the present as they dissolve the stubborn boundaries between them.

Rather than offering a plot, McElroy charts the murky flow of memory (many of the events—and the timeline—are not clear on first reading), the simultaneity of past and present represented symbolically in the text's use of geology (even the most unprepossessing rock testifies to layers of accumulated past). Although McElroy's creativity and narrative energies show no sign of dissipating, *Actress in the House* has a valedictory feel, the ultimate gift from a writer whose perplexing narratives have come, for better or worse, to represent for the lay reader the most excessive formal extravagances of postmodern experimentation. Here, McElroy offers the intricate narrative of two shattered lives rebuilt through the density of connection.

Steven Weisenburger; William Hoffman
Updated by Joseph Dewey

Bibliography

Hantke, Steffen. *Conspiracy and Paranoia in Contemporary American Fiction: The Works of Don DeLillo and Joseph McElroy*. New York: Peter Lang, 1994. Offers in-depth analysis and a comparative view of the postmodern themes of two leading American novelists.

LeClair, Tom. "Opening Up Joseph McElroy's *The Letter Left to Me*." *Review of Contemporary Fiction* 10 (Spring, 1990): 258-267. Presents critical commentary on the novel, noting that McElroy's use of language has "opened up sensibility for anyone to read." Also discusses how McElroy peels away layers and obstacles in *Women and Men*.

McElroy, Joseph. "Joseph McElroy." Interview by Tom LeClair. In *Anything Can Happen: Interviews with Contemporary American Novelists*, edited by Tom LeClair and Larry McCaffery. Urbana: University of Illinois Press, 1983. Thoughtful interview provides much valuable information and insight into McElroy's work and vision as a writer. Includes a brief introduction by LeClair that sums up the main themes in McElroy's writing.

McHale, Brian. "Women and Men and Angels: On Joseph McElroy's Fiction." In *Constructing Postmodernism*. New York: Routledge, 1992. Focuses on some of McElroy's less well-known novels as part of a larger discussion of the evolutionary aspect of the literary movement from modernism to postmodernism.

Mathews, Harry. "'We for One': An Introduction to Joseph McElroy's *Women and Men*." *Review of Contemporary Fiction* 10 (Spring, 1990): 199-226. Examines the novel's interchanges between men and women, noting its use of language and double entendres. Makes liberal use of extracts from the novel and diagrams to illustrate the commentary.

Porush, David. "The Imp in the Machine: Joseph McElroy's *Plus*." In *The Soft Machine: Cybernetic Fiction*. New York: Methuen, 1985. Careful analysis of *Plus* discusses the novel as science fiction that draws on the metaphors of computers and space technology.

Review of Contemporary Fiction 10 (Spring, 1990). Special issue devoted to McElroy is a valuable resource. Includes important critical essays as well as an informative introduction by Stanley Elkin, a bibliographical essay, a piece by McElroy titled "Midcourse Corrections," and an interview with McElroy conducted by John Graham.

Saltzman, Arthur. *The Novel in the Balance*. Columbia: University of South Carolina, 1993. Contains a highly readable and tightly organized reading of McElroy's *Plus* that recovers the novel's profound humanism despite its elaborate use of science and technology.

Tabbi, Joseph. "Literature as Technology: Joseph McElroy's *Plus*." In *Postmodern Sublime: Technology and American Writing from Mailer to Cyberpunk*. Ithaca, N.Y.: Cornell University Press, 1995. Presents a far-reaching, probing analysis of *Plus*, addressing the development of McElroy's use of science and how science, particularly chaos theory, is relevant to an understanding of the structural complexities of McElroy's novels. Essential reading.

Tanner, Tony. "Toward an Ultimate Topography: The Work of Joseph McElroy." *TriQuarterly* 36 (1976): 214-252. Early and remarkably prescient (and quite accessible) reading of McElroy is particularly strong on the first three novels, which Tanner views as a trilogy of complementary themes and structural experiments.

Ian McEwan

Born: Aldershot, England; June 21, 1948
Also known as: Ian Russell McEwan

Principal long fiction

The Cement Garden, 1978
The Comfort of Strangers, 1981
The Child in Time, 1987
The Innocent, 1990
Black Dogs, 1992
Enduring Love, 1997
Amsterdam, 1998
Atonement, 2001
Saturday, 2005
On Chesil Beach, 2007

Other literary forms

Ian McEwan's first two collections of short stories, *First Love, Last Rites* (1975) and *In Between the Sheets, and Other Stories* (1978), featuring grotesque characters, violence, and sexual perversion, earned him a reputation as a writer of shocking originality. McEwan finds the challenge of writing in the economical style needed for short fiction similar to that involved in screenwriting, at which he has tried his hand intermittently. Both the screenplays *The Ploughman's Lunch* (1983), set against the backdrop of the 1982 Falklands War, and *Soursweet* (1988), based on Timothy Mo's novel—about Chinese immigrants living in London in the 1960's—were made into respected films; *The Good Son* (1993), an adaptation of Joseph Ruben's novel, was made into a critically panned, though lucrative, film starring Macauley Culkin.

McEwan also wrote television plays, published together as *The Imitation Game: Three Plays for Television* (1981), with the eponymous play, set during World War II, anticipating the turn toward historical and political themes in his later fiction. While McEwan's writing for the screen reveals the dramatic aspects of his work, he also demonstrates an affinity for music through the libretto *Or Shall We Die?* (pr., pb. 1983; music by Michael Berkeley), a choral lament of the threat of nuclear devastation, and through the operatic libretto *For You* (pr., pb. 2008; music by Berkeley). His two forays into children's literature, *Rose Blanche* (1985; rewritten from translation of original by Roberto Innocenti) and *The Daydreamer* (1994), reflect his fascination with childhood and the transformative power of the imagination. His occasional journalistic pieces, such as those about climate change and terrorism, have established him as a leading public intellectual.

Achievements

Having outgrown his early nickname Ian Macabre, prompted by the dark subject matter of his early work, Ian McEwan is considered one of the world's best writers of contemporary fiction. Recognition of his work began with the Somerset Maugham Award in 1976 for *First Love, Last Rites*, and continued with the Whitbread Novel Award in 1987 and the Prix Femina Étranger in 1993, both for *The Child in Time*. Despite numerous nominations, the prestigious Booker Prize eluded him until 1998, when he won for *Amsterdam*, setting the stage for the enormous critical and commercial success of his next novels. *Atonement* earned him the W. H. Smith Literary Award (2002), the National Book Critics Circle Fiction Award (2003), the Los Angeles Times Book Prize for fiction (2003), and the Santiago Prize for the European Novel (2004); yet the book is undoubtedly best known for its adaptation as a highly successful, Oscar-winning film, released in 2007.

Saturday, which won the James Tait Black Memorial Prize for fiction in 2006, was already a best seller when its popularity was increased by its seemingly prescient anticipation of the 2005 terrorist bombings in London. McEwan's novels are eagerly awaited by critics and readers around the world, as witnessed by the positive reception of the short novel *On Chesil Beach*, which was named book of the year at the 2008 Galaxy British Book Awards. McEwan was named *Reader's Digest* Author of the Year in 2008. He also served as editor of the literary supplement to *The Guardian Review*.

Biography

Ian McEwan was born in Aldershot, England, in 1948 into a military family. His Scottish father, David, was a sergeant major in the British army, so the young McEwan spent much of his childhood on army bases in Singapore and Libya. He said that those experiences abroad opened his eyes to the importance of politics and history to ordinary people's lives. He has described his father as charming but domineering, and his mother as easily intimidated; this combination likely led to his parents' decision in 1942 to give away for adoption his only full sibling, David (Dave) Sharp. Sharp renewed contact with McEwan and his family in 2002 and wrote a memoir about his life, *Complete Surrender* (2008), for which McEwan wrote the foreword.

McEwan attended a boarding school in Sussex from 1959 to 1966, then studied English and French at the University of Sussex for three years before enrolling in a one-year master's degree program at the new University of East Anglia. He completed part of his course work in creative writing under the supervision of the well-known writer and critic Malcolm Bradbury. In 1971, McEwan began his career as a professional author, attracting critical attention in the mid-1970's and quickly gaining a reputation, along with his friend Martin Amis, as one of the enfants terribles of the British literary world.

McEwan was married to journalist Penny Allen, with whom he had two sons, from 1982 to 1997. Their divorce led to a bitter custody battle, which McEwan eventually won; the details of the case are protected by a nondisclosure agreement. In 1997, he married Annalena McAfee.

Throughout his career, McEwan has been active in various political causes, including the feminist and antinuclear movements in the 1980's and the later environmental movement. He has spoken against religious extremism as a leading cause of terrorism and world unrest. He is a declared atheist, with a keen interest in science, yet is fascinated by the imagination, myth, fantasy, and the power of "magical thinking."

Analysis

Like most contemporary fiction, Ian McEwan's work, too, combines compelling storytelling with literary self-consciousness in the form of overt intertextual references as well as the inclusion of artist figures, often writers, within his texts. Through these metafictional gestures, McEwan invites his readers to reflect on the power and limitations of language to depict reality. He frequently thematizes the difficulties of truthfully representing the past through the use of unreliable narrators, multileveled narratives, and passages focalized through subjective viewpoints. McEwan's pervasive use of irony encourages his readers to look beyond the surface of the story, and to consider carefully the meanings behind his characters and their actions.

While McEwan's ironic style remains distinctive, he has experimented with many generic forms, including the spy thriller, the satirical novel, the historical novel, and fantasy. His darkly comic, often grotesque early work focused on scenes of incest, sexual mutilation, dismembered corpses, and violence against women; his early characters were primarily children, adolescents, social outcasts, and deviants. As he matured as a writer, his novels became less insular and more socially and historically conscious, dealing with events from World War II and the Cold War to Thatcherism and London following September 11, 2001. At the same time, the sexual domination and misogyny central to his early work evolved into more nuanced representations of gender relationships, including marriage, parenthood, masculinity, and femininity.

All of McEwan's work shows a strong emphasis on the moral dimension of fiction. McEwan has stated repeatedly that novels play a valuable role in allowing readers to imagine the world from another person's point of view—the basis, he claims, of human morality. He frequently places characters in deliberately staged scenes where they are forced to work their way through ethical dilemmas, with the reader as audience and ultimate judge. These dramatic scenes help to create the narrative power that make his work so enjoyable for readers.

The Comfort of Strangers

The Comfort of Strangers perhaps is the most familiar of McEwan's early novels, and it epitomizes his fascination with dark themes of sexual violence. It is set in a city modeled on Venice, Italy, though without the canals. As British tourists Mary and Colin wander the streets, the labyrinthine urban setting serves as a projection of their growing psychological confusion. They are lured by a local man, Robert, and his Canadian wife, Caroline, into a perverse relationship that ends with the amputation of Colin's arms and legs, and his death.

Ian McEwan. (© Miriam Berkley)

While the brutal Robert, with his hatred of feminism, is the novel's villain, he is able to control the others only because his violence preys on their own repressed sadistic and masochistic desires. Caroline's desire to be hurt during sex symbolizes the female complicity required for patriarchal domination. The homoerotic victimization of Colin is complicated by his feminine characteristics, which figure in Mary's fantasies of mutilating him for her own sexual pleasure. The characters' tendency to objectify each other in visual terms is underscored by multiple images of voyeurism, including Robert's camera, which he uses to photograph Colin from afar.

Black Dogs

Black Dogs is a thoughtful meditation on the difficulties of knowing the past and rendering it faithfully into language. Like McEwan's bleakly comical *The Innocent*, *Black Dogs* is set partly in Germany, with the central event being the fall of the Berlin Wall in 1989. The history of Nazi totalitarianism haunts the text in the form of a concentration camp visited by the main character, Jeremy, and the titular black dogs, associated with Gestapo atrocities against women.

The novel is written as Jeremy's first-person memoir, recording not his own life but those of his in-laws. In a preface, Jeremy describes Bernard and June Tremaine as extreme opposites, a rationalist versus a mystic, whose views of the world, and memories of the past, are always in conflict. June's traumatic attack by two dogs in the French countryside as a young married woman takes on immense symbolic importance for her, while Bernard denies that the event ever took place and rejects her spiritual interpretation of the attack. Jeremy's goal as memoirist is not so much to reconcile these points of view but rather to give them equal voice. By listening carefully to and recording both perspectives, Jeremy recognizes and respects each individual's unique experience, a demonstration of compassionate understanding that is the antithesis of mass oppression.

Amsterdam

Amsterdam is a tightly constructed English comic novel in the tradition of Evelyn Waugh and Kingsley Amis. The third-person narrative voice creates a wry, ironic tone, and the book's ending has a delicious sense of moral inevitability as the two main characters, composer Clive Linley and tabloid editor Vernon Halliday, kill each other through their own selfish vindictiveness.

Like *The Child in Time*, *Amsterdam* reflects on the neo-Conservative period in England under Prime Ministers Margaret Thatcher and John Major. This is a fallen world characterized by greed, ambition, and heartless opportunism, and the physical setting, a trash-strewn London spreading its pollution into the Wordsworthian countryside, reflects the social decay. Clive and Vernon embody a kind of romantic, masculine, self-destructive egotism common in McEwan's novels, while the female characters, mostly off stage, represent a feminized ideal of compassion unheeded by the men. The staged scene in which Clive must choose between finding inspiration for his symphony and helping a woman being raped is one of the most dramatic ethical encounters in McEwan's fiction, while Vernon's decision to put personal gain above concern for the other in publishing salacious photographs of a prominent politician is the sort of moral lapse that the author takes open delight in punishing.

Atonement

Unquestionably, McEwan's most famous novel, *Atonement*, is also his most densely intertextual and intricately constructed. Beginning with an epigraph from Jane Austen's *Northanger Abbey* (1817) about the dangers of being carried away by a literary imagination, McEwan weaves a tale about a young girl, Briony Tallis, whose sense of her own powers as a writer leads her to falsely accuse her sister Cecilia's lover, Robbie Turner, of raping her cousin, Lola Quincey. This event is described in the novel's first section, set on the Tallis estate in 1935, from a seemingly omniscient narrative perspective.

The second and third sections of the novel leap ahead to World War II and relate Robbie's grueling experiences during the retreat to Dunkirk and Briony's service as a ward nurse in a London hospital, respectively. Again, these sections have the pretense of narrative objectivity, yet their gritty historical realism is shadowed by a peculiar sense of fantasy. Only after Briony has been reunited with Cecilia and Robbie in London, and has agreed to confess to her youthful crime, does the reader become aware that all that he or she has read to that point has actually been a novel written by Briony.

The novel's final section, set in London in 1999, provides a comic denouement, with the family's descendants reunited and Briony's literary career celebrated in her old age. However, McEwan leaves his reader wondering whether Briony, by giving a false happy ending to Cecilia and Robbie, both of whom she admits were killed during the war, has truly atoned, and whether her writing is just as much an act of childish self-indulgence as her original accusation.

Saturday

Saturday is McEwan's most topical novel, dealing with contemporary issues such as the anxieties of living in a major city after the 2001 terrorist attacks. The novel includes symbols that recall the attacks, including a burning plane streaking toward Heathrow Airport and a glass-paned tower (the British Telecom Tower), and McEwan deepens the political context by setting the action on Saturday, February 15, 2003—the day of the mass protest in London against the imminent invasion of Iraq by the United States and allies.

The novel is structured as an allegory of the confrontation between the West and the forces of terrorism. Henry Perowne is a successful neurosurgeon with all the advantages of his culture; he comes into conflict with Baxter, a mentally ill street thug, who represents the unruly outsiders, be they Islamic extremists or London's poor, who threaten the doctor's domestic security. Baxter's invasion into the Perowne home replays the horror of September 11, but he is ultimately vanquished and returned to the streets to die.

While *Saturday* is a deeply political novel, it is also very literary. It is openly modeled on Virginia Woolf's *Mrs. Dalloway* (1925) and James Joyce's *Ulysses* (1922), both texts played out during one day and centered on urban wanderers whose inner thoughts make up the narrative. *Saturday* is told entirely through Henry's point of view, which includes his preference for scientific analysis over artistic imagination. McEwan paints Henry as what Matthew Arnold called a middle-class philistine, one who rejects the civilizing power of art. However, the text has the violent Baxter subdued by a reading of Arnold's "Dover Beach," leaving the reader to ponder the novel's ultimate message about the ethical effect of all literature, and this piece in particular. Is the reader meant to identify with and celebrate Henry's triumph over the outsider, or to see in the novel's artificially happy ending an ironic message about the need to change Western attitudes to prevent future conflict?

Lynn Wells

Other major works

SHORT FICTION: *First Love, Last Rites*, 1975; *In Between the Sheets, and Other Stories*, 1978.

PLAYS: *Or Shall We Die?*, pr., pb. 1983 (libretto; music by Michael Berkeley); *For You*, pr., pb. 2008 (libretto; music by Berkeley).

SCREENPLAYS: *The Ploughman's Lunch*, 1983; *Soursweet*, 1988 (adaptation of Timothy Mo's novel *Sour Sweet*); *The Good Son*, 1993 (adaptation of Joseph Ruben's novel); *The Innocent*, 1995 (adaptation of his novel).

TELEPLAYS: *Jack Flea's Birthday Celebration*, 1976; *The Imitation Game*, 1980; *The Imitation Game: Three Plays for Television*, 1981 (also known as *The Imitation Game, and Other Plays*, 1981); *The Last Day of Summer*, 1983 (adaptation of his short story).

CHILDREN'S LITERATURE: *Rose Blanche*, 1985 (rewritten from translation of original by Roberto Innocenti); *The Daydreamer*, 1994.

Bibliography

Childs, Peter, ed. *The Fiction of Ian McEwan: A Reader's Guide to Essential Criticism*. New York: Palgrave Macmillan, 2006. An excellent resource for students of McEwan, providing excerpts from books, articles, and reviews examining his work through *Saturday*.

Head, Dominic. *Ian McEwan*. New York: Manchester University Press, 2007. A study of McEwan's aesthetics and themes through *Saturday*.

Malcolm, David. *Understanding Ian McEwan*. Columbia: University of South Carolina Press, 2002. This critical study covers McEwan's work up to *Amsterdam*. Each chapter is organized around what Malcolm sees as the five key issues in McEwan's work: textual self-consciousness, feminism, rationalism and science, moral perspective, and the "fragmentariness" of his novels.

Roger, Angela. "Ian McEwan's Portrayal of Women." *Forum for Modern Language Studies* 32, no. 1 (1996): 11-26. This article deals with the key issue of gender in McEwan's fiction. Roger argues that women in McEwan's fiction are always constructed from a male point of view.

Schemberg, Claudia. *Achieving 'At-one-ment': Storytelling and the Concept of the Self in Ian McEwan's "The Child in Time," "Black Dogs," "Enduring Love," and "Atonement."* New York: Peter Lang, 2004. This study relates four of McEwan's later novels to ethical criticism and emphasizes the role of storytelling in the creation of moral selfhood for McEwan's characters and readers.

Slay, Jack, Jr. *Ian McEwan*. New York: Twayne, 1996. A good thematic introduction to McEwan's work, up to *Black Dogs*. Part of Twayne's English Authors series.

Walkowitz, Rebecca L. "Ian McEwan." In *A Companion to the British and Irish Novel, 1945-2000*, edited by Brian W. Shaffer. Malden, Mass.: Blackwell, 2005. A ten-page biographical essay on McEwan in a literary companion examining British and Irish novelists writing from the end of World War II through the end of the twentieth century.

Patrick McGinley

Born: Glencolmcille, Donegal, Ireland; February 8, 1937

Also known as: Patrick Anthony McGinley

Principal long fiction

Bogmail, 1978
Goosefoot, 1982
Foggage, 1983
Foxprints, 1983
The Trick of the Ga Bolga, 1985
The Red Men, 1987
The Devil's Diary, 1988
The Lost Soldier's Song, 1994

Other literary forms

Patrick McGinley is known primarily for his long fiction.

Achievements

From the outset, Patrick McGinley's fiction enjoyed an enthusiastic reception from reviewers, particularly in the United States, where critics, inadequately acquainted with some of his background material, misleadingly drew attention to the work's Irishness. Reviews in England and Ireland, though less generous, were generally favorable, if somewhat resistant to McGinley's prolificity. McGinley's first novel, *Bogmail*, was nominated for several awards, including the prestigious Edgar Award for Best Novel of 1981, an award presented by the Mystery Writers of America.

Biography

Although his books received such popular success, little is known about Patrick Anthony McGinley's life; indeed, at a time when Irish fiction is receiving an increasing amount of academic attention, this author could be called the most anonymous Irish novelist of his generation. McGinley was born to a farming family in a comparatively remote area of county Donegal, Ireland's farthest northwest county. He was educated locally and at University College, Galway, from which he graduated with a bachelor's degree in commerce in 1957. For five years after his graduation he taught secondary school in Ireland before emigrating to England and entering the publishing profession. Apart from a year in Australia (1965-1966), he remained in publishing and became managing director of Europa Publications in 1980. McGinley married Kathleen Frances Cuddy in 1967 and had one son, Myles Peter. His family made its home in Kent, outside London.

Analysis

Because of lack of serious critical attention until the late 1990's, it had been difficult to assess Patrick McGinley's status as a contemporary Irish novelist. Beginning in the early 1960's, Irish writing in all forms underwent major self-interrogation, accompanied by the new thematic and formal considerations. While, unlike many Irish writers, McGinley was anything but vocal in this sustained period of reappraisal, it is instructive to see his work in such a context. Its individuality is arguably its most significant feature and, by a paradox more apparent than real, is the attribute that makes his novels symptomatic of new departures in Irish writing. At the same time, the representations of nature, the sense of the uncanny, the choice of traditional and relatively unchanging rural communities as settings, the focus on death, and the use of the romance form all reveal McGinley as being interestingly related to a long tradition of such preoccupations in Irish writing, from the seventh century writings of Saint Columkille, for whom McGinley's native place is named, to the modern era. More particularly, his fascination with reason's frailty and the fact of death makes his work an intriguing pendant to that of one of the most important Irish novelists of the twentieth century, Flann O'Brien.

Although McGinley is usually classified as a crime novelist, to consider him one in the conventional sense is both accurate and misleading. While it is true that, until the publication of *The Lost Soldier's Song* in 1994, McGinley had not deviated from the path signposted in the opening paragraph of his first published novel, *Bogmail*, where poisonous toadstools are being introduced to a mushroom omelette, and while it is also true that his publishers have tended to emphasize the murderous mysteriousness of his plots, there is both more and less than meets the eye to the convenient classification. This state of affairs is of significance because it draws attention to the fact that it is impossible to approach McGinley's work without drawing attention to its bifocal character.

McGinley's fiction evinces more interest in mystery than in solution—his work has only one detective, McMyler in *Goosefoot*, and the few police officers who crop up in the other novels are somewhat less than a credit to the force and have thoroughly earned their status as minor characters. The works' focus is directed gently but ineluctably toward those areas of existence that may not be brought within stable frameworks of perception. In particular, the unreasonable fact of death is so much more to the fore than is any power to counteract it that it is tempting to attach to the whole of this author's output the quotation from Robert Southey that is the epigraph to *Foggage*: "My name is Death: the last best friend am I."

Settings

For the most part, McGinley's novels are set in the author's native county Donegal. An exception to this general rule is *Foxprints*, which is largely set in the suburban Home Counties of England, a context that the author fails to enliven, perhaps because of its excessively social character. Typically, McGinley feels at home in remoteness, and Donegal settings possess a variety of strategic advantages for a writer of his proclivities. In the first place, by selecting Donegal as the scene of the action, McGinley is clearly presenting settings that he can treat with authority. So faithful is he to the fastidious re-creation of locales clearly maintained in his mind's eye by a deep attachment to his native area that he establishes a very palpable sense of place, and in every McGinley novel there are quietly rapturous descriptive passages that seem to hymn the landscapes they depict.

Situating his plots so squarely in a felt environment—in which the play of light, natural features, the oscillations of the sea, the weather's vagaries, and the presence of wildlife continually recur—seems to enable McGinley to virtually dispense with time. The exigencies of plot naturally require that time pass, but generally speaking there is little specific sense of period. Before *The Lost Soldier's Song*, which is set during the Black and Tan War and focuses on the events of the war itself, as well as its impact on character, long historical perspectives had little or no part to play in the assessing of the characters' problematic destinies. What exceptions there are to this rule—the setting of *The Trick of the Ga Bolga* in the early years of World War II, or the rather boldly stated observations on the spurious development of rural Ireland propounded by the protagonist of *The Devil's Diary*—seem rather to underline how watertight the rule is, since neither note of contemporaneity contributes significantly to the balance of forces at the center of either of these novels.

One effect of McGinley's obviation of cultural conceptions of time, and a general relaxation of time-consciousness, is that it assists in the creation of atmosphere but inhibits in the creation of thrills. Such a result accentuates the all-enveloping quality of the rural setting, while at the same time drawing both the characters' and the readers' attention from event to perception of event. The mystery deepens to the degree that it becomes as much part of the nature of things as the landscape in which it is situated. Any tension that results from the distressingly arbitrary and violent events of the plot—often as much the result of accidents as of articulated intentions—are to be found, unreleased, within the consciousness of McGinley's protagonists, and its psychological repercussions fail, with what the protagonists understandably find to be a maddening consistency, to have an objective correlative in the natural world around them. Remoteness of setting, therefore, is not merely an occasion of picturesqueness for McGinley. On the contrary, it is one of his fundamental means of lending plausibility to the sense of the inscrutable and uncanny that bedevils the mental landscapes of his protagonists, the majority of whom traverse the dual terrains of these novels like lost souls.

By virtue of its very naturalness, setting is experienced by McGinley's protagonists as a primary instance of otherness, of a set of conditions that are not comprehensible, tractable, alterable, or humanly amenable in any particular—conditions that are, strictly speaking, mysterious. Yet it is important to note that McGinley is sufficiently resourceful to prevent his approach from becoming too schematic. The rich farming country of county Tipperary, which provides the setting for *Foggage* and in which its main characters are ostensibly firmly established, engenders as much distress and destruction as county Donegal ever did, revealing unsuspected psychic remoteness. In *Goosefoot*, ungenial Dublin exposes the unsuspecting and vital Patricia Teeling to malevolences that are the antitheses of her winning sense of life.

McGinley's protagonists, settled or unsettled, are peculiarly susceptible to the atmosphere of their environments. For the most part they are unsettled, and it is generally this condition that has brought them to the locale of the story. Once arrived, they seem to believe, however, that they have found a secure haven: To a degree, the enclosed and remote character of their landfall—typified by the Glenkeel in *The Devil's Diary*, which has the same road into it as out—seduces them into thinking that now they are safe, they have come to the end of a particular phase of their lives and are permitted by their new circumstances to live lives that are at once both self-engrossed and detached. In a number of cases—*Foxprints* and *The Trick of the Ga Bolga* are the most significant—the protagonists are on the run from unsatisfactory marriages. The protagonists' status as outsiders, however, gives them novelty value to the locals, and before long they are involved in local affairs, often in a very literal sense, one of the principal means of involvement being that of sexual attraction. The inability to deny the presence of their sexuality has the effect of replicating in more intense form the substance of earlier distressing experiences, with the result that settings that seemed to be escapes end up as terminuses. Aiming for simplicity, McGinley's protagonists find it only to discover its essential mysteriousness.

Characters

The repetition and duplication of experience, the evidently unforgiving character of one's own nature, are particularly crucial in *The Devil's Diary* and *The Trick of the Ga Bolga*. Yet more important than their presence, and raising their significance beyond that of mere plot devices, is that the protagonists perceive their condition for what it is. The typical McGinley protagonist is well educated and sometimes dauntingly well read.

Not only do repetition and replication feature to a significant degree within each of McGinley's novels, but they are also notably present in his output as a whole. As a result, while resourceful variations in setting and protagonist occur—a female protagonist in *Goosefoot*, three protagonists in *The Red Men*, a suburban never-never land as the setting for *Foxprints*—and while these changes effectively vary the angle of approach from novel to novel, each work's ultimate preoccupations remain essentially unchanged. McGinley's output has a consistency of focus and pliability of approach that are crucially denied its characters. It hardly seems to matter that the English engineer Potter in *Bogmail* is a prototype for Coote, the protagonist of *The Trick of the Ga Bolga*, or that Coote's mistress has a formidable avatar in the insistently incestuous Maureen Hurley of *Foggage*. Story line is more ornament than staple, and while McGinley's plots are richly woven and colorfully peopled, they seem to be considered as no more than edifices of superficial plausibility to an investigation of whose inscrutable foundations the protagonist is, through no fault of his own (McGinley's fiction is resolutely amoral), condemned.

McGinley's sense of setting draws heavily on the elements—the motion of the seasons, the cloudscapes of the often protean Irish sky, the world of crag, pool, bog, and seashore. His sense of protagonist reproduces this concentration on the elemental. These characters seldom have a specific social role, or if they do—as in the case of Father Jerry in *The Devil's Diary*—it produces rather than defends against existential dread. On the other hand, the protagonists, for all the author's concentration on them and his use of them as both embodiments and victims of a unique optic on themselves and their world, are not sufficiently well endowed to render considerations of social role by functioning in a recognizable manner. Deprived of the safeguards that social and literary convention provide, they appear to have no choice but to assume a more fundamental, vulnerable, and elementary condition of selfhood—or rather, the plot lines of McGinley's novels show that fall taking place. In addition, the creation of mysteries without solution and the commissioning of crime without reproducing the social machinery of incrimination that is its normal, or generic, accompaniment, take at face value the genre to which these novels superficially belong, and by doing so subvert it, reducing it to such a bare embodiment of its elements that it only nominally maintains its presence.

Themes

The unemphatic but omnipresent concentration on a sense of the elemental in McGinley's fiction is nowhere seen to better advantage than in the works' recurring themes. Having brought his unsuspecting protagonists, who without knowing it are at the end of their tether, to what seems like the end of the world, the author subjects them to other experiences of the terminal. The most obvious one of these is death, yet although its literal presence is of prime importance to sustaining these works' fragmentary figment of plot, death is not merely present in a literal sense. It also exists as the pun for sexual climax familiar to students of English Renaissance poetry, where it helps to make a familiar and typically antithetical conjunction for McGinley (the fact of death is frequently deeply implicated in the act of love). In addition, its presence denotes a primary instance of the chaos and nullity to which a protagonist's perception of life may in any case be reduced—a state of perception that is frequently the aftermath of the violent and unexpected deaths that punctuate the duration of the McGinley protagonist's rustication.

Rather than describe McGinley as a writer of mysteries, it seems more appropriate to consider his works as those of a "parablist," who utters in story what cannot be otherwise so readily articulated. At least one McGinley novel, *The Red Men* (commonly taken as a retelling of the parable of the talents in the New Testament), seems to support such a view. More broadly, a strong case may be made for McGinley's novels to be considered as sophisticated romances of consciousness, in which the romantic quest, for all its pastoral trappings, is ironized by succeeding in finding that with which it cannot live.

What the quest locates reveals the philosophical undertow of McGinley's fiction. It would be misleading to consider McGinley a philosophical novelist of the school of, for example, Albert Camus, as is implied by his works' pleasing lightness of tone and deftness of manner. In all McGinley's works prior to *The Lost Soldier's Song*, philosophical themes, however fundamental to the extreme conditions to which action and character are reduced, are treated with no more intensity or deliberation than is any other feature of McGinley's fictional universe, possibly as a result of his having no ideological agenda. At the same time, the clearly existentialist scenarios, the manner in which action preys on the mind to elicit meaning, the emphasis on the mutability of fate as a standby of plot, the frequent epiphanic encounters between humanity and nature, the quietly satirical allusions to mind-body problems, and the impetus toward pattern forming and pattern recognition that initially stimulates and ultimately frustrates the inquirer all suggest works of a speculative, philosophizing, intellectual character.

This omnipresent preoccupation with perception, cognition, and the impossibility of stabilizing or normalizing them that bemuses McGinley's protagonists seems to amuse the author. Not only is his style, for the most part, wry, succinct, and supple, but its tone is also frequently one of comic detachment. A great strength of his work is his ability to create compelling minor characters, all of them gifted talkers, whose presence both diffuses and enhances the works' central preoccupations. In addition, McGinley is not averse to placing the reader in the lexical equivalent of his protagonists' opacity of perception by the inclusion of archaic and unfamiliar terminology. Here again, however, this tactic is employed in a spirit of play rather than one of dogmatism, just as his works as a whole resist to an exemplary degree didacticism and moralizing, preferring to articulate consciousness as a field of forces too vivid to be ignored and too broad to be disciplined. The greatest pleasure to be derived from McGinley's fiction, therefore, is not merely from its undoubtedly attractive and distracting stories, locales, and characters but also from the ruminative cast of mind that sets the various fictive effects in motion.

The Lost Soldier's Song

All these elements are present in part or in full before *The Lost Soldier's Song*, and many of them remain important even in this novel, which represents a departure from McGinley's previous fiction. Far from being a crime novel, except perhaps in the sense that the criminality of war is expressed in its pages, this novel focuses on the experiences of Declan Osborne and Maureen Sheehy during the Black and Tan War and the war's repercussions. As in his previous novels, however, McGinley continues his poetic attachment to place with his descriptions of locales such as the enchanted Chalice, his deft creation of minor characters in such figures as the enigmatic Owney Muldowney, his preoccupation with death, and his refusal to moralize.

Some of the most memorable and significant passages in this novel center on what is elemental, and they ably unite place, character, and philosophical concern. After having the prisoners he had taken at Loganboy murdered by McColl, for instance, Declan recalls the bog cotton that had attracted him one summer day with its whiteness from a distance. However, when viewed closely its corruption was revealed, giving him "a lesson in Irish history," for he had engrossed himself in the middle of something "best viewed from firm ground and from afar." Maureen's tale of the "shadow of redness in the air" left by a passing fox in the rural countryside brings to mind her dead brother, who would have made up a tale to explain the fox's phantom, making her recognize that "what you miss about people is the way they put things. When they've gone, you realise that they've left a little bit of their mind in yours." Declan's own vision of a running fox, "fully and superbly alive," forces him to realize that the courage he showed at Loganboy may never be duplicated; he can never again take anything for granted.

As this example shows and as is true of McGinley's earlier novels, his characters are totally cognizant of their true condition. This is especially true of Declan, who clearly understands his motive for becoming and remaining involved in the war—to find a place for himself in the world, ironically comparable to the safe haven sought by McGinley's characters in previous novels. He unmistakably realizes that luck, not courage, led to his spur-of-the-moment heroism at Fiachra's Well. Like

McGinley's other protagonists, Declan is an existential hero who relentlessly follows his course, despite the fact that he is never quite sure he believes in it.

What makes this novel different from McGinley's previous fiction is the necessary importance of the historical perspective, for none of the events would occur without the presence of the war. It is the war that also serves as the philosophical core of the book, as is seen when Declan and Ganly come to realize that they are "fighting high-handed imperialism with high-minded barbarism." Before she drowns herself in the Black Pool, the emotionally wounded Maureen appropriately writes the epitaph for the war: "It was a strange victory. . . . For some it was more like a defeat." Indeed, the final pages of the novel lead the reader to wonder what has improved for the heroes of the war who return to the brickyards or to the farms they had so wanted to escape. Sober, philosophical, poetic, and yet permeated with irony, *The Lost Soldier's Song* lies firmly in the mainstream of Irish fiction, while at the same time continuing to be stylistically and philosophically connected to McGinley's previous fiction.

George O'Brien
Updated by Jaquelyn W. Walsh

Bibliography

Brown, Richard E. "Patrick McGinley's Novels of Detection." *Colby Quarterly* 33 (September, 1997): 209-222. Brown discusses McGinley's mystery novels as parodies of the traditional detective novel.

Cahalan, James M. *The Irish Novel: A Critical History*. Boston: Twayne, 1988. The concluding chapter of this study is a survey of contemporary Irish fiction, which provides a good sense of McGinley's context. There are also stimulating, though necessarily brief, asides on McGinley's works up to and including *The Red Men*.

Clissmann, Anne. *Flann O'Brien: A Critical Introduction to His Writings*. New York: Barnes & Noble Books, 1975. Chapters 2 and 3 of this work offer a useful means of assessing the imaginative terrain upon which much of McGinley's fiction rests.

Kenner, Hugh. "A Deep and Lasting Mayonnaise." *The New York Times Book Review*, July 21, 1985. A review of *The Trick of the Ga Bolga* by an influential literary critic. Many of McGinley's interests and orientations are succinctly brought to the fore.

Knowles, Nancy. "Empty Rhetoric: Argument by Credibility in Patrick McGinley's *Bogmail*." *English Language Notes* 39 (March, 2002): 79-87. An analysis of the novel, commenting on the postmodern, poststructuralist nature of McGinley's representation of language as "empty," an endless chain of signifiers chasing an elusive signified.

Madden, David W. "Patrick McGinley." In *Critical Survey of Mystery and Detective Fiction*, edited by Carl Rollyson. Rev. ed. Pasadena, Calif.: Salem Press, 2008. Volume 3 of this survey includes an overview of McGinley's life and work, with analyses of *Bogmail*, *Goosefoot*, *The Trick of the Ga Bolga*, *The Red Men*, and *Foxprints* and a discussion about the general character of McGinley's detective fiction.

Patten, Eve. "Contemporary Irish Fiction." In *The Cambridge Companion to the Irish Novel*, edited by John Wilson Foster. New York: Cambridge University Press, 2006. Patten briefly discusses McGinley's novels *Bogmail*, *Goosefoot*, and *The Trick of the Ga Bolga* in her examination of contemporary Irish fiction, placing McGinley's work in a broader literary context

Shea, Thomas F. "Patrick McGinley's Impressions of Flann O'Brien: *The Devil's Diary* and *At Swim-Two-Birds*." *Twentieth Century Literature* 40 (Summer, 1994): 272-281. Taking a cue from Hugo McSharry, the novelist-character in the work, Shea examines McGinley's novel as a palimpsest, a parchment partially erased yet retaining traces of the original inscriptions, with the echoes of other writers, particularly Flann O'Brien.

THOMAS McGUANE

Born: Wyandotte, Michigan; December 11, 1939
Also known as: Thomas Francis McGuane III

Principal long fiction

The Sporting Club, 1969
The Bushwhacked Piano, 1971
Ninety-two in the Shade, 1973
Panama, 1978
Nobody's Angel, 1982
Something to Be Desired, 1984
Keep the Change, 1989
Nothing but Blue Skies, 1992
The Cadence of Grass, 2002

Other literary forms

In addition to writing novels, Thomas McGuane (muh-GWAYN) produced work for motion pictures and for popular magazines. He wrote the screenplay and directed the film version of *Ninety-two in the Shade* (1975), wrote the scripts for *Rancho DeLuxe* (1973) and *The Missouri Breaks* (1975), and shared credit with Bud Shrake for *Tom Horn* (1980) and with Jim Harrison for *Cold Feet* (1989). *An Outside Chance: Essays on Sport* (1980) contains many of his magazine pieces, and *The Longest Silence: A Life in Fishing* (1999) and *Some Horses* (1999) are collections of his nonfiction writings. His short fiction is collected in *To Skin a Cat* (1986) and *Gallatin Canyon* (2006). The year 2007 saw the publication of *Conversations with Thomas McGuane*, a book of interviews with the author.

Achievements

Early in his career, Thomas McGuane was heralded as one of the most promising writers of his generation, one with a good chance to become a major American writer. He appeared on the cover of *The New York Times Book Review* and was compared favorably with Ernest Hemingway, William Faulkner, and Saul Bellow. *The Bushwhacked Piano* won the Rosenthal Foundation Award, and *Ninety-two in the Shade* was nominated for a National Book Award. In the mid-1970's, however, when he began to devote the majority of his energies to writing for films, McGuane was dismissed as a sellout. In the late 1970's, his film career seemingly over, McGuane returned to publishing novels. Although Hollywood would continue to option screenplays written in the 1970's, McGuane maintained that novels were his true calling and that his goal was to be "a true man of literature, . . . a professional." *Something to Be Desired* and *Keep the Change* reaffirmed his position as a contender for inclusion in the American canon. In 1989, McGuane received the Montana Centennial Award for Literature.

Biography

Thomas McGuane was born in Wyandotte, Michigan, on December 11, 1939. He graduated with honors from Michigan State University in 1962, earned a master of fine arts degree from the Yale Drama School in 1965, and spent 1966-1967 at Stanford on a Wallace Stegner Fellowship. His parents were New England Irish who migrated to the Midwest, where his father became an auto-parts tycoon. McGuane once stated that he inherited his storytelling impulse from his mother's family, who loved verbal sparring and yarn spinning. Newspaper and magazine articles on McGuane often comment on the manic behavior, heavy drinking, and drug use that marked his film years, as well as on his eventual return to sobriety, family life, and hard work. McGuane chose to pursue a career as a writer apart from life in the academic world, believing that his chances of writing interesting novels would be diminished were he to confine himself to life in English departments.

McGuane developed an interest in raising and training cutting horses. He became a champion horse cutter, competing regularly in rodeos, and an accomplished sailor and fisherman, spending a part of every year at fishing haunts in Florida and Georgia. He also began to direct his energies toward conservation, working as director of American Rivers and of the Craighead Wildlife-Wildlands Institute.

Analysis

Thomas McGuane's fictional universe is a "man's world." His protagonists appear to do whatever they do for sport and to escape ordinary reality. They seek a world where they can, without restraint, be whoever they choose to be. This goal puts them at odds with prevailing social customs and middle-class ideas of morality and achievement. Unfortunately, most of these quests end in frustration. Finding themselves quite apart from the normal flow of society, McGuane's protagonists must try all the harder to fulfill themselves. As a result, they easily become self-absorbed and further jeopardize whatever ties they might once have had to conventional life. Usually this tie is to a woman, who, for her own self-fulfillment, must forsake the protagonist in the end.

The Sporting Club

McGuane's first novel, *The Sporting Club*, concerns the adventures of well-to-do Michiganders who maintain the exclusive and grand Centennial Club, to which they repair to fish and hunt. The story is limited to the point of view of James Quinn, who has emerged from a protracted adolescence to take over the family's auto-parts factory. Quinn's friend, Vernor Stanton, however, refuses to take up the ordinary life and spends his time in the pursuit of games. Stanton is bored by the elitist pretensions of the club members and the pride they take in its noble heritage, and he is frustrated with Quinn for outgrowing the need for freedom and frolic. Stanton engineers a series of adventures that ultimately result in the collapse of the club. The noble pretensions of the membership are exploded when Stanton unearths a photograph that shows their ancestors engaged in an outlandish "sexual circus at full progress." Once the current members see the photograph, the pretense on which they build their lives collapses, and they run rampant with, as Quinn puts it, "moral dubiousness," emulating the sexual circus of the forefathers.

In this way, McGuane manages to show that the established social order is rotten at its foundation, and the only sensible thing to do is to quest for a life in which one determines one's own values. Exposing this truth does nothing, however, for the survival of the McGuane protagonists. By the end of the aftermath occasioned by the photograph, Stanton is living under the surveillance of mental health workers at what is left of the club, and Quinn returns to the family business. They are no longer freewheeling protagonists able to make "the world tense."

The Bushwhacked Piano

In *The Bushwhacked Piano*, Nicholas Payne is more fortunate. Even though his father has the finest law practice in Detroit, Payne has no intention of doing anything respectable. He wants no part of his father's "declining snivelization" and "the pismire futilities of moguls." Payne does, however, want Ann Fitzgerald, an aspiring poet and photographer, whom he sees as almost a goddess.

Ann's parents do not approve of Payne; appearances, hard work, and achievement mean everything to them. They take Ann from Michigan to their ranch in Montana, but Payne follows because movement appeals to him, as well as the romantic idea of an almost unworldly mate. Ann is also sleeping with an establishment boyfriend whom she will not give up completely because she knows that someday she will have to behave like a conventional adult. For now, however, camera in hand, she joins Payne on an expedition to Florida

Thomas McGuane. (© Marion Ettlinger)

to sell fraudulent bat towers. She goes more for the experience than simply to be with Payne, and ultimately she leaves him.

Payne not only loses Ann but also is arrested for selling a useless bat tower. Still, breaking the law is not as serious as breaking conventions. Payne goes free when he agrees to reenact his trial for a television program. Life, McGuane seems to say, is indeed a bewildering proposition, and the only way to emerge victorious is to determine one's own goals and always keep them uppermost in mind. Indeed, neither the loss of Ann nor the scrape with the law has a lasting effect on Payne. Those who live the conventional life will never understand Payne, but he will not relent. The novel ends with Payne proclaiming, "I am at large," which is the same language used to describe an outlaw on the loose. Payne's movement outside conventional spheres will not stop. He is, for better or for worse, in charge of his own life, the artist of his own destiny.

Ninety-two in the Shade

In *Ninety-two in the Shade*, Thomas Skelton attempts to engineer his own fate when he tries to become a fishing guide with his own skiff off Key West. Nicole Dance, an established guide and murderer, forbids him to do so. When Dance plays a joke on Skelton, the young man burns Dance's skiff in retaliation. Dance vows to kill Skelton if he guides, but Skelton guides anyway, his fulfillment depending on it. The situation here is much the same as in earlier McGuane fiction. The protagonist must assert himself against the normal flow of life. With his life in danger, Skelton ought not to guide, but he knows that "when what you ought to do [has] become less than a kind of absentee ballot you [are] always in danger of lending yourself to the deadly farce that surrounds us." Couched in McGuane's wisecracking language is the idea that the deadly farce occurs when one absents oneself from vital energies and capitulates to the flow of ordinary life. Skelton must stand up for the self he desires to be and attempt the life he wants.

Ninety-two in the Shade could be considered McGuane's most optimistic book if it were not for the fact that when Skelton becomes a fishing guide, Dance kills him. Until the very end, Tom seems to have everything going his way. He has determined his own values and his own fulfillment. He has the support of family and a fulfilling love relationship with Miranda, a local schoolteacher. Yet he also has his feud with Nicole Dance, who shoots him "through the heart." In spite of the protagonist's courage to pursue goals and the conviction to stand up to adversity, life does not come equipped with happy endings.

Panama

McGuane's fourth novel, *Panama*, more clearly points up the frustrations of the unconventional life. Protagonist Chester Hunnicutt (Chet) Pomeroy has become an overnight sensation, performing loathsome acts of the imagination for audiences. He has, for example, crawled out of the anus of a frozen elephant and fought a duel in his underwear with a baseball batting-practice machine. He also vomited on the mayor of New York, which ended his career. As the novel opens, Chet has returned to Key West, Florida, in the hope of putting his life back together by reconciling with his wife, Catherine, who stuck by him until he became a national disgrace. Even though she still loves him, Catherine wants nothing to do with him because his behavior is still bizarre. At one point, he nails his hand to her door; at another, he snorts cocaine off the sidewalk. He has lost his memory and given up all hope. Catherine accepts that she cannot change him and leaves him for good to the emptiness he calls home.

Chet combats this emptiness by evoking a transcendent presence of Jesse James, who has the power to inhabit his loved ones. He prefers that James inhabit his father, a snack-foods tycoon. A typical McGuane protagonist, Chet is bothered by the security and ordinariness of his background. He insists that his father is dead and claims James as an ancestor, suggesting that Chester Hunnicutt Pomeroy really wishes he were someone else. Since the glories of the Old West are not available to him, he creates the myth of himself through bizarre behavior.

Chet's outlaw myth leads him nowhere. At the novel's conclusion, his father forces a reconciliation. Chet knows that all his father wants is for Chet to say hello, to acknowledge him as his father. To admit that his father lives will be to agree that Jesse James is dead. Chet will have to accept himself for who he is: the son of a packager of snack foods, the perfect symbol of conventional modern life.

Nobody's Angel

Nobody's Angel is McGuane's first novel to be set entirely in the West, a West that McGuane characterizes as "wrecked." In Deadrock, Montana, farmers abuse the land, cowboys are lazy, and American Indians are nowhere to be found. Returning to this damaged world is thirty-six-year-old Patrick Fitzpatrick. Patrick is as unconventional as earlier McGuane protagonists. As a whiskey addict and a professional soldier, he has been a tank captain in the Army for all of his adult life, most recently in Europe, and the only place he feels secure is inside his womblike tank. Suffering from "sadness for no reason," he has returned to the family ranch, which he will someday own. He feels stranded on the ranch because becoming a property owner is not a meaningful achievement for him. Patrick appears to be in the worst shape of any McGuane protagonist. He is not only without goals but also without any sense of himself, conventional or unconventional.

The effect of the wrecked West is seen in the character of Patrick's grandfather. The old man has been a cowboy all his life, has known real gunfighters, and has run the ranch like an old-time outfit. The West has changed, however, and everything from sonic booms to valleys cluttered with yard lights has got the old man down. The only things he feels good about are Australia, which he has heard is open country like Montana once was, and Western films. His one fit of excitement comes when he signs on to be an extra in a Western about to be filmed locally. Even that, however, is accompanied by overtones of sadness and ends in disappointment. The film is *Hondo's Last Move*, evocative of a legendary but nonexistent West popularized by actor John Wayne and writer Louis L'Amour. Even then, the "last move" refers to the dying of the West and perhaps Hondo himself. To make matters worse, the project folds when the distributor forsakes Westerns for science fiction.

In the end, the old man moves into town and takes an apartment from which he can see the local film theater, which plays old Westerns, and a little bar in which hangs the head of the best elk he ever shot. The open West has been reduced to one-bedroom apartments, yesterday's films, and mounted animals, which serve only to remind him of a glorious past.

In *Nobody's Angel*, McGuane continued to work the theme of unfulfilled love. Patrick hopes to bring purpose into his life by means of a love affair with Claire Burnett. Claire and her husband, Tio, are second-generation nouveau-riche Oklahomans summering in Montana. Not a genuine stockman like Patrick's grandfather, Tio is mainly interested in oil, cattle futures, row crops, and running horses. Since Tio's main hobby is pretending to be a good old boy, Patrick sees him as a personification of the substanceless modern West.

Patrick believes that "Claire could change it all" and wishes theirs could be a sentimental love story, the kind found in romantic books. Claire, however, will not become a part of Patrick's dream. Her commitment to Tio goes beyond Patrick's understanding. Her family provided the money to support their lifestyle. Tio's people are poor Okies, and this discrepancy in their backgrounds has driven him to incurable delusions of grandeur, to the point that Claire has promised that she will not abandon him. Even though she tells Patrick that she loves him, she never stops loving Tio, and Patrick's dream of a storybook romance crumbles. Even when Tio dies, Claire will not marry Patrick. She makes love to him one last time, explaining that love is "nothing you can do anything with." Patrick is not able to cope with Claire's pragmatic attitude about love and their relationship. She gives him a picture of herself, but he does not keep it with him, because it reminds him of the frustrations of his romantic hopes.

In the end, Patrick survives, but not in the West. When he was a teenager, Patrick invented an imaginary girlfriend named Marion Easterly. Even though he was eventually discovered, the fantasy has remained a part of his consciousness. He had hoped that Claire would replace Marion, but a living woman will never become the woman of a man's imagination, and when Claire dismisses him, Patrick rejoins the Army and finds fulfillment in his fantasy. Word filters back that he is now a blackout drinker in Madrid and that he is living with a woman named Marion Easterly. Patrick Fitzpatrick remains "at large"—in the sense that his heavy drinking and fantasy lover keep him outside the normal boundaries of life—but without the hope and energy of Nicholas Payne. The McGuane protagonist seemingly must find a way to accommodate himself, partially, to the concerns of conventional life.

Something to Be Desired

In *Something to Be Desired*, the McGuane protagonist combines both unconventional and conventional goals. Lucien Taylor grows tired of normality and destroys his perfectly fine marriage with self-absorbed erratic behavior. Once his single life becomes empty, he, like Chet, tries to put it back together again by reuniting with his former wife, Suzanne, and their son, James. Lucien's plight is not entirely the result of his disenchantment with conformity; he is victimized by his capricious lust.

Lucien's sense of sexual discipline was broken in college by Emily, who slept with him on their first meeting. Emily was engaged to a medical student and continued to sleep with both young men at the same time. Ultimately, she is abused by her surgeon husband and becomes totally self-absorbed and manipulating. Emily is a woman as selfish as Claire, and she continues her self-absorbed actions throughout the novel, exploiting everyone, including Lucien. However, Lucien married Suzanne, who "took the position that this was a decent world for an honest player." This basic decency is what Lucien eventually comes to value, but when he hears that Emily is free of her marriage, he thinks nothing of destroying his own and returning to Montana in quest of her. Lucien is troubled by the lack of romance in his life, an element that Suzanne and James cannot provide. Suzanne sums up Emily by calling her the queen of the whores, an assertion that is borne out when, on her penultimate appearance in the novel, she is seen sleeping naked next to her purse.

Such a portrayal of women who do not measure up to male ideals or fantasies is not rare in McGuane's fiction: Ann (in *The Bushwhacked Piano*) and Claire (in *Nobody's Angel*) are two other disappointing women. Lucien has dreamed of Emily since their first encounter. Not until he finally decides that he wants nothing more to do with her does she tell him that she regards his concern for her an infantile gesture, a thing she holds in contempt. Indeed, she does not even think enough of him to shoot him, which she has done to her husband and, by this time, another lover. Lucien, however, like Nicholas Payne in *The Bushwhacked Piano*, does not lose momentum. He pulls off a crackpot piece of venture capitalism. Through a series of exchanges, he comes to own Emily's ranch and develops its sulfur spring into a thriving health spa. In short, he becomes rich. In this way Lucien remains unconventional, at the same time—new for a McGuane protagonist—gaining that which is admired by conventional society.

Even though McGuane still maneuvers his protagonist through some outlandish paces because of his peripatetic penis, McGuane at the same time imbues Lucien with a sense of purpose higher than sport or making the world tense. Lucien, once his new wealth requires him to bring a semblance of order into his life, begins to want to think of himself as a workingman with a family to support.

When Suzanne and James come for a visit, Lucien first attempts to reach James from the security of his own masculine interests. He takes him out to band some hawks. He baits the trap with a live pigeon. When the hawk strikes the pigeon, James screams and crawls off. As Lucien bands the hawk, James shakes. While Lucien admires the hawk, James's natural inclination is to cradle the dead pigeon; he manifests a sense of compassion that his father lacks. The violent world of nature is awful to him. Lucien actually finds himself liking the fact that his son is timid and made of more delicate and sensitive stuff than his father. Still, McGuane is not becoming sentimental. Later, when he understands how nature works, James explains that killing pigeons is how hawks have to live, but the fact remains that James was terrified by the killing. His explanation is not so much an emulation of his father's more hard-boiled ways as it is an acceptance of them as his father's ways. James is actually reaching toward a relationship with his father.

What is important here is that Lucien is attempting to reestablish his family because such a reestablishment would be better for all of them, not only for him alone. Lucien's is one of the few unselfish acts by a McGuane protagonist. He would like not to see the child become a "hostage to oblivion." He wonders how he could leave him unguarded. His reward is that James begins not to fear his father.

Winning back Suzanne, however, is not as easy. She is too skeptical to welcome the sadder-but-wiser protagonist back into her arms. She tells him the truth about himself: He is self-absorbed, insensitive to those who love him, and not worth the effort of reconciliation.

Lucien is going to have to recognize her as an independent and worthy person. Before the novel's end, she works through her sense of him as a totally selfish person, but even though she admits to loving Lucien, she is not sure if she is ready to trust him. As she and James drive away from the ranch, she does not look back. She is charting her own course, which may or may not include Lucien.

The McGuane protagonist has progressed through the state of self-absorption with adventure and sport. He has begun to understand that what matters about life is not being at large to commit glorious exploits, but being a part of a larger whole that includes other people. The full life is not lived in furious battle with the forces of conventionality, but in achieving deep and lasting relationships with human beings.

Keep the Change

In *Keep the Change*, Joe Starling, Jr., an artist of limited talent, must come to understand this same truth. Chained by the ghost of his father, an overachiever who ultimately dies a failure, the young Starling's life is empty for no reason. He is not satisfied with his various successes as an artist, craftsperson, cowboy, or lover, because everything pales in comparison with his expectations for himself. He ricochets among Montana, Florida, and New York City without fully realizing that individual human meaning is something created rather than found.

Two of McGuane's most fully realized female characters offer Starling the possibility of a fully actualized life, but he is too full of himself to seize the opportunity. Ellen Overstreet, a rancher's daughter as wholesome as the new frontier, presents him with the vulnerability of awkward young love. The dynamic Cuban Astrid, whom Starling loves for her outlandishness, sticks by him until he is hopelessly lost in pointlessness. After she leaves him, Starling seems to be beginning to understand that sharing the routine concerns of daily life with Astrid may be the source of true meaning.

Keep the Change signals a new development in McGuane's perception of male competition. Games are no longer seen as means to make sport of conventionality. Joe Starling's rival here is Billy Kelton, an honest and simple, if luckless, cowboy who marries Ellen Overstreet. Kelton is Starling's physical superior and twice humiliates him with beatings. Violence here is real, not comic, and because it is real, it is bewildering and confusing. Kelton understands that his physical prowess is dehumanizing and, in facing the struggles of life with his wife and daughter, he shows Starling the importance of a deeper, if simpler, emotional life.

The key to the novel is found in a painting of Montana mountains, the white hills, which hangs in a decaying mansion that once belonged to the most powerful man in the territory. The work itself is indistinguishable: "It had seemed an unblemished canvas until the perplexity of shadows across its surface was seen to be part of the painting." Ultimately, Starling discovers that the shadows are in fact its only real feature. There is no painting; there never has been a painting. Yet "somewhere in the abyss something shone." That "something" is the meaning Starling seeks. He is the one who determined meaning in the painting and, by extension, in the hills themselves. He must then act to create a life for himself; he must determine his own meaning.

Nothing but Blue Skies

Nothing but Blue Skies, McGuane's eighth novel, continues the progression from self-absorption to maturity begun in *Something to Be Desired* and *Keep the Change*. Perhaps his most expansive work, it follows the breakdown and recovery of Frank Copenhaver after his separation from his wife, Gracie. A former hippie turned real estate speculator and cattle trader, Frank gradually loses control of his minor empire of rental properties, turning his scattered attention instead to awkward sexual encounters with the local travel agent and episodes of drunken self-destructiveness. Only a visit by his college-age daughter, Holly, can keep him momentarily in balance. Her brief stay includes an idyllic afternoon of fishing that buoys Frank's spirits, only to intensify the sense of loneliness and loss when she leaves again.

It is Holly who manages to suspend Frank's downward spin by creating a family crisis. She summons her estranged parents to Missoula to meet her new "boyfriend," Lane Lawlor, a gray-haired archconservative campaigning to "impound" the streams and rivers in Montana in order to retain the water that flows out of the state. Frank and Gracie meet to discuss the situation, but at each of the meetings Frank makes a fool of himself by failing to control his temper. The couple is finally brought together at a political rally where Lane Lawlor is the speaker and Holly his piano-playing assistant. The rally ends when Gracie, like Frank, secretly in attendance, attacks Lane and Frank joins the melee. In the aftermath they realize that Holly has engineered their reunion by pretending to fall for Lane. Frank also understands that Gracie has "nearly ruined" him in an attempt to break down his self-involvement and force him to see her and himself in a new way.

Nothing but Blue Skies is clearly McGuane's most optimistic and fully developed novel. In Frank Copenhaver, McGuane gives his typical protagonist a complexity and vulnerability that many of his earlier versions lack. Perhaps more notable, the novel's women show a richness of characterization often missing from earlier works. Gracie, Holly, and Lucy Dyer, the travel agent, all transcend easy generalities and stand firmly as independent, fully formed characters.

The core of *Nothing but Blue Skies* is Frank's bewilderment in the face of losing Gracie and his rehabilitation through public humiliation. McGuane's strength in creating such a character lies in his understanding of how life can be renewed through the comic downfall of the protagonist, his fall into public degradation a necessary starting point for rebuilding the life he has sold away through the soul-shrinking manipulations of business. Stripped of all attainments and pride, Frank Copenhaver can only start over. After all, as Gracie tells him, "There's nothing crazier than picking up exactly where you left off."

In Thomas McGuane's contemporary West, life is what you make it, nothing more, nothing less. His protagonists must work to fulfill hopes not by going against the grain of the conventional life, but by partaking of its normal flow and by building useful foundations on its undramatic but real joys.

Dexter Westrum
Updated by Clark Davis

Other major works

SHORT FICTION: *To Skin a Cat*, 1986; *Gallatin Canyon*, 2006.

SCREENPLAYS: *Rancho DeLuxe*, 1973; *The Missouri Breaks*, 1975; *Ninety-two in the Shade*, 1975 (adaptation of his novel); *Tom Horn*, 1980 (with Bud Shrake); *Cold Feet*, 1989 (with Jim Harrison).

NONFICTION: *An Outside Chance: Essays on Sport*, 1980; *The Longest Silence: A Life in Fishing*, 1999; *Some Horses*, 1999; *Conversations with Thomas McGuane*, 2007 (Beef Torrey, editor).

Bibliography

Carter, Albert Howard, III. "Thomas McGuane's First Three Novels: Games, Fun, Nemesis." *Critique* 17, no. 1 (August, 1975): 91-104. Although McGuane's use of the pathos and humor inherent in competition has become decidedly more sophisticated as he has matured, this article is essential for understanding his early novels.

Grant, J. Kerry. "Apocryphal America: Thomas McGuane's Troubled Republic." *Critique* 48, no. 1 (Fall, 2006): 103-111. Grant examines McGuane's bitter depiction of the United States as a country whose citizens are guided by undesirable cultural standards.

Ingram, David. "Thomas McGuane: Nature, Environmentalism, and the American West." *Journal of American Studies* 29, no. 3 (December, 1995): 423-459. Ingram analyzes the environmental and outdoors themes in McGuane's work, discussing his perspective on nature, his exploration of the contemporary West, and his traditional sense of masculinity.

Klinkowitz, Jerome. *The New American Novel of Manners: The Fiction of Richard Yates, Dan Wakefield, Thomas McGuane*. Athens: University of Georgia Press, 1986. Klinkowitz argues that a new, American novel of manners emerged from the experimental, twentieth century fiction of McGuane, Richard Yates, and Dan Wakefield. In these novels, the authors treat social behavior as a system of signs providing clues to the characters' lives.

McClintock, James I. "'Unextended Selves' and 'Unformed Visions': Roman Catholicism in Thomas McGuane's Novels." *Renascence* 49, no. 2 (Winter, 1997): 139-151. McClintock focuses on McGuane's works from *The Sporting Life* through *Nothing but Blue Skies* and compares him to a host of writers, most notably Flannery O'Connor.

Morris, Gregory L. "Thomas McGuane." In *Talking Up a Storm: Voices of the New West*. Lincoln: University of Nebraska Press, 1994. Includes a 1989 interview with the novelist, in which McGuane discusses his relationship to the West, his working methods, and the state of the American novel.

Rebein, Robert. *Hicks, Tribes, and Dirty Realists: American Fiction After Postmodernism*. Lexington: University Press of Kentucky, 2001. Rebein examines the works of McGuane, Dorothy Allison, Annie Proulx, Cormac McCarthy, Larry McMurtry, and Louise Erdrich, and asserts that these authors' gritty realism has gained ascendency over metafiction in American writing.

Smith, Carlton. "In the Shadows of the Crazies: The Omnipresent Father and Thomas McGuane's Deadrock Novels." In *Coyote Kills John Wayne: Postmodernism and Contemporary Fictions of the Transcultural Frontier*. Hanover, N.H.: University Press of New England, 2000. Smith analyzes contemporary fiction that subverts traditional visions of the American frontier. In his discussion of McGuane's Deadrock novels—*Keep the Change*, *Nobody's Angel*, *Nothing but Blue Skies*, and *Something to Be Desired*—Smith comments on the novels' representation of the West, the novel's protagonists, and the women in the novels.

Torrey, Beef, ed. *Conversations with Thomas McGuane*. Jackson: University Press of Mississippi, 2007. A collection of McGuane's interviews, some of which have appeared previously in *Publishers Weekly* and other periodicals. Among other topics, McGuane discusses his experiences as a screenwriter and his passions for ranching, fishing, and writing.

Wallace, Jon. *The Politics of Style: Language as Theme in the Fiction of Berger, McGuane, and McPherson*. Durango, Colo.: Hollowbrook, 1992. Wallace examines the use of language in works by McGuane, Thomas Berger, and James Alan McPherson. Includes a bibliography.

JOAQUIM MARIA MACHADO DE ASSIS

Born: Rio de Janeiro, Brazil; June 21, 1839
Died: Rio de Janeiro, Brazil; September 29, 1908
Also known as: Bruxo do Cosme Velho

Principal long fiction

Resurreicão, 1872
A mão e a luva, 1874 (*The Hand and the Glove*, 1970)
Helena, 1876 (English translation, 1984)
Iaiá Garcia, 1878 (*Yayá Garcia*, 1977)
Memórias póstumas de Brás Cubas, 1881 (*The Posthumous Memoirs of Brás Cubas*, 1951; better known as *Epitaph of a Small Winner*, 1952)
Quincas Borba, 1891 (*Philosopher or Dog?*, 1954; also known as *The Heritage of Quincas Borba*, 1954)
Dom Casmurro, 1899 (English translation, 1953)
Esaú e Jacob, 1904 (*Esau and Jacob*, 1965)
Memorial de Ayres, 1908 (*Counselor Ayres' Memorial*, 1972)

Other literary forms

Although Joaquim Maria Machado de Assis (muh-SHAH-dew dee ah-SEES) is best known for his novels, especially in the non-Portuguese-speaking world, he did not begin writing in this genre until comparatively late in life. He started with poetry at the age of fifteen and the short story at eighteen. During the first fifteen years of his writing career, Machado de Assis produced some six thousand lines of poetry, nineteen plays and opera librettos, twenty-four short stories, almost two hundred newspaper columns and articles, and a number of translations, chiefly from French and Spanish into Portuguese. Most of this work appeared in periodicals, but ten volumes were published in book form as well. Machado de Assis continued to work in other literary forms after he began to write novels.

ACHIEVEMENTS

Joaquim Maria Machado de Assis is so singular a figure in Brazilian literature, one who lends himself so little to inclusion in any school, that in any history of Brazilian literature he must be discussed in a separate chapter. He was a contemporary of the second generation of Romantics, who influenced him in his formative years, but during the succeeding generations of late Romantics, Parnassians, and Symbolists, he developed along highly personal lines. In addition, he merits special consideration because of his unquestionable supremacy in Brazilian letters, a supremacy that he exercised during his lifetime and that would continue to grow.

Machado de Assis's talent could not be contained by any one form or genre. His *Ocidentais* (Occidentals), first published in the *Revista brasileira* in 1879 and 1880, contains poems that in perfection of form were not to be surpassed by the Parnassians and whose thought sums up the bitter, disillusioned philosophy that seems to characterize Machado de Assis's prose work from 1881. Collections of short works such as *Papéis avulsos* (1882; miscellaneous papers), *Histórias sem data* (1884; undated stories), and *Várias histórias* (1896; various stories) include some of Machado de Assis's finest writing, among which are "Missa do galo" ("Midnight Mass") and "O alienista" ("The Psychiatrist").

Another important facet of Machado de Assis's oeuvre is the series of *crônicas* (columns) and articles of literary criticism that he wrote for the press over a period of some forty years. Collected, these pieces fill seven volumes; among them are some of the author's finest pages, such as those he wrote on "*o velho senado*" (the old senate). His critical essays and journalistic columns not only give intimate glimpses into Machado de Assis's life and his times but also serve as footnotes and marginalia to his fictional works.

Machado de Assis's first four novels, all written between 1872 and 1878, are marked by the spirit and devices of Romanticism. Their interest resides less in the observation of manners than in the analysis of a moral situation in which there is a clash of wills. In *Epitaph of a Small Winner*, his fifth novel, Machado de Assis introduced several devices that were to become characteristic of his novels thereafter: short chapters and short sentences; a humorous, skeptical, and ironic tone; and an intentionally disconnected narrative in which psychological analysis is effected through omissions, alternate assertions, and reservations. The reader sees the steady emergence of an intellect, of a conception of the art of writing and the role of the artist in human progress. Each of Machado de Assis's four novels that followed *Epitaph of a Small Winner* is a masterpiece as well—each in its own way, despite a similarity of manner. Outside Brazil or Portugal, critics who stumbled across Machado de Assis's novels only in Portuguese, or perhaps translated into a language other than English, did not hesitate to place their author among the world's greatest. Some expressed surprise that so subtle a genius could have sprung from the "jungles" of Latin America. Machado de Assis is by no means a wild jungle flower; however, his roots reach deep into Brazilian culture—and deeper still, into more than two millennia of Western culture.

Although shy and retiring, Machado de Assis was greatly interested in literary society and attended many meetings of various groups throughout his life. He was a member of the society that met at the offices of the *Revista brasileira*, which did not exclude Portugal. For his many years of hard work in the Brazilian Academy of Letters as well as his devotion to numerous duties in the service of his country and native city, not to mention his prodigious literary production, the Chamber of Deputies voted to give him a state funeral with civil and military honors. This was the first time in the history of Brazil that a man of letters was buried in the manner of a hero.

BIOGRAPHY

Joaquim Maria Machado de Assis was born on June 21, 1839, and was baptized on November 13, 1839, in the Senhora do Livramento (Our Lady of Deliverance) Chapel of the Church of Saint Rita in Rio de Janeiro. His father, Francisco Joze de Assis, was a native of Rio de Janeiro, and his mother, Maria Leopoldina Machado de Assis, came from São Miguel in the Azores. She was Portuguese, then, and not black, as had been reported prior to the discovery of the baptismal record. Other parish registries later revealed that the author's father was a mulatto born of freed slaves from Rio de Janeiro. The registries revealed other facts about the Assis family, including those given on the death certificates of Machado de Assis's younger sister, who died of measles at the age of four, and of his mother, who died of tuberculosis at thirty-four.

Patriarchal estates such as the one to which the Assis family was attached offered a better chance of education for former slaves and their offspring and for poor immigrants from Portugal than was possible in Rio de Janeiro itself. Humble by today's standards, the family's condition seems to have been good for the times. They were artisans, including Maria Leopoldina, who probably had black help for her heavy household chores; moreover, they were relatively literate and on their way up the social scale. Undoubtedly, they enjoyed a degree of intimacy, if not equality, with the proprietress's family. Machado de Assis's formal schooling, if any, was slight; however, in addition to what he was taught at home, he may well have been tutored by a loving godmother until her death (of measles, three months after that of Machado de Assis's sister) and thereafter by priests attached to the estate or to churches where the youngster served, perhaps as an altar boy, perhaps as a sacristan. There can be no question that Machado de Assis was largely self-taught, but without the basic learning acquired in the extended family situation, he could never have succeeded in his heroic task.

Machado de Assis's youth, from the time he left home at about fifteen until he married at thirty, was relatively normal in some respects, most extraordinary in others. In order to earn his living, never better than a precarious one, he tried a number of occupations, all of them connected in some way with the printed word. At first probably a clerk in a book or stationery shop, he became a typesetter, a proofreader, and eventually an editor and a staff writer. He entered the field of journalism enthusiastically, expecting to be able to live, more or less well, by his pen; he soon discovered how poorly remunerated this profession was. Not until 1867 would Machado de Assis achieve some measure of economic security in the bureaucracy of government service, where he worked first on the *Diário oficial* and, from 1874, as a functionary in the Ministry of Agriculture.

Machado de Assis was an astonishingly prolific writer. Although much of his work was published in periodicals and newspapers and was far from lucrative, he continued his frenetic production of such work even during the years in which he was producing his great and successful novels, at the same time that he was all but submerged in the bureaucratic paperwork of government service. Apart from his literary work, Machado de Assis participated in numerous other artistic and social endeavors. His considerable interest in and contribution to opera and theater in Rio de Janeiro and São Paulo, both in original works and in translations or adaptations, are evidenced by his work for the Conservatório Dramático Brasileiro, where for some years he served as censor, passing judgment on the moral and political propriety of manuscripts submitted to the conservatory and giving his literary opinions as well. During this period, Machado de Assis was assiduous in his attendance at the theater and at musical events in Rio de Janeiro, becoming personally or professionally acquainted with many artists and contributing numerous reviews to the periodicals of that city at the time. As though all of this activity were not enough, Machado de Assis held various positions in a number of literary societies and often contributed and even recited poems, his own or others'—despite his supposed timidity and severe stammering—and created short plays for special meetings and benefits. Machado de Assis's significant participation in the cultural life of Rio de Janeiro was recognized in 1867, when he was decorated with the Order of the Rose by Emperor Dom Pedro II.

Among Machado de Assis's many acquaintances before 1869 was a Portuguese poet, Faustino Xavier de Novaes, who, like others of his family, went to Brazil to seek his fortune. Beset by financial and marital problems, Faustino eventually suffered a severe nervous breakdown with serious physical manifestations. After his parents' death in Oporto, his youngest sister, Carolina, was sent to assist in caring for Faustino. Almost five years older than Machado de Assis, Carolina was intelligent, sensitive, and affectionate, and she and Machado de Assis fell in love. Her suffering, which Machado de Assis mentions as one of the reasons for his love, may have been caused by an earlier love affair and possibly influenced her departure for Portugal. Very little is known of the courtship of Machado de Assis and Carolina except for one letter and a substantial fragment of a second, written to "Carola" by her "Machadinho" during the de Novaeses' stay in Petrópolis, in which there is evidence of their great concern and love for each other.

Joaquim Maria Machado de Assis. (The Granger Collection, New York)

She chided him for not confiding in her. In response, Machado de Assis told her briefly of his earlier loves. The first was Corinna, who did not requite his love, and consequently there is nothing more to say (although in the tradition of such matters, Machado de Assis had published some 385 verses to Corinna). The second, who remains nameless but was possibly an actress and married, loved him in return and was the greater love. The situation was a painful one, however, and Machado de Assis was persuaded to break off the affair. Carolina was the one true love of his life. Despite a probable infidelity on the part of her husband—an "infidelity of the senses"—she was to be so always.

Against the wishes of some of her family, they were married November 12, 1869, a short time after the death of Faustino. In spite of some sorrow, it would seem that their marriage was a very happy one. In the style of the day, Carolina remained in the shadow of her husband, who was himself reserved and, in spite of fame, did not seek public acclaim. As has been mentioned, except for rare references to her in his correspondence, mostly very conventional in nature, Machado de Assis never wrote directly of his wife. Some of the feminine characters in the author's novels may well have Carolina's qualities, and a few of his poems were inspired by her, especially one sonnet, "A Carolina," published after her death. Her literary influence on him, grossly exaggerated by some critics, was at best very slight.

Once Machado de Assis was established as comptroller in the Ministry of Agriculture—later the Ministry of Transportation, as promotions and the evolution of ministries led him into related positions—and he and Carolina were settled in a chalet-style house on the Rua Cosme Velho in the city, they had no serious financial worries. Their great sorrow was to be childless. In addition, there were problems of health, first those of Machado de Assis, who for a time had an extremely serious eye ailment and later suffered from increasingly frequent and grave attacks of epilepsy, then Carolina's growing fragility and a tumor that eventually caused her death. Nothing, however, kept Machado de Assis from his literary production, which, if it did not bring him wealth, was a source of many satisfactions and gave him fame.

Machado de Assis was motivated in his activities by love for those who were close to him (especially promising young writers in need of encouragement), by deep interest in humanity and culture, and certainly by a desire to leave something lasting of himself, his thought, and his art. Posterity perhaps assumed greater importance for him than for other artists, because he had no children. Further, his works were not fully understood or appreciated in his day, often bringing him no more than a *succès d'estime*, and so posterity was probably all the more important to him.

Everything that Machado de Assis represents is embodied in the Brazilian Academy of Letters. When at last in 1905 its membership honored him, he was presented with the oak branch from the tree growing over Torquato

Tasso's tomb that Joaquim Nabuco, the famous statesman and man of letters who was a friend of Machado de Assis and a member of the Academy, had sent from Italy for such a symbolic ceremony. Machado de Assis treasured the branch and other mementos, leaving them to be housed in the Academy after his death, brought about by a variety of as yet poorly defined causes on September 29, 1908.

Analysis

The first four novels by Joaquim Maria Machado de Assis constitute his apprenticeship as a novelist, during which he refined the vision and the skills that came to focus in *Epitaph of a Small Winner* and the powerful novels that followed. In his famous criticism (1878) of José Maria Eça de Queiróz's *O Primo Basílio* (1878; *Dragon's Teeth*, 1889; better known as *Cousin Bazilio*, 1953), Machado de Assis states that the aim of the novel should be to describe action derived from the passions and ideas of its characters. He refers to William Shakespeare's *Othello, the Moor of Venice* (pr. 1604), in which the natures of Othello, Iago, and Desdemona are the chief ingredients of the action, not the handkerchief. Machado de Assis thus favors the tenets of realism and opposes naturalism as too often superficial and therefore artificial, not to mention tasteless.

Machado de Assis's persistent concern with character—his references to *Othello* and his creation of the figure of Felix in *Resurreicão*—leads one to think that he was interested above all in tragedy. Felix, torn between a sincere desire for love and cynical doubt regarding his and others' sincerity, is a tragic figure surrounded by characters drawn too much either from life or from less noble forms of literature. The whole, therefore, falls short of being tragic. In *The Hand and the Glove*, there is a clash between two strong-willed characters, developed in a structure of Romantic comedy. Some significant details are reminiscent of Shakespeare's *All's Well That Ends Well* (pr. c. 1602-1603) as well as the triumph rather than the defeat of love in the conclusion.

Helena, which also contains reminiscences of *All's Well That Ends Well*, is not a Romantic comedy; its main characters are fully developed. Unfortunately, their passions and consequent frustrations stem from a case of Rio de Janeiro etiquette largely regarding the status of women. The substance is so slight as to lack any claim to the universality required for genuine tragedy. The reader experiences both comic and tragic emotions, but at times he or she is incredulous and even impatient with what proves to be a melodramatic situation and conclusion. In *Yayá Garcia*, Machado de Assis uses classical allusions and symbolism to a high degree and elaborates on the class, family, and personal pride of women as never before. Above all, there is the theme of love thwarted by society, whose interference is caused by the evils of self-love. Ultimately it is love that triumphs in *Yayá Garcia*, both in the main plot and principal characters and in the figure of the ex-slave, Raymundo, a symbol of Brazilian civilization as opposed to that of Europe. In future novels, Machado de Assis was to stress the passions of individuals in their struggle to be true to themselves, which, for the author, meant to love. Social problems would reappear only whenever love became subordinate to vanity.

Epitaph of a Small Winner

In *Epitaph of a Small Winner*, for the first time in Machado de Assis's works, the main character is a man. Never again was a woman to be his principal subject. Self-love is the theme, and with it the several forms of evil and death to which vanity gives rise. Brás Cubas, the narrator of these memoirs, is dead, not only at the time of publication but also at the time of composition. Brás Cubas writes to pass time in eternity, still preoccupied with his fellows and in a detached mood much like the one that was his throughout life. Despite its seemingly misanthropic theme and its deep pessimism, the novel can be interpreted as profoundly comic.

There are many literary allusions and influences in *Epitaph of a Small Winner*. Very early in the novel, the reader is made aware of the importance of the picaresque genre, especially Charles Dickens's *Pickwick Papers* (1836-1837, serial; 1837, book), Laurence Sterne's *The Life and Opinions of Tristram Shandy, Gent.* (1759-1767), and Alain-René Lesage's *Histoire de Gil Blas de Santillane* (1715-1735; *The History of Gil Blas of Santillane*, 1716, 1735; better known as *Gil Blas*, 1749, 1962). The picaresque novel is comic in its parody, satire, and irony; at the same time, it may be very serious in its portrayal of manners, with philosophical implications, as is Miguel de Cervantes' *Don Quixote de la Mancha* (1605, 1615).

The traditional picaresque novel has one main character, usually male, who, whatever the circumstances of his birth, finds himself in the criminal or low class of society, rising after many adventures of all sorts to marry and settle down to lead a respectable if somewhat parasitic life. The life of the picaro is customarily traced in minute detail, from his origins through his childhood, adolescence, and early maturity and into middle age. Machado de Assis parodies his predecessors by having Brás Cubas begin his narrative after death and move backward through a series of regressions to his funeral and last illness. Contrary to the practice of his predecessors, however, Machado de Assis's is most economical and dramatic. Brás sees Virgília, his former mistress, when he is on his deathbed, not as she is, but as she was when they were lovers, and in his delirium he is taken back in time to his birth.

Brás has the proper genealogy for a picaro. The Cubas family is well-to-do—their wealth is based on the efforts of the founder of the family in Brazil, who was originally a mender of *cubas* (vats or barrels)—and Brás's father named his son after a famous early Brazilian patriot in the hope of associating his relatively humble family with the more distinguished one. The name of Brás further suggests Brazil, and there are numerous references and overtones to suggest that Brás may be taken as a kind of epic figure for Brazilians. Brás's upbringing is typical for the son of such a family in the Rio de Janeiro of the early nineteenth century. Spoiled by his parents and debauched by one uncle, he is little influenced by the ineffectual religious education of his other uncle. When Brás takes up with Marcella, a high-priced girl who promptly sets about depleting the Cubas fortune, his father has him abducted and sent off to the University of Coimbra. Typically, Brás forgets Marcella even before the ship reaches Portugal.

Although he claims to be inclined to melancholy, Brás never experiences serious emotion for very long. Like Jacques in Shakespeare's *As You Like It* (pr. c. 1599-1600), he leads a frivolous, empty life. Awareness of his apathy gives Brás the overtones of a tragic figure, but he does not struggle in the manner of an epic or tragic hero. Rather, he uses his great intelligence to observe, analyze, and write of his defects, which are also those of his fellows. He is thus primarily the comic author of a kind of comedy, human if not divine. The reader is occasionally led to expect more emotion of Brás, to no avail. During his long affair with Virgília, for example, she conceives a child by him but soon miscarries. He does not have time to feel emotion for mother or child. When Virgília at last passes out of his life, Brás, then in his forties, decides that it is time to marry. Alas, the lovely young Eulália dies of yellow fever before the wedding. Again there is no opportunity for very serious involvement.

Whether as the hero of a serious genre or of the picaresque, Brás must consider himself a failure. He lists his many defeats, including his one bid for fame, the invention of his medicinal plaster, which, instead of curing his melancholy, caused his death. When finally he balances the good against the evil in his life, Brás finds the only credit to be that, having had no child, he has bequeathed the legacy of human wretchedness to no one.

Despite the apparent pessimism of this last remark, often applied to Machado de Assis himself, Brás has the spirit if not the luck of a true picaro, both in his tour of life and in his tomb. Although he stresses pessimism and death, Brás is a most carefree corpse, and his tomb seems cozy enough. *Epitaph of a Small Winner* is a comedy of human vanity, of which almost all the characters are guilty, to the virtual exclusion of any other flaw. Vanity gives rise to ambition, which is the source of much that is good as well as evil. The point is that good, generous actions have the same source as vicious ones. Indeed, the latter are merely exaggerations of the former; as such, vice and virtue are one and the same.

"Humanitism"—the mad philosophy of Quincas (a nickname for Joaquim, Machado de Assis's given name) Borba, a secondary character in this novel—is a complete expression of egotism. In the elaboration of humanitism, Machado de Assis was no doubt satirizing many "isms" (and perhaps even himself as something of a philosopher). As he had previously criticized the determinism of naturalism in literature, Machado de Assis was now criticizing above all the positivism of Auguste Comte that had taken root as a religion in Brazil. Although Brás Cubas is sane and Quincas Borba insane, there is considerable similarity between their philosophies. Brás's determinism, expressed in his theory of "rolling balls," when projected in the action of the novel suggests that a combination of human will and chance governs life. The "pessimism" of Machado de Assis's work is thus relieved by a certain moral tone. Like much comedy, it has a moral purpose. Moreover, its author and its hero are not to be confused. If at times they bear some resemblance to each other—as posterity and the critics (to whom the novelist alluded as "worms") have not always understood—it must be understood that Machado de Assis often poked fun at himself, as he causes Brás to poke fun at himself and life in all of its aspects. Brás's true cure for melancholy is not his medicinal plaster but his book.

DOM CASMURRO

Machado de Assis's seventh novel, *Dom Casmurro*, both incorporates elements of its predecessors and is a more nearly perfect work of art than any of them. Especially impressive is Machado de Assis's progress in the use of symbolism. The narrator and chief character, Bento Santiago, explains early his nickname and the title of the work, but only partially. *Dom*, an honorary term applied only to the highest nobility and clergy, was given to him to ridicule his aristocratic pretensions. *Casmurro* meant "stubborn" in Machado de Assis's day, but was added to the *Dom* by an angry neighbor to signify "morose and withdrawn." This meaning has since found its way into Portuguese dictionaries; however, both meanings of the word characterize Santiago, his obstinacy making him morose and withdrawn.

Like other of Machado de Assis's characters, Santiago is two men in one. In his case, the combination comprises Othello and Iago, creating an almost purely tragic figure and one to bring about tragedy for others. Santiago is born into a family of wealth and rank, and he is handsome, well educated, and quite intelligent. Moreover, the narrator creates a semidivine aura for himself by telling the reader that his safe birth was considered miraculous by his mother and the family priest, and that in thanksgiving he was named Bento (blessed) and destined for the seminary. Santiago tells the reader directly that he is an Othello with a guilty Desdemona. Indirectly, because he likes to confide in his reader, he reveals that he is Iago as well, innately evil and determined to find an object for his jealousy.

Machado de Assis intrudes not at all. The reader must therefore be attentive to discover the real Santiago as, often with considerable wit, he narrates his life, describes the members of his family and his acquaintances, and above all paints a wonderful portrait of his lovely Capitu as a girl, young woman, and wife. Bento and Capitu conspire to persuade his mother to break her vow to make a priest of him, a vow that she does not wish to keep in any case. It is easy to see how Capitu captivates Bento, especially as he cleverly includes details that encourage the careless reader to accept the eventual adultery of which he accuses her. The real culprit, one learns, is Santiago, a man who refused to love and to be loved.

Again, the action in *Dom Casmurro* stems from the characters' passions, from a clash of opposing wills. Both are found in the principal character, the will to love and the will to deny that love. He is not without feelings of guilt, however, and must project that guilt onto others, especially Capitu. Again, the theme is self-love, evil, and death (albeit a living death) versus love, good, and life. Santiago suggests that it is Capitu and Escobar, her supposed lover, who murdered his love; even if they were guilty of adultery, however, the tragic jealousy was in him even before his wife and best friend met. At the end, Santiago, made to love, faces a terrible life without love. Any victory on the part of Capitu or the other characters pales before the tragedy of the dominant figure of the narrator.

COUNSELOR AYRES' MEMORIAL

Counselor Ayres' Memorial is a sequel to *Esau and Jacob*, an allegorical work the characters of which are largely abstractions. Ayres, the narrator of both novels, becomes a real human being in the sequel at the same time that he embodies Machado de Assis's customary theme. His heart desires love, and in order to attain it he must undergo the emotional evolution that others of the author's protagonists have failed to accomplish. An intimate diary aptly replaces the somewhat self-conscious narrative of *Esau and Jacob*.

The action of *Counselor Ayres' Memorial* takes place during 1888 and 1889, although the characters are so universal as to be of any period. Old Ayres and his sister, the faithful widow Rita, are the only characters taken from *Esau and Jacob*, but they are very different emotionally if not physically. In addition, there is the loving middle-aged couple Aguiar and Carmo—he a self-made banker but an honest and kindly man, she a homebody who, though childless, is a motherly type. These and other atypical characters reflect changing times in Brazil as well as a mellower attitude on the part of Machado de Assis favoring social and economic progress. Political change had been initiated under the empire, was continued through the period of emancipation, and brought about Dom Pedro II's abdication. A new nationalism prevailed during the Republic, and Brazilians loved their country as never before.

With most of Brazilian society, Ayres has been under foreign influence, particularly English. As the name suggests, he has been much like the stereotype of the cold, dry, rational, and detached Englishman. Not only has he preferred foreign authors and foreign women, but he has also traveled in Europe and, as a diplomat, has lived most of his life abroad. In early 1888, however, Ayres is glad to come home to Brazil. Among the first entries in his diary, Ayres reports a visit paid by him and his sister Rita to the cemetery, a symbol of nonexistent or dead love, where he notices a beautiful young woman in black.

As Rita tells him of the romantic and tragic love of Fidélia and Eduardo, Ayres compares them to Romeo and Juliet. Their story is similar to a point, but the outcome is quite different, for they are not English, but Portuguese. With Portuguese stubbornness on all sides, they were permitted to marry but were disowned by their fathers. After less than a year of happiness, Eduardo died, and Fidélia has been faithfully tending his grave for more than two years. Ayres is still cynical enough to remark that she may remarry, with which Rita, of course, disagrees, but says that, as her brother is a very well preserved sixty-two, he can try to woo Fidélia.

Ayres persists in his fondness for English literature, so that, when he meets Fidélia at the home of Aguiar and Carmo, he recalls the first line of a love sonnet by Percy Bysshe Shelley that he has been unable to translate into Portuguese with the passionate conclusion of the original. Now begins a new kind of odyssey, during the course of which Ayres composes his poem with the desired conclusion, as Bento Santiago could not. Unlike the latter, Ayres is successful in conquering coldness and achieving resurrection through love. He learns to love not only from Shelley but also from the happily married Aguiar and Carmo; behind them are Machado de Assis and his Carolina.

Unlike Rita, who gives her love for her dead husband to everyone around her, Ayres has never loved. He married for convenience and, when his wife died, buried her in Europe and forgot about her. None of the women with whom he has had affairs abroad means anything to him. He has never been a father and has no regrets in this matter. Yet in Europe he experienced nostalgia for home and for the warmth of Rio de Janeiro and his native language. His heart, it seems, was not entirely dead. When Ayres comes to know Fidélia, he first experiences sexual attraction, then appreciation of her beauty, later admiration for her intellectual and spiritual qualities, and finally a disinterested love for her happiness that includes everyone who made or could make her happy.

Much of the transformation in Ayres and similar ones in other characters are brought about by Aguiar and Carmo, not only in love with each other for twenty-five years but also full of love for all people and animals around them. Under Carmo's maternal love, Fidélia's heart comes alive again, at first symbolically when she resumes playing the piano, then more concretely when she falls in love with Tristão. Another of Carmo and Aguiar's foster children, Tristão has a cold heart, too, when he arrives from Portugal on an English ship. He, like most of the other characters, has fallen under Aguiar's spell, however, and comes to replace Eduardo for Fidélia.

The several resurrections developed in *Counselor Ayres' Memorial* are mutually influential, but the one that affects Ayres most is Fidélia's. Her return to love is his as well. The old habits die hard, however, and the cynical old diplomat is intermittently beset by doubts regarding the other's sincerity. It is only his own sincere love for Fidélia that makes him recognize that she loves Tristão just as sincerely. Eduardo continues to be remembered and loved, but life has its rights, the same as death. Fidélia's love for Tristão must therefore be understood as a continuation of her love for Eduardo. Ayres understands many seemingly contradictory things that escaped him as a skeptic. His new faith gives him a father's love for Fidélia, Tristão, and all children. Indeed, under the influence of love he has become like a child himself. With his attainment of the ideal of love, Ayres completes his sonnet and his odyssey.

Richard A. Mazzara
Updated by Stephen M. Hart

Other major works

short fiction: *Contos fluminenses*, 1870; *Histórias da meia-noite*, 1873; *Papéis avulsos*, 1882; *Histórias sem data*, 1884; *Várias histórias*, 1896; *Histórias românticas*, 1937; *The Psychiatrist, and Other Stories*, 1963; *What Went on at the Baroness'*, 1963; *The Devil's Church, and Other Stories*, 1977.

plays: *Desencantos*, pb. 1861; *Quase ministro*, pb. 1864; *Os deuses de casaca*, pb. 1866; *Tu só, tu, puro amor*, pb. 1880; *Teatro*, pb. 1910.

poetry: *Crisálidas*, 1864; *Falenas*, 1870; *Americanas*, 1875; *Poesias completas*, 1901.

nonfiction: *Páginas recolhidas (contos ensaios, crônicas)*, 1899; *Relíquias de Casa Velha (contos crônicas, comêdias)*, 1906; *A semana*, 1910; *Crítica*, 1910; *Crítica por Machado de Assis*, 1924; *Crítica literária*, 1937; *Crítica teatral*, 1937; *Correspondência*, 1938.

miscellaneous: *Outras relíquias*, 1908; *Obra completa*, 1959.

Bibliography

Caldwell, Helen. *The Brazilian Othello of Machado de Assis*. Berkeley: University of California Press, 1960. Focuses on Machado de Assis's masterpiece, *Dom Casmurro*, and shows how Machado apparently used a modified version of Othello's plot structure. Also discusses numerous other examples of the influence William Shakespeare had on Machado de Assis's work. Caldwell was the first critic to argue that the novel's heroine, Capitu, was not necessarily guilty of adultery, as generations of readers had assumed.

_______. *Machado de Assis: The Brazilian Master and His Novels*. Berkeley: University of California Press, 1970. Presents a concise survey of Machado de Assis's nine novels and his various narrative techniques. Includes discussions of his primary themes, a useful bibliography, and some comments on his plays, poems, and short stories.

Dixon, Paul. *Retired Dreams: "Dom Casmurro," Myth, and Modernity*. West Lafayette, Ind.: Purdue University Press, 1989. Critical discussion of *Dom Casmurro* enables readers to understand how Machado de Assis cultivated a radically new style of writing that featured ambiguity as the most "realistic" aspect of language and conceived of language as a system of tropes only arbitrarily connected to physical reality. Suggests that Machado de Assis was critical of his society's patriarchal codes and that, as evidenced in the relationship between the novel's two major characters, Bento and Capitu, he implies the virtues inherent in a more matriarchal approach to sociopolitical organization.

Fitz, Earl E. *Machado de Assis*. Boston: Twayne, 1989. First English-language book to examine all aspects of Machado de Assis's literary life—his novels, short stories, poetry, theater, critical theory, translations, and nonfiction. Includes sections on his life, his place in Brazilian and world literature, his style, and his themes. Features an annotated bibliography and argues that Machado de Assis—largely because of his ideas about the connections among language, meaning, and reality—is best appreciated as a modernist.

Gledson, John. *The Deceptive Realism of Machado de Assis: A Dissenting Interpretation of "Dom Casmurro."* Liverpool, England: Francis Cairns, 1984. Focuses on *Dom Casmurro* in arguing against the interpretation of Machado de Assis either as a modernist or as a precursor of the New Novel in Latin America. Asserts that the author should be regarded instead as a master (if unique) realist and as a subtle and artful stylist whose work accurately reflects the prevailing social and political tensions of his time.

Graham, Richard, ed. *Machado de Assis: Reflections on a Brazilian Master Writer*. Austin: University of Texas Press, 1999. Collection of four essays includes two that examine the novel *Dom Casmurro* and two that discuss the political dialogues in and English translations of Machado de Assis's works.

Kristal, Efraín, and José Luiz Passos. "Machado de Assis and the Question of Brazilian National Identity." In *Brazil in the Making: Facets of National Identity*, edited by Carmen Nava and Ludwig Lauerhass, Jr. Lanham, Md.: Rowman & Littlefield, 2006. Discussion of Machado de Assis's impact on Brazilian identity is included in a collection of essays examining the unique character of the country and the identity of its citizens.

Neto, José Raimundo Maia. *Machado de Assis, the Brazilian Pyrrhonian*. West Lafayette, Ind.: Purdue University Press, 1994. Part 1 of this study explores the first phase of Machado de Assis's career, from 1861 until 1878, during which he went from writing essays to writing stories and, eventually, his first novels. Part 2 concentrates on his second phase, 1879-1908, with separate chapters on *Epitaph of a Small Winner*, *Dom Casmurro*, and later fiction. Includes detailed notes and bibliography.

Nunes, Maria Luisa. *The Craft of an Absolute Winner: Characterization and Narratology in the Novels of Machado de Assis*. Westport, Conn.: Greenwood Press, 1983. Excellent study addresses Machado de Assis's novelistic techniques, his skill at characterization, and his primary themes. Offers good summaries of his novels and shows both how they compare to one another and how their author grew in sophistication and skill. Argues that the essence of Machado de Assis's genius, like that of all truly great writers, lies in his singular ability to create powerful and compelling characters.

Peixoto, Marta. "*Dom Casmurro* by Machado de Assis." In *The Cambridge Companion to the Latin American Novel*, edited by Efraín Kristal. New York: Cambridge University Press, 2005. Analysis of *Dom Casmurro* is included in a comprehensive historical survey that traces the development of the Latin American novel. Includes bibliography and chronology.

Schwarz, Roberto. *A Master on the Periphery of Capitalism: Machado de Assis*. Translated by John Gledson. Durham, N.C.: Duke University Press, 2001. Schwarz, a Brazilian literary theorist, applies a Marxist interpretation to his literary and cultural analysis of *Epitaph of a Small Winner*, discussing the novel's style and structure as well as its views of nineteenth century Brazilian society.

CLAUDE McKAY

Born: Sunny Ville, Jamaica; September 15, 1889
Died: Chicago, Illinois; May 22, 1948
Also known as: Festus Claudius McKay; Eli Edwards; Hugh Hope

Principal long fiction

Home to Harlem, 1928
Banjo: A Story Without a Plot, 1929
Banana Bottom, 1933

Other literary forms

Claude McKay's literary career started when he began writing poetry at an early age in his native Jamaica. In 1917, he published two poems in *Seven Arts* under the pen name Eli Edwards. Later in New York, when he was coeditor of the magazine *The Liberator*, he published one of his most famous poems, "If We Must Die" (1919), as well as essays and articles. A collection of McKay's short stories as well as a nonfiction volume were published in Russian in the early 1920's; English translations of these works did not appear until the late 1970's. *Gingertown*, a collection of short stories, was published in 1932, and McKay also wrote two autobiographical books: *A Long Way from Home* (1937) and *Harlem: Negro Metropolis* (1940). His poems have been published in several collections. A memoir of his youth, *My Green Hills of Jamaica*, was not published until 1979, when it appeared with some of his short fiction in *My Green Hills of Jamaica, and Five Jamaican Short Stories*.

Achievements

Claude McKay was always considered a talented writer, and for a time during his youth and early adulthood, his literary output brought him fame and popularity. In 1912, when he was only twenty-three years old, the Jamaican Institute of Arts and Sciences in Kingston awarded him a gold medal for his poetry published that year in two volumes, *Songs of Jamaica* and *Constab Ballads*. In 1922, as a representative of the American Workers Party, he attended the Third Communist International Conference in Moscow, Russia, and had the singular honor of addressing the assemblage. In 1928 he won the Harmon Gold Award for Literature, presented by the National Association for the Advancement of Colored People (NAACP), for his novel *Home to Harlem*. In 1937, when his memoir *A Long Way from Home* was published, he was the recipient of the James Weldon Johnson Literary Award.

Claude McKay. (Library of Congress)

Biography

Festus Claudius McKay was born to Hannah Ann Elizabeth McKay (née Edwards) and Thomas McKay, peasant farmers and landowners of Clarendon Parish, Jamaica. He was educated by his schoolteacher brother, Uriah Theodore, studying, among other things, British and classical literature. Encouraged in his early attempts to write poetry, by 1912 McKay had published two volumes of poetry, *Songs of Jamaica* and *Constab Ballads*. They were written in the dialect of Jamaica's folk culture and were based on peasant life and his experiences working for a brief time in 1911 as a policeman.

In 1912, McKay went to the United States to attend college, starting at Tuskegee Institute in Alabama but transferring to Kansas State College. After a year in Kansas, however, he dropped out and went to New York City, where he worked at various jobs, including that of railroad dining-car waiter. He married his childhood sweetheart, Imelda Lewars, in 1914, but she returned to Jamaica to have their daughter, who was named Ruth Hope, and McKay reportedly never saw his daughter. He and his wife divorced after only about a year of marriage.

He continued to write poetry, sometimes using the pseudonym Eli Edwards. He was also becoming more seriously involved with radical political and literary figures such as Hubert H. Harrison and Cyril V. Briggs, two West Indian writers with socialist and communist leanings, and Max and Crystal Eastman, siblings who were prominent in socialist activities. McKay's association with the Eastmans, who were editors of the radical journal *The Liberator*, led to the publication of his most famous poem, "If We Must Die," in the journal's July, 1919, issue.

McKay's fame from the popularity of "If We Must Die" led to many different opportunities for the writer. He got the chance in 1920 to travel to England, where he wrote articles, often under the name Hugh Hope, for the Socialist periodical *Worker's Dreadnought*. Later, in 1922, he went to Russia to attend a Communist congress. He was still writing poetry and published four volumes by 1922 as well as a series of articles that appeared in *The Liberator* and in the Soviet press.

For ten years, McKay traveled throughout Europe and North Africa, spending brief periods in Germany and Spain and more significant time in Paris and southern France, where he wrote his first novel, "Color Scheme"; unable to find a publisher for the work, he burned it. His second novel, *Home to Harlem*, not only found a publisher in 1928 but also received considerable acclaim. He next wrote *Banjo*, which was published in 1929. By 1932, McKay had moved to Tangier, Morocco, where he wrote several short stories that were published in a collection titled *Gingertown*. His last novel, *Banana Bottom*, was published in 1933. Neither of his last two novels was a commercial success, and when he returned to the United States in 1934, McKay was not only financially destitute but also sick, having contracted syphilis. Ever the writer, he continued writing, but only his articles were published with any consistency; they appeared in such periodicals as *The Catholic Worker* and *Interracial Review*.

McKay spent some time mostly unemployed, ill, and lonely, having been rescued by his friend Max Eastman from a federal government "welfare camp" in 1934, where he participated in the Federal Writers' Project. His autobiographical *A Long Way from Home* was published in New York in 1936, and by 1944 he had become an American citizen and joined the Catholic Church. He completed the memoir *My Green Hills of Jamaica*, which was not published until 1979.

McKay suffered from hypertension and edema in 1942, and in 1943 he had a stroke. A heart attack at age fifty-eight, on May 22, 1948, caused his death, and he was buried in Queens, New York.

Analysis

Claude McKay said about his writing, "I must write what I feel, what I know, what I think, what I have seen, what is true"; he also wrote, "Art is not a means of escape but a way to confront the world and expose the true nature of the human spirit." Having this philosophy and the personal experiences of an exiled Jamaican living first in the United States and then in Europe and North Africa, he found race, class, colonialism, communism, and capitalism to be themes that captured and held his attention throughout most of his career. That he was living during chaotic times—those of World War I and the Great Depression, when the influence of radical movements such as Black Nationalism was growing and spreading—only contributed to his ongoing interest in finding a distinctive black identity to complement his pride in his African heritage.

McKay was certainly a man of contradictions. In his search for his own distinctive identity and place in the world, he experienced various lifestyles and even philosophies, searching for one with which he could feel comfortable. He tried homosexuality even as he tried marriage. He tried Soviet communism, which did not appeal to him and was ultimately disillusioning. The leaders of the Black Nationalist movement did not meet his expectations. He abandoned even atheism and agnosticism finally, as he embraced Roman Catholicism at last.

McKay developed a prose writing style that included the beautiful imagery he had shown in his poetry, especially in his descriptions of the physical attributes of African American characters and of the sights and sites of the New York neighborhood of Harlem. He created natural and unforced dialogue for his characters and "brutally honest" narrative. Although by the standards of the early twenty-first century his style might be considered stilted, his works were ahead of their time in their realism. Some critics consider McKay to be the "first and most militant voice of the Harlem Renaissance."

He used picaresque elements in his novels, which show the working-class lives of African Americans in the 1920's. Because he tried to portray these lives in a realistic, even naturalistic manner, some critics at the time of their publication condemned what they saw as a "blatant focus on sex, drugs, alcohol and . . . prostitution." McKay's position, however, was that he was presenting black life not only as he lived it but also as he observed it, both in Harlem and, later, in France. He was not surprised that the black intelligentsia, so clamorously represented by Alain Locke and W. E. B. Du Bois, did not like his portrayal. McKay believed that his mission was to show life as he saw it, not as one might wish it to be. Through themes of dislocation, marginality, alienation, and disillusionment, he created stories about characters who were living in the midst of irreconcilable cultural clashes between two societies, one black, the other white.

Home to Harlem

Home to Harlem, McKay's most widely read novel, is the story of Jake, a black soldier who has gone absent without leave from his unit during World War I and returned to his home in Harlem. He almost immediately picks up a young woman in a cabaret and spends the night with her. The next morning, when he discovers that she has gone, leaving behind his last fifty dollars that he had given her and a sweet note, he is dismayed to realize he has no way to find her again. The rest of the story follows Jake as he encounters other women and finds work to support his various ways of entertaining himself in the many "metropolitan fleshpots" of Harlem. It ends happily with Jake once more finding the sweet girl he first met on his return to Harlem.

This novel has been described as "luxuriating" in the "sounds, sights, smells, language, and rhythms" of the African American community. Although Jake is the ostensible "hero" of the story, Harlem is actually the main character. Harlem comes to life with McKay's realistic depictions of cabarets, rent parties, and the poolrooms where his characters spend their days and nights. A character named Ray, thought by some critics to be the personification of McKay himself, provides insight into the many aspects of life among the working poor, whom he describes as "simple, earth-loving animals without aspiration." Such views, of course, added to criticisms at the time of publication that the novel only reinforced the negative stereotypes of black people that black leaders condemned. Nevertheless, either because of its depiction of African American life as mostly low life or in spite of that depiction, *Home to Harlem* was the first novel by a black writer to find a place on American best-seller lists.

Banjo

Banjo is a somewhat didactic episodic novel set in Marseilles, France, on the docks—an area with which McKay was familiar, having spent time there during his sojourn in southern France. Its black characters have drifted to Marseilles from many other parts of the world, and McKay's somewhat sentimentalized depictions of them as honest, natural, and even pure are similar to the depictions of Mexican and Spanish peasants as well as American "Okies" found in the writings of John Steinbeck and Ernest Hemingway. McKay's characters are vagabonds who have strayed to Marseilles from West and East Africa, from the West Indies, and from the southern and northern parts of the United States. They congregate in Marseilles on the beaches or at their work on the docks, where they engage in lengthy and occasionally far-fetched discourses on the issues that interested McKay.

The main character, Lincoln Agrippa Daily, is called "Banjo" because he plays the instrument. One of his friends, Goosey, a black racist who hates white people, derides his affinity for the instrument, which he sees as a symbol of slavery; Goosey argues that black people should not play the banjo because of its long connection with the degrading tradition of the minstrel show. Banjo contends that he plays the instrument because he likes its sharp, loud sound, which reminds him of what "American Negro" life is like. His character shows how a black man seeks the true meaning of human existence in a white society that excludes him.

A character probably patterned after McKay is Ray, a writer from the Caribbean who is in Marseilles after leaving New York City. Through him, McKay expounds many of his own views about Black Nationalism as an outgrowth of universal racial subordination. All the characters in *Banjo*, who are blacks from all over the world, discuss such issues as well as pan-Africanism, exposing those concerns significant to black men who wander the world searching for a home away from the homes from which they are exiled. The novel continues McKay's preoccupation with race and class and the influence that capitalism, communism, and colonialism have on them. *Banjo* reportedly had an impact on some of the pioneers of the negritude literary movement, such as Aimé Césaire in the French West Indies and Léopold Senghor in French West Africa.

Banana Bottom

Of McKay's three novels, *Banana Bottom* is generally considered his consummate achievement. Continuing his enduring theme of the black person's quest for a cultural identity in a white world, it tells the story of Bita Plant, a Jamaican girl educated in England by white missionaries. Bita returns after seven years to Banana Bottom, her native Jamaican village, to find her English-culture education at odds with her cultural heritage. Once home, where she is exposed to her more natural culture, with its festivals and West Indian superstitions, she embraces her roots and rejects what McKay portrays as a "colonial cultural ideology."

Banana Bottom is considered McKay's "mellowest" novel, rich in a lyrical style and in humor and melodrama. It shows that the peasant's own culture is to be preferred to the artificiality of an imposed Western culture.

Jane L. Ball

Other major works

SHORT FICTION: *Sudom lincha: Rasskazy o zhizni negrov v severnoi Amerike*, 1925 (*Trial by Lynching: Stories About Negro Life in America*, 1977); *Gingertown*, 1932.

POETRY: *Constab Ballads*, 1912; *Songs of Jamaica*, 1912; *Spring in New Hampshire, and Other Poems*, 1920; *Harlem Shadows*, 1922; *Selected Poems of Claude McKay*, 1953; *Complete Poems*, 2004.

NONFICTION: *Negry v Amerike*, 1923 (*The Negroes in America*, 1979); *A Long Way from Home*, 1937; *Harlem: Negro Metropolis*, 1940.

MISCELLANEOUS: *The Passion of Claude McKay: Selected Poetry and Prose, 1912-1948*, 1973 (Wayne F. Cooper, editor; contains social and literary criticism, letters, prose, fiction, and poetry); *My Green Hills of Jamaica, and Five Jamaican Short Stories*, 1979.

Bibliography

Cooper, Wayne F. *Claude McKay: Rebel Sojourner in the Harlem Renaissance—A Biography*. Baton Rouge: Louisiana State University Press, 1987. Describes McKay's life and career, providing insight into his complex personality. Discusses his social criticism as well as his poetry and his fiction.

Giles, James R. *Claude McKay*. Boston: Twayne, 1976. Critical study of McKay's fiction provides a good introduction to his work.

Gosciak, Josh. *The Shadowed Country: Claude McKay and the Romance of the Victorians*. New Brunswick, N.J.: Rutgers University Press, 2006. Examines McKay's contributions to literature beyond the Harlem Renaissance, with a focus on the context of his poetry and fiction within the late Victorian and early modern periods.

Hathaway, Heather. *Caribbean Waves: Relocating Claude McKay and Paule Marshall*. Bloomington: Indiana University Press, 1999. Explores the influence of McKay's and Marshall's immigrant status on the works of these two Caribbean authors. Presents analyses of their works that focus on issues of cultural dislocation.

Holcomb, Gary Edward. *Claude Mckay, Code Name Sasha: Queer Black Marxism and the Harlem Renaissance*. Gainesville: University Press of Florida, 2007. Discusses in depth McKay's novels *Home to Harlem* and *Banjo*, as wall as his unpublished work "Romance in Marseilles."

_______. "Diaspora Cruises: Queer Black Proletarianism in Claude McKay's *A Long Way from Home*." *Modern Fiction Studies* 49, no. 4 (Winter, 2003): 714-745. Presents discussion of McKay's role in the Harlem Renaissance, the black diaspora, Black Nationalism, and the black/white gay subculture of the era.

Maiwald, Michael. "Race, Capitalism, and the Third Sex Ideal: Claude McKay's *Home to Harlem* and the Legacy of Edward Carpenter." *Modern Fiction Studies* 48, no. 4 (Winter, 2002): 825-857. Discusses how *Home to Harlem* was influenced by Edward Carpenter's theories on sexuality, socialism, and gender.

Ramesh, Kotti Sree, and Kandula Nirupa Rani. *Claude McKay: The Literary Identity from Jamaica to Harlem and Beyond*. Jefferson, N.C.: McFarland, 2006. Explores McKay's life and writings with a focus on the author's cross-cultural experiences.

HUGH MacLENNAN

Born: Glace Bay, Nova Scotia, Canada; March 20, 1907
Died: Montreal, Quebec, Canada; November 7, 1990
Also known as: John Hugh MacLennan

Principal long fiction

Barometer Rising, 1941
Two Solitudes, 1945
The Precipice, 1948
Each Man's Son, 1951
The Watch That Ends the Night, 1959
Return of the Sphinx, 1967
Voices in Time, 1980

Other literary forms

Throughout his career, Hugh MacLennan was a prolific writer of nonfiction. Following his youthful attempts at poetry and the publication of his dissertation on a Roman colonial settlement in Egypt, *Oxyrhynchus: An Economic and Social Study* (1935, 1968), MacLennan began writing articles, reviews, autobiographical pieces, travel notes, and essays, publishing in a variety of magazines, including *The Montrealer*, *Maclean's*, and *Holiday*. Journalism sometimes served as a necessary supplement to his income and occasionally was used to try out material later incorporated into his novels. It has been claimed that his talent finds truer expression in his essays than in his novels; while this may be a questionable judgment, there is no denying the excellence of much of his nonfiction. Selections from the more than four hundred essays that he wrote have been collected in four books, the first two of which won Canada's Governor-General's Award: *Cross-Country* (1949), *Thirty and Three* (1954), *Scotchman's Return, and Other Essays* (1960), and *The Other Side of Hugh MacLennan: Selected Essays Old and New* (1978, Elspeth Cameron, editor). Additionally, his concern for Canada's history and geography found expression in his *Seven Rivers of Canada* (1961; revised as *Rivers of Canada*, 1974) and *The Colour of Canada* (1967). *Rivers of Canada*, in which MacLennan provided the text to accompany the beautiful photography of John de Visser, contains some of his best writing.

Achievements

Hugh MacLennan, as his biographer, Elspeth Cameron, has observed, "set out to be a writer, not a 'Canadian' writer," yet it was as a Canadian "nationalist" that he was first recognized, and in spite of his intermittent attempts to renounce this label, it was as a distinctively Canadian writer that his career and his reputation developed. He held a solid place as something like the dean of Canadian letters; for many years he was a public figure in Canada, appearing on radio and television, frequently being asked to comment not only on Canadian writing but also on culture generally and on politics. He made continual attempts to tap the American market (with some success, especially with *The Watch That Ends the Night*), his works have been translated into many languages, and his last novel, *Voices in Time*, is international in setting, yet MacLennan was thought of both in his own country and elsewhere as a, perhaps *the*, Canadian novelist.

Having written two unpublished novels with international settings, MacLennan turned to his own Halifax, Nova Scotia, when writing *Barometer Rising*. This first published novel was immediately successful and was praised for its Canadian nationalism. His next novel, *Two Solitudes*, treated the divisions between the English and French cultures in Quebec; the book's title, taken from Rainer Maria Rilke, entered popular usage as a convenient phrase to sum up this cultural schism. MacLennan continued to be hailed for his contributions to defining a Canadian identity. When his third novel, *The Precipice*, attempted to develop an international theme, presenting the love between a Canadian woman and an American man, he met with less critical acceptance. He returned to writing about Nova Scotia in *Each Man's Son* and followed this with a novel set primarily in Montreal, *The Watch That Ends the Night*. This work was both a critical success and a best seller, not only in Canada but also throughout the English-speaking world; it also sold well in translation. MacLennan's reputation as a major novelist was assured; it was bolstered by Edmund Wilson's lavish praise in *O Canada* (1965). Even the many unfavorable reviews of MacLennan's subsequent novel, *Return of the Sphinx*, which treated the Quebec independence movement, did not call into question his importance in Canadian writing. Those who thought this importance was only historical and that his novelistic powers had passed their peak were proven wrong by his subsequent and last novel, *Voices in Time*, which was well received even though it clearly transcended Canadian national issues.

As *Voices in Time* suggests, seeing MacLennan in the narrow focus of Canadian nationalism is too limiting. It is certainly true that his work was informed by his nationality and that younger Canadian writers owe a debt to his pioneering treatment of Canadian themes. It is also true that his achievement must be primarily judged thematically. While he was competent in plotting and occasionally excellent in characterization, these were not his strong points. He was a conservative novelist in craft, contributing no new forms to the genre, although his own technique did develop, especially in his use of point of view and manipulation of time.

Granting that MacLennan emphasized theme and wrote out of his Canadian experience, his relationship to Canada can be best understood, however, if he is seen not as a nationalist or a local colorist, but rather as a writer who used his Canadian background to put into perspective his political, social, and psychological ideas and to reinforce his sense of history. It is essentially as a creator of novels of ideas that MacLennan bids fair to appeal to future generations of readers around the world.

Biography

John Hugh MacLennan was born in Glace Bay, Cape Breton, Nova Scotia, on March 20, 1907. He drew on his memories of this birthplace, a coal-mining company town set at the edge of the Atlantic, explicitly in *Each Man's Son*, but his impressions of the seagirt land, a topography appropriate to the Scottish Highland character that was his heritage, entered, less directly, into much of his work. In this setting, his father practiced medicine among the miners. A dominating figure, "the Doctor" was to become the prototype of a number of characters in his son's novels.

In 1915, when MacLennan was eight, the family moved to Halifax, a venerable but lively port that fascinated the boy. The small city, with its sense of community, became a lifelong ideal for MacLennan, as did the contrasting beauty of the Cape Breton countryside where the family spent time in the summer, prefiguring the thematic retreat to the woods of many of MacLennan's fictional characters. As recounted in *Barometer Rising*, much of Halifax was destroyed by an explosion in 1917, but the city was rebuilt, and MacLennan was reared there, doing well in both studies and sports, and graduated from Dalhousie University in 1928.

Later in that year, a Rhodes scholarship allowed him to attend Oxford. While there he played rugby and tennis; an excellent athlete, MacLennan, as a novelist, frequently used sports to reveal character. At Oxford, he also wrote poetry and traveled extensively, during vacations, on the Continent. These holidays, especially those to Germany, were drawn upon in his first two, unpublished, novels and returned to in *Voices in Time*, and some of his own experiences from this time were used in creating those of his character, Paul, in *Two Solitudes*.

MacLennan also studied at Oxford, quite diligently in fact, and graduated in 1932, proceeding to graduate studies at Princeton. Returning to England, he met, on the ship, an American, Dorothy Duncan, who was to become his first wife. His developing love and his new devotion to becoming a novelist absorbed more of his attention than did his studies. While he did not find Princeton congenial, he completed his Ph.D. in history, with a dissertation discussing the Roman colonial settlement at Oxyrhynchus in Egypt.

In 1935, in the midst of the Depression, MacLennan's degree was not able to secure for him the university teaching position he desired; he accepted a job teaching at Lower Canada College, a boys' school in Montreal. (He was to give a fictionalized satiric portrait of the school in *The Watch That Ends the Night*.) After a year at the school, he married Dorothy Duncan and settled into a life of working as a schoolmaster during the day and writing at night, sinking in roots as a Montrealer, which he was to remain.

His first novel, *So All Their Praises*, had been completed while MacLennan was at Princeton; it was accepted by a publisher that ceased operation before the

Hugh MacLennan. (AP/Wide World Photos)

book was published. His second novel, *A Man Should Rejoice*, suffered a similar fate in 1938; its publication was postponed and finally dropped. These novels, the first owing a debt to Ernest Hemingway, the second to John Dos Passos, although never published, have their virtues. They both present comments on the political situation preceding World War II and employ international settings.

For his next novel, MacLennan turned, at his wife's suggestion, to Canada. *Barometer Rising* is set in Halifax in 1917. It was an immediate success. MacLennan continued his teaching and writing career in Montreal; an ear problem kept him out of the war. After the success of his second published novel, *Two Solitudes*, and the establishment, additionally, of his wife's successful career as a writer (Dorothy Duncan published nonfiction; one of her books, *Partner in Three Worlds*, 1944, won the Governor-General's Award for nonfiction), he resigned from Lower Canada College in 1945. Following a period of journalism and broadcasting and the publication of *The Precipice*, in 1951 he took a part-time position teaching in the English department at McGill University; he assumed a full-time post in 1964, becoming professor emeritus in 1979.

During the years in which he was establishing himself as a writer in Montreal, publishing *Cross-Country*, *Each Man's Son*, and *Thirty and Three* (a period described in *The Watch That Ends the Night*), his wife's declining health—she suffered a series of embolisms—added greatly to the pressures he experienced. Dorothy Duncan died in 1957. MacLennan dedicated *The Watch That Ends the Night* to her; the novel, originally titled *Requiem*, has as its heroine a figure whose characterization owes much to Dorothy Duncan. MacLennan married Frances Walker in 1959 and after a period of producing nonfiction—*Scotchman's Return, and Other Essays* and *Seven Rivers of Canada*—wrote *Return of the Sphinx*. This novel was unfavorably reviewed by a number of Canadian critics, but MacLennan continued to receive numerous honorary degrees and public recognition. He began consideration of another novel, but interrupted work on it to write *Rivers of Canada*. His last novel, *Voices in Time*, appeared to favorable reviews in 1980. In 1982, MacLennan retired from McGill, after more than thirty years of teaching there. He died in Montreal on November 7, 1990, at the age of eighty-three.

Analysis

Hugh MacLennan began as a historian, and, in a sense, he remained one throughout his long writing career. His doctoral dissertation, *Oxyrhynchus*, discussing the history of an area in Egypt during the seven hundred years that it was subject to the Roman Empire, foreshadowed such major themes in his novels as colonialism, the wanderer, the town-country antithesis, and geographical determinism. Underlying both the dissertation and the novels is a view of historical causality.

As Erich Auerbach has remarked, "Basically, the way in which we view human life and society is the same whether we are concerned with things of the past or things of the present"; a corollary of this may be that when a writer is, like MacLennan, both a historian and a novelist, his or her narratives of individual human lives will be shaped by larger forces that transcend the concerns of the psychological novelist. In MacLennan's fiction, geography is preeminently such a force.

In both his fiction and his nonfiction, MacLennan had a continual concern for the impact of geography on character, and thus, as people make history, on action, fictive or historical. That a Canadian, living in a frequently harsh terrain and climate, would appreciate the significance of geography is hardly surprising, but MacLennan went further, adopting a geographical theory of history. His sense of geography's interaction with psychology and history provides the ideological framework that, more than any other single factor, gives his work its distinctive character. This framework is especially useful to MacLennan as a way of putting into perspective his personal experience, for he drew less on "pure" invention than do many novelists. His method, in both his essays and his novels, was to use personal experience to support general and philosophical concepts.

This means that, fundamentally, MacLennan wrote novels of ideas; it does not mean, however, that his ideas were necessarily free from self-contradiction or that they remained entirely consistent throughout his career. His ideology, complex but ultimately growing from a sense of the fundamental importance of geography, is most explicit in his first three published novels, in which he worked toward a definition of Canadian identity by first contrasting Canada to England (*Barometer Rising*), then dealing with the potentials of Canadian unity (*Two Solitudes*), and finally differentiating Canada from the United States (*The Precipice*). The next novel, *Each Man's Son*, is transitional in that it conveys a strong sense of the land, Cape Breton in this case, while anticipating the greater interest in psychology that characterized his subsequent novels. Even in these later novels, however, history as geography remains a basic concept. While psychological concepts became more important to MacLennan, he employed topographical images to express this interest.

Character, then, in a MacLennan novel is closely related to theme, as is plot, and the theme is tied to setting. While he created a fairly wide range of characters, including some minor figures that are presented with Dickensian humor, the central focus in his characterization was either on the "love interest" or on a conflict of generations. Both of these recurring motifs are normally subservient to theme in that the characters, whether they come together in love, as, for example, Paul and Heather in *Two Solitudes*, or stand apart in years, as do Alan Ainslie and his son in *Return of the Sphinx*, represent different value systems or cultures. Their psychology, which motivates their interactions, is seen in terms of their conditioning by history and, ultimately, by geography.

Admittedly, this emphasis is modified, especially in the later novels, by MacLennan's concern with various ideological factors, such as Calvinism in *Each Man's Son*, and by his interest in psychological theories, especially Freudianism, particularly notable in *Return of the Sphinx*. Nevertheless, similar imagery and recurring motifs, reflecting a sense of historical causation, run through both his earlier and later works. One finds, for example, the antithesis between the city and the country; the retreat into the woods; the theme of the wanderer, exiled from his or her roots; frequent references to weather; and imagery of trees, gardens, and water, in all of his novels.

MacLennan's novelistic techniques did change, however, as he developed his craft, as can be seen in his plotting, use of point of view, and style. In plotting, as in many aspects of his craft, MacLennan was old-fashioned; he kept the reader interested in how the story will come out. MacLennan was by nature given to relatively happy endings, but after the upbeat conclusions characterizing his first three novels, his optimism became tempered, appearing more as a coda following climactic elements of tragedy in *Each Man's Son, The Watch That Ends the Night*, and *Return of the Sphinx. Voices in Time* has a series of climaxes occurring at different points in the novel and producing different effects on the reader. That MacLennan was able to unify the various narratives included in this, the most complex of his works in its plotting, is an indication of the development of his craftsmanship.

His ability to manipulate increasingly complex narrative patterns is closely related to his mastery of point of view. Although none of MacLennan's novels approaches a Jamesian concern for this aspect of the art of fiction, with *The Watch That Ends the Night*, as he moved away from straightforward chronological sequences, he slipped skillfully between first- and third-person narration. *Return of the Sphinx* uses third-person narration but with a shifting between the viewpoints of different characters. This novel, however, lacks what Henry James called "a fine central intelligence." Alan Ainslie does not provide this unifying quality as effectively as does John Wellfleet in *Voices in Time*; Wellfleet's perspective gives coherence to the novel's varied narrative strands.

As MacLennan's ability to structure his novels developed, slowly and within a fairly conventional framework, yet with increasing skill in his craft, so did his style mature. His earlier novels exhibited some tendency toward overwriting: *Barometer Rising* has "set pieces" that skirt the borders of sentimentality, *Two Solitudes* is sometimes verbose, and *The Precipice* is not free from clichéd expression. In *Each Man's Son*, the style, reflecting the dramatic structure, is tightened. *The Watch That Ends the Night* contains superior passages of description, although the dialogue (never one of MacLennan's strengths) occasionally shows some of the stilted qualities of the earlier novels. *Return of the Sphinx* is notable for its economy of style and in this respect prepares for *Voices in Time*, in which MacLennan's style is the most fully unselfconscious and "organic."

MacLennan, then, is a novelist whose works may be read for the pleasure to be found in an interesting story well told, but he remains a writer less likely to be remembered as a storyteller or fictional craftsperson than as a man of ideas, a dramatizer of history.

Barometer Rising

When, following his wife's advice to write about what he knew best, MacLennan turned to his hometown, Halifax; he used it not only as the novel's setting but also as its subject. In *Barometer Rising*, he was also writing of Canada; Halifax, with its colonial attitudes overlaying social and ideological divisions, is a microcosm of a new Canada. The book's title is in large part explained in a subsequent essay, in which MacLennan describes Halifax as a barometer for the whole country.

What goes up must have been down; if the barometer rises—if, by implication, Canada faces a halcyon future—it does so only after a great storm and a particularly violent stroke of lightning. The action of *Barometer Rising* is centered on an actual historical event, the blast that occurred when a munitions ship exploded in Halifax harbor on December 6, 1917. The largest single human-made explosion before the use of the atomic bomb at Hiroshima, it destroyed a major portion of the town and killed some two thousand people.

A result of Halifax's role in World War I, the explosion is also symbolically related to Canada's involvement in that bloody conflict. While the concurrent destruction of life, property, and outworn colonial beliefs—the old world dying with a monstrous bang—constitutes the core of the book, a number of other motifs are woven into its thematic patterns. The conflict of generations, the return of the wanderer and the Odysseus theme, the psychological aspects of technological change—these are all important elements of the novel that continued to reverberate in MacLennan's subsequent work. Underlying all the thematic strands is the author's view of historical process, a view that puts a strong emphasis on the conditioning significance of physical geography.

It is Halifax's geographical situation that underlies the book's basic contrast, that between old and new Canada, colony and country. The harbor gives the town its meaning; facing away from the rest of Canada, Halifax looks toward Britain and the Continent, in both a literal and a figurative sense. From the topographical facts, carefully elaborated at the beginning of the novel, derive the prevailing attitudes of the Haligonians: it is the preservation of England that motivates all of what happens in Halifax; the colonial mentality prevails. Had the geography been different, the town's development and activity would have been different, and, consequently, its people would have been different.

If geography is destiny, however, there is no rigid determinism in MacLennan's view of that destiny. Halifax, although pointed toward Britain physically and thus psychologically as well, is part of the New World and has, therefore, the potential for a different orientation. This reorientation follows from the book's central event, the explosion, an event that, while the result of accident, is influenced by topography in both cause and effect. The explosion is a result of the collision, in Halifax harbor, of a munitions ship with a Norwegian freighter; the crash occurs because the physical nature of the harbor limits visibility. As a result of the destruction, new values arise from the rubble of the old; Halifax is no longer dominated by the rigid ideas of its old colonial aristocracy.

While the story has this allegorical quality, with a message made explicit in a concluding passage on what might be termed Canada's "manifest destiny," its allegory is fleshed out with particular, three-dimensional characters, conditioned by geography and history, but living out their private lives within the interstices of that conditioning framework.

Neil Macrae, the book's hero, is, like Odysseus, a soldier returned from the war, bearing an assumed identity acquired after he was falsely accused of disobeying an order during an attack in which he was thought to have been killed. His accuser is the novel's villain, Colonel Wain, representative of the old order and father of Penelope—whose Homeric name is intentional—the heroine with whom Neil is in love. The cast is completed by a number of skillfully drawn secondary characters derived from MacLennan's memories, including Penny's younger brother Roddie, modeled on MacLennan himself, and Angus Murray, also in love with Penny, the first in a series of heroic doctors who appear in MacLennan's novels.

Following the explosion and the vindication of Neil's conduct during the attack in France (the outcome of the battle depending, just as does the collision in the harbor, on terrain), Neil and Penelope are finally united; the storm is over, and the future is bright. While the novel is marred by this rather facile happy ending and by its general didacticism, the basic interest in both action and character, reinforced with symbolism, makes *Barometer Rising* artistically satisfying. Although MacLennan was to write more subtly in future novels, *Barometer Rising*, representing clearly his basic approach, fiction as dramatized history, remains one of his best achievements.

Two Solitudes *and* The Precipice

MacLennan's next two novels also use love stories to express theme and continue to demonstrate his interest in the impact of geography on the character of a people. *Two Solitudes*, centered on the romance between Paul Tallard and Heather Methuen, begins with a description of the landscape of Quebec; throughout, the symbolism of the river, the forest, and the town reinforces the theme of the relationship of the English and French in Quebec.

The Precipice, with its love affair between a Canadian woman and an American man, contrasts Canada and the United States by relating the characters of the peoples to their respective terrains. Set primarily in Ontario, the novel uses Lake Ontario as a dominant symbol, reinforced by references to weather, gardens, the city, and other imagery prevalent in MacLennan's fiction.

Each Man's Son

Similar imagery informs *Each Man's Son*; thematic conflicts are drawn between two sides of the Scottish Highland character, between religion as a sense of sin and religion as inspiration, and between science and superstition, particularly focused through the contrast between the mines and the sea of Cape Breton. A major turning point in the plot occurs when Dr. Ainslie (whose name is taken from a Cape Breton place-name) gives his to-be-adopted son, Alan, a lesson in history, followed by one in geography.

The Watch That Ends the Night

Arguably MacLennan's best novel, *The Watch That Ends the Night* demonstrates a significant advance in his technique. The didactic quality of his earlier novels is reduced; the imagery becomes more involved, as does the handling of time; characters take on more interest, not as symbols, but in their own right. Concurrently, the sense of the formative power of geography on character is moved more to the background, as though Canada, having been conditioned by geography, is able to go beyond this conditioning. Nevertheless, in this, as in all his novels, MacLennan writes from essentially the same perspective on history and employs many of the same patterns in fictional construction.

Again, just as in the earlier novels, the book is based on a strong sense of place, in this case Montreal, described in memorable, often loving detail. Again, the plot centers on a love interest, a triangle involving George Stewart, who has autobiographical connections with MacLennan; Jerome Martell, a doctor with mythic qualities; and Catherine Carey, a remarkable woman (who takes on, for Canada, some of the symbolism Kathleen ni Houlihan does for Ireland) whose portrait owes something to MacLennan's wife Dorothy. George loves Catherine, but she marries Martell. After Martell is thought to have been killed by the Nazis, Catherine and George eventually marry, but, much later, Martell reappears. (The story begins at this point, and is told primarily through flashbacks.) Although Catherine stays with George, suffering a heart condition, she has little time left to live.

Within this framework, MacLennan presents a rich picture, with numerous well-realized minor characters, of Montreal during the Depression and during the time of the Korean War. For all his interest in psychology in this work, it is, as are all his novels, less a "novel of character" than a working out, through characters, of ideas, and a dramatization of social-historical processes. While the plot (except in the New Brunswick section) does not hinge on terrain, the imagery does. Images derived from nature control much of the book's tone, with references to rivers and oceans particularly important. In *The Watch That Ends the Night*, MacLennan moved beyond any mechanistic application of historical theory to the novel; he did not, however, change his fundamental view of the forces underlying human events.

Return of the Sphinx

His next novel, *Return of the Sphinx*, reintroduced Alan, from *Each Man's Son*, now a grown man with his own son. Dealing, on the surface, with events of the Quebec liberation movement in the 1960's, it is set mainly in Montreal and Ottawa but contains a "retreat to the woods" section and begins with an explicit statement of the impact of geography and weather on culture; it ends with images of the land. Beneath the political action lies a deeper psychological theme, in essence that of the Oedipus complex, as MacLennan extends in this novel his interest in psychological theory, begun in *Each Man's Son* and continued in *The Watch That Ends the Night*; he also extends his use of imagery derived from nature and geography to express psychological states.

Voices in Time

In MacLennan's final novel, *Voices in Time*, his lifelong interest in the perspective provided by history is obvious and central to the book's structure. Indeed, the direct, albeit complicated manner in which this interest informs the novel may be a key to its success. MacLennan's focus on history was always essentially pragmatic—to use the past to understand the present and anticipate the future; this is what *Voices in Time* undertakes.

The book intertwines the story of three men from three different generations: Conrad Dehmel, born in Germany in 1910, a concentration camp survivor; Timothy Wellfleet, a Canadian born in 1938 who becomes a television interviewer; and John Wellfleet, another Canadian, born in 1964. John Wellfleet is the central narrator. He is one of the few humans who has lived through the "destructions" of atomic explosions, and when the novel opens in 2039, he is approached by the young André Gervais, who has found materials related to Wellfleet's family and wants the old man to use them to reconstruct the past that has, in effect, been destroyed for Gervais and his friends. Wellfleet works out Dehmel's story, involving opposition to Hitler and love for a Jewish woman, and finds it subsequently connecting to Dehmel's stepson Timothy, who interviews Dehmel on television in 1970. As a result of the interview, during which Timothy accuses Dehmel of having been a Nazi, Dehmel is assassinated.

Obviously, the presentation of this material, these voices from different times, calls for a complicated structure: Timothy's story is told by John Wellfleet; Dehmel's is told both by Wellfleet and, through diaries, by himself; and Wellfleet's own story is concluded by Gervais. The time scheme moves from 2039, to the late 1960's, to 1909, to 1918-1919, to 1932-1945, to a climax in 1970, and finally to 2044.

Like the time scheme, MacLennan's view of causation that underlies this historical presentation is intricate, especially compared with *Barometer Rising* and his earlier novels. Nevertheless, his belief in the significance of geography, nature, and landscape in motivating character can still be seen, even though the landscape has become primarily urban, and character may be formed, or deformed, by *separation* from fundamental geography. Nature continues to provide MacLennan with a thematic contrast to the urban, technological environment and to be a source of much of his imagery. Timothy is cut off, in his technological world, from natural geography; at nineteen thousand feet, he flies over the woods his father's generation had known intimately. Dehmel finds a temporary salvation, in both the world wars, in Germany's Black Forest. John Wellfleet lives on the outskirts of what was once Montreal, with trees, flowers, and birds. Drawing on Walt Whitman, MacLennan uses lilacs and a star to make a contrast with urban technology and its sense of time; he has Wellfleet think of the "time-clocks" of plants and birds. In one key passage, civilization is compared to a garden. Most significantly, perhaps, when compared to the thoughts about civilization, its rise and fall, and time, which MacLennan presents in *Rivers of Canada*, is the mentioning of rivers, as when, for example, the cautious optimism that tempers the tragic events narrated in *Voices in Time* is symbolized by the return of salmon to the St. Lawrence River.

Voices in Time was MacLennan's final novel and was a fitting climax to a successful career. It indicated that although he assuredly has a major position in the history of Canadian letters, he was one of those novelists who, although solidly rooted in time and place, transcended both. His ability to dramatize his geographical sense of history suggests that MacLennan is a writer who will continue to speak to future generations, to be, himself, a voice not stilled by time.

William B. Stone

Other major works

NONFICTION: *Oxyrhynchus: An Economic and Social Study*, 1935, 1968; *Cross-Country*, 1949; *Thirty and Three*, 1954; *Scotchman's Return, and Other Essays*, 1960; *Seven Rivers of Canada*, 1961 (revised as *Rivers of Canada*, 1974); *The Colour of Canada*, 1967; *The Other Side of Hugh MacLennan: Selected Essays Old and New*, 1978 (Elspeth Cameron, editor); *On Being a Maritime Writer*, 1984; *Dear Marian, Dear Hugh: The MacLennan-Engel Correspondence*, 1995 (Christl Verduyn, editor).

EDITED TEXT: *McGill: The Story of a University*, 1960.

MISCELLANEOUS: *Hugh MacLennan's Best*, 1991 (Douglas M. Gibson, editor).

Bibliography

Bach, Susanne. "The Geography of Perception in Hugh MacLennan's Maritime Novels." In *Down East: Critical Essays on Contemporary Maritime Canadian Literature*, edited by Wolfgang Hochbruck and James O. Taylor. Trier, Germany: Wissenschaftlicher, 1996. Informative analysis of MacLennan's work is included in a collection of essays that analyze novels and dramatic works by authors from the Maritime Provinces of Canada. Includes bibliography.

Buitenhuis, Peter. *Hugh MacLennan*. Edited by William French. Toronto, Ont.: Forum House, 1969. Biography of MacLennan is accompanied by critical analyses of his first six novels and his nonfiction. Supports MacLennan's preoccupation with Canadian nationhood and provides an evenhanded, although somewhat academic, assessment of MacLennan's strengths and weaknesses. Includes bibliography.

Cameron, Elspeth. *Hugh MacLennan: A Writer's Life*. Toronto, Ont.: University of Toronto Press, 1981. Critical biography was written with MacLennan's cooperation. Presents assessments of MacLennan's work in addition to providing facts about his life, devoting a separate chapter to each of his seven novels.

Leith, Linda. *Introducing Hugh MacLennan's "Two Solitudes": A Reader's Guide*. Toronto, Ont.: ECW Press, 1990. Excellent resource for students includes an analysis of *Two Solitudes*, a chronology of MacLennan's life, information about the book's critical reception, a bibliography, and an index.

Lucas, Alec. *Hugh MacLennan*. Toronto, Ont.: McClelland & Stewart, 1970. Provides clear analysis of MacLennan's fiction and essays. Each chapter addresses a different component of MacLennan's vision in general and social morality in particular. Includes bibliography.

MacLennan, Hugh. Interview by Alan Twigg. In *Strong Voices: Conversations with Fifty Canadian Authors*. Madeira Park, B.C.: Harbour, 1988. In this absorbing interview conducted in 1979, MacLennan focuses mainly on his lifelong interest in Canadian nationhood and how that interest influenced his writing.

Pell, Barbara. *Faith and Fiction: A Theological Critique of the Narrative Strategies of Hugh MacLennan and Morley Callaghan*. Waterloo, Ont.: Wilfrid Laurier University Press, 1998. Analyzes MacLennan's works from a theological perspective. Demonstrates how the author's novels, particularly *The Watch That Ends the Night*, chart his journey from Calvinism to Christian existentialism.

Tierney, Frank M., ed. *Hugh MacLennan*. Ottawa, Ont.:

University of Ottawa Press, 1994. Solid critical study addresses MacLennan's works, personality, and character. Includes bibliographical references.

Woodcock, George. *Introducing Hugh MacLennan's "Barometer Rising": A Reader's Guide*. Toronto, Ont.: ECW Press, 1989. Offers careful, instructive methodology for reading the novel. Also includes a chronology of MacLennan's life and publications, biographical details, and an assessment of MacLennan's place in Canadian literature.

_______. "Surrogate Fathers and Orphan Sons: The Novels of Hugh MacLennan." In *Northern Spring: The Flowering of Canadian Literature*. Vancouver, B.C.: Douglas & McIntyre, 1987. Essay included in a two-part book on Canadian prose writers and poets examines what Woodcock perceives as MacLennan's central metaphor for the definition of "Canadian" nation: a generational theme. Also discusses the strongly didactic element that pervades MacLennan's works.

TERRY McMILLAN

Born: Port Huron, Michigan; October 18, 1951

Principal long fiction

Mama, 1987
Disappearing Acts, 1989
Waiting to Exhale, 1992
How Stella Got Her Groove Back, 1996
A Day Late and a Dollar Short, 2001
The Interruption of Everything, 2005

Other literary forms

Although she dabbled in poetry in her earliest attempts at writing, Terry McMillan's first publication was a short story, "The End," published in *Yardbird Reader* in 1976. Another short story, "Ma'Dear," originally published in *Callaloo*, is included in *Breaking Ice: An Anthology of Contemporary African-American Fiction*, which McMillan edited in 1990. McMillan has also collaborated on screenplays based on her novels, and in 2006 she published a collection of tips for high school students, *It's OK If You're Clueless: And Twenty-three More Tips for the College Bound*. She has also written articles for periodicals such as *Ebony* magazine.

Achievements

Terry McMillan has achieved considerable commercial success with her novels, three of which have been adapted into films that were received favorably. The film version of her novel *Waiting to Exhale*, which sold nearly four million copies and stayed on the *New York Times* best-seller list for months, was released in 1995; McMillan collaborated with Ronald Bass on the screenplay. The film adaptation of *How Stella Got Her Groove Back*, also written by McMillan and Bass, was released in 1998, and the adaptation of *Disappearing Acts* was made for cable television network HBO in 2000.

In an early literary effort, McMillan won the first *Essence* magazine college writing contest in 1974. In 1986 she received a New York Foundation of the Arts Fellowship and the Doubleday/Columbia University Literary Fellowship. She was a three-time fellow at the Yaddo Artist Colony and the MacDowell Colony. Her book *Mama* received the American Book Award from the Before Columbus Foundation in 1987. In 2008, the Essence Literary Awards presented McMillan with its Lifetime Achievement Award for "her contributions to contemporary African American literature."

Biography

Terry McMillan was born on October 18, 1951, in Port Huron, Michigan, to Madeline Washington Tillman, a domestic and auto factory worker, and Edward Lewis McMillan, a blue-collar worker. Her father suffered from tuberculosis and was in a sanitarium during his daughter's early years. The family included four other children, three girls and a boy. When McMillan was thirteen years old, her parents divorced, so she was essentially raised by her mother, a single parent.

McMillan's interest in writing began when, at age sixteen, she worked at a library and became an avid reader of such authors as Henry David Thoreau, Nathaniel Hawthorne, Charlotte and Emily Brontë, and Thomas Mann. When she discovered works by African American writer James Baldwin, she realized that black people could be authors, too. At age seventeen, she moved to Los Angeles and enrolled in an African American literature class at Los Angeles City College. There she studied the works of Zora Neale Hurston, Richard Wright, Jean Toomer, and, most significant, Ann Petry; Petry's novel *The Street* (1946), which depicts a black heroine's existence in a harsh urban environment, had an impact on McMillan's earliest writing.

Terry McMillan. (© Marion Ettlinger)

McMillan's first efforts at writing were in poetry, and when she was in college, some of her poems were published in campus newspapers. Her formal education included courses in journalism taken at the University of California at Berkeley. Then, when McMillan met black novelist and critic Ishmael Reed at a writing workshop at Berkeley, he encouraged her in her writing, and eventually Reed published her first short story, "The End," in 1976.

After McMillan completed her undergraduate studies with a bachelor of science degree from Berkeley in 1979, she moved to New York City. She enrolled at Columbia University to pursue a master of fine arts degree, joined the Harlem Writers Guild, and attended artists' colonies in upstate New York and in New Hampshire. At the urging and encouragement of other members of the Harlem Writers Guild, she expanded one of her short stories into the novel *Mama*, which was published in 1987.

Mama received little promotion from the publishing company, so McMillan undertook the promotion herself, writing more than three thousand letters to all the black organizations she could think of, including chain and independent bookstores and colleges. She offered to do readings and book signings and ultimately received enough favorable responses to develop a publicity tour. As a consequence, the first printing of *Mama* book sold quickly, and McMillan's successful efforts made an impression on her publisher, making her next book an easier sell.

Her personal life went through several shifts. She developed a drug and alcohol addiction but overcame it in 1981. In 1984 she gave birth to a son she named Solomon; McMillan's relationship with the child's father, Leonard Welch, ended soon after Solomon's birth. Later, Welch would take McMillan to court in a defamation suit, claiming that the main male character in her second novel, *Disappearing Acts*, was based on him and was disparaging and embarrassing. In the end, however, the court ruled in McMillan's favor. A second relationship, this time her marriage to Jonathan Plummer, also ended in divorce and legal conflict.

In addition to writing and promoting her books,

McMillan has held various teaching positions. From 1987 to 1990 she taught creative writing at the University of Wyoming in Laramie, and from 1990 to 1992, she was a tenured associate professor at the University of Arizona at Tucson.

Analysis

Terry McMillan's novels depict African American women whose lives are filled with personal crises, romantic entanglements, and conflicts as they aspire to upward mobility and professional success. The stories, written with honesty and humor and featuring engaging, interesting characters, chronicle the friendships between women and relationships between men and women. Considered autobiographical in tone, McMillan's novels explore African American urban family life in an episodic format, using an "earthy" vernacular that some critics have found distracting but that McMillan defends as accurate. She contends that the amount of profanity her characters use reflects the way women of her era actually talk—and she is quick to comment that male writers are rarely chastised for the language they use, suggesting the existence of a double standard.

In regard to style, McMillan has expressed her belief that every sentence does not have to be perfect, that in fact her first draft is usually the "most honest." She does not worry about how pretty her writing sounds or how lilting the imagery is, because most readers, she asserts, do not care about that sort of thing anyway. She believes that it is the people in the story who count; the human element and emotional responses are what make for interesting writing. Apparently, the critics' opinions about some of her work have not been shared by McMillan's fans, as most of her books have been commercial successes.

The themes of McMillan's novels reflect what critics consider to be the author's greater interest in material wealth and conspicuous consumption than in such unresolved issues as racial discrimination and women's rights. Most critics agree, however, that her stories cross the lines of race and sex to reveal universal lessons of life and love, and that their engaging narratives, appealing characters, and insights into the contemporary African American experience are a valuable contribution to popular literature. McMillan's upbeat novels about today's black women are in fact a new literary genre.

Because her novels have strong, feisty black heroines, McMillan is often compared favorably to such black writers as Zora Neale Hurston and Alice Walker. However flattering such comparisons may be, McMillan has stated her belief that African American women of her generation look at life differently from those earlier writers. Her heroines are intelligent, attractive, often unattached, often professionally successful middle-class black women who have strong, empowering relationships with each other and close ties with family. They also are often in disastrous relationships with the men in their lives.

Mama

The protagonist of *Mama* is Mildred Peacock, a twenty-seven-year-old mother of five who tries to hold things together when her abusive husband, Crooks, leaves her to deal with her own alcoholism and the bills that are piling up. To support her family, Mildred holds rent parties and takes all kinds of menial jobs, even working for a while as a prostitute. As her life sinks deeper and deeper into a morass of unpaid bills and increasing depression, she tries to escape more and more through alcohol. Finally, however, with her oldest daughter's support, she begins to turn things around, even deciding to go to a community college to improve herself and her lot.

Mama has been praised for its realistic detail and powerful characterizations, particularly of Mildred. Although it sometimes lacks focus and a clear point of view, this first novel clearly showed McMillan to be a writer with promise.

Disappearing Acts

The story of *Disappearing Acts* is told in alternating first-person monologues by the two main characters: Zora Banks is a music teacher who aspires to be a singer, and her lover, Franklin Swift, is a sometime construction worker. Theirs is a tumultuous relationship filled with passion, expectations, and disappointments. When Zora bears Franklin's child, she assumes full responsibility for raising the boy. At story's end, she has made it clear that she intends to leave Franklin behind and return to her family to raise her son.

Critics have described some of the writing in *Disappearing Acts* as wooden and have argued that occasionally McMillan states the obvious, but they have praised the dialogue as often lively and even explosive between the characters. The novel has been described as funny, earthy, and intensely realistic.

Waiting to Exhale

Waiting to Exhale may be McMillan's best-known work. The four women protagonists, all successful, independent black women in their late thirties, have a strong camaraderie based on their deep friendships with one another as well as on their disappointing relationships with men. They get together often to share their thoughts and feelings, revealing the pitfalls in their professional lives and the shortcomings of the men they meet and try to cultivate but usually discard. Because they so often find the black men they meet "sorry" and lacking for various reasons, some critics have accused McMillan of "bashing" African American men in general. The women in the story, however, never seem to give up on the notion of finding "Mr. Right," and even though the novel ends with two of the women still without significant others, two do find good men. The main point of the work, however, is that regardless of their success or failure in romance, the women are strong in their friendship and in their mutual support.

Spending months on the *New York Times* best-seller list, *Waiting to Exhale* resonated with African American readers in ways not seen since Alice Walker's *The Color Purple* (1982). It had sold about four million copies by the year 2000.

How Stella Got Her Groove Back

After McMillan took a vacation in Jamaica during which she met and fell in love with a young man about twenty years her junior, she wrote *How Stella Got Her Groove Back*, a novel more autobiographical than any of her previous ones. The main character, Stella Payne, is in her forties (as was McMillan at the time she was writing) and has gone to Jamaica on vacation in an attempt to "get her groove back"—to regain her zest for life. In Jamaica she meets Winston Shakespeare, a young man who charms her with his good looks and his directness and honesty. She is hesitant in her attraction to him because of the difference in their ages, but after a while she comes to believe that her hesitation is based not on her feelings but rather on what she thinks society expects of her. Throwing reservations about their relationship to the wind, she does the unorthodox and takes Shakespeare back to her home in California to live with her and her son. She loses her job as a security analyst and has to live for a while on her savings, but her main concerns arise from her ongoing questioning of her relationship with a man nearly half her age.

How Stella Got Her Groove Back was written in less than a month. It is written in a style similar to stream of consciousness, with free-flowing sentences and paragraphs and little punctuation. McMillan wanted the style to reflect the main character's desire to be free from slavish regard for what other people believe or think. Some critics have described the book as no better than a run-of-the-mill romance novel, but with a first printing of eight hundred thousand copies and the sale of film rights, it was clearly a huge commercial success.

The Interruption of Everything

The Interruption of Everything is the story of Marilyn Grimes, who, at forty-four years old, finds herself heading toward menopause and an unexpected, unwanted pregnancy. Already the mother of three grown children, she is also dealing with a live-in mother-in-law, Arthurine, who has an old pet dog named Snuffy. Marilyn's husband, Leon, is a hardworking man, but Marilyn suspects that he is handling a midlife crisis by having an affair. On top of these problems, her own mother, Lovey, seems to be slipping into dementia, and Marilyn's sister, Joy, a drug addict, is not raising her two children properly.

Marilyn has McMillan's trademark "best girlfriends" to listen to her complaints and concerns. There is also the man in her life, who, like many of McMillan's male characters, leaves a lot to be desired. Told with the author's usual irreverence, this is a story of a woman who must face and deal with her midlife dilemmas with little help from others. The result is a touching and often hilarious look at the way a contemporary woman manages the issues she faces when she reaches her forties.

Jane L. Ball

Other major works

Screenplays: *Waiting to Exhale*, 1995 (adaptation of her novel; with Ronald Bass); *How Stella Got Her Groove Back*, 1998 (adaptation of her novel; with Bass).

Nonfiction: *The Writer as Publicist*, 1993 (with Marcia Biederman and Gary Aspenberg); *It's OK If*

You're Clueless: And Twenty-three More Tips for the College Bound, 2006.

EDITED TEXT: *Breaking Ice: An Anthology of Contemporary African-American Fiction*, 1990.

Bibliography

Ellerby, Janet M. "Deposing the Man of the House: Terry McMillan Rewrites the Family." *MELUS* 22, no. 2 (Summer, 1997): 105-117. Uses McMillan's novels *Mama*, *Disappearing Acts*, and *Waiting to Exhale* as a basis for a discussion of how black families differ from white families. Addresses how McMillan's work contributes to an understanding of the evolving black family.

Fish, Bruce, and Becky D. Fish. *Terry McMillan*. Philadelphia: Chelsea House, 2002. Biography aimed at young readers provides informative discussion of McMillan's life and career. Includes photographs.

McMillan, Terry. "Author Spotlight: Terry McMillan." *Ebony*, July, 2005. McMillan focuses on discussion of her novel *The Interruption of Everything*.

_______. "Terry McMillan: The Novelist Explores African Americans from the Point of View of a New Generation." Interview by Wendy Smith. *Publishers Weekly*, May 11, 1992. McMillan reveals details of her early exposure to writing and of her experiences with publishers as a first-time novelist. Includes some discussion of her first three novels.

Patrick, Diane. *Terry McMillan: The Unauthorized Biography*. New York: St. Martin's Press, 1999. Emphasizes McMillan's achievement in rising from humble beginnings to become a best-selling author and argues that her success has changed the publishing industry's approach to works by black authors.

Richards, Paulette. *Terry McMillan: A Critical Companion*. Westport, Conn.: Greenwood Press, 1999. Presents analyses of McMillan's novels that place them within their cultural and literary contexts.

Larry McMurtry

Born: Wichita Falls, Texas; June 3, 1936
Also known as: Larry Jeff McMurtry

Principal long fiction

Horseman, Pass By, 1961
Leaving Cheyenne, 1963
The Last Picture Show, 1966
Moving On, 1970
All My Friends Are Going to Be Strangers, 1972
Terms of Endearment, 1975
Somebody's Darling, 1978
Cadillac Jack, 1982
The Desert Rose, 1983
Lonesome Dove, 1985
Texasville, 1987
Anything for Billy, 1988
Some Can Whistle, 1989
Buffalo Girls, 1990
The Evening Star, 1992
Streets of Laredo, 1993
Pretty Boy Floyd, 1994 (with Diana Ossana)
Dead Man's Walk, 1995
The Late Child, 1995
Comanche Moon, 1997
Zeke and Ned, 1997 (with Ossana)
Duane's Depressed, 1999
Boone's Lick, 2000
Sin Killer, 2002
By Sorrow's River, 2003
The Wandering Hill, 2003
Folly and Glory, 2004
Loop Group, 2004
Telegraph Days, 2006
When the Light Goes, 2007

Other literary forms

In addition to novels, Larry McMurtry has published a number of works of nonfiction as well as screenplays.

A respected critic and literary writer, he regularly contributes to *The New York Times Review of Books* and has been a contributing editor to *American Film* magazine since 1975. He has contributed articles and reviews to such periodicals as *The Atlantic Monthly*, *The New Republic*, *Playboy*, and *Saturday Review*. *In a Narrow Grave: Essays on Texas* (1968) is a collection of nine essays he wrote for various periodicals. In 1975-1976, McMurtry wrote monthly articles for *American Film*, some of which are collected in *Film Flam: Essays on Hollywood* (1987). He collaborated on the script for the 1971 motion-picture adaptation of his novel *The Last Picture Show* and has written or cowritten other scripts as well, notably for the made-for-television films *Memphis* (1992; with Cybill Shepherd and Susan Rhinehart) and *Johnson County War* (2002; with Diana Ossana) and for the 2005 feature film *Brokeback Mountain* (with Ossana). *Crazy Horse* (1999) is McMurtry's first foray into biography.

McMurtry's memoir *Books* (2008) offers invaluable insights into the author's lifelong love affair with books and reading, which inspired and shaped all of his writing. Born into a nonliterary ranching family in an isolated environment within a house devoid of books, McMurtry—who has grown to be more passionate about buying and selling books than about writing them—has worked tirelessly to change the very fabric of the hometown that nurtured him and served as the backdrop for much of his early fiction. In the process, he has transformed Archer City, Texas, into a book town. Filled with anecdotes about tracking and buying books, *Books* touches on incidents that fans of McMurtry's novels will recognize as having been incorporated into his fiction. In the memoir, McMurtry describes encounters with real people—such as Alice Roosevelt Longworth, daughter of Theodore Roosevelt—whose unique quirks he observed, captured, and blended into the personalities of his novels' characters.

Achievements

Larry McMurtry's early literary reputation was based on his depiction of hard modern times in North Texas. The novels *Horseman, Pass By*, *Leaving Cheyenne*, and *The Last Picture Show* are all set in that area, where the frontier and the old ranching way of life were disappearing while McMurtry was growing up. His second group of three novels, *Moving On*, *All My Friends Are Going to Be Strangers*, and *Terms of Endearment*, concerns an interrelated group of characters in the Houston area and focuses primarily on failed marriages. McMurtry's Pulitzer Prize and his greatest public success, however, came with his first venture into the traditional Western, his novel of the frontier past, *Lonesome Dove*, considered by many critics to be his finest achievement and the finest novel ever written in that form.

Biography

Larry Jeff McMurtry was born in Wichita Falls, Texas, on June 3, 1936, one of four children of ranchers Hazel Ruth McIver McMurtry and William Jefferson McMurtry, and the grandson of a pioneer cattleman in North Texas. McMurtry grew up on the ranch outside Archer City, Texas, and graduated in 1954 from high school in Archer City; the locale and surrounding setting served as the model for much of his early fiction. After one semester at Rice University, he attended North Texas State University, from which he earned a B.A. in 1958.

McMurtry was married to Josephine Scott "Jo" Ballard in 1959. The marriage, which produced one son, James Lawrence, ended in divorce in 1966. James McMurtry (born in 1962) lived with his father in Washington, D.C., until he graduated from high school; he has developed a successful career as a guitarist, singer, and songwriter. An occasional actor, he appeared in the made-for-television film adaptation of his father's novel *Lonesome Dove*. Larry McMurtry's former wife, Jo, is an English professor at the University of Richmond and has published several nonfiction books, including *Shakespeare Films in the Classroom: A Descriptive Guide* (1994).

McMurtry returned to Rice as a graduate student in English in 1958 and began work on his first two novels before earning his M.A. in 1960; he also wrote reviews for the *Houston Post*. *Horseman, Pass By* was accepted for publication while McMurtry was at Rice. The novel was published while he was a writing student as a Wallace Stegner Fellow at Stanford University in 1961, studying under Stegner alongside such later literary figures as Ken Kesey, Peter S. Beagle, and Gordon

Lish; McMurtry maintained a longtime friendship with Kesey, and when the latter embarked on a psychedelic cross-country trip in a bus with his Merry Pranksters, he stopped at McMurtry's home in Texas.

Between 1961 and 1969, McMurtry taught off and on at Texas Christian University and at Rice, while two more novels were published and he worked on his first long novel, *Moving On*. A dedicated reader whose early life had been greatly influenced by literature, McMurtry had worked occasionally as a rare-book scout for California bookstores while at Stanford, and in Houston he had managed Bookman, a well-known bookstore. In 1969, McMurtry left Houston and moved to Washington, D.C., where he wrote reviews for *The Washington Post* and served as a visiting professor at George Mason College and American University. In 1970, he became a partner (with Marcia Carter) in a Georgetown bookstore, Booked Up; another Booked Up was later established in Tucson, Arizona, and in 1988, McMurtry opened a Booked Up store in Archer City, Texas—it became one of the largest used-book stores in the United States. Since the early 1970's, McMurtry has divided his time between the stores and his writing.

McMurtry served from 1989 to 1991 as president of PEN American Center. In 1991, he suffered a heart attack and underwent quadruple bypass surgery; after his recovery, he plunged into a depression that lasted nearly four years.

Many of McMurtry's books have been made into motion pictures, most notably *Hud* (1963; the screen name of *Horseman, Pass By*), *The Last Picture Show*, which was filmed by Peter Bogdanovich in Archer City, and *Terms of Endearment* (1983). Actors in all these films (Patricia Neal, Cloris Leachman, Shirley MacLaine, and Jack Nicholson) won Oscars for their performances. *Lonesome Dove* was made into a miniseries for television, with Robert Duvall and Tommy Lee Jones in the major roles. A film version of *Texasville* was released in 1990. In 2005-2006, McMurtry and Diana Ossana—who has collaborated on various projects with the Texan since 1992, during his postsurgery depression—won many honors for their screenplay adaptation of E. Annie Proulx's short story "Brokeback Mountain," including the Academy Award for Best Adapted Screenplay and the Writers Guild of America Award for Best Adapted Screenplay. Beyond his memorable Oscar-accepting appearance in blue jeans, cowboy boots, and dinner jacket at the Academy Awards in 2006, McMurtry has chosen to lead a quiet life, devoted mostly to his two professions as writer and bookseller, and has avoided talk shows and gossip columns.

Analysis

Larry McMurtry's best fiction has used the American Southwest as its location and the characters typical of that area for its subjects. In the early years of his career, McMurtry dealt with life in the dying towns and decaying ranches of North and West Texas, often using as characters boys on the brink of manhood to provide perspective on a way of life that had reached a stage of corruption and betrayal. His trilogy that followed these early novels deals with the tangled relationships among somewhat older characters and reflects McMurtry's own move from Archer City to Houston. Later, he invested the Western novel with new vigor through two works, his classic *Lonesome Dove* and the satiric *Anything*

Larry McMurtry. (Lee Marmon)

for Billy, which holds the legend of Billy the Kid up to ridicule.

McMurtry has demonstrated the ability to change his locales and his subject matter when he feels the need for novelty, and he has been willing to revive characters from earlier novels to suit new purposes. He has been most successful in exploring the past and present of his native Texas, a state and a state of mind that provide seemingly inexhaustible material for his special blend of satire, romance, and tragedy.

McMurtry has used a variety of styles, from the elegiac to the rapid narrative, from the hilarious to the mournful. He has shown an unusual facility in depicting interesting and sometimes outrageous characters, especially women. While his fictional locales moved away from Texas for a time, in his later works he has returned to the settings and sometimes the characters of his earlier works. A regional writer, he has transcended the usual limitations of regional writers and attracted a broad audience.

Horseman, Pass By

McMurtry himself eventually said that *Horseman, Pass By*, written when he was in his early twenties, is an immature work. This first novel, a story of ranch life, narrated by a seventeen-year-old boy whose grandfather's livelihood and life are ended when his herd of cattle must be destroyed, sets many of McMurtry's themes: the ease with which people learn to betray others, in this case the old man's betrayal by Hud, his stepson; the mental and physical wear inflicted by the harsh Texas land; and the importance of the affection an older woman (in this case the Bannon family's black cook, Halmea) can give to a young man. This novel and McMurtry's next, *Leaving Cheyenne*, are clearly preparations for the success of *The Last Picture Show*.

The Last Picture Show

McMurtry's third novel is set in the early 1950's in the small, dying North Texas town of Thalia (there is a town with that name in Texas, but its geography does not fit the fictional town, which is clearly modeled on Archer City). Its central characters are Sonny Crawford and Duane Moore, two boys in their last year of high school. Neither is in fact an orphan, but neither lives with his surviving parent; both rent rooms in the town's rooming house, support themselves working in the oil fields, and hang out at the town's pool hall, run by their aging friend and mentor Sam the Lion. In the course of about six months, Duane and Sonny learn hard lessons about life and love.

Sonny is the more sensitive of the two. He falls into a passionate affair with Ruth Popper, the frustrated and lonely wife of the high school athletic coach—a stock figure whose homosexuality is masked by an aggressive masculinity in the presence of his athletes. Ruth begins the affair in desperation and is startled by the depth of her feeling for Sonny, while the boy is surprised and gratified by the experience. Both realize that the affair cannot last, but Ruth is devastated when Sonny leaves her at the invitation of the town's reigning beauty, Jacy Farrow.

Jacy has been Duane's girlfriend, a monster of selfishness who plays games with both Sonny and Duane, almost destroying their friendship. She keeps putting off Duane's demands that she marry him and insists on seeing another young man and going with him to wild parties in Wichita Falls. When Duane leaves town to work in the oil fields, Jacy decides to take Sonny away from Ruth Popper. Duane finds out, fights with Sonny, and blinds his friend in one eye by hitting him with a beer bottle. Jacy convinces Sonny to elope with her as an adventure, arranging matters so that her father will stop them before they are actually married. Jacy's wise and experienced mother, Lois, offers Sonny brief consolation and shows him that he must make peace with Ruth.

The boys' adventures have been made possible by the wise counsel and care of Sam the Lion. He has taught them about life, given them parental refuge, and shown them the limits of behavior by closing them out when they are involved in the mistreatment of his developmentally disabled ward, Billy. The safety of their world is shattered when Sam dies suddenly, leaving his pool hall and restaurant in the care of Sonny. The young man is forced to face the cruelty of the world when Billy, sweeping the streets of Thalia in his customary way, is hit and killed by a passing truck. The boys are reconciled when Duane leaves to join the Army and fight in Korea.

The Last Picture Show, named for the town's movie theater that is forced to close, symbolizing the decay of Thalia, is a compound of nostalgia, harsh realism, and tragedy. It deals with the inevitable loss of innocence of its central characters and with the hard realities of injury, loss, and death. It is frank about sex (Australian authorities banned the novel at one time), but it makes clear the price Sonny and Ruth pay for their affair. At the same time, its depiction of adolescence is often amusing and colorful; the boys take off on a wild adventure south through Texas and into Mexico, they enjoy playing bad basketball for an increasingly frustrated Coach Popper, they enjoy earning their own livings. With the exception of the incident involving the joke played on Billy, they do harm only to themselves.

The Last Picture Show also shows the meanness and small-mindedness of the people in a small town: Ruth Popper is scorned for loving a boy much younger than herself; the sheriff and other observers are callously indifferent when Billy is killed; Sam the Lion has had to live without the love of his life, Lois Farrow, because of the mores of the town; and the coach, despite his poor teams and his general ignorance and stupidity, is looked up to and admired by most of the town. Duane, the more conventional of the two central figures, is sometimes a bully and sometimes a fool. Nevertheless, there is a kind of soft quality to the novel. Most of those whom the boys encounter are sympathetic to them, including the waitress in Sam's café, the woman who is forced to close the theater, Ruth, and Sam himself. They have no parents, but there are plenty of surrogates to guide and care for them, and they seem always to be forgiven by those they have hurt. Billy carries no grudge against either of them, Sam eventually shows that Sonny has done his penance, and even Ruth forgives Sonny for leaving her. Duane is hard enough not to need forgiveness.

Texasville

McMurtry revives Thalia, Sonny, and Duane in *Texasville*, a comic look at Thalia after it has experienced the boom of high oil prices and then been hit by the oil depression of the early 1980's. In *Texasville*, Sonny recedes into the background, a forgetful and lonely middle-aged man who seems to suffer from something like premature Alzheimer's disease. The focus is on Duane, whose oil business has gone to pot, whose marriage to Karla (a new character) is in deep trouble, and whose love life and civic responsibilities provide material for comedy. His life is further complicated by the return to Thalia of Jacy, a thrice-married film starlet and mother of three children who has been saddened and made more human by the death of her young son. *Texasville* is longer, more comic, and more complicated than *The Last Picture Show*, but it is less affecting. Only an episode in which Sonny wanders off and is found sitting in the wreckage of the old theater recalls the tone of the earlier novel.

The Last Picture Show was McMurtry's sometimes bitter, sometimes nostalgic farewell to the North Texas setting of his early work. During the next stage in his career, he focused on young people in the Houston area, beginning with *Moving On*, a long depiction of the damage wrought by a marriage that is falling apart and a sad picture of university life and the lives of traveling rodeo performers. This second phase of McMurtry's career ended with *Terms of Endearment*, the story of a lively widow and her troubled daughter, who eventually dies of cancer.

All My Friends Are Going to Be Strangers

Typifying this second stage of McMurtry's career is *All My Friends Are Going to Be Strangers*, a novel held together only by the central character and narrator, Danny Deck, who was introduced in *Moving On*. Danny's experience is to some extent based on autobiographical events in the life of his creator. Early in the book, while he is a graduate student at Rice University, Danny has his first novel accepted for publication. In the euphoric mood that follows, he leaves Rice and marries Sally, a beautiful and sexy young woman who holds no other interest for Danny and who proves to be a monster. Her former lover accompanies them part of the way to California, leaving after they survive a flash flood in West Texas. After the couple has moved to San Francisco and Sally has become pregnant, she relieves her boredom by engaging in an affair with a blind musician and pushes Danny out of her life. Danny goes downhill, lives in a rundown hotel, and finds himself unable to do satisfactory work on his second novel.

Jill, a brilliant film cartoonist he meets on a brief excursion to Hollywood, pulls Danny out of his slump and lives with him for a while, setting his life in order. Temporarily he thinks that he has found the love of his life, and his writing is stimulated by an idea she has provided. Jill, however, has lost interest in sex (which seems to be Danny's chief interest), and their relationship deteriorates until she leaves him to return to Hollywood and Danny sets out for Texas.

The episodic nature of *All My Friends Are Going to Be Strangers* continues when Danny returns to Texas. He pays a visit to his Uncle L, providing a satiric picture of an old-time cowboy gone eccentric; he returns to Houston and makes love to various women, including Emma, the wife of his best friend, and Jenny, who had been his landlady; he goes through a nightmarish experience signing copies of his book at a bookstore; he has a horrible, violent encounter with Sally's parents, who prevent him from seeing his newborn daughter; and he is harassed and cruelly beaten by two Texas Rangers who take a dislike to his long hair. He goes for several days without any real sleep, and in the end he walks into the Rio Grande, pushing the manuscript pages of his new novel under the water and possibly intending to commit suicide by drowning (his intent is not made clear).

Danny's experiences are intended to show the dislocating effects of early success on a young man who has cut himself off from his roots and has become unable to establish real connections with any other human beings. He falls in love easily enough, but neither Sally nor Jill can return his love in the way he needs, and he has no way to extend his brief affair with Jenny. His encounter with Emma can lead only to guilty feelings for both of them.

Danny is just as much at sea in the other kinds of life he experiences. The editor of his publishing house takes him briefly into a world of authors and sophisticates in which he feels totally out of place. His brief experience in Hollywood exposes him to people who mystify and amaze him, but for whom he has no respect. He twice pays brief visits to the Stanford University campus, where McMurtry spent two years, but what he gets from those experiences is the knowledge that he enjoys taking drugs and that he is no scholar. Uncle L shows him that there is nothing for him in ranching life, and the professor from whom Danny took Sally in the beginning makes it clear that the professorial life is dull and unrewarding.

All My Friends Are Going to Be Strangers is a depressing book. Danny Deck is neither admirable nor particularly amusing. Two things save the novel, however. One is McMurtry's undoubted skill as a writer, which enables him to provide vivid and entertaining descriptions of scenes as disparate as the flash flood, Uncle L's encounter with his wife, and a literary party in a posh San Francisco suburb. The other is the presence of several interesting minor characters, from Wu, the exiled Chinese writer who admires Danny's work and plays table tennis with him, to Mr. Stay, the former-Communist bookstore owner and sonnet writer who hosts the book-signing party. Several of the women, including Jill, Emma, and Jenny, are memorable and distinctive. The novel suggests, however, that McMurtry's Houston years did not provide the material or the inspiration for his best fiction.

In a much later work, Danny Deck proves not to have killed himself: McMurtry brings him back in *Some Can Whistle* as a successful middle-aged writer who has chosen to live in relative isolation. He finds the daughter he has never known, T. R., and brings her and her two children to live with him. She is lively, engaging, and interesting; for a while she seems to be able to revive Danny's wish to be in closer touch with other human beings, but in the end, when T. R. is suddenly killed, the habits of his lifetime are too strong. He has not changed enough from his earlier self.

In the group of novels that followed *All My Friends Are Going to Be Strangers*, McMurtry seemed to be trying to demonstrate that he could write successful novels that have nothing to do with Texas or with the life of a writer. He expanded the brief satiric glimpse of Hollywood that appears in *All My Friends Are Going to Be Strangers* in *Somebody's Darling*, the central character of which is a film director trying to cope with her early success and the demands of two men she loves. The world McMurtry entered as a bookstore owner is reflected obliquely in *Cadillac Jack*, the protagonist of which is an itinerant antique dealer and the chief setting of which is Washington, D.C. The entertainment industry comes under further examination in *The Desert Rose*, which has as its heroine an aging topless dancer in Las Vegas. Each of these novels is entertaining and well written, but none of them did much to enhance McMurtry's reputation.

Lonesome Dove

That enhancement had to wait until McMurtry decided to write a novel in one of the oldest and most persistently popular of American fictional traditions, the

Western. With rare exceptions, critics have not treated Western novels as serious literature, since they have tended to follow hackneyed patterns of characterization and action. Patterns established by such writers as Ned Buntline and Doc Holliday in the nineteenth century were passed on almost intact to more recent writers such as Zane Grey and Louis L'Amour. What McMurtry did in *Lonesome Dove* was to reinvent the Western novel by taking its basic elements and elevating them to the level of epic. *Lonesome Dove* has attained the status of a classic of Western fiction.

The characters in *Lonesome Dove* are familiar to readers of Western fiction, here given new names: the silent hero, Woodrow Call, who cares more for horses than for women and who leads other men by example and by courage; the other hero, Augustus "Gus" McCrae, talkative and easygoing, always ready for emergencies; the prostitute with a heart of gold, Lorena "Lorie" Wood; the evil renegade half-breed, Blue Duck; the naïve but courageous boy, Newt; the strong almost-widow, Clara Allen; the handsome but weak gambler, destined to come to a bad end eventually, Jake Spoon; the unimaginative but dependable sheriff, July Johnson; the comic deputy, July's aide Roscoe; and a cast of thousands.

McMurtry's achievement in *Lonesome Dove* is twofold. First, he puts his huge cast of characters into motion. Beginning with a run-down livery stable and cattle-trading business in a tiny Texas town south of San Antonio called Lonesome Dove, the former Texas Rangers Call and Gus put together a herd by rustling from Mexican ranches across the Rio Grande, hire enough cowboys to run the drive, and set out for Montana, where Jake Spoon has told them there is a world of grass unclaimed by white men. Their journey is difficult and tragic, lightened at times by comedy, but it is never dull or ordinary. Lorie, whose beauty has been the only relief to the boredom of Lonesome Dove, makes Jake take her along, to the great disgust of Call, the former Ranger captain who can see no use for women anywhere, much less on a cattle drive. She and Jake are not part of the drive, but they stay close to it; many of the cowboys, in love with Lorie, are kept in a state of agitation—especially the top hand, Dish, who desperately wants to marry her.

McMurtry's approach to his material is leisurely. More than two hundred pages at the beginning, exceeding one-fourth of the long novel, are devoted to preliminary events in Lonesome Dove and the first stages of the drive: the arrival of Jake, a former Ranger on the run from a murder charge, with his news of Montana; Call's sudden and uncharacteristic decision to go, after ten years of relative inactivity; the raids into Mexico to steal horses and cattle; the gathering of an outfit to supplement Newt, Pea Eye, and Deets, the Hat Creek crew; Lorie's instant love for Jake, even though she quickly sees his weakness. Most of this material is humorous, largely because Gus is a man who refuses to take life seriously. The raid into Mexico is exciting and potentially dangerous, but even this adventure turns to comedy when the Hat Creek cowboys encounter two lost Irish brothers who left Ireland headed for Galveston and wound up missing their target by several hundred miles. The Irish brothers, despite their unfamiliarity with horses and cattle, are hired on.

The second major factor in McMurtry's success in *Lonesome Dove* is his ability to take stock characters and humanize them by making them recognizable and distinctive human beings while at the same time elevating them to mythic proportions. Call is a projection of the strong but silent type of frontiersman, quiet, self-contained, but restless and capable of angry outbursts. Despite his abilities, he is emotionally strangled. Gus McCrae is almost superhuman. When necessary, he can fight more effectively than other men, but he is also warm and sympathetic to women and to young boys in trouble, such as Call's unacknowledged bastard son, Newt. He brings Lorie out of her catatonic state and wins her love, but he is human enough to wish that he could have Clara instead. Newt Dobbs is the typical young man; subjected again and again to grief and strain, he grows and matures. The black scout, Deets, is everything a scout should be.

The pace of the novel accelerates once the herd is on the trail. As soon as the drive begins, disaster strikes. Two days out, the herd is hit by a storm, and the riders must stay up all night to keep the cattle from dispersing. The next day, crossing a stream roiled by the storm, the younger and sadder of the Irish brothers stirs up a nest of cottonmouth snakes and is horribly killed. It is the first of several deaths the men will encounter on their long odyssey.

Only late in this initial section does McMurtry introduce another set of characters: July Johnson, the sheriff of Fort Smith, Arkansas; his unhappy pregnant wife, Elmira, a former prostitute; her son, Joe; and the deputy Roscoe. In Fort Smith, July's brother, the town mayor, has been accidentally killed by a shot fired by Jake Spoon, and the mayor's widow is urging July to track down Jake and bring him back to hang. July, recovering from jaundice and convinced that the shooting was an accident, is reluctant to go, but eventually he sets out, at Elmira's insistence taking Joe along. Shortly thereafter, Elmira, pregnant with July's child, leaves town on a riverboat to seek out her former lover, the gambler Dee Boot, and July's sister-in-law insists that Roscoe track down July to tell him that his wife is gone.

All these characters, and others, eventually meet on the plains. Jake leaves Lorie to go to town to gamble, and while he is gone the Comanchero Blue Duck, a bitter, crafty, and resourceful renegade, kidnaps the terrified Lorie, takes her north to the plains, and keeps her barely alive only to sell her body to Kiowas and buffalo hunters, an experience that robs her of speech and very nearly of her sanity. She is rescued by Gus, but the cost of the rescue is high: July Johnson, still looking for Elmira, insists on helping Gus, and while they are dispatching the six Kiowas and two buffalo hunters who hold Lorie, Blue Duck sneaks into their small camp and murders Roscoe, July's stepson Joe, and a young girl who has been traveling with Roscoe.

Jake, in the meantime, has become entangled with the three Suggs brothers, hard cases who are getting harder. Jake accidentally kills another man and goes along with the Suggses, who kill several more, including the rancher Wilbarger, who has earlier befriended Gus. Call and Gus track down the Suggses and hang all three brothers; reluctantly, they also hang Jake.

Many of the elements of the plot resolve themselves in the Nebraska frontier town of Ogallala. Clara Allen, the only woman Gus has loved and lost, lives there with her comatose husband and two daughters. Elmira arrives first, has her baby, and departs with her buffalo-hunter escort, both soon to be killed by Sioux. Her lover, Dee Boot, is hanged. July Johnson comes next, sees his son, whom Clara has kept, and stays on as a hand at Clara's ranch. Gus and Call arrive with the herd, and Clara and Gus have a happy reunion, but she makes it clear that she will never marry him, even when her husband dies. Lorie finds herself welcomed by Clara, and she stays on when the herd moves north to Montana. Newt and the other young cowboys go to Ogallala and have their first experience with whores, and Newt decides to become a ladies' man like Gus.

In the final section, the herd moves north to Montana and to encounters with violent American Indians. Deets is killed by a desperate young warrior who fails to comprehend that Deets is not hostile. Gus and the cowboy Pea Eye, scouting ahead for a ranch site, are cut off by a roving band of Indians and attacked. Pea Eye gets away, but Gus is wounded. He escapes from the Indians but dies in Miles City after refusing to allow the doctor to amputate both of his gangrenous legs.

Call finds a spot for a ranch, and the men build a ranch house and corrals and spend a hard winter there. When spring comes, Call leaves Newt in charge of the remaining men and the cattle, tacitly acknowledging that he is Newt's father, but he cannot bring himself to call the boy his son. He fulfills his promise to take Gus's body and bury it in a Texas glen where Gus and Clara had picnicked years earlier. On his long and difficult journey, Call passes through Ogallala, where Clara's husband has died and she and Lorie are mourning for Gus. Later, he pauses long enough to witness Blue Duck's death. Call is shot and goes through numerous other trials, but he manages to bury Gus; at the end, he makes his way back to the deserted town of Lonesome Dove.

In *Lonesome Dove* McMurtry is at the height of his powers. The disparate strands of the plot are handled skillfully, as the story moves easily from the herd to July Johnson to Jake Spoon to Elmira and then back to the herd. McMurtry's ability to depict action comes into play often, as in the violent scenes of the young Irishman's death, Gus's explosion into the Kiowa camp where Lorie is held, the sudden thunderstorms that batter the cowboys and scatter the herd, and the sudden descent of a plague of grasshoppers. He is equally skilled at depicting character, not only major figures such as Call, Gus, Clara, and Lorie, but also young Newt and such minor characters as the cook Po Campo, Roscoe, Wilbarger, and Elmira. There is a leavening of humor, some of it hilarious, not only in the early sections of the novel but also throughout. At the same time, there is no attempt to downplay the violence and hardship of the lives of these men and women; the long journey is marked by one violent death after another. The hard life of the frontier is represented not only by Lorie's terrible experience at the hands of Blue Duck and the sudden deaths among the cowboys but also by Clara's loss of three sons and a husband to the harsh conditions of life on the prairie.

It is entirely fitting that the ending of the novel is grim. The most powerful scene in the final section is Clara's condemnation of Call when he returns to Ogallala with Gus's body, bringing the final notes that the dying Gus wrote to Clara and Lorie. Her scathing denunciation of his single-mindedness and the human sacrifice and misery the trip caused raises disturbing questions about the meaning of the heroic journey the men have accomplished. The surviving hands are left on the isolated ranch in Montana. Clara and Lorie remain on the ranch outside Ogallala, with July hoping to marry Clara and Dish hopelessly in love with Lorie. Call has no idea where to go after the trip back to Lonesome Dove is ended.

Other Western novels

The tone of McMurtry's next novel about the frontier, *Anything for Billy*, is very different. This book is a satiric retelling of the story of Billy the Kid, seen from the perspective of an easterner who has been addicted to dime novels of the West. The combination of humor and violent action that marks *Lonesome Dove* is present in the later novel but without the tragic undertone that gives *Lonesome Dove* its special power.

McMurtry's besetting weakness has clearly been his penchant for reviving characters and using them in sequels to novels that seem sufficient in themselves. Most of his novels can be classified as parts of trilogies, sometimes widely separated in their dates of publication. For example, *Duane's Depressed*, published in 1999, returns to the setting and characters introduced in *The Last Picture Show* and updated in *Texasville*. The pattern is stretched even further in the *Lonesome Dove* cycle. That very long novel, which fittingly concludes in tragedy and pathos, has since become the basis for a virtual library of sequels and prequels.

In *Streets of Laredo*, *Dead Man's Walk*, and *Comanche Moon*, the leading *Lonesome Dove* characters of Gus McCrae and Woodrow Call, as well as lesser figures, are revived. Adding to the confusion, the order of publication of the three later novels in the cycle does not follow the chronological stages in the characters' lives. *Streets of Laredo* is a true sequel that follows the career of Call after he has returned Gus's body to the nearly deserted village of Lonesome Dove. It ends with a crippled Call, minus an arm and a leg, dependent on Pea Eye and his wife Lorena and their many children. *Dead Man's Walk* jumps back in time to the years between the Mexican War and the Civil War, when McCrae and Call are about twenty years old and are new recruits to the Texas Rangers. It takes its title from the Spanish phrase *jornada del muerto*, which describes a barren stretch of land in what is now central New Mexico, where much of the action of the novel takes place. *Comanche Moon* takes the heroes through the years of the Civil War to their decision to leave the Rangers and settle in the village of Lonesome Dove.

As is the case with McMurtry's earlier novel cycles, the first book in the series is the most successful. One reason for this is that most of the salient facts are known. It is clear from *Lonesome Dove* that Gus never marries Clara Allen. The manners of his and Deets's deaths are presented in the earlier book, as are many other references to events earlier in time. Inevitably, this causes an absence of suspense. More important, however, there is in the later books of the series a sense of strain and a feeling that the author is adding incidents and plot lines simply to provide excitement. This is especially true of *Comanche Moon*, in which there is no clear, dominant plot line. Instead, several plots are interwoven in brief chapters, and much of the information is superfluous. It is enough to know that Blue Duck is a brutal savage, for example; the details of his early life add very little to the character.

The strain is more evident in the invention of two major new characters, Inish Scull and his wife, Inez. Scull is a Boston millionaire and Harvard graduate who is the captain of the company of Texas Rangers in which McCrae and Call are enrolled. His relentless search for adventure leads him to enter Mexico on foot with only a Kickapoo scout for company. He finds his enemy,

Ahumado, known as the Black Vaquero, but is taken prisoner. Subjected to a variety of tortures, climaxing with the removal of his eyelids, he manages to survive, although he temporarily goes crazy. Inez, while Inish is so engaged, is indulging her proclivities for young men and for spending Inish's and her own money. Their role in the story ends in farce, back in Boston. Inez continues to beat her husband with a bullwhip, and Inish turns down an invitation from Generals Sherman and Sheridan to take command of the western regiments that are crushing any remaining American Indian resistance. These exaggerated characters do not fit well into a realistic novel.

Duane's Depressed

After McMurtry's relative lack of success with the Western novels that followed *Lonesome Dove*, he returned to a contemporary setting in *Duane's Depressed*, which completes the trilogy begun with *The Last Picture Show* and continued in *Texasville*. Duane Moore, now on the brink of old age, is the mayor of Thalia. To the astonishment of the rest of the town, he abandons his pickup truck one day and begins to walk wherever he needs to go. His marriage in trouble again, he also breaks with convention by going for help to a young woman psychiatrist. *Duane's Depressed* is not McMurtry's finest novel, but it is fresher and less strained than the books that immediately preceded it and is a clear improvement over its predecessor in the trilogy, *Texasville*.

Loop Group

After revisiting the Old West for an extended period in the well-received Berrybender tetralogy, which deals with an ill-fated hunting trip in the 1830's, McMurtry returned to the present day once again in his 2005 novel *Loop Group*. The title of this slender contemporary novel covers several symbolic meanings. On one level, it defines the current existence of protagonist Maggie Clary, a businesswoman in her sixties. She operates Prime Loops, a successful Hollywood company that provides a small but vital service to the film industry. Maggie and her employees—a collection of eccentric personalities, including her childhood friend, Connie—supply audio "loops": sighs, grunts, and other vocal sounds for movie sound tracks.

"Out of the loop" also describes Maggie's current state of mind. Though she loves her work, her home, and her three grown, caring daughters, she feels out of sorts, incomplete. Her psychic discomfort stems from a recent hysterectomy and the symptoms of menopause, complete with depression and sexual cravings. Nothing, she decides, will cure her angst except a change of pace. A road trip with her best friend is called for. She and Connie will hop in a van and drive to Electric City, Texas, to visit eighty-year-old Aunt Cooney, living in the midst of two million chickens at her ranch.

Rather than the escape Maggie hoped for, the journey is instead merely the exchange of one loop group, one movielike milieu, for another. The two women, bolstered by a loaded pistol in the glove compartment, take foolish, unrealistic chances in search of physical, emotional, and mental sensations. The people they encounter are every bit as peculiar as those they have left behind. Virtually every temporary acquaintance has a quirk; worse, some of them are dangerously unstable.

Although *Loop Group* was mildly successful commercially thanks to the power of McMurtry's name and reputation based on his many previous novels, it was a critical failure. The author's strengths are in evidence in the work: well-drawn characters, tension-creating plot twists contrasted with chuckle-inducing slapstick situations, and cinematic, evocative descriptions. The whole exercise, however, seems pointless. Was this trip really necessary?

The plot of *Loop Group* is of necessity episodic, but the story becomes repetitive, as one weirdo after another parades by, interacts for a time with the two women, and is forgotten in the time it takes to vanish in the rearview mirror. Hitchhikers, car thieves, child molesters, and state troopers—all carry equal weight in their lack of lasting effect on Maggie's and Connie's lives. The novel provides nothing to hang on to, nothing memorable to take away as a lesson learned. None of the characters has much of importance to say; surprisingly, dialogue is a particular weakness in *Loop Group*. The women gain no valuable insights in their travels. They discover no newfound meaning of life. Maggie and Connie never appear to have benefited from their advanced years. They finish back virtually where they started, both in their location and in their understanding of who they are and what they want; in essence, they are part of a continuous loop with no beginning or end.

It is difficult to know what effect McMurtry was trying to achieve in *Loop Group*. Perhaps he intended nothing more profound than the concept that real life can be just as absurd as what is depicted on the big screen, or maybe the author was undergoing the same experiences as his main character—depression, a sense of loss, of being out of touch. It is possible that McMurtry, well into his sixties when he published this novel, was simply feeling his age.

John M. Muste
Updated by Jack Ewing

Other major works

SCREENPLAYS: *The Last Picture Show*, 1971 (based on his novel; with Peter Bogdanovich); *Falling from Grace*, 1992; *Brokeback Mountain*, 2005 (with Diana Ossana; based on E. Annie Proulx's short story).

TELEPLAYS: *Montana*, 1990; *Memphis*, 1992 (based on Shelby Foote's novel *September September*; with Cybill Shepherd and Susan Rhinehart); *Streets of Laredo*, 1995 (based on his novel; with Diana Ossana); *Dead Man's Walk*, 1996 (based on his novel; with Ossana); *Johnson County War*, 2002 (based on Frederick Manfred's novel *Riders of Judgement*; with Ossana); *Comanche Moon*, 2008 (based on his novel; with Ossana).

NONFICTION: *In a Narrow Grave: Essays on Texas*, 1968; *It's Always We Rambled: An Essay on Rodeo*, 1974; *Film Flam: Essays on Hollywood*, 1987; *Crazy Horse*, 1999; *Walter Benjamin at the Dairy Queen: Reflections at Sixty and Beyond*, 1999; *Roads: Driving America's Great Highways*, 2000; *Paradise*, 2001; *Sacagawea's Nickname: Essays on the American West*, 2001; *The Colonel and Little Missie: Buffalo Bill, Annie Oakley, and the Beginnings of Superstardom in America*, 2005; *Oh What a Slaughter: Massacres in the American West, 1846-1890*, 2006; *Books: A Memoir*, 2008.

EDITED TEXT: *Still Wild: Short Fiction of the American West*, 2000.

Bibliography

Busby, Mark. *Larry McMurtry and the West: An Ambivalent Relationship*. Denton: University of North Texas Press, 1995. Examines McMurtry's treatment of the West in his works. Includes bibliographical references and index.

Etulain, Richard W. *Telling Western Stories: From Buffalo Bill to Larry McMurtry*. Albuquerque: University of New Mexico Press, 1999. A cultural historian addresses how fiction has influenced the public's images of the American West. Places McMurtry's work within a period of fiction about the West that exhibits increasing complexity and ambiguity.

Jones, Malcolm. "The Poet Lariat." *Newsweek*, January 11, 1999, 62-63. Reviews *Duane's Depressed* and also provides a great deal of information about McMurtry's life and career.

Jones, Roger Walton. *Larry McMurtry and the Victorian Novel*. College Station: Texas A&M University Press, 1994. Presents a brief study of one of McMurtry's models for his fiction, the long and complex novel with easily recognizable heroes and villains.

McMurtry, Larry. "Capturing the Cowboys." Interview by Josh Tyrangiel. *Time*, January 30, 2006, 62-63. Brief interview focuses on McMurtry's adaptation of the Proulx short story "Brokeback Mountain" for the screen.

Nelson, Jane. "Larry McMurtry." In *A Literary History of the American West*, edited by Max Westbrook and James H. Maguire. Fort Worth: Texas Christian University Press, 1987. Places McMurtry's fiction within the context of the modern Western novel and shows some of the ways in which McMurtry has reinvented the form and given it more tragic shadings.

Olson, Theodore B. "Hats off to Larry." *American Spectator* 37, no. 9 (November, 2004): 38-39. Offers acknowledgment of McMurtry's contribution to literature, focusing specifically on the author's yeoman effort in reading and reviewing Bill Clinton's massive 999-page memoir, *My Life*.

Rebein, Robert. *Hicks, Tribes, and Dirty Realists: American Fiction After Postmodernism*. Lexington: University Press of Kentucky, 2001. Asserts that gritty realism has gained ascendancy over metafiction in American writing. Examines the works of McMurtry, Dorothy Allison, Annie Proulx, Thomas McGuane, Cormac McCarthy, and Louise Erdrich.

Reilly, John M. *Larry McMurtry: A Critical Companion*. Westport, Conn.: Greenwood Press, 2000. Provides an overview of McMurtry's work, supplemented by a biographical chapter. Looks at McMurtry's use of history, his uses of the conventions of the Western genre, and the relationships between his novels and their sequels.

Reynolds, Clay, ed. *Taking Stock: A Larry McMurtry Casebook*. Dallas: Southern Methodist University Press, 1989. Valuable collection of essays includes a bibliography edited by Charles Williams and important essays on McMurtry's work by Louise Erdrich and Ernestine P. Sewell.

DAVID MADDEN

Born: Knoxville, Tennessee; July 25, 1933
Also known as: Jerry David Madden

Principal long fiction

The Beautiful Greed, 1961
Cassandra Singing, 1969
Brothers in Confidence, 1972
Bijou, 1974
The Suicide's Wife, 1978
Pleasure-Dome, 1979
On the Big Wind, 1980
Sharpshooter: A Novel of the Civil War, 1996

Other literary forms

David Madden is a prolific writer who has worked in almost every literary genre. In addition to his novels, he has published numerous essays, short stories, and poems in a range of journals and magazines; short-story collections, *The Shadow Knows* (1970) and *The New Orleans of Possibilities* (1982); several plays, including both one-act and three-act versions of *Cassandra Singing* (1955); a number of book-length critical studies; as well as a film script for the television film of *The Suicide's Wife*. Additionally, Madden has edited more than ten volumes on such diverse subjects as the proletarian and tough-guy writers of the 1930's as well as on James Agee, Nathanael West, the short story, film and the commedia dell'arte, and the popular-culture explosion.

Achievements

David Madden's work has been unevenly recognized throughout his career. His early novels—*The Beautiful Greed*, a master's thesis project, and "Hair of the Dog," initially published in *Adam* but never reprinted as a book—received virtually no attention at the time of their publication. Although Harry T. Moore praised *Cassandra Singing*, *Brothers in Confidence*, and *Bijou* as "significant contributions to contemporary American fiction," other critics have not viewed Madden's work so favorably. While writer Walker Percy found *Bijou* "a triumphant, brutal story of growing up," some reviewers faulted it for lack of unity and excessive nostalgia. Mixed responses also greeted *Pleasure-Dome*. One critic praised it as a "lyrical, quite wonderful novel"; another found it too "demanding and sometimes a bore."

Madden's short stories, however, have received more consistent recognition. Two appeared in *The Best American Short Stories*, for 1969 and 1971, respectively, and *The Shadow Knows*, Madden's first collection of short fiction, was the National Arts Council selection for 1970. In 1969, he received a Rockefeller grant for fiction.

Madden's achievement in the novel form rests in his exploration of the oral storytelling tradition and his evocation of east Tennessee and Kentucky landscapes and experiences, especially those of his youth. He often reworks autobiographical material—the major exception is *The Suicide's Wife*—much of it found in earlier novels or stories. Characters and situations recur; earlier stories reappear as segments of a later novel. Though redundant and at times tedious for the reader engaged in surveying all of Madden's novels, the retelling of this material in different forms allows the novelist to experiment with narrative voice and to explore in depth the relationship between the storyteller and the listener, a subject that has fascinated Madden since his youth.

BIOGRAPHY

Jerry David Madden was born July 25, 1933, in Knoxville, Tennessee, to James Helvy and Emile Merrit, models for the parents of Lucius Hutchfield in *Bijou* and *Pleasure-Dome*. Madden's two brothers both figure in his fiction. As a child, Madden worked as a newsboy and a theater usher, two jobs also held by the autobiographical Lucius. Madden also was an avid storyteller, a trait inherited from his grandmother. "Telling stories as a child," he comments in *The Poetic Image in Six Genres* (1969), "acting out all the parts, doing all the voices, I was an actor on a stage, my spectators within reach. When I wasn't telling stories, I was day-dreaming them." Like the characters in his novels—Lucius, Hollis Weaver in *Brothers in Confidence*, Big Bob Travis in *On the Big Wind*—Madden "wanted to be able to affect people" with his stories: his "two brothers, curled under quilts . . . neighborhood kids, huddled on our high front steps, and later . . . classmates during recess in grammar school."

Inspired by the motion pictures he saw as an usher at the Bijou, Madden wrote his first story at age ten and thus discovered "the private, lonely thrill of affecting individual, absent readers—a relationship remote from the public, communal transaction of movies." With writers Thomas Wolfe as his "romantic," "nonliterary" model and Ernest Hemingway as the literary one, Madden launched himself in high school on a writing career that included sharing with Wolfe a nostalgic response to hometown and family and acquiring the same literary agent as detective novelist Raymond Chandler.

During high school, Madden worked as a radio announcer—an experience that figures in the Big Bob stories and *On the Big Wind*. He also wrote, acted in, and directed a number of radio plays, feeding his interest in narrative voice and the teller-listener relationship. "Radio drama," after all, as Madden has acknowledged, "demands that listeners see through their ears" and grants thereby enormous evocative power and control to the actors.

By the time he graduated from Knox High School in 1951, Madden already had won a state play contest that included having the award-winning play produced at the University of Tennessee. Madden enrolled for a time at Tennessee, but he interrupted his education for the sake of adventure: travel, work in New York, and a stint as a messman on a U.S. Merchant Marine ship, an experience that provided the basis for *The Beautiful Greed*. From 1955 to 1956, Madden also served in the Army in Alaska. He reenrolled in college in 1956, first at Iowa State Teachers College, then once again at Tennessee, where he received a bachelor of science degree in 1957.

In 1956, Madden married Roberta Margaret Young, whom he had met while working at a radio station in Iowa. During this period he continued to write, working on and off again on *Cassandra Singing* as a radio drama, a stage play, and a novel—a fourteen-year project. Indeed, the first one-act version of *Cassandra Singing* won third place in a contest at the University of Tennessee as early as 1954, and the planning of the novel was already under way in 1955 while Madden was stationed in Alaska.

In the fall of 1957, following completion of his undergraduate work at Tennessee, Madden enrolled at San Francisco State College (now university), where he continued to work on *Cassandra Singing* and completed a master of arts degree in creative writing. He then taught at Appalachian State Teachers College in Boone, North Carolina, for one year. From 1959 to 1960, he attended the Yale Drama School as a John Golden fellow in playwriting. After 1960, he taught in colleges and universities throughout the central, eastern, and southern United States: from 1960 to 1962 at Centre College in Danville, Kentucky; from 1962 to 1964 at the University of Louisville; from 1964 to 1966 at Kenyon College in Gambier, Ohio, where he was also assistant editor of the *Kenyon Review*; in 1966 at Ohio University in Athens; and in 1967 at the University of North Carolina, Chapel Hill. In 1968, he became writer-in-residence at Louisiana State University. He was named distinguished visiting professor of English at the University of Delaware in the spring of 1980. In 1988 he held the chair of excellence at Austin Peay State University in Tennessee. Beginning in 1992 he served as director of the U.S. Civil War Center at Louisiana State, and he was awarded a certificate of commendation from the American Association for State and Local History for his work at the center. From 1992 to 1994 he also served as the school's creative-writing program director.

Analysis

In *The Poetic Image in Six Genres*, David Madden acknowledges two principal influences on his work—his grandmother's storytelling and Hollywood films—both explored in the autobiographical novel *Bijou*. He considers both to be "extremes." Nevertheless, from his grandmother he learned the impact of the storyteller on his or her listeners and from motion pictures he learned the techniques for making his own "stories more vivid, the action more immediate." These two extremes or opposite forces—the oral storytelling tradition in the South and the visual realm of popular-culture films—combine in Madden's novels to produce an abiding fascination with the role of the narrator-performer and the contrast between the life of action, that of the speaker or storyteller, and the life of the imagination, that of the listener or audience. To some extent, most of Madden's novels explore this duality while also drawing on a nostalgia for old films and film heroes.

Because he comes out of the southern oral storytelling tradition, Madden, like William Faulkner, relies heavily on a fairly fixed source of raw material that he reworks in various forms. Thus, characters from one novel may reappear, sometimes under different names; situations may recur as well, in stories retold from a different point of view or stitched into a novel. All of *Brothers in Confidence*, for example, reappears as part of *Pleasure-Dome*, a much later work, with changes in the principal characters' names. Most notably, Hollis Weaver, the narrator in *Brothers in Confidence*, is replaced by Lucius Hutchfield, who narrates both *Pleasure-Dome* and the earlier work, *Bijou*. Retelling the material from *Brothers in Confidence* allows Madden to reshape this material into a sequel for *Bijou*. *On the Big Wind*, which appeared in 1980, combines stories appearing in magazines as early as 1966, including "The Singer," a variation on the *Cassandra Singing* material that Madden reworked for fourteen years.

Madden's justification for this reworking of material rests in his interest in the storytelling tradition, where repetition of a favorite story only enhances the storyteller-listener relationship, and in his interest in experimenting with point of view. "In this shifting from one perspective to another on the same material," he comments in *The Poetic Image in Six Genres*, "I have learned more about . . . my own interests, and about the teller-listener relationship."

One corollary of this fascination with the teller-listener relationship is Madden's concept of the artist-storyteller as "con man," an idea the novelist claims to have borrowed from Thomas Mann. In his 1980 essay "Let Me Tell You the Story," Madden speaks of this metaphor as one way of focusing his interest. "The relationship between the storyteller and the listener," he adds,

> is like that between the con man and his mark, who charge each other through phantom circuits of the imagination; the storyteller uses many of the same techniques for capturing attention, holding it, and projecting the reader into a totally different world from the one he is living in.

Such creation Madden calls the "pleasure-dome," the concept explored in his sixth novel.

Not surprisingly, most of Madden's novels involve some form of storytelling by central characters with listeners swayed or held captive by the magical words of the speakers. Often it is the con man, such as Travern Weaver in *Brothers in Confidence* or Lucius Hutchfield's corrupt older brother, Earl, who weaves these tales; often it is the artist-hero himself, Lucius in *Pleasure-Dome* or Hollis Weaver in *Brothers in Confidence*. Even a minor work such as "Hair of the Dog," a detective story showing the influence of the "tough-guy" writers of the 1930's on Madden's fiction, involves a story told in prison, as do *Brothers in Confidence* and *Pleasure-Dome*.

The two novels that do not explicitly explore this teller-listener relationship are *The Beautiful Greed* and *The Suicide's Wife*. Although both employ storytelling in at least one episode as a means of revealing character, even to some extent altering a relationship between the speaker and the listener, in neither novel is storytelling the focus of the book. Alvin Henderlight in *The Beautiful Greed* has shared a cabin for months with the mysterious Franco before Franco tells his story; in *The Suicide's Wife*, Ann Harrington's lack of inhibition in bed with her husband's colleague serves as a device for altering her life, not that of the listener.

Of these two novels, only *The Suicide's Wife* is not

autobiographical. While it grew from a dramatic monologue concerning a suicide that happened on "the periphery" of Madden's life, it does not concern the writer or a writer-hero, the autobiographical hero in most of Madden's novels. Incidents from *The Beautiful Greed*, perhaps because they are largely autobiographical, do appear elsewhere, notably in Lucius's artist-con man scheme in *Pleasure-Dome*. Only *The Suicide's Wife* remains outside this storytelling context, unique also in its treatment of the duality of passivity and action within one central character, Ann Harrington, the suicide's wife.

THE BEAUTIFUL GREED

Madden's first novel, *The Beautiful Greed*, was published by Random House in 1961 as part of the publisher's First Novel series. The book was Madden's master of arts thesis project at San Francisco State and drew heavily on his stint as a crewman aboard a Merchant Marine ship scheduled for Brazil but, in the novel at least, destined for Taltal, Chile, on a mercy mission to aid Chilean earthquake victims. The novel's protagonist, Alvin Henderlight, is clearly autobiographical. Aside from sharing with the novelist his Merchant Marine experience, Alvin is also from Knoxville, has motion-picture ideas about going to sea, reads voraciously (particularly Joseph Conrad and Herman Melville), and bears a physical resemblance to the novelist with his short stature and balding head. He also has a family much like Madden's own and that of other autobiographical heroes in Madden's novels: a father who drinks; a mother who works, most often as a maid or in a factory; and two vagabond brothers.

The Beautiful Greed is also a very conscious literary work strongly influenced by Conrad's sea fiction. The title comes from a passage from *Lord Jim* (1900) referring to the insatiable hunger of the seaman for experience and adventure, a passage that serves as the epigraph for Madden's book. Like Conrad's novel, *The Beautiful Greed* takes illusion and reality as its central theme, particularly Alvin's gradual disillusionment. As the novel progresses, so does Alvin's awakening to the brute reality of life. His spiritual and psychological journey parallels the ship's slow progress south, through the Panama Canal and eventually on to Chile and, for Alvin, to true knowledge and experience.

The ship is another conscious literary device, a microcosm of the world's society. Young, old, bestial, intelligent, all different nationalities and human types are represented on board. Using these varieties of human beings, Madden explores the conflict between intellect—Alvin is dubbed the "professor" for his reading habits—and brute, insensitive action. Alvin and his cabin mate—the mysterious, remote Franco—are pitted against a crew of men whose brutal jokes include pitilessly trapping a sea bird and mercilessly using Franco as a scapegoat. For the most part, the novel follows the pattern of the bildungsroman, but its message is clearly existential. When the enigmatic, falsely dignified Franco reveals the truth about himself in a compelling story, he also leaves Alvin to face the consequences of his choices and actions aboard ship. Once committed to staying on board the *Polestar*, Alvin must face the brutish men whom Franco escapes by returning to his home in Taltal. Alvin has passed the opportunity to leave with Franco; his change of mind comes too late to alter the implied course of events with which the novel ends: Alvin's own torture at the hands of the crew. While relying excessively on conscious literary devices and on the author's own experiences, *The Beautiful Greed* is nevertheless noteworthy as a first novel for the author's attempt to deal with important issues about people's relationship with themselves and others and the meaning of their actions.

CASSANDRA SINGING

In *Cassandra Singing*, Madden turned away from predominantly autobiographical material to work with a story originating in a conversation with a messman aboard the novelist's Merchant Marine ship—a tale of a girl who joined a motorcycle gang after "her brother was killed in a smashup." Analogies exist in several forms, including various play versions and at least two short stories, "The Singer" and "Lone Riding." Madden acknowledges being obsessed with the story for more than fourteen years.

Set in eastern Kentucky rather than the Knoxville of the novelist's childhood, the story revolves around what Madden has described in *The Poetic Image in Six Genres* as "the strange relationship between a motorcyclist named Lone and his invalid sister Cassie." Besides this nearly incestuous relationship, Madden also attempts to capture the life of the mountain people and the threat to their folk existence posed by progress represented in the novel by the steady encroachment of bulldozers that will raze Lone and Cassie's home. His efforts are successful, for he is able to depict in detail the violence and deceptive simplicity of the mountain people, particularly through their dialect and mannerisms.

Perhaps because the story existed in dramatic form first, the novel relies heavily on dialogue, making immediate the conflict between Lone, who represents action, and Cassie, who represents imagination. Through Lone's vivid retelling of his motorcycle adventures with his companion Boyd, Cassie, bedridden for years with rheumatic fever, is able to envision the life of action she has longed for but never had. Thus, she becomes one of the earliest of Madden's characters enchanted by the storyteller's art and imaginatively transported into a "pleasure-dome" of his own making. Lone likewise becomes one of the first of Madden's storytellers to dramatize the oral storytelling tradition prevalent among mountain and southern people.

Despite its successes, *Cassandra Singing* moves too slowly at times. It represents a testament to Madden's love of words, an essential trait in any writer, and his skill in capturing the speech of mountain people, yet the conversations become too repetitious, the action too prolonged. Like *The Beautiful Greed*, moreover, the novel draws heavily on other literary works and motifs. Cassie and Lone's relationship, as Madden has acknowledged in *The Poetic Image in Six Genres*, is "partly inspired" by the "brother-sister relationship in the *Oresteia* [458 B.C.E.], Eugene O'Neill's *Mourning Becomes Electra* [1931], Jean-Paul Sartre's *The Flies* [1943], and Jean Cocteau's *Les Enfants terribles* [1929]," and Cassie herself by Frankie in Carson McCullers's *The Member of the Wedding* (1950) and Cassandra, "the Greek prophetess of doom, who was condemned never to be believed." Coupled with the biblical allusions that accompany Boyd's attempted crucifixion and threatened castration of Lone near the end of the novel, these powerful literary antecedents overtake the meaning of Madden's tale, leaving it wanting for power and impact.

Brothers in Confidence

Brothers in Confidence, which appeared in part in the *Southern Review* four years before its publication as an Avon paperback, returns to largely autobiographical material. It is also one of the most playful and humorous of Madden's novels and the first to explore in depth the concept of the artist as con man. The first-person narrator, Hollis Weaver, is that artist.

Hollis's goal is to save his younger brother, Cody, from serving a sentence on a chain gang for forgery. Like his brothers—Cody and the older Travern, also a criminal and forger—Hollis, though a writer and teacher by profession, must act the con man to persuade several good citizens of east Tennessee to accept a token payment as promise that Cody will make retribution and to agree to drop all charges against him. To do this, Hollis must travel the countryside weaving tales of Cody's neglected childhood—his parents resemble Lone and Cassie's as well as Lucius Hutchfield's—and ensnaring his audience with his storytelling art. His success depends on his skill in playacting, manipulating his audience, and vividly dramatizing Cody's life in order to win pity—all talents that the oral storyteller must possess. Only Travern's pose as a fancy lawyer, Mr. French, outshines Hollis's art. Travern, a genuine rogue since his youth and a thief who steals from his own family, goes directly to the judge and, by using a soapy story about holding the judge's only son as he dies in combat, convinces the old man to release Cody and accept several bogus checks as payment for court costs and ready cash so the Weaver brothers can leave town.

Brothers in Confidence is a lively, quick-paced, humorous portrait of three witty con artists caught in the act of writing bad checks and weaving outrageous tales. Like Madden, they delight in holding their audiences, both listeners and readers, with the magic of their stories. Episodic in structure, the novel follows the exploits of the narrator-hero as he travels the countryside, attempting to stay out of jail while trying also to free his brother. In these two respects, *Brothers in Confidence* is a picaresque novel, though sexual adventures are noticeably absent, having been saved for abundant use in *Bijou*. Also noteworthy is Madden's reliance on Hollis's storytelling to handle exposition and family history—a dramatic device from oral storytelling—and his use of motion pictures as a means of enhancing action and character. Hollis, like the later Madden hero Lucius Hutchfield and the novelist himself, has worked as an usher in a film theater and served with the Merchant Marine. He envisions himself a romantic hero, an Alan Ladd figure acting out various roles assigned to him. Like Madden, he also has two brothers who have served time in prison.

BIJOU

In 1969, Madden received a Rockefeller grant in fiction to work on his fourth novel, *Bijou*. He wrote part of the novel in Yugoslavia, part in Venice—an "ideal place," he told Ruth Laney in an interview for the *Southern Review*. "When I got the grant," Madden continued, "I thought the best place to go to begin the book would be to a city that paralleled the exotic quality of the Bijou, both in the movies and in real life." In effect, through its focus on the aging theater at which its hero works, the novel duplicates the author's own nostalgia for the past. Its purpose is to capture the "seediness" of that theater, once a site for legitimate stage productions, now a place where pornographic films are shown.

Set in Cherokee, Tennessee, *Bijou* is another largely autobiographical bildungsroman, tracing the life and adventures of thirteen-year-old Lucius Hutchfield during one turbulent and painful year. The period is immediately after World War II, and the romantic Lucius is infatuated with film stars and the memorable and not-so-memorable motion pictures of Hollywood's so-called golden era. Like Madden, Lucius grows as an artist through two principal sources, both dramatized in the novel: his grandmother's storytelling and films.

Because the novel has little plot other than Lucius's growth over one year and his emergence as a young writer, it is highly episodic. *Bijou*, one critic complained, is "so long" (five hundred pages), "so unresponsive, and even irresponsible about itself" that the reader becomes bored and repulsed. Madden records virtually every intimate detail and every event, including bowel movements, every day of Lucius's life for a year. Some of the details are successful in capturing the formative factors in Lucius's growth; others are not. There is humor but also vulgarity and tedium.

Defending the novel, Madden told Laney that he had wanted "a concentration of effect, a sort of captivity in the Bijou" paralleling the enchantment the storyteller weaves through words and movements, here created by a place. The problem is that the book lacks the "unity of place [that] would have enabled [the author] to shorten the novel and to realize [his] original purpose." To accomplish his task, Madden dramatizes his own adolescence and growth as a writer, filtering every detail through Lucius's consciousness, yet Lucius is incapable of distinguishing the valuable from the useless in his experience.

Madden also experiments with several narrative patterns. Some work, others do not. Film sequences and bits of motion-picture dialogue blend with Lucius's thoughts and imaginings, successfully dramatizing the creative process and the impact of what Madden calls the "charged image" on the creative consciousness. Segments of night reveries in which Lucius nostalgically reviews his life, sections of the hero's diary, letters between him and his girlfriend, Raine—including one borrowed from a Joseph Cotton film—even whole stories written by the young Lucius appear as sections of narrative. Many of these bog down, particularly Lucius's and Raine's letters, which are often adolescent professions of love. The stories, though demonstrating the hero's early attempts at fiction writing, mirror the artist's growth only part of the time. Finally, *Bijou* is not a successful novel; Madden's long autobiographical piece testifies, as does *Cassandra Singing*, to his love of literature, but it is also an instance of the novelist's having been caught in his own storytelling trance and nostalgia for the past.

THE SUICIDE'S WIFE

The Suicide's Wife, which was made into a television film for which Madden wrote the script, is in many ways the novelist's most unusual—some might say successful and original—novel. It is unusual among his novels in focusing solely on a female character—*Cassandra Singing* does so only partially. Aside from a dramatic monologue by the wife, the novel has no predecessors in Madden's oeuvre, an unusual feature. It is also, in Madden's own words, "a very short novel inspired by something that happened" not in his own life but "on the periphery, a suicide." The novel is also unique in that it does not dramatize the oral storytelling tradition, as do Madden's other works, and is crisp and Hemingwayesque in style.

Filtered through the intelligence of the suicide's wife, Ann Harrington, the wife of an English teacher at a West Virginia university, the novel studies the struggle of "the wife" to acquire an identity of her own following her husband's apparent suicide. Her lack of knowledge about her husband and about herself is her source of motivation after her husband's death thrusts her into a world she is unprepared to confront. Set against the backdrop of the student riots and Civil Rights movement of the late 1960's, Ann's story becomes a parable for the women's movement, a tale of progression from passivity and emptiness toward action and self-fulfillment.

At the outset of the novel, Ann defines herself almost solely in terms of her vagina, an emptiness to be filled by her husband. Madden skillfully does not give his heroine a name in this opening section. Her identity is not yet established, either with the reader, or, more important, with herself. As the book progresses, however, Ann's painful growth is recorded increasingly in terms of herself, with the narrative moving in and out of her thoughts, at times allowing Ann to think in the first person as she develops some identity through action. The wife who is "still a wife" at the beginning of the novel "even though she doesn't have a husband" eventually realizes that the man to whom she felt inferior for years was in fact a nobody, as vague as she, as passive and purposeless and lost.

Pleasure-Dome

With *Pleasure-Dome*, Madden returned to the comic tone and first-person narrative voice he used in *Brothers in Confidence*, part of which is reworked here with Travern, Hollis, and Cody becoming Lucius Hutchfield of *Bijou* and his two brothers, Earl and Bucky. Like that earlier work, the novel is autobiographical and retells stories found in other forms and books. *Pleasure-Dome* is also a sequel to *Bijou*, with Lucius seven years older and experienced through travel and through time with the Merchant Marine. At twenty, Lucius is also seeking more than his own past, though he must deal with his troublesome family members who are frequently in trouble with the law.

Pleasure-Dome is an interesting novel for what James Park Sloan in *The New York Times Book Review* cited as its combination of "profligate storytelling with reflections on the storytelling process." The narrator's consciousness—seen to a lesser degree but very evident nevertheless in *Brothers in Confidence*—emerges on the first page when he invites the reader into his tale with the traditional storyteller's line, "Did I ever tell you about the time . . . ?" In this first half of the novel, Lucius adopts what he calls his Mark Twain persona, retelling, as he must to save Bucky, sad stories about his childhood in Tennessee, while at the same time he is reporting to the reader-listener the chronicle of his adventures in conning those citizens pressing charges against Bucky.

Pleasure-Dome also moves beyond *Brothers in Confidence* and *Bijou* by adding a segment on Lucius's quest for a past other than his own, that of the legendary Jesse and Frank James. His search involves the attempt to learn the tale of Zara Ransom, an old woman who reportedly had a brief romance with Jesse James when she was a girl. To get her story, Lucius must once again successfully con his audience, here by using Zara herself; one of the fascinating complications is that it is Zara who enchants Lucius by telling her own story. *Pleasure-Dome* then contains two or more stories: the autobiographical one concerning the Hutchfields, and another, a second tale, of Zara Ransom and her relationship with a figure from America's legendary past. Both stories concern the past; both are narrated by oral storytellers. Both create a pleasure-dome for the reader-listener.

Pleasure-Dome is clearly a more sophisticated work than Madden's earlier novels that experimented with point of view and narrative art. By adding Zara Ransom's story and having her tell that story as Lucius writes it, Madden captures the storytelling process and the transmission of a dying art to the writer. As in *Cassandra Singing*, progress in the form of razing bulldozers is threatening the folkways of which the oral storytelling tradition is a part. Without Lucius's written record of Zara's story, handled with what he calls his Henry James persona, and his interpretation of the ending, the tale would be lost. Zara may or may not have been Jesse James's lover, but she is a legend that reminds people, Lucius thinks, "that those who do not remember the past are doomed never to relive it in the imagination." Significantly, at the end of the novel, Zara is destroyed, and Lucius is moved to guilt and deep feelings of "something . . . for the first time besides nostalgia."

On the Big Wind

With *Pleasure-Dome*, *On the Big Wind* dramatizes more successfully than any other Madden novel what the writer has described in *The Poetic Image in Six Genres* as "the teller's compulsion to tell a story," "the oral tradition" and the process by which it depicts, renders, and stimulates the art of oral storytelling. The book consists of seven episodes, most of which were originally published as short stories in a variety of magazines. The tone is clearly comic, as indicated by the subtitle "Seven Comic Episodes in the Fitful Life of Big Bob Travis." What is especially fascinating here is that each episode explores a different dramatic relationship between the storyteller and his audience. Thus, Madden's major theme of the power of storytelling gains power itself through the variety of ways in which the narrative voice of radio announcer Big Bob manipulates his audience. As the novel's epigraph, taken from Charlotte Brontë's *Jane Eyre* (1847), observes, "The eagerness of a listener quickens the tongue of a narrator."

In the opening episode, Big Bob is a night-owl country music disc jockey in Nashville given to having affairs with the women who call him. The "magic" in his voice enthralls countless women, but Big Bob, married to a meek housewife, is honest enough to have only one affair at a time. Problems occur when his wife, Laura, masks her voice and calls and seduces him as the deep-throated Morina. When Bob cannot resist a rendezvous with the mythical Morina, the result of the confrontation is divorce.

In later episodes, Big Bob's status in the radio business declines, then rises again. In each episode he plays a different role, sometimes with a different professional name, including a Jewish one. As David Epstein, he becomes a spokesperson for environmental and social causes. As a rock-music disc jockey, he must fend off the attack of a menacing motorcycle gang by telling a story that mesmerizes the group. In another episode, he draws a huge crowd of people to a sleazy mobile-home sales park by narrating the activities of a van of hippies. In that scene, Big Bob, in the tradition of the oral storyteller, both creates and "narrates the news."

As in his other novels, Madden's concern in *On the Big Wind* is with narrative techniques more than with originality in character creation or invention in plot. Like the oral storyteller who draws on a seldom-changed repertoire, Madden is content to repeat a story if the retelling draws another member of the audience into his pleasure-dome.

Sharpshooter

Madden's storyteller-listener theme and allegiance to the southern oral tradition extend to his novel *Sharpshooter*, a fictional memoir of an American Civil War soldier, Willis Carr, who, at the age of thirteen, leaves his Tennessee home to accompany his father and brothers on a Union raid into Confederate territory. Captured, he agrees to join the rebel army rather than face execution. Soon, he becomes a sharpshooter while serving under General Longstreet during several major battles against Union forces. Eventually, he deserts but is recaptured by Confederate troops and ends up as a guard at the infamous Andersonville prison, where he is taught by a slave to read and write.

In recounting the experiences of the war through the eyes of the young Willis, Madden concentrates on a recurring theme: What is fact and what is fiction? Buffeted throughout the war by events he does not entirely understand, Willis comes to realize that his personal recollections are clouded, leaving him to contemplate at war's end not only the disconcerting effects of battle but also the meaning of his own participation. Troubled by his memories and the belief he may have missed something, he decides to put his experiences in writing. In so doing, he chooses to revisit the battlefields, examine photographs and memoirs, and listen to other veterans, as well as civilians, as they relate their experiences. However, he finds he is not alone in his difficulty in recalling events. Only a moment of intense personal recollection that brings everything into focus allows him to connect with what is essential to his imaginative and intellectual welfare.

In retracing his steps, Willis demonstrates another of Madden's favorite themes, that of a central character separated from the past, either mentally or physically, who as a consequence suffers from a loss of identity. It is only when Willis sees the war through the emotions, intellects, and imaginations of others that he is able to view it with a sense of completion. Yet, as he observes, the truth is never complete. He points to the legend-making inclinations of people to select actual incidents from the past and color them with imagined constructions. The retelling of tales by participants carries risks, because accounts can conflict, having been subjected to a variety of historical processes, some more reliable than others. While Willis's vantage point as a sharpshooter permitted him to see more than the infantryman, his mission was also single-minded, and no event played out on the battlefields, he concludes, could be solitary. There are other vantage points and other views that may or may not conflict but nevertheless must be considered if the past is to be interconnected. By connecting one experience with the other, especially the opposites, the participant integrates the pieces into a recognition and finally into a comprehension of the past. At this stage, Madden's storyteller operates in the realm of the impersonal with an omniscience that is able to accommodate simultaneous events, both real and imagined.

Unlike *Bijou*, Madden's *Sharpshooter* does not get bogged down in repetitive detail or gratuitous sentiments. Instead, it maintains an undercurrent of subdued thought and emotion that steadily steers the reader to the story's final moments of revelation. It is thus not surprising that, highly acclaimed by critics, the novel was nominated for a Pulitzer Prize.

Stella A. Nesanovich
Updated by William Hoffman

Other major works

short fiction: *The Shadow Knows*, 1970; *The New Orleans of Possibilities*, 1982.

plays: *Cassandra Singing*, pr. 1955; *From Rome to Damascus*, pr. 1959; *Casina*, pr. 1960; *Fugitive Masks*, pr. 1966; *The Day the Flowers Came*, pr. 1975; *Three Mean Fairy Tales*, pr. 1979.

nonfiction: *Wright Morris*, 1964; *The Poetic Image in Six Genres*, 1969; *James M. Cain*, 1970; *Harlequin's Stick, Charlie's Cane*, 1975; *A Primer of the Novel: For Readers and Writers*, 1980; *Writer's Revisions*, 1980 (with Richard Powers); *Cain's Craft*, 1985; *Revising Fiction: A Handbook for Writers*, 1988; *The Works of Carson McCullers*, 1988; *Fiction Tutor*, 1991; *Touching the Web of Southern Novelists*, 2006.

edited texts: *Proletarian Writers of the Thirties*, 1968; *Tough Guy Writers of the Thirties*, 1968; *American Dreams, American Nightmares*, 1970; *Rediscoveries: Informal Essays in Which Well-Known Novelists Rediscover Neglected Works of Fiction by One of Their Favorite Authors*, 1971; *The Popular Cultural Explosion: Experiencing Mass Media*, 1972 (with Ray B. Browne); *Nathanael West: The Cheaters and the Cheated*, 1973; *Remembering James Agee*, 1974; *Creative Choices: A Spectrum of Quality and Technique in Fiction*, 1975; *Studies in the Short Story*, 1975 (with Virgil Scott); *Classics of Civil War Fiction*, 1988 (with Peggy Bach); *Rediscoveries II*, 1988 (with Bach); *Eight Classic American Novels*, 1989; *The World of Fiction*, 1989; *A Pocketful of Prose: Contemporary Short Fiction*, 1991; *A Pocketful of Prose: Vintage Short Fiction*, 1992; *Critical Essays on Thomas Berger*, 1995; *A Pocketful of Plays: Vintage Drama*, 1996; *A Pocketful of Poems: Vintage Verse*, 1996; *Beyond the Battlefield: The Ordinary Life and Extraordinary Times of the Civil War Soldier*, 2000; *The Legacy of Robert Penn Warren*, 2000; *A Pocketful of Essays*, 2001 (2 volumes).

Bibliography

Bach, Peggy. "The Theatrical Image." *Southern Quarterly* 33 (Winter/Spring, 1995): 215-226. In this article, Bach offers her views on the adaptation of works of southern novelists, including Madden, to the stage and screen.

Hendricks, Randy, and James A. Perkins, eds. *David Madden: A Writer for All Genres*. Knoxville: University of Tennessee Press, 2006. Collection of essays examining the diversity of Madden's work that includes a discussion of his early novels, analyses of the novels *The Suicide's Wife* and *Sharpshooter*, and an interview with Madden.

Madden, David. Interview by Ruth Laney. *Southern Review* 11 (Winter, 1975): 167-180. This lengthy discussion with Madden during the second decade of his literary career explains much about his sources of inspiration, particularly his debt to folk tradition and popular culture.

_______. "Let Me Tell You the Story: Transforming Oral Tradition." *Appalachian Journal* 7 (1980): 210-229. Madden describes the influence of the southern tradition of storytelling on his own developing imagination during his childhood years and explains how oral anecdotes develop into the written works of a conscious artist.

Morrow, Mark. "David Madden." In *Images of the Southern Writer*. Athens: University of Georgia Press, 1985. Morrow's report of his visit with Madden at his Baton Rouge, Louisiana, home features Madden's own comments on the influences that shaped his work, influences that include events in his life and his historical and literary heroes.

Richards, Jeffrey. "David Madden." In *Contemporary Poets, Dramatists, Essayists, and Novelists of the South*. Westport, Conn.: Greenwood Press, 1994. In this profile of Madden, Richards examines the recurring themes of the author and notes that his diversity has not always served him well in being accepted as a serious writer of fiction.

NAGUIB MAHFOUZ

Born: Cairo, Egypt; December 11, 1911
Died: Cairo, Egypt; August 30, 2006

Principal long fiction

'Abath al-Aqdār, 1939 (*Khufu's Wisdom*, 2003)
Rādūbīs, 1943 (*Rhadopis of Nubia*, 2003)
Kifāh Tībā, 1944 (*Thebes at War*, 2003)
Khān al-Khalīli, 1945
Zuqāq al-Midaqq, 1947 (*Midaq Alley*, 1966, revised 1975)
Bidāya wa-nihāya, 1949 (*The Beginning and the End*, 1951)
Bayn al-qaṣrayn, 1956 (*Palace Walk*, 1990)
Qaṣr al-shawq, 1957 (*Palace of Desire*, 1991)
Al-Sukkariya, 1957 (*Sugar Street*, 1992; previous 3 titles collectively known as *Al-Thulāthiya* [*The Trilogy*])
Awlād ḥāratinā, 1959 (serial), 1967 (book; *Children of Gebelawi*, 1981; also known as *Children of the Alley*, 1996)
Al-Liṣṣ wa-al-kilāb, 1961 (*The Thief and the Dogs*, 1984)
Al-Summān wa-al-kharīf, 1962 (*Autumn Quail*, 1985)
Al-Ṭarīq, 1964 (*The Search*, 1987)
Al-Shaḥḥādh, 1965 (*The Beggar*, 1986)
Tharthara fawq al-Nīl, 1966 (*Adrift on the Nile*, 1993)
Mirāmār, 1967 (*Miramar*, 1978)
Al-Marāya, 1972 (*Mirrors*, 1977)
Al-Karnak, 1974 (*Karnak*, 1979; *Karnak Café*, 2007)
Ḥaḍrat al-muḥtaram, 1975 (*Respected Sir*, 1986)
Ḥikāyāt ḥāratinā, 1975 (*The Fountain and the Tomb*, 1988)
Malḥamat al-ḥarāfish, 1977 (*The Harafish*, 1994)
Afrāh al-qubbah, 1981 (*Wedding Song*, 1984)
Layālī alf Laylah, 1982 (*Arabian Nights and Days*, 1995)
Rihlat Ibn Fattumah, 1983 (*The Journey of Ibn Fattouma*, 1992)
Al-ā'ish fi al-ḥaqīqah, 1985 (*Akhenaten: Dweller in Truth*, 2000)
Yawm Qutila al-Za ʿīm, 1985 (*The Day the Leader Was Killed*, 1989)

Other literary forms

Naguib Mahfouz (mahkh-FEWS) is known primarily for his long fiction, although he wrote many short stories and some one-act plays, five of which he published with collections of his short stories in *Taḥta al-miẓalla* (1969). His first publication was a translation into Arabic from English, *Miṣr al-Qadīmah* (1931), of James Baikie's *Ancient Egypt* (1912). Mahfouz also published numerous pieces of popular journalism and his memoirs, including *Asda' al-sirah al-dhatiyah* in 1995 (*Echoes of an Autobiography*, 1997).

Achievements

In 1988, Naguib Mahfouz became the first Arab author to receive the Nobel Prize in Literature; he was cited by the Swedish Academy for works that are richly realistic. In his Nobel speech, he described himself as the son of two civilizations: Pharaonic and Islamic. He expressed his passion to transcend traditional barriers for a universal vision informed by a heightened sense of responsibility toward humanity. In 1989, Mahfouz received the Presidential Medal from the American University in Cairo. He was elected an honorary member of the American Academy and Institute of Arts and Letters in 1992, and he was presented with an honorary doctorate by the American University in Cairo in 1995, which established the Naguib Mahfouz Medal for Literature as an annual award for outstanding contributions to Arabic writing.

Mahfouz advanced the art of long fiction in Arabic through major works that are varied in their experimental approaches to narrative, and he captured the attention of many for his courageous defense of freedom from religious persecution. He brought to Arabic writing a new dedication to artistic integrity in a form that is recent and rare.

Biography

Naguib Mahfouz was the youngest of seven children born to his parents in the old Gamaliya quarter of Cairo, Egypt. When he was nine years old, his family moved to a suburban district called Abbasiya, where he had his first experience with love and where he began to write in imitation of Arabic fiction writers. The 1919 Revolution made a deep impression on the youth. The Revolution of 1952, which brought Colonel Gamal Abdel Nasser to power and ended the Egyptian monarchy, proved disillusioning to Mahfouz.

He studied philosophy at Fuad I (now Cairo) University from 1930 to 1934, concentrating on the French philosopher Henri Bergson. After graduating in 1934, he found employment as a civil servant, which he continued until his retirement in 1971. He worked in several different locations, from Cairo University to the Ministry of Religious Endowments, where he was working when, in 1939, he published his first novel, *Khufu's Wisdom*, a historical romance based on ancient Egyptian history. He returned to his old neighborhood in 1945, where he worked in the Ghuri library and read the works of Joseph Conrad, Herman Melville, Leo Tolstoy, Eugene O'Neill, Gustave Flaubert, and Marcel Proust. In 1950 he began work for the Ministry of National Guidance, held several positions, and at last became adviser to the minister of culture.

Mahfouz did not marry until 1954, when he was forty-three. Shortly after his marriage, he published the first volume of *The Trilogy*, *Palace Walk*, in 1956. In 1959, his novel *Children of the Alley* was serialized in the national newspaper *Al-Ahram*. It garnered severe criticism from religious fundamentalists. Sheik Omar Abdel Rahman called for the death of the author. Mahfouz was stabbed in the neck outside his house by an extremist on October 14, 1994, when he was eighty-two years old. The wound disrupted Mahfouz's writing career, but the following year he published his memoir *Echoes of an Autobiography*, causing yet another uproar in Egypt because of his criticism of Egyptian president Gamal Abdel Nasser.

On December 10, 1997, Mahfouz represented the Egyptian government at a ceremony on the West Bank of the Nile, where he expressed the nation's sorrow and sympathy for the victims of the Luxor terrorist attack on tourists shortly before. In 1999, after prolonged and intensive physiotherapy, Mahfouz resumed writing; he died in Cairo on August 30, 2006.

Analysis

After the end of World War II, Naguib Mahfouz published novels that represented life as he knew it when he was growing up, beginning with *Khān al-Khalīli* in 1945. Details of the neighborhood where he was born, Gamaliya, provided him with setting and symbols. *Midaq Alley* focuses on people struggling to survive amid the rapidly changing conditions of old Cairo. Mahfouz's disillusionment with President Nasser is reflected in many of the novels published after 1961, beginning with *The Thief and the Dogs*. These novels express the spiritual need and political discontent that had been suppressed in his previous works. *Autumn Quail* and *The Search* reflect the way Mahfouz expresses in his titles the symbolic images that crystallize the themes of these novels. *Miramar* presents an episode of romantic violence in a boardinghouse in Alexandria, Egypt, told by four boarders from their different points of view. Mahfouz would return to this narrative device in the later novel *Wedding Song*, with self-reflective characters who observe themselves in a drama with the same title as the novel.

Mahfouz's art varied in several different novels after *Respected Sir* in 1975, an ironic tale of a civil servant who sacrifices everything for career advancement. This includes the allegorical and anecdotal techniques of *Children of the Alley*, the epic adventures of *The Harafish*, and the romantic fantasies of *Arabian Nights and Days*. The first and third of these represent radical innovations by Mahfouz, in which he rewrites historical tales of religion and fable. *The Harafish*, on the other hand, is an extended version of the techniques used in *Children of the Alley*, with more irony and surface realism, and also with a conclusion that promises a return to original goodness.

While the romantic settings of ancient Egypt capture the majestic and the exotic in Mahfouz's fiction, his realistic scenes of twentieth century Cairo bring to life poor neighborhoods with complex entanglements amid sectarian and ideological differences, such as the English presence in Egypt, Shiahs, Sunnis, Islamic extremists, and Sufis. Mahfouz blends the Western art of fiction with the Islamic literary tradition of Sufism, which connects spirituality with folk culture. Even though the political environment in which he lived subjected Mahfouz to personal suffering and injustice, his artistic vision was not restrained by national politics. His vision of the human condition is guided by mystical dimensions that enrich his fiction with figurative language, infusing universal appeal. His use of symbols and allegorical devices may have served as a mask for his political criticism, but only a reductive approach would disregard the full scope of his fiction. It draws on both the Western tradition and the Sufi conventions of universal mystical appeal that connect the language of the heart and mind through feeling and meaning. Mahfouz also uses Sufism as a historical link with the grandeur of the Islamic past, beyond Arab-speaking countries, to integrate the magical or the miraculous, opening up his narratives to ambivalent interpretations. His recurrent references to Sufi sheikhs engaged in *dhikr*, or meditation, serve as a reminder of eternal hope and the spiritual path of love that unites the Creator and his creation.

THE TRILOGY

Mahfouz's major accomplishment is made up of three volumes: *Palace Walk*, *Palace of Desire*, and *Sugar Street*. Palace Walk is a street in Cairo on which Ahmad, a storekeeper, and his family live at the end of World War I. The head of the family is al-Sayyid Ahmad Abd al-Jawad, a religiously conservative middle-class merchant who finds pleasure in drinking with his friends and carousing with prostitutes. The lustful Yasin is his son by his first wife. Amina is Ahmad's devoted second wife and mother of four children. Fahmy is her elder son, a law student who becomes increasingly involved in the 1919 Revolution. Kamal is her younger son, who will grow to maturity over the course of the three novels, from a simple, innocent boy to a troubled, skeptical man. Khadija is the ugly elder daughter with a big heart. The beautiful younger sister, Aisha, marries first and goes to live on Sugar Street with her new family. Fahmy joins in a victory celebration at the end of *Palace Walk* and is killed by British soldiers.

Naguib Mahfouz. (© The Nobel Foundation)

Palace of Desire begins in 1924. The members of the family are portrayed after Fahmy's martyrdom. Yasin chases woman after woman, never satisfying his lust. Ahmad, relaxing his tyranny over his family, has a desperate affair with a prostitute, who marries Yasin. Amina becomes more outspoken. Kamal, in teachers' college, is disillusioned with love and loses his religious beliefs as he learns more science. At the end of this volume, in 1927, several characters are ill, and several die, as the hero of the revolution, Sa'd Zaghlul, also dies.

It is 1935 at the opening of *Sugar Street*, and the family is suffering from economic depression amid worries about war. At the end of the novel, in 1945, Ahmad is dead, Amina is dying, two grandsons are in a prison camp, and a granddaughter is about to have a child. Devastated by the deaths of her husband and children, Aisha is driven to madness and mysticism. Khadija is outraged when her sons—Abd al-Muni'm, a member of the Muslim Brethren, and Ahmad Ibrahim Shawkat, a communist—are arrested and imprisoned. Kamal, now an English teacher, believes life is a great cheat. Yasin is alarmed by signs of aging; he begins to reconstruct his memory, placing himself in a heroic light, thus casting *The Trilogy* in a comic attitude of ironic absurdity.

Children of the Alley

Children of the Alley centers on an Egyptian family confronted with trials and tribulations that suggest parallels with the patriarchs and religious leaders of Judaism, Christianity, and Islam. While the book has earned praise for its universal appeal, it has been condemned by Islamic extremists whose interpretation reduces the narrative to a disrespectful presentation of holy personages. It is a bold narrative in which the God-like Gabalawi chooses his youngest son, Adham, to manage his property. Adham, pressed by his satanic brother, violates his father's trust and is driven into a hostile world, where he is forced to peddle potatoes. After Adham's son Qadri murders his brother Humam, Adham is forgiven in a dream by Gabalawi. In the second tale, Gabal (a Moses-like figure) kills a henchman of Overseer, his foster father, and flees into the desert, where a snake charmer gives Gabal his daughter in marriage. Gabal returns home, and Gabalawi commands Gabal to oppose injustice. Gabal charms snakes away and becomes a lawgiver.

The Jesus-like Rifaa disappears into the desert to avoid marriage and returns, after a conversation with Gabalawi, preaching mercy. He protects a prostitute from a mob and then marries her. He acquires a reputation as a healer, but he is clubbed to death by gangsters and buried in the desert. There are rumors of his resurrection. The hero of the fourth tale is Qassem, who resembles the Prophet Muḥammad. He is visited by a servant of Gabalawi, who tells Qassem to bring justice to his people. He organizes athletic clubs to attract young men from the outcast tribe of Desert Rats, who train for combat; then he leads his men to overcome Overseer and establish peace. Arafa, a magician-scientist, and his brother Hanash arrive in the alley to avenge the death of their mother. Arafa steals into the house of Gabalawi and accidentally kills a servant, causing Gabalawi to die of shock. Arafa searches for magic to bring Gabalawi back to life. Arafa is summoned by Overseer, who forces him to share a bottle of explosive powder that Arafa has invented, but Arafa is kidnapped and buried alive in the desert, while his brother tries to protect the formula for the magic powder.

The Thief and the Dogs

The Thief and the Dogs alternates between interior monologues of the obsessed thief, Said Mahran, and objective descriptions of events in the days of his life after he is released from prison. Seeking revenge against his former friend and his former wife, he goes to the Sufi sheikh Ali al-Junaydi, who gives him aid and religious advice. Then Said searches for an old political comrade, journalist Rauf Ilwan, who tells Said to find a job. Said attempts to rob Rauf's home, but he is caught and thrown into the night. He obtains a gun and meets Nur, a prostitute and old friend, who takes him into her home. Said kills a stranger whom he mistakes for the husband of his ex-wife. He tries to kill Rauf, but again he kills the wrong man. The full fury of the police and public are launched, through Rauf's newspaper, to find and punish Said. He flees into a cemetery, and there, among the tombs, he is pursued by men and dogs; he opens fire and is cut down in a hail of bullets, raving at the dogs who have found him at last.

This novel incorporates elements of existentialism and psychological realism to show how social rejection—by his little daughter and then by his friend Rauf—leads to Said Mahran's alienation and inability to resist irresponsible actions. His mistaken killings are followed by a final mistake when he leaves the Sufi sheikh's sanctuary to retrieve his uniform, which provides a clue to the dogs who find him hiding in the cemetery. Said's final moment is open to differing interpretations: Are individuals inevitably defeated by sociopolitical forces, or do they rise in stature through the courageous acceptance of destiny? Surrounded by the police, Said is no longer afraid; he comes out "raving at the dogs." The dogs represent sociopolitical forces that are lacking in human understanding.

ARABIAN NIGHTS AND DAYS

Arabian Nights and Days is a retelling of the famous fifteenth century Arabic stories *The Arabian Nights' Entertainments*, also known as *The Thousand and One Nights*. Sultan Shahriyar announces he will no longer kill virgins. Gamasa al-Bulti, the chief of police, captures a genie, Singam, while fishing, then watches himself being beheaded because the genie has put a double in his place. The real Gamasa has assumed the form of Abdullah the porter. He begins a holy war, murdering people in the government. Abdullah confesses his murders, is ordered to a lunatic asylum, and disappears. Sakhrabout and Zarmabaha, drunken genies, scheme against people for fun. Foolish people are saved by Abdullah the madman, and the sultan becomes more righteous as he stalks the night streets to learn truth.

Aladdin is falsely arrested, then executed unjustly. The sultan is tricked, through a mock trial, into recognizing this injustice. Genies give a magic cap of invisibility to Fadil Sanaan, who can do anything except what his conscience dictates, yet he must not commit evil. He promptly violates these conditions, enjoying his powers and harassing people throughout the city, before he returns the cap, confesses his sins, and boldly meets his death. After the cobbler, Marouf, learns the limits of powers from genies, the sultan appoints him governor, and Marouf appoints the madman as police chief. Sindbad the Sailor teaches the sultan moral lessons, and in the final tale the sultan abandons his throne and family and finds a great rock, which opens to admit him to a beautiful eternal bride. However, he cannot resist opening a door that says, "Everything is clear except for this door." The door takes him back outside the rock, and he cannot return. In despair, he hears Abdullah saying there is no path to truth, and so it cannot be attained, but it cannot be escaped. The innovative twist of the title of this work implies a blend of magical tales from the past and spiritual parables that emphasize the theme of an individual's quest for truth that cannot be attained, either through "canonic laws" or through human perceptions.

Richard D. McGhee
Updated by Mabel Khawaja

OTHER MAJOR WORKS

SHORT FICTION: *Hams al-junūn*, 1939; *Dunyā Allāh*, 1963 (partial translation *God's World*, 1973); *Bayt sayyi' al-sumʿa*, 1965; *Khammārat al-qiṭṭ al-aswad*, 1968 (*The Tavern of the Black Cat*, 1976); *Hikaya bila bidaya wala nihaya*, 1971; *God's World*, 1973; *Al-Jarima*, 1973; *Al-ḥubb fawqa haðabat al-haram*, 1979; *Al-Shaytan Yaʿiz*, 1979; *Ra'aytu fīmā yarā al-nāʾim*, 1982; *Al-Tanẓīm al-sirri*, 1984; *Al-Fajr al-kādhib*, 1989; *The Time and the Place, and Other Stories*, 1991; *Voices from the Other World*, 2003; *The Dreams*, 2005; *The Seventh Heaven: Stories of the Supernatural*, 2005.

PLAYS: *One Act Plays*, 1989.

NONFICTION: *Asda' al-sirah al-dhatiyah*, 1995 (*Echoes of an Autobiography*, 1997); *Naguib Mahfouz at Sidi Gaber: Reflections of a Nobel Laureate, 1994-2001*, 2001.

TRANSLATION: *Miṣr al-Qadīmah*, 1931 (of James Baikie's *Ancient Egypt*).

MISCELLANEOUS: *Taḥta al-miẓalla*, 1969.

BIBLIOGRAPHY

Beard, Michael, and Adnan Haydar, eds. *Naguib Mahfouz: From Regional Fame to Global Recognition*. Syracuse, N.Y.: Syracuse University Press, 1993. Collection of essays is derived from a symposium held in recognition of Mahfouz's receipt of the Nobel Prize. Topics addressed include images of women in Mahfouz's fiction and critical reactions to his works.

Coetzee, J. M. "Fabulous Fabulist." *The New York Review of Books* 41 (September 22, 1994): 30-33. Argues that it was Mahfouz's example that spurred interest in the novel in Arabic in the 1950's and 1960's. Briefly discusses Mahfouz's fiction, describing the world of Cairo as he depicts it.

El-Enany, Rasheed. *Naguib Mahfouz: The Pursuit of Meaning*. New York: Routledge, 1993. Groups Mahfouz's novels according to their treatment of history, idealism, and episodic structural designs, with a detailed analysis of *Respected Sir*.

Gordon, Haim. *Naguib Mahfouz's Egypt: Existential Themes in His Writings*. New York: Greenwood Press, 1990. Examines the impressionistic view of Egyptian society in the writings of Mahfouz.

Kilpatrick, Hilary. *The Modern Egyptian Novel: A Study in Social Criticism*. London: Ithaca Press, 1974. Examines Mahfouz's novels in the context of contemporary Egyptian fiction.

Le Gassick, Trevor, ed. *Critical Perspectives on Naguib Mahfouz*. Washington, D.C.: Three Continents Press, 1991. Collection of essays on Mahfouz's work, four of which are in translation from Arabic, address a wide range of topics, including Mahfouz's contributions to the short story, the novel, and the Egyptian cinema. Complemented by bibliographies of materials in English.

Milson, Menahem. *Najib Mahfuz: The Novelist-Philosopher of Cairo*. New York: St. Martin's Press, 1998. Good introductory work for the beginning student of Mahfouz, offering insight into the author's works and life.

Moussa-Mahmoud, Fatma. "Depth of Vision: The Fiction of Naguib Mahfouz." *Third World Quarterly* 11 (April, 1989): 154-166. Presents a first-rate, comprehensive study of Mahfouz's life and work.

Stock, Raymond. "Naguib Mahfouz Dreams—and Departs." *Southwest Review* 92, no. 2 (2007): 172-179. Traces how Mahfouz's dreams blend realism and surrealism as a storytelling technique.

Weaver, Mary Anne. "The Novelist and the Sheikh." *The New Yorker*, January 30, 1995. Discusses how Mahfouz's characters debate issues of justice and injustice, expectation and disillusionment, and belief in God. Includes biographical information about the author.

NORMAN MAILER

Born: Long Branch, New Jersey; January 31, 1923
Died: New York, New York; November 10, 2007
Also known as: Norman Kingsley Mailer

Principal long fiction

The Naked and the Dead, 1948
Barbary Shore, 1951
The Deer Park, 1955
An American Dream, 1965
Why Are We in Vietnam?, 1967
The Armies of the Night: History as a Novel, the Novel as History, 1968
Marilyn, 1973
The Executioner's Song, 1979
Of Women and Their Elegance, 1980
Ancient Evenings, 1983
Tough Guys Don't Dance, 1984
Harlot's Ghost, 1991
Oswald's Tale: An American Mystery, 1995
The Gospel According to the Son, 1997
The Castle in the Forest, 2007

Other literary forms

Beginning with *The Armies of the Night*, Norman Mailer published several works that cross the conventional boundaries of fiction and nonfiction: a "novel biography," *Marilyn*; a "true life novel," *The Executioner's Song*; and an "imaginary memoir," *Of Women and Their Elegance*. Because of his sophisticated handling of style, structure, point of view, and characterization, many of Mailer's works of journalism and reportage approach the novel's complexity of language and form; examples include *Miami and the Siege of Chicago: An Informal History of the Republican and Democratic Conventions of 1968* (1969), *Of a Fire on the Moon* (1970), *The Prisoner of Sex* (1971), *St. George and the Godfather* (1972), and *The Fight* (1975). His essays, interviews, short stories, poems, and drawings have been collected in *Adver-*

tisements for Myself (1959), *Deaths for the Ladies and Other Disasters* (1962), *The Presidential Papers* (1963), *Cannibals and Christians* (1966), *The Short Fiction of Norman Mailer* (1967), *The Idol and the Octopus: Political Writings on the Kennedy and Johnson Administrations* (1968), *Existential Errands* (1972), *Pieces and Pontifications* (1982), *Modest Gifts: Poems and Drawings* (2003), *The Big Empty: Dialogues on Politics, Sex, God, Boxing, Morality, Myth, Poker, and Bad Conscience in America* (2006; with John Buffalo Mailer), and *On God: An Uncommon Conversation* (2007; with Michael Lennon). His work in drama and literary criticism appears in *The Deer Park: A Play* (pb. 1967) and *Genius and Lust: A Journey Through the Major Writings of Henry Miller* (1976).

Achievements

With the appearance of *The Naked and the Dead* in 1948, Norman Mailer was hailed by many critics as one of the most promising writers of the postwar generation. Since his early acclaim, Mailer's reputation has risen and fallen repeatedly—in part because of the unevenness of his writing and in part because of his intense participation in the causes and quarrels of his age. More important, however, his work has often been misunderstood because of its remarkably changing character and its innovative procedures, for Mailer relentlessly searched for the style and structure that could most effectively express his ambition to make "a revolution in the consciousness of our time."

By whatever standard Mailer is judged, it is clear that several of his books have a secure place not only in postwar literary history but also in the canon of significant American literary achievements. *The Naked and the Dead* and *The Armies of the Night* continue to receive attention as masterpieces, and his other novels have begun to benefit from the serious exploration accorded to the finest works of fiction. *The Executioner's Song*—very favorably reviewed when it first appeared—may eventually rank with Mailer's greatest writing because it contains a complexity of point of view and characterization rivaled only by *The Naked and the Dead*, *An American Dream*, and *Why Are We in Vietnam?* He believed that his last novel completed novel, *The Castle in the Forest*, was a major achievement, and certainly the reviews of this work were among the best Mailer had received in more than two decades.

In addition to receiving several literary honors and distinctions—including the National Book Award, the Pulitzer Prize, and election to the National Institute of Arts and Letters—Mailer has been the subject of more than a dozen book-length studies and hundreds of articles. His work is an essential part of college syllabi in contemporary literature, not only because it addresses crucial events, concerns, and institutions such as World War II, the Cold War, Hollywood, Vietnam, the Pentagon, and capital punishment but also because Mailer treats all of his important themes in the light of a deeply imaginative conception of literary form. As Robert Merrill has noted, far too many critics have treated Mailer's writing as simply a record of his opinions. They have taken his musings for assertions, and they have failed to see that he aims at conveying the "meaning" of characters and events with the fluidity of metaphor. What Mailer *imagines* rather than what he *believes* is important in assessing all of his prose—and what he imagines consists of entertaining several possible selves, and several sides of issues and events, simultaneously. In other words, he rejects fixity of thought in favor of the play of prose, which in turn parallels the complex play of characters and events.

Biography

Norman Kingsley Mailer grew up in Brooklyn, New York, and attended Harvard University (1939-1943), where he studied aeronautical engineering and became interested in writing. After he graduated from Harvard, he married Beatrice Silverman and was inducted into the U.S. Army, serving with the 112th Cavalry out of San Antonio, Texas. He was overseas for eighteen months in Leyte, Luzon, and with occupation forces in Japan. His varied experience as a field artillery surveyor, clerk, interpreter of aerial photographs, rifleman, and cook undoubtedly contributed to the comprehensive portrayal of the military in *The Naked and the Dead*.

After his discharge from the Army in May, 1946, Mailer immediately began work on *The Naked and the Dead* and completed the novel within fifteen months. In the next two years (1948-1950), he traveled in Europe, studied at the Sorbonne, wrote articles and delivered speeches, campaigned for presidential candidate Henry A. Wallace, worked briefly as a screenwriter in Hollywood, and finished his second novel, *Barbary Shore*, which was poorly received—in part because of Mailer's sympathetic engagement with Marxist ideas and his aggressive exploration of shifting political attitudes in the postwar years.

For the next ten years, Mailer was beset by various personal and professional traumas. He divorced his first wife—they had one daughter—in 1952. He married Adele Morales in 1954; he stabbed her with a penknife on November 19, 1960, after a party organized to launch his New York City mayoral campaign. The couple was divorced in 1962. During this period, Mailer had difficulty getting his third novel, *The Deer Park*, published, while he simultaneously struggled to complete another novel. After the births of his second and third daughters, Mailer married Lady Jeanne Campbell, who gave birth to his fourth daughter in 1962. With the publication of *Advertisements for Myself*, he began to find a way of rescuing the fragments and dead ends of his career, and with his essay "Superman Comes to the Supermarket" (1960), he evolved a supple way of dramatizing and musing on social and political issues that freed him from the constraints of his not entirely successful first-person narrators in *Barbary Shore* and *The Deer Park*.

Norman Mailer. (Library of Congress)

In many ways, the 1960's were Mailer's most productive years. Not only did he publish his two most sophisticated novels, *An American Dream* and *Why Are We in Vietnam?*, and adapt *The Deer Park* for the stage, but he also directed and acted in three films—*Wild 90* (January, 1968), *Beyond the Law* (October, 1968), and *Maidstone* (1971)—which provoked him to write important essays on the nature of film and prepared him for his innovative "novel biography," *Marilyn*. He was an active journalist during this period, covering political conventions and the moon shot, and out of his reportage he created a book, *The Armies of the Night*, that transcends the immediate occasion of its conception—a protest march on the Pentagon—in order to probe the shaping processes of history and fiction and their mutuality as human constructs. In 1963, Mailer divorced Lady Jeanne Campbell and married the actor Beverly Bentley, with whom he had two sons. He campaigned unsuccessfully for the office of mayor of New York City in 1969 and fathered a fifth daughter by Carol Stevens in 1971. He subsequently married and divorced her, taking Norris Church as his sixth wife.

In the 1970's and 1980's, Mailer continued to write nonfiction while working on his Egyptian novel, *Ancient Evenings*. Although he began in the mid-1970's to withdraw from public attention, his appearance in the film *Ragtime* (1981) and his defense of Jack Abbott, a writer-convict who committed a murder shortly after his release from prison, revived Mailer's image as a controversial, embattled author. As several reviewers pointed out, both *Ancient Evenings* and *Tough Guys Don't Dance* have first-person narrators who bear considerable resemblance to Mailer. His controversial tenure as president of the U.S. chapter of PEN (the International Association of Poets, Playwrights, Editors, Essayists, and Novelists), along with the 1987 film of

Tough Guys Don't Dance, which Mailer wrote and directed, once again focused public attention on him.

In the 1990's, Mailer produced three very different books, none of which seemed to enhance his reputation. *Harlot's Ghost*, a very long novel, is a compendium of his fictional themes—particularly Mailer's obsession with the Central Intelligence Agency (CIA) and with conspiracy theories. Nevertheless, this novel is a provocative reading of Cold War history and may yet be reevaluated favorably. *Oswald's Tale* again crosses the line between fact and fiction. It resembles *The Executioner's Song*, for once more Mailer worked with tape-recorded interviews, and he visited the former Soviet Union to collect material on his subject. Although *Oswald's Tale*, a very thorough investigation of Lee Harvey Oswald's period in the Soviet Union, received many good reviews when it appeared, it seems to have been lost in the flood of books on President John F. Kennedy's assassination. Finally, Mailer's nonfiction *Portrait of Picasso as a Young Man* (1995) received largely negative reviews, mainly because he was faulted for projecting too many of his own views onto the artist's life and because he did little primary research—borrowing instead from works such as John Richardson's acclaimed multivolume biography of Pablo Picasso. As with *Marilyn*, however, Mailer's *Portrait of Picasso* deserves more careful reading precisely because of the commonalities Mailer establishes between himself and his subjects.

In his later years, Mailer settled into an active, yet rather sober, literary life, continuing to devote himself to writing but shying away from the feuds and controversies that had marked so much of his career. He suffered various ailments, including gout and loss of hearing. In his last public appearances he had to walk with the aid of two canes. He remained, however, an active commentator on public affairs, expressing his harsh criticism of George W. Bush's presidential administration in *Why Are We at War?* (2003). He died of acute renal failure on November 10, 2007, in Mt. Sinai Hospital, New York City.

Analysis

Some of Norman Mailer's earliest writing, including "The Greatest Thing in the World," a prizewinner in a 1941 *Story* magazine contest, reveals that even at a very early age he could write accomplished, imitative apprentice fiction in the modes of Ernest Hemingway and John Dos Passos. Before his own service, Mailer was exploring the experience of war in "A Calculus at Heaven" (1942), which suggests his ambition to portray the sweep of his time, to show the psychological and sociological preconditions of war and the existential choices it demands.

The Naked and the Dead

Mailer advanced with astonishing rapidity from his first attempts at fiction to his own war experience to the writing of *The Naked and the Dead*. Although it is a very long novel, its coverage of so many diverse elements in remarkably fluid prose and in a compact four-part structure conveys a sense of a single complex concert of human motives and the vagaries of existence. *The Naked and the Dead* is far more than a war novel, more than a political novel, for it examines the way human experience is shaped and interpreted, and it establishes the ground out of which human character and belief arise.

Part 1, "Wave," concerns preparations for the invasion of Anopopei, an island held by the Japanese. The first wave of troops will assault the beaches by riding through the surf and charging ashore. One wave against another, humanity against the nature of its own enterprise, is one of the dominant themes of the novel, as its second paragraph indicates by describing an anonymous soldier who "lies flat on his bunk, closes his eyes, and remains wide-awake. All about him, like the soughing of surf, he hears the murmurs of men dozing fitfully." The poker game the soldiers play, like the war itself, has its meaning in "the margin of chance," in the calculation and skill that is nevertheless vulnerable to luck, good or bad. Much of what makes the novel fascinating is its persistent aligning of the interface between planning and probability; each soldier tries to gauge what his chances are of surviving, or—in Sergeant Croft's and General Cummings's cases—dominating the war, although almost every man, like Martinez, has at least one moment of fear, of total vulnerability, when he feels "naked" and almost certainly dead under fire.

Part 2, "Argil and Mold," shifts from the reactions of the combat soldiers to war to the grand strategy of General Cummings, who plans on shaping his army to fit his master design. For Cummings, the war—like history itself—must have a pattern, one that he can follow and channel in his direction. He disclaims the operations of chance; seeming accidents, he contends, are actually a result of a person's failure to capitalize on the opportunities life affords. If Cummings does not yet know the precise trajectory of history, he is confident that he will be percipient enough to discover it eventually. His game is not cards; it is chess. "The trick is to make yourself an instrument of your own policy," Cummings advises his resistant subordinate, Lieutenant Hearn, who refuses to credit the general's command not only over the forces of history but also over Hearn himself.

In the course of his conflict with Hearn, Cummings reveals his disdain for the liberal's "exaggerated idea of the rights due" to persons as individuals. In the general's reading of history, it is not the development of individuality but of power concentrations that counts in evaluating the causes of the war. As a result, he violates the integrity of much of the experience that is portrayed in the novel, for each character—including the general—is given a unique biography, a singularity of purpose that defies the notion that individuals can be permanently fashioned as part of a power bloc. After the initial success of his landing on Anopopei, Cummings is thwarted: "The campaign had gone sour. . . . his tactics were as well conceived as they had ever been, his staff performances as thorough, his patrols as carefully planned, but nothing happened. . . . A deep unshakable lethargy settled over the front-line troops." Like Hearn, Cummings finds he cannot argue his army into action for an indefinite period of time.

Each of the principal characters in the novel behaves not only in terms of his background (the "Time Machine" sections delineate prewar experiences) and his participation in a platoon (the "Chorus" sections suggest the extent to which individual experience can be collectivized) but also in terms of the power argument between Cummings and Hearn. That is why it is inevitable that Hearn will ultimately be placed at the head of Sergeant Croft's platoon, for Croft has often kept his men together by the force of his own will, by an invincible belief in the rightness of his position that is virtually identical to Cummings's self-assurance.

Like Cummings, Croft contends with a geographic and ethnic cross section of soldiers: Red Valsen, "the wandering minstrel" from Montana, who distrusts all permanent relationships; Gallagher, "the revolutionary reversed," an Irish Catholic from Boston who seems perpetually angry at the way the more privileged or the more conniving have deprived people of their dignity but who is also profoundly prejudiced against other groups, especially the Jews; Julio Martinez, the Mexican American, who desperately asserts his loyalty, his integrity, by taking pride in courageously executing Croft's dangerous orders; Joey Goldstein, who from his "cove in Brooklyn" tries to ingratiate himself in a world inhospitable to Jews; and Wilson, the affable southerner who traffics easily with women and the world, and who is without much sense of life's disparities and of how he has hurt as well as charmed others with his "fun." These characters and others are meant to convey the multiplicity of experience that Croft crushes in disciplining his platoon.

In one of the most telling scenes in the novel, Croft allows a captured Japanese soldier time to recover his composure, to express his humanity, to plead for his life, and to sense that he is in the presence of other compassionate human beings, before brutally shooting him in the very moment of his happiness. Croft's cruelty is the most extreme extension of Cummings's declaration that individuals do not count, that single lives are valued too highly. Ultimately, this kind of merciless wiping out of opposition does not make Croft a better soldier; his attempt to scale Mount Anaka has been futile from the beginning, and the Japanese are defeated without the imposition of either Croft's or Cummings's will. Just as Croft's men accidentally blunder into the hornets that drive them back down the mountain, so in part 3, Major Dalleson, a mediocre, timid officer, blunders into easy and rapid victory over the Japanese while Cummings is away from the campaign seeking naval support for an elaborate plan that in the end proves superfluous in the defeat of a Japanese army almost disintegrating by itself for lack of food and military supplies.

Part 3, "Plant and Phantom," prepares for the novel's abrupt denouement by exploring Friedrich Nietzsche's troubling premise that "even the wisest among you is only a disharmony and hybrid of plant and phantom. But do I bid you become phantoms or plants?" The question of human nature is unanswerable; human beings are divided creatures, both body and mind, and neither side of that nature can entirely suppress the other even in the shrewdest of individuals. In the novel, people live and die as plants and phantoms, as thinking and feeling beings who are bound by the conditions of nature and by the consequences of their own actions, over which they often have surprisingly little control. People are truncated, their lives are suddenly cut off, even as their thoughts appear to extend their hold over events. Thus, Hearn drives his men to the other side of the island so that they can reconnoiter the possibility of an invasion behind Japanese battle lines. He suffers from weariness, from the men's resistance, and from his own self-doubt, but he reasserts himself:

> As they moved along out of the hollow he felt good; it was a new morning, and it was impossible not to feel hopeful. The dejection, the decisions of the previous night seemed unimportant. He was enjoying this, but if he was, so much the better.
>
> A half hour later, Lieutenant Hearn was killed by a machine gun bullet which passed through his chest.

Hearn dies as swiftly as the Japanese defense crumbles, and in both cases the dissolution is all the more devastating when one considers their determination to survive.

Part 4, "Wake," is retrospective, a brief review of the invasion wave of part 1. The reality of the invasion has not conformed to expectations. Even after the fact, Major Dalleson deludes himself about the significance of the campaign, supposing that the forces Cummings finally deployed with naval support behind Japanese lines were decisive. Dalleson's self-deception is just like Martinez's delusion that Hearn did not heed reports of Japanese in the pass where he died. Martinez forgets that Croft had cautioned him not to mention the Japanese to Hearn. In taking a superior attitude to Brown, Stanley forgets, or never actually realizes, his former sycophancy that ensured, with Brown's help, his promotion to corporal. Wilson muddles his trickery of his buddies—getting them to pay more for their liquor so he can have an extra bottle—into a belief in his generous provision for them.

Even more self-conscious characters such as Hearn and Cummings catch themselves in self-deceptions. Hearn believes that he is rebelling against Cummings by crushing a cigarette on the general's immaculate floor when in fact he is playing his superior officer's game, getting himself into a position where Cummings is able to employ Hearn as just another pawn in his military strategy. Cummings, in turn, bitterly admits to himself that Hearn has a way of depriving him of his sense of command, for Hearn (who is something like a wayward son) represents the intractability of the fighting force Cummings wants to regard as an extension of himself. Mailer brilliantly reveals the ironies of Cummings's command in the general's discovery of the cigarette butt "mashed into the duckboards in a tangled ugly excrement of black ash, soiled paper, and brown tobacco." Cummings has been having bouts of diarrhea; what he sees on the floor is a manifestation of his lack of control, his inability to make his body, like his men, obey his rigorous schedule. In this encyclopedic novel—Mailer's attempt to write the equivalent of Leo Tolstoy's *Voyna i mir* (1865-1869; *War and Peace*, 1886) in his generation, to show that, like Napoleon, Cummings fails to reduce history to the curve of his desire—no character can claim mastery over himself or the world, for the interplay between individuals and events is too complex, too contingent, to be predictable, even though characters such as Cummings and Croft pursue their careers with the monomania of Herman Melville's Ahab in *Moby Dick* (1851).

The Naked and the Dead almost seemed to write itself, Mailer comments in *Advertisements for Myself*. In retrospect, Mailer felt he could not go on repeating a best-seller formula based on a skillful melding of Hemingway and Dos Passos. Given Mailer's ambition to be a great writer, it is not surprising that his obsession with style prompted him to devalue his first novel. If *The Naked and the Dead* is derived from the styles of other writers, it also conveys a sense of history that is almost entirely lacking in Hemingway and is diminished in Dos Passos by rather crude melodrama and determinism. In Mailer, there is no clear division of historical villains and heroes; on the contrary, he develops a dramatic dialogue of ideas that arise persuasively out of carefully delineated personalities. He did not equal this achievement for some time, perhaps because he had to go through various attempts at finding a style, a singular—even quirky—manner that is as individual as Dos Passos's "Camera Eye" sections in *U.S.A.* (1937) or the radically charged prose of William Faulkner's best work.

Barbary Shore

Mailer's next novel, *Barbary Shore*, was a disappointment to critics and to Mailer himself, even though he suggests in *Advertisements for Myself* that the novel helped to prepare him for becoming the kind of writer he would remain for the rest of his career. *Barbary Shore* seems detached from many of the basic assumptions of *The Naked and the Dead*, which has a naïve confidence when viewed from the perspective of its successor. Although history is not controllable in *The Naked and the Dead*, it is not even certain that history is knowable in *Barbary Shore*, where several characters and events have a phantasmagoric quality. Characters often speak in an allegorical dialogue, so that the Soviet Union, for example, is referred to as "the land beyond the sea."

One of the main characters, McLeod, has had a variety of identities, and it is never entirely clear what the truth of his life has been—not even to himself. The first-person narrator, Mike Lovett, is an amnesiac who vaguely recalls fragments of his past—most of them are memories of war—but is not sure that they are, in fact, his own. McLeod, at one time a foreign agent for the Communist Party, is pursued by Hollingsworth, who is some kind of government operative, an agent of the American status quo, on a mission to recover a "little object" (which is never identified) that McLeod is presumed to have stolen while working for what was probably a government agency—perhaps the same agency for which Hollingsworth works. The novel is further complicated by the presence of Guinevere, an apolitical sexual provocateur, who is discovered to be McLeod's wife. She attracts the amorous attentions not only of Lovett, Hollingsworth, and McLeod but also of Lannie, a bizarre, troubled woman who aligns herself first with Lovett, who befriends McLeod, and then with Hollingsworth. Hollingsworth alternately disputes and accedes to McLeod's hold over Lovett, for Lovett, with his lack of a past, represents the pure present over which conflicting personalities and ideologies contend.

Presumably, Mailer abandoned the realistic mode and third-person narration of *The Naked and the Dead* in favor of the ambiguities of *Barbary Shore* in order not only to suggest the Cold War period of shifting loyalties and competing ideologies but also to probe the divisions within his characters who suffer from crises of conviction. McLeod, for example, has tried but failed to follow the course of history, to remake the world into the fulfillment of revolutionary socialism. *Barbary Shore*, however, is unable to take the measure of McLeod in the way *The Naked and the Dead* judges Cummings, for McLeod's dialogue with others, in which the weaknesses of his position are diagnosed, becomes a monologue that upsets the balance of the novel and makes it seem as if McLeod has somehow rescued himself from his defeat. Lovett is unwilling to abandon him even though he is fairly sure that McLeod has murderously attempted to enforce his revolutionary purpose on others. It is true that his passing on of "the little object" to Lovett represents his final refusal to capitulate to the status quo, to the "two different exploitative systems," but his gesture to ameliorate "mankind in barbary," in a world where there is "war and preparation for new war," must be balanced by the novel's first historical parable.

Lovett describes his fantasy of a plump, complacent, middle-aged traveler who is anxious to get home. He is tired and "unaccountably depressed" after a long trip and suddenly shocked to find that while he recognizes the city in which he travels as his home, "the architecture is strange, and the people are dressed in unfamiliar clothing," and he cannot read the alphabet on the street sign. He tries to calm himself in the belief that he is dreaming, but Lovett shouts, "This city is the real city, the material city, and your vehicle is history." The fantasy aptly conveys the novel's contention that people think they know the course of their life, think that they can read the signs of history, when in fact what they have taken to be so familiar, so easily apprehended, is elusive, strange, and terrifying.

The Deer Park

It is not difficult to regard Mailer's third novel, *The Deer Park*, as a mature rewriting of *Barbary Shore*. Once again, there is a first-person narrator, Sergius O'Shaugnessy, who, like Lovett, is a writer. Although Sergius knows his past, he is an orphan who shares Lovett's sense of uncertainty: "I was never sure of myself. I never felt as if I came from any particular place, or that I was like other people." His feeling of being like a "spy or a fake" recalls Lovett's adamant refusal to become a spy for Guinevere. Sergius, however, is more self-aware, more active as a writer in this novel than Lovett is in *Bar-*

bary Shore, where his writing is a given but is not really explored. *The Deer Park*, on the other hand, is the product of Sergius's imagination; it represents his coming to terms with himself and the world. Although his friendship with Charles Eitel, a blacklisted Hollywood scriptwriter and director, is reminiscent of Lovett's friendship with McLeod, Eitel's story is framed in Sergius's words; Sergius contrasts Eitel's defeat with his victory.

Cold War politics play just as important a part in *The Deer Park* as in *Barbary Shore*, but the former eschews the strained allegorical rhetoric of the latter. Some of *The Deer Park*'s finest passages are the dialogues of Hollywood studio executives and politicians, in which the exploitative aspects of capitalist culture and government become apparent in the language, even in the physical gestures and tones of voice, the characters employ, so that Mailer avoids merely talking *about* political issues by demonstrating how they arise in careers such as Eitel's. He has been a Communist sympathizer, a fellow traveler, whose presence embarrasses his motion-picture bosses. He then alienates them by refusing to cooperate with a congressional committee investigating subversives. Eitel turns from Hollywood with the hope that he can recover his talent honestly as an artist but finds that the great film he had always dreamed of creating has been corrupted by his absorption of the cheap techniques of commercial filmmaking. Eventually, he capitulates by agreeing to testify about his Communist past and to construct his film according to Hollywood conventions.

At the same time, Sergius's own life story, from orphan to war hero, draws Hollywood interest, and he is sorely tempted to sell his biography—sell himself, in effect—to the studio, where he may also become a film star. What prevents him from doing so is Eitel's example, or rather Sergius's interpretation of Eitel's biography, for at the end of the novel it is Sergius who has made some meaning out of Eitel's career:

> "For you see," [Eitel] confessed in his mind, "I have lost the final desire of the artist, the desire which tells us that when all else is lost, when love is lost and adventure, pride of self, and pity, there still remains that world we may create, more real to us, more real to others, then the mummery of what happens, passes, and is gone."

Sergius goes on to imagine that Eitel equates the creative act with Sergius's rebellion, with "the small trumpet of your defiance."

Sergius invents an Eitel from whom he can learn, and his lessons are facilitated by his relationships with many of Eitel's friends and lovers. Lulu Meyers, for example, has been married to Eitel but now is free to engage in an affair with Sergius, which she eventually terminates, much to his despair. Sergius, however, avoids the extremes of self-pity and self-aggrandizement by reconstructing the affair between Elena Esposito and Eitel that is taking place during his pursuit of Lulu. Eitel's coldness, arrogance, and self-deceptiveness come through in Sergius's version of the affair, but, like McLeod, Eitel is essentially a sympathetic figure and more believably so than McLeod, since Eitel's tragic realization of his limitations is not muffled by the slightest self-justification at the end of the novel.

If the novel's Hollywood milieu is like Louis XV's Deer Park, that gorge in which innocents like Sergius are engulfed, Sergius barely escapes the gorge by imagining for himself the lives of its victims, of its pimps and prostitutes, of its sultans and sycophants. If *Barbary Shore* begins to put the first-person narrator, the writer as actor, in a paramount position, then *The Deer Park* examines the drama of that position, on which Mailer directly comments in *Advertisements for Myself*, where he acknowledges the increasingly autobiographical nature of his narrators. Not that Sergius is in any simple way Mailer—in fact, he is far less self-conscious about his style than Mailer usually is—but Sergius's quest as a writer who needs to find his words, his style, through direct involvement that tests him against his characters' actions, provided Mailer with the conception of himself and the process of literary creation that has become central to nearly all of his work. Indeed, the process of literary creation itself becomes his theme. In other words, the writer himself becomes his subject.

An American Dream

An American Dream, by its very title, points to Mailer's fascination with the notion that the United States is a complex fiction, a drama of reality that is captured in the dynamic language of its narrator, Steven Rojack, Mailer's hipster hero par excellence, a war hero, a college chum of John Kennedy, a congressman, college professor, psychologist, television personality, and actor resembling the Sergius O'Shaugnessy who was supposed to be the major figure in Mailer's uncompleted novel, delivered in the form of "Advertisement for Myself on the Way Out" at the conclusion of *Advertisements for Myself.* Rojack is also the first Mailer narrator to have an intellect, a vocabulary, and a multiplicity of roles that are commensurate with his author's own activities as soldier, writer, politician, film director, actor, and television personality. As a result, Rojack, like Mailer, registers and revalues his experience. Like his creator, he is never content with a single formulation of reality; on the contrary, he is a complex of shifting moods in response to the modulations of his environment. As Jennifer Bailey has noted, in Mailer's mature work, "identity is always a fiction insofar as it depends upon a constantly changing milieu for its definition."

All of Rojack's actions have to be viewed within the existential requirements of reality in the novel rather than within rigid moral codes applied by readers who want to keep "concepts firmly in category." For some readers, the novel's sense of absolute relativity, of moral fluidity, is repugnant, and *An American Dream* has been rejected out of hand as Mailer's most disturbing work, since Rojack as hipster does not merely live close to violence: He purges and cleanses himself through murdering his wife, Deborah.

In conventional fiction, Rojack's murder might be taken as the surest sign that he has lost control of himself. Quite the contrary is true in Mailer's daring fiction, however, for Rojack regains possession of himself in committing his crime. In some of his most sharply driven, economical prose, Mailer has Rojack explain in the first chapter that he doubts his perception of the world in terms of a rational paradigm. He notes that "the real difference between the President and myself may be that I ended with too large an appreciation of the moon, for I looked down the abyss of the first night I killed: four men, four very separate Germans, dead under a full moon—whereas Jack, for all I know, never saw the abyss." In other words, Rojack senses the occult nature of reality, of forces that terrorize him until he has the courage to act in harmony with them.

Until he reached a point of self-identification, Rojack "remained an actor. My personality was built upon a void." He quit politics "before I was separated from myself forever by the distance between my public appearance which had become vital on television, indeed nearly robust, and my secret frightened romance with the phases of the moon." Virtually the entire novel is written in a style that dramatizes Rojack's search for a new basis on which to live. After considering suicide, after literally expelling from his system the rotting, half-digested food and drink that signify a life he cannot ingest, he confronts his estranged wife, "an artist with the needle," a woman from an influential family who has represented his "leverage" on life. Doing away with Deborah means confronting his case by himself, and he has never had "the strength to stand alone."

Rojack begins to stand alone by following the hipster's course that Mailer sets out in *The White Negro* (1957). He recognizes, in the words of that essay, that "one must grow or else pay more for remaining the same (pay in sickness, or depression, or anguish for the lost opportunity), but pay or grow. . . . What he must do . . . is find his courage at the moment of violence, or equally make it in the act of love." Rojack finds his lover, Cherry, a blond with various qualities that remind him of Grace Kelly and Marilyn Monroe. More than that, however, is his sense that Cherry has "studied blondes," as if she has absorbed all of their styles. The multiplicity of her appeal is like the manifold manifestations of life that he intuits rather than grasps logically. Cherry, and many of the other characters in the novel, is viewed in a world of heightened senses, particularly the sense of smell. Rojack is constantly getting whiffs of things, of moods, of symbolic correspondences between people and ideas: "One kiss of flesh, one whiff of sweet was loose, sending life to the charnel house of my balls." The incredible number of smells that assault him prevent the novel from becoming mystical and abstract. Rather, the intangible linkages are permeated with the corporeality of bodies and beings. In this way, the world becomes an integral function in his psychic economy, and he is even able to face his wife's formidable father, Oswald Kelly, who would just as soon push Rojack to his death as to make him observe the proprieties of the funeral ceremony, where he expects Rojack's presence will help to subdue Kelly's embarrassment over the suspicious circumstances of Deborah's death.

Rojack's tie to Kelly becomes stronger when he discovers that Cherry has been Kelly's mistress—just one of those "coincidences" that rule Rojack's uncanny sense of the connections between lives. As he tries to save his integrity by confronting Kelly, he loses Cherry, who is murdered. He has been divided between returning to her and once again challenging the abyss, the drop from Kelly's high-rise apartment to the street, which represents the void Rojack must fill with his self-definition. At the end of the novel, in Las Vegas, he realizes that he has gambled for his life, that life is a gamble. If he has not been "good enough" to get it all, to have Cherry, he becomes "something like sane again" and departs for a "long trip to Guatemala and Yucatan," just two places, perhaps, on the itinerary of his voyage to selfhood.

Why Are We in Vietnam?

If the examples of Hemingway and Dos Passos prevail over *The Naked and the Dead* and Mailer's other early fiction, and if F. Scott Fitzgerald figures largely in the composition of *The Deer Park*, then the measure of Mailer's progress as a writer can be taken in *Why Are We in Vietnam?*, a novel that invites deliberate comparison with Faulkner. Mailer deftly describes a bear hunt, as does Faulkner in "The Bear," that explores the fundamental meanings of American identity inherent in the conquest of animals and environment. People must prove themselves no matter how much they override the intimate connections between humankind and nature. Rusty, the narrator D. J.'s father, "is fucked unless he gets that bear, for if he don't, white men are fucked more and they can take no more." This kind of reasoning leads to Vietnam, Mailer implies, just as the hunting of bear leads to slavery and other forms of subjugation in Faulkner. Both D. J. and Faulkner's Ike McCaslin come to identify with the animals whose lives they take and with the nature they usurp, so that they must also commune with their feeling of solidarity with life itself, as D. J. does in his remembrance of the mountain goat he has killed:

> It hit D. J. with a second blow on his heart from the exploding heart of the goat and he sat up in bed, in the bunk, listening to the snores, stole out to the night, got one breath of the sense of that *force* up in the North, of land North above him and dived back to the bed, his sixteen-year-old heart racing through the first spooks of an encounter with Herr Dread.

However close Mailer comes to Faulkner in terms of style and theme, *Why Are We in Vietnam?* is still an insistently original novel. In the passage quoted above, for example, the point of view is wholly that of D. J., of the Texan teenager who has never encountered the raw elements of life, who is a disc jockey in his ventriloquizing of many voices in the manner of a radio rock-music personality. Although the prose has Faulkner's relentless flow, its flippant and frenetic beat suggests the repetitive rhythms of technology that heat up D. J.'s talk.

Even more striking is Mailer's playful sport with his narrator's identity. Is D. J. "a Texas youth for sure or is he a genius of a crippled Spade up in Harlem making all this shit up?" Or is D. J. imitating a "high I.Q. Harlem Nigger"? "There is no security in this consciousness," he maintains, since much of what one takes to be reality is an American dream, or rather a "dream field," a "part of a circuit" with "you swinging on the inside of the deep mystery." Inevitably, one is reminded of Ralph Ellison's *Invisible Man* (1952), narrated by a shifting persona, a man of many guises who impersonates others, who like D. J. follows many channels, as if he is broadcasting to the world at large, a world he has somehow subsumed in his supple prose. D. J. brashly appropriates and transforms the styles of others; whereas Ellison's narrator mellowly hints that on the "lower frequencies" he speaks for "you," D. J. commands: "Goose your frequency"—in other words, rev up your sensibility, your reception of the totality D. J. imagines.

As in *An American Dream*, the tendency for the language to turn mystical is checked, even substantiated, by scatological images and metaphors. Some readers find the style offensive, but it is absolutely at the heart of Mailer's vision, since he wants to show on a visceral level how the ideology of consumption works. Because he believes that "the secrets of existence, or some of them anyway, are to be found in the constructions of language" ("The Metaphysics of the Belly"), his style must go to the scatological site of those secrets. To extend D. J.'s remark, the world is "shit" made up by human beings, and in America such "shit" prevails because of the incredible amount of resources that are used, turned into waste products, into refuse that Americans refuse to see. As Mailer sums it up in "The Metaphysics of the Belly": "Ambitious societies loathe scatological themes and are obsessed with them."

The last words of the novel, "Vietnam, hot dam," reflect D. J.'s anticipation; here is still another frontier on which to test himself, another territory for him to explore like Huckleberry Finn, to whom he compares himself at the beginning of the novel. D. J., "disc jockey to America," echoes the country's heated urge to dominate, to damn itself. Or is the minority voice mimicking the majority's will? "Which D. J. white or black would possibly be worse of a genius if Harlem or Dallas is guiding the other, and who knows which?" All the jive talk keeps the channels of possibility open at the end of *Why Are We in Vietnam?*, so that the question of the title has been answered in some ways but is still open-ended, like the identity of the narrator. The reader is left perfectly pitched between alternative readings, once again in the grip of the existential reality that Mailer has faultlessly articulated.

The Armies of the Night

The Armies of the Night climaxed a period of impressive creativity for Mailer in the mid-1960's. A culmination of the self-review he began in *Advertisements for Myself* and *Cannibals and Christians*, it is a definitive portrait of himself as writer and actor, a discovery of his nonfiction aesthetic, and a subtle amalgam of documentary notation and novelistic interpretation that convincingly captures the complexity and ambiguity of the march on the Pentagon. The book's authority is established by its point of view: Mailer's assessment of himself in the third person, sticking close to his own consciousness in the same way that Henry James sidles along Strether in *The Ambassadors* (1903). Mailer is thus able to preserve the spontaneity of historic moments in which he is free to act like a fool or a philosopher while reserving the right as an aloof narrator to judge himself and others with the benefit of hindsight and later research. Furthermore, as Richard Poirier has observed, Mailer "manages to be a witness of the present as if it were already the past. He experiences it from the perspective of his future talk and writing about it." The Mailer of the march is at various times "the Beast," "the Historian," "the Participant," "the Novelist," and "the Ruminant," all of which emphasize the many different guises he assumes depending on the evolving context of his actions.

As rich as a novel in its use of dialogue and characterization, *The Armies of the Night* humorously pursues the contentions of competing personalities—of the poet Robert Lowell and Mailer himself in this example:

> "I don't know, Cal, your speech really had a most amazing impact on me." Mailer drawled the last few words to drain any excessive sentimental infection, but Lowell seemed hardly to mind.
>
> "Well, Norman, I'm delighted," he said, taking Mailer's arm for a moment as if, God and kingdom willing, Mailer had finally become a Harvard dean and could be addressed by the appropriate limb. "I'm delighted because I liked *your* speech so much."

By using circular dialogue, the search for an agreeable exchange between very different personalities—Lowell, "at once virile and patrician," and Mailer, "the younger, presumptive, and self-elected prince"—they have made a story of their relationship that they can share and repeat. The fictive quality of real events—one of Mailer's major points—is ably demonstrated by his own style. As Mailer says before this dialogue, "the clue to discovery was not in the substance of one's idea, but in what was learned from the style of one's attack."

The book shuttles from such intimate dialogue and precise character delineation to panoramic sweeps of the crowds of the Pentagon march. Book 1, "History as a Novel," portrays Mailer as actor in order to show that history is understood only through a deep appreciation of the intersection of very personal feelings and public affairs. No episode, no idea, no impression remains unqualified by the circumstances out of which it arises, and chapter titles constantly emphasize the way in which the literary imagination shapes historical experience.

Book 2, "The Novel as History," goes even further than book 1 in suggesting that history as a whole can make sense only when the interpreter employs all the "instincts of the novelist," for the record of the march is contradictory, fragmentary, and skewed by various viewpoints. Only an act of profound imagination, a reading of the significance of the event itself, can possibly make its constituent parts coalesce, and Mailer convincingly shows that he has studied the record and found it wanting. History is essentially interior and intuitive, he avers. He then proceeds to elaborate a complex re-creation of events that concretely exposes the factitiousness of newspaper accounts.

Beyond the immediate causes and consequences of the march on the Pentagon, Mailer sees the event as a rite of passage for the young marchers, especially the ones who refuse to flee when their fellows are brutally beaten into submission in one of the most riveting and frightening pages in all of Mailer's writing. The coming of knowledge, of a historical fatalism, creeps into both Mailer's prose and his characters' weary postures as he recites events from America's past that reveal that the nation was founded on a rite of passage. It is as if these young people are suddenly imbued with historical consciousness, although Mailer's ruminations and their agony are kept separate on the page. Nevertheless, in his coda he suggests that if the march's end took place in the "isolation in which these last pacifists suffered naked in freezing cells, and gave up prayers for penance, then who was to say they were not saints? And who to say that the sins of America were not by their witness a tithe remitted?" His final words balance an earlier passage where he describes the marchers' opponents, "the gang of Marshals" who in their "collective spirit" emit "little which was good," and one of whom "paid tithe to ten parallel deep lines rising in ridges above his eye brows." Mailer achieves a harmony of form and an equilibrium of language that make the novel's ending seem as complex as the history it imagines, and as moving in its depiction of ignorance and confusion as the Matthew Arnold poem "Dover Beach" (1867), from which Mailer's title is taken.

MARILYN

While they are satisfactory in sections, *Of a Fire on the Moon*, *The Fight*, and Mailer's other writings from the late 1960's to the mid-1970's do not equal *Marilyn*, his follow-up study of the ambiguities of fiction and history so magnificently explored in *The Armies of the Night*. *Marilyn* has a twofold purpose: to measure faithfully and evaluate the obstacles that bar the biographer's way to a full understanding of his subject's life, and to suggest tentatively a biographical method that will aim at re-creating the whole person even though conceding that the search for wholeness is elusive and problematic.

Furthermore, Monroe ranks with Mailer's other major characters, such as General Cummings. Just as Cummings works to make himself an instrument of his own policy, so Monroe paints herself into the camera lens as an instrument of her own will. She is Napoleonic and yet divided against herself, a Dreiserian character who traverses the continent in quest of her true self in much the same way as Lovett, O'Shaugnessy, and Rojack do, detecting voids in themselves and voyaging to find their genuine identities. Much of Mailer's work in film, and his discussions of film in "Some Dirt in the Talk" and "A Course in Film-Making" (both collected in *Existential Errands*), leads directly to his perception of Monroe's disrupted sense of self. Although his later "imaginary memoir," *Of Women and Their Elegance*, in which Monroe recalls her last years, seems less substantial than *Marilyn*, he carries his concern with "twin personalities" a step further by integrating his narrative with Milton Greene's provocative photographs, which are studies in the doubling of personality in a divided world.

THE EXECUTIONER'S SONG

Set against the background of his reflexive writing of the 1960's and 1970's, *The Executioner's Song*, Mailer's next major work of fiction, is a startling book. Its sentences are simple and clear, with an occasionally striking but not elaborate metaphor. Absent from the narrative is Mailer's characteristic sentence or paragraph, which is long and comprehensive—an encyclopedic attempt to gather all of reality in one magnificent statement. There is no intrusive voice to sum up the life of Gary Gilmore, a convicted and executed murderer, and the age in which Gilmore grows to kill. Mailer does not explicitly explore a theory of biography and does not comment, except in his afterword, on his interaction with the life he has written. His book seems keyed to a new aesthetic.

In spite of its more than one thousand pages, *The Executioner's Song* is not a garrulous work; it is a quiet book punctuated by myriad silences. There is a double space following nearly every paragraph of the book, indicating the gap between events, the momentary pause that intervenes even in events that seemingly follow one another swiftly and smoothly. Reality is defined by these frequent intervals of silence, periods of stillness that intimate how much is left unsaid and how many characters fail to connect with one another. Gilmore is the most solitary character of all, cut off in large part from humanity and therefore able to murder.

A great deal of the book is dialogue or paraphrase of dialogue, which enhances the dramatic clash of details and conflicting points of view. Even the long descriptive passages and the evocations of characters' thoughts consist only of the results of the reporter who has interviewed these characters for their thoughts and who conveys what he has heard and observed. Hence, there is no privileged retrospective narrator to unify the book's disparate materials.

Mailer has called *The Executioner's Song* a "true life novel." By "novel" he seems to mean something somewhat different from his use of the term in *The Armies of the Night* and *Marilyn*, in which he employs a novelistic narrator to probe the unspoken motivations of his characters and to organize reality in creative metaphors. Of his unusual departure from past practice he remarked in 1979 in *The New York Times Magazine*,

> I was convinced from the start that the materials were exceptional; it had the structure of a novel. Whenever I needed a character for esthetic balance—a new character of imposing dimensions—one just appeared out of nowhere. If I had conceived *The Executioner's Song* as a novel entirely drawn from my own imagination, I doubt I could have improved on those characters.

Mailer conceives of the characters as revealing themselves to him, so that he does not have to serve as a mediating voice. Instead, he orchestrates their disclosures by surrounding them with a quiet space and spare style that preserves their individual integrity.

Reading such sparely created scenes, one is tempted to comb through the details over and over again in order to search for the pertinent clue that will point to the meaning of Gilmore's story, but as Joan Didion points out in her review in *The New York Times Book Review* (October 7, 1979), "the very subject of *The Executioner's Song* is that vast emptiness at the center of the Western experience, a nihilism antithetical not only to literature but to most other forms of human endeavor, a dread so close to zero that human voices fade out, trail off, like skywriting." Mailer has chosen, this time, to make a literature that is articulately mute, almost muzzled in its restrained revelations of actions that remain voiceless, dumb, and frighteningly uncommunicative:

> "Why'd you do it, Gary?" Nielsen asked again quietly.
>
> "I don't know," Gary said.
>
> "Are you sure?"
>
> "I'm not going to talk about that," Gilmore said. He shook his head delicately, and looked at Nielsen, and said, "I can't keep up with life."

For Mailer, *The Executioner's Song* is biography in a new key, since he attends to the integrity of individual lives without quickly elevating those lives into symbolic significance. At the same time, the continuity of his concerns is apparent in his ambitious desire to show that true life must be mediated through the imaginative power of a singular intelligence. He understood that *The Executioner's Song* required a voice, flexible and comprehensive, in order to embody the myriad voices that make up reality. There are patterns that can be perceived on rereading the book, yet no single pattern is definitive. Gilmore seems to reach some genuine self-understanding and consistency, but his behavior is still sometimes contradictory and enigmatic. He approaches his execution wanting to die, and yet he searches for every possible means of escape. *The Executioner's Song* remains faithful to the elusiveness of self, to both the revelation and the inscrutability of identity.

Ancient Evenings

Beginning with the opening sentence—"Crude thoughts and fierce forces are my state"—*Ancient Evenings* embarks on a style that is new to Mailer and to his readers who have been accustomed to an active voice transforming everything it articulates. Something very strange is happening to the passive voice of the novel's first narrator-protagonist, the ka (spiritual emanation) of Menenhetet II, who is undergoing the process of rebirth. The first book of the novel is awesome and quite wonderful in its depiction of a consciousness trying to differentiate itself from all that surrounds it.

After the first book, much of the novel is narrated by Menenhetet I, the great-grandfather of Menenhetet II. Menenhetet I is the great ancestor who has been able to live four lives (1290-1100 B.C.E.) by learning how to ejaculate into a woman at the very moment of his death, thereby conceiving himself anew in a lover who becomes his mother. Menenhetet I aspires in his first life to supplant his Pharaoh as ruler of Egypt and dies in the act of sexual intercourse with the Pharaoh's queen. Menenhetet I carries Mailer's conception of himself and of the hero in his fiction to the furthest extreme: He is a man of many ages, the self-invented avatar of Menenhetet II's quest for distinction. Menenhetet I has been a warrior and high priest, a scholar and man of action, a great lover of queens and yet a farmer of peasant origin. In his fourth life, Menenhetet I would like to be the vizier of Ramses IX (Ptahnem-hotep). In the very act of telling his four life histories to Ramses IX, however, Menenhetet I reveals an overweening ambition and fatal attraction to magical practices (including the repulsive eating of bat dung) that disqualify him for the role of Pharaonic confidant.

Ancient Evenings is embedded in the lush details of ancient Egypt, in the rhythms of an alien time. Even sympathetic readers have noted a numbing sameness in the prose that suggests that the author has striven too hard for unity, for the merging of the opposites that create so much exciting tension in *The Naked and the Dead, The Armies of the Night*, and *The Executioner's Song*. *Ancient Evenings* is Norman Mailer at his neatest, with the loose ends of his philosophy and his prose knit together rather impressively. Nevertheless, it seems static and too thoroughly thought-out; absent from it is the rough-edged stimulation of a writer on the make, who is best when he is suggestive rather than explicit, when he is promising to complete the circle and join the halves without ever quite doing so.

Tough Guys Don't Dance

Like Mikey Lovett in *Barbary Shore*, Tim Madden in *Tough Guys Don't Dance* is an amnesiac: He cannot remember what happened the night before, and he cannot account for the large amount of blood on his car seat. He is clearly kin to Stephen Rojack. More or less kept by his prized wife, the wealthy Patty Lareine, Madden, a writer, finds that he cannot work when she deserts him.

As her name suggests, Lareine has been Madden's imperious queen, and he seems at a loss when he is not in the service of his "medieval lady." At the same time, he has clearly chafed under her rule, for he regrets having broken his code of male self-sufficiency. As a result, the couple's marriage has been turbulent, and in its later stages, husband and wife seem most alike in their murderous inclinations. The novel begins with Madden wondering whether the severed head he discovers in his marijuana hideaway is the result of a drunken evening's debauchery with another woman, which turned violent when Patty Lareine returned home.

The characters in *Tough Guys Don't Dance* relate to one another as in an Arthurian romance. Madden discovers that his wife has had another lover, the deputy police chief, Alvin Luther Regency, a powerfully built, maniacal rival, who is part of the plot to set up Madden (who has already served a short term for possession of cocaine). Complicating matters further for Madden is the lurking presence of his envious former schoolmate, Meeks Wardly Hilby III, who was once married to Patty Lareine and from whom Madden stole her. If Madden can make sense of the two murders, he can also begin to put his life back together—including his failed relationship with Madeleine Falco, his witty, tough counterpart, who left him when he took up with Patty Lareine and who now finds herself mired in a bad marriage to the dangerous Regency.

Readers who prefer murder mysteries with taut, spare plots and prose may bristle at the complications of Mailer's syntax and philosophizing. The heads and bodies buried in different locations are indicative of the splits in the human psyche that Mailer has pursued in much of his writing. Usually Mailer is able to finesse the shifts between the novel's ideas and events, and his delineation of characters through clipped dialogue is convincing. At a few points, his narrative flags, perhaps because he has tried to do too much, to integrate characters, ideas, and plot simultaneously in a single narrative voice.

Harlot's Ghost

Harlot's Ghost is a mammoth and intermittently gripping novel of the CIA, charting the career of Harry Hubbard, protégé of the legendary Hugh Tremont Montague ("Harlot"), and a key participant in CIA operations in Berlin, Uruguay, Washington, D.C., Miami, and Cuba. The novel is based on a close reading of nearly one hundred books about the organization and on Mailer's vivid imagination, which often calls upon themes and characters he has rehearsed in several works of fiction and nonfiction, including speculations on the murder of Marilyn Monroe, Ernest Hemingway's suicide, and the nature of Cuban leader Fidel Castro's heroism.

Mailer's thesis is that a CIA operative is by definition a deceiver, a person who is always playing more than one role, an actor whose sense of reality is constantly shifting, making it difficult to maintain loyalties and friendships, never sure of his or her own ground. Harry Hubbard, the son of a fabled CIA agent, worries that he is not "tough enough" and takes on risky ventures such as the Bay of Pigs fiasco. As a matter of survival within the agency, he finds himself acting as a double agent—at one point reporting to both his mentor, Harlot, and to his father, Cal.

Through Harry's letters, diaries, and first-person narrative, Mailer manages to cover most of the dramatic events involving the CIA from 1955 to 1963. This very long novel (near thirteen hundred pages) is burdened with too much learning and too little plot—no detail is too trivial to include as long as it impinges on Harry's consciousness. There are some wonderfully realized characters (E. Howard Hunt and William King Harvey), but they do not quite redeem Mailer's turgid prose.

The Gospel According to the Son

By contrast, *The Gospel According to the Son* is a restrained retelling of the Christ story from Christ's point of view. Mailer successfully finds a voice quite different from his own for the first-person narrator. Christ is portrayed as very much of a man—driven by his divine mission but also doubting his ability to carry it out. Christ often compares himself to Moses, another reluctant prophet who feared he was not worthy of the Lord's trust.

Mailer's Christ gently but firmly takes issue with certain aspects of the Gospels. He is a miracle worker, yet he notes how often accounts of his powers have been exaggerated—the projections of those who fervently believe in him. Mailer ingeniously accounts for many of Christ's most famous sayings, such as "Render unto Caesar the things that are Caesar's." Such statements show a Jesus with a tactical and political sense—challenging the status quo, to be sure, but also adopting a diplomatic stance when it serves his purposes.

If Mailer can be faulted, it may be (surprisingly) for not being daring enough. His Jesus seems a little dull and not at all the charismatic figure who surely attracted Mailer in the first place. In Mailer's obvious desire to respect the Christ story while humanizing it, he has perhaps not risked quite enough in making Christ a believable character.

The Castle in the Forest

Why a novel on Adolf Hitler? Mailer's answer to several interviewers was that if it could be said that the angel Gabriel was present at the birth of Jesus, why could it also not be true that the devil presided over Hitler's nativity? The other standard interview answer Mailer gave was that his mother knew as early as 1932—a year before Hitler became Germany's chancellor—that Hitler was dead serious about killing the Jews. So, in Mailer's view, it was a just a matter of time until he confronted in a major novel (ten years in the making) the origins of Hitler's power.

There has always been something pre-Judeo-Christian about Mailer's imagination. His Homeric sensibility is also at home in ancient Egypt. Monotheism hardly appeals to the Manichaean Mailer. So it is not surprising that a devil (masquerading as an SS man) narrates *The Castle in the Forest*.

Modern psychology, Mailer implies, cannot account for the rise of Adolf Hitler. There are many explanations for Hitler's success, but no interpretation can really dominate the field. Mailer's novel reflects his study of the contemporary literature on the führer. The novel includes an extensive bibliography with asterisks identifying the books on which Mailer drew for inspiration and data.

Why the devil? Because no God-centered universe could possibly hold a Hitler, Mailer implies. Such evil is conceivable only in a divided cosmogony, in a contest between God and the E.O. (the acronym for the Evil One that Mailer's devil favors). This seesaw conflict between the forces of good and evil is a pet theory the novelist articulated for decades—at least as far back as *Advertisements for Myself* (1959). The devil in *The Castle in the Forest* is rather like one of those Greek gods who takes a special interest in a particular mortal and helps him out when it seems the human's strength of purpose may flag.

So Adolf—enabled but also enervated by mother

love—needs a dose of the devil to enhance his prospects. A biographer naturally thinks of Fanny Mailer, the maternal sentinel who presided over her son's rise to fame. To explain Mailer's choice of Hitler, perhaps the appropriate citation is the confession in *Advertisements for Myself*: "The sour truth is that I am imprisoned with a perception which will settle for nothing less than making a revolution in the consciousness of our time."

Norman Mailer's great contribution to American literature is his effort to encompass large subjects. His aspirations are so high he is bound to fail by any conventional standards. As soon as the SS man reveals he is a devil on assignment from the E.O., interest in his story slackens. Making Hitler a product of evil, rather than an originator of same, is troubling—at least in terms of the standards applied to biographical novels, where the subject reigns.

Much of *The Castle in the Forest* is really third-person narration recast in the voice of the devil. Mailer often found writing in the third person inauthentic—for him, at least—because he could not accept the authority of an omniscient narrator, and he wanted to distance himself from the contemporary historical novel. As he observes in *The Spooky Art: Thoughts on Writing* (2003),

> This Olympian third person, this Tolstoyan presence, needs experience, confidence, irony, insight, and lordly detachment. When it can be done, hurrah. Most of the great nineteenth century novels achieve just that tone. Today it's usually up to the novelists who can write best-sellers. In their case, God is always ready to offer an adjective adequate to their means. Teeming excitement, unendurable suspense, delightful joy, grim misery, dogged courage. But let me not froth at the mouth. There was a time when I used to do that myself.

Mailer abandoned the third-person narrator after *The Naked and the Dead.* To allay his qualms about omniscient narration, then, he invents a supernatural witness to Hitler's life.

Mailer's devil is not very engaging in his own right, however. Surely what matters in the narrator—third person or first—is the quality of the perceptions and the nature not of the devil but of the devil's beard, the SS man. What happens among the congregation of the devils (it has to be kept vague, lest trade secrets be revealed) is greeted with a virtual shrug. The devil's minion is factitious in a way that an astute third-person narrator, a literary convention after all, is not.

The novel's richly imagined terrestrial details—the depiction of Adolf's father, Alois, for example—marvelously re-create the Habsburg world in which Hitler grew up. The sex scenes have a ribald verve that is classic Mailer—and more humor than might be expected in the novelist's evocation of the petty despotisms of domestic life. This novel can be enjoyed for its deep learning and its well-wrought characters, if not for its factitious ontology.

Carl Rollyson

Other major works

SHORT FICTION: *New Short Novels 2*, 1956; *The Short Fiction of Norman Mailer*, 1967.

PLAY: *The Deer Park: A Play*, pb. 1967 (adaptation of his novel).

POETRY: *Deaths for the Ladies and Other Disasters*, 1962.

SCREENPLAY: *Tough Guys Don't Dance*, 1987 (adaptation of his novel).

NONFICTION: *The White Negro*, 1957; *The Presidential Papers*, 1963; *Cannibals and Christians*, 1966; *The Bullfight*, 1967; *The Idol and the Octopus: Political Writings on the Kennedy and Johnson Administrations*, 1968; *Miami and the Siege of Chicago: An Informal History of the Republican and Democratic Conventions of 1968*, 1969; *Of a Fire on the Moon*, 1970; *The Long Patrol: Twenty-five Years of Writing from the Work of Norman Mailer*, 1971 (Robert Lucid, editor); *The Prisoner of Sex*, 1971; *Existential Errands*, 1972; *St. George and the Godfather*, 1972; *The Faith of Graffiti*, 1974 (with Mervyn Kurlansky and Jon Naar); *Some Honorable Men: Political Conventions, 1960-1972*, 1975; *The Fight*, 1975; *Genius and Lust: A Journey Through the Major Writings of Henry Miller*, 1976; *Pieces and Pontifications*, 1982; *Portrait of Picasso as a Young Man*, 1995 (also known as *Pablo and Fernande: Portrait of Picasso as a Young Man*, 1994); *The Spooky Art: Thoughts on Writing*, 2003; *Why Are We at War?*, 2003; *The Big Empty: Dialogues on Politics, Sex, God, Boxing, Morality, Myth, Poker, and Bad Conscience in America*, 2006 (with John Buffalo Mailer); *On God: An Uncommon Conversation*, 2007 (with Michael Lennon).

MISCELLANEOUS: *Advertisements for Myself*, 1959; *The Time of Our Time*, 1998; *Modest Gifts: Poems and Drawings*, 2003.

Bibliography

Bloom, Harold, ed. *Norman Mailer*. Philadelphia: Chelsea House, 2003. Collection features essays by many of Mailer's most perceptive critics. Includes an informative editor's introduction, bibliographic references, and index.

Dearborn, Mary. *Mailer: A Biography*. Boston: Houghton Mifflin, 1999. Astute, full-scale biography presents penetrating discussion of Mailer's life and work as well as important interviews with his family and friends.

Leeds, Barry H. *The Enduring Vision of Norman Mailer*. Bainbridge Island, Wash.: Pleasure Boat Studio, 2002. Presents analysis of Mailer's works along with a 1987 interview that Leeds conducted with the author. Offers a good introduction to Mailer.

Lennon, J. Michael, ed. *Conversations with Norman Mailer*. Jackson: University Press of Mississippi, 1988. Collection features many of the most important interviews given by Mailer, in which he reveals his developing and changing attitudes toward his work.

_______. *Critical Essays on Norman Mailer*. Boston: G. K. Hall, 1986. Collection includes critical analyses of Mailer's work, important reviews, and an extremely valuable overview by Lennon of Mailer's reputation as it evolved.

Manso, Peter, ed. *Mailer, His Life and Times*. New York: Simon & Schuster, 1986. Oral biography benefits from significant contributions from Mailer's family and friends.

Merrill, Robert. *Norman Mailer Revisited*. New York: Twayne, 1992. One of the best introductory studies on Mailer available. Includes a chapter on Mailer's novels of the 1980's, a chapter on his biography and his legend, and a concluding assessment of his career. Supplemented by a chronology and an annotated bibliography.

Rollyson, Carl. *Norman Mailer: The Last Romantic*. New York: iUniverse, 2008. Revised and updated edition of *The Lives of Norman Mailer: A Biography* offers discussion of the author's writing as well as biographical information; new sections are devoted to his life and publications since 1991. Includes detailed notes and comprehensive bibliography.

BERNARD MALAMUD

Born: Brooklyn, New York; April 26, 1914
Died: New York, New York; March 18, 1986

Principal long fiction

The Natural, 1952
The Assistant, 1957
A New Life, 1961
The Fixer, 1966
The Tenants, 1971
Dubin's Lives, 1979
God's Grace, 1982
The People, 1989

Other literary forms

While acknowledging the significant achievements of Bernard Malamud (MAL-uh-muhd) as a novelist, many critics believe that the most distinctive and enduring contributions the author made to American fiction are to be found in his short stories, particularly those collected in *The Magic Barrel* (1958) and *Idiots First* (1963). Malamud published three more volumes of short fiction in his lifetime: *Pictures of Fidelman: An Exhibition* (1969), a collection of six linked stories featuring the same protagonist; *Rembrandt's Hat* (1973); and *The Stories of Bernard Malamud* (1983), twenty-five stories largely drawn from previously published volumes. The posthumously published volume *The People, and Uncollected Stories* (1989) gathers a number of previously uncollected stories, most of them early pieces from the 1940's but also including two from the 1980's.

Bernard Malamud. (© Jerry Bauer)

ACHIEVEMENTS

With novelists such as Saul Bellow and Philip Roth, Bernard Malamud is among the most distinguished of a number of Jewish writers who did much to set the tone of postwar American fiction. Malamud's singular achievement is to have captured the experience of Jews in the United States at a point of transition between cultures. His characters—not only the Jews but also their Gentile counterparts—are not yet quite a part of American culture, nor have they fully abandoned the old culture of which they are no longer members. Out of this sense of dislocation and the struggle to create a new life, Malamud created most of his early stories and novels. Although not all the novels have Jewish protagonists—the first two in fact do not—the dilemma is constant; the Gentile characters are as displaced and alienated as the Jewish ones. He received numerous awards for his fiction, including two National Book Awards and a Pulitzer Prize.

BIOGRAPHY

Bernard Malamud was born in Brooklyn to Russian immigrant parents. His father, like Morris Bober in *The Assistant*, was a small grocer, and the family moved around Brooklyn as business dictated. When Malamud was nine years old, he had pneumonia and began a period of intensive reading. Later, encouraged by his teachers, he also began writing short stories.

From 1932 to 1936, Malamud was a student at the City College of New York. He later began work on a master of arts degree at Columbia University, and, while teaching night school at Erasmus Hall, his own alma mater, he started writing in earnest. He married Ann de Chiara in 1945, and four years later he and his family moved to Corvallis, Oregon, where for twelve years Malamud taught English at Oregon State. A son was born before they left for Corvallis, a daughter after they arrived. While there, he published his first three books; after leaving, he wrote his satire of academic life in an English department, *A New Life*. Returning to the East in 1961, Malamud taught for many years at Bennington College in Vermont. He died in New York on March 18, 1986.

ANALYSIS

In *The Natural*, Iris Lemon tells the protagonist that all people have two lives, "the life we learn with and the life we live with after that. Suffering is what brings us toward happiness." Although her statement requires qualification, it is a suggestive summary of the major theme of Bernard Malamud's work: the journey toward a new life, a journey marked by suffering, which may or may not be redemptive. In fact, however, Malamud's characters usually have three lives: one from which they have not learned and that they are attempting to leave behind, a life the reader sees in flashbacks and confessions as well as in brief opening scenes; a middle life, the learning life, which is the substance of the books; and the new life promised to successful characters at the end. Malamud's novels, then, are in the tradition of the bildungsroman, but they have older protagonists than do most American novels of education. What Malamud depicts in each of his novels is a renewed attempt to find new life and to convert suffering to meaning, a second journey toward knowledge.

Of the old life, Malamud usually shows his readers little. *The Natural* opens with a brief pregame sketch that quickly shows Roy Hobbs's past. In *The Assistant*, the reader sees the robbery for which Frankie Alpine will try to atone, and in *The Fixer*, there is a short portrait of Yakov Bok's past in his village. Malamud's characters are trying to forget the past, so even when it enters their minds, they try to shove it away. Moreover, Malamud's novels usually begin with a journey away from a past life. Whether European Jews coming to America or moving from their shtetl to Kiev, or whether American Jews traveling from New York to Oregon or baseball players leaving the country for the big city, Malamud's protagonists are always travelers, uneasy with their past, uncertain of their future. In fact, they often try to conceal their past: Alpine and Hobbs work conscientiously to obliterate the stories of their earlier lives. Yakov Bok drops his prayer things, a reminder of his old life and its ways, into a river. One of Malamud's most frequent devices is to have characters change their names in an attempt to escape their past identity. Bok, trying to pass as a Gentile, becomes Yakov Ivanovitch Dologushev, his initials ironically spelling "yid."

What all of Malamud's characters must learn, however, is that they have to accept responsibility for their past actions. Paradoxically, while the evil that his characters have done remains with them and so must be acknowledged, the good can be erased. At the end of *The Natural*, Roy Hobbs, a failure in his quest for a new life, discovers that for his part in throwing the league playoffs, all of his baseball records will be expunged from the record books.

The journey is always a quest, as the mythological base of *The Natural*, Malamud's first and prototypal novel, makes clear. The public part of the quest takes place in the world of men, and its lesson is that of law, of the inner check, of renunciation. Hobbs is a natural hitter, but he lacks good judgment, both on the field and off. Frankie Alpine in *The Assistant* continually steals from Morris Bober. Saving Bober's daughter Helen from being raped, he is unable to control his own sexual appetite and rapes her himself. "Why do Jews suffer so much?" he asks Morris Bober, and after replying that to live is to suffer, Morris adds, "I think if a Jew don't suffer for the Law, he will suffer for nothing." Although Alpine is not yet a Jew, he does suffer for nothing.

Acceptance of the law, curbing one's appetite, is the first lesson. As Levin thinks in *A New Life*, "Renunciation was what he was now engaged in. It was a beginning that created a beginning." Law alone is not enough, however, and Malamud's questers must pass a second test as well for their journeys to be successful: the test of love, of dream, of acceptance of life in its fullness and ambiguity. Helen Bober could marry Nat Pearl, studying to be a lawyer but lacking dreams, or she could choose Louis Karp, pure appetite, lacking law. She chooses neither, and at the novel's conclusion a chance remains for Frankie Alpine, who is learning what W. H. Auden calls a "law like love." In *A New Life*, Levin first picks up Henry James's *The American* (1877), a book that makes a case for renunciation, but Pauline Gilley, another man's wife whom Levin first renounces but later accepts, moves the discussion to William Dean Howells, who, like Malamud, prefers the economy of pain.

Another qualification to Iris Lemon's statement is necessary: Suffering is what *may* bring one toward happiness. The quest is not successful for all of Malamud's characters. Many of them, already displaced from their European homelands, refuse to undertake another journey. Others learn the wrong lesson from their old life. "*Rachmones*, we say in Hebrew," says Yakov Bok. "Mercy, one oughtn't to forget it." Many, particularly women (there are no Jewish mothers in Malamud), do forget it and harden their hearts. Still others, having undertaken the journey, are, like Roy Hobbs, too selfish ever to move beyond themselves.

Not only do Malamud's novels tell and retell the same story, but they do so with similar casts and with the same images. The protagonist is typically without a close family, sometimes orphaned. He is often a *schlemiel* or a *schlemazl*, always wanting to escape his past, but unlucky and clumsy in the attempt. He is likely to be self-deceived. Early in *The Assistant*, while still stealing, Alpine tells himself that he is "an honest guy." Later he says, "Even when I am bad I am good," inaccurately viewing himself as a man of stern morality.

Especially in the early novels and short stories, there is a father figure, and the learning relationship is dramatized in terms of an apprenticeship. These figures become less important in the later novels. By *A New Life*, a transitional book, both would-be father figures, the inane Fairchild and the more scholarly but weak Fabrikant, are failures. After *A New Life*, the questers are orphaned even in this middle life.

Malamud also makes frequent use of doubles, figures both actual and dreamed. Roy and Bump Baily, the player he replaces, are identified with each other: They share the same girl and the same fault. Frankie Alpine enacts in his dreams the crimes Ward Minogue, his darker opposite, actually commits. In *The Tenants*, Harry Lesser and Willie Spearmint (born Bill Spear—blacks also change names in Malamud) act out the common racial stereotypes, reverse them, and then destroy each other's work and life. An image from William Shakespeare's *King Lear* (1605-1606), each as the other's shadow, dominates the book.

Women in Malamud's work are of two types: the dark ladies (Memo Paris, who betrays Roy Hobbs, and Harriet Bird, who shoots him; Avis Fliss, who spies on Levin; and Zenaida, who gives false testimony against Bok) and the potentially redemptive ladies of the lake (Iris Lemon, Helen Bober, Pauline Gilley, Fanny Bick in *Dubin's Lives*). The function of the good women is in part to hear the hero's confession, enabling him to acknowledge his past, but the women confess too, and, as in Nathaniel Hawthorne, an earlier fabulist, the protagonists have the obligation to accept the women's ambiguous moral nature, a test they often fail. Roy, for example, who wants Iris's sympathy, is disquieted when she tells him that at thirty-three she is a grandmother.

Malamud is also consistent in his metaphors. The journey is often from a prison to freedom. Stores are identified as prisons; Alpine feels both imprisoned and entombed in Bober's grocery. Bok exchanges a shtetl for a prison but learns the meaning of freedom while he is confined. Levin says that if you make the wrong basis for your life, "you spend your whole life in jail," though he later realizes that the prison is himself.

Another metaphor involves moving from a mirror to a window—and beyond. Characters must not reject the mirror, refuse to see themselves as they truly are, as Irene Bell, née Belinsky, does when she refuses to look into a dropped mirror in *The Tenants*. Unfortunately, after they know themselves, the characters sometimes become so fascinated with their own image that they cannot move on. *The Natural* opens with Roy Hobbs on a train, striking a match to look out the window but seeing only his own reflection; throughout the novel, he never achieves any higher values than those centered on himself.

Progress, the attempt to make contact with another, is often symbolized by gazing through a window—transparent, but still dividing, the attempt finally a failure. A common example of this failure is voyeurism; Levin eyes Pauline Gilley's house and watches her through binoculars at a basketball game, while Gerald, her husband, watches several characters through the viewfinder of his camera. Lesser in *The Tenants* is watched through a keyhole. Frankie Alpine climbs an air shaft to watch through a window as Helen Bober showers, and William Dubin in *Dubin's Lives* sneaks to Fanny Bick's house to spy on her and her boyfriend through a window.

Consistent images are linked in Malamud's novels. They must have about them a touch of red or black, a reminder of their human imperfection. They are associated, often by their names, with flowers (Iris, though with Lemon), with birds (Harriet Bird, Avis Fliss), and with trees. The bad women have sore breasts (Memo, Avis) and are like trapped birds and twisted trees.

If there is a conversion—an acceptance of the old life and a promise of a new—it takes place in an isolated, natural spot, such as the park in the urban world of *The Assistant*, where Alpine tells Helen that the best part of Leo Tolstoy's *Anna Karenina* (1875-1877; English translation, 1886) is Levin's conversion in the woods; the lake in *The Natural* (Memo, the bad woman, is, however, associated with polluted waters); the woods in *A New Life*, where Malamud's Levin is converted; and the artificial jungle of *The Tenants*, where the meeting of Lesser and Spearmint ends in death. In *Dubin's Lives*, Dubin is running through the countryside when he first meets Fanny, and it is there that they finally make love.

Despite this consistency of theme, character, and image, Malamud's fiction changed during his career. The early works, with their blend of romance and realism, represent Malamud's best writing. About midway through his career, however, he seemed to have tired of his form; his novels became more discursive, his protagonists more articulate. On one hand, he moved toward experimentalism, but on the other hand, toward the novel of ideas. Quoting Herman Melville that to have a mighty novel, one needs a mighty theme, suggesting that "the purpose of a writer is to keep civilization from destroying itself," Malamud in his later novels reached obtrusively for significance. The protagonists of these later works are frequently blocked artists: the writers in *The Tenants*, the biographer in *Dubin's Lives*.

The Natural

Malamud's first novel, *The Natural*, is a fanciful combination of American baseball lore with the myth of the wasteland. Here, the wasteland is a New York baseball team, the Knights, whose coach, Pop Fisher, is the fisher king of the legend. The quester and protagonist of the novel is Roy Hobbs, his name meaning rustic king. Roy undergoes a double-edged test to see if he can bring life to the baseball team, but the center of the novel is what Roy himself does—or does not—learn from the tests, the chance of a new life for the quester. Though *The Natural* is in many ways the least Jewish of Malamud's novels, it is the prototype for the rest of his fiction; the story it tells and the patterns it uses are those that persist through Malamud's work.

The pregame section of the novel, the brief history of the past life in which Hobbs does not learn and that he will attempt to leave behind, opens with the image of Hobbs staring at his own reflection in the train window. This inability to look beyond himself, his egocentric view of the world, is Hobbs's undoing. Both parts of Roy's testing are also prefigured in this section, which is a microcosm of the novel as a whole. In the public test, Roy, a pitcher, is challenged by an established batting king, whom Roy strikes out as Malamud draws the mythic parallels. The cost of that success is that Roy slays his first father figure, his mentor who catches the pitches without adequate chest protection, is injured, and dies.

If Roy is partially successful in his physical challenge, he is not at all so in the world of moral choice. In the pregame section, he is questioned by the first of the women in the novel, Harriet Bird. The episode is based on the real-life shooting of a ballplayer. Harriet invites Roy up to her hotel room. She tests him with a series of questions about the value of his ambitions, but when Roy's self-centered answers reveal the limits of his aspirations—he plays only for his own glory—his unalloyed confidence is rewarded with a bullet. The section ends with a fantastic tableau: Harriet Bird doing a grisly nude dance around the fallen body of Roy Hobbs.

The nine inninglike sections of the novel that follow repeat more spaciously the double test the quester has to undertake to revitalize the team and prove himself worthy of a new life. When Roy arrives, everything is dismal: The Knights are losing, the players are dispirited, Pop Fisher is ailing. Even the drinking fountain produces only rusty water. Once Roy begins to play, however, the team's luck changes. Armed with his mythic bat, Wonder Boy, Roy hits five home runs and energizes the team. Rain falls, and the process of restoring life-giving water to the land begins. Roy, however, gets his chance to play only when another player, Bump Baily, is injured. Again, Roy's success depends on the suffering of another, suffering on which Roy is too willing to capitalize. Roy and Bump are doubles, Bump a darker projection of many of Roy's faults. As the fans and team-members point out, they share a common limitation: They play for themselves rather than for the team. The high point of Roy's career is Roy Hobbs Day, an event that occurs in the middle of this symmetrical novel. He is given a white Mercedes, a symbolic lancer on which he proudly rides around the stadium.

Roy's acceptance speech has only one theme, his own greatness, and from this triumph, Roy's downward path, indicated by his batting slump, begins. Although there are short times of solid hitting, as when Roy agrees to play for another, the on-field slump is accompanied by Roy's involvement with the illegal off-the-field dealings of the team's owner, who is setting up the throwing of the league playoffs, a fictive event modeled on the notorious "Black Sox" scandal of the 1919 World Series. Roy is in a world beyond his experience. Baffled by the owner's oily, cliché-ridden speeches, Roy participates in the fix. Although at the end of the playoff game Roy tries to play well to reverse the evil he has already done, it is too late; he can no longer free himself and strikes out. The story that begins with Roy striking out an aging star comes full circle with a new young pitcher striking out Roy.

In the private half of the test, Roy once again fails. As he has earlier made the wrong choice with Harriet Bird, he once again makes the wrong moral choices in this section of the novel. He becomes involved with the dark lady, Memo Paris, and they drive off together to a beach, even though the sign cautions danger, warning them of polluted water. There can be no symbolic cleansing here. Memo tries to explain the values she has learned from the suffering in her past, but what she has learned is solely to look out for herself. Roy wants to say something comparable about his own life, but he can think of nothing except more boasting about his future. When he returns to the ballfield after this episode, his grim future is apparent and his lack of control is magnified. The mystic meal is transformed into a large banquet where Roy eats so much he becomes too sick to play.

Memo's counterpart, the redemptive lady of the lake, is Iris Lemon. Like Memo and Harriet, she is associated with birds, flowers, and water, and as with Memo, the key scene involves a journey to the lake; Iris's role, however, is as potential savior of Roy. They drive together to a lake sheltered from the outside world, and it is there that Iris, too, questions Roy about his values, but she tries to lead him beyond boasting. She begins a confession of her own life. Although she is a grandmother at thirty-three, she has learned from her suffering, has transformed it into meaning. Roy is thirty-four, but something about Iris's confession repels him. They make love, and Iris becomes pregnant—she is the only fruitful woman in the novel—but Roy finally rejects her. In the last game of the playoffs, he sees her in the stands, but he is intent on trying to hit a dwarf who habitually heckles him from the bleachers. The ball instead hits Iris, who has stood to cheer for Roy. In the final scene between them, Iris tells Roy that she is pregnant, that he has created a new life for another at least, and she asks Roy to hit one for their child. It is too late, and Roy strikes out. He thinks of all the wrong choices he has made and wants to undo them, but he cannot.

In addition to the myth of the wasteland and the quest for new life, a central image of the novel occurs in a dream Roy frequently has. It involves Roy and his dog in a forest, a secluded place where he can follow his innermost thoughts without shame. Driving once with Memo, Roy thinks he sees a boy and a dog emerging from a woods, a boy whom Memo seems to hit. Whether she has or not, Memo speeds on—leaving behind her destruction of Roy's innocence and his illusions. In the forest he thinks he will lose his directions in order to find himself, lose his life in order to save it, but for Roy, whose middle life is marked with nothing but wrong choices, there is no salvation, no learning. The boy and his dog have vanished along with Roy's innocence, and he has rejected Iris, who could have saved him.

THE ASSISTANT

In Malamud's second novel, *The Assistant*, the surface of the myth is quite different. The pastoral world of baseball gives way to an urban business setting. The rustic king gives way to the petty thief, and the myth of heroic action on which the fate of many depends is replaced by the legend of a saint. Spaciousness is superseded by narrowness, movement by confinement. *The Natural* is often humorous and always marked by energy; even evil is active. In *The Assistant*, gloom and lethargy hand over every scene, and the despair is oppressive. The mythic parallels in *The Natural* are elaborate and schematic; in *The Assistant*, implicit and suggestive.

These differences sketched, however, *The Assistant* remains another telling of Malamud's basic myth. For most critics, it is his most successful; the fusion of romance and realism, of surface accuracy with poetic evocation, is seamless and compelling. Like Roy Hobbs, Frankie Alpine, the protagonist of *The Assistant*, is without parents. Both find older men from whom to learn, and both are partially responsible for their deaths. When the lessons they encounter involve renunciation, a check on their passions, they refuse to heed the wisdom. Both learn the wrong lessons from their suffering, at least for a time, and both cheat for financial gain. The two novels are stories of their protagonists' education, and they both open with a glimpse of the old life: Frankie Alpine and a friend rob Morris Bober, the Jewish shopkeeper to whom Alpine apprentices himself. That old life indicated, Malamud settles into the central concern of his books: the middle life, the learning life, where suffering may promise the characters a new and better future.

Frankie returns to the scene of his robbery and begins to help Morris Bober in the grocery store. The relationship between the two is one of father and son, typically cast as master-assistant, an educational apprenticeship. There are three pairs of natural fathers and sons in the novel, and they contrast with Frankie and Morris in their inadequacy. The most promising of these is that of Nat Pearl, one of Frankie's rivals for Helen Bober's affection, with his father. Nat becomes a lawyer, but although he rises financially, he is shallow compared to Alpine, and his treatment of Helen is unkind. Less successful is the relationship of the loutish Louis Karp with his father, who is trying to arrange a marriage between Louis and Helen. The worst is that between Detective Minogue, who investigates the burglary, and his son Ward, who, with Frankie, has perpetrated it.

What Frankie must learn from his surrogate father is stated in a crucial scene in which Frankie asks Morris why Jews suffer so much. Morris first answers that suffering is a part of human existence: "If you live, you suffer." He goes on, however, to indicate that suffering can be meaningful if one suffers not only *from* but also *for*: "I think if a Jew don't suffer for the Law, he will suffer for nothing." Frankie's question is ironically self-directed, for it is Alpine himself, the non-Jew, who is suffering more than he has to: He is suffering not only the existential guilt that comes with living but also the contingent guilt that comes from his own stealing. Like Roy Hobbs, Alpine cannot check his appetite, and he continues to steal from Morris even while trying to atone for the earlier robbery. Though he steals only small amounts, though he promises himself he will repay Bober, and though he assures himself that he is really a good man, Alpine continues to violate the law, and he suffers unnecessarily for this violation. At the end of the novel, Alpine becomes a Jew and replaces Bober in the store. This action is not, as some critics have suggested, the pessimistic acceptance of a Jew's suffering or a masochistic embracing of Morris's despair; it is rather an acknowledgment of guilt for the suffering Alpine has imposed on others and on himself and the resolve to be like a Jew in suffering *for* something, in making suffering meaningful.

Alpine must learn more than just law, however, for human needs are more complex than that. When Helen Bober meets Nat Pearl on the subway, he is carrying a thick law book; her own book seems to her protection, and when he asks what it is, she replies, Miguel de Cervantes' *Don Quixote de la Mancha* (1605, 1615). Like Quixote, she is a dreamer, unsatisfied with her life as it is, and it is this quality that she will share with Frankie and that draws them together. The dialectic that informs Malamud's work is represented here: the law book, from a discipline that recognizes human limitations and demands attention to the responsibilities of this world, and *Don Quixote*, the book that allows one to look beyond these limits and provides a model for noble action. Helen rejects Nat Pearl because the law is insufficient by itself. Her action is not, of course, a rejection of the law, for she rejects Alpine too, when he lives in a world of dreams, unbound by law, for his dreams lead him into actions the law forbids. The generative force is a synthesis of the two.

Helen is, then, the other person from whom Frankie will learn. That he has the capacity for knowledge and for gentle action—as well as for the lawlessness that has marked his life—is shown by his constant identification with St. Francis. He is from San Francisco, and his name resembles that of the saint. He looks at pictures of and dreams about St. Francis, striving for his quality of goodness. With Helen, too, though, Frankie must learn to moderate his passions; with her, too, he violates the law. A voyeur, like so many Malamud characters, he climbs an air shaft to watch her showering. The mirror having been replaced by a glass, the glass remains itself a partition, separating the dreamer from the object of his desires. More serious is his rape of Helen in the park. It is the low point of the novel: Morris fires Frankie; his business is failing, and Morris tries to commit suicide. Frankie looks at himself in the mirror, finds himself trapped inside a prisonlike circle, and hates himself for always having done the wrong thing. He returns to the store and resolves to bring it back to life for the hospitalized Morris. Although Helen and her mother do not like Frankie's return, they have little choice but to accept him, and although Frankie occasionally backslides, he makes firmer progress at controlling his passions.

Helen never fully accepts Frankie in the course of the novel, but she does reject her other suitors, and in a series of dreams, the reader discovers a tentative acceptance of

Frankie: In his dreams, Frankie, like St. Francis, performs a miracle, turning a wooden rose he has carved and given to Helen into a real flower. In life, she has thrown the present away, but in the dream she accepts it. Helen, too, dreams of Frankie, out in the snow, making "a wife out of snowy moonlight."

Unlike *The Natural*, with its unambiguously pessimistic ending, *The Assistant* ends on a note of hope. Morris has died and Frankie has taken his place, and there is a suggestion that Frankie may be entrapped by the small grocery and the poverty of the Bobers' life, but there is also, in his conversion to Judaism and in his gradual winning of Helen's trust, a more powerful suggestion that he has learned the lessons of love and law, of dream and check, and that this middle life, for all its suffering, may indeed bring him toward happiness and offer him the promise of new life.

THE FIXER

The Fixer is Malamud's most ambitious novel, both because the reality he creates to embody his myth—the historical trial of a Russian Jew accused of murdering a Christian boy—is the most distant from his own experience and because the purposes of the tale, its philosophical underpinnings, are the most explicit and have the most scope.

As usual the novel opens with a journey. The main character, Yakov Bok, sees his travels, the leaving of his shtetl for a new life in Kiev, as an escape from his past. Bok attempts to strip away his Jewishness: He shaves his beard and cuts his earlocks. On the ferry across the river to his new hell, he drops his prayer things into the water. Like many of Malamud's characters, Bok is first adopted by an older man as an employee/foster son. This father figure, whom Yakov finds lying drunk in the snow, is without wisdom; indeed, he is a member of a militantly anti-Semitic organization. His daughter is the first woman with whom Bok becomes involved, but she also turns against Bok, accusing him of raping her. Because, however, she has written him letters avowing her love, even those who want to cannot believe her.

There are other dark women. On leaving the village, Bok is given a ride by a Jew-cursing Christian; he dreams of Lilith. The most powerful of these women is a member of a gang; she has killed her own son and accuses Bok of the deed and of a sexual assault on the boy. In this version of Malamud's story, not only does the father figure fail but there is also no redemptive counterpart of these betraying women to offer Bok hope or love.

Most of the novel takes place after the discovery of the murdered child's body and the imprisonment of Bok. The prison is a consistent metaphor in Malamud for the confined lives of his characters; Bok has left a figurative prison for a literal one. Malamud allows Bok escape through the agency of his mind, especially in his dreams. Like those of most of Malamud's characters, however, Yakov's dreams are full of bitterness and terror. If they provide him with a vision and a remembrance of life beyond the prison, they also remind him of the limits of his existence.

A second relief for Bok is that one of the Russian prosecutors, Bibikov, knows of Bok's innocence, and they share a philosophical discussion, its base in Baruch Spinoza, throughout the novel. Bok emphasizes that Spinoza, although he is a philosopher who asserts humanity's freedom, recognizes that people are limited; his name for that restrictive force is Necessity. The accumulated suffering in *The Fixer* is a powerful documentation of Necessity, and forces outside human control play a more significant role in this novel than in any other of Malamud's works.

If Necessity is so powerful, asks Bibikov, where does freedom enter? Bok replies that freedom lies within the mind: One rises to God when one can think oneself into nature. Bok also learns from one sympathetic guard, who quotes to him from the Bible that those who endure to the end will be saved. Yakov learns to endure, and he does so through the freedom his mind creates. He learns also that thoughtful endurance is not enough, for neither Bibikov nor that guard, Kogin, is allowed even to survive: Bibikov takes his own life, and Kogin is murdered.

Bibikov has explained to Bok that there is in Spinoza something Bok has missed, another kind of freedom, more limited but nonetheless real: "a certain freedom of political choice, similar to the freedom of electing to think." It is this freedom that Bok finally affirms. He has undergone the extreme suffering that Necessity entails. For most of the novel there is hope that in his mind he is at least free and can create new worlds, and there is hope that he will endure. The novel ends with a more political hope. Bok, at least in his dreams, elects to shoot the czar.

He has created political freedom by electing to think of himself as free. Again he cites Spinoza that if "the state acts in ways that are abhorrent to human nature, it's the lesser evil to destroy it."

Much of *The Fixer* is a moving dramatization of these ideas, and much of it as well conforms to the basic pattern of Malamud's myth, which he has developed so often and so well. *The Fixer* is marred, however, and its faults suggest those that damage many of Malamud's later works. The philosophy seems too often grafted onto a rather static tale, the story itself an excuse for the ideas rather than the ideas a product of the story. The historical events have been distorted to fit the ideas. There is no reason Malamud should be bound by fidelity to historical truth, but all of his revisions seem to be in the direction of simplicity—not the simplicity that allows the novelist focus, but a simplicity that reduces moral complexity to schematism. All the intellectual weight of *The Fixer* is given to one set of people who hold one set of values; it is not simply that the novel presents good versus evil, but that it presents eloquent and intelligent good versus inarticulate and stupid evil.

In the novels that followed *The Fixer*, Malamud's problems with form and with integrating form and meaning became more noticeable. *The Tenants* suffers from inadequately worked-out ideas. *Dubin's Lives* is marred by structural redundancy and by a facile ending, although it features an articulate and convincing hero, a failed artist's search to find himself. Dubin's own life is finally one of promise, and that is the story Malamud knew to tell.

God's Grace

God's Grace is the story of Calvin Cohn, the only surviving human after humankind has destroyed itself in a nuclear war. The novel opens with Cohn aboard a ship, where he discovers another survivor, a chimpanzee. Most of the book is set on an island where they discover other chimps, a reclusive gorilla, and some baboons. Unlike *Dubin's Lives*, *God's Grace* returns to the playfully fantastic style of Malamud's early stories, but like all of his work, it is another accounting of the middle life. For Cohn, the old life is completely dead; this is his new chance to re-create a life for himself—and for all the world. In part resembling Robinson Crusoe and his story of survival, *God's Grace* is more centrally a fable about Cohn's attempt to maintain his faith in a God who has allowed this destruction and his faith that humankind can develop order among the creatures that remain. He plays a record of his father singing, "They that sow in tears shall reap in joy," and that becomes Cohn's rationalistic credo.

When the chimpanzees begin talking, Cohn has a chance to verbalize his thoughts, but though this development would seem promising, Cohn's thoughts are insistently didactic. He is intent on teaching the animals to act morally, but his attempt fails: The tone darkens and the animals begin destroying each other and finally Cohn himself. His faith in the efficacy of reason to tame nature's cruelty is naïve, and just as he underestimates the darker passions, he omits love entirely from his list of virtues. In an ending reminiscent of the close of "The Magic Barrel," another story about the relationship of law and love, the gorilla George, who has remained outside the group, attracted only when Cohn is playing records of his cantor father's chanting, begins a Kaddish for the dead Cohn and his vanished dreams. Malamud asks perhaps too much of this work: The realism of survivorship does not always blend with the fantasy of animal speech; the playful beginning gives way too abruptly to the brutal ending, yet much that is sustained recalls Malamud's work at its best.

The People

At the time of his death, Malamud was working on a novel titled *The People*, having completed the first draft of sixteen of a projected twenty-one chapters. This unfinished work, published posthumously, is the story of a Jewish refugee who, like Levin in *A New Life*, is an anomalous figure set down in the American West. In *The People*, however, the time frame is the late nineteenth century, not the 1950's, and Malamud's protagonist is captured by a group of Native Americans whose chief and advocate he eventually becomes. Like *God's Grace*, *The People* is a fable, a darkly comic tale marked by the bleakness faintly laced with hope that characterizes Malamud's last works.

Howard Faulkner

Other major works

SHORT FICTION: *The Magic Barrel*, 1958; *Idiots First*, 1963; *Pictures of Fidelman: An Exhibition*, 1969; *Rem-*

brandt's Hat, 1973; *The Stories of Bernard Malamud*, 1983; *The People, and Uncollected Stories*, 1989; *The Complete Stories*, 1997 (Robert Giroux, editor).

NONFICTION: *Talking Horse: Bernard Malamud on Life and Work*, 1996 (Alan Cheuse and Nicholas Delbanco, editors).

BIBLIOGRAPHY

Abramson, Edward A. *Bernard Malamud Revisited.* New York: Twayne, 1993. Good general introduction to Malamud provides biographical information and individual chapters devoted to analyses of his first six novels. Includes selected bibliography and index.

Avery, Evelyn, ed. *The Magic Worlds of Bernard Malamud.* Albany: State University of New York Press, 2001. Wide-ranging collection of essays on Malamud and his writings includes personal memoirs by his friends and by members of his family as well as analyses of some of his novels.

Bloom, Harold, ed. *Bernard Malamud.* New York: Chelsea House, 2000. Collection of essays assesses the entire spectrum of Malamud's works, including analysis of *The Natural* and of Malamud's heroes. Includes a chronology of his life and a bibliography.

Cappell, Ezra. "Reflecting the World: Bernard Malamud's Post-Holocaust Judaism." In *American Talmud: The Cultural Work of Jewish American Fiction.* Albany: State University of New York Press, 2007. Chapter on Malamud is part of an examination of the fiction of American Jewish writers that focuses on how this fiction is linked to religious texts and traditions. Cappell argues that these writers can be viewed as creating a new form of Jewish rabbinic scripture.

Codde, Philippe. *The Jewish American Novel.* West Lafayette, Ind.: Purdue University Press, 2007. Malamud's novels are among those considered in this study of American Jewish novels that enjoyed unprecedented success in the post-World War II period. Discusses the possible reasons for this success.

Davis, Philip. *Bernard Malamud: A Writer's Life.* New York: Oxford University Press, 2007. First full-length biography of the author chronicles the events of his life, describes his writing methods, and connects the events of his life to his work. Also provides literary analysis of Malamud's novels and other fiction.

Field, Leslie A., and Joyce W. Field, eds. *Bernard Malamud and the Critics.* New York: New York University Press, 1970. Collection of critical essays addresses various topics, such as the Jewish tradition in Malamud's work and his use of myth, ritual, and folklore. Some contributors discuss specific novels and stories. A valuable resource for scholars interested in early Malamud criticism. Includes select bibliography and index.

Ochshorn, Kathleen. *The Heart's Essential Landscape: Bernard Malamud's Hero.* New York: Peter Lang, 1990. Presents discussion of each of Malamud's novels and his short-story collections. Ochshorn continues a trend in Malamud criticism that views his heroes as tending toward the *mensch* (good person) and away from the *schlemiel* (fool). Includes a bibliography.

Richman, Sidney. *Bernard Malamud.* Boston: Twayne, 1966. First book-length study of Malamud is a must for students who are starting to study the author's works. Systematically appraises each of Malamud's works through *A New Life* and devotes a chapter to Malamud's Jewishness. Includes some of Richman's personal correspondence with the writer and a select bibliography.

Smith, Janna Malamud. *My Father Is a Book: A Memoir of Bernard Malamud.* Boston: Houghton Mifflin, 2006. Malamud's daughter provides an intimate and candid account of her father's life and literary legacy, drawing on her own memories as well as on her father's letters and journals.

EDUARDO MALLEA

Born: Bahía Blanca, Argentina; August 14, 1903
Died: Buenos Aires, Argentina; November 12, 1982
Also known as: Eduardo Alberto Mallea

Principal long fiction

Nocturno europeo, 1935
Fiesta en noviembre, 1938 (*Fiesta in November*, 1942)
La bahía de silencio, 1940 (*The Bay of Silence*, 1944)
Todo verdor perecerá, 1941 (*All Green Shall Perish*, 1966)
El vínculo, Los Rembrandtes, La rosa de Cernobbio, 1946 (novellas)
Los enemigos del alma, 1950
Chaves, 1953 (English translation, 1966)
Simbad, 1957 (novella)
El resentimiento, 1966 (3 novellas)
La penúltima puerta, 1969 (novella)
Gabriel Andaral, 1971 (novella)
Triste piel del universo, 1971 (novella)

Other literary forms

In addition to his novels, Eduardo Mallea (mah-YAY-ah) published a number of short stories and novellas, as well as several volumes of essays and travel books. Critics have observed that the novellas and stories can be considered brief renditions of existentialist struggles, featuring solitary characters whose lives are aimless movements in anguish and alienation. Mallea's best-known collection of essays is *Conocimiento y expresión de la Argentina* (1935; knowledge and expression of Argentina), a slender volume whose point of departure is a series of lectures delivered in Italy. Essentially, it is an attempt to analyze and describe *homo americanus*. The writer's first literary effort, the collection of short narratives *Cuentos para una inglesa desesperada* (1926; stories for a desperate Englishwoman), gave early evidence of his aesthetic sensitivity and refinement.

In addition to short fiction and the essays on history, philosophy, and travel (some of which found their way into his long fiction), Mallea published literary criticism. *Historia de una pasión argentina* (1937; *History of an Argentine Passion*, 1983), his most important essay, stands as the cornerstone of his philosophical and literary credo. In this somewhat autobiographical volume, a troubled young Mallea investigates the authentic, invisible Argentina, submerged under its many ills, and attempts to expose them to find the spirit of the nation. The method is self-examination; the symptoms of the national illness include confusion of values, with ends more important than means; cultural snobbishness; feelings of inferiority; lack of authenticity, forcing people to don a mask to meet others; and an assault on the Spanish language, which Mallea perceived as continuously violated. *La vida blanca* (1960; the sterile life) reiterates the motif of a need for a national culture incorporating the spiritual foundations and traditional values already noticed in *History of an Argentine Passion. La guerra interior* (1963; the inner war) and *Poderío de la novela* (1965; the power of the novel) are critical essays in which Mallea treats his own works as well as those of American and European writers, particularly those of the beginning of the twentieth century.

Achievements

Eduardo Mallea was among Latin America's most prolific writers, with his novels and essays amounting to a total of more than thirty volumes, to which should be added his brief fiction. Both as an essayist and as a cultivator of fiction, he was prominent in Argentina during the 1930's and 1940's.

Mallea's significant literary activities also included editing the literary supplement of *La nación*, Argentina's most important and influential newspaper, by which he exercised considerable influence upon the country's literary scene up to 1955, when he accepted a position in Paris with the United Nations Educational, Scientific, and Cultural Organization (UNESCO).

From the 1940's onward, Mallea received many prestigious literary prizes, including the Primer Premio Nacional de Letras (1945) and the Gran Premio de Honor de la Sociedad Argentina de Escritores (1946).

He also won the Forti Glori Prize (1968) and the Gran Premio Nacional de las Artes (1970).

Biography

Eduardo Mallea was the second of three sons of Narciso S. Mallea, a physician, who endowed the boy with a sense of honesty, generosity, and compassion for the poor and who exercised a strong influence upon the future writer. In an autobiographical chapter of *History of an Argentine Passion*, Mallea expresses his admiration for his father and underscores his indebtedness to him for such important attributes as mental vigor, standing by his convictions, respect for education, and generosity; indeed, he indicates that family life centered on the father. When Eduardo was four, the family traveled to Europe, foreshadowing the many trips he would take as an adult and laying the foundation for his cosmopolitan perspective. Attending grammar school in Bahía Blanca, he was exposed to Anglo-Saxon discipline and the English language, which would be significant in his subsequent literary development.

Mallea abandoned law studies at the University of Buenos Aires after three years in favor of a literary career, perhaps as the result of his association with a group of young writers around 1922 who were planning to launch a magazine. This periodical, *Revista de América*, provided some of his apprenticeship editorial and writing experience and, although his contributions were limited, offered a forum for an exchange of literary views. Several short stories appeared in prestigious journals during the 1920's, and about 1927, Mallea commenced his association with the daily *La nación*, which would last until the mid-1950's and bring him considerable power among literary groups.

Mallea's first assignment for *La nación* was to cover the Olympic Games in Amsterdam in 1928, the same year he began to collaborate with Jorge Luis Borges in translating works of James Joyce. His rise to editorship of the literary supplement of *La nación* came in 1931. In 1944, he married Helena Muñóz Larreta, and in 1955 he resigned his editorial position to represent Argentina before UNESCO in Paris and in India the following year. His trip to India undoubtedly played a role in the inspiration of his novel *Triste piel del universo* (sad skin of the universe). Mallea died in Buenos Aires in 1982.

Analysis

An independent thinker and writer whose authentic expression diverges from the social realism that dominated Argentine literature in those years, Mallea developed on his own terms an ontological awareness that would become quite fashionable among French existentialists a few years later.

Undoubtedly, Mallea's existentialism has its roots in the Spanish thinker and author Miguel de Unamuno y Jugo, who is mentioned in the final pages of *History of an Argentine Passion*. The themes explored in Mallea's fiction are more fully developed in his essays, with this collection representing his search for the values and vital forces of authentic Argentine culture that Mallea viewed as betrayed, altered by waves of European immigrants, submerged beneath layers of urban congestion and an inauthentic way of life. The typical protagonist of Mallea's novels is cerebral, hermetic, anguished, yearning to transcend his unauthentic condition, and desirous of a Kierkegaardian leap of faith enabling discovery and communication of his true self. Nevertheless, Mallea did not consider himself an existentialist following the French model and often bitterly repudiated such labels.

Nocturno europeo

Critics are not in accord as to whether Eduardo Mallea's *Nocturno europeo* (European nocturne) ought to be termed a novel; it consists largely of impressions of the writer's travels, the most important of which are derived from a lecture tour of France and Italy taken the previous year. It might be classed a fictionalized travel book, with meditative and philosophical tendencies that impart an essaylike character.

The novel's main character—and in fact, the only one—Adrian, something of a globetrotter, has spent much of his life in travel (a symbolic voyage through this world), reaching old age without encountering the ontological objective of his search. On an individual plane, he seeks himself, his identity; on a more universal level, he seeks the meaning of life. Having abandoned his own country because he found no meaning there, he belongs spiritually to the "lost generation" (no gratuitous association, since Mallea quotes Gertrude Stein's comment to Ernest Hemingway: "You are the lost generation"). The search for identity frequently takes the form of comparisons and contrasts between Argentina and Europe and, given the protagonist's interest in art, includes much analysis of works in galleries that are explicitly or implicitly juxtaposed to his own heritage.

Lacking a plot in the traditional sense, the novel is saved from becoming a travelogue by virtue of the subthemes injected by Mallea, which add a valuable dimension of intellectual substance. Not only are contrasts established in the areas of art and the protagonist's heritage but also the sociopolitical situation of Europe during the 1930's provides material for comparisons with the Argentine background, much as occasional human encounters inspire a comparative view of mores and morality. The liberated females the protagonist finds in Paris prove much too threatening and his puritanical upbringing much too rigid to allow him to risk libidinal release: His alienation is thus even more pronounced. Adrian spends his evenings surrounded by the wealthy and their sycophants, silently watching the human comedy around him, unable to communicate, empty and bored. The novel's most important dimension is constituted by Adrian's constant self-analysis and search for identity, his efforts to transcend his confining middle-class origins and his own limited state.

FIESTA IN NOVEMBER

Fiesta in November is the work of an independent and contemplative intellectual, little indebted to the literary fashions of the day. During the 1930's, the vogue in Spanish America was the *criollista* novel, in which man appears as the victim of the mindless, overpowering forces of nature. *Fiesta in November*, in both a formal and a thematic departure, offered two juxtaposed yet seemingly unrelated story lines linked by problems of existential authenticity and the motif of art, artistic creation, and its meaning and value.

Some critics have suggested that part of *Fiesta in November* was inspired by the murder of Spanish poet and playwright Federico García Lorca at the outbreak of the Spanish Civil War in July of 1936 (an event that might well have coincided with the novel's genesis, for it appeared in 1938). Inasmuch as one of the two narratives relates the kidnapping and murder of a young poet, this interpretation acquires credence. Events in this story line—set against the background of civil strife in an unnamed European country—are intercalated between episodes of the other narrative, producing not a contrapuntal effect but an opportunity for the reader to observe the ironic contrast and to reflect upon what is "real" and important in life and what is not.

Fiesta in November is a title with different levels of meaning. First, it refers to the frivolous party on which the novel's second story line is centered; second, it refers to a celebration or rite and in Spain is used to denote the bullfight, so that its associations with violence and death are appropriate to the contrasting narrative. The party that is the title's primary referent is an elegant soiree given by the very wealthy Mrs. de Rague, to which the cream of *porteño* (Buenos Aires) society has been invited: ambassadors, financiers, judges, politicians, artists, and the landed gentry. Its atmosphere could hardly be more inane, with shallowness the norm among the guests and pseudo-artistic conversations the order of the evening, thanks to the de Ragues' collections of paintings. Lintas, the male protagonist, is an existential hero who has been to Europe and aspires to transcendence via his art. The de Ragues talk of the monetary rather than intrinsic artistic worth of their acquisitions, causing Lintas to commit the faux pas of telling the hostess that the prices of some paintings were inflated, with the result that he is forced to leave the party. Marta, daughter of the family, accompanies Lintas to his studio, where they engage in typical existentialist dialogues questioning the class structure, their place in life, and how to reach fulfillment.

In the novel's other story line, the poet, about to add a line to a poem in progress and holding a piece of bread in one hand, has his human and creative activity interrupted by the intrusion of his country's internal strife into his private domain. Soldiers invade the home of the nameless writer, taking him to the outskirts of the town, where he is executed. On the way, his sensations, his thoughts about dying, and the reflection that his white shirt will be covered with blood, together with his final perceptions, are detailed by an omniscient narrator. The tragic reality of this episode becomes even more stark in juxtaposition to the banality of the de Ragues' party, their meaningless existence and bourgeois decadence in contrast with humanity's need for physical and intellectual nourishment, as symbolized by the bread and poetry.

THE BAY OF SILENCE

Mallea's next novel, *The Bay of Silence*, established him as one of Argentina's most important writers. Probably one of his most autobiographical works, it reflects Mallea's constant struggle to convince his people of the need to espouse certain social ideals. The protagonist's suffering as he contemplates a misguided Argentina and perceives the reactions of an uncaring and impersonal public is the novel's most important and obsessive theme.

Mallea's attempt to encompass and portray a far more vast setting in time and space than in his previous novels, together with the work's complexity, has caused some critics to view it as too rambling and amorphous. The novel is divided into three parts, "Los jóvenes" ("The Young Men"), "Las islas" ("The Islands"), and "Los derrotados" ("The Defeated"), spanning the period between 1926 and 1939. Set both in Argentina and in Europe, it shares with *Nocturno europeo* a contrast between the two cultures, a search for identity, and political themes reflecting the crises of the 1930's. The novel is narrated in diary form by Martín Tregua, a former law student attempting to become a famous novelist (and thus a probable mask of Mallea). The coeditor of a magazine who is surrounded by intellectuals, he is working on a long novel titled *The Forty Nights of Juan Argentino*, suggesting incipient metaliterary elements and aspects of the self-aware novel.

Mallea apparently intends to present an Argentine archetype in the person of Tregua—ordinary, humble, filled with existential angst—as opposed to the corrupt oligarchy in power, a regime that is seen as not representative of the *homo argentinus* but intent only upon profit, even at the price of the country's being sacrificed in the international marketplace. Tregua's efforts to alter the status quo seem predestined to failure as they take the form of the publication of an avant-garde magazine, an undertaking not exempt of absurdity because of its inherent futility. The first part, "The Young Men," spanning eight years, portrays the young intellectual in Argentina in a constant groping for some meaning in life, agreeing with cohorts that the country has a problem but unable either to hit upon a solution or to try to do anything concrete and practical about it.

The second section, "The Islands," covers only a few months and is set in Europe, where Tregua stays at a friend's house in Brussels, discovers Joyce's *Ulysses* of 1922 (an echo of Mallea's encounter as a youthful translator), is overwhelmed by Joyce's prose, and from *Ulysses* takes the inspiration for the form—a novel within a novel—of his own work in progress, *The Forty Nights of Juan Argentino*.

Returning to Argentina, the third division extends over a period of roughly five years. Professor Donald Shaw has correctly indicated the resemblance between Mallea's novel and certain novels of the *generación del 1898*, or Generation of '98, in Spain, especially of Pío Baroja, in being essentially an autobiographical essay in which the protagonist is a spokesperson for the author, while other characters serving as interlocutors are handpicked to express ideas that allow the protagonist to propound his own philosophy.

The Bay of Silence closes with a quasi-mystical self-analysis. Tregua comes to believe that he is reaching further inside himself and is concurrently almost at one with the silent heart of his land as a result of his contacts with simple people and the reduction of his life to the most elementary essentials.

ALL GREEN SHALL PERISH

All Green Shall Perish was written almost simultaneously with *The Bay of Silence*, appearing the following year, in 1941. While such temporal proximity might suggest similarities between the two works, *All Green Shall Perish* is a novel of very different structure, theme, and nature. Gone are the amorphous structure, constant digressions, and almost anarchic form of *The Bay of Silence*.

All Green Shall Perish is a novel of action, dramatic intensity, and classic structure with a tight, well-developed plot. Furthermore, the protagonist and other characters of *The Bay of Silence* are drawn from real life, while those in the latter novel are completely fictitious. The settings, however, are not invented but are taken from places the novelist had visited or lived, most particularly from around his native region of Bahía Blanca. In seeking to find the true, invisible Argentina, Mallea abandons the city and its urban dwellers, commonplace in his previous novels, to turn to a land frequently barren and silent, so desolate that its desert nature is projected upon or reflected in the inhabitants. Strangely enough, this novel—which is probably Mallea's best-known work—is the one in which he comes closest to the thematics of the *criollista* novel (humankind's doomed struggle against overpowering natural forces) and at the same time most nearly approaches the French version of existentialism that he so often repudiated.

All Green Shall Perish opens with a cinematographic panorama of barren land, skeletal trees, dry river, and emaciated cattle at the point of becoming part of the bleached bones strewn across the burning land, devastated by a forty-five-day drought. The preface, quoting from Ecclesiastes, reminds the reader how ill winds will devastate humankind when it least expects it. Nicanor Cruz and his wife, Agata, the protagonists, blend well with this background (the symbolic surname, meaning "cross," suggests the burden the characters must bear in their struggle with nature). Agata's name, with its reference to stone, is also suggestive: Her drunken and embittered father named her for the agate on his desk, the object of her dying mother's stares. Her adolescence in Ingeniero White, near the large port of Bahía Blanca, is presented in a series of flashbacks that contrast the cosmopolitan milieu with her current isolation, the well-watered town with the arid desert, hopeful beginnings with the desperate present.

Husband and wife have been struggling in vain for fifteen years to produce green pastures and to bring the land to bear fruit; this failure parallels another, their inability to produce a child and to find a meaningful relationship in their marriage. Failing in all these efforts, they have succumbed physically and mentally to their environment. Unable to continue this miserable existence, Agata decides one winter when Nicanor is bedridden with pneumonia to end it all, opening doors and windows and disrobing as the freezing air rushes into the room. Field hands find them in the morning, but only Nicanor is dead; Agata's aborted suicide ends the first part.

Bahía Blanca, the setting of the second part, provides a strong physical, environmental, and cultural contrast. By returning Agata (and the reader) to this more vital area, Mallea seems to suggest hope for those wishing to escape ennui, isolation, and despair. The city, however, has undergone a metamorphosis since Agata's adolescence, and her attempts to retrace her steps, recapture her past, and thereby attain physical and spiritual rejuvenation are doomed to failure: Material change and technological progress have overwhelmed the past as she knew it, undermining its spiritual values.

The novelist presents a parade of characters—lawyers, physicians, accountants, merchants, single women, and others—all seeking the quickest means to make money and become a part of the boomtown prosperity. Entering this milieu, Agata becomes acquainted with a group of social butterflies and falls in love with one of them, a lawyer named Sotero. A nearly exact opposite of Agata, he is dynamic, loud, aggressive, and charming. The narrative viewpoint does not permit the reader to penetrate Agata's mind, but her entering into a love affair with Sotero suggests not only her wish to change her personality but also a willingness to give of herself beyond a mere sexual relationship. An apparent desire for continuity is visible when Agata refuses to leave Sotero's hotel room in the early morning hours. The lawyer is a self-centered hedonist, more interested in appearances than in Agata, and he has no wish for a permanent relationship with her. His decision to break off the relationship soon thereafter, by going to Buenos Aires, plunges Agata into a stupor; now certain of her failure and total isolation, she avoids all social contact.

At the novel's end, Agata appears alone against the backdrop of the deserted town and empty countryside, pursued by a menacing juvenile gang. The mood of *All Green Shall Perish* is not one of unremitting gloom, since there is a period of hope when Agata returns to Bahía Blanca, but she is not sufficiently aware to make the right existential choices and so once more plummets into pessimism and desolation. The denouement seems to suggest that humankind is condemned to loneliness, each person predestined by nature to become that which he or she ultimately proves to be.

Despite the novel's generally favorable critical reception, there has been adverse reaction by some critics to the limited autonomy accorded to Agata by the novelist. These observers perceive in her a monotonous personality, the result of a flat, one-dimensional character. Others, however, have seen in her suffering and state of mind a mystical experience comparable to that described by the Spanish mystic Saint John of the Cross in his *The Dark Night of the Soul* (1579).

LOS ENEMIGOS DEL ALMA

Los enemigos del alma (the enemies of the soul) was described by Mallea as a "sort of visual exultation that took hold of me." That visual fervor underlies one of his best descriptive achievements, and critics have singled out the descriptive element as perhaps the most significant aspect of the novel.

Set in Bahía Blanca in the 1930's, the novel provides a fascinating glimpse of the city by means of a large cast of marvelously well-described secondary characters. Against the backdrop of the city appear five protagonists belonging to two families: Three—Cora, Debora, and Mario—are descendants of José Guillén, and the remaining two are a married couple, Luis Ortigosa and his wife, Consuelo. Debora, the oldest of the Guillén offspring, is hermetic, antisocial, and puritanical in the extreme, while the younger brother and sister are hedonists who engage in every pleasure available in the town. Villa Rita, the mansion that was constructed by their father and in which they live, reflects the psychological and spiritual condition of its inhabitants: It is dilapidated and gloomy, humid and stale, often engulfed by fog and drizzle. José Guillén, their father, a vain and jealous man, had brutalized their mother, and their existence was nothing more than an affirmation of his machismo. As a result of living in a psychological atmosphere charged with hate, the three younger Guilléns become enemies of the spiritual realm.

The Ortigosas provide a counterpart to the inhabitants of Villa Rita. Consuelo married Luis to save her father, subsequently seizing on Luis's platonic relationship with a young girl (with whom he shared artistic ambitions) as a pretext for withdrawing into her own world and remaining estranged from her husband and perpetually unforgiving. Mario Guillén, bored and seeking amusement, sets out to seduce Consuelo, while his younger sister Cora flirts with Luis. Debora, suspecting the relationship among the four and outraged in her puritanical repression, sends a series of anonymous letters to the Ortigosas in the hope of putting an end to the presumptive affairs, but she is unable to provoke either spouse to act. Increasingly certain that their encounters are sexual, she considers leaving Villa Rita but is deterred by the realization that this would please them all. Rather than acknowledge defeat, Debora sets the living-room curtains afire, rapidly igniting the rest of the house, and perishes in the flames with her brother and sister.

Although she has occasional parodic points of contact with the avenging angel of the Apocalypse, Debora was not intended as an allegorical figure. Mallea, responding to criticism, indicated that she is a complex human being with a large number of contradictory and conflicting emotions just below the surface. Her behavior is allegedly the result of the cruel and emotionally sterile past that molded her character and predetermined her destiny (much like Agata in *All Green Shall Perish*, she is limited in her autonomy by the nature of the personality she possesses). Aware of her limitations and half-intuiting her emotional sterility, she resents humanity in general and rejects all psychological or spiritual growth.

As fictional creations, Mallea's heroines seem to lack the complexity of their more autobiographically inspired masculine counterparts, but male and female protagonists alike struggle, with generally little success, to meet the existential challenges of authenticity, communication, commitment, and self-realization. The discouraging conclusions to be drawn from their failures and frustrations are reinforced by the reiterated motif of predestination, a result not as much of social determinism (for, in the course of several novels, Mallea presents characters of varying classes of society—urban and rural, rich and poor, old and young) as of an inherent deficiency in the human condition, whereby the limits of one's personality, set early in life, conspire to annihilate freedom.

CHAVES

Perhaps Mallea's best-structured novel, *Chaves* contains few of the digressions present in earlier works that detract from the linear narrative: prolonged, erudite discussions of art, literature, philosophy, and history; the relentless focus on bourgeois manners and environment; the myriad soliloquies by "beautiful people" of wealth and family whose lives are an endless round of receptions, drinking, talking, and other accoutrements of the dolce vita. Thereby reduced to about one-third the length of the average Mallea novel, *Chaves* attains a dramatic impact appropriate to its subject that would have been lost by a more extended, rambling narrative.

A brief, intense character study of a withdrawn sawmill worker whose taciturnity is the result of profound grief and frustration, *Chaves* concentrates upon its grave, aloof, self-sufficient protagonist, who sometimes seems almost an allegorical figure. His refusal to socialize and participate in the pettiness of the primitive society of the sawmill community in Argentina's southwestern mountains arouses hostility and alienates him. Although Chaves is cast as an outsider, his behavior is not calculated arrogance or intellectual withdrawal, for he is rather a simple man.

From flashbacks, Chaves's psychological formation is reconstructed. Born, like the author, in Bahía Blanca, he grew up with nature and the ocean, amid sand dunes, without developing ambition or a competitive spirit. A change ensues when he meets a woman named Pura ("pure"), whom he marries. He then decides to compromise his ethical values to better support her: He sells worthless real estate while they live in a rented room. A daughter born to the couple dies at age four, underlining their failure and inability to conquer the sterile, dead environment. Moving from the hills of Córdoba to Tucumán, they settle in a small town where they live uneventfully for years, until fate intervenes and Pura dies of typhoid fever. Chaves's last attempt to communicate with other human beings is part of the futile effort to save Pura, but his recourse to the long-unused spoken word is to no avail. His silence deepens, and coworkers' attempts to force him to speak nearly degenerate into violence. Rescued by the foreman from an attack by coworkers, Chaves responds to his benefactor's request that he terminate his alienation with one word, "No." He is the existential outsider, a prototype of the hero so popular among French existentialists during the succeeding decade.

Some critics have suggested parallels between Chaves and Meursault in Albert Camus's *The Stranger* (1942). Both refuse to play by the rules and as a result become pariahs, but with certain differences. At the end of *The Stranger*, Meursault rises to denounce humankind's inhumanity to humans and points to humanity's eagerly awaiting death. Chaves, by contrast, refuses to speak, and his alienation is prolonged beyond the novel's end because he is not released by death.

Genaro J. Pérez

Other major works

SHORT FICTION: *Cuentos para una inglesa desesperada*, 1926; *La ciudad junto al río inmóvil*, 1936; *La sala de espera*, 1953; *Posesión*, 1957; *La barca de hielo*, 1967; *La red*, 1968.

NONFICTION: *Conocimiento y expresión de la Argentina*, 1935; *Historia de una pasión argentina*, 1937 (*History of an Argentine Passion*, 1983); *El sayal y la púrpura*, 1946; *Notas de un novelista*, 1954; *La vida blanca*, 1960; *Las Travesías*, 1961-1962; *La guerra interior*, 1963; *Poderío de la novela*, 1965.

MISCELLANEOUS: *Obras completas*, 1961, 1965 (2 volumes).

Bibliography

Chapman, Arnold. "Terms of Spiritual Isolation in Eduardo Mallea." *Modern Language Forum* 37 (1952): 21-27. An insightful study of Mallea's use of metaphor.

Dudgeon, Patrick. *Eduardo Mallea: A Personal Study of His Work*. Buenos Aires: Agonia, 1949. Brief and dated, but remains useful for its discussions of *Fiesta in November* and *The Bay of Silence*.

Levine, Suzanne Jill. "The Latin American Novel in English Translation." In *The Cambridge Companion to the Latin American Novel*, edited by Efraín Kristal. New York: Cambridge University Press, 2005. Levine includes three of Mallea's novels—*The Bay of Silence*, *Fiesta in November*, and *All Green Shall Perish*—in her discussion of Latin American novels that have been translated into English.

Lewald, H. Ernest. *Eduardo Mallea*. Boston: Twayne, 1977. A sound introduction covering Mallea's formative period, his handling of passion, his cosmopolitan spirit, his national cycle, and his last fictional works. Includes a chronology, notes, and an annotated bibliography.

Lichtblau, Myron I. *The Argentine Novel: An Annotated Bibliography—Supplement*. Lanham, Md.: Scarecrow Press, 2002. Lichtblau, who has critiqued and translated Mallea's work, has compiled bibliographies of all editions, reprints, and translations of Argentine novels published from 1788 through the end of the twentieth century. The book also includes critical commentary about the novels that originally appeared in American and Argentine newspapers and journals. This supplement expands the original 1997 edition.

______. Introduction to *History of an Argentine Passion*, by Eduardo Mallea. Pittsburgh, Pa.: Latin American Literary Review Press, 1983. This introduction to the first English translation of Mallea's *History of an Argentine Passion* provides an excellent overview of his place in Spanish American fiction. Includes an excellent bibliography

Polt, John H. *The Writings of Eduardo Mallea*. Berkeley: University of California Press, 1959. Polt discusses Mallea's essays and fiction through the mid-1950's. A dated yet thorough study.

Shaw, Donald L. Introduction to *Todo verdor perecerá*, by Eduardo Mallea. Oxford, England: Pergamon Press, 1968. Shaw's introduction to *All Green Shall Perish* offers an outstanding interpretation of Mallea's novel.

______. "Narrative Technique in Mallea's *La bahía de silencio*." *Symposium* 20 (1966): 50-55. One of the few studies in English of *The Bay of Silence*.

Stabb, Martin S. *In Quest of Identity: Patterns in the Spanish American Essay of Ideas, 1890-1960*. Chapel Hill: University of North Carolina Press, 1967. Although Stabb devotes a section mainly to Mallea's essays, his comments provide helpful background for Mallea's fiction as well.

SIR THOMAS MALORY

Born: Warwickshire, England; Early fifteenth century

Died: Newgate Prison, London, England; March 14, 1471

Principal long fiction

Le Morte d'Arthur, 1485 (the Winchester manuscript, 1934; discovered by W. F. Oakeshott)

Other literary forms

Le Morte d'Arthur is the only work attributed to Sir Thomas Malory. It was published in 1485 by William Caxton, England's first printer. The 1485 edition, for centuries the only source of Malory's tale, is a continuous narrative of twenty-one "books," though at the end of some books that clearly complete a larger grouping or "tale," Caxton included "explicits" (concluding comments) by the author. These explicits indicate that Malory may have intended the work to be organized in a fashion somewhat different from that of the published version. A manuscript of *Le Morte d'Arthur* discovered in 1934 at Winchester Cathedral indicates that Malory did not write it as a single long work, but rather as a series of eight separate tales, each of which deals with some aspect or character of the Arthurian legend.

Achievements

Any assessment of Sir Thomas Malory's achievement as a literary artist is inevitably bound up with a judgment of the form of *Le Morte d'Arthur*: Is it a single story or eight separate tales? As critic Stephen Knight points out, this question of form is central to critical inquiry, for "if we are not clear whether we have before us one book or eight, or something in between, then our attitude towards the work or works must be obscure and tentative."

That Malory's *Le Morte d'Arthur* should be considered a series of separate works is argued by Eugène Vinaver, editor of the modern standard edition, conspicuously titled *The Works of Sir Thomas Malory* (1947, 3 volumes). Vinaver argues in the introduction to his edition that the unity that scholars have found in *Le Morte d'Arthur* was imposed by Caxton and not intended by Malory. Vinaver's edited text, based on the Winchester manuscript, restores many passages excised by Caxton in the 1485 edition. Vinaver's opinion has been challenged by several critics, most notably by R. M. Lumiansky, who has argued that even in the Winchester manuscript one can see a unity of design and a progression from early to late tales, suggesting that Malory himself conceived of his eight tales as forming a single work.

Although this issue has been debated at length, it has not been settled with any real certainty, and any final judgment of Malory's talents as an original artist may remain in abeyance for some time. Yet, whether one considers the Caxton edition of *Le Morte d'Arthur*, where a stronger sense of unity is prevalent, or the Winchester manuscript, from which the argument for eight separate tales can be made more forcefully, one can see an unmistakable unity imparted by the ordering of the tales.

Malory's story moves progressively from the birth of Arthur to his assumption of kingship and defeat of all opposition, through the numerous stories depicting the adventures of knights in service to him, to his death at the hands of his traitorous, illegitimate son, Mordred. This kind of chronological progress is noticeably absent in the romances that Malory used as sources for his work. In the romances, especially that amorphous collection known as the French Vulgate cycle, from which Malory borrowed much of his materials, there is often little sense of direction or completeness to the knights' adventures. From the modern reader's point of view, Malory deserves special credit for unifying these disparate tales and arranging them in an order that lends motivation to certain characters' actions and—perhaps more important—gives the reader a sense of the cause-and-effect relationship between certain incidents that is lacking in the "French books" from which Malory says he has "drawn out" his tales.

Malory's achievement in condensing and organizing his sources has also been a matter of debate. Nineteenth century scholars, possessed of newly discovered Arthurian manuscripts of the twelfth through fifteenth centuries, were divided on the issue. Several noted medievalists branded Malory as a mere compiler; others, equally respected, praised him for his originality. Perhaps the most laudatory comment was offered by George Saintsbury, who claimed that in *Le Morte d'Arthur*, Malory made a significant advance over the romance tradition by developing a firm sense of narrative purpose, akin to that of the modern novelist. Saintsbury sees Malory exhibiting "the sense of *grasp*, the power to put his finger, and to keep it, on the central pulse and nerve of the story." Saintsbury and others, notably W. P. Ker, also praised Malory for his strong, original prose style. T. S. Eliot called Malory "a kind of crude Northern Homer," a fine prose stylist.

Regardless of the criticisms leveled at Malory's tale as an artistic achievement in its own right, there can be little question about the importance of *Le Morte d'Arthur* in literary history. Since its publication, it has stood as the preeminent English-language document to which readers of succeeding centuries have turned to learn of the Arthurian legend. Caxton's edition was followed by two others early in the sixteenth century, attesting to Malory's immediate popularity. Intellectuals during the Renaissance may have agreed with Roger Ascham, who commented in *The Scholemaster* (1570) that the chief pleasure of *Le Morte d'Arthur* lay in two points, "open manslaughter and bold bawdy."

Nevertheless, the appearance of still more editions of the work and the numerous references to the Arthurian legend in the literature of the period offer further proof of the influence of Malory's work long after its publication. When English society developed a renewed interest in chivalric materials and especially in the Arthurian legend, *Le Morte d'Arthur* was the work to which writers from Sir Walter Scott to Alfred, Lord Tennyson turned as the locus classicus of the legend. It was by comparison to Malory that Tennyson's *Idylls of the King* (1859-1885) and the Arthurian poems of Algernon Charles Swinburne, William Morris, and Matthew Arnold were judged by their contemporaries, and all openly acknowledged their debt to the author of *Le Morte d'Arthur*.

In part, *Le Morte d'Arthur*'s influence as a source for Arthurian adventure and chivalric virtue may be attributed to the good fortune of its having been printed, while hundreds or even thousands of Arthurian tales existed only in manuscript until the late nineteenth or even the twentieth century. Nevertheless, even after scholarly and popular bookshelves began to be filled with other versions, Malory's work continued to be regarded as the premier English rendition of the Arthurian story. In the twentieth century, T. H. White, who had at his disposal both medieval and modern accounts of the legend numbering in the hundreds, turned to Malory for inspiration in writing what is no doubt the most important twentieth century Arthurian tale, *The Once and Future King*. John Steinbeck, whose accomplishments as a novelist earned him the Nobel Prize, began a modern adaptation of Malory because he wanted to bring to "impatient" modern readers the "wonder and magic" of *Le Morte d'Arthur*. While the literary purist may question the value of modernizing Malory, one cannot quarrel too much with Steinbeck's motive, for he speaks truly when he observes that these stories "are alive even in those of us who have not read them." To write a work that becomes a part of the cultural heritage of one's country, and a classic of one's language and literature, is an achievement few writers accomplish; Malory is one of the exceptions.

BIOGRAPHY

Though it is clear that "Sir Thomas Malory, knight prisoner," wrote *Le Morte d'Arthur*, there is serious debate about which Thomas Malory actually authored the work. Records of fifteenth century England contain references to more than one dozen Thomas Malorys. Most modern scholars believe that the author of *Le Morte d'Arthur* was Sir Thomas Malory of Newbold Revell, Warwickshire, in southern England, but there are other candidates, most notably Thomas Malory of Hutton and Studley, Yorkshire, in the north.

That Thomas Malory of Newbold Revell was the author of *Le Morte d'Arthur* was first proposed in 1894 by George L. Kittredge, who examined both the Caxton text and historical records and deduced that the Newbold Revell knight met all the necessary criteria for authorship. From the explicit at the end of book 21 of *Le Morte d'Arthur*, Kittredge concluded that Thomas Malory was a knight, that he was in prison (he prays for "good delyveraunce"), and that the book was concluded in the ninth year of the reign of Edward IV (March, 1469-March, 1470). Extant records indicated that the Malory from Newbold Revell was the son of a gentleman and therefore probably received the education requisite to produce the work. He had been exposed to knightly virtues while in service to Richard Beauchamp, earl of Warwick, who was said to have embodied the knightly ideals of the age. Malory from Newbold Revell is reported to have died on March 14, 1471, after the *terminus ad quem* of the book's composition.

Kittredge's identification of Malory was reinforced when, in the early 1920's, Edward Cobb found an indictment consisting of eight charges against the Newbold Revell knight. Although it is not clear that Malory was ever found guilty on any of the charges, it is certain that he spent time in jail; in fact, it appears that between 1460 and 1471, the Newbold Revell knight spent most of his time at Newgate prison. His presence there would explain his having access to the books on which he based *Le Morte d'Arthur*, because Newgate was situated near a monastery with an excellent library. Malory may well have bribed his keepers to allow him to borrow the books.

The Winchester manuscript, discovered in 1934, contains several new explicits that provide additional information about the author. For example, at the end of the "Tale of Sir Gareth," Malory petitions his readers to pray that God will send him "good delyveraunce sone [soon] and hastely." Even more clear is the explicit at the end of the "Tale of King Arthur," in which the author says that "this was drawyn by a knyght presoner sir Thomas Malleorre." On this evidence, the knight from Newbold Revell has emerged as the leading candidate for the authorship of *Le Morte d'Arthur*.

The primary arguments discrediting the Newbold Revell knight have been made by William Matthews in *The Ill-Framed Knight* (1965). According to Matthews, no evidence suggests that this Malory had any familiarity with northern poetry, yet the dialect of *Le Morte d'Arthur* and its English sources (especially the alliterative *Morte Arthure*) are clearly northern. Further, none of the references to real places (many are mentioned in the text) are to locations near Warwickshire. Matthews contends, too, that it is doubtful that a criminal would have had access under any circumstances to the library near Newgate, and that there is no evidence that the monastery's library had the books on which *Le Morte d'Arthur* is based. At the time the work was completed, Thomas Malory of Newbold Revell could have been seventy-five years old, much too old to have completed such an arduous task. Finally, the Newbold Revell knight's political alliances were Yorkist, and *Le Morte d'Arthur* is distinctly Lancastrian in outlook. Kittredge had also cited two documents to support his claim, but this documentary evidence is discounted by Matthews. Matthews says that Kittredge's Malory was too old to have participated in a 1462 winter siege in which a Malory is recorded to have taken part. Similarly, the Newbold Revell knight could not have been the one named in the pardon made by Edward IV in 1468, since the pardon applied to political prisoners, and the Warwickshire man was a common criminal.

Matthews has proposed a second candidate, Thomas Malory of Hutton and Studley in Yorkshire. This Malory was a member of an eminent northern family; it is realistic to assume that he could read French, had access to the necessary source documents, was familiar with northern poetry and places, and spoke the northern dialect prominent in *Le Morte d'Arthur*. In addition, he supported the Lancastrian cause. The objections to his candidacy for authorship are that he is not described in family genealogies as a knight or chevalier, and there is no record of his ever being a prisoner. Matthews argues, however, that these are not serious discrepancies. Many men who could do so did not claim the title of knight. That there is no record of the Yorkshire Malory being a prisoner is also explainable. Although records abound detailing the imprisonment of criminals, it was not a fifteenth century custom to keep records of prisoners of war. These prisoners often had some measure of freedom and several wrote books while in captivity. It seems more likely that a work the scope of *Le Morte d'Arthur* would be written under these conditions than under those imposed on criminals. Further, the expression "knight-prisoner," used by Malory to refer to himself in the explicits, is applied in *Le Morte d'Arthur* to Lionel, Lancelot, and Tristram when they become prisoners of war. Similarly, "good deliverance" is used when Malory speaks of Tristram's trials in prison. Thus, the term "knight-prisoner" is used in a somewhat complimentary fashion as the epithet of a prisoner of war, not a common criminal. The claim for Thomas Malory of Studley and Hutton rests on these grounds.

Other candidates have been proposed as the author of *Le Morte d'Arthur*, but few can be considered seriously. Thomas Malorys appear in the records of English courts and parishes as laborers, armigers—and one as a member of parliament (though he is mentioned only once, and nothing else is known about him). What is known for certain about the author of *Le Morte d'Arthur* can only be gleaned from the text of the work itself, and then verified—with much conjecture—by searching the records of fifteenth century England.

Analysis: *Le Morte d'Arthur*

The modern reader approaching Sir Thomas Malory's *Le Morte d'Arthur* may be perplexed at first reading, for while the story of Arthur and his knights has the appearance of a novel, it is certainly far removed from representatives of the genre with which today's reader is more familiar. Though there is an overarching structure to the work, provided by the chronology of Arthur's reign, individual stories often seem mere appendages that add little to the major plot and seldom seem to have concrete beginnings or endings themselves. The "fault" for this apparent lapse into chaos lies not so much with Malory (though too close a reliance on his sources does tend to cause the story to branch off in several directions that lead nowhere), but rather with the reader who is not familiar with medieval techniques of storytelling.

It is not uncommon to find medieval romances that simply begin in medias res and seem to end there as well. That form of narrative technique has been supplanted in the modern literary world by the "well-made story," whose beginning, middle, and end are clearly defined, and whose parts are clearly integrated into the whole. The medieval audience demanded neither tight concentration on a single story line nor analysis of cause-and-effect relationships; to appreciate Malory and his achievement in the chain of events leading to the modern novel one must first appreciate that for writers before him, and for Malory himself, emphasis on the event itself, rather than on its consequences or on the role of characters, was of primary importance. Malory, in fact, was one of the first writers to delve into the minds of his characters and achieve a certain degree of verisimilitude in presenting the people who appear in his story.

Malory lacks originality in the modern sense, since almost everything he recounts in *Le Morte d'Arthur* is taken from medieval romances popular for centuries before his. His accomplishments as a storyteller and his claim to literary greatness lie in the artistry with which he wove together the elements of the Arthurian legend and in the insight he presents into the meaning of the story both for his contemporaries and for readers throughout the centuries. Beneath the surface chaos of the tales that make up the work, Malory has presented a unified vision of a society in triumph and in decay; his is a complex work with a complex purpose. As D. S. Brewer explains in his introduction to *Malory: The Morte Darthur* (1968), the work was "a part of the movement that transformed the medieval knight into the English gentleman." Through this story of the "ideal society," Malory presents the enduring dilemma of humankind's attempt to reconcile individual demands with those of the society and those of God.

Le Morte d'Arthur consists of eight tales, which Caxton divided into twenty-one books in his edition. The story itself divides into three large sections. The first, consisting of books 1 through 5 in the Caxton text, details the coming of Arthur and the establishment of the Round Table. It begins with the adulterous conception of the king, tells the now popular story of the sword in the stone, and continues with an account of the early battles and adventures of Arthur and his knights in their effort to subdue external threats to the realm. Always the careful craftsman where larger issues of plot and motivation are concerned, Malory skillfully interweaves into this larger story details that become important in later episodes: the "dolorous stroke" wielded by Balin that initiates in a curious way the Holy Grail quest, the hatred felt by Morgan le Fay for her brother Arthur, and the power of Excalibur and its symbolic significance. In the final book of this section, Arthur is hailed as the conqueror of Rome and welcomed into the city by the pope himself; the last great external challenge to this new order of society has been met and overcome.

The main books of *Le Morte d'Arthur* (11-17) deal with the adventures of Arthur's knights. Included are tales of the prowess of Sir Lancelot, the dedicated idealism of Sir Gareth ("Beaumains"), and the accomplishments and deceptions of Sir Tristram and his paramour, La Beal Isould. In these accounts, the court of King Mark is established as a kind of counterculture to that of Arthur, and the reader is made to feel the imminent doom that awaits Arthur's kingdom should the knights falter in their loyalty to their leader and the virtues he upholds. The final books of this section recount the quest of the Sangreal (Holy Grail), a devastating undertaking that strips Arthur of many of his knights and exposes the shortcomings of many of those considered the best in the realm. The quest marks the beginning of the end of the Round Table, for through vain pursuit of this holy artifact, the knights reveal their spiritual imperfection and perhaps their inherent imperfectability.

The third and final section of the work tells of the decay of Arthur's kingdom, a process that begins when the knights return from the unsuccessful Grail quest. Lancelot, by his actions, reveals that his dedication to the queen is greater than his devotion to God, his personal needs more important than his public duties. Arthur becomes unable to effect a suitable compromise between public and private life, and as incident after incident forces him to choose between his queen and his knights, he reluctantly is forced to opt for the latter. His sad statement after the civil war has begun in his kingdom reflects his inability to maintain a balance between his private and public lives: "Much more I am sorrier for my good knights' loss than for the loss of my fair queen; for queens I might have enough, but such a fellowship of good knights shall never be together in no company." This conflict between public and private virtues, a universal condition of humankind that Malory perceived at the heart of the Arthurian tale that he was transcribing, is the cause of the tragic development in the story.

The essence of the conflict Malory portrays in *Le Morte d'Arthur* has been described by D. S. Brewer as "the divergence of the values of honour and goodness from each other." The concept of honor is the paramount public virtue, informing the code of chivalry and motivating actions of those who were proponents of knighthood. Goodness, on the other hand, is a private virtue, and in *Le Morte d'Arthur* it is specifically identified as a Christian attribute. Hence, the conflict between honor and goodness is elevated beyond the level of individuals struggling within themselves to choose the proper path in life; it becomes, under Malory's skillful handling of individual tales from Arthurian romances, a larger conflict between two modes of living—the way of the good knight and the way of the good Christian.

The public virtue of honor had been the hallmark of chivalry for centuries before Malory brought it under scrutiny in *Le Morte d'Arthur*, and his characters all place great emphasis on winning and maintaining it. The promise of honor brings the knights to court; the chance to increase one's honor motivates them to accept the most impossible quests and to battle against the most insurmountable odds. The preservation of honor demands strict obedience to one's lord, unswerving fidelity to one's lady, and unshakable loyalty to one's brother knights. By striving for honor, the knights make the Round Table great, and paradoxically, by striving to maintain their honor, they destroy it.

In the society that Malory's Arthur imagines and attempts to build, honor and goodness are inseparable. In a passage not in any of Malory's sources, the king charges all his knights

> never to do outrageousity nor murder, and always to flee treason [that is, to avoid committing it]; also, by no mean to be cruel, but to give mercy unto him that asketh mercy, upon pain of forfeiture of their worship . . . and always to do ladies, damosels, and gentlewomen succour, upon pain of death.

By their honor, the knights are committed to doing good deeds. As the story progresses, however, the requirements of honor and goodness begin to diverge, and the inability of the knights and ladies to reconcile the two leads to the tragic demise of Arthur's society.

Malory highlights the growing divergence throughout a number of stories in *Le Morte d'Arthur*, but in none more clearly than "The Poisoned Apple" (book 18, chapters 1-7). In this vignette, Guinevere is accused by Sir Mador of poisoning Sir Patrice, his cousin. Mador demands justice: Either the queen is to be executed, or her champion must defeat Mador in battle. Arthur cannot fight, as he is to sit in judgment of the case, and Lancelot is not at court. Clearly this is a matter of honor—the king's lady is to be shamed, bringing dishonor on the entire court—and yet all of the knights present at court suspect Guinevere and refuse to fight in her behalf. In desperation, Arthur and Guinevere send for Sir Bors. They appeal to him to champion the queen not because she is to be shamed, and through her the court, but rather because he has an obligation to uphold the honor of his kinsman Lancelot, who no doubt would fight for the queen were he at court.

Bors tells Arthur he will fight "for my Lord Launcelot's sake, and for your sake." Bors then appeals to other knights, claiming that "it were great shame to us all" should the wife of Arthur be "shamed openly"; he is rebuked by many who, while acknowledging their respect for the king, have no love for Guinevere because she is a "destroyer of good knights." Though Lancelot eventually arrives in time to fight for Guinevere and save her from this charge, of which she is innocent, the implication here—borne out later in *Le Morte d'Arthur*—is that the prowess that wins honor may also allow one to win when the cause for which one is fighting is on the wrong side of justice; it might may indeed prevail for evil instead of goodness.

This sad fact is brought home to the reader in Malory's account of Lancelot's battles for the queen when she is accused of adultery. Lancelot is forced to come to Guinevere's rescue, even at the expense of creating strife within Arthur's realm, because his honor is at stake. "Whether ye did right or wrong," Bors advises him, "it is now your part to hold with the queen, that she be not slain . . . for and she so die the shame shall be yours." In the final chapters of *Le Morte d'Arthur*, Malory presents Lancelot fighting reluctantly against truth to preserve his honor. Arthur, too, fights reluctantly, even though he is on the side of truth, for he would rather preserve his noble society of knights than save his queen, and he appears willing to be cuckolded rather than have the Round Table destroyed by internal strife.

The clear dichotomy between knightly and Christian virtues is made evident at several points in *Le Morte d'Arthur*, but Malory makes his most forceful statement about the problem in "The Maid of Astolat" (book 18, chapters 9-20). Lancelot, fighting in disguise against his own kinsmen and the other knights of the Round Table, is wounded and taken to a hermitage to heal. The hermit attending him asks who this knight is, and when he learns it is one who fought against Arthur, remarks,

> I have seen the day . . . I would have loved him the worse because he was against my lord, King Arthur, for sometime I was one of the fellowship of the Round Table, but I thank God now I am otherwise disposed.

The hermit has renounced his former calling, perhaps because he has seen where the path of honor leads and has adopted a new path and a new Lord. Lancelot, who recovers from his wound while at the hermitage, comes to a momentary realization of his folly and bitterly acknowledges that his "pride" has led to his being thrown into this lowly condition. Only much later, however, does he abandon the pursuit of honor through the chivalric code, and by then Arthur is dead, Guinevere has entered a nunnery, and the kingdom is in ruins. The sense that one gets from reading Malory's account of the last days of Arthur's realm is that even the most chivalric society is doomed to failure, and that humanity's only hope lies in adopting values and goals that transcend worldly ideals.

What, then, has Malory accomplished in telling this tale? In the strife that tears Arthur's kingdom apart, fifteenth century readers saw mirrored their own griefs over the demise of feudal England, ravaged by the bloody struggle for the English throne that became known as the Wars of the Roses. *Le Morte d'Arthur* offered these readers faith, in a curious way, because in his work Malory has shown that, despite the collapse of an ideal society, lives and societies continue.

Even in their failures, the characters of *Le Morte d'Arthur* appear as larger-than-life personages who speak to the reader of the potential greatness of humankind. If honor can somehow be wedded to goodness, if the public virtues that gave the knights their sense of purpose can be married to the private virtues that cause people to rise above societal bonds when necessary, the ideal society can be created. To his contemporary readers, Malory's story no doubt offered this note of special hope. Thus, *Le Morte d'Arthur* speaks to not only its fifteenth century readers but also, through the story of Arthur and his knights, all peoples of all nations and times of the possibility of greatness, the inevitability of failure, and the glory that humankind achieves by striving for the impossible.

Laurence W. Mazzeno and Sarah B. Kovel

BIBLIOGRAPHY

Archibald, Elizabeth, and A. S. G. Edwards, eds. *A Companion to Malory*. Woodbridge, England, 1996. A collection of essays by medievalists, divided into three sections: Malory in context, the art of *Le Morte d'Arthur*, and the book's reception in later years. Includes discussion of the place of women and chivalry in Malory's book and of language and style in Malory.

Bennett, J. A. W., ed. *Essays on Malory*. Oxford, England: Clarendon Press, 1963. A collection of seven essays by scholars including C. S. Lewis, Derek Stanley Brewer, Eugène Vinaver, and W. F. Oakeshott. An essay on art and nature by Vinaver, written in the form of an open letter to Lewis, responds to many of the points made by Lewis in his own essay in this collection. The book also includes a lengthy examination of chivalry in *Le Morte d'Arthur*.

Field, P. J. C. *The Life and Times of Sir Thomas Malory*. Cambridge, England: D. S. Brewer, 1993. Field tries to unravel the mystery of Malory's identity, using documents that were unknown to previous biographers. He provides a detailed, scholarly retelling of Malory's life that is useful for advanced students and scholars.

Hanks, Dorrel Thomas, Jr., and Jessica Gentry Brogdon, eds. *The Social and Literary Contexts of Malory's "Morte Darthur."* Woodbridge, England: Boydell and Brewer, 2001. A collection of sociohistorical analyses of Malory's work.

Hardyment, Christina. *Malory: The Knight Who Became King Arthur's Chronicler*. New York: HarperCollins, 2005. Hardyment pored over the only known manuscript of Malory's novel to produce this biography. She finds evidence to suggest that *Le Morte d'Arthur* may have been influenced by Malory's reading of French romances, early English histories, and popular ballads, and she describes the originality with which Malory recounted the tales of Lancelot.

Ihle, Sandra Ness. *Malory's Grail Quest: Invention and Adaptation in Medieval Prose Romance*. Madison: University of Wisconsin Press, 1983. Examines "The Tale of the Sangreal" from *Le Morte d'Arthur*, looking both to its thirteenth century French source and to Malory's own structural and thematic adaptation. Discusses medieval literary theory and the underlying intentions of Malory's distinctive Grail quest.

Kennedy, Beverly. *Knighthood in the Morte Darthur*. Cambridge, England: D. S. Brewer, 1985. A comprehensive, detailed examination of knighthood and chivalry and a meticulous discussion of *Le Morte d'Arthur* in this light. Kennedy considers different facets of knighthood, such as "The High Order of Knighthood," "Worshipful Knighthood," and "True Knighthood."

McCarthy, Terence. *Reading the "Morte d'Arthur."* Wolfeboro, N.H.: Boydell and Brewer, 1988. An excellent introduction to *Le Morte d'Arthur*. McCarthy outlines the structure of the work, book by book, with plenty of background and analysis, then offers more discussions of chivalric tradition, historical background, Malory's style, and his method of storytelling. Also suggests a selection of passages for closer study to give the newcomer to Malory a representative and manageable introduction to the difficult text.

Merrill, Robert. *Sir Thomas Malory and the Cultural Crisis of the Late Middle Ages*. New York: Peter Lang, 1987. An original inquiry into the psychology of the knights of Arthurian romance and the impact of the Round Table on their lives. Traces the formation of medieval institutions and explores the personal and social tensions in the Middle Ages that led to the Protestant Reformation.

Parins, Marylyn Jackson. *Malory: The Critical Heritage*. 1988. Reprint. New York: Routledge, 1996. An important collection of early criticism and commentary on Malory's *Le Morte d'Arthur* in chronological order, beginning with Caxton's preface to the first edition and ending with remarks by influential literary critic George Saintsbury in 1912.

Svogun, Margaret duMais. *Reading Romance: Literacy, Psychology, and Malory's "Le Morte D'Arthur."* New York: Peter Lang, 2000. A new interpretation of the novel, focusing on the book's status as one of the first literary works to be mass produced typographically. Also analyzes the book's depiction of the personal fight to accommodate the conflicting demands of the divided self.

DAVID MALOUF

Born: Brisbane, Queensland, Australia; March 20, 1934
Also known as: David George Joseph Malouf

Principal long fiction

Johnno, 1975
An Imaginary Life, 1978
The Bread of Time to Come, 1981 (also known as *Fly Away Peter*, 1982)
Harland's Half Acre, 1984
The Great World, 1990
Remembering Babylon, 1993
The Conversations at Curlow Creek, 1996

Other literary forms

Because literary recognition came to him first for his verse collections, for quite some time David Malouf (mah-LOOF) was regarded primarily as a poet. His first published writings were poetry, and in addition to contributions to works featuring several authors, efforts such as *Neighbours in a Thicket* (1974), *Wild Lemons* (1980), *First Things Last* (1981), and *Typewriter Music* (2007) have sustained his reputation in this genre. Some critics have discerned varying levels of sophistication when his earlier verse is compared with his later verse.

Malouf has also experimented with the writing of short stories, an autobiographical narrative, and drama. His stories "Eustace" (1982) and "The Prowler" (1982) concern isolated and apparently unsociable characters who seem misplaced yet oddly adapted to Australian settings. The collection *Antipodes* (1985) comprises short stories that in the main deal with the troubles of immigrants and problems of adjustment in Australia as well as the culturally ambivalent situation of Australians in Europe. Malouf set down some of the personal sources behind themes and images in his fiction with the publication of *12 Edmondstone Street* (1985), a memoir that deals in part with the writer's childhood years in Brisbane and in part, somewhat impressionistically, with his work and travel during the 1980's. In addition, he has written librettos for several operas, including *Voss* (pr. 1986), based on Patrick White's novel, and *Jane Eyre* (pb. 2000), based on Charlotte Brontë's novel. He has explored another line of creative interest with his play *Blood Relations* (pr., pb. 1988).

Achievements

Many of David Malouf's works have won awards in his native country. In 1970, he published *Bicycle, and Other Poems*, for which he won the Australian Literature Society's Gold Medal. For the poetry collection *Neighbours in a Thicket*, he received the Grace Leven Prize and the Australian Literature Society's Gold Medal as well as an award from the James Cook University of North Queensland. He held an Australian Council fellowship in 1978, and his novel *An Imaginary Life* won the New South Wales Premier's Fiction Award in 1979. The short novel *The Bread of Time to Come* (published in Great Britain as *Fly Away Peter*) won two awards presented by the publication *The Age* in 1982, and his fiction was again honored with the Australian Literature Society's Gold Medal in 1983.

Malouf received the Victoria Premier's Award in 1985 for his short stories, and his play *Blood Relations* received the New South Wales Premier's Award for drama. *The Great World* received the Commonwealth Writers' Prize and the Miles Franklin Award in 1991 as well as the French Prix Femina Étranger. *Remembering Babylon*, which had already won the New South Wales Premier's Literary Award in 1993 and been short-listed for the 1994 Booker Prize, won the inaugural IMPAC Dublin Literary Award in June, 1996. In 2000, Malouf was awarded the Neustadt International Prize for Literature. In addition to such honors, Malouf frequently has been considered an important literary spokesman for his country, and much of his writing has been regarded as significant in indicating new trends in creative work.

David Malouf. (Jane Bown)

Biography

The name Malouf is Arabic and was handed on by the writer's paternal grandfather, who immigrated to Australia from Lebanon late in the nineteenth century; other relatives were from England and were of Portuguese Jewish ancestry. David George Joseph Malouf, the son of George Malouf, a Lebanese Christian, and Welcome Mendoza Malouf, a British-born Portuguese Jewish mother, was born in Brisbane on March 20, 1934. He attended Brisbane Grammar School and graduated in 1950. He earned a bachelor's degree, with honors in English, from the University of Queensland in 1954. For two years he taught there, and evidently during that period he also began to write poetry. Along with the work of other writers, his verse was published as part of the collection *Four Poets* in 1962.

Malouf left Australia when he was twenty-four years old and lived in Britain from 1959 until 1968. Between 1962 and 1968 he was a schoolmaster in England at St. Anselm's College, Birkenhead, Cheshire. When he returned to Australia, he served as a lecturer in English at the University of Sydney until 1977. He was also a member of the Literature Board of the Australia Council for two years, beginning in 1972. He gained recognition and several awards for his poetry written during his teaching years. The increasing recognition accorded his work encouraged him particularly to devote time to his writing, and in 1978 he began spending part of each year in Australia and part in Grosseto, Italy. Appropriately, much of his writing has tended to deal with cultural confluences and differences that are felt in lands on two sides of the world.

Analysis

Many reviewers have commented on the finely honed language and the delicately etched descriptive passages that have distinguished David Malouf's important works. Often, affinities have been found between his poetry and prose writing, which possess similar lyrical traits. Certain thematic concerns—such as the effects of history, time, and memory, and the distinctive cultural position of Australia with respect to other nations—have also received comment. On the other hand, some readers have regarded Malouf's prose as somewhat coy and elusive, as hinting at meanings that are sometimes obscure or incompletely developed; indeed, some of his narrative works are told through highly oblique means and finish on rather inconclusive notes. In this view, Malouf's achievements in long fiction must be weighed against structural problems to the extent that the manner of his narration at times has threatened to overshadow the stories he has chosen to recount.

Malouf has received increasing critical attention over the course of his career, much of which has been concerned primarily with the unity of his fiction and poetry. His works testify to his defined and preserved individual identity, focused through humanist values in terms of language, mapping, art, and imagination.

Johnno

Malouf's first novel, *Johnno*, is a haunting and evocative depiction of youth and friendship in Australia and abroad during World War II. The narrator, Dante, an outwardly decent and somewhat impressionable young man, has become intrigued with the wayward habits of Johnno, a fatherless boy who possesses a strange, attractive charm. Although Johnno's propensity for drinking and revelry has a darkly appealing side to it, Dante is unable quite to enter into the spirit of his companion's conduct, and later he becomes somewhat more suspicious and withdrawn from his friend. After some travels that bring them together in Paris, Dante returns home and learns that Johnno has drowned under circumstances that suggest suicide. He learns later, from a note that his friend has written, that Johnno indeed intended to take his own life, partly because he came to regard Dante as unsympathetic and uncaring. This early novel introduces a theme that preoccupies Malouf: the way oppositional forces within individuals function and the manner in which these forces determine human behavior.

An Imaginary Life

Although much of Malouf's writing has dealt with settings and historical periods that have had some significance in his own life, *An Imaginary Life* aroused interest precisely because it represents a venture into an area that is remote in time and is all but unknown to historians and literary scholars. The famous Roman poet Ovid was sent into exile to an isolated outpost on the Black Sea in the year 8 C.E.; the reasons for his banishment remain somewhat unclear. Apart from what can be gathered from his epistles in verse, the *Tristia* (after 8 C.E.; *Sorrows*, 1859), which pleaded for his release, essentially nothing is known about the final decade of his life. From this point of departure, Malouf commenced with his own version of Ovid's last years, into which he also incorporated material from an account of the eighteenth century "wild child" of Aveyron.

The story is told in stark, spare, measured prose, and indeed the setting in which the fictional Ovid finds himself seems gloomy and desolate. His existence among the people of a small, primitive village would appear at the outset to be drab and monotonous, but after a while he has come to regard his life in exile with something more than resignation. As Malouf portrays the classical poet, Ovid feels the stirrings of new life even as he has become accustomed to surroundings that have little in common with the metropolis of imperial Rome. He regards himself as thrown back upon the most elemental and rudimentary sensations, when the most ordinary objects of the natural world arouse in him a wonderment that he has not felt before. Time and change seem recast as they operate in a fashion much different from what he knew before; with only the most basic temporal points of reference, he finds it difficult to keep track of passing days, and only transitions in the seasons serve to remind him that years have passed during the period of his banishment.

When the villagers, who are accustomed to hunting wild animals in the open fields, bring in a small boy they have captured, Ovid takes an immediate interest in the child's welfare and for that matter believes that, though the boy may appear backward and inarticulate, the poet himself still may learn from the gradual development of his speech and manual skills. His affection reflects in some form memories of his own childhood; indeed, so captivated does he become by the boy's companionship that he ceases hoping for a return to Rome and becomes reconciled to his fate. Nevertheless, the villagers, who follow a form of shamanism and believe that malevolent spirits are constantly lurking about them, are not quite so tolerant of the boy from the wild; when it is thought that the child is responsible for a mysterious illness that afflicts the local headman, Ovid concludes that he and the boy must leave the family with which they have been staying and venture off into the trackless steppes to the north. His story ends in the open spaces, where, far from other human habitations but without regrets or unhappiness, he and the child have found safety.

An Imaginary Life attracted much favorable comment for its originality in supplying what was possibly a plausible ending in fictional form to what otherwise was a sizable lacuna in the literary history of classical times. Some have objected, however, that Malouf's depiction of Ovid is at odds with what is actually known about the earlier life of the Roman poet; Ovid, after all, made a name for himself in Rome for the elegance, wit, and virtuosity of his verse works, and to portray him as accepting a simpler and more austere way of life arguably is out of character with the historical figure.

CHILD'S PLAY

Malouf uses a contemporary Italian setting in his short novel *Child's Play*, which deals with a young man who believes that his chosen calling deserves a better term than what the newspapers call "terrorism." The novel reconstructs, ostensibly from the inside, a hired gunman's characteristic mode of operation, and indeed the narrator's story of preparations for a planned assassination is gripping and engrossing in an eerie, offbeat way. This curiously sympathetic evocation of the mind of a terrorist—moreover, one who takes a distinctly impersonal view of his work (the narrator is moved by no sense of political commitment)—may be taken perhaps as an oblique commentary on violent acts that seemingly defy specific explanation.

The narrator, who maintains that for security reasons he must be reticent about his own past life and identity, nevertheless is willing to provide some glimpses of the inner operations of his group. His planned victim is a venerable literary man, about eighty years old. As part of his assignment, the narrator has learned much about the man's publications and other aspects of his life. The great man has nothing really villainous about him; rather, he is merely recognized and successful. He was a political émigré during World War II, and his subsequent activities have hardly been of a sort that would provoke social or ideological hatred. Nevertheless, because he is well known, he is considered a suitable target by the organization that has employed the narrator. In the course of the narrator's methodical planning, which requires him to know precisely certain details of the victim's daily habits, the narrator has come to regard the old man as somehow a necessary component of a task he must accomplish.

THE BREAD OF TIME TO COME

Much of Malouf's writing has a retrospective tendency, where events from earlier portions of the twentieth century are called back in an effort to delineate the effects of historical change and upheaval on Australia and its people. *The Bread of Time to Come*, also known as *Fly Away Peter*, is one such work. The novel concerns two young men in their early twenties, Ashley Crowther and Jim Saddler, who are drawn together by a common interest in the birds that gather at a local refuge. Strange, exotic birds of every sort, from as far away as Siberia and Norway, put in an appearance in the course of their elongated migratory flights. Just as it has become a destination for such journeys from afar, the island continent seems isolated yet a part of the greater pattern of events in the world at large. Having lived at the bird sanctuary as a guide, Saddler has been protected from the harsh realities of the wider world. His perception changes as he finds himself fighting during World War I along with his friend Crowther.

The outbreak of World War I in Europe sets in motion a delayed reaction in Australia. The men are packed off to the western front in France, feeling perhaps at first some tug of patriotism, but the harsh realities of trench warfare leave them troubled and hardened. After one soldier, as part of a foolish bet, shows himself to snipers and is shot down, and an enemy shell leaves others dead or maimed, the grim, mindless, and destructive underside of armed conflict becomes apparent to them. When the news eventually reaches Australia that, in another engagement, Saddler has been killed and Crowther wounded, it brings home finally the senseless and brutal waste the war has brought.

In this novel, Malouf uses symbolism, repetition, and contrasts between the "natural" and "civilized" worlds, between birds and biplanes, and between the edenic bird sanctuary and the violence of war. Through Jim Saddler, who sees birds migrating even during war, Malouf reveals a character who comes to terms with the universe he lives in and the realities in it.

Harland's Half Acre

One of Malouf's most highly regarded works of fiction is *Harland's Half Acre*, which portrays the development of an Australian artist against a historical backdrop that embraces much of the twentieth century. The title character, Frank Harland, is a crotchety, reclusive person who wears his aspirations lightly. Harland is loosely based on the life of Ian Fairweather (1891-1974), a painter who settled on an island off the coast of Brisbane. Like Harland, he was reclusive and ignored the demands of fame.

During the early portions of his career in the difficult years of the Great Depression, when he has been beset by economic hardships, Harland finds odd ways to support himself. He also becomes acquainted with others who have become impoverished by the onset of hard times. Later, during World War II, he comes to know refugees who have left Europe and learns that older established nations have cultural traditions with historical dimensions that Australia cannot yet share; on the other hand, Europe is also subject to political turmoil and upheaval that has not affected the island continent.

Much of Harland's story is told indirectly, through the accounts of others who have known him. It would appear that he has remained fiercely independent and stubbornly dedicated to his efforts at painting during bad times and good; much of his later work is done on a small plot of land where he can preserve some sense of solitude. He has, however, acquired land elsewhere, partly in an effort to regain holdings that one of his ancestors lost in a card game during the nineteenth century. At times, some of Harland's paintings are sold for relatively little; even toward the end, when he has become well known and his works have become of some value to investors, he does little to exploit the reputation he has earned.

Critics have discussed the story that Malouf tells in *Harland's Half Acre* as in some ways symbolic of the problematic position of creative art in Australia, which began with little legacy of its own. It seems likely as well that Malouf intended his title character's situation to suggest in some sense the personal isolation that may accompany any creative quest.

The Great World

In *The Great World*, Malouf takes up various themes again in depicting the response to historical change that is felt among Australian men who grew up before World War II. Their uncomplicated existence is abruptly altered when war with Japan brings the men to Malaya with other Australian fighting forces. After their units have surrendered to the enemy, the men, who have been trained in combat, are ill prepared for captivity, and waves of memories from the past sweep over them during the difficult early days of their confinement as prisoners of war. Their lot is hard but not quite unbearable, though there are numerous discomforts and indignities. One of them fights with a guard and a full-scale riot erupts; even then, the prisoners are not mistreated as seriously as they had feared. Even wearying labor in a work camp set up along the lines of a railway into Burma does not daunt them entirely, though some among them fall victim to any of a multitude of diseases. In time, however, exhaustion and fevers begin to tell on them, and their lives seem reduced to a few relatively simple elements. The men feel a common bond with one another; they also cherish the few letters they have received from the outside world.

Toward the end of the war, weakened by privations and troubled that they have become little more than coolie labor for their captors, they have nearly lost track of the passage of time, and when peace comes, they are somewhat taken by surprise. Even after they have been repatriated, afterimages from their years of ordeal haunt the men occasionally. Nevertheless, there is also a sense of tedium and sameness to the routine into which they are cast in their civilian work. Renewing old acquaintanceships holds some fascination for them, but even this becomes tiresome after a while. Settled patterns of doing things eventually become habits that are followed almost instinctively.

After the war, time seems to pass quickly and stealthily, sometimes in leaps of years at a time, and change engulfs Australia in odd, ironic ways. The Japanese, once feared as enemies, become known for their commercial acumen; another war, in Vietnam, comes and goes; and business expansion takes hold for a while. Toward the end of the novel, the men who began as friends some decades before look back on a bewildering array of images from the past even as financial reverses seem to have laid them low.

Remembering Babylon

Malouf returns to the Australian colonial period in *Remembering Babylon*, which recounts the lives of Scottish pioneers in a remote settlement. Their hardscrabble but contented existence in the northern Queensland tropics is disrupted by the appearance of a near-naked Englishman named Gemmy Fairley, who has spent sixteen years with a tribe of Aborigines after being cast away off the coast of Queensland as a boy. When confronted by the stalwart Scots, he shouts, "Do not shoot . . . I am a B-b-british object!" Gemmy gains reluctant acceptance in the community of Scots until two men from the tribe he has left visit him. The settlers' deep-seated fear of the Aborigines and of anyone tainted by them is so strong that the settlers eventually drive Gemmy back to the bush, where he is killed during a raid on the tribe he has joined. The narrative also follows into adulthood some of the children who knew Gemmy and reveals how their contact with his exile affected their lives.

Fragmented in structure and abbreviated in its development, *Remembering Babylon* falters as a precise depiction of pioneer life and as a sympathetic account of the hapless Gemmy. Instead, it has been read as a symbolic representation of exile—in particular, artistic and linguistic exile, which brings to mind Malouf's earlier books *An Imaginary Life* and *Harland's Half Acre*. On this level, the narrative questions obliquely, through the experiences of the pioneers, how the Australian artist can grasp the fresh experience that the new continent offers and reshape it in untried forms apart from inherited European culture. Gemmy appears to represent the artist's answer to this dilemma. He realizes that there exists a connection between language and landscape. At least metaphorically, by forgetting his English and replacing it with a native language, he is better able to reach an understanding of the new world.

The Conversations at Curlow Creek

In *The Conversations at Curlow Creek*, Malouf again finds a rich source of metaphor in colonial Australia and the great emptiness of the continent. Set in 1827, this work examines the growing bond created as conversations take place between Michael Adair, a policeman, and Daniel Carney, a bush ranger. They meet in a desolate area, where Carney, the remaining member of a gang, awaits hanging. The two men spend the night before the execution in a hut, intermittently talking, remembering, sleeping, and dreaming. About half of the book is devoted to actual conversations, the rest to flashbacks of the two men's lives in Ireland. Although the direct exchanges are stronger than the extended forays into memory, revelation of the men's disparate backgrounds intensifies the immediate situation.

The two men take opposite views of the colony, reflecting a dichotomy that has long dominated Australian thinking. The doomed one sees the barren land as a source of punishment, a place that makes life hard, while the policeman imagines settlers prospering there. Along with this exploration of colonialism, the novel focuses on a timeless question: Which takes precedence in human affairs, human justice or a higher justice? As usual in Malouf's work, no clear-cut answer emerges. The reader must unravel the plot and then contemplate the themes that have been left unrealized.

J. R. Broadus; Robert L. Ross
Updated by Tel Asiado

Other major works

SHORT FICTION: *"Child's Play," "The Bread of Time to Come": Two Novellas*, 1981; *"Child's Play," with "Eustace" and "The Prowler,"* 1982; *Antipodes*, 1985; *Untold Tales*, 1999; *Dream Stuff*, 2000; *The Complete Stories*, 2007.

PLAYS: *Voss*, pr. 1986 (libretto); *Blood Relations*, pr., pb. 1988; *Mer de Glace*, pr. 1991 (libretto; with Richard

Meale); *Baa Baa Black Sheep: A Jungle Tale*, pr. 1993 (libretto; music by Michael Berkeley); *Jane Eyre*, pb. 2000 (libretto; music by Berkeley).

POETRY: "Interiors," in *Four Poets*, 1962; *Bicycle, and Other Poems*, 1970 (also known as *The Year of the Foxes, and Other Poems*, 1979); *Neighbours in a Thicket*, 1974; *Poems, 1975-1976*, 1976; *Wild Lemons: Poems*, 1980; *First Things Last*, 1981; *Selected Poems*, 1981; *Selected Poems*, 1991; *Poems, 1959-1989*, 1992; *Typewriter Music*, 2007.

NONFICTION: *12 Edmondstone Street*, 1985 (autobiography); *A Spirit of Play: The Making of Australian Consciousness*, 1998.

EDITED TEXTS: *We Took Their Orders and Are Dead: An Anti-war Anthology*, 1971 (with Shirley Cass, Ros Cheney, and Michael Wilding); *Gesture of a Hand*, 1975; *New Currents in Australian Writing*, 1978 (with Katharine Brisbane and R. F. Brissenden).

MISCELLANEOUS: *David Malouf: "Johnno," Short Stories, Poems, Essays, and Interview*, 1990 (James Tulip, editor).

Bibliography

Brittan, Alice. "B-b-british Objects: Possession, Naming, and Translation in David Malouf's *Remembering Babylon*." *Publications of the Modern Language Association* 117 (October, 2002): 1158-1171. Focuses on the relationships between names and objects, racial violence on the Australian frontier, and the nature of commerce in a cashless society in Malouf's novel.

Doty, Kathleen, and Riston Hiltunen. "The Power of Communicating Without Words—David Malouf's *An Imaginary Life* and *Remembering Babylon*." *Antipodes* 10 (1996): 99-105. Two linguists draw comparisons between the two novels, stressing how Malouf employs nonverbal experiences to construct human identity. Densely written but rewarding.

Indyk, Ivor. *David Malouf*. New York: Oxford University Press, 1993. Provides a brief but substantial and original discussion of Malouf's essays, poetry, and fiction through *The Great World*, with emphasis on *An Imaginary Life* as the pivotal work. Notes the absence of strong female characters in the fiction and explores the question of homosexual desire as a subversive theme.

Malouf, David. "David Malouf." Interview by Ray Willbanks. In *Australian Voices: Writers and Their Work*. Austin: University of Texas Press, 1991. Provides an excellent introduction to Malouf and his work. Topics covered include the author's approach to writing, especially fiction, and how he got the ideas for various novels through *The Great World*. Includes full discussion of the genesis of *An Imaginary Life* as well as Malouf's use of autobiographical materials.

Nettelbeck, Amanda. *Reading David Malouf*. Sydney: Sydney University Press, 1995. Perceptive study examines Malouf's novels *Fly Away Peter*, *Johnno*, *An Imaginary Life*, and *The Great World*. Recurring themes in the works are discussed in the context of debates about Australian identity.

_______, ed. *Provisional Maps: Critical Essays on David Malouf*. Nedlands: Centre for Studies in Australian Literature, University of Western Australia, 1994. Collection of essays provides a wide range of discussion of Malouf's work.

Nielsen, Philip. *Imagined Lives: A Study of David Malouf*. Brisbane: University of Queensland Press, 1996. Offers a detailed study of Malouf's poetry and fiction through *Remembering Babylon*, with extensive interpretation of each novel discussed. Also provides biographical information and primary and secondary bibliographies.

Randall, Don. *David Malouf*. Manchester, England: Manchester University Press, 2007. Analyzes Malouf's fiction from the vantage point of postcolonial theory as the works progress toward narrative sophistication and thematic universality.

Taylor, Andrew. "Origin, Identity, and the Body in David Malouf's Fiction." *Australian Literary Studies* 19 (May, 1999): 3-14. Looks at several of Malouf's works, commenting especially on the author's use of Australian history.

World Literature Today 74 (Autumn, 2000). Special issue devoted to Malouf includes seven essays on his work, a chronology of his life, and a select bibliography.

ANDRÉ MALRAUX

Born: Paris, France; November 3, 1901
Died: Paris, France; November 23, 1976
Also known as: André Georges Malraux

Principal long fiction

Les Conquérants, 1928, 1949 (*The Conquerors*, 1929, 1956)
La Voie royale, 1930 (*The Royal Way*, 1935)
La Condition humaine, 1933 (*Man's Fate*, 1934; also known as *Storm in Shanghai* and *Man's Estate*)
Le Temps du mépris, 1935 (*Days of Wrath*, 1936; also known as *Days of Contempt*)
L'Espoir, 1937 (*Man's Hope*, 1938; also known as *Days of Hope*)
Les Noyers de l'Altenburg, 1943 (*The Walnut Trees of Altenburg*, 1952)

Other literary forms

In 1921, André Malraux (mal-ROH) published the fictional text *Lunes en papier*, a Surrealist composition. In addition to his novels, Malraux wrote several books on art, the most significant of which is the three-volume *La Psychologie de l'art* (1947-1950; *The Psychology of Art*, 1949-1950). Other volumes on art include *Le Musée imaginaire de la sculpture mondiale* (1952-1954, 3 volumes) and *La Métamorphose des dieux* (1976, 3 volumes). Malraux wrote two significant essays on painters: *Saturne: Essai sur Goya* (1950; *Saturn: An Essay on Goya*, 1957) and *La Tête d'obsidienne* (1974; *Picasso's Mask*, 1976), published as the third volume of *Le Miroir des limbes* (1976). The latter work also contains meditations unrelated to art, notably what Malraux has called his *Antimémoires* (1967; *Anti-Memoires*, 1968) and *Les Chênes qu'on abat* (1971; *Felled Oaks: Conversation with de Gaulle*, 1972), a tribute to the memory of Charles de Gaulle.

At the end of his writing career, Malraux wrote *L'Homme précaire et la littérature* (precarious man and literature), a critical work in which he reevaluated the evolution of literature. This volume was published posthumously in 1977.

Achievements

André Malraux is known principally for his novels rather than for his writings on art. In all of his books and essays, however, Malraux's composition is bold and extremely dense. His style frequently reaches epic dimensions and is often characterized by an abrupt journalistic form. Whereas Malraux's works on art have been given a lukewarm reception, his novels, from the beginning, have elicited the enthusiasm of readers and critics alike. General recognition of his literary genius came with Malraux's third novel, *Man's Fate*, awarded the Prix Goncourt in 1933 and considered a masterpiece.

Despite early critical acclaim, however, Malraux's fictional works were not interpreted in the same way during the ten to twenty years after their publication as they are today. *Man's Fate*, translated in England in 1934 as *Storm in Shanghai*, was at first taken to be a political thriller based on the Chinese Revolution. *The Conquerors* also was misunderstood, perhaps because of its journalistic style. Originally seen to be more truth than fiction, it was interpreted as a kind of documentary on the 1925 Canton uprising, which eventually was to lead to the 1927 Shanghai massacre of China's Communists by Chiang Kai-shek. Malraux was suspected of taking sides in the Communist-capitalist struggle he portrayed. Today, critics generally agree that the political fanaticism of Malraux's heroes should be seen in a different light.

Malraux's novels, including *Man's Hope*—based on the Spanish Civil War, in which Malraux himself actively participated—are not vehicles for political ideology. Indeed, the realistic political struggle portrayed in his fiction is now viewed as only a backdrop for the metaphysical conflict confronting Malraux's characters. In short, Malraux's portrayal of humankind is what is most valued by serious readers; this compelling picture calls up questions that critics and thinkers will continue to ponder.

Biography

André Georges Malraux was born in Paris, France, on November 3, 1901, the only child of young working-class parents. When Malraux was about eight years old, his parents separated, and his mother took him with her to live with her mother and sister above a grocery store in Bondy, a northeastern suburb of Paris. One of Malraux's favorite pastimes was reading, and the close proximity of Paris and the Louvre allowed him to discover art at a fairly early age. For a time, Malraux commuted to school in Paris. He was judged to be an exceptionally good student, but, when he turned eighteen, he abruptly lost interest in formal education. He dropped out of school and rented an apartment in Paris. To supplement the allowance given him by his father, Malraux worked for a bookstore, buying rare books. Gradually, he turned to writing articles for magazines, and his interests drew him into Parisian literary circles.

At the age of twenty, Malraux met and married Clara Goldschmidt, an intelligent woman, somewhat older than he, from a wealthy Jewish family. Their impetuous wedding and liberal marriage were like a romantic adventure. What appears to have united Malraux and Goldschmidt was their mutual interest in art and their desire to travel around the world. All the women who were closely associated with Malraux were writers or artists; all were intelligent and endowed with dynamic personalities. Goldschmidt spoke German, French, English, and Italian and would later write six volumes of memoirs, *Le Bruit de nos pas* (1963, 1966; *Memoirs*, 1967), about her life with Malraux.

In 1923, the young married couple undertook an archaeological trip to Indochina (now mainland Southeast Asia). This expedition led to Malraux's arrest for trying to take bas-reliefs from a Khmer temple. Eventually, Malraux was released because of the protestations of many French writers, including Louis Aragon, André Breton, André Gide, Max Jacob, and François Mauriac. In a second trip to Indochina, Malraux and Goldschmidt attempted to publish a French-language, antigovernment newspaper in Saigon. When one newspaper, *L'Indochine*, was forced out of business, another, *L'Indochine enchaînée* (Indochina in chains), was started, only to be suppressed by the government in 1926. Malraux's first four novels are based on his readings about Asia and some of his experiences there.

In 1936, a year before the publication of *Man's Hope*, Malraux volunteered to fight in the Spanish Civil War, in which he commanded an international air squadron. Subsequently, Malraux and Goldschmidt officially separated; their marriage had been strained for some time. Goldschmidt, who had given birth to their daughter, Florence, did not want a divorce.

After his separation from Goldschmidt, Malraux had a seven-year liaison with Josette Clotis, a young, vivacious writer who had been working for *Marianne*, a magazine for which Malraux was writing at that time, when the two met. During World War II, Malraux enlisted in a French tank regiment; he was taken prisoner in Sens in 1940 but escaped. Later, he worked for the French Resistance. Clotis and Malraux had two sons, Pierre-Gauthier and Vincent. When the children were still quite young, in 1944, Clotis was killed when she accidentally fell in front of a moving train.

In 1945, Malraux became minister of information for the first de Gaulle government. Now that the war, with its persecution of Jews, was over, the divorce from Goldschmidt could finally be settled. In 1950, Malraux was married again, this time to Madeleine Lieux Malraux, a former concert pianist. She had been married to Malraux's half brother, Roland, who was killed in the war.

From 1959 to 1969, Malraux became minister for cultural affairs in the second de Gaulle government. During this time, he made several trips within Europe and to the United States, China, and parts of Asia to give speeches on culture and art and to talk with foreign dignitaries, including John F. Kennedy, Mao Zedong, and Indira Gandhi.

In 1961, the two sons that Malraux had with Clotis were killed in an automobile accident. Malraux was deeply depressed following the accident, but in 1966, when he was sixty-five years old, he met an old acquaintance, Louise de Vilmorin, who subsequently changed his life. She and Malraux had had an affair more than thirty years earlier, in 1933. A poet and novelist, she also was a romantic aristocrat. Their reunion sparked off all the madness of a first love. After Vilmorin's death in 1969, Malraux stayed at the Vilmorin family estate, located not far from Paris, in Verrières, where he spent his later years writing. After he died of a pulmonary embolism on November 23, 1976, Malraux was given national homage at the Louvre.

Analysis

André Malraux's novels immediately come alive by means of their style. The literary text gives one the impression of capturing a series of fleeting moments as a recent newspaper headline, a dispatch, a radio transmission, or a telephone call is urgently related. Passing time is often officially noted by date and time. Scenes are cinematically condensed. Malraux's heroes are already enmeshed in a struggle in which they have chosen to fight. Even the most insignificant gestures and movements are now powerful and carry with them the urgency of a crisis. When events occur or communiqués are released, Malraux's characters grope to understand what is really happening in the conflict surrounding them—what is false and what is true. With Malraux's heroes, the reader plunges into a void of uncertainty that encompasses not only the happenings related in the novel but also the inner turmoil of the heroes themselves.

In this crucial situation, Malraux's protagonists experience a loss of equilibrium and ask themselves questions that, under normal circumstances, they would not ask. Why are they fighting, who is the enemy, and who are they? Regarded by many critics as a precursor of the existentialists, Malraux often causes his heroes to confront death—an important theme in his fiction, because the novelist can thereby question the very essence of humanity.

According to Malraux, the greatest tragedy of human destiny in the contemporary world is not the meaninglessness of human existence, with all doomed to be defeated by death. Rather, Malraux believes that humanity's real tragedy lies within people themselves and, more specifically, in modern notions of individualism. The novelist's brief encounter with the Surrealist movement proved to him that individuals do not know themselves. Contrary to Surrealist thought, however, Malraux believed that one's inner being could never be understood. Thus, the ego of Malraux's characters is portrayed as an incongruous monster. Moreover, his protagonists' preoccupation with themselves as individuals only leads them to draw closer to madness and increasingly to isolate themselves from others. Individualism, then, is at the heart of the most significant theme of Malraux's fiction: solitude. Absolute solitude, in which one becomes alienated from others as well as from oneself, represents, for Malraux, the most tormenting of human conditions.

To counteract human solitude and give meaning to human existence, faced by the inevitability of death, another theme appears in Malraux's fiction: *fraternité virile*, or virile fraternity, a term that denotes a special bond between men, a solidarity of such strength that individual solitude and metaphysical anguish are overcome. Malraux's service during World War II and in an air squadron in the Spanish Civil War confirmed his conviction that the comradeship between soldiers can sometimes approximate this ideal of fraternal love.

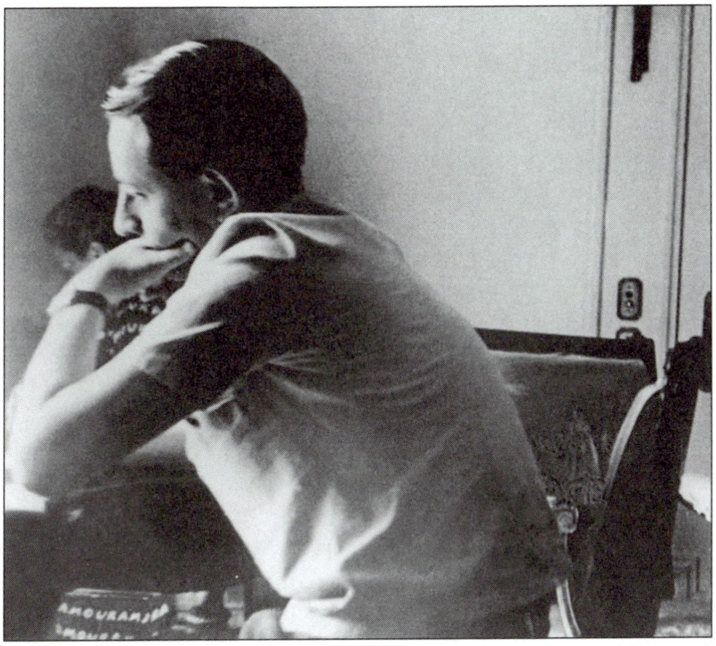

André Malraux. (Library of Congress)

Himself an avowed agnostic, Malraux painted in his fiction the tragic picture not of humanity's loss of God, but rather of the loss of humankind's belief in humanity. Particularly in *Man's Fate* and *Man's Hope*, Malraux proposed that humans can recapture the latter conviction through what may be termed a personal revolution. When some of Malraux's heroes revolt against the dominance of the ego and succeed in defeating its power over them, their unity with others shows that mutual love between human beings is possible.

The Conquerors

Published in 1928, *The Conquerors* introduced the journalistic style that became characteristic of Malraux's fiction. The novel begins with a radioed news flash, "A general strike is decreed in Canton," and updates about political upheaval in Canton and Hong Kong punctuate the entire book. From the beginning, the narrator—who remains nameless—writes down dates, places, and whatever factual impressions he can record. In the first part of the novel, his boat draws near Canton, where he intends to meet and work with an old friend, Pierre Garin, now called Garine. The narrator has not seen Pierre for five years; when he comes across verbal and written reports about him, he strives to find once again the man he used to know so well. Garine, however, has become so different that he might as well be a stranger. Garine had always been a gambler and an adventurer; now, in charge of the propaganda bureau in Canton, he is obsessed by a power struggle over the expulsion of the British from Hong Kong.

When the narrator finally sees Garine face-to-face, it is obvious that the latter can think of nothing but his struggle for power and his enigmatic adversary, Tcheng-Daï. The latter is an old Chinese leader whose conservative, altruistic philosophy opposes the liberal individualism of Garine. In a way, Malraux continues in *The Conquerors* a debate that was at the heart of his philosophical tale *La Tentation de l'Occident* (1926; *The Temptation of the West*, 1961), in which the letters exchanged between a European in China and a Chinese traveler in France contrast Western and Eastern philosophical beliefs. More important in *The Conquerors* than the revealing questions to which such a contrast leads, however, is the notion of solitude, which Malraux presents primarily through his hero, Garine.

Solitude, probably the most compelling theme in Malraux's fiction, is often portrayed, as Malraux depicts it in *The Conquerors*, as the result of a break of ties to another—a break caused by an individual's personal ambition and by the egocentric image he has of himself. It is significant that, before going to China, Garine had already totally rebelled against society as a result of a brush with the law. The brief account of the trial in which Garine was found guilty of financing illegal abortions, although undoubtedly based on Malraux's own trial for having attempted to take several bas-reliefs of an Indochinese temple out of the country, also prefigures in many ways Albert Camus's well-known novel *The Stranger* (1942). Like the trial of Camus's hero, Meursault, Garine's court judgment is shown to be an absurd ritual. In Garine's eyes, his trial was a ludicrous comedy, since the process of "judging" him only proved the refusal of the jurors to understand what he had done. Although Garine knew that what he had done was not legal, he had spent his own money to help destitute women pay for their abortions.

Since the trial, Garine's hatred for society has led him to think only of himself. With pride, he declares to the narrator at one point that he is completely asocial and hates all humanity, including himself. What his ego demands is power. Even the political struggle in which Garine is now engaged, where it is a question of the expulsion of the British from Hong Kong, is a highly personal fight in which he sees himself as having to emerge as conqueror. This image of himself has isolated him from not only the social establishment but also himself. Dominated by his quest for power, Garine willfully ignores the signs of tropical disease that he knows is slowly eroding his vitality and about which his doctor has alerted him in vain. Garine will get necessary medical help later.

Finally, the friendship between Garine and the narrator has likewise broken down because of Garine's obsession. Malraux shows by his narrator's continual physical presence during nearly every minute of Garine's day—logically explained by the fact that he is Garine's secretary and Chinese interpreter—that the bond of friendship that united them in the past has been destroyed. The narrator's cautious attempts to reach Pierre Garin are only rebuffed.

It is somewhat ironic that a secondary character in the novel, Hong, who is as obsessed with terrorism as Garine is by political power, should, in one scene, explain to a group of shocked observers—which includes Garine and the narrator—that he kills, not for politics or to change the social order, but rather to prove something to himself.

In the final pages of the novel, Malraux suggests the need for fraternal love when Garine, upon learning of the successful advance of the Red Army, spontaneously embraces the narrator. This embrace causes all the latent fraternal emotions of the narrator to burst forth, but when he looks at Garine again, the latter seems to be as distant as ever. Although Garine is now closer than ever to death, he is already thinking about going to England to continue his conqueror's fight.

The Royal Way

Even though Malraux had not yet visited China when he wrote about it in *The Conquerors*, the Cambodian jungle where he situates the characters of *The Royal Way* was all too familiar to him. Published in 1930, *The Royal Way* is linked to the author in two ways.

First, through one of his protagonists, Claude Vannec, Malraux retraces his own footsteps to Indochina, where he had uncovered stone engravings and tried to remove them. Malraux conceals the motivations of his hero and also his own when two different arguments are proposed for the dangerous archaeological trip. Claude is aware that the bas-reliefs he secures will yield him a fine sum of money, but, even so, it is difficult to conclude that he is nothing more than a fortune hunter, because of the argument he makes to the director of the French Institute in Saigon. His venture, Claude explains, will ultimately benefit all humankind. Someone must uncover the bas-reliefs and statues of Khmer art so that they can be preserved for history. The government does not propose to track them down; other adventurers are turned away by the perilousness of the enterprise. It is therefore possible to conclude that Claude is a courageous man, willing to risk his life for the sake of art.

Through his second protagonist, Perken, Malraux portrays a legendary middle-aged hero, supposedly modeled on the adventurer David de Mayrena, who, in the tradition of Lawrence of Arabia, had made himself king of the Sedangs. The link between Perken and the author occurs through the theme of death, which dominates the novel and which is clearly associated with Perken.

It is probable that Perken—faced by an inevitable death—is, to some extent, a fictionalized shadow of Malraux's own father, who, only a year before the publication of *The Royal Way*, had suffered a massive stroke. The relationship between the two protagonists of Malraux's book can be seen as a mythical association—perhaps as much imaginary as real—between the novelist and his father. Claude strongly admires Perken, for not only what he has done but also the aura of grandeur that seems to surround him. Moreover, Claude feels a strong affinity between himself and Perken, Malraux explaining, for example, that Claude, like his older companion, has been obsessed with death ever since his grandfather accidentally killed himself with an ax (Malraux's own grandfather had died in this way).

Near the end of the book, when Perken is slowly dying from having fallen on an arrowhead planted in the ground by Stieng warriors, Claude has the choice of staying with his companion or leaving him behind in order to secure the bas-reliefs they have managed to collect and transport them to Bangkok. Although he was not with his father after the latter suffered his stroke, Malraux causes his fictional counterpart, Claude, to abandon the bas-reliefs in order to stay with Perken. In the final pages, with the approach of Perken's death, Claude cries out in rage that nothing can justify the end of a human's existence, and he embraces Perken out of a desperate sense of *fraternité*. This gesture is similar to the one that occurs at the end of *The Conquerors* and evokes a theme that Malraux developed more fully in his subsequent fiction. Despite the love that Malraux—through his hero, Claude—expressed for his father, represented by the figure of Perken, two months after the publication of *The Royal Way*, Malraux's father, whose condition was worsening, committed suicide.

Man's Fate

Most of the key themes seen in Malraux's fiction before 1933 can be found again in *Man's Fate*, which is considered his masterpiece. The novel's background is the Chinese Revolution—a setting of outward hostility that, like the Canton uprising in *The Conquerors*, complements the inner turmoil of Malraux's characters. *Man's Fate*, however, is not the story of one man, such as Garine, who transfers the war raging within himself onto the stage of current historical events. Rather, in *Man's Fate*, Malraux portrays a large number of characters of various nationalities, political beliefs, and obsessive drives who in interacting with one another, dramatically illustrate Malraux's notion of solitude. Not only is there an acute tension between the characters of *Man's Fate* but also, when the protagonists look within themselves, they find only chaos and confusion.

Kyo Gisors—of Japanese and French descent—makes a significant personal discovery when, upon hearing a recording of his own voice, he finds he cannot recognize it. Like virtually all of Malraux's heroes, Kyo is a stranger to himself. In a scene of confrontation between himself and his wife, May, Kyo decides not only that the "inner monster" of his ego is incomprehensible but also that he feels more alienated by himself than he does by his wife's unfaithfulness.

In the opening pages of the novel, the reader follows the fearful inner thoughts of Tchen, another protagonist of *Man's Fate*. Chinese by birth but reared and educated according to European values, the young Tchen kills a sleeping man in a dark hotel bedroom. It is his first assassination. Like Hong, who plays a minor role in *The Conquerors*, Tchen quickly becomes a terrorist obsessed by killing. Tchen's terrorism, however, is more powerfully portrayed as an inner madness when Malraux shows that, with his chosen final victim, Chiang Kai-shek, Tchen also has decided to kill himself.

In portraying Ferral, another protagonist of *Man's Fate*, Malraux shows his continued interest in the blind obsession with egotistical power that he had illustrated previously through Garine in *The Conquerors*. Like Garine, Ferral—a French entrepreneur who attempts to construct, for his own glory, a commercial consortium between France and China—is totally obsessed by his quest for power. Unlike Garine, however, Ferral is absurdly unsuccessful. Malraux shows the vanity of Ferral's ambitions to become a "conqueror" by having his character face failure on all sides: not only with the consortium and the French government but also with his mistress, Valérie.

Another interesting figure in *Man's Fate* wages war against himself. The fascinating Baron de Clappique is a Frenchman who wears a patch over one eye and whose obsession, mythomania, is caused by an exceedingly strong aversion to himself. The baron habitually invents new identities for himself in an attempt to defeat, if only temporarily, his own inner being. Clappique, always in disguise and always living out a mythical existence, may reflect more than that part of the human psyche inclined toward acting out illusions and lies: He may also reflect a facet of Malraux's own personality. Malraux at least implies as much when he causes Clappique to reappear, unchanged, in his *Anti-Memoires*.

In no other novel does Malraux paint such a sharp picture of discord within and between his characters; in no other novel is humankind's agonizing loneliness more strongly described. In *Man's Fate*, however, Malraux also develops the theme of fraternity, which is suggested in his two previous novels principally by the final momentary embrace of his characters.

In a powerful scene, Kyo Gisors and a Russian, Katow, face death with many other prisoners. All the men are doomed to be burned alive in the boiler of a locomotive. In the mind of each prisoner, the concept of death attains horrendous dimensions; dominated by it, they become like frightened animals. Kyo and Katow, however, both succeed in overcoming their inner fear by expressing fraternal love for humankind. When Kyo takes his cyanide pill, he dies with peace because he dies for all the men to whose dignity he has devoted his life. Katow, more graphically and certainly more spontaneously, demonstrates his love for all the prisoners surrounding him by giving his cyanide to two of them whom he does not know, so that they will not have to be burned alive. This gesture unites all the men and causes each man's personal fear of dying to be replaced by feelings of love and brotherhood. Malraux portrays virile fraternity as a miracle, for most of the characters of *Man's Fate* remain not only troubled by their inner selves but also estranged from others. The notion of brotherhood is nevertheless made into a reality in this novel. It is no longer depicted as an ephemeral embrace or a totally inconceivable wish.

Man's Hope

Malraux's participation in the Spanish Civil War for six months in 1936 was the impetus for *Man's Hope*, published in 1937. As critics and biographers point out, by volunteering to command an international squadron of airmen, Malraux was, in a sense, assuming the role of his fictional heroes. The protagonists of *Man's Hope*, however, have very little in common with Garine, Tchen, or Ferral. The characters in *Man's Hope* leave their individual selves behind them when they decide to fight in the war. Scali used to be an art historian; Garcia, an anthropologist; Manuel, a sound engineer for a film studio; but the pasts of many others remain unaccounted for, because the former lives of these fighting men are not important. Like Malraux, who was to take on a new identity when he was given the title of colonel and assumed command of the España Squadron, the heroes of *Man's Hope* are now soldiers whose existence is defined by their common fight and by their unity. The opposing army they battle is composed of faceless and nameless "fascists," and their greatest metaphysical enemy is not death but rather the elements of nature: snow, rain, and fire.

In *Man's Hope*, Malraux causes his protagonists to experience or witness many scenes of fraternal love. The rescue of wounded flyers whose bomber had crash-landed on the mountain above Linares is often cited for its moving description of human solidarity; there are many other scenes of communion in this, the most epic of any of Malraux's novels.

There remains, however, amid all the manifestations of fraternal love depicted in the novel, a significant remnant of the notion of solitude. A number of characters in *Man's Hope* recognize that, however genuine their unity with others may be, their identity as soldiers is only temporary. When the war is over, everyone will lose this "fraternal existence" and may be thrown back into individual solitude again. The novelist calls attention to this danger by describing his characters as though they were actors, wearing costumes and playing out a role.

In the final pages of the book, Malraux, indeed, brings the war to an end, but through his lyricism, his protagonists are not shown reverting immediately to their isolated, prewar selves. In a springtime of new beginnings, one of Malraux's heroes, Manuel, stripped of his position as commander of a brigade, witnesses the awesome miracle of life around him. Clearly representative of all the other soldiers, Manuel sees his life as totally new and infinite in possibilities. Through this hero, Malraux proposed metaphorically that humanity can choose to modify its existence. As the experience of human solidarity in the war has proved, a being has more than one possible destiny.

Instead of returning to the tragic isolation of his inner self, Manuel can try to guide his steps in harmony with the fraternal bond he shares with others. As Ximénès, Manuel's old, respected adviser, has told him earlier in the novel, the real battle starts when one must fight a part of oneself.

Sonja G. Stary

Other major works

SHORT FICTION: *Lunes en papier*, 1921; *Le Royaume farfelu*, 1922, 1928.

NONFICTION: *La Tentation de l'Occident*, 1926 (criticism; *The Temptation of the West*, 1961); *Le Musée imaginaire*, 1947 (*Museum Without Walls*, 1949); *La Psychologie de l'art*, 1947-1950 (collective title for the following 3 works: *The Psychology of Art*, 1949-1950; *La Création artistique*, 1949 [*The Creative Act*, 1949]; and *La Monnaie de l'absolu*, 1950 [*The Twilight of the Absolute*, 1950; revised as *Les Voix du silence*, 1951; *The Voices of Silence*, 1953]); *Saturne: Essai sur Goya*, 1950 (*Saturn: An Essay on Goya*, 1957); *La Statuaire*, 1952; *Des bas-reliefs aux grottes sacrées*, 1954; *Le Monde chrétien*, 1954 (previous 3 titles collectively known as *Le Musée imaginaire de la sculpture mondiale*); *Le Surnaturel*, 1957; *Antimémoires*, 1967 (*Anti-Memoirs*, 1968); *Les Chênes qu'on abat*, 1971 (*Felled Oaks: Conversation with de Gaulle*, 1972); *Lazare*, 1974 (*Lazarus*, 1977); *La Tête d'obsidienne*, 1974 (*Picasso's Mask*, 1976); *L'Irréel*, 1974; *L'Intemporel*, 1975; *La Métamorphose des dieux*, 1976 (collective title for *Le Surnaturel*, *L'Irréel*, and *L'Intemporel*; *The Metamorphosis of the Gods*, 1960); *Le Miroir des limbes*, 1976 (collective title for *Antimémoires*, *Les Chênes qu'on abat*, *La Tête d'obsidienne*, and *Lazare*); *L'Homme précaire et la littérature*, 1977.

MISCELLANEOUS: *Œuvres complètes*, 1989-1996 (3 volumes).

Bibliography

Bloom, Harold, ed. *André Malraux*. New York: Chelsea House, 1988. Essays on Malraux's major novels, on the writer and his critics, on his creation of a Bolshevik hero, on his philosophy of art, and on his treatment of violence and Asians. Includes an introduction, a chronology, and a bibliography.

Cate, Curtis. *André Malraux: A Biography*. New York: Fromm International, 1995. A solid, scholarly work.

In her helpful preface, Cate assesses earlier biographies of Malraux. Includes detailed notes and a bibliography.

De Courcel, Martine, ed. *Malraux: Life and Work*. New York: Harcourt Brace Jovanovich, 1976. Divided into sections on Malraux's life and work. The first section includes essays on his early novels and his experience in Indochina and Spain. The second section explores Malraux's "unity of purpose through art and action," the myth he established of himself as a writer, and his philosophy and creative process. Includes a chronology, notes, and a bibliography.

Harris, Geoffrey T. *André Malraux: A Reassessment*. New York: St. Martin's Press, 1996. A balanced look at Malraux's works. Harris argues that Malraux's writings are "nonideological," express an "elitist humanism," and strive to transform mundane human activity into something more sublime. Includes bibliographical references and an index.

_______. *André Malraux: Across Boundaries*. Atlanta: Rodopi, 2000. Collection of essays, including pieces analyzing Malraux's early fiction, his novel *The Walnut Trees of Altenburg*, and Malraux and the "crisis of narrative form." Includes a bibliography.

Hewitt, James Robert. *André Malraux*. New York: Ungar, 1978. A short, clear introduction to Malraux's life and work. Hewitt analyzes Malraux's six novels, discusses how the author developed his concept of the hero, and considers Malraux's memoirs and writings about art. Includes a useful bibliography.

Jenkins, Cecil. *André Malraux*. New York: Twayne, 1972. Chapters on the writer and the myth, on Malraux's career as an antifascist, and on his major novels and memoirs. A useful introduction to his life and work. Includes a chronology, notes, and an annotated bibliography.

Lebovics, Herman. *Mona Lisa's Escort: André Malraux and the Reinvention of French Culture*. Ithaca, N.Y.: Cornell University Press, 1999. Focuses on Malraux's role as French minister of cultural affairs. During his ten-year tenure, Malraux sought to make French citizens more aware of French culture and to restore his nation's place as a major artistic center.

Lewis, R. W. B. *Malraux: A Collection of Critical Essays*. Englewood Cliffs, N.J.: Prentice-Hall, 1964. Contains a useful introduction, "Malraux and His Critics," and an essay on Malraux's image of humankind. An especially good collection with representative work by Malraux's best critics. Includes a chronology and a bibliography.

Lyotard, Jean François. *Signed, Malraux*. Translated by Robert Harvey. Minneapolis: University of Minnesota Press, 1999. A complex, intellectual, and unconventional biography by an important French critic. Lyotard attempts to deconstruct Malraux's life by demythologizing his image, and he describes the contrasts between Malraux's life and work.

Todd, Olivier. *Malraux: A Life*. Translated by Joseph West. New York: Alfred A. Knopf, 2005. Originally published in French in 2001, this biography is a critical analysis of the writer's life and work. Todd is especially good at describing Malraux's charismatic personality and his confused relationships with women.

THOMAS MANN

Born: Lübeck, Germany; June 6, 1875
Died: Zurich, Switzerland; August 12, 1955
Also known as: Paul Thomas Mann

PRINCIPAL LONG FICTION

Buddenbrooks: Verfall einer Familie, 1901 (English translation, 1924)
Tonio Kröger, 1903 (novella; English translation, 1914)
Tristan, 1903 (novella; English translation, 1925)
Königliche Hoheit, 1909 (*Royal Highness*, 1916)
Der Tod in Venedig, 1912 (novella; *Death in Venice*, 1925)
Herr und Hund, 1919 (novella; *Bashan and I*, 1923; also known as *A Man and His Dog*, 1930)
Der Zauberberg, 1924 (*The Magic Mountain*, 1927)
Unordnung und frühes Leid, 1926 (novella; *Disorder and Early Sorrow*, 1929)
Mario und der Zauberer, 1930 (novella; *Mario and the Magician*, 1930)
Die Geschichten Jaakobs, 1933 (*Joseph and His Brothers*, 1934; also known as *The Tales of Jacob*, 1934)
Joseph und seine Brüder, 1933-1943 (*Joseph and His Brothers*, 1948)
Der junge Joseph, 1934 (*The Young Joseph*, 1935)
Joseph in Ägypten, 1936 (*Joseph in Egypt*, 1938)
Lotte in Weimar, 1939 (*The Beloved Returns*, 1940)
Die vertauschten Köpfe: Eine indische Legende, 1940 (novella; *The Transposed Heads: A Legend of India*, 1941)
Joseph, der Ernährer, 1943 (*Joseph the Provider*, 1944)
Doktor Faustus: Das Leben des deutschen Tonsetzers Adrian Leverkühn, erzählt von einem Freunde, 1947 (*Doctor Faustus: The Life of the German Composer Adrian Leverkühn as Told by a Friend*, 1948)
Der Erwählte, 1951 (*The Holy Sinner*, 1951)
Die Betrogene, 1953 (novella; *The Black Swan*, 1954)
Bekenntnisse des Hochstaplers Felix Krull: Der Memoiren erster Teil, 1954 (*Confessions of Felix Krull, Confidence Man: The Early Years*, 1955)

OTHER LITERARY FORMS

Thomas Mann (mahn) presents a complex intellectual and aesthetic physiognomy, primarily in the area of long and short fiction, though for many he is equally powerful as an autobiographical, literary-critical, or political essayist. Alongside his novels and novelettes stand his novellas and short stories; the two types of fiction are often mixed in collections such as *Ausgewahlte Erzählungen* (1945).

A true twentieth century classical author, Mann spanned all the restless philosophical issues of his day, obsessed with the notion of decay and nothingness, with the concept of beauty superhumanly understood and melancholically associated with death, and with the shifting verities of political, social, and moral existence in a decadent world. On one hand, with the exception of the World War I period, during his early and middle years he guarded jealously his posture of intellectual independence and impartiality before historical events, retaining the objectivity of a witnessing spectator and artist, either acquiescing or rejecting (and doing so often, given the distance he maintained) with ironic glances. On the other hand, this stance did not preclude (particularly toward the end of his life) a strong ideological, idealistic commitment. These qualities of fundamental impartiality and occasional engagement spilled over into his noncreative writing, from the essays later collected in *Adel des Geistes: Sechzehn Versuche zum Problem der Humanität* (1945; *Essays of Three Decades*, 1947) and *Neue Studien* (1948) to more openly political tracts and those pieces collected in *Altes und Neues: Kleine Prosa aus fünf Jahrzehnten* (1953). The latter collection contains some of Mann's best autobiographical and autocritical writings.

The intimate relationship between some of Mann's nonfiction and his fiction creates a thought network that unifies his total production, which is that of an author less interested in conventional narrative than in analytical discourse. Thus, Mann's thoughts on writers Johann Wolfgang von Goethe and Leo Tolstoy relate to *The Magic Mountain*, as those on philosopher Friedrich Nietzsche and writer Fyodor Dostoevski relate to *Doctor Faustus* or as, conversely, his autocritical comments on the tetralogy *Joseph and His Brothers* grow out of a lecture on psychoanalyst Sigmund Freud. As a result, Mann's narrative fiction contains little plot, as plot is narrowly understood. A document that stands on its own is *Betrachtungen eines Unpolitischen* (1918; *Reflections of a Nonpolitical Man*, 1983), with its self-examining reflections mingled with a polemic against Western civilization and democracy (note the war-year dates).

Finally, to round out his writer's profile and not to be overlooked are pieces such as his charming and sentimental (if unsuccessful) attempt at poetry, "Gesang vom Kindchen" (1919), on the occasion of the birth of his last child; his letter about matrimony, "Über die Ehe: Brief an den Grafen Keyserling" (1923), affirming the moral and religious validity of the institution; and his one attempt at drama, *Fiorenza* (pb. 1906), dealing with the supposed confrontation between the paganizing, art-loving Lorenzo de' Medici and the moralistic, religious fanatic Girolamo Savonarola. In 1956, one year after his death, Mann's *Nachlese: Prosa, 1951-1955* appeared.

Achievements

While concerned primarily with the problem of Germany, however socially, politically, artistically, or morally perceived, Thomas Mann's focus always benefited from an awareness of spatial and temporal considerations, from the geographical and the historical. Holland and London, Valparaiso and Florence, Russia and Venice, Palestrina and Switzerland, Italy and the Near East, Mesopotamia and Egypt, Torre di Venere and Davos, India and Lisbon—all these settings round out a worldview that is in no way restricted to the Rhineland or Thuringia or Munich or Lübeck, Hamburg, Weimar, or Bremen. Similarly, the historical dimension shifts broadly, from the Napoleonic wars in *Buddenbrooks* and the Italian Renaissance in *Fiorenza* or the Lutheran Reformation in *Betrachtungen eines Unpolitischen* to medieval society in *The Holy Sinner*, the Greek civilization in passages from *Death in Venice*, the Judeo-Egyptian world in *Joseph and His Brothers*, even the prehistorical world, in passages from *Confessions of Felix Krull, Confidence Man*. All was designed to arrive at a better understanding not only of Germany but also of the human condition, of what it means to be human.

The sheer breadth of his perspective facilitated, perhaps even inspired, one of Mann's major analytical devices: contrast and antithesis. The Dionysian of Italy and the arts, of profane love and the irrational, is juxtaposed to the Apollonian of Germany and the mercantile, of sacred love and the rational. Like Johann Wolfgang von Goethe and many other "Teutons" before him, Mann felt acutely the lure of southern Europe, the so-called *Drang nach Süden*, whereby Italy (and Greece, sometimes translated into what is Latin, French, or even Russian) beckons like a Siren of art, music, and poetry the efficient and practical will of the northerner. The bohemian attracts the bourgeois. With the attraction, interwoven with the whole question of genius or the superior creative spirit, come the notions of disease, sickness, and death as they counterbalance soundness, health, and life.

If the names and origins of the characters mislead at times in this regard, the antithetical premise remains the same. Tonio Kröger (Italian-German)—like the German engineer Hans Castorp in *The Magic Mountain*, who falls in love with the French-named Russian Clavdia Chauchat—is torn between the two poles, very much like the author himself. The Germanic Hans Hansen and Ingeborg, in *Tonio Kröger*, are juxtaposed to the Slavic and more romantic Lisabeta Ivanovna; in *The Magic Mountain*, the rational Italian humanist scholar Settembrini opposes the mystical, Jesuit-trained Jew Naphta; and in *Doctor Faustus*, the staid, conservative bourgeois Professor Serenus Zeitblom contrasts only too obviously with the genial hedonist composer Adrian Leverkühn. The same kind of dialectic obtains outside Mann's novels and novellas, for example, in "Gesang vom Kindchen," with the Nordic father and the southern/eastern mother; in *Fiorenza*, with the hedonistic Lorenzo and the ascetic Savonarola; indeed, even in "A Man and His Dog," with the mongrel Bauschan and the purebred

Percy. This contrasting technique usually makes for character delineations that project Mann's own views through the protagonists or that portray eccentricities through the secondary characters.

Most often people are dealing with artist figures, creators concerned with beauty, and the sound of music is generally audible. According to the nineteenth century philosopher Arthur Schopenhauer, music is the central energy of life; according to Nietzsche, it gives birth to the spirit of literature. Along with Goethe, Freud and Carl Jung, Tolstoy and Dostoevski, and the aestheticist Stefan George, Nietzsche in particular moved Mann to a number of speculations. For Mann, the superior artist is touched with madness and the devil, ecstasy and disease; isolated, he does not achieve the modest comforts and simple expectations of life—not even the love of a woman. One of Mann's finest achievements lies in his representation of this concept in *Doctor Faustus*, a novel that readers and critics, unless they are versed in the art of music, will never fully understand. With its analyses of Johann Sebastian Bach, Franz Joseph Haydn, Ludwig van Beethoven, Frédéric Chopin, twelve-tone composition, and modern music generally, it is a culmination of a process that had begun years before, with the later generations in *Buddenbrooks*, the Wagnerian presence in *Tristan*, and the musical observations in *The Magic Mountain*, and that had been abetted by Mann's association with conductor Bruno Walter and composer Arnold Schönberg. More than Honoré de Balzac, E. T. A. Hoffmann, Romain Rolland, or Gabriele D'Annunzio, whose utterances on music have left a mark in novelistic history, Mann developed a unique facility to grasp the essence of the musical experience, theoretically and historically, and to communicate it in a way the art of the novel has never known before or since (Alejo Carpentier notwithstanding). Though associated with disease and therefore inhabited by a diabolism that places the mystique-powered Richard Wagner and Gustav Mahler at the threshold of Nazism, music, however suspect to Mann, is nevertheless the centrifugal core of the free human impulse.

Mann preferred opportunities to meditate to opportunities to contemplate. Music is meditation, a landscape is contemplation, and it has often been noted that, outside the mountain (see *The Magic Mountain*) and the sea (see *Death in Venice*), Mann rarely paints landscapes, despite *Joseph and His Brothers*. What he excels in depicting is human nature, the portrait over the landscape, in all of its most intricate and elusive details—a talent that made him appreciate Albrecht Dürer, as Leverkühn's soulful fascination with the painter clearly indicates.

Mann's other achievement lies in his penetrating understanding of all that is human, the vagaries of sublimity and grotesqueness, of hedonism, passion, and violence, and of measure, Puritanism, and gentility. He discovers the stimulation of sickness and the relation between disease and genius, and he combines his observations with a keen interest in myth (there are archetypal reminiscences in all of his works) and its recurrence in the human experience; most obviously, the Faust archetype reemerges in *Doctor Faustus*. In line with Mann's psychological/psychoanalytical preoccupations, one must mention his concern with eroticism, an almost sui generis eroticism, not one of pseudopornographic titillation but one derived from Nietzsche's, and then Freud's, views on erotic phenomena. Concealed at first, in such works as "Der kleine Herr Friedemann" (1897; "Little Herr Friedemann," 1936) and *Confessions of Felix Krull* (which was actually begun as early as 1911), sensual love surfaces finally in *The Magic Mountain*, when, upon contracting tuberculosis, Hans Castorp develops a passionate love for Clavdia Chauchat, just as Leverkühn achieves stature as a composer after contracting syphilis. *The Transposed Heads* and *The Holy Sinner* (dealing with incest) sink even deeper into the erotic. If the psychoanalyst Dr. Krokowski in *The Magic Mountain* or his counterpart in *The Holy Sinner* does not fare well under Mann's ironic pen, the author is more than well disposed toward the theory of a subconscious existence as an essential factor in assessing one's true self.

Taking his clue from Nietzschean symptomatology, and studying with detachment but at close range the complex infirmities of modern society, Mann became the novelist of decadence. His attitude of study sometimes impinged on the fundamental humanity of his characterizations: Abstract hypotheses and experimental ideas often confer an intellectual quality on his protagonists, who, like Kröger and Leverkühn, tend to hover in their "realism" between observable reality and conceptual supposition. His guiding premise was psycho-

Thomas Mann. (© The Nobel Foundation)

physiologically real enough to be acceptable and, more than that, significant: the interrelationship of the physical and the moral—put otherwise, medicine and the soul. (Mann once admitted that medicine and music were the two spheres closest to his art.) This coherence of the two pathologies, that of the body as well as that of the spirit, enabled Mann to use one as the metaphor of the other. Various layers of interpretation emerge for the attentive reader, who finds analogies between cancer, typhoid fever, or meningitis and social, economic, or political conditions. "Mario und der Zauberer" (1929; "Mario and the Magician," 1936) gives off overtones of ruler Benito Mussolini's totalitarian Italy; *Buddenbrooks* and *Doctor Faustus* reflect social evolution in Germany; and, as has been pointed out often, Leverkühn's illness symbolizes (the word "symbolism" has been used in this context frequently) German (Teutonic?) decadence under leader Adolf Hitler.

All of this is accomplished with a consummate sense of style. Mann uses his native language not like a sculptor fighting marble but like a painter washing his canvas with a subtle variety of colors. He is analytical, but suggestively rather than pedantically; he is descriptive with selectivity of detail rather than with effusiveness; and he is haunting in the moods he establishes, from the snows of Switzerland to the waters of Venice to the wastelands of North Africa. In 1929 Mann won the Nobel Prize in Literature for his work.

BIOGRAPHY

A comparison of Thomas Mann's parents suggests immediately the sense of ambiguity or contrast that marks his works. His father was a rich middle-class merchant, a solid citizen of the patrician bourgeoisie of the North German, Hanseatic trading town of Lübeck; his mother, Julia da Silva-Bruhns, was a fiery, artistic woman with a passion for music, of South American (Brazilian) origin and Creole stock. Of the five children, in addition to Thomas, Heinrich, the oldest, also became a fine writer. Thomas was both proud and mocking of his own staid, honored ancestry: He saw the decadence taking place. When he was nineteen, in 1894, after the death of his father, the Mann enterprise in Lübeck fell apart and the family moved south to Munich. By this time, Mann had given up on the puritanism of middle-class respectability, though he never transgressed too noticeably in the opposite direction. The tension sparked his desire to become a writer—an artist with many reservations about his vocation, like Tonio Kröger—and after entering and exiting various schools, he traveled with Heinrich, winding up in Rome, where he began to work on the novel that brought him fame: *Buddenbrooks*, a story of the decadence of a bourgeois family. Then with *Tristan* and *Tonio Kröger*, he confirmed his reputation, expanding the focus, adumbrated in the later *Buddenbrooks*, from the sociological to the artistic-musical. Now Mann meditated on the contrast between life and art, between the one's necessity for involvement and the other's need for isolation. Like the former one, this new tension resulted in a kind of pervasive irony, aimed in both directions. As an artist in search of beauty, Mann had variously mocked political venality, but "Beim Propheten" (1904; "At the Prophet's," 1936) also mocks the artist's solitude, in this case that of the poet Stefan George and his disciples.

Instinctively, Mann determined that the expansion of tensions necessitated an evolution of literary style, from the basically naturalistic vein of a writer steeped in the novelistic literature of Russia to the more intellectualistic manner of a writer interested both in realistic characterization and in a more direct exposition of his own views. Mann mastered the art not only of open, contrastive dialogue between characters but also of "inner" dialogue between character and author. The novella *Death in Venice* illustrates the new manner in a context of disintegration and solitude. It appeared immediately before the eruption of World War I. In an effort to defy his would-be solitude as an artist, Mann surprised his contemporaries by embracing with passionate patriotism the nationalistic cause of Germany and of Wilhelm II. His essay on Frederick II of Prussia, "Friedrich und die grosse Koalition" (1915; "Frederick and the Great Coalition," 1929), led to *Betrachtungen eines Unpolitischen*, which was immediately attacked by his democratic critics as Germany succumbed. In the totality of Mann's life, this political stance was an aberration. Recovering from his error, he established his true posture: the impartial democrat (rather than plain observer) commenting through antithesis and irony. He was now ready for his masterpiece, his "ideal farewell to many dangerous sympathies and seductions and enchantments that still pervaded Europe": *The Magic Mountain*. Largely because of this novel, Mann received the Nobel Prize in Literature in 1929.

A corner of Mann's family life in Munich is revealed, always under the aegis of antithesis, in the postwar inflation tale of a father who looks with consternation on the disruptive new mores of the younger generation and who can only accept them understandingly and amicably: *Disorder and Early Sorrow*. This very sense of dialectics culminates in the tetralogy *Joseph and His Brothers*, whose publication began in 1933 and concluded in 1943. Between the war and 1932, with his faith in democratic and liberal values strengthened, Mann had reason to fear on both material and moral grounds the course of events in Germany. An adversary of National Socialism, he believed it best, after Hitler came to power, to leave Germany with his devoted and supportive wife, Katia Pringsheim, and their six children.

That was in February, 1932. They lived in France, then Switzerland, then Princeton, New Jersey, and from 1940 to 1952 in Pacific Palisades, California. Like Joseph, Mann had become an exile, albeit voluntary; the biblical tale, clearly, had archetypal roots and contemporary ramifications as well. Through Hans Castorp and Joseph, let alone through the evil historical events, Mann came to grips with the fact that there is no such thing for the artist as isolation—especially from the common man. His early fascination with the heroic but also elite moralities of Wagner, Nietzsche, and Schopenhauer distorted, through their halo of dissolution, the service-to-fellow humans principle of a sounder intellect, Goethe's (though until this point, Mann had retained a very ambivalent impression of the author of *Faust*; see his Schiller-oriented "Schwere Stunde" of 1905). *The Beloved Returns*, utilizing Goethe's old love for Charlotte Buff (one recalls Goethe's *The Sorrows of Young Werther*, 1774) and her visit to the aging poet in Weimar, permanently fixed Mann's admiration.

Mann opposed the Fascist regimes in Europe; a series of political tracts in 1938 and 1939 left no doubt of where he stood ideologically. World War II delayed for many years *Joseph the Provider*, but he devoted much time to speaking out on political, social, and moral issues. From 1940 to 1945, he made frequent radio broadcasts, through the British Broadcasting Corporation, to fellow Germans. During the later years of the Holocaust of World War II, he began penning what he considered his crowning work, the politically undertoned and artistically exegetical novel *Doctor Faustus*, published in 1947. After this heavy effort, he was understandably tired; he had written creatively even for distraction (*The Transposed Heads* and "Das Gesetz," 1945). The writing impulse could not be suppressed. One would say that he amused himself putting together *Die Entstehung des "Doktor Faustus": Roman eines Romans* (1949; *The Story of a Novel: The Genesis of "Doctor Faustus,"* 1961), a piece on the novel's genesis. A few years later came the wittily narrated, curious fantasy *The Holy Sinner*, an implausible Nordic tale of the incest-begotten Gregorius, whose long career, like a parody of medieval romance, ends in the papacy.

However, the new political situation of the world, the United States in the foreground, inspired in Mann no cause for happiness, much less for wit. The future of American culture, as he saw it, chilled him; indeed, he said that in the New World he felt an imposition on his freedom. He returned permanently to Europe, to Switzerland, in 1953, living first in Erlenbach, then in Kilchberg, and finally in Zurich. Not to leave anything undone, he returned to work on *Confessions of Felix Krull*, begun more than two score years before and temporarily resumed in 1923, which he finally finished in 1954—the lighthearted story of a handsome and intelligent man who lives day by day and derives maximum pleasure from his attributes. On the threshold of his eightieth year, Mann fittingly composed his last work for the May 9, 1955, anniversary of Friedrich Schiller's death, commemorated on both sides of the Iron Curtain, *Versuch über Schiller*—fitting because this poet, too, as the critic Bonaventura Tecchi suggests, had ultimately found an abiding solace not in dialectics but in the ideal, not in intellectual play but in human duty. After a brief illness, Mann died in Zurich three months later. In the long run, then, Mann remains the classical modern writer because he was able to dissect the neuroses and reveal the inquietudes of the human condition of the twentieth century by staying close to it.

Analysis

In *Meine Zeit* (1950), Thomas Mann wrote,

> If Christian means to consider life, one's own life, as a guilt, a debt, an invoice to pay, as a subject of religious uneasiness requiring immediate remission, redemption, and justification, then those theologians who see me as the type of un-Christian author are not at all correct. For rarely has the work of a lifetime, even when it appeared to be a skeptical, artistic, and humorous game, been born totally and from the outset of an anxious desire for reparation, for purification, and for justification as was my personal—and so modestly exemplary—attempt to practice the art.

More than that of most writers, Mann's own literary production can come under the heading of a quest.

Buddenbrooks

As its German subtitle indicates, *Buddenbrooks* tells of the decadence of a family—by extension, the nineteenth century bourgeoisie, which socially and politically lost to the lower classes it had worked to advance, and aesthetically so enriched the spirit with inner life that no practical energy was left for the outer life of action. In 1835, in Hanseatic Lübeck, the clan of the old grain merchant Johann Buddenbrook appeared wealthy and solid when it inaugurated its economic prominence with a grand banquet (Mann describes it in no fewer than sixty pages) in its seventeenth century palace on Mengstrasse, with offices on the ground floor. Four generations later, the process of weakening and disintegration ends, in 1876, when the delicate and artistic Hanno dies of typhus in a modest house outside Porta.

The decadence, like an uncontrollable germ inside the family body organism, is ineluctable. Mann does not present what is commonly referred to in Marxist terms as class struggle, nor does he base his perspective either on the French, naturalistic tradition or on the historical manner that informs John Galsworthy's *The Forsyte Saga* (1922). There is something less scientific or legendary than personal about *Buddenbrooks*, for it was the chronicle of Mann's own family as seen by him, an aesthete doting on the fantasies of the inner life yet a bourgeois with a keen sense of reality and of observation. Hence, Mann's sensibility and understanding are interpenetrated with his irony and detachment. Men and women, relatives and friends, their conversations and values, dress and habits, food and furniture provoke the author's sarcastic smile, but at the same time he senses in them something solid and virtuous. The banquet sets the stage, like a skillful overture adumbrating many coming themes. Not many events occupy the novel's six hundred pages, but a whole way of life does.

Johann Senior is orderly and self-assured; Johann Junior (the Consul) is self-satisfied, without his father's daring and vision; his older brother Gotthold, whose marriage has never received his father's sanction, finds himself nearly dispossessed. Of the Consul's children, only Thomas keeps up the family name by being made consul and elected senator, but, though intelligent and elegant, he continues the business lazily and irresponsibly, without self-criticism, dabbling in aesthetics and philosophy, morbidly and nervously concerned with "subconscious needs," and in the long run ruinously alone in his palace, his wife, business, and future gone. His brother

Christian has some of the old Buddenbrook energy, but he cannot harness it, failing repeatedly in business ventures, trying to "find somehow his place in the world," and finally becoming insane. Their sister Annette inspires no assurance with her impulsiveness and frivolousness. She does not marry the older, unattractive Herr Grünlich, but her elder sister, Tony, who fills the novel, develops both interest and pride in the family genealogy, does not wait for the medical student, Mortens, with whom she has fallen in love at the beach, and marries Grünlich, who turns out to be a self-seeking bankrupt. Tony, on the other hand, is a fine echo of the good bourgeois, sentimental and dutiful, vivacious and supportive, but she must undergo divorce, another marriage, and another divorce, and see her daughter Erika do the same (Erika's man is jailed for fraud). The other marriage was to Herr Permaneder, a man "as good as bread" but who does not have enough "for home and beer"; he is caught with his arms around the cook Babette, and all breaks up again.

Tony's school-year friend is the Dutch Gerda, whom her brother Thomas married in Holland and who thinks only about her attractiveness, music (Bach and Wagner), and her relationship with the impetuous Lieutenant von Trotha, who is equally interested in music. The semblance of riches continues; Thomas acquires an even grander mansion, on Fischerstrasse, but, as he tells Tony: "Often the outward and visible material signs and symbols of happiness and success only show themselves when the process of decline has already set in." Even the tender devotion of the "eternal tutor" of three generations of Buddenbrooks, Ida Jungmann, or the correct and attentive teacher of all proper young ladies in town, Sesemi Weichbrodt (whom Mann has conclude the novel with a philosophical observation about life after death: "Es ist so!"—"So it is!"), cannot stem the creeping disintegration. When the last of Thomas's children, Johann (known familiarly as Hanno), comes along, he is frail and dreamy, musically gifted, a violinist, and he dies in young manhood.

In this context, a natural event such as death assumes symbolic proportions, and retrospectively, through its recurrence, functions almost as a leitmotif. As each character lives his or her life, so does each die his or her death: Johann Senior quietly, with dignity; his daughter Klara, ingenuously; Johann Junior, unexpectedly; Johann Junior's wife, Elisabeth, deliberately and slowly (the agony takes twenty pages); Consul Kröger, on his outdoor marble steps; Senator Thomas, on the pavement, where two passersby recognize him; and Hanno, exhausted and drained of the little vitality that his music had afforded him. This atmosphere cuts through all social strata encountered in the novel, and through it, the novel rises philosophically above the narrower confines of the decadence of Thomas Mann's own family.

TONIO KRÖGER

The story of *Tonio Kröger* is related to that of *Buddenbrooks*; even the protagonist's surname derives from the earlier novel. Unlike Hanno, however, Tonio is a vigorous young writer, strongly reminiscent of Mann; indeed, the autobiographical thrust of the story is only too clear: a temperamental, artistic mother; a practical Lübeck businessman for a father; and a shy, sensitive adolescent poet who feels "inferior" to his companions, such as the normal, healthy, athletic, and popular Hans Hansen, who, though a fine scholar, is not interested in Schiller's *Don Carlos* and is far more at ease, and less awkward, on the dancing floor with the Germanic blond Ingeborg Holm, whom Tonio would like to befriend—this is the basic situation. Years later, well known in Munich, Tonio is rejected by the romantic young painter Lisbeta Ivanovna, who deems him incapable of shedding his middle-class background. Several queries plague him: Can a true artist ever feel like a normal, honest person? How can modern art reach simple folk? What is it to be an artist? Disillusioned, he returns to Lübeck, where, as a result of the family's financial woes, the ancestral home has been sold; after he is almost arrested, he continues to Denmark where, in an isolated hotel, Hans and Ingeborg arrive on their honeymoon. Tonio sees his life as a failure; deprived of the simple joys and "tired out with envy," he gives up the possibility of living in order to understand it.

Most of this sounds familiar, but the narration is less naturalistic and more impressionistic than in *Buddenbrooks*, and the artistic motif is more pronounced: the contrast between the modern artist's need to transcend the human dimension and his attachment to safer and more traditional ways. Tonio is destined to wander forever between these two poles. Corresponding to Tonio's nature, a musical sense underscores the wandering, displaying Mann's strong musical consciousness. The work is structured along the lines of the A-B-A sonata form while being punctuated with many nearly word-for-word repetitions of descriptive phrases serving as leitmotifs: a "gentleman with the wild-flower in his buttonhole" (the father); "not being gypsies living in a green wagon" (a metaphor for propriety).

Tristan

What Mann later referred to as "a certain fascination with decadence" continued in *Tristan*, which also derived spiritually from *Buddenbrooks*—from the whole fin de siècle syndrome in relation to the effect that Wagnerian music can have on society—while presaging *The Magic Mountain* with its sanatorium atmosphere of doctors, attendants, guests, visitors, isolation, and quiet, and the Directress, Fraülein von Osterloh. In *Tristan*, the monotony of the Einfried Sanatorium for consumptives is broken when the prosperous, robust merchant Klöterjahn takes his fragile, lovely wife there—a pianist and the daughter of a patrician of Bremen who is a violinist and whose high culture suggests, in Mann's context, a setting of decadence. She became enfeebled giving birth to a sound son, Anton. In her, a melancholy writer, seeker of beauty, and neurotic intellectual named Detlev Spinell, who cannot shake off, as he would like to, his bourgeois ties, sees a wonderful woman living an ill-designed life with her merchant husband. He induces her, against the doctors' stern orders, to play the piano; the score of Wagner's *Tristan und Isolde* is intoned, exuding the voluptuousness of death. Now she becomes herself, not just "the wife of Herr Klöterjahn," but Gabriele Eckhof. Thereafter, however, her health deteriorates rapidly. Spinell infuriates Klöterjahn by suggesting that at least now Gabriele may die basking in her musical beauty, and he exits into the garden, humming the *Sehnsuchtsmotiv* that accompanies the death of Tristan, though nauseated at the sight of the healthful, "sheer animal spirits" of Anton.

Death in Venice

No more decadent piece can be found among Mann's works than *Death in Venice*. Another Mann-like protagonist and (successful) writer, Gustav von Aschenbach, exhausted by his labors and his art's artifice, journeys to Venice to seek invigoration and renewal. On the beach and in a Lido hotel lounge, he notices four Polish children with a governess, the sole boy, Tadzio (about fourteen years old), "astonishing, even terrifying" him with his "really godlike beauty." He felt an "unending delicate appeal to his senses" as he devised all kinds of ways to espy him, in the hotel and streets, on boats and sand. All of this takes place without a word of communication between them. The lad who naturally stands for beauty contrasts with the writer who has to strain to create it; Homer and Plato are invoked to help explain Aschenbach's insane love for the boy (he resorts to cosmetics to look younger); rather than invigoration, Aschenbach cultivates a further weakening of his being. Learning of an outbreak of cholera in the city, he neither informs the Polish family nor departs to safety. He falls victim to the disease, and on the day the family is due to leave and Tadzio is dipping a final time into the sea, waving as if beckoning to him, Aschenbach dies.

Mann's exceptionally symbolic, even precious style drags the Greek gods into Byzantine Venice (Dionysus ultimately dispatches Aschenbach), makes Tadzio represent degeneration and death, and plays fluidly with antitheses: youth and old age, Christianity and classicism, Germany (the north) and Italy (the south), health and disease, voluptuous aestheticism and moral conscience, love and death.

The Magic Mountain

Symbols, motifs, and antitheses interweave in the unusual and complex novel of life and treatment in a sanatorium, *The Magic Mountain*, which moves toward a greater equilibrium and understanding with reference to the totality of living, including its simpler aspects, by stepping away somewhat from the gravitational themes of decadence and dissolution. Hans Castorp, a German engineer from Hamburg, visits his cousin Joachim (who dies after leaving and returning to the institution) in the Alpine valley at Davos, Switzerland. Feeling fatigued with a slight chest oppression in this "magic" realm, Castorp decides to take the cure, extending his sojourn of three weeks to a stay of seven years, losing all track of time until the 1914 "thunderclap" of World War I breaks the spell. In the end, the author hints that Castorp lost his life as a soldier, yet the magic spell opens up to him a new world of spirit as he comes in contact with various people representing various living forces; in the aggregate, his mountaintop experience brings into view all shades of European culture.

The Magic Mountain has been called a bildungsroman, that is, a novel of individual development; more than this, however, it is a novel of ideological adventure (through long discussions on every conceivable subject, Mann attempts a *summa* of modern knowledge—impossible, of course, but still impressive). It functions on various levels. To begin with, there is the naturalistic description of pathological realities revolving around the illnesses, as well as the presence of many European nationalities, which together suggest embryonically a future society, thanks to the institution's isolated elevation. Then there is the evolution of Castorp as he undergoes many influences: his erotic awakening, immaturely with Pribislav Hippe and passionately (though Mann never had a flair for overwhelming passion) for the sensual and divine Russian redhead, Clavdia Chauchat, representing Eastern eroticism; the intellectual discourses with the Enlightenment humanist and nineteenth century libertarian, the clear rationalist Settembrini, as opposed to the irrational, instinctive, medievally mystic and romantic "apostle of darkness," Naphta, the lawyer who wins the arguments. Naphta shoots himself in a duel with Settembrini. Castorp does not choose between them; they are less characters than ideas in dialogue, ideas blowing through Germany at the time, and their duel was to rend the world.

There is also the unsavory psychiatrist Dr. Krokowski, who probes the recesses of the mind, and the Director, Dr. Hofret Behrens, detached and cynical with his explanations of human anatomy; these influences shape the intellectual and emotional mosaic of Castorp's formation. Finally, there is Time, which emerges as a passive yet instrumental force whose rhythm beats at a different pace (it nearly stands still) amid the rarefied snows and allows ideas to acquire personalities, as if they were characters.

In this shuttling back and forth between life and death, Castorp would not be able to take stock of himself and his position in the world without the constant drama of oppositions and without being surrounded by all types of personalities. This includes the magnificent and grotesque Dutchman, the friend of Madame Chauchat, Mynherr Pepperkolm, who becomes the ruling spirit of the group but burns himself out in Dionysian fervor. Thanks to all these "events," Castorp gains experience of the world and a balanced view of it, as in the revelation in chapter 5 ("Snow"), when, drowsy in a snowstorm, he dreams of the Apollonian "people of the Sun" (the Greeks), whose moderation and serenity counterbalance the concealed but coexisting Dionysian, elemental, evil forces of life; the dream sets forth the dual structure underlying civilization and art.

THE JOSEPH AND HIS BROTHERS TETRALOGY

Dreams assume prominence in the tetralogy *Joseph and His Brothers*. Mann's familiarity with Freud's theories of the subconscious and dreams, with Jung's archetypes, with Goethe's primal types, and with Nietzsche's Eternal Return was brought to bear on the Genesis story of Joseph—very faithfully retold, but with a clear concern for its mythological import. Thanks to his intellectual mentors, Mann was able to retell the story for the moderns and for future generations, humanize the myth, and make it contemporary. A "prelude" to the first volume, *The Tales of Jacob*, establishes the mythological motifs. Then comes the story, without particular concern for chronology: Jacob's special love for Joseph, God's favorite; Jacob's reverence for the God (Adonai) who subjects him to many trials; Jacob's seven years' work to obtain the hand of Rachel from the "devilish" Laban; the nuptial-bed substitution of Leah for Rachel; Jacob's acquisition of the birthright from Esau; his childbearing relationships with Laban's daughters and their maids; Dinah's denial by Simon and Levi and her rape; and Jacob's flight to Hebron and Rachel's death as she gives birth to Benjamin.

The Young Joseph highlights the brother-feud motif. Joseph's normal human weaknesses; his youthful pride in being the elect; his referral of his brothers' misdeeds to his father; his recounting of his flattering dreams to all; his brothers' fear of the loss of birthright and voluntary exile; Joseph's seeking them out, immodestly donning the multicolored cloak; his brothers' revenge by throwing him into the pit from which he is "resurrected" (a common motif) by the Midianite merchant and then sold into slavery—all these events make Jacob wonder about the fulfillment of Abraham's sacrifice. Mann's masterful characterization endows each brother with distinct psychological attributes.

The Eternal Mother motif—the Oedipus complex—appears in the third volume, *Joseph in Egypt*. Here Joseph becomes a servant of Potiphar (who, contrary to the biblical version, is a cultivated and complex man); Joseph earns Potiphar's favors, being now a true Egyptian named Osarsif. The volume's main action revolves around Potiphar's wife, Mut-em-enet, who falls in love with Joseph and falsely accuses him to her husband when he rejects her. Mann studies the woman psychomedically, from her self-struggle through her covert revelation to her open and indecorous self-offering. Sensing the real situation, the sympathetic Potiphar sentences Joseph with the mild punishment of detention in an island fort.

Finally, in *Joseph the Provider*, the mythic significance of the dream emerges, as Joseph acquires the reputation of a dream interpreter and is called back to Pharaoh (Amenhotep IV) to explain the dream of the seven fat and seven lean cows. Episodes of his marriage to the virgin daughter of the High Priest, Amun, introduce historical and cultural descriptions, a process dear to Mann, who then blends in, after the birth of Manasses and Ephraim, an account of Joseph's successful welfare program and administrative system generally. Then, circularly, the novel returns to Hebron, to the last years of Jacob, the idyll with Tamar, the brothers' journey to Egypt without Benjamin, the recognition and the reunion of father and son in Goshen, and the membership of Manasses and Ephraim in the Twelve Tribes.

Mann's measured view of human nature, exaggerating neither the goodness of the good nor the evil of the evil, brings into relief, in more than two thousand pages, the story of Joseph as an archetypal situation; at the same time, the work, appearing between 1933 and 1943, called attention to what might be termed the "mission of Israel"—signifying metaphorically, through the eternal mythology, Mann's faith in democratic principles and the values of liberty.

Doctor Faustus

Like other works by Mann, *Joseph and His Brothers*, through its pattern of themes, may be seen in terms of a musical structure. The great outpouring of musical ideas in Mann's works, however, came with *Doctor Faustus*. Only personal taste and private affinity can choose among the early *Buddenbrooks*, the middle *The Magic Mountain*, and the late *Doctor Faustus* for the award of the golden pome, but surely the latter is a highly significant creation. Again, as in Mann's earlier work, symbols commingle with intricate motifs to make for a complex multidimensionality—Mann's hallmark—that, by its very nature, manages to make contact with any number of contemporary concerns. The motifs involve political allegory, eternal return (the Faust theme itself), the artist versus society, and music—in other words, the political, the mythical, the personal, and the artistic.

The period covered by the novel is from 1930 to 1940, a morbid decade in German history, symbolized by the demoniac composer Adrian Leverkühn. His lifetime friend, the respectable and somewhat naïve bourgeois Serenus Zeitblum, narrates the biography. The opening, set in Thuringia and presenting Adrian's formative years, introduces enough elements, like a musical overture, to suggest future developments, something the protagonist's studies in Halle (law) and Leipzig (music) also do. The promptings of art make the creative and demoniac Leverkühn a rebel, condemned to personal, loveless unhappiness as he "condemns" himself to his art, which favors a higher order of existence, an ecstasy rising above bourgeois mediocrity, and which, in Nietzschean fashion, belongs to an elite of suffering. Such suffering Leverkühn willfully invites (not unlike Nietzsche) by disregarding the warnings of his prostitute friend, Esmeralda, and contracting syphilis through her—a disease that, as he had surmised, will excite his creative imagination. In Italy, in Palestrina, the decisive encounter occurs: Whether through reality, sick imagination, hallucination, or vision, Leverkühn meets the Devil, with whom he signs a twenty-four-year pact that will enable the composer to pen impressively futuristic scores in exchange for a frigid renunciation of all meaningful human contacts, including love. In Pfeiffering, near Munich, Leverkühn composes his great *Lamentatio Doctoris Faustis*, an apocalyptic oratorio making use of extraordinary musical ideas and devices. After playing it on the piano for his gathered friends, Leverkühn confesses his terrible story, wild with folly. This happens in about 1930. He dies insane, in 1940, in his native village.

German history, from Bismarckian 1870 to Hitlerian 1940, the year of the Blitzkrieg, figures in the reader's mind as more than mere innuendo; Germany, too, had made a pact with the Devil. For this, Mann summons a recurrence of the Faust legend—the *Faustbuch* of 1587—rather than the elevating Goethean version. Mann's modern Faust, then, comes to stand also for the artist who in the twentieth century must (or believes he must) assume demoniac traits—indeed, invite the repulsion of disease, with its human isolation and aridity—to attain a privileged status.

Leverkühn's good and admiring biographer Zeitblum is startled at both the political and the biographical events, which he narrates with a sadness typical of an intelligent but stolid bourgeois incapable of action. The honest recounter cannot fathom the gelid genius of his friend. One of the novel's fascinating devices is the use of this narrator, which, combined with the author's manipulation of his fiction, produces an expressive, dual perspective. It is the author, however, who is responsible for the technical discussions on music (as in chapter 8, for example, concerning Beethoven's Piano Sonata, Opus 111) and, obviously, for the novel's symphonic pattern (the early exposition of musical motifs, their development, and their climactic recapitulation). Leverkühn's twelve-tone "invention" is Schönberg's *Tonreihe*, and many of his philosophical reflections relate to Theodor Adorno's comments on modern music. The new artist—shaping abstractions and stressing reason over instinct, seeking unusual combinations that, through their ambiguity, direct themselves less to the traditional human ear than to a "cosmic order" of aesthetic experience—invites, in his diseased ecstasy, his own tragic demise. Perhaps art, having become metacerebral, can no longer claim to be a human verity. As with art, so with modern life. Zeitblum can only ask, "When, out of extreme despair, will a new dawn of hope arise?"

Doctor Faustus thus can be seen as Mann's final call for serenity and balance, for a shaking off of the morbid decadence and apocalyptic fanaticisms to which the twentieth century is heir. This appeal to sanity remains his legacy.

Jean-Pierre Barricelli

Other major works

SHORT FICTION: *Der kleine Herr Friedemann*, 1898; *Das Wunderkind*, 1914; *Erzählung*, 1922; *Children and Fools*, 1928; *Stories of Three Decades*, 1936; *Ausgewahlte Erzählungen*, 1945; *Death in Venice, and Seven Other Stories*, 1954; *Stories of a Lifetime*, 1961; *Collected Stories*, 2001.

PLAY: *Fiorenza*, pb. 1906.

POETRY: "Gesang vom Kindchen," 1919.

NONFICTION: "Friedrich und die grosse Koalition," 1915 ("Frederick and the Great Coalition," 1929); *Betrachtungen eines Unpolitischen*, 1918 (*Reflections of a Nonpolitical Man*, 1983); *Rede und Antwort*, 1922; *Bemühungen*, 1925; *Die Forderung des Tages*, 1930; *Lebensabriss*, 1930 (*A Sketch of My Life*, 1960); *Three Essays*, 1932; *Past Masters, and Other Papers*, 1933; *Leiden und Grösse der Meister*, 1935; *Freud, Goethe, Wagner*, 1937; *Achtung, Europa!*, 1938; *Dieser Friede*, 1938 (*This Peace*, 1938); *Vom künftigen Sieg der Demokratie*, 1938 (*The Coming of Victory of Democracy*, 1938); *Deutsche Hörer!*, 1942 (*Listen, Germany!*, 1943); *Order of the Day: Political Essays and Speeches of Two Decades*, 1942; *Adel des Geistes: Sechzehn Versuche zum Problem der Humanität*, 1945 (*Essays of Three Decades*, 1947); *Neue Studien*, 1948; *Die Entstehung des "Doktor Faustus": Roman eines Romans*, 1949 (*The Story of a Novel: The Genesis of "Doctor Faustus,"* 1961); *Altes und Neues: Kleine Prosa aus fünf Jahrzehnten*, 1953; *Versuch über Schiller*, 1955; *Nachlese: Prosa, 1951-1955*, 1956; *Last Essays*, 1958; *Briefe*, 1961-1965 (3 volumes; partial translation *Letters of Thomas Mann, 1889-1955*, 1970); *Addresses Delivered at the Library of Congress*, 1963; *Wagner und unsere Zeit*, 1963 (*Pro and Contra Wagner*, 1985); *Reden und Aufsätze*, 1965 (2 volumes); *Essays*, 1977-1978 (3 volumes); *Tagebücher*, 1977-1986 (6 volumes; partial translation *Diaries 1918-1939*, 1982); *Goethes Laufbahn als Schriftsteller: Zwölf Essays und Reden zu Goethe*, 1982; *Frage und Antwort: Interviews mit Thomas Mann 1909-1955*, 1983; *Thomas Mann's "Goethe and Tolstoy": Notes and Sources*, 1984.

MISCELLANEOUS: *Gesammelte Werke*, 1956 (12 volumes; includes critical writings in volumes 10-11); *Gesammelte Werke*, 1960-1974 (13 volumes; includes critical writings in volumes 9-11); *Werkausgabe*, 1980-1986 (20 volumes; includes 3 volumes of critical writings).

Bibliography

Feurlicht, Ignace. *Thomas Mann*. Boston: Twayne, 1968. Provides a critical introduction to Mann through analysis of the plots, characters, ideas, and styles of his novels and stories against the background of his life. Notes that most of his early stories focus on marked men, individuals who are weak, sick, or odd, outsiders who cannot endure everyday life.

Hayman, Ronald. *Thomas Mann: A Biography*. New York: Charles Scribner's Sons, 1995. As the first biographer to have access to Mann's unexpurgated diaries, Hayman provides a revealing look at the German author. Describes how in his public appearances and writing, Mann presented himself as self-controlled and dignified, when in reality he was subject to nervousness and feelings of guilt and sexual embarrassment.

Heilbut, Anthony. *Thomas Mann: Eros and Literature*. New York: Alfred A. Knopf, 1996. One of the most commanding biographies of Mann available in English presents a carefully detailed narrative of his life and work. Includes detailed informative notes and an extensive bibliography.

Heller, Erich. *The Ironic German: A Study of Thomas Mann*. Boston: Little, Brown, 1958. Stimulating and influential study examines Mann's intellectual ancestry and provides analysis of his fiction.

Hollingdale, R. J. *Thomas Mann: A Critical Study*. Lewisburg, Pa.: Bucknell University Press, 1971. Rather than presenting analyses of individual novels and stories, this work discusses the basic philosophical assumptions in Mann's works, especially as these relate to the philosophy of Friedrich Nietzsche. Focuses on such themes as crime, sickness, decadence, irony, and myth.

Kurzke, Hermann. *Thomas Mann: Life as a Work of Art*. Translated by Leslie Willson. Princeton, N.J.: Princeton University Press, 2002. Biography takes a balanced approach to Mann's life and work. Among the areas addressed are Mann's homosexuality and his relationship to Judaism. Includes an index.

Lehnert, Herbert, and Eva Wessell, eds. *A Companion to the Works of Thomas Mann*. Rochester, N.Y.: Camden House, 2004. Collection of essays covers the range of Mann's work, including analyses of the major novels and the novella *Death in Venice*.

Mann, Thomas. *Death in Venice*. Edited by Naomi Ritter. Boston: Bedford Books, 1998. This edition of a widely acclaimed translation of Mann's novella includes five critical essays that serve to help students understand the work in depth.

Mundt, Hannelore. *Understanding Thomas Mann*. Columbia: University of South Carolina Press, 2004. Discusses the themes, concerns, presentation, and meanings of many of Mann's works, drawing in part on information found in Mann's recently published diaries. Among the works considered are *Buddenbrooks*, *The Magic Mountain*, *Joseph and His Brothers*, and *Doctor Faustus*.

Reed, T. J. *Thomas Mann: The Uses of Tradition*. 2d ed. New York: Oxford University Press, 1996. Meticulously researched and well-documented study on Mann's thought and fiction. Presents analysis of some of Mann's works, including *Buddenbrooks*, *The Magic Mountain*, and *Doctor Faustus*. Includes bibliographical references and an index.

Robertson, Ritchie, ed. *The Cambridge Companion to Thomas Mann*. New York: Cambridge University Press, 2002. Collection of essays on Mann's works presents analyses of individual works as well as discussion of such topics as Mann and history, Mann's intellectual world, his literary techniques, and his representations of gender and sexuality. Includes a bibliography and an index.

Shookman, Ellis. *Thomas Mann's "Death in Venice": A Novella and Its Critics*. Rochester, N.Y.: Camden House, 2003. Offers a chronicle of the literary reception of Mann's novella from its initial publication in 1912 to criticism appearing from 1996 through 2001. Among the critics whose commentaries are included are authors D. H. Lawrence, Mario Vargas Llosa, and Mann himself.

Travers, Martin. *Thomas Mann*. New York: St. Martin's Press, 1992. Excellent, short introductory study contains chapters on Mann's life, the autobiographical elements of his first novels and early stories, and separate chapters on the novels. A concluding chapter assesses Mann as a modern novelist. Includes notes and an excellent annotated bibliography.

ALESSANDRO MANZONI

Born: Milan, Lombardy, Austria (now in Italy); March 7, 1785
Died: Milan, Italy; May 22, 1873
Also known as: Alessandro Francesco Tommaso Antonio Manzoni

Principal long fiction

I promessi sposi, 1827 (revised 1840-1842; *The Betrothed*, 1828, revised 1951)

Other literary forms

Alessandro Manzoni's vast range of intellectual endeavor is astonishing. He was a scholar and thinker in the best sense of the words, respecting thoroughness of documentation and clarity of analysis. His novel maintains an epic quality throughout, not simply because of the constantly expanding tableaux and narrative but also because of the breadth of knowledge that informs it. It is a historical novel because Manzoni was a historian, the author of such works as the *Discorso sopra alcuni punti della storia longobardica in Italia* (1822), the *Lettre à Alphonse de Lamartine* (1848), and the jurisprudential and humanitarian *La storia della colonna infame* (1842; *The Column of Infamy*, 1964). The best known of his philosophical and religious works include *Lettre à Victor Cousin* (1829), *Dell'invenzione* (1850), and *Osservazioni sulla morale cattolica* (1819). His two historical tragedies, *Il conte di Carmagnola* (pb. 1820; *Count of Carmagnola*, 2002) and *Adelchi* (pr., pb. 1822), were much admired by Charles-Augustin de Sainte-Beuve and Johann Wolfgang von Goethe. To round out his accomplishments, it must be added that as an agronomist he performed a number of experiments at his country retreat in northern Lombardy, some of which yielded positive and enduring results. For all these reasons, his published correspondence, *Epistolario* (1882), makes fascinating reading.

Finally, as a poet, Manzoni's fame rests primarily on his religious poetry, the *Inni sacri* (1812-1815; *The Sacred Hymns*, 1904), an occasional political piece such as "Marzo 1821" (1821, 1848), and "Il cinque maggio" (1821; "The Napoleonic Ode," 1904), the historico-philosophico-religious ode on the emperor Napoleon Bonaparte, perhaps the most dispassionate view (compared to the poems of Victor Hugo and Henrik Wergeland on the same subject) of the emperor.

Achievements

Alessandro Manzoni understood many of his era's religious and moral, historical and political, and aesthetic and linguistic problems, all of which he synthesized in different ways in his various works, particularly in his salient achievement of *The Betrothed*, judged by literary critics around the turn of the century in Geneva to be the greatest novel of the nineteenth century. In its pluralism of modes, it surpasses generic classification: It is at once historical, philosophical, sociological, metaphysical, psychological, realistic, naturalistic, idealistic, lyric, epic, dramatic, religious, optimistic, pessimistic, moralistic, ironical, oratorical, and both classical and Romantic—in short, universal. For the first time (aside from the picaresque, which exists in a class by itself), the "heroes" are peasants who are battered by historical events and yet around whom all historical events turn. Along with this, it may be said with justification that after Dante's *The Divine Comedy* (c. 1320), *The Betrothed* established the literary Italian language, for there has been no better stylist to dispute this claim.

As a playwright, Manzoni has been credited with composing, in *Adelchi*, a truly Christian tragedy, regardless of the pronouncements of theorists that such a tragedy amounts to a contradiction in terms. *The Column of Infamy* stands out as a remarkable example of that two-edged combination of legal literature and literary jurisprudence, a provocative merging of both disciplines. Manzoni must be recognized as a fine Christian apologist and a democratic philosopher, and his historical works will be seen to take their rightful place in the area of historiography, documented as they are with objective rigor.

Biography

Alessandro Francesco Tommaso Antonio Manzoni's putative father was Count Pietro Manzoni, and his mother, Giulia Beccaria, the daughter of the famous author of *Dei delitti e delle pene* (1764; *An Essay on Crimes and Punishments*, 1767). His early schooling took place in Lugano and Merate (under the Somaschi brothers) and in Milan (under the Barnabites), where he was born on March 7, 1785. Reacting against religion and sympathetic to the libertarianism of the French Revolution, at sixteen years old he wrote a Jacobin poem, "Il trionfo della libertà" (1801). Such liberal ideas attracted him to Paris, where his mother, legally separated from her husband since 1792, went to live with Carlo Imbonati in 1795. Manzoni returned to Paris in 1805 after traveling to Switzerland, Piedmont, Lombardy, and Venetia; Imbonati died, leaving Manzoni a goodly inheritance, to which Manzoni added the estate left him by his father, who died two years later.

During this period, still under the dictates of a classical aesthetic, Manzoni wrote a number of poems, including "In morte di Carlo Imbonati" (1805-1806). The Imbonati piece does not suggest that he was troubled by his mother's questionable morality (as he was to be later); his close—and what was to become lifetime—friendship with the French historian Claude Fauriel, who lived with Sophie de Condorcet, may have had something to do with his acceptance of the situation. In fact, in "divine Paris," he met many ideologues, freethinking philosophers and politicians such as Constantin-François de Volney, Marie-François Maine de Biran, Antoine-Louis Destutt de Tracy, Benjamin Constant, Pierre-Jean-Georges Cabanis, and François Guizot, who filled his head with theories of skepticism, atheism, materialism, and other notions then in vogue.

How much this intellectual ferment actually shaped Manzoni's mind is hard to say. A heightened awareness of history and historical studies, thanks to Vincenzo Cuoco in Milan and Fauriel in Paris, remained with him to a degree significant enough to guide his research interests, but the philosophical currents of the Enlightenment were already in decline, and Manzoni always found more attraction in matters of the spirit. He frequented Jansenist circles and, his conscience in turmoil, underwent a spiritual crisis—his so-called conversion—after which he settled on a more serene, almost devotional view of life. Supposedly, the process began in the Church of Saint Roche, to which he had repaired in a state of confusion one day. Still in Paris, he met a "very sweet, very proper" young woman, "an angelic creature" of Calvinist background, Henriette Blondel, whom he married in Milan in 1808. Enrichetta, as he then called her, and to whom he remained devoted all of her life, was only sixteen when they married. Two years later, the marriage rite, originally evangelical, was celebrated in Roman Catholic fashion. About the conversion, Attilio Momigliano says,

> Manzoni's religious conversion is the definitive settlement of his moral conscience, the moment in which his scrupulous honesty finds an unwavering basis. . . . The deist becomes theist, and his humanitarian morality becomes Catholic morality. . . . Hence, in life: modesty, love of meditative solitude, charity, a reluctance to speak ill of his neighbor, and an acute and indulgent penetration into the motivations for human actions; in art: the portrayal of these and similar virtues, and of the opposite defects, so rendered as to induce approval of the former and revulsion of the latter; in criticism: the struggle against poetry that is of no use to the loftiest interests of the soul.

In this development, the learned clerics Eustachio Dègola and Luigi Tosi played a key role. Manzoni's mother also returned to Catholicism.

In Italian Romanticism, compared with the more mystically oriented German strain, Manzoni detected Christian indications—an inspiration that resulted, in 1812-1815, in *The Sacred Hymns*. When he read Jean-Charles-Léonard de Sismondi's *Histoire des républiques italiennes du moyen-âge* (1807-1818; *A History of the Italian Republics*, 1832), in which Catholicism is accused of having corrupted Italian life, he wrote the *Osservazioni sulla morale cattolica*, a rationalistic apology that relies on his keen historical sense and on his knowledge of seventeenth and eighteenth century texts. During the next few years, he wrote prodigiously. *Count of Carmagnola*, begun in 1816 and continued in 1819, was readied for publication in 1820, along with its scrupulously documented historical introduction and a preface similar to the 1823 *Lettre à M. C*** [Chauvet] sur l'unité de temps et de lieu dans la tragédie*.

Wishing to give his historical inclinations further avenues, Manzoni began *The Betrothed* in 1821, also writing "Marzo 1821" and "The Napoleonic Ode." In 1822

Alessandro Manzoni. (Library of Congress)

came the historical tragedy *Adelchi* with its companion piece, the scrupulous historical investigation *Discorso sopra alcuni punti della storia longobardica in Italia*; the latter develops Augustin Thierry's dualism between the conquerors and the conquered, the oppressors and the oppressed, a favorite perspective of Manzoni, whose instinctive sympathy always resided with life's humble. *Lettera sul romanticismo* is a letter written in 1823 to Marquis Cesare D'Azeglio and published without Manzoni's knowledge in 1846; it advances the notion that poetry and literature must aim at usefulness as a goal, truth as a subject, and what is interesting as a means.

Frequently in his country estate in Brusuglio and deep into the historical works of Giuseppe Ripamonti and the economic treatises of Melchiorre Gioia, Manzoni continued to compose his novel, the first version of which appeared in 1823 as *Fermo e Lucia*. He eliminated the excessive Romanticism of this version in a revised edition of 1827, at first titled *Gli sposi promessi*, just before he left for Florence "in order to rinse [his linguistic] clothes in the Arno [River]." The final version, hailed by Goethe and Edgar Allan Poe, among others, eventually saw light in its present form in 1840-1842.

The last forty years of Manzoni's life were beset with sorrow. He described the passing away of his beloved Enrichetta in 1833 as "a great and irreparable misfortune." His mother died in 1841; his second wife, Teresa Borri, whom he married in 1837, died in 1861; he was survived by only two of his eleven children. His close friend, philosopher Antonio Rosmini, the celebrated author of *Della enducazione cristian* (1837), *Filosofia del diritto* (1841-1843), *Psicologia* (1846-1848; *Psychology*, 1884-1888), *Teosofia* (1837), and many other works that influenced Manzoni, also died, in 1855; even his brother-in-law, writer Massimo D'Azeglio (*Ettore Fieramosca*, 1833; *I miei ricordi*, 1861, and other works), died during Manzoni's lifetime. Thus it is understandable that after *The Betrothed*, Manzoni restricted himself to philosophy, linguistics, history, and criticism, publishing no more fiction or poetry.

From all corners of Europe, Manzoni's fame received recognition, from Sir Walter Scott to Archduke Maximilian of Austria, John Henry Newman, and William Ewart Gladstone. He turned down many honors, including acceptance to the French Legion of Honor, the grand duke of Tuscany's Order of Merit, and a deputyship in the Piedmont chamber. Other honors he accepted include a life pension by King Victor Emanuel II of twelve thousand lire annually, the senatorship of the kingdom, and the prestige of Roman citizenship. Though reserved and withdrawn by temperament, not given to fiery political leadership, he exercised a visible role in forging the national consciousness of several generations of Italians: In 1814, he joined the group that refused to ask Frenchman Eugène de Beauharnais to become king of Italy; in 1838, he did not participate in the Milanese celebrations for the despotic Bourbon Ferdinand I; he rejected Austrian honors; and as one dissatisfied with Austrian rule, he signed the document by Lombard moderates asking Carlo Alberto to intervene from Piedmont-Sardinia in 1848. In 1860, he voted to transfer the Italian capital from Florence to Rome.

Manzoni's life, however, was primarily a life of thought and art, transcending Romantic literary squabbles as well as the arena of national politics. His retirement to Brusuglio to carry on agricultural experiments typifies his posture of serenity, of working on behalf of humanity, of finding solace in the beauties and miracles of nature. In his vision of life, he integrated all elements—political, literary, historical, religious, and artistic—so that whatever he wrote, in whatever category of thought or discipline, the personal stamp of his overall synthesis was always identifiable. All Italy mourned at the news of his death in Milan on May 22, 1873, and the event inspired composer Giuseppe Verdi to return to work on the *Messa da Requiem*, which he had put aside; it was dedicated to Manzoni and performed in Milan's Church of San Marco on the first anniversary of his death.

Analysis: The Betrothed

The premise of Alessandro Manzoni's only novel is a timeworn one: The author claims to have discovered an interesting, but primitive, anonymous manuscript of the seventeenth century dealing with the war, famine, and pestilence occasioned by the occupation of Lombardy by Spanish troops; because this narrative is poorly written, he has decided to retell the story in his own words.

Somewhere in the Milanese region, the story begins, around Lecco and Lake Como, two young peasants wish to marry and seek the services of the village priest. Renzo Tramaglino and Lucia Mondella are good, honest people, and at first they cannot understand Don Abbondio's equivocation followed by a refusal, until it becomes known that the local tyrant, the evil and feared Don Rodrigo, wants Lucia for his own pleasures and through his *bravi* (ruffians) has threatened the priest accordingly. Eight hundred pages later, the two finally marry. The epic of *The Betrothed* lies in between.

From the microcosm of Lecco, the events swell into a macrocosmic panorama of life itself, with all its confusion and wandering, suffering and barbarism, death and destruction. The simple threads of private events weave into ever more complex fabrics until the tapestry of calamities reaches fateful public proportions. The lives of Renzo and Lucia fork at the outset. Fra Cristoforo, a sternly upright monk, arranges for the latter to leave her town and seek shelter in a convent directed by a nun with a dark past, Sister Gertrude, whose story shows Manzoni to be one of the finest psychologists in literature. For his part, Renzo looks for help from a crooked lawyer, Azzeccagarbugli; travels to Milan, where he is greeted by bread riots and other difficulties; and escapes to the Adda River after talking too long at an inn.

Meanwhile, angry Don Rodrigo requests assistance in his wrongdoing from a powerful and enigmatic figure, a kind of regional overlord whose name is never told but who goes under the appellation of the Unnamed (*l'innominato*). This spirit of evil (and as such he acquires impressive literary stature, to be considered along with Honoré de Balzac's Vautrin, William Shakespeare's Iago, and the like) has Lucia kidnapped and brought to his secluded castle. One of the most debated issues in literature occurs here: the conversion of this formidable figure to good, seemingly occurring overnight in the presence of the purity and radiance of the innocent peasant girl, but actually occurring over a period of time preceding the novel's action. A famous colloquy takes place between him and the historical cardinal of legendary sanctity, Federico Borromeo.

The ills continue, however—indeed, multiply: drought, famine, war (a ramification of the Thirty Years' War), infection introduced by the Spanish army, and the devastating plague of 1630, which decimated the population of the Milanese, whose bodies were carried off by hooded *monatti* to the hospital camp known as the *lazzeretto* or to burial ditches. Manzoni's description of the terror of the "greasers," or *untori*, the supposed spreaders of disease, and of the horrible plague itself, must be considered literary landmarks. Many characters perish: Don Rodrigo; his henchman, Il Griso; Fra Cristoforo; the village priest's gossipy housekeeper, Perpetua; the ostentatious intellectual, Don Ferrante; and his wife, Donna Prassede. Lucia recovers miraculously, and her mother, Agnese, is spared. Fires burn the evil out, rains purify the land, and Renzo and Lucia are finally united in humble marriage.

The novel blends aesthetico-poetic and ethico-religious elements in a creative synthesis that conceals Manzoni's concern to separate artistic invention from historical document. History is not a convenient mold into which to pour the vicissitudes surrounding the lives of Renzo and Lucia but a vehicle to expand the reader's humanitarian consciousness, which must then outweigh narrowly political, social, or economic issues. Rocco Montano put it this way: The unity of the novel consists

> in its universality, which on the level of moral vision absorbs the historical and realistic particular; it consists in the profound accord between man's autonomy and the existence of an Absolute which transcends us; it consists in the dialectic of historical truth, which becomes myth and with which corresponds that other dialectic of feeling and linguistic objectivity.

Critics have put a great deal of emphasis—possibly too much emphasis—on Manzoni's Catholic persuasion and have thereby failed to grasp his true universality. There is no denying his religious conviction, but this conviction never reached such doctrinaire proportions as to preclude a transcending commitment to poetry, in the broadest sense of the word. If the ending of the novel suggests the working of Providence, the fact is that, as in *Adelchi*, Providence comes not from without but from within and is something that people work out for and by themselves. If the Unnamed converts, he or she does so after long self-questioning that emerges from an existential anguish of loneliness and dread and self-doubt. If Fra Cristoforo appears at times hard to believe in his total unselfishness, like Victor Hugo's Bishop Myriel in *Les Misérables* (1862), it is because, unlike Myriel, he is atoning for his former sinful ways, driven by a guilty conscience.

More than anything else, Manzoni embraced closely the fundamental attitudes of the Christian tradition—love, humility, forgiveness, and charity—in such a way as to seem to make Christianity itself a metaphor for the superior life of the spirit, the universal spirit. This was his true Absolute, a moral vision that, in the context of art, becomes poetic, even mythical. More than a "religious" novel, then, *The Betrothed* is a human novel, well worth its place in the original Harvard classics series.

Hence Manzoni's profound feeling for the humble and the suffering who give history a *common* sense; hence, too, the absence of any protagonist of exalted individualism. Manzoni "deheroizes" the novel, yet every character stands out with recognizable humanity: Renzo, candid, ingenuous, excited, generous, like the perdurance of the human race; Lucia, pious, sensible, good, like a creature of light; Agnese, enterprising, affectionate, energetic, a woman of the people; Perpetua, protective, brash, the perpetual gossip; Don Abbondio, fearful, confused, vacuous, the model of a coward; Don Rodrigo, mean, capricious, vainglorious, an impenitent rascal; Fra Cristoforo, altruistic, concerned, impulsive, a fiery saint; the Unnamed, mysterious, awesome, demoniac, like an emanation of evil; Cardinal Borromeo, exemplary, firm, a noble figure of persuasive serenity; Sister Gertrude, proud, agonized, gloomy, a tragic victim of misguided parents; Azzeccagarbugli, false and niggardly; Don Ferrante and Donna Prassede, the pedant in his artificial world and the presumptuous Christian. All these characters need more than a few adjectives to describe them, for not one of them is two-dimensional. Each is greater than the sum of his or her parts, each is portrayed with the understanding and compassion of an author who has long observed humankind, and each is subjected to a delicately comic assessment. Manzoni's is an art of indulgence.

This art is expressed in exquisite prose, highly sophisticated and precise. Action, commentary, soliloquy, dialogue—all are finely honed to the needs of analysis, humor, irony, or moral example. The style engages many tonalities—"rather a chorus," says Giorgio Petrocchi, "a concert of languages." Many passages have remained classics, such as the opening paragraph (an interesting adumbration of the novel in imagistic terms), Lucia's farewell to her hometown as she escapes to the convent, Don Abbondio's humorous donkey ride up the mountainside to the Unnamed's castle, the bread riots in Milan (Manzoni handles crowds adroitly), and the agony of death in the throes of the plague. In Manzoni's prose, the word has a communicative vitality, always contained, fitting, and significant. This virtue more than makes up for the repeated digressions, which have not gone uncriticized, even if they ultimately fit the tale's epic dimensions, completing the background of the events, and are presented in a style consistent with the tenor of those events. Furthermore, images planted here and there structure the novel expressively and create desired tonalities. Individual words become word-symbols that interrelate within the novel, stimulating in the reader an associative process that gives certain images their own "plot." (Bread, as juxtaposed to wine, is one such image.) They become the lifeblood of the novel and its characters; at the same time, through them, the human situations achieve an artistic dimension.

The Betrothed is unquestionably a unique novel. It will retain its power so long as human beings can read it, because in it, heroic measure is taken not in accomplishing great deeds in the face of danger but in unassuming strength of character in the middle of human suffering.

Jean-Pierre Barricelli

Other major works

PLAYS: *Il conte di Carmagnola*, pb. 1820 (*Count of Carmagnola*, 2002); *Adelchi*, pr., pb. 1822 (English translation, 2002); *Alessando Manzoni: Two Plays*, pb. 2002 (includes *Count of Carmagnola* and *Adelchi*).

POETRY: "Il trionfo della libertà," 1801; *Sermoni*, 1801-1804; "A Francesco Lomonaco," 1802; "Ode," 1802-1803; "L'Adda," 1803; "In morte di Carlo Imbonati," 1805-1806; "Urania," 1808-1809; *Inni sacri*, 1812-1815 (*The Sacred Hymns*, 1904); "Il cinque maggio," 1821 ("The Napoleonic Ode," 1904); "Marzo 1821," 1821, 1848.

NONFICTION: *Osservazioni sulla morale cattolica*, 1819; *Discorso sopra alcuni punti della storia longobardica in Italia*, 1822; *Lettre à M. C*** [Chauvet] sur l'unité de temps et de lieu dans la tragédie*, 1823; *Lettre à Victor Cousin*, 1829; *La storia della colonna infame*, 1842 (*The Column of Infamy*, 1964); *Del romanzo storico*, 1845; *Lettera sul romanticismo*, 1846; *Lettre à Alphonse de Lamartine*, 1848; *Dell'invenzione*, 1850; *Sulla lingua italiana*, 1850; *Dell'unità della lingua e dei mezzi di diffonderla*, 1868; *Lettera intorno al vocabolario*, 1868; *Epistolario*, 1882; *Saggio comparativo su la rivoluzione francese del 1789 e la rivoluzione italiana del 1859*, 1889; *Sentir Messa*, 1923.

Bibliography

Barricelli, Gian Piero. *Alessandro Manzoni*. Boston: Twayne, 1976. An introductory biography and critical study of selected works by Manzoni, including *The Betrothed*. Includes bibliographic references and an index.

Colquhoun, Archibald. *Manzoni and His Times: A Biography of the Author of "The Betrothed" ("I promessi sposi")*. 1954. Reprint. Westport, Conn.: Hyperion Press, 1979. A useful resource, this biography was written by one of the best-known scholars of Italian literature. Includes illustrations.

Ferlito, Susanna F. "Fear of the Mother's Tongue: Secrecy and Gossip in Manzoni's *I promessi sposi*." *MLN* 113, no. 1 (January, 1998): 30-51. Ferlito discusses how Manzoni's representation of the mother-daughter bond in *The Betrothed* implicitly recognizes and keeps at bay the critical potential of that bond and, by extension, a female alliance among the peasants.

_______. *Topographies of Desire: Manzoni, Cultural Practices, and Colonial Scars*. New York: Peter Lang, 2000. Drawing upon a wide range of disciplinary debates in the fields of comparative politics, anthropology, cultural studies, and comparative literature, this book examines how Manzoni's French and Italian writings produced differences between cultural discourses in a nineteenth century Europe that was not yet thought of as "naturally" divided between nation-states. Includes a bibliography and an index.

Ginzburg, Natalia. *The Manzoni Family*. Translated by Marie Evans. New York: Arcade, 1989. An especially good background study of the tradition and the history out of which Manzoni's work was created. Ginzburg includes a family tree, a list of characters, and a map of Italy during the Risorgimento.

Godt, Clareece G. *The Mobile Spectacle: Variable Perspective in Manzoni's "I promessi sposi."* New York: Peter Lang, 1998. Godt describes how Manzoni consistently represents what the eye sees (landscape, cityscape) and the mind conceives (characters' plans, history) under different and often paradoxical aspects. Includes notes and a comprehensive bibliography.

Matteo, Sante, and Larry H. Peer, eds. *The Reasonable Romantic: Essays on Alessandro Manzoni*. New York: Peter Lang, 1986. An anthology of seventeen original essays, a few using deconstruction, written by new and established Manzoni scholars to introduce Manzoni to readers. The first section is a general introduction, followed by sections on Manzoni and Romanticism, language, history, and religion.

Pierce, Glenn. *Manzoni and the Aesthetics of the Lombard Seicento: Art Assimilating into the Narrative of "I promessi sposi."* Lewisburg, Pa.: Bucknell University Press, 1998. Pierce examines *The Be-*

trothed in terms of seventeenth century aesthetics, arguing that Manzoni used artistic and dramatic works from that period as historical documents with which to create his novel. Contains numerous illustrations.

Ragusa, Olga. "Alessandro Manzoni and Developments in the Historical Novel." In *The Cambridge Companion to the Italian Novel*, edited by Peter Bondanella and Andrea Ciccarelli. New York: Cambridge University Press, 2003. Ragusa's essay is included in this historical overview of the Italian novel. While referring to many of his works, she focuses on *The Betrothed* and provides a broader context of his place in Italian literature.

Wall, Bernard. *Alessandro Manzoni*. New Haven, Conn.: Yale University Press, 1954. Contains chapters on Manzoni's life and times, his work as a poet and dramatist, and *The Betrothed* and its place in literature. Also features discussions of Manzoni's religion, the problem of language, and Romanticism. Includes biographical and bibliographical notes.

MARIVAUX

Born: Paris, France; February 4, 1688
Died: Paris, France; February 12, 1763
Also known as: Pierre Carlet de Chamblain de Marivaux; Pierre Carlet

Principal long fiction

Les Effets surprenants de la sympathie, 1713-1714
La Voiture embourbée, 1714
La Vie de Marianne, 1731-1741 (*The Life of Marianne*, 1736-1742; also known as *The Virtuous Orphan: Or, The Life of Marianne*, 1979)
Le Paysan parvenu, 1734-1735 (*The Fortunate Peasant*, 1735)
Le Télémaque travesti, 1736
Pharsamon, 1737 (*Pharsamond: Or, The New Knight-Errant*, 1750)

Other literary forms

Œuvres complètes de Marivaux, the complete works of Marivaux (ma-rih-VOH), were published in twelve volumes in 1781 and again in 1825-1830 in ten volumes. In addition to his novels, thirty-one of his plays are included in these early editions, as well as the speech he gave upon his reception into the French Academy. Also included are issues of the periodicals *Le Spectateur français*, *Le Cabinet du philosophe*, and *L'Indigent philosophe*; *Homère travesti: Ou, L'Iliade en vers burlesques (a travesty of Homer, or the Iliad* in burlesque verse), a mock epic in verse, in 1716; *L'Éducation d'un prince* (a prince's education), written upon the occasion of the birth of Louis XVI in 1754; *Le Miroir* (the mirror), a philosophical essay, in 1755; and various *Réflexions* (1744-1755; comments).

Marivaux's *Théâtre complet* (1878, 1964, 1968, 2000) has often been republished, but there is no modern edition of his complete works. A few critical editions with notable commentaries are available in large part because of the efforts of Frédéric Deloffre.

Achievements

One of Marivaux's great achievements is the enrichment of the French vocabulary with the terms *marivaudage* and *marivauder*, which appeared while the author was still alive. The noun is defined in *Encyclopedia Britannica* as verbal preciousness reflecting the sensitivity and sophistication of Marivaux's era. Nowadays, the lightly interpreted verb and noun suggest badinage, but Deloffre, in his *Marivaux et le Marivaudage* (1955, 1967), sees *marivaudage* as serious in intent, an alliance of sensibility and wit. In *The Novel of Worldliness* (1969), Peter Brooks analyzes *marivaudage* and explains it as

> a style which seeks to move from a state of semi-awareness and confusion to a clear and total knowledge of the self, while concomitantly refusing to ver-

> balize that which cannot be spoken without a resultant loss of subtlety. . . . Marivaux is notoriously interested in states of semi-awareness, ambiguity of emotion, sentimental limbos; and *marivaudage* is a style elaborated to render these states while making progress toward a greater clarity and distinction.

Deloffre's and Brooks's fine descriptions provide a corrective to the idea that *marivaudage* precludes insight and is merely amusing, never profound.

For a long time, Marivaux was appreciated more as a dramatist than as a novelist, and today, Molière is the only author whose plays are represented on the stage of the Comédie-Française more often than those of Marivaux. While he was still trying to find himself as a novelist, Marivaux experienced his first great success on the stage with his *Arlequin poli par l'amour* (pr. 1720; *Robin, Bachelor of Love*, 1968). *La Surprise de l'amour* (pr. 1722; *The Agreeable Surprise*, 1766) revealed an author very sure of his art, capable of mixing his knowledge of dramatic culture with a real originality in the domains of plot, dialogue, and mise-en-scène. It is not surprising, then, that his masterpieces, as those of other great dramatists, are well received in foreign countries. French theatrical companies have taken his plays through Europe, North and South America, the Soviet Union, the Middle East, and Japan.

In order to understand Marivaux, it is essential to read his essays and miscellaneous writings, published in *Nouveau Mercure* and in his own periodicals, because he set forth in them many of the principles that his plays and novels illustrate. He persevered in cultivating the journalistic genre from 1717 to 1734, writing articles that occupy more than 750 pages in the first edition of his works. In his *Pensées sur la clarté du discours* (1719; thoughts on clear expression), Marivaux declares that "the modern conception of style . . . springs less from the idea of clarity than from the ideal of suggestive and subjective writing." As Oscar Haac writes in *Marivaux* (1973), "It posits a style which is appropriate to its subject rather than conforming to standards of rhetoric."

In the first issue of the *Le Spectateur français*, Marivaux showed his interest in interpreting the faces that people wear in public; mask-wearing became a necessity for many of his heroines, because innocence and virtue were in constant danger. *Le Cabinet du philosophe* includes a dialogue, "Le Chemin de la fortune" (the path to fortune), in which are found sketches of a number of characters on their way to wealth and position, representing aspects of Marianne in *The Life of Marianne* and Jacob in *The Fortunate Peasant*.

Despite the increasing availability of Marivaux's prose works, readers who are familiar with him know him primarily as a dramatist, although André Gide placed *The Life of Marianne* among France's ten best novels—a fair indication of Marivaux's importance in the development of the novel in France.

Biography

Few authors have been as discreet about their private lives as Pierre Carlet de Chamblain de Marivaux. Born Pierre Carlet in Paris on February 4, 1688, he left practically no correspondence, and an analysis of his writings does not help much. The most elementary facts of his biography have been established recently through scholarly scrutiny of legal documents. His father, Nicolas Carlet, was a naval officer, then a supply officer, before becoming director of the royal mint in Riom, a small town in central France. His mother was Marie-Anne Bullet; his maternal uncle, Pierre Bullet, and a cousin, Jean-Baptiste Bullet de Chamblain, were well-known and successful architects.

Marivaux probably spent half of his first twenty years in the provinces and the other half in Paris visiting relatives and friends. He may have attended the Collège de Riom, run by Oratorian monks; he studied Latin but admitted having no knowledge of Greek. In 1710, he registered at the Faculty of Law in Paris while still a resident of Riom. His first comedy, *Le Père prudent et équitable: Ou, Crispin l'heureux fourbe* (pr. c. 1709; the careful and just father), was performed in Limoges in 1712 and published with a preface signed "M***." The same year, he moved to Paris, where he was welcome in the fashionable salon of Madame de Lambert and later of Madame de Tencin. He embraced the cause of the "Moderns" with Bernard le Bovier de Fontenelle and Antoine Houdar de La Motte, and he adopted the name Marivaux, with which he signed his *Homère travesti* in 1716. The following year, he married Colombe Bollogne, who was five years older than he and who had a substantial dowry. In 1719, the couple had a daughter, Colombe-Prospère.

Most of the family's wealth was lost in John Law's Louisiana speculations, and the author had to rely on the success of his publications to live fairly independently. Marivaux's wife died in 1723 when their daughter was barely four years old. Colombe-Prospère was reared in a convent and, in 1746, became a nun with an annuity of 110 francs given by the duke of Orléans.

In February, 1743, Marivaux became a member of the French Academy, not because his confreres recognized his literary talents, but rather because he was appreciated for his pleasant and easygoing temperament; at that time, a rejected candidate for this much-coveted position was Voltaire. From then on, Marivaux attended faithfully the meetings of the academy and wrote very little. In April, 1744, he moved into the apartment of an unmarried woman, Mademoiselle Angélique Gabrielle Anquetin de la Chapelle Saint-Jean. Biographers disagree about the relationship between the two quinquagenarians; it seems that their age kept contemporaries from believing they were lovers, while some modern critics consider that a purely platonic cohabitation is, at the age of fifty-six, rather unlikely.

Marivaux died on February 12, 1763. Because his will, which made Mademoiselle de Saint-Jean his sole heir, was dated January 20, 1758, and because he had not written for some time, it is assumed that he suffered a prolonged illness. His death was almost unnoticed publicly.

ANALYSIS

The early works of Marivaux show the young author's interest in the way his protagonists react to the conventional twists of fate, a preoccupation showing up as early as 1713-1714 in *Les Effets surprenants de la sympathie* (the surprising results of affection) and recurring in his other novels. Another predilection of theme is found in Marivaux's first novel, in which love comes by surprise very rapidly and is reciprocated. Though "love at first sight" is a more frequent theme in Marivaux's plays, it manifests itself in the novels as well.

In *Les Effets surprenants de la sympathie*, Clorante sees Caliste at a window and is "surprised by love." When Marianne meets Valville and is helped by him, she reflects that "he did not cast a glance at me which did not clearly say 'I love you': nor did I know what to do with mine, because it would have told him the same." At the beginning of the novel, in a twenty-nine-page "Avis" (admonition to the reader), Marivaux criticizes novels that tell a story with a haste that may amuse the reader but does not move him or her; he stresses the right of the author's "reflections" to suspend the action and interpret its significance. Marianne is only one of Marivaux's many characters who grasp all opportunities and excuses for sharing their thoughts with the reader. She says explicitly

> I was afraid the first part of my life contained so few events, and such long reflections, that you would already think me tedious. However you are pleased to say the contrary, and to press me to go on. I shall therefore proceed.

Marivaux. (Getty Images)

Reflections automatically involve a judgment on the milieu in which the heroes evolve. His reflective analyses make of Marivaux a moralist, but one who amuses rather than one who preaches; he is conscious of the bad faith of some of his characters; he absolves them but is never blind, never unaware of the bruises their "virtue" suffers, virtue that is often a mask.

"The mirror and the mask," writes William S. Rogers, "are two themes which recur with frequency in the writings of Marivaux, and represent vividly his close observation of the human comedy, his desire to probe the reality that lies behind appearances." In *The Life of Marianne* and in *The Fortunate Peasant*, the heroes' constant preoccupation is to achieve the most flattering possible picture in the mirrors of others by wearing a mask. That is how Jacob wins Mademoiselle Habert, her money, and pseudonobility.

Les Effets surprenants de la sympathie

For his first novel, *Les Effets surprenants de la sympathie*, Marivaux looked for inspiration to the successful writers of the preceding century, Mademoiselle de Scudery and Gautier de Costes de La Calprenède. It is almost impossible to give a summary of *Les Effets surprenants de la sympathie*, in which every character's story is interpolated into someone else's story, all accounts being given in the first person. Caliste tells Clarice about her ancestors; she speaks for her father, who makes his own wife, Parménie, tell her story; she, in turn, listens to Merville's misfortunes. The plot is complex: Clorante is loved by Clarice, but he does not love her; he loves Caliste. Clarice is loved by Turcamène, from whom she flees. Caliste, pursued by Périande, whom she despises, loves Clorante but cannot find him. Fights, abductions, murders, and treasons follow one another; people thought to be dead suddenly reappear at the end of the story, one announcing that he is Clorante's father, the other, that he is Caliste's.

Some critics see in Marivaux's first novel not a mere imitation of seventeenth century novels, but a parody. It is more likely that the young author was experimenting and searching for his own style through imitation. In the "Avis," he expresses his ideas about the problems he sees in the writing of novels at the beginning of the eighteenth century. He opposes "reason," which establishes rules, to "nature," which is instinct, the base of spontaneous feeling of pleasures of the heart. He praises "feminine intuition" and castigates male pedantry. Another question raised by Marivaux is that of truth in writing when he remarks that fiction is capable of moving readers more agreeably than reality. A novelist should not worry about realism, so long as the effect is successful. The writer appeals to the emotions rather than to the intellect.

This first novel by Marivaux is interesting from a thematic point of view. Ronald Rosbottom points out that it includes elements that "presage some of Marivaux's more serious preoccupations in his later works," namely, the psychological complications of initial love, the specific subject of the young orphaned girl, and the role of mask, disguise, and subterfuge in social relations.

Pharsamond

During the time he was writing his first novel, Marivaux was also working on his second one, *Pharsamond*, definitely a parody, sometimes referred to as "The Modern Don Quixote." The hero, Pierre Bagnol, is eighteen years old; he has read many heroic stories and wants to experience similar adventures. He and his servant, Cliton, meet Cidalise and her *suivante*, Fatime, who want to be treated like heroines in a novel. Pharsamond-Pierre fights for his lady, Cliton does the same in the kitchen, and Cidalise's mother throws them out. They return home, where they are scolded by Pierre's uncle, but leave again in search of new adventures, which they find in an old castle. A lady, Clorine, dressed in a man's clothes, and her *suivante* tell their story and fall madly in love with the pseudo-Don Quixote and Sancho Panza, who flee, pursued unsuccessfully by their high-spirited mistresses. The two men find their first loves, are chased away once more by the mother, and arrive at a house where a marriage is being celebrated; this gives Cliton another opportunity to create havoc in the kitchen and in the reception room. Both heroes are finally cured by a magician and settle down to a much more prosaic life.

In *Pharsamond*, Marivaux studies again the relationships between reality and imagination as the four main characters move among the down-to-earth country people. Clorine is another precursor of Marianne; she is an orphan loved by a young nobleman whom she refuses to marry because of his family's opposition and her lack of wealth. Marivaux's favorite theme, that of a young girl facing a moral and a psychological dilemma while analyzing the initial feelings of love, is more developed in *Pharsamond* than it is in his first novel.

La Voiture embourbée

Marivaux's preoccupation with the theme of reality and illusion continues to show in *La Voiture embourbée* (the stagecoach stuck in the mud), a short novel that begins like Marguerite de Navarre's *L'Heptamerón* (1559; *The Queene of Navarres Tales*, 1597; also known as *The Heptameron*, 1959). To pass the time while the coach is being repaired, a group of travelers agree to tell stories, but instead of different stories, as in *The Heptameron*, the characters—who include the author himself, a middle-aged lady, her daughter, a *bel esprit* (or witty person), and an aging but gallant financier—are each going to add an episode to the story proposed by the author about Amandor and Ariobarsane, revealing their personalities through their contributions to the narration.

The frame story shows the passengers making their way at night to an inn in a country village. The heroes of the story started by the narrator are again readers of novels who wish to become characters in a novel. When the middle-aged lady takes over, she fills the story with disguises, kidnappings, and separations of lovers that show her taste for the romances of the previous centuries. She tells her audience that she tried to give them what they requested, something tragic, something magical, and something astonishing. The *bel esprit* adds murder, prisons, and torture. The young girl ends the horror story of her predecessor by waking up the heroine, Ariobarsane, from her nightmare and adding everyday risqué situations that show that, at fifteen years of age, she knows the facts of life. The financier then shows his romantic dreams by reuniting Amandor and Ariobarsane, and the local curate's nephew, who has been asked to join in, wraps up the story with a celebration in which all the characters drink too much and fall asleep. They find, then, that the coach has been repaired; the travelers go on their way, and when the author reaches his destination, he decides to write down what happened on his trip.

The interest of *La Voiture embourbée* rests in the formula used by Marivaux, combining his parodies of romantic fiction with a great share of realism. In this work, he developed the technique that he perfected in *The Life of Marianne* and *The Fortunate Peasant*, the use of a participant narrator. Marivaux thus shifted his authorial interventions to the narrative voice; the narrator is part of the story, yet, at the same time, he is above it; he can look inside himself and be looked at.

Le Télémaque travesti

Marivaux wrote one more novel around 1714, *Le Télémaque travesti*, which shows a young peasant, Brideron, and his uncle, Phocion, trying to relive the adventures of Telemachus because the young man's father went to war and never came back. François Fénelon's *Télémaque* (1699; *The Adventures of Telemachus*, 1720) is their bible and their travel guide; they plan each step according to its outline, making each one of their many adventures fit those of Ulysses' son. Part of the interest in this work comes from the transposition of the Greek heroes' experiences to those of Brideron and Phocion, who do not venture very far from their own French province. The constant references to the wars of Louis XIV, the satires of petty provincial tyrants, and the fights between Catholics and Huguenots make of the long novel a social document. Of interest also is the growing ability shown by Marivaux in depicting the reality of the exterior world and its effect on heroes who "have considerable difficulty in distinguishing between appearance and reality, even on the most obvious level," as Rosbottom points out. Most of the novel is made up of dialogues between Brideron and Phocion, as Marivaux honed his skills to write for the stage.

From 1714 to 1727, Marivaux devoted most of his time to the theater, writing sixteen plays during this period, including a fragment of "Mahomet Second" and "L'Amour et la vérité" (love and truth). During those years, he married, had a child, and lost his wife and his money. When he returned to the novel with *The Life of Marianne*, he was no longer an author in search of a personal style but a successful writer in the prime of life, ready to produce what some consider not only his masterpiece but also one of the best novels of the eighteenth century.

The Life of Marianne

Marivaux's interest in the theme of the young orphaned girl was evident from the time he wrote his first novel. *The Life of Marianne* is the story of a poor young girl on a quest for identity. She knows nothing about her origins, but she is convinced that her parents belonged to the high nobility. The aim of the fifteen-year-old Marianne is to force people to recognize her value. Because birth gives and even dictates the moral qualities that define a human being, Marianne uses her virtue to prove her worth. (A more recent edition of Marivaux's novel had for its title *The Virtuous Orphan: Or, The Life of Marianne*.) She in turn uses her moral qualities to reflect her high birth because, as the French proverb goes, good blood cannot lie.

Upon the death of the old people who brought her up, Marianne finds herself in the humiliating position of having to accept a job in a laundry. Though she refuses the offer of an old gentleman, Monsieur de Climal, to provide her with a small apartment and a pension, her virtue does not prevent her from accepting, temporarily, the beautiful clothes he has bought for her. Marianne wears them to church, where she catches the eye, and the heart, of a young, handsome, and rich count named Valville. Coincidences play a large part in Marivaux's novel. Marianne tries to keep Valville from finding out that she lives with a common laundress, but he has her followed by one of his servants. When he comes to pay his respects, he finds his own uncle, Monsieur de Climal, at Marianne's feet. In great danger of losing her reputation, Marianne has to convince the people around her that Monsieur de Climal is not the pure and generous philanthropist everyone thinks he is, but an old Tartuffe. She congratulates herself for having kept the dress as proof of his immoral designs.

Not wanting to return to the laundress, Marianne is totally distraught and is crying in a church where a kind lady notices her. Madame de Miran, touched by the orphan's misfortunes and her obvious fine qualities, takes her in charge, pays her pension in a convent, and soon considers herself Marianne's adoptive mother. Having followed the path of virtue, Marianne is rewarded by moving closer to the man she loves, as Valville is Madame de Miran's son. For the love of her new mother, however, even more than for the love of Valville's reputation, she declares herself ready to forget him and to force him to forget her, all the time expecting her great sacrifice to be well rewarded. Madame de Miran is so impressed that she soon gives her consent to her son's and Marianne's marriage. Relatives who learn, in spite of all precautions taken, of Marianne's unknown origins are determined to save Valville from himself; they kidnap Marianne and try to force her to marry, on the spot, a lower-class citizen. Fortunately, Marianne has a gift for long speeches that prove her virtue, her disinterest, and her self-sacrificing nature. Once more, she makes such a favorable impression that she convinces everybody of her moral nobility, which can come only from a noble ancestry.

Obstacles having been removed, the novel could end happily, but it is now discovered that Valville is not a constant lover; he is susceptible to damsels in distress, and Marianne—no longer in distress—has lost that certain charm. When he sees in his fiancé's convent an attractive girl, Mademoiselle Varthon, who has just fainted, the sight overwhelms him. This girl is most cooperative, and Marianne faces once more the danger of losing Valville and her identity, inasmuch as being allowed to marry him was a proof of her nobility:

> I might well be reduced to a smart lass, an adventurer, and a little creature beneath their notice, who was no longer worthy of their care and who had been very bold to presume to wound the heart of a gentleman.

She wonders whether she should become a nun, and her story is now interrupted by the long one of Tervire, a nun in the convent, a melodramatic and bitter tale aimed presumably at proving to Marianne that knowing one's aristocratic parents does not ensure happiness, and that one should not become a nun without being sure of one's vocation.

Marivaux never finished *The Life of Marianne*, and critics have thought of several reasons for the author's loss of interest. He may have been sensitive to contemporary criticism, which alleged that he would never catch up with his heroine's story because it took him ten years, from 1731 to 1741, to account for less than fourteen weeks of her life. He had given one of his characters the honor of stating the moral of his tale: "I am not concerned about your family, for if you were of royal extraction, would it add anything to your personal merit?" Marivaux may have lost interest in Marianne as he was working at the same time on *The Fortunate Peasant*.

More significant is that Marianne had painted herself into a corner. If she allows Valville to marry someone else, the world will know he has found someone better than she, an unbearable thought for someone who considers that the quality of her virtue places her above all around her. There is no doubt in her mind that she can recapture Valville's love, but she does not want anybody to think she lowered herself to compete with Mademoiselle Varthon, morally so inferior to her. She would also have to fight off all the ladies in distress that her flighty husband might find on his path. Marrying the old officer, who does not care about her unknown ancestors, or becoming a nun will show the world that Valville broke her heart. All that Marivaux lets the reader know about his heroine is that she eventually becomes a countess.

From traditional novels with their lost princesses in search of parents, *The Life of Marianne* draws its love story characterized by obstacles impossible to overcome. It is in the memoir form, as old Marianne, now a countess, reconstructs her life for the benefit of a close friend, by means of a long letter, which makes this novel one of the many eighteenth century epistolary novels. At the same time, *The Life of Marianne* is a new type of novel in its point of view. With a recall of some thirty-five years, the now worldly-wise and experienced Marianne explains and rationalizes her past actions, words, and intimate thoughts as she sets out to prove that she is the kind of person she thinks she is. "She consults the aristocratic principle within herself," writes Peter Brooks, "and brings to light the kind of behavior it dictates to her." Her story is a series of interior recognition scenes in which Marianne discovers in herself aristocratic origins. She feels at home when in high society, while she records her instinctive repugnance for the laundress and her shop.

Marivaux describes his novel as a "tissue of events which have given [Marianne] a certain knowledge of the human heart and character." Jean Rousset uses the term "structure of the double register" to explain Marivaux's innovation, Marianne being, at the same time, the one who lives her adventures and the one who tells them, inheriting the double roles of heroine and narrator, which until then were distributed between separate persons. The two registers remain distinct and disjointed; the older Marianne who narrates is not the young Marianne living her isolation and her love; she looks at her from afar; she has for young Marianne the feeling of an author who knows the fate of the character whose life he is writing and who is at the same time somewhat of a stranger. The structure of the double register, as Brooks explains it, "permits a complex play between the tone of experience and that of freshness, the worldly and the spontaneous, the lucid and the indefinite, what Marianne will become and what she is" at fifteen.

Beyond her introspection lies Marianne's acute ability to perceive what others think of her and to act in a manner that always puts her at her best, imposing on all the image that she has of herself, but using different "masks" for the different kinds of persons she sets out to impress. The church episode in which she first sees Valville is one of many examples. She knows she is beautiful because of the way the other young ladies look at her; they show their feelings of spite and jealousy all the more when they try to conceal them. The way Marianne is looked at provides her with an identity. After having lost sight of Valville and walking home, Marianne does not feel the necessity of acting and puts down her mask: "My thoughts were no longer full of myself, and I did not even wish to be agreeable: indifferent to all but him, I neglected my charms, and took no care to display them to the best advantage."

One of the worst things that can happen is being unmasked by the enemy. While visiting Madame de Fare and wearing her mask of the young lady from a good background, Marianne runs into the laundress. Marianne tries to avoid exposure to Madame de Fare by pretending to be sick, but "every impression of those emotions with which I had been agitated remained still on my countenance; there might be seen there an air of grief and consternation which I could not remove." Everyone in Marivaux's novels is so aware of the necessity of wearing a mask that Marianne is encouraged to do so by one of her benefactors. In order to discourage Valville's assiduities at first, she must feign indifference and "persuade him, even with the appearance of regret, that he will love her in vain and that she is not in a condition to return his affection." When Madame de Miran accepts Marianne as a daughter-in-law, she knows she will have to wear a mask. "If my son marries you and the world can be convinced it was against my consent . . . I shall not fail to appear angry; but at last I shall be reconciled and forgive all."

Mask-wearing may be considered an instinctive

means of survival in a hostile society, but it does not exclude a certain dose of hypocrisy, and the title *The Virtuous Orphan* does not give a true picture of Marianne. Practically every move she makes is the result of calculation. When she has an extreme desire to see Valville, she says "I restrained myself; I refused to go to him, because if Mme de Miran should know it, it would add to her esteem. Thus my refusal was only a laudable piece of artifice." The winner of this human comedy is the one who unmasks others without allowing himself to be unmasked.

The Fortunate Peasant

Written at the same time as the second and third parts of *The Life of Marianne*, Marivaux's *The Fortunate Peasant* has much in common with that novel in themes as well as in techniques. The memoir form again allows a fifty-year-old narrator to establish a distance between himself and Jacob the protagonist. Even as Marianne refuses Monsieur de Climal's offer to set her up in a room and is rewarded by meeting Madame de Miran, so Jacob refuses to marry his master's girlfriend and is rewarded by meeting Mademoiselle Habert. Both Marianne and Jacob succeed in their endeavors with the help of their physical attractiveness. Their reasons for choosing the moral path do not stem so much from rigid codes of ethics as from pride; they feel that they deserve something better. Jacob has no need to settle with his master's servant when he is sure of being able to seduce his master's wife.

After working on the novel for two years, Marivaux left it unfinished, with the implication that Jacob would be successful in his quest for money and respectability. Unlike Marianne, Jacob knows that his father is a simple farmer, but he is handsome, intelligent, and adaptable. After some three months of apprenticeship in Paris, he has the good fortune of coming to the rescue of Mademoiselle Habert, a well-preserved "spinster" of about fifty years of age who gives up for him a life devoted to her sister as well as to piety and obedience to a confessor. As well-intentioned relatives had tried to prevent Marianne from marrying Valville, so Jacob has to plead his case to show he is worthy of Mademoiselle Habert. Where Marianne wins by proving the nobility of her soul, Jacob claims he is the social equal of the Habert sisters by bringing them down to his level, because their grandparents were also farmers; from this point of view, Jacob can well be considered the male counterpart of Marianne.

Reflections and examples of mask-wearing abound. Jacob uses two different modes of expression, switching at will the mask of the somewhat sophisticated Parisian for that of the naïve peasant. He says that he always guards his language when he is in the company of men, while he purposely uses provincial expressions with the women, who think of them as cute. Sometimes the mask sticks, and Jacob not only dupes others but also dupes himself: "I acted my part so well," he says when Mademoiselle Habert asks him if he does not exaggerate his attachment for her, "that I deceived myself." The narrator, in this instance, tries to excuse the young protagonist, who uses his masks with such expertise that, flirting at dinner simultaneously with three women, he gives each one the impression that he sees only her. This apparently innocent game, with his soon-to-be wife, the landlady, and her daughter, prepares Jacob for bigger catches. His affairs with Madame de Ferval and Madame de Fecour flatter his ego and give him confidence in his abilities; he admits to not loving them but to loving their rank, so much above his.

Jacob the peasant acquires from his devoted wife the title of Monsieur de la Vallée, with the clothes and sword to complete the picture of a gentleman: Clothes make the man in Marivaux's novels. Without her pretty dress and hat, Marianne would not have been noticed by Valville. Wearing nice clothes is another form of mask-wearing. Jacob, who describes himself as a handsome lad, adds: "What's a handsome lad in an ordinary dress? Why, he is buried alive, such dupes are our eyes in that respect."

Jacob loses all countenance when his mask is torn off by one of those coincidences that is reminiscent of Marianne being recognized by the laundress. Having joined Madame de Ferval for an intimate rendezvous in a house in Versailles, Jacob is interrupted by the intrusion of a chevalier who thinks his own mistress is entertaining another man. The chevalier knew Jacob when he was a servant, and suddenly the hero feels no longer like Monsieur de la Vallée, a gentleman worthy of having a liaison with an important lady; he returns instantly to the status of the bowing and scraping servant, unable to utter a sound. The novel ends with another unmasking experience: Invited by a count to go to the Comédie-Française, the elegance he finds there overwhelms the poor Jacob, who again bows each time he is addressed by one of the count's friends.

Marivaux is now recognized as a pioneer of the novel, even though never completely freed of the romanesque of the preceding century. He made use of the well-worn schemes of the memoir and of the epistolary novel and even of the device of the manuscript-found-in-the-attic, as in *The Life of Marianne*. His originality is evidenced in an imaginative though convoluted style that is appropriate to the motifs of nearness and distance developed in his fiction, permitting the author to enter into the action as both observer and participant. Marivaux does not reduce the novel to purely psychological analysis, although he is an adept analyst of the heart with all its caprices of feeling and motive. The sensitivities of his protagonists, the subtle retrospective expositions of thoughts and actions experienced long ago but still acutely felt and delineated, give Marivaux the right to insist on his singularity. The subtlety, tonality, and coloring that he gives to his writing allow the reader to understand the total complex of the characters in his novels and plays. His adroit and light style diffuses the fictive picture into charming vignettes and vistas. The smile of pleasure evoked in the reader is as well a smile of rueful understanding.

Marivaux was aware of the newness of his enterprise and made a personal cult of its originality. His most appreciated novels, those placed among the best examples of French fiction, are his unfinished ones. They stand apart and defy the definition of their genre.

Marie-France Hilgar

Other major works

SHORT FICTION: *Le Bilbouquet*, 1714.

PLAYS: *Le Père prudent et équitable: Ou, Crispin l'heureux fourbe*, pr. c. 1709; *Arlequin poli par l'amour*, pr. 1720 (*Robin, Bachelor of Love*, 1968); *La Surprise de l'amour*, pr. 1722 (*The Agreeable Surprise*, 1766); *La Double Inconstance*, pr. 1723 (*Double Infidelity*, 1968); *Le Prince travesti: Ou, L'Illustre aventurier*, pr. 1724; *L'Île des esclaves*, pr., pb. 1725 (*Slave Island*, 1988); *Le Triomphe de Plutus*, pr. 1728 (*Money Makes the World Go Round*, 1968); *Le Jeu de l'amour et du hasard*, pr., pb. 1730 (*The Game of Love and Chance*, 1907); *L'École des mères*, pr., pb. 1732; *L'Heureux stratagème*, pr., pb. 1733 (*The Wiles of Love*, 1968); *Les Fausses Confidences*, pr. 1737 (*The False Confessions*, 1961); *L'Épreuve*, pr., pb. 1740 (*The Test*, 1924); *La Femme fidèle*, pb. 1746; *Théâtre complet*, 1878 (revised 2000); *Théâtre de Marivaux*, 1929-1930; *Seven Comedies*, 1968.

POETRY: *Homère travesti: Ou, L'Iliade en vers burlesques*, 1716.

NONFICTION: *Pensées sur la clarté du discours*, 1719; *Le Spectateur français*, 1721-1724 (25 issues); *L'Indigent Philosophe*, 1727 (7 issues); *Le Cabinet du philosophe*, 1734 (11 issues); *Réflexions*, 1744-1755; *L'Éducation d'un prince*, 1754; *Le Miroir*, 1755 (essay); *Journaux et œuvres diverses*, 1969; *Œuvres de jeunesse*, 1972.

Bibliography

Badir, Magdy Gabriel, and Vivien Elizabeth Bosley, eds. *Le Triomphe de Marivaux: A Colloquium Commemorating the Tricentenary of the Birth of Marivaux, 1688-1988*. Edmonton: Department of Romance Languages, University of Alberta, 1989. A collection of papers on Marivaux, covering his life and work. Includes a bibliography.

Brady, Patrick. "Chaos, Complexity, Catastrophe, and Control in Marivaux's *La Vie de Marianne*." In *Disrupted Patterns: On Chaos and Order in the Enlightenment*, edited by Theodore E. D. Braun and John A. McCarthy. Amsterdam: Rodopi, 2000. This analysis of Marivaux's novel *The Life of Marianne* is included in a collection of essays that interpret European Enlightenment texts from the perspective of modern chaos theory. Useful for advanced students.

Culpin, D. J. *Marivaux and Reason: A Study in Early Enlightenment Thought*. New York: Peter Lang, 1993. Culpin examines Marivaux's ideas, his place in the Enlightenment, and his place in the history of philosophy. Includes discussions of Marivaux's thinking about metaphysics, morality, religion, and politics. Contains a bibliography and an index.

Foster, James R. "Sentiment from Aphra Behn to Marivaux." In *The Eighteenth Century English Novel*, edited by Harold Bloom. Philadelphia: Chelsea House, 2004. Although this book mainly covers the English novel, it includes this essay by Foster, in which he discusses Marivaux's work within the context of the eighteenth century sentimental novel.

Jamieson, Ruth Kirby. *Marivaux: A Study in Sensibility*. 1941. Reprint. New York: Octagon Books, 1969. Jamieson approaches Marivaux's career from the point of view of artistic and linguistic merit.

Lynch, Lawrence W. *Eighteenth Century French Novelists and the Novel*. York, S.C.: French Literature, 1979. Lynch's general study contains insightful commentary on the stylistic unity of Marivaux's novels. Includes a bibliography.

Mander, Jenny. *Circles of Learning: Narratology and the Eighteenth Century French Novel*. Oxford, England: Voltaire Foundation, 1999. Mander's study of narration and autobiography in the eighteenth century French novel focuses on works by Marivaux and the Abbé Prévost. Includes bibliographical references and an index.

Mylne, Vivienne. *The Eighteenth Century French Novel: Techniques of Illusion*. 2d ed. New York: Cambridge University Press, 1981. Mylne's study focuses on illusion as a literary device and comments on its use by Marivaux and other novelists. Includes a bibliography.

Russo, Elena. In *Styles of Enlightenment: Taste, Politics, and Authorship in Eighteenth-Century France*. Baltimore: Johns Hopkins University Press, 2007. Russo analyzes works by Marivaux and others to prove that while French Enlightenment writers and philosophers espoused theories of democracy, they also established strict and elitist standards of literary style and artistic expression.

JOHN P. MARQUAND

Born: Wilmington, Delaware; November 10, 1893
Died: Newburyport, Massachusetts; July 16, 1960
Also known as: John Phillips Marquand

Principal long fiction

The Unspeakable Gentleman, 1922
The Black Cargo, 1925
Warning Hill, 1930
Ming Yellow, 1935
No Hero, 1935
Thank You, Mr. Moto, 1936
The Late George Apley: A Novel in the Form of a Memoir, 1937
Think Fast, Mr. Moto, 1937
Mr. Moto Is So Sorry, 1938
Wickford Point, 1939
Don't Ask Questions, 1941
H. M. Pulham, Esquire, 1941
Last Laugh, Mr. Moto, 1942
So Little Time, 1943
Repent in Haste, 1945
B. F.'s Daughter, 1946
It's Loaded, Mr. Bauer, 1949
Point of No Return, 1949
Melville Goodwin, U.S.A., 1951
Sincerely, Willis Wayde, 1955
North of Grand Central, 1956 (includes *The Late George Apley*, *Wickford Point*, and *H. M. Pulham, Esquire*)
Stopover: Tokyo, 1957
Women and Thomas Harrow, 1958

Other literary forms

John P. Marquand (mahr-KWAHND) was a prolific writer of short stories, especially for such mass-circulation magazines as the *Ladies' Home Journal*, *Collier's*, *Sports Illustrated*, and *The Saturday Evening Post*, as well as novels, many of which were serialized in these same magazines before book publication. Two of the serials, *3-3-8* (1937) for *The Saturday Evening Post* and *Castle Sinister* (1938) for *Collier's*, never did appear between covers. Marquand reprinted some of his short stories in *Four of a Kind* (1923), *Haven's End* (1933), and *Life at Happy Knoll* (1957). In addition, he published in 1954 a collection of sketches, travel pieces, lectures, and short stories, *Thirty Years*.

Several of Marquand's novels were dramatized; the most successful dramatization of his work was *The Late George Apley: A Play* (pr. 1944), the result of a collaboration between Marquand and George S. Kaufman. Marquand's one foray into biography, *Lord Timothy Dexter of Newburyport, Mass.*, was originally published in 1925 and reissued and much revised in 1960 as *Timothy Dexter Revisited*. Finally, there is *Prince and Boatswain: Sea Tales from the Recollection of Rear-Admiral Charles E. Clark* (1915), a volume of nonfiction Marquand compiled with James Morris Morgan while in the U.S. Navy.

Several of Marquand's novels were scripted for Hollywood films, and the Moto books inspired an entire series, starring Peter Lorre, patterned on the popular Charlie Chan mysteries. Unlike other novelists who were lured to the West Coast, Marquand worked on only a few of the scripts. Marquand also occasionally wrote for magazines such as *Harper's*, *The Atlantic*, and *Saturday Review of Literature*, contributing fiction and essays.

Achievements

John P. Marquand is known primarily as a writer of slick magazine fiction and long popular novels dealing with upper-middle-class life. His reputation as a magazine writer, not only of short stories but also of longer, serialized fiction, rests on his association with middlebrow magazines that have come to represent the mainstream in American culture. It is all too often forgotten that Ernest Hemingway, F. Scott Fitzgerald, and William Faulkner, to name only a select few, also wrote for such mass-circulation periodicals. Although Marquand's prominence as a writer of serious fiction dates from the publication of *The Late George Apley*, the popularity of the Mr. Moto books, *No Hero* and *Thank You, Mr. Moto*, had already established him with a wide audience. In spite of a sizable output of additional serious fiction, he has been unable to shake his early reputation as a writer of merely popular novels and short stories.

In spite of his lack of critical standing, however, Marquand's literary achievement was substantial. In 1949, near the beginning of the final phase of his career, he wrote that what he had been trying to do was to write a series of novels that would depict a "segment of America during the last fifty years." Scholars are now realizing how successful Marquand was in capturing that fifty-year segment of American life, and his reputation as a novelist of manners has risen dramatically. He is now considered among the finest social critics of his time, one to compare with Charles Dickens, William Makepeace Thackeray, and Anthony Trollope as an accurate recorder of manners and customs. The nine serious novels that he wrote between 1937 and 1960 have secured for Marquand an important place in contemporary American fiction.

Since his death, Marquand's work has undergone a steady reappraisal. Scholarly monographs and biographies have appeared as well as a flow of articles dealing with his role in American letters. This reexamination has resulted in a growing appreciation of Marquand's novels of manners. C. Hugh Holman and John J. Gross, in two major critical works, have called for a reassessment of Marquand's standing in American literary history, and the final judgment of Marquand's work has yet to be written.

Biography

John Phillips Marquand was born in Wilmington, Delaware, on November 10, 1893. The history of his family reaches back into the precolonial world of the Puritans: he was a descendant on his mother's side of Thomas and Joseph Dudley, early governors of the Massachusetts Bay Colony, and he was a grand-nephew of Margaret Fuller. The Marquands, of Norman-French ancestry, emigrated from the Guernsey islands to New England in 1732, where they settled in Newburyport, north of Boston. Marquand came from a long line of shipbuilders, mariners, and Harvard men. During his early years, he lived in New York City, where his father made a comfortable living as a stockbroker. The family went broke during the Panic of 1907, and young Marquand was sent to live with two aunts and a great-aunt at the family home at Curzon's Mill, Kent's Island, west of Newburyport; his parents moved to the Panama Canal Zone when his father returned to a career in civil engineering.

Although he was unable to attend preparatory school,

because of a lack of funds, Marquand did receive a scholarship to attend Harvard after he completed public high school. He felt keenly the class differences at Harvard and passed rather lonely years there devoting himself to reading and writing. With the exception of working on the *Lampoon*, he did not join any clubs.

After his graduation in 1915, Marquand went to work for the *Boston Evening Transcript* at fifteen dollars per week. During this time, he enlisted in a local battery of the Massachusetts National Guard, which was soon mobilized and sent to El Paso, Texas, for duty on the Mexican border. Originally mustered in as a private, he was sent in April, 1917, to Officers' Training Camp at Plattsburg, New York, where he headed the class of candidates. After receiving his commission in August, Marquand was shipped overseas with the Fourth Army to join the Allied Expeditionary Force in France, where he fought with the 77th Field Artillery at Saint-Michel, at the Vesle River, and in the Argonne. He returned to the United States in November, 1918, and was demobilized as a captain. Marquand returned to journalism when he got a job with the magazine section of *The New York Herald Tribune*; he soon left, however, for a copywriting job in advertising with the J. Walter Thompson Agency.

John P. Marquand and his wife. (Time & Life Pictures/Getty Images)

In 1921, with four hundred dollars saved from his job, Marquand moved back to Curzon's Mill to write a historical romance based on an early nineteenth century gentleman, Henry Shelton. Set in Newburyport, the novel, of little consequence now, was of considerable importance to Marquand. In the novel, he introduced a number of those large themes, such as the New England past and the protagonist as a member of the upper class brought low by changing social and/or economic circumstances, which later provided such strong bonds among his novels. The acceptance of the novel for serialization by the *Ladies' Home Journal* and its subsequent publication as a book by Scribner's launched Marquand as a professional writer. In the same year, he sold stories to George Horace Lorimer of *The Saturday Evening Post* and to Ray Long of *Cosmopolitan*, beginning a long and profitable association with both periodicals.

On the proceeds from his first novel, Marquand traveled to Europe, where he became engaged to Christina Sedgwick, whose uncle was editor of *The Atlantic* and one of the literary arbiters of Boston. The couple was married on September 8, 1922, and moved to an old house on Beacon Hill in Cambridge, where they joined the social set. A son, John, Jr., was born in 1923 and a daughter, Christine, in 1927. Between 1921 and 1931, Marquand published five serials and fifty-nine short stories in the "slicks." As he was to write later, it was a period of apprenticeship during which he learned the craft of writing fiction. His second book, *Four of a Kind*, appeared in 1923. In 1925, Marquand published two books set at least in part in Newburyport. The first, *The Black Cargo*, originally a serial, dealt with the romantic exploits of a Yankee clipper-ship captain and his adventures in the Pacific. The second was a historical biography of an eccentric New Englander, *Lord Timothy Dexter of Newburyport, Mass.*, and proved to be of lasting interest to Marquand; a revised version of it was the last thing he published before his death.

In addition to the historical books, Marquand was also beginning to move toward the themes of his later and more important works. In *Warning Hill*, another serial published as a book in 1930, Marquand introduced a protagonist who because of the financial failure of his father is denied his rightful position in the class structure of a New England town. The setting, attitude, and even the tone of this work are repeated in his later novels. The second of the books of this period was *Haven's End*, which consists of fourteen stories, some of them revised from versions previously published in *The Saturday Evening Post*. These tales, which range in period from the seventeenth to the twentieth centuries, deal with the rising new fortunes of the Scarlet family poised against the decline of the Swales, who built the town in which they are set. Apparent in these stories is Marquand's growing interest in the processes of social change.

For a variety of reasons both personal and professional, Marquand left for China in 1934, where he remained for nearly a year. As a result of his travels, Marquand wrote a serial, *Ming Yellow*, in which he combined local color with the usual materials of a novel of manners, and introduced his readers into the Asian world that would provide the background for perhaps Marquand's most famous creation, Mr. Moto. While on his tour, he was divorced by Christina. He met Adelaide Hooker, a wealthy woman related by marriage to the Rockefellers, who was on tour with her mother; they later married, in 1937. Marquand followed up the success of the first of his Asian books with *No Hero*, which had been serialized in *The Saturday Evening Post* the spring following *Ming Yellow*. "Mr. Moto Takes a Hand" introduced the Japanese intelligence agent who was to figure in five additional adventure stories. The Moto novels were to prove extremely popular, and the serials and short stories generated a sizable income for Marquand and may have been partly responsible for the gamble in more serious fiction that he took when he published *The Late George Apley* in 1937.

Marquand began the novel in 1934 but did not complete it until 1936. It was a breakthrough period for him, in which he not only published a portion of *The Late George Apley* but also serialized two of the Moto books and published five short stories. *The Late George Apley* won the Pulitzer Prize for 1938 and also won unprecedented praise for Marquand's work from the critics. Although the writing of *The Late George Apley* marked a turning point in his career and would ultimately move him away from slick fiction, Marquand continued to write serials during the late 1930's. In 1937, *3-3-8* appeared in *The Saturday Evening Post*, the same journal that ran *Mr. Moto Is So Sorry* in 1938. *Castle Sinister* came out in *Collier's* in the same year. A version of *Wickford Point* was serialized in *The Saturday Evening Post* in 1939, as was the adventure tale, *Don't Ask Questions*. *Wickford Point*, which also appeared as a book in 1939, forms a trilogy with *H. M. Pulham, Esquire*, which was published in 1941, and *The Late George Apley*. All three novels are connected insofar as they provide Marquand's contrasting views of Boston.

In 1940, Marquand's second daughter, Blanch Ferry, was born. Timothy Fuller, his second son, was born in 1942. A third son, Elon Huntington Hooker, was born in 1943. Marquand joined Army intelligence and traveled extensively in the Pacific war zones during 1941. In 1942, he went to Hollywood to work on the film version of *H. M. Pulham, Esquire*, directed by King Vidor. In addition, he collaborated with Kaufman on a stage adaptation of *The Late George Apley*, which enjoyed a successful run for a year in 1946. In 1944, he accepted a position on the board of editors of the Book-of-the-Month Club. Marquand became a special adviser to the U.S. secretary of war and spent the bulk of 1944 and 1945 in Washington D.C. Finally, he traveled for a portion of 1945 as a war correspondent in the Pacific.

Marquand did not give up his writing during the war years. He rounded out his adventure stories with a rather average thriller, *It's Loaded, Mr. Bauer*, which ran as a serial in *Collier's* but never appeared as a book in the United States. The war years also produced another of Marquand's trilogies. Using his extensive traveling around the United States during the war, Marquand wrote three novels concerning the home-side reaction to the global conflict and the accelerated social change brought on by the war. *So Little Time* is set in Hollywood and deals with a playwright who is trying to write a successful drama and to come to grips with his fleeting life. *Repent in Haste* is about Navy fliers in the Pacific, and *B. F.'s Daughter* is a Washington, D.C., novel concerned with an industrialist and his daughter in an almost painful re-creation of wartime society. The novel points the way to the series of brilliant portraits of American life Marquand produced following the war.

In 1949, Marquand published *Point of No Return*, generally considered one of his best novels, which he adapted for the stage with Paul Osborne in 1951. With this novel, Marquand inaugurated a tetralogy of books each dealing with a central character set against an organization. *Melville Goodwin, U.S.A.* was the second of this loose series and is centered on Goodwin, a general in the Army, who is subjected to the "opinion molders" that make him into a hero. In 1952, Marquand was profiled in *The New Yorker* by Philip Hamburger. A collection of short fiction and nonfiction, *Thirty Years*, which was published in 1954, contains a summary of his reflections on his craft and provides the only statement of his theory of fiction. Marquand continued his analysis of the organization man in *Sincerely, Willis Wayde*, which contains a generally unsympathetic portrait of a lower-middle-class boy who becomes a successful and unscrupulous businessman. In 1956, *North of Grand Central*, an omnibus volume containing the first three New England books, appeared with notes on each of the novels by Marquand. *Stopover: Tokyo*, the last of the Moto books, was published in 1957, as was a collection of pieces from *Sports Illustrated* dealing with a country club and titled *Life at Happy Knoll*. In 1958, Marquand divorced Adelaide and published his last novel, *Women and Thomas Harrow*, the story of a thrice-married playwright whose success and talent fail to provide him with a happy or fulfilled life.

During the last years of his life, Marquand enjoyed the comfort provided by his considerable income. It has been estimated that he made some ten million dollars during the 1950's. He lived and worked in the family home at Curzon's Mill and made trips to Bermuda and the Bahamas. In 1960, he published his last book, *Timothy Dexter Revisited*, a revised version of the volume he had written thirty-five years earlier. Marquand died in his sleep at his home in Massachusetts on July 16, 1960.

ANALYSIS

Although debate continues over the merits of John P. Marquand's writing, there is little question that collectively, his novels provide a comprehensive and accurate picture of changes in American society from the end of World War I to the beginnings of the 1960's, a *comédie humaine* of modern American life. Marquand was a realist and was largely conservative in style; his accuracy of detail gives his best work an uncanny sense of reality. He was a transitional figure in postwar American letters, and his adherence to the novel of manners, never very central to the American literary experience, dates his fiction. Since his death, his type of realism, with its emphasis on the public scene, has been relegated to the writers of popular fiction.

The world depicted by Marquand's novels seems irretrievably gone. His characters' need for loyalty and decency and courage in everyday life, out of which they constructed standards capable of withstanding the flux of their lives, seems antiquated now. Perhaps even his accurate sense of the havoc wreaked by the rapid social change of his time will eventually lose its impact as the generations for which he wrote pass on. His novels will remain valuable, however, for the understanding with which Marquand portrayed the American male, with "accuracy, compassion, incisive perception, and wry love." As a recent critic of Marquand's work has written, Marquand's American male is "obsessed with the material trivia of his daily needs and confused personal diplomacy that his marriage demands, trying frantically to find something meaningful somewhere to fill the hollowness at the core of his life."

THE LATE GEORGE APLEY

The Late George Apley was the first of Marquand's major novels, has remained his most famous, and is considered by many to be his finest. In it, he set the pattern for the major novels that followed over the next twenty years. Briefly, the point of the book is to show how even though the community of Boston dominates George Apley, it nevertheless provides a comfortable social code within which he finds a measure of security.

The novel itself begins with a "Foreword and Apology" by Horatio Willing, who has been chosen by Apley's son to write a "Life in Letters" study of his father. Marquand's pen was never sharper than in this novel, which parodies the honorific biography. The novel traces Apley's life from youth to old age and death, and is concerned with the individual's place within a society and the possibility of remaining organically connected to a community but not smothered by social conformity. Marquand described the novel as "a savage attack on the old water side of Beacon Street." In spite of the satire, the reader's attitude toward Apley is one of affection. Willing appears smug and the society itself is stifling, but Apley remains a deeply human figure wrestling with himself to accommodate his own desires and dreams with the values of the community to which he feels such loyalty. Although Apley's values are for the most part admirable (for example, the Puritan attitude of responsible stewardship with which he distributes the family money), it becomes increasingly clear that he is a man out of touch with the changing society around him. It is his simple adherence to his values that renders him both a commendable product of his community and heritage and an increasingly embarrassing anachronism within that community.

Wickford Point *and* H. M. Pulham, Esquire

The tenacity of the past, which molds and influences the current generation, provides one of the central themes for Marquand's next two Boston novels as well. If *The Late George Apley* deals with the Boston of the past, *Wickford Point* is concerned with a contemporary, decaying New England family once dimly connected with the tradition of transcendentalism through a minor nature poet. The traditions and values that often rendered Apley merely silly are carried in this novel to grotesqueness. The story, filtered through the consciousness of a popular magazine writer, describes the Brills, an old family once of some prominence, who now are reduced to a quirky eccentricity, and it deals in particular with the narrator's relationship, both past and present, with Bella Brill, Marquand's study of the consummate "bitch." In her, Marquand introduces the first of many "old-money" women who are denied to his middle-class protagonists.

The third of the Boston novels, *H. M. Pulham, Esquire*, records the ineffectual efforts of Pulham, a businessman of post-World War I Boston, to rebel against the customs and background of his youth. This is a novel, as one critic described it, of "inexorable time, of mutability, of the flood of the largely wasted years" that make up the lives of so many of Marquand's central characters. In spite of Pulham's insistence that he did the right thing by not marrying the "wrong" girl or digging up his cultural roots and moving to New York, the reader understands, as is so often true in Marquand's books, the depth of the emptiness of Pulham's life. It is a portrait done with understanding, however, for in spite of his social obtuseness, Pulham remains a sympathetic character, one who retains a sense of decency and tenacity in the face of a shifting social order.

These three books, later issued in a single volume titled *North of Grand Central*, were a critical as well as popular success; two of the novels were made into movies and one became a long-running play, and they did much to dispel Marquand's standing as a writer of slick magazine fiction. The trilogy also did much to label Marquand as a New England writer, a tag that annoyed him almost as much as the earlier designation as simply a writer of popular fiction. His next series of novels was set in a variety of American locations, in part in an attempt to dislodge the notion that he had become "merely" a writer of satiric regional books.

So Little Time, Repent in Haste, *and* B. F.'s Daughter

The three Marquand novels to come out of World War II exhibit the variety of activities that occupied him during these years. *So Little Time* is set in the worlds of the theater and of Hollywood and focuses on a playwright, Jeff Wilson, who must grapple with his failure as a writer, a father, and a husband. The war provides the necessary pressure to motivate him to rethink his life. Ranging from Wilson's recollections of the small New England town of his boyhood, to his experiences as an American aviator in World War I, his various jobs as a newspaperman, play "doctor," and scriptwriter, and the story of his married life, the novel offers a panorama of American life between the wars.

The second of Marquand's war novels, *Repent in Haste*, originally serialized in *Harper's Magazine*, is a short work about Navy fliers in the Pacific. The theme of this novel is the inexorable passing of time and the uncertainty of the future. It is an attempt to portray a generation at war and its search for values amid the flux of the modern world. As in *So Little Time*, there is a tentativeness about the conclusions drawn in this novel that reflects Marquand's growing uncertainty about values that could provide a stay against the chaos that he saw as increasingly characteristic of modern life.

Marquand's last novel of the war period, *B. F.'s Daughter*, was more ambitious stylistically and contains Marquand's only female protagonist, Polly Fulton. The portrait of B. F. Fulton, Polly's father, provides a prologue for Marquand's full-scale exploration of the businessman in *Sincerely, Willis Wayde* and points to the attention he will pay to organizations in the novels of his last period. Although none of the war novels is entirely successful, as a group they do represent a transition between the New England novels of the 1930's, with their search for contemporary values in the past, and the nihilistic tone of the books of the 1950's, with their despair and emptiness. Whether the relative failure of these novels was caused by a lack of perspective, as some critics have argued, or merely a lack of commitment on Marquand's part, is of minor concern, because these works of fiction provide the background against which were written the last four major novels, books that are considered by some critics to be the best of his career.

POINT OF NO RETURN

Point of No Return was Marquand's first postwar novel, and it captures with all of his old assurance the spirit of the late 1940's. In fact, it is so accurate in its depiction of the postwar world that it provides a more satisfactory study of American society of that period than can be found in such later sociological classics as William H. Whyte's *The Organization Man* (1956) and David Riesman's *The Lonely Crowd* (1969).

Point of No Return, borrowing an aviator's term from the war for its title, deals with Charles Gray, once a native of New England and now a banker who lives in New York City, as he sifts through his memories while waiting to learn whether he is to be promoted to the vice presidency of his bank. It is the comprehensive sweep of the book, Marquand's broadest, and the thoroughness of the depiction of Gray's small hometown in Maine that give the book its sociological accuracy. Once again, Marquand's protagonist must wrestle with the humiliation of his past social failure and the emptiness of his present financial success. Security seems as illusory as the past, and in Marquand's fictional world, where there are no second chances, Nancy and Charles Gray can only wonder at their lack of triumph in the promotion that comes at last. There is no "out-of-breath feeling" in success, only a continuation of the anxiety that propelled the effort in the first place.

MELVILLE GOODWIN, U.S.A.

Although Marquand wrote about military types in some of his wartime pieces, *Melville Goodwin, U.S.A.* is his only full-length book about the Army. Written at the height of the Cold War, it is a satiric look at the power of mass communications to elevate a rather ordinary professional soldier to the role of a demigod. Both the military and the world of journalism are treated ironically in this novel, which has been proclaimed as Marquand's greatest stylistic triumph. The complexity of the work opened it up to misinterpretation, and the satiric point of the book eluded many readers. It is instructive that Marquand writes about a man who is bound by the traditions and social rigidity of the military in order to explore a civilian world that he characterizes as irresponsible, self-indulgent, and morally adrift. Although the military always provides General Goodwin with a code of behavior, if nothing else, even he wonders what it would be like to share in the postwar world of which he is nor really a part. It is remarkable that Sid Skelton, the journalist, and Goodwin can live in such different worlds yet be nevertheless capable of coexisting in something approaching harmony, and that Marquand can capture both the differences and the harmony with a measure of sympathetic understanding for each.

SINCERELY, WILLIS WAYDE

Marquand's next novel, *Sincerely, Willis Wayde*, was a thoroughgoing "business novel," written in the mid-1950's when such novels were in vogue. Marquand's special gift for close social observation, however, elevates Willis Wayde far above the other "organization man" ventures of the period. This study of the struggles of a lower-middle-class boy to achieve financial success is harsh and unsympathetic. Marquand anatomizes the process by which Wayde, the son of an independent-minded factory worker, becomes, in the words of his father, "a son-of-a-bitch." The conflict, by now a familiar one in Marquand's fictional world, is between old and new money, with the successful protagonist denied the social acceptance he needs to marry the right girl. In this novel, however, the business competence of Willis

Wayde allows him to usurp the power of the old-money Harcourt family.

Although he still pays lip service to their values of loyalty, family, and place, Wayde is easily capable of circumventing them in favor of a new set of ethics based on the business world, where everything is relative. The old Harcourts, incapacitated by their leisure, must rely for their very survival on a quintessential organization man, a representative of the modern business community who is responsible for destroying their world. There is a further irony in that while Wayde is betraying the old values of his past and the way of life most associated with those values, he is unaware of what he is doing. He simply feels that he is streamlining the old to fit in with the new. By the time of the writing of his last novels, Marquand could only look backward in his search for an explanation of the modern world; it was only in retrospect that he could find meaning.

Women and Thomas Harrow

Women and Thomas Harrow is Marquand's exit work from the world of letters. The novel was not only Marquand's last novel but also was a dark summary work, full of pessimism and regret. It is the story of Thomas Harrow, a successful playwright, and his three marriages. Harrow, fundamentally a decent man, finds himself at odds with the modern world, a world that through no fault or action of his own has become alien to him. No longer can Marquand's protagonist retrieve even the vestiges of a value-system from within the community; values are all past and unreachable. Harrow becomes the repository of all the doubts that plague contemporary humans, who acknowledge the inaccessibility of the past and realize that there is no buttress against the vulgarity of the present. Like many of Marquand's protagonists, Harrow discovers that success and money are ultimately not enough. In the absence of a meaningful relationship with place or community, there is no safe haven in contemporary society. What Harrow discovers about life might well be applied to the other central characters of Marquand's fiction: "There was no safety in living, and in the end, about all you got out of life was learning how to face truth without side-stepping to avoid it."

Marquand once wrote that the aspect that interested him most in the phenomena of human nature was the individual caught in a pattern of social change. The principal characters in his novels are caught in a world undergoing rapid alteration: moral securities erode before them, the social order collapses, moral commitments pale, religious sureties evaporate. Perhaps, as one critic has suggested, modern society can best be portrayed by examining what it stifles in able, good, but weak people. Marquand's protagonists become standards for measuring society, and, lacking direction, they search the past for a meaningful order, for standards of value against which to judge the highly relativistic American culture of the present. Marquand as a novelist provided his readers with an incisive examination of the modern world, exposing the hollowness of contemporary life, and dramatizing the spiritual search prompted by the recognition of that emptiness. Hugh Holman has summed up Marquand's place in contemporary American literature as follows: "To our age, at least, he speaks with ease and skill, with irony and wit, but above all with the authority of unsentimental knowledge."

Charles L. P. Silet

Other major works

PLAY: *The Late George Apley: A Play*, pr. 1944 (with George S. Kaufman).

SHORT FICTION: *Four of a Kind*, 1923; *Haven's End*, 1933; *Life at Happy Knoll*, 1957.

NONFICTION: *Prince and Boatswain: Sea Tales from the Recollection of Rear-Admiral Charles E. Clark*, 1915 (with James Morris Morgan); *Lord Timothy Dexter of Newburyport, Mass.*, 1925 (revised as *Timothy Dexter Revisited*, 1960); *Thirty Years*, 1954.

Bibliography

Auchincloss, Louis "John P. Marquand." In *Writers and Personality*. Columbia, S.C.: University of South Carolina Press, 2005. Novelist Auchincloss includes a chapter about Marquand in this examination of how writers' temperaments, interests, and other personality traits are reflected in their fiction.

Bell, Millicent. *J. P. Marquand: An American Life*. Boston: Little, Brown, 1979. A comprehensive account of Marquand's life, with a biographical rather than a critical emphasis. In the prologue, Bell describes Marquand's work as belonging to "the novel of manners" genre and compares him to William Dean Howells, Edith Wharton, Sinclair Lewis, John Updike, and John O'Hara, among others.

Birmingham, Stephen. *The Late John Marquand: A Biography*. Philadelphia: J. B. Lippincott, 1972. A sympathetic biography of Marquand by a writer who had frequent contact with him. Includes personal background about Marquand's life and some review of his writing.

Gross, John J. *John P. Marquand*. New York: Twayne, 1963. This full-length study examines Marquand's success in his day and gives critical acknowledgment of his expertise as a social novelist. Gross discusses the action in his later novels, written in the last twenty-five years of his life. Includes a useful but dated bibliography.

Gura, Philip P., and Joel Myerson. *Critical Essays on American Transcendentalism*. Boston: G. K. Hall, 1982. Briefly mentions Marquand and the hero of his novel *H. M. Pulham, Esquire*. Gura and Myerson consider this character as one exemplifying the genteel tradition of American humanism, a tradition that becomes reactionary only when it is divorced from renewal and change.

Hamburger, Philip. *J. P. Marquand, Esquire: A Portrait in the Form of a Novel*. Boston: Houghton Mifflin, 1952. An unusual approach in which Hamburger unfolds aspects of Marquand's life in the form of a novel. Contains little critical reference to his writings.

Hoffman, Daniel, ed. *Harvard Guide to Contemporary Writing*. Cambridge, Mass.: Harvard University Press, 1979. Discusses Marquand in the context of novelists of manners. Hoffman provides commentary on his novels, which is appreciative, but he also faults Marquand for becoming an emblem of the "trap of popular success."

Teachout, Terry. "Justice to John P. Marquand." *Commentary* 84, no. 4 (October, 1987): 54-59. A reassessment of Marquand's literary legacy more than twenty years after his death, in which Teachout explains why Marquand has been overlooked by critics and academics.

Whipple, Robert D., Jr., ed. *Essays on the Literature of American Novelist John P. Marquand, 1893-1960*. Lewiston, N.Y.: Edwin Mellen Press, 2004. This collection, intended for a general academic audience, includes essays on Marquand and success, the role of women in his fiction, his Mr. Moto series, and analyses of *The Late George Apley* and *H. M. Pulham, Esquire*.

PAULE MARSHALL

Born: Brooklyn, New York; April 9, 1929
Also known as: Valenza Pauline Burke

Principal long fiction

Brown Girl, Brownstones, 1959
The Chosen Place, the Timeless People, 1969
Praisesong for the Widow, 1983
Daughters, 1991
The Fisher King, 2000

Other literary forms

In addition to her novels and the four novellas contained in *Soul Clap Hands and Sing* (1961), Paule Marshall has written a number of short stories, the most important of which are "Reena," "To Da-Duh, in Memoriam," and "Some Get Wasted." In "To Da-Duh, in Memoriam," a young girl growing up in Brooklyn discovers her Barbadian roots on her first trip to Barbados. Her struggle to integrate the two sides of her heritage is a theme that Marshall develops more fully in her first novel, *Brown Girl, Brownstones*. In "Reena," the middle-aged, middle-class woman who shares her experiences with a friend at the wake of her aunt seems the woman that Selina of *Brown Girl, Brownstones* might have become. Each of these stories reveals a stage in Marshall's development of character analysis and theme. The major theme that runs through all Marshall's novels is the search for identity—the idea that individuals cannot really know who they are until they know who they *were*, and that it is only as they become connected with their ancestral heritage that they are able to become whole and complete human beings. In her short stories, the author also introduces some of the minor themes—marriage and family relationships, interracial relationships, and political issues—developed in her novels.

Paule Marshall. (Courtesy, Augusta State University)

Achievements

Only in the 1990's did Paule Marshall's work begin to receive the critical attention it deserves. While most of her novels have received high praise when they were first published, they have not always been commercially successful. Marshall nevertheless has received the Guggenheim Fellowship (1960), the Rosenthal Foundation Award (1962), a Ford Foundation Grant for poets and fiction writers (1964-1965), and a National Endowment for the Arts Fellowship (1984). She has also received the Langston Hughes Medallion Award (1986), the New York State Governor's Award for Literature (1987), the John Dos Passos Award for Literature (1989), and the John D. and Catherine T. MacArthur Fellowship (1992). In 2001, she was awarded the Black Caucus of the American Library Association Award for Fiction.

Marshall's major contribution to the novel is her deep understanding of the human psyche, which allows her to create characters that are movingly sympathetic. She gives careful attention to female characters—especially the black female, whom she feels has been long neglected in literature. She destroys stereotypes, creating black women who are neither "sensual, primitive, pleasure-seeking, or immoral, nor sinner, siren or matriarch (strong, humble, devoutly religious and patient)." Her women are complex, with deep reservoirs of strength that can be called upon when needed.

Biography

Paule Marshall was born Valenza Pauline Burke in Brooklyn, New York, to Samuel Burke and Ada Clement Burke, who migrated to New York from Barbados shortly after World War I and joined the growing community of West Indian immigrants in Brooklyn. Her parents brought with them to the United States the strong sense of pride and tradition that was an integral part of West Indian culture, and she was nourished by a community of people who revered their West Indian heritage even as they embraced the advantages that their new country afforded them. Her parents returned often to their homeland of Barbados, taking their small daughter with them. Thus, from her earliest years, Marshall began to develop an understanding of the two worlds to which she belonged and to appreciate the differences between those worlds—a fact that is immediately recognizable in her fiction.

Marshall attended Brooklyn College, where she received a bachelor's degree in 1953, graduating magna cum laude and Phi Beta Kappa. She subsequently went to work as a researcher and later as a feature writer for *Our World* magazine. In 1955, she enrolled as a graduate student at Hunter College (City University of New York) but continued to write for *Our World*, where her assignments carried her to Brazil and the West Indies. In 1957, she married Kenneth Marshall, with whom she had one son, Evan Keith. Her trips to the Caribbean islands were rewarding in that they provided her an opportunity to return to the land of her ancestors. While there, she immersed herself in the culture, absorbing the nuances of language, customs, and traditions that were to figure so prominently in her novels.

In 1959, Marshall published her first novel, *Brown Girl, Brownstones*, and in 1960 she received a Guggenheim Fellowship, which allowed her to complete the collection of novellas *Soul Clap Hands and Sing*. More than eight years passed, however, before the publication of her second novel. In that interim, she worked for *New World*, a Caribbean magazine, produced several short stories, and continued work on her novel. So committed was she to her craft that she would often hire a babysitter to watch her son (over her husband's objections) and go to the home of a friend in order to continue her writing. She divorced Kenneth Marshall in 1963, and in 1970 she married for the second time, to a Haitian businessman—a man with whom she has said she had an "open and innovative marriage," one that gave her the time and freedom to pursue her work.

Marshall has combined a writing career with teaching. Among other positions, she has held a professorship at Virginia Commonwealth University and was for some years the Helen Gould Sheppard Chair of Literature and Culture in the Creative Writing Program at New York University.

Analysis

Being of both African American and Caribbean ancestry helped to shape Paule Marshall as a woman and as a writer. She first visited Barbados as a nine-year-old child. When she visited the island as a young woman just starting out on a writing career, she began to develop a deeper appreciation for the West Indian culture—its rituals, its customs, its people and language—and a greater sense of pride in her West Indian heritage. She was most impressed with the strength and character she observed in West Indian women, qualities she saw reflected in the women of the Brooklyn community where she had grown up.

The lives of these women, whom Marshall has called her "literary foremothers," were to become the major focus of her novels. They were primarily domestic workers who would sit around her mother's kitchen table in the evenings after a hard day's labor, talking endlessly about everything from the white women for whom they worked to politics to their own husbands and families. Because of their creative use of language, Marshall considered these women poets, though they had never written a line. They had their special cadences and rhythms, they played with syntax, and they introduced certain Africanisms into their speech and sprinkled it with a generous smattering of French Creole expressions, biblical quotations, and colorful proverbs.

Their use of language and their storytelling skills influenced Marshall's style, and their strength and deep sense of pride are the essential qualities of the female characters she creates. The protagonists of Marshall's novels are almost always women and are the products of dual cultures. In her characterization of these women, Marshall explores the ways in which their psyches are affected by their cultural heritages and by the societies in which they live. She also focuses on the difficulties that they encounter in trying to integrate their two worlds.

Brown Girl, Brownstones

In *Brown Girl, Brownstones*, Marshall begins to develop the self-identity theme through the character of Selina Boyce, a girl moving from childhood into adolescence in Brooklyn and caught between two cultures, the American culture in which she lives and the Barbadian culture of her ancestors, the customs of which are carefully observed in her household. The novel treats the problems that Selina encounters in trying to reconcile these two disparate parts of herself. She is a "divided self," feeling little connection with either the "bajan" community or the larger white community. She rejects her Barbadian heritage and its "differentness" and yearns to be a part of the white community, which rejects her. The sense of isolation that she feels is the source of all her problems.

At the climax of the novel, the "divided self" is integrated as Selina finally accepts her heritage and discovers that with acceptance comes wholeness. She resolves her conflict with her mother, makes peace with the Barbadian Association, and leaves Brooklyn to begin her travels. As she passes through her old neighborhood, she feels psychically connected to all the people who helped create her integrated self. As a final symbolic act, she tosses behind her one of her two Barbadian bangle bracelets and retains the other as a reminder of her link with the past. Selina has finally learned that true selfhood begins with the acceptance of one's own history.

The Chosen Place, the Timeless People

Marshall's second novel, *The Chosen Place, the Timeless People*, is set in the West Indies, specifically Bournehills, a remote part of one of the Caribbean islands. Here, Marshall expands the identity theme, focusing not on the individual self but rather on the collective self of a community of people in search of a common bond. Although Merle Kimbona—a mulatto who has returned to Bournehills after many adventuresome years in Europe to become mistress of a large estate left her by her white father—is the protagonist of the novel and a strong female character, she is really not the central figure of the novel. At the center of the novel are the people of Bournehills, who, having been oppressed first by slavery and then by their own people, search for some common thread of unity. They discover this in Carnival, an annual ritual in which the people reenact the story of Cuffee Ned, who led a slave revolt against the slaveholder Percy Byram.

The plot turns with a visit by a team from an American philanthropic organization sent to Bournehills to provide aid to this underdeveloped country. The team consists of a Jewish American social scientist, Saul Amron; his wife, Harriet; and two returning natives of Bournehills, Allen Fuso and Vere. During their stay on the island, the outsiders interact with the natives, observing their rituals and customs, and contrasting them with their American experience. As guests at the estate of Merle Kimbona, now a political activist, they also become involved in the political affairs of Bournehills.

The contrasts between the two cultures are apparent throughout the novel. The high-tech white society, represented by the machine (in this case the machines in the sugarcane factory), enslaves the people of Bournehills in much the same way they had been enslaved by Percy Byram. Also it is the machine—the American automobile—that takes the life of the Bournehills native Vere.

In the novel, Marshall brings together characters from many backgrounds and classes—black and white; upper, middle, and lower classes; natives and outsiders—in this "chosen place." The ritual reenactment of their history at Carnival is the common thread that binds all classes of people in Bournehills, and it also connects them to their African ancestry and Western culture.

Praisesong for the Widow

In *Praisesong for the Widow*, Marshall continues the theme of self-discovery through her protagonist, Avey Johnson, a middle-aged, middle-class black woman who is on a Caribbean cruise with two of her women friends. Avey is haunted by a recurring dream about a story told to her by her great-aunt, with whom she had spent summers in Tatem, South Carolina, of how the African slaves who landed at Tatem had immediately turned back toward the sea, walking across the water back to their home in Africa.

Deciding to leave the ship before the cruise is over and return home, Avey misses her flight to New York and is stranded in Grenada just at the time of the annual excursion to the island of Carriocou. Here, again, Marshall uses ritual to reveal to Avey the importance of connecting to her African ancestry. In a scene that is almost surreal, she is transported to Carriocou, where this annual ritual is to take place. Reluctant to participate at first, Avey eventually joins in the ritual and discovers the meaning of her recurring dream. The landing of the Ibos in South Carolina and their return to Africa by the mythic walk on water symbolize the link between Africa and all black people of the diaspora. In participating in this ritual, Avey becomes aware that she can achieve wholeness only if she becomes reconnected to her African roots.

Daughters

Like the protagonists of most of Marshall's other novels, the protagonist of *Daughters*, Ursa MacKensie, is a woman caught between two cultures: the African American culture of her mother, Estelle, and the Caribbean culture of her father, Primus. The action of the novel is divided almost equally between New York City, where Ursa lives, and Triunion, the West Indian island where her parents reside and her father is a leading politician, known from his boyhood as the PM (prime minister). Although firmly rooted in the urban culture of New York, where she is pursuing a professional career, Ursa keeps one foot planted in the small Caribbean island through her relationship with her doting father, a relationship strengthened by frequent letters and periodic visits.

In this novel, Marshall again explores the themes of identity and the attempt to bridge the gap between two cultures. The novel addresses the integration of the two cultures on several levels, the first being the marriage of Ursa's parents—her African American mother to her West Indian father. The second is the birth of their daughter, Ursa-Mae, who physically integrates the two cultures. Then, the African American and West Indian cultures are geographically and spiritually linked as Ursa's mother moves to Barbados with her husband and becomes integrated into that community.

Much of the novel is devoted to the workings of Triunion politics and their effects on the Triunion people, the marriage of Primus and Estelle, and Ursa. Its setting and wide array of characters provide Marshall the opportunity to explore the theme of self-discovery from a number of perspectives.

The Fisher King

With *The Fisher King*, Marshall seems to signal a departure from her focus on female characters. Grounded in personal memory as well as in Arthurian legend, *The Fisher King* focuses on Sonny-Rett Payne, a deceased jazz musician who left the United States to live in Paris, and on his eight-year-old namesake grandson, Sonny Payne, born and raised in Paris, who has been brought to the United States by his caretaker, Hattie Carmichael, for a concert to be produced on the occasion of the fiftieth anniversary of his grandfather's death. They arrive to find the long-standing family feud between Sonny's great-grandmothers, one West Indian and the other African American, still in place.

In *The Fisher King*, Marshall creates a story that takes the reader on a journey through the life of a jazz musician as seen against the backdrop of the Great Migration of African Americans from the South to the North in the period from 1910 to 1940, the influx of West Indian immigrants to 1920's New York, and black expatriates leaving the country for better opportunities in Europe. The story is fueled by Marshall's memory of a first cousin whom she never met because of a family feud, but whose picture stayed atop the piano in her home. This memory, taken with details she heard about the cousin over time, provided the catalyst for her novel. The title of the book, however, is taken from the Arthurian legend of a wounded king imprisoned in his castle, awaiting the knight who will heal and protect him. In the novel, young Sonny Payne draws pictures of castles that include an armed miniature knight constantly standing guard. When Sonny shows his American cousins his drawings, he divulges that he is the knight who is always guarding his grandfather inside the castle.

The Fisher King relates the story of Sonny's grandfather's youth. He endures beatings by his mother when she catches him playing jazz instead of classical music. He becomes a brilliant musician as a teenager and then is drafted by the military and goes to war; when he returns from the fighting, his mother refuses him entrance to the family home when he acknowledges that he is still playing jazz. During his subsequent exile in France, he lives the life of a drug-plagued musician and ultimately dies in a Paris subway. Although the details of Sonny-Rett's life might indicate his need for protection on a literal level, Marshall uses the legend of the Fisher King as a metaphor for the need to protect black culture.

Memory may have been the catalyst for this novel, but in it Marshall still returns to themes found in previous works. *The Fisher King* has been described as a jazz novel, but the work puts the spotlight not only on the musician but also on the women behind his music. In this respect, Hattie Carmichael, Sonny-Rett's close friend and business confidant, is central. Secretly in love with him for years, Hattie is involved in a complicated relationship with Sonny-Rett, his wife, his daughter, and ultimately his grandson, continuing Marshall's exploration of themes of self-discovery and identity.

Gladys J. Washington
Updated by Jacquelyn Benton

Other major works

SHORT FICTION: *Soul Clap Hands and Sing*, 1961; *Reena, and Other Stories*, 1983 (also known as *Merle: A Novella and Other Stories*, 1985).

Bibliography

Alexander, Simone A. James. *Mother Imagery in the Novels of Afro-Caribbean Women*. Columbia: University of Missouri Press, 2001. Compares Marshall's representation of mothers and the mother-daughter relationship with those found in the works of writers Jamaica Kincaid and Maryse Condé.

Anatol, Giselle Liza. "Caribbean Migration, Ex-Isles, and the New World Novel." In *The Cambridge Companion to the African American Novel*, edited by Maryemma Graham. New York: Cambridge University Press, 2004. Examines the works of Paule Marshall and Haitian American writer Edwidge Danticat as literary representations of the dynamics between African diasporic populations in the United States.

Coser, Stelamaris. *Bridging the Americas: The Literature of Paule Marshall, Toni Morrison, and Gayl Jones*. Philadelphia: Temple University Press, 1995. Compares and contrasts the fiction of these three authors, taking their respective cultural heritages into consideration.

Denniston, Dorothy Hamer. *The Fiction of Paule Marshall*. Knoxville: University of Tennessee Press, 1995. Examines Marshall's novels as imaginative reconstructions of African history and culture. Provides close readings of individual works along with biographical information.

Gnage, Marie Foster. "Reconfiguring Self: A Matter of Place in Selected Novels by Paule Marshall." In *Middle Passages and the Healing Place of History: Migration and Identity in Black Women's Literature*, edited by Elizabeth Brown-Guillory. Columbus: Ohio State University Press, 2006. Focuses on Marshall's treatment of women on their journeys to selfhood, examining how those journeys cause or shape their migrations. Novels discussed are *Praisesong for the Widow*, *Daughters*, *The Chosen Place, the Timeless People*, and *The Fisher King*.

Hathaway, Heather. *Caribbean Waves: Relocating Claude McKay and Paule Marshall*. Bloomington: Indiana University Press, 1999. Presents discussion of Marshall's fiction within the context of the black diaspora, emphasizing the West Indian themes in her work.

Macpherson, Heidi Slettedahl. "Perception of Place: Geopolitical and Cultural Positioning in Paule Marshall's Novels." In *Caribbean Women Writers*, edited by Mary Condé and Thorunn Lonsdale. New York: St. Martin's Press, 1999. Offers informative discussion of Marshall's use of fictionalized island backdrops in her novels. Argues that while Marshall acknowledges geopolitical place, her representation of place moves beyond any specific locale.

Rogers, Susan. "Embodying Cultural Memory in Paule Marshall's *Praisesong for the Widow*." *African American Review* 34, no. 1 (Spring, 2000): 77-93. Identifies protagonist Avey Johnson as a repository of memory who must restore awareness of her cultural inheritance. Asserts that Avey's embrace of her African inheritance is essential to her being.

Ropero, Lourdes López. "'Some of All of Us in You': Intra-racial Relations, Pan-Africanism, and Diaspora in Paule Marshall's *The Fisher King*." *Miscelánea* 26 (2002): 39-57. Discusses *The Fisher King* as an excellent companion to Marshall's first novel, *Brown Girls, Brownstone*, because it brings the Afro-Caribbean and African American conflict to the forefront.

Smith, Maria T. *African Religious Influences on Three Black Women Novelists: The Aesthetics of Vodun: Zora Neale Hurston, Simone Schwarz-Bart, and Paule Marshall*. Lewiston, N.Y.: Edwin Mellen Press, 2007. Examines the ways in which Marshall's *Praisesong for the Widow* as well as the works of the other two authors allude to the Vodun pantheon and ancestor veneration that recognizes the interconnectedness of all living things but also functions as a source of cultural resistance.

ROGER MARTIN DU GARD

Born: Neuilly-sur-Seine, France; March 23, 1881
Died: Bellême, France; August 22, 1958

Principal long fiction

Devenir!, 1908
L'Une de nous, 1910
Jean Barois, 1913 (English translation, 1949)
Le Cahier gris, 1922
Le Pénitencier, 1922
La Belle Saison, 1923
La Consultation, 1928
La Sorellina, 1928
La Mort du père, 1929
L'Été 1914, 1936
Épilogue, 1940
Les Thibault, 1922-1940 (collective title for the previous 8 novels; *The World of the Thibaults*, collective title for *The Thibaults*, 1939 [parts 1-6] and *Summer 1914*, 1941 [parts 7-8])
Le Lieutenant-Colonel de Maumort, 1983 (*Lieutenant-Colonel de Maumort*, 2000)

Other literary forms

Roger Martin du Gard (mahr-tan-dew-GAHR) published three plays, all of which were produced as well: *Le Testament du père Leleu* (old Leleu's will), in 1914 (pr. 1914); another farce, *La Gonfle* (the swelling), in 1928 (pr. 1988); and *Un Taciturne*, in 1932 (pr. 1931). He also published the short-fiction work *Confidence africaine* (1931; English translation, 1983) and sketches of provincial life, *Vieille France* (1933; *The Postman*, 1954). All these works are available in the two-volume Pléiade edition of Martin du Gard's complete works. In 1951, a portion of his extensive journal was published under the title *Notes sur André Gide* (*Recollections of André Gide*, 1953). Of his letters, only his exchanges with André Gide and Jacques Copeau have appeared.

Achievements

Success came rather early to Roger Martin du Gard. Even his first novel, *Devenir!* (becoming), published in 1908, earned for him a *succès d'estime* at the age of twenty-seven. The publication of *Jean Barois*, in 1913, and the reception of his first play, *Le Testament du père Leleu*, earned the esteem of the new literary establishment developing around *La Nouvelle Revue française*. After World War I, when he began to publish the eight volumes of *The World of the Thibaults*, his readership continued to grow steadily.

Although leading a discreet life and shying away from the Parisian literary scene, Martin du Gard maintained at least an epistolary contact with numerous confreres among the established and the young, who frequently sought and received his advice. He was respected by all for his integrity, moderation, and dedication to friendship. His readers admired the solidity and ingenuity of the structure of his novels, his knowledge of contemporary society and his insight into the period covered, and his ability to cast his characters into a well-understood historical context. Like Marcel Proust, he wrote about the quarter-century preceding World War I. Whereas Proust painted aristocratic society in its decadence and decline, replaced at the top of the social pyramid by the bourgeoisie, Martin du Gard studied the fate of individuals in the bourgeois family and society, as well as the challenge to their class posed by demands for social justice and by historical accidents such as wars.

In his other works, such as *Le Testament du père Leleu*, *La Gonfle*, and *Vieille France*, Martin du Gard pays special attention, though with a sense of humor, to the mentality and mores, as well as the backward conditions, of French rural life during the first half of the twentieth century. Although many writers of his generation were quite aloof to social and political problems, Martin du Gard was keenly aware of them. Even later, however, when commitment became almost unavoidable, especially after he received the Nobel Prize in Literature in 1937, he strove to remain scrupulously objective. Except for his total and pronounced atheism, he avoided philosophical dogmatism.

Although Martin du Gard's reputation declined sharply in the postwar years, the publication of his vast journal, his extensive correspondence, and his unfinished last novel may reawaken interest in his work and bring about a reevaluation of his French and world literature of the twentieth century.

Biography

Roger Martin du Gard was born in Neuilly-sur-Seine, a town near Paris, on March 23, 1881. Both of his parents were of the upper middle class. Although he benefited from that circumstance and lived all of his life in material comfort without having to work for it, he did realize the weakness of the ethical foundation of his class and sought to bring about social and economic change.

Because of his discreet way of life and because most of his private papers remain unpublished and unavailable to scholars, much is left unknown about Martin du Gard. He grew up in Paris, where he attended the École Fénelon, a private Catholic school, and later Condorcet, one of the better Parisian *lycées*. While still a child, he was fascinated with literature and felt the urge to write.

Roger Martin du Gard. (© The Nobel Foundation)

At Fénelon, his adviser, the Abbé Hébert, gave him Leo Tolstoy's *War and Peace* (1865-1869) to read. Martin du Gard always acknowledged the great impact Tolstoy's masterpiece had on his concept of the novel and his understanding of the place of history in fiction. Hébert, a Modernist priest, also had a considerable influence on Martin du Gard's spiritual evolution.

After taking his *baccalauréat* degrees, Martin du Gard enrolled at the École des Chartes at the Sorbonne. There, he studied historiography and paleography. This experience taught him the importance of history and documentation as well as a sense of discipline in writing, which was to serve him in good stead throughout his career.

In 1906, Martin du Gard married Hélène Foucault, the daughter of a wealthy Parisian lawyer. In spite of the similarity of their backgrounds, his agnosticism, which began in adolescence, and her continued adherence to her Catholic faith caused a deepening rift between them. Shortly after his marriage, he traveled with Foucault in North Africa and began his writing career. He abandoned his first work, "Une Vie de Saint" (a saint's life), after having written two volumes of it. In 1908, he wrote rapidly and published his first novel, *Devenir!* It received some favorable critical attention, although even the author later recognized its weaknesses. Martin du Gard next worked on a novel titled *Marise*, which was to encompass the entire life of a woman. This project was also abandoned. He wrote his first major work, *Jean Barois*, between 1910 and 1913. Martin du Gard had also the good fortune of publishing it in *La Nouvelle Revue française*, which introduced him to Gide's circle. This group was to include most of the major writers of the rising generation.

Jacques Copeau, a member of this group, soon drew Martin du Gard into his theatrical venture, the foundation of the Théâtre du Vieux-Colombier. Martin du Gard, who from the beginning of his career had shown a predilection for dialogue, became fascinated by the theater and wrote his first play, *Le Testament du père Leleu*, in 1914. During the war, which he spent in the service, and a year after, he remained keenly interested in theater, imagining a new kind of theater: "la Comédie des Tréteaux." In 1920, he left Copeau's group and began his masterpiece, *The World of the Thibaults*, which occupied him for almost two decades. During this period, he attended the Décades de Pontigny, yearly gatherings of artists and intellectuals. After the death of his parents, he moved to a new property, Le Tertre, in Normandy. In 1931, he had a serious automobile accident that caused him to modify the plan of *The World of the Thibaults*. It began to appear in 1922, and the last volume, *Épilogue*, was published in 1940. Martin du Gard also wrote two more plays, *La Gonfle* and *Un Taciturne*; a short story, *Confidence africaine*; and *Vieille France*, a volume of sketches of country life thinly connected by the activities of a character. In 1937, he received the Nobel Prize in Literature. Shortly after receiving that honor, he took a cruise with his wife to the Caribbean, at the end of which he spent three weeks in the United States.

During the Occupation of France, Martin du Gard lived in Nice. After the war, he continued to spend winters on the French Riviera and summers in Normandy. His wife died in 1949. Between 1940 and his death in 1958, his only new work to be published was a selection from his journal, titled *Recollections of André Gide*. His last work, "Souvenirs du Colonel de Maumort," begun in 1941 and left unfinished at his death, was donated along with his personal papers to the Bibliothèque Nationale, where they were earlier kept under seal. Some of them were made available to scholars by 1983. The work was published in French as *Le Lieutenant-Colonel de Maumort* and in English as *Lieutenant-Colonel de Maumort*.

Analysis

Roger Martin du Gard, who admired such novelists as Tolstoy, attempted in his works to depict an individual or a family in as comprehensive a cultural and historical context as possible. This explains his continued attempt to embrace a large historical period in its totality. He uses antithetical characters (for example, Antoine and Jacques in *The World of the Thibaults*) as a structural device to illustrate the two sides of his principal views. Dominant among Martin du Gard's ideological preoccupations is the concept of the liberation of the individual—most important, liberation from religion and from family—and from social taboos such as those concerning homosexuality. Although he enjoyed the advantages of his birth into the high bourgeoisie, he was keenly interested in socialism; his social concerns, especially his leanings toward socialism and pacifism, correspond to those of many leading French intellectuals of the day. That he received the Nobel Prize in 1937, when France was governed by the Popular Front, may be more than coincidental.

Martin du Gard's first two works, *Marise*, part of which was published under the title *L'Une de nous* (one of us), and *Devenir!*, provide insight into the literary beginnings of the author of *The World of the Thibaults*. According to Albert Camus, *Devenir!* is the story of an individual who wants to become a writer but fails for lack of character. Although in *Devenir!*, Martin du Gard draws too directly upon his own experience, already the author expresses his deterministic view of the human condition and senses the tragic in human destiny.

Jean Barois

Jean Barois was written at the apogee of a period during which positivism and scientism held sway. The year of its publication, 1913, was also the eve of the catastrophe that was to bring about an anguished and nihilistic questioning of the premises of scientific positivism. Fittingly enough, *Jean Barois* has the appearance of a scholarly text. Camus remarked that this novel "consists of dialogues and documents. It is the only novel of the scientist age." While writing this work, Martin du Gard was very much under the spell of the theater, as he was several times later during his career. Earlier, he had considered writing a novel consisting of dialogues connected only with comments similar to stage directions in a play. Several novels of this type had been written during the early part of the century. What led Martin du Gard to choose such a structure was his concern with verisimilitude more than literary fashion. He was striving to remove the voice of the narrator in order to present characters and ideas impersonally. This led him to employ the cinematographic technique that was widely used in the 1930's.

The themes of *Jean Barois* can be summarized as a human's evolution from his (or her) traditional faith to a faith in science, provided the reader realizes that this individual evolution is associated with and brought about by that of history. Human liberation from religious belief is a recurring theme in Martin du Gard's works. Socialism is seen as one of the most dynamic forces of contemporary history, and it separates itself from religion. It enables humans not to expect any hope or help from God. The hero, Jean Barois, is carried quite far by those historical forces, but because of his heredity and the imprint left on him by the milieu in which he grew up, he dies ironically in the end, reconciled with his church as his father had been before him. As a child, Jean Barois is the object of opposition between positivism and religion: Medicine is rejected by his grandmother in favor of faith healing. As an adolescent, he questions his spiritual adviser, Abbé Joziers, about the problem of evil. Several years later, the young man is troubled by the contradictions between science and faith as well as by contradictions within Christianity. Soon he is in conflict with Cécile, his thoroughly faithful wife.

The second part of *Jean Barois* is dominated by the Dreyfus affair. A primary concern of the protagonist as well as the author, this crisis in French political, intellectual, and moral life was described by Martin du Gard in a way that is accurate, authentic, and yet artistic. By temperament and by training, Martin du Gard meticulously gathered, analyzed, and synthesized lengthy documentation, which he incorporated into his novel. Among Martin du Gard's contemporaries, all major parties, groups, ideologies, and institutions were involved on one side or the other of this issue. Having become an unbeliever and a liberal—a member of a group of humanistic Socialists—Jean dedicates himself to Dreyfus's cause. The reader is able to follow the unfolding of the drama as the author alternately focuses on both sides of the issue and on all major adversaries. In spite of his desire to be objective, Martin du Gard does favor his own Dreyfusard point of view.

In the third part of the novel, after having experienced disappointments and especially a confrontation with his eighteen-year-old daughter, who has decided to become a nun, Jean, the protagonist, tired and ill, begins to see the shortcomings of his summary rejection of religion. He is also shaken by the reactions of his rising generation to his own beliefs—especially the response of those who returned to Catholicism. Though his character Jean returns to the religion of his youth, throughout the novel, Martin du Gard strongly favors rationalism over Christianity—especially Catholicism—and attacks religion or shows it in a poor light on all traditional controversial points. The author was fully aware of this dominant aspect of his novel, aware that he had not achieved impartiality. His first readers, Gide and Jean Schlumberger, who held similarly anti-Catholic views, were delighted by it at once.

In 1920, while deeply involved in Copeau's Théâtre du Vieux-Colombier—a venture in regenerated theater—Martin du Gard first conceived of writing a novel about two brothers as different as possible from each other. Yet they were to be "deeply marked by the hidden similarities which a powerful common heredity creates between two beings of the same blood." Again, one notices the great importance Martin du Gard attributed to heredity throughout his writings, expressed with special clarity in his unfinished *Souvenirs de Colonel de Maumort* and his letters. He decided to place his characters in the turmoil of powerful forces and in a society headed toward a catastrophic war. Martin du Gard clearly stated his growing interest in various types of ideology and his preoccupation with the challenging problems of his time. Significantly, while planning his new work, he wanted to entitle it "Good and Evil."

THE WORLD OF THE THIBAULTS

The structure of *The World of the Thibaults* is that of a *roman-fleuve*, a long, multivolume novel. It is divided into eight parts of uneven length covering periods of various durations. The author focuses on certain events and scenes within rather brief periods of time, leaving long intervals between them, which he then connects with narrative. Description, exposition, and summarization of events and ideas abound. Thus, Martin du Gard chose a time-tested fictional structure, although at first he had attempted to adapt the purely dramatic technique that he had used so successfully in *Jean Barois*. He explained his rejection of the dramatic approach based exclusively on the use of dialogue, saying that, for the work he was contemplating, it would have required excessive and ultimately unrealistic circumvolutions. By employing conventional rather than innovative techniques of dialogue and narration, Martin du Gard revealed his artistry within an otherwise conservative framework.

The World of the Thibaults is essentially the history of a family of several individuals belonging to different generations, interacting with one another and various members of a society caught up in the movement of history. Using this combination of factors, Martin du Gard seeks to give his novel a deep philosophical meaning. The existence of numerous characters, however, poses the problem of point of view. Martin du Gard solved it by playing the role of an omniscient narrator whose presence is intermittently eclipsed by the characters. This technique was all the more practical because it enabled him to dramatize the lives of principal characters Antoine and Jacques and to create the impression of psychological truth. Martin du Gard's characters are as unusual as some of those of Gide or Proust. They are strongly individualized and realistic representatives of society, yet they are common members of the upper middle class who would realistically come in contact with one another. They are studied, however, not as members of a class but as individuals, and this method is reinforced by each character's inclination to self-study.

The first part of *The World of the Thibaults* depicts a short crisis lasting only a week. It is caused by Jacques Thibault and Daniel de Fontanin, two adolescents who run away from home one fine Sunday under the pretext of having to attend a special class. Soon they are caught and returned to their families. Daniel is welcomed home by his mother with understanding and affection, whereas Jacques is sent to a reform school by his father for having failed to show any repentance. Through the reactions of the two families, Martin du Gard presents his protagonists along with their particular milieu and ethos. Madame de Fontanin, a Protestant, is a person of integrity, and she is stronger and calmer than the bigoted, self-righteous, and authoritarian Monsieur Thibault. Martin du Gard's lifelong anti-Catholic bias, of which he was perhaps the strongest exponent since Voltaire, is only weakly balanced by Madame de Fontanin's implausible belief in her pastor's faith-healing powers.

Le Cahier gris

Through *Le Cahier gris*, Jacques's private notebook, which is a lyric expression of adolescent friendship, the reader becomes acquainted with Jacques and Daniel. There is nothing abnormal or reprehensible in this friendship, as the priests in Jacques's school wrongly suspect. From their flight, the reader discovers Daniel's sentimental nature and Jacques's decisive nature. Both have inherited these traits from their fathers. Readers also notice Jacques's capacity for sympathy and his resilience in near despair. His father's punishment pushes him deeper into rebellion and wins for him the reader's sympathy. At this point, he attempts to liberate himself from the oppression of the family. Later, he will take on bourgeois society on an international scale.

Le Pénitencier

The second volume, *Le Pénitencier* (reform school), focuses on Jacques. He is subjected to an especially harsh regimen; he is alone, deprived of companions his age and of good teachers, under a guard who shows him obscene pictures and has him copy them and another guard who clearly has pederastic inclinations. These two experiences awaken the adolescent's sexuality in a sordid fashion. Rather than a punishment, however, this experience turns out to be a trial of adolescence. Suspicious of his brother's fate, Antoine visits him and, thanks to the intervention of the sympathetic and reasonable Abbé Vécard, succeeds in freeing Jacques. The two brothers will live together in Antoine's apartment.

While together, the two brothers are contrasted. Antoine is mature, is practical, and leads a purposeful life, whereas Jacques remains moody, idealistic, and uncertain of his future. These differences are illustrated in their respective attitudes toward Lisbeth, the concierge's daughter. While having an affair with her, Antoine urges her to initiate his brother. The latter, however, begins by having a Platonic infatuation with her.

Erotic awakening at the beginning of *Le Pénitencier* is associated with adolescent rebellion, and sexual initiation with the beginning of maturation and socialization. In this novel on adolescence, Martin du Gard does not abandon one of his major themes and biases, namely, the evils and consequences of religious faith: Father Thibault founded the reform school with the approval of the Paris archbishop, and the fanatical Protestant minister preaches to Madame Fontanin to forgive her husband's extreme infidelity. These elements are contrasted with Antoine's humane attitude, which derives from his faith in science and reason.

La Belle Saison

La Belle Saison (the beautiful season) is the longest volume of *The World of the Thibaults* before *L'Été 1914*. Focused on two families, the Thibaults and the Fontanins, it is also complex and includes a great deal of action. Each of the two families owns a summer home in

Maisons-Lafitte, which becomes the point of departure and return for many episodes.

The three young men, Daniel, Jacques, and Antoine, have leading roles. They have become adults and now encounter a variety of people through their discoveries, and through them the author broadens his exploration of society. It is the beautiful season because it is the season of youth, which holds out limitless possibilities for the young men. They will not approach these possibilities, however, with total freedom. Again, heredity manifests itself as an important force, as does the conditioning of their respective childhoods. Daniel clearly has artistic talent but is a philanderer like his father. Jacques, who wins admission to the École Normale Supérieure, a door to professional and social success, is elated. Instead of pursuing this promising path, he is drawn to socialism, which, interestingly, is his own extension of his father's preoccupation with philanthropy. For most of the novel, however, he is searching for himself and remains confused about both his attraction to Jenny and her rejection of him. Antoine emerges as a liberated positivist, a man of science who exercises his profession most competently. In the eyes of the reader, he is adorned with the prestige of one who saves lives. The protection of human life was for Martin du Gard a fundamental value. While saving a child's life, Antoine meets Rachel, with whom he has a genuine and beautiful love affair. In the end, however, she returns to her former lover, Hirsch, to whom she is irresistibly drawn despite his bizarre character and sordid past.

As a departure from his usual thematic concerns, Martin du Gard treats in this volume the influence a literary work may have on its readers. Jacques becomes enthralled by Gide's *Les Nourritures terrestres* (1897; *Fruits of the Earth*, 1949). Both he and Daniel are drawn to Gide's urging to reject bourgeois morality and family. It is not purely coincidental that none of the three young men will have families. For that, their fathers bear some responsibility: Jérôme de Fontanin for having neglected all of his responsibilities toward his family, and Oscar Thibault for having placed the interests of religion and society above paternal love.

LA CONSULTATION

Antoine, the medical doctor, is at the center of *La Consultation* (the doctor's visit) and dominates the action even more than Jacques did in *La Belle Saison*. He is presented during a day of consultation, October 13, 1913. The day begins for him with a visit to his father, who is critically ill. Not only does Antoine struggle to sustain life, but he also must face the question of whether to hasten death. These alternatives, within the power and responsibility of doctors, appear as goals of science and the culminating point of philosophy. In all professional circumstances, Antoine is prepared to do what he believes to be right; thus he accepts the possibility of euthanasia, without reference to the dictates of religion or even medical ethics.

Throughout this phase, Antoine's life is dominated by medicine and his service to others. He appears somewhat interested in Gise. His major concern, however, is Jacques's disappearance. Depicting the way Antoine spends his time enables Martin du Gard to present him as the mature man and professional he has become. Although he leads a quieter and even more prosaic life, Antoine is assuming a more important role in the novel.

Antoine's friendly concern for two adolescent brothers who struggle to survive alone, without the support of a family, is the means through which the reader catches a glimpse of the harsh economic conditions faced by the working class. Similarly, through his conversation with his patient Rumelles, who works at the Foreign Ministry, the reader becomes aware of the intensifying crisis about to culminate in World War I.

LA SORELLINA

La Sorellina, a somewhat longer volume, relates the events of one week. Monsieur Thibault continues to decline after the serious operation he has undergone. His desire to die in an edifying manner makes him appear ridiculous. It is at this time that Antoine discovers a story, "La Sorellina," written by Jacques. As he reads it, he soon understands that it is based on circumstances in Jacques's life. Through "La Sorellina," the reader learns that Jacques did not commit suicide, as his father thought; that he loved both Jenny and Gise; and why he disappeared. As soon as he learns of his brother's precise whereabouts in Lausanne, Antoine goes there to bring Jacques back to their father's deathbed. As the two brothers converse, Jacques rectifies some of the inaccuracies in Antoine's interpretation of events in his life as seen transposed in "La Sorellina."

La Mort du père

In *La Mort du père* (the death of the father), Antoine, on returning from Lausanne, discovers that his father's condition has worsened. Martin du Gard is not only precise but also quite technical in his description of Thibault's illness and of its treatment. Death becomes the focal point of Thibault's thoughts and of life itself. As he rejects the consolation of religion, it is clear that Thibault does not accept death, that he desperately wants to live. Seeing their father suffer to a degrading extent, "like an animal," his sons agree to resort to euthanasia.

After Thibault's death, Antoine's attitude toward him changes, especially as he discovers, by reading his father's papers, how humane he had been. Too late, Antoine realizes that he could have understood and loved his father. On the other hand, Jacques's attitude does not change. He continues to hate his father, and he remains awkward toward Gise. Again, thoughts of suicide and destruction increase his violent and nihilistic sentiments.

As they travel back to Paris after the funeral, Abbé Vécard and Antoine engage in a discussion on religious faith. Martin du Gard strives to advance the strongest arguments on each side. In the end, while not conceding, Antoine simply admits that he may lack a religious sense—as Martin du Gard felt he himself did.

L'Été 1914

L'Été 1914 deals in detail with events that took place between June 28, 1914—the date of the assassination of the Austrian archduke Ferdinand in Sarajevo—and August, 1914. This volume is almost as long as all previous volumes together. For all the major characters, the outbreak of World War I is a climactic event, as indeed it was for all Europeans. Although Martin du Gard wrote at least a decade after that war, he respects the perspective of his characters. As the diplomatic tension intensifies and the threat of war grows, people become increasingly preoccupied with the crisis. In *L'Été 1914*, the psychological analysis of adolescents or young adults and the study of tensions within middle-class families are overshadowed by the focus on national and international tensions of vast proportions. The change of viewpoint corresponds to a natural evolution from personal concerns to the broader spheres of the momentous crisis.

At the beginning of *L'Été 1914*, the reader resumes contact with Jacques, who lives in the cosmopolitan Socialist milieu in Geneva. The total commitment of the young bourgeois to the Socialist cause may first seem surprising. In spite of Martin du Gard's long and keen interest in socialism, his emphasis on the movement in that chronological framework was probably increased by subsequent events. Like most intellectuals of the 1920's and 1930's, he was convinced that the coming to power of socialism in at least one major country on the globe, Russia, was the single most important event of the first half of the century.

Jacques is observed within a cross section of revolutionaries. Their respective ideas and plans on the eve of the war are studied from their perspective. Jacques's return to Paris on a special mission coincides with Jérôme de Fontanin's suicide. Jacques also finds Antoine preoccupied by his affair with Anne de Battaincourt. The doctor appears rather out of touch and unconcerned with the alarming political situation threatening Europe. By temperament and habit, however, he opposes Socialist ideals.

While paying a visit to the dying Jérôme, Jacques sees Jenny—four years after his unexplained departure. This encounter does not bring about a reconciliation. At first, Jenny, who has suffered much from the separation, feels resentful toward Jacques. In subsequent days, they see each other frequently, and Jacques explains to her his feelings about the past and his present commitment to socialism and pacifism. Jenny comes to share his idealism and his commitment. Perhaps Martin du Gard knew that Jenny was also the name of one of socialist Karl Marx's daughters; his choice of such an un-French name is significant.

In the meantime, the political situation worsens, and Jacques accomplishes clandestine liaison missions in Paris, Antwerp, Berlin, and Brussels for his revolutionary leader, Meynestrel. The reader becomes aware of the lack of a unified view among Socialists on such vital issues as whether to try to prevent war or to hope war will result in progress for socialism. Martin du Gard succeeds in re-creating the tension and the confusion in the days preceding the declaration of war. Antoine's belief that reason and science are the foundations of life is pushed aside by the momentum of the war movement. Jacques decides to give his inheritance to the Socialist Party and plans to refuse to be conscripted. He still hopes French and German Socialists will be able to organize a general strike to prevent the war. At this critical point, Jacques and Jenny witness the assassination of Jean Jaurès, the only leader capable of inspiring a strong pacifist following.

Before departing, Jacques tells Antoine of his love for Jenny. This causes the two brothers to quarrel in very unfortunate circumstances. The same day, war is declared by Germany on Russia. During that night, Jacques and Jenny consummate their love, but not very happily. Perhaps as a result of her puritanical upbringing, Jenny feels humiliated, while Jacques feels remorse for having drawn her into his tragic destiny. Jenny's mother is strongly opposed to their marriage. As a consequence of an argument with her mother, Jenny decides to postpone settling in Geneva with Jacques. That suits him well, for he has decided to make an ultimate attempt to interrupt the war. With Meynestrel, he plans to drop a million leaflets urging soldiers and workers not to fight. The mission, however, fails pathetically. Their plane crashes, the leaflets are burned, the two Socialists are killed, and the war continues. In spite of his useless death, Jacques appears as a hero who embodies an ideal of justice and the vision of a better world.

Épilogue

The World of the Thibaults could have ended with Jacques's death, as it begins with his misadventure. Accustomed, however, to the regular reappearance of all major characters, readers do not expect to know about their fate—especially that of Antoine, the other known heir of the Thibault spirit. The final volume, *Épilogue*, picks up the thread of history in the spring of 1918 as Antoine is being treated for toxic gas inhalation in a hospital in the south of France. He spends all of his time reflecting on his own condition and the human condition in general. On a visit to Paris, he returns to the family house there and the summer home in Maisons-Lafitte; he sees Jenny and Gise, both caring for Jean-Paul, Jenny's child by Jacques. Daniel has been completely transformed by a castrating wound. He has lost all interest in life and contemplates suicide. Antoine also pays Dr. Philip a visit. After his professor has examined him, he realizes he will not recover.

Épilogue ends with letters and Antoine's journal. During the last four months of his life, Antoine has kept a diary. Through it readers learn of his anguish and the solitude of the ending of his life. He takes a keen interest in the Allies' progress, although he will die a week after the Armistice. His attitude alternates between despair at the thought of his death and his thoughts of Jean-Paul's future in a world of peace that is full of possibilities. He hopes that when his nephew reaches full manhood—ironically, in 1940—it will be a more propitious time. Finally, Antoine refuses the consolation of religion and hastens his own death. In spite of his cruel fate, however, he dies believing in human progress.

The World of the Thibaults is something of an anomaly in twentieth century literature. Like the even more ambitious *roman-fleuve* by Jules Romains, *Les Hommes de bonne volonté* (1932-1936; *Men of Good Will*, 1933-1946), it recalls the sweeping vision of Honoré de Balzac and Émile Zola. Martin du Gard, however, lacks Balzac's energy, psychological acuity, and sheer narrative genius, and his treatment of social issues cannot match Zola's brutal force. Time has not been kind to writers who, in the first half of the twentieth century, wrote as if they were living in the nineteenth.

Jean-Pierre Cap

Other major works

SHORT FICTION: *Confidence africaine*, 1931 (English translation, 1983); *Vieille France*, 1933 (*The Postman*, 1954).

PLAYS: *Le Testament du père Leleu*, pr., pb. 1914; *La Gonfle*, pb. 1928; *Un Taciturne*, pr. 1931.

NONFICTION: *Notes sur André Gide*, 1951 (*Recollections of André Gide*, 1953); *Correspondance, 1913-1951*, 1968; *Correspondance*, 1972.

MISCELLANEOUS: *Œuvres complètes*, 1955 (2 volumes).

Bibliography

Boak, Denis. *Roger Martin du Gard*. Oxford, England: Clarendon Press, 1963. An informative study of Martin du Gard's artistic vision. Boak emphasizes the tragic overtones, symphonic orchestration, and transcendental qualities of *The World of the Thibaults*.

O'Nan, Martha, ed. *Roger Martin du Gard Centennial*. Brockport: Department of Foreign Languages, State University of New York, 1981. A special collection commemorating the anniversary of the author's birth. The nine featured essays are wide-ranging and comprehensive.

Ru, Yi-Ling. *The Family Novel: Toward a Generic Definition*. New York: Peter Lang, 1992. Ru argues that the family novel is a distinct literary genre, proving her contention by analyzing *The World of the Thibaults*, *The Forsyte Saga* by John Galsworthy, and *The Turbulent Trilogy* by Chinese author Pa Chin.

Schalk, David L. *Roger Martin du Gard: The Novelist and History*. Ithaca, N.Y.: Cornell University Press, 1967. Schalk evaluates Martin du Gard's historical perspective and includes an impressive collection of critical comments from other scholars. Includes a bibliography.

Stern, Richard Clarke. *Dark Mirror: The Sense of Injustice in Modern European and American Literature*. New York: Fordham University Press, 1994. A substantial discussion of *Jean Barois* is included in this book, which analyzes literature that demonstrates the decline of universal or "natural" ethical law in Western culture.

Sturrock, John. "The Man Who Believed in Nothing." *The New York Times Book Review*, January 23, 2000. Sturrock's review was one of several that appeared in American newspapers and journals after the English translation *Lieutenant-Colonel de Maumort* in 1999. Sturrock places that novel within the context of Martin du Gard's other writings, his literary style, and his career.

PETER MATTHIESSEN

Born: New York, New York; May 22, 1927

Principal long fiction

Race Rock, 1954
Partisans, 1955
Raditzer, 1961
At Play in the Fields of the Lord, 1965
Far Tortuga, 1975
Killing Mister Watson, 1990
Lost Man's River, 1997
Bone by Bone, 1999
Shadow Country: A New Rendering of the Watson Legend, 2008

Other literary forms

Peter Matthiessen (MATH-eh-suhn) is perhaps better known, and certainly far more prolific, as a writer of nonfiction than as a novelist. He has produced numerous volumes of nonfiction, beginning with *Wildlife in America* (1959). Many are chronicles of Matthiessen's trips to distant and barely accessible areas of the earth, such as *The Cloud Forest: A Chronicle of the South American Wilderness* (1961), *Under the Mountain Wall: A Chronicle of Two Seasons in the Stone Age* (1962), *Oomingmak: The Expedition to the Musk Ox Island in the Bering Sea* (1967), *Blue Meridian: The Search for the Great White Shark* (1971), *The Tree Where Man Was Born: The African Experience* (1972), *The Snow Leopard* (1978), *Sand Rivers* (1981), *African Silences* (1991), and *End of the Earth: Voyaging to Antarctica* (2003). *The Shorebirds of North America* (1967) and *The Birds of Heaven: Travels with Cranes* (2001) are straight natural history, and *Sal Si Puedes: Cesar Chavez and the New American Revolution* (1970) is a biographical essay and political commentary on the California labor leader.

Among Matthiessen's other works of nonfiction are *In the Spirit of Crazy Horse* (1983), *Indian Country* (1984), *Nine-Headed Dragon River: Zen Journals, 1969-1982* (1985), and *Men's Lives: The Surfmen and Baymen of the South Fork* (1986). He has also published two volumes of overlapping short fiction, *Midnight Turning Gray* (1984) and *On the River Styx, and Other Stories* (1989), and a children's book, *Seal Pool* (1972).

Achievements

Peter Matthiessen's achievements lie in two distinct but interrelated genres: the personal essay, similar in many respects to the writings of Henry David Thoreau, and the novel. Two of his most distinguished works of fiction, *At Play in the Fields of the Lord* and *Far Tortuga*, draw heavily on the author's evocation of the natural world: the Amazon rain forest in the first case and the open sea and Caribbean islands in the second. Both novels are extended studies of humanity's interrelation with these wild environments, and much of their effectiveness lies in Matthiessen's ability to place the reader within the primeval setting, projecting the smell, taste, and feel of the jungle and the sea. Similarly, Matthiessen's nonfiction relies for its power on transporting the reader to a remote natural world and making that world live, impressing indelibly nature's importance. Matthiessen stresses the value of nature to humankind, as a fountainhead of fundamental impulses and as an avenue of self-exploration, a means of cutting away the confusions of the "civilized" world and probing the essential elements of human nature. Matthiessen is not, however, a naïve romantic, finding in nature a Rousseauistic panacea for all the ills of society. His essays, whether book-length or merely brief sketches, have a gritty objectivity that precludes any superficial romanticizing of the natural world.

In 1973, Matthiessen was named to the American Academy of Arts and Letters. He won both the American Book Award and the National Book Award for *The Snow Leopard*. He received the John Burroughs Medal and the African Wildlife Leadership Foundation Award for *Sand Rivers*, and his nonfiction book *Wildlife in America* can be found in the White House's permanent collection. In 2008, Matthiessen received both the National Book Award for *Shadow Country* and *The Paris Review*'s Hadada Award for his lifetime commitment to the literary arts.

Biography

Peter Matthiessen was born in New York City on May 22, 1927, of a well-to-do, if not wealthy, family. His father, Erard A. Matthiessen, was a well-known architect and for many years a trustee of the National Audubon Society. His interest in nature and conservation was passed on to his son, and many of Peter Matthiessen's essays were eventually published in the society's magazine, *Audubon*. From childhood, Matthiessen was exposed to the New York world of literature and the arts. By the time he was sixteen, he had decided to become a writer. Following the path of many boys from prominent families, he was first educated at the Hotchkiss School, then at Yale University. He spent many of his summers on the Connecticut shore in the relatively exclusive society of friends from the New York intellectual world. "My first story," he later said casually, "was published by my girl's father"—Cass Canfield, then editor of *Harper's* magazine.

Late in World War II, Matthiessen interrupted his education to join the U.S. Navy, an experience of mixed success, since he was demoted for disciplinary reasons, but one that gave him his first real experience of the life of the common man. He returned to Yale in 1947, continued his creative writing, and wrote about hunting and fishing for the *Yale Daily News*. He graduated from Yale in 1950, spent a year there as an instructor in creative writing, and moved to Paris, by then married to Patsy Southgate, the daughter of a socially prominent diplomat. The Matthiessens soon became the center of a glittering crowd of American expatriate intellectuals, including William Styron, James Jones, George Plimpton, James Baldwin, and Irwin Shaw. In 1951, with Harold L. Humes, Plimpton, and others, Matthiessen founded *The Paris Review*, which became one of the most influential literary magazines of the postwar era; for four decades, Matthiessen served as fiction editor for the magazine.

Matthiessen's first novel, *Race Rock*, was written in Paris. It looks back to the world of Matthiessen's youth: The characters are a group of disillusioned, upper-middle-class young people living on the New England coast. Aimless and confused by their meaningless lives, they stagnate, wallowing in their angst and neuroses. A reunion of childhood friends degenerates into an overflow of emotions and finally violence. Sadder but wiser, the survivors face an uncertain future, vowing to profit from their past mistakes and show maturity in the future.

In 1953, the Matthiessens returned to the United States and settled in East Hampton, Long Island, where Matthiessen divided his time between writing in bad weather and commercial fishing in good. His second novel, *Partisans*, appeared in 1955. It was an obvious product of Matthiessen's knowledge of the avant-garde left wing that infested expatriate intellectual circles in the 1950's. (Ironically, in the light of his later political

Peter Matthiessen. (© Nancy Crampton)

commitments, it was rumored among the *Paris Review* crowd that Matthiessen was an agent of the U.S. Central Intelligence Agency, which would hardly have been surprising, considering his background and contacts.) The protagonist of *Partisans* is Barney Sand, a young American journalist and son of a diplomat, who is searching for a cause to which he can commit himself. With the pure idealism of a Grail knight, he scours the Paris slums seeking Jacobi, an old and deposed revolutionary who has been rejected by the Communist Party but who is the emblem of purity and integrity to Sand. Like *Race Rock*, *Partisans* is a kind of bildungsroman—that is, a novel in which a young person grows into maturity. In this case, the young man comes to realize that his naïve vision is unattainable.

The Matthiessens' marriage ended in divorce in 1957, but by that time Matthiessen had already begun the series of "world wanderings" that would provide him with the subjects of his major works. With little formal scientific training, he spent three years studying American animals and birds, with particular attention to endangered species. The result was *Wildlife in America*, a book widely praised for showing, as one reviewer wrote, "the skill of a novelist and the accuracy of a zoologist." In 1959 and 1961, Matthiessen made the two difficult journeys that eventually provided him with the setting for *At Play in the Fields of the Lord*, the first to South America and the second to New Guinea. On both expeditions, Matthiessen penetrated the wilderness as deeply and thoroughly as possible, at times at considerable personal risk, and lived with the native tribes in an effort to come to know them.

Between these travels, Matthiessen produced a third "conventional" novel, *Raditzer*, drawing this time on the naval experience of his young manhood for material. The novel is the study of a pariah, Raditzer, a sailor who embodies virtually every human vice. A product of the slums, Raditzer is dishonest, paranoid, sadistic, servile, and bullying by turns—a more unpleasant version of James Wait of Joseph Conrad's *The Nigger of the Narcissus* (1897). Matthiessen has pointed to Conrad and to Fyodor Dostoevski as two important influences on his fiction. An instinctive parasite, Raditzer attaches himself to the hero, a young intellectual sailor of good family who, like the protagonists of *Race Rock* and *Partisans*, bears considerable resemblance to the author as a young man. When Raditzer becomes such a Jonah that his shipmates plot to kill him, the sailor-hero finds himself in the disagreeable position of having his courage tested in the defense of a man he loathes. He comes to realize—as Barney Sand does, despising the poor whose cause he has championed—that moral action does not come in neat, sanitized packages, and that good and evil are peculiarly muddled in the real world. Unlike most of Matthiessen's works, *Raditzer* does not concern itself integrally with nature, and it is particularly interesting for the success with which it explores the lives of common working men, a topic of increasing interest to the author.

At Play in the Fields of the Lord signaled Matthiessen's coming of age as a writer and thinker. In it, and in the rest of his mature work, he fuses the speculative insight of a philosopher, the lyricism of a poet, and the scrupulous observation of a scientist to produce a broad statement about the relationship between humanity and the natural world as profound as any in Western literature. His fifth novel, *Far Tortuga*, published in 1975, is a stylistic and structural tour de force as well as a profoundly moving elegy for the doomed world of the Caribbean turtle fishers. It followed a remarkable book-length essay, *The Tree Where Man Was Born: The African Experience*, an extended philosophical commentary on life and death in East Africa that contains some of Matthiessen's finest and most thoughtful observations concerning humanity's place in the natural world.

Matthiessen remarried in 1963, but his second wife, Deborah Love Matthiessen, died ten years later after a long struggle with cancer. Toward the end of her life, both she and her husband had been moving deeply into the study of Zen Buddhism, convinced that it offers an alternative to the emptiness of the modern world. After his wife's death, Matthiessen undertook a difficult and dangerous trip on foot into the heart of Nepal to visit the Crystal Monastery, a center of Zen meditation and reverence; his companion on the trip was the noted naturalist George Schaller, who was studying Nepalese blue sheep. Matthiessen was specifically hoping for a sight of the real but mystical snow leopard, an animal so rarely seen that is has become a Zen symbol for everything possible and unattainable. *The Snow Leopard*, based on his journey, was published in 1978. This very personal account of Matthiessen's spiritual pilgrimage in the Himalayas was honored with the National Book Award.

In the early 1980's, Matthiessen published two books dealing with the fate of the American Indian: *In the Spirit of Crazy Horse* and *Indian Country*. The former, which argues for the innocence of Leonard Peltier, a member of the American Indian Movement who was convicted of murdering two agents of the Federal Bureau of Investigation, embroiled Matthiessen and his publisher, the Viking Press, in two libel suits that lasted for six years. The result was the virtual suppression of the book, despite the fact that the suits were ultimately found to be without merit.

In 1990, Matthiessen published his first novel in fifteen years, *Killing Mister Watson*, which was the beginning of an ambitious trilogy, or one "monster novel," as Matthiessen referred to it. The second part, *Lost Man's River*, was published in 1997, and the third, *Bone by Bone*, was released in 1999. A film adaptation of Matthiessen's book *At Play in the Fields of the Lord* was finally released in 1991, twenty-five years after it was first optioned in 1966 and after passing through the hands of many celebrated directors, producers, and actors, including John Huston, Paul Newman, and Richard Gere.

Matthiessen settled in Sagaponack, New York, with his third wife, Maria, whom he married in 1980. He is a Buddhist priest of the White Plum Asanga and is a frequent speaker on the topics of ecology and writing.

Analysis

Peter Matthiessen is a latter-day Henry David Thoreau. There are other fine contemporary nature writers, such as Edward Hoagland and John McPhee, but no other writers bring to their observations of the natural world and humankind's place in it the philosophical depth and poetic command of the language displayed by Matthiessen. His two finest novels, *At Play in the Fields of the Lord* and *Far Tortuga*, combine his experience as a naturalist with the felt immediacy that only a deeply persuasive work of fiction can provide.

Matthiessen's first twenty years as a novelist can be divided into two phases, one comprising his first three novels—*Race Rock*, *Partisans*, and *Raditzer*—and the other, the major works *At Play in the Fields of the Lord* and *Far Tortuga*. The first three are thoroughly competent novels, and they certainly show the promise of the writer Matthiessen became. All exhibit a young man's fascination with the maturing process and the loss of innocence—with "rites of passage." All center on protagonists who are obviously surrogates for the author himself, idealistic but troubled young men of good family, aimless and seeking direction and commitment in a world of inexplicable evil and suffering. Although *Race Rock*, in particular, is rather complex in its presentation of multiple levels of time, all three books are essentially traditional narratives, accomplished but unextraordinary.

Matthiessen's next two novels, however, are fundamentally philosophical meditations on the human condition. As such, they join the company of Herman Melville's *Moby Dick* (1851), Joseph Conrad's *Heart of Darkness* (1902), and Stendhal's *Le Rouge et le noir* (1830; *The Red and the Black*, 1898), all works in which the narrative impulse, however strong, is essentially a vehicle for metaphysical statement. Matthiessen is concerned with *things*, but he is more concerned with the meanings of things. This is hardly to say that he is a didactic writer (although unequivocal pleas for environmentalism fill his nonfiction), but he is insistently an explorer of the meaning of life. In both *At Play in the Fields of the Lord* and *Far Tortuga*, that meaning is manifested in terms of humanity's place in the continuum of natural life on earth. In the former, Lewis Meriwether Moon deliberately and consciously projects himself into the world of the Niaruna, and his discovery of his identity as a natural man is the result of an act of will. In contrast, in *Far Tortuga*, Raib Avers and the crew of the *Lillias Eden* are in harmony with the sea and its creatures but have little opportunity to determine the lives they lead.

Unlike philosophical writers who persistently project humans as purely social or psychological beings, Matthiessen insists that people are animals, although not primarily in the naturalistic terms of Theodore Dreiser or Jack London, who write of people as victims of fate, the pawns of uncontrollable chemical and biological impulses. Matthiessen's human beings, as animals, share a common heritage and destiny with all the living world. Both *At Play in the Fields of the Lord* and *Far Tortuga* exhibit a fatalism, however, that suggests affinities with literary naturalism. An unavoidable destruction hangs over and overtakes the Niaruna, regardless of the efforts of the missionaries and Moon. Similarly in *Far Tortuga*, the last voyage of the *Lillias Eden* has a predestined quality about it, and the novel is full of omens and foreshadowings.

There is, in Matthiessen's art, an ominous skepticism about the possibility of survival for traditional patterns of life. Men such as Moon and Avers, who cast their lot with the natural world, through choice or chance, are destined to go down with the ship; the smug, technocratic modern society has little place or tolerance for them. Still, there are survivors. These two novels are too open-ended to be tied up with certainties and happy endings, but both hold out the possibility of hope. Moon soldiers on, "in celebration of the only man beneath the eye of Heaven," himself. Speedy, the most decent and heroic of the turtlers, survives the wreck, like Melville's Ishmael. The reader is unsure that he will live but sure that the novel does not explicitly have him die with the rest of the crew.

Both *At Play in the Fields of the Lord* and *Far Tortuga* present the possibility of human fulfillment through the apprehension and acceptance of humanity's proper role in the natural world. That world is constantly threatened, however, by the values of "civilization." Still, Matthiessen believes, there is a chance of avoiding the spiritual damnation implicit in the destruction of the Niaruna and the turtlers. "I hope we'll be forced into a new value system," he has stated. "But I think we're going to be forced to the edge of the cliff first. It's going to be so close."

AT PLAY IN THE FIELDS OF THE LORD

More than a decade after he published *At Play in the Fields of the Lord*, Matthiessen remarked that he thought of it as a "conventional novel . . . full of fine writing." Critics, however, have seen the novel as extraordinary in theme, structure, and style, as well as in quality. "A most unusual novel," wrote Emile Capouya in *The New York Times*; Granville Hicks wrote of the book's "power over the imagination" and its "astonishing assortment of characters." More than any other work, *At Play in the Fields of the Lord* established Matthiessen, in fellow novelist and poet Jim Harrison's words, as "our most eccentric major writer."

Superficially, the novel is an obvious outgrowth of Matthiessen's years as a wandering naturalist in obscure areas of the world. He had already produced two nonfiction studies of the tropical wilderness and its native inhabitants, both of which explore in depth the implications of the contact between the "civilized" world and the "primitive." *At Play in the Fields of the Lord* is set in the Amazon, and it is a study of the interpenetration, and ultimately the irreconcilability, of cultures.

At the center of the novel, more a presence than a group of characters, are the Niaruna, a tiny Stone Age Indian tribe precariously clinging to life on the banks of a jungle river. Matthiessen does not romanticize the natives. They are crude, unthinking, dirty, and addicted to drugs and occasional violence; there are no noble savages here. Still, there is a kind of purity and integrity in their lives that the more "civilized" characters lack. The greatest threat to the existence of the Niaruna is the local governor, Guzman, "El Comandante," a petty dictator with a handful of bestial troops at his disposal. This vanguard of civilization is engaged in a "pacification" of the Niaruna bordering on genocide; only drinking and whoring in the squalid fleshpots of Madre de Dios, the little jungle town that provides much of the novel's early locale, and self-indulgent incompetence have kept these representatives of law and order from exterminating the Indians long since. A third cultural bloc is formed by an earnest pair of American missionary families, the Hubens and the Quarriers. Humorless hustlers for God's will as they see fit to interpret it, the missionaries seek to convert and uplift the Niaruna before El Comandante uses the tribe's savagery as an excuse for its liquidation or dispersal. For the missionaries, the salvation of the Niarunas' souls, as well as their bodies, is synonymous with the abandonment of the tribe's primitive, natural culture.

Caught between these groups, and emphatically not of any of them, are Lewis Meriwether Moon and his partner Wolfie. These two American soldiers of fortune are stranded in the jungle after El Comandante impounds their small plane, gaudily plastered with a sign reading "Wolfie and Moon, Inc.—Small Wars and Demolition." When Martin Quarrier sees it, he says, disbelieving, "It's a joke." So it is, and one of the aspects of *At Play in the Fields of the Lord* most frequently ignored is the pervasive comic irony of the novel. Wolfie is only a richly sketched bit player in the panorama of the novel, but Moon is the most thoroughly developed and complex character in all Matthiessen's fiction, and one of the most interesting in modern American writing; it is his novel. Part American Indian and something of a cynical philosopher, Moon masquerades as an amoral pragmatist. In fact, he is a closet mystic who practices introspection that borders on meditation (foreshadowing Matthiessen's own developing interest in Zen, which culminated in *The Snow Leopard*).

El Comandante wants Moon and Wolfie to bomb the Indians for him, and at first Moon is tempted. Gradually, however, circumstances and powerful but obscure forces in his own psychology impel him to cast himself in the role of a savior to the tribe. The native hallucinogen *ayahuasca* projects Moon into a weird and frightening drug trip, an exploration into the depths of his psyche, rendered with astonishing effectiveness by Matthiessen's surrealistic prose. (Matthiessen may have used his own experiences with hallucinogens to inform this scene.) Moon goes to live among the Indians, his civilized persona dissolving as he adopts their simple ways. As he sheds his Western cultural skin and melds himself into the ethos of the tribe, Moon also discovers a new self lurking under his civilized mask—that of the Indian he comes to believe he truly has always been.

Walls of misunderstanding rise between the characters of this novel. The members of each group struggle against what they perceive to be the challenges of the others, crippled by a myopia that makes it impossible for any of the characters but Moon to see beyond their own values. Doomed by their lack of knowledge and by the narrowness of their specialized world, the Niaruna tremble on the brink of extinction. Blinded to their own bigotry by their faith and by the arrogance of religious Babbittry, the missionaries seek to do everything for the Indians at Niaruna Station except understand and accept them for what they are. The missionary leader, Les Huben, is, in his own way, nearly as sinister an embodiment of progress as the soulless and corrupt representatives of the state, who are at least more candid in acknowledging their desire to destroy the Indians.

Society, whether the elemental one of the Niaruna tribe or the neurotic and more complex one of the other characters, is only one pole of the action of *At Play in the Fields of the Lord*. The human world is counterpointed throughout by the natural world. The jungle hangs persistently about the characters, purifying some, driving others to the verge of insanity. The lushness of Matthiessen's rhetoric (which eventually led him to describe the novel as "ornate") complements the scrupulous accuracy of his observations, so that the forest is rendered with a rich immediacy unmatched in modern fiction. Matthiessen's jungle is *alive* and the equal of the jungles of Conrad or of Melville in *Typee: A Peep at Polynesian Life* (1846). So vividly is the natural world painted that it assumes a thematic weight and aesthetic value that makes it superior to its foil, the world of society and civilization. At the end of the novel, appropriately, the Niaruna are all killed or scattered, and Moon finds himself alone and naked in the jungle. Momentarily, at least, civilization has fallen away and the forest primeval has reassumed the land.

The jungle for Matthiessen is much more than simply a setting. So great is the power of his evocation of it that it becomes almost a character, and a character with a particular personality. It is schizophrenic—alternately rich and nurturing, then corrupt and threatening. The life with which it swarms is emblematic of degeneration and filth to Hazel Quarrier but represents vitality and sustenance to the life-affirming Niaruna. As their chief says, "We have our river and our forest, we have fish and birds and animals to eat. . . . Surely we are living in a golden time!"

The jungle setting gradually absorbs, or rather subsumes, the other elements of the novel. The psychological, social, political, and religious forces that seethe through the early pages subside, replaced by an almost beatific peace that Moon finds by withdrawing into the forest life of the Indians. Certainly, the threat of annihilation from outside society hangs over the book to the end, but it becomes a threat external to the organic integrity of the jungle life. By the time the Niaruna have been dispersed, all the characters have faded, and only the jungle earth remains.

The jungle earth remains, and Moon tenaciously endures. He finds himself with only his own soul for sustenance in the face of the awesomeness of nature. It is he alone, and not the Niaruna, who represents the force that counterpoints the rich, beautiful, but inhuman breadth of nature: the individual human mind. Matthiessen's fundamental apposition is not the traditional one between nature and society but that between the individual human consciousness and the great natural world within which it exists. Matthiessen maintains, in fact, that the true genesis of *At Play in the Fields of the Lord* was an image of isolation in nature: "I wanted to get at what I consider to be the essential human condition, which is solitude under a big sky. I think it's when we run away from that that we miss the whole reverberation of life."

This basic "reverberation of life" is the ultimate subject of the novel. In the end, Moon and the natural world vibrate to a common chord. Thematically, the civilized world falls away, and the individual human psychology forms a continuum with the natural world it inhabits. In this sense, *At Play in the Fields of the Lord* is a Romantic novel, with overtones of William Wordsworth and Percy Bysshe Shelley. Humanity for Matthiessen becomes something like the "mind that feeds upon infinity" of Wordsworth's *The Prelude: Or, The Growth of a Poet's Mind* (1850), and nature assumes its traditional Romantic role as the path to transcendental experience.

In his developing power to interpret that experience, Moon becomes a priest of nature without portfolio, or, to use one of Matthiessen's favorite words, a shaman. Ultimately, *At Play in the Fields of the Lord* is a novel of religious conflict. On one side is the sterile and lifeless theology of the missionaries, on the other the natural celebration of life, biological and spiritual, practiced daily by the Niaruna. For the Indians, the jungle, and their existence therein, is truly sacramental—the external and visible manifestation of an inward and invisible state of grace. For the missionaries, God is extrinsic to the corrupt world of the tropical wilderness. Martin Quarrier, the most decent and conscientious of the group, tries to come to grips with natural instinct as embodied both by the Indians and by his own lust for another missionary's wife, but he cannot bridge the gap between his rigid intellectualized Western mind and the elemental life of the jungle world. Only the part-Indian Moon can gain the natural world and not lose his individual soul in the process.

FAR TORTUGA

If Matthiessen could claim of *At Play in the Fields of the Lord* that it is a conventional novel, he could hardly say the same of the radical *Far Tortuga*, which novelist James Dickey called a turning point in the evolution of the novel, "creating a new vision." *Far Tortuga* was widely hailed at its publication for its experimentalism in style and structure, reaping high praise even from the reclusive novelist Thomas Pynchon. If the novel is not entirely unique, its departures from conventionality mark it as an impressionistic tour de force. Going beyond even the metaphor-free, plain style of writers such as Ernest Hemingway, Matthiessen trimmed his book of superfluities. Quotation marks, indicators such as "he said" and "there was," adjectives, and adverbs were left out. Further, he used the physical form of the book itself and of words and sentences on the page to create visual impressions analogous to the typographic effects of E. E. Cummings. At times, the verbal yields to the ideographic in *Far Tortuga*: A black smudge represents the death of a man, a meandering line marks the horizon or the edge of the sea. Often, words or lines are accented by sweeps of empty white paper. Matthiessen has said that if he had the novel to do over, he would have written it even more like a musical score or an illuminated manuscript, with a much larger format and more dramatic utilization of space.

The form of the novel was an organic outgrowth of its subject, the dying world of a Caribbean turtle-fishing boat on its last voyage. The crew's world is a primitive one, like that of the Niaruna, an unintellectual existence of sea and sky, of superstitions, myths, and folktales, and of a rich cultural tradition succumbing to the modern world. The objective particulars of the turtlers' lives—the boat, the creatures of the sea, the shifting weather—parade through the novel without authorial comment, producing a stark, powerful texture that gives an impression of overwhelming physicality.

Like the cetology sections of *Moby Dick*, the action of *Far Tortuga* is rooted in a solidly constructed core of informational specifics delineating the turtlers' trade. The characters themselves, the doomed sailors of the decrepit boat *Lillias Eden*, live only in their speech and their actions, for Matthiessen never penetrates their minds. The novel's unique oral quality derives from its swell of dialect, which seems increasingly natural as the book progresses. Rhythm is everything in *Far Tortuga*, rhythm and basic image (there is only a single simile in the entire work). As on the pages of Walt Whitman, Ezra Pound, or Charles Olsen, the basic elements of poetic evocation, words, raise up their images as *things*, hung together with a kind of narrative glue, the speech and stories of the turtlers. The dialogue is of a rich and variegated texture. As William Kennedy observed, the great strength of *Far Tortuga* is its use of detail, and both the dialogue and the narrative swarm with a wealth of objective particulars.

Like Matthiessen's Amazonian rain forest, this Caribbean setting is a singular one. Again, the book presents a simple people living close to nature and comfortable with it. Again, the protagonists' culture is threatened, on the brink of extinction. "The Modern World," as the turtlers bitterly call it, is a more distant enemy in this book, lurking outside the visual and verbal matrix that defines the narrative space of *Far Tortuga*, but the reader is well aware that it will soon bring the end of this culture. Modernity is distant only because, within the context of this novel, what is, what is done, and what is said on the *Lillias Eden* is everything. On one hand are the specific objects and actions that define activity on the boat. On the other hand is a kind of spirit world bodied forth in the talk of the men. Legends, ghost stories, and, most of all, tales of the past give the sense of an existence lived always in the shadow of the unseen. For these men, the sea turtle itself, like all animate and inanimate nature, is imbued with a spiritual character, akin to a soul. The line "Green turtle very mysterious, mon" runs through the novel like a chorus. Very mysterious, indeed—sacred, in fact.

The characterization in *Far Tortuga* is one of Matthiessen's most remarkable achievements. As the novel progresses, the reader is able to distinguish among the various speakers, and, gradually, individual personalities emerge. The sailors are rendered only in terms of their verbal expression of the world in which they work and live. There are no narrative threads or subplots unrelated to the immediate action of the book. One character stands out, the captain of the *Lillias Eden*, "Copm" Raib Avers. He is a full-bodied creature, irascible, arrogant, and energetic. He is also the embodiment of the integrity of the turtlers' trade, for he is rightfully proud of his skill as a sailor and passionate in his desire to be as good as "de copms of old"—men to whom sailing and turtle fishing were a calling rather than a way of just getting by. Avers's character is totally a function of the sea-swept world in which he lives. He seems to be related to half the people in the story, and his speech is a continual tale of the folk. To listen to him is to hear a kind of cultural history of the Caribbean, in which the living and the dead, the real and the fanciful, the past and the present are interwoven to create a vivid tapestry. Avers is the voice of the *paideuma*, the wisdom, knowledge, and heritage of his people. "I really do know what working men talk like," Matthiessen said once. In *Far Tortuga*, he proves it.

If Avers is the mouthpiece of a communal voice, he is also, like Moon, an individual voice. Doomed to defeat and death, all the men on the *Lillias Eden* share a common fate. If Avers's voice stands out, it is still the choral effect that dominates the novel. The group of men move as a unit toward their destiny, borne relentlessly by the tides and their own impulses, like the characters in a

Greek tragedy. Avers repeatedly asserts his belief that he is the master of his fate and captain of his soul as well as of the ship. He is more aggressive and less introspective than Moon, more of an activist, and he sees his role in the natural world as confrontational, a constant struggle between himself and the sea. He accepts the struggle, even celebrates it in his rough way, but he does not dominate the novel. Ultimately, his life and death are merged into the total picture of the turtlers as a group.

Avers is not even the last to survive the wreck of the *Lillias Eden* after the ship strikes a reef and sinks. The last forty pages of the novel are a remarkable finale in which the turtlers, adrift and unprotected in catboats, die one by one. The furious, frenetic rush of sounds and images subsides as the life goes out of the men. Finally, only a few hesitant words scattered on otherwise empty pages remain, and finally only the last image—of a man, presumably Speedy, on a beach. One has escaped to tell the tale, to plunge again into the natural continuum of humankind and sea that is the turtler's life, the brilliant portrait of which is the ultimate achievement of this remarkable novel.

The Watson trilogy

In the long hiatus between *Far Tortuga* and *Killing Mister Watson*, Matthiessen was hardly idle, publishing a number of nonfiction works. He has said, however, "I have always considered myself primarily a novelist." His next novel began a trilogy that has come to be called the Watson trilogy or the Everglades trilogy.

In some ways, the first novel in the trilogy, *Killing Mister Watson*, strongly resembles *Far Tortuga*. Set in the Florida Everglades, the book revolves around Edgar J. Watson, who was, by various accounts, a murderer and rogue or a pioneering planter and entrepreneur. He was rumored to have killed Belle Starr and many others. E. J. Watson was a real historical character, and Matthiessen found that "he killed at least seven" people before being shot down by his neighbors in a communal act of murder (and justice). Matthiessen called *Killing Mister Watson* and its sequels, *Lost Man's River* and *Bone by Bone*, a "reimagined life." Though the structural frame of the trilogy is factual, the work is fictional. Matthiessen said only that "there is nothing that could not have happened—nothing inconsistent . . . with the very little that is actually on record."

For *Killing Mister Watson*, Matthiessen adapted nonfiction techniques to his fiction, two forms of writing in which he excels. The book has a documentary feel and departs from most conventional novels as radically in its way as does *Far Tortuga*. E. J. Watson is never seen directly. He is killed "behind the scenes" in the prologue, and the remainder of the book consists of reminiscences by people who knew him or knew about him. The book is leavened with letters, commentary, and newspaper reports that create a sense of history, but it is the sharply rendered and distinctive voices of the characters, like the voices of the turtlers in *Far Tortuga*, that are the heart of the novel.

Like most of Matthiessen's work, *Killing Mister Watson* evokes the natural world in extraordinary detail and with a strong sense of the losses caused by human encroachment. Of the overharvesting that has devastated many species in the Everglades, one character says: "A broke-up rookery, that ain't a picture you want to think about. . . . The pile of carcasses left behind when you strip the plumes and move on to the next place is just pitiful, and it's a piss-poor way to harvest, cause there ain't no adults left to feed them starving young 'uns." This is, in microcosm, what Matthiessen has been saying about environmental destruction across most of his career.

Beginning with *At Play in the Fields of the Lord*, all of Matthiessen's fiction has moved relentlessly against this backdrop of human assault on the natural world. *Lost Man's River*, the second book of the trilogy centered on E. J. Watson's murder, is presented less as a documentary and more as the personal story of Lucius Watson, E. J.'s youngest son from a second marriage. (Lucius appears in *Killing Mister Watson* but is well hidden in that novel.) Lucius is searching for the truth of his father's life and death, though he often seems to reject the more unpleasant facts he finds.

Born in 1889, Lucius was twenty-one when his father was shot. He did not see the murder, and the circumstances surrounding it have haunted him for nearly fifty years by the time of *Lost Man's River*. He had, at one point, even compiled a list of those supposedly present at the killing, earning himself many enemies. Lucius's obsession keeps him from marriage and family and drives him from one career path to another. He has worked primarily as a fisherman, but he starts, abandons, and later completes a university degree. He struggles to finish a history of southwest Florida, and at the beginning of *Lost Man's River* he has decided to write a biography that will redeem his father. Lucius advertises for information for his biography and is brought an urn that supposedly holds his father's bones. He is also invited to visit the man who owned the urn, and Lucius sets off, serving as a researcher-investigator throughout the rest of the book—though he often seems destined to observe rather than act. He is accompanied at various times by Sally Brown, a young assistant who also provides a love interest, and by two men, the drunk Arbie Collins and the blind Andy House, who act almost as "spirit guides." Lucius finds the man who fired the first shot to kill his father, a man whose identity he would have never guessed, a man he could not blame. Andy asks Lucius, "Feel any better?" Lucius never answers, and the reader is never certain if he does.

Henry Short killed E. J. Watson in self-defense. He was the only black man in the armed crowd that day, and, even though dying himself now, he still recalls the murder and the accompanying fear. Matthiessen's sympathetic portrayal of Short embodies another theme of *Lost Man's River* and of much of this writer's work: the deep-seated racism that pervades U.S. society. Although *Lost Man's River* is lyrical and evocative, an occasional ponderousness slows the novel's pace. For example, the complicated family relationships, detailed at length, tend to cause confusion, especially concerning secondary characters. The book is certainly no "quick read," but Matthiessen has long been known for demanding much of his readers and of himself.

The final volume of the trilogy, *Bone by Bone*, is told from the point of view of E. J. Watson himself. Edgar is not a bad man, though he has a bad side and has done bad things. He is a man who was shaped by the sins of his drunken and cowardly father, Elijah Watson, and whose life has been a series of exiles that end only with his death in the Everglades in 1910. He recounts tales of his early life in the Indian Territory of Oklahoma and his experiences with racism. Watson's goal is to find the answers to the mystery surrounding Edgar's life and death as well as the meaning of life in general.

Bone by Bone completes the tale of Edgar Watson and strips away the "myth" that made up so much of the first two books in the series. Watson is revealed rather than concealed. The reader may not like Mr. Watson very much, but the character is certainly unforgettable, as unforgettable as the novel's setting in the beautiful but damaged Florida Everglades.

Shadow Country

When Matthiessen set out to create a fictionalized telling of the life and murder of E. J. Watson, he produced a fifteen-hundred-word manuscript that his publishers determined would be better presented as three separate novels: *Killing Mister Watson*, *Lost Man's River*, and *Bone by Bone*. Nine years after the publication of the third novel, Matthiessen returned to his original vision, completely reworking the Watson trilogy into a single novel, *Shadow Country: A New Rendering of the Watson Legend*. The new work, which involved both significant trimming and significant rewriting, compresses the trilogy from its more than thirteen hundred pages down to a still-substantial nine hundred. The book was enthusiastically received, with many reviewers calling the new novel a monumental achievement that would become known as Matthiessen's best work of fiction. *Shadow Country* earned for Matthiessen the National Book Award for fiction in 2008.

Shadow Country is divided into three books that roughly correlate with the original three novels in the trilogy. Book 1 opens, as *Killing Mister Watson* does, with the murder of the central character, Florida entrepreneur E. J. Watson. What follows is the story of Watson's arrival in coastal Florida in the late nineteenth century and his ruthless rise to fortune as he despoils the lushly described Ten Thousand Islands to plant sugarcane. This story is told in more than fifty monologues spoken by more than a dozen voices—those of the neighbors who in 1910 organized to gun Watson down openly. As the pieces of narrative gradually resolve into a portrait, Watson emerges as the archetypal American desperado: enterprising, beyond the law, charming, greedy, brave, and single-minded. The various narrators reveal conflicting tendencies between admiration and repulsion as they give Watson the nicknames "Emperor Watson," for his success, and "Bloody Watson," for the murders he reputedly commits to succeed.

Book 2, the most drastically revised of the three sections, is narrated by Watson's son Lucius, a historian who returns to Florida years after the killing, determined to write a redemptive biography of his father. Lucius conducts archival research that mirrors the decades of work that Matthiessen himself did to craft his novel. In revising book 1, Matthiessen has stripped away several third-person pieces, emphasizing orality; here, he has removed several first-person accounts, leaving book 2 more of a history lesson. Matthiessen himself has noted that he considers *Lost Man's River*, which relates the story of Lucius, to be the weakest novel of the trilogy. For *Shadow Country*, Lucius's story has been reduced by half, but reviewers continue to find it most effective as a bridge to the last section.

Watson himself narrates book 3, recounting his story from childhood until his death. His savage adulthood is partially explained by the brutal childhood he endured, and the Watson who emerges from book 3 is more complex—introspective and learned, tender and violent—than his killers could have imagined. Watson's complexity, it is clear, resides not just in one man but in the heart of every American pioneer and in American national myths of settlement and development.

In this revision of the Watson story, Matthiessen places greater emphasis on the historical record and on undercurrents of racism. He retains his focus on an exploration of the connection between landscape and psychology, and the novel displays the attention to descriptive detail that informs all of his work.

John L. Cobbs; Charles A. Gramlich
Updated by Cynthia A. Bily

Other major works

SHORT FICTION: *Midnight Turning Gray*, 1984; *On the River Styx, and Other Stories*, 1989.

NONFICTION: *Wildlife in America*, 1959; *The Cloud Forest: A Chronicle of the South American Wilderness*, 1961; *Under the Mountain Wall: A Chronicle of Two Seasons in the Stone Age*, 1962; *Oomingmak: The Expedition to the Musk Ox Island in the Bering Sea*, 1967; *The Shorebirds of North America*, 1967; *Sal Si Puedes: Cesar Chavez and the New American Revolution*, 1970; *Blue Meridian: The Search for the Great White Shark*, 1971; *Everglades: Selections from the Writings of Peter Matthiessen*, 1971 (Paul Brooks, editor); *The Tree Where Man Was Born: The African Experience*, 1972; *The Wind Birds*, 1973; *The Snow Leopard*, 1978; *Sand Rivers*, 1981; *In the Spirit of Crazy Horse*, 1983; *Indian Country*, 1984; *Nine-Headed Dragon River: Zen Journals, 1969-1982*, 1985; *Men's Lives: The Surfmen and Baymen of the South Fork*, 1986; *African Silences*, 1991; *Baikal: Sacred Sea of Siberia*, 1992; *Shadows of Africa*, 1992; *East of Lo Monthang: In the Land of Mustang*, 1995; *An African Trilogy*, 2000 (includes extracts from *The Tree Where Man Was Born*, *African Silences*, and *Sand Rivers*); *The Peter Matthiessen Reader: Nonfiction, 1959-1961*, 2000 (McKay Jenkins, editor); *Tigers in the Snow*, 2000; *The Birds of Heaven: Travels with Cranes*, 2001; *End of the Earth: Voyaging to Antarctica*, 2003.

CHILDREN'S LITERATURE: *Seal Pool*, 1972.

Bibliography

Bawer, Bruce. "Peter Matthiessen, Nature Boy." In *The Aspect of Eternity: Essays*. St. Paul, Minn.: Graywolf Press, 1993. Presents a generally unflattering critique of Matthiessen's novels prior to *Killing Mister Watson*. Argues that Matthiessen romanticizes the primitive and hypocritically attacks American and Western civilization. Also traces an "antagonism toward fathers" in Matthiessen's work.

Bishop, Peter. "The Geography of Hope and Despair: Peter Matthiessen's *The Snow Leopard*." *Critique* 26, no. 4 (1984): 203-216. Places Matthiessen alongside other literary travelers such as Graham Greene, Evelyn Waugh, and D. H. Lawrence. Discusses *The Snow Leopard* in depth and compares it to the novels *Far Tortuga* and *At Play in the Fields of the Lord*. Asserts that the book's lack of conclusion is its success.

Dowie, William. *Peter Matthiessen*. Boston: Twayne, 1991. Provides a good introduction to Matthiessen for the beginning student of his fiction. Includes bibliographical references and index.

Grove, James P. "Pastoralism and Anti-pastoralism in Peter Matthiessen's *Far Tortuga*." *Critique* 21, no. 2 (1979): 15-29. Discusses this highly praised novel and reflects on the influence of Zen Buddhism on Matthiessen's views. Provides an in-depth treatment of the content and intent of the novel within the theme of pastoralism.

Jenkins, McKay. "'Thinking Like a Mountain': Death and Deep Ecology in the Work of Peter Matthiessen." In *Reading under the Sign of Nature: New Essays in Ecocriticism*, edited by John Tallmadge and Henry Harrington. Salt Lake City: University of Utah Press, 2000. Explores the relationships between Aldo Leopold's ecological awareness and Matthiessen's practice of Zen Buddhism as reflected in his writings.

Raglon, Rebecca. "Fact and Fiction: The Development of Ecological Form in Peter Matthiessen's *Far Tortuga*." *Critique* 35, no. 4 (1994): 245-259. Looks at Matthiessen's work, *Far Tortuga* especially, as a criticism of the dualistic view of nature and humanity. Argues that Matthiessen sees no separation between nature and humanity and writes instead of their necessary interrelatedness.

Roberson, William. *Peter Matthiessen: An Annotated Bibliography*. Jefferson, N.C.: McFarland, 2001. Useful guide to resources on Matthiessen's work provides listings of primary and secondary source literature.

Tredinnick, Mark. "The Long Coastline: Peter Matthiessen." In *The Land's Wild Music: Encounters with Barry Lopez, Peter Matthiessen, Terry Tempest Williams, and James Galvin*. San Antonio, Tex.: Trinity University Press, 2005. Presents a profile of Matthiessen and reflections on his writings, interwoven with an extended interview conducted as Matthiessen guides Tredinnick through his home landscape.

Watson, James G. "Man Writing: The Watson Trilogy—Peter Matthiessen in Archive." *Texas Studies in Literature and Language* 46, no. 2 (July, 2004): 245-270. Reveals Matthiessen's research and writing process through an examination of the twenty-five boxes of manuscripts and notes related to the Watson trilogy in the Peter Matthiessen Collection at the University of Texas at Austin.

CHARLES ROBERT MATURIN

Born: Dublin, Ireland; September 25, 1780
Died: Dublin, Ireland; October 30, 1824
Also known as: Dennis Jasper Murphy

Principal long fiction

Fatal Revenge: Or, The Family of Montorio, 1807 (as Dennis Jasper Murphy)
The Wild Irish Boy, 1808 (as Murphy)
The Milesian Chief, 1812 (as Murphy)
Women: Or, Pour et Contre, 1818
Melmoth the Wanderer, 1820
The Albigenses, 1824

Other literary forms

In addition to his novels, Charles Robert Maturin (MAT-choo-rihn) also wrote plays, three of which were performed and published during his lifetime: *Bertram: Or, The Castle of St. Aldobrand, a Tragedy* (pr., pb. 1816), *Manuel* (pr., pb. 1817), and *Fredolfo* (pr., pb. 1819). A fourth, *Osmyn, the Renegade: Or, The Siege of Salerno, a Tragedy*, written sometime between 1817 and 1821, was produced in Dublin in 1830. It was never published in its entirety; excerpts were printed in *The Edinburgh Literary Journal* (April 24, 1830). Of these plays, only *Bertram* was financially successful. When it first appeared, it was one of the most talked about plays of the season, and today it is noted for being one of the first dramatic portrayals of the brooding, sinned against, and sinning figure who has come to be called the Byronic hero.

Two short fictional pieces were published posthumously: "Leixlip Castle: An Irish Family Legend" appeared in *The Literary Souvenir: Or, Cabinet of Poetry and Romance* of 1825, and "The Sybil's Prophecy: A Dramatic Fragment" was printed in the 1826 edition of the same publication. Both these pieces are in the gothic style.

Achievements

Charles Robert Maturin is best known for *Melmoth the Wanderer*, the fifth of his six novels. Although, when it first appeared, many critics viewed it merely as an unfortunate attempt to revive the gothic novel, a form earlier made popular by such authors as Ann Radcliffe and Matthew Gregory Lewis, scholars now consider *Melmoth the Wanderer* one of the finest examples of its genre. It is judged to be not only a culmination of the gothic novel but also a forerunner of the psychological novels of such writers as Fyodor Dostoevski and Franz Kafka. Although Maturin's handling of narrative structure is often awkward and confusing, and although he borrowed so closely from the works of others that he can be accused of plagiarism, his novels are original in their depiction of extreme states of mind, especially those engendered by fear.

Maturin himself was aware of his major strength. In the prefatory pages of *The Milesian Chief*, he wrote

> If I possess any talent, it is that of darkening the gloomy, and of deepening the sad; of painting life in extremes, and representing those struggles of passion when the soul trembles on the verge of the unlawful and the unhallowed.

His settings of mazelike madhouses and dungeons lead the reader into the dark places of the human soul. This particular aspect of his novels fascinated and influenced many other authors. Edgar Allan Poe, Robert Louis Stevenson, Oscar Wilde, Christina and Dante Gabriel Rossetti, Honoré de Balzac, and Charles Baudelaire were all impressed by Maturin's attempt to penetrate the mystery of evil.

Critical attention also has been given to Maturin's role in Irish literary history. In such novels as *The Milesian Chief* and *The Wild Irish Boy*, descriptions of Irish settings and character play an important part. More study needs to be done to evaluate fully this contribution to the development of the Irish regional novel; whatever the outcome, Maturin's place among the significant writers of the English gothic novel is assured.

Biography

Charles Robert Maturin was born in 1780, one of several children born to William Maturin and Fidelia Watson. The Maturin family was of French descent. One of their ancestors was a Huguenot priest who was forced to leave France because of religious persecution during the reign of Louis XIV. This aspect of his family history strongly impressed the young Maturin, and throughout his life he was fond of relating how his ancestors had suffered for their faith. He himself was strongly anti-Catholic and especially opposed to the rule of monastic life, which he considered dangerously repressive. His novels contain many scenes and descriptions of monasteries as sadistic places where virtue turns to vice.

When in Ireland, Maturin's family became closely connected with the Anglican Church. Maturin's great-grandfather, Peter Maturin, was dean of Killala from 1724 to 1741, and his grandfather, Gabriel James Maturin, succeeded Jonathan Swift as dean of St. Patrick's in Dublin in 1745. Following this tradition, Maturin entered Trinity College in 1795 to study theology, and in 1803 he took holy orders. In the same year, he married Henrietta Kingsbury, a daughter of the archdeacon of Killala. From all reports, the couple were well suited and happily married. After ordination, Maturin served as curate in Loughrea, Galway, for two years. He then returned to Dublin to become curate of St. Peter's, a position he held for the rest of his life. His small income from this curacy was insufficient to support his family, especially after his father was accused of fraud and dismissed from his position with the Irish post office in 1809. Later, he was cleared and given another position, but for a time, the family struggled in severe poverty. In fact, Maturin was continually troubled by financial difficulties. To supplement his income, he ran a school to prepare boys for college, and later he turned to novel writing.

The prefaces of his novels and the styles of romance he chose to employ indicate that he wanted very much to become a popular writer. Because he realized that many of his parishioners and superiors might not approve of a minister writing novels, he used the pseudonym Dennis Jasper Murphy, publishing three novels under that name. When it was discovered that he was the author of the play *Bertram*, a play involving adultery and an amoral hero, he was for a time in danger of losing his curacy. Apparently, friends intervened to soothe the necessary bishops. After this incident, since his identity was known, he published his next novels and plays under his own name. It is quite possible that his literary activities did prevent his advancement in the clerical profession. There were those

Charles Robert Maturin. (Library of Congress)

who interpreted the beliefs of his characters, some of which were atheistic and heretical, as Maturin's own.

Maturin's novels did gain him one very influential friend, Sir Walter Scott. In 1810, Scott wrote a generally favorable review of *Fatal Revenge* for *The Quarterly Review*. Encouraged, Maturin wrote to him, and a correspondence was begun that lasted until Maturin's death. Although the two never actually met, Scott did assist Maturin with encouragement and advice, and he was instrumental in Maturin's one financial success; he recommended *Bertram* to Lord Byron, who was then responsible for play selection at Drury Lane Theatre. Byron was favorably impressed, and the famous actor Edmund Kean agreed to play the lead. The play's success earned Maturin one thousand pounds, most of which paid a relative's debt. Earlier, Maturin had been able to sell the copyright of his third novel, *The Milesian Chief*, for eighty pounds (the first two novels he had printed at his own expense), and later he was advanced five hundred pounds for *Melmoth the Wanderer*, but his literary efforts never brought the long-sought and often desperately needed financial stability.

Up until his death, Maturin continually tried to write in a style that would sell. *The Albigenses* is a historical romance, a type Scott had established and made quite popular. This novel was the first in what was to be a trilogy depicting European manners in ancient, medieval, and modern times. Soon after *The Albigenses* was completed, Maturin died in his home on October 30, 1824, apparently after a long period of ill health. The exact cause of his death is not known. He left his wife and four children, who were still in desperate need of financial assistance.

ANALYSIS

In his preface to *Fatal Revenge*, Charles Robert Maturin stresses the fear of the unknown as essential in the emotional and spiritual lives of humans:

> It is *not* the weak and trivial impulse of the nursery, to be forgotten and scorned by manhood. It is the aspiration of a spirit; 'it is the passion of immortals,' that dread and desire of their final habitation.

In one of his sermons, he focuses on the same theme:

> The very first sounds of childhood are tales of another life—foolishly are they called tales of superstition; for, however disguised by the vulgarity of narration, and the distortion of fiction, they tell him of those whom he is hastening from the threshold of life to join, the inhabitants of the invisible world, with whom he must soon be, and be for ever.

These quotations indicate a major aspect of Maturin's perception of human existence; the haunted and the sacred are interwoven and share a common ground. Human fascination with the supernatural, the world of demons and ghosts, springs from the same source as the desire to believe in salvation and a return to paradise. In fact, the road to salvation leads through the dark places of the soul where individuals must admit their fallen state, their own guilt.

The theme of guilt is common in all of Maturin's novels. His major characters must struggle with the serpents in their own hearts, their own original sin. In keeping with this theme, the settings of his novels are generally those of a fallen world; dungeons and underground passages are common backgrounds for the action. Even in those novels that contain descriptions of more natural surroundings, storms and earthquakes are common occurrences, always reminding people that they have been exiled from paradise. Harmony with nature, with humanity, and with God has been lost.

Maturin develops this theme of guilt, which brings exile and separation, through his handling of character. The divided nature of humanity is represented by the pairing of characters, especially brothers: Ippolito and Annibal in *Fatal Revenge*, Connal and Desmond in *The Milesian Chief*, Paladour and Amirald in *The Albigenses*. These brothers are described in such a way as to suggest one identity fragmented into two opposing selves. Ippolito is passionate, Annibal rational; Desmond is the soft flower, Connal the proud oak. Often a character is torn in two opposing directions and does not know how to reconcile them: Connal between his Irish pride and his realization that the Irish peasants are not yet ready to govern themselves; Charles in *Women* between his love for Eva, a shy quiet girl, and Zaira, a worldly and more accomplished woman. At times, a character seems pursued by a dark, sinister double: Montorio by Schemoli in *Fatal Revenge*; Alonzo by the parricide in *Melmoth the Wanderer*. By far the most striking and powerful example of this is the character of the wanderer himself. Melmoth represents the potential for evil that can be found in all humans. In developing Melmoth's character, Maturin echoes the warning in Genesis against too much curiosity about the tree of knowledge of good and evil. Melmoth has sold his soul for increased knowledge; his sin is one of "pride and intellectual glorying," the sin of Lucifer and of the first mortals.

As Maturin's characters wander in a fallen world, little guidance is provided. Especially weak and ineffective are the parental figures. In fact, a distinguishing trait of this fallen world is the disintegration of the family. In all of Maturin's six novels, there are parents who are woefully irresponsible. They are often self-centered, putting their own greedy desires before their children's welfare, or they seek to expiate their own guilt by placing the burden of their sin upon their children. This selfish turning inward and transference of guilt to another is also found in Maturin's representations of larger structures of authority, especially the Catholic Church. As the divided soul wanders in a fallen world, parent and church offer little hope.

Maturin reserves the role of spiritual guide for the female characters who either love or are loved by the hero (such love is not always fulfilled or requited). Often his women are idealized creatures who can reconcile within themselves all conflicting opposites: in *Melmoth the Wanderer*, Immalee embodies passion and purity; in *The Albigenses*, Genevieve is a "mixture of strength and purity that is never to be found but in woman." Even if a woman finds herself hurled into a world of experience and corruption, as Zaira is in *Women*, her heart remains pure. At times, Maturin uses his female characters to symbolize self-sacrificing love that, although never placing the beloved before God, does place the beloved before the self. Despite Maturin's emphasis on such redeeming love, however, when domestic happiness is found by his characters it seems contrived and imposed upon them by others. Maturin is undoubtedly at his best when depicting people lost and searching for wholeness, not in actually finding it.

Fatal Revenge

Maturin titled his first novel *The Family of Montorio*, but the publisher changed the title to *Fatal Revenge*, hoping to attract readers who would be interested in a gothic tale. The novel is definitely written in the style of Radcliffe—one of its central figures, a ghostlike monk who calls himself Schemoli, is clearly patterned on Radcliffe's Schoedoni in 1797's *The Italian*—but Maturin uses what he borrows to develop his own characteristic theme with originality. Although he follows Radcliffe's technique of revealing the supernatural events as merely the result of disguise and charade, his descriptions of aberrant states of mind, to which all are subject, go beyond her handling of evil, and beyond the mere cataloging of grotesque horrors used by those writers who chose to imitate the more sensational style of Matthew Gregory Lewis. Annibal concludes after a brief period of solitary confinement that an "inward acquaintance" delights one not with tranquillity but, on the contrary, with "the grave of the mind." In describing the anguish of his guilt, Montorio cries, "the worm within me never dieth; and every thought and object it converts into its own morbid food." In Maturin, the evil within is quite real.

The plot of this novel is complicated, and Maturin's narrative is at times twisted and confusing. The tale relates the vengeful machinations of Schemoli, the once noble Count Montorio. He is seeking revenge for the wrongs his younger brother committed against him by manipulating Ippolito and Annibal, two young men he believes are his brother's sons, into believing that they are fated to murder their father. In part, the novel's convoluted structure works to Maturin's advantage, for it helps create a nightmare quality that suits this theme of revenge and guilt. By the end of the novel, after several brutal crimes, it is clear that the words of Ippolito to the Inquisition accurately represent human nature as portrayed in the novel:

> There is no human being fully known to another. . . . To his own consciousness and recollection, a man will not dare to reveal every thought that visits his mind; there are some which he almost hopes are concealed from the Deity.

THE WILD IRISH BOY

Maturin's second novel, *The Wild Irish Boy*, although often following the style of the sentimental, regional novel, still has some of the same motifs and themes as those of the gothic *Fatal Revenge*. The novel does have many flaws and is probably Maturin's poorest work: There are long pointless digressions, a decidedly awkward handling of point of view, and an ineffective mixture of literary techniques. Nevertheless, when Maturin touches upon those subjects that most fascinated him, he does so with some success. The novel's most interesting character is Lady Montrevor, a strong, compelling woman who through her own foolish vanity allows herself to be trapped into a loveless marriage, thus sacrificing the sincere love of a good man. She must bear the anguish of her loss and the knowledge of her guilt. She does so grandly, wanting no man's pity. Maturin often alludes to John Milton's fallen angel when describing her: She is "no less than archangel ruined." In many ways, she is a female Byronic hero who knows that evil is more than appearance. This type of female character clearly interested Maturin. Zaira in *Women* and Armida in *The Milesian Chief* are similarly delineated, and all three are quite unlike the sentimental heroines so typical of the other novelists of the day.

THE MILESIAN CHIEF

In Maturin's third novel, *The Milesian Chief*, his interest in the anguish of the proud heart reveals itself in his portrayal of the hero as well as of the heroine. Connal, the Irish rebel, is the once-great angelic chief fallen among lesser spirits, an appropriate male partner for the melancholy Armida, who is shaded by a "proud dejection, like that of an abdicated monarch." The novel is set in Ireland during an uprising against the British in 1798. As the plot unfolds, it becomes clear that Maturin is more successful in handling narrative structure and point of view than in his previous works, and although the final scene, in which the four major characters (Connal, Armida, Desmond, and Ines) all die more or less at the same time in the same place, seems contrived, it is psychologically appropriate. Throughout the novel, these four personalities have been interwoven. Connal and Desmond function as opposites linked in one identity, and each female character both mirrors and complements her male counterpart. Again, even when trying to write a regional novel, Maturin shows that his main interest lies in depicting the individual lost and searching for a way back to some longed-for paradise.

WOMEN

In his preface to *Women*, Maturin writes that he believes his previous novels failed to win popular approval because they lacked reality. He indicates that in this novel he has fashioned his characters to resemble those of "common life." This intention does not, however, cause any significant change in his major theme. Again, through his three central characters, Maturin depicts human nature as torn and guilt ridden. Charles vacillates between his love for Eva, a shy innocent girl, and Zaira, the older, more accomplished woman. He is never able to commit himself fully to loving one or the other until it is too late. Only when Eva is dying of consumption brought on by Charles's abandoning her for Zaira does he desert Zaira to return to Eva.

Throughout the novel, Eva has struggled with her love for Charles, for in her heart it conflicts with her love for God. On her deathbed, she rejects Charles completely, refusing even to see him, and she dies at peace with God. Zaira undergoes a similar ordeal after Charles abandons her. She turns to God, hoping for consolation, yet she continues to see Charles's image before her eyes. After Eva's death, Charles dies from fever and madness. As the novel closes, Zaira becomes the primary figure of guilt. She lives on, always holding her hand to her heart, accusing herself of having murdered her daughter. She has discovered that Eva was the child taken from her at birth, the child she has been trying to find. This discovery is not made until it is too late to remedy the painful consequences of the mother and daughter loving the same man. Maturin concludes the novel with an image typical of his style: "The serpents that devour us, are generated out of our own vitals."

Melmoth the Wanderer

Although Maturin's preface to *Melmoth the Wanderer* suggests that what follows will show the reader the enemy of humankind in the form of Satan, the tales within tales that constitute the novel show instead that this enemy lies within each individual. By combining the qualities of Faust, Mephistopheles, and the Wandering Jew, Maturin fashioned a hero-villain suitable for leading the reader through the maze of tales that takes him into the obscure recesses of the human soul.

Melmoth is Maturin's most compelling and powerful character; he is an embodiment of the dark side of each human being, the shadow that each person casts. Thus, it is particularly appropriate that in the narrative frame of these tales of human malignity, John Melmoth, who bears the same name as the mysterious wanderer, inherits the task of dealing with the molding manuscript that will set him on his own journey into the mystery of evil. His withdrawal at midnight into a closed room, sealed off from society, to read the manuscript, disregarding his uncle's warning that perhaps he should destroy it unread, suggests a type of original sin. Indeed, as he pursues knowledge of the wanderer's life, he learns that all humans are potential agents of Satan. After all, Melmoth the Wanderer did not spring from the fires of hell, but from his own family.

The hope that Maturin offers in his guilty state is to be found in self-sacrificing love; yet to love in this manner one must believe in the potential for goodness in humankind, the possibility of redemption. Melmoth is finally damned not because of his original bargain to sell his soul but because of his own misanthropy. He believes in nothing but the hostility and evil of human nature. Immalee, the island maiden who learns of suffering by loving him, was his hope. If he had chosen to trust in her love, seeing in it the essence of the greater self-sacrificing love of Christ, he might have been saved.

The Albigenses

Maturin's last work, *The Albigenses*, is a historical novel that focuses on the crusade in 1208 against the Albigenses, a Manichaean sect declared heretical by the Catholic Church. Maturin, however, follows the historical facts only roughly, altering events and chronology to suit plot and character. Again, he portrays two brothers, Paladour and Amirald, and their two loves, Isebelle and Genevieve. Although the theme of the fragmented self is not as predominant as in his previous novels, it is present. Paladour and Amirald were separated at birth, and for most of the novel neither knows the other is his brother; they are characterized in such a way as to suggest differing aspects of one personality. Paladour is associated with iron and Amirald with flowers, yet they are bound together through suffering. In choosing their brides, they also reveal complementary personality traits: Paladour marries the noble Lady Isebelle, and Amirald chooses the simple peasant girl Genevieve. When the novel ends, the reader is left with the impression that all four live together in absolute harmony.

Such an easy resolution does seemed contrived, for *The Albigenses* begins with Paladour's sinister encounter with a seemingly demoniac lady of the lake. He believes there is a curse upon him and that he is fated to murder his bride on their wedding night. When the effects of these dark tones are no longer wanted, Maturin quickly resolves all with rational explanations. Paladour is then free to live as a very natural husband. Part of the dissatisfaction the reader feels with this happy ending may be accounted for by the fact that the novel bristles with gothic motifs that are not smoothly integrated into the historical aspects of the novel.

Despite Maturin's own belief that the day of the gothic novel had already passed when he began writing, and his repeated attempts to use whatever narrative form might suit the reading public, he was continually drawn to the techniques of the gothic tale. Whether it be a mysterious monk haunting underground passages or a madwoman raving prophetic truths, all his novels have gothic elements. The gothic novel provided him with a literary world suitable for the images of evil and suffering that populated his own mind, a mind repeatedly drawn to the problems of human guilt and the divided soul. The body of Maturin's work, although uneven, offers ample proof of his ability to shape these dark themes with power and originality.

Diane D'Amico

Other major works

SHORT FICTION: "Leixlip Castle: An Irish Family Legend," 1825 (in *The Literary Souvenir: Or, Cabinet of Poetry and Romance*); "The Sybil's Prophecy: A Dramatic Fragment" 1826 (in *The Literary Souvenir*).

PLAYS: *Bertram: Or, The Castle of St. Aldobrand, a Tragedy*, pr., pb. 1816; *Manuel*, pr., pb. 1817; *Fredolfo*, pr., pb. 1819; *Osmyn, the Renegade: Or, The Siege of Salerno, a Tragedy*, pr. 1830.

Bibliography

Bayer-Berenbaum, Linda. *The Gothic Imagination: Expansion in Gothic Literature and Art.* Rutherford, N.J.: Fairleigh Dickinson University Press, 1982. A sympathetic study of gothicism, the essence of which is its confrontation with evil and feelings of doom. Contains chapters on literary gothicism and Gothic art's relationship to literature as well as focused analyses of particular works of literature. Maturin is given considerable attention, including an extensive analysis of *Melmoth the Wanderer*.

Jeffares, A. Norman, and Peter van de Kamp. *Irish Literature: The Nineteenth Century*. Dublin: Irish Academic Press, 2006-2007. A three-volume reference set that contains critical essays about the lives and works of numerous Irish writers. Includes an essay on Maturin in the first volume.

Johnson, Anthony. "Gaps and Gothic Sensibility: Walpole, Lewis, Mary Shelley, and Maturin." In *Exhibited by Candlelight: Sources and Developments in the Gothic Tradition*, edited by Valeria Tinkler-Villani, Peter Davidson, and Jane Stevenson. Amsterdam: Rodopi, 1995. This study of gothic literature includes Johnson's learned and clear discussion of how Maturin handles the gaps in reality that are exploited in gothic fiction.

Kiely, Robert. *The Romantic Novel in England*. Cambridge, Mass.: Harvard University Press, 1972. An important book about Romantic prose fiction, including Maturin's gothic romances, which analyzes twelve Romantic novels. *Melmoth the Wanderer* is covered in detail; this novel is found to be more emotionally involved with Catholicism and rebellion against authoritarian political systems than other gothic fiction.

Kosok, Heinz. "Charles Robert Maturin and Colonialism." In *Literary Inter-Relations: Ireland, Egypt, and the Far East*, edited by Mary Massoud. Gerrards Cross, England: C. Smythe, 1996. Kosok's paper, initially delivered in 1993 at a conference examining Ireland's literary relationships with countries in the Middle and Far East, focuses on Maturin's representation of colonialism.

Kramer, Dale. *Charles Robert Maturin.* New York: Twayne, 1973. Analyzes Maturin's personality, describes the conditions of his life, and indicates his innovations in the gothic tradition. Includes a chronology, notes and references, a selected annotated bibliography, and an index.

Lougy, Robert E. *Charles Robert Maturin.* Lewisburg, Pa.: Bucknell University Press, 1975. An insightful review of Maturin's life and writings, dividing his career into early, middle, and later years. Includes a chronology and a selected bibliography of primary and secondary works.

Moynahan, Julian. "The Politics of Anglo-Irish Gothic: Charles Robert Maturin, Joseph Sheridan Le Fanu, and the Return of the Repressed." In *Anglo-Irish: The Literary Imagination in a Hyphenated Culture*. Princeton, N.J.: Princeton University Press, 1995. Moynahan's analysis of gothic literature by the two authors is included in his study of literary works written by Anglo-Irish authors during the nineteenth century.

Norton, Rictor, ed. *Gothic Readings: The First Wave, 1764-1840.* London: Leicester University Press, 2000. This study of gothic literature includes an excerpt from *Melmoth the Wanderer*, which is defined as belonging to "the German school of horror," and two contemporary reviews of the novel, including one by Sir Walter Scott. Useful for placing Maturin within the larger context of the gothic and Romantic novel.

W. SOMERSET MAUGHAM

Born: Paris, France; January 25, 1874
Died: Nice, France; December 16, 1965
Also known as: William Somerset Maugham

Principal long fiction

Liza of Lambeth, 1897
The Making of a Saint, 1898
The Hero, 1901
Mrs. Craddock, 1902
The Merry-Go-Round, 1904
The Bishop's Apron, 1906
The Explorer, 1907
The Magician, 1908
Of Human Bondage, 1915
The Moon and Sixpence, 1919
The Painted Veil, 1925
Cakes and Ale: Or, The Skeleton in the Cupboard, 1930
The Narrow Corner, 1932
Theatre, 1937
Christmas Holiday, 1939
Up at the Villa, 1941
The Hour Before Dawn, 1942
The Razor's Edge, 1944
Then and Now, 1946
Catalina, 1948
Selected Novels, 1953

Other literary forms

A professional man of letters whose work spanned more than six decades, W. Somerset Maugham (mawm) published in a wide range of literary forms, the significant exception being poetry. He first won success, fame, and wealth in the theater; his most acclaimed dramas were performed on the London stage during the first three decades of the twentieth century. He produced more than a hundred short stories, largely written during the period from 1921 to 1950; his collected short stories include four of the best-known stories of the twentieth century: "Rain," "The Outstation," "The Letter," and "The Colonel's Lady." Fifteen or more additional volumes are devoted to autobiography, literary and aesthetic criticism, and travel. Among these, the most useful for students are *The Summing Up* (1938), *Ten Novels and Their Authors* (1954), and *A Writer's Notebook* (1949).

Achievements

W. Somerset Maugham's twenty novels are exceptionally uneven; the first eight, though interesting, suggest the efforts of a young novelist to discover where his talent lies. Between the publication of *Of Human Bondage* in 1915 through *The Razor's Edge* in 1944, he produced his most significant prose works. During this period, he was a world-famous man of letters with a following of many thousands who would buy and read anything he wrote; however, a few novels that he produced, such as *Then and Now* and *Up at the Villa*, were not in his best vein.

The novels brought Maugham acclaim and recognition both from a general audience and from the intelligentsia. Among common readers, he was perhaps the most successful English novelist of the twentieth century, and, as Samuel Johnson pointed out, the common reader is not often wrong. It must be admitted, however, that Maugham's detractors, such as Edmund Wilson, present valid criticism: One expects a serious artist to exert an important influence, either thematic or formal, on his or her medium. The symphony was forever altered by Ludwig van Beethoven; no similar statement can be made about Maugham and the novel. He sought to tell a story with clarity and grace, to embody a set of attitudes and values, and to entertain his readers with insights into character and life.

Biography

William Somerset Maugham, son of an English solicitor, was born in the British embassy in Paris and spent his early childhood in France, learning French as his first language. Following the early death of both parents, Maugham went at age ten to England to live with his uncle, the Reverend Henry Maugham, Vicar of Whitstable, and his German-born wife. The rigid routine and disciplined family life of the Whitstable rectory contrasted with the casual, carefree existence and close warmth that Maugham had known in France. He was enrolled in the King's School, Canterbury, where he spent several unhappy years. A permanent stammer that developed during this period of his life destroyed any possibility of following the profession of his father and two of his brothers. Instead of enrolling in a university, Maugham chose to travel abroad to Germany, where at Heidelberg he saw Henrik Ibsen's dramas and attended lectures by Kuno Fischer on the philosophy of Arthur Schopenhauer. Returning to London, he enrolled in the medical school at St. Thomas's Hospital, where he received his M.D. in 1897.

Maugham's stronger interests, however, were literary and aesthetic, and when his first novel, *Liza of Lambeth*, achieved a modest success, he resolved to enter upon a career as a writer. None of the novels that Maugham wrote during the following decade repeated the success of *Liza of Lambeth*, yet he achieved sudden and unexpected acclaim through a series of plays, modern comedies of manners, beginning with *Lady Frederick* (1907). In 1908, four of his plays were running in London simultaneously. During World War I, Maugham served with British Intelligence in Switzerland and Russia. In 1915, he married Syrie Bernardo Wellcome, a marriage that ended in divorce in 1927. Following World War I, Maugham traveled to more remote areas of the world: the South Seas, Southeast Asia, and America, accompanied by his secretary, a gregarious American named Gerald Haxton, who aided the author in finding material for his fiction. Maugham acquired the Villa Mauresque on the French Riviera in 1928, an estate that became his home for the remainder of his life, though he continued his frequent travels and spent several years during World War II living in the United States. Creative work during his later years centered principally on short stories, novels, and autobiography.

Analysis

W. Somerset Maugham's novels are written in a style highly idiomatic and fluent, revealing the qualities of simplicity, lucidity, and euphony that the author sought to attain. Content to narrate an interesting story from his own unique angle of vision, he brought to the genre a gift for creating interesting characters who reflect life's ironies. In his later works, Maugham's narrative persona is a character interested in people, yet detached and somewhat clinical in his analysis of their actions and motives. The narrator demonstrates an unusual degree of tolerance for human peccadillos and incongruities and is reluctant to judge the actions of human beings. He writes primarily of adults in conflict with one another and with social mores. Frequently, his characters grow in tolerance and acceptance of human life, which is portrayed somewhat pessimistically. Maugham based his characters on people whom he had known or whose lives he had somehow come to know; their actions are presented with consummate realism. They are motivated by their passions or emotions and by their attempts to control their destinies, not by an ideology or set of ideals. Though they may experience inner turmoil and conflict, they are seldom tormented by such emotions. Like their creator-narrator, the characters often have the ability to view themselves with clinical detachment and objectivity, to cast a cold eye on life.

W. Somerset Maugham. (Library of Congress)

LIZA OF LAMBETH

Among the early novels of Maugham, *Liza of Lambeth*, published when the author was only twenty-three, is probably the best known. Set in the Lambeth slum along Vere Street, London, it depicts naturalistically the lives of people in a state of poverty, characters such as those whom the author had come to know at first hand as an obstetric clerk at St. Thomas's Hospital. In its depiction of character, *Liza of Lambeth* fits the tradition of the naturalistic novel, somewhat in the manner of George Gissing, whose work Maugham knew well. The Cockney dialogue that pervades the novel is accurately represented, both in its pronunciation and in its slang or colloquial expressions. As is typical of naturalistic fiction, the characters are generally without hope, yet even in a naturalistic tradition Maugham reveals an original perspective. Unlike much naturalism, *Liza of Lambeth* does not urge social reform; the characters exhibit more hostility toward one another than toward any system. They generally accept their lot, which would be bearable but for their own mistakes. Liza Kemp's friend Sally enters marriage with hope, only to find her chances for happiness shattered owing to her husband's bad temper following drinking bouts, a weakness he had previously concealed. Liza, brimming with life and energy, spurns the devotion of a staid suitor, Tom, and finds excitement in an affair with an older, married neighbor, Jim Blakeston. By allowing passion to dominate their lives, the characters create undue hardships for themselves. This theme is commonly found in Maugham's work.

Just as *Liza of Lambeth* represented an effort at producing a naturalistic novel, Maugham's other early novels give the impression of deliberate attempts at imitating well-established forms. In *The Making of a Saint*, he wrote a brief historical novel with a late fifteenth century Florentine setting. A story of intrigue, assassination, and revenge, it is derived from a brief passage in a work by Niccolò Machiavelli. *Mrs. Craddock* is set in rural England of the late nineteenth century, a novel of manners depicting provincial life, much in the manner of Arnold Bennett; *The Merry-Go-Round* belongs to a similar tradition. In *The Magician*, Maugham incorporates the conventions of the gothic genre, though there is perhaps too much realism for this work to be designated a true gothic novel.

OF HUMAN BONDAGE

In *Of Human Bondage*, Maugham's longest novel and his masterpiece, he turned to the well-known form of the bildungsroman, the novel of a young person growing to maturity. *Of Human Bondage* is highly autobiographical, although it departs significantly from autobiographical accuracy in places. With the aid of an omniscient narrator, the reader follows the life of Philip Carey from his mother's death when he was only nine until he becomes a doctor and resolves to marry. Numerous characters in the novel are based on people the author knew. The Reverend William Carey and his wife Louisa are based on Maugham's uncle and aunt with whom he lived; Lawson is his friend Sir Gerald Kelly; Cronshaw derives from the eccentric poet Aleister Crowley, who had also been the model for Oliver Haddo in *The Magician*; and Hayward is based on Maugham's friend Ellington Brooks. In a similar manner, Maugham incorporates descriptions of places that he knew well, with names only slightly altered (Whitstable to Blackstable, Canterbury to Tercanbury) or not altered at all, as the countryside of Kent or the cities of London and Paris.

In *Of Human Bondage*, Maugham sees three forces impinging on Philip, shaping and influencing his life, forces that the novel emphasizes strongly: passion, disillusionment, and the quest for purpose in life. Philip is ill-equipped to cope with passion. Having been born with a clubfoot, which becomes a source of ridicule among school boys, and having lost both parents in childhood, he becomes overly sensitive. He takes pleasure in the solitary pursuit of reading and is less in the company of others than most boys; as a result, he has little understanding of the world at large. He finds that women who adore him arouse in him no passion in return, whereas he falls irrationally and inexplicably in love with the common and venal Mildred Rogers. Only after a long period of bondage, humiliation, and pain can he free himself from this attachment, which he comes to regard as degrading. At the end of the novel, he proposes marriage to Sally Athelney, not because he feels passion for her but because he believes she will be a good wife. Maugham's view of romance in this work is consistent with the view presented in his other works and with Arthur Schopenhauer's pessimistic outlook—that romantic passion is a kind of trick played on people by nature to foster procreation, that it does not last, that it is irrational, and that it represents a poor basis for marriage.

To express the necessity for disillusionment, Maugham depicts Philip as growing up in an atmosphere of illusion involving religious beliefs and assumptions about the code of an English gentleman. When Philip arrives in Germany, it becomes awkward to continue to maintain that a gentleman necessarily belongs to the Church of England. He encounters a diversity of religious beliefs, all sincerely held and advocated through conflicting arguments. The result is that he loses his religious faith, though he assumes that the actual cause of the loss is that he lacks the religious temperament. Losing a framework so basic, he experiences a sense of liberation, yet he finds his new freedom uncomfortable as well, lacking in certainties.

Philip clings to one certainty: He assumes without question that he must earn his living through some profession, and he begins to explore various unsuitable paths. He rejects the idea of becoming a clergyman, quits a career in accounting, abandons the struggle to become an artist after studying in Paris, and finally decides to pursue medicine. He does not escape hardship, for at one point he loses the money provided for his education and must work at a department store until his uncle's death brings a small inheritance.

Reflecting on happiness, Philip is puzzled as to how this quality fits as a purpose in life, since his own is unhappy. He observes that happiness eludes people, such as the dancers at the Bal Bullier in Paris, who pursue it frenetically. Those who seek happiness through the enjoyment of art waste their lives, and those who struggle to create art seldom find happiness, even when they succeed. The paintings of El Greco suggest to Philip, however, that the human will is powerful, that life can be made meaningful through struggle. After this realization, Philip comes to understand the secret of a piece of Persian rug given him by an eccentric poet. The poet told him that the rug held the key to the meaning of life, but he refused to explain the puzzle to Philip. The solution becomes apparent to Philip years later, after much searching for it: Life has no meaning. There is no set of obligations by which a person must live, no certain path to follow. With this bleak conclusion, Philip comes to another realization: Like the weaver of the carpet, a person may choose the strands that please his aesthetic sense and make a pattern of his life satisfying to his own taste. Happiness and pain are important only as strands in the design. Though people are under no obligation to create a design, they are free to do so if they choose; or, if they reject freedom of the will, it may seem that they are free. Life for Philip, then, has purpose because he wills to endow it with purpose—a conclusion primarily existential but also in accord with Schopenhauer's view of the human will.

THE MOON AND SIXPENCE

In *The Moon and Sixpence*, a novel that relies somewhat on autobiographical materials used in *Of Human Bondage*, Maugham narrates a portion of the life of his hero Charles Strickland, a stockbroker turned artist whose character is based on that of the artist Paul Gauguin. The narrator, or the Maugham persona, is a successful author who enjoys access to high society and, like Maugham, travels extensively around the world. He is detached and analytical in his attitudes, revealing a fondness for the maxims of Blaise Pascal and La Rochefoucauld. He prefers to permit the story to unfold in an episodic way by letting others whom he meets tell him what they know or think about Strickland. Maugham sees in Strickland the frustrated genius, a moderately successful businessman who, at age forty, decides to become an artist, ruthlessly throwing over everything to pursue his ambition, and succeeding.

The action occurs over a period of more than twenty years, with the setting shifting from London to Paris to Tahiti and back to London. As in the earlier *Of Human Bondage* and later in *Christmas Holiday*, art is an important theme, and allusions to paintings and painters are numerous. At the beginning of the novel, Maugham invents a "scholarly" tradition on Strickland, complete with footnotes, to enhance the realism. In the concluding segment set in Tahiti, he introduces characters who had known Strickland during his final years and who report on his decline and death. They are modeled on characters whom Maugham met in Tahiti and who told him about Gauguin. With references to actual people whose identities the author does not very much bother to conceal, *The Moon and Sixpence*, then, is a roman à clef, as are its two most important successors, *Cakes and Ale* and *The Razor's Edge*.

CAKES AND ALE

In *Cakes and Ale*, the most "literary" of Maugham's novels, the narrator assumes the name Willie Ashenden, one that Maugham had used in his collection of short stories based on his work as an intelligence agent (*Ashenden*, 1928). Ashenden is a novelist in his fifties who during the course of the narrative has several meetings with another novelist and critic, Alroy Kear. Kear, about the same age as Willie Ashenden, represents the Edwardian novelist Hugh Walpole. (The unflattering portrait of Walpole, recognizable to many contemporaries and to Walpole himself, contributed to an attack on Maugham by Elinor Mordaunt in the 1931 novel *Gin and Bitters*, where he is given the name Leverson Hurle.) In addition to the narrator and Kear, another author plays a major role in the novel. Edward Driffield, the grand old man of Victorian literature, is based on the character of Thomas Hardy. Rosie Gann, Driffield's first wife, is modeled on the actor Ethelwyn Sylvia Jones, to whom Maugham once proposed.

Alroy Kear, who is writing a biography of Driffield, discovers that Ashenden has been a longtime acquaintance of the Driffields. The Driffields once lived in Ashenden's village of Blackstable, where they were regarded with suspicion by the villagers, especially by Ashenden's uncle, the vicar, who represents the epitome of Victorian propriety and prudery. The villagers' suspicions are confirmed when the Driffields move to London, leaving behind debts to most of the merchants.

Later, Ashenden renews his acquaintance with the Driffields in London, gradually losing touch with them after Rosie leaves Driffield for a Blackstable coal merchant, Lord George Kemp. Ashenden's knowledge of all these details merges in flashbacks that go back as far as his childhood. Ashenden knows that a tactful biographer such as Kear, who has secured the approval of Driffield's second wife, cannot include such revealing recollections, and thus he tells them to the reader. He concludes his narrative with an account of meeting Rosie, then more than seventy years old, in New York. She confesses to Ashenden that she ran off with Lord George because "He was always such a perfect gentleman," a judgment with which every other character in the novel would have disagreed.

Except for one brief episode that occurs in New York, the novel is set either in London or in the nearby villages and countryside. Maugham relies heavily on flashbacks ranging over a period of some forty years; *Cakes and Ale* is a novel cast in the form of reminiscences of a character, which assuredly would conflict with the "official" biography of Driffield as recorded by Alroy Kear. Its appeal lies primarily in its allusions to actual persons, its behind-the-scenes literary gossip, and the creation of Rosie Gann, probably the most appealing of Maugham's female characters—a wholesome, agreeable, and vivacious woman utterly lacking in pretense.

THE RAZOR'S EDGE

In *The Razor's Edge*, the narrator becomes "Mr. Maugham," a celebrated author and world traveler. With characters such as the urbane and aristocratic art agent, Elliott Templeton, he exchanges views and pleasantries in an attitude of amusement and tolerance. To younger characters such as Sophie Macdonald he offers sage advice. To readers he offers a variety of wry comments on the art and craft of the novel. He speculates as to why people whom he barely knows divulge their life stories so readily to him. He admits the reader behind the scenes of the writer's study with such unguarded comments as the famous opening, "I have never begun a novel with more misgiving," and such wry asides as "I feel it right to warn the reader that he can very well skip this chapter without losing the thread of [the] . . . story. . . . I should add, however, that except for this conversation I should perhaps not have thought it worthwhile to write this book." Usually "Mr. Maugham" limits his involvement to conversation; his own actions, where they are noted (as when he withdraws to write a novel or takes his boat to Toulon), do not advance the plot. Occasionally, he does involve himself in the plot in some minor way. He contrives for the dying Elliott Templeton to receive an invitation to a party given by the Princess Novemali after she had deliberately snubbed Elliott, and he is on hand to identify the body of Sophie Macdonald.

"Mr. Maugham" reports the story as the major characters reveal it in their conversations. Isabel Bradley is in love with Larry Darrel but sensibly marries the successful Gray Maturin, only to find that after Gray loses his assets during the Depression, she and her husband and their two daughters must live on the generosity of her uncle Elliott. Larry, whose main interest in life is the study of philosophy and religion, attempts to marry Sophie Macdonald to save her from a dissolute life, an effort that Isabel shrewdly thwarts. Larry goes to a Benedictine monastery in France, later leaving it to study the Hindu religion in India. Returning from India at the end of the novel, he gives up his independent income and resolves to find work in New York driving a taxi. The Maturins move from Paris to Dallas, where Gray has secured an executive position in an oil company. The plot covers more than a decade, with the settings in France, England, and America. "Mr. Maugham," like the young Philip Carey, seeks a pattern in the lives of those he has met, and he finds that each life in *The Razor's Edge* has been a success. Even Sophie Macdonald, whose trauma caused her to seek death, found what she was seeking.

Maugham's three most significant novels following *Of Human Bondage* explore ideals that he considered in the final chapters of his autobiography, *The Summing Up*—truth, beauty, goodness. In *The Moon and Sixpence*, Charles Strickland represents the true genius whose work survives and speaks to posterity, even though his talent surfaced late in life and he violated accepted standards to advance it. In him, truth is neither obvious nor pleasant, but its existence can be confirmed by those who have felt the power of his work. Even the wife he abandoned displays reproductions of his paintings in her home and takes pride in his attainments. In *Cakes and Ale*, the ideal is beauty, which readers and critics find in the style, characters, and descriptions of Edward Driffield's novels. The narrator Willie Ashenden rejects this aesthetic beauty in favor of a more realistic beauty. He discovers the ideal in the warmth and charm of Rosie Gann, Driffield's first wife, who possessed neither fidelity nor business ethics but whose character brought others a wholesome sense of well-being. In *The Razor's Edge*, Larry Darrel reveals a basic goodness, a difficult quality to depict, partly because it may be attributed to the absence of either appetites or temptations. Though not an ascetic, Larry keeps passion and ambition in check and pursues his own spiritual development. He readily sacrifices himself for others, making a futile effort to save Sophie Macdonald from self-destruction through an offer of marriage, yet his sacrifices do not appear quixotic. A generous amount of modesty enables him to make the best of a life that reveals only goodness as an extraordinary element.

In each character, the ideal is neither obvious nor probable in the conventional sense. Its existence is ironic, and it might be overlooked were not the Maugham persona on hand to define it. Not even the narrator, however, can explain or account for it; the reader savors its presence without fully understanding its origin.

Among Maugham's remaining novels are works of literary merit and appeal, but they represent lesser achievements than his earlier work. A reader of Maugham would not want to miss novels such as *The Painted Veil* and *The Narrow Corner*, which narrate suspenseful and intense conflicts. Works such as these differ from the better-known novels in several important respects. First, the Maugham persona is either absent or less intrusive. In *The Narrow Corner*, for example, the author's viewpoint is usually expressed through Dr. Saunders, who lives on a Pacific island and has no literary interests or ambitions. Further, the settings are usually foreign or exotic—European or Asian rather than American or English. Instead of spanning decades, the plots narrate events that occur during a few months; novels such as *Up at the Villa*, for example, differ little from some of Maugham's short stories.

Significantly, in Maugham's major novels, the important characters—Philip Carey, Larry Darrel, Rosie Gann, and Charles Strickland—either embody an ideal or achieve some measure of success in pursuit of an ideal, whereas idealism in the minor works is usually crushed and defeated. Fred Blake and Erik Christensen in *The Narrow Corner* find only disappointment, disillusionment, and early death, as does the unfortunate Karl Richter in *Up at the Villa*. Those who survive are worldly-wise and detached characters who can regard life as Maugham's spokesman Dr. Saunders does:

> Life is short, nature is hostile, and man is ridiculous but oddly enough most misfortunes have their compensations and with a certain humour and a good deal of horse-sense one can make a fairly good job of what is after all a matter of very small consequence.

The minor works reward the reader with their depiction of the ironies of human life, the eccentricities of human beings and the unusual settings and universal conflicts, yet, however rewarding, they lack the thematic richness and emotional concentration of Maugham's best novels.

Stanley Archer

Other major works

SHORT FICTION: *Orientations*, 1899; *The Trembling of a Leaf: Little Stories of the South Sea Islands*, 1921; *The Casuarina Tree: Six Stories*, 1926; *Ashenden: Or, The British Agent*, 1928; *Six Stories Written in the First Person Singular*, 1931; *Ah King: Six Stories*, 1933; *East and West: The Collected Short Stories*, 1934; *Cosmopolitans*, 1936; *The Favorite Short Stories of W. Somerset Maugham*, 1937; *The Round Dozen*, 1939; *The Mixture as Before: Short Stories*, 1940; *Creatures of Circumstances: Short Stories*, 1947; *East of Suez: Great Stories of the Tropics*, 1948; *Here and There: Selected Short Stories*, 1948; *The Complete Short Stories*, 1951; *The World Over*, 1952; *Seventeen Lost Stories*, 1969.

PLAYS: *A Man of Honor*, pr., pb. 1903 (wr. 1898-1899); *Lady Frederick*, pr. 1907; *The Explorer*, pr. 1908; *Jack Straw*, pr. 1908; *Mrs. Dot*, pr. 1908; *The Noble Spaniard*, pr. 1909; *Penelope*, pr. 1909; *Smith*, pr. 1909; *Landed Gentry*, pr. 1910 (as *Grace*); *The Tenth Man*, pr. 1910; *Loaves and Fishes*, pr. 1911 (wr. 1903); *The Land of Promise*, pr. 1913; *Caroline*, pr. 1916 (as *The Unattainable*); *Our Betters*, pr. 1917; *Caesar's Wife*, pr. 1919; *Home and Beauty*, pr. 1919 (also known as *Too Many Husbands*); *The Unknown*, pr., pb. 1920; *The Circle*, pr., pb. 1921; *East of Suez*, pr., pb. 1922; *The Constant Wife*, pr., pb. 1926; *The Letter*, pr., pb. 1927; *The Sacred Flame*, pr., pb. 1928; *The Breadwinner*, pr., pb. 1930; *The Collected Plays of W. Somerset Maugham*, 1931-1934 (6 volumes; revised 1952, 3 volumes); *For Services Rendered*, pr., pb. 1932; *Sheppey*, pr., pb. 1933.

SCREENPLAY: *Trio*, 1950 (with R. C. Sherriff and Noel Langley).

NONFICTION: *The Land of the Blessed Virgin: Sketches and Impressions in Andalusia*, 1905 (also known as *Andalusia*, 1920); *On a Chinese Screen*, 1922; *The Gentleman in the Parlour: A Record of a Journey from Rangoon to Haiphong*, 1930; *Don Fernando*, 1935; *The Summing Up*, 1938; *Books and You*, 1940; *France at War*, 1940; *Strictly Personal*, 1941; *Great Novelists and Their Novels*, 1948; *A Writer's Notebook*, 1949; *The Writer's Point of View*, 1951; *The Vagrant Mood: Six Essays*, 1952; *The Partial View*, 1954 (includes *The Summing Up* and *A Writer's Notebook*); *Ten Novels and Their Authors*, 1954 (revision of *Great Novelists and Their Novels*); *The Travel Books*, 1955; *Points of View*, 1958; *Looking Back*, 1962; *Purely for My Pleasure*, 1962; *Selected Prefaces and Introductions*, 1963.

MISCELLANEOUS: *The Great Exotic Novels and Short Stories of Somerset Maugham*, 2001; *The W. Somerset Maugham Reader: Novels, Stories, Travel Writing*, 2004 (Jeffrey Meyers, editor).

Bibliography

Burt, Forrest D. *W. Somerset Maugham*. Boston: Twayne, 1985. Presents some biographical background and then focuses on Maugham's literary works from a critical standpoint. Asserts that Maugham has long been an underestimated and neglected writer in terms of an assessment of his value and position in the literary canon and that a more serious appraisal of his works began to take place following his death. Includes a chronology.

Calder, Robert. *W. Somerset Maugham and the Quest for Freedom*. London: Heinemann, 1972. Impressive study primarily emphasizes critical and thematic assessment of Maugham's novels, breaking them down into categories by genre, such as novels of apprenticeship, or categories of thematic focus, such as artist-hero novels. Also exhaustively delineates several of the important issues with which Maugham was concerned, including the absolute importance of money, the nature of marriage and bondage, and the nature of individual freedom. Includes four informative appendixes, one containing material on Maugham's role in Allied espionage in 1917.

_______. *Willie*. London: Heinemann, 1989. Offers an informed account of the novelist and playwright, drawing on interviews with Maugham's friends and letters made available for the first time and published here. Includes photographs, bibliography, and index.

Connon, Bryan. *Somerset Maugham and the Maugham Dynasty*. London: Sinclair-Stevenson, 1997. Examines the influence of the Maugham family on the life and works of W. Somerset Maugham. Includes bibliography and index.

Cordell, Richard A. *Somerset Maugham: A Writer for All Seasons*. 2d ed. Bloomington: Indiana University Press, 1969. A friend and confidant of Maugham provides an in-depth examination of the writer's life and works. Disputes the labeling of Maugham as "enigmatic" and "inscrutable," charging instead that Maugham was just the opposite. Includes chapters on three of Maugham's "autobiographical novels" as well as on his other fiction.

Holden, Philip. *Orienting Masculinity, Orienting Nation: W. Somerset Maugham's Exotic Fiction*. Westport, Conn.: Greenwood Press, 1996. Examines the themes of homosexuality, gender identity, and race relations in Maugham's works. Maintains that Maugham's writing was a way for him to negotiate between two different masculine identities: the private gay man and the public writer.

Meyers, Jeffrey. *Somerset Maugham*. New York: Alfred A. Knopf, 2004. Biography emphasizes Maugham's "otherness," particularly his homosexuality. Unlike other critics who have dismissed Maugham's work, Meyers defends Maugham as a great writer who influenced George Orwell, V. S. Naipaul, and other authors.

Morgan, Ted. *Maugham*. New York: Simon & Schuster, 1980. The first full-scale biography of Maugham and therefore an essential text in all studies of the man and his work. Unlike previous biographers, Morgan enjoyed the cooperation of Maugham's literary executor and so was able to correct many distortions in previous studies. Offers a comprehensive account of the private man, including photographs, a complete primary bibliography, and an index.

Rogal, Samuel J. *A Companion to the Characters in the Fiction and Drama of W. Somerset Maugham*. Westport, Conn.: Greenwood Press, 1996. Reference resource provides an alphabetical listing of the characters—animal and human, unnamed and named—in Maugham's fiction and drama. Each entry identifies the work in which a character appears and the character's role in the overall work.

_______. *A William Somerset Maugham Encyclopedia*. Westport, Conn.: Greenwood Press, 1997. Alphabetically arranged entries provide information on Maugham's writings, family members, friends, settings, and the historical, cultural, social, and political issues associated with his life and work. Includes bibliography and index.

FRANÇOIS MAURIAC

Born: Bordeaux, France; October 11, 1885
Died: Paris, France; September 1, 1970
Also known as: Forez

PRINCIPAL LONG FICTION

L'Enfant chargé de chaînes, 1913 (*Young Man in Chains*, 1961)
La Robe prétexte, 1914 (*The Stuff of Youth*, 1960)
La Chair et le sang, 1920 (*Flesh and Blood*, 1954)
Préséances, 1921 (*Questions of Precedence*, 1958)
Le Baiser au lépreux, 1922 (*A Kiss for the Leper*, 1923, 1950)
Genitrix, 1923 (English translation, 1950)
Le Fleuve du feu, 1923 (*The River of Fire*, 1954)
Le Désert de l'amour, 1925 (*The Desert of Love*, 1929)
Thérèse Desqueyroux, 1927 (*Thérèse*, 1928)
Destins, 1928 (*Destinies*, 1929)
Le Nœud de vipères, 1932 (*Vipers' Tangle*, 1933)
Le Mystère Frontenac, 1933 (*The Frontenac Mystery*, 1952)
La Fin de la nuit, 1935 (*The End of the Night*, 1947)
Les Anges noirs, 1936 (*The Dark Angels*, 1950)
Les Chemins de la mer, 1939 (*The Unknown Sea*, 1948)

La Pharisienne, 1941 (*Woman of the Pharisees*, 1946)
Galigaï, 1952 (*The Loved and the Unloved*, 1952)
L'Agneau, 1954 (*The Lamb*, 1955)
Un Adolescent d'autrefoix, 1969 (*Maltaverne*, 1970)

Other literary forms

François Mauriac (mawr-YAHK) is known primarily for his fiction, although, like many other French novelists both before and after him, he began his career in letters as a poet (with *Les Mains jointes*, 1909). In his fifties, long after reaching maturity as a novelist, he tried his hand at writing plays, encouraged in that effort by the popular playwright Édouard Bourdet, who was also chief administrator of the Comédie-Française. The first of Mauriac's plays, *Asmodée* (pr. 1937; *Asmodée: Or, The Intruder*, 1939), achieved considerable success on the Parisian stage, a success nearly matched by that of *Les Mal Aimés* (pr., pb. 1945), which the author himself considered to have been his finest play. *Passage du malin* (pr. 1947) was somewhat less well received. Gradually losing interest in the stage after the death of Bourdet, Mauriac nevertheless persevered with one more, generally successful, play: *Le Feu sur la terre: Ou, Le Pays sans chemin* was first performed, to considerable critical acclaim, in 1950. Mauriac is also remembered as the author of short stories (most of them an outgrowth of his novels), as a biographer of Blaise Pascal and Jean Racine, and as an essayist.

Achievements

François Mauriac is generally considered to have been the preeminent Roman Catholic novelist of the twentieth century, his accomplishments rivaled only by those of his presumed British disciple, Graham Greene. For a long time, however, Mauriac's novels sustained strong attack from conservative Catholic critics, who argued with some justice that in Mauriac's novels God is most conspicuous by His absence. Aided in his strongest works by a keen gift for social observation, Mauriac habitually portrays a fictional universe of almost unrelieved human meanness, with frequent incidence of avarice and lust; the most sympathetic among his characters are those who rebel, however ineffectually, against the drab conformity of their frequently privileged backgrounds.

Although primarily concerned with the inner spiritual state of his principal characters, Mauriac derives considerable effect, and credibility, from his evocation of the social and geographical milieu in which those characters exist. Admittedly influenced by Honoré de Balzac in his portrayal of property and its effects, Mauriac, in his strongest efforts, combines the concerns of the Catholic novel with those of the novel of manners, showing frequent flashes of bitter satire. Set almost exclusively in his native Bordeaux and the surrounding countryside, Mauriac's novels nevertheless transcend their geographical boundaries to reach a worldwide audience, speaking eloquently of the individual at odds with him- or herself and with society. God, however conspicuous by His absence, emerges from the structure of Mauriac's novels as the only "reasonable" refuge for those whose pleas for love and understanding go unheard. Despite Mauriac's notoriously uneven production, the stronger of his novels continue to be read as exemplary studies of human character and destiny, notable also for their influence upon the works of Greene and upon the younger British novelist Piers Paul Read, whose frequently startling works sustain Mauriac's probing analysis of character and society within a Christian (and specifically Catholic) context.

Biography

The youngest of five well-derived children destined for the professions, François Mauriac was born in Bordeaux on October 11, 1885. Following the death of her husband when the young Mauriac was less than two years old, Madame Mauriac and her children moved to the affluent but forbidding household of her mother, an atmosphere that was to loom large in the young novelist's developing consciousness. Educated at first by the Marianite fathers and later at the University of Bordeaux, Mauriac moved to Paris in 1906 to prepare for study at the École Nationale des Chartes. By that time, however, he had already begun to travel in literary circles and was beginning to attract attention as a poet. Less affluent, perhaps, than his older contemporaries Marcel Proust and André Gide, Mauriac was nevertheless suffi-

François Mauriac. (© The Nobel Foundation)

ciently well-off to be able to write and eat without the constraints of regular employment.

Soon after the acclaimed appearance of his first volume of poetry, Mauriac began work on *Young Man in Chains*, the first of several "apprentice" novels that in subsequent years would be all but repudiated by their author. Married in 1913 to Jeanne Lafont, Mauriac continued writing both poetry and novels with regularity but without distinction until 1922, when he at last achieved acknowledged success with *A Kiss for the Leper*. From then on, he was justly hailed as the major novelistic talent of his generation, consolidating his reputation with such remarkable works as *The Desert of Love*, *Thérèse*, *Vipers' Tangle*, and *Woman of the Pharisees*. Although his output remained decidedly uneven, with a number of lesser, even regrettable novels interspersed among his good or great ones, by 1932, Mauriac's stature as a novelist was such as to withstand the critical impact of occasional failure, and in the following year, he was elected to the prestigious French Academy; twenty years later, he received the Nobel Prize in Literature.

Shortly before his election to the French Academy, Mauriac had nearly lost his life to throat cancer; for the nearly forty years of life that remained to him after successful therapy, he was barely able to speak above a hoarse whisper. No sooner had he returned to writing than the growing threat of fascism in Germany and elsewhere turned his attention increasingly toward politics; during the Spanish Civil War of 1936 to 1939, for example, Mauriac engaged actively in journalistic support of the Republican cause, in open opposition to the Roman Catholic orthodoxy. During World War II, writing partially under the Resistance pseudonym Forez, Mauriac continued to oppose the fascist forces, both in the periodical *Les Lettres françaises* and in the clandestine volume *Le Cahier noir* (1943; *The Black Notebook*, 1944). After the war, however, he frequently advocated compassionate treatment of those collaborators whom he had once opposed.

A vigorous supporter of General Charles de Gaulle, Mauriac, in the late 1950's and early 1960's, again antagonized political conservatives with his advocacy of President de Gaulle's policies concerning self-determination for French colonies in North Africa; as late as 1962, there were threats against Mauriac's life because of his outspoken liberal views. Thereafter, until his death in the summer of 1970 (just weeks before that of de Gaulle), Mauriac lived peacefully in Paris, writing several volumes of memoirs and a regular column for the magazine *Le Figaro littéraire*.

Analysis

Among the major novelists of the twentieth century, perhaps only Ernest Hemingway may be said to have produced an oeuvre as uneven as that of François Mauriac. To an even greater degree than Hemingway, Mauriac appears to have been almost constitutionally incapable of distinguishing between treasure and trash in his work, leaving that task to several generations of able scholars and critics. Decades after Mauriac's first true success with *A Kiss for the Leper*, most critics have reached agreement on the relative merits of his various works, citing the decade between 1922 and 1932 as the period of his richest, if not his most prolific, activity. To this period belong such acknowledged masterpieces as *Genitrix*, *The Desert of Love*, *Thérèse*, and *Vipers' Tangle*. Characteristically, however, Mauriac also produced several lesser, even mediocre, novels during that same period, among them *The River of Fire* and *Destinies*. To the list of Mauriac's five great novels many critics would add a later title: *Woman of the Pharisees*, published in 1941 after a long succession of minor efforts, is surely the finest of Mauriac's later novels and closely approaches his best work of the 1920's.

It is well known that Mauriac wrote even the best of his novels in great haste, often in a matter of weeks; as a consequence, his works are frequently flawed by contrived or hasty endings suggesting that the author had exhausted his interest or patience. Fortunately, the almost visceral vigor of Mauriac's strongest writing usually suffices to sustain the reader's interest in a credible, well-drawn cast of characters, both major and minor. Mauriac, incidentally, while eschewing the *roman-fleuve*, or multivolume novel, favored by many of his contemporaries, nevertheless features continuing or overlapping characters in a number of his works, suggesting bonds of kinship and friendship similar to those in Balzac's *The Human Comedy* (1829-1848). Thérèse Desqueyroux, for example, turns up in several narratives other than the one bearing her name; so, also, does Brigitte Pian of *Woman of the Pharisees*.

Even considering the uneven quality of Mauriac's mature work, the four first, or apprentice, novels, published between 1913 and 1921, must by any standard be viewed as his weakest, offering little promise of better things to come. Differing widely in form, style, and construction, these initial efforts are frankly autobiographical in tone and content, of interest to scholars mainly for what they reveal of the author's early life. Although included in both the original and the translated collections of Mauriac's work, *Young Man in Chains*, *The Stuff of Youth*, *Flesh and Blood*, and *Questions of Precedence* never sold well and were among the few of Mauriac's works to be all but repudiated by their author. *The River of Fire* fared hardly better, although by the time it was published, Mauriac had presumably "hit his stride" with *A Kiss for the Leper* and *Genitrix*.

"God is no novelist," wrote Jean-Paul Sartre in 1939, "and neither is François Mauriac." Sartre, then evolving the aesthetic theories later to be propounded in *Qu'est-ce que la littérature?* (1948; *What Is Literature?*, 1949) and other works, was particularly bothered by Mauriac's omniscient, indeed almost authoritarian, stance with regard to characters whom he would transparently manipulate at will, claiming intimate knowledge of their inmost thoughts and actions. Indeed, with or without Sartre's help, omniscience in narration was by the 1930's becoming increasingly obsolete, at least in the "serious" novel, harking inevitably back to the implied complacency of such nineteenth century masters as Gustave Flaubert and Balzac. For Sartre, who did not share Mauriac's belief in God, the middle-aged novelist had compounded his transgressions in a then recent essay by describing novelists, again complacently, as "the apes of God."

After Sartre's original attack and with both authors long since deceased, it is possible to distinguish merit on both sides; it is possible, moreover, that Mauriac was beneficially influenced by Sartre's criticism as he prepared the manuscript of *Woman of the Pharisees*, considered by some critics to have been the last of his truly great novels. In any case, the power of *Vipers' Tangle* derives in no small measure from Mauriac's extensive, effective, and uncharacteristic use of the first-person viewpoint, with perceptions generally limited to those of the aging lawyer and miser Louis, who commences the narrative as a letter to astonish and confound his uncomprehending wife of forty years. Although somewhat marred at the end by the inclusion of epistolary aftermatter over which Louis could have had no control, *Vipers' Tangle* nevertheless ranks among Mauriac's finest achievements precisely because of the way he handles his limited-viewpoint, self-revealing principal narrator. With the additional exception of *Woman of the Pharisees* (narrated by an interested observer), the bulk of Mauriac's narratives are recounted in the third person, with varying degrees of success.

Throughout his long career, Mauriac chafed repeatedly under the label of "Catholic novelist," preferring to describe himself as "a Catholic who writes novels." As many Catholic critics were quick to note, Mauriac's novels are quite unlike traditional devotional literature, with the sinners far outnumbering the saints. Unlike his eminent contemporary Georges Bernanos, whose narrator-protagonists are invariably priests, Mauriac features members of the clergy only in minor or supporting roles and rarely, if ever, explores their thoughts or motivations. His preferred characters are to be found among the laity, people with some religious upbringing and sufficient latent faith to expect more of life than has been offered to them. God, unseen or barely glimpsed, presumably waits patiently to fill the void that Mauriac's mortals have discovered in their lives. Also, unlike the poet and playwright Paul Claudel, his only true rival as a Catholic interpreter of the human experience, Mauriac stops short of portraying human suffering as somehow willed by God or as part of His cosmic scheme ("God," Claudel once said, "writes straight with crooked lines," and Claudel often did the same). Mauriac prefers to portray "the desert of love" in a heart still closed to its Creator. For many readers, however, the states in which Mauriac leaves some of his characters suggest forms of cruel, unusual, and perhaps undeserved punishment.

A Kiss for the Leper

Generally agreed to be the first of Mauriac's truly great novels, *A Kiss for the Leper* offers an almost unrelieved exemplary spectacle of renunciation, sacrifice, and suffering that may well suffice to alienate all but the most devout among Mauriac's readers. Even the skeptic, however, cannot fail to appreciate the deftness of Mauriac's social satire and the evocative power of his nature scenes.

Set in the Gascon region that was Mauriac's boyhood home and that became his literary trademark, *A Kiss for the Leper* takes as its point of departure the disastrous "arranged" marriage of two basically decent people whose paths might otherwise never have crossed. Jean Péloueyre, doubly burdened by physical ugliness and by a large potential inheritance, has little say in the matter when his father, Jérôme, suddenly decides to divert the fortune from his own sister and nephew by marrying off his only son. The object of Jérôme's vicarious choice turns out to be Noémi d'Artiailh, a healthy peasant girl whose parents, although poor, are no less materialistic and avaricious than Jérôme himself. Jean and Noémi thus find themselves bound in marriage with little choice and less fault, each incommunicably sensitive to the other's needs and disappointments.

Jean, conditioned by his diminutive stature and ill-favored appearance to expect little of his fellow mortals, soon senses Noémi's revulsion and departs for Paris at the urging of his priest, ostensibly on an errand of scholarly research but actually to spare Noémi his bothersome presence. Noémi tries hard to overcome the aversion that she feels but finds it difficult to communicate with a near hermit who, for want of human companionship, has done most of his living through books.

Straightforward and sturdily built, Noémi is intelligent but undereducated, hopelessly out of phase with her reticent, scholarly husband. Upon Jean's return from Paris, his already frail constitution mined by overwork and undernourishment, he is placed in the care of a young physician, with whom Noémi falls secretly in love. Jean, intuitively aware of Noémi's unexpressed feelings, contrives to expose himself to certain infection by spending most of his spare time at the bedside of a consumptive friend. During his resulting fatal illness, Noémi finds herself genuinely torn between her feelings for the handsome young doctor and a developing, if belated, tenderness toward Jean. When Jean dies, Noémi wholeheartedly commits herself to faithful widowhood, doubly bound by Jérôme's stipulation that his son's widow (and her family) would forfeit the inheritance were she to remarry. A brief appended chapter included in collected editions of Mauriac's work portrays Noémi only a few years later, overweight and still in widow's weeds, displaying the qualities of sainthood.

To today's reader or critic, *A Kiss for the Leper* may seem an unlikely vehicle to have lifted its thirty-six-year-old author from not only his early mediocrity but also well above the rank and file of his contemporaries. Even in the Catholic tradition, tastes have changed considerably since Mauriac wrote the novel, and such unmitigated suffering may be hard to accept, even when justified by faith. At the time the novel was written, however, Mauriac's deft descriptions and economy of style sufficed to render his bleak tale both credible and satisfying, with a good sense of place and character. Especially skilled is Mauriac's portrayal of the unlovable, unlovely Jean, a thoroughly credible personage who, if he had been ill presented, might well have emerged as a caricature. Somewhat closer to caricature yet still authentic is the presentation of Jean's father, Jérôme, which recalls both the miser and the imaginary "invalid" immortalized in the plays of Molière. In Mauriac's fictional universe, however, there is no room for comic relief; as ridiculous as he may seem, Jérôme is both serious and ultimately dangerous, jeopardizing through his utter thoughtlessness the sanity of those around him.

Throughout *A Kiss for the Leper*, carefully chosen similes and metaphors contribute to the author's establishment of mood. Jean, for example, is often perceived both by Noémi and by the unseen narrator in terms appropriate to the description of an insect; like the insect he presumably resembles, Jean is predictably more in his element outdoors with nature than indoors with his fellow human beings. As elsewhere in Mauriac's better fiction, evocations and descriptions of nature convey both the isolation of the characters and their rare moments of freedom or release. The smell of the air or the feel of the air upon the skin is often used to "frame" the characters within a given situation, offering insight into their feelings; Noémi, for example, becomes viscerally aware of her ample healthy body as she contemplates the unwelcome prospect of offering herself to Jean. Jean, for his part, is all the more keenly aware of Noémi's charms as he senses instinctively that they will forever be denied to him. Undeniably, however, the accumulation of such excruciating pain often results in novelistic beauty, and, in its finest moments, *A Kiss for the Leper* is a starkly beautiful narrative, recalling the best work of Mauriac's seventeenth century mentors Pascal and Racine. Indeed, the prevailing mood of the novel is never too far removed from that of classical tragedy. Only in the next life, suggests Mauriac, will such hapless mortals as Noémi and Jean reach mutual understanding through the will of God.

Genitrix

If *A Kiss for the Leper* may be seen as portraying the hopelessness of marriage, Mauriac's next major novel, *Genitrix*, may likewise be interpreted, at least on one level, as a scathing attack upon the supposedly hallowed institution of motherhood. Like her brother Jérôme Péloueyre, featured in *A Kiss for the Leper*, Félicité Cazenave narrowly escapes caricature to emerge as a credible and most convincing monster, dominating the action of the novel as she dominates the life and marriage of her son, Fernand. Perceived as "the enemy" by her daughter-in-law, Mathilde (who soon dies of childbed fever as an indirect result of Félicité's mismanagement), Madame Cazenave successfully prevented her son from marrying until he was past fifty, having interfered also to abort a once-promising political career that she perceived as a potential threat to Fernand's precarious health. Not until after the death of his much-maligned wife does Fernand begin to perceive the nature and extent of his mother's domination, and even then, the realization does him little good; after Félicité's death, little remains of Fernand but a shell capable only of childish and impotent rages.

As elsewhere in his fiction, Mauriac in *Genitrix* derives considerable power from physical description, either of nature or of human-made "improvements" upon the land itself. Particularly striking is his portrayal of the vast and gloomy old house that shelters the three main characters and their faithful servants. At the start of the novel, Mathilde lies mortally ill in "her" wing of the house, which she and Fernand were to have shared but is now hers alone, Fernand having long since retreated to the shelter of his mother's wing at the other end of the house. Few images, in Mauriac's fiction or elsewhere, are as effective in illustrating separation as the cavernous Cazenave dwelling, clearly divided into "zones" ill-served by drafty corridors. Nature, perceived through the window, offers welcome solace to the dying Mathilde, as it did to the ailing Jean Péloueyre, Fernand's cousin, in *A Kiss for the Leper*. On other occasions, as in the earlier book, evocations of blinding sun or suffocating heat serve both to illustrate and to justify the anger and frustration of the characters.

To a number of contemporary critics and reviewers, *Genitrix* seemed an even bleaker and more unrelenting tale than its predecessor, no doubt because its characters (with the possible exception of the hapless Mathilde) have even less to recommend them than the ill-matched Jean and Noémi of *A Kiss for the Leper*. Fernand and his mother, however, remain no less credible for being thoughtlessly cruel, and *Genitrix* may well emerge as the more plausible of Mauriac's first two major novels.

The Desert of Love

More than once in his career, Mauriac agreed with critics that the title of *The Desert of Love* might well summarize the overriding thematic concern of his entire literary output. In any case, the novel itself is well named and quite representative of Mauriac's mature power and talent. Developing the technique of flashback borrowed from the cinema and first used effectively in *Genitrix*, *The Desert of Love* spans nearly twenty years of often-troubled relations between the eminent Dr. Courrèges and his playboy son, Raymond, who, without each other's knowledge, are ironically united in their unrequited love for the same woman. The woman, to whom Mauriac has given the heavily ironic and symbolic name Maria Cross, is a young widow who, with some justification, has acquired a reputation for loose morals; nevertheless, she rebuffs the clumsy and crude advances of the seventeen-year-old Raymond, nine years her junior, unwittingly inflicting upon him a scar that he carries well into adulthood. Raymond's physician father, meanwhile, finds himself unable to declare his physical love to a woman who venerates her healer as a saintly father figure. Maria, unaware of the doctor's feelings, eventually marries the rich businessman Larousselle, who has been supporting her. With considerable economy of means and style, Mauriac convincingly evokes the stifling atmosphere of noncommunication and, indeed, unexpressed love between father and son, exploring the parent-child relationship even more deeply and plausibly than in *Genitrix*.

THÉRÈSE

In his next major novel, *Thérèse*, Mauriac again turned his attention to the impossibility of communication within marriage. Since the novel's publication, Thérèse Desqueyroux has become quite probably the best-remembered of Mauriac's characters and the short novel bearing her name the most frequently reprinted of his many narratives. For some time, apparently, the enigmatic character of Thérèse had been intruding upon the author's consciousness, demanding that her tale be told. Throughout Mauriac's maturity, moreover, Thérèse remained his "favorite" character, her further adventures pursued in whole or in part in various lesser works. To be sure, she is one of Mauriac's most intriguing and representative creations—representative of alienation and estrangement as observed in modern society.

Based, in part, upon a sensational trial that took place in Bordeaux during 1906, *Thérèse* begins immediately after the title character has been acquitted, with some political intervention, of attempting to poison her husband, Bernard. As in *The Desert of Love* and *Genitrix*, judicious use of the flashback technique serves to illuminate both Thérèse's earlier life and the circumstances leading to the crime of which she has been accused. Thérèse, like Noémi of *A Kiss for the Leper*, finds herself married to a man chosen by her family rather than by herself; unlike Noémi, however, Thérèse springs from a family fully as privileged (and as stifling) as that of her husband. The act of which she stands accused in fact begins by accident, when she watches Bernard inadvertently swallow a double portion of a prescription drug containing arsenic. Thereafter, only half-aware of what she is doing, Thérèse continues to increase his dosage, never quite allowing her resentment of Bernard to form fully in her own mind. Bernard, indeed, is a rather unlikely victim, an affectionate husband, according to his own dim lights, who never fully understands what has happened and is more than willing not to press charges against his wife.

As elsewhere in Mauriac's fiction, the true drama of *Thérèse* lies in the unspoken and perhaps unspeakable loneliness of the principal characters. Bernard, in fact, is neither stupid nor insensitive; passably well educated in keeping with the demands of his social position, he is at worst placid and nonreflective, given, if not addicted, to such simple sensual pleasures as eating and hunting. Thérèse, by contrast, is pensive, sensitive, and high-strung in the manner of Jean Péloueyre of *A Kiss for the Leper*, hopelessly ill suited to the role in which society and family have placed her. Indeed, matters do not come to a head in her life until she is asked by Bernard to break up a love match that threatens his sister's impending arranged marriage to a wealthy landowner. Thérèse, sensing in Anne's love idyll the passion that she herself has missed, is thus highly suggestible when she watches Bernard swallow an accidental overdose and makes no effort to stop him. Thereafter, in an almost childlike exploration of cause and effect, she increases the dosage until Bernard is hospitalized and his family brings charges against her. Fearing publicity at all costs, however, both families soon arrange for the charges to be dropped in exchange for Thérèse's discreet "disappearance" from their lives. At first, she is all but imprisoned in her own home, enjoined to stay out of her husband's sight; later, she is "exiled" to Paris, where she will continue to receive a modest income.

Like Mauriac's earlier fiction, *Thérèse* derives no small part of its effect from the author's skillful evocation of nature, in particular the pinewoods in which Thérèse feels herself imprisoned and the raging forest fire during which Bernard accidentally swallows his first overdose of arsenic. The family homes, like that of the Cazenaves in *Genitrix*, likewise loom large, suggesting imprisonment. A subsequent novel, *The End of the Night*, continues the story of Thérèse some fifteen years later in Paris but falls considerably short of the earlier narrative's total effect. In the meantime, however, Mauriac had met or surpassed the accomplishment of *Thérèse* with *Vipers' Tangle*, considered by many critics to be the finest of his novels.

Vipers' Tangle

All but abandoning the omniscient narrative stance with which Sartre was later to find fault, Mauriac in *Vipers' Tangle* exposes most of the action through the eyes and carefully chosen words of one Louis, retired from a brilliant and lucrative career in criminal law. In failing health, all but confined to one wing of his rambling, cavernous old house, Louis eavesdrops with mounting revulsion as his wife and children conspire to confiscate his lifelong hoard by having him declared incompetent. Combining in his distinguished but disagreeable person the most salient features of William Shakespeare's King Lear and Molière's miser, Harpagon, Louis has spent most of his nearly seventy years living up to the hate and fear that he believes himself to inspire in those around him. Like Jean Péloueyre of *A Kiss for the Leper* (and presumably, the reader is told, like the author himself), Louis perceived himself early in life to be ill-favored and unprepossessing, endowed only with high intelligence and a nearly photographic memory.

Accustomed to rebuff from his schoolmates and later from the opposite gender as well, Louis soon developed a gruff and forbidding demeanor behind which he continued to hide his true feelings, feelings of which even those closest to him would have considered him incapable. A product of secular education, as opposed to that of the Church, Louis has defended himself to a large extent by using his militant anticlericalism—often mistaken for atheism—as a weapon; one of the novel's more memorable scenes is one in which, as usual, Louis defiantly shocks his family by eating veal chops on Good Friday. Like Thérèse Desqueyroux, however, Louis soon emerges as a truly sensitive soul, one of the few who has somehow managed to resist the dehumanizing effects of his conformist bourgeois milieu. Arguably, the basic conflict of *Vipers' Tangle* is one between form and substance, with the unlikely Louis defending, in his gruff voice, the same values to which his outwardly pious relatives pay little more than lip service.

In ironic replication of his career, Louis has, in fact, conducted his marriage according to the adversary method ever since a late-night conversation, soon after his honeymoon, that his wife, Isa, doubtless has long since forgotten. In any case, one feels, Isa would be hard put to believe that her childish confidences of an earlier love affair would suffice to poison her marriage, as indeed they have. Louis, at first unable to believe his good fortune in winning the rich and charming Isa Fondaudège as his bride, takes her words as definitive proof that he has been fooled. Thus wounded in the darkest recesses of his pride, he resolves never to be fooled again; over the years, the wound festers into a palpable bitterness (perhaps the vipers' tangle of the title) that isolates him even from his own children and grandchildren.

Knowing that his family eagerly anticipates his death, Louis begins his narrative as a letter to Isa, pouring out a confession of hatred much as a presumably saner man might pour out a confession of love. His intention, it seems, is to place the letter atop the pile of stock certificates that he knows she will be looking for within hours or even minutes after his death. Until recently, he admits, he had planned to divest himself of everything but the house and land, thus depriving Isa and their children of his entire inheritance, but has since managed "to survive his hatred." As he writes—intensely sensitive (like most of Mauriac's characters) to the sights, sounds, and smells outside his window—the various members of his family sneak around the house and garden, audibly plotting against him even as they are afraid to meet him face-to-face; failing to understand Louis, Isa and the others have immunized themselves against his rantings with the comforting assurance that he is probably insane.

Throughout the novel, Mauriac spares little effort to assure the reader that Louis is indeed quite sane, probably more stable than his habitual detractors. Although never lovable, Louis is increasingly sympathetic, a man of keen intelligence and rare integrity whose most visible fault is that he implicitly demands of others the same lucidity and honesty that he has come to value in himself. As seen through his eyes, his children and in-laws border upon caricatures, fawning and posturing in hollow imitations of real life. Toward Isa, however, Louis still harbors the vestige of his early, frustrated love; her unexpected death, while Louis is in Paris attempting to frustrate a conspiracy mounted against him by his son and son-in-law, permanently alters both Louis's plans and the structure of the novel. Even as he has been pouring out his hatred in the lengthy letter, he seems never to have anticipated the possibility that his wife might predecease him, and his children are even further confounded by the spectacle of genuine grief that he displays at Isa's funeral. Thereafter, truly drained of his hatred, Louis "proves" his insanity by releasing all claim to his property, reserving only the right to live in the house for the remainder of his life. At the time of his death, not long thereafter, Louis is observed (through letters included as an epilogue) to have been rediscovering a long-buried faith in God.

To a number of contemporary critics, Louis's apparent "deathbed conversion" appeared implausible at best, a clumsy attempt on the part of the author to rectify, with one ill-aimed masterstroke, the bad habits of a lifetime. In certain of his earlier novels, Mauriac had often angered critics with hasty and apparently contrived conclusions, and to some of these critics, *Vipers' Tangle* appeared to be no exception. With time, however, the denouement of Louis's frustrated life has emerged as one of Mauriac's more plausible and satisfying conclusions, more than adequately justified by what, in Louis's mind, has gone before.

The central drama of Louis's life is indeed one of intense passion deflected from its object (Isa) and gone haywire; the initial purpose of his rambling account is to blurt out the passion that remains, in whatever distorted form. Once Isa has died, Louis's passion soon dissipates for want of a target, his attention refocusing on those people and incidents (already mentioned in the narrative) that have commended themselves to his subconscious mind. Louis's life, to an even greater degree than that of Dr. Courrèges and his son, has been a "desert of love," occasioned by the massive lack of communication between him and his wife. Only her death, it seems, can liberate him from the bondage of his frustrated passion, allowing him to seek satisfaction elsewhere. Indeed, Louis's peculiar blend of passion, lucidity, and intellectual curiosity (established early in the novel) would appear to predispose him toward belief, if not toward consolation. For today's reader, Louis's change of heart thus seems quite plausible, given the facts of his character as established.

After the general success of *Vipers' Tangle* (which accounted, at least in part, for Mauriac's election to the French Academy in the year following the novel's publication), Mauriac underwent a serious health crisis that was soon followed by a period of intense antifascist political activity. Although he continued to write novels, most of them concerned, as usual, with the lack of communication among mortals, his true interests during the 1930's and 1940's appeared to lie elsewhere. Of his later works, only *Woman of the Pharisees*, published in 1941, approaches in quality or power the best of his earlier works, and even in that novel the power is somehow dissipated, spread among too many characters.

WOMAN OF THE PHARISEES

Presented as a retrospective memoir of the aging Louis Pian, *Woman of the Pharisees* focuses primarily upon the title character, Louis's stepmother, Brigitte, a headstrong woman whose apparently well-intentioned meddling all but sufficed to ruin several lives during the narrator's youth and early adulthood. In order to show the nature and extent of Brigitte's meddling, Mauriac introduces an unusually large cast of significant characters, often at the risk of losing the reader's interest and attention. Brigitte Pian herself, however, emerges as one of Mauriac's most plausible, complex, and satisfying characters, a would-be saint who, after considerable reflection, honestly believes that her outwardly destructive behavior will serve to fulfill the will of God. In few other works of literature has the age-old debate between good works and divine grace been pursued so effectively as in *Woman of the Pharisees*; Brigitte Pian, moreover, is a considerably more credible, multidimensional, and engrossing creation than her immediate literary ancestor in Mauriac's oeuvres, Félicité Cazenave of *Genitrix*.

Mauriac's literary accomplishment thus stood complete, if not quite finished, by his fifty-seventh year, enviable for its portrayal of human alienation even among those readers who reject the author's implicit promise (and premise) of a better life to come in the next world, and quite deserving of the Nobel Prize in Literature conferred upon Mauriac in 1952.

David B. Parsell

Other major works

PLAYS: *Asmodée*, pr. 1937 (*Asmodée: Or, The Intruder*, 1939); *Les Mal Aimés*, pr., pb. 1945; *Passage du malin*, pr. 1947; *Le Feu sur la terre: Ou, Le Pays sans chemin*, pr. 1950.

POETRY: *Les Mains jointes*, 1909; *L'Adieu à l'adolescence*, 1911; *Orages*, 1925; *Le Sang d'Atys*, 1940.

NONFICTION: *Souffrances du chrétien*, 1928 (translated in *Anguish and Joy of the Christian Life*, 1964); *La Vie de Jean Racine*, 1928; *Bonheur du chrétien*, 1929 (translated in *Anguish and Joy of the Christian Life*); *Dieu et Mammon*, 1929 (*God and Mammon*, 1936); *Blaise Pascal et sa sœur Jacqueline*, 1931; *Le Romancier et ses personnages*, 1933; *Journal*, 1934-1953 (memoir); *Vie de Jésus*, 1936 (*Life of Jesus*, 1937); *Le Cahier noir*, 1943 (*The Black Notebook*, 1944); *Mes Grands Hommes*, 1949 (memoir; *Great Men*, 1952); *Écrits intimes*, 1953 (memoir); *Bloc-notes, 1952-1957*, 1958 (memoir); *Mémoires intérieurs*, 1959 (memoir; English translation, 1960); *Le Nouveau Bloc-notes*, 1961-1970 (memoir); *Ce que je crois*, 1962 (memoir; *What I Believe*, 1963); *De Gaulle*, 1964 (English translation, 1966); *Nouveaux Mémoires intérieurs*, 1965 (memoir; *The Inner Presence*, 1968); *Mémoires politiques*, 1967 (memoir); *Le Dernier Bloc-notes, 1968-1970*, 1971 (memoir); *Correspondance, 1925-1967*, 2001.

Bibliography

Brée, Germaine, and Margaret Guiton. "François Mauriac." In *The French Novel from Gide to Camus*. 1957. Reprint. New York: Harcourt, Brace & World, 1962. Although dated, this collection offers an excellent introduction for students. The chapter on Mauriac places his works in the broader context of French literature of the twentieth century.

Flower, John E. *Intention and Achievement: A Study of the Novels of François Mauriac*. Oxford, England: Clarendon Press, 1969. An especially useful introduction to and analysis of the author's life and works.

Flower, John E., and Bernard Swift, eds. *François Mauriac: Visions and Reappraisals*. New York: Berg, 1991. This book looks at new ways of interpreting Mauriac's work and career; it presents what is perhaps a more nuanced picture of the author and his work than the appraisals found in pre-1960's criticism.

Moloney, Michael Francis. *Francois Mauriac: A Critical Study*. 1958. Reprint. Whitefish, Mont.: Kessinger, 2006. An excellent critical treatment of Mauriac's poetic imagery. Includes an index.

O'Connell, David. *François Mauriac Revisited*. New York: Twayne, 1995. O'Connell provides a useful introduction to Mauriac, with information about the author's life and analyses of his novels and other works. Includes a bibliography and an index.

Wansink, Susan. *Female Victims and Oppressors in Novels by Theodore Fontane and François Mauriac*. New York: Peter Lang, 1998. Wansink compares the depiction of female characters as both victims and oppressors in Mauriac's novels, focusing on *Thérèse* and *Genitrix*.

Welch, Edward. *François Mauriac: The Making of an Intellectual*. Amsterdam: Rodopi, 2006. Welch examines Mauriac's career, tracing his evolution from a novelist in the 1920's and 1930's to a major French intellectual and journalist in the years following World War II. Welch also describes how the arc of Mauriac's career reflected broader changes in French culture.

Williams, Timothy J. *Desire and Persecution in "Thérèse Desqueyroux" and Other Selected Novels of François Mauriac*. Lewiston, N.Y.: Edwin Mellen Press, 2007. Williams uses French literary critic René Girard's concept of scapegoating to analyze Mauriac's novel *Thérèse*, arguing that the character Thérèse is both oppressor and victim. Welch compares *Thérèse* to other novels by Mauriac to describe how scapegoating and persecution are common themes in the author's long fiction.

WILLIAM MAXWELL

Born: Lincoln, Illinois; August 16, 1908
Died: New York, New York; July 31, 2000
Also known as: William Keepers Maxwell, Jr.

PRINCIPAL LONG FICTION

Bright Center of Heaven, 1934
They Came Like Swallows, 1937
The Folded Leaf, 1945
Time Will Darken It, 1948
The Château, 1961
So Long, See You Tomorrow, 1980

OTHER LITERARY FORMS

In his memoir *Ancestors* (1971), William Maxwell provides a history of his family, tracing his ancestry on both his mother's and father's sides to American pioneers and presenting much of the autobiographical material that is reflected in his fiction. In addition to his novels, Maxwell is well known for his short stories and for the reviews he wrote during his long career (1936-1976) on the editorial staff of *The New Yorker*. Some of his stories have been collected in *The Old Man at the Railroad Crossing, and Other Tales* (1966), *Over by the River, and Other Stories* (1977), and *All the Days and Nights: The Collected Stories of William Maxwell* (1995). He also wrote two works for children: *The Heavenly Tenants* (1946) and *Mrs. Donald's Dog Bun and His Home Away from Home* (1995).

ACHIEVEMENTS

William Maxwell was probably best known as a writer and fiction editor for *The New Yorker*, where he edited the works of John Cheever, Irwin Shaw, John O'Hara, and others. Although not well known among general readers, Maxwell received much critical acclaim for his own fiction, earning many awards, including the Friends of American Writers Award in 1938 and the William Dean Howells Award for Fiction for *So Long, See You Tomorrow* in 1980. He received a grant from the National Institute of Arts and Letters in 1958 and served as that organization's president from 1969 to 1972. Maxwell was consistently praised for the realism of his dialogue, his deep and sensitive insights into characters, especially children, and his depiction of the American Midwest.

BIOGRAPHY

Born in the small midwestern town of Lincoln, Illinois, in 1908, William Keepers Maxwell, Jr., was the second of three sons of William Keepers Maxwell, a traveling fire-insurance salesman, and Eva Blossom (Blinn) Maxwell. In his memoir *Ancestors*, Maxwell remembers his parents' marriage and his childhood as being extremely happy. Maxwell was especially close to his mother, who died of Spanish influenza in 1918, only three days after giving birth to Maxwell's younger brother. This event, frequently recalled in Maxwell's novels, is a focal point in *They Came Like Swallows* and *So Long, See You Tomorrow*. He relates that his family members never really discussed their grief with one another and therefore never fully recovered from the loss. His father's decision to remarry and move the family to Chicago four years later created more problems, for, although Maxwell's stepmother was pretty and kind, he resented her taking the place of his mother. The move to Chicago brought Maxwell, a small, bookish child who had no interest in sports, to the Nicholas Senn High School, where for the first time he was encouraged to study literature and music.

Maxwell received a B.A. from the University of Illinois in 1930 and an M.A. from Harvard University in 1931. He taught in the English department at the University of Illinois from 1931 to 1933. Shortly after the publication of his first novel, *Bright Center of Heaven*, Maxwell joined the editorial staff of *The New Yorker*, where he remained as fiction editor for forty years. Maxwell was married to Emily Gilman Noyes on May 17, 1945, and they had two daughters. He died in New York City on July 31, 2000.

ANALYSIS

William Maxwell's fiction has a strong autobiographical basis. Especially noted for accurate and vivid depiction of small midwestern towns in the first half of the twentieth century, Maxwell frequently drew from his early childhood in Lincoln, Illinois. Consequently, his novels deal with recurring themes and events that reflect his own experiences. The most common of these is the absence of one parent, stemming either from the death of Maxwell's mother or from estrangement from a father who never understood him, a condition that contributed to the loneliness of a child who had a reserved and intellectual temperament. Maxwell's sharp and insightful character delineations have consistently been praised by critics.

Bright Center of Heaven

Maxwell's first novel, *Bright Center of Heaven*, is set on a farm called Meadowland near Thisbe, Wisconsin. The farm is run by Mrs. Susan West, a generous but absentminded and disorganized widow who, finding her husband's estate insufficient to support her family, takes in a number of boarders. Paul McKenzie is a former schoolteacher who is searching for meaningful work. His lover is actor Nigel Foley, who fears that she may be pregnant. Also staying at the house are a brokenhearted pianist, Josefa Marchand, and a depressed painter, Cynthia Damon. Mrs. West's two teenage sons, Thorn and Whitey, are of opposite temperaments. Thorn loves the farm and is very much like his father; he is also in love for the first time, with Nigel. Whitey spends most of his time running errands for his mother. Also living at Meadowland is Mrs. West's sister, Miss Amelia Bascom, who has eaten nothing but cottage cheese and weak tea for three years and is easily upset and offended. Completing the family is nephew Bascom, who disturbs the tenants and talks incessantly. Most of the other characters suspect that Bascom is mentally unsound. The house is maintained by two servants: Johanna, the German cook, whose mother is dying overseas, and Gust, the old caretaker, who has worked for Mrs. West's family for many years and whose loyalty prevents him from retiring as soon as he would like.

William Maxwell. (Getty Images)

It is an eccentric household, and Maxwell moves among the points of view of all the characters before finally viewing the action through the eyes of Jefferson Carter, a Negro lecturer whom Mrs. West has invited to stay at the house—an act that almost guarantees a scandal. The novel runs through the course of one day, from breakfast to bedtime, and the simple, realistic dialogue, the ordinary daily tasks, and the exceptional circumstance of Carter's visit combine to permit great insight into the characters. Although the novel deals with subjects normally treated only in serious novels—subjects such as unwanted pregnancy, suicide, and racism—the novel is essentially a comic one and displays Maxwell's great potential as a novelist.

They Came Like Swallows

In *They Came Like Swallows*, Maxwell again presents his story through various points of view. Beginning in November, 1918, and covering a period of about two months, the novel examines the effect that the death of Elizabeth Morison has on her husband and her two young sons. The novel is divided into three sections, each devoted to the point of view of one of these three characters. Eight-year-old Peter Morison, known as Bunny and clearly Maxwell's fictional alter ego, is exceptionally close to his mother and suffers his father's cold detachment, both common elements in Maxwell's novels. Bunny also experiences some sibling rivalry with his thirteen-year-old brother, Robert, who, despite having lost a leg in an accident, continues to participate actively in sports. In the beginning of the novel Bunny's mother is pregnant and reads the first newspaper reports on the mysterious Spanish influenza. World War I comes to an end and all seems well, but Bunny contracts the disease. When two sparrows accidentally become trapped in Bunny's room, his mother impetuously enters, although she has been banished from the room because of her pregnancy.

Because of the complications she experienced with her first two pregnancies, Elizabeth goes to Decatur with her husband, James, to have the baby. Original plans to stay with their favorite aunt, Irene, fall through, so the boys stay with their Aunt Clara; there Robert feels isolated and finally comes down with the flu as well. During their illness, the boys learn that both parents have also contracted the disease, and, shortly after the birth of a frail son, Robert and Bunny's mother dies. Each of her remaining family members has grief and feelings of guilt to confront. James fears that his rushing to get on a crowded train may have unnecessarily exposed his wife to the illness; Robert blames himself for allowing his mother into Bunny's room. James is completely helpless and considers sending the children permanently to Aunt Clara's. Through their shared grief, their reliance on one another, and the guidance of Elizabeth's sister Irene, who commits herself to helping James care for the three children, however, the Morison family will be able to survive their loss. The novel has been commended for its insights into children's perceptions and its avoidance of excessive sentimentality.

The Folded Leaf

A child's loss of his mother and his subsequent loneliness, as well as his father's inability to deal with the loss, are also integral to the conflicts in *The Folded Leaf*. Lymie Peters is a small, unathletic, lonely fifteen-year-old boy who, following his mother's death, has recently moved with his father to Chicago from a small town in Illinois. Lymie's father is neglectful, drinks excessively, and spends time with prostitutes. One day Lymie is rescued at the swimming pool by Spud Latham, who, despite his abilities in sports and making friends, also feels out of place, having just moved to Chicago from a small town in Wisconsin. The boys become good friends. Craving the attention and warmth he receives from Spud's family, Lymie frequently stays at the Lathams' home, a tacky and cramped apartment.

After the boys eventually go to college in Indiana, their relationship is strained when Spud joins a fraternity. Spud also finds a girlfriend, Sally Forbes, and Lymie is both attracted to Sally and resentful of the attention she gets from Spud. Feeling rejected, Lymie attempts suicide. In the hospital, he is visited by his father, whose main concern is why Lymie did not leave a note for him. The novel ends with Spud and Sally entertaining Lymie, but their childish games are stopped by a nurse. Lymie assures everyone that he has learned valuable lessons. Several critics have argued that this ending is unsatisfactory and that Lymie's change is unconvincing, as the reader is not presented with sufficient evidence of his maturity. Despite this criticism, *The Folded Leaf* is generally considered Maxwell's finest novel, and his portrayal of the Midwest in the 1920's in this work is considered unparalleled.

Time Will Darken It

Also an especially effective novel in terms of its nostalgic and accurate depiction of time and place is *Time Will Darken It*, set in 1912 in fictional Draperville, Illinois. Austin King, a lawyer in Draperville, and his wife, Martha, have one daughter and have just learned that they are to have another child. Austin has invited the Potter family from Mississippi to visit, honoring a family obligation (Austin's father was reared by Mr. Potter's grandfather). The invitation proves to have been a serious mistake, and the visit changes the lives of all concerned. The Potters and their grown children—Nora, intelligent and bored with southern life, and Randolph, charming but cruel—stay for more than a month. The visit puts a great strain on the marriage of Austin and the beautiful Martha, who has never had a strong love for her husband and at times fantasizes about running away. Mr. Potter engages many of Austin's associates in a business scheme that, when it later fails, causes some of the men to question Austin's honesty.

When the Potters finally return home, Nora, who has fallen in love with Austin, decides to stay on with a nearby family, start a kindergarten, and read law in Austin's office. Flattered by Nora's devotion and stimulated by her intelligence, Austin irresponsibly encourages the girl. Not surprisingly, gossip runs rampant in the small town. After Nora is horribly disfigured in a fire, she returns to Mississippi to be with her family. She is both physically and emotionally scarred. Martha King gives birth to her second child, but the labor is difficult, and she almost dies. The King marriage, however, though strained, apparently will survive.

The Château

The Château again exposes midwesterners to another culture, but, unlike Maxwell's other novels, the work is set elsewhere. A young married American couple, Harold and Barbara Rhodes, are visiting Europe on a four-month holiday in 1948. They spend most of this time at the château of Madame Viénot. Though the Rhodeses speak some French, they have considerable difficulty overcoming the linguistic and cultural barriers between themselves and the French people. France still shows the ravages of World War II, and there are shortages of food and other supplies. The French also have considerable resentment toward American wealth and the late involvement of the United States in the war.

The Rhodeses fall in love with France, however, and despite the French people, whom they find moody—sometimes warm and generous, sometimes distant and rude—they form lasting friendships with members of Madame Viénot's household. Among those they meet are Eugène and Alix Boisgaillard, the son-in-law and daughter of Madame Cestre, Madame Viénot's sister. Eugène's moods alternate drastically, and Alix is similarly unpredictable. The Rhodeses also become quite fond of an old woman, Madame Straus, but as she often talks about associations with people who say that they have never heard of her, the Rhodeses wonder about her sanity and her integrity. When they return to the United States, however, Madame Straus continues to write them passionate letters, and they see her again when they return to France in 1953. The Rhodeses' closest alliance is formed, however, with Madame Viénot's daughter, Sabine, a kind and bright young woman who is isolated by her family's loss of wealth and status.

The Viénot family has clearly experienced a dramatic and tragic change of fortune, and the Rhodeses view their French friends with a sense of mystery. How did the Viénots lose their money? Where is Monsieur Viénot? Why does Eugène's mood change so frequently and so abruptly? Is Madame Straus really who she says she is? In an unusual epilogue, Maxwell engages in a dialogue with an imaginary reader who asks these questions and demands answers. He obliges, but only after assuring the reader that the answers are unimportant and that all mysteries cannot be solved.

So Long, See You Tomorrow

Maxwell's final novel, *So Long, See You Tomorrow*, is clearly based on events from the author's own life; in fact, the first half of the short novel reads more like autobiography than like fiction. Maxwell recalls a scandal in his hometown of Lincoln, Illinois, involving the family of his only boyhood friend, Cletus Smith. Maxwell was a frail child who would rather stay inside reading, close to his mother, than engage in sports. His father, who did not understand him, made him go outside to play; however, he had no friends, and the other boys teased him. He meets Cletus Smith, and they play together on the scaffolding of an unfinished house. Cletus's mother, Fern Smith, has been having an affair with Lloyd Wilson, who owns an adjacent farm and who is a good friend of the family. After she divorces her husband, Clarence, the truth of the affair comes out, and Clarence murders Lloyd and then kills himself. Maxwell does not see Cletus again until years later, after his mother's death, his father's remarriage, and his family's relocation to Chicago. Seeing Cletus in the hall of the high school, Maxwell snubs his friend rather than speaking to him. Nearly sixty years later, Maxwell still feels guilty and wishes to make amends.

In the first half of the novel Maxwell attempts to reconstruct the facts of the case, relying on the memory of witnesses and even obtaining information from court records. He digresses often to discuss his own early difficulties, including the loss of his mother and his general feelings of isolation. In the second half of the novel he attempts to reconstruct the scene by examining it through the varying points of view of the characters involved. Although *So Long, See You Tomorrow* contains the expected elements of Maxwell's fiction, critics have insisted that this novel represents a culmination rather than a rehashing of old ideas. Maxwell's careful honing produced a work whose tight construction and poetic language reflect the author's development as one of the twentieth century's distinguished writers.

Lou Thompson

Other major works

SHORT FICTION: *Stories*, 1956; *The Old Man at the Railroad Crossing, and Other Tales*, 1966; *Over by the River, and Other Stories*, 1977; *Five Tales*, 1988; *Billy Dyer, and Other Stories*, 1992; *All the Days and Nights: The Collected Stories of William Maxwell*, 1995.

NONFICTION: *Ancestors*, 1971; *The Outermost Dream: Essays and Reviews*, 1989; *The Happiness of Getting It Down Right: The Letters of Frank O'Connor and William Maxwell, 1945-1966*, 1996 (Michael Steinman, editor); *The Element of Lavishness: The Letters of Sylvia Townsend Warner and William Maxwell, 1938-1978*, 2001 (Michael Steinman, editor).

CHILDREN'S LITERATURE: *The Heavenly Tenants*, 1946; *Mrs. Donald's Dog Bun and His Home Away from Home*, 1995.

EDITED TEXTS: *The Garden and the Wilderness*, 1980; *Letters*, 1982 (of Sylvia Townsend Warner).

MISCELLANEOUS: *Early Novels and Stories*, 2008; *Later Novels and Stories*, 2008.

Bibliography

Baxter, Charles, Michael Collier, and Edward Hirsch, eds. *A William Maxwell Portrait: Memories and Appreciations*. New York: W. W. Norton, 2004. Collection of essays, analyses of Maxwell's works, and biographical sketches is more of a celebration of Maxwell than a critical study of the author.

Burkhardt, Barbara A. *William Maxwell: A Literary Life*. Urbana: University of Illinois Press, 2005. Combines biography and literary criticism, drawing on Burkhardt's interviews with Maxwell and access to Maxwell's writings and correspondence. Includes bibliography and index.

Campbell, James. "William Maxwell's Lives." In *Syncopations: Beats, New Yorkers, and Writers in the Dark*. Berkeley: University of California Press, 2008. Chapter on Maxwell is part of a collection of profiles and essays about writers working in the United States in the years after 1950.

Maxfield, James F. "The Child, the Adolescent, and the Adult: Stages of Consciousness in Three Early Novels of William Maxwell." *Midwest Quarterly* 24 (1983): 315-335. Uses primarily a psychoanalytic approach to examine *They Came like Swallows*, *The Folded Leaf*, and *Time Will Darken It*, arguing that these works form a trilogy that reflects the maturing of Maxwell as he confronts the loss of his mother and his father's remarriage. Asserts that the three early novels represent the wish fulfillment of the author at three stages of life.

_______ "Memory and Imagination in William Maxwell's *So Long, See You Tomorrow*." *Critique* 24, no. 1 (Fall, 1982): 21-37. Argues that in *So Long, See You Tomorrow* Maxwell combines factual and imagined elements to reconstruct the past in order to assuage his guilt for snubbing his friend Cletus and also to work out Oedipal conflicts with his father.

Maxwell, William. Interview. *Publishers Weekly*, December 10, 1979. Interview published shortly before the release of *So Long, See You Tomorrow* shows how Maxwell viewed his career as fiction editor for *The New Yorker* and describes his writing process. Maxwell also discusses the importance of his midwestern heritage in his writing.

Shereikis, Richard. "William Maxwell's Lincoln, Illinois." *Midamerica: The Yearbook of the Society for the Study of Midwestern Literature* 14 (1987): 101-112. Contrasts Maxwell with other midwestern writers, such as Sherwood Anderson and Edgar Lee Masters, and praises Maxwell for shunning extremes and portraying realistically the balance between the intolerance and generosity of the inhabitants of small midwestern towns. Notes Maxwell's ability to depict vividly these small, constricted worlds and still give them universal significance.

Updike, John. "The Imperishable Maxwell." *The New Yorker*, September 8, 2008. Reviews Maxwell's literary career and analyzes his novels and some of the short stories.

Wilkinson, Alec. *My Mentor: A Young Man's Friendship with William Maxwell*. New York: Houghton Mifflin, 2002. Memoir by a younger writer, a son of one of Maxwell's friends, sheds light on Maxwell's life. Wilkinson knew Maxwell for twenty-five years and credits him with teaching him the craft of writing.

HERMAN MELVILLE

Born: New York, New York; August 1, 1819
Died: New York, New York; September 28, 1891

Principal long fiction

Typee: A Peep at Polynesian Life, 1846
Omoo: A Narrative of Adventures in the South Seas, 1847
Mardi, and a Voyage Thither, 1849
Redburn: His First Voyage, 1849
White-Jacket: Or, The World in a Man-of-War, 1850
Moby Dick: Or, The Whale, 1851
Pierre: Or, The Ambiguities, 1852
Israel Potter: His Fifty Years of Exile, 1855
The Confidence Man: His Masquerade, 1857
Billy Budd, Foretopman, 1924

Other literary forms

Herman Melville, as if turning a new corner in his literary career, began a series of short stories after the financial failures of the novels *Moby Dick* and *Pierre*. The tales, which present an enigmatic addition to Melville's artistry, were published between 1853 and 1856, either in a collection (*The Piazza Tales*, 1856) or individually in journals such as *Putnam's Monthly Magazine* and *Harper's Monthly* magazine. Melville had difficulty with the short forms, and he seemed unable to work out the plot and characters in the space required. His best stories are novella length: "Benito Cereno," "The Encantadas," and "Bartleby the Scrivener." With the publication of *The Apple-Tree Table, and Other Sketches* (1922), all of Melville's stories became available in collection.

Melville also wrote poetry, which suffers from the same unevenness that plagues his short fiction. A handful of poems, gathered selectively from *Battle-Pieces and Aspects of the War* (1866), *John Marr and Other Sailors* (1888), and *Timoleon* (1891), are worthy of being anthologized with the best poetry of the nineteenth century. His worst poem, *Clarel: A Poem and Pilgrimage in the Holy Land* (1876), a long, flawed reflection on Melville's travels in the Holy Land, continues to be of interest only for its revealing autobiographical and philosophical content. "Hawthorne and His Mosses," Melville's only serious attempt at criticism and analysis, is important as an assessment of Hawthorne's first important sketches.

Achievements

Herman Melville's achievements, before the discovery of *Billy Budd, Foretopman* and the subsequent revival of Melville studies, were viewed simply as writings from "a man who lived among the cannibals." He was remembered only for *Typee* and *Omoo*, his slight but extremely popular South Seas adventures. While important as the beginnings of the popular tradition of exotic romances, *Typee* and *Omoo* are not classics. Only with the publication of *Billy Budd, Foretopman*, and the critical scrutiny that its publication encouraged, were *Moby Dick*, *Pierre*, and the rest reassessed, and Melville's reputation as a leader among giants affirmed.

Apart from introducing the South Seas tale to the American public, *Pierre* is arguably the first important work of psychological realism, and *Moby Dick* is a masterpiece of metaphysics, allegory, philosophy, and literature. The assessment of Melville's work was not realized until years after his death and almost seventy years after Melville had given up the novel form for the quick money of short stories, the personal introspection of poetry, and the security of a government post in the New York customs office. Melville was never psychologically or ideologically attuned to the demands of his reading public and, thus, popularity eluded him in his lifetime.

Biography

Herman Melville was born in New York City, August 1, 1819, the third child of a modestly wealthy family. His father, a successful merchant, traced his lineage back to Major Thomas Melville, one of the "Indians" at the Boston Tea Party. His mother, Maria Gansevoort Melville, was the only daughter of General Peter Gansevoort, also a revolutionary war hero. Melville had a happy childhood in a home where there was affluence and love. He had access to the arts and books, and he was educated in some of the city's finest private institutions. His father, however, considered young Melville to be somewhat backward, despite his early penchant for public speaking, and marked him for a trade rather than law or a similar professional pursuit.

The prosperity that the Melvilles enjoyed from before the young Melville's birth came to an end in the economic panic of 1830. Unable to meet creditors' demands, despite the financial aid of his family, Melville's father lost his business and was forced into bankruptcy. After attempts to save the business, he moved the family to Albany and assumed the management of a fur company's branch office. The move seemed to settle the Melvilles' financial problems until the cycle repeated itself in 1831. Melville's father again suffered a financial reversal, went into physical and mental decline, and died on January 28, 1832.

After his father's death, Melville became, successively, a bank clerk and accountant, a farmworker, a schoolteacher, and, after another economic failure—this time his brother Gansevoort's fur business—an unemployed, but genteel, young man seeking a job in New York City. With the aid of his brothers, Melville secured a berth on a Liverpool packet and thus launched his sea career and, indirectly, his literary fortunes. After one cruise, however, Melville returned to teaching. When the school closed for lack of funds, he and a friend determined to go West to visit Melville's uncle in Illinois, hoping to find some type of financially satisfying arrangement there. Failing to find work, Melville returned to New York City and signed aboard the *Acushnet*, a new whaler making its maiden voyage. From 1841 to 1844, Melville was to participate in seafaring adventures that would change American literature.

On his return to New York in 1844, Melville found his family's fortunes somewhat improved. He also found that the stories he had to tell of his travels were enthusiastically received by his friends and relatives. Finally persuaded to write them, he produced *Typee* and published it in 1846. The immediate success and acclaim that followed the publication assured Melville that he had finally found his place in life. He followed *Typee* with its sequel, *Omoo*, which achieved a similar success, and resolutely set out to make his living by his pen. He found the financial return of two popular novels was not sufficient to support him, however, and he applied for a government position and was rejected. Melville married Elizabeth Shaw, moved to New York City with most of his family, and started a third novel that became *Mardi, and a Voyage Thither*.

The visionary and allegorical structure of *Mardi, and a Voyage Thither* did not appeal to the readers of his previous successes, and its failure frustrated Melville. In need of ready funds, he began two quick potboilers, or inferior works, to produce those funds. After the publication and success of *Redburn* and *White-Jacket*, Melville moved his family to a farm in the Berkshires of New York State, which he dubbed Arrowhead because of Indian artifacts he found there, and assumed the life of a country gentleman and a member of the loosely knit literary society that included Oliver Wendell Holmes, Sr., Nathaniel Hawthorne, and others living in the vicinity of Pittsfield, Massachusetts.

How Hawthorne and Melville met is not known, but that they met is witnessed by the production of *Moby*

Herman Melville. (Library of Congress)

Dick. It was likely that Hawthorne encouraged Melville to write as he saw fit, not as the public demanded. Their correspondence reveals an intense, cordial friendship that was of immense value to Melville during this time of his greatest personal, emotional, and artistic development. Hawthorne was one of the first, not to mention the few, to praise Melville's whaling story. Despite Hawthorne's praise, *Moby Dick* was a financial and critical failure. *Pierre*, the "rural bowl of milk" that followed *Moby Dick*, defied Melville's predictions for its success and was also a failure. The dual failure caused Melville considerable pain and bitterness. As a result of the failures and the debt to his publishers, Melville turned away from the novel to the short-story form.

Melville was to publish two more novels in his lifetime, but neither was commercially successful. He began writing poetry in addition to the short story, but his poetry was even more introspective than his fiction, and by the time he was appointed to the customs office of New York City in 1866, he had virtually stopped publishing for public consumption.

The security of the customs office eliminated Melville's need for the slim financial return of publication, and he no longer felt compelled to write for an unwilling public. Yet, he continued to write. At his death, he left a box full of manuscripts of his unpublished work during the years from 1866 to his death (he had published some poetry). When the box was opened, it was found to contain one more novel. *Billy Budd, Foretopman*, published in 1924, was the final piece of Melville's frustration. He never finished it and never attempted to publish it, but since its discovery and publication it has been recognized as one of Melville's masterpieces. When Melville died in 1891, his obituaries recalled him not only as one who wrote novels of adventure but also one who had "fallen into a literary decline." It was left for another generation to appreciate and revere him.

Analysis

Herman Melville's career as a novelist breaks down, somewhat too neatly, into a three-part voyage of frustration and disappointment. The first part of his career is characterized by the heady successes of *Typee* and *Omoo*; the second by the frustrating failure of, among others, *Moby Dick*; and the third by his increasing withdrawal from publication and the final discovery of and acclaim for *Billy Budd, Foretopman*, thirty-two years after Melville's death. After the initial successes of *Typee* and *Omoo*, Melville never again achieved anything approaching popular success, but it was the acclaim over those two novels that assured Melville that he should attempt to make his way as a novelist. It probably did not occur to Melville at the time, but he was introducing a new genre into American literature.

Typee struck the American public like a ray of sunshine falling into a darkened room. The fresh descriptions and intriguing narrative of an American sailor trapped among the Rousseauesque natives of the Marquesas Islands were hailed on both sides of the Atlantic Ocean, and its sequel, *Omoo*, was received even more enthusiastically. The problems inherent in Melville's harsh treatment of missionaries and imperialism and the general disbelief of the veracity in the author's tale aside, the works satiated a public thirst for exotic places. That *Typee* and *Omoo* have survived in the estimation of critics is testimony to Melville's art even in those early stages of his development.

Typee

Whether it is the simple narrative or the dramatic suspense of impending doom that holds the reader, *Typee* offers a flowing romantic atmosphere of timeless days, pointless endeavor, and mindless existence. The Happy Valley in which Melville's Tommo finds himself trapped is an idyllic setting for the lovely Fayaway and Tommo to live and love. In *Typee* there is none of the agonizing speculation on life, humanity, philosophy, or the cosmos, which readers later came to expect of Melville. With only slight exaggeration and minimal research, Melville created the picture of a world that was beyond the ken of his readers but that would never die in his memories.

Omoo

Omoo, a sequel to *Typee*, is only an extension of that idyll. There is a basic difference between *Typee* and *Omoo*, however. *Typee* is a tightly woven dramatic narrative, incorporating the day-to-day suspense of whether Tommo would be the Marquesan cannibals' next meal; *Omoo* is a more picaresque representation of the events, the charm in *Omoo* depending solely on the loosely tied chain of events encountered by the narrator and his companion, Dr. Long Ghost, among the indigenous of Tahiti. There is no threat hanging over them, as in *Typee*, and there is no necessity for escape. *Omoo* also differs in that it takes place in a tainted paradise. Tahiti has been, in *Omoo*, Christianized and settled and, thus, the natives are familiar with the white sailor and his games. This reduction of innocence colors *Omoo* in a way not reflected in *Typee*.

There is an inescapable glow of romance throughout Melville's two Polynesian novels. The record of missionary abuse and the encroachment of civilization does not make an overbearing appearance, but it does lay the groundwork for the reflections of Melville's despair and convoluted indictments of humans and their world in later, more mature works.

Mardi, *Redburn*, and *White-Jacket* rapidly followed Melville's early successes. *Mardi*, opening like a continuation of *Typee* and *Omoo*, shocked readers when it lapsed into philosophical allegory. *Mardi*'s subsequent failure prompted Melville, in search of fame and funds, to return to sea narrative in *Redburn* and *White-Jacket*, but despite their modest successes, Melville reviled them as hackwork.

Moby Dick

With *Moby Dick*, there is evidence that Melville intended the work to be little more than a factual account of the whale fisheries in the South Pacific detailed with firsthand tales of adventures on a whaler. When completed two years after its beginning, it was a puzzling, intricately devised literary work in which a white whale is the central character. Around this central figure, Melville weaves symbolism, speculation, philosophy, and allegory on life, God, humanity, and the human condition. In short, Melville had created an epic romance that stood at the brink of becoming mythology.

The plot of *Moby Dick*, when not interrupted by authorial asides and digressions, is relatively direct. A young man, Ishmael, comes to the sea seeking a berth on a whaling ship. He finds the *Pequod*; falls into a friendship with the cannibal harpooner, Queequeg; discovers that the ship is captained by a madman, Ahab, who is driven to wreak vengeance on the white whale that took his leg off on a previous voyage; finds himself in a crew that is a microcosm of the world's peoples; watches as Ahab drives the ship and crew in pursuit of Moby Dick; and is the sole survivor when Ahab is killed in a direct confrontation with the whale. By itself, the plot is thrilling but does not have the ingredients of greatness. The layers of fiction—the levels that the reader must traverse in order to rend the novel for all its substance—make the work magnificent. To the surface adventure, Melville adds gleanings from volumes of cetological and marine lore, his own observations on human psychology, and, finally, his ultimate speculations on good and evil—the basic morality of humanity and humankind's place in the universe.

Melville's frequent displays of marine erudition are often cursed as flaws in an otherwise closely woven fabric. They seem to do little for the on-rushing spectacle of Ahab and his monomania, and they almost function as literary irritants designed to interrupt the reader's chain of thought. They are not intended to enhance the characterization of Ahab or his crew, nor are they an integral part of the narrative; they are, however, the essence of the novel's central character, the whale. Without Melville's lore, there is no reality to the ominously ethereal presence of Moby Dick. The periodic chapters of information and background are the author's reminders to the reader of the whale's presence and that the whale drives the story forward. The lore is also the foundation of belief in the whale. It promotes and maintains the physical presence of the whale by the sheer weight of scientific or pseudoscientific data. When the whale finally appears, the reader has been sufficiently educated and prepared. Melville creates the whale, vicariously, with his lore and trivia and sets the stage for its appearance.

In describing Ahab, his ship, and the crew, Melville employs a nonnarrative form of characterization, where each individual is the subject of an inquiry or is an example of a human type. Of the major characters, Ahab is the most complex, but the others form a society in which that complexity can best be displayed. First Mate Starbuck, Second Mate Stubb, and Third Mate Flask are only the closest of several layers of the crew around Ahab. Queequeg, Tashtego, and Daggoo, the harpooners, form the next layer, and the rest of the crew fill out Ahab's world. Like Fleece, the ship's cook, and Pip, the mad cabin boy, they all perform vignettes that enlarge and enhance the magnitude of Ahab and his quest. For example, Ahab feels compelled to explain the real reasons behind his insane search for the white whale only to Starbuck, the conscientious, scrupulous first mate. Rather than simple revenge, as Starbuck supposes it to be, Ahab proposes to strike through the "pasteboard masks" of reality by striking at the whale. In his reasoning with Starbuck, Ahab demonstrates a side of himself that is otherwise hidden; there is purpose, calculation, and preparation in his madness. Ahab's insanity, thereby, becomes a divine sort of madness, and he transcends mere earthly logic to become an epic madman jousting with creation. It is through Starbuck and the others that the reader learns most about Ahab, and it is in such relationships that one sees the mastery of Melville's artistry.

Ahab becomes more than a simple villain when viewed against the backdrop of Starbuck and the other characters. He becomes a monolithic character testing a universe that he sees as perverse and unkind toward human existence. He dares to confront nature itself and to challenge it to single combat. It is Queequeg who unwittingly provides the clues to the venture's outcome. He has a coffin built when he fears he will die of a fever, and when Moby Dick rams the *Pequod*, it is the coffin that supports Ishmael, the only survivor. The coffin becomes the symbolic remainder of Ahab's world. Humans and their science cannot stand against nature and hope to survive. It is Ahab's tragic flaw to believe that he can survive, and his belief is the final sign of his ultimately evil nature.

Ahab would, he tells Starbuck, "strike the sun if he offended me," and he considers himself as the equal of any other force in nature. He forgets that he is limited by human frailty—or he believes he is no longer subject to the laws of temporal existence or his own physical shortcomings. He is, in one sense, a blighted Prometheus who can offer nothing but his vision to his fellow humans, and they blindly accept it. Ahab's greatest evil is the corruption of his relatively innocent world, and its ultimate destruction is his sole responsibility.

Melville used many symbols and devices in *Moby Dick*, and they are important strands by which the story is held together. The names alone are important enough to demand attention. Ishmael, Ahab, Jereboam, and Rachel carry biblical significance. Starbuck, Stubb, and Flask all have significance when examined symbolically. The mythical ramifications of a voyage beginning on Christmas night enlarge as the story unfolds. The ultimate device is Ishmael himself. Ostensibly the story's narrator, he only appears in about every fourth chapter after the first twenty-five. When he does appear, it is difficult to keep track of whether the narrator or author is speaking. Ishmael, however, is never used in an omnipotent, obtrusive manner that would belie his place on the *Pequod*, and, thus, the point of view remains clear. Ishmael opens the novel and announces "and I only am escaped alone to tell thee," but he is there primarily to provide a frame for the story. This very flexible point of view is an adroit device by which the author can distance himself from the story while still involving himself in a story as few authors have or will. When Melville finds Ishmael to be an encumbrance, he sheds him and speaks for himself. It remains an open question whether the story is Ishmael's, Ahab's, the whale's, or Melville's. It is not necessary, however, that the dilemma be resolved in order to appreciate and acknowledge the massive achievement in *Moby Dick*.

Billy Budd, Foretopman

After *Moby Dick* failed commercially, Melville's increasingly sour approach to novel writing produced *Pierre*, perhaps the first psychological novel in American literature but also a miserable failure; *Israel Potter*, a rewriting and fictionalizing of a Revolutionary War diary; *The Confidence Man*, a sardonic, rambling, loosely constructed allegory on American society; and *Billy Budd, Foretopman*. The last of Melville's attempts in the novel form, *Billy Budd, Foretopman* was never offered for publication by the author and was discovered and published in the mid-1920's. Despite its checkered publication history (it has appeared in any number of flawed or badly edited forms), *Billy Budd, Foretopman* has come to be recognized as Melville's final word on the great problems with which he first grappled in *Moby Dick*. Its form and simplicity make it the perfect companion for the epic proportions of *Moby Dick*. Its message is such that it seems Melville created it as a catharsis for the unanswered questions in the greater work.

Billy Budd, Foretopman is a masterful twisting of historical event into fiction to maintain the tension of a gripping story. While so doing, Melville explores the stirring, but somewhat less exciting, problems of the conflict between humans, good and evil, and the law.

Melville uses a blend of the historically significant British mutinies of the Nore and at Spithead in 1797 and the 1842 execution of three alleged mutineers of the U.S. ship *Somers*, in which his cousin, Guert Gansevoort, played a significant part, to mold the setting and motive for his story leading to the trial and execution of the "handsome sailor." The events leading to the trial are relatively unadorned, and there is little question prior to the trial where the reader's sympathies should be and which characters embody which attributes of human nature.

There is a slightly melodramatic air about the principal characters in *Billy Budd, Foretopman*. Claggart, by shrewd characterization and description, is the evil master-at-arms who is in direct conflict with the innocent, pure, guileless Billy Budd. Melville never makes clear why Claggart develops his seemingly perverse prejudice against Billy, but a definite line of good and evil is drawn between the two men. The evil is magnified by the mysterious impetus for Claggart's antipathy toward Billy; the good is intensified by Billy's naïve ignorance of Claggart's malice, even though the entire crew seems to know of it and understand the reasons for it, and by his cheerful mien not only in the face of Claggart's bullying but also in spite of the circumstances that brought him to the *Indomitable*.

Billy is wronged from the beginning, when he is impressed from the U.S. ship *Rights of Man* to the British *Indomitable* (the names of the ships being a sly piece of Melville commentary on the British navy, the War of 1812, and Billy Budd's predicament, among other things). He is instantly recognized and accepted by his new mates on board the *Indomitable* and becomes a full and useful member of the crew and a good shipmate. Claggart, who has the unenviable job of policing a British man-of-war, or combat ship, and administering the British crown's maritime justice, seems to extend himself to bring charges against the new man. When Billy is implicated in a mutiny rumor, Claggart seizes the opportunity to bring him before a drumhead court-martial. At the hearing, Claggart concentrates all of his inexplicable venom against Billy Budd in false charges, innuendo, and lies calculated to ensure a guilty verdict for which Billy will be hanged.

The wonder of Billy Budd and Claggart is that Melville, while portraying the two extremes of human morality in human forms, avoids creating flat caricatures. Billy and Claggart seemingly are real people operating in a real world, and they develop in very believable ways, even given Claggart's behavior toward Billy. At the climax of the trial, perhaps the most fantastic moment in the novel, there is no appreciable relaxation of the verisimilitude Melville creates, even though Billy strikes Claggart dead with one crashing blow of his fist. The other major character of the novel fills the momentary gap in the credibility of the story after Claggart's death. Captain Vere commands not only the *Indomitable* but also the trial, and it is he who pushes the novel through its climactic scene and who, in essence, takes the message of the novel from Billy Budd and develops it to its fruition.

Edward Fairfax "Starry" Vere appears at length only from the trial to the end of the novel, but, despite the title character and his antagonist, Vere is the heart of the novel. He is everything Billy and Claggart are not. He is a complex character—a philosophical ship's captain—and a man who is caught between many pressures as he decides the fate of a man whom he evidently likes. Faced with the precedent of the historical mutinies that Melville introduces into the novel's background, Vere feels the necessity of creating Billy Budd as an example to other prospective mutineers. Seeing Billy's innocence, and understanding part of Claggart's fulsome character, Vere is loath to condemn a man who probably was within his moral right to strike his superior. Even so, the need for order and the maritime sense of justice force Vere to send Billy to the yardarm. Vere, more than anyone, recognizes that he is sacrificing an innocent man for the good of his ship, its crew, and, ultimately, his society. He sentences Billy under the prescription of law, but he begs his forgiveness as a moral human being.

The sacrifice of the innocent is a theme that pervades Western literature, but in *Billy Budd, Foretopman*, Melville confronts the struggle between chaos and order, law and morality, and humankind and society. There is no clear decision as Vere dies in battle; Billy haunts him to his end. Yet the society, the system for which Billy was sacrificed, survives and prevails. Vere remains incomprehensible except to the man he condemns. Billy Budd understands but does not have the capacity or the will to exert himself in order to save himself. He is reminiscent, in some respects, of the Christ figure he has universally been called. In the final analysis, Vere, Claggart, and Billy are all sacrificed, and the initial skirmishes between good and evil become almost trivial when compared to the moral and philosophical riddles Melville poses.

From *Omoo* and *Typee* to *Moby Dick* and *Billy Budd, Foretopman*, Melville traverses the paths to maturity and complexity not only in prose fiction but also in philosophical and spiritual understanding. Nevertheless, there is little difference between Tommo and Billy Budd, the two innocents of civilization. Ahab and Vere are similar enough to be recognized as brothers of the quarterdeck and of humankind. While facing different problems and decisions, they both meet them and deal with them similarly—and both die for their causes. The thread of the sea is unmistakable in Melville, but he recognized the function of the ship at sea as a symbol or as an experimental station, isolated and representative of the world he examined. Melville had his causes and injected them into his stories, but he is primarily interested in the human condition. He inspects all facets of each character ruthlessly and meticulously, without judgment and without prejudice, and he allows the results of his inspection to speak for themselves without gratuitous commentary. Since the revival of Melville studies with the discovery of *Billy Budd, Foretopman*, Melville's reputation as one of America's most significant authors is secure.

Clarence O. Johnson

Other major works

SHORT FICTION: *The Piazza Tales*, 1856; *The Apple-Tree Table, and Other Sketches*, 1922; *Great Short Works of Herman Melville*, 1969 (Warner Berthoff, editor).

POETRY: *Battle-Pieces and Aspects of the War*, 1866; *Clarel: A Poem and Pilgrimage in the Holy Land*, 1876; *John Marr and Other Sailors*, 1888; *Timoleon*, 1891; *Collected Poems of Herman Melville*, 1947; *The Poems of Herman Melville*, 1976 (revised 2000; Douglas Robillard, editor).

NONFICTION: *Journal up the Straits*, 1935; *Journal of a Visit to London and the Continent*, 1948; *The Letters of Herman Melville*, 1960 (Merrell R. Davis and William H. Gilman, editors); *Journals*, 1989 (text revised with historical note and annotations by Howard C. Horsford with Lynn Horth); *Correspondence*, 1993 (Horth, editor).

MISCELLANEOUS: *The Works of Herman Melville*, 1922-1924 (16 volumes); *The Writings*, 1968-1993 (15 volumes; Harrison Hayford, Hershel Parker, and G. Thomas Tanselle, editors); *Tales, Poems, and Other Writings*, 2001 (John Bryant, editor).

Bibliography

Arvin, Newton. *Herman Melville*. Reprint. New York: Grove Press, 2002. Still the definitive biography, originally published in 1950. Arvin provides a balanced, critical study of Melville's life and work. This book received the National Book Award for Best Nonfiction Book in 1951.

Bryant, John, ed. *A Companion to Melville Studies*. New York: Greenwood Press, 1986. Collection of essays about Melville's life and work. Includes a biography; analyses of his novels; discussions of his thoughts on aesthetics, philosophy, and religion; and examinations of Melville and the myth of modernism and on his impact on popular culture.

_______. *Melville Unfolding: Sexuality, Politics, and the Versions of "Typee," a Fluid-Text Analysis, with an Edition of the "Typee" Manuscript*. Ann Arbor: University of Michigan Press, 2008. The manuscript of *Typee*, Melville's most popular novel during his lifetime, was discovered in 1983. Bryant focuses on the "invisible text of revision" in the manuscript, describing how Melville altered his text to create the final version of the novel. This book is linked to an electronic edition of *Typee* to enable readers to chart Melville's process of creating his novel.

Delbanco, Andrew. *Melville: His World and Work*. New York: Alfred A. Knopf, 2005. Delbanco's critically acclaimed biography places Melville in his time and features discussion about the debate over slavery and life in 1840's New York.

Hardwick, Elizabeth. *Herman Melville*. New York: Viking Press, 2000. A short biographical study that hits all the high points and some low ones in Melville's life, from his early seagoing expeditions to his settling down in middle age and finally his languishing in his job as a New York customs inspector.

Higgins, Brian, and Hershel Parker, eds. *Critical Essays*

on Herman Melville's "Moby Dick." New York: G. K. Hall, 1992. A comprehensive selection of contemporary reviews and later essays about Melville's themes and techniques, his literary influences and affinities, the characters of Ahab and Ishmael, and Melville in the context of antebellum culture.

Kirby, David. *Herman Melville*. New York: Ungar, 1993. A short yet comprehensive guide to Melville's career, including chapters on his life, his early novels, *Moby Dick*, the later novels, and the tales and poems. Includes a chronology and a bibliography.

Levine, Robert S., ed. *The Cambridge Companion to Herman Melville*. New York: Cambridge University Press, 1998. An indispensable tool for the student of Melville, this collection of essays includes analyses of *Typee*, *Moby Dick*, and *The Confidence Man*; a discussion of Melville and sexuality; and a chronology of Melville's life. Includes a bibliography and an index.

Parker, Hershel. *Herman Melville: A Biography*. Vol. 1, 1819-1851, Vol. 2, 1851-1891. Baltimore: Johns Hopkins University Press, 1997-2002. This two-volume biography of Melville written by a distinguished authority on his life and art is especially helpful on the early life of Melville and the controversies that arose from his early novel's being labeled obscene and blasphemous.

Renker, Elizabeth. *Strike Through the Mask: Herman Melville and the Scene of Writing*. Baltimore: Johns Hopkins University Press, 1996. Renker argues that Melville was obsessed with the difficulties of the material act of writing, as reflected in his repeated themes and leitmotifs, such as the face or mask; she maintains that Melville's depression, violent nature, and abuse of his wife are reflected in his writings. Includes notes, a list of works cited, and an index.

Robertson-Lorant, Laurie. *Melville: A Biography*. New York: Clarkson N. Potter, 1996. Robertson's biography examines the personal, psychological, social, and intellectual aspects of Melville's life, as well as his travels and adventures in the South Seas and Europe.

Rollyson, Carl E., and Lisa Paddock. *Herman Melville A to Z: The Essential Reference to His Life and Work*. New York: Checkmark Books, 2001. Comprehensive and encyclopedic coverage of Melville's life, works, and times. The 675 detailed entries discuss the characters, settings, allusions, and references in his fiction as well as discuss his friends and associates and the critics and scholars who have studied his work.

GEORGE MEREDITH

Born: Portsmouth, England; February 12, 1828
Died: Flint Cottage, near Box Hill, Surrey, England; May 18, 1909

PRINCIPAL LONG FICTION

The Shaving of Shagpat, 1855
Farina, 1857
The Ordeal of Richard Feverel, 1859
Evan Harrington, 1861
Emilia in England, 1864 (also known as *Sandra Belloni: Or, Emilia in England*, 1886)
Rhoda Fleming, 1865
Vittoria, 1867
The Adventures of Harry Richmond, 1871
Beauchamp's Career, 1874-1875 (serial), 1876 (book)
The Egoist: A Comedy in Narrative, 1879
The Tragic Comedians, 1880
Diana of the Crossways, 1885
One of Our Conquerors, 1891
Lord Ormont and His Aminta, 1894
The Amazing Marriage, 1895
Celt and Saxon, 1910 (unfinished)

OTHER LITERARY FORMS

Ironically, George Meredith, one of nineteenth century England's greatest novelists, actually considered himself a poet. Regrettably, the several volumes of poetry he published during his lifetime went largely unnoticed. Even though Alfred, Lord Tennyson, praised "Love in the Valley," published in his first volume, *Poems* (1851), dedicated to his then father-in-law, Thomas Love Peacock, it was as a novelist that Meredith achieved recognition in his own time. Undaunted, nevertheless, Meredith continued to write poems and, in keeping with his stated vocation and with his aspiration, both his first and his last published books were collections of poems.

Modern Love and Poems of the English Roadside (1862) represents Meredith's lyric and dramatic power at its height, especially in the sequence of fifty sixteen-line lyrics, *Modern Love*. In these poems, Meredith traces the dissolution of a marriage with an unrestrained candor that is more like the attitudes toward marital relationships of the late twentieth century than the straight-faced, closed-lipped Victorian notions. At the lowest point in the sequence, the persona exclaims, "In tragic life, God wot,/ No villain need be! Passions spin the plot;/ We are betrayed by what is false within." Herein Meredith seems to capture with great precision the essence of tragedy. Meredith's poetic vision is not always dark; light imagery, in fact, plays a significant role in his poetry.

The thinking man appears often in Meredith's works, but he is perhaps most prominent in the 1877 work *On the Idea of Comedy and of the Uses of the Comic Spirit*. This essay is significant enough to be included in many contemporary collections of criticism, especially in those that pertain to drama. Acknowledging that the muse of comedy has never been "one of the most honored of the Muses," Meredith submits that it is the "Comic Spirit" that civilizes humans. By means of thoughtful laughter, the Comic Spirit corrects and checks the foibles of all those who exceed the bounds of temperance and indulge by excessive behavior. Although Meredith opened himself to censure in his own day, his ideas about women and their roles in comedy are particularly interesting to today's readers. Indeed, comedy, "the fountain of common sense," teaches that men and women are social equals and that women are often men's superiors.

Achievements

In the late nineteenth century, George Meredith achieved the status of a literary dictator or arbiter of taste. The path toward this recognition was, however, a long and arduous one. For years, Meredith received little to no recognition, and he had to wait for the publication of *The Ordeal of Richard Feverel* before he enjoyed the limited appreciation of Algernon Charles Swinburne, Dante Gabriel Rossetti, and others among the Pre-Raphaelites. Not until the appearance of *The Egoist* in 1879 did Meredith's literary reputation reach its zenith.

During his last years, Meredith received many awards and honors, including the succession of Alfred, Lord Tennyson, as the president of the Society of British Authors and election as one of the original members of the Order of Merit. Within twenty years after Meredith's death in 1909, nevertheless, his literary reputation began to suffer a partial eclipse, from which it began to recover in the 1970's. One explanation for Meredith's decline in reputation is simple: His turgid style and complex plots demand more from the average reader than he or she is often willing to give.

C. L. Cline's three-volume edition of *The Letters of George Meredith*, which appeared in 1970, and Phyllis B. Bartlett's two-volume collection of *The Poems of George Meredith* (1978) have done much to reawaken interest in Meredith's work, particularly in his poetry, which seems to appeal to modern readers much more markedly than it had to those of his own time. Even so, the influence of Meredith the novelist on such younger writers as Thomas Hardy was decisive, and Meredith's theory of the Comic Spirit as the civilizing force of all thoughtful persons speaks to all cultures of all times.

Biography

Born the son and grandson of tailors, George Meredith appears to have rejected his humble origins. Indeed, he once threatened that he would "most horribly haunt" any who attempted to reconstruct his biography. Despite his modest heritage, legacies from his mother and an aunt permitted him to attend private schools, St. Paul's Church School, Southsea, and the Moravian School of Neuwied, Germany. His objective in formal training was to become a lawyer, and he was apprenticed to a London solicitor in 1845. Young Meredith soon became dissatisfied with the legal profession, however, and began to seek a career as a journalist, a vocation that he pursued throughout most of his life, since he was never quite able to survive financially as an author of novels and poems.

From at least 1845 until his marriage in 1849 to Mary Ellen Nicolls, a widow and the daughter of Thomas Love Peacock, Meredith appears to have read widely and deeply in the literature of Greece, Rome, Germany, France, and England. The first few years of his marriage appear to have been ones of continued intellectual growth. The Merediths lived either with or near the aspiring young author's famous father-in-law. Meredith made good use of Peacock's extensive and often arcane library, whose shelves included volumes on such Near Eastern religions as Zoroastrianism, a faith that was later to have a profound influence on Meredith's novels and poems.

George Meredith. (Library of Congress)

The first few years of apparent bliss were soon terminated, however, when Mary eloped in 1858 with the painter Henry Wallis to the isle of Capri. Meredith was consequently left alone to rear his son, Arthur; the author later wrote about these unhappy times both in the novel *The Ordeal of Richard Feverel* and in the lyric sequence *Modern Love*. After Mary's death in 1861, Meredith married, within three years, Marie Vulliamy; this match proved to be both enduring and much happier. After serving as war correspondent, he and Marie moved to Flint Cottage, Box Hill, Surrey. Box Hill is where admiring and enthusiastic young authors went to seek Meredith's sage counsel.

ANALYSIS

Although George Meredith's works all emphasize the corrective, civilizing influences of the Comic Spirit, his novels, as well as his poems, forcefully work out a sort of theodicy that is consistently informed by the Near Eastern religion Zoroastrianism. This philosophy that treats the being and government of God and the immortality of the soul displays the theme of the struggle between good and evil in the early work *Farina*.

Surrounded by the trappings of medieval Germany, Farina, the hero of the tale, is left to contend with the evil effects of a bout between a monk and Satan. The monk represents the Zoroastrian god of light or good, Ormuzd, and Satan, the god of darkness or evil, Ahriman.

THE ORDEAL OF RICHARD FEVEREL

In the later, much more successful novel *The Ordeal of Richard Feverel*, this dialectic is seen in the sixth chapter, "The Magian Conflict" (the magi were ancient priests of Zoroaster). In this case, Meredith assigns the roles of the two opposing parties of the struggle to a Tinker and a Yeoman; the witness to this debate is the adolescent Richard Feverel, whose father, Sir Austin, has attempted unsuccessfully to shield him from any introduction to the world's forces of good and evil.

The Tinker, who appears to be a faithful follower of Zoroaster, the ancient prophet of the faith, asserts that the Good Spirit reigns supreme. The Yeoman, whom Meredith playfully calls Speed-the-Plough, protests, because of his recent misfortune of having lost several jobs, that the Evil Spirit dominates. The Yeoman is particularly hostile to Farmer Blaize, with whom Richard and a companion have also had an unpleasant encounter. Farmer Blaize is responsible for the beginning of the Yeoman's misfortunes. Tinker and Yeoman discuss the universal strife between good and evil in Zoroastrian terms, wherein the Good Spirit is supposed to hold dominion for a two-thousand-year period and the Evil Spirit is believed to assume dominion for a like period of two thousand years. Clearly, then, this debate challenges the young Richard to side with Ahriman (darkness) or to join the legions of Ormuzd (light).

Richard later relates the details of this encounter to Adrian Harley, a sort of tutor and confidant of the young Mr. Feverel, who is actually a disciple of the Comic Spirit and whom the narrator addresses as the Wise Youth. Adrian explains to Richard that "I'm perfectly aware that Zoroaster is not dead. You have been listening to a common creed. Drink the Fire-worshippers, if you will." Adrian recognizes the nature of the timeless controversy and applies to it the synecdoche, "Zoroaster," to point out the age of the struggle. Adrian also emphasizes that this struggle is a universal one, the result of a "common creed," regardless of Sir Austin's refusal to acknowledge it.

Adrian's comic toast to the Fire-worshippers is also ironic in that Richard and Tom Bakewell, the plowman, have plotted to burn Farmer Blaize's hayracks. That night, Richard and his friend Ripton Thompson watch the fiery destruction resulting from the match of Tom Bakewell, whose last name is comically appropriate to his role. This "Bakewell Comedy," however, has serious overtones when seen in the light of the Zoroastrian metaphor. The fire of the boys' vision is not a pure one, for there are "dense masses of smoke" amid the flames that leap into the darkness like "snakes of fire." In Zoroastrianism, Ahriman (Evil) is responsible for this corruption of the pure flame.

The chapter's title, "Arson," which initiates the Bakewell Comedy, effectively points out the boys' error. The boys are, like Tom Bakewell, not good Zoroastrians because the fire they are worshiping reflects the evil nature of their revenge. Adrian sees through their conspiracy; however, he does not expose the boys. Rather, in the true manner of the Zoroastrians, he believes that the most effective punishment would be a spiritual, inner conflict. "The farmer's whip had reduced them to bodily contortions; these were decorous compared with the spiritual writhings they had to perform under Adrian's skillful manipulation." Adrian knows the true value of fire to the Zoroastrians: it is a symbol of the inner light of the soul, which glows brightest when fired by Ormuzd. If the soul is possessed by the evil Ahriman, the spiritual light is contaminated and burns, if at all, with a dim, impure glimmer.

Richard's next crucial encounter intensifies the glow of the purer fire burning within him. He meets Lucy Desborough, destined to be his wife. The imagery used to describe this encounter is filled with references to light. Nature herself has provided "a Temple for the flame" of love. From a boat, Richard first sees Lucy pictured in an idyllic scene of radiant sunshine reflecting from the "green-flashing plunges of a weir." Lucy's face is shaded from the sun's illumination mysteriously but compellingly "by a broad straw hat with a flexible brim that left her lips and chin in the sun, and sometimes nodding, sent forth a light of promising eyes." Her hair was "golden where the ray touched" it. Even her name is derived from the Latin word for light: *lux*. Richard's soul is filled with the light of passionate love, but he has another journey to the vision of the celestial light of the Zoroastrians.

Other references to Zoroastrianism abound in the novel. For example, at a later point, Sir Austin yields to the dark force of Ahriman when he chooses to "do nothing" at a time when his son needs his counsel most. Consequently, he turns his son away from him, perhaps forever, thus proving that a father with a "system" for child rearing cannot meet that system on its own terms.

Viewed within the bounds of the magian conflict, *The Ordeal of Richard Feverel* is seen as a novel about the inevitability of the human strife between good and evil, both of which are inextricably mixed within the soul of every human being. Some measure of hope is given the novel, however, when the reader learns that, finally, Richard does view, if but for a moment, the celestial light of Ormuzd through the aid of a truly devoted wife.

It is this hope that raises *The Ordeal of Richard Feverel* to the level of true tragedy, which must in some measure be positive. Although Sir Austin falls victim to Ahriman, his son, Richard, has seen the vision of Ormuzd. By the use of Zoroastrian imagery, Meredith has greatly intensified his conviction that the ultimate destiny of humankind is unity with the light of the spirit or, more realistically for Meredith, unity with the great "Over Reason" of the universe. This unity directs humans along the path of spiritual evolution and is the apex of Meredith's developing doctrine about humanity: blood (perfection of the body), brain (perfection of the mind), and spirit (perfection of the needs of human spiritual consciousness by means of realizing one's intrinsic independence and freedom).

The tone of the first half of *The Ordeal of Richard Feverel* is predominantly one of comic irony; the latter half of the novel, however, assumes tragic dimensions. Meredith's later novels display a much greater reliance upon the comic mood. Even so, the essence of "The Magian Conflict" is never lost; rather, Meredith wields the forces of darkness against those of light to accentuate the balancing, equalizing role of his emerging Comic Spirit, whose seeds have been planted in the wise youth, Adrian Harley. The struggle to reach the evolutionary apex, the light of the spirit, assumes a background role in the novels following *The Ordeal of Richard Feverel* and is treated later most directly in the poetry. In his novels, Meredith becomes increasingly more concerned with the question of how one should meet the vicissitudes of everyday life.

Meredith published his essay *On the Idea of Comedy and of the Uses of the Comic Spirit* in 1877. *Beauchamp's Career* appeared the year before; the novel portrays many of the theories Meredith proposed in his essay. In 1879, Meredith completed *The Egoist*, which the author named "a comedy in narrative." Meredith's last great achievement in the novel genre appeared in 1885 and was titled *Diana of the Crossways*. The novels provide interesting examples of the working out of Meredith's theories centered in the Comic Spirit, and they demonstrate some degree of the use of Zoroastrian imagery. *Beauchamp's Career* employs the Zoroastrian contrast of light and dark to a much greater extent than the other two novels. Meredith draws from Zoroastrianism to a noticeable degree, however, in each of these three novels in order to make the instructive character of his Comic Spirit more emphatic.

Beauchamp's Career

Meredith makes repeated references to fire, sun, and light throughout *Beauchamp's Career*, which undoubtedly reflects his prior use of Zoroastrianism in *The Ordeal of Richard Feverel*. Meredith's dependence upon Zoroastrianism is most pronounced, however, in his characterization of Dr. Shrapnel. Nevil Beauchamp is ambitious and wants to be a politician; he plans to exercise his philanthropic desire to "save the world." He joins a radical political party in order to battle the more conservative Tory Party and to oppose the vehement objections of his Uncle Everard Romfrey, a hater of radicals. After Nevil loses an election for a seat in Parliament, he comes under the tutelage of Dr. Shrapnel, a professed Fire-worshipper.

As "Fire-worshippers" is a name that Zoroastrians were often mistakenly called, when Dr. Shrapnel testifies, "I am a Fire-worshipper," the reader perceives already an element of Meredith's comedy. Dr. Shrapnel, whose name calls to mind a number of images, all of which indicate either potential destruction or active destruction, has obviously become enamored of the mystic, esoteric nature of the religion and hence has adopted certain of its tenets to his own philosophy. Basically Shrapnel's personal doctrine is, in his own words: "That is our republic: each one to his work; all in union! There's the motto for us! *Then* you have music, harmony, the highest, fullest, finest!"

Admittedly, Shrapnel's philosophy is good, or superior in its idealism, and it represents a direct restatement of Meredith's own philosophy (expressed in many of his poems). At this point in the novel, however, the philosophy is stated by an extremist; hence, there is a touch of the comic, which becomes more apparent as the novel progresses. Meredith's infrequent use of the exclamation point and his almost negative use of italics make this particular passage stand out as the radical view of an extremist.

Rosamund Culling, the future wife of Nevil's uncle, thinks of Shrapnel as "a black malignant . . . with his . . . talk of flying to the sun." As may be expected from Rosamund's tone, Dr. Shrapnel has at some time in her company been overzealous in the expression of his republican sentiments. News of Dr. Shrapnel's inflammatory radicalism soon reaches Nevil's Uncle Romfrey, who proceeds to horsewhip Shrapnel to the point of severe injury. Lack of understanding by his fellowman appears to be Shrapnel's failing and provides the occasion for comment from the Comic Spirit, who judges that

Shrapnel must suffer for his intemperance, for his imbalance. Compromise should be humankind's objective.

Both in *The Egoist* and in *Diana of the Crossways*, the part played by Zoroastrian imagery is greatly reduced from that it played in *The Ordeal of Richard Feverel* and *Beauchamp's Career*. Meredith's Comic Spirit, however, comes to the front in full array; the increased subordination of Zoroastrian imagery to Meredith's portrayal of his Comic Spirit indicates that Meredith's theories and understanding of the purpose of his literary art were expanding and maturing. In the later novels, Meredith's Zoroastrian and classical images become frequently and inseparably fused, a combination that further exemplifies Meredith's artistry and more significantly indicates that Meredith's philosophy was progressively becoming more distinct. His thinking was beginning to become a cultivated doctrine.

The Egoist

The Egoist characterizes the egocentric element in Meredith's theory of high comedy. Sir Willoughby Patterne, who thinks himself the epitome of goodness and excellence in the world, surrounds himself with admirers and sycophants who satisfy his compulsion to be adored. In creating Patterne, Meredith has taken the next logical step from his production of Beauchamp. Patterne does not merely aspire to goodness and excellence; he actually believes himself to be the embodiment of these qualities.

Patterne attempts to satisfy his ego chiefly by involving himself with three women whom he manipulates with promises of marriage. His first "pretender," Constance Durham, sees through Patterne's facade of greatness with some degree of alacrity and leaves him. The lovely Clara Middleton, however, is not so insightful. She experiences a great deal of emotional turmoil, first in ascertaining the truth of Patterne's pose and then in distinguishing the light of "her sun" from that of Patterne's less self-assured cousin, Vernon Whitford, "a Phoebus Apollo turned Fasting Friar."

Here, Meredith gives more attention to extravagances so that he may better reveal the necessity for the corrective influence of his Comic Spirit. Sir Willoughby Patterne burns; he does not merely reflect. His fire is the product of his own egotism, which burns with an outer brilliance but promises no inner flame. Meredith may well be recalling satirically the Western world's traditional misconception of the importance of fire to the Zoroastrians, who do not worship fire for itself but only as a symbol of the light of the inner spirit.

The character of Vernon presents a striking contrast to that of Patterne. His light is the light of Apollo, who is not only the Greek god of poetry but also the classical god of the sun. Meredith has fused classical allusion with the Zoroastrian importance placed upon fire. Vernon's flame is one of inner strength, for he burns with the light of poetic truth as well as with physical fire. He is also a Fasting Friar, however, a characteristic that raises doubt about the nature of his fire, since Meredith was not an ascetic. In effect, he has achieved in the characterization of Vernon the moderation that Dr. Shrapnel's explosive goals denied him, since Vernon's flame is tempered with some degree of asceticism. Vernon has measured life for what it is, but he has not given up the light of hope for what life can become. Meredith has achieved in his image of the contrast of the two fires the blending of Zoroastrian, classical, and Christian elements.

Laetitia Dale, the third of Patterne's "adorers," presents an interesting foil to Patterne's character. At the beginning of the novel, she is described as a delicate, misled woman, a "soft cherishable Parsee." The Zoroastrian connection is obvious: The Parsees are a modern sect of the Zoroastrians. Indeed, within Meredith's comic framework, Laetitia worships "her sun" much as the Parsees were reputed to worship a "god of fire."

Laetitia gradually becomes a strong, practical Parsee, however, as she, like the other two women in Patterne's egotistic design, begins to see that the source of Patterne's fire is not from within. Patterne is left in the end with Laetitia and is forced to accept her on her own terms. No reader of *The Egoist* can claim its conclusion as romantic or condemn it as pessimistic; rather, Meredith has achieved a noble expression of the corrective power of his Comic Spirit.

Diana of the Crossways

Meredith creates in *Diana of the Crossways* a character who faces decisions similar to those of the women in *The Egoist*. Even Diana's superior wit and intellect do not prevent her from battling the forces of darkness. Meredith prepares the reader for Diana's struggle in the introductory chapter of the novel. He develops a light image, "rose pink," which "is rebuked by hideous revelations of filthy foul," a likeness of darkness. Meredith opens this novel with a discussion of the same subject he had treated in his other novels. For man to think himself already a part of the celestial light at his present step on the evolutionary ladder is surreptitious folly. The future holds for him only "hideous revelations of filthy foul." The narrator further asserts that it is not within the capacity of man to suppress completely the evil forces of darkness. The duality of good and evil inevitably creeps into life.

Having established an atmosphere of foreboding, the narrator sets out to explore Diana's mental processes. Diana quickly becomes disillusioned by a mismatched marriage. Her husband, Warwick, is a man of limited intelligence. As a consequence, Diana becomes drawn to ideas outside the rigid, Victorian system of mores. Her desires strongly urge her to take leave of her witless, insensitive husband, who has accused her of infidelity. She experiences a night of conflict in which she fights like "the Diana of the pride in her power of fencing with evil."

Meredith's presentation of the strife between good and evil by his mixing of classical mythology with overtones of the Zoroastrian duality creates a sense of the universal nature of Diana's struggle. Diana must decide whether to remain loyal to her marriage vows or to strike out on her own and obey her inner compulsions. She finds the impetus for her escape in Dacier, a character who is associated with devil imagery. Indeed, Dacier is the embodiment of Meredith's assertion that there is "an active Devil about the world."

Dacier is a lure to Diana in her desire to escape. His devilish character, however, is ironically exposed by his sanctimonious friend, Sir Lukin. Lukin declares that no man should be fooled by masks of goodness that seem to cover the bad in the world. Dacier, who presents every indication of virtuous conduct, is compared to the old Jewish Prince of Devils, Asmodeus, who spurs on appetite and uproarious activities of all sorts. Although the name Asmodeus appears in the Apocrypha, it also bears connotations to Eshina-Dewa, a wicked spirit of ancient Persian mythology. This is one of Meredith's clearest fusions of Zoroastrianism with Christianity.

Dacier is thwarted in his evil intentions to seduce Diana. An acceptable guide appears for Diana in Thomas Redworth, a character capable of controlling Diana's energetic impulses. Dacier does obtain a prize, however, in the lovely but naïve Constance Asper. Constance is "all for symbols, harps, effigies, what not" and believes that brains in women are "devilish." Constance is perhaps the ideal mate for *The Egoist*'s Sir Willoughby Patterne, and she presents no problems for Dacier's devious motivations. Constance, along with Dr. Shrapnel and Patterne, has failed to see the smoke for the fire. All three are so enamored of the physical brilliance of the flames that they cannot see the subtle glow of spiritual truth within the heart of the blaze.

In *Diana of the Crossways*, Meredith suggests that the endurance of life is perhaps more replete with task than with play. The individual is forced to make a distinction between good and bad, which life seldom presents in a clear-cut fashion. Constance and Dacier somewhat ironically indulge each other in their ostensibly opposing forces. The subtle comment of the Comic Spirit is that both approach life with attitudes of excess; hence, both have lost contact with the steady movement toward self-improvement. Diana and Redworth offer hope to the reader, however, because they have accepted the moderation that the Comic Spirit has taught them and that is necessary for the future success of the human spirit.

These novels present Meredith's concern with the inevitability of "The Magian Conflict" in the life of each man. They also present Meredith's keen observation that this conflict is never one from which one emerges successfully with ease. The struggle makes man's attempt to choose an acceptable path—a way that is acceptable both to him and to his society—extremely difficult. The conflict is presented in terms of Zoroastrian, Christian, and classical myth; Meredith borrows from each in order to make his presentation of this undeniable, unavoidable battle assume universal dimensions. Meredith's Comic Spirit attempts to aid man in his struggle, but it is not always successful in exposing man's shortcomings, excesses, and refusal to see himself in a true light. In the fullest meaning of Meredith's doctrine, however, the individual is also instrumental in the greater, universal struggle of humankind to move up the evolutionary ladder.

Meredith demonstrates in his attitude toward humankind and nature the belief that humans can achieve their evolutionary destiny by conforming to the lessons and demands of nature. His philosophy is universal in scope and implies a comprehensive fusion of nearly all the ethical ideals that people have gathered from the beginning of time. Although Meredith does not discard all the dogma or the moral ideals of the many religious philosophies he studied, he does select with careful scrutiny those elements that he feels contribute to his own doctrines. Indeed, he demonstrates that he is vitally affected by all the religious thought known to him.

John C. Shields

Other major works

SHORT FICTION: *The Case of General Ople and Lady Camper*, 1890; *The Tale of Chloe*, 1890.

PLAYS: *Bertram: Or, The Castle of St. Aldobrand*, pr., pb. 1816; *Manuel*, pb. 1817; *Fredolfo*, pb. 1819.

POETRY: *Poems*, 1851; *Modern Love and Poems of the English Roadside*, 1862; *Poems and Lyrics of the Joy of Earth*, 1883; *Ballads and Poems of Tragic Life*, 1887; *A Reading of Earth*, 1888; *Poems: The Empty Purse*, 1892; *Odes in Contribution to the Song of French History*, 1898; *A Reading of Life, with Other Poems*, 1901; *Last Poems*, 1909; *The Poetical Works of George Meredith*, 1912 (3 volumes); *The Poems of George Meredith*, 1978 (2 volumes; Phyllis B. Bartlett, editor).

NONFICTION: *On the Idea of Comedy and of the Uses of the Comic Spirit*, 1877; *The Letters of George Meredith*, 1970 (3 volumes; C. L. Cline, editor).

Bibliography

Beer, Gillian. *Meredith: A Change of Masks*. London: Athlone Press, 1970. Beer attempts one of the first modern appraisals of Meredith's art, seeing him as a novelist anticipating twentieth century concerns and techniques, as well as questioning Victorian certitudes. Includes an index.

Fraser, Robert. "Nineteenth-Century Adventure and Fantasy: James Morier, George Meredith, Lewis Carroll, and Robert Louis Stevenson." In *A Companion to Romance: From Classical to Contemporary*, edited by Corinne Saunders. Malden, Mass.: Blackwell, 2004. Fraser's essay about Meredith and three other British writers is included in this study of romance literature, which charts the genre from its beginnings through the twenty-first century.

Harris, Margaret. "George Meredith at the Crossways." In *A Companion to the Victorian Novel*, edited by William Baker and Kenneth Womack. Westport, Conn.: Greenwood Press, 2002. An introductory overview of the Victorian novel. Contains essays about Meredith and other authors and discussions of the historical and social context of the Victorian novel, the growth of serialization, and the different genres of Victorian fiction.

Jones, Mervyn. *The Amazing Victorian: A Life of George Meredith*. London: Constable, 1999. Jones's biography aims to recover Meredith from obscurity and introduce the author to a new generation of readers. He links Meredith life to his writing and includes a forty-page appendix recounting the plot summaries of all of Meredith's novels.

Muendel, Renate. *George Meredith*. Boston: Twayne, 1986. Chapters on Meredith's poetry, his early fiction, his novels of the 1870's and 1880's, and his last novels. A beginning chapter provides a brief biography. Includes a chronology, notes, and an annotated bibliography.

Roberts, Neil. *Meredith and the Novel*. New York: St. Martin's Press, 1997. Roberts employs twentieth century literary criticism, especially the ideas of literary critic Mikhail Bakhtin, to analyze all of Meredith's novels. Includes bibliographical references and an index.

Shaheen, Mohammad. *George Meredith: A Re-Appraisal of the Novels*. Totowa, N.J.: Barnes & Noble Books, 1981. Shaheen suggests that traditional Meredith criticism has viewed his fiction too much in the light of *The Egoist*. He concentrates on Meredith's other major works as more representative of the author's true independent mind and specifically explores how character expresses theme for Meredith. Contains a bibliography.

Stevenson, Richard C. *The Experimental Impulse in George Meredith's Fiction*. Lewisburg, Pa.: Bucknell University Press, 2004. Stevenson focuses on the novels he considers most representative of Meredith's experimental fiction—*The Ordeal of Richard*

Feverel, *The Adventures of Harry Richmond*, *The Egoist*, *One of Our Conquerors*, *Lord Ormont and His Aminta*, and *The Amazing Marriage*. He demonstrates how these books feature controversial contemporary themes, innovative narrative structures, representations of human consciousness, and other unconventional elements.

Tague, Gregory. *Ethos and Behavior: The English Novel from Jane Austen to Henry James (including George Meredith, W. M. Thackeray, George Eliot, and Thomas Hardy)*. Bethesda, Md.: Academica Press, 2008. *The Ordeal of Richard Feverel* and *The Egoist* are among the novels Tague analyzes in his examination of English didactic literature. His study includes a discussion of the ethical aspects of these novels and the conduct of their fictional characters.

Williams, Ioan, ed. *Meredith: The Critical Heritage*. London: Routledge & Kegan Paul, 1971. A collection of reviews and essays showing the critical reception of Meredith's work from 1851 through 1911. Contains indexes of his work, periodicals, and newspapers.

DMITRY MEREZHKOVSKY

Born: St. Petersburg, Russia; August 14, 1865
Died: Paris, France; December 9, 1941
Also known as: Dmitry Sergeyevich Merezhkovsky

Principal long fiction

Smert bogov: Yulian Otstupnik, 1896 (*The Death of the Gods*, 1901; also known as *The Death of the Gods: Or, Julian the Apostate*, 1929)
Khristos i Antikhrist, 1896-1905 (collective title for *Smert bogov*, *Voskresshiye bogi*, and *Antikhrist*; *Christ and Antichrist*, 1901-1905)
Voskresshiye bogi: Leonardo da Vinci, 1901 (*The Forerunner*, 1902; better known as *The Romance of Leonardo da Vinci*, 1928, 1953)
Antikhrist: Pyotri Aleksey, 1905 (*Peter and Alexis*, 1905)
Aleksandr I, 1913
Chetyrnadtsatoye dekabrya, 1918 (*December the Fourteenth*, 1923)
Rozhdeniye bogov: Tutankamon na Krite, 1925 (*The Birth of the Gods*, 1925)
Messiya, 1926-1927 (*Akhnaton, King of Egypt*, 1927)

Other literary forms

Although famous in the Western world primarily for his historical romances, Dmitry Merezhkovsky (mehr-ehsh-KAWF-skee) was known among his Russian peers as a critic as well—and a particularly harsh one at that. His first critical work, a collection of essays published under the title *O prichinakh upadka i o novykh techeniyakh sovremennoy russkoy literatury* (1893; on the causes of the present decline and the new currents of contemporary Russian literature), was followed a decade later by perhaps his most important work of criticism and nonfiction, *L. Tolstoy i Dostoyevsky* (1901-1902; *Tolstoi as Man and Artist, with an Essay on Dostoievski*, 1902).

Throughout his life, Merezhkovsky would remain an essayist and critic, choosing as his subjects such wide and varied topics as the Acropolis, Michel de Montaigne, Marcus Aurelius, Gustave Flaubert, Henrik Ibsen, Alexander Pushkin, and Maxim Gorky. After the Bolshevik Revolution, his criticism became especially vitriolic, culminating in *Tsarstvo Antikhrista* (1921, with Z. N. Gippius and others), an indictment of Russia as a whole.

In addition, Merezhkovsky was a classicist, thus enabling him to translate Longus's idyll *Daphnis and Chloë* (c. mid-second century C.E.) as well as numerous tragedies of Aeschylus, Sophocles, and Euripides, into Russian for the first time. Finally, in the early stages of his career, Merezhkovsky published two collections of poetry, *Stikhotvoreniya, 1883-1887* (1888) and *Simvoly* (1892), and one play, *Pavel I* (1908).

Achievements

To understand Dimitry Merezhkovsky's importance, one must look beyond the source of his international reputation, his historical romances, into prerevolutionary Russia itself, for in a confused yet profound way, he reflected a current of thought and belief common to members of the intelligentsia of that day. Steeped in years of czarist tyranny, prey to feelings of cultural inferiority brought on by the legacy of Russian isolationism, trying desperately to discover and solidify a national identity, trapped within the heated polemics of the Westerners, who followed the lead of their patron saint, Peter the Great, and the Slavophiles, who refused to have anything to do with Europe's cultural "corruption," it was no wonder that the artists and writers of turn-of-the-century Russia should accuse themselves and one another of floundering in history and finally standing still. This was not only a political crisis but also a deeply felt spiritual one. Was Russia merely a reflection of Europe with nothing original to say? Or was it blessed with a culture and message of its own that would save its own land, Europe, and eventually the world?

Concurrent with this was the central position of the Russian Orthodox Church in shaping the philosophy and action of its homeland. From time immemorial, the Russian Church had existed in a kind of grand and splendid isolation from Western Christianity; after the fall of Constantinople to the Turks in 1453, however, a belief arose that would show itself, with slight modifications, time and again—the conception of Moscow as the third Rome, the spiritual center of a Russia that would lead the world out of sin and darkness. This notion caused the Russian Church to regard "heretical" Europe with pride, condescension, and fear.

Finally, in the 1890's—the decade of Merezhkovsky's rise to fame—changes inspired by literary experimentation and new aesthetic trends were in the wind. Stéphane Mallarmé, Paul Verlaine, Arthur Rimbaud, and Charles Baudelaire were the ascendant stars, yet, simultaneously, a renewed interest in Fyodor Dostoevski and everything Russian could not help but modify such "decadent" foreign trends. These early modernists were quickly superseded by the Russian Symbolists, who sought to transform art into a mystical theurgy—the ultimate purpose of which was the transfiguration of consciousness for humans and humankind. In time, even this would be replaced—by Maxim Gorky and his Znaniye school of violent Social Realists.

From a historical perspective, Merezhkovsky stands in the center of this whirlwind. Though never actually considered a literary great, he was, for nearly a decade, the central figure of Russia's early modern period; he was particularly popular among the avant-garde and the young. His mysticism—based on a system of Hegelian opposites (thesis and antithesis, pagan and Christian, old and new)—attracted the attention of a public grown weary of the stagnation and oppression of the Russian Church. His aesthetics—a peculiar combination of modernism and symbolism—attracted the tastes of those fed up with generations of simplistic and idealistically colored positivism. Though to modern readers his symbolism seems rather artificial and shallow, lacking in those qualities that made the true symbolists' works more than mere patchworks composed of intersecting lines drawn between obvious dualities, Merezhkovsky's works were—for the time and place—both important and beneficial. They brought to the Russian reader a wealth of new ideas; they stirred up controversy and in many ways, notwithstanding their unidimensionality, served as an important catalyst for a religious revival in Russia.

Finally, Merezhkovsky's criticism had a lasting influence on the Russian mind, which has perhaps been ignored in the West. His interpretation of the lives, personalities, and works of Tolstoy and Dostoevski in *Tolstoi as Man and Artist, with an Essay on Dostoievski* dominated not only Russian but also German discussion of the subject for years, focusing in minute detail on the religions of the two great writers as the prime movers of their works. To Merezhkovsky, Tolstoy was the great pagan and pantheist, the "seer of the flesh," while Dostoevski was the opposite—the great Christian of Russian letters, the "seer of the spirit." *Tolstoi as Man and Artist, with an Essay on Dostoievski* marked Merezhkovsky's transition from the West to the East, from Europe back to Russia—from the Hellenic ideal of his classical studies back to the mystical, though primarily Christian, ideal of his Russian roots. The "great Christian" Dostoevski was consistently lauded at the expense of the "great Pagan" Tolstoy, and throughout the work,

Russia's messianic destiny is stressed and supposedly revealed. After *Tolstoi as Man and Artist, with an Essay on Dostoievski*, Merezhkovsky would frequently return to this mystical and antithetical theme, but never quite so lucidly as he did in the original critical work.

Biography

Dmitry Sergeyevich Merezhkovsky was born in St. Petersburg, Russia, on August 14, 1865. His father, Serge Ivanovich Merezhkovsky, an inspector of buildings for the Imperial Court, was known to be stern and puritanical—he was even supposed to have thrown one of young Dmitry's older brothers out of the house for expressing sympathy for a woman nihilist who recently had been executed. The father was proud of his youngest son, however, and when, at the age of fifteen, Dmitry began his first efforts at writing verse, Serge dragged the youth to Dostoevski to read his work aloud. After the reading, Dostoevski's response was reportedly that "to write, one must suffer."

On entering the University of St. Petersburg, Merezhkovsky proved to be a brilliant student. He immersed himself in the Greek and Roman classics and completed his studies in two years. He grew fascinated by the works of Herbert Spencer, John Stuart Mill, Auguste Comte, and Charles Darwin, as well as that of Friedrich Nietzsche, but soon found that such readings left the religious urge fostered in him since childhood unsatisfied. Turning to literature instead, he joined a student-formed Molière club; so reactionary and suspicious was the czarist government at this time, however, that the club was suppressed, and if it had not been for the intervention of his aristocratic father, Merezhkovsky would have been exiled. This, in addition to his frail health, led to his spending the year after graduation in the Caucasus and Crimea.

While there, Merezhkovsky met Zinaida Hippius, at that time the best-known woman poet in Russia. They were married in 1889. Soon afterward, Zinaida fell gravely ill; before she recovered, Merezhkovsky's beloved mother died, and he found himself unwillingly following Dostoevski's dictum. His response to these trials was mysticism, and as he grew older his mysticism correspondingly deepened. He and his wife began traveling throughout Greece, Turkey, and the Near East, and this experience, linked to his newfound beliefs, eventually resulted in the trilogy of philosophical novels focusing on Julian the Apostate, Leonardo da Vinci, and Peter the Great, collectively titled *Christ and Antichrist*.

After his return to St. Petersburg, Merezhkovsky began pursuing his literary career in earnest. As early as 1883, he had published verse in the "civic" style (*Stikhotvoreniya, 1883-1887*) but had found no real success. Nearly a decade later, he published the first book of symbolist poetry written in Russian, *Simvoly*, followed immediately by his first collection of critical essays, *O prichinakh upadka i o novykh techeniyakh sovremennoy russkoy literatury*. Soon thereafter appeared his first work of classicism, *Vechnye sputniki* (1897; eternal companions), and Merezhkovsky's reputation as a modernist critic, classical scholar, and symbolist poet was fixed. It was not until the release of the *Christ and Antichrist* trilogy, however, that Merezhkovsky's reputation became international and he found himself a true celebrity in his own land.

Like many other artists cast suddenly into the limelight, Merezhkovsky began to take himself too seriously. His mysticism intensified and, as a result, his criticism became more virulent and dogmatic. His fiction developed into a pulpit from which he proselytized the heathen, and he subjugated plot and characterization to turgid philosophy. After 1900, he founded a religion known as the New Road, with which he tried to reconcile Nietzsche's egoism with Tolstoy's altruism and synthesize the pagan, Hellenic cult of the flesh with the Christian cult of the spirit—all into one new entity. For a time, Merezhkovsky and his wife conducted salons devoted to the spreading of this new religion, and shortly devotees of this Society of Religion and Philosophy began to appear. Merezhkovsky rejected in his teachings the "heresy" of historical Christianity and preached instead a personal, apocalyptic Christianity of the "Third Testament," in which Hellenism and Christ would be synthesized when history came to an end—which, he asserted, would be soon. Over time, his doctrine evolved into the worship of an Eternal Woman-Mother as the Holy Spirit, the third person of the Trinity and simultaneously an embodiment of Russia's destiny. He also exalted hermaphrodites as symbols of a Being who would eventually unite the sexes on Judgment Day. Thus, as his religion became more arcane, his fiction became more unreadable.

Merezhkovsky supported the abortive Revolution of 1905 in the hope that it would become a religious revolution overthrowing Russia's established church and state, leading in turn to the Kingdom of God on earth. The revolution, however, did not achieve this goal, and he and his wife fled to Paris. In 1910, they returned to Russia and subsequently opposed World War I. Merezhkovsky opposed the Bolsheviks even more zealously, and, in 1918, he was sent to Siberia. In 1920, he and Zinaida escaped, settling first in Poland and then in Paris, where they spent the remainder of their lives as émigrés. There he produced bitter tracts against the Soviets and books (which were generally ignored) attempting to explain the New Road. Merezhkovsky died in Paris on December 9, 1941, of a brain hemorrhage.

Analysis

Once, in 1905, at the peak of his literary success, Dmitry Merezhkovsky complained that "in Russia they did not like me and upbraided me; abroad they like me and praised me; but equally here and there they failed to comprehend 'what is mine.'" Indeed, most writers, in their darkest moments, will bewail what they consider the low comprehension levels of critics and the general reading public; few, however, are caught doing this at the time of their triumph, and perhaps, in a circuitous manner, this very complaint provides an insight into the complex and often tumultuous art and life of Merezhkovsky. How does one finally interpret his phrase "what is mine"? In the final analysis, one must conclude that he does not mean his fiction, poetry, or criticism, but rather his religious beliefs and his messianic attempt to give the world what was in his opinion the true means for its salvation.

This discovery of the absolute religious truth was the motivating force behind all of Merezhkovsky's work. At the beginning of his career, he valued above all else the "liberation of life through Beauty" and dreamed of Hellenic perfection. Over time, however, this worship of the beautiful narrowed, away from the general sense intended by most idealists, toward a more limited definition—a more sensual and erotic one in which beauty came to mean the aesthetics of the leisured class. Merezhkovsky's other beliefs and theories also narrowed as his age increased, so that eventually he cut himself off from all but a very select group of initiates—and finally from them also.

What makes an understanding of Merezhkovsky's life and art even more difficult is that, though his search for truth was unswerving, his choice of vehicles for that search swung wildly from one end of the pendulum's arc to the other. He first sought truth through the populist ideal of service to the people; soon, however, he discovered that this would be an impossibility, because at heart he never could love individuals. Again and again this problem springs up in Merezhkovsky: He is more enamored of generalities, the "big ideas," than he is of "little truths" or individuals. In even his best works of fiction, his main characters are not characters at all, but rather embodiments of ideals.

After populism, Merezhkovsky swung to the opposite extreme. He extolled the classical virtues and posited a Nietzschean "superhumanity" as humankind's ultimate goal. Eventually, he would abandon even this, concluding that this system denied God. Merezhkovsky would always be torn by these swings in his philosophy and allegiance—his love for Russia and Europe, for God and humanity, for the old and new, for Christian spiritualism and Hellenic hedonism—and never reconciled the fundamental duality of his nature.

Up to a point, this duality informs and strengthens his work; after that point, when his religious beliefs finally gelled, this same duality tore his creations down. The dividing line seems to be the early 1990's, before the publication of *Peter and Alexis*, and indeed it is only his first two novels, *The Death of the Gods* and *The Romance of Leonardo da Vinci*, which are still read today. After that, his writing became too polemical, too mystical, and finally too hysterical and arcane to be enjoyed or even understood, increasingly bogged down in a gamesmanship of Hegelian dialectics in which he tried unsuccessfully to reconcile his dual truths—so much so, in fact, that one seems to be reading a new type of philosophical formula writing.

The Death of the Gods and *The Romance of Leonardo da Vinci* are masterpieces of historical romance, however, and the international renown that sprang from them was well deserved. Though sometimes clumsily constructed, the two novels do possess a kind of raw power in the depiction of the historical panorama, usually executed in mosaic form. Original documents, excerpts, quotes, and other historical tidbits are employed to re-create the life and spirit of fourth century Rome or fifteenth century Italy: Merezhkovsky was even dubbed by one critic as the "Napoleon of Quotes." Oddly enough, though his protagonists Julian and Leonardo seem little more than abstractions, his minor characters—Caesar Constantius, Gallus Flavius, Arsinoe, Cesare Borgia, Machiavelli, Pope Leo X, Mona Lisa (La Gioconda), and others—all live. Once again, this is indicative of the fact that when Merezhkovsky tries to prove a thesis, he stumbles, but when he simply writes, his narrative flies.

CHRIST AND ANTICHRIST TRILOGY

Merezhkovsky's trilogy *Christ and Antichrist*, which includes the novels *The Death of the Gods*, *The Romance of Leonardo da Vinci*, and *Peter and Alexis*, presents in partly Nietzschean, partly mystical terms the advance of European history as an ongoing battle between the forces of paganism and Christianity. Julian is presented as torn between Christ and Apollo: He is a monk at first, but adores the nude, white beauty of a marble Aphrodite and seeks the divinity and understanding of Apollo. When Julian becomes Emperor of Rome, he returns Hellenic paganism to its lost splendor, but a mob of fanatic Christians destroys a new temple. The collapse of the temple's columns symbolizes the death of the old gods. Merezhkovsky presents this as a tragic event; however, his spirits rise once more when he shows the Renaissance's resurrection of these Olympians, who are now beyond good and evil. Leonardo, who never takes sides, is seen as half Christian, half pagan—and the highest embodiment of the two. He realizes that perfect knowledge leads to perfect love and yet, like Merezhkovsky, is unable to reconcile the two extremes. Finally, Christ and Antichrist wage war in Russia at the turn of the eighteenth century: Peter the Great, shown as a Leonardo of action, clashes with his superstitious and doctrinaire son, Alexis. In the end, Merezhkovsky's message is that the struggle to achieve a balance between the flesh and the spirit is a terrible, never-ending one.

LATER NOVELS

The later novels—*December the Fourteenth*, *The Birth of the Gods*, and *Akhnaton, King of Egypt*—explore the same themes but are never as well realized. *December the Fourteenth* is the story of the unsuccessful Decembrist Revolution against the newly crowned Nicholas I, and the harsh treatment meted out by the czar against those implicated. That this book was published in 1918 gives it some historical interest: The Bolshevik Revolution had already taken place by then, but at the end of this book, Merezhkovsky seems to hint that a more pervasive revolt of the spirit based on a belief in Russia as the "Holy Mother" will sweep the nation and eventually the world.

Merezhkovsky's last two works of fiction, *The Birth of the Gods* and *Akhnaton, King of Egypt*, are a pair of connected stories, the first taking place in Crete, the second in Egypt. In *The Birth of the Gods*, Tutankhamon, son-in-law and envoy of the Egyptian pharaoh, arrives in Minoan Crete, where he meets the virginal Dio, priestess of the sacred bull. Through Tutankhamon, Dio comes to realize that her native religion is evil, and so kills the sacred bull. In the second book, Dio is now associated with King Akhnaton and his mystical plans to reform the world and establish universal peace. Both characters die in the end, but Akhnaton is revealed as one who will somehow rise again and save the world.

The Death of the Gods and its sequel, *The Romance of Leonardo da Vinci*, cannot, like Merezhkovsky's other works of fiction, be called second-rate. In many ways, *The Death of the Gods* is similar to another famous work of historical fiction—Robert Graves's *I, Claudius* (1934)—in that all the intricate plots, counterplots, and court intrigues of Imperial Rome are related in superb detail. Julian Flavius, the protagonist and cousin to Caesar Constantius, the Emperor of Rome, survives to become Caesar himself simply by staying out of his cousin's reach. In fact, he does lose a brother, Gallus Flavius, to the Emperor and wonders how much longer he himself has to live.

After Julian's ascension to power, the book spends less time with temporal affairs and begins instead to establish the mystical blueprint on which the rest of the trilogy is based. The goal of the trilogy *Christ and Antichrist*, as stated earlier, was to establish a synthesis between flesh and spirit, life and faith. To Merezhkovsky, life, as represented by the Olympian gods (Dionysius in particular), and faith, as symbolized by Christ, were inseparable: One without the other was incomplete. Recorded history was to be interpreted as a dialectic of these two opposing yet complementary forces.

In *The Death of the Gods*, this synthesis is not yet explicitly presented—it is still too early in the scheme of the trilogy. Instead, the reader is meant to glean hints of it. Near the beginning of the novel, one notices such a hint in the representation of Christ as the Good Shepherd, hidden away in a dark corner of the church where Julian goes to pray as a child. Later, it is revealed in the dying words of a secondary character when she states that everyone—the righteous and the sinners—will be redeemed by Christ's love and that everything, even Bacchic celebrations, is sacred. This idea of the holiness of Bacchus is a recurring one in Merezhkovsky's work; in many ways he seems to believe that Christ's return to earth will be as a combination of the Bacchic and the divine. Finally, Merezhkovsky's theme can be seen near the novel's end when a hymn to Pan and a monkish chant to God are symbolically merged. As the curtain falls on the death of Julian and the triumph of historical Christianity, one is left with the feeling that something irreplaceable has been lost.

All is not completely lost, however, for in the beginning of *The Romance of Leonardo da Vinci* the resurrection of the Olympians is signified by the discovery of a marble Venus that had been hidden away for centuries. The time is the late fifteenth century, during the Italian Renaissance; the Middle Ages—a period of ignorance and superstition in which the Church reigned supreme—has passed. With the Olympians' resurrection comes a resurrection of knowledge, and presiding over it all is that Nietzschean patron saint of knowledge, Leonardo da Vinci.

To Merezhkovsky, Leonardo is beyond good and evil: He is willing to serve any master, simply because he exists on a plane above earthly concerns. Merezhkovsky wants his reader to believe that Leonardo embodies the hoped-for synthesis of paganism and Christianity, though it is also posited that he is too advanced for his time. Thus, Leonardo is drawn to prove a thesis and, as is often the case in Merezhkovsky's work, ends up a pale shadow compared to those fleshed-out others who do not straddle such philosophical fences. The purely Christian characters (Savonarola, the Grand High Inquisitor), purely pagan ones (Cesare Borgia, Duke Moro), or even those who aspire to Leonardo's greatness yet remain caught in the old webs of belief, all seem more real than Leonardo himself—which in itself is perhaps revealing of the conflict between Merezhkovsky's stated beliefs and his true ones. In any case, Leonardo seems an abstraction until the point when he falls in love with his model Mona Lisa (La Gioconda); even then, however, he hesitates and loses her to an early death.

Perhaps it is because Merezhkovsky fails to portray convincingly Leonardo as this prophesied synthesis that the character gains stature as an artist instead, for it is during Leonardo's search for truth, rather than during his supposedly otherworldly contemplation of it, that Leonardo becomes real. That everything in nature reveals God is the ultimate answer lying at the bottom of the abyss for both Leonardo and Merezhkovsky; furthermore, both are convinced that perfect knowledge leads to God. Instead of detracting from faith and love, knowledge increases their power. In the end, this seems to be Merezhkovsky's final conclusion—a conclusion that leaves considerable room for artistic elaboration. It is unfortunate that he failed to recognize this and became bogged down in mysticism instead.

Joe W. Jackson, Jr.

Other major works

PLAYS: *Makov tsvet*, pb. 1908; *Pavel I*, pb. 1908; *Budet radost'*, pb. 1916; *Romantiki*, pb. 1917; *Tsarevich Aleksey*, pb. 1920.

POETRY: *Stikhotvoreniya, 1883-1887*, 1888; *Simvoly*, 1892.

NONFICTION: *Flober v svolkh pis' makh*, 1888 (*The Life Work of Flaubert*, 1908); *Kal'deron*, 1891 (*The Life Work of Calderon*, 1908); *Mark Avreliy*, 1891 (*The Life Work of Marcus Aurelius*, 1909); *Montan*, 1893 (*The Life Work of Montaigne*, 1907); *O prichinakh upadka i o novykh techeniyakh sovremennoy russkoy literatury*, 1893; *Vechnye sputniki*, 1897; *L. Tolstoy i Dostoyevsky*, 1901-1902 (*Tolstoi as Man and Artist, with an Essay on Dostoievski*, 1902); *Akropol'*, 1897 (*The Acropolis*, 1909); *Joseph Pilsudski*, 1920 (English translation, 1921); *Tsarstvo Antikhrista*, 1921 (with Z. N. Gippius, D. V. Filosofov, and N. V. Zlobin); *Napoleon*, 1929 (2 volumes; includes *Napoleon, cheloviek* [*Napoleon, the Man*, 1928; also known as *Napoleon: A Study*, 1929] and *Zhizn' Napoleona* [*The Life of Napoleon*, 1929]); *Atlantida-Yevropa*, 1930 (*The Secret of the West*, 1933); *Michael Angelo, and Other Sketches*, 1930.

TRANSLATION: *Dafnis i Khloya*, 1897 (of Longus).

Bibliography

Bedford, C. Harold. *The Seeker: D. S. Merezhkovsky*. Lawrence: University Press of Kansas, 1975. Bedford provides a detailed analysis of Merezhkovsky's religious beliefs. Includes a bibliography, an index, and a list of Merezhkovsky's works.

Frajlich, Anna. "The Contradictions of the Northern Pilgrim: Dmitry Merezhkovsky." In *The Legacy of Ancient Rome in the Russian Silver Age*. Amsterdam: Rodopi, 2007. Frajlich discusses how the renewal of classical scholarship in nineteenth century Russia led Merezhkovsky and other Russian symbolists to find inspiration in ancient Rome. Includes examinations of some of Merezhkovsky's novels and poems.

Hellman, Ben. *Poets of Hope and Despair: The Russian Symbolists in War and Revolution, 1914-1918*. Helsinki, Finland: Institute for Russian and East European Studies, 1995. This study of Russian symbolism includes a chapter on Merezhkovsky. Analyzes how he and other symbolists interpreted the deeper meaning of the events of World War I and the Russian Revolution.

Pachmuss, Temira. *D. S. Merezhkovsky in Exile: The Master of the Genre of Biographie Romancée*. New York: Peter Lang, 1990. Pachmuss focuses on 1919 through 1941, the years Merezhkovsky spent in exile. She analyzes the unpublished fictionalized biographies and the other works he wrote during this period.

Rosenthal, Bernice Glatzer. *Dmitri Sergeevich Merezhkovsky and the Silver Age: The Development of a Revolutionary Mentality*. The Hague, the Netherlands: Martinus Nijhoff, 1975. Rosenthal examines Merezhkovsky's role in the Russian cultural renaissance at the turn of the twentieth century and discusses the political implications of the renaissance's aesthetics.

PROSPER MÉRIMÉE

Born: Paris, France; September 28, 1803
Died: Cannes, France; September 23, 1870

Principal long fiction

La Famille de Carçajal, 1828
Chronique du règne de Charles IX, 1829 (*A Chronicle of the Times of Charles the Ninth*, 1830)
La Double Méprise, 1833 (novella; *The Double Mistake*, 1905; better known as *A Slight Misunderstanding*, 1959)
Les Âmes du Purgatoire, 1834 (novella; *Souls in Purgatory*, 1905)
Colomba, 1840 (novella; English translation, 1853)
Arsène Guillot, 1844 (novella; English translation, 1905)
Carmen, 1845 (revised 1847; novella; English translation, 1878)
Lokis, 1869 (novella; English translation, 1905)

Other literary forms

Prosper Mérimée (MEHR-ih-may) experimented with various literary forms at the start of his career, before discovering that fiction was his true artistic vocation. His first composition, never published, was a tragedy in the Romantic style concerning Oliver Cromwell, and the first work published was a set of four critical articles on the theater of Spain's Golden Age.

Mérimée's debut as an author of books was made in disguise, in the form of two literary hoaxes, one volume purporting to be a group of six plays translated from the Spanish, the other a collection of Illyrian folk poetry translated from the Serbian. The contents of both volumes were actually clever pastiches of Mérimée's own invention. Under his own name, he then published a volume containing two plays based on historical material before publishing as a novelist, at the age of twenty-six, a well-received historical romance constructed around the episode of the Saint Bartholomew's Day massacre of Huguenots in 1572.

Mérimée's first novel was followed almost immediately by a brilliant group of short stories that are generally credited with having established the short story in France as a valid new genre and that definitively confirmed Mérimée's primary calling in literature as that of storyteller. Thereafter, he devoted his creative efforts almost exclusively to the writing of fiction, the only exceptions being two brief closet dramas that he allowed to be published in periodicals during the 1850's.

Creative efforts, however, were not Mérimée's central preoccupation as a man of letters. Indeed, his works of the imagination were to prove to be the smallest part of his very substantial output. Mérimée himself tended to think of his vocation as that of historian and regarded his drama and fiction as avocational. He was, after all, a civil servant for nearly thirty years, and that work often entailed writing of a professional kind. As inspector of historical monuments, for example, Mérimée had to prepare scholarly reports, travel accounts, and historical studies, many of which were commercially published, in somewhat altered form.

In addition to that kind of writing, Mérimée found time, regularly, to contribute articles to the best-known journals of the day, some on literature, some on art, but most on historical subjects. Several collections of such articles appeared in book form during his lifetime, as did several historical monographs expanded from journal articles, such as his histories of Don Pedro I of Castille and Peter the Great of Russia. Late in life, Mérimée took up the study of the Russian language and published important translations of Alexander Pushkin and Ivan Turgenev that helped to make those authors more widely known in France.

Finally, it must be noted that Mérimée was a gifted and indefatigable letter writer. His published correspondence, in seventeen volumes, is perhaps the richest and most important part of his literary legacy for modern readers. Thus, Mérimée's writings cover an unusually wide range of forms, from scholarly historiography to popular theater. There was hardly a time in his adult years when he was not engaged in some kind of writing, though the personal letter was perhaps his most characteristic and persistent form. It was his fiction, to be sure, which brought him lasting fame, but in his own eyes, that work was not more than an occasional pastime. It never constituted a career.

Achievements

Perhaps the rarest of Prosper Mérimée's public distinctions was his election, at the age of forty, to the Academy of Inscriptions and Belles-Lettres, in recognition of his scholarly work as a student of antiquity, followed within a year by his election to the most prestigious of all such bodies, the French Academy, in recognition of his literary achievements. Yet, with characteristic irony, Mérimée was wont to mock this unusual honor of election to two such elite bodies and remarked to one interviewer that, if asked what had been the most painful day of his life, he would not name the day he had been forced to go to jail (for a published attack on the judiciary), but the day he had been inducted into the French Academy. Mérimée's mockery of his double electoral triumph is, in the long view, perhaps justified, but the achievement is unmistakable evidence, nevertheless, of his stature in French cultural life during his lifetime.

One of Mérimée's most significant contributions to French culture was certainly the preservation and restoration of many major architectural monuments that would otherwise have been allowed to decay or disappear. This heritage is still visible, in every corner of France.

Mérimée's first novel, *A Chronicle of the Times of Charles the Ninth*, still ranks as one of the best French examples of the historical romance in the manner of Sir Walter Scott, and at least two of Mérimée's plays have taken their place as classics in the permanent repertory. It is as a writer of lean and powerful realistic fiction, however, that Mérimée made his greatest contribution. Brevity was the essential characteristic of all of his fiction. His first novel, relatively short as historical romances go, was his longest work of fiction. His best-known works of fiction, *Carmen* and *Colomba*, are unusually short for the genre—perhaps one-third to one-half of what is regarded as normal length for the average novel. It is that brevity that gives them their stark, dramatic, and memorable impact. In the character of Carmen, Mérimée created one of the most unforgettable figures of world literature.

There is no doubt about Mérimée's most lasting claim to importance in the history of literature: It is the invention of the modern short story as a literary genre. The famous tale "Mateo Falcone," first published in 1829, is generally recognized as the prototype of a new kind of fiction in France. Those who value the modern short story, which is so vital a part of contemporary literary culture, have Mérimée to thank as its creator.

Biography

Prosper Mérimée was the only child of a comfortable middle-class couple, both of whom were artists by profession and freethinking republicans in outlook. Growing up in Paris, and in such a family, Mérimée came naturally by his attraction to the arts and his inveterate skepticism about religion, politics, and human behavior. The influence of that family atmosphere was also largely responsible for the central paradox of Mérimée's personality: the profoundly sensitive and romantic soul who concealed his tender response to the world under a public mask of ironic wit and cold detachment.

There is an oft-told anecdote about Mérimée, that at the age of only five years—feeling so humiliated by his mother's laughter when he begged her forgiveness, on his knees, for some trivial misbehavior—he vowed on the spot never to expose himself again to the mockery of others; this illustrates clearly the origins of that public mask of insensitivity in the atmosphere of his childhood. Yet it was, on the whole, a happy childhood, and Mérimée's relationship with his parents was always a positive and affectionate one. His parents carefully nurtured both his artistic and his intellectual interests, seeing him through his legal studies while introducing him to the social circles frequented by painters, writers, and scholars. Mérimée never used his training in the law directly, but it undoubtedly helped him gain entry into the government circles where he eventually made his career.

His legal studies completed, the young Mérimée devoted himself at first to the literary life, producing some journalism, some works for the theater, and a tribute to Scott in the form of a historical romance—all activities appropriate to a youth of the 1820's who aspired to a role among the rising generation of the Romantics. Although he had some successes and met the leading literary lights of the era—Stendhal, Victor Hugo, and Alfred de Musset—he grew restless by 1830 and, spurred by an unhappy love affair, he left Paris for a lengthy tour of Spain. When he returned, at the end of 1830, he found France changed by the July Revolution, and he himself was changed, ready for a serious career. He entered the service of a prominent minister in the government of Louis-Philippe, early in 1831, beginning the career as a

Prosper Mérimée. (Library of Congress)

civil servant that soon brought him the title and duties of inspector general of historical monuments; he filled that position for more than a quarter of a century, resigning for reasons of health in 1860.

From 1831 on, Mérimée's life was comparatively uneventful and only intermittently devoted to literature, for his principal occupations were of a bureaucratic and scholarly nature. He carefully maintained his friendships in the literary world, published occasional works of fiction or literary criticism, and kept his name before the public actively enough to have become one of the forty "Immortals" of the French Academy in 1844.

Mérimée never married but had numerous relationships, both platonic and passionate, including one great love, Madame Valentine Delessert, whom he worshiped for nearly twenty years and regarded as his source of literary inspiration. The most significant among his many platonic friendships with women was his close relationship with Eugénie de Montijo, whom he first met in Spain when she was a small child, and who, in 1853, married the emperor Louis Napoleon, thus becoming empress of France and ensuring Mérimée a ready welcome at the imperial court whenever he wished it.

Ill health made social life difficult for Mérimée, and his declining years proved a lonely time. After resigning from government service in 1860, Mérimée took to spending more and more time in the warmth of Cannes, on the Riviera, and much less time in Paris. His death came after the outbreak of the Franco-Prussian War in 1870, while he was in Cannes. The home he had maintained in Paris was burned in 1871 by fanatics of the Commune who resented his close political and personal ties to Napoleon III. The fire destroyed all of Mérimée's books, paintings, papers, and letters, depriving posterity of much significant documentation of his life and career.

Analysis

For a Parisian born and bred, Prosper Mérimée's most obvious distinguishing characteristic as a writer is indeed an odd and almost inexplicable one: All of his life he was irresistibly attracted to the exotic, in both setting and theme. For Mérimée, however, "exotic" seldom meant the truly remote, in location or time, but only that which was sharply different from his own familiar culture. Geographically, it would not be Asia or America that he would choose to write about, but places closer to home such as Spain and Corsica. He was an admirer of Sir Walter Scott but found the age of chivalry too remote and too demanding of specialized research for his taste as a writer. Renaissance France was historically the most remote culture he ever attempted to evoke. The one subject he seemed almost pointedly to avoid—with but two exceptions—was that of Parisian life in his own day. That subject, which had made his contemporary Honoré de Balzac so famous, seemed to have little appeal for Mérimée.

Perhaps because literature was, for him, a way of escaping from reality, he preferred, whenever he had a story to tell, to set it in any time and any place other than nineteenth century Paris. To judge by the kind of theme he tended to choose, moreover, Mérimée's choice of an exotic setting seemed designed to make plausible, in his story, the two qualities he seemed to find most necessary: an element of the enigmatic or unexpected in human behavior, and the opportunity to shock his reader with a drama of violence, whether physical, emotional, or moral. Finally, in order for the exotic setting, the unexpected behavior, and the shock of violence to be combined in a narrative bearing the unmistakable stamp of a Mérimée creation, it was necessary for a tone of ironic detachment to be present in its telling. These traits of exoticism, violence, and irony were the hallmarks of almost all of Mérimée's fiction and his theater, doubtless because they correspond to basic traits that we know to have marked Mérimée's own character: the impulse toward escapism, simultaneous fascination with and fear of strong emotions, and timidity that often expressed itself as indifference, disdain, or mockery.

Mérimée's distinctive characteristics as a creator were already fully visible in his first publication, the literary hoax that he published in 1825 under the title *Le Théâtre de Clara Gazul* (*The Plays of Clara Gazul*, 1825). At the front of the volume appeared the portrait of a haughty Spanish lady, shrouded in a black mantilla, identified as the celebrated Spanish actor and playwright Clara Gazul. Mérimée's friends could recognize, in the stern countenance of the fiery actor, the actual features of Mérimée himself, who had posed for the fake portrait painted by a friend. The six plays presented in the volume, exaggerated dramas of passion and honor parodying the classic Spanish manner with such themes, tended to leave a stage strewn with dead bodies at the denouement and to bring down the curtain with a burlesque of the traditional Spanish "apology" asking the audience to "excuse the faults of the author." The variety of exotic settings (from Denmark to Peru), the plots involving almost every known form of human violence, and the mocking, parodic tone that flaunted the volume's nature as a hoax all combined to establish the identifying traits that Mérimée's creative writing would thereafter always display.

The second hoax, published two years later and purporting to be a collection of popular ballads and folk poetry translated from the Serbian, bore the title *La Guzla* (1827), impudently evoking the previous hoax with its transparent anagram of the name of the invented Spanish playwright. The invented poems leaned heavily toward themes of dark passion, including that newly popular Balkan specialty, vampirism. It is hard to understand why the readers of 1827 did not recognize instantly that the author of *La Guzla* was also the author of *The Plays of Clara Gazul*, yet the historical fact is that *La Guzla* was a much more successful hoax than its predecessor. That very success perhaps encouraged Mérimée to trust his powers of invention enough to make his next undertaking a single, book-length narrative to which he would sign his own name. It was wholly in character for Mérimée that that narrative, conceived as a historical novel of the kind then favored by his fellow Romantics, should have focused on one of the most violent events of French history, the Saint Bartholomew's Day massacre of 1572.

A Chronicle of the Times of Charles the Ninth

The longest work of the imagination Mérimée ever composed, *A Chronicle of the Times of Charles the Ninth* continues to be read because of its witty style and sparkling characterizations rather than because of its depiction of real events and real people in sixteenth century France. Mérimée's lengthy preface to the novel explicitly declines to place the accurate retelling of history at the center of his artistic concerns, arguing that it is more important to give an accurate impression of ordinary daily life by means of invented characters than to recount actual historical happenings in which the principal actors are the powerful and the famous.

In a historical novel, according to Mérimée, real events and real people should be relegated to the background and used sparingly, for verisimilitude only. In this novel, the central figures are indeed invented: Bernard Mergy, a Protestant gentleman, and his brother, Georges, a convert to Catholicism, represent the religious divisions of French society in that era. The consequences of those divisions are dramatized in the troubled love between Bernard Mergy and the Catholic countess Diane de Turgis, who excuses her own guilty passion by her constant efforts to convert her lover to the "true faith." There are furtive glimpses of the actions of the king, Charles IX, and of the massacre's instigator, the duc de Guise, but the reader's attention is kept constantly riveted on the fate of the Mergy brothers and of Diane de Turgis, as it is played out against the violent backdrop of the religious wars of the period.

In spite of the intense seriousness of the events depicted, there are deft comic scenes leavening the drama at regular intervals. Mérimée's personal interventions into the narrative—once, in the middle, to argue with his readers about a narrator's obligation to satisfy the readers' craving for accurate historical portraits and settings, and once, at the end, to invite the reader to imagine his (or her) own denouement, since the author has no intention of supplying one—contrive to lighten the tone of the novel and keep the reader at some emotional distance from the grim and sometimes gory drama being recounted. Indeed, so evenhanded is the depiction of the warring factions that some critics have complained of the book's seeming failure to denounce the massacre in forthright and unambiguous terms.

Anticipating the criticism, Mérimée asserts in his preface to the novel that the massacre was a great crime even by the standards of its era, but he insists that it must be evaluated by those standards and not our higher modern ones. He goes on to note, mischievously, that the great majority of the French, in 1572, sympathized with the massacre, viewing the Huguenots as impious aliens and feeling that the destruction of heretics was God's good work. It should be added that the actual massacre scenes in the novel are portrayed with undisguised horror, even though the general atmosphere of the wars of religion is rendered with an evident effort at neutrality.

The critical debate about the novel's morality, however, seems beside the point inasmuch as Mérimée carefully avoided interpreting or judging history, wishing only to tell a story that would entertain without falsifying the reality of the times in which it was set. Most modern readers agree that Mérimée has succeeded in his purpose. The plot is lively and unfolds swiftly through many unexpected twists; the love story is intense and moving and is made especially memorable by the capricious and unpredictable character of Diane de Turgis, who manages to be at once passionately sinful and sincerely devout, while remaining serenely unruffled by the contradiction; the period detail is rendered sharply and vigorously, giving an excellent "feel" for the daily life of that time. These virtues more than offset the unsatisfying ending and the frequent tone of persiflage that systematically discourage any impulse on the part of readers to become emotionally involved with the characters or events. *A Chronicle of the Times of Charles the Ninth* ranks with Hugo's *Notre-Dame de Paris* (1831; *The Hunchback of Notre Dame*, 1833) as the best of the historical romances produced by the French Romantics.

Following his success with *A Chronicle of the Times of Charles the Ninth*, Mérimée took to cultivating the vein of fiction, in preference to theater or poetry, publishing a series of remarkable short stories in journals in 1829 and 1830, which he then polished and arranged as a book with the artistic title *Mosaïque* (1833; *The Mosaic*, 1905), and composing two remarkable short novels that appeared at about the same time as *The Mosaic*, the one in 1833, the other in 1834. The earlier of the two, *A Slight Misunderstanding*, is a penetrating psychological study with a contemporary Parisian setting, rare in Mérimée's work. The essential matter of this work is a case study of a woman who prides herself on the strictness of her fidelity to an aging and disagreeable husband, but who, one day, abruptly allows herself to be seduced in a carriage by a man she hardly knows, then dies of remorse a few days later, having recognized that both she and her lover had misread each other's feelings. The painful truth of the analysis makes *A Slight Misunderstanding* one of Mérimée's most affecting and impressive tales about the vagaries of the human heart.

The second short novel of that period, *Souls in Purgatory*, is a curious reworking of the Don Juan legend, in which the great seducer is suddenly smitten with remorse, is converted to Christianity, and dies a saint. The somber pessimism of the narrative tone makes *Souls in Purgatory* the only work by Mérimée in which humor is almost wholly lacking, and in that respect it is an atypical work, apparently the product of a period of severe but temporary depression in Mérimée's personal life. His appointment as inspector general of historical monuments, at about that time, seems to have helped pull him out of his state of depression, and a few years later, following an inspection trip to Corsica, he produced a novel about Corsican life that was to become one of the most widely admired works of his career. That was the dramatic account of a Corsican *vendetta*, or blood feud, titled *Colomba*, which was first published in installments in 1840 and in book form the next year.

Colomba

In its length, *Colomba* ranks second to *A Chronicle of the Times of Charles the Ninth* among Mérimée's works of fiction—an extended composition by his standards, but rather a short novel of some fifty thousand words by normal measure. It is hard to deny a certain artificiality in this composition, since it was plainly devised as a showcase for the exotic aspects of Corsican primitivism and not for its exciting plot or subtle psychology, neither element being in this instance especially remarkable.

The plot is serviceable but without complexity or surprise: The hero, Orso della Rebbia, returns to his native Corsican village after many years of service in the French military and finds that his sister, Colomba, is intent on avenging the death of their father two years earlier. While Orso had accepted the official verdict that the father had been killed by a bandit, Colomba feels sure the deed had been done by the rival Barricini family, and she demands that Orso act in accordance with the ancient traditions of Corsican vendettas, to avenge this affront. Because Orso had met and fallen in love with a pretty English lady, Miss Lydia Nevil, while en route back to Corsica, he now finds himself caught between the demands of civilized culture, represented by Lydia, and those of primitive culture, represented by his sister. The clash of cultures within Orso constitutes the psychological drama of the novel, though it is never resolved as an inner conflict, because events force Orso's hand before he can make a choice.

Fearing that the trumped-up nature of the evidence disguising their guilt has been discovered, the two Barricini sons ambush Orso and wound him, forcing Orso into the vendetta. In the ensuing battle, both Barricini sons are killed, and Orso hides from the law while recovering from his wounds. Proof of the guilt of the Barricinis is then promptly produced, permitting a happy ending in which Orso and Lydia are married and a satisfied Colomba accompanies them on their wedding trip to Italy. In a powerful concluding scene, however, Colomba encounters the grieving old Barricini father in Italy, who complains to her that it was not necessary to take *both* of his sons. At this, Colomba shows not the slightest sign of pity, reminding the old man that his suffering will soon end, since he is dying, whereas she had to suffer more than two years before attaining revenge for her father's death.

It is the steely determination and primitive single-mindedness of Colomba that have the most potent appeal for the reader in this novel. The other main characters—Orso, Lydia, and Lydia's father—are rather pale figures by comparison. Colomba is another in Mérimée's small but memorable portrait gallery of fascinating females—strong characters of passionate nature and faintly mysterious motivation who live in the reader's recollection long after their stories have been read. There are many colorful descriptions of Corsican customs in the novel and a few scenes of high drama, all of which contribute to the novel's popularity. It is, without question, the stunning portrait of Colomba herself that makes this work a distinguished achievement.

The success of *Colomba* demonstrated that Mérimée was at the peak of his creative powers around the year 1840. *Colomba* had been preceded by a strikingly skillful short story on a supernatural theme titled "La Vénus d'Ille" (1837; "The Venus of Ille," 1905) and was followed by an unusually touching tale of a poor but sensitive courtesan, titled *Arsène Guillot*, that Mérimée called a *nouvelle* and that qualifies, by its intricate plot and oddly interconnected characters, as a novella. The distinguishing feature of this work is its unaffected absence of sentimentality, not its display of honest pity for a humble prostitute; it is one of the few works in which Mérimée did not hide his emotions under a mask of cynicism or irony. His finest creative achievement during this particularly fecund period was the work that followed *Arsène Guillot*: the celebrated tale of the Spanish Gypsy, *Carmen*, destined to become his most widely known work.

Carmen

As with *Colomba*, so with *Carmen*: The source of its powerful attraction is the complex and elusive character of the title figure. Carmen, like Mérimée's other women of passion and mystery, exerts an unbreakable hold on the imagination, but in this instance Mérimée has the courage to follow Carmen's story to its inexorably tragic conclusion, a courage he did not have in the case of Diane de Turgis in *A Chronicle of the Times of Charles the Ninth* or in that of the title character in *Colomba*. There is a feeling of completeness, of resolution, to the story of Carmen, which his other stories centered on a "fatal woman" do not have. That sense of closure, painful but aesthetically satisfying, is perhaps the principal artistic superiority of *Carmen* and the element that has made it Mérimée's most popular creation.

It is true that Georges Bizet's very successful opera based on Mérimée's story has contributed greatly to the popularity and fame of the work. In the twentieth century, there are more people who know the story through the opera than know it from having read the original. Since the opera takes considerable liberties with the original, adding new characters and diluting its starkly tragic tone with extraneous sentimentality, it must be said that many who admire the work do not really know it. Whatever its artistic value as music-drama, Bizet's *Carmen* (1875) is simply not the same work as Mérimée's *Carmen*. A major factor in the difference, no doubt, is that the opera allows the story to be acted out as a spectacle, whereas Mérimée concentrates his effects by having the story told, in the first person, by Don José Navarro while he awaits his own execution for having murdered Carmen. Mérimée's device imprints deeply felt passion and pain on the very language of the narration, an effect impossible to achieve on the stage, and focuses attention exclusively on the highly charged emotions created by the relationship between Carmen and Don José, while the opera, by the very nature of the medium, must broaden and diffuse the focus to include musical and theatrical "values" as well.

The power of Don José's narrative, in Mérimée's

text, is that it affords the reader the most direct experience possible of the irresistible fascination exerted by the personality and presence of Carmen. Don José's words, spontaneous, rapid, and forceful, are at once a confession of his own weakness and an involuntary tribute to the aura of demoniac attraction to Carmen's being. The reader feels, with urgent immediacy, the force of the passion Carmen can inspire and the menace inherent in her strong-willed need for independence combined with a strangely passive fatalism. When Don José reaches the climax of his narration, depicting his own exasperation upon realizing that he can never hold Carmen's love, and Carmen's silent submission to his murderous assault on her with a knife, the reader is not only prepared for the moment, having sensed its inevitability long since, but also actually relieved to have the mounting tension resolved. At that moment in the tale, Mérimée achieves for the reader the full impact of the emotions of tragedy, the purging of pity and fear prescribed by Aristotle. Therein lies the greatness of the artistic skill that Mérimée brought to *Carmen*.

Don José's first-person narration occupies more than two-thirds of a text that runs to some thirty thousand words. This "confessional" text is framed by an opening passage in which Mérimée himself serves as narrator, explaining how he met Don José and Carmen in the course of his archaeological researches in Spain, and by a concluding chapter, also in Mérimée's own words, in which he discusses philological aspects of the language of Gypsies. These "framing" passages have aroused critical debate—particularly the concluding chapter, which seems almost impudently irrelevant as well as anticlimactic in effect and which is known to have been added later, in 1847, since the text printed in 1845 ended with the last words of Don José. Some critics believe that the framing device undercuts the story and is a mistake, while others see it as Mérimée's habitual "distancing" mechanism, a variant of the ironic mask he always affected as a protection against strong emotion. We cannot know, definitively, what Mérimée's intentions were in this regard, but it is perhaps worth pointing out that the extreme contrast between the dry pedantry of the opening and closing passages and the violently passionate confession in the middle can affect the reader's response. Like a well-made picture frame, the opening and closing passages in *Carmen* hold the unruly passions of the story within acceptable bounds, unobtrusively focusing and setting limits on the viewer's attention and thereby heightening the emotional impact of the experience. It seems at least possible that Mérimée had some such effect in mind when he added the learned disquisition on Gypsy dialects to the text of *Carmen*.

The publication of the revised *Carmen* in 1847 marked the effective end of Mérimée's career as a serious writer of fiction. For the next twenty years, he busied himself with the writing of history and with translations from Russian but showed no interest in further exploiting the storyteller's art, which he had developed to such a high level. Briefly, in the late 1860's, he was coaxed into composing a short story and reading it aloud for the entertainment of Empress Eugénie and her friends. A year before his death, in 1869, he allowed to be published another story he had composed, inspired by a real-life incident told to him by a Polish countess. That story, *Lokis*, was the only work of fiction Mérimée permitted to appear in print between the 1847 edition of *Carmen* and his death in 1870. After his death, in 1873, a small volume called *Dernières Nouvelles* (*Last Stories*, 1905) appeared that contained *Lokis*; the short story "La Chambre bleue," prepared for the empress; and two other stories, written in the 1840's but never printed.

Mérimée's talent was clearly not for the complex compositions that the novel became in the hands of his great contemporaries, Stendhal and Balzac. A shorter and more compact formula suited his abilities and his temperament far better. His narrative manner was crisp, spare, and direct, for the most part stripped of adornment and digressive excursions. His was the talent for the concentrated and compressed art of the short story—an art of which he was the generally recognized inventor in France. Occasionally, when the matter of his narrative was richer and more substantial, he wrote what must be called a novel, for it filled much more space than a short story, though it was still far short of the dimensions that had become standard in his day for a novel. Compositions such as *A Slight Misunderstanding*, *Colomba*, *Arsène Guillot*, and *Carmen*, which are the cream of Mérimée's production in this longer format, may be viewed as the kind of novel a gifted storyteller would write. They are marked by a concentration on the main action, a small cast of characters, and a vivid, efficient, and rapid prose style.

Conspicuous in every Mérimée narrative is the theme of violence, physical or emotional, and the preoccupation with the unfathomable and unpredictable in human nature. The uneasiness aroused by these insistent themes is, however, invariably tempered for the reader by a skeptical viewpoint and ironic tone provided by the narrator. At their best, Mérimée's fictions afford memorable insights into the stranger workings of the human heart and create characters, such as Colomba and Carmen, which haunt the imagination of the reader long after the details of their story have been forgotten. The creation of such characters is perhaps Mérimée's most durable achievement in the art of fiction.

Murray Sachs

Other major works

SHORT FICTION: *Mosaïque*, 1833 (*The Mosaic*, 1905); "La Vénus d'Ille," 1837 ("The Venus of Ille," 1905); *Nouvelles*, 1852 (*Stories*, 1905); *Dernières Nouvelles*, 1873 (*Last Stories*, 1905); *Carmen, and Other Stories*, 1998.

PLAYS: *Le Théâtre de Clara Gazul*, pb. 1825 (*The Plays of Clara Gazul*, 1825); *La Jaquerie*, pb. 1828; *La Carrosse du Saint-Sacrement*, pb. 1829; *L'Occasion*, pb. 1829; *Les Deux Héritages*, pb. 1850.

POETRY: *La Guzla*, 1827.

NONFICTION: *Histoire de don Pedre Ier, roi de Castille*, 1848 (2 volumes; *The History of Peter the Cruel*, 1849); *Les Faux Démétrius*, 1852 (*Demetrius, the Impostor*, 1853); *Lettres à une inconnue*, 1874 (*Letters to an Unknown*, 1874); *Correspondance générale*, 1941-1964 (17 volumes).

MISCELLANEOUS: *The Writings of Prosper Mérimée*, 1905 (8 volumes).

Bibliography

Auchincloss, Louis. "Prosper Mérimée." In *Writers and Personality*. Columbia: University of South Carolina Press, 2005. Mérimée is one of the authors whom Auchincloss, himself a novelist, discusses in his examination of writers' personalities and how their temperaments, interests, and other personal traits are linked to their fiction.

Bowman, F. P. *Prosper Mérimée: Heroism, Pessimism, and Irony*. Berkeley: University of California Press, 1962. Provides an analysis of the heroes depicted in Mérimée's works, a study of his basically pessimistic ideas about life and human fate, and a discussion of the way Mérimée's concepts of hero and life express themselves in the formal aspects of his writing. Includes a bibliographic note and extensive references.

Dale, Robert C. *The Poetics of Prosper Mérimée*. The Hague, the Netherlands: Mouton, 1966. An exploration of the creative theory that underlies Mérimée's writing. Although the focus is more on Mérimée's theory as revealed in his letters and criticism than on his fictional works, the study does offer a number of insights that can be applied to the fiction. According to Mérimée, Dale concludes, the writer's fictional works incorporate a worldview that reflects his own psyche or inner self.

Raitt, A. W. *Prosper Mérimée*. London: Eyre and Spottiswoode, 1970. An essential study of the life, times, and works of Mérimée, for both the specialist and the general reader. Raitt combines a biography with critical chapters analyzing Mérimée's major writings. Includes illustrations, appendixes, a comprehensive bibliography, and an index.

Smith, Maxwell A. *Prosper Mérimée*. New York: Twayne, 1972. A readable introductory study of the author's life and works. Biographical and critical material are supplemented by a chronology of Mérimée's life, a select bibliography, and an index.

Stowe, Richard. "Prosper Mérimée." In *European Writers*. Vol. 6 in *The Romantic Century*, edited by Jacques Barzun and George Stade. New York: Charles Scribner's Sons, 1985. This brief study combines a biographical overview with a discussion of the style and content of Mérimée's major works. The select bibliography includes editions, collected works, bibliographies, translations, correspondence, and biographical critical studies.

JAMES A. MICHENER

Born: New York, New York; February 3, 1907(?)
Died: Austin, Texas; October 16, 1997
Also known as: James Albert Michener

PRINCIPAL LONG FICTION

Tales of the South Pacific, 1947
The Fires of Spring, 1949
The Bridges at Toko-Ri, 1953
The Bridge at Andau, 1954
Sayonara, 1954
Hawaii, 1959
Caravans, 1963
The Source, 1965
The Drifters, 1971
Centennial, 1974
Chesapeake, 1978
The Covenant, 1980
Space, 1982
Poland, 1983
Texas, 1985
Legacy, 1987
Alaska, 1988
Journey, 1988
Caribbean, 1989
The Eagle and the Raven, 1990
The Novel, 1991
Mexico, 1992
Recessional, 1994
Miracle in Seville, 1995
Matecumbe, 2007

OTHER LITERARY FORMS

Although James A. Michener (MIHCH-nuhr) considered himself primarily a novelist, he also was an accomplished short-story writer, essayist, art historian, and editor. Major themes in his nonfiction are travel and American politics. *The Voice of Asia* (1951) is also in the political tradition. *The Floating World* (1954) is a philosophical essay on Japanese art, a theme he treats in four other works, most notably in *Japanese Prints from the Early Masters to the Modern* (1959).

ACHIEVEMENTS

In the early 1950's, James A. Michener was heralded as the new voice in American fiction. Still basking in the considerable praise that followed his first book, *Tales of the South Pacific*, and the Pulitzer Prize that accompanied it, he shared the reflected glow of Richard Rodgers and Oscar Hammerstein's musical adaptation, *South Pacific* (1949). Although critics objected to the romantic cast of his early novels, they also found much to praise. Critical reaction to his later novels has also been mixed: While some consider them brilliant for their sweeping panoramic scope, others have condemned the novels for their mass of information, undeveloped characters, and lack of depth. Despite the doubts of literary critics as to the merits of Michener's novels, an eager public has responded to them enthusiastically.

In addition to the Pulitzer Prize, Michener's writing earned for him a number of honorary degrees and awards, including the appointment to several government committees. His work on two of these committees—the Centennial Commission and the National Aeronautics and Space Administration (NASA) Advisory Council—contributed to research for his fiction. In 1977, President Gerald R. Ford awarded Michener the Medal of Honor, America's highest civilian award.

BIOGRAPHY

Although standard references state that James Albert Michener was born on February 3, 1907, in New York City to Edwin and Mabel Michener, the facts of his birth are unknown; he was a foundling whom Mabel Michener reared from birth, moving at times to the county poorhouse to help the family through poverty and illness. On a scholarship, he attended Swarthmore College, from which he graduated summa cum laude in 1929. For ten years, he taught at a variety of schools and universities, including the School of Education at Harvard, and in the early 1940's he became an editor at Macmillan. He was a practicing member of the Society of Friends (Quakers) and might have been exempted from combat, but in 1942 he volunteered for active duty in the U.S. Navy and was sent to the Pacific.

Royalties and a small percentage of ownership in the musical *South Pacific*, which opened in April, 1949, assured Michener financial freedom to travel and write. He thus became an independent writer and scholar, publishing more than forty books, and an even greater number of articles, from his home base in Bucks County, Pennsylvania. He also wrote shortened versions of many of his novels for inclusion in the *Reader's Digest* series of condensed books.

Overcoming serious heart problems in the 1980's, Michener remained active until his death, writing and traveling. In addition, he was generous in support of literature and the arts, endowing a fellowship for young writers and contributing in many other ways to the benefit of individual artists and arts institutions. In particular, Michener donated more than one million dollars to the Bucks County Free Library, more than three million dollars to the James A. Michener Art Museum in Doylestown, Pennsylvania, and more than seven million dollars to his alma mater, Swarthmore, part of which was used to teach students discipline-specific ways of writing. For his numerous contributions to benefit humanity, Michener was named Outstanding Philanthropist in 1996 by the National Society of Fund-raising Executives.

Michener built a legacy as a storytelling phenomenon. He was a world traveler who was at home on virtually every continent, having reportedly lived in 121 different states and countries where he gathered background for his novels. His secrets to success were determination, hard work, self-reliance, and an incredible memory. Unlike many other novelists who imagined their plots and characters, Michener was a meticulous researcher, a craftsman who would not begin to write until he had absorbed the details of the culture, the history, the geography, and the people of the country he had chosen for his next work.

In his books, Michener emphasized the importance of harmonious relationships among people and the continuing need to overcome ignorance and prejudice. While the critics were often unkind to Michener, he was adored by the public, who have bought tens of millions of copies of his books. Plagued by numerous health problems in the 1990's, Michener died on October 16, 1997, after declining to continue receiving dialysis treatments for kidney failure. Until the end of his life, Michener remained productive, completing *This Noble Land* in 1996 and *A Century of Sonnets* in 1997.

Analysis

In almost all of James A. Michener's novels, the story line is a loosely woven thread, a framework, a context in which to tell tales and provide geographic and historic detail. Although in his notes on *Centennial* Michener explains four different narrative devices he developed in the course of his writing career, each is still a framing device for a series of related events or information. Throughout all of his work Michener is the social-science editor and teacher, using quantities of well-researched data and imaginative incidents to explain issues from his particular point of view. In many of his writings, it is apparent that Michener is not only a very competent writer, historian, and geographer but also a competent psychologist and geologist. While each of his

James A. Michener. (Library of Congress)

novels has a historical basis that covers hundreds or thousands of years, each is rooted in its own time as well.

Much of Michener's writing, both fiction and nonfiction, is journalistic in style, but his staccato rhythms are interrupted from time to time by florid descriptions and precise diversions, such as recipes and statistical contrasts. All of his writing is permeated by an unmistakable creed that affirms human values and a deep concern for the United States. The harsh facts of his early life shaped his career, and his writing is that of a grateful man driven to repay society for the chances he was given in life. There is more to his writing, however, than a need to express gratitude: His broad panoramas are peopled with Dickensian characters from every part of society, although his sympathies remain with the sad and the unfortunate—even rogues such as Oliver Wendell in *Centennial* and Jake Turlock in *Chesapeake*—who can get by on their wits.

Underscoring all of Michener's work is a strong statement of human courage and human tolerance, coupled with a driving concern for humanity's relationship with its environment. Many of his novels focus on racial discrimination of some kind, and each teaches the value of hard work and the necessity for change. As in his nonfiction, Michener does not hesitate to portray society's weaknesses. While critics have frequently panned both his style and the values it embodies, particularly in his later work, these same late novels have consistently been best sellers.

Tales of the South Pacific

Ironically, *Tales of the South Pacific* was not a best seller, even though of all Michener's works it is perhaps the most familiar. Although it continues to sell as many copies today as when it was originally published and has won the Pulitzer Prize, the book was first printed on the cheapest paper with the poorest binding available—so little did the publisher think of its chances—and new chapters did not even begin at the tops of new pages. Even after its award, the novel would have continued to die a slow death were it not for the musical comedy based on it. Few successful writers have had a less auspicious beginning.

Tales of the South Pacific is a framing story that sets up many of Michener's themes; with it the author began a literary romance with the Pacific islands that would last for more than fifteen years and characterize much of his work. In this work, nineteen related episodes tell the story of the commitment of the United States to the Pacific theater during World War II. The treatment of character as well as setting is significant to the body of Michener's work. No one character can be called the protagonist, although Tony Fry (a Navy lieutenant) and the narrator are most central to the plot. By not having a protagonist, Michener implies that this is not the story of one person but rather the shared experience of all those who were in the Pacific during the war years. The narrator makes no moral judgments: Men and women are presented at their finest and their weakest moments; some die in war, but life somehow goes on.

The Bridges at Toko-Ri

With the exception of *The Fires of Spring*, a semiautobiographical novel that develops much of Michener's personal life through 1929, both the fiction and nonfiction that followed *Tales of the South Pacific* are steeped in Pacific history and Michener's own war experience. All are connected as part of a cumulative statement; the collection *Return to Paradise* (1951), for example, with its alternating essays and stories, begins with the description of islands emerging from the sea, the same technique Michener employs in the first of his blockbuster novels, *Hawaii*. Of these early works, *The Bridges at Toko-Ri* is particularly significant. The novel exemplifies Michener's typical blend of fact and fiction, as he exposes his reader to the Asian world and the Korean War experience. With the publication of the novel, the author observed that it was the "purest writing" he had done so far.

Although *The Bridges at Toko-Ri* is a short novel and neatly divided into sections—"Sea," "Land," and "Sky"—in it, Michener provides his strongest development of character. The protagonist is Harry Brubaker, a twenty-nine-year-old veteran of World War II and promising Denver, Colorado, lawyer, who resents fighting in Korea. In the first section, Brubaker is rescued from the frozen sea by another three-dimensional character, Mike Forney, a cocky Irishman from Chicago. Michener included an expanded version of both these characters in his later novel *Space*. The "Land" interlude takes place in Japan, a liberty stop, where Brubaker must rescue Forney and his friend from jail before he can visit with his family, who has come to see him there. In a human brotherhood scene typical of Michener, the Brubakers meet a Japanese family in a private pool at their hotel; paddling naked, the families intermingle and converse, resolving any conflict left over from the days before. At this point, the major conflict of the novel begins, however, as the carrier crew starts to plan its assault on four bridges across the canyon of the enemy center at Toko-Ri. Connected to the questions about the attack are more rhetorical ones, addressed to the reader: Will the flyers knock out the bridges? Will this make the Communists stop the war? Have Americans lost the strength to make this sacrifice? Where will America's last stand against the Communists come—in California, or Colorado, on the banks of the Mississippi?

The climax of the novel comes in "Sky," when the heroic Brubaker and Forney destroy the bridges but are killed in the aftermath of the attack. The action reaffirms that the United States has produced fighters who will always "fly against bridges." The energy of this short section is powerful, deeply rooted in Michener's own naval air experience and the passion of his convictions.

Caravans

Caravans is a transitional novel for Michener; while the setting is still Asia, it marks a western movement in both action and thought. Precursor to *The Drifters*, *The Source*, and to a lesser extent *Poland*, *Caravans* begins in 1946, in the aftermath of World War II. Here, the journalistic style that marks much of Michener's fiction is handled through a first-person narrator, Mark Miller, a junior-grade State Department officer stationed in Afghanistan. During the opening pages of the novel, Miller is sent on a mission to locate Ellen Jaspar, a high-spirited college student from Dorset, Pennsylvania, who left Bryn Mawr College to marry an Afghan exchange student named Nazrullah. The plot is a series of adventures laced with romance, even after Ellen is found with a nomad caravan in the desert. The connecting link for the related incidents is the ancient route of the Kochis, whom Miller joins in the hope of convincing Ellen to return to her parents. Again, in usual Michener fashion, the plot provides a context within which to describe geographic and historic detail and argue thematic questions.

In his excellent discussion of Michener's major works, George J. Becker points out that for more than twenty years the author was concerned with the "stresses and false values that beset American youth"; Becker applies his insight to *The Drifters*, but it is equally true of *Caravans*. Although the time of the story is 1946, Ellen is almost a stereotype of college youth in the early 1960's—when the novel was written—in her dress, ideas, and lifestyle. For the last third of the book, she and Miller articulate the fiery rhetoric of campuses across America.

The thematic substance of *Caravans* goes further than any of Michener's previous work in its discussion of racial and religious prejudice. The dark-skinned Nazrullah explains his educational experience in Germany and America, infuriating Miller by comparing the American treatment of blacks to the German treatment of Jews. Although the reader's sympathy is with Miller, Nazrullah's point is well made. It is underscored in the climactic moment of the novel, when Miller—a Yale man, perhaps the most civilized member of the cast—announces that he is Jewish and nearly kills Dr. Stiglitz for his wartime Nazi efforts.

The majority of characters in the novel are Muslim, and a few are Christian. Repeatedly, however, the novel turns on a Jewish element, directly anticipating Michener's next major novel, *The Source*. Even Kabul, the Afghan capital, is used to show "what Palestine was like at the time of Jesus."

Chesapeake

Chesapeake was the first of Michener's highly popular novels to deal with an indigenously American subject (one might take exception here with *Hawaii*, but that work seems clearly to belong to his earlier preoccupation with the Pacific). As in *Centennial* and later in *Texas*, Michener hoped to chronicle the making of America and to celebrate the courage of those who took part in that achievement. Spanning nearly four hundred years, the novel moves from the first indigenous peoples who settled the land to the funeral, in 1978, of one of the Quaker descendants of the earliest Caucasians. In part, it is an instructive, political book, dealing with governments in Great Britain and France as well as the United States, culminating with Pusey Paxmore's suicide over his involvement in the Watergate scandal. For the most part, the focus is narrow—the eastern shore of Chesapeake Bay—despite the long roster of historical characters, from John Smith and George Washington to Daniel Webster and Henry Clay.

Here the episodes are organized in a fairly straightforward pattern—allowing for slight digression with a chapter devoted to a family of geese and another to a batch of crabs—and the third-person omniscient point of view does not shift. Four fictional families provide the substance of the book: the Catholic family of Edmund Steed who flees religious persecution in England and joins John Smith in exploring the land in 1607; the family of London thief and indentured servant Timothy Turlock, who arrives a generation later; the Quaker family of Edward Paxmore, who comes in search of religious freedom by way of Barbados and ironically receives the first slaves in the area; and the Caters, a family of former slaves, who build their contribution to the novel from the time just before the American Civil War. Although there is great discussion of loyalties, each of the first three families fares well in the American Revolution: Steed is an interpreter for the French, Turlock a sharpshooter, Paxmore a builder of fine ships. The War of 1812 continues the tension that creates the climax of the novel, with the Emancipation Proclamation and the American Civil War. Certain characters are given focus—Rosalind Steed, for example—but Michener does not slow down to develop any of them fully; many are types used to maintain the human element while the narrative sweeps over succeeding generations. This large movement does not, however, mitigate the value of the novel.

From the outset, Michener's emphasis is on human courage and tolerance and humanity's relationship with its environment. Ample descriptions build a love for the land and for the watermen who work it; later chapters deal with ecological concerns—erosion, litter, and landfill. Early chapters ennoble the Native American and lament his passing. Perhaps the greatest weight throughout is given to the issues of racial and religious freedom.

The suffering of both the Steeds and the Paxmores offers compelling insight into the theocracy of Puritan New England and those who came to America seeking religious freedom. In ironic contrast, both the Steeds and the Paxmores own slaves. The final struggle for black freedom comes at the start of the twentieth century, with an amendment to the Maryland constitution intended to disenfranchise blacks. Although the Steed and Turlock clans support it, Emily Paxmore champions the defeat of the bill by arguing that it can be applied equally to all European immigrants after 1869, and the campaign becomes her own personal Armageddon.

Chesapeake is a big novel (it even includes a recipe for oyster stew). The fragments that fill the end are the unresolved conflicts of modern time—except for an account of the passing of Devon Island. As the scene of much of the action slips into the sea, Michener affirms that it will come again and again until at last the "great world-ocean" reclaims it.

Space

Although his other novels touch on the twentieth century, *Space* and *Recessional* are Michener's two pieces of fiction that concentrate solely on life in twentieth century America. In *Space*, he chronicles the U.S. space program from its inception in 1944 to an ebb in 1982 through a series of incidents that connect neatly to his work before and after it. The novel begins on October 24, 1944, with scenes that introduce four major characters. The first is Stanley Mott, an American engineer, who is in London at the request of the U.S. president, whose job it is to see that the German installation at Peenemünde is not bombed before three of the chief scientists can be captured alive. The second is Norman Grant, drawn much like Harry Brubaker, in the climactic naval battle of Leyte Gulf. The third is John Pope, a seventeen-year-old football hero from Grant's hometown of Clay. Finally, there is Dieter Kolff, one of the scientists whom Mott must rescue, who survives the bombing because he is away with his girlfriend, Leisl.

The next part of the novel introduces the women who are loved by these men and advances the story through them. Because of the ingenuity of a Nazi officer who later becomes a leader of the U.S. aerospace industry, Kolff and Leisl come to the United States, shepherded by Mott and his wife, Rachel. Pope gets appointed to Annapolis, on the recommendation of Grant, who has become senator from the state of Fremont; Pope's wife, Penny, earns a law degree and goes to work for Grant when he is appointed to the space committee; Grant's wife, Elinor, preoccupied with little green men, becomes the principal supporter of Leopold Strabismus and the Universal Space Associates.

These characters, and those who flesh out their stories, create the substance of the novel. While Michener's focus is on the space program, his characters are among the most fully developed in all of his work. Systematically moving through the various stages of America's efforts in outer space, he keeps the weight of his research in careful balance with the stories of human lives. This is particularly true in the second half of the novel, which centers on six fictional astronauts (Pope among them). While the reader is drawn into the explorations (particularly the Gemini flight, which Pope shares with his likable opposite, Randy Claggett, and their adventures on the dark side of the moon), one's interest is held by the characters at least as much as by the technology. This is particularly true of the capable con man Strabismus.

At first Strabismus seems an unnecessary diversion—similar to the recipes Michener offers for Polish sausage or oyster stew—but as the story builds, he becomes an integral part of the work. Playing off the initials U.S.A., Strabismus moves through a series of lucrative rackets until he sets himself up as a preacher with the United Salvation Alliance. As he panders to the fears of the uneducated, he crusades against "atheistic humanism" and advocates a return to fundamentalism that will prohibit the teaching of evolution and forbid National Park rangers from describing the geological history of their areas. He launches impassioned attacks on homosexuals and fosters a virulent anti-Semitism. Michener clarifies his point of view in the final confrontation between Strabismus and the "heroes" of his novel. Finally, Michener suggests, the conflict is part of the long march of history and will continue thousands of years hence.

Poland

Two massive novels are representative of Michener's later works: *Poland* and *Texas*. The first is a well-researched chronicle of Polish history that moves backward and forward, connecting the Communist country of modern time to the thirteenth century raids of Genghis Khan through the development of three fictional families. In the acknowledgments section, in which the author explains his reasons for choosing this particular subject, he sounds very much as he did three decades before, when clarifying his interest in Asia. In both instances, the geographical and ideological positions of the areas indicate that they will become political focal points. Again, Michener is using his fiction to educate readers of his time, moving through history to explain the present.

Texas

Texas is perhaps Michener's largest novel: More than two hundred characters are involved in its story, a number of whom are historical figures, and dialogue is the primary vehicle through which their story is told. Michener tracks the major events in Texas history, including the struggle for independence from Mexico. The battles of the Alamo, Goliad, and San Jacinto form the backdrop for fictional characters who illustrate the migrations of the Spanish, Europeans, and Americans to Texas. With its narrative framework and blending of fact and fiction, the novel compares neatly with many of its predecessors. Despite its scope, however, one would be hard-pressed to claim that *Texas* is among the finest of Michener's works.

Mexico

Mexico traces the history of Mexico from fictional pre-Columbian Indians to modern Mexico through the eyes of an American reporter. Begun by Michener in the 1950's, *Mexico* was set aside because of negative comments by the publisher, eventually was lost, and then was rediscovered and completed by Michener in 1992. The narrative's structure differs from Michener's previous novels, with more concentration on the present than the past. Norman Clay, the central character, is a Princeton-educated Virginian whose family roots have been in Mexico since the 1840's. Clay is sent to Mexico as a Spanish-speaking journalist to cover a series of bullfights between two celebrated matadors, Victoriano Leal and Juan Gomez. Through Clay's eyes, the readers discover Mexico, its turbulent history, and the part played in that history by Clay's family. A variety of conflicts are portrayed, including Spaniard versus Indian, Catholic versus pagan, and the quest for the exploitation of gold and silver, as well as war, civil war, and revolution in the twentieth century.

A gripping story unfolds that becomes a vivid portrait of a fascinating country. The cultural conflicts of a class-torn society are epitomized through the tale of the sad, bitter, dirty, sometimes lucrative business of being a matador. In Mexico, bullfighting not only is a sport but also an art form, big business, and festival, mirroring the sordid, grisly, and violent aspects of Mexican culture.

Mexico shows that Michener had not lost any of his ability to tell a great story while providing his readers with interesting information about how different cultures live, think, and interact.

Miracle in Seville

As in *Mexico*, Michener uses a journalist as the narrator and participant in *Miracle in Seville*. The narrator, Shenstone, is sent by his editor to Seville, Spain, to write the story of Don Cayetano Mota, owner of a famous ranch where fighting bulls have been raised for decades. However, Shenstone never writes the story, because he believes that he will lose his credibility as a journalist if he reports the unbelievable events that he witnessed while in Seville.

By using a journalist as the narrator, Michener provides a realistic framework for detailing the classical Spanish bullfight with its four distinct parts, as well as the context for describing the appearance, personalities, and techniques of four matadors who will fight in Seville after Easter. Michener places the reader in Seville, seeing, smelling, hearing, and experiencing the bullfights, the processions, and the parade. Character development becomes secondary in the narrative, as Michener is much more interested in telling the story of Don Cayetano, who is seeking to restore the lost honor and glory of his ranch with the help of the Virgin Mary. Through Shenstone, Michener paints a portrait of Spain as a country where bullfighting is an art form, where religious faith is sincere and often dramatic in its expression, and where constant effort is required to sustain personal and family honor.

Miracle in Seville stands apart from Michener's other novels. Although it resembles his previous novels in its focus on the culture of a particular place, it is his only novel that presents events that cannot be rationally explained, creating a strong aura of fantasy. However, even though it is an adult fairy tale, this novel exhibits a well-developed story and a vivid sense of location.

Whatever the critical verdict on Michener the novelist may be, it is clear that Michener the educator-through-fiction has been a great success. To a popular audience numbering in the millions, he has communicated the uniquely modern sense of the long view of history.

Joan Corey Semonella
Updated by Alvin K. Benson

Other major works

SHORT FICTION: *Return to Paradise*, 1951; *Creatures of the Kingdom: Stories of Animals*, 1993.

NONFICTION: *Proposals for an Experimental Future of the Social Sciences: Proposals for an Experimental Social Studies Curriculum*, 1939 (with Harold Long); *The Unit in the Social Studies*, 1940; *The Voice of Asia*, 1951; *The Floating World*, 1954; *Rascals in Paradise*, 1957 (with A. Grove Day); *Selected Writings*, 1957; *Japanese Prints from the Early Masters to the Modern*, 1959; *Report of the County Chairman*, 1961; *The Modern Japanese Print: An Appreciation*, 1962; *Iberia: Spanish Travels and Reflections*, 1968; *Presidential Lottery: The Reckless Gamble in Our Electoral System*, 1969; *Facing East: The Art of Jack Levine*, 1970; *The Quality of Life*, 1970; *Kent State: What Happened and Why*, 1971; *A Michener Miscellany, 1950-1970*, 1973; *About Centennial: Some Notes on the Novel*, 1974; *Sports in America*, 1976; *In Search of Centennial: A Journey*, 1978; *Collectors, Forgers, and a Writer: A Memoir*, 1983; *Testimony*, 1983; *Six Days in Havana*, 1989; *Pilgrimage: A Memoir of Poland and Rome*, 1990; *My Lost Mexico*, 1992; *The World Is My Home: A Memoir*, 1992; *Literary Reflections: Michener on Michener, Hemingway, Capote, and Others*, 1993; *William Penn*, 1994; *This Noble Land: My Vision for America*, 1996; *A Century of Sonnets*, 1997; *Talking with Michener*, 1999 (interviews; with Lawrence Grobel).

EDITED TEXT: *The Hokusai Sketchbooks: Selections from the Manga*, 1958.

Bibliography

Day, A. Grove. *James A. Michener*. 2d ed. New York: Twayne, 1977. This overview of Michener's life and works is written from the point of view of one who knew and worked with Michener. Contains an excellent biography and index.

Grobel, Lawrence. *Talking with Michener*. Jackson: University Press of Mississippi, 1999. Grobel, a friend of Michener's, conducted a series of interviews with the writer from 1980 through 1997 that are published here. Michener reminisces about his life and discusses the status of publishing, the position of the artist in society, and many other topics. Includes an index.

Groseclose, Karen, and David A. Groseclose. *James A.*

Michener: A Bibliography. Austin, Tex.: State House Press, 1996. A detailed chronology of Michener's life, including the most important events, his publications, honors, awards, and his contributions to society, education, and politics. Contains a comprehensive bibliography about Michener and presents an informative synopsis of each of Michener's novels, as well as a compilation of Michener's works.

Hayes, John P. *James A. Michener: A Biography*. Indianapolis, Ind.: Bobbs-Merrill, 1984. A useful biography. Hayes depicts Michener as one who is plagued by doubts and insecurities, who apparently was born an illegitimate child. Michener initially cooperated with Hayes, but he ended their association when he deemed Hayes's questions too personal.

Lyons, Paul. "Redeeming Hawai'i (and Oceania) in Cold War Terms: A. Grove Day, James Michener, and Historicism" In *American Pacificism: Oceania in the U.S. Imagination*. New York: Routledge, 2006. Lyons analyzes how Americans since the nineteenth century have misrepresented the historical realities of Oceania and Oceanians. His study includes an analysis of Michener's novels *Hawaii* and *Tales of the South Pacific* and his short-story collection *Return to Paradise*.

May, Stephen J. *Michener: A Writer's Journey*. Norman: University of Oklahoma Press, 2005. Michener's own writing is used to paint a portrait of him as a journalist and popular writer who never achieved the literary acclaim that he craved. Includes nineteen black-and-white photographs.

Michener, James A. *The World Is My Home*. New York: Random House, 1992. A memoir, in which Michener recalls the people, events, and ideas that influenced his life and work and describes both the "headaches and rewards" of being a writer.

Severson, Marilyn S. *James A. Michener*. Westport, Conn.: Greenwood Press, 1996. Severson's book, part of the Critical Companions to Popular Contemporary Writers series, presents a complete overview of Michener's life, including his writing style, themes, ideas, and concerns. Also provides an excellent, detailed analysis of nine of Michener's books. Includes a partial bibliography of works by Michener, of information and criticism about Michener, and of reviews of some of Michener's books.

Silverman, Herman. *Michener and Me: A Memoir*. Philadelphia: Running Press, 1999. Silverman, who first met Michener before the latter's literary success, recounts his memories of more than fifty years of friendship, providing many revealing details about Michener's personality.

HENRY MILLER

Born: New York, New York; December 26, 1891
Died: Pacific Palisades, California; June 7, 1980
Also known as: Henry Valentine Miller

Principal long fiction

Tropic of Cancer, 1934
Black Spring, 1936
Tropic of Capricorn, 1939
The Rosy Crucifixion, 1949-1960, 1965 (includes *Sexus*, 1949, 2 volumes; *Plexus*, 1953, 2 volumes; *Nexus*, 1960)
Quiet Days in Clichy, 1956
Crazy Cock, 1991

Other literary forms

In an interview, Henry Miller once described himself as one part a writer of tales and one part a man electrified by ideas. This simple dichotomy provides a way to classify Miller's work, but, in truth, his whole canon is autobiographical. The many collections of his shorter pieces—portraits, essays, stories, travel sketches, reviews, letters—are all of value in ascertaining the truth of his life, his admitted literary goal. For example, *The Colossus of Maroussi: Or, The Spirit of Greece* (1941), Miller's first book about Greece, is ostensibly about George Katsimbalis, a leading figure in modern Greek letters. Katsimbalis, however, turns out to be Miller's alter ego, a fascinating monologuist, and the book becomes the record of Miller's attaining peace of heart through the elemental beauty of Greece. *The Time of the Assassins: A Study of Rimbaud* (1956) is less about Arthur Rimbaud than about the romantic affinities between Miller's and Rimbaud's lives. In Miller's books, all things become translated into images of his own mental landscape.

Achievements

When Henry Miller repatriated in 1940, only *The Cosmological Eye* (1939), a collection of short pieces drawn from *Max and the White Phagocytes* (1938), had been published in the United States; all of his fiction was deemed too obscene for publication. In France, *Tropic of Cancer* and *Tropic of Capricorn* had been seized in 1946, and Miller was convicted as a pornographer. After an outcry of French writers, this conviction was reversed, but in 1950, *Sexus* was banned in France, and in 1957, it was condemned as obscene in Norway. When *Tropic of Cancer* was finally published in the United States, in 1961, by Barney Rosset of Grove Press, more than sixty lawsuits were instituted against Miller and the book. Miller became the most litigated-against author in history, and the book was allowed to circulate only after a U.S. Supreme Court decision in 1965.

The furor over Miller's books' alleged obscenity prevented dispassionate evaluation of his literary merit for many years, and Miller feared that he would be dismissed as the king of smut. He was, however, inducted into the National Institute of Arts and Letters in 1957, and he received a citation from the Formentor Prize Committee, in France, in 1961 and the French Legion of Honor in 1975.

These memberships and citations, however, do not mark Miller's true achievement. His true quest and calling was to narrow the gap between art and life. That he—or his public persona of Paris expatriate, Big Sur prophet, desperado, clown, artist-hero, satyr—was the focus of critical attention throughout his life, rather than his books, testifies to the measure of success he achieved. Miller wanted to become free, as free as the young boy of the streets he had been in his childhood, in the face of a culture he saw as sterile, mechanical, and death-driven. He also wanted to discover and embody the truth of his life in art, in his "autobiographical romances." His defiant spit in the face of art in his first book, *Tropic of Cancer*, prompted critics to label his works as "antiliterature." Rather than deprecating literature, however, Miller saw art as a means to life more abundant. He conceived of his work as enlightening, as offering his vision of reality.

Often described as a *roman-fleuve* of the life of Miller, his fiction is neither strictly autobiographical nor realistic in method. As an artist, he notes in *The Wisdom of the Heart* (1941), he must give his reader "a vital, singing universe, alive in all its parts"; to accomplish this, he relied on the verbal pyrotechnics of Surrealism and the temporal discontinuities of stream of consciousness. The result was a series of works full of contradictions, repetitions, incongruities, and rhetorical flights, all documenting his growth as a person and as an artist.

Biography

Henry Valentine Miller was born on December 26, 1891, in the Yorkville section of New York City. Both of his parents were of German stock: His father, a gentleman's tailor, came from jovial people; his mother and her family typified the austere, industrious, respectable bourgeois life against which Miller was to rebel so vehemently. For the first nine years of his life, the family lived in the Williamsburg section of Brooklyn, the Fourteenth Ward. For Miller, this was a child's paradise.

When Miller was ten years old, his family moved to Decatur Street, the so-called Street of Early Sorrows, in Brooklyn's Bushwick section. His teenage experiences there helped form his attitudes on life, literature, and women. Miller was an affable young man; his special friends at this time were members of the Xerxes Society, a musical crowd. Male conviviality would be important to Miller throughout his life.

Miller was a model student and graduated as salutatorian from high school, but his formal education ended after a few months at the City College of New York. Always an avid reader—he had read through the Harvard classics as well as many romantic and adventure tales—Miller became an autodidact. By the time he was twenty years old, he had devoured such diverse authors as Joseph Conrad, Madame Blavatsky, and François Rabelais and had decided that he wanted to be a writer—about what, he did not know. Besides frequenting theaters in New York and Brooklyn, Miller was often seen at burlesque shows and in brothels. If his mother seemed cold and difficult to please, these women were open for sexual pleasure. Despite these experiences, Miller developed an intense idealism about love and the perfect woman, centering his longing on a school classmate, Cora Seward. At the same time, though, he began in 1910 an affair with a widow, Pauline Chouteau, closer to his mother's age.

In an effort to escape this passionate entanglement, Miller went to California in 1913, winding up miserable as a ranch hand near Chula Vista. Only hearing Emma Goldman in nearby San Diego, extolling anarchism, redeemed the trip. The next year Miller was back in New York, working in his father's tailor shop (described in *Black Spring*) and reading omnivorously. He was attracted to universalizing ideas and grander interpretations of the meaning of life than those of his Brooklyn milieu. During the years 1914-1915, Miller began to study piano seriously; through this enthusiasm, he met Beatrice Sylvas Wickens, whom he married in 1917. Their stormy courtship and marriage is depicted graphically in *The World of Sex* (1940, 1957), *Tropic of Capricorn*, and *Sexus*.

Drifting through many jobs, Miller found his way to the bottom—Western Union. His experience as a messenger employment manager opened his eyes to the underlying misery in America. His sympathy with these victims, adrift in a dehumanized urban landscape, was responsible for his unpublished first novel, *Clipped Wings*, dedicated to Horatio Alger. Miller's disillusionment with the American Dream came at a time when his marriage was also foundering. His response, rather than despair or self-pity, was to begin keeping a journal and extensive files of material for later use. He was beginning to become a writer, establishing an aesthetic distance from life and from himself.

Miller's delivery as a full-fledged artist was through the agency of his second wife, June Edith Smith, the Mona, Mara, She, or Her of his fiction. They met at a Broadway dance hall in 1923 and married the next year. June was a creative artist—of herself and her life story—who showed Miller the bridge between life and the imagination. Convinced that he was a great writer, she made him quit his job and devote his life to his work. This metamorphosis is recorded in *Tropic of Capricorn* and *Plexus*. To relieve their desperate poverty, June began peddling a series of brief prose sketches Miller had written called "Mezzotints," signed "June E. Mansfield." Miller might have freed himself from a conventional American life, but June—her schemes, her stories, her lovers, herself—held him completely in thrall. When June eloped with her lover, Jean Kronski, to Paris in 1927, Miller began to record notes of his obsessional attachment to her. His life with June was to be the book he tried to write throughout his life, culminating in *The Rosy Crucifixion*. His second unpublished novel, *Moloch*, the story of Miller's experiences in the year 1923, was written under unique pressure: One of June's admirers promised her a year in Europe if she completed a book. *Moloch* was their ticket to Paris.

Henry Miller. (Larry Colwell)

The trip to Paris in 1928-1929 was unproductive; Miller painted watercolors instead of writing books. Only when he returned alone to Paris in 1930 and ran out of resources did he begin to live and write truly. Living a marginal life, he not only completed his novel about June and Jean, *Crazy Cock*, but he also discovered "Henry Miller," the voice and main character of his "autobiographical romances." Alfred Perlès—"Joey"—contributed his bohemian lifestyle and epicurism to Miller's new persona. The French Surrealists gave artistic form to Miller's sense of incongruity. The Hungarian photographer Brassaï helped him see the poetry of the sordid side of Paris. American journalist-poets Walter Lowenfels and Michael Fraenkel converted him to the "death school"—although Miller knew that he, for one, remained very much alive. French writer Anaïs Nin became his ministering angel. Her love restored his faith in both himself and womankind. Her own journals confirmed him in the belief that his true subject was himself. Through her, he met the psychoanalyst Otto Rank: Miller's interest in psychology (and Nin) brought him back to New York for a brief period in 1936 to work as an analyst, but more important, it helped him understand his past and himself, which were to become the central concerns of his life.

Miller kept a dream book in this period, some of which reappears in his fiction. *Tropic of Cancer* and *Quiet Days in Clichy* draw on Miller's first two years in France. By 1936, his apartment in Villa Seurat had become the center of an industrious artistic circle, which was joined in 1937 by British writer Lawrence Durrell, Miller's first disciple. Far from Wambly Bald's Paris *Tribune* picture of the great American hobo artist, Miller in his Paris years worked with Germanic regularity and thoroughness on his fiction and essays.

By 1939, Miller was able to finish *Tropic of Capricorn*. With its completion, his furious literary activity abated. He began to lose interest in the narrative of his life and became engrossed in spiritual literature—in astrology, Zen, and Theosophy as well as in Krishnamurti and the I Ching. When he left Paris in 1939, at the advent of World War II, to visit Durrell in Corfu, Greece, the stage was set for his third metamorphosis. He records in *The Colossus of Maroussi* that in Greece he discovered a new goal in life: not to be a writer but, simply, to be. Images of simplicity—the land, sea, and silences of Greece—awakened in Miller, the city lover, a response to the allure of nature.

Back in the United States in 1940, Miller continued his autobiographical saga, but his only major fictional endeavor in the next forty years was to be *The Rosy Crucifixion*, written between 1942 and 1959, in which he tried to capture the elusive truth of his relationship with June. Most of his writing during this period was nonfiction. On an advance from publisher Doubleday, Miller and the painter Abraham Rattner went on a tour of the United States from 1940 to 1941. The resulting book, *The Air-Conditioned Nightmare* (1945), turned out to be a jeremiad rather than a travelogue.

In 1942, Miller moved to California, settling into a cabin in Big Sur in 1944. There, amid natural splendor, he found his Walden. Miller was again the center of a circle of painters and writers, a group that came to national attention through a 1947 *Harper's* magazine article, "Sex and Anarchy in Big Sur." Life, however, was not an orgy for Miller. He still remained in poverty, supporting himself by selling his watercolors and begging from his friends. In 1944, he married his third wife, Janina M. Lepska, who attempted to introduce domestic order into his life, but by 1948, she had left him. She and Conrad Moricand, an astrologer friend from Miller's Paris days, were castigated as "devils" in his account of his life at Big Sur, *Big Sur and the Oranges of Hieronymous Bosch* (1957). In 1953, he married Eve McClure; their marriage was dissolved in 1962.

In 1967, Miller married Hiroko "Hoki" Tokuda, a twenty-nine-year-old cabaret singer from Tokyo; that marriage ended in divorce in 1978. His later travails in love are described in *Insomnia: Or, The Devil at Large* (1970). Indeed, his later works seem to have been written to cleanse himself of the demons that possessed him. His final days were spent in Pacific Palisades, California. The acclaimed father of the sexual revolution of the 1960's died on June 7, 1980. He was eighty-eight years old.

Analysis

Henry Miller's books, in their frank sexual description, pushed back the last frontier of American literary realism. Sex was, for Miller, a means by which to study the cosmos: He noted in *The World of Sex* that

> to enter life by way of the vagina is as good a way as any. If you enter deep enough, remain long enough,

> you will find what you seek. But you've got to enter with your heart and soul—and check your belongings outside.

Whatever he sought, women became his connection to the universal. Although women are often depicted as sexual objects in his fiction, sex, he insisted, is "an elemental force. It's just as mysterious and magical as talking about God or the nature of the universe." The way in which Miller used obscenity against the bourgeoisie is telling: that sex was considered "dirty" reflected the puritanical nature of the culture he was attacking.

Because of his use of the obscene, the world of Miller's books is often repulsive and degrading, filled with grotesque characters living on the margin of society. The harsh reality of life must be accepted, he felt, before it could be transcended. In *My Life and Times* (1971), he explained, "The only way you can prove you are not of it is by entering into it fully. . . . When you fully accept something, you are no longer victimized by it." Savoring the dregs of civilization, Miller castigated its pretensions with anarchic glee. Indeed, Miller's value lies not in a depiction of some salvific (redemptive) vision (reality always remains a bit hazy in his fiction), but in his searing indictment of the modern world's impoverishment of "soul life." Miller shared D. H. Lawrence's horror of the mechanical modern world and endorsed Lawrence's response—the instinctual life—yet for all his apocalyptic prophecies, Miller was no Lawrentian messiah. Indeed, the "Henry Miller" of the novels is a flâneur, an American picaro.

TROPIC OF CANCER

Miller admitted in an interview at age eighty-four that Ernest Hemingway's *The Sun Also Rises* (1926) was the impetus for his own journey to Paris, the artists' mecca. What Miller found there in the 1930's forms the basis of his first and best novel, *Tropic of Cancer*. Paris, which provided both the impetus and the substance of his disjointed narrative, is, Miller writes, like a whore, "ravishing" from a distance; but "five minutes later you feel empty, disgusted with yourself. You feel tricked." Whores—Germaine, Claude, Llona, and others—and their hangouts dominate Miller's Paris, suggesting the debunking of romantic ideals, which was necessary for Miller before he could write. This is apparent in the evolving nature of his relationship to his wife Mona in the book.

The book begins with Miller's anticipation of their reunion, which proves blissful but short-lived. Although he claims that "for seven years I went about, day and night, with only one thing in my mind—*her*," after she returns to America, her image—like all the rest of his old life—"seems to have fallen into the sea," until he can only wonder "in a vague way" at the novel's conclusion whatever happened to her. Paris has replaced her as the center of his attention, and Paris makes far fewer demands on his inner self. Like his superficial relationships with whores, his stay in Paris is a fruitful form of self-destruction out of which a new self emerges.

The predominant metaphor in *Tropic of Cancer* is that of the river, of all that flows, in contrast to the stultifying conceptions and conventions of modern civilization. Early in the book, the sight of the Seine, and the great unconscious life that it represents, is inspirational. He later learns to see the world without "boundaries" or preconceived notions and recognizes it "for the mad slaughterhouse it is." His two trips outside Paris demonstrate his acclimatization and the death of his illusions. Returning from Le Havre, he recognizes the essential attraction of Paris for him, and he demonstrates in his outwitting of a whore his adjustment to the scene. Returning from Dijon, that bastion of medievalism that reminds him of the north (a bad place in Miller's geography, redolent of the coldness and sterility of his German ancestors), where everybody is constipated and even the toilet pipes freeze, he recognizes his previous dependence on women, "a fear of living separate, of staying born." This realization enables him to free Fillmore from the clutches of the rapacious Ginette and himself from Mona. The climax of the episode, and of the book as well, takes him again to the River Seine. He has already announced his love for everything that flows—"rivers, sewers, lava, semen, blood, bile, words, sentences"—and in this climax, he surrenders himself with religious intensity to the flux of time and space: "I feel this river flowing through me—its past, its ancient soul, the changing climate."

While a parade of other displaced persons in Paris passes through the book, they are all, like Moldorf, a "sieve through which my anarchy strains, resolves itself into words." Unlike the Jews Boris and Moldorf, the reborn Miller enjoys his suffering, because it confirms his sense of this world as a "putrid sink." Van Norden exists as a foil to Miller, both in relation to women and to himself. Van Norden is a neurotic egotist who uses women to try to forget himself, personifying the lovelessness of the modern world, where passion is removed from sex. As he watches Van Norden and his fifteen-franc whore grinding away, Miller compares him to a runaway machine or a maimed war hero: The human reality that gives meaning to the act is missing. Fillmore is another foil to Miller; like the typical American expatriate, he has come to France for wine, women, and song. Miller helps him escape Ginette and a marriage into the French bourgeoisie, and he returns to America disillusioned. Miller stays behind, his illusions gone, replaced by an appetite for life. The women characters of the book are negligible—with Mona's disappearance from his world, the woman has been replaced by her pudendum.

Tropic of Cancer is Miller's gleeful song over the corpse of the twentieth century: "I will sing while you croak." The comedy, sexual and otherwise, is at the expense of everyone, himself included. The novel played a decisive role in Miller's career: In the book he found the distinctive voice that he never thereafter abandoned. Miller describes the realization of the insufficiency of all ideas and the justification for the abandonment of conventional beliefs: "I am only spiritually dead. Physically I am alive. Morally I am free. . . . The dawn is breaking on a new world." The book ends on this note of openness to a better life.

Tropic of Capricorn

Tropic of Capricorn is Miller's *Künstlerroman*, depicting his own development as an artist. It records his struggle to achieve detachment from America and from his past life and become an angel, "pure and inhuman," in possession of his spiritual core. It is written from the perspective of one who has awakened from the "nightmare" of history, an achievement at first inspired by his friend Ulric and by the works of Lawrence and Fyodor Dostoevski, and later catalyzed by Her—Mara.

The book opens "on the ovarian trolly," when the persona of Miller is still unclear, mired in the chaos of his surroundings. America is a "cesspool of the spirit" and its statistical wealth and happiness is a sham: Everywhere, there is testimony to humankind's inhumanity to humans. This inferno is revealed to him through his job as employment manager at a branch of the Cosmodemonic (or Cosmococcic) Telegraphic Company of North America. His own persona might still be gestating, but those of the messengers, Carnahan, Guptal, Dave Olinski, Clausen, Schuldig—with clipped wings all—are surely in focus. Their stories, as well as those of Miller's "merry crew," reveal the underside of America and constitute Miller's anti-Horatio Alger story. Determined to escape being a "failure or ridiculous," Miller sees art as a way out.

At the beginning of the second part, Miller's friend Kronski advises him that good writers must first really suffer. Miller scoffs at this "Jewish" advice, preferring the "terrific animal sense of adjustment" of his German milieu, but the experience with Mara that is to come—in this book only intimated surrealistically—will leave him a marked man. For the moment, eating is all, and his reminiscences of good food take him back to his "wonderful past" when his Aunt Caroline gave him a thick slice of sour rye bread. The bread, through the lenses of Miller's nostalgia, becomes transformed into the "communion loaf." Adulthood can only be a diminished realm: "The taste goes out of bread as it goes out of life. Getting the bread becomes more important than the eating of it."

The next section of the book, "An Interlude," depicts "general sexual confusion." It is clear that, in some sense, sex is the agent for Miller's regeneration—at least it provides him with an escape from the workaday world that is death in life. Sex is ultimately disappointing to Miller, however, and his thinking "via the penis" leads absolutely nowhere. It only helps him to establish his first mask—that of Capricorn or the Goat—to deal with his life: "In this strange Capricornian condition of embryosis God the he-goat ruminates in stolid bliss among the mountain peaks." Moreover, sex puts Miller in touch with natural vitality.

What Miller really wants is love, the "Real Thing." From a wistful description of Una, his first love, Miller proceeds to the Amarillo Dance Hall: His encounter there with Mara is volcanic. Henceforth, he will be Gottlieb Leberecht Müller, a man who has lost his identity. Mara, a fabulous creature whose life is a web of illusion, resembles a figure of mythology, a Juno or a Circe, or an archetype, a Terrible Mother.

Together with Mara in their black hole of Calcutta, Miller hibernates, "a blazing seed hidden in the heart of death." She is fascinating but terrible—"a dead black sun without aspect," a "great plunder-bird." In the coda, reflecting on this book as "a tomb in which to bury her—and the me which had belonged to her," Miller makes another attempt to explain how she became the Beatrice who led him to the paradise of the imagination. The language he uses reveals that she might actually represent his unconscious life, the life whose very existence America denied. United with Mara, "the inner and the outer ego are in equilibrium. . . . Henceforth I take on two sexes. . . . I shall seek the end in myself."

As an artist, Miller achieves personal harmony and, more important, power. He feels a kinship with Norwegian writer Knut Hamsun's Herr Nagel, the artist as unacknowledged saint, driven to art "because the world refuses to recognize his proper leadership." Like Abelard, like Christ, Miller sees his life as instructive, an object lesson in self-fulfillment: "All my Calvaries were rosy crucifixions, pseudotragedies to keep the fires of hell burning brightly for the real sinners who are in danger of being forgotten."

The value of Miller's work transcends the expression of his personality, however vital and unique that was. In his essay "Defense of the Freedom to Read" (1957), Miller notes, "Whatever I may say about my own life which is only a life, is merely a means of talking about life itself." Like Walt Whitman, Miller extended the literary terrain of American literature, democratizing it as well. Besides his direct influence on Durrell and the Beat generation of the 1950's—Jack Kerouac, Allen Ginsberg, Lawrence Ferlinghetti, and Gregory Corso—Miller's influence can be detected in much postwar American fiction, with its blending of colloquial, surreal, obscene, fantastic, and desperate rhetoric. Miller's confessions provided a voice for the alienated individual who, against all odds, remains sure of his own humanity.

Honora Rankine Galloway

Other major works

play: *Just Wild About Harry: A Melo-Melo in Seven Scenes*, pb. 1963.

nonfiction: *Aller Retour New York*, 1935; *What Are You Going to Do About Alf?*, 1935; *Max and the White Phagocytes*, 1938; *Money and How It Gets That Way*, 1938; *The Cosmological Eye*, 1939; *Hamlet*, 1939, 1941 (2 volumes; with Michael Fraenkel); *The World of Sex*, 1940, 1957; *The Colossus of Maroussi: Or, The Spirit of Greece*, 1941; *The Wisdom of the Heart*, 1941; *The Angel Is My Watermark*, 1944 (originally published in *Black Spring*); *Murder the Murderer*, 1944; *The Plight of the Creative Artist in the United States of America*, 1944; *Semblance of a Devoted Past*, 1944; *The Air-Conditioned Nightmare*, 1945; *The Amazing and Invariable Beauford Delaney*, 1945; *Echolalis: Reproductions of Water Colors by Henry Miller*, 1945; *Henry Miller Miscellanea*, 1945; *Maurizius Forever*, 1945; *Obscenity and the Law of Reflection*, 1945; *Why Abstract?*, 1945 (with Hilaire Hiler and William Saroyan); *Patchen: Man of Anger and Light, with a Letter to God by Kenneth Patchen*, 1946; *Of, by and About Henry Miller: A Collection of Pieces by Miller, Herbert Read, and Others*, 1947; *Portrait of General Grant*, 1947; *Remember to Remember*, 1947; *Varda: The Master Builder*, 1947; *The Smile at the Foot of the Ladder*, 1948; *The Waters Reglitterized*, 1950; *The Books in My Life*, 1952; *Nights of Love and Laughter*, 1955 (Kenneth Rexroth, editor); *Argument About Astrology*, 1956; *A Devil in Paradise: The Story of Conrad Mourand, Born Paris, 7 or 7:15 P.M., January 17, 1887, Died Paris, 10:30 P.M., August 31, 1954*, 1956; *The Time of the Assassins: A Story of Rimbaud*, 1956; *Big Sur and the Oranges of Hieronymus Bosch*, 1957; *The Red Notebook*, 1958; *The Henry Miller Reader*, 1959 (Lawrence Durrell, editor); *The Intimate Henry Miller*, 1959 (Lawrence Clark Powell, editor); *Reunion in Barcelona: A Letter to Alfred Perlès*, 1959; *To Paint Is to Love Again*, 1960; *The Michael Fraenkel-Henry Miller Correspondence, Called Hamlet*, 1962 (2 volumes); *Stand Still Like the Hummingbird*, 1962; *Watercolors, Drawings, and His Essay "The Angel Is My Watermark,"* 1962; *Books Tangent to Circle: Reviews*, 1963; *Lawrence Durrell and Henry Miller: A Private Correspondence*, 1963 (George Wickes, editor); *Greece*, 1964; *Henry Miller on Writing*, 1964 (Thomas H. Moore, editor); *Letters to Anaïs Nin*, 1965; *Selected Prose*, 1965 (2 volumes); *Order and Chaos chez Hans Reichel*, 1966; *Collector's Quest: The Correspondence of Henry Miller and J. Rivers Childs, 1947-1965*, 1968; *Writer and Critic: A Correspondence*, 1968 (with W. A. Gordon); *Insomnia: Or, The Devil at Large*, 1970; *My Life and Times*, 1971 (Bradley Smith, editor); *Henry Miller in Conversation with Georges Belmont*, 1972; *Journey to an Unknown Land*, 1972; *On Turning Eighty*, 1972; *Reflections on the Death of Mishima*, 1972; *First Impressions of Greece*, 1973; *Reflections on the Maurizius Case*, 1974; *Letters of Henry Miller and Wallace Fowlie, 1943-1972*, 1975; *The Nightmare Notebook*, 1975; *Books of Friends: A Tribute to Friends of Long Ago*, 1976; *Four Visions of America*, 1977 (with others); *Gliding into the Everglades, and Other Essays*, 1977; *Sextet*, 1977; *Henry Miller: Years of Trial and Triumph*, 1978; *My Bike and Other Friends*, 1978; *An Open Letter to Stroker!*, 1978 (Irving Stetner, editor); *Some Friends*, 1978; *Joey: A Loving Portrait of Alfred Perlès Together with Some Bizarre Episodes Relating to the Other Sex*, 1979; *Notes on "Aaron's Rod" and Other Notes on Lawrence from the Paris Notebooks of Henry Miller*, 1980 (Seamus Cooney, editor); *The World of Lawrence: A Passionate Appreciation*, 1980 (Evelyn J. Hinz and John J. Teumissen, editors); *Reflections*, 1981; *The Paintings of Henry Miller*, 1982; *From Your Capricorn Friend: Henry Miller and the "Stroker," 1978-1980*, 1984; *Dear, Dear Brenda*, 1986; *Letters from Henry Miller to Hoki Tokuda Miller*, 1986 (Joyce Howard, editor); *A Literate Passion: Letters of Anaïs Nin and Henry Miller*, 1987; *The Durrell-Miller Letters, 1935-1980*, 1988; *Henry Miller's Hamlet Letters*, 1988; *Henry Miller and James Laughlin: Selected Letters*, 1996 (Wickes, editor).

Bibliography

Balliet, Gay Louise. *Henry Miller and Surrealist Metaphor: "Riding the Ovarian Trolley."* New York: Peter Lang, 1996. Describes the origins, aesthetics, and other characteristics of twentieth century French Surrealism, focusing on how Miller uses Surrealistic images and other techniques in his fiction. Individual chapters analyze the novels *Black Spring*, *Tropic of Cancer*, and *Tropic of Capricorn*.

Blinder, Caroline. *A Self-Made Surrealist: Ideology and Aesthetics in the Work of Henry Miller*. Rochester, N.Y.: Camden House, 2000. Blinder reevaluates Miller's work, examining how he was influenced by the French Surrealists and French culture during his years in Paris. Although she addresses the "obscene" and sexual nature of his work, she seeks to transcend feminist critiques defining Miller as a sexist; instead, she focuses on Miller's more general concerns with mass psychology and politics and their relation to art.

Bloshteyn, Maria R. *The Making of a Counter-culture Icon: Henry Miller's Dostoevsky*. Toronto, Ont.: University of Toronto Press, 2007. Examines the enormous influence of Fyodor Dostoevski on Miller's writing and worldview. Miller and his friends Lawrence Durrell and Anaïs Nin were especially impressed with Dostoevski's psychological treatment of characters, and they sought to similarly depict characters in their own fiction.

Brown, J. D. *Henry Miller*. New York: Frederick Ungar, 1986. A concise assessment of Miller's work in relation to the events of his life, with a good summary chapter entitled "Autobiography in America." Brown writes with clarity and knows the material well. Includes a chronology of the events of Miller's life, a bibliography of his writing through 1980, and useful sections listing interviews, bibliographical collections, biographies, and selected criticism.

Dearborn, Mary V. *The Happiest Man Alive: A Biography of Henry Miller*. New York: Simon & Schuster, 1991. Dearborn provides an objective and comprehensive account of Miller's life and is generally sympathetic to her subject, comparing his literary life to that of Walt Whitman.

Ferguson, Robert. *Henry Miller: A Life*. New York: W. W. Norton, 1991. A full and sensitive treatment of Miller's life and work. The first chapter is especially good, providing information about the problems involved in interpreting Miller, the response of feminist critics, and the difficulties of evaluating Miller's memoirs. Includes notes and a bibliography.

Gottesman, Ronald, ed. *Critical Essays on Henry Miller*. New York: G. K. Hall, 1992. Divided into sections on the early Miller, including the "phallic" Miller, featuring conflicting interpretations by Norman Mailer and Kate Millett; the "orphic" Miller; the "American" Miller; and various retrospectives of his life and career, including memoirs.

Jahshan, Paul. *Henry Miller and the Surrealist Discourse of Excess: A Poststructuralist Reading*. New York: Peter Lang, 2001. Jahshan argues that descriptions of Miller's literary style as Surrealist evade a serious analysis of the work. He shows that Miller's texts share with those of the French Surrealists an imagery of excess, but one which is economically and masterfully geared toward readers whose responses help to construct a peculiarly Millerian version of stylistic deviation.

Lewis, Leon. *Henry Miller: The Major Writings*. New York: Schocken Books/Random House, 1986. Concentrates on the seven books regarded as the heart of Miller's achievement as a writer. Lewis offers detailed critical analysis of each book as well as a comprehensive estimate of Miller's entire life as an artist. Relates Miller to the American writers he admired and to Albert Camus and the Surrealists of the 1920's to locate him within literary and cultural traditions.

Mitchel, Edward, ed. *Henry Miller: Three Decades of Criticism*. New York: New York University Press, 1971. A representative compilation that indicates just how much controversy and personal response Miller's work elicited during the first three decades after *Tropic of Cancer* was published.

Widmer, Kingsley. *Henry Miller*. Rev. ed. Boston: Twayne, 1990. Updates Widmer's 1962 work, taking into account the final years of Miller's career and the criticism that appeared after Widmer's study. A succinct yet comprehensive introduction. Includes a chronology, notes, and an annotated bibliography.

SUE MILLER

Born: Chicago, Illinois; November 29, 1943

Principal long fiction

The Good Mother, 1986
Family Pictures, 1990
For Love, 1993
The Distinguished Guest, 1995
While I Was Gone, 1999
The World Below, 2001
Lost in the Forest, 2005
The Senator's Wife, 2008

Other literary forms

Sue Miller writes short stories as well as novels. A film adaptation of the title story from her collection *Inventing the Abbotts, and Other Stories* (1987) was released in 1997. Her short stories have been published in magazines such as *The Atlantic Monthly*, *Mademoiselle*, and *Ploughshares*. Miller has also written a memoir about her father's struggle with Alzheimer's disease in which she reveals her frustration that she could do nothing to stop his deterioration and her difficult reconciliation as he succumbed.

Achievements

Sue Miller received a Boston University Creative Writing Fellowship in 1979. Her writing won her a Bunting Institute Fellowship in 1983, and the extended time to focus that the fellowship provided made it possible for her to write *The Good Mother*. Miller received a Pushcart Honorable Mention for a short story in 1984, and in that same year the Massachusetts Art Council also gave her an award. She has been the recipient of both Guggenheim and MacDowell fellowships as well.

Miller's career as a novelist was launched by her very public success with *The Good Mother*. *Family Pictures* was a National Book Critics Circle Award nominee in 1991, and in 1999, Miller's visibility as a writer was further enhanced when her novel *While I Was Gone* became an Oprah's Book Club selection. Miller's work merits recognition as it continually grapples with problems central to family life and intimate personal relationships, including the state of marriage. American social practices have changed markedly in the decades since the 1960's, and Miller crafts stories that capture the vitality and challenges of those alterations.

Biography

Sue Miller, the second of four children, was born and grew up in Chicago. Her father taught religion at the University of Chicago, and her mother was a full-time homemaker. The Miller family had ministers in their lineage for three generations, and Miller grew up in an atmosphere steeped in the language of sermons and serious thinking about issues of right and wrong. Miller was a quiet child and read avidly. Finishing high school early, she entered Harvard University at the age of sixteen. She has stated that she was overwhelmed by the situation and glided through her time at the university without really reaping the benefits.

After graduating at twenty, she married a medical student and worked to support him. They had a son, Ben, in 1968, and the marriage ended in 1971. For the next thirteen years, Miller worked at many jobs and continued her education, eventually earning a master's degree in creative writing from Boston University, an M.A. in education from Harvard University, and an M.A. in teaching from Wesleyan University. In 1985 she married writer Michael Bauer, but they later divorced. As her reputation as an American realist author has grown, Miller has taught at universities in the Boston area, has done guest editing for anthologies, and has written short stories for magazines, in addition to continuing to work on her novels.

Analysis

Sue Miller's *The Good Mother*, the story of a divorced woman who openly takes a lover into her life even though she is living with a small daughter, dramatized the end of an era in American social mores and customs. Anna Dunlap's existence gave names and faces to the upheavals in domestic living arrangements of the 1960's and 1970's. Through Anna's struggle to support herself and her daughter, Miller exposes the difficult and lonely world of single parenting. In the novel, Anna's seemingly casual attitude toward sex and physicality in her daily life leads to a custody battle that costs her her daughter. Few books before *The Good Mother* had taken such a frank look at how the law and traditional expectations could clash with a woman's finding a new direction for love and life. Miller's work filled a void in American fiction; it explored life from a woman's internal perspective, sparing none of the uncertainties or struggles that beset Anna as she tries to forge her new existence.

This relentless search for balance and meaning in women's lives has come to be a hallmark of Miller's fiction. Her women search for answers without abandoning hope even when they seem to have failed. Her women are not always sure of their direction, but they keep thinking and working out possible solutions as they move through their experiences. Jo Becker (in *While I Was Gone*) flirts with the romantic memory of her youthful rebellion, and twice-divorced Catherine Hubbard (in *The World Below*) grapples with trying to find a new direction as she returns to her grandparents' Vermont home. Both these women question their daily decisions and measure the present in the light of the past. They are acutely aware of how their actions may inspire hurt or disappointment in those close to them, but they need to follow their own questions to the end regardless.

All of Miller's characters embrace family history directly, in houses or towns from their childhoods or through the weight of memory on thoughts and motives. Whether bickering about shared memories (*Family Pictures*) or trying to sort out the importance of past actions (*The Distinguished Guest*), Miller's people site themselves in family dynamics that affect their actions and decisions. In this way, Miller brings time into every situation, even if obliquely. For instance, a relationship from the deep past prompts the foolish mistake that leads to the tragic death of a teenage babysitter in *For Love*, and Catherine Hubbard's dead grandmother's youthful love, revealed in her newly discovered diary, helps Catherine come to terms with both her deep past and her present situation.

Miller's novels, set in periods stretching from the 1960's to the 1990's and beyond, reflect the time when the public conversation about women's lives and family life in the United States was remade to include the word "choice." When American women began returning to work after having children, began entering the workforce without first getting married and having children, and began deciding not to marry in favor of careers, new choices confronted American families. New approaches to child-care responsibilities and child custody, new reproductive options, and new approaches to work, such as flextime, emerged as domestic life assumed new shapes. Miller's books give faces to the social issues swirling around family and the search for values in a shifting world. Her books look at the intimate side of public discourse about marriage, family, and personal identity.

When the rules and ways of being that we know shift by circumstance or choice, we must invent or translate new ways to survive without guidelines. Miller believes in the integrity of individual vision, no matter how flawed or contradictory it may be. As her characters seek self-knowledge and strategies for life in new locales or new relationships, they also seek their places in families and their relation to the American Dream of hope and prosperity for all. They never stop trying to understand what is happening to them and around them. Sometimes this leads to surprises. In *Lost in the Forest*, Daisy becomes entangled in a perverted sexual situation from which she must be rescued. Her father, Mark, estranged and formerly distant, rises to the occasion, reentering her life decisively just when he is needed, against expectation and past history.

Miller's plots include situations in which the past and the present pressure characters to act wisely on their own behalf or on behalf of their families. The best course of action is often hard to see, complicated by the interaction of public expectation and personal need. People are all public people with private selves, part of the way society moves, breathes, and thinks. Miller captures the complexity of women's stories in particular. She reminds us that if we break the rules we become part of what society judges, but she also clearly believes that some rules need changing. Her sense of this is completely contemporary. At the same time, she ponders the cost and the morality of the new arrangements.

In Miller's stories, circumstances often evoke urges and situations that are beyond the characters' power to cope, despite their wanting to do the right thing. There are always the questions: Did I do the right thing? Can I find my balance and a new direction alone? What next? Miller's women always ask such questions, and they arrive at their answers one day at a time. Miller's characters meet the frontier daily in their life decisions. Like many American authors before her, Miller sets the stage for characters to reinvent themselves, to inhabit the realm of what might be possible. They embody American optimism despite their setbacks. Her women do not "head out for the territories." They stay put, emotionally if not physically, and keep on working on relationships, building their worlds.

The Good Mother

Sue Miller's wildly and unexpectedly successful first novel lays out the existence of Anna Dunlap and her young daughter, Molly. After leaving an unsatisfying marriage to a minister's son, Anna envisions a life of new hopes fulfilled. Instead she finds herself strapped for cash and struggling to find ways to support herself and Molly.

Sue Miller. (© Miriam Berkley)

This situation, in which a woman has left a marriage because she is looking for more in her life, still seemed an outrage to many in 1986, when the book appeared. Feminism was accused of weakening the American family and destroying the domestic traditions that had helped make America strong. Public opinion condemned "unnatural" mothers or bad mothers who left their families to pursue careers; women who remained with their families but returned to work after having children were also criticized. In this climate, writing *The Good Mother* took nerve, and Miller created a story that was not a polemic against tradition or a propaganda piece for women's liberation.

The Good Mother avoids shrill tones by meeting issues head-on, without inflated language. Anna adopts a matter-of-fact approach as she relates what she thinks about women's lives. As a child, she says, she listened to her aunts talk "about things that mattered—love, death, mutilation." Later, she learned that "the preoccupation with [these things] kept women from doing anything of consequence in the world," and she listened instead to her father and the other men of the family. Anna's recognition of where power resided changed her idea of what she wanted and how she should proceed to get it.

When she decides to ask her grandparents for financial help, she meets a solid wall of disapproval. Her grandfather objects to Molly's being put in day care and reminds Anna that Molly "is not the child of factory workers," a comment that escalates tension. His insistence that Anna is inflicting poverty on her daughter, that this is all Anna's fault, prompts an emphatic retort: "It's not poverty I care about, Grandfather. . . . It's independence. It's being my own person." For this overreaching, Anna's grandfather does not forgive her, and many Americans shared his views. After she leaves her grandfather, Anna wonders, "How much could I love [Molly] without damaging her. . . . Not too much, not too little. Is there such a love?" These questions, about personal independence, responsibility, and the dangers and rewards of motherly love, form the core of the book's drama.

The catalyst for the unraveling of Anna's life is her relationship with her lover, Leo. Their casual cohabitation and his helping to care for Molly lead to a situation involving what Anna's ex-husband calls sexual irregularities. The resulting court battle for custody of Molly embodies layers of judgment, debates about ethical behavior, and discussion of the purview of the law that Miller handles with dexterity.

Anna pays for her liberation. She loses in court and in the court of public opinion, as signaled by her grandfather's rebukes. Anna's new parenting style and her open relationship have jeopardized her custody of Molly because the outside world, and the law, question their appropriateness. Can she be a good mother? How far must society move toward accepting the shifts in values concerning parenting? Such questions were often on the minds of Americans in the 1980's. Miller's book asks these questions and gives hard answers, all poignant and still relevant.

The World Below

In contrast to Anna Dunlap, Catherine Hubbard is well along in her life. She has had two failed marriages. Her children are older and out of the house. Like Anna, however, she feels the weight of disapproval. People judge her when they find out that she is twice divorced. "Everyone's allowed one marital mistake, it seems, but two is over the top." Even her children are "slightly *pissed* about it." Catherine must deal with the same kind of public censure that Anna experiences.

Her grandmother's death precipitates a return to rural Vermont. Catherine has inherited the house where she spent a good bit of her childhood. Facing uncertainty in California, Catherine heads east to see if she can find her way to some order and plan to move ahead. The book starts with a longing for peace and understanding in the midst of change, a possible new direction.

Catherine is a pragmatist. She stops in Boston to contact an old lover because she "missed sex." Her straightforwardness reminds readers of Anna, but her unapologetic sexuality is evidence that the public practices and expectations about intimate relations have changed markedly in America since 1986. Miller lets Catherine go further. "I found I had missed more simply lying next to someone and talking in that postcoital way." Frank expression of sexual need is a product of women's liberation and appears without fanfare in *The World Below*. Miller's comfort with and acceptance of the new status quo puts her in the forefront of women writing about the "new world" a decade or more after the upheavals of opinion faced by Anna. Like Anna, Catherine neither crusades nor proselytizes. She exercises sexual freedom.

At her grandmother's house, Catherine finds old photos and miraculously happens upon her grandmother's diary. Its story of a young girl's sojourn and love affair in a tuberculosis sanitorium and the confession of why she married Catherine's grandfather reveal a world below the calm and ordered surface of life in Vermont that Catherine has cherished. Taking it in, she compares her life to the surprising revelations about her grandmother. Catherine has banished secrets. "My children understood my life. There was not the constant division between the surface and the depths of it; and I'd been careful to explain the difference to them if there was."

Catherine continually juggles a budding relationship, her own confusion, and relationships with her children and tries to integrate what she is learning about her grandmother into the developing dynamic of her own life. When she returns to her world the future is not certain, but she reconnects with her daughter Karen when her granddaughter is born and the family moves into a new generation. The past comes forward on another coast, and the dead towns of the east are far behind, literally. A town underwater after a dam was built makes the perfect metaphor for how Catherine will sail above her recognizable past, charting a new course to arrive at a new beginning.

The Senator's Wife

Never one to walk away from controversy, Miller framed *The Senator's Wife* in the wake of the scandal involving President Bill Clinton and Monica Lewinsky, amid widespread questions about how Hillary Clinton could remain in her marriage. In this tale, Delia Naughton, aging wife of a retired U.S. senator, Tom Naughton, who is still handsome and known for philandering, becomes a neighbor to Meri and Nathan Fowler. The narrative spins out the parallel paths of the two couples' relationships as they share a duplex in a recognizably New England town called Williston.

Nathan proceeds to disappear into his university job, hoping to make a name for himself. Meri takes up her role as new wife, finds it not enough, and gets a job with a campus radio station to anchor her in the new place. Her unexpected pregnancy throws everything off-kilter, even more than Nathan's indifference to her presence except for their steamy lovemaking, which also becomes clouded with the pregnancy and resentment as the book progresses. Readers can sense trouble ahead.

Delia and Tom Naughton have had their trouble before the story begins and have worked out amicable, separate existences. The arrival of the young couple in the duplex brings back memories of better times for Delia, however, as well as memories of the cataclysmic affair that signaled the end of making up in the Naughton's marriage. Delia and Meri like one another and develop an accepting and congenial relationship.

When Meri watches over the Naughtons' home while Delia takes her annual extended stay in Paris, she plunders Delia's letters and discovers secrets and history that change her view of the Naughtons. At the same time, Nathan and Meri are no longer connected to each other in the same intense way they were before the baby's arrival.

Delia and Tom Naughton become entwined with Nathan and Meri because Tom's health declines and Delia takes him into their Williston home to care for him. It gives her a perverse sense of justice that he is at her mercy, but the situation also deeply satisfies her need to be important to him again. She has never stopped loving him, despite years of disappointment and hurtful affairs. She feels that perhaps these last months or years will pay her back for endless separations. In a perverse turn that involves Meri nursing her child and watching over Tom so Delia can run some errands or carry on some of her community work, the final betrayal of marriage and friendship occurs.

Meri and Nathan go on to have more children and build a successful life, but Meri knows that she lied on the day of the final betrayal. She had to, to keep baby Asa safe and to keep her life with Nathan. The Naughtons' lives unravel, and they separate for good after that day. Meri carries the secret past inside without regret, thinking that she did what she did for love. As this novel, published more than twenty years after *The Good Mother*, shows, Miller's women continue to struggle with their own sexual natures as well as with those of their partners. The terms of the discussion are different, the times in the characters' lives and marriages are different, but the dilemmas of personal faithfulness and ethical behavior seem much the same.

Karen L. Arnold

Other major works

short fiction: "Given Names," 1981; "Leaving Home," 1982; "Tyler and Brina," 1985; "Calling," 1986; "The Lover of Women," 1986; *Inventing the Abbotts, and Other Stories*, 1987; "The Moms of Summer," 1991.

nonfiction: *The Story of My Father: A Memoir*, 2003.

edited texts: *The Best American Short Stories 2002*, 2003; *Best New American Voices 2007*, 2007.

Bibliography

Miller, Sue. "A Conversation with Sue Miller." Interview by Lewis Burke Frumkes. *The Writer* 112, no. 6 (June, 1999). In-depth interview focuses on Miller's writing of *While I Was Gone*. Miller discusses the characters in the book, her reading habits, and a bit about her own writing routines.

_______. "Diving Deep: Sue Miller Explores Submerged Emotional Worlds." Interview by Elfrieda Abbe. *The Writer* 115, no. 4 (April, 2002): 26-31. In a conversational and probing interview about *The World Below*, Miller discusses the source of the story and how she views her characters. Other topics covered include Miller's writing habits and the questions her books have helped her explore.

Pritchard, William H. "Sue Miller." In *American Writers: A Collection of Literary Biographies*, edited by Jay Parini. New York: Charles Scribner's Sons, 2003. Thorough essay covers Miller's biography and presents critical evaluations and synopses of her major works.

Smiley, Jane. "Someone's in the Kitchen with Freud." *The New York Times Book Review*, April 22, 1990. Thoughtful review of *Family Pictures* praises the work as "profoundly honest, shapely, ambitious, engrossing, original and true."

Warner, Judith. "Stand by Your Man." *The New York Times Book Review*, January 13, 2008. Comprehensive review of *The Senator's Wife* provides an overview of the novel.

ANCHEE MIN

Born: Shanghai, China; January 14, 1957

Principal long fiction

Katherine, 1995
Becoming Madame Mao, 2000
Wild Ginger, 2002
Empress Orchid, 2004
The Last Empress, 2007

Other literary forms

Anchee Min's first publication, "Red Fire Farm," was a short story based on her experiences on a Communist collective farm in the People's Republic of China; it was published in *Granta* magazine in 1992. The short story formed the basis of Min's successful 1994 memoir, *Red Azalea*, which chronicles her early life in mainland China during Mao Zedong's catastrophic Cultural Revolution. In addition to her memoir and her novels, Min has written, together with Jie Zhang and Duoduo, the text for the 2003 book *Chinese Propaganda Posters*, which collects reproductions of the mass art of the Mao years in China.

Achievements

Anchee Min's memoir *Red Azalea* won the Carl Sandburg Literary Award and was named a Notable Book of the Year in 1994 by *The New York Times*. This work established Min's status as a contemporary writer, and shortly after its publication she turned to writing long fiction. Her novels have fascinated a large audience with their depiction of extraordinary women protagonists who struggle against the hardships of contemporary and historical Chinese society. Min's first three novels are strong contributions to the growing body of literature about the inhumanity of the Chinese Cultural Revolution. Min approaches this topic from the perspective of female protagonists who are outsiders, followers, or prime architects of the disaster. From this group of novels, Min's work about Madame Mao represents a bridge leading to Min's next two novels about the life of China's last empress. Here, Min succeeds in offering her readers a fascinating life story.

Min's refusal of easy stereotypes in her complex descriptions of women wielding power is a key achievement of her historical fiction. Her interest as a storyteller is in depicting the ambiguous motivations that drive her characters to make controversial choices. As her work is based on close analysis of actual historical sources and documents, Min's two novels about China's last empress also support a strong claim for a serious reassessment of the historical person. Written in English, the author's second language, Min's novels have been translated internationally, albeit not yet into Chinese.

Biography

Anchee Min was born on January 14, 1957, in Shanghai, People's Republic of China. Her father, astronomy and industrial design instructor Naishi Min, and her mother, middle school teacher Dinyun Min, would have three more children. Anchee Min grew up in Shanghai and was a schoolgirl when Mao launched the disastrous Cultural Revolution in 1966. Min was sent as a teenage laborer to the Communist collective Red Fire Farm near the East China Sea in 1974.

By extraordinary luck and supported by her determination to leave the miserable collective, Min was chosen in 1976 as a possible actor for the central role in Jiang Qing's final revolutionary film, *Red Azalea*. Min was promoted from understudy to star, but her fortunes fell with the death of Mao on September 9, 1976, and the arrest of his widow on October 6. The film project was abandoned, and a vengeful Communist Party secretary assigned Min to work as a set clerk, including stage-sweeping duties. Through her friendship with actor Joan Chen, Anchee Min managed to emigrate to the United States. Upon arriving in the United States on September 1, 1984, Min spoke no English, but she was admitted to the School of the Art Institute of Chicago under the condition that she learn the basics of English in six months. Min succeeded and painstakingly acquired the language in which she has written all of her published works. In 1991, she married the painter Qigu Jiang, whom she had dated since 1988, and received her master of fine arts degree.

As Min started to write, she drew heavily on her personal experiences as a teenager during the Cultural Revolution. Her first short story, "Red Fire Farm," won a local American prize and was published in the British *Granta* magazine in April, 1992. The story caught the eye of literary agent Sandra Dijkstra, who secured Min a contract for her first book. In 1993, Min and Jiang's daughter Lauryan was born. In 1994, Pantheon Books published Min's memoir of her teenage years in Mao's China, *Red Azalea*. The book, which took Min eight years to write, became an international success. In 1994, she and Jiang were divorced, and Lauryan stayed with her mother.

Min succeeded in shifting her writing career to long fiction and published her first novel, *Katherine*, in 1995. Min's next work took some time to be published, both because of the intensity of her research and because of publishers' reluctance. In December, 1999, Min married author and former high school teacher Lloyd Lofthouse. Finally, Houghton Mifflin bought and published *Becoming Madame Mao* in 2000. The same publisher brought out Min's subsequent novels *Wild Ginger* in 2002, *Empress Orchid* in 2004 and *The Last Empress* in 2007. Min, her daughter, and her husband live in Northern California.

Analysis

Anchee Min's novels center on strong, morally ambiguous women who are affected by the vicissitudes of present and past life in China. All of Min's protagonists suffer from an oppressive, often violent society that seeks to circumscribe their lives with tight rules and rituals that stifle their free personal, and especially sexual, development. Her characters have to learn to live under these rules and try to adapt to them as best they can, for the penalties for violating the rules are brutal, whether the rules are those of Mao's Communist regime unleashing the Cultural Revolution, which lasted from 1966 to 1976, or the tight court rules of the imperial Qing Dynasty, which was extinguished in 1912.

Min's first three novels are told against the backdrop of the Cultural Revolution and its aftermath, an era Min personally experienced and suffered through. Her first novel, *Katherine*, brings an outsider to Communist China, a European American woman who quickly falls into the traps sprung by a society hostile to any acts of individualism. Characteristic of Min's fiction, individualism is ultimately expressed by a woman's right to enjoy and self-determine her sexuality. Her protagonist Katherine quickly encounters social and personal jealousy, and Katherine's opponents use the strict, puritanical dictates of official Communist society to avenge themselves. In *Katherine*, return or emigration to the United States serves as the solution to the dilemma posed by rigid Chinese society. In Min's third novel, *Wild Ginger*, such an escape is no longer possible, and tragedy is the foreordained outcome.

For her second novel, Min chooses a powerful historical woman as protagonist, just as she does in later novels. In *Becoming Madame Mao*, Min envisions in great psychological detail the woman who would become Mao Zedong's last wife. Min's Jiang Qing is presented as an ambiguous character who undergoes a vast personal development that her author has called a journey from innocence to hell, with hell partially of her own making.

From writing about a historical person whose acts personally affected the author, Min moved to two novels telling of the life of the woman who would become China's last empress. With *Empress Orchid* and *The Last Empress*, Min's efforts to resurrect a historical person are successful and force a genuine reassessment of that person's vilified life. Critics have worried that Min's meticulous research distracts from the literary development of her protagonist, but this objection appears misguided; it may be related to the fact that Min's character is very ambiguous—any reader looking for a fully sympathetic protagonist, or a purely evil one, will find her difficult to like.

Stylistically, Min's fiction is very descriptive and at times has the quality of a painting or a historical film. Her choice of the old Wade-Giles system for transliterating Chinese names of the imperial age, rather than the Pinyin system generally in use since the late twentieth century, forces readers to keep in mind that her empress Tzu-Hsi is more familiar to the modern world as Cixi. The same is true for all the other names in the two novels about her. At the time her characters lived, however, Wade-Giles was in use in the West, so there is some justification for Min's choice.

Katherine

When Min's somehow underrated first novel, *Katherine*, appeared, many readers and critics were unsure of how to read the work, as it did not fall easily into any category. The novel tells of a European American woman, Katherine, who is invited to teach English in Shanghai after the Mao era is over. One of her enraptured students, Zebra Wong, tells the story from her point of view. Katherine's Chinese students, male and female, come to look upon Katherine as the epitome of sexual liberation still lacking in their socially oppressed and austere lives. As Katherine nonchalantly engages in sexual affairs with some of her students, perhaps of both sexes, jealous forces conspire to expose her and have her expelled. Before her departure, however, Katherine adopts an unwanted, sickly Chinese girl named Little Rabbit. With the help of a sympathetic U.S. congressman, Katherine gets Zebra and Little Rabbit to follow her to the freedom that the United States represents in Min's novel.

Becoming Madame Mao

With *Becoming Madame Mao*, her striking novel about the woman who, as Jiang Qing, became the last of Mao Zedong's wives, Min turned to one of China's most hated historical persons. Min's goal was to show the person behind the popular image, and her novel showcases her protagonist's development from early rebellion and misfortune to triumph and eventual downfall. For each stage of her life she passes through, the protagonist acquires a new name. The girl Yunhe refuses foot binding and runs away, the young actor Lan Ping moves toward the Communists, and Jiang Qing becomes Mao's wife. Min has called her protagonist's fate a journey from innocence to hell, and it is captivatingly told. With a narrative structure that shifts from first to third person and between past and present, *Becoming Madame Mao* seeks to underline how a private person acquires a public image and how early events affect later decisions.

It is during her youth and after Jiang Qing's fall from power after Mao dies that Min's character shows her most sympathetic qualities. Sentenced to death but kept alive in prison, Jiang Qing, in a moving scene that speaks of her unbending will to assert herself, is caught having stitched her name in tiny characters on the shirts she must sew together. In Min's novel even a notorious woman has a personal, vulnerable side.

Wild Ginger

Wild Ginger takes the reader straight to the horrors of the Cultural Revolution as experienced by a trio of teenagers. With extreme clarity, Min depicts the absurdities of a totalitarian system that turns society into an Orwellian nightmare where today's outcasts are tomorrow's heroines and vice versa.

As the novel opens, Wild Ginger, a teenage girl, is an outcast because of her father's partially French heritage in Mao's xenophobic People's Republic. Her spirit refuses to be subdued, however; she even rescues her friend Maple, narrator of the novel, from the girl bully Red Pepper, who uses politics as an excuse to torment her adversaries. Symptomatic of the wild political swings of the chaotic era, Wild Ginger suddenly becomes a Communist heroine and even meets Chairman Mao. Her downfall comes when both she and Maple fall in love with a boy named Evergreen. In the vicious political climate of the day, Wild Ginger commits suicide out of desperation as the tide turns against her again.

Although some critics have objected to this novel's dramatic emotions and improbable coincidences, which put the characters' fates on a roller-coaster ride, it was exactly such emotional chaos and turmoil that Mao and his wife unleashed on China from 1966 to 1976. *Wild Ginger* can be seen as a worthy fictional counterpart to Min's celebrated memoir *Red Azalea*, which covers the same era.

Empress Orchid *and* The Last Empress

In two historical novels based on meticulous research, Min renders the life of China's final empress in the most sympathetic light possible. Her focus is on the rigid imperial rules and court intrigues that made her protagonist struggle for her life. Opposing the traditional negative view of Empress Tzu-Hsi (in Pinyin, Cixi), Min's two novels offer an alternative.

Empress Orchid features the desperate struggle of the young Manchu girl Orchid Yehonala, who chooses life as one of Emperor Hsien Feng's (in Pinyin, Xianfeng) seven imperial consorts next to three thousand concubines. To lead a meaningful existence, she must capture the attention of the emperor. Min is particularly effective in her description of the means Orchid employs in her carefully crafted dance of seduction.

By bearing the emperor's son and by participating in political decision making, Orchid incurs the jealousy of others, and, as in all of Min's novels, the woman protagonist has to fight for her life. Choosing allies wisely, Orchid manages to avoid being put to death in the young emperor's tomb after his untimely death. She succeeds in turning tables and becomes coregent for her baby boy, the new emperor. *Empress Orchid* closes as the young widow is torn by her desires for General Yung Lu. In Min's novel, Orchid remains chaste, contrary to historical malicious gossip.

The Last Empress tells of Tzu-Hsi's reign as regent, first for her young son and then, after his early death, for her nephew. In Min's extremely sympathetic rendition, Tzu-Hsi's historical actions are all motivated by her love for her family and by her recognition of China's weakness against militarily superior Western and Japanese forces. Where hostile historical propaganda has implicated Tzu-Hsi in the murder of her son to regain power, for example, in the novel the son dies of an illness exacerbated by venereal disease. There are moments when Min's Empress Orchid is near despair at the limitations imposed on her by her gender and by ancient traditions. She is shown disconsolate at the betrayals of those close to her.

What gives Min's two novels about China's last empress their particular power as fiction is the author's uncompromising decision to portray a historical person in a sympathetic yet still accurate and thus ambiguous light. Perhaps because Min stays so close to history, some readers and critics have found themselves unable to connect with her protagonist. The presence of an authentically ambiguous protagonist, however, is the very strength of Min's historical fiction.

R. C. Lutz

Other major works

nonfiction: *Red Azalea*, 1994; *Chinese Propaganda Posters*, 2003 (with Jie Zhang and Duoduo).

Bibliography

Farmanfarmaian, Roxane. "Anchee Min: After the Revolution." *Publishers Weekly*, June 5, 2000. Excellent article provides a sympathetic portrayal of Min, describing her road to becoming a writer. Praises Min for her determination as a writer, the scope and quality of her historical research, and the emotional force of her novels.

Hayot, Eric. "Immigrating Fictions: Unfailing Mediation in *Dictée* and *Becoming Madame Mao*." *Contemporary Literature* 47, no. 4 (Winter, 2006): 601-635. Presents scholarly comparative analysis of Theresa Hak Kyung Cha's novel *Dictée* (1982) and Min's second novel. Asserts that both works resist successful assimilation to American values and that both evaluate how art is crafted at the interface of politics and literature.

Kakutani, Michiko. "For Maoists, Love Became a Many-Frenzied Thing." Review of *Wild Ginger*, by Anchee Min. *The New York Times*, April 5, 2002. Acknowledges Min's eye for detail and the horrors of the Cultural Revolution as they affect the novel's three characters; argues that the narrative suffers because Min packs into the novel too much high-pitched emotion and too many impossible circumstances.

Lai, Amy Tak-yee. *Chinese Women Writers in Diaspora: Jung Chang, Xinran, Hong Ying, Anchee Min, Adeline Yen Mah*. Newcastle, England: Cambridge Scholars Publishing, 2007. Examines the work of Chinese women writers who live and work in the United States and England, including Min. Discussion of Min's work concerns her use of theatrical conventions in depicting her protagonists' entrapment.

Min, Anchee. "Interview with Anchee Min." Interview by Brendan Dowling. *Public Libraries* 45, no. 2 (March/April, 2006): 29-31. Focuses on Min's becoming a writer, her historical novels, her relation to contemporary China, and her dedication to research. Also discusses the challenges Min faced in writing novels about Mao's wife and China's last empress.

Tsang, Lori. "The Last of Everything." Review of *The Last Empress*, by Anchee Min. *Women's Review of Books* 25, no. 1 (January/February, 2008). Provides a good overview of the novel. Argues that the book is more valuable for its fresh historical look at its imperial protagonist than for its literary accomplishments.

_______. "People's Enemy? Feminist Hero?" Review of *Empress Orchid*, by Anchee Min. *Women's Review of Books* 21, nos. 10/11 (July, 2004). Presents a thorough overview of the novel. Discusses the historical controversies associated with the real-life Chinese ruler depicted in the book and stresses how Min turns the remote historical person into a sympathetic young woman coping with a stifling society.

YUKIO MISHIMA

Kimitake Hiraoka

Born: Tokyo, Japan; January 14, 1925
Died: Tokyo, Japan; November 25, 1970
Also known as: Kimitake Hiraoka

Principal long fiction

Kamen no kokuhaku, 1949 (*Confessions of a Mask*, 1958)
Ai no kawaki, 1950 (*Thirst for Love*, 1969)
Kinjiki, 1951 (English translation in *Forbidden Colors*, 1968)
Higyō, 1953 (English translation in *Forbidden Colors*, 1968)
Shiosai, 1954 (*The Sound of Waves*, 1956)
Kinkakuji, 1956 (*The Temple of the Golden Pavilion*, 1959)
Kyōko no ie, 1959
Utage no ato, 1960 (*After the Banquet*, 1963)
Gogo no eikō, 1963 (*The Sailor Who Fell from Grace with the Sea*, 1965)
Kinu to meisatsu, 1964 (*Silk and Insight*, 1998)
Haru no yuki, 1969 (*Spring Snow*, 1972)
Homba, 1969 (*Runaway Horses*, 1973)
Akatsuki no tera, 1970 (*The Temple of Dawn*, 1973)
Tennin gosui, 1971 (*The Decay of the Angel*, 1974)

Hōjō no umi, 1969-1971 (collective title for previous 4 novels; *The Sea of Fertility: A Cycle of Four Novels*, 1972-1974)

Other literary forms

In addition to serious novels and his lighter fictional "entertainments," Yukio Mishima (mee-shee-mah) wrote a number of works in a variety of genres and styles. His short stories, particularly "Yūkoku" ("Patriotism"), written in 1961, are among his most sharply etched and emotionally charged works of narrative fiction. Mishima's writing for the stage earned for him an important reputation as a dramatist in Japan, both in the older forms of twentieth century drama such as *shimpa* (a hybrid between Kabuki and modern theater), for which he created a masterful melodrama of nineteenth century Japan, *Rokumeikan*, in 1956, and in the contemporary theater, perhaps most effectively for the play *Sado kōshaku fujin* (pr., pb. 1965; *Madame de Sade*, 1967). He also wrote dramas specifically composed for performance by traditional *bunraku* puppet troupes. Mishima's modern versions of traditional Japanese No plays, reconceived for modern actors, were also widely admired.

In addition, Mishima earned considerable fame as an essayist, particularly for his confessional *Taiyō to tetsu* (1968; *Sun and Steel*, 1970), in which he explored his newfound commitment to and trust in his body, superseding what he had come to see as the limitations inherent in the life of the mind.

Achievements

Many Japanese readers and critics, and a large number of enthusiastic readers of Yukio Mishima in translation, are willing to place him at the forefront of postwar Japanese writers, perhaps even among the best writers of the entire modern period in Japanese literature. There remains, however, a certain disparity between foreign and Japanese views of Mishima and his accomplishments. Many intellectuals in Japan view Mishima's talents and attitudes with a certain reserve. For many Japanese, Mishima's flamboyant life and death lacked the dignity appropriate to a great writer, yet his often sensational subject matter (homosexuality, right-wing patriotism, mental derangement) was not necessarily frowned upon per se. Nevertheless, the posture frequently adopted in Mishima's writings of the novelist/narrator as a kind of voyeur seemed to some critics self-indulgent and inappropriate. It should be noted, however, that the very levels of emotional and erotic life that Mishima sought to chronicle were and are a part of human, specifically Japanese, mentality, and he bears genuine witness to aspects of Japanese life that may well make his novels and other works outlive their first popularity and attain a classic status.

One Japanese critic has remarked that Japan needed Mishima in the same way that Victorian England needed Oscar Wilde: Both writers used the beauty of the perverse to reveal crucial aspects of life in their societies that were tacitly banned from examination or open discussion. In many ways, Mishima was a man living out of his time, particularly because of his seemingly total lack of interest in social and political issues. The postwar literary scene in Japan has had at its center a considerable number of distinguished writers who show a genuine social commitment, often of a Marxist orientation. To such writers, Mishima merely seemed self-absorbed and narcissistic. The fact that Mishima, toward the end of his life, combined his aesthetic responses to life with a highly charged personal sort of homoerotic militarism that resulted in his own suicide remains distasteful and disturbing to many. In other ways, however, Mishima was the very prototype of the best-educated Japanese of his period—cosmopolitan, sophisticated, and often intellectually daring.

The legend of Mishima the man will doubtless continue to fascinate the general public, but at the same time, a certain amount of his work will surely continue to find an important place in the literary history of the twentieth century, for its beautiful language, psychological insights, and the close ties many of the works show with the techniques and philosophies of the great Japanese classical masterpieces so much admired and made use of by this most artful and self-aware of modern Japanese novelists.

Biography

Born Kimitake Hiraoka in 1925, the eldest son of a government bureaucrat, Mishima (who took the pen name of Yukio Mishima in 1941) was reared largely by his grandmother Natsuko, a woman of artistic tastes and neurotic temperament. During his childhood and early

Yukio Mishima. (Time & Life Pictures/Getty Images)

adolescence, Mishima, by his own admission, spent much of his time in a kind of fantasy world. He pursued his studies at the Gakushuin (Peers School), where he began to write, in a highly precocious manner, for the school literary magazine. Mishima's interest in European, particularly French, literature began during this period. Graduated from the Peers School in 1944, he was not drafted and was able to begin his studies at Tokyo University. In 1947, he began working at the Ministry of Finance but soon resigned on the strength of his early literary successes to devote his full energies to writing. As his novels became more and more successful, he turned as well to writing for the stage, where he met with both critical and popular success.

Mishima made his first trip abroad during 1951 and 1952, visiting the United States, Europe, and Brazil. These visits gave him both another sense of the world and an increasing understanding of the appeal that his works had in translation for readers outside Japan.

Mishima married in 1958 and remained close to his wife and two children until his death twelve years later. At the same time, his strenuous cult of bodybuilding and his growing association with what came to be his own private army, the Tatenokai, suggest a homoerotic side of his nature first revealed in his early writings.

Mishima embarked on the composition of his tetralogy, *The Sea of Fertility*, while engaging in military maneuvers with his private army. To many critics and readers in Japan, Mishima seemed to have become something of a right-wing extremist, and by 1970, he had made the decision to kill himself upon completion of the manuscript of the fourth and final novel of the series. On November 25, 1970, after making a speech to the Self-Defense forces, he committed ritual suicide in the traditional Japanese manner.

Analysis

Yukio Mishima's work covers a wide spectrum of subject matter and themes. On one hand, he drew on the first-person confessional style familiar in Japanese literature since the time of the court diaries of the late Heian period (794-1185) right up to the works of such earlier twentieth century modern Japanese masters as Shimazaki Tōson (1872-1943). To that existing style, however, Mishima added a confessional eroticism seldom if ever before employed within the canon of serious literature in Japan. Mishima also admired Western literature, particularly such French novelists as Raymond Radiguet and François Mauriac and the classical playwright Jean Racine, finding in them models of a style that involved an elegant surface control of language that could permit glimpses of powerful passions underneath. Mishima's often baroque style and florid vocabulary tend to flatten out in translation, but the surfaces of his works in the original are usually highly polished and, in the context of the kind of naturalism so much a part of the postwar literary scene around the world, perhaps a bit artificial. Still, in novels dealing indirectly with social issues, notably in *After the Banquet*, Mishima the stylist was able to find an idiom both contemporary and altogether appropriate to his relatively public subject matter.

Confessions of a Mask

The confessional aspects of Mishima's writing can best be seen in his early *Confessions of a Mask*, the book that made him famous and is often regarded as his masterpiece. The device of the mask and the face, a frozen image shown to society that stands in opposition to the truth of the inner psyche, is an image so often employed that it may seem merely banal. In this novel, however, the title represents a powerful and entirely appropriate symbol for the narrator as he slowly comes to grasp his profound attraction to other men, and perhaps to violence as well. The unwinding of this theme is so skillfully carried out by means of his first-person narrative technique that the structures Mishima has conceived present a cumulative effect altogether authentic, both in emotional and literary terms. Then too, while Mishima creates a narrator who is principally concerned with chronicling, understanding, and analyzing his emotional development, he was careful to include in the novel enough suggestions concerning the narrator's surroundings that the reader can gain a real sense of what it was like to have grown up as a sensitive child during the difficult years when Japan was at war.

Still, the major themes of the book are indisputably eros and (at least by occasional implication) death. The powerful vision contained in the final pages of the book, when the narrator takes full cognizance of his erotic responses to a bare-chested hoodlum, certainly represents for the author a moment of truth that cannot be emotionally denied, and any sympathetic reader will surely be drawn in to the power of that sudden and revelatory instant of self-understanding.

The Temple of the Golden Pavilion

In *The Temple of the Golden Pavilion*, published seven years later, in 1956, Mishima again draws on the possibilities of psychological confession in the first person, but on this occasion, he uses his skill to employ newspaper accounts and trial documents as a means to penetrate the mind of another; in this sense, the book maintains a powerful objectivity. In the novel, Mishima sets out to reconstruct the psychology of a young Buddhist acolyte who, in 1950, burned down the famous Zen temple Kinkakuji, the Golden Pavilion of the title, one of the great masterpieces of traditional Japanese architecture and an important site in the ancient capital of Kyoto. In his own way, Mishima took over the techniques of such traditional writers as the great Tokugawa playwright Chikamatsu Monzaemon (1653-1724), who, particularly in his famous love-suicide plays, took an actual event for his theme and attempted to reconstruct the psychological states that might have plausibly led up to the event portrayed.

In the case of a gifted writer such as Mishima, reportage was quickly subsumed in a masterful evocation of psychological imbalance. As in *Confessions of a Mask*, Mishima limits himself to the construction of a first-person psychological and introspective narrative, in which the acolyte reveals his self-disgust, his growing obsession with beauty, and his final decision (here Mishima seems to be inadvertently imitating themes in the work of Oscar Wilde, whom he admired) to destroy the thing he loves the most—the beautiful temple itself. Like Salomé, after she has done away with John the Baptist, the acolyte lives on, satiated and at peace, at least until traditional morality reasserts itself.

In an even more effective manner than in the earlier novel, however, Mishima took great care to include in the narrative details of setting and milieu as well as to create a series of well-sketched additional characters, thus providing the reader with both a relief and a diversion from the obsessive quality of the narrator's personality. In particular, the temple superior, a remarkably worldly and opportunistic Buddhist priest, is portrayed with shrewdness and a sardonic humor, so that he might assume the role of a kind of foil for the young acolyte, psychologically speaking. By employing such a series of delicate balances in his narrative, Mishima makes certain that the reader always has a means to look objectively at the world of the acolyte, permitting the book to stand as a disturbing artistic vision of derangement, rather than as a case history.

After the Banquet

Reportage of another sort provides the material employed by Mishima in composing *After the Banquet*, in which the author drew on the circumstances surrounding the Tokyo mayoral elections in the late 1950's. He based his account on certain events surrounding the candidacy of a prominent Socialist politician, who, because of his attachment to the proprietress of a fashionable restaurant, suffered a good deal of criticism and, among other things, lost the election. The novel caused a considerable scandal itself because of the supposedly revelatory nature of certain details in his account, but again, Mishima used the materials he had at hand to evoke his own authentic image of a contemporary Japan, catching both crucial details of the milieu and a beautifully realized delineation of the psychology of his two main characters, the stiff politician Noguchi and the earthy, yet somehow winning, Kazu, the owner of the restaurant.

The novel offers as revealing a glimpse into the somewhat despoiled yet remarkably vigorous life of politicians in Tokyo as any postwar author has been able to manage. The success of the novel results in part from the fact that Mishima's thrust is psychological, not political; he espouses no causes but plays instead the role of a humane and astute observer. The moral of the novel lies thus within the structures of the narrative itself. The development of the relationship between the pair, in which money and opportunity signally affect the changing nature of the affection each feels for the other, make *After the Banquet* perhaps the most objectively rendered and humanly satisfying of Mishima's novels.

The Sound of Waves

Mishima's attraction to European literature is particularly apparent in his novel *The Sound of Waves*, published in 1954 after his European trip four years earlier. Here Mishima drew directly on the Greek pastoral romance of Daphnis and Chloë (used also in the twentieth century by Maurice Ravel in his celebrated 1911 ballet), couching the famous account of the antique shepherd and shepherdess in Japanese terms. Quite popular at first, and immediately a success abroad when translated into English, the work has not worn well. The style is doubtless brilliant, yet the world of classical Greece and timeless, rural Japan are too far apart to merge effectively. The result now seems a sort of artificial pastiche. On the other hand, Mishima could blend classical Japanese sources into his work with enormous skill. A work such as the modern No play *Dōjōji* (pb. 1953; English translation, 1966) shows a remarkable blending of ancient form and subject matter with a thoroughly modern sensibility. In Mishima's version, a young woman, spurned in love, decides to take her revenge in a fashion that, while paying homage to the medieval play, allows a thoroughly contemporary and, for the reader or spectator, altogether intimidating moment of psychological truth.

The Sea of Fertility

Mishima's tetralogy *The Sea of Fertility*, which occupied him from the mid-1960's until his death in 1970, was to be for him the summing up of his life, art, and belief. Although the tetralogy has been widely read in the original and in translation, the critical response to these four books has remained mixed. The highest praise has been reserved for the first volume, *Spring Snow*, which begins an account of a reincarnation in four separate personalities, all to be witnessed by Honda, a subsidiary character whose own growth of self-awareness and spiritual insight stands as one of the accompanying themes of this vast fable.

In *Spring Snow*, Honda is shown as a friend and confidant of Kiyoaki, a beautiful and willful young man who only manages to fall in love with his fiancé Satoko when he finds it necessary to force his way to see her in secret. At the end of the novel, Satoko flees their difficult situation and becomes a Buddhist nun. Kiyoaki dies, with an intimation that he and his friend Honda will meet again. The novel is elegiac in its emotional tone and contains a moving re-creation of the atmosphere of late nineteenth century Japan that can surely stand among Mishima's finest accomplishments.

The three remaining volumes find Kiyoaki reborn as a young fencer turned political extremist in *Runaway Horses*, then reappearing as a Thai princess in *The Temple of Dawn*, and, in the final volume, *The Decay of the Angel*, as a selfish, and perhaps empty-spirited, working-class youth. The plan and conception of this work is surely grand, perhaps grandiose. Some readers find the series, with its increasingly powerful Buddhist references, too far removed from the realities of the present-day Japanese consciousness. Some critics have also commented on the fact that the later volumes are spottily written. In any case, it is still too soon to say whether this last and most ambitious effort on Mishima's part will take its place at the head of his oeuvre or will merely remain a last ingenious experiment in the career of this gifted, adventuresome, and sometimes perverse genius of modern Japanese letters.

J. Thomas Rimer

Other major works

SHORT FICTION: *Kaibutsu*, 1950; *Tōnorikai*, 1951; *Manatsu no shi*, 1953 (*Death in Midsummer, and Other Stories*, 1966).

PLAYS: *Dōjōji*, pb. 1953 (English translation, 1966);

Yoro no himawari, pr., pb. 1953 (*Twilight Sunflower*, 1958); *Aya no tsuzumu*, pr. 1955 (*The Damask Drum*, 1957); *Shiroari no su*, pr., pb. 1955; *Aoi no ue*, pr., pb. 1956 (*The Lady Aoi*, 1957); *Hanjo*, pb. 1956 (English translation, 1957); *Kantan*, pb. 1956 (wr. 1950; English translation, 1957); *Kindai nōgakushū*, 1956 (includes *Kantan*, *The Damask Drum*, *The Lady Aoi*, *Hanjo*, and *Sotoba Komachi*; *Five Modern Nō Plays*, 1957); *Sotoba Komachi*, pb. 1956 (English translation, 1957); *Tōka no kiku*, pr., pb. 1961; *Sado kōshaku fujin*, pr., pb. 1965 (*Madame de Sade*, 1967); *Suzakuke no metsubō*, pr., pb. 1967; *Waga tomo Hittorā*, pb. 1968 (*My Friend Hitler*, 1977); *Chinsetsu yumiharizuki*, pr., pb. 1969.

NONFICTION: *Hagakure nyūmon*, 1967 (*The Way of the Samurai*, 1977); *Taiyō to tetsu*, 1968 (*Sun and Steel*, 1970); *Yukio Mishima on "Hagakure": The Samurai Ethic and Modern Japan*, 1978.

EDITED TEXT: *New Writing in Japan*, 1972 (with Geoffrey Bownas).

MISCELLANEOUS: *Hanazakari no mori*, 1944 (short fiction and plays); *Eirei no Koe*, 1966 (short fiction and essays).

Bibliography

Keene, Donald. *Dawn to the West: Japanese Literature of the Modern Era, Fiction*. New York: Holt, Rinehart and Winston, 1984. Massive study of the fiction produced in Japan from the time of the Japanese "enlightenment" in the nineteenth century closes with discussion of Mishima's work.

_______. *Five Modern Japanese Novelists*. New York: Columbia University Press, 2003. Keene devotes a chapter to Mishima in this examination of five Japanese novelists with whom he was acquainted. Provides his personal recollections of the writers as well as literary and cultural analyses of their works.

_______. *Landscapes and Portraits: Appreciation of Japanese Culture*. Tokyo: Kodansha International, 1971. Devotes a section to Mishima and his writings, commenting on a variety of his works but especially on *Confessions of a Mask*, because, atypically, this novel is autobiographical and so provides insight into the author's thinking and his relation to his own work. Mishima's preoccupation with death also is explored.

Miyoshi, Masao. *Accomplices of Silence: The Modern Japanese Novel*. Berkeley: University of California Press, 1974. Chapter 6 in part 2, "Mute's Rage," provides studies of two of Mishima's major novels, *Confessions of a Mask* and *The Temple of the Golden Pavilion*, as well as comments on other works. Includes notes and an index.

Nathan, John. *Mishima: A Biography*. 1974. Reprint. Cambridge, Mass.: Da Capo Press, 2000. Classic biography includes a new preface in this reprint edition. Nathan knew Mishima personally and professionally, and he presents a detailed and balanced portrait of the writer.

Piven, Jerry S. *The Madness and Perversion of Yukio Mishima*. Westport, Conn.: Praeger, 2004. Psychological study of Mishima traces the events of his life—most notably his early childhood, spent largely in his grandmother's sickroom—to provide a better understanding of the author and his works.

Scott-Stokes, Henry. *The Life and Death of Yukio Mishima*. Rev. ed. New York: Noonday Press, 1995. Following a personal impression of Mishima, presents a five-part account of Mishima's life, beginning with its last day, then returns to his early life and the making of the young man as a writer. Part 4, "The Four Rivers," identifies the rivers of writing, theater, body, and action, discussing in each subsection relevant events and works. Supplemented by glossary, chronology, bibliography, and index.

Starrs, Roy. *Deadly Dialectics: Sex, Violence, and Nihilism in the World of Yukio Mishima*. Honolulu: University of Hawaii Press, 1994. Critical and interpretive look at Mishima's work focuses on its elements of sex, violence, and nihilism. Examines Mishima's intellectual background, including the influences of Thomas Mann and Friedrich Nietzsche, and describes the quality of Mishima's thought. Includes bibliography and index.

Yourcenar, Marguerite. *Mishima: A Vision of the Void*. 1986. Reprint. Chicago: University of Chicago Press, 2001. Yourcenar, herself a novelist, analyzes Mishima's works and his role as a suicide in a film to argue that his life was "an exhausting climb" toward what he perceived as its proper end.

ROHINTON MISTRY

Born: Bombay (now Mumbai), India; July 3, 1952

Principal long fiction

Such a Long Journey, 1991
A Fine Balance, 1995
Family Matters, 2001

Other literary forms

Rohinton Mistry is known primarily for his novels, but he began his writing career as a short-story writer, publishing the collection *Tales from Firozsha Baag* in 1987. Like his novels, his short stories focus on life in India, specifically Bombay (now Mumbai). However, three of the published stories, including "Squatter," about the difficulty an immigrant from Bombay has in adapting to Western toilet customs, deal with the immigrant experience in Canada, something not dealt with in his long fiction, which focuses entirely on life in India.

Achievements

Rohinton Mistry won acclaim with his very first writings, two short stories he entered into literary competitions in Canada (the 1983 and 1984 Hart House Literary Prizes), both of which took first prize. In 1985, he won the annual Contributor's Award from *Canadian Fiction Magazine*. He continued to receive honors when he turned to longer fiction. His first novel, *Such a Long Journey*, won the Canadian Governor-General's Award for fiction, the W. H. Smith/*Books in Canada* First Novel Award, and the Commonwealth Writers' Prize; it was also short-listed for the Booker Prize in England, as were both of his next two novels. In 1998, *Such a Long Journey* was made into a film of the same title.

In 2001, talk-show host Oprah Winfrey chose Mistry's second novel, *A Fine Balance*, as one of her featured book-club works, and Mistry appeared on her show; the book then sold an additional one-half million copies. *A Fine Balance* also won the Giller Prize for the best Canadian novel of 1995, the 1996 Commonwealth Writers' Prize, and the 1996 Los Angeles Times Book Prize for fiction. In 1996, Mistry was awarded an honorary doctorate from the University of Ottawa.

Biography

Rohinton Mistry was born on July 3, 1952, into the Parsi community in Bombay. The Parsi are a small ethnic minority in India whose ancestors originally came from Iran centuries ago. During British rule over India, which ended just five years before Mistry was born, the Parsi had relatively high status and identified with the British. After Indian independence their situation became more difficult, and many of them emigrated.

Mistry became part of the emigration in 1975, the year he turned twenty-three. He followed his wife-to-be, Freny Elavia, to Toronto, Canada, and found work there in a bank. Before leaving India he had attended the University of Bombay, obtaining a degree in mathematics and economics, but he was more interested in music, performing as a folksinger in the style of Bob Dylan and even releasing an album.

Unable to pursue his musical career in Canada, Mistry eventually turned to literature, studying part time for a degree in English and philosophy at the University of Toronto and beginning to write short stories. In 1985, he obtained a Canada Council grant, which enabled him to leave his job at the bank and write full time. He also became a Canadian citizen and remained in Canada, though his writing continued to be almost entirely about India.

Analysis

Rohinton Mistry became one of a number of well-respected writers in Canada, including Michael Ondaatje, M. G. Vassanji, and Neil Bissoondath, who are associated with India or other parts of South Asia. What sets Mistry apart is his Parsi identity and his focus on Parsi life in his writings. At the same time, though, he is praised for speaking to universal human concerns in his fiction. He himself has said that since the Parsi are a dwindling minority, his works are documents bearing witness to their way of life, but he added that the Parsi way of life has not been his major concern. Similarly, although politics plays a major role in his fiction, he insists that he is only secondarily writing about politics.

Critics disagree about the importance to attribute to

politics and Parsi life in Mistry's works and also over his relation to traditional realism. Some even refer to him as an antirealist or a postcolonial subverter of such traditions as realism. However, others consider his works to tend toward realism, presenting a true-to-life portrayal of Parsi life in particular and the human condition in general, with a special emphasis on the politics of India in the years after independence. Mistry writes about suffering and the oppressed, and is quite critical of what he describes as the corruption and brutality in India under the rule of Prime Minister Indira Gandhi.

As a Parsi from Bombay now living in Toronto, Mistry is sometimes seen as doubly displaced, having been a minority first in India and then in Canada. Mistry himself says being in Canada gives him the perspective to write about India, but some Indian critics have said he is out of touch with Indian reality in general and the Hindu experience in particular. He is often praised, however, for presenting an outsider's view and for being sensitive to human frailties.

Mistry is sometimes associated with literary modernism, that is, with a view of the universe in which inexplicable forces hold sway over humans, unable to control their own destinies. Modernist poets William Butler Yeats and T. S. Eliot are sometimes cited as influences, and Mistry quotes from Eliot in an epigraph to *Such a Long Journey*. Mistry is also generally considered a writer much interested in memory, loss, and the patterns people impose on existence. He is much given to literary allusions and flashbacks, and he wins praise for his gently ironic tone.

Such a Long Journey

Such a Long Journey is the novel in which Mistry most successfully combines the specifics of Parsi life with universal human concerns. Gustad Noble, a Parsi bank clerk in Bombay, says his daily Zoroastrian prayers (Zoroastrianism being the religion of the Parsi community) and tries to cope with the difficulties of life amid bothersome mosquitoes, arguments with his wife, a son who will not obey him, a daughter who is perhaps seriously ill, and a good friend who seems to have abandoned him. This friend then involves him in a dangerous government mission.

Through the first part of the novel, Gustad feels betrayed and mistreated, and he seeks to retreat behind blackout papers on his windows and a large wall surrounding his apartment building. By the end of the novel, however, his basic decency and growing maturity overcome his feelings of bitterness and betrayal, and he is able to recognize friendship where it exists and to move on with his life, finally tearing down the blackout papers and reaching out to his estranged son. He is able to put aside his obsession with the past, and seems ready to agree with the modernist view of his friend the pavement artist, who is happy to escape from an attempt at permanence and settling down, and who says it is the journey that matters.

The book presents a detailed picture of Parsi and Zoroastrian life, from funeral practices to some very odd superstitions to the decline in social status of the Parsi and their fear of what the Hindu majority may do to

Rohinton Mistry. (AP/Wide World Photos)

them. There is also a clear reference, in the adventure plot in the second half of the novel, to a specific scandal in Gandhi's India. However, despite all these specifics, the underlying theme is the universal one of coping with misfortune, and Mistry's success in this novel is to make the reader feel both the anguish of Gustad and the power of his qualified triumph over that anguish at the end of the story. The story itself, in a sense, is a journey and a discovery, in which the reader, along with Gustad, learns that it is impossible to live in the past and make time stand still, impossible to hold on to what has been done, and yet possible to accept change and loss and carry on.

A Fine Balance

A Fine Balance is more political and historical than Mistry's first novel. Whereas politics and history in *Such a Long Journey* form a backdrop to Gustad's personal problems, in *A Fine Balance* the political situation is much more central, and the problems the characters face often stem directly from actual historical events, notably the Emergency Measures declared by Gandhi in 1975.

A Fine Balance is also a much more sweeping work than *Such a Long Journey*. Through the frequent use of flashbacks, it lays out the prehistory as well as the current actions of the novel's four major characters. The novel also depicts the larger Hindu community beyond the Parsi minority, and even includes a minor but significant Muslim character. This is the part of the novel that some critics said lacks authenticity.

Two of the central characters, Om Darji and his uncle, Ishvar, are Hindus originally from a low caste of tanners whose family sought to break through caste barriers; Ishvar's father sent him and his brother to a nearby town to train to be tailors. The eventual price of this revolt against the caste system was the murder of Ishvar's father and brother (Om's father) and of all the other members of their family. However, Ishvar and Om continue to work as tailors, though they have difficulty making a living and eventually move to Bombay. In Bombay they meet the other two central characters, Dina Dalal and the son of one of Dina's friends, Maneck Kohlah, who are both Parsi.

The tailors at first simply work for Dina, who keeps them at a distance, but eventually a friendship springs up among the four characters, who become a sort of artificial family enjoying much happiness—until the government's Emergency and the continuing enmity of upper-caste Hindus for the renegade tailors lead to various tragedies. The tragedies are too much for Maneck, who breaks under their weight, but the other three carry on.

The message of *A Fine Balance* is expressed by a minor character: When circumstances change, especially when they change for the worse, one must change with them and adapt. This message is similar to that of Mistry's first novel, persevering in the face of adversity, primarily by maintaining connections with others. This perseverance is symbolized in *A Fine Balance* by the giant quilt that Dina Dalal is always working on. The novel also suggests that telling stories about your own life helps you maintain some control of your life, that a person must not lose him- or herself in his or her own memories, as Gustad Noble did in the first part of *Such a Long Journey*; yet people should not renounce all memory and past events as useless, as the pessimistic Maneck does in *A Fine Balance*; the answer seems to be to use one's memories and the stories of one's past to connect to others.

Uplifting as this message is in *A Fine Balance*, it seems to sit uneasily atop a book full of tragedies, deaths, disfigurements, and misery. *Such a Long Journey*, however, emerges more organically.

Sheldon Goldfarb

Other major works

short fiction: *Tales from Firozsha Baag*, 1987 (also known as *Swimming Lessons, and Other Stories from Firozsha Baag*, 1989).

Bibliography

Barucha, Nilufer E. *Rohinton Mistry: Ethnic Enclosures and Transcultural Spaces*. New Delhi, India: Rawat, 2003. Examines Mistry's work in relation to postcolonialism, and explores the issue of whether Mistry is a Parsi writer or a writer of universal themes. Criticizes Mistry's portrayal of Hindus in *A Fine Balance* but praises the compassion of *Such a Long Journey*.

Dodiya, Jaydipsinh. *The Fiction of Rohinton Mistry: Critical Studies*. New Delhi, India: Prestige, 1998. An uneven collection, but useful for seeing how critics in India view Mistry's portrayal of the country.

Genetsch, Martin. *The Texture of Identity: The Fiction*

of M. G. Vassanji, Neil Bissoondath, and Rohinton Mistry. Toronto, Ont.: Tsar, 2007. Includes useful background on the Parsi and on Zoroastrianism, and seeks to place Mistry in a Canadian context among other Canadian writers with South Asian connections. Provides useful analyses of Mistry's first three books.

Morey, Peter. *Rohinton Mistry*. New York: Manchester University Press, 2004. Includes biographical information, analyses of Mistry's four books, a summary of critical opinion, and an attempt to categorize Mistry in terms of realism and postcolonialism. Also includes useful background material on the Parsi and on Zoroastrianism.

BRIAN MOORE

Born: Belfast, Northern Ireland; August 25, 1921
Died: Malibu, California; January 11, 1999
Also known as: Michael Bryan; Bernard Mara

Principal long fiction

Judith Hearne, 1955 (also known as *The Lonely Passion of Judith Hearne*)
The Feast of Lupercal, 1957
The Luck of Ginger Coffey, 1960
An Answer from Limbo, 1962
The Emperor of Ice-Cream, 1965
I Am Mary Dunne, 1968
Fergus, 1970
Catholics, 1972
The Great Victorian Collection, 1975
The Doctor's Wife, 1976
The Mangan Inheritance, 1979
The Temptation of Eileen Hughes, 1981
Cold Heaven, 1983
Black Robe, 1985
The Colour of Blood, 1987 (also known as *The Color of Blood*)
Lies of Silence, 1990
No Other Life, 1993
The Statement, 1995
The Magician's Wife, 1997

Other literary forms

In addition to his novels, Brian Moore wrote a travel book, *Canada*, with the editors of *Life* magazine in 1963. A number of his works were regarded by Moore himself as hackwork, written to support his serious fiction; these include romances and mysteries, some published under the pseudonym Michael Bryan. His dozens of short stories appeared in a wide range of periodicals, from *Weekend Review* to *The Atlantic*, and in anthologies including *The Irish Genius*, edited by Devin A. Garrity (1960); *Canadian Writing Today*, edited by Mordecai Richler (1970); and *The Best American Short Stories, 1967* (1967), edited by Martha Foley and David Burnett. Throughout his writing career, he published many articles and reviews. Several of Moore's books have been adapted for films and television, and he wrote screenplays and teleplays produced in the United States, Canada, and Great Britain.

Achievements

Brian Moore's first novel, published both as *Judith Hearne* and as *The Lonely Passion of Judith Hearne*, established him as a contemporary novelist of the first order. He has appealed to many readers as a novelist who writes without embarrassment in the realistic tradition of the Victorians about distinctively modern topics: spiritual and erotic crises, the reality of the objective world, ethnic conflict, relationships between men and women, and the place of women in the societies of the old world and the new. Modern themes of alienation and estrangement are rooted firmly in Moore's work by a sense of place and of time. His evocation of Montreal in *The Luck of Ginger Coffey* has been compared to James Joyce's portrayal of Dublin on "Bloomsday." The bleak urban environment of Belfast of the earlier works and the windswept Irish coast of *The Mangan Inheritance* strike responsive chords in readers conditioned to the blank landscapes of much modernist literature.

Just as Moore's geographical terrain changes, however, so do his characters and his stylistic formats. From the almost naturalistic treatment of the unfortunate Judith Hearne to the ghostly dialogues of Fergus and the magical creation of *The Great Victorian Collection*, from the Jesuit missionaries in *Black Robe* to the terrorists in *Lies of Silence*, Moore's unpredictable inventiveness and his sure hand in storytelling and character development kept him in the forward ranks of late twentieth century novelists.

Among the honors Moore received were a Guggenheim Fellowship, an award from the American National Institute of Arts and Letters, a Canada Council Fellowship, the Author's Club of Great Britain First Novel Award, the Governor-General Award of Canada for fiction, and honorary literature degrees from Queens University, Belfast (1989) and National University of Ireland, Dublin (1991). He was three times short-listed for the Booker Prize, for *The Doctor's Wife*, *The Color of Blood*, and *Lies of Silence*. *Catholics* won the W. H. Smith Award in 1973, and *The Great Victorian Collection* won the James Tait Black Memorial Prize in 1975. *Black Robe* was given the Heinemann Award from the Royal Society of Literature in 1986.

Brian Moore. (Doubleday)

Biography

The basic facts of Brian Moore's life are familiar to anyone who knows his work, for he has mined heavily his own experiences for his novels. Moore was born in Belfast, in 1921, to James Bernard Moore, a fellow of the Royal College of Surgeons, and Eileen McFadden Moore. His childhood was a stable and fundamentally happy one; the warm and well-ordered O'Neill family in *Judith Hearne* was in fact identified by Moore in an interview as "a sort of facsimile of my own." Although his work reveals a continuing ambivalence about the order and protection of the family, as about other highly ordered forms of community, he clearly finds much to admire in the sort of family structure that provided his early nurturing.

Moore was educated in Catholic schools, leaving St. Malachi's College, Belfast, in 1940 to join the Air Raid Precautions Unit in Belfast. He served with that unit until 1942, when he left Belfast to serve as a civilian employee of the British Ministry of War Transport in North Africa, Italy, and France. Immediately after the war, he served as a port officer in Warsaw, and then remained for some time in Scandinavia, where he was a freelance reporter in Sweden, Finland, and Norway until he emigrated to Canada in 1948. From 1948 to 1952, he continued his career as a journalist in Montreal. His Canadian newspaper career began humbly; he was first a proofreader for the *Montreal Gazette*. He was promoted to reporter, an occupation he continued until he began writing pulp fiction to finance his serious work. Although some of his serious short fiction was published in the early 1950's, Moore was forced to continue to write pulp fiction until the appearance of *Judith Hearne* in 1955, and even after, under the pseudonym Michael Bryan.

The early stages of Moore's life and work essentially came to a close two years after the publication of *Judith*

Hearne with the appearance of his second novel, *The Feast of Lupercal*. Shortly thereafter, he moved to the United States from Canada, and in 1959, received the Guggenheim Fellowship that allowed him to complete one of his most highly regarded works, *The Luck of Ginger Coffey* (1960). Between 1960 and the publication of *The Emperor of Ice-Cream* in 1965, he published *An Answer from Limbo*. Moore said, in an interview with Hallvard Dahlie, that a dramatic change in his life occurred in the years between the publication of the latter two novels: "I am much happier now than I was when I was thirty-five or forty. *Emperor* was written at a crucial time in my life—it was the first book after I changed." That change was demonstrated also in his personal life during the year of *The Emperor of Ice-Cream*'s publication. In 1966, Moore married his second wife, Jean Denny, his first marriage having been to Jacqueline Sirois.

From 1966 until his death in 1999, Moore continued to publish at the rate of a novel every one to three years. Although he maintained Canadian citizenship, he continued to live in the United States, in a house overlooking the Pacific Ocean, near Oxnard, California.

Analysis

Although he became increasingly cosmopolitan in his adult life, Brian Moore's work is very much rooted in the place of his origin—Northern Ireland—in his middle-class Irish Catholic upbringing, and in concerns readers have learned to recognize in the work of several generations of Irish writers, from John Millington Synge, William Butler Yeats, and James Joyce to the present. In his earlier work at least, Moore was fettered by the ghost of Evelyn Waugh's Irishman, "dragging everywhere with him his ancient rancours and the melancholy of the bogs." That Irishman, however, is transformed by the multiplicity of thematic and structural interests of the inventive Moore.

Beginning with *Judith Hearne*, the themes that primarily occupied Moore throughout his literary career emerge. There is the struggle with the fathers—fathers embodied in the family, in the Church, in the community, and in Ireland itself, which Moore portrays as a restrictively ordered world isolated from the freer West by Joyce's "dark, mutinous Shannon waves" ("The Dead"). Against the protective but stultifying structures that order life, the individual spirit struggles. On the one side is safety and security, but with the prospect of extended childhood, with its continuing demands for obedience and submission. On the other is adulthood, individual responsibility, the possibility of liberation through the imagination beyond the childish fantasizing that characterizes life within the restricted community—but also on that side is the threat of the void.

The tension between these conflicting choices provides both form and substance to nearly all of Moore's serious fiction. In the earlier works, the struggle is overt and played out in simple correspondences. Judith Hearne, middle-aged, unmarried, and without real personal attachments, except in fantasy, faces literal extinction in her crisis of faith. Diarmud Devine is left sexually and morally powerless as he submits to the hierarchy of the fathers at St. Michan's, and Ginger Coffey is a man without country or community as he severs all ties that bind him to his Irish past.

The tension that characterizes Moore's work is a familiar one, as is the resulting ironic tone that several generations of modern critics since Allen Tate have described. Perhaps in no literature, however, is either the tension or the ironic tone more pervasive than in the Irish tradition to which Moore so clearly belongs. Certainly, the conflict between the desire to identify with and belong to the community on one hand and the need, on the other hand, to define oneself as an individual is nearly universal in Irish literature. Moreover, as Andrew Carpenter has noted, many Irish writers seem to have a double vision that derives "from a view of life that is continually probing the different values which exist in Ireland and testing them one against the other" and from immersion in "interrelationships between values, philosophies and cultures antipathetic if not downright hostile to one another." Irish writers thus come naturally to multiple points of view as well as to the idea that opposing points of view are equally acceptable; they "see two things at once," but "with one eye at a time." This peculiar double vision is manifestly present in Moore's fiction.

Judith Hearne

Explaining the protagonist of the same name of his first novel, *Judith Hearne*, Moore told Hallvard Dahlie that "I wanted my major character to be someone who wasn't me—who could never be mistaken for me. . . . And yet, I was lonely for much of my life, and so I put something of myself into her." This lonely spinster on the brink of middle age with her "chances" all behind her is bedeviled by the same Irish ghosts that confront nearly all of Moore's protagonists, male and female.

Judith Hearne is a true daughter of Catholic Ireland. The "real" world in which she lives is bounded by Church, family—or the idea of family—and sexual mores so restrictive that fantasy life becomes a compelling escape. In Moore's later novels, beginning with *Fergus*, this fantasy life imposed by the Irish past finds an outlet in art; Moore's protagonists become novelists, poets, and even, in *The Great Victorian Collection*, necromancers. For Judith, however, there are only pitiful and predictable adolescent fantasies. Nearly forty years old, Judith has found herself penniless, without home or family or prospects for either. Wherever she wanders in her penury and displacement after her aunt's death, she anchors herself with two objects: a photograph of her aunt and a picture of the Sacred Heart. Like a child, she ritualistically bids good night to these images of the only protective forces she knows as she turns off the light in her latest bed-sitter, and she is comforted by the knowledge that they are there for her in the darkness.

As her imaginary romance with Madden, the returned emigrant to America, unfolds, the childishness of Judith's fantasy life is revealed. Absorbed in personal ritual, she sits before her glass transforming through her imagination her plain, sallow face and angular figure into the "delightful illusion of beauty." Perhaps legitimately led to believe in Madden's interest in her—an interest later revealed to be motivated by a plan for a joint investment in a hamburger stand—Judith abandons herself to her fantasies. Her arrested sexual development and the debased view she, like nearly all of Moore's characters, has of the possibilities for relationships between men and women are demonstrated in a painful series of encounters with Madden, as in her daydreams about him: "He kissed her," she imagines, "Or, enraged about some silly thing she had done, he struck out with his great fist and sent her reeling, the brute. But, contrite afterwards, he sank to his knees and begged forgiveness."

Sexuality framed in violence, or tied to power struggles, is a hallmark of the identity crises that form the substance of so much of Moore's work. The submission and obedience demanded by religion and family preclude the assertiveness and self-confidence required for adult sexuality, or for any adult relationship. In the early novels, childish sexual fantasies, shaped by cheap romances and shadowed by disapproval of the fathers, are shattered in encounters with real men and women. Spiritual and erotic crises are thus established by Moore as essential to the search for identity in the restrictive world about which he writes.

Judith's passion is sexual, but it is the passion of religious suffering as well. When Judith's frantic search for meaning ends in her challenge to God in the tabernacle, even that door is locked against her. "In the old Irish choice between accepting actuality and retreating from it," Jeanne Flood observes, "the old Irish mistake is choosing the latter alternative." Judith's ultimate fiction at that moment of truth is to transform the scene into a pietà. Her imaginary salvation, like her crisis, is both religious and sexual:

> His mother ran up the altar steps, her painted face still sadly smiling, lifted her as she lay broken on the steps. . . . And He, His fingers uplifted in blessing, bent over her, His bleeding heart held against His white tunic. Lifted her in His arms and His face was close to hers.

In fantasy alone, Judith Hearne is able to have it all—the sheltering arms of family and religion, and the romantic encounter that can exist nowhere but in the adolescent imagination.

The Feast of Lupercal

Though more obviously autobiographical, Moore's second novel, *The Feast of Lupercal*, is essentially a variation on the themes established in *Judith Hearne*. Set also in contemporary Belfast, the novel follows the ill-fated adventures of Diarmud Devine, a master at St. Michan's, the same Catholic school that Devine attended as a boy. Devine, now thirty-seven, has spent his entire life within the academic hierarchy of the Church. The family persists as a central force in his life as well, for Diarmud lives in a rented room furnished with the accoutrements of his parents' home. He sleeps in his boyhood bed and is watched over in his daily routines by his dead mother and father posed stiffly in their wedding picture.

The Feast of Lupercal, from which the novel takes its name, was a Roman festival celebrating the god of fertility. Against the ironic backdrop of a study of the festival with his sex-obsessed, leering, adolescent pupils, Diarmud is offered a chance at adult sexuality. The challenge is to abandon childish fantasy and to accept the demands of an adult relationship with its dimensions of sexuality, responsibility, and power. The nearly middle-aged man is unable, however, to bring the moment to its close. At the crucial moment, Dev sees the real Una not as a sinful temptress but as a young girl in a white slip "so unlike his sinful imaginings . . . the sinful imagination which atrophied reality."

The repressive moral world from which Dev has been unable to manage even the slightest distance requires only the simple judgments of childhood, uncluttered by the ambiguities of adult life. So long as Una remained a "hot Protestant," a representative of the sex who were "mockers, character assassins, every single one of them," the simple equations on which Moore's Catholic Ireland rests could be sustained. "Fancy putting yourself in a position where a woman could laugh at you. An intimate moment, a ridiculous posture—a declaration of love, for instance. Or on your wedding night, to hear a girl laugh at you." In the tradition of the early Church Fathers, man is the spirit and woman the body—the defiling physical presence. The sight of a real and vulnerable young woman, however, undoes the myth, and him, in a culturally caused sexual dysfunction suffered by heroes throughout Moore's work.

Dev makes the "Irish choice," retreating from actuality. Afraid of censure from the hierarchy of the fathers, who are embroiled in a power struggle of their own that threatens Dev, he abandons Una to the consequences of the morally compromising position in which he has placed her, and resigns himself to his narrow and deprived existence. The

> boy who dreamed of marrying Madeleine Carroll, the film actress, and taking her to the Riviera where they would commit unknown flesh sins the priests warned about in sermons . . . [was] now a man of thirty-seven [who] had not lived a real life; he had been dreaming.

The Luck of Ginger Coffey

Moore's third novel, *The Luck of Ginger Coffey*, is set in Montreal, and its title character is a man who has nominally extricated himself from the ties of religion, family, and community that bind Judith Hearne and Dev. Still very much a son of Ireland, however, Ginger dreams of success in the New World, just as Judith dreams of love and marriage and Devine fantasizes sexual conquest. The affliction of the "Irish choice" makes Ginger a man for whom, as for Dev, real life is obscured by dreaming.

In Moore's later expatriate novels—and even at the end of *The Emperor of Ice-Cream*, when young Gavin Burke decides to leave Belfast—there is hope of fulfillment for his dreaming Irish men and women. Tierney in *An Answer from Limbo*, and the confused *poète maudit* of *The Mangan Inheritance*, Jamie Mangan, are endowed with the potentially transforming and liberating force of imagination. They are possessed of a creative power denied Ginger Coffey, as it had been denied to Judith and Dev.

Trapped in a series of cheap fictional images of success rooted in his Irish past, Ginger affects a Dublin squire look, and he thinks of himself as being in his soldierly prime, handsomely mustachioed and booted. A Canadian employer to whom he appeals sees him otherwise: "A limely type . . . with his tiny green hat, short bulky car coat and suede boots." Nor is he otherwise successful in adapting to his adopted country. The uniform of a diaper service delivery man is a mockery of his early dreams of military adventure. His dreams of an adventurous career as a journalist shrink in the cellar of the building where he works as a proofreader, and evaporate finally in the words of a dying coworker: "Irish. An immigrant same as you," the dying man tells him. Nearly forty, he looks at his dying compatriot and realizes what he has abandoned, and how little he has gained. Will he so end his days, "his voice nasal and reedy, all accent gone"? Coffey denies such a fate: "Yes, I'm Irish. James Francis Coffey. Fine Irish name."

In the end, though, Coffey is without country or community, and nearly without family, as his wife and daughter yield to the attractions of the vulgar materialism of the country to which he has brought them, in which he has insisted they stay, and where at last he resigns himself to life with them in "humble circs." His marriage to Veronica, née Shannon, whom he calls by a name for Ireland, "Dark Rosaleen," is his only tie to his native land. He must pay a dear price to sustain that tie, his only protection from the chaos that threatened Judith Hearne, and that Dev could not even contemplate. The price is to be what he most feared—an Irish failure, living with a wife he no longer wants, and working at a job worse than the one he left behind in the scorned Ulster.

An Answer from Limbo

Ginger Coffey represents to Moore, as he told Robert Fulford, "what I was terrified would happen to me. I've always felt myself to be a misfit, I still do." By contrast, Brendan Tierney, the protagonist of *An Answer from Limbo*, is the first of Moore's protagonists to possess the creative power that seems to have been Moore's salvation. Curiously, however, Tierney is a less sympathetic character than any of the three doomed and powerless protagonists who precede him in Moore's work. The hapless Judith, who suffers a woman's fate along with the burden of the Irish cross; the tragicomic Dev; and the feckless Ginger, who befriends the lonely child of his landlady in the middle of his troubles—all are caught in the grip of social circumstances, and all struggle to maintain dignity and humanity in spite of those circumstances. That humanity is absent in Brendan Tierney.

The theme of *An Answer from Limbo*, repeated in *Fergus* and in *I Am Mary Dunne*, is a problematic repudiation of the Irish past with its shackles of family, religion, and community in favor of a freer identity, shaped by the personal power of the imagination. Moore's disapproval of Tierney, as of later artist heroes, warns the reader, however, not to expect simple solutions to the conflict.

No childlike victim, no futile fantasizer, Brendan Tierney is a hard-eyed young writer who seems destined to achieve the success and fame for which he hungers. Replete with the self-confidence absent in Judith and Dev, and possessed of talent and purpose sadly lacking in Ginger, Brendan expects his future work to find a place among the ranks of "Kierkegaard and Camus, Dostoyevsky and Gide." As John Scanlan has observed, the theme here is Faustian. Tierney is the artist who sacrifices not only his own happiness for his art but also the well-being of those who have loved him or depended on him in the past. He drives his wife, Jane, into miserable infidelity; his rejected mother dies alone, waiting to return to Ireland. Mrs. Tierney is effectively "killed" by Brendan, who rejects her overtly and puts her out of his mind. In his single-minded devotion to his art, Brendan denies his past, the emotional solace and protection offered by Ireland, his family, and his religion. At the novel's end, he is overcome by the self-loathing that even Ginger Coffey was spared. Ginger was able to say at least, as he sought to reconcile himself to his failures, "Life itself is a victory." Brendan, even with the real prospect of attaining his dreams of success, is left with the knowledge that "I have altered beyond all self-recognition. I have lost and sacrificed myself."

I Am Mary Dunne

I Am Mary Dunne marked a shift in direction for Moore. Having achieved a kind of resolution of his old material with the altered—and happier—perspective of *The Emperor of Ice-Cream*, Moore was ready in this sixth novel to move into new territory. It is significant that the protagonist of the first novel in this less traditional phase is, like that of his first novel, a woman. Just as he wanted to ensure that his first major character "wasn't me—could never be mistaken for me," so *I Am Mary Dunne* is determined to avoid the appearance of autobiography. Despite its innovative style, the novel takes up many of Moore's familiar themes. Mary is an artist—a failed one, perhaps—and an Irish expatriate whose haunted past is full of the old ghosts of religion, a troublesome father, and an identity and community that elude her in both Canada and New York.

Moore, whose insights into female psychology as well as sexual politics were demonstrated in *Judith Hearne*, makes clear the importance of Mary's gender in her search for identity. She has fitted herself to each of her husbands, adopting a new identity with each name change. The novel's epigraph from Yeats is apt: It is no longer possible for Mary to tell the "dancer from the dance." She is threatened by the void that froze the earlier Moore characters into childhood, and drives the quest of the later characters for meaning through acts of the imagination. For Mary, though, the possibilities of the creative imagination have been discarded; her life as an actor is over, her potential as a writer and a painter lie fallow. Her current identity is defined by the successful playwright to whom she is now married. Thus, she tries to find herself by remembering who she once was—her mother's daughter, Mary Dunne.

Catholics

In *Catholics*, Moore's eighth novel and one of his best, the religious commitment that was a major hedge against the void for the victimized early characters regains center stage. For the first time, however, the struggles are sexless. Neither the relationship between men and women nor the exercise of sexual power is at issue here. The confrontation with the empty tabernacle is drawn pure and simple. On a remote rocky island in Kerry, a priest's personal crisis of faith is played out against the clinical relativism of a twenty-first century world, represented by James Kinsella, a young priest sent by Rome to obliterate the last vestiges of the old order to which the priests and parishioners of Muck Abbey still cling.

Unlike Judith Hearne, whose ultimate capacity for childlike fantasy offered her protection against the void, the Abbott has no defenses. He had chosen long ago to forsake all else for his God, and now he has found that "there is no Father in Heaven." When he tries to pray, he "enters null." When the young priest, Kinsella, arrives, the Abbott has not prayed in years. He sees his role as a manager of the Abbey, and also as a human bulwark for others against the void he has confronted. The Abbott knows, just as the behaviorist friend of young Kinsella knows, that "People don't want truth or justice. They want certainties. The old parish priest promised them that." Thus, the Abbott tries to deliver certainty, although it is lost to him. The past, however, is irredeemable. Its loss began long ago with "that righteous prig at Wittenberg nailing his defiance to the church door." The Abbott's attempt to recall it is doomed, as is he.

While those last lines absolve Moore of any suspicion of romanticizing the past of which he once despaired, the earlier faith in the possibilities of the imagination to liberate and to create its own enduring reality seems all but lost here. *The Great Victorian Collection*, Moore's next novel, continues that dark view of the power of the individual spirit and the creative imagination.

The Great Victorian Collection

Moore's increasingly pessimistic vision is expressed in the central conceit of *The Great Victorian Collection*: Anthony Maloney, an undistinguished young professor and student of Victorian life, dreams into existence an authentic and unprecedented collection of Victoriana, an opportunity for the creative synthesis of past and present, of tradition and the imagination, that would resolve the fundamental conflict Moore presents. Significantly, however, the Collection is dreamed into existence in California, a land of hollow dreams. Moreover, it appears in a motel parking lot in that precious California tourist mecca, Carmel-by-the-Sea, with its "galleries filled with local paintings, arcade shops selling homemade candles, and bookstores displaying the complete works of Kahil Gibran."

The California tourist town becomes, in this most imaginative of Moore's novels, a world that, however far in form and principle from Belfast, has an equivalent capacity to thwart the individual spirit and to stultify the creative process. Tony is trapped by the Collection, which begins to deteriorate as he allows his attention to waver from it. Trapped in the dilemma of the successful artist, he must involve other people in his work. Other people include, notably, a commercial agent whose efforts to "market" the Collection lead to great commercial success, but the real "success" is a facsimile of the Collection at a place and in a form more palatable to the public. Tony's own investment in his creation becomes increasingly detached, until the pieces of it become artificial, and his caretaking is mechanistic. His dreams are reduced to soul-deadening surveillance by a black-and-white television camera. Finally, he tries to destroy his deteriorated creation, but it has assumed a life of its own and is indestructible.

This parable of the failure of the imagination to liberate or to sustain the spirit includes Moore's familiar erotic crisis. The creation of The Great Victorian Collection seems to be connected with Maloney's relationship with the beautiful young girl who comes into his life almost immediately after the Collection appears. A Dutch clairvoyant warns him that she is important to what has happened, and indeed, Mary Ann McKelvey soon emerges as Tony's anchor to reality in the feverish life of the imagination in which he finds himself. In a scene highly reminiscent of Moore's early works, their first and only sexual encounter ends in disaster, with Mary Ann thinking she has "failed" Tony. In fact, as with Dev, the apprehension of Mary Ann as a real woman "undid him." Tony "was, and always would be, a dreamer. . . . No longer a man and maid in those far-off wicked times, they were now equals, contestants, almost enemies." Unable to live with the human challenges of the real world or with women who are real people, and faced in his life as an artist with a choice between commercial exploitation of his gifts or the caretaking of deteriorating museum pieces, Maloney chooses to end his own life.

The Mangan Inheritance

The connection between Moore's concern with a particular male inability to form adult sexual relationships and the failure of the imagination to craft a synthesis of tradition and the individual creative spirit is treated most directly in *The Mangan Inheritance*. In this novel the connection, at least in outline, is simplistic. Jamie Mangan, failed poet, failed husband, perhaps even failed son, uses the windfall from his wife's sudden death to try to bury his failures in a return to a romanticized past. His search in the Irish village of his ancestors for confirmation of his relationship to the nineteenth century *poète maudit* James Clarence Mangan is a search for validation by the past, and is as doomed to failure as that of the Abbott in *Catholics*.

Unlike some of Moore's previous protagonists, however, Jamie is able to acknowledge his failures and learn from them. He refuses to succumb to the romantic fantasies that have spoiled the lives of past and present members of his Irish family. The excesses of the *poète maudit* are revealed to him in their sordid reality in the lives of his Irish cousins. He even comes to see his sexual infatuation with the beautiful but slovenly teenage Kathleen for the destructive fantasy it is in the light of the story of incest and sexual abuse he hears from his Irish doppelgänger, Michael Mangan. In the end, Jamie is able to repudiate his fantasies, literary and sexual, and return to his dying father and to responsibility to a future generation. In the daguerreotype of James Clarence Mangan lying smashed beyond repair against the stones of a ruined Irish castle, Jamie sees the features of his dying father and "wished that those features were his own." Implicit is the promise that his father's unborn child, whom he has promised to protect, will be welcomed into a family free of romantic illusion about itself, and that Jamie has a chance at fulfillment in the real world. The resolution is not unshadowed, however, for Jamie was a poet, and apparently will be no longer.

The Temptation of Eileen Hughes

The note of guarded optimism on which *The Mangan Inheritance* ends is not repeated in Moore's next novel, *The Temptation of Eileen Hughes*. Bernard McAuley, the novel's "artist," is a strange admixture of Moore's earlier protagonists. Sexually paralyzed, though married to Mona, a beautiful woman who loves him, Bernard searches for identity and meaning in his life, ranging from "offering [himself] to God" as a priest and finding he "wasn't wanted," through studies of history, art, music, and business, and finally to his bizarre attempt to force his strangely celibate relationship with young Eileen Hughes into his sordid household.

The themes of sexual power and the act of the imagination attain a distorted unity in this novel. Bernard enacts an evolution into decadence, and in a confirmation of Moore's recurrent tendency to find healthy self-knowledge in women targeted as victims by male identity-seekers, Eileen ultimately understands the manipulative and powerful McAuleys: "It was not she who had been in their power but they in hers. She had escaped them. Would they escape her?" Like Mary Ann McKelvey, or Diarmud Devine's Una, Eileen is anchored in a reality to which men such as Bernard (and the women whose lives they steal) will be forever denied admission.

The four novels that followed *The Temptation of Eileen Hughes* are diverse in setting and character, yet they are linked both stylistically and thematically; together they mark a new phase in Moore's work. In three of the four—*Cold Heaven*, *The Color of Blood*, and *Lies of Silence*—Moore adopts the plot-scaffolding and many of the generic conventions of the thriller, while in *Black Robe*, set in the 1630's in the Canadian wilderness, he adopts the conventions of the historical adventure novel.

Some reviewers have seen in this shift an attempt on Moore's part to win a larger audience. If that is the case, the attempt must be judged a failure, for while these works have been well received by critics, they did not make Moore a best-selling author. It seems just as likely, though, that Moore turned to the thriller for other reasons. In *Black Robe*, which centers on the physical hardships and spiritual conflicts of a Jesuit missionary to the Indians, in *The Color of Blood*, a pre-glasnost novel set in Eastern Europe and focusing on a Roman Catholic cardinal and the prime minister of an unnamed nation closely resembling Poland, and in *Lies of Silence*, about a man who is inadvertently drawn into a plot by Irish Republican Army terrorists, Moore grounds individual moral conflicts in the context of larger social and political struggles.

THE STATEMENT

Moore's concern with history is evident in his last two novels, *The Statement* and *The Magician's Wife*. In the first of these he chooses as his subject the French government and Catholic Church's protection of and complicity with Nazi war criminals. The protagonist, Pierre Broussard, is based on Paul Touvier, a functionary of the Vichy government who was found guilty of war crimes and who spends twenty-five years hiding in monasteries and avoiding Jewish agents hired to assassinate him. To save the government embarrassment, he is eventually betrayed by a former police commissioner who has been aiding him in his flight.

Once again Moore finds a way to use the conventions of a popular thriller to present probing moral and political observations. However, the most compelling and challenging aspect of the novel is its concentration on the thoughts and torment of a monstrous individual. Broussard was an adroitly expert killing machine during the war, and he remains one after, as he eludes captors and assassins. In these ways the novel is oddly Dostoevskian in presenting a despicable person, in all his turpitude, yet showing him to be deeply pathetic.

Moore long wrestled with his own conflicted feelings about the Catholic Church, feelings he candidly expressed in interviews, and his books often represent oscillations in his attitudes toward issues of faith and dogma. *Cold Heaven* is a perfect example of literary agnosticism, wherein a woman is forced to deal with rationally inexplicable phenomena that priests and nuns have no trouble accepting as signs of divine intervention. *The Statement*, however, offers a bleaker vision of religion; here the Church, the putative exemplar of moral authority, is run by self-serving hypocrites bent on protecting their own political power before all else.

THE MAGICIAN'S WIFE

The Magician's Wife extends Moore's concerns with history, and once again he seizes on a tiny incident to reveal the workings of power and coercion. The setting is 1856 at Napoleon III's winter palace. The foremost magician of the day, Henri Lambert, and his wife, Emmeline, have been called for mysterious but presumably high purposes. The emperor informs him that he is to travel to Algiers, dazzle and terrify the local authorities with his illusions, and aid France in its conquest of this foreign territory. When the magician's assistant dies of cholera, his wife assumes that role; she becomes fascinated with the local Muslim leader, eventually seeking a clandestine audience and convincing him to forestall a planned jihad. Although he is successful, the magician is permanently injured when an outraged spectator shoots and paralyzes him.

Once again Moore's concerns with religion and faith are paramount, and the novel offers numerous comparisons between Christianity and Islam, with the deck stacked squarely in favor of the latter. When Emmeline contemplates these differences, she comes to profound personal realizations about cultures, politics, her marriage, and most sweepingly, the place of women in her world. She realizes that she is the sum of everyone else's projection of who she should be, and her experience emboldens her to begin defining herself in her own terms.

Moore wrote with grace, felicity, and remarkable insight; his novels do not obviously pontificate. He was deeply concerned with moral conflicts and the individual's search for identity and authenticity, and his characters are typically figures who endure profound crises. Moore manipulates otherwise humble forms, such as the thriller and the historical novel, to reach an audience and then to interrogate assumptions subtly.

Michele Wender Zak
Updated by David W. Madden

OTHER MAJOR WORKS

SCREENPLAYS: *The Luck of Ginger Coffey*, 1963 (adaptation of his novel); *Torn Curtain*, 1966; *The Slave*, 1967; *Catholics*, 1973 (adaptation of his novel); *Black Robe*, 1991 (adaptation of his novel).

NONFICTION: *Canada*, 1963; *The Revolution Script*, 1971.

Bibliography

Craig, Patricia. *Brian Moore: A Biography*. London: Bloomsbury, 2002. An authorized biography of Moore, which recounts the events and influences in his life that led him to create his fiction.

Dahlie, Hallvard. *Brian Moore*. Boston: Twayne, 1981. This comprehensive study of Moore discusses his short stories and nonfiction as well as his novels. Dahlie addresses the metaphysical dilemmas presented in some of Moore's characters who struggle for identity and meaning. Selected bibliography and chronology.

Flood, Jeanne A. *Brian Moore*. Lewisburg, Pa.: Bucknell University Press, 1974. Covers Moore's work until 1973, with some emphasis on *Catholics*. Each chapter looks at a different position taken by the novelist. This slim volume is a solid piece of criticism and contains much insight into Moore's narrative technique and purpose. Includes a chronology and bibliography.

Gearon, Liam. *Landscapes of Encounter: The Portrayal of Catholicism in the Novels of Brian Moore*. Calgary, Alta.: University of Calgary Press, 2002. Gearon analyzes Moore's novels to examine his treatment of Catholicism, showing how this depiction was altered after the Church initiated its Vatican II reforms. This study also includes a discussion of Moore's portrayal of the Catholic Church in the modern world.

O'Donoghue, Jo. *Brian Moore: A Critical Study*. Montreal: McGill-Queen's University Press, 1991. Examines sixteen novels in terms of Moore's spiritual questioning and the personal search for freedom. Although the study examines each novel, particular emphasis is given to his novels dealing with female protagonists.

Sampson, Denis. *Brian Moore: The Chameleon Novelist*. Dublin: Marino Books, 1998. Sampson interviewed Moore and members of his family, as well as friends and colleagues, to write this biography, which chronicles Moore's life and discusses his literary works.

Sullivan, Robert. *A Matter of Faith: The Fiction of Brian Moore*. Westport, Conn.: Greenwood Press, 1996. An extensive and detailed treatment of Moore's fiction, examining novels up to *No Other Life*. Concentrates on the themes of love and faith and suggests that the writer's oeuvre is a cohesive master narrative. Sullivan is equally concerned with issues of craft and reveals the author's dedication to the art of fiction.

GEORGE MOORE

Born: Moore Hall, County Mayo, Ireland; February 24, 1852
Died: London, England; January 21, 1933
Also known as: George Augustus Moore

Principal long fiction

A Modern Lover, 1883
A Mummer's Wife, 1884
A Drama in Muslin, 1886
A Mere Accident, 1887
Spring Days, 1888
Mike Fletcher, 1889
Vain Fortune, 1891
Esther Waters, 1894
Evelyn Innes, 1898
Sister Teresa, 1901
The Lake, 1905
Muslin, 1915
The Brook Kerith, 1916
Lewis Seymour and Some Women, 1917
Héloise and Abélard, 1921
Ulick and Soracha, 1926
Aphrodite in Aulis, 1930

Other literary forms

George Moore was a man of letters rather than purely a novelist. He published seven collections of short fiction, and all but the first of his eight plays were produced in London or Dublin. He published two volumes of poetry in 1877 and 1881. Moore published numerous nonfictional works, and more than one thousand of his periodical writings have been located in English, Irish, French, and American journals. In addition, he published a notable translation of Longus's *Daphnis and Chloë* in 1924.

Achievements

George Moore's fiction was at all times innovative and influential. Amid much controversy in the early 1880's, he adapted the methods of French realism to the English novel. His earliest goals were to liberate the novel from Victorian conventions of subject and treatment and from commercial constraints imposed by a monopolistic book trade.

By the middle 1880's, Moore began to turn from realism to aestheticism. Under the influence of his friend Walter Pater and the rising Symbolist poets of France, Moore anticipated the "decadence" of the 1890's by eschewing the conflict between realism and popular Romanticism that had formerly absorbed him. He realized that these schools of writing were generally organized and evaluated on moral and social grounds. In regard to prose narrative, Moore's increasing and then sole preoccupation became literary art.

As an aesthete in the early 1890's, he composed his masterpiece *Esther Waters*. He also wrote some of the short stories that later contributed to his reputation as an inventor of modern Irish fiction. The large income generated by his books allowed him to quit his second career as one of England's leading art critics. He cofounded the Independent Theatre and Irish Literary Theatre and by the turn of the century he became a leading polemicist of the Irish revival.

The major achievement of Moore's Irish involvement was the composition of *Hail and Farewell: A Trilogy* (1911-1914). In the tradition of Laurence Sterne, Thomas De Quincey, and George Borrow, Moore wrote the story of his life using the conceptual framework of fiction rather than history. The trilogy contains an account of artistic movements of the late Victorian era, but attention is concentrated on the intellectual life of Dublin in the early years of the twentieth century.

During the 1910's and 1920's, Moore retreated from the popular literary market to the composition of prose epics. Biblical history in *The Brook Kerith*, medieval history in *Héloise and Abélard*, and classical history in *Aphrodite in Aulis* offered structural premises for a new exploration of human problems and for the development of a modern, rarefied aestheticism. Reviewers greeted the novels as exemplars of composition and elevated Moore to the status of Ireland's senior man of letters.

Biography

The Moores of Moore Hall were a prominent Catholic family in the west of Ireland. Their home, a large, gray, stone mansion presiding over 12,500 acres, was built in 1795 by George Moore, the novelist's great-grandfather. The founder of Moore Hall was a businessman. His eldest son, Peter, was certified insane for most of his life; the second son, John, was martyred in the 1798 rebellion (see Thomas Flanagan's novel *The Year of the French*, 1979); the youngest son, George, the novelist's grandfather, was a scholarly historian. George inherited the estate and through marriage established an intimate connection with the Brownes of Westport. His eldest son was George Henry Moore (1810-1870), a keeper of excellent racing stables and member of Parliament for the nationalist cause. In 1851, he married Mary Blake (1829-1895), daughter of a neighboring landlord.

George Augustus Moore, the eldest of G. H. Moore's five children, was born at Moore Hall on February 24, 1852. He was a robust but rather backward child: a late talker, then an endearing but poor pupil under a succession of governesses. Beginning in 1861, he attended Oscott College, Birmingham, a famous preparatory school designed as the Catholic complement of Eton or Harrow. He remained at Oscott until 1868, when his learning disabilities finally convinced the headmaster that further attempts at instruction would be futile.

After leaving Oscott, Moore lived with his parents in London while Parliament was in session. His time was divided between military tutors and amusements, including betting shops, music halls, and painting studios. When his father died suddenly in 1870, the quest for an army commission was dropped, and soon Moore was devoting most of his energy to the study of painting.

From 1873 until 1879, he lived mostly in Paris, first as a student painter at the École des Beaux Arts and

Académie Julian. Before setting aside his brushes in 1875, he had received instruction from James Whistler, John Millais, Alexandre Cabanel, and several less famous painters in France and England. Education did not make a painter of him, but it did help make him a sensitive art critic later in life. His first steps in literature during the later 1870's were likewise tentative. He was enraptured with French Romantic drama and Parnassian poetry. By the time the income from his property suddenly failed and he was forced to leave France, he had published two volumes of exotic juvenile verse and a large Romantic drama that was intended for but declined by Henry Irving.

Moore's literary career properly began in London in 1881. He was then settled in inexpensive rooms near the Strand and determined to make a living by his pen. While developing the plan of a naturalistic novel, he contributed paragraphs and reviews to the weekly press. Among his friends he numbered several poets and critics of the Pre-Raphaelite circle, but these receded as his friendship with Émile Zola became a discipleship. "When I attacked the Philistine," Algernon Charles Swinburne commented after reading *A Mummer's Wife*, "it was not with a chamber pot for a buckler and a dung fork for a spear." Moore's first two novels and his early journalism, although consonant with the ideals of the French avant-garde, drew charges of indecency from English readers. Although he moderated his style as his aestheticism changed, the reputation he earned at the start of his career remained with him, and all of his fiction until the turn of the century was banned from the circulating libraries.

Moore continued to live in the vicinity of the Strand until 1886, when he moved to a village near Brighton and afterward to a house atop the Sussex downs. In the English countryside he found an almost idyllic refuge from the distractions of London. His fiction of the period shows an increasing tolerance of ordinary life, and his literary theories, which he collected for *Confessions of a Young Man* (1888), reveal a firmer, more self-reliant mind than was evident before. He returned to London in 1889, engaged to write art criticism for his brother's magazine *The Hawk* and, more important, with the plan for a novel that became *Esther Waters*.

George Moore. (Library of Congress)

From 1889 until 1895, Moore contributed columns of art criticism briefly to *The Hawk* and then to *The Speaker*, both weekly reviews of politics and the arts. He was the first Impressionist art critic in England. Aside from writing fiction and criticism, he became deeply involved in theater reform and in 1890 cofounded the Independent Theatre, where Henrik Ibsen and George Bernard Shaw had their London premieres. With the publication of *Esther Waters*, Moore was soon able to leave the staff of *The Speaker*.

During the rest of the 1890's, Moore was prominent among the aesthetes and Decadents generally associated with *The Yellow Book*. He also took a publicized interest in the revival of early music, begun by his friend Arnold Dolmetsch, and in Wagnerism. His annual pilgrimage to Bayreuth began at this time, and his last novel of the century is permeated with musical theory. Drawn by the ideas of William Butler Yeats and others concerning the artistic possibilities of Gaelic, he also became involved in the Irish revival. With Yeats and Edward Martyn he founded the Irish Literary Theatre (precursor of the Abbey). In 1901, enamored of the "new Ireland" and bitterly depressed by British conduct of the Boer War, Moore leased a house in Upper Ely Place, near St. Stephen's Green in Dublin. He remained there until 1911.

Owing mainly to aesthetic and religious convictions, Moore's return to Ireland was characterized more by frustration than success. Having learned his profession in Paris and London, he could feel little sympathy for the relatively parochial challenges that writers of the movement faced. His advocacy of intellectual freedom for the artist was inappropriate to prevailing ideology. Worse, his notion that a politically free Ireland was one that would disown both Westminster and the Vatican virtually exiled him from the cause he tried to embrace. Though he made several friends among literary Dubliners, wrote polemics in the Irish press, and published important fiction, his greatest achievement was the comic indictment of the movement that appeared, after he left Dublin, in *Hail and Farewell*.

From 1911 until his death, Moore lived in Ebury Street, London. For the first time he was associated with no movement but instead practiced his art purely as an individual. His fiction and books of theory were welcomed by an elite readership of a few thousand. His best friends were the English Impressionist painters who lived in nearby Chelsea. Turning about-face on the six-shilling format he had invented with publisher Henry Vizetelly in 1884, he issued his books in limited, sometimes elegantly illustrated editions that took him entirely out of the popular market. He died in his home on January 21, 1933, and was buried on an island in Lough Carra, in front of Moore Hall. Because the rites of burial were pagan, a police guard was called to protect the funeral. George Russell composed the oration and the epitaph of George Moore: "He forsook his family and friends for his art. But because he was faithful to his art his family and friends reclaimed his ashes for Ireland. VALE."

ANALYSIS

Thirty of George Moore's fifty years as a novelist postdate the Victorian era, yet he is not generally remembered as a modern writer. To some extent this is because his aestheticism was the outcome of inspiration rather than experiment. "I desire above all things," he wrote in 1892, "to tell the story of life in grave simple phrases, so grave and simple that the method, the execution would disappear, and the reader, with bating breath, would remain a prey to an absorbing emotion."

Complexity and diversity are striking characteristics of the Moore corpus. He told "the story of life" ranging from classical Greece (*Aphrodite in Aulis*) to industrial England (*A Mummer's Wife*). His changing style reflected the influence of diverse writers, including Gustave Flaubert, Ivan Turgenev, and Walter Pater. Confused by such diversity, Arthur Symons reached the conclusion that Moore had no style, and James Whistler believed that he had no conscience. In a curious way this is true. He achieved not style, but expression. As an artist he avoided moral judgments and ceased his endeavors after discovering the soul in the body, the idea in action. The nature of his critical theories and the evolution of his fiction confirm that he was not a modernist, but a classicist.

A MODERN LOVER

Moore's first novel, *A Modern Lover*, like his last, is a study of artistic temperament. The chief protagonist is Lewis Seymour, a young painter of middling talent whose problem is to advance his career. He is attracted to a fraternity of avant-garde artists called the moderns, who advocate a radical departure from academic painting. However, he realizes that to achieve success in the sense of worldly recognition, he must be conventional and flatter the tastes of an ignorant public. The narrative traces Lewis's development as a painter with a "market" that expands in proportion to the distance between himself and personal integrity.

A Modern Lover represents the first conscious attempt to write a naturalistic novel in English. Reviewers noticed its power. In addition to its literary qualities, the novel offers an account of conflicting trends in art: The moderns are painters modeled on the French Impressionists; the medievalists are modeled on the Pre-Raphaelites; the Royal Academy appears as a copy of the original. Through the character of John Harding, Moore expounded his own views as a critic of Victorian culture and advocated reforms that prepared the way for a new definition of modern art.

Susan Mitchell noted in her study of Moore that he had an uncanny ability to understand women. *A Mummer's Wife* and *A Drama in Muslin* may be regarded as portraits of women: the first novel rather sinister and tragic, the second almost feminist and deeply encouraging.

A Mummer's Wife

Kate Ede is introduced in *A Mummer's Wife* as the wife of a shopkeeper living in the industrial town of Hanley. She is a young woman of sober character and dry religious convictions. Dick Lennox, the actor-manager of a touring company, rents lodgings in her house and seduces her. She is persuaded to leave her unhappy marriage and to accompany Dick on his travels. In Moravia, Kate's self-discipline gives way to a sensuous dreaminess. After becoming an actor, she marries Dick and has a baby by him, but her course runs steadily downward. As the moral underpinnings of her life are loosened, she slips almost unawares into depravity and dies in the end, an alcoholic among prostitutes.

A Drama in Muslin

Alice Barton, the heroine of *A Drama in Muslin*, is the daughter of an Irish landlord. She is an intellectual girl and rather homely; consequently she is unfitted for the grotesque "marriage market" of the Castle season in Dublin. Her sister and acquaintances spend their energy and sometimes dignity in preparing for the most important event of their lives: the entrapment of a moneyed young man in matrimony. All the innocence, loveliness, and promise of girlhood are publicly and somewhat brutally bartered for the passing illusions of title and fortune. Alice remains aloof, quietly preparing herself for a literary career. In the end, because of her intelligence and self-reliance, she alone makes a happy marriage.

Apart from many distinguishing features, the one shared by Kate Ede and Alice Barton is a departure from the common rut of experience. When Kate becomes the mummer's mistress, she breaks free from the paralyzing control of her husband and mother-in-law. During the months before conscience prods her to become the mummer's wife, she achieves sexual and emotional fulfillment and finds herself on the verge of a career and independence. Kate's is not a social tragedy: The opportunity to change her life was offered, but for personal reasons she neglected it. Alice's success is likewise of her own making. The reader finds soon after beginning *A Drama in Muslin* that the heroine is set apart less by her lack of beauty than by her strength of character. By virtue of a correct perception of Vanity Fair, Alice disentangles herself from the fatal bonds of family, class, and background to secure a hopeful future.

Esther Waters

Esther Waters, properly regarded as one of the greater novels in English literature, is also one of the least understood. From the year of its publication, reviewers and scholars have persisted in classing it as a realistic novel, using "realism" to mean an imitation of nature.

Esther Waters has been bound in its reputation of realism because Moore's choice of a subject from nature was powerful enough to be blinding. His protagonists were servants, characters whose place in English fiction had been confined to doing odd jobs and providing comic entertainment. Now they were comprehended as full human beings and their vast subculture moved from the periphery to the center of consciousness. The force of Moore's decision to write about servants was increased by the novel's central problem: the struggle of an unmarried mother to rear her child. By making Esther Waters his heroine, Moore overturned an array of Victorian sexual mores and political assumptions.

It is not surprising that the controversy that greeted publication of the novel distracted readers from its artistic merits. It must be emphasized, however, that Moore was no champion of the working class; he was neither a sociologist nor a philanthropist. He was only what he claimed to be: an artist. Essentially, he was no more interested in servant girls than his friend Edgar Degas was interested in ballerinas: They merely represented new opportunities for artistic expression. To think otherwise is to obscure the development of Moore's fiction and to ignore his many explanations of his aestheticism.

The quality of beauty Moore captured in *Esther Waters* may be summarized in its theme: the drama of motherhood, the presence in human nature of maternal instincts that create and protect life in a threatening environment. Rising from numerous realistic scenes in mansion, tenement, hospital, and public house, at racecourses and in the streets of London, the ineffable mystery of human love and self-sacrifice irradiates the text. At the conclusion of the novel Esther does not inherit a fortune; her son does not grow up to be prime minister; the villains are not punished and the heroes are not rewarded. A life of dedicated struggle is simply allowed to come to rest with a mild sense of achievement. In so doing, this ordinary life becomes a thing of extraordinary beauty.

Evelyn Innes

Evelyn Innes is another study of a woman seeking independence from stifling conventions and expectations. Evelyn, the daughter of a musicologist, carries on relationships with two men, each representing a principle of her life. Sir Owen Asher, the patron of her opera singing career, is the carnal. Ulick Dean, a musician and mystic, is the intellectual. The contradictory emotions these men inspire make her anxious about personal morality. The narrative traces her meditations until they reach a logical though drastic conclusion: religious vocation. Evelyn abandons love, career, and society, entering a convent in a desperate attempt to reconcile her life with her conscience. The novel concludes with a statement of her mature beliefs, which might be characterized as a somewhat secularized Christianity.

Moore did not explain why an author who cherished personal freedom, did not believe in God, and hated Catholicism should feel compelled to write the story of Evelyn Innes. Compelled by his imagination he certainly was, for he continued to revise the work for ten years until putting it aside, unsatisfied. It is possible that the trappings of Catholicism and musical theory were as incidental to his purpose as the kitchen and garret were in *Esther Waters*. He was essentially concerned about the problem posed by a woman's liberation from traditional restraint and the use to which she puts her freedom. Kate Ede in *A Mummer's Wife* shared Evelyn's dilemma, though in a different setting.

During the last twenty-five years of Moore's career, his longer fiction was historical. Ancient and medieval landscapes of Greece, Palestine, and France were more capable of supporting his literary ideas, though he continued to view the twentieth century in Great Britain through the media of essay and autobiography.

Moore's turn from modern subjects was accompanied by a turn from modern spoken English. In regard to both subject and treatment, he wished to emulate Pater, whose pure literary English was free of associations carried over from worldly usage and whose setting, in the much admired *Marius the Epicurean* (1885), was remote enough from mundane reality to assume more easily the aura of myth.

The Brook Kerith

The Brook Kerith retells the story of Christ in accordance with the Synoptic Gospels and later histories but adds an enormous new dimension by allowing him to survive the crucifixion and live, in thoughtful retirement, at an Essene monastery. Christ in the Bible struck Moore as an unfinished man, a visionary glimpsed only in his immaturity. As Christ matures he develops a more generous and sympathetic morality as part of a better understanding of humanity. At the conclusion of the novel, St. Paul comes to the monastery. Messiah and apostle are brought face-to-face. When Christ hears about the founding of the bellicose Christian tradition, he is horrified. When Paul learns the identity of his auditor, he rages and strikes Christ to the ground. Their paths soon part, Paul to carry his dogma to Europe and Christ to carry the truth to Jerusalem.

Héloise and Abélard

The process of humanizing religious history and of faulting dogma in favor of free intelligence is continued in *Héloise and Abélard*. The figure of Abélard as perhaps the first Renaissance man was profoundly attractive to Moore, but he was equally moved by his conception of Héloise, who is his chief protagonist. The novel pits intellectual freedom and its complement, wholesome sexual love, against the rigors of doctrine and medieval customs of chastity and celibacy. In its blending of landscape and character, idea and expression, *Héloise and Abélard* might well be ranked the most nearly perfect "aesthetic novel" ever written.

Aphrodite in Aulis

In order to strengthen his sense of place in *The Brook Kerith* and *Héloise and Abélard*, Moore had traveled over Palestine and France and "assimilated" culture. By the time he had the plan for *Aphrodite in Aulis*, however, he was too old and frail to make a tour of Greece. Illness for the first time settled in his body, and, though his mind remained vigorous, he was forced to live with a great deal of pain. Despite these obstacles, he achieved a final novel of abundant mystery and flawed but engrossing beauty.

The story is set in Greece of the fifth century B.C.E. Kebren, a young Athenian actor and rhapsodist, settles in Aulis as the husband of Biote and business partner of her father, Otanes. Biote gives birth to two sons, Rhesos the sculptor and Thrasillos the architect. After a period of training under Phidias in Athens, the brothers return to Aulis and marry their cousins Earine and Melissa. Earine is the inspiration for the figure of Aphrodite that Rhesos carves for a temple in Aulis. Following her role of inspiration, at the conclusion of the novel she embraces a new role as the mother of his children.

The book may be read as an act of devotion to art and thus a fitting conclusion to Moore's career. Throughout the narrative, art and life are almost hypnotically counterpointed. Each recovers the continuing theme from the other, seeming for a moment to frustrate the other's aims. In the end an exquisite harmony occurs: Art is animated by life, while life is beautified and ennobled by art. That harmony characterizes the oeuvre of George Moore.

Robert Becker

Other major works

SHORT FICTION: *Parnell and His Island*, 1887; *Celibates*, 1895; *The Untilled Field*, 1903; *Memoirs of My Dead Life*, 1906; *A Story-Teller's Holiday*, 1918; *In Single Strictness*, 1922; *Peronnik the Fool*, 1924; *Celibate Lives*, 1927; *A Flood*, 1930; *In Minor Keys: The Uncollected Short Stories of George Moore*, 1985 (David B. Eakin and Helmut E. Gerber, editors).

PLAYS: *Martin Luther*, pb. 1879 (with Bernard Lopez); *The Strike at Arlingford*, pr., pb. 1893; *The Bending of the Bough*, pr., pb. 1900; *Diarmuid and Grania*, pr. 1901 (with William Butler Yeats); *Esther Waters*, pr. 1911; *The Apostle*, pb. 1911; *Elizabeth Cooper*, pr., pb. 1913; *The Making of Immortal*, pb. 1927; *The Passing of the Essenes*, pr., pb. 1930 (revision of *The Apostle*).

POETRY: *Flowers of Passion*, 1878; *Pagan Poems*, 1881.

NONFICTION: *Confessions of a Young Man*, 1888; *Impressions and Opinions*, 1891; *Modern Painting*, 1893; *Hail and Farewell: A Trilogy*, 1911-1914 (*Ave*, 1911; *Salve*, 1912; *Vale*, 1914); *Avowals*, 1919; *Conversations in Ebury Street*, 1924; *Letters from George Moore to Edouard Dujardin, 1886-1922*, 1929; *The Talking Pine*, 1931; *A Communication to My Friends*, 1933; *Letters of George Moore*, 1942; *Letters to Lady Cunard*, 1957 (Rupert Hart-Davis, editor); *George Moore in Transition: Letters to T. Fisher Unwin and Lena Milman, 1894-1910*, 1968 (Gerber, editor).

TRANSLATION: *Daphnis and Chloë*, 1924 (of Longus).

Bibliography

Dorré, Gina M. "Reading and Riding: Late-Century Aesthetics and the Cultural Economy of the Turf in George Moore's *Esther Waters*." In *Victorian Fiction and the Cult of the Horse*. Burlington, Vt.: Ashgate, 2006. Dorré analyzes *Esther Waters* and other Victorian-age novels to describe their inclusion of horses to reflect Victorian society during a period of massive technological, economic, and social change.

Dunleavy, Janet Egleson. *George Moore: The Artist's Vision, the Storyteller's Art*. Lewisburg, Pa.: Bucknell University Press, 1973. A review of Moore's writings, presented in chronological form, with particularly useful commentary on his earlier novels. Dunleavy describes the societal influences on Moore's work and his changing ideas about literary form, style, theme, and characterization.

_______, ed. *George Moore in Perspective*. New York: Barnes & Noble Books, 1983. A compilation of critical essays on Moore that discuss his Irish background and the Irish Literary Renaissance, his connections with Samuel Beckett, and his relationship to James Joyce. The appendix includes a bibliographical essay by Edwin Gilcher.

Fratantaro, Sal. *The Methodology of G. E. Moore*. Brookfield, Vt.: Ashgate, 1998. Part of the Avebury series in philosophy, this volume presents a comprehensive description of Moore's complex philosophy and the methodology he used in his fiction.

Frazier, Adrian. *George Moore, 1852-1933*. New Haven, Conn.: Yale University Press, 2000. A thorough biography, drawing on much previously unpublished material and emphasizing Moore's historical and cultural context. This is not a critical examination of his works but a narrative of his life, including his time in Paris during the era of Impressionism and in Dublin during the Irish Literary Renaissance.

Gray, Tony. *A Peculiar Man: A Life of George Moore*. London: Sinclair-Stevenson, 1996. A good, updated biography of Moore, which takes into account his different vocations, such as art critic and landowner. Includes a short bibliography and an index.

Grubgeld, Elizabeth. *George Moore and the Autogenous Self: The Autobiography and Fiction*. Syracuse, N.Y.: Syracuse University Press, 1994. As Grubgeld's title suggests, she explores the interdependence of Moore's fiction and autobiography; her discussion of narrating and remembering is especially good. Includes detailed notes and an extensive bibliography.

Jeffares, A. Norman. *George Moore*. London: Longmans, 1965. Part of the British Council series and one of the best short introductions to the author and his work. Jeffares devotes a chapter to Moore's life and another to a discussion of his novels.

Pierse, Mary, ed. *George Moore: Artistic Visions and Literary Worlds*. Newcastle, England: Cambridge Scholars Press, 2006. A collection of papers delivered at a 2005 international conference on Moore. The papers analyze Moore's works, discussing, among other topics, his literary innovations, avant-garde feminism, and his literary significance and legacy.

Swafford, Kevin. "Reification and Respectability in Thomas Hardy's *Tess of the D'urbervilles* and George Moore's *Esther Waters*." In *Class in Late-Victorian Britain: The Narrative Concern with Social Hierarchy and Its Representation*. Youngstown, N.Y.: Cambria Press, 2007. Swafford's study of how social-class distinctions were depicted by late nineteenth century British authors includes this comparison of *Esther Waters* with a famous novel by Thomas Hardy.

ALBERTO MORAVIA

Born: Rome, Italy; November 28, 1907
Died: Rome, Italy; September 26, 1990
Also known as: Alberto Pincherle Moravia

Principal long fiction

Gli indifferenti, 1929 (*The Indifferent Ones*, 1932; also known as *The Time of Indifference*, 1953)
Le ambizioni sbagliate, 1935 (*The Wheel of Fortune*, 1937; also known as *Mistaken Ambitions*)
La mascherata, 1941 (*The Fancy Dress Party*, 1947)
Agostino, 1944 (English translation, 1947)
La romana, 1947 (*The Woman of Rome*, 1949)
La disubbidienza, 1948 (*Disobedience*, 1950)
L'amore coniugale, 1949 (*Conjugal Love*, 1951)
Il conformista, 1951 (*The Conformist*, 1951)
Il disprezzo, 1954 (*A Ghost at Noon*, 1955)
La ciociara, 1957 (*Two Women*, 1958)
La noia, 1960 (*The Empty Canvas*, 1961)
L'attenzione, 1965 (*The Lie*, 1966)
Io e lui, 1971 (*Two: A Phallic Novel*, 1972)
La vita interiore, 1978 (*Time of Desecration*, 1980)
1934, 1982 (English translation, 1983)
L'uomo che guarda, 1985 (*The Voyeur*, 1986)
Il viaggio a Roma, 1988 (*Journey to Rome*, 1990)

Other literary forms

Though he is known primarily as a novelist, especially outside Italy, Alberto Moravia was equally productive as a short-story writer. Not available in translation until the 1950's, Moravia's short stories brought him considerable recognition in his own country. The majority of Moravia's short stories appeared in collected form, usually after an initial publication in a literary journal or newspaper, in the following volumes: *La bella vita* (1935), *L'epidema: Racconti surrealistici e satirici* (1944), *Due cortigiane* (1945), *Racconti romani* (1954; *Roman Tales*, 1956), *Nuovi racconti romani* (1959;

More Roman Tales, 1963), *L'automa* (1963; *The Fetish*, 1964), *Una cosa è una cosa* (1967; *Command and I Will Obey You*, 1969), *Il paradisio* (1970; *Paradise, and Other Stories*, 1971; also known as *Bought and Sold*, 1973), *Un'altra vita* (1973; *Lady Godiva, and Other Stories*, 1975; also known as *Mother Love*, 1976), and *Boh* (1976; *The Voice of the Sea, and Other Stories*, 1978). Two useful comprehensive editions of Moravia's stories are *I racconti, 1927-1951* (1952) and *I racconti di Alberto Moravia* (1968), though they must be supplemented by the collections published subsequently.

In addition to his fiction, Moravia also published and produced a number of plays, including dramatic versions of *Gli indifferenti* (pr., pb. 1948) and *La mascherata* (pr. 1954), as well as several original dramas: *Beatrice Cenci* (pr. 1955; English translation, 1965), *Il mondo è quello che è* (pr., pb. 1966; *The World's the World*, 1970), *Il dio Kurt* (pr., pb. 1968), and *La vita è gioco* (pb. 1969). The collected edition of his plays is published as *Teatro* (1998; 2 volumes).

Moravia's travel essays appeared in four collections: *Un mese in U.R.S.S.* (1958), *Un'idea dell'India* (1962), *La rivoluzione culturale in Cina* (1967; *The Red Book and the Great Wall*, 1968), and *A quale tribù appartieni?* (1972; *Which Tribe Do You Belong To?*, 1974).

Moravia also wrote a large body of polemical essays on literature, politics, religion, and other topics. These appear in *Saggi italiani del 1959* (1960) and *L'uomo come fine, e altri saggi* (1964; *Man as an End: A Defence of Humanism—Literary, Social, and Political Essays*, 1965). They are collected in a comprehensive edition, along with other, previously uncollected, polemical writings, in *Impegno controvoglia: Saggi, articoli, interviste* (1980).

Numerous film adaptations of Moravia's work have been made, not only in Italy but also in other countries, by some of Europe's leading filmmakers. Among the best-known of them are Vittorio De Sica's *La ciociara* (1960; *Two Women*, 1961), Michelangelo Antonioni's *L'avventura* (1960), Damiano Damiani's *La noia* (1964; *The Empty Canvas*, 1964), Jean-Luc Godard's *Le mépris* (1964; *Contempt*, 1964), Bernardo Bertolucci's *Il conformista* (1969; *The Conformist*, 1970), and *L'amore coniugale* (1970), directed by Moravia's wife, Dacia Maraini.

Achievements

Alberto Moravia is an important figure in the history of modern Italian literature for several reasons. First, and for some literary historians most important, is Moravia's popularity with a large, widely dispersed international reading audience. He is, by far, the most widely translated modern Italian novelist. Every one of his novels has been translated into English, for example, as well as nearly all of his shorter fiction. This international popularity is, no doubt, helped by the frequent practice of marketing his works as soft-core pornography in paperback editions, so that his work is made to appeal to an audience much wider than those who would read it solely for its literary qualities. This practice is made possible by the prominence of sexuality in Moravia's fiction, but it would be misleading to think of this erotic content as an end in itself.

In his own country, Moravia's reputation is based primarily upon his relation to the neorealist movement in the arts, in which he occupies a key position. The neorealist aesthetic was first defined in a critical essay published by Arnaldo Bocelli in 1930. In this essay, Bocelli used Moravia's first novel, *The Time of Indifference*, as an example of the advent of a neorealist aesthetic that—in attempting to present the everyday experience of typical, representative characters in a concrete, realistic way—opposed the convention-bound formalism of the Hermetic tradition. In the eyes of the public, however, it was not so much Moravia's first novel that established him as an important neorealist as it was the popular series of tales he wrote describing the life of the Roman working classes. These stories—most of which first appeared in the Milan newspaper *Il corriere della sera*—were told by lower-class characters themselves in their Roman vernacular. It was these Roman tales that brought Moravia widespread recognition as a leading neorealist and won for him the Strega Prize in 1952.

Biography

Alberto Pincherle Moravia was born in Rome on November 28, 1907. His father, Carlo Pincherle Moravia, was a successful architect in Rome. A native of Venice, he had been reared in a family of Jewish heritage, though—as Moravia later described him—he did not practice that or any other faith. Moravia's mother, Teresa de Marsanich, reared in Ancona, carried the title of countess, her family being of Dalmatian noble extraction. Along with his brother and his two sisters, Moravia was reared in his mother's faith, Roman Catholicism.

It is commonly believed that Moravia's real name is Alberto Pincherle and that the name with which he signed his work, Alberto Moravia, is a pseudonym. According to Moravia himself, this is not true. In an interview given to Luciano Rebay in 1968 and later confirmed in a letter, Moravia explained that his legal name, as it appears on his birth certificate, passport, and other official documents, is Alberto Pincherle Moravia.

Moravia's family was fairly affluent, belonging to the upper middle class. His family had high expectations for Moravia, planning for him from childhood a career in the diplomatic service. Toward this end, Moravia was tutored in French, English, and German. At the age of nine, however, he was stricken with tubercular osteomyelitis, which affected his legs and gradually worsened until he was unable to walk. First stricken with the disease in 1916, Moravia continued to suffer its effects for almost ten years. For a time, he continued in school, managing to complete his elementary education, but as his condition worsened and he became increasingly bedridden, he was forced to abandon his formal education, as well as his parents' plans for a career in the diplomatic service. In 1923, when Moravia was sixteen years old, a new cure was tried, and he was sent to the Istituto Codivilla, a sanatorium at Cortina d'Ampezzo in the Italian Alps. Finally, in 1925, Moravia was pronounced cured and was sent for a period of rest to Bressanone, near Bolzano on the Austrian border. It was there that he began to write *The Time of Indifference*, his first novel, which was published four years later.

In 1927, Moravia's first published story, "Il cortigiana stanca" ("Tired Courtesan"), appeared in *900*, an Italian avant-garde review that was published in French. Later that same year, and in the years that followed, stories in Italian appeared with increasing frequency.

The other decisive influence on Moravia's career was the rise to power of the Italian Fascist Party under Benito Mussolini. In October of 1922, the Fascists seized control of Rome, where Moravia lived, and began waging an increasingly repressive campaign of terror against those who refused to support them. Speaking of these two experiences—his extended childhood illness and the rise of fascism—Moravia later observed,

Alberto Moravia. (Library of Congress)

> Because of them I had to suffer much and did many things that I otherwise would not have done. It is what we are forced to do that forms our character, not what we do of our own free will.

Moravia's difficulties with Fascist censorship began after the publication of his first novel in 1929. Fascist authorities resented the critical view he presented of the Italian middle class, from whom their strongest support derived. During the decade following *The Time of Indifference*, Moravia traveled widely as a foreign correspondent for *La stampa* and *Gazetta del popolo*, two prominent Italian newspapers. His assignments took him to England, France, Greece, China, and Mexico, places where he could live and work relatively free of the influence of the Fascist tyranny at home.

At the beginning of World War II, Moravia returned to Italy, living in retreat from 1940 to 1943 on the island of Capri. In 1941, he published his third novel, *The Fancy Dress Party*, a thinly disguised satire of Mussolini's regime. Shortly afterward, the book was suppressed by the censors, and Moravia was forbidden to publish anything at all. The same year, he married Elsa Morante, also an Italian novelist, with whom he returned to Rome following the collapse of Mussolini's government in July of 1943. By the fall of that year, however, Moravia and his wife were forced to flee Rome once again when it was occupied by German forces. Moravia had been warned that his name was on the list of those opponents of Fascism who were to be arrested, so he and his wife fled south toward the Allied liberation—which by then had reached Naples. Unable to cross the front, however, they took refuge in Fondi, a small town in the Ciociara region south of Rome. There they spent nine months living in a stable, waiting for the Allied forces to reach them.

After the liberation of Rome in June of 1944, the couple returned to the city, and Moravia resumed his publication in journals and newspapers with accelerated intensity. During this postwar period, his leftist political orientation became apparent, though he remained independent of the powerful Italian Communist Party, which assimilated so many of the antifascist intellectuals at that time.

Between 1944 and 1946, Moravia served as film critic for *La nuova Europa* and began to publish the series of Roman tales for which he is best known in his own country. In 1952, he was awarded the prestigious Strega Prize for *I racconti, 1927-1951*. The following year, he founded the literary review *Nuovi argomenti* with Alberto Carocci. In 1955, he again served as a film critic, this time for the Roman weekly *L'espresso*. During the period from 1958 to 1970, he undertook another extensive series of travels—to the United States, Turkey, the Soviet Union, India, Egypt, Greece, Japan, China, and Africa—that were reported in the essays collected in his four travel books.

In 1962, Moravia divorced Elsa Morante, and in the following year, he married Dacia Maraini, another Italian novelist. In 1967, he was at last awarded a high school diploma when he passed an equivalency test, and in 1968 he undertook a lecture tour of colleges in the United States. Thereafter, he returned to the city where he was born, continuing to produce an abundant variety of novels, stories, and plays. He died there on September 26, 1990.

Analysis

Alberto Moravia's popularity and continuing recognition as a literary artist are based on the universality of his insights into the dilemmas that plague the divided consciousness of modern humanity. These dilemmas are presented and explored through the basic elements of Moravia's fiction: his use of characterization, style, and form, as well as his presentation of themes that express a distinctly modern view of the world.

The treatment of character in Moravia's fiction has been much discussed by critics. One of the most important aspects of Moravia's characterization is what might be called "the method of exhaustion." Sergio Pacifici, one of Moravia's critics, has effectively described this aspect of his work: "Moravia's greatest gift consists precisely in his ability to leave his reader with the distinct feeling that he has said all that could possibly be said about his characters." For Pacifici, this quality of Moravia's work is clearly an asset, though it has often been criticized by others as belaboring the obvious, usurping the modern reader's participation in constructing the text. Whatever judgment one may pass on this "method of exhaustion," it is a quality that Moravia's work shares with that of other important modern novelists, such as Alain Robbe-Grillet, who raises the technique to the status of a phenomenological analysis of existence.

Another important aspect of Moravia's characterization is the frequent recurrence of certain character types, an element that again has elicited both negative and positive responses. Those who dislike this element of Moravia's work point to the sameness of his alienated middle-class male protagonists, who go through a predictable pattern of development that is always essentially the same. To these critics, Moravia's work seems to lack the dynamism that arises from a hero who is capable of growth and change. More sympathetic critics have shown, however, that the dynamism of Moravia's novels lies not within the protagonists themselves but in the conflict between characters who are capable of making choices and gratifying their desires through physical action and those who are caught up in narcissistic reflection that does not lead to action and therefore cannot change their situation in the world. More important than the description of this pattern of conflict, however, is that Moravia's characters rarely come to any recognition themselves; the recognition almost always takes place within the reader, who reflects upon the meaning of the characters' successes and failures in the novel.

Two other aspects of Moravia's characterization that are frequently commented upon are his portrayals of women and of human sexuality. By unsympathetic critics, he is accused of creating nothing but mindless women whose sole trait seems to be a powerful erotic drive. Sympathetic critics see these flat women as catalytic agents whose function is to expose the hero's character. The same is true of Moravia's use of sexuality. To unsympathetic critics, it is simply exploitative titillation or an unwitting reflection of the author's own prurient or voyeuristic sensibility. To sympathetic critics, such as Donald Heiney, however, sex is an "encounter in which the conflict of human egos is seen more simply," while for others it assumes the status of a symbol for the alienation of modern humans, a demonstration of the fundamental isolation from others that characterizes the life of individuals in modern industrial societies.

One of the most distinctive elements of Moravia's fiction is his narrative style and form. The unnamed narrators who dominate Moravia's early work speak in an unadorned, journalistic style that has frequently been compared to Ernest Hemingway's in its emotional reticence, objective detachment, and avoidance of value-laden diction. The narrative stance in these works often seems to approach the extreme objective detachment of Hemingway's famous story "The Killers," which Moravia translated in 1934.

Following World War II, Moravia began to abandon the omniscient perspective in favor of first-person narrators. *The Woman of Rome* and *Conjugal Love* are both told from this new perspective, as are all his novels following *The Conformist*, which uses the omniscient point of view. The reasons for this change in strategy are complex, as are its effects. Beginning with *The Woman of Rome*, Moravia's principal subject—the analysis and critique of middle-class life in modern Italy—is rivaled by a growing interest in the lives of the lower class. Moravia himself said this change of interest was stimulated by his experiences with the peasants among whom he and his wife lived during the German Occupation. An equally strong influence, however, was the developing neorealist aesthetic, which encouraged the employment of participating narrators speaking in the informal diction of regional vernaculars as a much-needed relief from the convention-bound *lingua pura* dialect traditionally employed in literary works.

Another aspect of Moravia's work that has elicited mixed reaction from his critics is the repetitiveness of subject and theme. Moravia himself acknowledged this aspect, but he saw it as an artistic necessity, not a creative shortcoming: "Good writers are monotonous, like good composers. Their truth is self-repeating. They keep . . . trying to perfect their expression of the one problem they were born to understand." The central theme of Moravia's work is the human relationship to reality, which he sees as "the fundamental problem of our time." In Moravia's work, the relationship of people to the world and to others is an amoral one, for clearly defined conceptions of good and evil based on traditional ethics no longer apply to these relationships. In the modern world, humankind, according to Moravia, "is no longer the end but the means," and in the face of this, it adopts the attitude of indifference, becoming alienated from the external world.

Modern human alienation is expressed in many ways in Moravia's work. One of the most prominent of these methods is his portrayal of the decadence and irresponsibility of the affluent Italian middle class, whose desire to protect their vested interests in a world of crumbling social, political, and economic values paved the way for the rise of fascism in Italy. Many of Moravia's protagonists, being intellectuals, come from this class, as did Moravia himself. As Jane Cottrell says, "Painfully aware of the hypocrisy and false values of middle-class society, the Moravian hero rejects his own class and turns to the lower classes, which he sees as more authentic." This myth of the lower classes is an important theme that recurs throughout the course of Moravia's career.

Another symptom of modern alienation is expressed in Moravia's portrayal of the family. Like capitalistic economics and totalitarian politics, the institution of the family, in Moravia's analysis, robs people of their freedom, making them an end instead of a means. In a 1965 essay, he stated the thoughts that are often voiced less coherently by his alienated protagonists: "The most mistaken teachings are those given by the family . . . worship of such divinities as Prudence, Self-interest, Ignorance, Hedonism. . . . Any school at all, even the worst, is better than the family."

Underlying Moravia's central concerns is his particular philosophical orientation toward the world, which mingles elements of Freudianism, Marxism, existentialism, and phenomenology. In Freudian thought, Moravia found a confirmation of the idea of the primacy of sexual experience in humanity's relation to the world. Marxism, as Heiney says, "provided Moravia with an explanation of the decadence of his own social class," helping him to put his analysis of modern human position in the world into a historical framework. In existentialism, he found a philosophical context for his own conception of people's alienation from the world, which he had formulated—not by systematic reasoning but by the unconscious processes of intuition—years before it was elaborated by Jean-Paul Sartre. In phenomenology, he found confirmation for the idea of the intentionality of consciousness, which is reflected in the method of exhaustion employed in his work. These basic patterns of thought inform Moravia's fictional world.

The Time of Indifference

Alberto Moravia wrote *The Time of Indifference*, his first published novel, between October, 1925, and March, 1928. It was Moravia's third attempt at the genre, according to him, for he had already completed two novels that failed because "they were imitations of this or that author with whom I had become infatuated as I went along." *The Time of Indifference* is certainly not open to this charge; it contains many of the distinctive characteristics of Moravia's subsequent work. Despite its remarkable maturity and originality, the novel was turned down by three reputable publishers before being accepted by Alpes, an obscure publishing house in Milan, which issued the novel at Moravia's expense in July of 1929. The novel was an immediate popular success and received high praise from many critics. By the following year, Moravia was already being identified as one of the leading innovators of the developing neorealist aesthetic in literature. Though the novel was strongly attacked by the Fascist press for its negative portrayal of the life of comfortable affluence led by the Italian middle class, to other critics this was precisely the value of the novel—its portrayal of the moral corruption and social irresponsibility of the middle class for the first time in an unsentimental and realistic way.

The novel's protagonist, Michele Ardengo, suffers from that form of modern alienation that Moravia calls "indifference." Michele observes, from this position of detachment, the struggles of his mother, Mariagrazia, to hold on to her bored lover, Leo Merumeci, and the growing willingness of his sister, Carla, to sacrifice her innocence to Leo in order to ensure the continued affluence of the family in the face of their sagging fortunes. As the narrator's description of her thoughts reveals, Carla's own actions arise from this same feeling of indifference: "Why should she refuse Leo? Virtue would merely throw her back into the arms of boredom." Helpless to escape his detachment from life, Michele is only able to protest feebly the absurdity of his own condition. In this novel, Moravia's critique of the family as an institution for the perpetuation of decadent social values is prominent.

The Time of Indifference is also an important example of Moravia's use of novelistic form. Like *Mistaken Ambitions*, *The Fancy Dress Party*, *Agostino*, *Disobedience*, and *The Conformist*, this first novel employs the objective detachment of third-person narrative. His later shift to first-person narration marks an important division in his work and arises in part from the radical questioning of the objective nature of reality that is first expressed through the thoughts and actions of Michele Ardengo. In its use of the alienated protagonist-hero, the middle-class Roman background, and the objectification of reality through the omniscient point of view, *The Time of Indifference* is perhaps the best representative of the work Moravia published before the end of World War II.

The Woman of Rome

The Woman of Rome marks the next, and for many critics the most important, step in Moravia's development as a literary artist, for this novel was the first work in which he employed the first-person narrative perspective that dominates his later fiction. Moreover, the novel was his first to be written in the Roman vernacular. In this respect, it is related to his Roman tales, in which he brought the use of the lower-class vernacular narrator to stylistic perfection. *The Woman of Rome* marks the beginning of this phase of Moravia's work, which concluded with *Two Women*, the last of his novels written in the vernacular.

The Woman of Rome, which Moravia began writing shortly after his return to Rome in 1944, grew from its original conception as a short story to a massive, five-hundred-page novel comprising the "memoirs" of a Roman prostitute, Adriana. This expansion of scope, and the perspective from which the novel is told, indicated an important change of orientation in Moravia's aesthetic, which he later expressed in an interview: "The third person is a way of telling a story of a time when people believed in objective reality. Nowadays we believe in subjective reality. Everybody is his own reality and your reality is not mine."

This novel also marked the beginning of Moravia's re-creation of the authentic, uncorrupted life of the lower classes. Adriana, the working-class heroine of this novel, is unlike the alienated middle-class heroes of his early work in that she represents "a triumph of the life force," as Luciano Rebay has put it. To a large degree, the great popular success the novel enjoyed resulted from the vitality of its heroine. Moravia himself later said that "in identifying myself with Adriana I thought for a while that I had found the key to my own rapport with reality, with life." This myth of the renewing vitality of the life of the lower classes, as well as his interest in the Roman vernacular, was stimulated by his experiences at Fondi during the period he spent in hiding from the Fascist authorities. Here, for the first time, Moravia was removed from the social milieu and material comforts of the affluent middle-class existence he had always known. Though it is certain that, given a choice, Moravia would not have spent this period of nine months living in a peasant's stable, it is also certain that without this experience, *The Woman of Rome*, *Two Women*, and the Roman tales that won him the Strega Prize would never have been written.

Moravia had become accustomed to portraying in his fiction, for almost twenty years, the life of the affluent middle class. Because this social milieu was identical with his own experience, his use of an educated, literate narrator speaking in the third person seemed unobtrusive enough; it created little conflict between the omniscient consciousness and the mentality of the principal characters. The literate style would seem very artificial in presenting the experiences and thoughts of his uneducated, working-class heroine, however, and it is most likely for this reason that Moravia finally decided to cast the novel into the form of a memoir, allowing Adriana to tell her own story in her own speech, employing the vernacular with which he had become familiar during his stay at Fondi.

The abandonment of the omniscient point of view also reflects, in retrospect, a more radical shift in Moravia's conception of fictional representation, which was retained even in the later novels that return to portraying the alienation of the Italian middle class. In "Notes on the Novel," an essay later collected in *Man as an End*, Moravia argued that "the omniscience of the nineteenth-century novelist turned finally into a trick, a lifeless convention. Today we can no longer write 'He thought.' . . . We can only write 'I thought.'" Elaborating on Moravia's statement, Heiney observes that the omniscient perspective does not correspond to the epistemological need of the modern novel to be realistic, because it does not correspond to the radically subjective way in which modern humanity regards the phenomena of consciousness or the external world. It is above all this particular aesthetic principle that is retained and developed in Moravia's subsequent fiction.

The Conformist

To many critics, *The Conformist* is an embarrassing anachronism in Moravia's oeuvre, because it employs the third-person omniscient narrative perspective he had abandoned four years earlier in *The Woman of Rome*. Though it is true that Moravia did not return to the objective point of view that he used in *The Conformist*, the novel is not by any means the miserable failure that many critics, in an effort to mold Moravia's technical development into a neat but oversimplified pattern, have asserted.

There are, in fact, a number of conditions in this particular case that make the omniscient perspective an effective choice. The first is Moravia's desire to put the totalitarian era, with which the novel deals, into a historical perspective, so that he can explore and analyze its effects on particular types of individuals. In addition, *The Conformist* employs irony very differently from the way it is used in most of Moravia's other work. The novel has as its central character a hero who is exceptional, not representative, whom the reader is expected to dislike and from whom he is expected to distance himself—not one with whom the reader can sympathize and identify. The irony is conveyed by the comments of the omniscient narrator, who condemns and satirizes Marcello's behavior.

Unlike the heroes and heroines of his other novels, who usually suffer from an excess of self-consciousness, Marcello does not reflect at all but only responds mechanically to external stimuli. In *The Conformist*, unlike most of Moravia's other novels, it is the narrator rather than the characters who does most of the thinking. For these reasons, *The Conformist* is not only Moravia's most uncharacteristic novel but also the one most suited to the use of third-person narrative. The objectification Moravia achieves through the use of viewpoint is reinforced by the form of the novel, which—as several critics have pointed out—resembles that of a classical tragedy. Cottrell has even attempted to show the similarity of Marcello's fate to that of Oedipus.

Undeniably, *The Conformist* has faults. This is so mainly because of the same devices of objectification, which Moravia used effectively to help guide the reader's response to the material. The hero, Marcello, who becomes a Fascist agent out of a desire to prove himself "normal" through submission and conformity, is, in fact, so "spineless"—as one critic put it—that it is difficult for the reader to care much about his fate. There is an unsettling discontinuity between the various parts of the novel, which cover events ranging from 1920 to 1943, as well as the artificiality of the deus ex machina ending. The events of the prologue, which covers Marcello's childhood, often remind one of the sensational case histories Freud recounted in formulating his theory of infantile sexuality. The intrusive moralizing of the narrator, while seen by some critics as an artistic defect, seems more a matter of personal taste, because it does serve a useful function in the narrative.

Despite these shortcomings, the novel does effectively present to the reader an analysis of the phenomenon of conformity—the roots from which it arises and the effects it has upon the relation of humans to the world. In this respect, *The Conformist* is not a failure at all, since it addresses one of the central ethical dilemmas of the modern era.

The Empty Canvas

In *The Empty Canvas*, Moravia returned to the portrayal of the alienated, middle-class hero, yet in this mature novel, there are two new elements present: the subjective narrative perspective afforded by the use of the first-person point of view and the close relationship of the thoughts of the hero, Dino, to those of the author himself. This latter characteristic led some critics, following Moravia's own use of the term, to call *The Empty Canvas* an "essay-novel," a novel in which the emphasis falls not on the plot but on the ideas of the central character, who attempts to convey a particular view of the world.

The Empty Canvas tells the story of a young painter, Dino, who encounters a creative block. Suddenly becoming disgusted one day with an abstract composition on which he is working, he destroys the painting and replaces it with a new canvas, which will remain "empty" throughout the novel. Having symbolically destroyed the past, he turns in the prologue to an examination of his present life in an attempt to define and understand the feeling of *noia*, or boredom, which has overwhelmed him.

In the increasing abstractness of his recent paintings, Dino sees a progressive loss of reality, because, as he observes, "I felt that my pictures did not permit me to express myself, in other words, to deceive myself into imagining that I had some contact with external things." He makes several attempts to describe the boredom that plagues him. He describes it alternately as a feeling of absurdity, insufficiency, or lack of reality—like a sickness of inanimate objects that causes them to wither, or the effect of a too-short blanket upon a sleepy man on a cold winter night, or a sudden and mysterious interruption of the electric current in a house.

In reflecting upon the onset of this feeling, Dino also comes upon the question of his own authenticity as an artist. Because of the affluence of his mother, he gradually comes to feel that he is only "playing" at the role of artist. It is his mother's wealth, not his own talent, that pays for his studio and provides him with living expenses. Because of his dependence upon a way of life he wishes to reject, he finds himself in a position of inauthenticity, not choosing his own destiny. As many critics have observed, *The Empty Canvas* presents one of Moravia's strongest critiques of the alienating effect of wealth upon the individual.

In this novel, the decadence of the affluent Italian middle class comes under attack, particularly in those episodes in which Dino visits his mother, who lives in a villa on the Via Appia. Dino's mother has been effectively characterized in two details by Jane Cottrell: "Money is her only link with reality. . . . Above her bed is a picture of Danäe reclining nude on a bed, watching with pleasure the rain of golden coins fall into her lap." Moravia's ironic presentation of this privileged way of life reaches a climax in a scene describing a cocktail party in which Dino acts out, with his girlfriend, Cecilia, the myth of Danäe and the golden coins.

The irony in this novel arises not from a contrast between the author's opinions and the actions of his characters, but rather from the contrast between the apparently concrete, "realistic" details of the plot and the abstract ideas of the author to which they refer. The scene in which Dino covers the nude body of Cecilia with his mother's money on the bed beneath the painting of Danäe, to which his act refers symbolically, is a striking example of the method by which Moravia expresses his own conception of the relationship between money and power in this essay-novel.

The ultimate question for the reader of *The Empty Canvas* must be, as Heiney observes, whether this portrait of boredom is in itself boring or is an effective method of conveying the author's particular view of reality. Though Moravia's view of humankind's alienated existence in the modern world remained consistent throughout the course of his career, the methods by which he presented this particular experience underwent considerable development. He began by adopting the stance of narrative objectivity, employing the omniscient point of view to distance himself from the materials of his fiction. With the publication of *The Woman of Rome*, the first novel in which Moravia employed the first-person point of view, a new element of narrative subjectivity entered his work; in *Conjugal Love*, *A Ghost at Noon*, and *Two Women*, the author adopted the perspective of a character inside the work and so disappeared from the text, which became a mere document he presented without judgment to the reader. In *The Empty Canvas*, Moravia took a new approach, abandoning the authorial effacement of the conventional first-person narrative for the more limited subjectivity of the essay-novel. Using this form, Moravia maintained the psychological realism of the first-person narrative while retaining direct access to the reader through the essayistic portions of the novel. This method was further developed and refined in *The Lie*, *Two*, and *Time of Desecration*.

Steven E. Colburn

Other major works

SHORT FICTION: *La bella vita*, 1935; *L'imbroglio*, 1937; *I sogni del pigro*, 1940; *L'amante infelice*, 1943; *L'epidemia: Racconti surrealistici e satirici*, 1944; *Due cortigiane*, 1945; *L'amore coniugale, e altri racconti*, 1949; *I racconti, 1927-1951*, 1952; *Bitter Honeymoon, and Other Stories*, 1954 (selections from *I racconti*); *Racconti romani*, 1954 (*Roman Tales*, 1956); *Nuovi racconti romani*, 1959 (*More Roman Tales*, 1963); *The Wayward Wife, and Other Stories*, 1960 (selections from *I racconti*); *L'automa*, 1963 (*The Fetish*, 1964); *Una cosa è una cosa*, 1967 (*Command and I Will Obey You*, 1969); *I racconti di Alberto Moravia*, 1968; *Il paradiso*, 1970 (*Paradise, and Other Stories*, 1971; also known as *Bought and Sold*, 1973); *Un'altra vita*, 1973 (*Lady Godiva, and Other Stories*, 1975; also known as *Mother Love*, 1976); *Boh*, 1976 (*The Voice of the Sea, and Other Stories*, 1978); *La cosa, e altri racconti*, 1983 (*Erotic Tales*, 1985).

PLAYS: *Gli indifferenti*, pr., pb. 1948; *La mascherata*, pr. 1954; *Beatrice Cenci*, pr. 1955 (English translation, 1965); *L'intervista*, pr., pb. 1966; *Il mondo è quello che è*, pr., pb. 1966 (*The World's the World*, 1970); *Il dio Kurt*, pr., pb. 1968; *La vita è gioco*, pb. 1969; *L'angelo dell'informazione, e altri testi teatrali*, pb. 1986; *Teatro*, 1998 (2 volumes).

NONFICTION: *Un mese in U.R.S.S.*, 1958 (travel sketch); *Saggi italiani del 1959*, 1960; *Un'idea dell'India*, 1962 (travel sketch); *L'uomo come fine, e altri saggi*, 1964 (*Man as an End: A Defence of Humanism—Literary, Social, and Political Essays*, 1965); *La rivoluzione culturale in Cina*, 1967 (travel sketch; *The Red Book and the Great Wall*, 1968); *A quale tribù appartieni?*, 1972 (travel sketch; *Which Tribe Do You Belong To?*, 1974); *Impegno controvoglia: Saggi, articoli, interviste*, 1980; *Lettere dal Sahara*, 1981; *L'inverno nucleare*, 1986; *Passeggiate africane*, 1987; *Vita de Moravia*, 1990 (with Alain Elkann; *Life of Moravia*, 2000).

children's/young adult literature: *Tre storie della preistoria*, 1977; *Quando Ba Lena era tanto piccola*, 1978; *Un miliardo di anni fa*, 1979; *Cosma e i briganti*, 1980; *Cama Leonte diventò verde lilla blu*, 1981; *Storie della preistoria*, 1982.

Bibliography

Dego, Giuliano. *Writers and Critics: Moravia*. New York: Barnes & Noble Books, 1967. A valuable overview of Moravia's early work, with discussion centering on his naturalistic presentation, his remarkable descriptive ability, his major theme of alienation, and his ceaseless exploration of crises.

Heiney, Donald. *Three Italian Novelists: Moravia, Pavese, Vittorini*. Ann Arbor: University of Michigan Press, 1968. Concentrates on Moravia as creator and craftsman, not as political thinker, psychologist, sociologist, or philosopher. Discusses characters, themes, and techniques in the novels. Includes notes, a bibliography, and an index.

Kozma, Janice M. *The Architecture of Imagery in Alberto Moravia's Fiction*. Chapel Hill: University of North Carolina Press, 1993. Kozma carefully examines how Moravia organizes his imagery into simple and complex forms, and into "discrete and seemingly discrete" categories. A set of appendixes analyzes the imagery of women, men, war, nature, architecture, machines, the body, food, and sex. Includes a bibliography.

Lewis, R. W. B. "Alberto Moravia: Eros and Existence." In *From "Verismo" to Experimentalism*. Bloomington: Indiana University Press, 1969. Lewis, describing Moravia as a minor master of the strategy of "*artistic* conversion, of the transformation of one set of values into another," succinctly analyzes the "sexualization" of objects, values, and relationships in Moravia's fiction.

Peterson, Thomas Erling. *Alberto Moravia*. New York: Twayne, 1996. Comprehensive coverage of the life and works of Moravia. Includes critical analysis of major works, as well as information on personal and public activities. Describes the political climate in Italy and its relevance to Moravia's life.

Rebay, Luciano. *Alberto Moravia*. New York: Columbia University Press, 1970. An abbreviated but useful introduction to Moravia's life and novels. Rebay emphasizes that Moravia gladly accepted the charge of being "monotonous" in his concentration on tragic human emptiness, spiritual crisis, and sex. Includes a bibliography.

Ross, Joan, and Donald Freed. *The Existentialism of Alberto Moravia*. Carbondale: Southern Illinois University Press, 1972. Placing Moravia in the context of the literature and philosophy of existentialism, this thoroughly conducted analysis underscores the considerable significance of the concepts of love, suffering, and reality in Moravia's work within this broader framework. Includes notes and an index.

Stella, M. John. *Self and Self-Compromise in the Narratives of Pirandello and Moravia*. New York: Peter Lang, 2000. Stella analyzes works by Moravia, including *The Empty Canvas*, and by Luigi Pirandello to examine how they treat issues of identity, focusing on how the two writers' concepts of individual identity were influenced by Buddhist doctrines.

Weaver, William. "Roman Candle." *The New York Review of Books*, June 25, 1998. Discusses the life and works of Moravia, whom Weaver befriended for four decades. He notes that Moravia claimed the determining factors in his life were his aversion to fascism and a childhood illness that denied him both a normal adolescence and a traditional education. Weaver also explains how the antifascist stance and sexual candor of Moravia's novels antagonized both the Church and Italy's wartime government.

Wood, Sharon. *Woman as Object: Language and Gender in the Work of Alberto Moravia*. London: Pluto Press, 1990. Cogent and sensitive, this excellent study explores the relationship of language to sex and power, and to experience—both gender bound and intimately individual—in Moravia's work. Wood concludes that Moravia's attempts at representing experience from the female perspective ultimately fail. Includes excellent, extensive notes, a bibliography, and an index.

WRIGHT MORRIS

Born: Central City, Nebraska; January 6, 1910
Died: Mill Valley, California; April 25, 1998
Also known as: Wright Marion Morris

Principal long fiction

My Uncle Dudley, 1942
The Man Who Was There, 1945
The Home Place, 1948
The World in the Attic, 1949
Man and Boy, 1951
The Works of Love, 1952
The Deep Sleep, 1953
The Huge Season, 1954
The Field of Vision, 1956
Love Among the Cannibals, 1957
Ceremony in Lone Tree, 1960
What a Way to Go, 1962
Cause for Wonder, 1963
One Day, 1965
In Orbit, 1967
Fire Sermon, 1971
War Games, 1972
A Life, 1973
The Fork River Space Project, 1977
Plains Song, for Female Voices, 1980

Other literary forms

Several of Wright Morris's books, including *The Inhabitants* (1946), *God's Country and My People* (1968), and *Love Affair: A Venetian Journal* (1972), are photo-texts. They feature photographs accompanied by brief prose passages. In the first of these, Morris describes the "inhabitants" of the United States from coast to coast through photographs of their structures—buildings that have affected the "indwellers." Pictures of porch fronts in the West, for example, reveal New England influences, as do the inhabitants of the dwellings. The photographs, although not synchronized with the text, appear on facing pages and combine with it to make a larger statement than would be possible from either medium used alone—a statement about America and its people and their place in the changing world. Fences, privies, and churches are among the other artifacts pictured on unnumbered pages and bearing a poetic relationship to the human characters described in the text; it is up to the reader to determine the truths thereby conveyed.

God's Country and My People, more autobiographical yet less nostalgic than its predecessors, suggests present-day values and their usefulness to a later generation. *Love Affair*, utilizing color photographs taken in Venice in 1969, presents the problem of "shouting" that everything is of interest, while the black-and-white pictures of the photo-texts of the plains are more selective in their emphasis. Morris also published several collections of photographs: *Wright Morris: Structures and Artifacts, Photographs, 1933-1954* (1975), *Photographs and Words* (1982), and *Picture America* (1982). A meditation on photography and writing, *Time Pieces: Photographs, Writings, and Memory*, appeared in 1989.

Morris's books of essays include *The Territory Ahead* (1958, 1963), a work of criticism expressing his admiration for the artistry of Henry James and the vitality of D. H. Lawrence, and his concern about the misuse of the past by sentimental illustrators or writers. *A Bill of Rites, a Bill of Wrongs, a Bill of Goods* (1968) contains more critical essays deploring the practices of professional reviewers, of speed readers, and of symbol hunters, and the passing of the reader who simply wants to establish a dialogue with the writer. The writer's duty, says Morris, is to bring the real world into a field of vision that will give it meaning and to stir the readers' imagination. In this sometimes angry book, Morris also denounces advertising, which has created the consumer culture with its longing for possessions, and technological expertise, which allows humankind to explore space without at all improving life on Earth. In his third book of essays, *About Fiction* (1975), Morris describes the ideal reader, discusses point of view, and compares realism with "fabulation"—a more artistic, shapely, idea-filled narrative, exemplified by the works of John Barth, Thomas Pynchon, and Vladimir Nabokov.

Earthly Delights, Unearthly Adornments: American Writers as Image-Makers (1978) surveys Morris's own career and the course of American writing through quotations, recollections, and pictures. Perhaps the best summation of these books of essays is to be found in *About Fiction*'s subtitle: *Reverent Reflections on the Nature of Fiction with Irreverent Observations on Writers, Readers, and Other Abuses*.

Morris's other works include an anthology, *Wright Morris: A Reader* (1970), which contains two short novels, *The Works of Love* and *The Field of Vision*, two short stories, and selections from eight other novels. *Real Losses, Imaginary Gains* (1976) is a collection of thirteen short stories; another volume of Morris's short fiction appeared in 1986, *Collected Stories: 1948-1986*. The memoir *Will's Boy* (1981) was followed by two other autobiographical works: *Solo: An American Dreamer in Europe, 1933-1934* (1983) and *A Cloak of Light: Writing My Life* (1985).

Achievements

While a few of Wright Morris's books have European settings, he is most effective when writing about his native Nebraska and characters returning home to try to recapture memories or relive the past. That Morris was unusually concerned with his craft is evidenced by his several books of essays on the writing of fiction and the readers thereof. A prolific writer, Morris was primarily a delineator of character, rather than a constructor of intricate plots. He pays considerable attention to the "artifacts" of his characters' worlds and to the workings of their minds, most particularly to the kinds of thoughts that are never expressed aloud.

Morris is inevitably compared to both James Agee and Walker Evans because of his poetic, reflective prose about the dignity of rural life and because his photography is reminiscent of Evans's in *Let Us Now Praise Famous Men* (1941). Morris combines the talents of both Agee and Evans in his photo-texts, conducting a search for the meaning of America through word and picture.

Although Morris always received critical acclaim, he did not enjoy popular success. Robert Knoll suggested that the reason may be Morris's failure to involve the reader in the exciting events of his fiction. He rather invites the reader casually, as did Robert Frost, to come along and clear the leaves away. His poetic style is as far removed as prose can be from the popular journalistic narrative mode. Although Morris knew that readers do not want fictive distance, he created novels that question rather than confess, that disturb rather than reassure.

Morris received three Guggenheim awards, two of them for photography and the third for fiction (*The Deep Sleep*); the National Book Award for *The Field of Vision* and *Plains Song, for Female Voices*; and the National Institute for Arts and Letters Award for *Ceremony in Lone Tree*. He received a National Institute Grant in 1960 and was fiction judge for the National Book Award in 1969.

Biography

After his birth in Central City, Nebraska, Wright Marion Morris lived with his father in Schuyler, Kearney, and other small Nebraska towns along the Platte River before moving to Omaha. (His mother died six days after his birth.) He worked for two summers on his uncle Harry's farm in Norfolk, Nebraska, but the move to Chicago in 1924 brought him a different kind of employment at the YMCA. He attended college in California for five weeks, then worked for several months on the Texas ranch of his uncle Dwight Osborn. He entered Pomona College in Claremont, California, but withdrew to spend a year in Austria, Italy, Germany, and France. He had written some brief prose sketches while at Pomona, and he returned to California to begin his first novel.

Morris married Mary Ellen Finfrock of Cleveland, Ohio, in 1934. Between 1935 and 1938, he wrote two novels and the sketches for *The Inhabitants* and developed the interest in photography that flourished during two summers at Wellfleet, Massachusetts. In 1940-1941, he toured the United States, taking pictures to be used in *The Inhabitants*. He lived in California two more years before moving to Haverford, Pennsylvania, in 1944. In 1954, he began spending more time in Venice, Italy, Mexico, and Greece, returning intermittently to California. He lectured at the University of Southern California and at Amherst College and taught at California State University, Los Angeles. He was a professor of English at San Francisco State University from 1962 until his retirement in 1975.

In 1961, Morris and his first wife were divorced, and Morris married Josephine Kantor. He was selected in 1983 to occupy the visiting writer's chair at the University of Alabama. In 1992, an exhibition of Morris's photography was held in San Francisco. Morris died of unreported causes in Mill Valley, California, where he had lived since the early 1960's, on April 25, 1998. In the obituary in *The New York Times*, Ralph Blumenthal noted that Morris is "often called one of the nation's most unrecognized recognized writers."

Analysis

A novelist who has been read more—and surely appreciated more—in Europe than in his own country, Wright Morris explored the legacies of heroism and nostalgia, the dreams and delusions examined by earlier twentieth century American writers. Another concern of Morris, whose novels seldom display violence, is the rise of violence in America. His narratives often take place within a twenty-four-hour time period, suggesting the capture of a finite period of time as the photographer captures a finite space with a camera. This limitation of time unifies Morris's novels, which are more intimately related by the device of recurring characters. Indeed, David Madden and other critics have suggested that one must read Morris's entire canon in order to understand any one novel.

The spirit of place, whether it be the central plains, a California beach, a Philadelphia suburb, or an Alpine château, is central to Morris's novels, and the impingement of objects or places upon humanity a major facet of Morris's imagination, as they had been to James, who believed that places gave out a "mystic meaning." Admittedly influenced by James and by Lawrence, Morris was his own man for five prolific decades. Fortunate to have as his birthplace the "navel of the universe," the central United States, from that vantage point he "salvaged" meaningful artifacts that represent an earlier American life and, concomitantly, the values of that life.

Accused by critic Alfred Kazin of overloading his fiction with symbols, Morris disavowed any conscious symbolic creation, noting that symbols may appear without the author's deliberate intent in any good work of fiction. Obsessed by the cliché, which he considered a dead repository for something once alive, he peopled his fiction with stereotypes and challenged himself to bring them back to life. Wayne Booth described Morris's transformation of clichés as "toying" with them. David Madden saw the characters' coming to terms with clichés as absolutely essential to their knowledge of the enjoyment of love, sex, their bodies—even of travel. He added that after Morris, clichés are never the same, because they are killed and resurrected in the same moment, reappearing in an improved form.

It is not easy to generalize about an oeuvre as varied as Morris's, but his works frequently disregard chronology, an attempt to possess time and understand it being one of his obsessions. A recurring relationship, as Madden pointed out, is that of the hero and his "witnesses"—the characters who are transformed because their lives have intersected his. The contact, strangely enough, is often more meaningful after the death of the hero. Booth noted that the novels of Morris begin with a problem or a misunderstanding and conclude with a solution or a clarification. While this statement could be made about most plots, it is not the beginnings and the endings that occupy Morris's inventive mind, but what is in between. The

Wright Morris. (Jo Morris)

resolutions that he works toward require especially appropriate intervening incidents that require "a lot of doing." Morris, added Booth, approaches his introductions not as promises to the reader but as problems to be solved by the author himself. What is important in this kind of plot progression is the quality of the middle, and here Morris excels.

Believing that the fiction writer must do more than reproduce facts, Morris transmuted his raw material, particularly his experience of the Midwest, through his imagination into something that he saw as more real than life itself.

My Uncle Dudley

My Uncle Dudley, Morris's somewhat autobiographical first novel, concerns an odyssey in an old Marmon touring car from California to the banks of the Mississippi. The central character, Uncle Dudley, a cross between a modern-day Odysseus and Don Quixote, describes himself as a "horseless knight." His impossible dream of committing one single audacious act is realized when he spits a stream of brown tobacco juice accurately into the eye of a sadistic, perverted police officer.

What is experimental about this novel is the use of the unnamed adolescent narrator, known only as the Kid, who records no emotion at all, thereby enabling the author himself to remain detached. As Madden noted, the heroic act requires a witness. The Kid is Uncle Dudley's witness, through whose imagination the reader recognizes heroism and an unexpressed affection.

Morris acknowledges a debt to Mark Twain's *Adventures of Huckleberry Finn* (1884), although he had not then read the Twain work "as a writer." The Kid is the Huck figure, Uncle Dudley the Jim-father, and the journey in the Marmon a flight from repressive civilization similar to the downriver trip of the raft. The unifying element in Morris's narrative is not the river or the road, however, but Uncle Dudley himself, whose final foolhardy act qualifies him as the first in a long line of heroes.

The Man Who Was There

Agee Ward, the "protagonist" of *The Man Who Was There*, has gone to war and has been reported missing in action; he makes his presence felt through his absence, and he is a hero not of action, as was Uncle Dudley, but of imagination. In the novel's first section, he is remembered at Grandmother Herkimer's funeral by Private Reagan, a boyhood friend, whose stare causes the minister to change his sermon subject to the desire for immortality. The middle section of the book, titled "The Three Agee Wards," re-presents the hero through the media of family photographs, sketches, and letters, through knowledge about his ancestors, and through the mind of the village barber, who has seen him in the eyes of his now deceased mother. Her gravestone inscription announces, "She died that he might live."

The unity of the novel results from the hero's power to transform others. Agee has become a painter and a writer, whose notebooks contain drawings of such artifacts as a pump and a privy; his perspective is faulty because his memory fails and because he cannot reconcile the real and the imaginary in his own mind.

The last witness to be transformed is his spinster landlady Gussie Newcomb, who becomes Agee's symbolic next-of-kin when she is notified by the War Department that he is missing. She barely remembers her lodger, but when the people who do remember him want to look at his belongings, Gussie moves into the apartment herself. Peter Spavic, who has kept up Agee's album and who is obviously a witness, enables Gussie to absorb Agee's personality, the transformation assisted by her communion with the missing man's personal artifacts. Gussie begins to drink, to tell Agee jokes, to dress in some of his costumes, and to take the initiative in her relationship with her suitor, Mr. Bloom. She sits in the dark, as Agee had sat, and she agrees with Peter to name his first son Ward while she will name her first child Agee.

The book explores an idea that was then a cliché: the effect of a dead or missing-in-action soldier on those left at home. Agee, a hero in the literal sense because he actually wants to combat fascism, transforms his witnesses by his very absence, at the same time suggesting the problems of an artist who tries to filter reality through his imagination.

Man and Boy

The first few chapters of Morris's novel *Man and Boy* have been widely anthologized, with slight changes, as the short story "The Ram in the Thicket." The first of Morris's novels to depart from the plains tradition, *Man and Boy* takes place in Philadelphia and New York and describes a single day in the life of the remnants of a family. The Navy is to name a destroyer in honor of the Boy, who has died a hero. His father, Warren, recollects the day he gave the Boy an air rifle, a gift that caused his mother to abolish Christmas henceforth and the Boy to become a hunter, who perhaps wanted to die. Recalling the diverse impressions of Agee Ward in *The Man Who Was There*, the Boy Virgil appears to his parents in different ways, transforming them both, but not improving their relationship.

Warren Ormsby, the Man, is a westerner who boasts that his pioneer grandfather used to eat three rabbits as a meal. He soon learns, however, that his wife, Violet, is not very "feminine." She has, in fact, appropriated to herself the virtues once attributed to pioneer men. Warren has to call her Mother and allows her to dominate the household. She rids the house of germs and bathroom sounds, and even of conversation. While Ormsby cares for the birds in a way that is to him a form of worship, a "Eucharist," Mother insists on calling them by their Latin names. After the Boy is dead, he appears to his father in a dream, wearing "bright, exotic plumage" and accompanied by a flock of birds. When the father tries to join the birds, they attack him. Even in his dream, he recognizes the Mother's effort to destroy the Boy's love for his father, who has been systematically unmanned by Mother.

Indirectly responsible for her son's death, Mother is selected to christen the boat named for her son, thus ironically ensuring the continuation of killing, to which she has been so opposed. The Boy lives on in the imagination of the Man, but Mother's power may extend over that realm eventually; it has embodied the sanitized house and defeated the Navy on the day of the ceremony.

The Works of Love

Morris has admitted that he gave an inordinate amount of time to writing *The Works of Love*. In his first novel, he had set out to make a hero of a nonheroic figure, in the second to allow a man who was not present to dominate the action, and in the third, to allow a man to be dominated by a ruthless female, who finally won his grudging respect, if not admiration. In *The Works of Love*, the protagonist, Will Brady, learns to love in a prodigious, self-conscious, almost methodical manner, even though he has not himself been loved or found suitable recipients for his own works of love. The self-centered women in his life have not appreciated his fumbling, inarticulate efforts at communication. Two of them have been prostitutes, one of whom laughed when he proposed marriage; the other ran away and mailed him another man's baby son to adopt. After his marriage to the widow Ethel Bassett, who sleeps like a mummy tightly wrapped in a sheet, he lies beside her listing in his incipiently loving mind her reasons for doing so. The last woman to whom he tries to become a father-husband is a cigar-counter girl turned alcoholic streetwalker. In an effort to understand and grow closer to his adopted son Willy, Will searches the pages of Booth Tarkington's *Penrod* (1914) and Twain's *The Adventures of Tom Sawyer* (1876) for enlightenment. His final role, that of a department store Santa Claus, allows him to touch and love little children, at the same time distributing some of the works of his abundant love.

Will handles the eggs that he sells with the same gentle touch that he reserves for women, sensing perhaps that both species contain the miracle of life. He is more at home, however, with the eggs than with the women, always a stranger in his own house. In his pursuit of love, he finally cuts himself off from all midwestern, rural roots and heads for Chicago on a quest to fill his emotional void. His incapacity to receive love, his failure to understand himself, and especially his inability to communicate his feelings have set up an almost insurmountable barrier between Will and his love objects. Significantly more at home in a hotel than in his house, he has, for most of his life, failed to connect with the rest of humankind.

The Deep Sleep

In *The Deep Sleep*, Morris again presents a hero who has died, this time Judge Howard Porter. Porter's "witnesses" include the hired man Parson, who has worked for the Porter family for thirty years and loves the almost unlovable Mrs. Porter; the Judge's son-in-law Paul Webb, who gets to know him well just before the funeral, and the Judge's mother, who communicates by tapping her cane and never became acquainted with her son at all. Mrs. Porter had known her husband twice—once in the biblical sense, when their first child was conceived, and a second time just before the funeral, when she told their daughter Katherine that she missed him.

Paul Webb discovers that Mrs. Porter had not ruled her husband as iron-handedly as she had thought. Like Violet Ormsby's husband, the Judge had found a basement-toilet retreat where he stashed his whiskey. In addition, Paul discovers, Judge Porter had an attic hide-out where he smoked cigars and admired his expensive Swiss watch, while he carried a cheap, loud, dollar watch in public. The artist Webb is objective enough to get a balanced picture of the Porter family as he studies the house, room by room. While his wife Katherine fears that he cannot show her mother the sympathy she deserves, the fact that the two finally arrive at the same conclusion about Judge and Mrs. Porter suggests that both are fair in their appraisal.

Like Gussie in *The Man Who Was There*, Webb takes on an additional characteristic of the dead man every time he gains a new insight. As Webb becomes the Judge's spiritual son, he reaches a better understanding of Mrs. Porter. The two watches become the artifacts that connect Webb and his mother-in-law, whose sense of order ("never go to bed with dirty dishes in the house") leads to an understanding with daughter Katherine. Webb finds satisfaction in a compassionate act: He places the gold watch in the cabinet, where Mrs. Porter will have the pleasure of finding it herself.

Madden explains that the novel's title refers to the deep sleep into which American males of the twentieth century have allowed themselves to fall. Like the sleep induced in Adam before God created Eve from his rib, it is so deep that the man never awakens. Woman is born; she dominates, and man sleeps on. That this is a twentieth century phenomenon is demonstrated in Morris's 1980 novel *Plains Song, for Female Voices*, whose character Cora carries out her wifely duties with such distaste that she bites herself on her wedding night. Her husband Emerson feels obliged to explain to the frontier doctor that Cora suffers from the bite of a horse; the uncomplaining Cora finds most of her life as a Nebraska farm wife distasteful, but rebellion never occurs to her.

The Huge Season

Another novel with a dead hero, *The Huge Season* is different because it is told from the single viewpoint of Peter Foley, a professor of classics in a small Pennsylvania college and himself a fully developed character. Foley attempts to escape the bondage of two experiences from the past. The first took place at Colton College in California: Foley shared a suite with several other young men, among them Charles Lawrence, a would-be great tennis player who later committed suicide. The second experience was a single day spent in New York after one of his other suite mates, Jesse Proctor, testified before the U.S. House Committee on Un-American Activities.

Lawrence, the hero who affects all the other men, is another midwesterner with an audacious grandfather. Lawrence himself tries to be audacious, both in the bullring and on the tennis court. He succeeds at tennis, not because he plays well but because he wills himself to win. As is to be expected, the hero strongly influences the lives of his witnesses—three of them actually write books about him.

Foley finally frees himself from captivity by recreating the past in his mind while wearing his hero's jacket around the house. As he achieves his own freedom, Foley at the same time understands more about America. The title of the novel refers to the past—the youth—that Foley realizes is over when he is released into the present. Lawrence, however, continues to live in the imagination of his witness, who has also acquired the tennis player's audacity.

Love Among the Cannibals

The past, so important in *The Huge Season*, is missing in *Love Among the Cannibals*. Macgregor and Horter, two middle-aged Hollywood songwriters, take two girls to Acapulco: Billie, a Memphis "chick" who reads Norman Vincent Peale, and Eva the Greek. The story is about people who live to the tune of "What Next?," a song in progress when Horter and Eva meet. Their car, a fire-engine-red convertible with green leather upholstery, has a built-in record player. Macgregor, a true Hollywood cliché and composer of sentimental popular music, insists that what he is looking for in a woman is "the real thing." Horter, who writes clichéd lyrics because that is what Hollywood demands, persuades Billie, Eva, and Mac that they can write a Mexican musical if they have the proper setting. Mac and Billie find romance in Acapulco and swear to be true to each other, but Eva leaves with a ladybug-shaped biologist, Dr. Leggett.

The Hollywood beach, with its suntan oil and portable radios, symbolizes the artificial present with no traditions or values, the Mexican beach the real present, unspoiled, honest, and authentic. The two "artists" deal in clichés of the kind demanded by mass culture, but Horter recognizes that even clichés can be powerful. He is transformed in Mexico by the natural, physical powers of the Greek, who is unabashedly tanned all over. As he appreciates her vitality and audacity, he even considers returning to the life of a serious poet. He has been stripped to essentials and returned to a wholeness and a recognition of his past that bring with them a hope for the future.

The Field of Vision

Morris's critics generally agree that *The Field of Vision* and *Ceremony in Lone Tree*, both dealing with the same central characters, are his most successful novels. Both employ several narrators viewing the same events and interpreting them differently. The actions of the main character, Gordon Boyd, are witnessed by his best friend, Walter McKee. The two are in love with the same woman, but Lois chooses the more stable Walter.

In *The Field of Vision*, Nebraskans Gordon and Walter recall their experiences while attending a bullfight in Mexico. More than any Morris character, Gordon, a failed writer, is a prisoner of his past, formed by three pivotal events. As a boy, Gordon tries to walk on water but ends by trying to drag himself out in a feeble effort at convincing Walter he can at least swim. The second is Gordon's ripping the back pocket off Ty Cobb's pants during an exhibition baseball game in Omaha, yet another incident witnessed by Walter. When Walter introduces Lois, Gordon kisses her. They fall in love, but she marries Walter anyway, feeling constant guilt afterward. The passive, ineffectual Walter realizes how she feels but is unable to help her.

These events are repeated from several points of view until they take on almost mythic dimensions. The walk represents Gordon's penchant for audacity and accompanying failure. The pocket, which Gordon always carries with him, becomes a tattered emblem of his unattained dreams. The kiss suggests the characters' lack of romantic fulfillment, the kind of emotional austerity all too typical of the residents of Morris's Midwest. Gordon attempts an exorcism of sorts by tossing the imitation coonskin cap of McKee's young grandson into the bullring and lowering the boy, named Gordon, down to retrieve it.

Ceremony in Lone Tree

Ceremony in Lone Tree gathers four generations in a small Nebraska town, their birthday celebration for Lois's elderly father contrasting with a backdrop of contemporary violence. While an atomic bomb failed to go off at a Nevada testing site the day before, two other "bombs" exploded: The nephew of one character runs down three bullies with his hot rod, killing two of them, and Charlie Munger murders ten people during a shooting spree in nearby Lincoln because he wants to be somebody. Morris's America seems capable of only two extremes of behavior: violence or enervating nostalgia. The protagonists have sunk into a stultifying slumber from which even irrational murder and the threat of nuclear annihilation cannot arouse them.

Gordon, accompanied by a tawdry young woman he calls Daughter, arrives to seek a final break with his past through dying a symbolic death. Walter, on the other hand, finally awakens from his deep sleep to stand up to his friend for the first time. Stirred to action by a subconscious recognition of her emotional paralysis, Lois fires her father's ancient six-shooter, the shot ironically causing the old man to drop dead on the morning of his ninetieth birthday. These acts seem to free the McKees from the past somewhat, though the novel, as is typical of Morris, ends ambiguously. *Ceremony in Lone Tree* is the most detailed of Morris's many explorations of Americans' need to free themselves both from the tenacious hold of the past and the banality of the present so that the future can unfold without encumbrance.

Plains Song, for Female Voices

After several decades of novels about women who dominated their men, lured them into sex, and left them, or who married them and honeymooned shrouded in a sheet, Morris's *Plains Song, for Female Voices* should perhaps have redressed some grievances. Madge, however, the only happy wife in the novel, is content with being a bearer of children and smelling Fels-Naptha soap. Cora, a plain Ohio girl who marries Emerson to move to Nebraska, becomes Madge's mother. Cora's world is Emerson's farm, and although she finds enjoyment only with her chickens and her garden, she never considers widening her horizon. Sharon Rose, Madge's cousin, is the modern woman and artist who shuns men altogether, finding her happiness in fleeing Nebraska for Chicago and music study. Sharon cannot understand her past and cannot understand why her relatives are content with their bleak lives, but she does attain a certain amount of self-knowledge.

Like so many of Morris's protagonists, Sharon tries to go home again. What startles her memory is not the paint scaling off Emerson's house but the absence of people. The dipper (a marvelous artifact) floats in a bucket of water, and Sharon smells scorched ironing. Displeased that Madge's husband Ned refers to his car as a "good girl," Sharon becomes ill when Avery, who plans to be a veterinarian, chips tartar off the teeth of a Maltese cat with his thumbnail while she is at the dinner table. On the train on the way back to Chicago, however, Sharon is ashamed of disliking these friendly, decent people. She writes Madge's daughter to suggest that Blanche attend a private school for girls in Waukegan and spend her weekends in Chicago, because Sharon cannot bear the "thought of Blanche thick with child by some loutish youth."

When the pretty girl arrives, Sharon deliberately dresses her in a way to "emphasize her adolescence" so that the "idling males" will not be tempted to molest her. When she finds Blanche with a "beardless, oafish" young man, his arm about the girl's waist, she knows that her efforts to "citify" Blanche—actually to make her independent—have been in vain, and she allows her to return home to her daddy, whom she has missed a great deal.

Sharon finally teaches at Wellesley, more respected than liked by her students. On her last trip home, for Cora's funeral, Madge's daughter Caroline assures Sharon that because of her example, the girls "don't get married anymore unless [they] want to." All that is left of her parents' farm is a pitted field of stumps. "There was nothing worth saving," says Caroline, who adds that she would never forgive Cora for her failure to complain about the hard farm life.

Funerals and eggs, an unlikely combination, continue to recur in Morris's fiction—unlikely until one realizes that, in a Morris novel, the dying will "connect" with and transform many characters, perhaps even achieving resurrection through them, and that eggs, important to Morris since his father sold them, represent not only a new and ongoing life but also the rural Midwest to which he returns again and again for his fictional world.

The wasteland motif, actually verbalized in some of the novels, is to be found in a society without imagination, as on the Los Angeles beach where women wear bathing caps that look like fake hair. The one who can deliver others from such a wasteland is a man or woman with a creative heart—an audacious artist who dares to transform the clichés of the past into the wonders of the present and future, who can convert the raw material of America into values that enable humanity to endure.

Sue L. Kimball
Updated by Michael Adams

Other major works

SHORT FICTION: *Green Grass, Blue Sky, White House*, 1970; *Here Is Einbaum*, 1973; *The Cat's Meow*, 1975; *Real Losses, Imaginary Gains*, 1976; *Collected Stories, 1948-1986*, 1986.

NONFICTION: *The Inhabitants*, 1946; *The Territory Ahead*, 1958, 1963; *A Bill of Rites, a Bill of Wrongs, a Bill of Goods*, 1968; *God's Country and My People*, 1968; *Love Affair: A Venetian Journal*, 1972; *About Fiction: Reverent Reflections on the Nature of Fiction with Irreverent Observations on Writers, Readers, and Other Abuses*, 1975; *Wright Morris: Structures and Artifacts, Photographs, 1933-1954*, 1975; *Earthly Delights, Unearthly Adornments: American Writers as Image-Makers*, 1978; *Will's Boy*, 1981; *Photographs and Words*, 1982; *Picture America*, 1982; *Solo: An American Dreamer in Europe, 1933-1934*, 1983; *A Cloak of Light: Writing My Life*, 1985; *Time Pieces: Photographs, Writing, and Memory*, 1989.

MISCELLANEOUS: *Wright Morris: A Reader*, 1970.

Bibliography

Bird, Roy K. *Wright Morris: Memory and Imagination*. New York: Peter Lang, 1985. An excellent appraisal of self-consciousness in Morris's fiction. Bird moves from a discussion of Morris's use of the past, namely the author's ambivalence toward it, to an analysis of his linguistic technique. The final chapter contains a detailed analysis of *The Fork River Space Project* and *Plains Song, for Female Voices*. Includes a bibliography.

Crump, G. B. *The Novels of Wright Morris: A Critical Interpretation.* Lincoln: University of Nebraska Press, 1978. In an effort to demonstrate Morris's importance and clarify his contribution to modern fiction, Crump begins his study by addressing the major critical positions toward Morris's writing, thus isolating significant features of the author's work. Then he offers a new theoretical groundwork for criticizing the author's fiction: a major dualism between the real and the ideal.

Hollander, John. "The Figure on the Page: Words and Images in Wright Morris's *The Home Place*." *Yale Journal of Criticism* 9 (Spring, 1996): 93-108. Discusses how Morris's *The Home Place* mixes text and photographs. Examines the work's original way of presenting word and image in a mode that appears to mix ekphrasis and illustration.

Howard, Leon. *Wright Morris.* Minneapolis: University of Minnesota Press, 1968. In this brief but insightful pamphlet surveying Morris's novels, Howard asserts that no other American novelist has approached Morris in the variety and shaping of the raw materials. According to Howard, the novelist's unique medium is the high seriousness of brilliant comedy in which the absurd is laid bare with neither bitterness nor hope.

Knoll, Robert E., ed. *Conversations with Wright Morris: Critical Views and Responses.* Lincoln: University of Nebraska Press, 1977. This collection of lectures, interviews, critical essays, and photographs is one of the best sources of information about Morris and his work for the general reader. Much is illuminated in the discussions of Morris the novelist and Morris the photographer. Extensive bibliography.

Madden, David. *Wright Morris.* New York: Twayne, 1964. This work assumes little or no prior knowledge of Morris's writing. Examines each of Morris's novels (ending with *Cause for Wonder*) in order for the reader to see how Wright's themes and methods develop from novel to novel. Madden also discusses characterization and the influence of setting (the Midwest) on Morris's work. Includes a bibliography of primary and secondary sources.

Morris, Wright. *A Cloak of Light: Writing My Life.* New York: Harper & Row, 1985. In this extremely informative and insightful autobiography, Morris sheds light not only on the formation of his character but also on his writing. Among other things, Morris discusses his talent for image-making or what he calls time retrieval—a faculty that has served him well both as a photographer and as a writer.

Trachtenberg, Alan. "Home Place." *Raritan* 26, no. 1 (Summer, 2006): 64-87. Trachtenberg, who has written a book about Morris's photography, discusses two of Morris's books—*The Home Place* and *The Inhabitants*—to describe how they integrate words and photographs to examine the meanings of home and place. He argues that Morris's novels can be well described by the word "photographic."

Wydeven, Joseph J. "Images and Icons: The Fiction and Photography of Wright Morris." In *Under the Sun: Myth and Realism in Western American Literature*, edited by Barbara Howard Meldrum. Troy, N.Y.: Whitston, 1985. This lengthy essay is one of best examinations of the relation between Morris's photography and his fiction.

_______. *Wright Morris Revisited.* New York: Twayne, 1998. A scholar who has written often about Morris updates Madden's study (above). Wydeven argues that Morris's works are about American dreamers who viewed the West as the place where they could fulfill their desires. Includes a portfolio of Morris's photographs.

TONI MORRISON

Born: Lorain, Ohio; February 18, 1931
Also known as: Chloe Anthony Wofford

Principal long fiction

The Bluest Eye, 1970
Sula, 1973
Song of Solomon, 1977
Tar Baby, 1981
Beloved, 1987
Jazz, 1992
Paradise, 1998
Love, 2003
A Mercy, 2008

Other literary forms

Although primarily a novelist, Toni Morrison has published some short fiction, a few works of nonfiction, some edited volumes, and some children's books. Among her edited volumes are *The Black Book: Three Hundred Years of African American Life* (1974), a collection of documents and articles on African American history compiled by Middleton Harris, and a collection of Toni Cade Bambara's writings titled *Deep Sightings and Rescue Missions: Fiction, Essays, and Conversations* (1996). Among Morrison's notable nonfiction works are many essays, such as "The Site of Memory," published in *Inventing the Truth: The Art and Craft of Memoir*, edited by William Zinsser (1987), and "Unspeakable Things Unspoken: The Afro-American Presence in American Literature," which first appeared in the winter, 1989, issue of the *Michigan Quarterly Review*. She has also published the nonfiction works *Remember: The Journey to School Integration* (2004) and *What Moves at the Margin: Selected Nonfiction* (2008).

With her son, Slade Morrison, she has produced several children's books in a series titled Who's Got Game?; titles in the series include *The Ant or the Grasshopper?* (2003) and *The Lion or the Mouse?* (2003). Morrison's first play, *Dreaming Emmett* (pr. 1986), was commissioned by the New York State Writers Institute of the State University of New York. *Honey and Rue*, a musical piece with lyrics by Toni Morrison and music by André Previn, was commissioned by Carnegie Hall for soprano Kathleen Battle and premiered in January, 1992.

Achievements

Toni Morrison is widely regarded as one of the most significant African American novelists to have emerged in the 1970's. Her novel *Sula* was nominated for the National Book Award in 1975, and in 1977, *Song of Solomon* won the National Book Critics Circle Award. The former was a Book-of-the-Month Club alternate and the latter, a main selection. In 1988, *Beloved* was awarded the Pulitzer Prize, and in 1993, Morrison became the first black woman to be honored with the Nobel Prize in Literature.

Morrison's fiction, especially *Song of Solomon*, has been compared to Ralph Ellison's *Invisible Man* (1952) for its mixture of the literal and the fantastic, the real and the surreal. Morrison has been praised for her use of language and for the sense of voice that emerges not only in her dialogue but also in the movement of her narratives. Morrison's novels are also remarkable for their sense of place, for the detailed, coherent physical worlds she creates. Finally, her fiction is noteworthy for its depiction of the deep psychic realities of women's experience.

Biography

Toni Morrison was born Chloe Anthony Wofford, the second of four children. Morrison's father was a shipyard welder. When she was in the first grade, she was the only black student in her class and the only child who was already able to read. Her early literary influences include Leo Tolstoy, Gustave Flaubert, and Jane Austen. Later, as a student at Howard University, Morrison toured the South with the Howard University Players. She married Harold Morrison in 1958; they had two children before divorcing in 1964.

Morrison received her B.A. in English and minored in classics. She taught at the State University of New York at Purchase as a professor of English in 1971-1972 and was the Albert Schweitzer Chair in the Humanities at State University of New York at Albany from 1984 to

1989. From 1989 until she retired in 2006, Morrison was Robert F. Goheen Professor in the Council of the Humanities at Princeton University. During her career, she has also served as trustee of the National Humanities Center and as cochair of the Schomberg Commission for the Preservation of Black Culture. She is a member of the American Academy and Institute of Arts and Letters, the National Council on the Arts, the Authors Guild, and the Authors League of America. In addition to her writing, Morrison has become a popular public lecturer, focusing on African American literature.

ANALYSIS

In all of her fiction, Toni Morrison explores the conflict between society and the individual. She shows how the individual who defies social pressures can forge a self by drawing on the resources of the natural world, on a sense of continuity within the family and within the history of a people, and on dreams and other unaccountable sources of psychic power. Many of her works also confront some sort of sexual depravity that has become a controlling influence on the lives of the characters.

THE BLUEST EYE

In *The Bluest Eye*, Morrison shows how society inflicts on its members an inappropriate standard of beauty and worth, a standard that mandates that to be loved one must meet the absolute "white" standard of blond hair and blue eyes. Morrison's narrator says that two of the most destructive ideas in history are the idea of romantic love (canceling both lust and caring) and the idea of an absolute, univocal standard of beauty.

In the novel, the most extreme victim of these destructive ideas is Pecola, a young African American girl who finds refuge in madness after she has been thoroughly convinced of her own ugliness (confirmed when she is raped by her own father, Cholly). Mrs. Breedlove, Pecola's mother, is another victim who gets her idea of an unvarying standard of beauty from romantic motion pictures that glorify white film stars. When she realizes the impassable gap between that ideal and her physical self (she has a deformed foot and two missing teeth), she also gives up any hope of maintaining a relationship with Cholly, her husband, except one of complete antagonism and opposition. Mrs. Breedlove even comes to prefer the little white girl she takes care of at work to her own daughter, Pecola, whom she has always perceived as ugly.

The ideal of unattainable physical beauty is reinforced by the sugary, unattainable world of the family depicted in school readers—of Mother and Father and Dick and Jane and their middle-class, suburban existence. The contrast between that false standard of life and the reality lived by the African American children in the novel makes them ashamed of their reality, of the physical intimacy of families in which the children have seen their fathers naked.

Although Pecola is thoroughly victimized, Freida and Claudia MacTeer, schoolmates of Pecola, do survive with some integrity and richness. Freida seems to accept Shirley Temple as the ideal of cuteness, but her sister Claudia, a center of consciousness in the novel, responds with anger and defiance, dismembering the hard, cold, smirking baby dolls she receives at Christmas. What Claudia really desires at Christmas is simply an experience of family closeness in the kitchen, an experience of flowers, fruit, and music, of security.

Claudia's anger at the white baby dolls springs from a conviction of her own reality and her own worth. In defense of her own individuality, Claudia rejects Shirley Temple and "Meringue Pie," the "high yellow" princess, Maureen Peal. It is that defense of her own reality that makes Claudia sympathize with Pecola and try to defend her, even to the point of sacrificing Freida's money and her own.

Claudia is especially puzzled and regretful that nobody says "poor baby" to the raped Pecola, that nobody wants to welcome her unborn baby into the world. It would be only natural, "human nature," it seems, for people to sympathize with a victim and rejoice at the creation of a human life. Instead, the springs of human sympathy have been dammed up by social disapproval. Suffering from the self-hatred they have absorbed from the society around them, the members of the black community maintain inflexible social standards and achieve respectability by looking down on Pecola. The two MacTeer sisters appeal to nature to help Pecola and her unborn baby, but nature fails them just as prayer did: No marigolds sprout and grow that year. The earth is unyielding. The baby is stillborn. Eventually, even the two girls become distanced from Pecola, whose only friend

Toni Morrison. (Maria Mulas)

is an imaginary one, a part of herself who can see the blue eyes she was promised. Pecola functions as a scapegoat for the society around her, and Claudia's sympathy later grows into an understanding of how the members of the black community used Pecola to protect themselves from scorn and insult. What finally flowers in Claudia is insight and a more conscious respect for her own reality.

Sula

Sula also explores the oppressive nature of white society toward African Americans, evident in the very name of the "Bottom," a hillside community that had its origin in the duplicitous white treatment of an emancipated black slave who was promised fertile "bottom land" along with his freedom. In a bitterly ironic twist, the whites take over the hillside again when they want suburban houses that will catch the breeze. In taking back the Bottom, they destroy a place, a community with its own identity. In turn, the black community, corrupted by white society, rejects Sula for her experimenting with her life, for trying to live free like a man instead of accepting the restrictions of the traditional female role.

Sula provokes the reader to question socially accepted concepts of good and evil. As Sula is dying, she asks her girlhood friend Nel, "How do you know that you were the good one?" Although considered morally loose and a witch by the townspeople, the unconventional Sula cannot believe herself to be an inferior individual. Contrasting the traditional role of mother and churchwoman that Nel has embraced, Sula's individuality is refreshing and intriguing. Despite her death, Sula maintains an independence that ultimately stands in proud opposition to the established network of relationships that exists within conventional society.

The novel shows that the Bottom society encompasses both good and evil. The people are accustomed to suffering and enduring evil. In varying degrees, they accept Eva's murder of her drug-addict son, Plum, and Hannah's seduction of their husbands, one after another. The community, nevertheless, cannot encompass Sula, a woman who thinks for herself without conforming to their sensibilities. They have to turn her into a witch, so that they can mobilize themselves against her "evil" and cherish their goodness. Without the witch, their goodness grows faint again. Like Pecola, Sula is made a scapegoat.

Growing up in the Bottom, Sula creates an identity for herself, first from the reality of physical experience. When she sees her mother, Hannah, burning up in front of her eyes, she feels curiosity. Her curiosity is as honest as Hannah's admission that she loves her daughter Sula the way any mother would, but that she does not like her. Hearing her mother reject her individuality, Sula concludes that she has no one to count on except herself.

In forging a self, Sula also draws on sexual experience as a means of feeling both joy and sadness and as a means of feeling her own power. Sula does not substitute a romantic dream for the reality of that physical experience. She does finally desire a widening of that sexual experience into a continuing relationship with Ajax, but the role of nurturing and possession is fatal to her. Ajax leaves, and Sula sickens and dies.

A closeness to the elemental processes of nature gives a depth to the lives of the Bottom-dwellers, although nature does not act with benevolence or even with consistency. Plum and Hannah, two of Eva's children, die by fire, one sacrificed by Eva and one ignited by capricious accident. Chicken Little and several of those who follow Shadrack on National Suicide Day drown because acts of play go wrong and inexplicably lead to their destruction. Sula's supposed identity as a witch is connected to the plague of robins that coincides with her return to the Bottom. The people of the Bottom live within nature and try to make some sense of it, even though their constructions are strained and self-serving.

On one level, Sula refuses any connection with history and family continuity. Her grandmother Eva says that Sula should get a man and make babies, but Sula says that she would rather make herself. On the other hand, Sula is a descendant of the independent women Eva and Hannah, both of whom did what they had to do. It is at least rumored that Eva let her leg be cut off by a train so that she could get insurance money to take care of her three children when BoyBoy, her husband, abandoned her. When her husband died, Hannah needed "manlove," and she got it from her neighbors' husbands, despite community disapproval. In their mold, Sula is independent enough to threaten Eva with fire and to assert her own right to live, even if her grandmother does not like Sula's way of living.

To flourish, Morrison suggests, conventional society needs an opposite pole. A richness comes from the opposition and the balance—from the difference—and an acceptance of that difference would make scapegoats unnecessary. The world of the Bottom becomes poorer when Sula dies.

Song of Solomon

In *Song of Solomon*, Morrison again traces the making of a self. The novel is a departure for Morrison in that the protagonist is not female but a young man, Milkman Dead. Milkman grows up in a comfortable, insulated, middle-class African American family, the grandson of a doctor on his mother's side and the son of a businessman, whose father owned his own farm. Son of a doting mother, Milkman is breast-fed a long time, the reason for his nickname, and is sent to school in velvet knickers. Guitar Baines, a Southside black, becomes Milkman's friend and an ally against the other children's teasing.

As the novel progresses, and as Milkman discovers the reality of his family and friends as separate people with their own griefs and torments, Milkman comes to feel that everyone wants him dead. (Ironically, Milkman's last name actually is "Dead," the result of a drunken clerk's error when Milkman's grandfather was registering with the Freedmen's Bureau.) Milkman learns that his mere existence is extraordinary, as even before his birth, his father tried to kill him. Milkman survived that threat through the intercession of his mother and, especially, of his aunt, Pilate, a woman with no navel. After having been conjured by Pilate into making love to his wife again, years after he had turned against her, Macon Dead wanted the resulting baby aborted. Ruth, the baby's mother, out of fear of her husband, took measures to bring about an abortion, but Pilate intervened again and helped Ruth to find the courage to save the child and bear him.

In the present action of the novel, Hagar, Milkman's cousin, his first love and his first lover, pursues him month after month with whatever weapon she can find to kill him. Hagar wants Milkman's living life, not his dead life, but Milkman has rejected her, out of boredom and out of fear that he will be maneuvered into marrying her. At this point, he does not want to be tied down—he wants freedom and escape.

Hagar, like Pecola of *The Bluest Eye*, feels unlovely and unloved, rejected because Milkman does not like her black, curly hair. Pilate says that Milkman cannot *not* love her hair without *not* loving himself because it is the same hair that grows from his own body. Hagar is another victim of an absolutely univocal standard of beauty, and she is a character who needs a supporting society, a chorus of aunts and cousins and sisters to surround her with advice and protection. Instead, she has only Pilate and Reba, grandmother and mother, two women so strong and independent that they do not understand her weakness. Unhinged by Milkman's rejection of her, Hagar chases Milkman with various weapons, is repeatedly disarmed, and finally dies in total discouragement.

Trying to find out about his family's past, Milkman travels to Virginia, to Shalimar, a black town, where the men in the general store challenge him to fight, and one attacks him with a knife. Milkman does not understand why these people want his life, but they think he has insulted and denied their masculinity with his powerful northern money and his brusque treatment of them, by not asking their names and not offering his own.

The most serious threat to Milkman's life, however, turns out to be Guitar, Milkman's friend and spiritual brother. When Guitar tries to kill Milkman, he is betraying the reality of their friendship for the idea of revenge against whites and compensation for the personal deprivation he has suffered. Guitar thinks that Milkman has a cache of gold that he is not sharing with him, so he decides to kill him. Guitar rationalizes his decision by saying that the money is for the cause, for the work of the Seven Days, a group of seven black men sworn to avenge the deaths of innocent blacks at the hands of the whites.

Milkman's being alive at all, then, is a triumph, a victory that he slowly comes to appreciate after coming out of his comfortable shell of self-involvement. Unwillingly, Milkman comes to know the suffering and grief of his mother and father and even his sisters Magdalene and Corinthians. The decisive experience in his self-making, however, is the quest for Pilate's gold on which his father sets him. In the first stage, the men are convinced that Pilate's gold hangs in a green sack from the ceiling of her house, and Guitar and Milkman attempt to steal it. The two friends succeed in taking the sack because the women in the house are simply puzzled, wondering why the men want a sack that is really full of old bones. In leaving the house, however, the two men are arrested, and Pilate must rescue them and the bones by doing an Aunt Jemima act for the white policemen. Milkman's father, Macon, is convinced that the gold still exists somewhere, and Milkman sets out to find it by going back to Pennsylvania, where Macon and Pilate grew up, and later to Virginia, where the previous generation lived.

Milkman's making of a self includes many of the archetypal adventures of the heroes of legend and myth. Like other heroes of legend, Milkman limps, with one leg shorter than the other, a mark of his specialness. Like Oedipus's parents, his parents try to kill him early in his life. There is a wise old lady who gives him help and advice. He goes on a quest for a treasure, and he hopes for gold and the hand of a beautiful princess. He solves a puzzle or riddle to achieve his quest and confirm his identity. He has a transcendent experience and reaches heights of prowess (he can fly). When his people turn against him, he gives his life for them.

Like Sula, too, Milkman creates a self from the reality of physical experience, the processes of nature, a connection to history and family continuity, and springs of human possibility through myth, dreams, legends, and other sources of psychic power. Milkman reaches an understanding of physical experience and the processes of nature in a struggle against the physical environment. As a rich city boy, Milkman was insulated from nature, but in his trip south to try to get the gold, he overcomes a series of physical obstacles to reach the cave where Macon and Pilate in their youth encountered white people and gold. Milkman gets there only after falling into the river and climbing up twenty feet of rock, splitting his shoes and the clothes that mark him as a city man. During the trip, Milkman loses his possessions—trunk, clothes, and whiskey—and he makes it on his own, in a place where his father's name and father's money do not protect him. Milkman succeeds in finding Circe, who years ago sheltered Pilate and Macon when their father was killed, and he reaches the cave, where there is no longer any gold.

Milkman also encounters nature as an obstacle to be overcome when, after the knife fight in Shalimar, he is invited to go on a coon hunt into the woods with the older men of Shalimar. Again, Milkman undergoes a test, having to move through the woods in the dark, having to show the courage and physical endurance necessary to be one of the hunters. Milkman also experiences the music of the hunt, the communication between the men and the dogs, the language before language, of a time when people were so close to their physical reality that they were in harmony with all creatures.

Milkman also creates himself in searching for his origins. In searching for his fathers, he discovers himself; like Telemachus of Greek mythology and James Joyce's Stephen Dedalus, Milkman must find the reality of his fathers to know his own potential. Milkman's original pursuit of the gold seems to be an impulse he gets from his father, the man of business, and even from his father's father, who was a lover of property. The quest, however, changes as Milkman pursues it, finding the thread of his family's history. Stopping in Pennsylvania, Milkman hears the stories of the men who knew his father and grandfather and who rejoice in their successes. The story of the Dead family dramatizes the dream and the failure of that dream for blacks in America. When the older Macon Dead was killed by white men for his flourishing farm, the possibilities of his neighbors were narrowed and their lives scarred. Seeing his father and grandfather through their former neighbors' eyes helps Milkman to understand better the pride that Macon had when he said that his father had let Macon work side by side with him and trusted him to share in his achievements.

In Shalimar, Milkman also learns about his great-grandfather by piecing together the memories of people there and by deciphering a children's game and song, a song about Solomon and Rynah that seems to be interspersed with nonsense words. Milkman matches this song to a song that he had heard Pilate sing about Sugarman. He solves the riddle of the song, and he even figures out what the ghost of Pilate's father meant when he said, "Sing," and when he told Pilate to go get the bones. Finally, he discovers that his grandmother was an American Indian, Singing Bird, and that his great-grandfather, Solomon, was one of the legendary flying Africans, the father of twenty-one sons, a slave who one day flew back to Africa. His grandfather Jake had fallen through the branches of a tree when Solomon dropped him, trying to take his last baby son back with him. Learning about that magic enables Milkman himself to fly when he surrenders to the air and lets himself be upheld.

Milkman creates a self so that he can share it and even sacrifice it for a friend. With Pilate, Milkman buries the bones of Jake, his grandfather, on Solomon's Leap. Guitar, who has continued to stalk Milkman, shoots and kills Pilate, but Milkman, saying to Guitar, "Do you want my life? Take it if it is any good to you," leaps into the air and flies. Guitar is free to kill his friend, but Milkman soars. The ending of the novel shows the transcendence of the spirit, as the hero achieves his destiny. The satisfaction of the ending, which also soars into legend, comes from the triumph of the human spirit, the triumph that even death cannot destroy. *Song of Solomon* is a beautiful, serious, funny novel that moves beyond the social to the mythic.

Tar Baby

Tar Baby explores three kinds of relationships: the relationships between blacks and whites; the relationships within families, especially between parents and children; and the relationships between African American men and women. In the epigraph to the novel, Saint Paul reproaches the Corinthians for allowing contentions to exist among their ranks; the quotation serves to foreshadow the discord that abounds in the novel's relationships.

In *Tar Baby*, Morrison depicts not a self-contained black society but an onstage interaction between blacks and whites. The novel juxtaposes two families, a white family of masters and a black family of servants. The white family includes a retired candy maker, Valerian Street, and his wife, Margaret, once the "Principal Beauty of Maine," who is now in her fifties. The couple's only son, Michael, lives abroad; his arrival for Christmas is expected and denied by various characters. The black family consists of Sydney Childs, who is Valerian's valet and butler, and Sydney's wife, Ondine, who serves as cook and housekeeper. They are childless, but their orphan niece, Jadine, plays the role of their daughter. (Valerian has acted as Jadine's patron, paying for her education at the Sorbonne.)

The pivotal character in the novel, who enters and changes the balance of power and the habitual responses of the families, is a black man who rises out of the sea. His true name is Son, although he has gone by several aliases. The veneer of politeness and familiarity between the characters is shaken by Son's abrupt appearance. Uncomfortable racial and personal assumptions are put into words and cannot be retracted. The Principal Beauty is convinced that Son has come to rape her: What else would a black man want? (Jadine is convinced that if Son wants to rape anyone, it is she, not Margaret.) Sydney finds Son a threat to his respectability as a Philadelphia black, because when Son appears, the white people lump all blacks together. Ondine seems less threatened, but most of her energy goes into her running battle with the Principal Beauty. Jadine is apprehensive at Son's wild appearance, and later she is affronted by his direct sexual approach. Only Valerian welcomes Son. He sees Son as a vision of his absent son, Michael, and he invites him to sit down at the dining table and be a guest.

Son's coming is the catalyst that causes timeworn relationships to explode when Michael does not come for Christmas. His failure to appear leads to the revelation that the Principal Beauty abused her son as a child, pricking him with pins and burning him with cigarettes. Ondine, the black woman, finally hurls this accusation at Margaret, the white, and makes explicit what the two women have known mutually since the beginning. Valerian, who has been haunted by the memory of Michael as a lonely child who would hide under the sink and sing to himself, is hit with a reality much harsher than he has known or admitted.

Structured as it is in terms of families, the whole novel revolves around family responsibilities, especially between parents and children. Michael Street does not come home for Christmas, but the abuse he suffered as a child seems to justify his absence. Thus, the undutiful mother Margaret has thrown the whole family off balance. In the black family, later in the novel, attention is drawn to the undutiful daughter Jadine, although it seems implied that she has learned this undutifulness, partly at least, from whites, wanting her individual success to be separate from family ties and responsibilities. This undutifulness also springs from a question of identity. In Paris, even before she comes to Valerian's island, Jadine feels affronted by a beautiful, proud, contemptuous African woman in yellow who buys three eggs and carries them on her head. She is herself and embodies her tradition consummately, exhibiting balance and physical grace that symbolize spiritual poise. Jadine feels diminished and threatened by the African woman, who spits at her. The scorn sends Jadine back to her family, Sydney and Ondine.

Jadine is similarly disturbed by her dream of the women with breasts, the mothers, who reproach her for not joining that chain of mothers and daughters who become mothers with daughters. Although Jadine herself is an orphan, reared by Ondine and Sydney and owing much to their care, she refuses to take the self-sacrificing role of the woman who cares for her family. Jadine wants money and the power it brings in the white world. Eventually she wants to run her own business, perhaps a boutique. Also, she may choose a white husband, like the man who bought her a seductive sealskin coat.

Jadine is the Tar Baby of the novel, and Son is Br'er Rabbit from the Uncle Remus stories. As the Tar Baby, Jadine acts as a possible trap for Son set by his enemies, white society. Jadine, who has absorbed many white values, wants money and success. Son wants something purer, something associated with nature (he is associated with the sea and the beauty of the savannahs) and with family tradition. Nature, direct physical experience, and family traditions that are integral to personal identity are all important values in Son's existence. Son has a home—the completely black town of Eloe—and there he abides by the ideas of respectability held by his father and his aunt Rosa. (He asks Jadine to sleep at Aunt Rosa's, apart from him, and he comes to her secretly only when she threatens to leave if he does not.) To amuse herself in the traditional town, in which she is uncomfortable, Jadine takes photographs of the people and steals their souls, stealing their individual beauty and grace. In the photographs, they seem graceless, poor, and stupid, even to Son, who usually sees them with loving eyes.

Individually, Son and Jadine love each other, but they seem unable to find a world in which they can both thrive. Son is an undaunted lover, however, unwilling to let Jadine go, even when she flees from him. Son tries to return to Isle de Chevaliers, Valerian's island, to get news of Jadine, but the only way he can get there seems to be through the help of Thérèse, a half-blind, fifty-year-old black woman who says that her breasts still give milk. Thérèse takes him by boat to the island of the horsemen. Son has said that he cannot give up Jadine, but Thérèse tells him to join the fabled black horsemen who see with the mind. At the end of the novel, Son is running toward his destiny, whether that be Jadine and some way to make her part of his world or the black horsemen who ride free through the hills. Readers do not know what Son's fate is to be; they only know that Son is running toward it, just as Br'er Rabbit ran from his enemy Br'er Fox and from the Tar Baby. Like Milkman Dead at the end of *Song of Solomon*, Son leaps into mythic possibility; like Br'er Rabbit, Son, the black man, is a figure with the power to survive.

Beloved

In editing *The Black Book*, a collection of African American historical memorabilia, Toni Morrison discovered an article that would serve as the foundation of her fifth novel. *Beloved* is based on a true account of a runaway slave mother who, rather than allowing her children to be taken back into slavery, murders three of the four. As the novel begins, Sethe's sons, Buglar and Howard, have already run away, while Denver, the youngest child, has survived the murder attempt and still lives with her mother in a house beset by the spirit of her murdered sister, Beloved. Morrison deliberately disorients the reader as she delves into the "interior life" of slavery, creating an experience similar to that of slavery as the narrative breaks apart, shifts, and confounds.

The house at 124 Bluestone Road is personified as a tormented being when Beloved returns, emerging from a lake, fully clothed, the same age she would have been had she survived the infanticide. What the spirit wants initially is unclear. Morrison uses metaphorical imagery with tremendous skill, such as in her description of Sethe's back, a relief map of scars from savage beatings, as resembling the branches of a chokecherry tree. When Paul D, a former slave whom Sethe once knew, moves in, Beloved wreaks havoc. The spirit behaves like an enraged toddler, but the damage she does is that of a full-grown woman. As the ghost continues to threaten her mother and sister, the characters' thoughts intertwine until the reader cannot be certain which character is which.

Jazz

Morrison intended *Jazz*, another novel inspired by a news article, to follow *Beloved* as the second of a trilogy, although the narrative does not pick up where *Beloved* ends. Joe Trace, a married man and cosmetics salesman, shoots his teenage lover, Dorcas, at a party. She dies refusing to reveal his name. At her funeral, Violet, Joe's wife, a hairdresser, defaces the girl's corpse. Set in 1926, *Jazz* begins after Violet has cut the dead girl's face, twenty years after she and Joe arrived in Harlem from the South, where they scraped out a living as sharecroppers. After Dorcas's funeral, Violet returns home and releases her caged parrot, the only creature in her life who says "I love you" anymore.

The deep, unrealized passion for human contact that Morrison depicts in *Beloved* takes root in *Jazz*, but it too becomes messy, dangerous, and out of control. Violet's mind unravels, and, strangely, she turns to Alice Manfred, Dorcas's aunt, for comfort. The theme of mother loss, profound and frustrated, also continues in *Jazz*: Dorcas's mother burns to death in an intentionally set fire; Violet's mother throws herself down a well because of her despair over not providing for her children. Years later, Violet longs so achingly for a child that she considers stealing one. It is only at the end of *Jazz*, when Violet and Joe reconcile and Violet buys a sick parrot that she nurses back to health by playing jazz for it, that there is some hope of a lasting human connection.

Paradise

Paradise, Morrison's seventh novel, like her previous two, was inspired by a little-known event in African American history, this time the post-Civil War westward migration of former slaves set on establishing their own all-black utopias. The all-black town in the book is named Ruby. Shifting back and forth across a century of time, *Paradise* begins in 1976, when a group of Ruby's settlers' male descendants attack a mansion-turned-convent of women, convinced that the town's survival is threatened by the women's eschewing of male companionship and their questionable pasts.

The story of Ruby's establishment is related: The town is founded as a response not only to white racism but also to other African Americans who turned away would-be settlers in other towns for having skin that was "too black." Twin brothers Deacon and Steward, the town's elders, are deeply committed to keeping Ruby as pristine and trouble-free as possible. Together, they symbolize Ruby's twin identity and conscience.

Initially, Ruby has no crime and therefore needs no police. There is no hunger; those who have resources assist those in need. However, the town's total isolation from the outside world proves to be its undoing as the rebellion of the 1960's youth movement seeps into Ruby. A ragtag group of women, most escaping either abusive relationships or the responsibilities of motherhood, settle outside Ruby. Among others, there is Consolata, the maternal leader; Seneca, abandoned as a child by her teenage mother; and Pallas, a white woman fleeing her wealthy but negligent parents. The violent confrontation between the men of Ruby and the self-exiled women is brought on, in part, by the black men's anger at women who have willfully chosen a life without men.

Love

In *Love*, Morrison deconstructs familial relationships in an African American community that has been strongly influenced by the presence of Bill Cosey, a wealthy black man who owned a resort hotel that catered to both blacks and whites during the years just before and during the Civil Rights movement of the 1960's. Christine, Cosey's granddaughter, and Heed are the main characters; as old women, they have an intense hatred for each other. Their animosity seems to be based on Heed's marriage to Cosey—Heed was an uneducated, poverty-stricken eleven-year-old child when she was sold into marriage with Cosey. Until late in the novel, readers are led to believe that, with the marriage, Heed usurped Christine's place in her grandfather's affections.

As in many of Morrison's novels, a shifting narrative perspective provides insight into the characters, in this case the women and the man around whose life theirs seemingly revolved. Monologues from L, the spirit for whom the novel is named, provide what seem to be the most strongly objective point of view on the women's past. L is able to understand what motivates Christine, the granddaughter who was thrown aside by her best friend's marriage to her grandfather, as well as the confusion and insecurity of Heed, the child tied to a fifty-two-year-old man. Additionally, L provides insight into May, Christine's mother and Bill Cosey's daughter-in-law.

Sandler and Vida Gibbons are comparatively minor characters whose memories of Cosey provide more insight into the depraved man who had such a strong hold over the community. Though introduced early, Sandler reveals his true connection to Cosey only a little at a time. Sandler reminisces about fishing trips with Cosey but neglects to reveal that those fishing trips included sexual escapades. Heed and Christine both add their own flashbacks to the narrative, clarifying that their adult hatred of each other stems more from the devastation that Heed and Cosey's marriage wrought on both than from a problem between the girls. Intertwined with the stories of the other characters is the story of Romen, the Gibbonses' grandson, and Junior Viviane, a troubled young woman who answers Heed's advertisement for a companion. Junior's ravenous hunger for food, shelter, and sex reflect Bill Cosey in many ways.

Bill Cosey seems to be the central axis around which all of the women's lives revolve. His sexual appetite is seemingly boundless. He is well known for his affairs with women during and between his marriages, including a relationship with his daughter-in-law, but a darker side emerges as readers recognize that his marriage to an eleven-year-old child is just the tip of his depravity. There is also the suggestion that he has molested his granddaughter and had homosexual relations not only with Sandler Gibbons but also with rich and influential white men in the community. Cosey's significance is primarily as an agent of separation and of unity. His depraved sexual behavior started a rift between the girls that his marriage to Heed increased. Each lost her best friend as a result of fear that the other would see the manner in which Cosey's depravity had shadowed her own soul. Though the story is really about Christine and Heed, Cosey unifies the characters in complicated ways that leave readers wondering whether he was good or bad.

Kate Begnal; Nika Hoffman
Updated by Theresa L. Stowell

Other major works

PLAY: *Dreaming Emmett*, pr. 1986.

NONFICTION: *Playing in the Dark: Whiteness and the Literary Imagination*, 1992; *Conversations with Toni Morrison*, 1994 (Danille Taylor-Guthrie, editor); *Remember: The Journey to School Integration*, 2004; *What Moves at the Margin: Selected Nonfiction*, 2008 (Carolyn C. Denard, editor).

CHILDREN'S LITERATURE: *The Big Box*, 1999 (with Slade Morrison); *The Book of Mean People*, 2002 (with Slade Morrison); *The Ant or the Grasshopper?*, 2003 (with Slade Morrison); *The Lion or the Mouse?*, 2003 (with Slade Morrison); *Poppy or the Snake?*, 2003 (with Slade Morrison); *The Mirror or the Glass?*, 2004 (with Slade Morrison).

EDITED TEXTS: *To Die for the People: The Writings of Huey P. Newton*, 1972; *The Black Book: Three Hundred Years of African American Life*, 1974; *Race-ing Justice, En-gendering Power: Essays on Anita Hill, Clarence Thomas, and the Construction of Social Reality*, 1992; *Deep Sightings and Rescue Missions: Fiction, Essays, and Conversations*, 1996 (of Toni Cade Bambara's writings); *Birth of a Nation'hood: Gaze, Script, and Spectacle in the O. J. Simpson Case*, 1997 (with Claudia Brodsky Lacour).

Bibliography

Bloom, Harold, ed. *Toni Morrison*. New York: Chelsea House, 1990. Provides a fine selection of critical essays on Morrison's works, with an excellent introduction by Bloom and an extensive bibliography.

Conner, Marc C., ed. *The Aesthetics of Toni Morrison: Speaking the Unspeakable*. Jackson: University Press of Mississippi, 2000. Collection of essays concentrates on the imagery and stylistics of Morrison's writings and her ability to convey the "unspeakable" aspects of African American experience.

Decker, James M. "Toni Morrison's Sula and Subjective Ideology." In *Ideology*. New York: Palgrave Macmillan, 2004. Scholarly work provides a close reading of *Sula* from an ideological viewpoint.

Denard, Carolyn C., ed. *Toni Morrison: Conversations*. Jackson: University Press of Mississippi, 2008. Collection of previously published interviews with Morrison covers topics such as her early life, her teaching philosophy, and her perspectives on American society, American literature, and her own work, including the evolution of her writing style.

Fultz, Lucille P. *Toni Morrison: Playing with Difference*. Urbana: University of Illinois Press, 2003. Examines Morrison's approach to differences (for example, black and white, male and female, wealth and poverty) in her intricate narratives.

Furman, Jan, ed. *Toni Morrison's "Song of Solomon."* New York: Oxford University Press, 2003. Collection of essays presents the major critical responses to Morrison's novel; intended as a starting point for students first encountering the book.

Harris, Trudier. *Fiction and Folklore: The Novels of Toni Morrison*. Knoxville: University of Tennessee Press, 1991. Examines the use of African and African American myth and folklore in Morrison's novels through *Beloved*, with a focus on the archetypes and antiheroes that pervade the stories. An important scholarly guide to understanding the subtext of Morrison's work.

O'Reilly, Andrea. *Toni Morrison and Motherhood: A Politics of the Heart*. Albany: State University of New York Press, 2004. Discusses the ways in which Morrison depicts mothers and motherhood in her works. Considers Morrison's connection between mothering and racism, sexism, and culture.

Otten, Terry. *The Crime of Innocence in the Fiction of Toni Morrison*. Columbia: University of Missouri Press, 1989. Groundbreaking study of Morrison's first five novels explores the mythic substance in the writings by tracing the motif of the biblical Fall. Provides insightful readings and unflagging attention to the historical and literary backdrop.

Tully, Justine, ed. *The Cambridge Companion to Toni Morrison*. New York: Cambridge University Press, 2007. Collection of essays offers an excellent introduction to and examination of Morrison's whole body of work. Covers all aspects of her writings, from narrative sequences to themes to political philosophy. Includes a chronology and critical guide for further reading.

WALTER MOSLEY

Born: Los Angeles, California; January 12, 1952
Also known as: Walter Ellis Mosley

Principal long fiction

Devil in a Blue Dress, 1990
A Red Death, 1991
White Butterfly, 1992
Black Betty, 1994
RL's Dream, 1995
Gone Fishin', 1996
A Little Yellow Dog, 1996
Always Outnumbered, Always Outgunned, 1998
Blue Light, 1998
Walkin' the Dog, 1999
Fearless Jones, 2001
Bad Boy Brawly Brown, 2002
Fear Itself, 2003
Little Scarlet, 2004
The Man in My Basement, 2004
Cinnamon Kiss, 2005
Fear of the Dark, 2006
Fortunate Son, 2006

The Wave, 2006
Blonde Faith, 2007
Killing Johnny Fry, 2007
Diablerie, 2008
The Right Mistake: The Further Philosophical Investigations of Socrates Fortlow, 2008
The Tempest Tales, 2008

OTHER LITERARY FORMS

In addition to his novels, Walter Mosley (MOHZ-lee) has coedited *Black Genius: African American Solutions to African American Problems* (1999) and has written a critical analysis of capitalism, *Workin' on the Chain Gang: Shaking Off the Dead Hand of History* (2000). In *What Next: A Memoir Toward World Peace* (2003), he contends that the African American experience provides a unique and helpful perspective on the way to achieve world peace. As in his novels, in his nonfiction Mosley transforms social problems into palpable personal ones—in this case by drawing on his own family history. Mosley attacks American provincialism and provides his own idiosyncratic solutions to the problem in *Life Out of Context: Which Includes a Proposal for the Non-violent Takeover of the House of Representatives* (2006). *This Year You Write Your Novel* (2007) provides practical advice for starting and completing a novel within a year. Mosley's short stories have been published in several collections, including *Futureland: Nine Stories of an Imminent World* (2001).

ACHIEVEMENTS

A prolific author of mystery, young adult, and science-fiction novels, Walter Mosley has become one of the most successful African American authors whose work has crossed over into mainstream fiction. His work has been compared favorably to that of classic African American authors such as Chester Himes and John Edgar Wideman. As Frances Smith Foster has observed, however, Mosley surpasses these authors and others in his ability to dramatize the lives of ordinary African Americans with a political consciousness and a sense of social history.

Mosley's first novel, *Devil in a Blue Dress*, was nominated for the prestigious Edgar Award, presented by the Mystery Writers of America, as well as the Shamus Award of the Private Eye Writers of America. In 1996, Mosley won an award from the Black Caucus of the American Library Association as well as an O. Henry Award. *Bad Boy Brawly Brown* was nominated for the International Association of Crime Writers' Hammett Prize. In 2005, Mosley received several honors: the Sundance Institute's Risk-Takers Award; a Lifetime Achievement Award presented at the Twenty-first Annual Celebration of Black Writing, held by the Art Sanctuary of Philadelphia; and an honorary doctorate presented by the City College of the City University of New York.

BIOGRAPHY

Walter Ellis Mosley was born in January, 1952, and grew up in South Central Los Angeles, which became the setting of many of his novels. Early in his life he became acutely aware of social and political issues, hearing stories from his African American father about life in the American South and from his Jewish mother about anti-Semitism.

Mosley earned a bachelor's degree in political science from Johnson State College in Vermont and then worked as a computer programmer for fifteen years (an experience he puts to good use in his novel *Diablerie*) before enrolling in a creative-writing program at City College of the City University of New York, where he was taught by Edna O'Brien and other important writers. He had long been a keen reader of detective stories, and it is not surprising that he turned to the genre in his first novel—although the initial inspiration for his work was Alice Walker's novel *The Color Purple* (1982). One of Mosley's teachers showed an early draft of Mosley's first novel to her literary agent, who was able to sell it to the publishing company W. W. Norton.

Mosley's most famous character, Easy Rawlins, belongs to Mosley's father's generation, and many of Rawlins's experiences are based on stories that Mosley's father told him about the lives of black people of his generation in both northern and southern areas of the United States. Los Angeles, the main setting of the Rawlins novels, represents the promise and the peril that Mosley's father found in a wide-open and yet highly stratified society full of opportunity but also dangerous for African Americans.

Analysis

Walter Mosley has been praised for his powerful evocation of African Americans and their milieu. His novels show African Americans interacting with each other, creating their own problems and solutions. While the white power structure certainly impinges on these characters, they are not victims. On the contrary, they are accorded their full humanity and the right, so to speak, to commit their own mistakes and achieve their own successes as individuals and as a people.

RL's Dream

RL's Dream has been compared favorably with Ralph Ellison's classic novel *Invisible Man* (1952), an apt comparison, since Mosley, like his illustrious predecessor, writes a prose that is suffused with the rhythms of the blues. Like Ellison, Mosley does not blink at the harshness of the African American experience, and he finds a meaning in suffering, a definition of humanity, that triumphs over degradation.

Robert "RL" Johnson, a legendary blues musician, is the presiding presence in the novel. Atwater "Soupspoon" Wise is an aging African American musician obsessed with memories of RL and determined to recover for posterity the role of the blues in African American life. Kiki Waters, a white girl from Arkansas, befriends the aging Soupspoon, takes care of him, and helps to ensure that he is able to tell his life story.

RL exists only in the memories of those he touched with his music. By dreaming of RL, Soupspoon provides the geography of the blues, explaining to the young Kiki how it was for talented musicians who had to disguise their genius by playing the slack-jawed, clownish Negro—except that RL refused to bow to this form of degradation, paying the physical and mental price for his independence: "Ain't no start to his misery," Soupspoon's book says of RL, "An' death could not never ease his kinda pain."

Life is a tragedy and full of pain, and yet it is a story that is redeemable in the beauty of the blues. This is the story of the blues that Soupspoon conveys to Kiki and a story that he is determined to share with the world. Years earlier, he was asked to provide an account of his career, but his life was too complicated and his suffering too great for him to contemplate telling his own tale. Now confronting certain death, Soupspoon finds that he has the motivation and the perspective to organize his experience into a narrative, which he composes on a tape recorder as he relates his memories to Kiki and others.

Soupspoon regards RL's music as the essence of the blues—perhaps because RL did not permit any event or experience to distract him from the making of music. He is, then, the blues personified, always beset with suffering and yet indomitable and inimitable. The latter point is what Soupspoon emphasizes; that is, he regards himself as a pale imitation of RL because RL is the epitome of a form of music that has allowed a whole people to endure suffering and even to prevail by creating great art.

RL is a "dream" in the sense that he represents the artist's aspirations, the ideal of a great music that transcends life's limitations and the frailties of the artists who perform that music. By recounting his "dream" of RL, Soupspoon is ennobling not only his life but also the strivings of the people blues artists muse about in their music.

Walkin' the Dog

Walkin' the Dog is Mosley's second novel in his series featuring Socrates Fortlow, an ex-convict who has

Walter Mosley. (Courtesy, Allen & Unwin)

settled down to make his quiet way in the world but who is constantly challenged by events in his neighborhood and community that make it difficult for him to remain a peaceful man. Fortlow's difficulty is that he cannot ignore injustice. At the same time, he realizes that for the first time in his life he may actually have the opportunity to live like a normal person with a decent job and home, although he can hardly accept his good fortune—even when he is offered a promotion at the produce market. Fortlow wonders if he wants more responsibility. He values his independence, and a part of him would prefer not to take on more in the form of employment.

Fortlow lives in a high-crime neighborhood but has managed to stay out of jail for nine years. He has a modest and very circumscribed domestic life, which includes a two-legged dog named Killer. It is hard for him to live on an even keel, however, when the police continue to pester him, trying to link him to various crimes in his area. Inured to police suspicion, Fortlow just barely manages to keep his temper—although he stands up for his rights and will not be bullied.

The novel takes the form of various incidents, complete in themselves as short stories but linked by Fortlow's continual troubles with the law, that culminate in his campaign to protest the violent crimes of a cop who has abused and even killed African Americans. Fortlow turns himself into a walking billboard, and though at first he seems destined to be arrested, others who share his concerns soon join him. Ultimately, one man's protest becomes a community's cause, which in turn generates media attention and pressure on the police department to discipline and punish its own. This story is a triumph for Fortlow, since his first impulse was simply to murder the cop. Now he seeks ways to channel his rage into socially responsible behavior. At the same time, he refuses to accept the status quo; he still takes risks that he knows may land him in jail once more.

Mosley has emphasized that in Socrates Fortlow he has created a black thinker, a kind of representative of African American consciousness. This is probably why the Fortlow stories have relatively little plot and action. They are centered, instead, on the development of character and theme. As a result, Mosley's main character does indeed seem like the skeptical philosopher for whom he is named. He doubts the certitudes that others express because he is aware of the precariousness not only of his own position but also that of others, who might, like himself, end up in prison precisely because their worldviews are flawed and do not take in account so many of the forces in society over which they have no control. In this respect, Fortlow has been compared with Tom Joad, the philosopher/common man of John Steinbeck's *The Grapes of Wrath* (1939). Both men, hemmed in by societal pressures, commit murder, and yet they conceive of a redemptive vision of humanity that transcends their individual fates.

Bad Boy Brawly Brown

In *Bad Boy Brawly Brown*, Easy Rawlins is out to find the title character and keep him out of trouble. The boy's mother and his stepfather (an old friend of Easy) are concerned that Brawly has become involved with a group of black revolutionaries. The setting is the Los Angeles neighborhood of Watts in 1964, the year before the riots that alarmed both the city and the nation. Easy—not a man susceptible to the rhetoric of black power—has to negotiate his way through the duplicity of the black revolutionaries, Brawly's naïve faith in them, and the machinations of law-enforcement agents attempting to infiltrate and destroy political protest groups.

Very much an individualist, Easy is wary of the movement leaders and their zealous lieutenants, but he is hardly any more sanguine about the motives of the white establishment and the police. Easy is no rebel (indeed, he is a World War II combat veteran), but he is also not complacent about the status quo. He provides a critical perspective on all sides of this engrossing political novel, never forsaking his unique experience as a black man but also not overlooking the opportunities his country does offer—provided bitterness, bigotry, and fanaticism do not blind the individual to reality. In this work Mosley skillfully employs the form of the detective novel to get at the psychological roots of radicalism and reaction, since Easy has to keep a clear-eyed, objective attitude if he is to understand the people who have enthralled Brawly and discover how to disengage the young man from his conspiratorial cohort.

Diablerie

The title of Mosley's 2008 novel *Diablerie* is also the name of a new magazine that the main character's wife is promoting. Ben Dibbuk is a computer programmer stuck in a rut. He is bored with his routine job, and, even worse, he has withdrawn from his wife, Mona, and is cheating on her even as she herself has taken a lover. Dibbuk reluctantly shows up at the party held to celebrate publication of *Diablerie* and is accosted by a woman who claims knowledge of a murder he committed more than twenty years earlier in Colorado. Dibbuk does not remember the woman or the crime but is disturbed by her allegation because he was drinking heavily at that time in his life and was prone to memory lapses and blackouts.

Acting like a detective, Dibbuk seeks to expose his own life and to come to terms with what has happened to him emotionally. Why has he closed himself off? Why has he settled for such a routine job? His rather heroic self-analysis and his refusal to accept anything less than the truth about himself are the most compelling aspects of the novel. Dibbuk's plight, at least in some respects, is informed by Mosley's own experience of life-changing events that took him out of his dull computer programming job and propelled him toward a writing career.

Carl Rollyson

Other major works

SHORT FICTION: *Futureland: Nine Stories of an Imminent World*, 2001; *Six Easy Pieces: Easy Rawlins Stories*, 2003.

NONFICTION: *Workin' on the Chain Gang: Shaking Off the Dead Hand of History*, 2000; *What Next: A Memoir Toward World Peace*, 2003; *Life Out of Context: Which Includes a Proposal for the Non-violent Takeover of the House of Representatives*, 2006; *This Year You Write Your Novel*, 2007.

YOUNG ADULT LITERATURE: *Forty-seven*, 2005.

EDITED TEXTS: *Black Genius: African American Solutions to African American Problems*, 1999 (with others); *The Best American Short Stories, 2003*, 2003 (with Katrina Kenison).

Bibliography

Berger, Roger A. "'The Black Dick': Race, Sexuality, and Discourse in the L.A. Novels of Walter Mosley." *African American Review* 31 (Summer, 1997): 281-295. Provides a thoughtful and comprehensive discussion of the Easy Rawlins novels.

Brady, Owen E., and Derek C. Maus, eds. *Finding a Way Home: A Critical Assessment of Walter Mosley's Fiction*. Jackson: University Press of Mississippi, 2008. Collection of essays focuses on the meaning of the concept of home in Mosley's novels and other writings.

Coale, Samuel. "Race, Region, and Rite in Mosley's Mysteries." In *The Mystery of Mysteries: Cultural Differences and Designs*. Bowling Green, Ohio: Bowling Green State University Popular Press, 2000. Examines Mosley's use of black characters within the mystery and detective genre, which has traditionally been dominated by white characters.

Foster, Frances Smith. "Mosley, Walter." In *The Oxford Companion to African American Literature*. New York: Oxford University Press, 1997. Provides a brief biography and discusses the significance of the Easy Rawlins novels, comparing them to works by other notable detective and mystery writers.

Gussow, Adam. "'Fingering the Jagged Grain': Ellison's Wright and the Southern Blues Violences." *Boundary* 30, no. 2 (2003): 137-155. Presents historical background that is essential for an understanding of Mosley's work.

Mosley, Walter. "Anger and Hope Mosley's Formula for Success." Interview by Greg Burchall. *The Age* (Melbourne, Australia), January 31, 1996. Mosley discusses his career, growing up in south Los Angeles, and his belief in the heroism of the black struggle. He also provides information on the literary influences on his work and describes the process he uses in drafting his novels.

Mvuyekure, Pierre-Damien. "Mosley, Walter." In *St. James Encyclopedia of Popular Culture*. Vol. 3. Farmington Hill, Mich.: St. James Press, 2000. Focuses on the importance of the first Easy Rawlins novel, *Devil in a Blue Dress*, with a very brief discussion of Mosley's later work.

Wilson, Charles E., Jr. *Walter Mosley: A Critical Companion*. Westport, Conn.: Greenwood Press, 2003. Good introduction to Mosley's fiction presents discussion of several of his novels, including an analysis of *RL's Dream* that explores the novel's treatment of the blues. A biographical chapter provides background on Mosley's life.

BHARATI MUKHERJEE

Born: Calcutta (now Kolkata), West Bengal, India; July 27, 1940

Principal long fiction

The Tiger's Daughter, 1972
Wife, 1975
Jasmine, 1989
The Holder of the World, 1993
Leave It to Me, 1997
Desirable Daughters, 2002
The Tree Bride, 2004

Other literary forms

Bharati Mukherjee was initially propelled to literary fame with the publication of short stories that provide intense portraits of "immigrant experiences" and cultural collisions through her kaleidoscopic characters; these stories have been published in the collections *Darkness* (1985) and *The Middleman, and Other Stories* (1988). In these brilliant and multifaceted stories, Mukherjee depicts the harsh realities of the "stranger in a strange land" who may find him- or herself confronted with the challenges of understanding new cultures, coping with "otherness," and learning new ways of being. An immigrant herself, Mukherjee delineates in these stories the hardship of and the need for transforming oneself that is inherent in the immigrant experience.

Mukherjee is also recognized for her nonfiction works that deal with the immigrant experience from both political and social perspectives. Her *Days and Nights in Calcutta* (1977), coauthored with her husband, Clark Blaise, demonstrates a bipartite perspective on India: from a returning native (the author) and a foreigner (American-born Blaise). Such a perspective allows for a complex and multilayered look at the complications of being a "citizen" in transition.

Mukherjee has written several studies on political issues and India—studies that demonstrate her continuing interest in placing her fictional concerns within a historical perspective. *The Sorrow and the Terror: The Haunting Legacy of the Air India Tragedy* (1987), coauthored with Blaise, not only examines the personal tragedy of the families involved in the suspected terrorist bombing of an Air India flight in 1985 (to New Delhi from Toronto) but also scrutinizes the role played in the event by the Canadian government's shortsighted immigration policies. Mukherjee also has produced a significant body of work that consists of uncollected essays and articles on women's issues, the intersection of politics and multiculturalism, and the history of India.

Achievements

In addition to blazing a path for female Indian writers, Bharati Mukherjee has succeeded in initiating a new focus for an entire group of writers: the impact and importance of the immigrant experience. It is an experience that is relevant not only to the immigrant but also to the population of the receiving culture. Mukherjee has been cited as "embracing" American culture and "hopeful" at the regenerative effects of amalgamating her Indian heritage with a constantly metamorphosing American culture.

For both her scholarship and her literary production, Mukherjee has received fellowships, awards, and other recognition, most notably a P.E.O. International Peace Scholarship to the University of Iowa's Writers' Workshop and the National Book Critics Circle Award for fiction (1988) for *The Middleman, and Other Stories*—a work of superbly crafted portraits of a multitude of characters in conflict while acculturating to new homes, families, or cultures. Mukherjee has become known worldwide for her works that somehow define what it means to be an American and, as Radha Chakravarty has noted, what it means to "find a voice to express a complex, cross-cultural sensibility."

Biography

Although born in India to parents of a Bengali Brahman (upper-class) caste, Bharati Mukherjee became a citizen of the world early in life. Born in July, 1940, to a father who was a prosperous pharmaceutical chemist and business owner and to a freethinking mother, both of whom wanted education and freedom of action for their daughters, Mukherjee experienced a rather cosmopolitan education. In 1947, after India won its independence from Great Britain, she was enrolled in boarding schools in England and Switzerland, where she perfected her English. Her native Bengali language and customs were marginalized by her educators, and she returned to Calcutta (now known as Kolkata) somewhat a cultural "outsider" to her native India. There she completed her secondary education at Loreto House, taught by Irish nuns.

Mukherjee continued her education, obtaining a bachelor's degree in English at the University of Calcutta and a master's degree in both English and ancient Indian culture at the University of Baroda (1961). Subsequently, she was part of the Writers' Workshop at the University of Iowa and began her literary and teaching career, the latter of which included positions at Marquette University in Milwaukee, the University of Wisconsin at Madison, McGill University in Montreal, Columbia University in New York, and the University of California at Berkeley.

It was at the University of Iowa that Mukherjee received both an M.F.A. and a Ph.D. In 1963, she married Clark Blaise, with whom she migrated to Toronto. Issues with local racism caused Mukherjee to reevaluate her adopted country and seek residence in the United States. In her essay "An Invisible Woman," published in the Toronto magazine *Saturday Night* in 1981, Mukherjee decried the racism she felt there, presenting a negative picture of Canada's attitude toward its burgeoning immigrant population. As a result, she and her husband sought a more amenable environment for teaching and writing in the United States, which Mukherjee has described as a more fluid environment—one that does not demand passive accommodation but instead allows the immigrant to "help build a culture."

While teaching at McGill, Mukherjee completed her first novel, *The Tiger's Daughter*. It is the story of a conflicted female protagonist who returns to India and is disillusioned by the gap between her memories of her homeland and its reality—a reality even more striking after her sojourn in the West. In the following years, Mukherjee returned repeatedly to India, spending the year 1973 there with her husband on sabbatical. In 1980, the two settled permanently in the United States, and Mukherjee began teaching at a number of institutions while writing. She held the position of writer-in-residence at Emory University in 1984, and her first collection of short fiction, *Darkness*, was published the following year. Many works followed as Mukherjee progressed in her craft and in her vision—the two novels *Wife* and *Jasmine*, short stories, articles, and nonfiction books that entered more directly into political arenas. In 1989, Mukherjee accepted the position of distinguished professor at the University of California at Berkeley, where she has continued to pursue her writing.

Analysis

Bharati Mukherjee has spent many years as a writer and commentator on social issues that involve her native India, immigrants, and the developing "face" of the United States—designating herself first and foremost as an American writer. She has carefully distinguished be-

Bharati Mukherjee. (©Tom Victor/Courtesy, Grove Press)

tween herself as an immigrant writer and what is termed an "expatriate writer"; the latter may still be involved in "nostalgia" for a home country instead of redefining him- or herself in an innovative and mutating cultural sense. In fact, some critics have described Mukherjee as both a postcolonialist writer and a feminist writer, but these two "agendas" are not her prime focus, although in redefining their identities in new environments, her protagonists and characters may be shedding "old thought" perceptions of themselves endemic to colonial or gender-oppressive societies. Mukherjee's writing goes beyond these two narrowly defined categories, and her ideas always entail the identity and individuality of transmigrating people and their interactions with old and new worlds.

Furthermore, in her later novels, Mukherjee abandons linear progression and traditional points of view to interweave tales that span centuries, continents, and personal histories. In her long fiction, Mukherjee has progressed from the omnisciently narrated novel (*The Tiger's Daughter*) that, the author has admitted, attempted to imitate British models such as Jane Austen to the intense stream-of-consciousness and first-person personas in *Wife* and *Jasmine*, respectively. This progression of narrative style has been accompanied by greater emphasis on her characters' abilities to negotiate (or attempt to negotiate) the very necessary transformations that form the central focus of her fiction; as she states in her introduction to the short-story collection *Darkness*, "We are a series of fluid identities . . . culture never stops."

Thus, despite violence, racism, and destruction of psychic "selves," the underlying message of Mukherjee's fiction is hope—for a new America, a transformative one, that allows its citizens to create and re-create themselves in myriad ways. Such an attitude characteristically informs her female protagonists, who often take on multiple identities (*Jasmine*, *The Holder of the World*, *Desirable Daughters*, *Leave It to Me*) and liberate themselves metaphorically through separation, expatriation, divorce, and even murder.

Mukherjee's themes, therefore, deal with the forging of identity—both personal and national. For the author, this forging is insistently constant and self-altering, and this state of flux must be accepted, even embraced. This flux and complexity are increasingly mirrored in Mukherjee's long fiction, as the works become progressively more layered and more complex—intermixing time frames and personalities from strikingly different cultures. Mukherjee herself seems to have expanded and extended her narrative goals even further—her two novels *Desirable Daughters* and *The Tree Bride* are in fact a continuing story, the latter a sequel and perhaps the middle of a trilogy that circumscribes an even larger reality, amalgamating history, myth, tradition, and change.

Another aspect explored in Mukherjee's fiction is the nature of female self-identity, which often reflects the larger society in which her heroines are positioned. India, her homeland, has been cited as a constant presence in her work, but it informs her work not merely as a singular cultural stance but also as a particular background of an individual human being. In a 2003 interview, Mukherjee stated that "the writer can only write about the individual self." Mukherjee's themes, however, encompass, paradoxically, both a global and a personal consciousness, and it is this intersection that makes her works so valuable and engrossing. Her style—in both short and long fiction—tends to mix opposites, shuffle ironies, and connect past with present. Mukherjee has been cited as a masterful writer of immigrant literature, but certainly, in the United States, she speaks for all.

Wife

The narrative of Mukherjee's second novel, *Wife*, focuses on Dimple Dasgupta, who is traditionally united with her husband in an arranged marriage and yet untraditionally transplanted to New York City. Without a support system, Dimple becomes increasingly alienated, an alienation that leaves her as a double outsider—outside her current new culture and outside her old culture. Dimple progressively loses touch with reality until, almost instinctively, she "knows" that to survive she must kill herself (to release herself from the world) or kill her husband (to release herself from incongruent old-world traditions). She chooses the latter, stabbing her husband while he prosaically consumes a bowl of cereal.

The novel is written in the third person, but Mukherjee's focus and tone are deeply personal and totally internal (unlike the more stilted and classic style of *The Tiger's Daughter*), and the only clear, unified perspective received is that of Dimple, who becomes a tragic heroine. Dimple's story depicts one woman's struggle to maintain her sense of self—and her ultimate defeat. Dimple is a victim because she no longer clearly understands her "role" in the world: She has not the strength, stamina, or status of Tara, the heroine of *The Tiger's Daughter*.

Mukherjee emphatically portrays the inner workings of the claustrophobic, paranoid psyche of a culturally deprived young woman who cannot deal with her strange external world. In addition, she does not love her husband, Amit, and subsequently floats between cultures, immersed in a liberating, yet distancing, culture while her partner will not let her partake in it—he denies her freedom to work and, incidentally, to wear slacks. Finally, having nothing with which to fill her "gaps" (except American television), Dimple infuses reality with fantasy and psychically collapses. Deftly, Mukherjee creates a world in which "cultural collisions" have impacts on feminist issues and indicate, in a striking way, the destructiveness of moving from one culture to another—as immigrant, human being, and woman.

JASMINE

Mukherjee's quintessential novel of exploration and self-actualization, *Jasmine* depicts a woman capable of transforming into many selves, assuming a new name that alternately signifies another identity that the heroine is able to assume in her metamorphosis of self. In *Jasmine* Mukherjee departs from linear construction and intermingles time frames and physical space. The protagonist travels from violence in her native village to the United States, where she is raped, where she murders, where she marries, and where she adopts children who, like her, are both global and time travelers.

Jasmine seeks ultimate freedom (a by-product of the American mentality), and in her quest she leaves much behind (her losses) but gains integration of self. Certainly, Jasmine's immigrating self also metaphorically represents the larger self of all humans in their "immigration" through life. Culturally, Jasmine may also adumbrate the Hindu belief in the transmigration of souls. In any case, Jasmine is a survivor and an emblem of the modern immigrant who must "die" in many ways, submit to violence (external racism, emotional loss, or both), and reinvent him- or herself in the "fusion chamber" of a new culture. A masterful, perfect novel, full of lyrical prose, *Jasmine* portrays the odyssey of one woman who is, by extension, all immigrants.

THE HOLDER OF THE WORLD

Mukherjee's supremely complex and intellectual novel *The Holder of the World* takes on the United States and India, juxtaposing them in two narrators: one (of Indian descent) in the form of a researcher or "asset-hunter" who stumbles upon her ancestor in the search for the perfect diamond and the other a Puritan woman (reminiscent of Nathaniel Hawthorne's Hester Prynne—an American woman ahead of her time) who becomes the lover of an Indian raja and transforms herself into "Salem Bibi." This novel displays Mukherjee's powers at an admirable high: Intermixing history and fantasy (verging on Magical Realism) with dual narrators (Beigh Masters and her ancestor Hannah Easton), the author creates a sense of a journey through time—with two cultures contrapuntally commenting on adaptation and the complexity of self. Mysteries abound and discoveries are made—most important, that across time and geography people are indeed interconnected. Critics have described *The Holder of the World* as a "luminous gem of a novel" that possesses "staggering originality"; it allows readers to glimpse a multifaceted reality of self that has infinite permutations amid a discourse on the magical properties of storytelling (diaries and letters), art (Mughal miniature paintings), and the modern world of computers and virtual reality.

Sherry Morton-Mollo

OTHER MAJOR WORKS

SHORT FICTION: *Darkness*, 1985; *The Middleman, and Other Stories*, 1988.

NONFICTION: *Kautilya's Concept of Diplomacy*, 1976; *Days and Nights in Calcutta*, 1977 (with Clark Blaise); *The Sorrow and the Terror: The Haunting Legacy of the Air India Tragedy*, 1987 (with Blaise); *Political Culture and Leadership in India: A Study of West Bengal*, 1991; *Regionalism in Indian Perspective*, 1992.

BIBLIOGRAPHY

Alam, Fakrul. *Bharati Mukherjee*. New York: Twayne, 1996. Provides a good introduction to the author's life, works, and accomplishments.

Chakravarty, Radha. "Bharati Mukherjee." In *South*

Asian Writers in English, edited by Fakrul Alam. Vol. 323 in *Dictionary of Literary Biography*. Detroit, Mich.: Gale Group, 2006. Biographical essay explores Mukherjee's progression thematically and examines her longer works through *Desirable Daughters*.

Chua, C. L. "Passages from India: Migrating to America in the Fiction of V. S. Naipaul and Bharati Mukherjee." In *Reworlding: The Literature of the Indian Diaspora*, edited by Emmanuel S. Nelson. Westport, Conn.: Greenwood Press, 1992. Discussion of Mukherjee's and Naipaul's work is part of a collection of essays that analyze a variety of Indian expatriate writing, scrutinizing the major areas of the diaspora and the "haunting presence" of India in the process of "reworlding."

Dascalu, Cristina Emanuela. *Imaginary Homelands of Writers in Exile: Salman Rushdie, Bharati Mukherjee, and V. S. Naipaul*. Youngstown, N.Y.: Cambria Press, 2007. Places Mukherjee's fiction within the category of the literature of exile, analyzing it along with the works of other postcolonial authors.

Mathur, Suchitra. "Bharati Mukherjee: An Overview." In *Feminist Writers*, edited by Pamela Kester-Shelton. Detroit, Mich.: St. James Press, 1996. Provides an overview of Mukherjee's thematic concerns and examines her position in the canon of American immigrant writers. Briefly discusses her four major novels as well as her short-story collections.

Morton-Mollo, Sherry. "Bharati Mukherjee." In *A Reader's Companion to the Short Story in English*, edited by Erin Fallon et al. Westport, Conn.: Greenwood Press, 2001. Presents biographical information, an overview of Mukherjee's work, and critical analysis of her fiction.

Nelson, Emmanuel S., ed. *Bharati Mukherjee: Critical Perspectives*. New York: Garland, 1993. Collection of essays on Mukherjee's work addresses various topics, including the uses of violence and eroticism in her fiction. Also provides biographical information.

HARUKI MURAKAMI

Born: Kyōto, Japan; January 12, 1949

Principal long fiction

Kaze no uta o kike, 1979 (*Hear the Wind Sing*, 1987)

1973: Nen no pinbōru, 1980 (*Pinball, 1973*, 1985)

Hitsuji o meguru bōken, 1982 (*A Wild Sheep Chase*, 1989)

Sekai no owari to hādoboirudo wandārando, 1985 (*Hard-Boiled Wonderland and the End of the World*, 1991)

Noruwei no mori, 1987 (*Norwegian Wood*, 2000)

Dansu dansu dansu, 1988 (*Dance, Dance, Dance*, 1993)

Kokkyō no minami, taiyō no nishi, 1992 (*South of the Border, West of the Sun*, 1999)

Nejimaki-dori kuronikuru, 1994-1995 (3 volumes; *The Wind-Up Bird Chronicle*, 1997)

Supūtoniku no koibito, 1999 (*Sputnik Sweetheart*, 2001)

Umibe no Kafuka, 2002 (*Kafka on the Shore*, 2005)

Afutādāku, 2004 (*After Dark*, 2007)

Other literary forms

Haruki Murakami (myur-ah-kah-mee) is also an accomplished writer of short fiction, and English translations of his many stories are collected in *The Elephant Vanishes* (1993), *Kami no kodomotachi wa mina odoru* (2000; *After the Quake: Stories*, 2002), and *Blind Willow, Sleeping Woman* (2006). Murakami is also a translator of international reputation, translating the works of American writers such as Raymond Carver, F. Scott Fitzgerald, Truman Capote, Raymond Chandler, Tim O'Brien, and Paul Theroux into Japanese. Finally, Murakami's significant contributions as a journalist should not be overlooked, particularly *Andaguraundo*

(1997; *Underground: The Tokyo Gas Attack and the Japanese Psyche*, 2000), his moving account of the 1995 sarin gas attack in a Tokyo subway by members of the religious group Aum Shinrikyo. Considered to be journalistic literature, *Underground* includes a series of interviews with victims and perpetrators of the attacks.

ACHIEVEMENTS

In 1994, for his three-volume novel *The Wind-Up Bird Chronicle*, Haruki Murakami won the Gunzo Literature Prize; he also won the Noma Literary Prize for New Writers for his first novel, *Hear the Wind Sing*, and the Yomiuri Prize for Literature—a prestigious Japanese literary award whose previous recipients included Yukio Mishima and Kōbō Abe. The Yomiuri Prize was awarded to him by Nobel Prize winner Kenzaburō Ōe, who had long been critical of Murakami. Murakami also received the Tanizaki Prize in 1985 for *Hard-Boiled Wonderland and the End of the World*, and he was a teaching fellow at Princeton University and Tufts University in the United States.

Murakami was awarded the Franz Kafka Prize from the Czech Republic in 2006 for *Kafka on the Shore*, the Frank O'Connor International Short Story Award from Ireland in 2006, the Asahi Prize from Japan in 2006, and honorary doctorates from the University of Liège in 2007 and Princeton in 2008. In 2007, Murakami won the Kiriyama Prize—a literary award given annually to books that encourage greater understanding of and among the peoples and nations of the Pacific Rim and South Asia—for his collection of short stories *Blind Willow, Sleeping Woman*; he declined the award "for reasons of personal principle." Murakami's works have been translated into more than forty languages, including Arabic, Estonian, Icelandic, Russian, Thai, and Vietnamese.

Haruki Murakami. (AP/Wide World Photos)

BIOGRAPHY

Born in Kyōto in 1949, Haruki Murakami spent most of his youth in Kōbe. Both his father and mother taught Japanese literature, igniting a passion for literature early on in their son. Murakami's father was also a Buddhist priest (meditations on religion and spirituality are key themes in Murakami's work), and his mother was the daughter of a merchant. Murakami showed an affinity for Western culture from an early age, particularly Western literature and music. His favorite writers were Kurt Vonnegut and Richard Brautigan, and his favorite musicians were the Beatles, Bob Dylan, Radiohead, Charlie Parker, and countless jazz and classical musicians, particularly Ludwig van Beethoven. Murakami graduated from Waseda University in Tokyo in 1973, where he studied theater arts, and his first job was at a record store. Just before graduating, Murakami opened a coffeehouse (which served as a jazz bar in the evenings) called Peter Cat in Okobunji, Tokyo, with his wife, Yoko. He is a collector of vinyl records, a full-marathon runner and triathlete, and obsessed with cats (all interests that weigh heavily on his fiction).

Murakami did not start writing until he was twenty-nine years old. Legend has it that he was attending a baseball game in Tokyo when he had a revelation regarding writing. Murakami suddenly realized that he was capable of writing a book after seeing American ballplayer Dave Hilton (playing for the Hiroshima Carps) hit a double. Murakami started working on a novel immediately following the game. After several months he had finished *Hear the Wind Sing*, a short, fragmented book (modeled on Brautigan and written in fits and starts) that introduced many elements that would come to dominate Murakami's style: an embrace of Western influences (especially writers Brautigan and Vonnegut, and Western music), dark humor, anonymity, relationships, loss, and alienation. His success—he won the Gunzo Literature Prize for the novel—encouraged him to keep at it. He next published *Pinball, 1973* and then *A Wild Sheep Chase*, the last two works of what came to be known as the trilogy of the rat.

Hard-Boiled Wonderland and the End of the World marked the beginning of Murakami's career as a writer of international reputation, but it was *Norwegian Wood* that made him a star of the literary world. Initially published in two installments, *Norwegian Wood* sold millions of copies among the youth of Japan, catapulting Murakami to superstar status. Murakami initially was not pleased with the sort of fame he had attained, and he left Japan to travel through Europe, before settling in the United States. He became a writing fellow at Princeton and Tufts, where he worked on and completed *South of the Border, West of the Sun* and *The Wind-Up Bird Chronicle*.

Murakami returned to Japan after the Hanshin earthquake and the poison gas attack in the Tokyo subway in 1995. He worked on two nonfiction books about the gas attack, which were combined to form the English edition of *Underground*. *Sputnik Sweetheart*, *Kafka on the Shore*, and *After Dark* cemented Murakami's reputation as one of the world's most popular and critically successful novelists. Several of his stories and novels have been adapted into films, and *Hashiru koto ni tsuite kataru toki ni boku no kataru koto* (2007; *What I Talk About When I Talk About Running: A Memoir*, 2008), Murakami's memoir about his life as a marathon runner and triathlete, was a highly anticipated step in a new direction for the successful novelist.

Analysis

If it is true that writers and artists should spend their entire lives and careers investigating, examining, and trying to understand the same themes, then Haruki Murakami is a prime example of how to do this successfully. Like a jazz musician building on the same note, Murakami has—from the start—been obsessed with issues of sexual identity and love, loss and detachment, history and war, and nostalgia and fate. He has been deeply influenced by Western culture, and his themes, in some ways, are distilled from his favorite writers and musicians. Murakami changed the face of Japanese fiction. He was the first to incorporate Western influences in such an immediate way and he introduced a broad, spare, and raw style that Japanese readers had never before seen. His flirtation with Magical Realism, surrealism, and the fantastic is evidence of his fearlessness as a writer. Never one to be pigeonholed, Murakami is that rarest of literary figures, a writer who revels in telling a good and exciting story without sacrificing his severe vision of what literature is and should be.

Notably, Murakami's novels often have musical themes and often speak of the power and beauty of music. More than that, his titles are often taken directly from songs. The three volumes comprising *The Wind-Up Bird Chronicle* refer to works by Gioachino Antonio Rossini, Robert Schumann, and Wolfgang Amadeus Mozart. *Norwegian Wood*, possibly Murakami's most famous work, is named after a song by the Beatles, and *Dance Dance Dance*, a sort of sequel to *A Wild Sheep Chase*, is named after a song by the Beach Boys.

Murakami's work is the highwater mark at the intersection of popular culture and serious literature. As a writer who has filtered such a variety of influences into his work, he is a complete original. He is also a writer who has sought to understand Japanese history (especially Japan's role in World War II), but he has done so without attempting to make political statements. He examines, explores, and dissects history, war, love, and identity with the same complex (and sometimes confusing) gracefulness. Murakami, like Georges Simenon and Charles Bukowski, has become his own brand name. Though his work has been described in many different ways—as Magical Realism, surrealism, hard-boiled mystery, love story, cyberpunk—it is almost entirely impossible to identify one of his books as anything other than a "Murakami."

Murakami goes where a novel takes him, where history takes him. He goes to the place where love and memory and fear take him. As an independent artist with a singular vision, he is unrivaled in this generation of world writers.

Hard-Boiled Wonderland and the End of the World

A complex and playful novel, *Hard-Boiled Wonderland and the End of the World* features two separate narratives. The odd-numbered chapters are set in the Hard-Boiled Wonderland and feature a narrator who is a Calcutec, a human data-processing system. The even-numbered chapters take place in a strange, walled-off village called The End of the World, removed from the rest of civilization. The narrator of this story becomes the village's dream reader. Eventually, the two stories merge, and the deep influences here—American hard-boiled detective fiction, cyberpunk, Franz Kafka—come together to make this one of the most complex and yet accessible examples of Magical Realism in world literature.

Norwegian Wood

Norwegian Wood, the book that made Murakami into a superstar, is a nostalgic story of love and loss. It is also Murakami's most straightforward work. Told from the perspective of Toru Watanabe, who looks back on his days as a college freshman, the novel details Toru's relationships with two beautiful, electric, and unusual women, Naoko and Midori. The title of the book is taken from a 1965 song by the Beatles—"Norwegian Wood (This Bird Has Flown)," which appears several times in the novel's narrative (alongside other allusions to Western music and literature). Set in Tokyo in the late 1960's, the novel also portrays a changing Japan, as students protest against the establishment. While Murakami identifies the student movement as naïve and phony, the setting is just the backdrop for a real and complex love story that—while not supernatural or fantastic like much of Murakami's other work—nonetheless reveals a unique vision of how to live and survive in the world.

South of the Border, West of the Sun

South of the Border, West of the Sun also takes part of its title from a song, this time from one sung by Nat King Cole, "South of the Border." The title comes to mean something wholly mystical and mysterious to the novel's two main characters, Hajime and Shimamoto. The second part of the title is a psychological condition known as "*hysteria siberiana*," which is, as Shimamoto explains to Hajime, something that happens to Siberian farmers when they lose their minds and walk west toward the setting sun until they fall down and die. A melancholic novel rooted in the same sense of nostalgia as *Norwegian Wood*, *South of the Border, West of the Sun* is a meditation on love, choices, and mystery.

The Wind-up Bird Chronicle

Widely considered to be Murakami's finest achievement, *The Wind-Up Bird Chronicle* tells the story of Toru Okada, an unemployed man whose cat disappears. Toru is married to Kumiko, who has a successful career in the publishing business. A bizarre chain of events leads him to strange encounters with May Kasahara, a young girl who is obsessed with death and deterioration, and Nutmeg Akasaka, a writer who shares a few strange coincidences with Toru. The novel explores typical Murakami themes, and it is also a story of war and history. Particularly relevant to the story are the Manchukuo war crimes before and during World War II and their deep significance in Japanese history. As always, Murakami revels in mystery—both the mystical and hard-boiled varieties—and his crisp, sharp, and accessible style is at its peak here.

Kafka on the Shore

Kafka on the Shore is another epic Murakami novel with two different narratives—told in alternating chapters—that eventually come together. The odd-numbered chapters tell the story of Kafka, a fifteen-year-old runaway bent on escaping an Oedipal curse, who takes shelter in a library until police arrest him in connection with an unsolved murder. The even-numbered chapters tell the story of Nakata, a mystical cat finder. Nakata and Kafka move toward each other until their stories combine in a thunderclap.

Murakami examines many of the prominent themes readers have come to expect from him—love, loss, spirituality, dreams, the power of music, redemption, and sexual identity—but he also further investigates Japan's World War II heritage, the notion of reality, and the authority of prophecy, fate, and nature.

William Boyle

Other major works

SHORT FICTION: *The Elephant Vanishes*, 1993; *Kami no kodomotachi wa mina odoru*, 2000 (*After the Quake: Stories*, 2002); *Blind Willow, Sleeping Woman*, 2006.

NONFICTION: *Andaguraundo*, 1997 (*Underground: The Tokyo Gas Attack and the Japanese Psyche*, 2000); *Hashiru koto ni tsuite kataru toki ni boku no kataru koto*, 2007 (*What I Talk About When I Talk About Running: A Memoir*, 2008).

Bibliography

Amitrano, Giorgio. *The New Japanese Novel: Popular Culture and Literary Tradition in the Work of Murakami Haruki and Yoshimoto Banana*. Boston: Cheng and Tsui, 1996. An accessible introduction to the work of Japan's most famous contemporary novelists, Murakami and Yoshimoto Banana.

Japan Foundation. *A Wild Haruki Chase: Reading Murakami Around the World*. Berkeley, Calif.: Stone Bridge Press, 2008. A collection of essays exploring the "Murakami phenomenon," namely, how Murakami is read and translated throughout the world.

Napier, Susan J. *The Fantastic in Modern Japanese Literature: The Subversion of Modernity*. Florence, Ky.: Routledge, 1996. An examination of the fantastic in contemporary Japanese fiction, film, and comics and how it relates to the nation's anxieties and fears. Part of the Nissan Institute/Routledge Japanese Studies series.

Rubin, Jay. *Haruki Murakami and the Music of Words*. New York: Random House, 2001. Rubin, a professor of Japanese literature at Harvard and one of Murakami's translators, takes an exhaustive look at Murakami's life and works. A concise and complete critical introduction to Murakami's books.

Seats, Michael. *Murakami Haruki: The Simulacrum in Contemporary Japanese Culture*. Lanham, Md.: Lexington Books, 2006. Seats discusses the relationship between contemporary Japanese culture and Murakami's fiction, concluding that there are glaring comparisons to be made between Murakami's works and Japanese modernity and technology.

Strecher, Matthew. *Dances with Sheep: The Quest for Identity in the Fiction of Murakami Haruki*. Flint: University of Michigan, Center for Japanese Studies, 2002. Strecher's critical study argues for Murakami's relevance (rejecting the notion of Murakami as a pop author). Relying heavily on theory, Strecher aims to begin a serious critical discussion of Murakami's work.

_______. *Haruki Murakami's "The Wind-Up Bird Chronicle": A Reader's Guide*. New York: Continuum International, 2002. An accessible and informative guide and companion to Murakami's best-received novel.

Suter, Rebecca. *The Japanization of Modernity: Murakami Haruki Between Japan and the United States*. Cambridge, Mass.: Harvard University, Asia Center, 2008. Discusses Murakami's role as a kind of "mediator" between Japanese and American literature.

MURASAKI SHIKIBU

Born: Kyōto, Japan; c. 978
Died: Kyōto, Japan; c. 1030
Also known as: Tō Shikibu

Principal long fiction

Genji monogatari, c. 1004 (*The Tale of Genji*, 1925-1933)

Other literary forms

In addition to *The Tale of Genji*, Murasaki Shikibu (mur-ah-sah-kee shee-kee-boo) is credited with two other works: her diary, *Murasaki Shikibu nikki* (eleventh century), and a collection of her poetry, *Murasaki Shikibu-shū* (eleventh century). Both of these works are translated and annotated in full in Richard Bowring's *Murasaki Shikibu: Her Diary and Poetic Memoirs* (1982); a partial translation of the diary may be found in Annie Shepley Omori and Kochi Doi's *Diaries of Court Ladies of Old Japan* (1920), excerpted in Donald Keene's *Anthology of Japanese Literature* (1955).

In common with other Japanese diaries by court women of the period, Lady Murasaki's diary is both of high literary quality and of importance as a social-historical document. It is not a daily journal, but rather a collection of entries, made erratically between the years 1008 and 1010, that record significant events in Murasaki's life as a lady in the court of Empress Fujiwara no Shōshi, consort of Emperor Ichijō. Like other diaries of the period, also, this one includes poetry, both by the author and by other people in her life, and thus helps document the role of poetry composition in the daily life of the imperial court. Of greatest importance, however, is the insight the diary provides into the personality of Murasaki Shikibu; while the diary is not an intensely self-revealing, confessional work, it is helpful in understanding how *The Tale of Genji* came into being because it reveals the way in which Murasaki processed real life into literary art and her finely tuned sensitivity to human relationships. Murasaki's collected poems are not regarded as being of great literary quality or consequence in themselves; rather, as in the case of her diary, the poems are looked to largely for the light they might shed on Murasaki as the author of *The Tale of Genji*.

ACHIEVEMENTS

Murasaki Shikibu's premier achievement is, without question, *The Tale of Genji*, which stands as perhaps the greatest monument of Japanese fiction. The work followed a tradition of several generations' standing of romances depicting life among the court nobility of Japan, most of which were written by women of rank, but in its length (more than one thousand pages in English translation), realism, psychological depth, and literary distinction, *The Tale of Genji* stands far above its predecessors and has subsequently been imitated but never equaled.

Prior to the advent of printing on a large scale in the seventeenth century, *The Tale of Genji* was circulated only in manuscript, but its influence was nevertheless immense. Its situations and the poetry exchanged by its characters quickly became a vital part of the literary canon, sources often exploited in later Japanese poetry, which was highly dependent on allusion and reference. It became an important source for dramatists of the No theater in the fifteenth and subsequent centuries. By the seventeenth century, it had become the object of scholarly commentary and analysis and was seen by Motoori Norinaga (1730-1801), the foremost eighteenth century scholar of the native literature, as the *locus classicus* of ancient aesthetic, literary, and spiritual values.

Orthodox moralists of both the Confucian and the Buddhist schools condemned *The Tale of Genji* throughout the premodern period: What was fiction, after all, but a seductive tissue of lies? It was, moreover, a work steeped in carnality and moral inconsistency. Nevertheless, the work remained at the center of the Japanese literary tradition, and by the Tokugawa, or Edo, period (1603-1868), its influence was firmly embedded in popular culture as well. It was often retold and parodied, its characters were depicted in wood-block prints, it was the source of a popular card game, and the names of its characters were even taken as pseudonyms by courtesans in the urban brothel districts.

In more recent times, Murasaki and *The Tale of Genji* have continued to occupy a prominent place in Japanese letters. In the twentieth century, the poet Yosano Akiko and the novelists Jun'ichirō Tanizaki and Fumiko Enchi produced modern Japanese translations for a public no longer able to read the language of the original, and through translations into other languages, Murasaki's special vision of the world of the classical imperial court has shaped readers' perceptions of Japan around the world.

BIOGRAPHY

Lamentably, little is known of the life of Murasaki Shikibu. Scholars generally date her birth to sometime in the mid-970's, and guesses about the year of her death range between 1014 and about 1030. Even her real name is a mystery: "Murasaki" seems to have been taken from *The Tale of Genji* itself, where it is a name attached to one of the novel's most affecting female characters, and "Shikibu" (meaning "Bureau of Rights") is a court title that was borne by her father, Tametoki, a member of one of the lesser branches of the Fujiwara clan, which dominated court life and politics in Murasaki's day. (Court women were frequently referred to publicly in this way, by titles derived from those of male relatives; it is not unusual for a woman's real name not to have survived.)

On the evidence of her diary, Murasaki seems to have had a somewhat unusual upbringing from the perspective of the highest reaches of court society. She may have spent some time away from the imperial capital, Kyōto, in the company of her father, who served as a provincial governor in the late 990's; more important, she appears to have been unusually well educated in comparison with her peers, having acquired some knowledge of Chinese in addition to the facility in written Japanese that was expected of any aristocratic woman.

Murasaki appears to have married a nobleman and distant kinsman, Fujiwara no Nobutaka, in about 998. Nobutaka was nearly her father's age, and Murasaki was by that time well past the customary age for marriage, facts that suggest she had been married briefly before. In any case, in 999 she and Nobutaka had a daughter, who would become a poet in her own right under the names Echigo no Ben and Daini no Sammi, and who lived at least until 1078. Nobutaka, however, died in 1001, and it was as a widow that Murasaki became a lady-in-waiting to the empress in 1005 or 1006.

Murasaki was far from being plebeian, but it is probable that neither her rank nor her family connections would alone have been sufficient to account for her being called into service at the court of the empress, who was doubly to be honored, not only as the emperor's consort but also as the daughter of the most powerful noble in the land, Fujiwara no Michinaga. (One reason the birth of the crown prince, to which Murasaki devotes a great deal of space in her diary, was of such interest in the court was that it had the important consequence of tightening Michinaga's control over the imperial line.) It seems likely, therefore, that it was Murasaki's literary abilities that made her attractive as an attendant to the young empress, who inhabited a rarefied and stylized subculture that had made poetry a principal mode of public and private expression. Empress Fujiwara no Shōshi was at the most eighteen years old when Murasaki joined her retinue, presumably in need of a mature mentor in literary matters. Most scholars agree that it may well have been the repute of *The Tale of Genji* itself, or some early portion of it, that originally gave Murasaki her entrée at court.

How long Murasaki stayed with the empress is a matter of scholarly debate. Emperor Ichijō died in 1011, and his widow moved to different quarters, but Murasaki seems to have stayed with her at least until 1014, which is the earliest of several dates suggested by scholars for her death. Rather clear evidence exists that Murasaki was no longer in the empress's retinue in 1031, but only shaky evidence supports any earlier date for her death.

While the lack of certain knowledge of the details of Murasaki's life helps her modern critics avoid the pitfalls of an autobiographical interpretation of *The Tale of Genji*, it is otherwise a frustrating lacuna in the historical record. Working from a small number of surviving pre-*Genji* texts, it is possible to reconstruct something of the tradition of courtly romances within which Murasaki wrote. It is likewise possible to look at the much better-preserved poetic tradition of her day as a guide to the human and literary values of her world. Important as they are, however, such circumstantial approaches to the literary surroundings of *The Tale of Genji* cannot help with many questions that only a biography of Murasaki might answer: Are the people and settings of *The Tale of Genji* portraits from life or from imagination (and literary models) alone? In what ways might Murasaki's understanding of her own life story have shaped the telling of her fiction? When and where were the pieces of the tale written and knit together? Why did her readers so identify the author with her fictional Murasaki that the name became her sobriquet? The lack of final answers may keep many doors closed, but it does not diminish Murasaki's achievement, for *The Tale of Genji* is a work that can stand alone.

Analysis: *The Tale of Genji*

Murasaki Shikibu's novel *The Tale of Genji* both epitomizes and transcends the world of letters in which it found its origin. It is emphatically of its period, a work that has its roots in a highly stylized literary, primarily poetic, subculture, yet it is also a work of sufficient universality and psychological depth to have a claim to be called the world's earliest novel. To read *The Tale of Genji* is not simply to acquit oneself of some imagined duty to cross-cultural understanding but to step inside a fully realized fictional world. It should not be thought surprising that even to modern Japanese, that world is indisputably an alien one—the passage of nearly a millennium puts Murasaki and her fiction irretrievably in a place that even the remarkable continuity of Japanese literary culture cannot bring very close. It is a measure of Murasaki's art that *The Tale of Genji* can, nevertheless, still arouse the emotions of non-Japanese and Japanese alike.

PLOT AND THEMES

The Tale of Genji, as its title implies, is on its face the story of the princeling Genji, the son of an emperor by a concubine, who is so favored by nature with beauty and other, subtler gifts of character that he bids fair to replace in his father's favor the proximate heir to the imperial throne. To forestall disputes over the succession, the beautiful boy-child is given the nonimperial surname Genji and thus, in the prevailing political scheme, is removed from consideration as heir to the throne. It is therefore technically incorrect to refer to the hero of the novel as the "prince" Genji, but in every other respect, he is indeed princely, the very embodiment of royal virtues: He is beautiful, so beautiful, indeed, that his sobriquet is *hikaru*, or "shining," Genji; his skills as a dancer in the highly disciplined court style are unchallengeable; he is a consummate musician on strings and flute, a specialist in the compounding of exotic fragrances, and a master of popular song—and of poetry, the primary and essential art of the courtier of the Heian era, the real-life period in which Murasaki wrote and that historians have named after the imperial capital of the time, Heian-kyō, the "capital of peace," modern Kyōto.

Above all, Genji is a lover. He is not a Don Juan, driven by a neurotic need to prove his virility to himself and to the world, but rather a man who, from puberty forward, is both free and almost obliged to bestow his favors on the women with whom he comes in contact. His first love, significantly, is his own father's concubine Fujitsubo, a woman who, the world acknowledges, bears a strong resemblance to the kinswoman who was Genji's mother. Genji has a succession of affairs with women of varying degrees of quality, but his deepest and most enduring love is for Murasaki, who enters his life a waif in need of protection but whose first claim in Genji's affections derives from her resemblance to her cousin Fujitsubo, who takes her name from the "wisteria courtyard" that adjoins her quarters. As no reader of the original story would fail to note, *murasaki* is an herb whose roots yield a dye that mimics the hue of the wisteria in bloom. (Associations such as these and other clues lead some modern critics to suggest that a primary theme of the novel might be described as a search for the lost parent, with Oedipal complications.)

Murasaki becomes the love of Genji's life but was not originally his principal consort. That honor went to the noblewoman known as Aoi, the daughter of a high minister of the emperor. The marriage was arranged, as was proper, with a careful eye to the disposition of power in the court. A certain uneasy distance always prevails between Genji and Aoi. She is several years his senior when they marry, and Genji is then still young enough to find the difference in age disconcerting. As time goes by and Genji begins spending more and more of his nights away from her father's palace (highborn women of Heian lived under their fathers' roofs and received their husbands as guests), Aoi, in her turn, retreats from Genji into a mood of jealousy compounded with despairing yearning.

If the compelling power of beauty is one theme that is introduced early in the novel, another and more vivid one is jealousy, quite intertwined with the first. Aoi's jealousy is perhaps mitigated by her awareness of the circumstances of her marriage to Genji, but for another of Genji's early amours, the Rokujō lady, jealousy becomes literally a murderous passion. The first to suffer is Yūgao, the lady of the "evening faces" (a kind of flower), who is a mysterious woman of lesser rank who passively succumbs to Genji's courtship and allows him to spirit her off to a deserted mansion; a dreamlike interlude of lovemaking and deepening intimacy—the lovers engage in one of the subtlest poetic exchanges in the novel in trying to uncover each other's secrets—is shattered by Yūgao's sudden, inexplicable death. The second death is that of Aoi herself, less violent but no less devastating to Genji.

It becomes clear that both deaths resulted from possession by the avenging spirit of the Rokujō lady, whose jealous passion at her felt neglect by Genji is so strong that it has effected, quite without her knowledge, a separation of body and soul in life. In this respect, *The Tale of Genji* reveals itself to be something of a cautionary tale: Although love and sexual relations are a natural part of life, and a man, at least, need not restrict himself to a single partner, the bond between lovers is of such strength and durability that it must not be taken lightly.

The moral has its roots in Buddhism, specifically in the concept of karma. In this instance, the intense emotional attachments formed in sexual union constitute a karmic bond of great strength; the stronger the emotion, the tighter the bond. In Buddhism as it was known to Murasaki, emotional attachments of any kind translate into karmic ties that bind the individual to the cycle of birth, death, and rebirth, an undesirable state but one that is the common human lot. Normal emotional ties may keep the unassisted individual from Nirvana, final liberation from the cycle of rebirth, but they cannot be avoided. The lesson of the horrific tale of the Rokujō lady, however, is that passions of an abnormal intensity are dangerous. In common belief, they not only impede a gradual progress, lifetime by lifetime, toward the goal of liberation but also can actually tether the soul of the departed in a limbo between this world and the next, hovering as a ghost near the object of the passion. The Rokujō lady had not died, but her jealous passion was so strong that it drew her soul from her body into destructive encounters with its objects, Yūgao and Aoi.

Genji himself recognizes that he bears some responsibility in these deaths, but he is not shown to mend his ways, for, in the world of the novel, they are not in any particular need of repair. His subsequent conquests, however, are not so much conquests as they are, in a sense, adoptions or quasi marriages in which he is scrupulously attentive to his lovers' material and—insofar as possible—emotional needs. The maturing Genji, chastened by Rokujō's excesses and sobered by his responsibilities to the young Murasaki, does not embrace monogamy, but he is careful to see that his attentions are spread among his dependent women in accordance with their respective expectations; none is simply ravished and then abandoned. Throughout his part of the novel, Genji remains a creature of his time and place, a man whose sex, social position, and physical and intellectual gifts allow him to make almost any woman his own, but he is almost invariably portrayed as a paragon of Heian virtue.

Genji's behavior does not by any means escape censure—he is banished for a time from Kyōto to the wild coast of Suma (near the modern city of Kōbe) for a particularly indiscreet liaison—but his character is his redemption. He is sincere in his remorse and steadfast in fulfilling his responsibilities to his growing harem; above all, he matures into a gentleman of immense sensitivity to what the eighteenth century scholar Motoori Norinaga identified as the central aesthetic and spiritual value of the court subculture, *mono no aware*. The term has no precise translation, but to "know" *mono no aware* is to understand the sweet pathos of things, to realize that the only unchanging reality is that all is change and transience, that beauty is the most ephemeral of all phenomena and for that reason is all the more precious and profoundly moving. *Mono no aware* is thus congruent with the Buddhist metaphysical vision of the phenomenal world as absolute illusion, as nothing more than an arbitrary projection of consciousness; to feel this "pathos of things" as profoundly as Genji does, then, is to reveal a sensibility that is fundamentally akin to religiosity, and that is what makes him something other than an imperious swaggerer whose wealth, power, and sexual attractiveness grant him sway over the women of his choosing. Modern Western readers sometimes find those virtues unredeeming. Genji is not a cad, but neither do his sensitivities keep him from imposing himself on women in ways that are no longer quite acceptable.

Nevertheless, as Genji and Murasaki age, and as they mature in their ability to sympathize with their surroundings, the reader can begin, at least, to enter respectfully into their world of values. Among Genji's women, Murasaki in particular is a graceful model of adjustment to an awareness of the mutability and fragility of life; in her last appearances in the novel, she is on the verge of middle age, a gentle but somewhat troubled woman whose concern for the next life leads her to a nunnery to begin the necessary process of weakening and then severing the worldly bonds of karma that will otherwise impede her movement toward rebirth on a higher plane. Genji himself remains something of an abstraction to the end, a bit too good to be true, perhaps. The reader can nevertheless share his grief at losing Murasaki, and his death, which comes unheralded (its abruptness suggests to some a lacuna in the text) some three-quarters of the way through the novel, leaves a void that is felt by the reader almost as strongly as by Genji's survivors.

The Uji chapters

The world Genji leaves behind seems sometimes to be inhabited by a diminished race. It is a place of muted colors, dark, moody, and sometimes tormented. Its principal male characters are the young Niou and Kaoru, whose names translate as "glow" and "be fragrant," respectively—allusions, surely, to the "shining" Genji himself, so often described as possessing an ineffably sweet natural fragrance. The young nobles appear in the novel as products of a very complicated web of sexual liaisons and deceptions involving Genji and the boon companion of his youth, Middle Captain Tō no Chujō, who was the brother of Aoi. They seem to split between them the vanished, larger-than-life Genji: Niou is impetuous, more than occasionally irresponsible, and inclined to force himself on women; Kaoru is old beyond his years, sensitive to *mono no aware* to a painful degree, and so far from being impetuous as to be nearly paralyzed in his dealings with women. A trio of sisters, the protected, unworldly daughters of an aged and reclusive prince, are the primary female characters in this part of the novel, called the Uji chapters for the location of much of the action, in and around the old prince's villa by the Uji River outside Kyōto.

The principal overt plot action in the Uji chapters centers on the conflict between Niou and Kaoru, which in turn revolves around their relationships to the sisters. A subtler theme, however, is once again the matter of coping with the radical inconstancy of the things of this world—love, beauty, life itself. The theme is more starkly presented here than in the pages devoted to the life of Genji himself. There, the physical world is for the most part benign; except for a few interludes—such as Genji's exile to Suma and his harrowing expedition with Yūgao's corpse to a mountain temple—nature is seen at a distance or in the confines of an elegant garden. Here, the primary symbol of the natural world is the swirling water of the Uji River, the sound of whose roaring current is a constant feature of life in the prince's villa. It is into these waters, the name of which poets have always associated with the adjective *ushi* (sorrowful), that the most sensitive of the prince's daughters throws herself; the daughter's name, in the traditional reading of the novel, is Ukifune—"floating boat," but containing also *uki*, the attributive form of the same mournful word, *ushi*.

Appropriately enough, the Uji chapters end inconclusively. There is no wrapping up of the multiple stories of the scores of characters whose lives intersected with those of Genji and his dilute reincarnation in Niou and Kaoru, no resolution, really, of the latter's inability to choose between life in the world and in the cloister; the novel seems to end simply with a drawing of the blinds. The title of its final chapter is probably not Murasaki's own, but it is apposite: "the floating bridge of dreams" (*yume no ukihashi*), taken from a poem in the chapter that belongs to a long tradition of contrasting while still conflating "dream" and "reality." A floating bridge (*uki* yet again) or pontoon bridge (*hashi*) offers only insecure footing, and this one is more insubstantial still, seen in or made of dreams; it is a metaphor here both for the tenuous links between people in this world and for this world in its insubstantial entirety, which is a mere fantasy connecting the next life with the ones that have gone before. Some scholars argue that the tale is unfinished, that its ending has been lost or that Murasaki was for some reason unable to continue it; others find the indefiniteness of the ending, whether it was intentional or not, to be wholly satisfying.

The Uji chapters are of a gray and melancholy cast, and it is certainly possible to see the work as a whole as embodying a decidedly uncheerful and pessimistic statement of the futility of any but the contemplative life. There is, in fact, a world-denying ideology that underlies *The Tale of Genji*, that of *mappō*, or the "end of the law," in Buddhist doctrine the name of an age in which humankind has become entirely estranged from the teachings of the historical Buddha. This estrangement results in an absolute human inability to perceive clearly the metaphysical truth or law (Sanskrit *dharma*) regarding, among other things, the utter insubstantiality of the phenomenal world; the spiritual life becomes a never-ending but ultimately futile struggle to escape the delusive certainty that the concerns of this world are of genuine moment while at the same time recognizing the responsibilities that go with participation in human society. *Mappō* ideology shares with millenarian thought a conviction that the present age is essentially corrupt, but the era of *mappō* is open-ended, not to be climaxed in any human comprehensible future time by a new order of existence. *The Tale of Genji* is the product of a time, then, of a kind of religious radicalism, when the only escape from an effectively infinite cycle of painful rebirths was offered by a relatively new doctrine of salvation through faith in

Amida (Sanskrit Amitabha), a disciple of the Buddha who relinquished his claim to Nirvana in exchange for his vow to bring salvation to any sentient being who sincerely invokes his name.

Here, in the radical pessimism of *mappō* ideology and the promise of Amida's vow, are to be found some, at least, of the motivations underlying the behavior of the principals of *The Tale of Genji:* The ineluctable drift toward the cloister shown by so many is symptomatic not only of a yearning for monastic simplicity as an aid to severing worldly bonds of karma but also of efforts to demonstrate a single-minded faith in the redemptive power of Amida to effect one's salvation. It has been noted also that *mappō* ideology may account in part for the backward-looking tone of the latter chapters of *The Tale of Genji*—the past can only have been better if the earthly future, at least, is so devoid of promise.

It should not be imagined, however, that reading *The Tale of Genji* is a grim experience, for the novel is also a colorful artistic tapestry of life in a world that achieved a uniquely fine appreciation of the satisfactions of the life of the senses, even if the aesthetic pleasures of color, fragrance, the calligraphic line, and the magic of poetry and of the changing seasons are conventionally called only "consolations" in the face of the unavoidable sorrows of existence. Like any novel of substance, *The Tale of Genji* deals with serious and sometimes unpleasant truths, but like the best of her modern counterparts, Murasaki Shikibu was an author who knew as well the importance of a well-told tale. Her novel is a literary achievement of the highest order, worthy of inclusion in any short list of masterpieces of world fiction; it is also a precious document that preserves a vanished way of life of astonishing refinement with a degree of detail and three-dimensionality that is simply not to be found in any fictional work of remotely comparable antiquity.

Robert W. Leutner

Other major works

POETRY: *Murasaki shikibu-shū*, eleventh century (poetry; included in *Murasaki Shikibu: Her Diary and Poetic Memoirs*, 1982).

NONFICTION: *Murasaki Shikibu nikki*, eleventh century (diary; included in *Murasaki Shikibu: Her Diary and Poetic Memoirs*, 1982).

Bibliography

Bargen, Doris G. *A Woman's Weapon: Spirit Possession in "The Tale of Genji."* Honolulu: University of Hawaii Press, 1997. Provides a feminist interpretation of the "possessing spirits" in the novel, arguing that spirit possession was a female strategy to counter male empowerment and redress the imbalance of power between the sexes.

Bloom, Harold, ed. *Murasaki Shikibu's "The Tale of Genji."* Philadelphia: Chelsea House, 2004. Collection of essays contains important twentieth century criticism and analysis of various aspects of the novel. Includes an informative editor's introduction.

Bowring, Richard. *Murasaki Shikibu: "The Tale of Genji."* 2d ed. New York: Cambridge University Press, 2004. Provides a brief overview of the novel and discusses the work's cultural background, language, style, impact, influence, and reception. Includes bibliography.

Caddeau, Patrick W. *Appraising "Genji": Literary Criticism and Cultural Anxiety in the Age of the Last Samurai*. Albany: State University of New York Press, 2006. Assesses the novel's impact on Japanese culture through diaries, critical treatises, newspaper accounts, film adaptations, and stage productions. Focuses on a treatise by Hagiwara Hiromichi, a nineteenth century samurai whose massive study of the novel challenged traditional interpretations of the book and conventional beliefs about the nation's culture.

Field, Norma. *The Splendor of Longing in "The Tale of Genji."* Ann Arbor: Center for Japanese Studies, University of Michigan, 2001. Focuses on many of the women characters in the novel to show how these heroines "make" and "unmake" the hero, Genji. Includes discussions of the social, psychological, political, and aesthetic aspects of the novel.

Keene, Donald. *Landscapes and Portraits: Appreciations of Japanese Culture*. Palo Alto, Calif.: Kodansha International, 1971. Reprints Keene's 1967 essay "Feminine Sensibility in the Heian Era," which explores the emergence of women writers and the *kana* writing system, and analyzes *The Tale of Genji* as part of this phenomenon. Includes illustrations and bibliography.

Morris, Ivan. *The World of the Shining Prince: Court Life in Ancient Japan*. 1964. Reprint. New York: Kodansha International, 1994. One of the best interpretive works available on the historical and cultural milieu of *The Tale of Genji*. Chapter 9 offers an excellent biographical account of Murasaki. Includes a complete glossary listing historical figures in Murasaki's life.

Pekarik, Andrew, ed. *Ukifune: Love in "The Tale of Genji."* New York: Columbia University Press, 1982. Collection of essays focuses on Ukifune, the central character in one of the chapters in Murasaki's novel. Murasaki scholars discuss the role of poetry, narrative conceptions, the lyrical mode, and romance in Ukifune's story and the novel as a whole.

Puette, William J. *"The Tale of Genji" by Murasaki Shikibu: A Reader's Guide*. 1983. Reprint. Rutland, Vt.: Charles Tuttle, 1992. Provides a useful précis plot of *The Tale of Genji*, supplemented by background chapters on topics relevant to understanding the novel. Chapter 4 presents a brief biography of Murasaki. Includes a good bibliography.

Seidensticker, Edward G. "Eminent Women Writers of the Court: Murasaki Shikibu and Sei Shōnagon." In *Great Historical Figures of Japan*, edited by Hyoe Murakami and Thomas J. Harper. Tokyo: Japan Cultural Institute, 1978. Authoritative essay by a respected translator of *The Tale of Genji* compares and contrasts the lives and literary works of Murasaki and her court rival.

IRIS MURDOCH

Born: Dublin, Ireland; July 15, 1919
Died: Oxford, England; February 8, 1999
Also known as: Jean Iris Murdoch

Principal long fiction

Under the Net, 1954
The Flight from the Enchanter, 1956
The Sandcastle, 1957
The Bell, 1958
A Severed Head, 1961
An Unofficial Rose, 1962
The Unicorn, 1963
The Italian Girl, 1964
The Red and the Green, 1965
The Time of the Angels, 1966
The Nice and the Good, 1968
Bruno's Dream, 1969
A Fairly Honourable Defeat, 1970
An Accidental Man, 1971
The Black Prince, 1973
The Sacred and Profane Love Machine, 1974
A Word Child, 1975
Henry and Cato, 1976
The Sea, the Sea, 1978
Nuns and Soldiers, 1980
The Philosopher's Pupil, 1983
The Good Apprentice, 1985
The Book and the Brotherhood, 1987
The Message to the Planet, 1989
The Green Knight, 1993
Jackson's Dilemma, 1995

Other literary forms

Iris Murdoch (MUR-dok) produced a considerable amount of work in areas other than fiction, particularly in literary criticism, drama, and, most important, philosophy. Her first book, *Sartre: Romantic Rationalist* (1953), was a critique of Jean-Paul Sartre's philosophy as it appears in his novels. She wrote three plays for the theater and adapted several of her novels for the stage. *The Servants and the Snow* was first performed at the Greenwich Theatre in 1970, and *The Three Arrows* at the Arts Theatre, Cambridge, in 1972; the two plays were published together in 1973. Another play, *Art and Eros*, was performed at the National Theatre in 1980. Murdoch collaborated with J. B. Priestley to adapt her novel *A Severed*

Head for the stage (pr. 1963) and with James Saunders to adapt *The Italian Girl* (pr. 1967). *The Black Prince* was also adapted for the stage, first performed at the Aldwych Theatre in 1989.

Murdoch also produced books on the subject of philosophy: *The Sovereignty of Good* (1970), which consists of three essays on moral philosophy, "The Idea of Perfection," "On 'God' and 'Good,'" and "The Sovereignty of Good over Other Concepts"; and *The Fire and the Sun: Why Plato Banished the Artists* (1977), a study of Plato's objections to art and artists. Murdoch added to her work on Plato in the form of two "platonic dialogues" titled "Art and Eros: A Dialogue about Art" and "Above the Gods: A Dialogue about Religion," which she combined in a book titled *Acastos: Two Platonic Dialogues*, published in 1986. *Metaphysics as a Guide to Morals* appeared in 1992, and a collection of essays titled *Existentialists and Mystics: Writings on Philosophy and Literature* was published in 1997. Murdoch also published several philosophical papers in the Proceedings of the Aristotelian Society and other important articles on philosophy and aesthetics, including "The Sublime and the Good" (*Chicago Review*) and "The Sublime and the Beautiful Revisited" (*Yale Review*). Her best-known essay, "Against Dryness: A Polemical Sketch," which appeared in the January, 1961, issue of *Encounter*, is a work of literary criticism that urges a return to the capacious realism of the great nineteenth century novelists.

Achievements

Universally acknowledged as one of the most important novelists of postwar Britain, Iris Murdoch combined a prolific output with a consistently high level of fictional achievement. From the beginning of her career as a novelist, she was a critical and popular success in both Great Britain and the United States. In general, Murdoch is thought of as a "philosophical novelist," and despite her objections to this description, she attempted a fusion of aesthetic and philosophical ideas in her fiction. Including her first novel, *Under the Net*, published in 1954, she published twenty-six novels and received a variety of literary awards and honors. In 1973, she was awarded the James Tait Black Memorial Prize for Fiction for *The Black Prince*, and in 1974 she received the Whitbread Literary Award for Fiction for *The Sacred and Profane Love Machine*. *The Sea, the Sea* won the Man Booker Prize for Fiction in 1978. Murdoch became a member of the Irish Academy in 1970 and an honorary member of the American Academy of Arts and Letters in 1975; she was awarded the honorary title of Commander of the Order of the British Empire in 1976. She was made a Dame of the Order of the British Empire in 1987, and in 1990 she received the Medal of Honor for Literature from the National Arts Club in New York.

Biography

Jean Iris Murdoch was born in Dublin, Ireland, on July 15, 1919, to Anglo-Irish parents, Wills John Hughes Murdoch and Irene Alice Richardson. The family later moved to London, where Murdoch attended the Froebel Education Institute; she finished her secondary education at the Badminton School, Bristol, in 1937. From 1938 to 1942, she attended Somerville College at Oxford University, studying classical literature, ancient history, and philosophy. After obtaining a first-class honors degree, she worked from 1942 to 1944 as the assistant principal in the British Treasury, and from 1944 to 1946 she served as an administrative officer with the United Nations Relief and Rehabilitation Administration in England, Austria, and Belgium.

After World War II, an interest in existentialism led Murdoch to turn her attention to philosophy. She was unable to accept a scholarship to study in the United States because she had become a member of the Communist Party while an undergraduate at Oxford, and instead attended Newnham College at Cambridge University from 1947 to 1948 after receiving the Sarah Smithson Studentship in philosophy. In 1948, she was made a fellow of St. Anne's College, Oxford, where she lectured in philosophy until 1963, when she was named an honorary fellow of the college. In 1956, she married John Bayley, the author of many books of literary criticism as well as book reviews. For many years Bayley was the Thomas Warton Professor of English Literature at Oxford. He has also written several novels, including *The Queer Captain* (1995).

From 1963 to 1967, Murdoch lectured at the Royal College of Art in London, after which she stopped teaching to devote all her time to writing fiction and philosophy. Her novels have won many awards, including the

Book of the Year Award from the *Yorkshire Post* (1969), the James Tait Black Memorial Prize (1974), and the Booker Prize (1978). Murdoch became a Commander of the Order of the British Empire in 1976 and a Dame of the same order in 1987. Oxford University awarded her an honorary D. Litt. in 1987; Cambridge University followed in 1993. In 1992, she published her major philosophical work, *Metaphysics as a Guide to Morals*, a brilliant and sometimes garrulous survey of her ideas about many more topics than its title indicates. In 1997, many of her writings on philosophy and literature were collected in *Existentialists and Mystics*.

Iris Murdoch. (Thomas Victor)

At one time Murdoch maintained a London flat in the Earls Court area, but she and her husband always had their primary residence in or near Oxford. In the mid-1990's, Murdoch was diagnosed with Alzheimer's disease. Her husband described their life together, including how they coped with her mental condition, in *Iris: A Memoir* (1998), published in the United States as *An Elegy for Iris* in 1999, the year Murdoch died.

Analysis

A knowledge of Iris Murdoch's philosophical and critical essays is invaluable for the reader wishing to understand her fiction. Her moral philosophy, which entails a rejection of existentialism, behaviorism, and linguistic empiricism, informs her fiction throughout and provides a basis for an interpretation of both the content and the form of her work. Although early influenced by Sartrean existentialism, she developed a radically different view of the human condition. The major disagreement she had with the existentialist position was its emphasis on choice, a belief Murdoch characterized as "unrealistic, over-optimistic, romantic" because it fails to consider the true nature of human consciousness and what she called "a sort of continuous background with a life of its own." Existentialism, which she called "the last fling of liberal Romanticism in philosophy," presents humanity with "too grand" a conception of itself as isolated from its surroundings and capable of rational, free choice. She described this picture of humankind as "Kantian man-gods" who are "free, independent, lonely, powerful, rational, responsible, and brave." Although Murdoch denied being a Freudian, Sigmund Freud's "realistic and detailed picture of the fallen man" is much closer to her own conception of human nature, and she agreed with what she called Freud's "thoroughly pessimistic view" in which the psyche is described as an "egocentric system of quasi-mechanical energy" determined by its individual history; the natural attachments of this psyche are "sexual, ambiguous, and hard for the subject to control." The most important dimension of this description of the individual is his lack of rational free will, and Murdoch's statement in "Against Dryness" that "we are not isolated free choosers, monarchs of all we survey, but benighted creatures sunk in a reality whose nature we are constantly and overwhelmingly tempted to deform by fantasy" is perhaps her tersest summary of the human condition.

Murdoch's philosophical position was the basis for her choice of prose fiction as the most realistic literary genre. The novelist's advantage is a "blessed freedom from rationalism," and she saw the novel as the literary form that, because of its lack of formal restrictions, could best portray the "open world, a world of absurdity and loose ends and ignorance." Although she had reservations about modern literature and believed that the twentieth century novel tends either to be "crystalline" (self-contained, mythic, sometimes allegorical, and frequently neurotic) or "journalistic" (semidocumentary, descriptive, and factual), the nineteenth century novel as written by Leo Tolstoy, Jane Austen, and George Eliot remains the best example of how fiction can create free, independent characters who are not "merely puppets in the exteriorization of some closely-locked psychological conflict" of the author. The nineteenth century novel, because it "throve upon a dynamic merging of the idea of person with the idea of class," was not simply a representation of the human condition but rather contained "real various individuals struggling in society"; in other words, it presented characters *and* the "continuous background with a life of its own."

Murdoch believed that the most important obligation for the novelist is the creation of particularized, unique, and ultimately indefinable human beings, characters who move outside the novelist's consciousness into an independent ontological status. This aesthetic theory has its corollary in Murdoch's moral philosophy, in which she stresses the need for the individual to recognize the "otherness" of other individuals. The great novelist, like the "good" person, has an "apprehension of the absurd irreducible uniqueness of people and of their relations with each other," an apprehension she castigated Sartre for lacking. Recognition of otherness is, to a degree, dependent on the individual's ability to "attend to" other individuals, a concept Murdoch derived from the philosophy of Simone Weil. Murdoch described attention as a "patient, loving regard, directed upon a person, a thing, a situation" and believed that we "*grow by looking*"; morality, both for the individual and the novelist who is attempting a realistic portrayal of human beings in the world, is an endless process of attending to a reality outside the individual consciousness. Attention is seeing, "a just and loving gaze directed upon an individual reality," and as such is an effort to counteract "states of illusion" brought about by selfish fantasy. For Murdoch, attention is also another name for love, and "the ability to direct attention is love." Imaginative prose literature, Murdoch believed, is the best medium in which to focus attention on the individual because it is "*par excellence* the form of art most concerned with the existence of other persons."

In "The Sublime and the Good," Murdoch defines love as "the perception of individuals. Love is the extremely difficult realization that something other than oneself is real. Love, and so art and morals, is the discovery of reality." She has also said that the main subject of her fiction is love, and her novels usually depict the difficulties involved in recognizing the uniqueness and independence of other human beings. In *The Bell*, the Abbess tells Michael Meade that "all of our failures are ultimately failures in love," a statement that neatly describes Murdoch's fictional world. The enemy of love in her novels is the propensity of the individual to fantasize and to create false pictures of reality, particularly distorted conceptions of other people. As a result, her novels frequently present situations in which characters are forced to confront the "otherness" of those around them, situations that often involve a realization of the past or present sexual involvements of other persons. The comfort and safety of the "old world," as it is called by many Murdoch characters, is destroyed by a discovery about the past or by characters suddenly falling passionately in love with each other. *A Severed Head*, in which Martin Lynch-Gibbon is shocked by a series of revelations about his wife and friends and falls precipitately and unpredictably in love with Honor Klein, is one of the best examples of this recurring pattern in Murdoch's work.

Murdoch believed that the experience of art can serve to shock the individual into an awareness of a reality outside the personal psyche, and her novels contain several scenes in which characters who gaze upon paintings are able to escape temporarily from solipsistic fantasy. Dora Greenfield in *The Bell*, Harriet Gavender in *The Sacred and Profane Love Machine*, and Tim Reede in *Nuns and Soldiers* each experience what Murdoch calls "unselfing" and Harriet Gavender describes as "not being myself any more"; in fact, Dora Greenfield notes that paintings give her "something which her consciousness could not wretchedly devour. . . . The pictures were something real outside herself." Murdoch, in "The Sublime and the Beautiful Revisited," calls art "spiritual experience" because it can bring out this radical change in perception, and in *The Fire and the Sun: Why Plato*

Banished the Artists, she claims that in an unreligious age good art provides people with "their clearest experience of something grasped as separate and precious and beneficial and held quietly and unpossessively in the attention."

Murdoch's ambivalent attitudes about the role of art and artists are present in both her fiction and her philosophy. In an interview with Michael Bellamy, in *Contemporary Literature* (1977), she described art as a "temptation to impose from where perhaps it isn't always appropriate," and in the same discussion noted that "morality has to do with not imposing form, except appropriately and cautiously and carefully and with attention to appropriate detail." Murdoch suggested to several interviewers that the basis of her novels is what she calls the conflict between "the saint and the artist," or the dichotomy between the "truthful, formless figure" and the "form-maker." She mentioned Tallis Browne and Julius King in *A Fairly Honourable Defeat*, Ann and Randall Peronett in *An Unofficial Rose*, and Hugo Belfounder and Jake Donaghue in *Under the Net* as examples. She believed that Plato's life exemplifies this conflict: "We can see played out in that great spirit the peculiarly distressing struggle between the artist and the saint." The true or "good" artist must avoid the "ruthless subjection of characters" to his will and should use symbolism judiciously in a "natural, subordinate way" that attempts to be "perfectly realistic." In her fiction, Murdoch's artist figures are often demonic individuals who manipulate people in real life without regard for their well-being or independence as persons. Her "saint" figures have a corresponding lack of form, or sense of self, and are frequently unable or unwilling to act in any way. Douglas Swann's comment in *An Unofficial Rose* that "nothing is more fatal to love than to want everything to have form" is also true of Murdoch's attitude toward art.

Many of Murdoch's characters attempt to find form in their own lives in order to explain the apparent chaos that surrounds them. In her essay "Vision and Choice in Morality," Murdoch talks about the need at times to stress "not the comprehensibility of the world but its incomprehensibility" and says that "there are even moments when understanding *ought* to be withheld." In *The Flight from the Enchanter*, John Rainborough experiences a moment of joy when he feels "how little I know, and how little it is possible to know," but this happiness in a lack of knowledge is rare in Murdoch's fiction. In the same novel, Rosa Keepe, a much more representative Murdoch character, listens to the sound of the machines in the factory, hoping to hear a "harmonious and repetitive pattern," just as Michael Meade in *The Bell* expects to find "the emergence in his life of patterns and signs." At the end of the novel, he regretfully concludes that the apparent pattern he had observed in his life was merely his own "romantic imagination. At the human level there was no pattern."

The search for rational, discernible causal relationships is the major structuring principle in *An Accidental Man*, a novel concerned with the discovery of, in Gracie Tisbourne's words, "a world . . . quite without order." In "The Sovereignty of Good over Other Concepts," Murdoch says that "there are properly many patterns and purposes within life, but there is no general and as it were externally guaranteed pattern or purpose of the kind for which philosophers and theologians used to search," and she has also stated her desire to write novels that, because they contain more of the contingent, accidental dimensions of life, are more realistic than "patterned" fiction.

Murdoch's reservations about form in life and art are paralleled by her suspicions about language. A fervent defender of literature and language who said in "Salvation by Words" that "words constitute the ultimate texture and stuff of our moral being. . . . The fundamental distinctions can only be made in words" and in *The Fire and the Sun* that "the careful responsible skillful use of words is our highest instrument of thought and one of our highest modes of being," Murdoch also voiced suspicions about the ironic nature of language, its potential to distort the truth and to create false pictures of reality. This distrust of language is evident in her first novel, *Under the Net*, and continued to inform her fiction. In this respect, Murdoch was greatly influenced by Ludwig Wittgenstein; direct references and sly, sometimes ironic allusions to Wittgenstein appear repeatedly in her novels.

In spite of these reservations, however, Murdoch mounts one of the most eloquent defenses of art and literature in modern times in *The Sovereignty of Good* and *The Fire and the Sun*. She claims in "The Sovereignty of Good over Other Concepts" that art "can enlarge the sensibility of its consumer. It is a kind of goodness by proxy," and in "On 'God' and 'Good,'" she asserts that art, rather than being any kind of playful diversion for the human race, is "the place of its most fundamental insight." According to Murdoch, literature is the most important art because of its unique ability to shed light on the human condition: "The most essential and fundamental aspect of culture is the study of literature, since this is an education in how to picture and understand human situations." This statement in "The Idea of Perfection" obviously places an enormous burden on the novelist, a burden that Murdoch's prolific output, technical virtuosity, and moral vision appear to be capable of bearing.

Under the Net

Jake Donaghue, the narrator-protagonist of *Under the Net*, informs the reader early in the novel that the story's central theme is his acquaintance with Hugo Belfounder. The relationship between the two men illustrates Murdoch's philosophical and aesthetic concerns, for the Hugo-Jake friendship represents the saint-artist dichotomy; this "philosophical novel" allows her to explore the problem of theoretical approaches to reality, the issue of contingency, the realization of the otherness of individuals, and the ambiguities of language and art.

The character of Hugo Belfounder is based in part on that of the enigmatic Elias Canetti, winner of the Nobel Prize in Literature in 1981; the Bulgarian-born Canetti, who settled in England in 1939, appears in various guises in several of Murdoch's early novels. Hugo, some of whose precepts also suggest the influence of Wittgenstein, is Murdoch's first "saint" figure, and he embodies many of the qualities of the "good" characters who appear later in her fiction. Hugo's saintliness is a result of his truthfulness and his lack of desire for form or structure in life and art. Opposed to him is Jake, who, fearing that he may actually tell the truth to Mrs. Tinckham about being evicted by Madge, delays telling his story until he can present it in a "more dramatic way . . . as yet it lacked form." Form, as Jake tacitly admits, is a kind of lying, an imposition of structure that distorts reality. Hugo, on the other hand, is attracted by the ephemerality and formlessness of the firework displays he has created, and he abandons them when they receive the attention of art critics who begin to classify his work into styles. Hugo is also characterized by a selflessness that Jake finds astonishing: It does not occur to him that he is responsible for the concepts discussed in Jake's book *The Silencer*, or that Anna Quentin's mime theater is based on her interpretation of his beliefs.

The difference between the two men is also evident in their attitude toward theory. After his conversations with Hugo, Jake concedes that his own approach to life is "blurred by generalities," and he is entranced by Hugo's refusal to classify the world around him or to adopt any kind of theory about it. Annandine, Hugo's persona in *The Silencer*, says that "the movement away from theory and generality is the movement towards truth. All theorizing is flight. We must be ruled by the situation itself and this is unutterably particular." Theories, like form, distort what they attempt to explain and understand. Hugo's lack of a general theoretical framework for his ideas, the "net" of the novel's title, makes everything he encounters "astonishing, delightful, complicated, and mysterious."

Part of Jake's education and development as a potential artist is dependent on his relinquishing the need for theories and generalizations. In his first meeting with Anna, he notices that she is in "the grip of a theory," and one of the most important episodes in the novel is Jake's realization that Jean-Pierre Breteuil, whose work he has previously translated into English, has finally written a good novel—a feat Jake had believed impossible. He understands that he has incorrectly "classed" Jean-Pierre and says that "It wrenched me, like the changing of a fundamental category." Similarly, when Jake becomes aware that Hugo is in love with Sadie Quentin rather than Anna, he says that "a pattern in my mind was suddenly scattered and the pieces of it went flying about me like birds." At the end of the novel, Jake has abandoned attempts to impose his own ideas onto his environment; rather, he decides to sit quietly and "let things take shape deeply within me," noting that he can "sense," beneath the level of his attention and without his conscious aid, "great forms moving in the darkness."

Jake's initial need to perceive form and to create theories is paralleled by his fear of contingency. One of Murdoch's major quarrels with Sartre is his inability to deal with the contingent, or, in her words, the "messiness" and "muddle" of human existence. Rather than rejecting

Sartre's concept of viscosity, Murdoch frequently forces her characters to come to terms with the physical world and the accidental and apparently chaotic nature of reality. Early in the novel, Jake announces that "I hate contingency. I want everything in my life to have a sufficient reason," and later, in a reference to Sartre's *La Nausée* (1938; *Nausea*, 1949), observes that Hugo's Bounty Belfounder film studio is situated in a part of London "where contingency reaches the point of nausea." The novel ends with Jake laughingly admitting that he does not know why Mrs. Tinckham's kittens look as they do. "I don't know why it is," he says. "It's just one of the wonders of the world." In this scene, Jake focuses on the particular—the kittens—and is able to accept that their appearance cannot be explained by him, two actions that show that he has moved much closer to Hugo's position. Hugo had earlier advised Jake that "some situations can't be unravelled" and, as a result, should be "dropped."

This acceptance of contingency implies a realization that life cannot be completely controlled by human will. Jake also learns that other individuals exist independent of him and resist his efforts to explain and categorize their behavior. When he introduces his close friend Peter O'Finney to the reader, he claims that "Finn has very little inner life" and that, while Finn is an inhabitant of his universe, "I . . . cannot conceive that he has one containing me." Events in the novel force Jake to move out of his solipsistic consciousness, and at the conclusion he acknowledges that for the first time Anna exists "as a separate being and not as a part of myself," an experience he finds "extremely painful." She becomes "something which had to be learnt afresh," and he then asks if it is possible ever to know another human being. He answers himself in a statement that clearly belongs to his author: "Perhaps only after one has realized the impossibility of knowledge and renounced the desire for it and finally ceased to feel even the need of it." In the same way, Jake also grants Hugo a final mysteriousness and impenetrability, comparing him to a monolith whose purpose remains obscure.

Murdoch's suspicions about the nature of language are also evident in *Under the Net*. In a conversation between Hugo and Jake, Hugo maintains that, by definition, language lies: "The whole language is a machine for making falsehoods." Language is also vulnerable because of humanity's tendency to distort and to exaggerate experiences when attempting to articulate them; Hugo notes that when he speaks he does not state precisely what he thinks but rather what will impress Jake and force him to respond. Only actions, says Hugo, do not lie. This is not, however, Murdoch's final word on language and literature, for Jake's development as a human being during the course of the novel culminates in his realization that he will be able to write creatively. The "shiver of possibility" that he feels at the novel's conclusion is his knowledge that his earlier writing has been merely a preparation for his emergence as a novelist.

Murdoch's first novel is clearly a *Künstlerroman* and her most overtly "philosophical" novel. In an interview in 1978 with Jack Biles, in *Studies in the Literary Imagination*, she said that she does not want to "promote" her philosophical views in her novels or to allow them to "intrude into the novel world." This attitude certainly seems more descriptive of the novels written after *Under the Net*. Although she paints an ironically amusing portrait of the novel's only professional philosopher, Dave Gellman, her major concerns in her first novel are clearly philosophical; *Under the Net* contains in more obvious form the philosophical issues that are transmuted into the fictional material of her subsequent work.

A Fairly Honourable Defeat

Speaking of *A Fairly Honourable Defeat* in her interview with Michael Bellamy, Murdoch said that the "defeat" of the novel's title is the defeat of good by evil. She calls the novel a "theological myth" in which Julius King is Satan, Tallis Browne is a Christ figure, and Leonard Browne is God the Father. Another trichotomy, however, is suggested in *A Fairly Honourable Defeat*, for Julius and Tallis, like Ann and Randall Peronett in *An Unofficial Rose*, embody the saint-artist opposition that is so common in Murdoch's fiction, and Rupert Foster represents the rationalist philosopher's approach to experience, an approach that ultimately fails because it does not take into consideration the reality of evil and the formlessness of good. The relationships among these three men form one of the most important thematic concerns of the novel.

A Fairly Honourable Defeat begins with Hilda and Rupert Foster enacting a scene common in Murdoch's fiction, that of the happily married couple whose contentment has insulated them from their less fortunate friends. Like Kate and Octavian Gray in *The Nice and the Good*, Rupert and Hilda feel as if their happiness has granted them a privileged and protected status. Rupert's statement that "anything is permitted to us," ominously similar to Friedrich Nietzsche's "all is permitted," signals that for the moment they live in the "old world" of pleasure and stability that is so frequently shattered in the course of a Murdoch novel. The agent of destruction in *A Fairly Honourable Defeat* is Julius King, a scientist who considers himself an "artist" whose artworks consist of manipulating the lives of people around him, forcing them to "act parts" and in the process become "educated" about their moral failures.

Julius King's reaction to Rupert's philosophy of life is the catalyst for the events of the novel. Although Rupert, like Murdoch, calls human existence "jumble" and castigates his sister-in-law Morgan Browne for her "love and do as you please" attitude toward people, Rupert believes that "complete information and straight answers and unambiguous positions . . . clarifications and rational policies" are possible and desirable; for Rupert, goodness is a fairly simplistic concept that can be experienced directly and articulated eloquently. His statement to Morgan after Julius has orchestrated their ostensible "love affair" that "nothing awful can happen" summarizes his inability to grasp the kind of evil that Julius represents, and the destruction of the manuscript of his book on moral philosophy symbolizes the fragility of his worldview, a fragility underscored by his death. Rupert's major error is believing that his own rationality can prevail; he hypocritically thinks that "the top of the moral structure was no dream, and he had proved this by exercises in loving attention: loving people, loving art, loving work, loving paving stones and leaves on trees." In reality, as Julius later observes, Rupert is in love with his own image of himself as a good, loving, and rational man who can control any urge that threatens the "moral structure" of his world; while he espouses many theories about the nature of love, he lacks the "direct language of love" that makes real action possible.

Unlike Rupert, who believes that his duty is to love others, Julius's attitude toward human beings is one of contempt, an emotion the narrator describes as "the opposite extreme from love: the cynicism of a deliberate contemptuous diminution of another person." One of the major reasons for his low valuation of people is the very quality that makes them vulnerable to his manipulation—their malleability, or, as he phrases it, the easiness with which they are "beguiled." In a conversation with Tallis, Julius says that most individuals, motivated by fear and egotism, will cooperate in almost any deception. The most obvious examples of his theory in *A Fairly Honourable Defeat* are Morgan Browne and Simon Foster. Morgan, titillated by Julius's boast that he can "divide anybody from anybody," first encourages him in his plan to separate Simon and Axel and later unknowingly becomes one of his victims; Simon, afraid that Julius will destroy his relationship with Axel, unwillingly allows Julius to "arrange" a relationship between Rupert and Morgan. In fact, Julius's claim that he is an "artist" and a "magician" depends on the moral weaknesses of the characters whose lives he carefully "plots."

Both Leonard Browne and Julius King mount verbal assaults on the world; in some respects, their diatribes sound remarkably similar. Like Leonard, Julius believes that the human race is a "loathsome crew" who inhabit a "paltry planet"; he goes further than Leonard, however, in his statement that human beings "don't deserve to survive" and, more important, in his desire to see the reification of his ideas. Julius's theory that people are merely puppets who need to be educated becomes, in practice, a tragedy. Like Hugo Belfounder, he claims that philosophy is the subtlest "method of flight" from consciousness and that its attempted truths are "tissues of illusions." In *Theories*, he is entranced with his own theorizing, as is Rupert. Good, he says, is dull, and what passes for human goodness is a "tiny phenomenon" that is "messy, limited, truncated." Evil, by comparison, "reaches far far away into the depths of the human spirit and is connected with the deepest springs of human vitality." Good, according to Julius, is not even a "coherent concept; it is unimaginable for human beings, like certain things in physics."

One of Murdoch's saintlike characters, James Tayper Pace in *The Bell*, also discusses the difficulty of comprehending goodness while he emphasizes the need for individuals to seek the good beyond the confines of their own consciousness: "And where do we look for perfection? Not in some imaginary concoction out of our own idea of our own character—but in something so external and so remote that we can get only now and then a distant hint of it." In "The Sovereignty of Good over Other Concepts," Murdoch writes about contemplating goodness, and, like James Tayper Pace, defines it as "an attempt to look right away from self towards a distant transcendent perfection, a source of uncontaminated energy, a source of *new* and quite undreamt-of virtue." Unlike Pace and Murdoch, Julius is unwilling to waste his energies in the contemplation of a concept so "remote" and "transcendent" and is instead beguiled by the immediacy and vitality of evil.

Tallis Browne, the "saint" of *A Fairly Honourable Defeat*, is one of the strangest characters in Murdoch's fiction. Early in the novel, his wife Morgan, talking about the human psyche, complains that "it stretches away and away to the ends of the world and it's soft and sticky and warm. There's nothing real, no hard parts, no centre." This description of human consciousness also explains Morgan's dissatisfaction with her husband, who is completely lacking in the qualities she so admires in Julius King: form and myth. With Tallis, says Morgan, "there were no forms and limits, things had no boundaries"; he lacks any kind of personal "myth," while she characterizes Julius as "almost all myth." Like Julius, Tallis does not believe in theories, and at one point he correctly accuses Morgan of being "theory-ridden" and chasing "empty abstractions"; unlike Julius, however, he has no theories about human nature or behavior, a fact that Julius acknowledges when he tells Tallis that Rupert probably feels that "theorizing would be quite out of place with you." While Julius manipulates the relationships of those around him according to his ideas about human weakness and Rupert writes a text on morality and goodness, Tallis nurses his dying father and helps to feed and shelter the poverty-stricken immigrants in his neighborhood.

The formlessness of Tallis's goodness causes him to have no desire to analyze the tragedy of Rupert's death or to assign reasons or blame. He grieves "blankly" over what appears to have been a "disastrous compound" of human failure, muddle, and sheer chance, and mourns Rupert by attempting to remember him simply with a kind of mindless pain. His reaction to the loss of his wife is similar. Rather than indulging in anger, grief, or speculations about their future relationship, he simply lets her "continue to occupy his heart." His unwillingness to impose any kind of form or to structure his surroundings in any way extends to his feelings for his father Leonard, who is dying of cancer. Tallis cannot find the appropriate moment to tell his father of his impending death because, as he tells Julius, "It seems so arbitrary, at any particular instant of time, to change the world to that degree." Rather than seeing human beings as puppets, as does Julius, Tallis has reached a crisis state in which he fears that any action may have a deleterious effect on those around him. Significantly, however, in spite of Tallis's passivity he is the only character in the novel who is capable of positive action. As Axel phrases it, he is "the only person about the place with really sound instincts." In the Chinese restaurant, he strikes the young man who is abusing the Jamaican, and later he forces Julius to telephone Hilda Foster to explain that it is Julius who has created the "affair" between Morgan and Rupert.

At the end of the novel, Tallis has abandoned the idea of prayer, which the narrator notes could only be a "superstition" for him at that point, and has instead become a completely passive and receptive consciousness. He catches hold of objects "not so as to perform any act himself, but so as to immobilize himself for a moment to be, if that were possible, perhaps acted upon, perhaps touched." The similarity of this statement to Simone Weil's definition of "attention" in *Waiting for God* (1951), where she describes the act of attention as "suspending our thought, leaving it detached, empty, and ready to be penetrated by the object . . . our thought should be empty, waiting, not seeking anything," is clear. Much earlier in the novel, Morgan has grabbed an object, a green paperweight belonging to Rupert, in an attempt to escape from the formlessness of the psyche. Tallis, on the other hand, uses objects as a way to attend to reality, as a means of opening himself up to the world outside himself.

A Fairly Honourable Defeat ends with Tallis weeping over his father's approaching death and Julius, after contemplating his choices of Parisian restaurants, concluding that "life was good." The conversation between the two men that precedes this, however, is much more ambiguous. Julius, in an apparent attempt to win Tallis's approbation for his actions, reveals a great deal about himself personally and asks Tallis to agree that he is "an instrument of justice." Tallis's attitude toward Julius is one of detached tolerance, and his response to Julius's statement is merely to smile. A parallel to his calm acceptance of Julius's evil is his response to the "weird crawling things," apparently rats, mice, and insects, which inhabit his house; he feels for them "pity rather than disgust" and has advanced far beyond Rupert's claim to love "paving stones and leaves on trees." Tallis's acceptance of the world, which has grown to embrace even its most despicable and horrible elements, makes him the most saintlike character in Murdoch's fiction. He is her answer to Sartre's Roquentin in *Nausea*: Instead of becoming nauseated by the world's plethora of objects and the muddle of existence, as does Roquentin, Tallis, at the end of *A Fairly Honourable Defeat*, is capable of feeling only pity and acceptance for everything that surrounds him.

An Accidental Man

In *An Accidental Man*, Murdoch presents a chaotic world of accident and unpredictability in which several of her characters search for—and fail to find—any kind of pattern or causal relationships in their lives. Perhaps Murdoch's fear that form in fiction can hinder the characters' development as complex and fully realized individuals and that intricately patterned fiction sometimes prevents the author from exploring "the contradictions or paradoxes or more painful aspects of the subject matter" led her to write a novel in which the narrative voice is almost completely absent: In *An Accidental Man*, the characters appear to have taken over the novel. In an interview with W. K. Rose, in *Shenandoah* (Winter, 1968), Murdoch expressed the desire to write a novel "made up entirely of peripheral characters, sort of accidental people like Dickens's people," and mentioned that the author "might go so far as starting to invent the novel and then abolishing the central characters." *An Accidental Man* is the result of these speculations about fiction, for it contains a Dickensian sweep of characters and lacks any kind of "protagonist." The inclusion of more "accident" in Murdoch's work is one aspect of her wish to write realistic fiction, for she believes that the novelist should portray the world as "aimless, chancy, and huge." *An Accidental Man*, a brittle comedy of manners that contains four deaths, two attempted suicides, and more than twenty characters, some of whom are suffering from mental retardation, schizophrenia, and brain damage, is Murdoch's vision of a contingent, random, and godless world.

Many characters in the novel share this vision. At the conclusion, Matthew Gibson Grey notes that Austin's appropriation of Mavis Argyll "has been, like so many other things in the story, accidental." Charlotte Ledgard, contemplating suicide, sees herself as "the slave of chance" and the world as being made up of "chaos upon which everything rested and out of which it was made." Ludwig Leferrier senses that "human life perches always on the brink of dissolution," and Gracie Tisbourne, who is usually not given to philosophical speculations, has "a sense of the world being quite without order and of other things looking through." The characters in *An Accidental Man* wander through mazes in which they lack important information about their own and others' lives, or they become the victims of "accidents" that radically transform their existence. London's labyrinthine streets become symbolic of their ignorance and blindness as they pass and miss one another, and, in the instance of Rosalind Monkley, symbolic of accidental death itself. Garth Gibson Grey, Matthew Gibson Grey, Ludwig Leferrier, and Mavis Argyll all hope to find some kind of logical order and rationality in the world, but are finally defeated by the "absolute contradiction . . . at the heart of things," and instead encounter what Garth calls "the rhetoric of the casually absent god."

Although Murdoch is generally not interested in experimentation in form, *An Accidental Man* shows her moving beyond the traditional narrative form of her earlier work in search of new structures to embody the philosophical assumptions that underlie the novel. Conspicuously missing in this novel is an authoritative narrative voice; instead, one-tenth of the book is in epistolary form and a significant portion consists of chapters of untagged dialogue. In *An Accidental Man*, Murdoch, who has stated her wish to expel herself from her fiction in order to avoid imposing "the form of one's own mind" on the characters, creates a work in which the narrator is frequently not privy to the inner thoughts or reactions of the characters and can only report their spoken and written words without comment or elucidation. The disappearance of the narrator in certain sections of the novel parallels the absence of god; Murdoch creates a novelistic world in which readers must search for their own patterns and conclusions without the guiding presence of the authorial voice that was present in her earlier fiction. In addition, the narrator's refusal to pass judgments or give information about the thoughts of the characters, despite the fact that the narrator has been shown to be omniscient in certain situations, results in a coldly detached tone that refuses to grant a fundamental importance to any act.

Like the chapters of dialogue, the epistolary sections of the novel create a voyeuristic situation for the reader that parallels the voyeurism that takes place several times during the narrative. The reader is privileged to read correspondence and to overhear important conversations while being denied access to the characters' thoughts, just as the characters in *An Accidental Man* have a noticeable penchant for eavesdropping on one another's conversations and reading other people's letters. The epistolary sections also create comically ironic effects because the reader knows more about the entire situation than any of the individual letter writers, and the ignorance, lies, and exaggerations of the writers are juxtaposed in ways that underscore the limited and fallacious viewpoint of each individual. These chapters also give Murdoch an opportunity to open up the novel, expanding its boundaries to encompass more and more territory—a narrative technique that corresponds to her desire to write fiction that depicts reality as "a rich receding background" with "a life of its own."

The widening framework of the novel creates a constantly changing perspective, for when the narrator withdraws from a direct presentation of events in order to present the reactions of peripheral or uninvolved characters, the importance of these events is reduced through distancing and in the process rendered comic. The same technique is used in the chapters of pure dialogue, where events that have been treated seriously in earlier episodes become the subject of comically trivial cocktail-party conversations. The dialogic and epistolary sections are central elements in the novel, for Murdoch uses them to advance the narrative through fragmentary bits of information that are often necessary for a complete understanding of what is happening; her belief that "reality is not given whole" is expressed in her narrative technique.

The self-acknowledged "accidental man" of the novel's title is Austin Gibson Grey. Neurotically obsessed with his older brother, Matthew, and unable to keep either his wife or his job, Austin is nevertheless a survivor who depends on his own egotism for his continued well-being. One aspect of Austin's ability to survive is his refusal to allow the catastrophes of others to affect him. He observes that "a man can see himself becoming more callous to events because he has to survive," and his reaction to the death of Rosalind Monkley, whom he has killed in an automobile accident, is typical. He writes to his wife, Dorina, that "I will survive and recover, I have had worse blows than this"; he does not mention any guilt he may feel about the incident or the pain Rosalind's death may have caused her family. Similarly, after Dorina's accidental death, Austin tells Matthew that "Poor old Dorina was just a sort of half person really, a maimed creature, she had to die, like certain kinds of cripples have to. They can't last." In spite of Austin's selfishness, however, he is merely the most exaggerated example of egotism in *An Accidental Man*. The statement by an unnamed character at the novel's conclusion that "Austin is like all of us only more so" is, unfortunately, correct.

Austin Gibson Grey resembles several other characters in Murdoch's fiction, all of whom show a talent for survival and an ability to turn unfortunate incidents to their account. In the same way, Austin's wife Dorina is representative of another character type that recurs throughout Murdoch's novels: the individual who functions as a scapegoat or assumes the consequences of the sins of others. Frequently, through no fault of their own, such characters cannot cope with the events happening around them and either choose suicide or become the victims of an "accidental" death that appears to be inevitable. Traditionally, the scapegoat or *pharmakos* figure is an individual who must be expelled from society in order to maintain its continued existence and vitality. Dorina Gibson Grey is a *pharmakos* who manifests all of these characteristics. Early in the novel, she feels as if "something were closing in for the kill," and after her death, her sister Mavis voices the opinion that "she has died for me," telling Matthew that "she has somehow died for us, for you and me, taking herself away, clearing herself away, so that our world should be easier and simpler." Dorina's death enables Garth Gibson Grey to feel love once again for his father. Her death also rejuvenates her husband, as Matthew ironically observes: "Something or other had . . . done Austin good. Perhaps it was simply Dorina's death." Her death has an almost ritualistic dimension in *An Accidental Man*, and it ensures the rejuvenation of several of the characters.

The ending of *An Accidental Man* is one of the darkest in Murdoch's fiction, and very few of the defeats suffered in this novel can be termed "honourable." In fact, several characters, including Matthew Gibson Grey, Garth Gibson Grey, and Charlotte Ledgard, appear to have settled for what Julius King in *A Fairly Honourable Defeat* calls a "sensible acceptance of the second rate." Matthew, en route with Ludwig Leferrier to the United States, where Ludwig will receive a prison sentence for refusing to fight in Vietnam, realizes that "he would never be a hero. . . . He would be until the end of his life a man looking forward to his next drink"; Garth is metamorphosed into a self-satisfied, successful novelist whose former social conscience and pursuit of goodness have been abandoned in favor of marriage to Gracie Tisbourne and all that she represents; and Charlotte chooses to remain with Mitzi Ricardo in spite of her knowledge that what she feels for Mitzi is merely "a fake dream love." These failures contrast with the fates of Austin and Clara Tisbourne, both of whom are described as looking "radiantly juvenile." Austin, in particular, has been completely rejuvenated by the misfortunes of others and is finally able to move his fingers, which have been rigid since his childhood "accident"; his inability to do this heretofore has symbolized his problems with dealing with the world, just as his new physical flexibility reflects the rebirth of his psyche.

The darkly comic final chapter of *An Accidental Man*, which consists solely of untagged dialogue, furnishes important information while it trivializes the events of the entire novel. The fact that Ludwig Leferrier is now in prison in the United States after his decision to leave his idyllic and protected situation in England, the real moral dilemma of the novel, is mentioned in passing and then dropped by an unnamed character who incorrectly says that he has been imprisoned for "Drugs or something." In this final section of the novel, unlike the earlier chapters of letters and dialogue, the reader becomes less and less certain about who is actually speaking. In fact, the dialogue appears to be spoken by a group of eerie, disembodied voices that create an ominous atmosphere from which the narrator and the main characters have departed, leaving the reader to overhear the mindless gossiping of strangers. At the conclusion of *An Accidental Man*, contingency and "the rhetoric of the casually absent god" have triumphed.

The Sea, the Sea

In *The Sea, the Sea*, Murdoch focuses on a type of character who has appeared throughout her fiction, the artist or would-be artist who confuses life and art with unfortunate (and sometimes tragic) consequences. In Murdoch's earlier novel, *The Black Prince*, Bradley Pearson's quiet life is suddenly shattered by a series of revelations and catastrophes that include an affair with the teenage daughter of his best friend. These real-life events cause Bradley to create the novel he had been unable to write previously; at the same time, Bradley is consciously aware of his movement from experience to the expression of experience in aesthetic form and realizes the difference between the two, even though he takes great pride in his "artistic" consciousness throughout the story. In *The Sea, the Sea*, however, Charles Arrowby, the famous and ostensibly "retired" theatrical director who is unable to leave behind the artifice and dramatic structure of the stage, begins to "direct" life offstage, ignoring the boundaries between fact and fiction. His theater becomes the small seaside village to which he has moved, and his actors are the people around him.

Published one year before *The Sea, the Sea*, *The Fire and the Sun*, Murdoch's study of Plato's objections to art and artists, is instructive to read in the light of her portrayal of Charles Arrowby. Although Murdoch disagrees with several of Plato's fundamental assumptions about the nature of art, her narrator in *The Sea, the Sea* embodies many of Plato's—and Murdoch's—suspicions about the artistic sensibility. In *The Fire and the Sun*, Murdoch discusses the Platonic doctrine that art and the artist "exhibit the lowest and most irrational kind of awareness, *eikasia*, a state of vague image-ridden illusion"; in Plato's myth of the cave, this state corresponds to the prisoners who, facing the wall, can see only the shadows cast by the fire. Charles Arrowby, called the "king of shadows" several times in the novel, exemplifies the "bad" artist, the "naive fantasist" who "sees only moving shadows and construes the world in accordance with the easy unresisted mechanical 'causality' of his personal dream life." Throughout the novel, James Arrowby, Charles's cousin and the "saint" figure in *The Sea, the Sea*, tries to convince Charles that the woman he is pursuing is only a "dream figure," just as Hartley Fitch, the sixty-year-old woman who was Charles's adolescent girlfriend and is now married to another man, tells Charles that their love is a "dream" that does not belong in the real world. Near the end of the novel, Charles acknowledges the truth of their interpretations, calling his novel "my own dream text."

Charles Arrowby's psychological state, one that combines tremendous egotism with an obsessional need to control other people while remaining almost completely deluded about what is happening around him, closely resembles Murdoch's description of Plato's idea of the "bad" man. The "bad" or mediocre man is "in a state of illusion, of which egoism is the most general name. . . . Obsession, prejudice, envy, anxiety, ignorance, greed, neurosis, and so on *veil* reality." Similarly, Plato says that the human soul desires "omnipotence" and erects barriers between itself and reality so that it can remain comfortably within a "self-directed dream world." Although on the novel's first page Charles claims that he has come to his retirement home "to repent of egoism," his realization that Hartley is living in the same village results in his jealously obsessional need to "capture" her from her husband. Although he views himself as a Prospero-like magician-artist who can effect any kind of magical transformation, he gradually reveals his incorrect evaluations of himself and others. Charles's novel, the chronicle of his delusions and errors, is a portrait of the "bad" man who refuses to acknowledge the unpredictability and intransigence of reality.

Charles tells the reader that his last great role as an actor was as Prospero in William Shakespeare's *The Tempest* (1611), and he believes he has much in common with Shakespeare's magician. Despite his statement early in the novel that "Now I shall abjure magic and become a hermit," he soon begins the direction of his final "drama." His theatrical vision of the world often obscures reality; not surprisingly, he is overjoyed to discover that what he first called a "diary," "memoir," and "autobiography" has become a novel. The change from a journalistic mode of writing to a fictional one parallels his growing tendency to dramatize and fictionalize events, and soon after his announcement that he is indeed writing a novel, he begins to construct an elaborate "story" about Hartley and her marriage. James fails in his attempt to convince his cousin that he is fighting for a "phantom Helen" and that his wish to rescue her is "pure imagination, pure fiction." Although Charles later admits to the reader that he has created an "image" of Hartley that does not correspond to reality, he denies that his "image" is untrue. His kidnapping of Hartley reveals his need to hold her prisoner in his imagination, to create an aesthetic image he can manipulate for his own purposes. Unlike Bradley Pearson, who finally admits that any kind of final possession of human beings is impossible, Charles continues to believe that he can force Hartley to concede to the planned denouement of his "drama."

Charles's attitude toward his novel is related to his dramatic theories, and both have implications for the way his story is interpreted by the reader. He defines the theater as "an attack on mankind carried on by magic," and its function as being "to victimize an audience every night, to make them laugh and cry and suffer and miss their trains. Of course actors regard audiences as enemies, to be deceived, drugged, incarcerated, stupefied." Although he claims to take painstaking care to relate events in his novel as truthfully as possible, at one point even reassuring the reader that he is rendering the dialogue almost verbatim, he is delighted by his sudden discovery that language, like dramatic art, can create illusion and veil truth. He says that anything written down is "true in a way" and gloats over the fact that he could write down "all sorts of fantastic nonsense" in his memoir and be believed because of "human credulity" and the power of the written word. He takes an increasing pleasure in fictionalizing his life and in transforming the people around him into "stylish sketches," acts that reveal his desire to cast his friends and enemies into a drama he can both write and direct. Like Bradley Pearson in *The Black Prince*, he finds that verbalizing experience can be a way to control what is happening; he also believes that he can dramatically intensify his feelings by writing them out "as a story." When he writes out his account of the visit of another former girlfriend, Lizzie Scherer, he observes that it would be "rewarding" to "write the whole of one's life thus bit by bit as a novel. . . . The pleasant parts would be doubly pleasant, the funny parts funnier, and sin and grief would be softened by a light of philosophic consolation." Murdoch, who has said that the function of art is to reveal reality rather than to console its creator or consumer, portrays Charles as the "bad" artist who attempts to use art and the creative process for solace instead of revelation.

Just as Murdoch's characters often misuse art and their own creative impulses, they frequently fall in love suddenly and violently, an experience that produces a state of delusion and neurotic obsession. Although she says in *The Fire and the Sun* that the "lover" can be shocked into an awareness of "an entirely separate reality" during the experience of love, the lover's ego usually causes him to wish to "dominate and possess" the beloved. The lover, rather than wishing to "serve and adore," instead wants "to de-realize the other, devour and absorb him, subject him to the mechanism of . . . fantasy." Charles Arrowby's "Quest of the Bearded Lady," as one character terms his pursuit of Hartley, exemplifies this dimension of falling in love; his feelings for her are typical of the obsessive, self-centered, fantasy-ridden love that Murdoch believes is antithetical to an objective, free apprehension of others. He admits that he is "like a madman" and compares himself to a "frenzied animal." Later, he says that "I was sane enough to know that I was in a state of total obsession and that I . . . *could only* run continually along the same rat-paths of fantasy and intent." Unlike his cousin James, who has cultivated the intellectual and spiritual detachment of Eastern philosophy combined with a concern for the well-being and "otherness" of individuals, Charles has a passion for Hartley Fitch that is, at bottom, an obsession with his own past and loss of innocence.

In two earlier novels, *An Accidental Man* and *The Black Prince*, Murdoch uses narrative devices such as epistolary and dialogic chapters and the addition of "postscripts" by other characters to alter the reader's perspective and interpretation of events. In *The Sea, the Sea*, she allows Charles Arrowby to add a "revision" to his novel that qualifies and contradicts much of his earlier narrative. At the end of the "History" section of *The Sea, the Sea*, he closes his story on a note of repentance and revelation, goes to sleep hearing "singing," and awakens to see the seals he had previously been unable to sight.

Murdoch believes that fiction should reflect the "muddle" of reality, and thus she adds a postscript by the narrator appropriately titled "Life Goes On." Charles begins by mocking his "conclusion" and observing that life, unlike art, "has an irritating way of bumping and limping on, undoing conversions, casting doubt on solutions"; he then decides to continue his story a while longer, this time in the form of a "diary" in which he alters his own version of events and reveals that he has learned very little from them. In this way, Murdoch further reduces the stature of her "failed Prospero," and the picture of Charles that emerges in the postscript is that of a rapidly aging man with an incipient heart condition. Another addition to the group of "power figures" in Murdoch's fiction who believe that they can "invent" reality and manipulate other people for aesthetic purposes, Charles Arrowby represents Murdoch's belief in the final impossibility of one human being's controlling another. In *The Sea, the Sea*, the would-be director who thought himself a "god" or "king" is revealed as a relatively powerless individual over whom the formlessness and unpredictability of "transcendent reality" triumphs.

The Good Apprentice

Murdoch's most critically acclaimed novel of the 1980's is *The Good Apprentice*, a novel that reflects her continuing desire to write fiction whose length and complexity embody her belief in a contingent, infinitely particularized universe in which goodness is easily discussed but achieved, if at all, with great difficulty and pain. The "good apprentice" can refer to either of two characters in the novel. Edward Baltram has recently been responsible for the death of his best friend and is attempting to deal with his resulting guilt and self-hatred; Stuart Cuno, his stepbrother, is, like many other Murdochian characters, seeking goodness and finding it a problematical goal.

Murdoch make Stuart Cuno the mouthpiece of some of her most cherished ideas about the nature of goodness. Like Murdoch, Stuart acknowledges that goodness is often an unimaginable concept that involves inaction rather than action, and several times in the story he is referred to as a "negative presence." Stuart has rejected the entire concept of God and instead attempts to meditate blankly, to empty his mind in order to perceive clearly, what Murdoch calls "an instinctive craving for nothingness which was also a desire to be able to love and enjoy and 'touch' everything, to *help* everything." Psychoanalyst Thomas McCaskerville, who stands in direct opposition to Stuart's nontheoretical approach to goodness, catechizes the younger man at length in an important conversation that reveals Thomas's dependence on the cozy theories of psychoanalysis that Murdoch had mocked in her earlier novels. Thomas has a conceptual framework for almost any idea or event, and his discovery that his wife Midge has been having an affair with Stuart's father Harry Cuno only temporarily shocks him out of his comfortable mental and emotional world. His further realization that his supposedly psychotic patient Mr. Blinnet is actually quite sane and has been faking mental illness for years is another blow at Thomas's carefully constructed theoretical world.

It is the artist Jesse Baltram, Edward's father, who best represents one of the most enduring and interesting figures in Murdoch's fiction, the magician-artist power figure who mysteriously spellbinds those around him and functions as a catalyst for many important events. Edward goes to Seegard, Jesse's home, to be "healed" and "purified" of his friend's death. In the process he meets May Baltram, Jesse's wife, his two half sisters, and, finally, his father, who has been reduced by an unspecified illness to childlike behavior and incoherence. Jesse's difficulty in making rational conversation is another alternative in the novel to Stuart's "blankness" and "whiteness" and Thomas's frenziedly articulate philosophizing: It signifies that the logical ordering principle of language ultimately cannot describe or explain a reality that is always "boiling over" with energy and creativity. Jesse's description of the world and the relationship between good and evil, in which syntax and logic break down, is directly opposed to the other characters' slick facility with language. He tells Edward,

> "What I knew once—about good and evil and those—all *those* things—people don't really have them, meet them—in their lives at all, most people don't—only a few—want that—that fight, you know—think they want—good—have to have evil—not real, either—of course—all inside something else—it's a dance—you see—world needs power—always round and round—it's all power and—energy—which sometimes—rears up its beautiful head—like a dragon—that's the meaning of it all—I think—in the shadows now—can't remember—doesn't matter—what I need—is a long sleep—so as to dream it all—over again."

Jesse's connection with the supernatural and paranormal dimension of Edward's stay at Seegard reveals Murdoch again experimenting with the limits of realistic fiction. As in *The Sea, the Sea*, she is willing to force the reader to accept the unexplained and acknowledge the thin line between the natural and the supernatural, between distortion of perception and a glimpse into another world where the usual rational rules no longer apply. *The Good Apprentice* shows Murdoch at the height of her powers as a novelist, combining her "moral psychology" with her long-held aesthetic theories in a work that proves the undiminished fecundity of her imagination and intelligence.

The Book and the Brotherhood

In another important novel of the 1980's, *The Book and the Brotherhood*, Murdoch's power figure is as charismatic as Jesse but is neither impotent nor incoherent. David Crimond is an intellectual of the far Left (the communists kicked him out for being too radical). Years ago at Oxford, a group of Crimond's friends pledged to support him while he wrote the volume of revolutionary economic and social philosophy they thought world needed. Years later, although Crimond's book remains unpublished, his intellectual, personal, and even sexual power over the group remains undiminished. The novel shows how the friends try to define their moderating political views in relation to Crimond's.

The novel also shows how the friends and *their* friends try to make peace with the world. Each yearns for fulfillment, though in widely different ways—some of them touching, some admirable, some reprehensible. Gerard, perhaps the novel's central character, yearns for a vague something (his yearning began with his affection for his pet parrot, as described in one of Murdoch's most brilliant passages). Rose, a passive woman, yearns for Gerard. Duncan yearns for his wife, who yearns for Crimond. Jenkins, a saintly schoolmaster, yearns for a perfect act. Other characters are less important but stranger. At the end of an Oxford party, Gulliver is awakened by a deer's kiss; later he has a paranormal experience in a London railway station. Other inexplicable forces are exerted by buried Roman roads and by Church rituals performed by an unbelieving priest.

The Book and the Brotherhood offers no certainties, for neither Crimond's ideas nor Gerard's refutations are convincing. It shows a wide spectrum of memorable characters yearning earnestly and sometimes comically toward some things they cannot fully define.

The Green Knight

Murdoch's last great novel, *The Green Knight*, is one of her most perplexing. The story is bizarre. It often resembles (but does not strictly parallel) that of the medieval narrative poem *Sir Gawain and the Green Knight*. In its central act, Murdoch once again pushes the bounds of realism. One dark night in a public park, Lucas Graffe, while attempting to kill his brother Clement with a baseball bat, hits a third man instead and kills him. Later, like the medieval Green Knight, the supposedly dead man reappears. His name is Peter Mir, and he is this novel's powerful magician; he is alive and demands justice. His demand is worked out in a way that also recalls *Sir Gawain and the Green Knight*. (Mir also is said to resemble Mr. Pickwick, Prospero, the Minotaur, and Mephistopheles.)

The stories of other characters encircle the central one. Clement hopelessly loves Louise Anderson, whose magical house contains three wonderful daughters about to begin life's journey. The most mysterious is Moy, who can move small stones at a distance. The Andersons keep a dog named Anax, one of Murdoch's finest animal creations. His master, Bellamy, gave him away to embark on a spiritual quest for which he is ill suited. At one point Anax, who may embody the goodness of the flesh, escapes and tries to find his master in an anxious lope through the streets of London.

Murdoch's conclusion of this novel may not satisfy everyone, but the journey through the novel is exciting and rewarding. Her last novel, *Jackson's Dilemma*, has many high spots, but it is often confusing. By the time the reviews appeared, her Alzheimer's disease had progressed so far that she could not understand them.

Angela Hague
Updated by George Soule

Other major works

short fiction: *Something Special: A Story*, pb. 1999 (wr. 1955).

plays: *A Severed Head*, pr. 1963 (with J. B. Priestley); *The Italian Girl*, pr. 1967 (with James Saunders); *The Servants and the Snow*, pr. 1970; *The Three Arrows*, pr. 1972; *Art and Eros*, pr. 1980; *The Black Prince*, pr. 1989; *Joanna Joanna*, pb. 1994; *The One Alone*, pb. 1995.

poetry: *A Year of Birds*, 1978 (limited edition), 1984 (engravings by Reynolds Stone).

nonfiction: *Sartre: Romantic Rationalist*, 1953; *The Sovereignty of Good*, 1970; *The Fire and the Sun: Why Plato Banished the Artists*, 1977; *Acastos: Two Platonic Dialogues*, 1986; *Metaphysics as a Guide to Morals*, 1992; *Existentialists and Mystics: Writings on Philosophy and Literature*, 1997 (Peter Conradi, editor).

Bibliography

Antonacchio, Maria. *Picturing the Human: The Moral Thought of Iris Murdoch*. New York: Oxford University Press, 2000. Focuses on Murdoch's moral philosophy and describes the significant role Murdoch continues to play in debates about ethics. Offers a framework with which to assess Murdoch's ideas.

Baldanza, Frank. *Iris Murdoch*. New York: Twayne, 1974. Provides both biographical information and discussion of Murdoch's novels and the plays adapted from *A Severed Head* and *The Italian Girl*. Covers significant details about Murdoch's life and writing before 1970.

Bayley, John. *Elegy for Iris*. New York: St. Martin's Press, 1999. Poignant and loving memoir by Murdoch's husband of forty-two years. Describes the final years of Murdoch's life, when she was afflicted with Alzheimer's disease.

Bove, Cheryl K. *Understanding Iris Murdoch*. Columbia: University of South Carolina Press, 1993. Lucid and valuable handbook for college students separates Murdoch's works into two broad categories—the ironic tragedy and the bittersweet comedy—to explain how the writings express her philosophy, depict human relationships, and handle plot and theme.

Conradi, Peter J. *Iris Murdoch*. New York: W. W. Norton, 2001. Biography of the novelist examines her early life as an imaginative only child, through the trauma of World War II, up to her final years. Describes Murdoch's life as a search for good in a particularly evil century.

Dipple, Elizabeth. *Iris Murdoch: Work for the Spirit.* Chicago: University of Chicago Press, 1982. Valuable study examines the aesthetic, moral, and philosophical dimensions of Murdoch's works through *Nuns and Soldiers*. Discusses Murdoch's use of Plato's concept of the good and perhaps overemphasizes the bleak Buddhist elements in the novels.

Grimshaw, Tammy. *Sexuality, Gender, and Power in Iris Murdoch's Fiction.* Madison, N.J.: Fairleigh Dickinson University Press, 2005. Examines representations of power, sexuality, and gender in Murdoch's fiction, providing a feminist reading of the work and describing how Murdoch's treatment of homosexuality, bisexuality, cross-dressing, and related issues reflect her preoccupations with reality and morality.

Nolan, Bran. *Iris Murdoch: The Retrospective Fiction.* 2d ed. New York: Palgrave Macmillan, 2004. Takes a psychological approach to Murdoch's work, focusing on how she represents past events and their effects on her characters. Includes analysis of novels that were not discussed in the first edition, published in 1999; also includes a new preface, an updated bibliography, and three additional chapters covering Murdoch's most important and popular novels.

Rowe, Anne, ed. *Iris Murdoch: A Reassessment.* New York: Palgrave Macmillan, 2007. Collection of essays reinterprets Murdoch's work in terms of twenty-first century debates about the aesthetic impulse, moral philosophy, gender and sexuality, literature, and authorship. Includes comparisons of Murdoch's work with works by other authors.

Spear, Hilda D. *Iris Murdoch.* New York: Palgrave Macmillan, 2007. Provides an introduction to Murdoch's novels, tracing how she progressively used the plots of her books to address philosophical issues such as the nature of reality, good, and evil.

Todd, Richard. *Iris Murdoch.* London: Methuen, 1984. Focuses on Murdoch's novels up to *The Philosopher's Pupil*, providing interpretations that are incisive and occasionally profound. Shows how Murdoch's novels developed basic themes about which she wrote in her philosophical volumes.

Tucker, Lindsey, ed. *Critical Essays on Iris Murdoch.* New York: G. K. Hall, 1992. Useful collection of twelve essays by Murdoch scholars. Four essays consider Murdoch's work generally, while the rest focus on individual works, including *An Accidental Man* and *The Sea, the Sea*.

ROBERT MUSIL

Born: Klagenfurt, Austria; November 6, 1880
Died: Geneva, Switzerland; April 15, 1942
Also known as: Robert Edler von Musil

PRINCIPAL LONG FICTION

Die Verwirrungen des Zöglings Törless, 1906 (*Young Törless*, 1955)

Der Mann ohne Eigenschaften, 1930-1943 (unfinished; 3 volumes; *The Man Without Qualities*, 1953-1960 [3 volumes], 1995 [2 volumes])

OTHER LITERARY FORMS

In addition to the short novel with which he began his literary career and the massive unfinished work that occupied the later years of his life, Robert Musil (MEW-zihl) wrote a dissertation on the Austrian philosopher Ernst Mach, *Beitrag zur Beurteilung der Lehren Machs* (1908; *On Mach's Theories*, 1982); a number of short stories and novellas, including those published in *Vereinigungen* (1911; partial translation *Unions*, 1965) and *Drei Frauen* (1924; *Tonka, and Other Stories*, 1965) and later published in English under the title *Five Women*

(1966); two plays, *Die Schwärmer* (pb. 1921; *The Enthusiasts*, 1983) and a farce titled *Vinzenz und die Freundin bedeutender Männer* (1923; Vinzenz and the girlfriend of important men); and many essays, reviews, and newspaper pieces, some of which were revised and published in *Nachlass zu Lebzeiten* (1936; *Posthumous Papers of a Living Author*, 1987). Two multivolume collections of Musil's diaries and letters have also been edited and published in German, and a selection of his writings was collected and published in English in 1986.

Achievements

Neither in his life nor in his work was Robert Musil ever willing to accept the necessity of choosing between the "two worlds" of science and culture. He was trained as a scientist, but he abandoned a promising scientific career in favor of literature, which he regarded as a serious instrument for exploring the social and philosophical problems of his time. Although his work was praised by such prominent writers as Thomas Mann, Hermann Broch, and Alfred Döblin, the extreme precision of Musil's style and the "essayistic" density of his method made for difficult reading. As a result, he was never a popular success, and he was even forced in his later years to live on charitable contributions provided by small groups of friends and supporters. Plagued by financial worries during his last years, spent in exile in Switzerland, Musil would often wonder—with characteristic irony—how it had happened that he had become the object of such universal esteem and such utter neglect.

In a sense, this awkward situation has continued to the present day: Because *The Man Without Qualities* remained unfinished at the time of Musil's death, scholars and critics have been largely preoccupied with editorial problems connected with the question of how the novel was supposed to end. In any event, Musil's work has yet to receive the international recognition it deserves, and much of it remains unavailable except in German. More than ten thousand pages of Musil's manuscripts are housed in the Austrian National Library in Vienna, and three research centers devoted to Musil studies have been established, at the University of Klagenfurt (Austria), Reading University (England), and the University of the Saarland (Saarbrücken, Germany).

Biography

Robert Musil was the child of Hermine and Alfred Musil; his father was an engineer and later a professor at the Technical Institute in Brno (now in the Czech Republic). At the age of twelve, young Musil was sent away from home to military schools in Eisenstadt and then Mährisch-Weisskirchen, which later were to provide the setting for *Young Törless*. He became increasingly interested in technical subjects, and he continued his studies in mechanical engineering at Brno, where he passed state examinations in mathematics, physics, mechanics, and statistics. He was such a promising student that, after he completed his military service in 1902, he was invited to work at the Technical Institute in Stuttgart, which was then the most modern laboratory for mechanical engineering in Europe. A year later, in 1903, he moved from Stuttgart to the University of Berlin, where he took up the study of philosophy and experimental psychology. He also invented a device for use in the psychological testing of the perception of colors. Musil completed his first novel in 1905, made contacts among members of the literary circles in Berlin, and, upon completing his doctoral dissertation on Ernst Mach in 1908, decided not to pursue an academic career, but instead to try to live as a writer. He returned to an archivist's job in Vienna in 1911, where he married Martha Marcovaldi (née Heimann), who remained his lifelong companion.

During World War I, Musil served as a captain on the Italian front and as a writer and editor for Austrian military newspapers. After the war, his time was divided between Vienna and Berlin; he was active as a playwright and essayist and as a member of various literary and journalistic organizations. The first two volumes of *The Man Without Qualities* appeared in 1930 and 1933. When Adolf Hitler came to power, Musil left Berlin for Vienna and continued working on his novel. He suffered a mild stroke in 1936, and in 1938, following the Anschluss (Nazi Germany's annexation of Austria), he went into exile, by way of Italy—first to Zurich and then to Geneva. His books were banned in Germany and Austria. Musil's last years in Geneva were troubled with financial and passport worries and with the problem of carrying his novel forward. He died suddenly of a stroke in 1942. The first "complete" English-language edition of *The Man Without Qualities* appeared ten years later.

ANALYSIS

The full German title of Robert Musil's early novel *Young Törless* translates literally as "the perplexities of Cadet Törless," which echoes the title of Johann Wolfgang von Goethe's first novel, *Die Leiden des jungen Werthers* (1774; *The Sorrows of Young Werther*, 1779). *Young Törless* is, on one level, a story of adolescent intrigue among cadets at the most prestigious military academy in the Austro-Hungarian Empire, but it has also been read as an early and prophetic vision of the sadistic and irrational tendencies that were later to find expression in Hitler's Third Reich.

YOUNG TÖRLESS

The plot of the novel is fairly simple. Törless, a young and lonely new cadet in an academy in a remote setting on the Russian frontier of the empire, gravitates toward his more forceful older classmates, Beineberg, a would-be Eastern mystic, and Reiting, a Machiavellian schemer. When Beineberg and Reiting accidentally discover that a third cadet, a pudgy and effeminate boy named Basini, has been stealing from other boys' lockers, they blackmail Basini into becoming their virtual slave; in a secret "Red Chamber" in the attic of their dormitory, they regularly subject Basini to psychological and sexual abuse that grows increasingly severe. Törless watches Basini's degradation from the sidelines until finally, when Beineberg and Reiting threaten to kill Basini, the school authorities are notified and the scandal is exposed. Törless is asked to explain himself before the headmaster, but he can only try to express the impossibility of all explanation, since language only skims the surface and is inadequate for exploring the irrational depths that house things like Basini's torture: "There's something dark in me, deep under all my thoughts, something I can't measure out with thoughts, a sort of life that can't be expressed in words and which is my life, all the same." In the final scene, Törless leaves the school, accompanied by his mother.

The moral of this story, as Törless puts it, is the cynical realization that "things just happen: that's the sum total of wisdom." Underneath this superficial cynicism, however, lies Törless's more challenging recognition that conventions cannot be accepted merely for the sake of comfort and that much of human reality indeed lies outside the realm of the expressible. For these reasons, *Young Törless* was hailed as an important contribution to German Expressionism when the book first appeared in 1906. In view of the unity of Musil's approach throughout his career, it is also possible to see this novel as an early sketch for his later work; Törless is a "cadet without qualities" who is unwilling to take a stand on any foundations that cannot themselves bear the burden of close scrutiny. An excellent German film version of the novel, directed by Volker Schlöndorff, was released in 1966.

THE MAN WITHOUT QUALITIES

The Man Without Qualities (the German title of which, *Der Mann ohne Eigenschaften*, could perhaps be rendered more accurately as "the man without anything of his own") is the magnum opus on which, or toward which, Musil was working throughout his life, in which he sought to bring together and integrate all the various strands of his experience by subjecting them to a rigorous and ironic analysis. Thematic sketches for such a novel appear even in Musil's earliest known diary entries, dating back to around 1899. He finally settled

Robert Musil. (Getty Images)

down to work on the novel in the 1920's, and he continued working on it for the rest of his life. Although the novel was not yet finished when Musil died, the first two volumes, together amounting to more than one thousand printed pages, were published by 1933; until 1995, these were the only portions of the novel available in English, in three volumes published from 1953 to 1960. The 1978 German edition of the novel is more than two thousand pages long because it includes a large selection of materials from what was "left behind": drafts of chapters, unfinished sketches, notes and projects, and so on. The two-volume 1995 English translation also includes many such additional materials.

The Man Without Qualities is the story of Ulrich, a brilliant and well-to-do young Viennese intellectual who decides, in August, 1913, to take a year's "vacation from life" in order to make a final attempt to become a "meaningful man," one whose life has a meaning that can be proved. Ulrich (like Musil) has already broken off possible careers as a military officer, a mechanical engineer, and a mathematician. For Ulrich, it is important not simply to discover the right profession but also to find a way of life that does not exclude any of the other possibilities of which he is constantly aware. He is described as a man with a "sense of possibility":

> Whoever has this sense doesn't say, for example: Here this or that happened, will happen, must happen; instead he considers: Here could, should, or might happen; and if someone tells him that something is the way it is, he thinks: Well, it could probably also be some other way. So the sense of possibility could be defined as the ability to think of all that could just as well be otherwise, and of not regarding what *is* as more important than what *isn't*.

If this is fantasy, it is fantasy with a purpose, for this approach enables Ulrich to find the flaw in all the ready-made attitudes and conventions that are presented to him.

The structure of the novel is fundamentally ironic, because the end of Ulrich's yearlong experiment will coincide with the thunder of the guns of August, 1914. No sooner has Ulrich decided to undertake this project than his father arranges for him to serve as honorary secretary to the Parallel Action, a group composed of the best minds in the Austro-Hungarian Empire. The group has been asked by Count Leinsdorf, an enlightened aristocrat and representative of the old order, to decide how the seventieth anniversary of the reign of the Austrian emperor, Francis Joseph I, should best be celebrated five years later, in 1918 (in "parallel" competition with the thirtieth anniversary of the German emperor being celebrated that same year). This group of high-minded and patriotic experts meets regularly in the salon of Ulrich's cousin Diotima, where they seek to discover the "Austrian idea," the spiritual essence of the empire that was in political fact a patchwork conglomeration of many diverse peoples, all with their own languages, cultural traditions, and national interests.

Musil calls the empire "Kakania," a nickname based on the ubiquitous abbreviation of a phrase describing the double nature of Austro-Hungarian sovereignty, which was both imperial and royal ("*kaiserlich und königlich*": *k.u.k.*). He portrays Kakanian society with loving irony as a muddling, quasi-imaginary world in which things are regularly—as an old Austrian proverb puts it—"hopeless, but not serious." Musil was not alone in noting the "dreamlike" aspects of life in the doddering empire. Writers otherwise as diverse as Hugo von Hofmannsthal, Hermann Broch, and Franz Kafka had also approached this theme, and it is perhaps no accident that the renowned investigator of dreams, Sigmund Freud, was a product of this culture. What made Musil's work different was the rigor and consistency with which he applied the tools of fiction to the conquest of his chosen theme.

Musil saw the Austrian dilemma as "a particularly clear case of the modern world," and historians have often agreed that if the empire could only have solved its problem of the "nationalities," this solution could perhaps have helped pave the way for such later utopian endeavors as the League of Nations or the United Nations. In Musil's work, however, the "nationalities" are presented less as a political problem than as an image of a more general dilemma: Not only do different peoples fail to understand one another, but also even those who speak the same language are unable to reach agreement on issues of basic concern. In the novel, the Parallel Action's quest for the great "idea" that will unify Austria reflects, on social and historical levels, Ulrich's own personal search for an idea that will enable him to integrate his own life and give it meaning. Both quests end in failure, but along the way, Musil portrays an enormous range of modern attitudes in the characters who frequent Diotima's salon, and he engages in brilliant—and still very relevant—satire of these attitudes as he describes the futile attempts of the group to reach a consensus.

Among the frequent visitors to the salon is Dr. Paul Arnheim, a Prussian industrialist and a "great writer" who offers, in contrast to Ulrich, the image of a powerful and successful man *with* qualities, whose achievements are recognized by all. Musil acknowledged that the character of Arnheim owed much to that of Walther Rathenau, whom he had met in Berlin. The critic Peter Gay has described Rathenau as an "industrialist, economist, and Utopian"; as minister for reconstruction and then as foreign minister of the postwar Weimar Republic, Rathenau worked to reconstruct the German economy until his assassination in 1922. Some of the other characters are similarly based on identifiable persons: The guru Meingast is modeled on the philosopher Ludwig Klages, and the poet Friedel Feuermaul is a caricature of Franz Werfel. Musil, however, indulges in satire less for the sake of entertainment than as what he called a "positive construction," a means of exposing and refuting the assumptions inherent in the worldviews represented by these figures.

Often the satire remains implicit: When Arnheim has an affair with Diotima, their relationship is reflected and gently parodied in a corresponding affair between their servants. The novel also features a good many episodes that are simply hilarious, as, for example, when the genial General Stumm (who, together with Arnheim, represents a kind of "military-industrial complex") goes to the library in search of the essential gist of all the knowledge contained there, only to be handed the "Bibliography of Bibliographies." There are also a number of subplots involving Ulrich's various love affairs and the attempts of Clarisse, a sort of Nietzschean emotional extremist, to bring about the release of the mass murderer Moosbrugger from the mental asylum in which he is confined. As always with Musil, these stories are told not only for their dramatic effect but also for the sake of the social and philosophical issues they raise: Is Moosbrugger—or anyone else—ever "mentally competent"?

By the end of the first volume of *The Man Without Qualities*, the public has grown angry with the Parallel Action, having misunderstood it in a variety of ways, and a mob stages a noisy demonstration in protest. Ulrich, discouraged, walks home one evening wishing he were a character in a novel, because in that case all the inessential and superfluous aspects of his life would be left out: "It occurred to him that the law of life we dream of when overburdened and longing for simplicity might be none other than the law of narrative sequence! . . . Happy the man who can say 'before,' 'during,' and 'after'!" When he reaches home, he finds a telegram announcing "the passing of his progenitor"—the death of his father.

The second volume, which bears the subtitle, more ominous in retrospect, *Ins tausendjährige Reich: Die Verbrecher* (*Into the Millennium: The Criminals*), begins as Ulrich, having left Vienna to attend his father's funeral, encounters his younger sister Agathe for the first time in years. They become close friends, and their closeness is reflected in the fact that they refer to themselves as "twins" and even as "Siamese twins." Most of this volume centers on the relationship that develops between Ulrich and Agathe, although they continue to receive progress reports (or, rather, lack-of-progress reports) about the Parallel Action from General Stumm. In effect, the friendship of Ulrich and Agathe amounts to a metaphysical love affair, an intense attempt to achieve a utopian "other condition," a perfect otherworldliness of peace and limitless possibility. Ulrich once refers to Agathe as his "self-love," and she is indeed, in many respects, a female double or complementary mirror image of himself, so that his relationship with her is a reflection of his own search for an inner and lasting harmony apart from the disintegrating world of the Parallel Action.

This volume concludes with a gala reunion of all the participants in the Parallel Action, at which two newcomers, a pacifist poet and a proto-Nazi Brownshirt, reach agreement on a final resolution: "Let each person get himself killed for the sake of his own ideas; but whoever leads men to die for the ideas of others is a murderer." This interesting resolution confirms once and for all the impossibility of arriving at a utopian synthesis of ideas or a consistent program of social action by means of consensus. When General Stumm asks Ulrich for help in finding an optimistic way to report this outcome to his superiors, Ulrich tells him: "Just report . . . that it's the Thousand-Year Holy War. And never has mankind been so poorly armed for it as now." The posthumous chapters contain references indicating that all the money donated to the Parallel Action later goes toward building up the army (the only patriotic purpose with which no one could argue), while the celebration planned for 1918 will amount only to an elaborate costume parade.

Even though the experiments of Ulrich and the Parallel Action prove unsuccessful, the ultimate value of the endeavor may rest not as much in the final results as in the method used to reach them, or to reach toward them. As Musil said, "I keep on with my work even though I know that it is only part of the truth, and I would keep on with it all the same even if I knew that it is false, because certain mistakes are way-stations along the road to truth." For Musil, the utopia of unlimited possibility is less a goal than a direction. If the medium is always in some sense the message, in *The Man Without Qualities* the method is also the moral. In other words, the fact that life inevitably fails to "make sense" does not mean that one should abandon the task of searching for its sense with all the means at one's disposal, including the novel. Moreover, Musil regarded fiction as a privileged mode in which to explore these philosophical issues, because in fiction he was able to bridge the gulf that usually exists between the attitudes and methods of science and those of art—between rationality and emotion, the head and the heart. He strove to understand and unite both in a fictional (that is, hypothetical) synthesis of critical importance to the spiritual well-being of the modern world. In so doing, Musil explored the potential of the novel as a genre to serve as a vehicle for analysis on both an individual and a social level; at the same time, he produced a magnificent "anatomy" of the decline and fall of the Austrian Empire. He provides a diagnosis rather than a cure, but, as his fellow countryman Freud discovered, the diagnosis is itself a kind of cure.

Musil regarded his "essayistic" method as a form of "active passivity" in which the story or plot is at the service of a discussion of ideas, while the passage of time tends to be replaced by the uneven or circular flow of an ongoing argument. In Musil's hands, the novel becomes a kind of critique of analogical reason: On the fictional terrain where art and science meet, laws are understood as metaphors, and metaphors are accorded the gravity of law. Given that Musil regarded fiction as the setting for an analytic process, like an endless Platonic symposium, one is tempted to wonder whether a novel so conceived could ever be concluded without injury to some of those very possibilities in the spirit of which it was written. The Great War, which cost some 800,000 Kakanian lives, was in fact the great denier of possibility; it looms beyond the novel as the inevitable end to Ulrich's story. As Musil explained in an interview in 1926, "That the war happened, had to happen, is the sum total of all the contradictory streams and influences and movements I am depicting."

How might the outcome have been different? Musil's work represents an enormous effort to construct a synthesis able to stand as an answer to this question. The "prevention" of World War I is thus the ironic and hidden intention of *The Man Without Qualities*, for it would mean the retroactive undoing of Austria's destruction. Should the war prove evitable in the novel's "world of possibility," Musil was convinced, this possibility could offer a model for the resolution of present and future conflicts in the world of reality. This "saving idea" is a matter not of individual salvation but of a collective salvation to be shared by all; as Ulrich tells Agathe, "I'm not pious: I look at the road to Heaven and wonder if one could also drive along it in a truck!" The novels of Robert Musil stand as a demonstration of the fact that, whatever else they may be, works of fiction are also instruments to be used in the search for answers to the conflicts and quandaries that plague our modern world no less than they plagued his.

Gene M. Moore

Other major works

SHORT FICTION: *Vereinigungen*, 1911 (partial translation *Unions*, 1965); *Drei Frauen*, 1924 (*Tonka, and Other Stories*, 1965); *Five Women*, 1966 (includes stories from *Vereinigungen* and *Drei Frauen*).

PLAYS: *Die Schwärmer*, pb. 1921 (*The Enthusiasts*, 1983); *Vinzenz und die Freundin bedeutender Männer*, pr. 1923.

NONFICTION: *Beitrag zur Beurteilung der Lehren Machs*, 1908 (*On Mach's Theories*, 1982); *Das hilflose Europa*, 1922; *Nachlass zu Lebzeiten*, 1936 (*Posthumous*

Papers of a Living Author, 1987); *Theater: Kritisches und Theoretisches*, 1965; *Der deutsche Mensch als Symptom*, 1967; *Tagebücher*, 1976 (2 volumes; partial translation *Diaries, 1899-1941*, 1998).

MISCELLANEOUS: *Gesammelte Werke in Einzelausgaben*, 1952-1957 (3 volumes); *Gesammelte Werke*, 1978-1981 (9 volumes; volumes 8 and 9 translated as *Precision and Soul: Essays and Addresses*, 1990); *Selected Writings*, 1986 (Burton Pike, editor).

Bibliography

Bartram, Graham, ed. *The Cambridge Companion to the Modern German Novel*. New York: Cambridge University Press, 2004. Collection of essays includes many references to Musil's works, but the majority of information about the author can be found in two chapters: chapter 4, "Gender Anxiety and the Shaping of the Self in Some Modernist Writers: Musil, Hesse, Hofmannsthal, Jahnn," by Ritchie Robertson; and chapter 7, "Apocalypse and Utopia in the Austrian Novel of the 1930's: Hermann Broch and Robert Musil," by Graham Bartram and Philip Payne.

Bernstein, Michael André. "Robert Musil: Precision and Soul." In *Five Portraits: Modernity and the Imagination in Twentieth-Century German Writing*. Evanston, Ill.: Northwestern University Press, 2000. Essay on Musil expresses great admiration for the novelist's narrative abilities. Part of a larger examination of the work of five modernist German writers—Musil, poets Rainer Maria Rilke and Paul Celan, philosopher Martin Heidegger, and literary and cultural theorist Walter Benjamin.

Hickman, Hannah. *Robert Musil and the Culture of Vienna*. La Salle, Ill.: Open Court, 1991. Traces the "development of Musil's mind" by examining his literary works, notebooks, essays, and personal biography.

Jonsson, Stefan. *Subject Without Nation: Robert Musil and the History of Modern Identity*. Durham, N.C.: Duke University Press, 2000. Analyzes *The Man Without Qualities*, demonstrating how Musil's novel expressed a new concept of identity in Western culture. Maintains that the novel's protagonist is a "new human being" who refuses to become part of Austria's imperialist, nationalist, and fascist communities.

Luft, David S. *Robert Musil and the Crisis of European Culture, 1880-1942*. Berkeley: University of California Press, 1980. Places Musil's work in the larger cultural context from which it emerged, drawing parallels between the events of Musil's life and Europe's transformation. Includes bibliography and index.

McBride, Patrizia C. *The Void of Ethics: Robert Musil and the Experience of Modernity*. Evanston, Ill.: Northwestern University Press, 2006. Examines Musil's fiction and his other works to analyze his ideas about ethics. Argues that for Musil, ethics is a void, or a "realm of experience that eludes language and thought," and describes how this idea was Musil's response to events in Europe following World War I.

Payne, Philip. *Robert Musil's "The Man Without Qualities": A Critical Study*. New York: Cambridge University Press, 1988. Provides a thorough, theme-by-theme analysis of the novel that is generally considered Musil's masterpiece.

Payne, Philip, Graham Bartram, and Galin Tihanov, eds. *A Companion to the Works of Robert Musil*. Rochester, N.Y.: Camden House, 2007. Collection of essays includes several that focus on various elements of *The Man Without Qualities*. Others examine *Young Törless* and Musil's other works and provide information on his life, his position as an intellectual, and his politics. Includes chronology of Musil's life, bibliography, and index.

Rogowski, Christian. *Distinguished Outsider: Robert Musil and His Critics*. Columbia, S.C.: Camden House, 1994. Chronicles the scholarly reception of Musil's works, describing how critics both during and after his lifetime viewed Musil's writings from a multitude of different perspectives. Includes index and bibliography.

Stoehr, Ingo R. *German Literature of the Twentieth Century: From Aestheticism to Postmodernism*. Rochester, N.Y.: Camden House, 2001. Historical overview of German literature places it within the context of artistic and political developments in Western Europe during the twentieth century. Includes information about Musil's work and German modernism in the 1920's and 1930's.

WALTER DEAN MYERS

Born: Martinsburg, West Virginia; August 12, 1937
Also known as: Walter Milton Myers

Principal long fiction

Fast Sam, Cool Clyde, and Stuff, 1975
Mojo and the Russians, 1977
It Ain't All for Nothin', 1978
The Young Landlords, 1979
Hoops, 1981
The Legend of Tarik, 1981
Won't Know Till I Get There, 1982
The Nicholas Factor, 1983
Motown and Didi: A Love Story, 1984
The Outside Shot, 1984
Crystal, 1987
Fallen Angels, 1988
Scorpions, 1988
The Mouse Rap, 1990
Somewhere in the Darkness, 1992
The Righteous Revenge of Artemis Bonner, 1992
The Glory Field, 1994
Slam!, 1996
Monster, 1999
Handbook for Boys, 2002
The Beast, 2003
The Dream Bearer, 2003
Shooter, 2004
Autobiography of My Dead Brother, 2005 (illustrated by Christopher Myers)
Game, 2008
Sunrise over Fallujah, 2008

Other literary forms

One of the most prolific writers of fiction for young adults in the United States, Walter Dean Myers has also made numerous forays into other genres, including children's picture books, historical biographies intended for students at both elementary and high school levels, short stories, and poetry that celebrates not only his childhood Harlem community (as in *Here in Harlem: Poems in Many Voices*, 2004) but also such diverse topics as the heroism of African American patriots and the unique rhythms of black music (as in *Blues Journey*, 2003, and *Jazz*, 2006). Myers has collaborated with his son Christopher (as illustrator) on many of these projects, including works that defy classification, such as the uniquely formatted *Street Love* (2006), which tells its story of young love across class lines in short lines of free verse, and the first-person perspectives of biblical personages in *A Time to Love: Stories from the Old Testament* (2003). Myers has also written a series of historical informational texts on prominent African American figures and topics. Additionally, he has produced a highly acclaimed memoir of his life titled *Bad Boy* (2001). Certainly a multifaceted talent, Myers has produced more than seventy works that appeal to readers of all age groups and sensibilities.

Achievements

Walter Dean Myers has repeatedly been cited as a sole "voice in the wilderness" for the African American youth and teenager. Myers has provided a voice for many who did not previously have one—becoming a writer for so many who have needed to see themselves represented in a literature bereft of that representation. For his unique contribution to literature, Myers has received many honors: He is a two-time Newbery Honor Book winner, for *Scorpions* and *Somewhere in the Darkness*, and has been cited five times as a Coretta Scott King Award winner, for his novels *The Young Landlords*, *Motown and Didi*, *Fallen Angels*, and *Slam!* and for the nonfiction work *Now Is Your Time! The African-American Struggle for Freedom* (1991). In 1994, Myers was presented with the American Library Award for "lifetime contribution to Young Adult Literature" for four of his novels. He has also been recognized twice as a National Book Award finalist, for *Monster* and *Autobiography of My Dead Brother*. *Monster* was also selected as the first recipient of the Michael L. Printz Award for Excellence in Young Adult Literature in 1999. Truly a pioneer in the genre, Myers continues to create relevant and powerful stories that explore the experiences of young African Americans.

Biography

Walter Dean Myers was born Walter Milton Myers in Martinsburg, West Virginia, in 1937. His life was irrevocably altered when he lost his mother at a young age. His foster family (the Deans, whose name he adopted) moved to Harlem in New York City before his third birthday. Myers reportedly had a happy childhood, but he encountered problems in school because of a slight speech defect that hampered his pronunciation. His teachers, however, promoted and nurtured in him a love for reading and writing that fulfilled the young author-to-be.

Because the concept of actually supporting himself through writing did not occur to Myers until later, he left Stuyvesant High School at age seventeen to join the U.S. Army, in which he served from 1954 to 1957. This was an auspicious decision, as his military experience would provide the background that Myers would later use in several books, most notably *Fallen Angels*. After he was discharged from the Army, Myers obtained a bachelor of arts degree from Empire State College. He worked at several jobs, but the one that provided fortuitous insight for his future career was with the publishing company Bobbs-Merrill. Myers has stated that it was this experience that taught him the inner workings of the "book business" and informed him of the reality of writing—a reality that finally seemed possible to him.

The major impetus for Myers's success in writing books was his winning of a contest for his children's picture book *Where Does the Day Go?* (1969). Encouraged, Myers went on to publish several more children's books before he moved on to full-length novels geared for young adults. In 1975, his first novel, *Fast Sam, Cool Clyde, and Stuff*, appeared—after which it seems Myers began a full-time writing career and never looked back. What has followed is a cornucopia of works and artistic productions that give testament to a major literary talent who has not only filled a gap for young adult readers but also created a universe of inspiration for his audience. Myers frequently collaborates with his youngest son, Christopher, who is an artist and illustrator.

Analysis

Walter Dean Myers has been described as having a genius for creating realistic, gritty settings that serve as backdrops for his frequently dark dramas involving inner-city youth attempting to escape the destructive effects of the ghetto, urban life, and poverty that have plagued young African Americans. Myers's novels tend to focus on young male characters (although female characters play supporting roles) and their confrontations with hopelessness and the forging of their identities—most often in a world where they lack role models, paths to freedom, and any vision of reality other than that determined by their environment. This "literary naturalism" in settings sometimes involves the battlefield (as in *Fallen Angels* and *Sunrise over Fallujah*), but the protagonists usually hail from Myers's own Harlem. Harlem itself is a paradoxical metaphor in many of Myers' novels: a place of both damnation and redemption. In the crucible of inner-city poverty, his protagonists are made or broken.

A prominent theme recognized by critics in Myers's fiction is the desperate need for male bonding in some

Walter Dean Myers. (Courtesy, HarperCollins)

form—through surrogate father figures (in the absence of effective parents), through characters' reinvention of themselves as fathers or older brothers, or through the negotiation of friendship—for the male hero to self-actualize and create a moral core that transcends environment. In his analysis of four of Myers's novels, literary critic Dennis Vellucci asserts that within such settings, Myers's protagonists face crises that threaten their self-growth and the building of moral character and yet, more often than not, they muster the strength "to retain an innate sensitivity . . . and to avoid or reject the gang membership, violent behavior, and illegal activity" characteristic of their milieu. In their conflicts with their environment, Myers's central characters define who they are, mature, and discover internal truths. Myers thus offers hope and a possible blueprint for young black readers.

A particular strength of Myers's style is his unerring ear for the resonances of the street life, which he portrays through his characters' voices. Characters are clearly delineated not only by what they say but also by how they speak. Rudine Sims Bishop notes Myers's ability to "capture the way urban African-American teenagers . . . talk to each other." Furthermore, she asserts that "these kinds of oral expressions come out of traditional African American discourse styles." In short, through his characters, Myers replicates the rhythms and cadences of black teenage culture—a culture overlooked both by its participants and by other, nonblack, youths.

Another aspect of Myers's engaging style is his ability to create characters who evoke the reader's sympathy and empathy, often through humor. Even though sometimes crass, with a tough-guy persona, Pee Wee Gates in *Fallen Angels* is a supremely endearing character whose humor enables him and the protagonist to "get through" combat—and their lives. Finally, Myers's novels present realistic plots with complex and layered themes that touch on issues that are important for black youth today: how one connects to oneself and one's culture in a social milieu that builds failure and almost insurmountable obstacles into the process of growing up.

Scorpions

Scorpions, a novel widely read in middle schools and high schools, chronicles the coming-of-age of seventh-grader Jamal, who he is forced to define his "manhood" without the examples of any truly upright role models. Jamal must decide—under negative duress—whether to assume his now-imprisoned brother's role in a gang. In his descent into desperation, Jamal allows a gun, rather than his conscience or his moral friend Tito, to define his budding manhood.

The novel is dark, providing no true resolution for the hero and leaving the reader with a sense of both boys' terrible price for misguided behavior: a profound loss of innocence. The boys have become "men" in the worst sense of the word—stripped of illusions about themselves and the world's possibilities. This Newbery Honor Book serves as an unrelenting and stark cautionary tale.

Fallen Angels

Often termed Myers's "classic" war story, *Fallen Angels* is taught in many high schools in the United States despite controversies that have arisen about its graphic violence and use of "indecent" language. Students are captivated by the novel's vivid characters, realistic portrayal of the Vietnam War, and powerful themes. The title invites complex interpretation: It refers to the innocent soldiers (angels) who have "fallen" (died), but it also illuminates the protagonist's sense of falling from grace once he has killed other human beings. A subordinate theme is revealed by the paralleling (via flashbacks) of the graphic violence of the war with the terrible violence of the urban Harlem neighborhood in which protagonist Richard Perry grew up.

Perry is a thoughtful hero who naïvely accepts being drafted into the Army (despite a misplaced medical release that would have prevented him from serving) as a way out of crushing poverty and a means to be a role model for his younger brother, Kenny, back home. As the war progresses, Perry experiences his own coming-of-age, reaching a rather ambivalent peace within himself about life, right and wrong, and the importance of vulnerability and dependence in friendship—while witnessing for the reader the disturbing aspects of a war that was undefined and ultimately seen as fruitless. It is interesting to note that Myers later produced a "sequel" of sorts in *Sunrise over Fallujah*, with another year, another war (Iraq), and another narrator—Perry's nephew, Robin.

Monster

In its style, *Monster* is something of a departure for Myers. The novel presents a complex, ambiguous representation of "reality," forcing the reader to interact with the differing layers of text—one is a handwritten journal/memoir retelling of events, and the other a neatly typed developing screenplay that is not only stylized (as opposed to the raw, seemingly honest handwritten text) but also utilizes the language of film (long shot, close-up, panning across the room) that the budding screenwriter places as part of the text. Thus, from the outset, the "text" and its "truth" are presented as ambiguous in the most basic sense of that word (capable of two meanings). This ambiguity underscores the lack of a definitive meaning of "guilt" as seen through the eyes of both the reader and the protagonist, who ponders if he is truly the "monster" he is accused of being.

Steve Harmon, the protagonist, is being tried for complicity in a murder that took place while Steve was standing as lookout on a robbery. During the trial and his incarceration, Steve ruminates on the desperate plight of the accused—susceptible to the constant threat of violence by other prisoners—while creating cinematically (through the screenplay) an ever-changing physical scenario that questions what the image (artificially created or envisioned) means. This questioning further ripples into questions about how society views the accused (especially the black youth) and, by extension, how the accused comes to terms with his "guilt"—be it actual guilt or simply submitting to an image (tough guy, criminal) that society demands of its oppressed. Myers does not solve the problem for readers, producing a suspenseful, confounding drama that allows no heroes to emerge.

One of Myers's prominent themes—how young African Americans build their identities in an image-laden, socially antagonistic society—rears its head here in a more provocative and thought-provoking manner than in his other novels. Steve's "guilt" remains open-ended and, as John Staunton asserts in a review of *Monster*, "the novel confronts the white middle-class fear of black youth as public menace and places Steve's story within the troubled history of that image."

Sherry Morton-Mollo

Other major works

SHORT FICTION: *Smiffy Blue, Ace Crime Detective: The Case of the Missing Ruby, and Other Stories*, 1996; *145th Street*, 2000; *A Time to Love: Stories from the Old Testament*, 2003; *What They Found: Love on 145th Street*, 2007.

POETRY: *Brown Angels: An Album of Pictures and Verse*, 1993; *The Great Migration: An American Story*, 1993; *Glorious Angels: A Celebration of Children*, 1995; *Harlem*, 1997; *Angel to Angel: A Mother's Gift of Love*, 1998; *Blues Journey*, 2003 (Christopher Myers, illustrator); *Here in Harlem: Poems in Many Voices*, 2004; *Jazz*, 2006 (poetry; illustrated by Christopher Myers); *Street Love*, 2006; *Tribute*, 2008.

NONFICTION: *The World of Work: A Guide to Choosing a Career*, 1975; *Social Welfare*, 1976; *Now Is Your Time! The African-American Struggle for Freedom*, 1991; *A Place Called Heartbreak: A Story of Vietnam*, 1993; *Malcolm X: By Any Means Necessary*, 1993; *Young Martin's Promise*, 1993; *Toussaint L'Ouverture: The Fight for Haiti's Freedom*, 1996; *One More River to Cross: An African-American Photograph Album*, 1995; *Amistad: A Long Road of Freedom*, 1998; *At Her Majesty's Request: An African Princess in Victorian England*, 1999; *Malcolm X: A Fire Burning Brightly*, 2000; *Bad Boy: A Memoir*, 2001; *The Greatest: Muhammad Ali*, 2001; *Antarctica: Journeys to the South Pole*, 2004; *I've Seen the Promised Land: The Life of Dr. Martin Luther King, Jr.*, 2004 (illustrated by Leonard Jenkins); *USS Constellation: Pride of the American Navy*, 2004; *The Harlem Hellfighters: When Pride Met Courage*, 2006 (with William Miles); *Ida B. Wells: Let the Truth Be Told*, 2008.

CHILDREN'S/YOUNG ADULT LITERATURE: *Where Does the Day Go?*, 1969; *The Dancers*, 1972; *The Dragon Takes a Wife*, 1972; *Fly, Jimmy, Fly!*, 1974; *Brainstorm*, 1977; *Victory for Jamie*, 1977; *The Black Pearl and the Ghost: Or, One Mystery After Another*, 1980; *The Golden Serpent*, 1980; *Tales of a Dead King*, 1983; *Mr. Monkey and the Gotcha Bird*, 1984; *Sweet Illusions*, 1987; *Me, Mop, and the Moondance Kid*, 1988; *Mop, Moondance, and the Nagasaki Knights*, 1992; *Darnell Rock Reporting*, 1994; *Shadow of the Red Moon*, 1995; *The Story of the Three Kingdoms*, 1995; *How Mr. Monkey Saw the Whole World*, 1996; *The Journal of Joshua Loper: A Black Cowboy*, 1999; *The Journal of Scott Pendleton Collins: A World War II Soldier*, 1999; *The Blues of Flats Brown*, 2000; *The Journal of Biddy Owens: The Negro Leagues*, 2001; *Three Swords for Granada*, 2002.

Bibliography

Bishop, Rudine Sims. *Presenting Walter Dean Myers.* Boston: G. K. Hall, 1990. Provides an introduction to the author and his works through the 1980's, addressing Myers's unique contribution as the only African American writer of fiction for young adults who worked to fill an obvious gap in literature relevant to young black readers.

Marler, Myrna Dee. *Walter Dean Myers.* New York: Greenwood Press, 2008. Reference work aimed at both students and teachers provides insights into Myers's themes and characters.

Murray, Beth. "Defending *Fallen Angels* by Walter Dean Myers: Framing—Not Taming—Controversy." In *Censored Books II: Critical Viewpoints, 1985-2000*, edited by Nicholas J. Karolides. Lanham, Md.: Scarecrow Press, 2002. Examines the controversy surrounding teaching the novel in high school because of its depiction of violence and graphic language among soldiers. Asserts that Myers's "mission" is not wanton brutality but a presentation of a coming-of-age story that reflects the global issues involved.

Patrick-Wexler, Diane. *Walter Dean Myers.* Portsmouth, N.H.: Heinemann, 1996. Offers a glowing description of the author in words and pictures formulated for the elementary to middle school reader.

Sickels, Amy. *Walter Dean Myers.* New York: Chelsea House, 2008. Volume aimed at young readers (part of a series titled Who Wrote That?) provides biographical information and a chronology of Myers's life. Includes photographs.

Snodgrass, Mary Ellen. *Walter Dean Myers: A Literary Companion.* Jefferson, N.C.: McFarland, 2006. Provides a good introduction to Myers's work. Alphabetically arranged entries cover characters, events, and themes in Myers's fiction. Includes informative appendixes.

Vellucci, Dennis. "Man to Man: Portraits of the Male Adolescent in the Novels of Walter Dean Myers." In *African-American Voices in Young Adult Literature: Tradition, Transition, Transformation*, edited by Karen Patricia Smith. Metuchen, N.J.: Scarecrow Press, 1994. Essay on Myers's work is part of a collection of essays devoted to the issues addressed in the works of prominent writers of young adult literature.

Zitlow, Connie S. *Teaching the Selected Works of Walter Dean Myers.* Portsmouth, N.H.: Heinemann, 2007. Work designed for high school teachers provides ideas for connecting students with the text. Students can also benefit from the examination of Myers's imagery, poetic language, and form. In-depth analyses are provided for *Monster*, *Street Love*, and *Fallen Angels*, among other works.

VLADIMIR NABOKOV

Born: St. Petersburg, Russia; April 23, 1899
Died: Montreux, Switzerland; July 2, 1977
Also known as: Vladimir Vladimirovich Nabokov; V. Sirin

Principal long fiction

Mashenka, 1926 (*Mary*, 1970)
Korol', dama, valet, 1928 (*King, Queen, Knave*, 1968)
Zashchita Luzhina, 1929 (serial), 1930 (book; *The Defense*, 1964)
Kamera obskura, 1932 (*Camera Obscura*, 1936; revised as *Laughter in the Dark*, 1938)
Podvig, 1932 (*Glory*, 1971)
Otchayanie, 1934 (serial), 1936 (book; *Despair*, 1937; revised 1966)
Priglashenie na kazn', 1935-1936 (serial), 1938 (book; *Invitation to a Beheading*, 1959)
Dar, 1937-1938 (serial), 1952 (book; *The Gift*, 1963)
The Real Life of Sebastian Knight, 1941
Bend Sinister, 1947
Lolita, 1955
Pnin, 1957
Pale Fire, 1962
Ada or Ardor: A Family Chronicle, 1969
Transparent Things, 1972
Look at the Harlequins!, 1974

Other literary forms

Vladimir Nabokov (nah-BO-kof) began, as many novelists do, as a poet. As a youth, he published privately what now would be called a chapbook and a full book of poetry before emigrating from Russia. Throughout his life, he continued to publish poetry in periodicals and several book-length collections, including *Stikhotvorenia, 1929-1951* (1952), *Poems* (1959), and *Poems and Problems* (1970). Some critics even consider the long poem "Pale Fire" (an integral part of the novel *Pale Fire*) a worthy neo-Romantic poem in itself. Nabokov also published a good deal of short fiction, first in a variety of short-lived émigré publications such as *Rul'*, *Sovremennye Zapiski*, and *Russkoe ekho*, and later in such prominent magazines as *The New Yorker*, *The Atlantic Monthly*, *Playboy*, *Harper's Bazaar*, and *Tri-Quarterly*. His stories were collected in *Vozrashchenie Chorba* (1930; the return of Chorb), which also included twenty-four poems, *Soglyadatay* (1938; the eye), *Nine Stories* (1947), and *Nabokov's Dozen* (1958), among others. His plays include *Smert'* (pb. 1923; death), *Tragediya gospodina Morna* (pb. 1924; the tragedy of Mister Morn), *Chelovek iz SSSR* (pb. 1927; the man from the USSR), *Sobytiye* (pr., pb. 1938; the event), and *Izobretenie Val'sa* (pb. 1938; *The Waltz Invention*, 1966). He also worked on a screenplay for the film version of *Lolita* (1962). In addition to translating his own works from Russian to English (and vice versa, as well as occasionally from French to Russian to English), he often translated the works of other writers, including Lewis Carroll's *Alice's Adventures in Wonderland* (1865) and poetry of Rupert Brooke, Alexander Pushkin, Arthur Rimbaud, William Shakespeare, and Alfred de Musset. In nonfiction prose, Nabokov's fascinating life is recalled in three volumes of memoirs, *Conclusive Evidence* (1951), *Drugie Berega* (1954; other shores), and *Speak, Memory: An Autobiography Revisited* (1966, a revision and expansion of the earlier works). Throughout his life, his often idiosyncratic criticism was widely published, and the publication after his death of several volumes of his lectures on world literature provoked much discussion among literary scholars. As a lepidopterist, Nabokov published a number of scholarly articles in such journals as *The En-*

tomologist, Journal of the New York Entomological Society, Psyche, and *The Lepidopterists' News*.

Achievements

Vladimir Nabokov's strength as a writer lay in his control and mastery of style. Writers are sometimes successful in a language other than their native language, but only a select few are capable of writing equally well in two languages, and Nabokov may be alone in his ability to master the insinuations of two such extraordinarily different and subtle languages as Russian and English. Under the pen name "V. Sirin," Nabokov was recognized as a noteworthy émigré novelist and poet in Berlin and Paris. After fleeing the rise of Nazism and settling in the United States, he became recognized as a major English-language author with the publication of *Lolita* in 1955. As was the case with Gustave Flaubert, James Joyce, and D. H. Lawrence, all of whose international sales were aided by the controversies surrounding their works, Nabokov received worldwide attention as critics debated the morality of *Lolita*, prompting the republication and translation of many of his earlier works. Few writers with such an uncompromising style achieve such popularity. Nabokov was often in financial difficulty before *Lolita*, yet he always remained the consummate craftsman. He has come to be regarded as one of the literary giants of his generation.

Biography

Vladimir Vladimirovich Nabokov was born to Vladimir Dmitrievich and Elena Rukavishnikov Nabokov in St. Petersburg, Russia, the eldest of five children. He grew up in comfortable circumstances, tracing his ancestry back to a Tartar prince of the 1380's and through a number of military men, statesmen, Siberian merchants, and the first president of the Russian Imperial Academy of Medicine. His father was a noted liberal who had helped found the Constitutional Democratic Party, was elected to the first Duma, and coedited the sole liberal newspaper in St. Petersburg. In his childhood, the young Nabokov was taken on trips to France, Italy, and Spain, and he summered on the country estate of Vyra, accumulating memories that would become woven into his later writings. His father, an Anglophile, provided governesses who taught the boy English at a very early age. He once remarked that he had learned to read English even before he had learned Russian. He was also taught French.

Entering puberty, Nabokov attended the liberal Prince Tenishev School, where he first developed a hatred of coercion but played soccer and chess, started collecting butterflies, and showed some artistic talent. He began writing poetry, and a now lost brochure of a single poem "in a violet paper cover" was privately published in 1914. In 1916, he privately published a recollection that provoked his cousin to beg him to "never, never be a writer," and in 1918, he collaborated on a collection with Andrei Balashov. Nabokov inherited an estate and the equivalent of two million dollars when his Uncle Ruka died and seemed to be on his way to the comfortable life of a Russian bourgeois when history intervened. His father became part of the Provisional Government in the March Revolution of 1917, but in October, when the Bolsheviks displaced the Alexander Kerensky government, the Nabokov family fled, first to the Crimea and then, in 1919, into permanent exile in the West on an old Greek ship ironically named *Nadezhda* ("Hope").

Nabokov studied at Trinity College, Cambridge University, paying little attention to anything but soccer, tennis, and girls. He did, however, do many translations (of Rupert Brooke, Seumas O'Sullivan, William Butler Yeats, Lord Byron, and others) and came under the influence of English poetry. He also read and was influenced by James Joyce. Despite his claim that he never once visited the library, he graduated with honors in French and Russian literature in 1923. This was shortly following his father's assassination in Berlin in March, 1922, as two reactionaries shot the elder Nabokov in error as he was introducing their intended victim. After Cambridge, the twenty-five-year-old Nabokov moved to Berlin, where, in 1925, he married Vera Evseevna Slonim, and a year later he published his first novel, *Mary*, under a pseudonym. He felt that his father had prior claim to the name "Vladimir Nabokov," and he wrote all of his early Russian works as "V. Sirin."

With very little money, Nabokov published poems, stories, and essays in Berlin's émigré newspapers, and later, as the Nazis grew in power (his wife was Jewish), in similar Parisian publications. He survived by teaching tennis, devising crossword puzzles in Russian, making up chess problems, teaching Russian, and translating. He sold the Russian translation of *Alice's Adventures in Wonderland* (*Anya v strane chudes*, 1923), for example, for the equivalent of five dollars. In 1934, his only son, Dmitri, was born, and four years later, Nabokov fled to Paris. As early as 1935, he decided to immigrate to the United States, probably recognizing that Europe was no longer safe. He was invited by the Soviet government during the 1930's to return to Russia several times, but he refused.

Nabokov's novels published in Berlin and Paris had been relatively successful, and several had been translated into English with and without his assistance. He made the remarkable and difficult decision to abandon the language in which he had written so well. "My private tragedy," he later wrote, "which cannot, indeed should not, be anybody's concern, is that I had to abandon my natural idiom, my untrammeled, rich, and infinitely docile Russian tongue for a second-rate brand of English." Stanford University invited him to teach in the summer of 1940, and he set sail for the United States on the liner *Champlain* in May, just ahead of the German invasion. He had already begun writing his first English novel, *The Real Life of Sebastian Knight*, while in Paris, and, in 1941, it was published in the United States after several friends helped him edit it. He taught Russian grammar and literature at Wellesley College from 1941 to 1948, also serving as a research fellow at the Museum of Comparative Zoology at Harvard University. He became a prominent lepidopterist, publishing many monographs, articles, and reviews. He spent summers roaming the United States searching for butterflies and discovered several species and subspecies, including one that came to be called Nabokov's wood nymph. After seeing praise for his work on the *Lycaeides* genus in a field guide, Nabokov is said to have remarked, "That's real fame. That means more than anything a literary critic could say."

Vladimir Nabokov. (Library of Congress)

In 1944, Nabokov published a critical book on Nikolai Gogol, and in 1947, his first novel written in the United States, *Bend Sinister*, appeared. From 1948 to 1959, he taught at Cornell University, carefully writing out his lectures, combining his attacks on such intellectual touchstones as Karl Marx, Charles Darwin, and especially Sigmund Freud with dramatic classroom readings. Well before the publication of *Lolita*, he was recognized as a remarkable talent in certain quarters, as is indicated by his receipt of grants from the Guggenheim Foundation in 1943 and 1953 and by an award from the American Academy of Arts and Letters in 1953; students in his classes at Cornell, however, were often unaware that their teacher was also a writer, although he published stories and articles in *The New Yorker*, *The Atlantic Monthly*, *Hudson Review*, and other periodicals. *Lolita* changed all that. Rejected by several American publishers, it was brought out by publisher Maurice Girodias's Olympia Press in Paris in 1955. As one of the most controversial books ever published—banned for a while in France, debated in Parliament in England, and forbidden in many American libraries—it swept the best-seller lists and freed Nabokov from teaching. In addition to the royalties, he received $150,000 and a percentage from the sale of the film rights. He also wrote a screenplay (which was later substantially changed) for the film version to be directed by Stanley Kubrick, which was released in 1962. (A second film version of *Lolita*, directed by Adrian Lyne, was released in 1997.)

In 1960, Nabokov moved to Montreux, Switzerland, where he and his wife lived in a sixth-floor apartment in the Palace Hotel overlooking Lake Geneva, in order to be near their son Dmitri, who was having some success as an opera singer. In the wake of *Lolita*, Nabokov and his son translated many of his earlier novels into English and introduced several collections of his short stories to American readers. His novels *Pale Fire*, *Ada or Ardor*, *Transparent Things*, and *Look at the Harlequins!* were all published during this period. He was regularly discussed as a possible recipient of the Nobel Prize until his death of a viral infection in 1977.

Analysis

In 1937, Vladeslav Khodasevich, an émigré poet and champion of "V. Sirin's" work, wrote, "Sirin [Nabokov] proves for the most part to be an artist of form, of the writer's device, and not only in that . . . sense of which . . . his writing is distinguished by exceptional diversity, complexity, brilliance, and novelty." Khodasevich went on to say that the key to all Sirin's work was his ability to put all his literary devices on display, with little or no attempt to conceal them, thus entertaining his readers more with the revelation of how the magician performs his tricks, than with the trick itself. "The life of the artist and the life of a device in the consciousness of an artist—this is Sirin's theme." Khodasevich, although he had not yet read *The Gift*—purported to be Vladimir Nabokov's greatest Russian novel—had discovered the most important element of Nabokov's fiction.

Throughout his entire life, although Nabokov underwent great changes in his circumstances, he was consistent, whether writing in Russian or English, in his unflagging delight in literary devices of all sorts, art for its own sake, and a contempt for mimetic conventions, simplistic psychological motivation, ordinary plot structure, and anything that inhibits the literary imagination. He can, in many respects, be called an aesthete, but his rejection of most schools of thought makes him difficult to classify. He strove for and achieved a uniqueness that runs as a thread throughout his oeuvre. Clarence Brown once commented in a critical essay that "for well over a quarter of a century now . . . [Nabokov] has been writing in book after book about the same thing," and Nabokov is said to have admitted that Brown was probably correct.

Mary *and* King, Queen, Knave

Nabokov's first novel, *Mary*, is rather sentimental and probably based on Nabokov's regret for a lost love, but it already contains two elements he would use repeatedly—the love triangle and uncertain identity. *King, Queen, Knave*, however, is an even more obvious reflection of the Nabokov canon. In it, a character named Franz Bubendorf, a country bumpkin on his way to the city, apparently to be corrupted by the bourgeois life, is, in fact, already corrupted by his distaste for his own class, which distorts his perception. As if to emphasize this distortion of perception, Franz steps on his glasses and Berlin becomes a blur. Again, there is a love triangle, and each of the participants is, in his or her own way, unable to perceive reality. The melodrama of a love triangle and a planned murder is handled with the authorial detachment that is one of Nabokov's hallmarks. The novel becomes a parody of traditional forms, and the characters become obvious contrivances of the author. Derived from a Hans Christian Andersen work of the same title, the novel consists of thirteen chapters, as there are thirteen cards in each suit in a deck of cards. The card metaphor is carried throughout the work, even in the description of clothes.

Laughter in the Dark

Laughter in the Dark opens with a parody of the fairy tale revealing the entire plot, here a relatively conventional bourgeois love story that Nabokov typically manipulates. The main character, blinded by love, becomes literally blinded and trapped in a love triangle, which results in his murder (accomplished in a scene that is a parody of motion-picture melodrama). This type of parody, which partially represents Nabokov's delight in mocking inferior art, can also be seen as a parody of the reader's expectations. Nabokov constantly thwarts the reader who wants a nice, comfortable, conventional novel. The writer is always in control, always tugging the reader this way and that, never allowing a moment of certainty. Perceptions are distorted on all levels. The characters have distorted perceptions of one another. The reader's perception of events is teasingly distorted by the author. Nabokov operates a house of mirrors. If a reader expects realism, there will be no pleasure in the warped mirrors Nabokov presents. One must delight instead in the odd shapes and obvious deformities in the mirrors he has shaped.

Nabokov's characters

Character types in the Russian novels also recur throughout Nabokov's career, so much so that some critics have attempted to pair earlier Russian novels with later English ones. Usually, the central figure is an outsider, an unusual person in his milieu. Bubendorf of *King, Queen, Knave* is a country boy in the city. In *The Defense*, the chess master Luzhin does not fit in with his family or his school, and is sent into exile after the Revolution. Martin Edelweiss of *Glory* is in exile in London.

What is more important, however, is that these and many more of Nabokov's characters are isolated as much by their mental states as by their physical surroundings. Their fantasies, dreams, ambitions, and obsessions set them utterly apart from the ordinary world. Luzhin, for example, is so obsessed with chess that he cannot deal with the disorder of life. Cincinnatus in *Invitation to a Beheading* is thought peculiar by his fellow workers in the doll factory. In later English novels, immigrant Timofey Pnin is thought mad by his academic colleagues, Humbert Humbert and Adam Krug are seen as dangers to society, and Charles Kinbote intrudes and imposes on people. Generally, the main characters of Nabokov's novels are perceived as talented men, in some sense more valuable than the soulless people and society that persecute them. They are outsiders because they are extraordinary. They are free, imaginative, and capable of a kind of heroism that ordinary people lack: the ability to remake the world according to their own obsessions.

The Gift

The Gift is generally thought of as Nabokov's best Russian novel. It was originally published serially in *Sovremennye Zapiski*, an émigré periodical, and the fourth section was not included (for political reasons) in a complete edition until 1952. In *The Gift*, the central figure is Fyodor Godunov-Cherdyntsev, a brilliant émigré poet. As the book opens, he has just published a collection of poems, and much of the early part concerns his literary career. Later, his obsession with the memory of his father begins to dominate his everyday life, and he becomes caught in the typical confusions of the biographer: What is the truth and how can one see it? He feels an obligation to write a biography of his father but becomes trapped in assessing the various versions of his father's life. Later, he does succeed in writing a biography of Nikolai Gavrilovich Chernyshevski, a so-called poetic history based on the idea that reconstructing the past is essentially a creative act—history exists only in the historian's imagination—and that the best biographies are literary creations.

The Gift has been seen as the summing up of Nabokov's experiences as an émigré writer, and similarities have been seen between the author's biography and the events and people in the novel. The book is heavy with allusions to Russian literature and has been called the Russian counterpart to *Ada or Ardor*, an extremely allusive and complex book that also focuses on the nature of the writer. In *The Gift*, many of Nabokov's favorite devices are employed: the love triangle, the ironic suicide, and the heightened perception of the hero, in which he imagines conversations with the dead.

The Real Life of Sebastian Knight

After his decision to begin writing in English, Nabokov produced two novels before the *succès de scandale* of *Lolita*. *The Real Life of Sebastian Knight* was begun in Paris and is ostensibly the biography of a fiction writer, Sebastian, narrated by his brother, "V." V. is shocked to discover upon his brother's death in 1936 that there was more to learn of Sebastian from his novels than he had learned in person. Once again, Nabokov introduces the theme that art surpasses reality. V. fights the various distortions of Sebastian's life yet, at the end of his biography, confesses that "Sebastian's mask clings to my face." V. created Sebastian, so Sebastian is V. (as both characters were created by Nabokov). Again, the novel is characterized by the use of parodistic techniques and distorted characters. One can easily recognize this novel as a Nabokov work, yet because of Nabokov's uncertainty at writing in the English language at this stage, the work is not completely satisfying. Nabokov admitted, for example, to having had native speakers help him with the editing, something he would never permit later.

Bend Sinister

Many resemblances have been noted between Nabokov and his brother Sergei, and V. and his brother Sebastian. Sergei, unlike Vladimir, stayed in Europe during the Nazi period and died of starvation in a concentration camp near Hamburg on January 10, 1945. These events perhaps explain the harsh allegorical tone of *Bend Sinister*, a novel that is, in some ways, better than its predecessor and perhaps one of the most accessible of Nabokov's novels. The hero, Adam Krug, is an intellectual whose ideas are largely responsible for the new regime in an Eastern European country. Krug, however, refuses to swear allegiance to the ruler of the regime, a fellow student from childhood named Paduk. "I am not interested in politics," he says. Inexorably, the ring of tyranny tightens around Krug, resulting in the arrest of friends, the death of his son, and Krug's death as he attempts to attack Paduk in a mad vision of schoolyard life.

The artist, the literary craftsman in Nabokov, was incapable, however, of writing a straightforward novel of outrage against Fascists or Communists. The country is not specified; numerous vague descriptions of setting give the work a Kafkaesque flavor. The regime is tyrannical—it wants the souls of its people as well as their cooperation (not unlike Big Brother in George Orwell's *Nineteen Eighty-Four*, 1949)—yet it is not a specific ideology that is being attacked. Any form of coercion that limits the imagination of the artist or the intellectual is the target. Although some critics have argued that Krug's flaw is that he refuses to become involved in politics, it is difficult to imagine *Bend Sinister*, in the light of other works, as being a call to commitment. Krug has made a commitment to his own intellectual life. He, like many Nabokov heroes, does not "fit in" and, like many Nabokov heroes, comes to a tragic end. The supremacy of the individual imagination is Nabokov's "message"; art is his morality. There is an abundant helping of satire and parody directed against the intellectual community and the "great" political leaders of the world. Paduk is shown as a sniveling, ugly weakling who craves Krug's approval, but the alternatives to his tyranny are shown to be equally preposterous. Even in reacting to the horrors of dictatorship, Nabokov remains the detached artist.

Lolita

Lolita, the novel that would provide a comfortable living for the author for the rest of his life, has been called everything from pornography to one of the greatest novels of the twentieth century. Today, when virtually every sexual predilection has been the subject of motion pictures and television, it is hard to appreciate the whirlwind of controversy that was stirred up by *Lolita*'s publication. Humbert Humbert, the central character and narrator, has an obsession with young girls that he has hidden by unhappy affairs with older women. He comes to the United States after inheriting a business and separating from his childish wife Valeria. Eventually, he becomes the boarder of Charlotte Haze and becomes sexually obsessed with her twelve-year-old daughter, Lolita. He marries Mrs. Haze to be near Lolita, and when the mother is killed, he takes the girl on a trip across the United States. She is eventually stolen by Clare Quilty, who is, in many ways, Humbert's double, and Humbert goes on a two-year quest to rescue the girl. He finds the sad, pregnant Lolita married to a man named Richard Schiller and, in revenge, shoots Quilty. The novel is allegedly Humbert's manuscript, written as he awaits trial. According to the foreword, Humbert died in jail of a coronary thrombosis, and the manuscript was transmitted to one John Ray, Jr., Ph.D., who prepared it for publication.

As in all of Nabokov's works, however, a plot summary is absurdly inadequate in characterizing the book. *Lolita* is protean in its directions and effects. It has been seen as a satire on the United States (though Nabokov denied it), as a psychological study (although Nabokov called Freud a "medieval mind"), and as a parody of the Romantic novel. Lionel Trilling argued that, since adultery was such a commonplace in the modern world, only a perverse love could cause the adequate passion mixed with suffering characteristic of great Romantic loves: Tristan and Isolde, Abélard and Héloise, Dante and Beatrice, Petrarch and Laura. Humbert often justifies his pedophilia by references to the courtly love tradition. There is also much reference to the story of Edgar Allan Poe's love for Virginia Clemm (Humbert's first teenage love was a girl named Annabel Leigh).

Although many critics attempted to justify *Lolita* as having an important moral message, Nabokov rebuked the notion by saying, "I am no messenger boy." His aesthetic philosophy would never have permitted him to subordinate his art to a moral. He once said that Lolita was about his love for the English language, but even that is an oversimplification of an immensely complex book. Among the various elements critics have noted are the doppelgänger relation of Quilty to Humbert, chess metaphors, puns on names, the question of the masks of the narrator (the probably unreliable Humbert through the clinical Ray through the mischievous Nabokov), and the supposed immortality of Humbert's love, a love that becomes timeless through a work of art. It has even been argued that Nabokov's description of Lolita very much resembles his description of a certain species of butterfly in his scientific studies. While *Lolita*'s place in the canon of world literature is still debated, there is little doubt that it may be the finest example of the author's "game-playing" method of artistic creation.

PALE FIRE

With the publication of *Pale Fire*, readers were once again amused, perplexed, or horrified by Nabokov's ironic wit. This experimental novel inspired extremes of praise—such as Mary McCarthy's judgment that "it is one of the great works of art of this century"—and mockery. The novel is presented in the form of a scholarly edition of a poem titled "Pale Fire" by John Shade, with commentary by Charles Kinbote. Both worked at Wordsmith University, where Kinbote seems to have believed that Shade was writing a poem about Kinbote's obsession with Charles Xavier Vseslav, "The Beloved," the king of Zembla who was forced to flee the revolution that replaced him.

Pale Fire can be described as a series of Russian dolls, one enclosed within another. John Shade's poem (as edited by Kinbote) is explained by Kinbote, who intends to give life to the extraordinary personality of Shade. He writes in the foreword, "Without my notes Shade's text simply has no human reality at all," but the reader soon recognizes that Kinbote is a madman who either is or imagines himself to be the displaced king of Zembla, and whatever human reality Shade may have exists only through his colleague's warped interpretation of events. On another level, the reader finds some of Shade's "reality" in the text of his poem and reads much into and between Kinbote's lines as the madman gradually exposes his own madness.

Nabokov never wants his reader to forget, however, that all this invention is entirely of his making. The author intends much more in *Pale Fire* than a mere parody of scholarly editions, scholars, and neo-Romantic poetry. Once more, Nabokov wittily develops his lifelong theme that reality exists only in the eyes of its interpreter.

J. Madison Davis

OTHER MAJOR WORKS

SHORT FICTION: *Vozrashchenie Chorba*, 1930; *Soglyadatay*, 1938 (title novella and short stories); *Nine Stories*, 1947; *Vesna v Fialte i drugie rasskazy*, 1956; *Nabokov's Dozen: A Collection of Thirteen Stories*, 1958; *Nabokov's Quartet*, 1966; *A Russian Beauty, and Other Stories*, 1973; *Tyrants Destroyed, and Other Stories*, 1975; *Details of a Sunset, and Other Stories*, 1976; *The Stories of Vladimir Nabokov*, 1995.

PLAYS: *Dedushka*, pb. 1923; *Smert'*, pb. 1923; *Polius*, pb. 1924; *Tragediya gospodina Morna*, pb. 1924; *Chelovek iz SSSR*, pb. 1927; *Izobretenie Val'sa*, pb. 1938 (*The Waltz Invention*, 1966); *Sobytiye*, pr., pb. 1938.

POETRY: *Stikhi*, 1916; *Dva puti*, 1918; *Gorny put*, 1923; *Grozd'*, 1923; *Stikhotvorenia, 1929-1951*, 1952; *Poems*, 1959; *Poems and Problems*, 1970.

SCREENPLAY: *Lolita*, 1962 (adaptation of his novel).

NONFICTION: *Nikolai Gogol*, 1944; *Conclusive Evidence: A Memoir*, 1951; *Drugie berega*, 1954; *Speak, Memory: An Autobiography Revisited*, 1966 (revision of *Conclusive Evidence* and *Drugie berega*); *Strong Opinions*, 1973; *The Nabokov-Wilson Letters: Correspondence Between Vladimir Nabokov and Edmund Wilson, 1940-1971*, 1979 (Simon Karlinsky, editor); *Lectures on Literature*, 1980; *Lectures on Russian Literature*, 1981; *Lectures on Don Quixote*, 1983; *Vladimir Nabokov: Selected Letters, 1940-1977*, 1989.

TRANSLATIONS: *Anya v strane chudes*, 1923 (of Lewis Carroll's novel *Alice's Adventures in Wonderland*); *Three Russian Poets: Translations of Pushkin, Lermontov, and Tiutchev*, 1944 (with Dmitri Nabokov); *A Hero of Our Time*, 1958 (with Dmitri Nabokov; of Mikhail Lermontov's novel); *The Song of Igor's Campaign*, 1960 (of the twelfth century epic); *Eugene Onegin*, 1964 (of Alexander Pushkin's novel).

BIBLIOGRAPHY

Alexandrov, Vladimir E. *Nabokov's Otherworld*. Princeton, N.J.: Princeton University Press, 1991. Argues that "the central fact of both Nabokov's life and his art was something that could be described as an intuition about a transcendent realm of being." Shows how an awareness of this "otherworld" informs Nabokov's works, focusing on the autobiography

Speak, Memory and on six of Nabokov's novels. Seeks to correct the widely accepted view of Nabokov as an aloof gamesman preoccupied with verbal artifice for its own sake. Includes notes, a secondary bibliography, and an index.

Bloom, Harold, ed. *Vladimir Nabokov*. New York: Chelsea House, 1987. Collection of essays addresses such topics as Nabokov's handling of time, illusion and reality, and art. Includes an informative editor's introduction, essays on Nabokov's major novels, chronology, and bibliography.

Boyd, Brian. *Vladimir Nabokov: The Russian Years*. Princeton, N.J.: Princeton University Press, 1990.

_______. *Vladimir Nabokov: The American Years*. Princeton, N.J.: Princeton University Press, 1991. Prodigiously researched two-volume biography is based in part on material found in Nabokov's archives, to which Boyd gained unprecedented access. Recounts the events of Nabokov's life and charts his development as a writer. Each volume includes illustrations, extensive notes, and an exceptionally thorough index.

Connolly, Julian W., ed. *The Cambridge Companion to Nabokov*. New York: Cambridge University Press, 2005. Collection of essays offers a good introduction to Nabokov's life and writings. Topics addressed include Nabokov as a storyteller, a Russian writer, a modernist, and a poet; also covered are his transition to writing in English and the reception of *Lolita*.

De la Durantaye, Leland. *Style Is Matter: The Moral Art of Vladimir Nabokov*. Ithaca, N.Y.: Cornell University Press, 2007. Focuses on *Lolita* but also looks at some of Nabokov's other works to discuss the ethics of art in Nabokov's fiction. Asserts that although some readers find Nabokov to be cruel, his works contain a moral message—albeit one that is skillfully hidden.

Field, Andrew. *VN: The Life and Art of Vladimir Nabokov*. New York: Crown, 1986. Critical biography recounts the events of Nabokov's life and places his works within personal and historical context. Includes discussion of *Lolita*, *Pale Fire*, *The Gift*, and other works.

Foster, John Burt. *Nabokov's Art of Memory and European Modernism*. Princeton, N.J.: Princeton University Press, 1993. Scholarly work divides discussion of Nabokov's work into three parts: Nabokov's early years in Russia, his period in Europe, and his prolonged period in the United States. Intended for advanced students.

Glynn, Michael. *Vladimir Nabokov: Bergsonian and Russian Formalist Influences in His Novels*. New York: Palgrave Macmillan, 2007. Glynn disagrees with other critics who have called Nabokov a Symbolist writer, arguing that he was an anti-Symbolist who was influenced by the philosopher Henri Bergson and by Russian Formalism. Useful for advanced students of Russian literature and philosophy.

Grayson, Jane, Arnold B. McMillin, and Priscilla Meyer, eds. *Nabokov's World: Reading Nabokov*. New York: Palgrave Macmillan, 2002.

_______. *Nabokov's World: The Shape of Nabokov's World*. New York: Palgrave Macmillan, 2002. Two-volume collection of essays written by an international group of Nabokov scholars provides comprehensive discussion of his work. Presents analyses of individual novels as well as coverage of topics such as intertextuality in Nabokov's works and the literary reception of his writings.

Parker, Stephen Jan. *Understanding Vladimir Nabokov*. Columbia: University of South Carolina Press, 1987. Introductory guide to Nabokov for students and non-academic readers focuses on individual analyses of five of his Russian novels and four of his American novels. Begins with a chapter on the self-reflexive aspects of Nabokov's narrative technique.

Pifer, Ellen, ed. *Vladimir Nabokov's "Lolita": A Casebook*. New York: Oxford University Press, 2002. An interview with Nabokov and a collection of essays provide a range of approaches to the reading of *Lolita*, including discussions of the novel and the art of persuasion, the Americanization of Humbert Humbert, and *Lolita* and the poetry of advertising.

Wood, Michael. *The Magician's Doubts: Nabokov and the Risks of Fiction*. Princeton, N.J.: Princeton University Press, 1995. Close readings of Nabokov's works show the power and beauty of his language and subtlety of his art. This examination also reveals the ethical and moral foundations of his work, which Nabokov denied existed.

V. S. NAIPAUL

Born: Chaguanas, Trinidad and Tobago; August 17, 1932
Also known as: Vidiadhar Surajprasad Naipaul

Principal long fiction

The Mystic Masseur, 1957
The Suffrage of Elvira, 1958
Miguel Street, 1959
A House for Mr. Biswas, 1961
Mr. Stone and the Knights Companion, 1963
The Mimic Men, 1967
In a Free State, 1971
Guerrillas, 1975
A Bend in the River, 1979
The Enigma of Arrival, 1987
A Way in the World, 1994
Half a Life, 2001
Magic Seeds, 2004

Other literary forms

V. S. Naipaul (ni-POL) is a rarity among writers in that he enjoys equal recognition for his novels and for his works of nonfiction. Indeed, had Naipaul never published a novel, his works of nonfiction would in themselves be sufficient to ensure his reputation as a major writer. As a writer of nonfiction, Naipaul has specialized in a distinctive blend of travelogue, reportage, and autobiography, offering penetrating accounts of regions as diverse as his native Trinidad, India (the home of his ancestors and the subject of several of his books), Africa, the Middle East, Southeast Asia, and the American South.

Naipaul is a prolific writer, and, as a journalist and fiction editor for the *New Statesman*, he wrote a considerable number of articles, book reviews, and short stories for a variety of magazines in both the United States and the United Kingdom. Most of these have not been collected in any form, but *A Flag on the Island* (1967) contains some of Naipaul's stories on the impact of Christianity on Hindus, culture clashes between boardinghouse tenants and owners, and even the cleverness of West Indian business practices. *Literary Occasions* (2003) collects his literary essays and reviews.

Achievements

In his own author's note to the Penguin editions of his books, V. S. Naipaul, who began to write in London in 1954, states, "He has followed no other profession." In *Naipaul: An Introduction to His Work*, Paul Theroux describes Naipaul as completely dedicated to his art. Naipaul's characters Ganesh (*The Mystic Masseur*), Biswas (*A House for Mr. Biswas*), Ralph Kirpal Singh (*The Mimic Men*), and Mr. Stone (*Mr. Stone and the Knights Companion*) are all writers who, like Naipaul himself, participate in the "thrilling, tedious struggle with the agony and discouraging, exhilarating process of making a book." Naipaul considers extensive travel essential to sustaining his writing and to releasing his imagination from deadeningly familiar scenes.

Starting his career as a comic/satiric interpreter of Trinidadian society, Naipaul gradually developed into a serious novelist with human concerns: an interpreter of global issues, culture conflicts, and change. *The Mystic Masseur*, his first novel, has a regional flavor, while *In a Free State*, written fourteen years later, has an international cast. His landscapes have shifted from the alleys and lanes of Miguel Street (Trinidad) to East Africa, French Africa, South America, and India. From the Dickensian comedy and irony of *A House for Mr. Biswas*, he moved to probing the heart of universal darkness in *Guerrillas* and *A Bend in the River*. As John C. Hawley has observed, Naipaul has a compassion and appreciation for the vulnerable "man in the street."

Consequently, Naipaul has received wide critical attention. He is the subject of a number of full-length critical studies and innumerable articles, and his books have received front-page reviews. Irving Howe has called him "the world's writer, a master of language and perception, our sardonic blessing." Writer Elizabeth Hardwick considers the sweep of Naipaul's imagination and the brilliant fictional frame it encompasses unique and without equal in contemporary literature. Writer Paul Theroux considers him superior to existentialist author Albert Camus in his treatment of the theme of displacement. Critics and students of Naipaul place him in the company of such masters of fiction as Joseph Conrad—

whom Naipaul admires intensely—and Graham Greene. In fact, critic Michael Thorpe has stated that Naipaul is Joseph Conrad's heir as a political novelist. Moreover, even his critics praise his mastery of English prose. For example, in 1987 Nobel laureate Derek Walcott, a Caribbean-born poet who rejects many of Naipaul's views, described Naipaul as "our finest writer of the English sentence."

In his nonfiction, Naipaul has proven adept at the scholar's meticulous research, and his travelogues display a journalist's brilliant reportage coupled with the novelist's narrative skill at dramatizing human concerns. Naipaul's canon confirms his uncompromising standards and values, relentless inquiry, and tough judgment, and thereby establishes him as one of the foremost masters of contemporary fiction. The Nobel Foundation, upon awarding him the Nobel Prize in Literature in 2001, epitomized Naipaul as "a modern philosophe," carrying on an eighteenth century satiric tradition, transforming "rage into precision," and allowing "events to speak with their own inherent irony."

Biography

Vidiadhar Surajprasad Naipaul, a third-generation West Indian of East Indian ancestry, was born in Lion House (reincarnated as Hanuman House in his fourth novel, *A House for Mr. Biswas*) into a Hindu Brahman family in Chaguanas, Trinidad, on August 17, 1932. He grew up in a large Indian joint family with a brother, five sisters, and more than fifty cousins (author Neil Bissoondath is his nephew). Naipaul has called his family "a microcosm of the authoritarian state," with power struggles and the seamy side of human behavior.

Naipaul's father, Seepersad Naipaul, a correspondent for the *Trinidad Guardian* and an avid Charles Dickens fan, wrote *Gurudeva, and Other Indian Tales* (1943, 1946), a collection of short stories that Naipaul used as a model to discover what he calls "the trick of writing." Naipaul captures his tender affection for his father in the father-son relationship in his first major novel, *A House for Mr. Biswas*. Even so, Naipaul, speaking about his Trinidad childhood in a 1972 interview, described his father as "a defeated man" who, like Mr. Biswas, felt alienated from the family hierarchy and solaced himself with "easy contempt." His mother's side of the family was prominent in Trinidadian society; his father's was not.

Naipaul spent two years at Chaguanas Government School, a school his father had attended twenty years earlier, when it was the Canadian Mission School. In 1938, when his father was transferred to the capital city, Port-of-Spain, Naipaul transferred to Tranquillity Boys' School, where he distinguished himself and thus won a free place at the prestigious Queens Royal College, a secondary school, where he studied for six years, specializing in French and English; the school has featured in three of Naipaul's novels. In 1948, Naipaul wrote an article for the *Queens Royal College Chronicle* on the origins of W. Somerset Maugham's novelistic skill and Maugham's study of slum life in his first novel, *Liza of Lambeth* (1897); Naipaul later tackled Trinidadian slum life in his third novel, *Miguel Street*.

Naipaul longed to leave Trinidad, and he did so at age seventeen, when he entered Oxford University's University College in 1950. Although his studies were uninspiring, his biggest nightmare was of returning to Trinidad. While he was at Oxford, his father died. After graduating in 1955 with a second-class degree in English, Naipaul married fellow student Patricia Ann Hale and settled in London; he had a number of extramarital affairs, including one with Margaret Gooding that lasted twenty-four years. In 1957, he published his first novel, *The Mystic Masseur*, for which he received the John Llewellyn Rhys Prize in 1958.

Naipaul served as editor of the British Broadcasting Corporation's *Caribbean Voices* program and as fiction reviewer on the staff of the *New Statesman* until 1961, reviewing perhaps sixty-one novels during his tenure. He thought so little of these reviews that he included none of them in *The Overcrowded Barracoon, and Other Articles* (1972), a collection in which he reflects negatively on his eight-year stay in London, his travels to unstable island nations, and his fear of intellectual sterility.

To overcome this fear, Naipaul traveled, first to Trinidad for seven months (his first visit home) and then to India for a year to research his cultural heritage. The Trinidad visit resulted in *The Middle Passage: Impressions of Five Societies—British, French, and Dutch—in the West Indies and South America* (1962), a book of travel essays whose title evokes the slave trade and whose content confirmed his deep-seated desire to leave the tropical island of his birth, a land blighted by a legacy of slavery and imperialism, its native heritage lost. The India visit produced *An Area of Darkness: An Experience of India* (1964), with its negative images of a crowded, filthy, barbaric, alien land. Later visits led to more objective, more optimistic studies: *India: A Wounded Civilization* (1977) and *India: A Million Mutinies Now* (1990). While in Kashmir, Naipaul wrote his first novel about London, *Mr. Stone and the Knights Companion*, which won the Hawthornden Prize.

Despite this literary productivity, travel only fueled Naipaul's restlessness and intensified his sense of displacement and his difficulty in responding positively to London. Naipaul's next novel, *The Mimic Men*, completed in Uganda and awarded the W. H. Smith Prize, brilliantly articulated this mood of "being physically lost." Four years later, in 1971, Naipaul signed a petition supporting the birth of Bangladesh, an active commitment that clearly reflected a new trend in his works. For example, in *The Loss of El Dorado: A History* (1969), a meticulously researched historical study of Trinidad (selected by *Time* magazine as one of the ten best nonfiction books of 1969), Naipaul concludes that, as the indigenous peoples of all Caribbean islands are defunct, the contemporary populations of the islands are immigrants.

In a Free State, Naipaul's next book, won England's highest literary award, the Booker Prize. Its series of linked stories eloquently expresses his realization that homelessness is not merely an Indian or West Indian trait but a universal feature of the modern world. *Guerrillas*, which *The New York Times* named the best novel of 1975, and *A Bend in the River* portray "the ordeals and absurdities of living in the third world." Seven months of travel to visit the Ayatollah Khomeini's Iran, General Mohammad Zia-ul-Haq's Pakistan, and Muslim Indonesia and Malaysia resulted in *Among the Believers: An Islamic Journey* (1981), a journalistic account of the new Islamic energy sweeping these nations. In the early 1980's, Naipaul, who had been renting a Wiltshire cottage in the 1970's, purchased his own house, Dairy Cottage, Sallerton, Wiltshire, and took up gardening. A trip to the United States inspired *A Turn in the South* (1989), which provides an outsider's take on the American southern way of life, southern Protestantism, country music, and Elvis Presley.

In April, 1996, following the death of his first wife in February, Naipaul married journalist Nadira Khannum Alvi, who was born in Kenya of Pakistani descent; the couple settled in London. In 1994 and 1995, Naipaul, who often asserts his lack of religious belief, returned to the countries discussed in *Among the Believers* to produce *Beyond Belief: Islamic Excursions Among the Converted Peoples* (1998), which traces the development of Islam-dominated politics during the fifteen-year interval between the two works, based on interviews with many people in the first book. Naipaul's studies of developing-world countries inspired both admiration and indignation, receiving praise in the United States and Great Britain and vilification in Middle Eastern, Asian, and

V. S. Naipaul. (Thomas Victor)

Caribbean nations, where nationalists found his pro-Western orientation and contempt for postcolonial cultures elitist and even misanthropic.

A controversial figure in England because of his acerbic, unconventional remarks on politics and culture, Naipaul was nevertheless knighted in 1990 and has won every major literary prize presented in Great Britain, including the David Cohen Literature Prize in 1993 for lifetime achievement, in addition to the Nobel Prize in Literature in 2001. In writing acceptance speeches for these awards, Naipaul began to consider the influences on his writing, which led to *A Writer's People: Ways of Looking and Feeling* (2007). In this work, he uncompromisingly examines the flawed and limited visions of his literary mentors, decrying the insular community for which his father wrote, contrasting the magnificence of Gustave Flaubert's *Madame Bovary* (1857; English translation, 1886) with the artificiality of his *Salammbô* (1862; English translation, 1886), confessing his friendship with Anthony Powell and yet his final contempt for Powell's writing, struggling with the paradoxes of India, and pointing out the limitations of colonial and mainstream perceptions. Piercing illusions and self-deceit thus remains Naipaul's central goal. In early 2007, he returned to Trinidad, where he was warmly received; comments he made there, urging citizens to reject the notions of "Indian" and "African" and to concentrate on being "Trinidadian," suggest that he has come full circle, finally attaining closure with his island origins.

Analysis

"The novel is my main delight," V. S. Naipaul has asserted, although in a brief prefatory note to *"The Return of Eva Perón" with "The Killings in Trinidad"* (1980) he admits that when a novel fails to emerge, he travels and turns to nonfiction. In *India: A Wounded Civilization*, Naipaul calls the novel a form of social inquiry, and in *An Area of Darkness* he insists that it must respond to the here-and-now conditions of humanity. He equates the novel in its finest form to truth. Such comments shed light on his artistry.

Growing up in the multiracial, multireligious society of Trinidad, with migrants from four continents, Naipaul was a part of a joint Hindu family: rigid, clannish, suffocating. An alien amid aliens, he observed that the various migrant groups, including his own, failed to maintain their own identities because they were uncertain about what truly constituted those identities and either remained ignorant of their cultural backgrounds or conjured up romantic fantasies about the past. When their ethnic identities eluded them, they often rejected their pasts and aped their colonial masters, acquiring in the process a hodgepodge of pseudo-Westernization. Ganesh Ramsumair in *The Mystic Masseur* is a classic example; East Indian by tradition, Trinidadian by birth, he champions Hinduism, but when that fails, he swings to the other extreme, changing his name to G. Ramsay Muir, Esq., M.B.E., and completely rejecting his past, in particular by cruelly rejecting an admiring student from back home. Over the course of the novel, he transforms himself from masseur to mystic to pamphleteer to politician and statesman, trapping himself in roles whose expectations box him in.

Like the characters in Salman Rushdie's *The Satanic Verses* (1988), Naipaul's characters pursue pseudo-Westernization, a pursuit itself symptomatic of their rootlessness. This theme of displacement and its consequences, comically absurd at first, later tragic, dominates Naipaul's works. Having desperately sought to escape Trinidad as a youth, Naipaul felt stifled and alone in London, a stranger in search of tradition, feeling the burden of his double displacement from India and Trinidad. In order to find a resting place for his imagination, Naipaul undertook a voyage of self-discovery to India, journeying to the very village from which his ancestors had migrated to Trinidad, but instead of clarifying the past, the trip left him even more alienated from his heritage, his life broken. On his return to England, to confront his own empty sense of dark negation, Naipaul unflinchingly distilled these life experiences into his novels. Like Albert Camus, Naipaul is quintessentially the voice of exile and alienation.

Naipaul's three early novels of his apprentice years, *The Mystic Masseur*, *The Suffrage of Elvira*, and *Miguel Street*, are comedies of Trinidadian manners, dependent on satire and irony to portray eccentric citizens of Trinidad: Ganesh Ramsumair, "the great belcher," who rises "from laughing-stock to success" with his political poster "A vote for Ganesh is a vote for God," in *The Mys-*

tic Masseur; Surujpat "Pat" Harbans, in *The Suffrage of Elvira*, with its political theme (a contested election) and setting in Elvira, "the smallest, most isolated and most neglected of the nine counties of Trinidad"; and the colorful, loosely picaresque Caribbean characters in *Miguel Street* (such as Titus Hoyt, who teaches "Latin," a language he invents). Such satire is Dickensian in detail and grotesquery.

A serious thinker, Naipaul began as a social satirist, examining the rootless, homeless, nomadic migrant world, but transformed his novels into social inquiries, probing the ethos of the half societies in which the members of his gallery of misfits and nomadic exiles (the debris of wounded civilizations) drift. His Trinidad, India, French Africa, and Latin America are not romantic lands of primitive innocence but rather harsh and inhospitable, barbaric and cruel, the very opposite of the fantasy images found in slick travel brochures. Naipaul uncompromisingly portrays life in the developing world.

A House for Mr. Biswas

A House for Mr. Biswas is Naipaul's first serious work, the book in which he claims to have discovered "the trick of writing." Dickensian in approach, it meticulously and leisurely chronicles one man's lifetime obsession with establishing his identity: Mohun Biswas's desire to own a house in order to give himself a physical and spiritual home. Herein, his comic tone muted, Naipaul moves from the regional character portraits of his early novels to a universal theme.

The reader follows Biswas's point of view: his trials and tribulations within the Tulsi family and his attempts to be a writer. Despite Naipaul's protest that the work is not autobiographical, he modeled Biswas on his father, Seepersad Naipaul, and the love between Biswas and his son at the heart of the novel echoes the affection Naipaul and his father shared. Biswas, however, for all his yearning, is doomed to an ordinary life, limited by family realities and colonial models. He dies owning his desired house, but that house is not a home.

Naipaul's narrative style parallels the story line: lyrical when describing the environment, short and crisp when expressing Biswas's frustrations and disappointments. Social and personal history, comedy, and tragedy all blend in the novel, making it "indistinguishable from truth."

Mr. Stone and the Knights Companion

Mr. Stone and the Knights Companion, with its allegorical elements, has a completely English setting. Naipaul's character Mr. Stone echoes the rootlessness, emptiness, and identity crisis the former colonial faces upon returning to England. His immediate environment seems hostile, and his colonial memories are secondhand. The novel explores the three years before Stone's mandatory retirement at age sixty-five, as he faces insecurity and apprehension about the approaching "experience of nothingness, an experience of death." The novel focuses on Stone's attempt to avoid this emptiness by establishing a commune for old men (hence the idea of the Knights Companion). Seeking to give old men like himself something to do, he perfects the idea by writing about it, and the act of writing gives him deep satisfaction. Passages describing Stone wrestling with the challenge of writing with full concentration are some of the most forceful in the novel.

Bill Whymper, a colleague of Stone who has a knack for "licking things into shape," takes away from Stone the project on which he has worked so devotedly. Insensitive to the human concern for old age that motivated Stone's proposal, Whymper turns Stone's idea into a slick public relations project, thereby leaving Stone heartbroken and enraged and yet, alienated, unable to share his frustration with anyone. Gradually, Stone calms down and stoically takes consolation from having survived.

The Mimic Men

The Mimic Men, a fictional autobiography and Naipaul's darkest novel, tells the story of Ranjit "Ralph" Kirpal Singh, a forty-year-old West Indies Indian, who expresses an unrelieved sense of emptiness even more intensely than does Mr. Stone. One of Naipaul's most complex novels, *The Mimic Men* follows no real chronological sequence. Closeted in an old hotel in London, Kirpal Singh writes the story of his life, attempting to order the four periods of his life as "student, householder, man of affairs [a London dandy, a maneuverer, an organizer], recluse." His remembrance of events is episodic and constantly shifting, depending on the intensity of his feelings. He alternates between fantasy and reality as he moves from India to London and back to Isabella, the West Indian island where he grew up. Like Naipaul, Kirpal Singh is drawn to London. There, his marriage to Sandra, an English girl, fails, so he returns to Isabella, where he succeeds in real estate and runs for political office. He perceives these actions as "roles" that he plays, imitating others. He has become one of the mimic men. They are absurd; he is absurd and, he concludes, "shipwrecked." He wants to escape "to a place unknown, among people whose lives and even language" he need never enter. The best he can do is escape to an old hotel.

Kirpal Singh is *the* Naipaul man: educated, sophisticated, complex, forever conscious of his physical and spiritual rootlessness. He echoes Naipaul's own belief that one cannot return to an ordered harmony or hope for magical moments of tranquillity. One must accept what one has, since the pursuit of illusions is the absurd role of mimic men.

IN A FREE STATE

Purposefully nontraditional in form, *In a Free State*, which contains a short novel—a series of interconnected stories—and two fragments of a travel diary, marks an important stage in Naipaul's career. After its publication, Naipaul described the novel as a "final statement" of themes he had already exhausted.

Set in postindependence Africa, *In a Free State* depicts five different kinds of wandering, represented by a group of international characters, all in middle passage—in a free state. They are not truly free, however, in that they do not belong in the countries they are in and are unable to belong in the countries from which they come. The title suggests the aimless drift of contemporary aliens. The varied characters include an Indian in the United States ("one out of many"), a displaced Indian from the West Indies ("tell me who to kill"), a West Indian in London, and an Englishman and Englishwoman in Africa ("in a free state").

The work's prologue ("The Tramp at Piraeus") and the epilogue ("The Circus at Luxor") make an important statement about Naipaul himself. In the prologue, Naipaul only watches a fat Egyptian student harass a tramp, but in the epilogue, when an Arab boy whips a group of Arab beggar boys for a group of Italians to photograph, Naipaul puts a stop to it. His action demonstrates the quality missing in his characters in *In a Free State*; they have surrendered without protest. The writer, however, must protest against injustice, violence, and anarchy and remind the world of its responsibility to humanity.

GUERRILLAS

Like *In a Free State* and *A Bend in the River*, Naipaul's 1975 Booker Prize-winning novel *Guerrillas*, which was written "in five months of controlled frenzy," realistically presents "the ordeals and absurdities of living in the third world." The title is ironic because none of the major characters in the novel engages in any revolutionary action, only a pretension to guerrilla activity, resulting in a murder produced by sexual shame. The epigraph summarizes the philosophical core of the novel—it quotes "revolutionary" Jimmy Ahmed: "When everybody wants to fight there's nothing to fight for. Everybody wants to fight his own little war, everybody is a guerrilla."

Jimmy Ahmed is another of Naipaul's rootless heroes. He is half black and half Chinese, and even his name is assumed, an imitation of the Black Muslims; he has no authentic identity at all. Michael de Freitas, alias Michael X, the Trinidadian black power leader hanged for murder, provided the inspiration for Jimmy Ahmed.

Jimmy Ahmed's fantasy is to be the true hero. He lives in an imaginary world, talking a lot about revolutionary guerrilla activity, playacting in much the same way as Kirpal Singh in *The Mimic Men* and various characters in *In a Free State*. Jimmy, who fled a rape case in England, has an army of slum rejects who make his attempt at a peaceful commune seem pathetic.

Peter Roche, a white South African who had been tortured and imprisoned because of his opposition to the apartheid regime, and Roche's girlfriend, Jane, one of those "liberals who come flashing their milk white thighs and think they're contributing to the cause," travel to Jimmy's commune to help him. All three are homeless; none really trusts the others or is committed to any cause, but their pretensions to guerrilla activity give them a needed facade.

The generic city of an unspecified emerging Caribbean island bristles with political corruption and greedy men from multinational corporations. Naipaul brilliantly evokes the locale, "a place at the end of the world, a place that had exhausted its possibilities," capturing the smell and substance of the developing world, with its irritations, bureaucracy, and nightmarish fantasies. When the city reaches its breaking point and snaps, anger and violence take over. The trio—Jimmy, Peter, and Jane—are jolted from their fantasy and the result is a disturbingly savage sexual violation, explicitly described, and brutal murder, the end result of Jane's masochist sexual games. In *Guerrillas*, Naipaul demonstrates how far he has traveled from the Dickensian irony and comedy of *The Mystic Masseur* and from the regionalism of Trinidad to the global tragedy of rootlessness.

A BEND IN THE RIVER

A Bend in the River is set in Africa, in a country resembling Zaire under General Mobutu Sese Seko, its colonial terrain similar to that explored by Joseph Conrad in *Heart of Darkness* (1902). Salim, a young Indian shopkeeper from the eastern coast of Africa, tells the story. He is the quintessential Naipaul hero: an outsider, an exile in a damaged land. Salim's ancestors came from northern India, and Salim has traveled to the interior of the country, about a thousand miles from the capital, to set up shop "at a bend in the great river," a place "where the future had come and gone." The novel describes approximately seven years in his life, during which time he carries on his modest trade in pencils, copybooks, toothbrushes, and pots and pans. He keeps to himself, limiting his wanderings to "flat, shop, club, bar, the river embankment at sunset."

Independence comes to the country, and it emerges from its own past, but in spite of all the trappings of modern civilization—tall buildings, schools and universities, long radio broadcasts by the "Big" man who has elected himself for life—the country has a hard time becoming a part of the contemporary world. Naipaul sketches this absurd, violent, corrupt, twilight world. The capital has the Big man, with his army, sorcery, and terrorism, while in the bush lurk the Liberation Army guerrillas and the ghosts of an ancestral past. In Salim's town at the bend of the river, refugees, impoverished Africans, and corrupt officials are all anxious about the bloodshed that precedes independence.

Each character contributes to the tension and the rage: Raymond, the French scholar, once a close adviser to the Big man, "the Big man's white man"; Metty, "someone of mixed race," Salim's lifelong servant, whose relationship with Salim disintegrates because Metty no longer gets the traditional protection from his master; Father Huisman, the Belgian priest who collects African tribal masks, whose steady decay reflects his failure to recognize their cultural value; Yvette, Raymond's wife, whose affair with Salim makes him say, "I felt blessed and remade"; and Ferdinand, the son of a bush woman, a student who vociferously repeats the Big man's sayings on national pride. As part of the Big man's radicalization, the government confiscates Salim's shop and gives it to citizen Theotime, who then hires Salim as his manager. Next Salim is arrested and imprisoned but then released by Ferdinand, who sums up events in this attempt to impress order on disorder: "We're all going to hell, and every man knows this in his bones. . . . Everyone wants to make his money and run away. But where?" He answers that question cryptically: "The bush burns itself. But there is no place to go."

To make the darkness even more intense, Naipaul creates an incident in which Salim visits his friend Nazruddin in London before deciding to leave Africa. Nazruddin warns Salim that people are stampeding—Argentineans, Chinese, blacks, Koreans—all on the run, all frightened of the fire: "You mustn't think it's only Africa people are running from." Naipaul thus confirms rootlessness and wandering as worldwide phenomena, although Salim embraces his past by marrying a fellow Muslim.

THE ENIGMA OF ARRIVAL

In 1987, Naipaul published *The Enigma of Arrival*, his first novel in almost a decade. In several ways this book marked a change of direction for him. Set primarily in Wiltshire and spanning the period from 1950 to 1984, *The Enigma of Arrival* is by far Naipaul's most autobiographical novel. The protagonist, like Naipaul himself, is a middle-aged writer, a Trinidadian who came to England on a scholarship to study at Oxford University. Like Naipaul, too, he has settled in the English countryside. Indeed, so close are the parallels between author and protagonist that some reviewers have wondered why Naipaul published the book as a novel. In its reflective tone and its relative lack of novelistic incident, *The Enigma of Arrival* could easily be mistaken for a memoir about rites of passage and shifts of perception along the unanchored journey of Naipaul's life.

Nevertheless, Naipaul chose to treat his experience from the distance a novel provides. Quietly developed scenes—reflections on his Wiltshire neighbors, memories of his early years in England, luxurious descriptions of the English landscape, and an account of a return to Trinidad for a memorial service after the death of his elder sister—sound a note new in his work: a sense of reconciliation, of serenity even, growing out of an awareness of the endless cycles of life and death. Furthermore, Naipaul's interest in colorful individuals led to insightful depictions of rural working-class Englishmen. Naipaul seems to have found in the English countryside a vision central to the Indian heritage he left behind.

A Way in the World

In 1994 Naipaul published his eleventh novel, *A Way in the World*, a difficult book to categorize within established genres. The publisher listed it as a novel, but critics demurred, finding it a mixture of short stories, history, and autobiography, with a structure resembling that of *In a Free State*: nine narratives, some clearly fictional and involving historical persons (English navigator Sir Walter Raleigh and Venezuelan revolutionary Francisco de Miranda) and some ostensibly factual, involving historical figures or people supposedly known by Naipaul (such as novelist Foster Morris), and reminiscences, which seem factual in spirit if not in every detail. Together, the narratives examine various types of cultural displacement—how the principal characters find their way in a world in which cultures meet, clash, and mingle.

In the opening narrative Naipaul mulls over his youth in the mixed society of Trinidad. He meets an ambitious black man, Blair, who represents the successful postcolonial Trinidadian. Whereas the young Naipaul leaves Trinidad to become an expatriate in England, Blair remains in Trinidad and becomes a successful politician. In the book's last section, the two meet again, decades later, in East Africa, where Blair is advising a fledgling government on economic policy. In the book's most touching scene, the two men, with mutual empathy, recognize the different sorts of alienation their careers have brought them, one as a writer, the other as a political consultant for the Third World. Soon afterward, Blair is brutally murdered. Although African in heritage, a Caribbean-born man such as Blair, Naipaul intimates, cannot return to his ancestral roots.

The other narratives also show that returns are perilous, if not impossible, for the culturally displaced. Raleigh, for instance, finds that, after staking his future on discovering gold in the Orinoco region of South America, he cannot return to England without facing derision and execution because of his failure. By contrast, Francisco de Miranda, part revolutionary, part confidence man, devotes his life to freeing his homeland Venezuela from Spain, traveling the United States and Europe to gain support for his cause, but when his chance finally comes, he too fails in his attempt to return home, betrayed by his own protégé, revolutionary Simón Bolívar, and imprisoned in Spain.

A Way in the World shows how people adrift in the world make their way by redefining themselves. The result is a psychological chimera, composed partly of inherited traits, often poorly understood; partly of acquired interests, as from education; and partly of experience from random incidents in foreign contexts. This plunges the book's culturally displaced characters into, at best, eventual irrelevance and, at worst, disaster. Its elegiac tone confirms that the product of postcolonial displacement is often tragedy.

Half a Life

Naipaul's next novel, *Half a Life*, conflates ideas from his early works (such as *The Mimic Men* and *A Bend in the River*), blending autobiography and fiction, Dickensian characters, and sociopolitical observations to explore the "half lives" of those raised in English colonies and educated abroad. It traces the life of protagonist Willie Somerset Chandran, born in India in the 1930's and named after W. Somerset Maugham (his silent father provided Maugham material on Indian mysticism), from childhood to middle age. Initially, Willie follows in Naipaul's footsteps. His ascetic Brahman father chooses to express solidarity with Mahatma Gandhi by marrying a lower-caste "untouchable" on scholarship at the university and thereby to liberate himself from ignorant class distinctions. In doing so, he effectively casts his son out of a secure classification in Indian society and finds himself bound to a woman whose potential for self-betterment ended with marriage and whose touch he finds repulsive.

In rebellion against the hollowness of his father's political/personal acts, Willie flees to England in the 1950's to study, to find authentic experiences, and to become a writer. His experiences with the "bohemian-immigrant" London life, reflecting Naipaul's own, make him realize that every place has its own caste system and that he has fallen into a colonial pattern, writing short stories for white liberals like the newspaper editor who writes his own obituary and shares it with others. Consequently, he strives to forge for himself a new identity, to remake himself through writing a novel, which he does. Ironically, publishing a book proves more stultifying than liberating, too facile to be satisfying.

Willie's life thereafter departs from Naipaul's own, a sort of alternative possibility the author toys with. Willie's sister marries a left-wing film director and moves to West Berlin, while Willie decries his "half and half world." He marries a fan, Ana, a half-African, half-Portuguese woman who has read his one published book. He moves to her estate in Portuguese East Africa—colonial Mozambique—and begins an adulterous "half life." Through Willie's observations and reactions, Naipaul examines the dying days of Portuguese colonialism—its grandeur and pretensions, its trivialities and boredom—and then the Marxist creation of new illusions, equally damaging to human psyche. Tiring of the tedium of plantation life (and even of the sexual adventures and brothels it offers) after eighteen years and tired of living Ana's life, Willie flees to Germany just as a Marxist government replaces the colonial one. His comment on his life is, "I've done nothing. . . . I have been hiding for too long." Once again Naipaul, dealing with class, race, and maturation, portrays with cutting irony the negative personal consequences of postwar decolonization as father and son live lives not fully their own, make fraudulent compromises that prevent them from fully engaging in life, and so remain blind to their own realities.

MAGIC SEEDS

Magic Seeds continues the story begun in *Half a Life*, following Willie to Berlin, where he takes refuge with his sister, Sarojini, whom he has not seen for more than eighteen years. She is actively engaged in the political world of 1970's Berlin and pushes him to break out of his listlessness and engage in meaningful action. Through her, he connects with a guerrilla group in India (the planting of "magic seeds") and returns there, seeking a cause to give meaning to his basically empty life. Ironically, the cause is what drove him from India in the first place, caste prejudice: The guerillas are engaged in revolutionary action to free the lower castes from the limitations placed on them by class prejudice. His new associates (mediocre intellectuals playing revolutionaries) claim to be engaged in war, with the police and government the enemy, ambush the preferred method, and the civilians who perish simply collateral damage.

As reviewer Brad Hooper has observed, the novel is "an anatomy of revolution," as Naipaul takes readers behind the scenes of a "terrorist" group and shows the motivations that produce recruitment and the obsessions that drive acts of terror. Although Willie describes these guerrillas as "absolute maniacs," he nonetheless stays with them for seven years, enduring the discomfort of their jungle life as they shift from locale to locale before choosing surrender and jail to escape them. His disillusioning discovery is that his attempts to create an idealized vision of society does not match the reality, for the guerrillas are actually killing indiscriminately and are opposed by the very peasants they claim to support.

A former London friend, Roger (now a lawyer), helps Willie get his book of short stories republished while he is incarcerated, so that, ironically, his status changes from terrorist to postcolonial author, and embarrassed authorities rush to free him. Returning to London, Willie repays Roger by seducing his wife, Perdita, then takes a staff position with an architecture magazine funded by a rich banker (who is also sleeping with Perdita). Once again, Naipaul depicts the nowhere man, the mimic man, the homeless, rootless, self-made wanderer, the stateless man searching for an individual identity but in between potential roles to which he never fully commits.

This continual state of nonbelonging and noncommitment, and the negative directions in which it might lead one, is the central theme of this novel. Willie Chandran thus devolves into a mouthpiece for Naipaul's anticommunist complaints and for his disturbing images of kinky cross-racial sex. Having begun his life in an Indian ashram, experienced the lifestyle of the London bohemian, and luxuriated in the gated community of a decaying colonial nation, in *Magic Seeds* he suffers the physical and psychological discomfort of jungle life amid psychopaths who demand sacrifices and acts whose value he questions; he learns the precariousness of civilization as the magical cause turns nasty. The novel is pessimistic, its study of how terrorists are recruited and engage communities disturbing: Naipaul makes Willie the reader's concrete face of abstract terrorism, while Willie himself dismisses his personal guilt, asserting that political mischief starts whenever one has an idealized worldview.

K. Bhaskara Rao; Roger Smith
Updated by Gina Macdonald

Other major works

short fiction: *A Flag on the Island*, 1967.

nonfiction: *The Middle Passage: Impressions of Five Societies—British, French, and Dutch—in the West Indies and South America*, 1962; *An Area of Darkness: An Experience of India*, 1964; *The Loss of El Dorado: A History*, 1969; *The Overcrowded Barracoon, and Other Articles*, 1972; *India: A Wounded Civilization*, 1977; *"The Return of Eva Perón" with "The Killings in Trinidad,"* 1980; *Among the Believers: An Islamic Journey*, 1981; *Finding the Center: Two Narratives*, 1984; *A Turn in the South*, 1989; *India: A Million Mutinies Now*, 1990; *Beyond Belief: Islamic Excursions Among the Converted Peoples*, 1998; *Between Father and Son: Family Letters—Selected Correspondence of V. S. Naipaul and His Family, 1949-1953*, 2000 (also known as *Letters Between a Father and Son*, 1999); *Reading and Writing: A Personal Account*, 2000; *The Writer and the World: Essays*, 2002 (Pankaj Mishra, editor); *Literary Occasions: Essays*, 2003 (Mishra, editor); *A Writer's People: Ways of Looking and Feeling*, 2007.

miscellaneous: *The Nightwatchman's Occurrence Book, and Other Comic Inventions*, 2002.

Bibliography

Ball, John Clem. *Satire and the Postcolonial Novel: V. S. Naipaul, Chinua Achebe, Salman Rushdie*. New York: Routledge, 2003. Applies the perceptions of postcolonial comparative theories to a reconsideration of Western constructs of the satiric and an exploration of the complex and multidirectional ways these three writers employ satire.

Barnouw, Dagmar. *Naipaul's Strangers*. Bloomington: Indiana University Press, 2003. Praises Naipaul's nonfiction in particular for demonstrating a growing sense of the complexities of cultural difference and the difficulties that human beings have in understanding those different from themselves. Explores the sophisticated strategies on which Naipaul relies to communicate existentialist images of humankind's enduring strangeness.

Dooley, Gillian. *V. S. Naipaul, Man and Writer*. Columbia: University of South Carolina Press, 2006. Provides a scholarly, concise, readable analysis of Naipaul's oeuvre. Includes bibliography and index.

French, Patrick. *The World Is What It Is: The Authorized Biography of V. S. Naipaul*. New York: Alfred A. Knopf, 2008. First authoritative biography of the enigmatic author draws on Naipaul's personal papers and personal reminiscences. Presents a richly detailed portrait of his life, travels, contrarian stance, affairs, depression, and powerful creative impulse.

Gorra, Michael. *After Empire: Scott, Naipaul, Rushdie*. Chicago: University of Chicago Press, 1997. Argues that, like novelists Paul Scott and Salman Rushdie, Naipaul explores his English education against the backdrop of a culturally blurred society left behind by British imperialism. Asserts that Naipaul concerns himself with history, the nature of identity, and the mimicry inherent in postcolonial society.

Hayward, Helen. *The Enigma of V. S. Naipaul*. New York: Palgrave Macmillan, 2002. Well-researched, objective study identifies and traces recurring themes that shed light on Naipaul's creative process and the ties between his factual life and his artistic creations. Among the themes explored in forty years of his writing are cultural alienation, detachment, and anxiety.

Khan, Akhtar Jamal. *V. S. Naipaul: A Critical Study*. New Delhi: Creative Books, 1998. Provides a non-Western perspective on Naipaul's works. Khan expresses his offense at Naipaul's negative portrayal of Islam.

King, Bruce. *V. S. Naipaul*. 2d ed. New York: Macmillan, 2003. Analyzes Naipaul's fiction and also discusses his nonfiction. King notes that he finds a moral honesty in Naipaul's writing that brings freshness to his fiction. Includes informative appendixes concerning Naipaul's family and experiences in Trinidad and Africa.

Mustafa, Fawzia. *V. S. Naipaul*. New York: Cambridge University Press, 1995. Stresses the influence on

Naipaul of Joseph Conrad, for whom, like Naipaul, English literature was a borrowed tradition. Divides Naipaul's work into four decades and examines the novelistic techniques the author uses to understand the postcolonial condition of developing nations through his fiction and nonfiction.

Theroux, Paul. *Sir Vidia's Shadow: A Friendship Across Five Continents*. London: Hamilton, 1998. Presents a contrarian account of a ruptured friendship: Naipaul as a self-centered racist, hostile to women, but also a worthy author in his early and middle years, though now in decline.

R. K. NARAYAN

Born: Madras, India; October 10, 1906
Died: Madras, India; May 13, 2001
Also known as: Rasipuram Krishnaswami Narayan

Principal long fiction

Swami and Friends, 1935
The Bachelor of Arts, 1937
The Dark Room, 1938
The English Teacher, 1945 (also known as *Grateful to Life and Death*, 1953)
Mr. Sampath, 1949 (also known as *The Printer of Malgudi*, 1957)
The Financial Expert, 1952
Waiting for the Mahatma, 1955
The Guide, 1958
The Man-Eater of Malgudi, 1961
The Sweet-Vendor, 1967 (also known as *The Vendor of Sweets*)
The Painter of Signs, 1976
A Tiger for Malgudi, 1983
Talkative Man: A Novel of Malgudi, 1987
The World of Nagaraj, 1990

Other literary forms

In addition to his novels, R. K. Narayan (nuh-RI-yuhn) published a number of volumes of short stories. The title of his first collection of short stories, *Malgudi Days* (1941), is also the title of a later, expanded collection published by Viking in 1982. Other collections include *Dodu, and Other Stories* (1943), *Cyclone, and Other Stories* (1944), *Lawley Road: Thirty-two Short Stories* (1956), *A Horse and Two Goats, and Other Stories* (1970), *Old and New* (1981), *Under the Banyan Tree, and Other Stories* (1985), and *The Grandmother's Tale, and Selected Stories* (1994). Two autobiographical works are *My Days* (1974), which covers four decades of Narayan's career as a writer, and *My Dateless Diary* (1960), a journal of his travels through the United States. "Gods, Demons, and Modern Times," a talk given at Columbia University in 1972, is collected together with tales from Indian mythology in *Gods, Demons, and Others* (1964). Narayan also published translations of two Indian epics: *The Ramayana* (1972) and *The Mahabharata* (1978). During the war years, he edited *Indian Thought*, and his weekly newspaper "middles" were collected in *Next Sunday: Sketches and Essays* (1960). A film adaptation of Narayan's novel *The Guide* was released in 1965, but Harvey Breit and Patricia Rinehart's stage adaptation of the novel only incurred Narayan's displeasure. Despite his attempt to withhold permission for the production, *The Guide* opened on Broadway in March, 1968.

Achievements

R. K. Narayan was inducted into the American Academy of Arts and Letters in 1982. He was also made a member of the Sahitya Academy (Literary Academy) in India.

Biography

Rasipuram Krishnaswami Narayan was born in Madras on October 10, 1906. During his early years he was reared by his grandmother in Madras. Very early in his autobiography, *My Days*, he records his dislike of education, of the mission schools, of the British colleges, and of his short-lived adventure as a schoolteacher. All these experiences permeate his writing and serve as the subject matter of his fiction. His literary education was predominantly Victorian in flavor. Francis Turner Palgrave's *The Golden Treasury of the Best Songs and Lyrical Poems in the English Language* (1861), the works of Sir Walter Scott, and reading William Shakespeare's plays aloud were its staples.

In 1933, Narayan fell in love with a woman named Rajam, whom he married only after great difficulties because their horoscopes showed theirs was not an auspicious match; she died of typhoid in 1939. The trauma of this loss, his inability to come to terms with his fate, and his effort to defy his destiny led to Narayan's interest in purported psychic communication with the dead and provided the inspiration for *The English Teacher*. A feeling of helplessness in the face of destiny takes sometimes comic and sometimes tragic turns throughout Narayan's work.

Narayan was commissioned to write a travel book on Mysore, and after several years of writing for *The Hindu* and other journalistic experiences, he began publishing *Indian Thought*, a quarterly of literature, philosophy, and culture. Not until October, 1956, did Narayan travel outside the boundaries of the three-city area of Madras, Mysore, and Coimbatore. He went to Berkeley, California, on a Rockefeller Foundation grant to write a novel, *The Guide*. Subsequently, he visited the United States several times while living and writing in Mysore and Madras. The death of his daughter Hema in the early 1990's caused him to become extremely reclusive. Narayan died on May 13, 2001 in Madras, India.

Analysis

On January 18, 1982, R. K. Narayan was inducted into the American Academy of Arts and Letters. He received a similar honor in India from the Sahitya Academy (Literary Academy), but the induction was not without debate. Could a South Indian writer who had never stirred outside his home region, who was writing in English rather than his mother tongue, whose fiction was not concerned with lofty nationalistic issues, actually be worthy of such a literary honor? Indeed, it is to Narayan's credit that he continued to write in English. His writing is neither imitative nor experimental. Never feeling compelled to work within the boundaries of large literary or nationalistic trends, Narayan did not find it necessary to vary the English language or to describe moments of nationalistic history as a means of establishing his identity. Joycean word coinage, attempts to introduce the rhythms of various Indian languages in his English style, and the use of Indian-English dialect are not Narayan's tools. Rather, it is through character description and his characters' worldviews that Narayan expresses a distinctly Indian sensibility. For him, Standard English is the most effective medium for conveying this sensibility. To Narayan, English is so opaque that it can take on the "tint of any country."

Narayan's bilingual situation thus was not a handicap. It provided him with the means to know and use English while keeping him in touch with his own roots and cultural wisdom. It kept him aware of English literary history, yet his style does not show "the marks of a labored acquisition." On the contrary, it reflects the English language in its "process of transmutation," as Narayan described the adoption of English in India. Most of Narayan's characters speak and use the sort of Standard English Narayan himself spoke in India. Occasionally, an Indian-English idiom reflects a character's situation.

Narayan's consistent use of Standard English is, more often than not, appropriate to the circumstances of his fiction. Swami and his cricket-playing cohorts, reading the Messrs. Binn's catalog of cricket equipment, are not likely to be speaking in a native language, nor are the boys educated at Albert Mission College. In *The Guide*, Raju, providing instruction to Velan the villager, is not likely to be speaking English or Indian English, yet his Tamil is best translated into straightforward, crisp, Standard English. Narayan thus does not provide any superfluous Tamil lilt to the English prose of these passages. The characters and situations are more than sufficient expressions of Indianness.

Narayan was often criticized for being immune to the stylistic experimentation that other Commonwealth writers seem to have found necessary. He was also criticized for the very sentence structure for which Ernest Hemingway was praised. William Walsh, for example, while admiring Narayan's style for "its pure and easy flow," found it lacking in the "adventitiously injected" energy that "marks the writing of the West Indians." A number of Indian critics objected that Narayan's prose seems oblivious to the tradition of English literary style. What they meant is that it lacks a "Macaulayan amplitude of phrase." Narayan's distance from the centers where the language is changing and developing is seen as yet another handicap to the development of his style.

Such criticism fails to recognize Narayan's supreme achievement as an Indian writer in English: his refusal to heed critical stereotypes and his development of an individual style based on his understanding of the process of the English language's transmutation in India. By his rejection of both an overt Indian idiom and a self-conscious literary English, Narayan is able to maintain his unobtrusive authorial stance. His style is far from monotonous; it often changes pace to reflect action and character. Both in *The Guide* and in *The Painter of Signs*, it reflects the breathlessness with which the action takes place but slows down as it reflects moments of repose in the consciousness of his characters.

By using simple sentence constructions, Narayan was known for bending the English language to describe suitably the languorous quality of South Indian life. Ironically, this effect is achieved with short, crisp, Hemingwayesque sentences with simple variations on the subject-object construction. While for Hemingway this technique would yield "sparse and muscular prose" that conveys the American character, in Narayan's prose it conveys the leisurely nature characteristic of the Indian's ordinary life and daily conversation.

In elevating ordinary life through style, character, and situation, Narayan's fiction is like a prism that reflects a many-colored Indianness. Ignoring the obvious means of providing his work with an Indian identity, Narayan focuses instead on quintessential situations in which Indian character develops. "Episode and escapade," "moment and mood," in their peculiarly Indian contexts of a belief in destiny, astrology, and arranged marriages, give Narayan's fictional locale, Malgudi, its own postage stamp that says, "In India we trust."

The common man in his passage toward self-knowledge, in his sometimes comic and sometimes tragic struggle against destiny, is the subject of Narayan's fiction. Narayan's recurring preoccupations are universal, but they are given form in an intensely particularized fictional world, as palpable and idiosyncratic as William Faulkner's Yoknapatawpha County. The reality of Narayan's Malgudi is established in his first novel, *Swami and Friends*.

R. K. Narayan. (Library of Congress)

Swami and Friends

With *Swami and Friends*, the Malgudi town became reality. Lawley extension was laid out at a perfect distance from the Sarayu river, just enough distance to be comfortable for the Westernized Indian and the British Sahibs. The railway station made civilized connections possible, while an old trunk road wound through the forest. It is through following the trunk road and spending a night out in the cold that Swami comes to an understanding of himself. He makes the passage from innocence to experience, very much like Mark Twain's Huck Finn.

British and Indian critics have compared him to Richmal Crompton's William and Jennings, both very young British schoolboys who, through several volumes, fail to mature. It is the universal experience of childhood, the process of "growing up," that *Swami and Friends* captures, and yet Swami's misadventures are played out in uniquely Indian settings. The cricket games and cricket bat catalogs are as Indian and real to the bicultural situation as grandmother, the monkey, and mango chutney.

The Bachelor of Arts

In another work, the teenage years become a time of learning and realization, and Chandran, in *The Bachelor of Arts*, learns about the importance of success and failure. Although this success and failure are centered on seemingly trivial issues—the passing of college examinations, the winning of college elections, and the gaining of attention from the opposite sex—these situations are tremendously important in the life of the Indian college student. At the same time, however, they are infused with the general human yearning for success at any cost, the debating of the ethics of such situations, and the human fear of failure. Each little question of conscience holds its own cathartic tragicomedy. Narayan's preeminence among Indian writers in English lies in his ability to capture moments in time that are as much a part of his readers' lives as they are of the lives of his characters, and to depict both the comic and tragic aspects of those moments.

The English Teacher

The English Teacher, also known as *Grateful to Life and Death*, describes the existential moments through which almost any individual faces the "eternal now." The Malgudi adolescent moves to the householder stage yet cannot procure the woman whom he loves in marriage—the horoscopes do not match; the astrologers will not give their consent. The English teacher, however, is able to persuade the astrologer that the girl's horoscope has some adverse stars that might cancel out those in the boy's horoscope. He then triumphantly brings his wife home to an idyllic happiness, a happiness that reigns despite an unsuccessful teaching career and rejected manuscripts.

Every individual, however, must face the disparity between "hope" and "fate." The karmic wheel turns, and the English teacher is helpless in the face of merciless fate, in this case, typhoid. Intensely personal, it is a private tragedy of the "felt experience"—the tragedy that no human being can fully accept. In his refusal of his destiny, the English teacher attempts to transcend his fate. His struggle against death and his eventual acceptance of it take the form of efforts to communicate with the dead. While this second half of the novel seems melodramatic and purposeless, it is the "still point" on which Narayan's philosophy of humanity turns and is developed in his later novels. The ring of cosmic laughter surrounds the English teacher's struggles against that external force that "moves" and "mates" and "slays."

The struggle against humankind's destiny in this uniquely personal, human, small, and yet heroic way pervades *The Guide*, *The Financial Expert*, *The Vendor of Sweets*, and *The Painter of Signs*.

The Guide

Railway Raju in *The Guide* is clearly an individual caught on the wheel of fortune. Raju starts out attempting to be as successful as his father with a magazine stand in the Malgudi railway station; he also has a side business in guiding tours of Malgudi, the caves, the Mempi Hills, and the source of the Sarayu for tourists. On one such tour, he falls in love with a professor's dancer-wife, gives her shelter to escape from her boring husband, and, eventually, foolishly falls into a trap devised by the professor. Raju ends up in the Malgudi jail accused of forgery.

Upon his release from prison, accident and his fortune confer on him the important position of a holy man. Raju, who knows himself well as a foolhardy scoundrel, makes every attempt to shun this position. He is hungry, however, and in return for gifts of food from the villagers he gives them the words of wisdom he learned from his mother's bedtime stories and from the magazines and books he has read at his magazine stand. When famine returns and rages through Malgudi and the surrounding villages, a chance conversation with the village idiot leads Raju to undertake a fast to bring on the rains. This happens while Raju himself is yearning for a particular Indian delicacy—*bondas*. Although he wants to ask for food, he finds himself trapped. Raju attempts to be honest and describe to Velan, the villager, his ordinary humanness. "Greatness," however, cannot be revoked. Furthermore, a television crew from California is photographing the last days of the fast of this mahatma, or great soul. "Have you always been a yogi?" asks the reporter. "Yes, more or less," Raju replies.

Raju does his penance, his yoga, and moves toward the self-knowledge of a Sanyasi. The question remains whether his penance is real or merely a form of self-delusion. As the dancer's manager, he had attained a newfound importance that ended in a crushing fall. Perhaps he is to meet a similar fall from his swamihood. Through all his adventures, even his last, Raju is painstakingly honest. Is Narayan's ironic vision saying something about the power of delusion? It is in that last scene, in which the fasting Raju/swami sinks to his knees and believes that his fast has in fact caused it to rain in the hills, that the reader feels the fall of a great man—an ordinary, common man, struggling against destiny.

In *The Guide*, readers hear "cosmic laughter" not only at the individual's struggle against his fate but also at the setting in which the struggle takes place. In a sense, Malgudi has lost its innocence; the changing destiny, the town's sudden growth, has brought it only famine and criminals. It is no longer the Malgudi of Swami and his friends, of cricket fields, of the Lawley extension bungalows, and "the club." In *The Dark Room*, corruption slowly begins to appear in Malgudi. By the time of *The Guide*, technology has worked its evil magic. Underneath the crust of technology, change, and evil, however, the essence of Malgudi remains the same. The people remain innocent, gullible, and incapable of acting against their destinies.

The Financial Expert

The rise and fall of the "fortunes" of the title character in *The Financial Expert*, Margayya, follow more closely the classic tragic pattern. In fact, critics have often seen in this novel's five chapters the five parts in an Elizabethan tragedy. Narayan's vision, however, does not permit him a "tragic hero." Margayya seems more and more of a buffoon as he is driven by his blind passion for money, and Narayan's readers continue laughing with him as he shows what fools mortals can be.

The disparity between Margayya's "hope" and his "fate" is a wide chasm, and Margayya is a man continually on the brink of an abyss. He begins as a small-time moneylender working under a banyan tree across from an established bank. The bankers try to drive him away so that he will not take the villagers' business, but Margayya persists. An astrologer has told him that the goddess Lakashmi will be kind to him if certain *pujas* are carried out. When he comes in contact with Dr. Pal, who has the manuscript of a sex manual, he seizes the opportunity to make more money. With the aid of a publisher, he markets this book on "domestic harmony."

Margayya invests all his energy and affection and hope in his son, Balu. He works hard to provide for Balu the best opportunities in the hope of having a highly educated, supportive son. The more Margayya gives Balu, however—the best schools and the best clothes—the more recalcitrant Balu becomes. He is unable to pass his high school exam, and he falls into a life of lust and debauchery with Dr. Pal, as Margayya appears more and more to be a blundering fool. Both Balu and Margayya see themselves as "men of consequence." An attempt to support their style of living, more particularly Balu's debauchery, results in financial difficulties, and Balu begins to demand his share of his father's wealth.

When Margayya discovers that Dr. Pal is responsible for his son's corruption, a hostile exchange of words follows. To avenge himself, Dr. Pal spreads a rumor that Margayya is insolvent. His investors demand the return of their investments, which leaves Margayya without any money. He has it in him to consider his beginnings, however, whereas his son does not. Balu refuses to go back to his father's humble origins. With his hopes for wealth dashed, Margayya goes back to being the financial expert under the banyan tree. Like other Narayan characters, he has come full circle to his destiny.

The Painter of Signs

Among this portrait gallery of Malgudiwalas who have kept their "trysts" with their destinies are Jagan, the "vendor of sweets," and Raman, "the painter of signs," in *The Painter of Signs*. Their destinies lock them in a battle with modernity and change. With the flow of time, Malgudi has grown far beyond the limits of Lawley extension and even the central cooperative land mortgage bank. Computers, the story-writing machine that Jagan's son wants to develop, and the family planning clinic that Daisy develops have become part of this growing, bustling city.

Incapable of controlling the changes that surround him, Jagan also finds himself disappointed by his son, of whom he expected so much. The reader, however, questions how fair it is for Jagan to expect his Americanized son, who holds a master's degree in business administration, to follow in the footsteps of Jagan's Gandhism and to sit at his candy shop. It is Jagan, whose Gandhism would not let him permit his wife to take aspirin, who remains the absurd focus of this tragicomic situation.

Raman, the painter of signs, whose hope is to marry Daisy, the independent manager of the family planning clinic, is left similarly baffled. Daisy evades him in much the same way as the concept of an independent woman eludes him. The passionate tiger, prowling under the bullock cart on the desolate trunk road where the female government official must travel to spread the enlightenment of family planning, is surprised to find not only that the modern woman is quick to escape but also that she is willing to spend the night on a high tamarind treé branch. In the same way, the modern woman is puzzled and unable to come to terms with the barren women of the village who must visit the swami on the hill in order to bear children.

While their changing destinies continue to thwart them, Malgudiwalas remain essentially innocent. Their tragedy is in their bewilderment at their fate, and Malgudi remains a very accurate microcosm of the sociopolitical scene in contemporary India.

Much of Narayan's success as a novelist lies in his ability to capture the tragicomedy of the human situation. Like F. Scott Fitzgerald, Narayan appeals to two different audiences—the popular and the literary elite—with only one difference: He appeals to the literary elite only outside his own country. The Indian literary elite generally do not go beyond Narayan's undecorated English and structured plots to experience his celebration of moment and character. These so-called literary mistakes, however, lead to his popularity with the popular audience in India and the literary elite abroad. Graham Greene, who first championed Narayan's cause, referred to him as the "Indian Chekhov." In *My Days*, Narayan records that a rumor circulated in Mysore that W. Somerset Maugham, during a visit, wanted to meet the great Indian novelist, and no one within Mysore's bureaucracy could think of who it could be. Such is the dichotomy of Narayan's reception.

Appellations such as the "Indian Chekhov" and the "Indian Jane Austen" fall short of Narayan's achievement. He is *the* "Indian Narayan," as Indian as William Faulkner is American. His concern is the heroic quality of the ordinary Indian individual's struggle with destiny, as it is portrayed through personal, seemingly trivial experiences. This is what makes Narayan's fiction "moral art."

Feroza Jussawalla
Updated by Geralyn Strecker

Other major works

SHORT FICTION: *Malgudi Days*, 1941 (expanded 1982); *Dodu, and Other Stories*, 1943; *Cyclone, and Other Stories*, 1944; *An Astrologer's Day, and Other Stories*, 1947; *Lawley Road: Thirty-two Short Stories*, 1956; *Gods, Demons, and Others*, 1964; *A Horse and Two Goats, and Other Stories*, 1970; *Old and New*, 1981; *Under the Banyan Tree, and Other Stories*, 1985; *The Grandmother's Tale, and Selected Stories*, 1994.

NONFICTION: *Mysore*, 1944; *My Dateless Diary*, 1960; *Next Sunday: Sketches and Essays*, 1960; *My Days*, 1974; *Reluctant Guru*, 1974; *The Emerald Route*, 1977; *A Writer's Nightmare: Selected Essays, 1958-1988*, 1988; *The Writerly Life: Selected Nonfiction*, 2001 (includes essays from *My Dateless Diary*, *A Writer's Nightmare*, *A Story-Teller's World*, and *Salt and Sawdust*; S. Krishnan, editor).

TRANSLATIONS: *The Ramayana: A Shortened Modern Prose Version of the Indian Epic*, 1972; *The Mahabharata: A Shortened Prose Version of the Indian Epic*, 1978.

MISCELLANEOUS: *A Story-Teller's World*, 1989 (stories, essays, and sketches); *Salt and Sawdust: Stories and Table Talk*, 1993.

Bibliography

Bery, Ashok. "'Changing the Script': R. K. Narayan and Hinduism." *Ariel* 28, no. 2 (April, 1997): 7-20. Argues that Narayan often probes limitations and contradictions in Hindu worldviews and identities. Analyzes how Narayan challenges Hindu doctrines, particularly those that teach that the individual self and the phenomenal world are unimportant.

Holstrom, Lakshmi. *The Novels of R. K. Narayan*. Calcutta: Writers Workshop, 1973. An early study of

Narayan's first ten novels addresses his themes and narrative technique. Attempts to place Narayan in the tradition of Indian fiction. Includes a bibliography.

Kain, Geoffrey, ed. *R. K. Narayan: Contemporary Critical Perspectives*. East Lansing: Michigan State University Press, 1993. Collection of essays discusses primarily Narayan's novels, with contributors taking feminist, cultural, postcolonial, and other contemporary approaches to the works. Other topics addressed include irony, satire, transcendence, self-reflexivity, and mythmaking in Narayan's fiction.

Khatri, Chhote Lal, ed. *R. K. Narayan: Reflections and Re-Evaluation*. New Delhi: Sarup & Sons, 2006. Collection of essays by Indian scholars examines Narayan's work. Includes discussions of his depiction of women, male-female relationships, British characters, and love and marriage, as well as analysis of individual novels.

Naik, M. K. *The Ironic Vision: A Study of the Fiction of R. K. Narayan*. New Delhi: Sterling, 1983. Perceptive study demonstrates Narayan's use of irony, in its various forms, to portray human character and situations and to project his total vision of life. Includes a depiction of the layout of Malgudi and its surroundings, a select bibliography, and an index.

Ram, Susan, and N. Ram. *R. K. Narayan: The Early Years, 1906-1945*. New Delhi: Viking Press, 1996. First volume of a projected multivolume biography offers an excellent recounting of Narayan's early life. Prepared with the cooperation of Narayan's family members and friends.

Sankaran, Chitra. *Myth Connections: The Use of Hindu Myths and Philosophies in R. K. Narayan and Raja Rao*. 2d rev. ed. New York: Peter Lang, 2007. Comparative study of four novels by each of the authors—including Narayan's *The Man-Eater of Malgudi*, *Mr. Sampath*, *The Guide*, and *The Painter of Signs*—describes how the novels are based on Hindu mythology and philosophy.

Sundaram, P. S. *R. K. Narayan*. New Delhi: Arnold-Heinemann, 1973. Introductory work aims, according to its author, "to acquaint the Common Reader with the works of an outstanding writer and to suggest what makes the writing outstanding." Supplemented by notes and references, select bibliography, and index.

Thieme, John. *R. K. Narayan*. New York: Manchester University Press, 2007. Reexamination of Narayan's work focuses on his novels. Argues that Narayan is not a chronicler of "authentic Indianness," describes the influences on his fiction, and discusses his depiction of Malgudi.

Walsh, William. *R. K. Narayan*. London: Longman, 1971. Provides a general critical appraisal of Narayan as a novelist. Discusses Narayan's novels as "comedies of sadness" and argues that "his work is an original blend of Western method and Eastern material." Includes a select bibliography.

GLORIA NAYLOR

Born: New York, New York; January 25, 1950

Principal long fiction

The Women of Brewster Place: A Novel in Seven Stories, 1982
Linden Hills, 1985
Mama Day, 1988
Bailey's Café, 1992
The Men of Brewster Place, 1998
1996, 2005

Other literary forms

In 1986, Gloria Naylor wrote a column, *Hers*, for *The New York Times*. She is also the writer of a number of screenplays, short stories, and articles for various periodicals. She is known primarily, however, for her novels.

Achievements

Enjoying both critical and popular acclaim, Gloria Naylor's work has reached a wide audience. *The Women of Brewster Place* won the 1983 American Book Award for best first novel and was later made into a television miniseries. Naylor's other awards include a National Endowment for the Arts Fellowship in 1985 and a Guggenheim Fellowship in 1988.

Surveying the range of African American life in the United States, from poor ghetto to affluent suburb to southern offshore island, Naylor's work examines questions of black identity and, in particular, celebrates black women. In the face of enormous problems and frequent victimization, black women are shown coping through their sense of community and their special powers. Male readers might find less to cheer about in Naylor's early works, as she writes from a feminist perspective. Later works, however, recognize the plight of black males, acknowledging their struggles and celebrating their achievements. Though Naylor's focus is the black experience, her depictions of courage, community, and cultural identity have universal appeal.

Biography

The oldest child of parents who had migrated from Mississippi, Gloria Naylor was born and reared in New York City, her parents having left the South the year before her birth. An avid reader as a child, Naylor seemed to have inherited her passion for reading from her mother, a woman who would go to great lengths to purchase books to which she was denied access in Mississippi libraries because blacks were not allowed inside. The year Naylor graduated from high school, Martin Luther King, Jr., was assassinated, and the shock of this event caused Naylor to delay her college education. She chose instead to become a missionary for the Jehovah's Witnesses in New York, North Carolina, and Florida. She eventually found missionary life too strict, but her zeal apparently carried over into her later feminism. Although her writings are not religious, a fundamentalist pattern of thinking pervades them. She tends to separate her characters into the sheep and the goats (the latter mostly men), the saved and the damned, with one whole book, *Linden Hills*, being modeled on Dante's *Inferno* (c. 1320).

In high school Naylor read widely in the nineteenth century British novelists, but later in a creative writing course at Brooklyn College she came across the book that influenced her most—*The Bluest Eye* (1970), by the black American novelist Toni Morrison. The example of Morrison inspired Naylor to write fiction and to focus on the lives of black women, who Naylor felt were underrepresented (if not ignored) in American literature. Naylor began work on *The Women of Brewster Place*, which was published the year after her graduation from Brooklyn College with a bachelor of arts degree in English. By that time, Naylor was studying on a fellowship at Yale University, from which she received a master of arts degree in African American studies in 1983.

Naylor's background and literary achievements won for her numerous invitations for lectureships or other appointments in academia. She held visiting posts at George Washington University, the University of Pennsylvania, Princeton, New York University, Boston University, Brandeis, and Cornell. Diverse in her pursuits, Naylor wrote a stage adaptation of *Bailey's Café*. She founded One Way Productions, an independent film company, and became involved in a literacy program in the Bronx. She settled in Brooklyn, New York.

Analysis

White people do not appear often and are not featured in the work of Gloria Naylor, yet their presence can be felt like a white background noise, or like the boulevard traffic on the other side of the wall from Brewster Place. White culture is simply another fact of life, like a nearby nuclear reactor or toxic waste dump, and the effects of racism and discrimination are omnipresent in Naylor's work. Against these stifling effects her characters live their lives and try to define their sense of black identity, from the ghetto dwellers of Brewster Place to the social climbers of Linden Hills to the denizens of Willow Springs, a pristine southern island relatively untouched by slavery and segregation.

Naylor writes about these settings and characters in a romantic mode that sometimes verges on the melodramatic or gothic. The influence of her earlier reading—such authors as Charlotte Brontë and Emily Brontë, Charles Dickens, William Faulkner, and Morrison—is apparent. The settings have heavy but obvious symbolic meanings, some derived from literary references: Brewster Place is a dead-end street, Linden Hills is a modern version of Dante's Hell, and Willow Springs recalls the magical isle of William Shakespeare's *The*

Gloria Naylor.

Tempest (1611). The weather and numerous details also carry symbolic freight, almost as much as they do for such an emblematic writer as Nathaniel Hawthorne. In addition to literary influences, the symbolism seems to draw on Hollywood, particularly Hollywood's gothic genre, horror films; for example, in *Linden Hills* the character Norman Anderson suffers from attacks of "the pinks"—imaginary blobs of pink slime—while the rich undertaker Luther Nedeed locks his wife and child away in the basement.

These two examples also show, in an exaggerated fashion, how Naylor's characters fit into the Romantic mode. Her characters tend to go to extremes, to be emotional and obsessive, or to have a single trait or commit a single act that determines their whole life course. While rather one-dimensional and melodramatic, they nevertheless linger in the memory. Such is the case with Luther Nedeed, who represents Satan in *Linden Hills*, and with the old conjure woman Miranda "Mama" Day, who represents Satan's usual opposition in the scheme of things.

In Naylor, this scheme of things illustrates how she has transferred her former missionary fervor, along with the framework of religious thought, to her feminism. Luther Nedeed's behavior is only the most sensational example of men's cruelty to women in Naylor's work; he has a large following. On the other hand, the mystical ability of Mama Day, the Prospero of women's rights, to command the forces of nature and the spirit world is only the most sensational example of women's special powers in Naylor's thinking. Even the women of Brewster Place demonstrate these powers through their mutual love and support, enabling them to triumph over devastating personal tragedies and demeaning circumstances.

Naylor's men are another story: If not outright demons or headed that way, they seem to lack some vital force. Even the best men are fatally flawed—they are subject to the pinks, are addicted to wine, or have weak hearts. Failing at key moments, they are useful only as sacrifices to the feminine mystique. A prime example is the engineer George Andrews of *Mama Day*, who, for all his masculine rationality and New York smarts, does not know how to handle (significantly) a brooding hen. A close reading of Naylor's works reveals the men's victimization, along with the women's; however, Naylor is concerned with the women in her earlier novels. Naylor's later works indicate that she has expanded her vision to include men.

The Women of Brewster Place

Naylor began fulfilling her commitment to make black women more prominent in American fiction with *The Women of Brewster Place: A Novel in Seven Stories*. The seven stories, featuring seven women, can be read separately, but they are connected by their setting of Brewster Place and by characters who appear, or are mentioned, in more than one story. The women arrive on the dead-end street by different routes that exhibit the variety of lives of black women, but on Brewster Place they unite into a community.

The middle-aged bastion of Brewster Street is Mattie Michael, who over the course of her life was betrayed by each of the three men she loved—her seducer, her father, and her son. She mothers Lucielia Louise Turner (whose grandmother once sheltered Mattie) when Ciel's abusive boyfriend destroys her life. In addition, Mattie welcomes her close friend Etta Mae Johnson, who also once gave Mattie refuge. Etta Mae is a fading beauty who has used men all of her life but is now herself used by a sleazy preacher for a one-night stand. The other women featured are the young unwed Cora Lee, a baby factory; Kiswana Browne, an aspiring social reformer who hails from the affluent suburb of Linden Hills; and Lorraine and Theresa, two lesbians seeking privacy for their love.

Few men are in evidence on Brewster Place, and these few inspire little confidence. C. C. Baker and his youth gang lurk about the alleyway and, in the novel's brutal climax, rape Lorraine. The crazed Lorraine in turn kills the wino Ben, the old janitor who earlier had befriended her. Naylor acknowledges the plight of the men, however. In her description of the gang members, she says,

> Born with the appendages of power, circumcised by a guillotine, and baptized with the steam of a million nonreflective mirrors, these young men wouldn't be called upon to thrust a bayonet into an Asian farmer, target a torpedo, scatter their iron seed from a B-52 into the wound of the earth, point a finger to move a nation, or stick a pole into the moon—and they knew it. They only had that three-hundred-foot alley to serve them as stateroom, armored tank, and executioner's chamber.

As these scenes suggest, Brewster Place is located in a ghetto plagued by social ills. The women must face these on a daily basis in addition to their personal tragedies and dislocations. Instead of being overcome by their sufferings, however, the women find within themselves a common fate and a basis for community. They gain strength and hope from their mutual caring and support. In addition to their informal support system, they form a block association to address larger problems. The ability of women to unite in such a community inspires admiration for their courage and their special powers.

LINDEN HILLS

The community feelings of Brewster Place, from which the women gain a positive sense of identity, somehow make the ghetto's problems seem less awesome, paradoxically, than those of Linden Hills, an affluent suburb. If Brewster Place is a ghetto, Linden Hills is a hell. Naylor underlines this metaphor by deliberately modeling *Linden Hills* after Dante Alighieri's *Inferno*. Linden Hills is not a group of hills, but only a V-shaped area on a hillside intersected by eight streets. As one travels down the hill, the residents become richer but lower on the moral scale. Lester and Willie, two young unemployed poets who perform odd jobs for Christmas money (they are the modern counterparts of Vergil and Dante), take the reader on a guided tour.

Lester's sister Roxanne deems black Africans in Zimbabwe unready for independence; one young executive, Maxwell Smyth, encourages another, Xavier Donnell, no longer to consider Roxanne as a prospective corporate bride; and Dr. Daniel Braithwaite has written the authorized twelve-volume history of Linden Hills without making a single moral judgment. Other sellouts are more personal: The young lawyer Winston Alcott leaves his gay lover to marry, and Chester Parker is eager to bury his dead wife in order to remarry.

Significantly, Linden Hills is ruled by men. The archfiend is Luther Nedeed, the local undertaker and real estate tycoon who occupies the lowest point in Linden Hills. Speaking against a low-income housing project planned for an adjacent poor black neighborhood, Nedeed urges outraged Linden Hills property owners to make common cause with the racist Wayne County Citizens Alliance. Most damning of all, however, is that Nedeed disowns his own wife and child and imprisons them in an old basement morgue; the child starves, but the wife climbs up to confront the archfiend on Christmas Eve.

MAMA DAY

It is clear that, while examining problems of middle-class black identity in *Linden Hills*, Naylor has not overlooked the plight of black women. In *Mama Day*, Naylor returns to a more celebratory mood on both subjects. The setting of *Mama Day* is a unique black American culture presided over by a woman with even more unique powers.

The coastal island of Willow Springs, located off South Carolina and Georgia but belonging to no state, has been largely bypassed by the tides of American history, particularly racism. The island was originally owned by a white person, Bascombe Wade, who also owned slaves. Bascombe married Sapphira, one of his slaves, and they had seven sons. In 1823, Bascombe freed his other slaves and deeded the island to them, his sons, and their respective descendants in perpetuity (the land cannot be sold, only inherited). Bascombe was more or less assimilated, and a black culture grew up on the island that was closely tied to the land, to the culture's beginnings, and to African roots. In other words, Willow Springs is definitely a mythical island—a tiny but free black state flourishing unnoticed under the nose of the Confederacy. Naylor underlines the island's mythic qualities by drawing parallels between it and the magical isle of *The Tempest*.

If Prospero presides over Shakespeare's island, then Prospero's daughter, Miranda "Mama" Day (actually a great-granddaughter of the Wades), presides over Willow Springs. Known and respected locally as an old conjure woman, Mama Day is a repository and embodiment of the culture's wisdom. In particular, she is versed in herbs and other natural phenomena, but she also speaks with the island's spirits. Mama Day uses her powers to heal and aid new life, but other island people who have similar powers are not so benevolent. One such person is Ruby, who stirs her knowledge with hoodoo to kill any woman who might take her man.

Unhappily, Mama Day's grandniece, Cocoa, down from New York on a visit with her husband, George, arouses Ruby's jealousy. By pretending to be friendly, Ruby is able to give Cocoa a deadly nightshade rinse, scalp massage, and hairdo. Just as a big hurricane hits the island, Cocoa begins to feel the effects of the poison. George, an engineer, native New Yorker, and football fan, works frantically to save Cocoa, but he is overmatched. With his urbanized, masculine rationality, he cannot conceive of what he is up against or how to oppose it. Suffering from exhaustion and a weak heart, he is eventually killed in an encounter with a brooding hen.

Meanwhile, Mama Day has been working her powers. She confronts Ruby in a conjuring match, good magic versus bad magic, just as in Mali's oral epic tradition of the thirteenth century ruler Sundjata and in other traditions of modern Africa. Ruby is destroyed by lightning strikes, and Cocoa is saved. It is too late for George the doubter, however, who learns about the mystical powers of women the hard way.

BAILEY'S CAFÉ

In each of Naylor's first three novels, clear links to the work that follow it are evident. The character Kiswana Browne in *The Women of Brewster Place* serves as the connection to *Linden Hills*, having moved from that bourgeois community to Brewster Place to stay in touch with the struggles of her people. Willa Prescott Nedeed, the imprisoned wife in *Linden Hills*, points the way to *Mama Day*, since she is grandniece to Mama Day and first cousin to Cocoa. It is George, Cocoa's husband, who provides the link to *Bailey's Café*, Naylor's fourth novel.

In perhaps her most ambitious work yet, Naylor moves her readers from the magical island of Willow Springs to an equally intriguing site, for Bailey's Café is both nowhere and everywhere. It is sitting at the edge of the world yet is found in every town. As the café's proprietor, Bailey (though that is not his real name), tells readers,

> Even though this planet is round, there are just too many spots where you can find yourself hanging onto the edge . . . and unless there's some place, some space, to take a breather for a while, the edge of the world—frightening as it is—could be the end of the world.

Bailey's Café offers that breather, though some who enter the front door decide not to take it, instead going right through the café out the back door and dropping off into the void.

Like the inhabitants of Brewster Place, the customers in Bailey's Café are marginalized people. Their lives have taken them beyond the poverty and hard times of their urban sisters and brothers to the very edge of despair. However, for the women who people this extraordinary novel, Bailey's is simply a place to get directions to Eve's boardinghouse. Sweet Esther, abused to the point that she will receive visitors only in the dark; Peaches, whose effect on men drives her to mutilate her face with a can opener; Jesse, whose loss of marriage, child, and good name lead her to female lovers and heroin; and the pregnant virgin Mariam, ostracized from her village and bearing the effects of female circumcision—all find at Eve's a haven for their battered souls.

Throughout the individual stories of these women, Naylor uses unifying imagery: flower imagery, since each woman is associated with a particular bloom; musical imagery, jazz mostly, though the chords of the broken lives suggest the blues; and religious imagery, figuring heavily in Eve and her garden, but most noticeably in the virgin birth at the end of the novel. This birth is where the connection to *Mama Day* is made clear. Explaining the circumstances of his birth to Cocoa, George told of being left as an infant outside Bailey's Café by his mother, who was later found drowned. The last few pages of *Bailey's Café* reveal George as the drowned Mariam's child, recursively pointing back to *Mama Day*.

Similar to Naylor's other novels in its concentration on the diverse lives of black people, *Bailey's Café* nonetheless marks a shift for Naylor. This shift is evident in her inclusion of Mariam, from Ethiopia, who broadens the depiction of the black experience by encompassing an African one. Mariam is also Jewish, a fact that links her to the Jewish shopkeeper, Gabriel, in the novel. The coming together of the characters in celebration of the baby's birth—a celebration that intermixes different cultural and religious beliefs—brings a multicultural component to the novel absent in Naylor's other works.

Another notable change is Naylor's foregrounding of male characters. Bailey himself, the novel's narrator, is an example. His running commentary on the customers who find themselves in his establishment, his knowledge of Negro Leagues Baseball, and his narration of his courtship of his wife, Nadine, make him a central and engaging figure throughout the book. Another example is Miss Maples, the cross-dressing male housekeeper at Eve's boardinghouse. His rather lengthy individual story is included with those of the women; it points to Naylor's intention to portray a different kind of male identity as well as her desire to cultivate a different relationship with her male characters. This shift links *Bailey's Café* to *The Men of Brewster Place*, Naylor's fifth novel.

The Men of Brewster Place

Naylor's return to Brewster Place gives readers the opportunity to revisit the male characters introduced in the first book (generally portrayed negatively) and see them in a different light. No longer assuming background roles, they are up front, giving an account of their actions in the first book. In *The Women of Brewster Place*, Mattie's son Basil skipped town while awaiting sentencing, causing his mother to lose the property she had put up for his bail. Here Basil does return, check in hand, to repay his mother for her loss; however, she is dead, and his unfulfilled desire to make amends leads him into a detrimental relationship and a prison sentence. Eugene, absent from his daughter's funeral in the first book, is in fact on site. His grief compels him to undergo a harsh punishment, one that has much to do with the fact that he could never tell Ciel that he is gay. C. C. Baker, responsible for the vicious gang rape of Lorraine, executes another heinous crime in this book but gives the reader insight into his tragic character. When he squeezes the trigger to kill his brother, he does so with eyes closed, thanking God "for giving him the courage to do it. The courage to be a man."

In *The Men of Brewster Place*, Naylor seems to be acknowledging that there is after all more than one side to a story and that she is ready to let the whole story be known. Passages from the first book provide continuity between the two works, as does the resurrected voice of Ben, the janitor killed by Lorraine. Reminiscent of the character Bailey in *Bailey's Café*, Ben is both character and narrator.

However, Naylor brings some new voices to Brewster Place when she introduces Brother Jerome and Greasy. These characters link together the lives of the men living in Brewster Place. Brother Jerome is a retarded child with an ability to play the piano that speaks of genius. The blues that pour from his fingers speak to the lives of each man, rendering their conditions tangible. Greasy makes his brief but memorable appearance in the story called "The Barbershop," leaving the men to carry the burden of his self-inflicted demise. Naylor's portrayals of these two characters are perhaps the most moving of the book. These characterizations, along with the complexity of all the male characters, point to a Naylor who is taking a broader view. She had prefaced *The Women of Brewster Place* with a poem by Langston Hughes that asked the question, "What happens to a dream deferred?" In *The Men of Brewster Place*, she seems ready to acknowledge that deferred dreams are not only the province of women.

Harold Branam
Updated by Jacquelyn Benton

Other major works

nonfiction: *Conversations with Gloria Naylor*, 2004 (Maxine Lavon Montgomery, editor).

EDITED TEXT: *Children of the Night: The Best Short Stories by Black Writers, 1967 to the Present*, 1995.

BIBLIOGRAPHY

Braxton, Joanne M., and Andrée Nicola McLaughlin, eds. *Wild Women in the Whirlwind: Afro-American Culture and the Contemporary Literary Renaissance*. New Brunswick, N.J.: Rutgers University Press, 1990. This wide-ranging collection of critical articles brings the cultural history of black women's writing to the 1980's. Barbara Smith's article "The Truth That Never Hurts: Black Lesbians in Fiction in the 1980's" discusses the section of *The Women of Brewster Place* entitled "The Two," but other articles also bear indirectly on Naylor's important themes.

Felton, Sharon, and Michelle C. Loris, eds. *The Critical Response to Gloria Naylor*. Westport, Conn.: Greenwood Press, 1997. A collection of essays analyzing four of Naylor's novels—*The Women of Brewster Place*, *Linden Hills*, *Mama Day*, and *Bailey's Café*—from a wide variety of perspectives.

Fowler, Virginia C. *Gloria Naylor: In Search of Sanctuary*. New York: Twayne, 1996. Fowler analyzes Naylor's first four novels; she also explains how Jehovah's Witnesses, of which Naylor was a member until she was twenty-five years old, and Naylor's feminism have influenced her fiction. Includes an interview that Fowler conducted with Naylor, a bibliography, and a chronology of Naylor's life.

Gates, Henry Louis, Jr., and K. Anthony Appiah, eds. *Gloria Naylor: Critical Perspectives Past and Present*. New York: Amistad, 1993. Focuses on Naylor's first four novels, with reviews of each book and essays analyzing her work. Two of the essays examine the role of William Shakespeare and of black sisterhood in Naylor's novels.

Kelley, Margot Anne, ed. *Gloria Naylor's Early Novels*. Gainesville: University Press of Florida, 1999. A collection of essays analyzing Naylor's first four novels, with several essays examining her work from a feminist perspective. Includes bibliographical references and an index.

Montgomery, Maxine Lavon. "Authority, Multivocality, and the New World Order in Gloria Naylor's *Bailey's Café*." *African American Review* 29, no. 1 (Spring, 1995): 27. Montgomery discusses *Bailey's Café* as a woman-centered work that draws on black art forms and biblical allusions. Though she fails to recognize the true identity of Mariam's child (George of *Mama Day*), Montgomery otherwise provides a valid reading of *Bailey's Café*, commenting on the "more mature voice" with which Naylor addresses the concerns of her earlier novels.

_______, ed. *Conversations with Gloria Naylor*. Jackson: University Press of Mississippi, 2004. A compilation of previously conducted interviews and conversations with Naylor, in which Naylor addresses a wide range of topics. Includes Naylor's conversations with writers Toni Morrison and Nikki Giovanni.

Puhr, Kathleen M. "Healers in Gloria Naylor's Fiction." *Twentieth Century Literature* 40, no. 4 (Winter, 1994). Puhr discusses the healing powers of Naylor's female characters, principally Mattie Michael (*The Women of Brewster Place*), Willa Nedeed (*Linden Hills*), and Miranda (*Mama Day*), as well as Naylor's healing places, particularly the café and Eve's garden in *Bailey's Café*. She also discusses Naylor's works in terms of African American ancestry, generational conflicts, and broken dreams.

Stave, Shirley A., ed. *Gloria Naylor: Strategy and Technique, Magic and Myth*. Newark: University of Delaware Press, 2001. A collection of essays focusing on *Mama Day* and *Bailey's Café*. Stave argues that Naylor deserves an elevated position in the American literary canon.

Whitt, Margaret Earley. *Understanding Gloria Naylor*. Columbia: University of South Carolina Press, 1998. A thoughtful examination of Naylor's novels, through *The Men of Brewster Place*, that discusses major themes, symbolism, character development, Naylor's critical reputation, and her literary influences.

Wilson, Charles E., Jr. *Gloria Naylor: A Critical Companion*. Westport, Conn.: Greenwood Press, 2001. An analysis of Naylor's first five novels, with a separate chapter devoted to an examination of each book. The first chapter chronicles the events of Naylor's life, including information obtained in an interview conducted for this book, while another chapter establishes Naylor's place within African American literature.

NGUGI WA THIONG'O

Born: Kamiriithu village, near Limuru, Kenya; January 5, 1938

Also known as: James Ngugi

Principal long fiction

Weep Not, Child, 1964
The River Between, 1965
A Grain of Wheat, 1967
Secret Lives, 1974
Petals of Blood, 1977
Caitaani Mũtharaba-Inĩ, 1980 (*Devil on the Cross*, 1982)
Matigari ma Njiruungi, 1986 (*Matigari*, 1989)
Mũrogi wa Kagogo, 2004 (*Wizard of the Crow*, 2006)

Other literary forms

In addition to his novels, Ngugi wa Thiong'o (ehn-GEW-gee wah tee-ONG-goh) has published short stories, numerous plays, and several works of nonfiction. His plays include *The Black Hermit* (pr. 1962); *The Trial of Dedan Kimathi* (pr. 1974), written with Micere Githae-Mugo; and, with Ngugi wa Mirii, *Ngaahika Ndeenda* (pr. 1977; *I Will Marry When I Want*, 1982) and *Maitu Njugira* (pb. 1982; *Mother, Sing for Me*, 1986). Ngugi has expressed his commitment to his political responsibility as a writer in numerous works of literary, political, and social criticism, including *Homecoming: Essays on African and Caribbean Literature, Culture, and Politics* (1972), *Writers in Politics* (1981; enlarged, revised, and subtitled *A Re-engagement with Issues of Literature and Society* in a 1997 edition), *Detained: A Writer's Prison Diary* (1981), *Decolonising the Mind: The Politics of Language in African Literature* (1986), and *Penpoints, Gunpoints, and Dreams: Toward a Critical Theory of the Arts and the State in Africa* (1998). In the 1980's, he pursued his interest in African-based educational curricula by recasting stories of the Mau Mau resistance, many of which had appeared in his novels, as works for children, written first in his native Kikuyu and later translated into English. A collection of Ngugi's essays and talks written between 1985 and 1990 appeared in 1993 under the title *Moving the Centre: The Struggle for Cultural Freedoms*.

Achievements

With the publication of his first three novels, Ngugi wa Thiong'o quickly established himself as the major East African writer of the anglophone literary movement that began in Africa in the late 1950's and early 1960's. This anglophone literary school, which must be distinguished from the preceding romantic francophone movement called "negritude" because of its different political assumptions and its stress on realism, coincided with the bitter political and at times military struggle and the eventual achievement of independence by most African countries that had been under British colonial rule. Given the political situation, this literary movement was naturally preoccupied with assessing the impact of colonialism and with defining independent and syncretic African cultures. With a handful of other African writers, Ngugi stands out as a literary pioneer in this movement.

Ngugi's systematic examination of the manner in which indigenous cultures were destroyed by colonialism has distinguished him from many of his colleagues, while his depiction of these cultures' attempts to reconstitute themselves has made him unique. His refusal to divorce literature from politics and his acerbic portrayal of corruption in independent Kenya—first in *Petals of Blood* and then in his play *Ngaahika Ndeenda*, which was considered more dangerous by the government because it was performed in an indigenous language—earned him the wrath of political leaders and a year in prison without a trial. Building on his reputation as a fearless critic of African dictatorships, Ngugi produced *Wizard of the Crow*, which takes up where *Petals of Blood* left off—sparing readers nothing by graphically depicting the carnage wrought by these murderous regimes, yet all the while employing his characteristic whimsy and humorous satire to highlight the surreal world the dictators create for their subjects.

Ngugi has also been concerned with the implications entailed in the use of English language by African writers, and he has supplemented his theoretical reflections by switching to Kikuyu as his primary literary language. Ngugi is widely recognized as Africa's foremost revolutionary writer and is one of the world's most read African writers.

Biography

Ngugi wa Thiong'o, who published as James Ngugi until 1970, was born in 1938 near Limuru, a Kikuyu region of Kenya. He received a varied education, alternating between mission schools and an institution that grew out of the independence schools movement, the aim of which was to prepare Kenya's young people for freedom from British rule. The Mau Mau war disrupted Ngugi's education and had a profound impact on his family: His brother Walter fought with the Mau Mau, and his parents were detained as subversives. Ngugi's experiences during the war made a lasting impression on him and served as the basis for his first three novels.

In 1955, Ngugi entered Alliance High School, a missionary institution from which he graduated. His literary career developed rapidly once he became a student at Makerere University College in Kampala, Uganda. There he edited the student literary magazine, *Penpoint*, and wrote *The Black Hermit*, a play celebrating Uganda's independence.

In 1964, Ngugi published his first novel, which won two prizes, one from the 1965 Dakar Festival of Negro Arts and one from the East African Literature Bureau. After working for the *Sunday Nation*, a Nairobi newspaper, he attended graduate school at the University of Leeds in England. He returned to Kenya in 1968 to take up a lectureship in the English department at University College, Nairobi, and in 1969 he resigned that post in protest against government interference with academic freedom and in sympathy with a student strike. That same year, he accepted a teaching position at Northwestern University in Illinois, where he remained until 1971, when he returned to University College in Nairobi.

On December 31, 1977, the police detained Ngugi for his political views, a charge stemming from his involvement with an educational theater project in a Kenyan village. He remained in prison until December 12, 1978. On his release, he went back to teaching and again worked with a theater group, which was banned by Kenyan authorities in 1982. Ngugi, anticipating further restrictions on his artistic freedom, entered self-imposed exile, first in London, then in the United States. He took a teaching job at Yale University. In the following decade, he taught at New York University and traveled back to Nairobi, where he and his wife were attacked by progovernment forces. In 2002, he became director of the International Center for Writing and Translation at the University of California at Irvine.

Although Ngugi wrote little in the 1990's, he continued to speak against and write about the widespread corruption and injustice in Kenya. In particular, he stresses what he calls "the politics of language," insisting that the continued use of English, French, and Portuguese in Africa rather than the native languages separates the people from their culture.

Analysis

Ngugi wa Thiong'o's fiction, like that of many contemporary African novelists, is highly political: It por-

Ngugi wa Thiong'o. (Antony Njuguna/Reuters/Landov)

trays the traumatic transition from colonized culture to an independent African society. His novels illustrate with unmatched clarity the problems created by this period of rapid change. Superior European technology introduced into Africa at the beginning of the twentieth century undercut traditional cultural values, and colonial domination (denunciation of indigenous cultures and religions, appropriation of native lands, forced labor) led to a disintegration of indigenous societies.

The major themes of Ngugi's novels derive from his characters' attempts to overcome the confusion caused by the peripeteia of values and to reintegrate and revitalize their new syncretic culture. Faced with the drastic dissolution of his family in the Mau Mau war from 1952 to 1958, Njoroge, the protagonist of *Weep Not, Child*, tenaciously adheres to his beliefs in education and messianic deliverance in a vain attempt to maintain some cohesion in his life. Waiyaki, the hero of *The River Between*, believing that he is the new messiah, also attempts in vain to reunite the Christian and traditional Kikuyu factions of his village. *A Grain of Wheat* is experimental in form: The novel's meaning is available not through the character and experiences of a single protagonist but through the complex interrelationships of five major and many minor characters. The theme, however, remains the same—the attempt of the members of a Kikuyu village to reintegrate themselves and to reorder their priorities after the devastation of the Mau Mau war. *Petals of Blood*, set in postcolonial Kenya, once more depicts a group of peasants who are trying to fashion a meaningful life for themselves in the context of economic exploitation by the new black leaders of the country.

Ngugi's preoccupation with this theme is best understood in the historical context of the conflict between the Kikuyus and British colonizers that culminated in the Mau Mau war of 1952 and that was provoked by three important factors: the economic and cultural effects of land appropriation, the importance of education for the Kikuyus and consequently the impact of its deprivation, and the messianic fervor that characterized Kikuyu politics at the time. Ngugi focuses on various combinations of these three factors in his novels, and his repeated concern with these issues is largely determined by his traumatic experiences during the war.

When the British settled in Kenya, they expropriated large areas of the best arable land from the Kikuyus (who were then crowded into reserves). The land was given, at little or no cost, to English syndicates, investors, and farmers. Piecemeal appropriation of Kikuyu land was finally systematized by a 1921 court ruling in which all land, even that which had been put aside for "reserves," was declared to be owned by the British government. The natives were thus considered squatters on land they had owned for generations. In exchange for squatting "rights," the Kikuyus had to provide 180 days of free labor per annum. Such manipulation, along with coercive tax laws and punitive raids, put tremendous pressure on the Kikuyus and eventually led to the Mau Mau war. Although independence was achieved in 1962, the war was a particularly bitter experience for the Kikuyus because they were divided—some fought for and some against the British.

While being deprived of their land, the Kikuyus focused their attention on education, only to find themselves once more at odds with the colonial government, which, with the aim of promoting agricultural and vocational training, limited African education to the primary level and prohibited the use of English as the medium of instruction. The Kikuyus, however, preferred liberal, humanistic secondary education because it permitted access to civil service jobs and, more important, because English was the language of technology and power. They reasoned, quite accurately, that mastery of English was crucial for their nationalistic aspirations. The Kikuyus responded by mercilessly taxing themselves in order to build their own schools, only to have them shut down repeatedly by the government. This struggle continued until the outbreak of the Mau Mau war, when all Kikuyu schools were closed for several years.

Knowledge of another element of Kenyan history is also important to an appreciation of Ngugi's fiction. Mugo wa Kibiro, a Kikuyu prophet, predicted that a messianic leader would come to deliver the tribe from colonial bondage. Jomo Kenyatta, the leader of the independence movement and the first president of Kenya, skillfully used this prophecy to coalesce the social and religious sentiments of the Kikuyu around himself during the Mau Mau war. Hence the atmosphere at that time was charged by powerful contradictory feelings: Fear, uncertainty, bitterness, and despair produced by colonial oppression were balanced by fervent feelings of loyalty, sacrifice, and elation resulting from messianic expectations and hopes for independence, freedom, and recovery of the land.

At the age of fifteen, Ngugi was caught up in this historical and emotional drama, and its effects on him were profound. He had experienced extreme poverty and thus clearly sympathized with the economic and political predicament of the peasants. At the age of ten or eleven, he witnessed the forced evacuation of Kikuyu farmers from their land. As they were being moved, they sang about their hopes of reclaiming their property and about their educated children who might attain this goal some day. Ngugi's memory of this scene explains his preoccupation with the war: "They sang of a common loss and hope and I felt their voice rock the earth where I stood literally unable to move." Ngugi's burden was exacerbated by the closing of schools. Young Kikuyus were being exhorted to master Western knowledge and use it as a weapon of liberation, but the political and military crises blocked access to education and therefore to the possibility of leadership. This deprivation was rendered even more painful by the sustained messianic fervor that reemphasized the role of leadership.

This, then, was the nexus of forces that composed the sociopolitical and religious ambience in which Ngugi reached maturity. Because he was so young when he began writing, his early fiction shows an imperfect understanding of his predicament. His first two novels graphically depict his entanglement in the peripeteia of values, whereas his third and fourth novels, written after he had studied Frantz Fanon's psychopolitical analysis of colonialism, show a sudden and clearer understanding of the ambiguities and contradictions of colonial society.

WEEP NOT, CHILD

Set in Kenya in the 1940's and 1950's and ending in the midst of the Mau Mau war, *Weep Not, Child* is Ngugi's most autobiographical novel; Njoroge, its child protagonist, is about the same age as Ngugi would have been at that time. The novel is an anticlimactic, truncated bildungsroman in that it follows the development of a child into adolescence but does not adequately resolve the question of what precisely the hero has learned by the end.

The novel rapidly and cogently focuses on Njoroge's preoccupation with education and messianism. Ngotho, Njoroge's father, is confused and emasculated by his inability to comprehend and resist the appropriation of his land by an English settler named Howlands, so the family begins to disintegrate, reflecting in microcosm the general social fragmentation. The family's burden passes to Njoroge, who is fortunate enough to be receiving a formal education (which annually consumes the wages of two brothers). When Njoroge graduates into secondary school, the entire village contributes to his tuition, and thus the hero is transformed from the "son of Ngotho to the son of the land." He begins to feel that through his education he will become a great leader, and Kenyatta's imprisonment further fuels his grandiose fantasies: He even envisions himself as the new messiah.

Njoroge's self-image, however, remains insubstantial. His love of "education" is abstract: He does not care for particular subjects, nor does his vision encompass specific goals or projects. His messianic delusions are equally empty, and his egocentric world crumbles as soon as he is confronted with the reality of the war. When his father dies as the result of severe torture and castration, when his brothers are either imprisoned or killed, and when he too is tortured in spite of his innocence, his illusions are shattered. Finally, the girl he loves rejects him, and he attempts suicide but is easily dissuaded by his mother. The novel ends with his recognition that he is a coward.

Ngotho's rapid descent from the height of self-importance to the nadir of self-negation is enacted against the backdrop of a society in violent turmoil, which Ngugi depicts in effective detail. The complex social entanglements and contradictions—the different political views and the conflict between generations within Ngotho's family; the enmity between Ngotho and Jacobo, whose loyalty to the British is rewarded with wealth and political power; the mixture of fear, hatred, and respect that Howlands harbors for Ngotho because he has occupied the latter's land; the Englishman's desire to torture and kill Ngotho, which leads to the retaliatory murder of Howlands by Ngotho's son; Howlands's contempt for Jacobo's collaboration; Njoroge's love for Mwihaki, Jacobo's daughter, and his brief friendship with Howlands's son—as well as the descriptions of torture and summary executions by the British and the Mau Mau—create a powerful microcosmic picture of a whole society being ripped apart by economic and political conflict. The novel brilliantly depicts the trauma and the ambiguities of a revolution. Njoroge's actual experience is not derived from active involvement in this upheaval, however; rather, he functions as a passive, reluctant witness. His experience is that of a highly suggestible and solitary adolescent who easily internalizes the hopes, frustrations, and anguish of his society and then soothes his own trauma with self-aggrandizing fantasies.

The violence and trauma to which Njoroge is subject only partially account for the oscillation of his self-image. The rest of the explanation lies in the abrupt change of values that engulfs the hero and the narrator. Njoroge's early subscription to English values includes a naïve belief in biblical messianic prophecies that supplement the Kikuyu myth. As a self-styled messiah, he attempts to soothe the fears of a "weeping child"; thus his attitude toward others exactly parallels the narrator's depiction of Njoroge as the weeping child. This profound sympathy and parallelism between the narrator's and the hero's views underscore the complete absence of irony in Ngugi's portrayal of Njoroge.

The denouement of the novel also confirms this underlying problem. Without any justification, Njoroge assumes all the guilt of the trauma suffered by several families and accuses the girl he loves of betraying him before he tries to commit suicide. He is thus still following the model of Christ, of a messiah who assumed all human guilt, was betrayed, and was then turned into a scapegoat. By allowing his hero to transform his self-image from that of a savior to that of a scapegoat, Ngugi allows him to retain his original egocentricity. This essential continuity in Njoroge's characterization testifies to the powerful influence of Christianity on Ngugi himself. If Njoroge's fantasies are a product of the sociopolitical and religious factors in this specific colonial situation, then the ambiguity in the narrative attitude toward Njoroge can be ascribed to the same forces. In the final analysis, it is Ngugi's inability to define adequately his stand toward these factors that is responsible for the narrative ambiguity. The novel, then, can be seen simultaneously as a portrayal and a product of changing values. The persistence of this confusion led Ngugi to a reworking of the same issues in his next novel.

The River Between

The plot of *The River Between*, set in the late 1920's and 1930's, is centered once more on a combination of education and messianism, while the subplot examines the clash of values through the emotionally and culturally charged controversy over female circumcision. The geographic setting is allegorical: The events take place in the "heart and soul" of Kikuyu land and culture among the communities on two ridges ranged on either side of the river Honia (which means "regeneration" in Kikuyu). Both ridges, Kameno and Makuyu, claim to be the source of Kikuyu culture, but as the novel progresses, Kameno, home of the Kikuyu prophet Mugo wa Kibiro and his descendant Waiyaki, the novel's protagonist, becomes the base for those who want to retain the purity of Kikuyu culture, whereas Makuyu becomes the home of those who have converted to Christianity and have renounced various "evil" aspects of their original tradition. The ensuing conflict thus becomes emblematic of the problems of upheaval experienced by the entire culture. The stylized characterization reflects this antagonism between the desire for cultural purity and the desire to abrogate traditional values.

Among the older generation, which provides the secondary characters, the opposition is embodied in Chege and Joshua. Chege, Waiyaki's father, a minor prophet embittered by the people's disregard for his claims, is realistically aware of the specific cultural and technological superiority of European society and thus, in spite of inherent dangers, commands his son to attend the missionary school and master Western knowledge without absorbing its vices. He is simultaneously concerned with preserving Kikuyu purity and with ensuring its survival through the absorption of clearly efficacious aspects of Western culture. On the other hand, Joshua, a zealous convert who has become a self-righteous, puritanical minister, renounces Kikuyu culture as dirty, heathen, and evil. He has entirely dedicated himself to his own and other people's salvation through Christianity. Ngugi balances these static and absolute oppositions with the dynamic and relativistic attitudes of Waiyaki and Joshua's two daughters, Muthoni and Nyambura, who attempt in their different ways to synthesize the two cultures.

The subplot depicts Muthoni's disastrous attempt to combine what she considers to be the best aspects of both cultures. Even though her parents will not permit her to undergo circumcision because the church has forbidden this rite of purification and rebirth in Kikuyu culture, Muthoni decides that she must be circumcised. By becoming a circumcised Christian she hopes to combine the two cultures within herself. Unfortunately, an infection contracted during the ceremony kills Muthoni. In addition to radicalizing the two factions, her apostasy and death reveal the more profound problems of cultural transition. The fact that her notion of womanhood is predicated on circumcision shows that peripeteia involves not only physical and social changes but also ontological ones; specific modifications of a culture become meaningless unless the entire cultural gestalt is altered to accommodate particular infusions. Waiyaki sees Muthoni as a sacrifice to the clash of cultures, and when he falls in love with her uncircumcised sister, Nyambura, the subplot is deftly woven into the main plot—Waiyaki's attempt to become a messiah and an educator.

Unlike *Weep Not, Child*, where the messianic possibility is entirely confined to Njoroge's fantasies, *The River Between* presents it as an actual, unambiguous fact: While Waiyaki is still a child, his "mission" to master Western knowledge and unite the Kikuyus is revealed to him. When, along with many other students, he resigns from the Christian mission school, he gets his chance to fulfill his destiny. With the help of the people and his colleagues he establishes an independent Kikuyu school that flourishes and thus earns him the respect befitting a messiah; by successfully mediating between the English and Kikuyu cultures and by making the positive aspects of the former available to the latter, he seems to have fulfilled the prophecy. His success, however, is short-lived. Jealousy and political ambition spur a faction from Kemano to accuse him of treason and spiritual contamination because he loves an uncircumcised woman. Since he is unwilling to renounce Nyambura, Waiyaki is forced to relinquish his leadership, and his personal fate remains ominously ambiguous at the end of the novel.

The River Between is a better bildungsroman than Ngugi's first novel because Waiyaki does realize that he is a product of shifting values and that cultural synthesis is an ambiguous, complex, and even dangerous undertaking. This education of the hero is not sufficient, however, to save the novel from the confusion caused by a double narrative intention. Overtly, the narrator clearly intends to present Waiyaki as a man constantly concerned with communal welfare, yet the rhetoric of Waiyaki's contemplation demonstrates that he is entirely engrossed in his own messianic potentiality: All his dealings with people always revert to questions about his status and leadership. Furthermore, the divine source of his authority, by providing him with *transcendent* knowledge, severs him from the Kikuyu to the extent that his vision of the future, and actions based on that vision, need not rely on mundane familiarity with the people's social and political desires.

The major problem of the novel is that Ngugi seems unable to decide whether to treat his protagonist as a real messiah or to portray him as a character whose prophetic calling is a self-delusion: Waiyaki is simultaneously subjected to divine surety and human fallibility. At the end of the novel, Ngugi seems to sympathize with two incompatible feelings—with Waiyaki's decision to choose a personal relationship over communal obligation, a private cultural synthesis over a larger social synthesis, and with the people's decision to protect their culture by sacrificing a promising individual. The persistent ambiguity about Waiyaki and the final recourse to scapegoating, which resembles so closely the pattern of grandiose self-delusion and vindication through persecution in *Weep Not, Child*, reveal once more that *The River Between* is a product of subjective anxiety. Waiyaki's insight into the anxiety caused by the peripeteia of values is applicable to the novel as a whole. According to him, this anxiety can cause a person to cling fanatically to whatever promises security. For Waiyaki and Ngugi, messianism provides that security. If one considers Ngugi's predicament at the age of fifteen, when he internalized the social preoccupation with education, leadership, and messianism, one can see that the ambiguity and ambivalence of *The River Between* are a literary transformation of the author's own traumatic experience.

A Grain of Wheat

Before writing his next novel, *A Grain of Wheat*, Ngugi studied Frantz Fanon's *The Wretched of the Earth* (1961), an experience that unmistakably altered his understanding of the psychological and cultural changes that take place in the process of anticolonial revolutions. The view that education and messianism are panaceas is entirely displaced by a clear and deep comprehension of the way out of the psychological bind produced by colonial subjugation. In *A Grain of Wheat*, Ngugi is still concerned with the reintegration of Kikuyu society, but his method has changed drastically. Instead of focusing on a single protagonist, Ngugi uses five major characters—Mugo, Karanja, Kihika, Gikonyo, and Mumbi—and a host of minor ones to contrast different kinds of personal isolation, love, and sympathy for others, and then he orchestrates a complex pattern wherein some characters move from isolation to community, some move in the opposite direction, and still others remain relatively static. By contrasting and interweaving these movements, Ngugi creates a polyphonic novel in which the experience of social regeneration and communal cohesiveness lies not in the awareness of any single character but in the interactions between various individuals and in the reader's experience of these interactions.

The novel's plot concerns an intriguing search for the traitor who betrayed Kihika, a leader of the Mau Mau guerrillas. The war is over, and, just prior to independence day, Kihika's comrades emerge from the forests in order to seek the traitor. The search, however, is really a vehicle for investigating various characters' motives and actions during the war that has destroyed the village of Thabai. The actual time encompassed by the novel is only six days, but through retrospection the reader is allowed to experience the whole Mau Mau revolution and even the prerevolutionary childhood of the protagonists as well as the mythic past of the Kikuyus. The multiplicity of viewpoints through which the reader is led to understand the characters conveys admirably Ngugi's notion that an organic community can be apprehended only through its historical and interpersonal interactions.

Ngugi's investigation of patterns of isolation and communality is focused on four men and one woman. Two of the men, Mugo and Karanja, are motivated by an almost pathological desire for isolation, and the other two, Kihika and Gikonyo, are deeply dependent on their different views of communality. Mugo, deprived of human warmth since childhood, attempts in vain to avoid all involvement. His isolation is repeatedly shattered, first by Kihika, who is seeking shelter from the colonial soldiers and whom Mugo betrays, and then by the whole village of Thabai, which, having mistaken Mugo for a supporter of Kihika and a staunch patriot, ironically invites him to become the village chief on independence day.

While Mugo gradually journeys from isolation to social integration, Karanja moves in the opposite direction. In order to remain with Mumbi, who had earlier rejected him for Gikonyo, Karanja joins the colonial police when Gikonyo is sent to a concentration camp. His collaboration with the British naturally earns him the enmity of the entire village, which expels him on independence day. While Karanja betrays the community as an abstract entity in order to remain with a specific woman, Kihika abandons his pregnant lover in order to become a guerrilla fighter and plays an important part in winning the freedom of his society. In contrast to Kihika, Gikonyo has always been dependent on concrete relationships with his mother and Mumbi. His personality and the very meaning of existence crumble when he is forcibly isolated from them. He confesses his involvement with the Mau Mau so that he can return to his village, only to find when he arrives that Mumbi has given birth to Karanja's child.

Ngugi explores these labyrinthine relationships with great skill. The retrospections, juxtapositions, and multiple interpretations of events, and the gradual, interrupted revelation of the truth represent in a concrete and poignant manner the actual reintegration of a community that has been destroyed. Ngugi's main objective, admirably realized, is to show that strength in one character can be a weakness in another and that what is constructive and desirable at one stage in a community's history is harmful at another—that all forms of fortitude and lapses are necessary for social cohesion. Even Mugo's betrayal performs a vital function in the end. His confession of the betrayal fits into the pattern of complementary wills that is essential for the cohesion of a community. Thus, where Kihika's callousness toward individuals may be undesirable in itself, its reverse, his concern for abstract humanity, proves invaluable for the freedom of his country. Where Kihika's self-sacrifice, in spite of its eventual usefulness, causes a great deal of pain to the community (because of his assassination of a British district officer, Thabai is burnt to the ground), Mugo's self-sacrifice, through his confession, is ultimately soothing. It comes to symbolize the depth of misunderstanding and the renewal of honest and open communication.

In a different manner, Kihika and Gikonyo form a complementary unit that is equally vital for the society. Kihika's disregard for the individual and concern for people in general are balanced by Gikonyo's lack of concern for an abstract conception of community, his betrayal of the Mau Mau covenant, and his powerful desire for concrete individual relations with Mumbi and his mother. Whereas Kihika's attitude is necessary for society's struggle to free itself, Gikonyo's attitude is necessary for its survival. Similarly, even Karanja's defection can be seen as a complementary necessity because he is responsible for keeping Mumbi alive while the rest of the men are either guerrillas hiding in the forests or prisoners in the camps. People are thus tied to one another in ways that they themselves fail to understand. By focusing on these interconnections, Ngugi demonstrates that relationships between individuals are more important than individual character.

The bulk of *A Grain of Wheat* represents the reintegration of Thabai through keen and accurate realism, but in order to emphasize that he is depicting the entire Kikuyu culture, Ngugi resorts to symbolism at the end of the novel. Gikonyo and Mumbi clearly symbolize the mythic ancestors of their society, Kikuyu and Mumbi. Gikonyo feels that his "reunion with Mumbi would see the rebirth of a new Kenya." In light of this symbolism, Karanja's protection of Mumbi and Mugo's confession, which is responsible for the reunion of Gikonyo and Mumbi, become significant contributions to their society. Finally, the iconography—a father, a pregnant mother, a child, a field ready for harvest, and a stool that Gikonyo intends to carve and present to Mumbi as a gift of reconciliation—implies the regeneration of community that is so central to all Ngugi's fiction. The formal structure of *A Grain of Wheat*, a perfect emblem of an actual viable society, and Ngugi's definition of community make this a unique novel in African fiction.

Petals of Blood

Toward the end of *A Grain of Wheat* there are signs that after political "independence" has been won, the struggle between British colonizers and Africans that has dominated the country and the novel will be displaced gradually by a conflict between the native political-economic elite and the peasants, who will be disinherited once again. *Petals of Blood*, set in independent Kenya in the mid-1970's, examines in depth the problem that Ngugi's previous novel has accurately predicted. In *Petals of Blood*, Kenya is drastically, perhaps too schematically, divided between the rich capitalists, portrayed as two-dimensional, greedy, conniving predators, and their peasant victims, depicted as complex individuals who become prey to a modern world they cannot control. The problem with this dichotomy is that the opposition between the poor and the rich lacks any dramatic tension, because the latter are shallow characters minimally and symbolically represented through their expensive automobiles, lavish parties, and deceptive contracts. Thus, even though Ngugi's portrayal of the economic and political situation in Kenya is broadly accurate, it is not entirely convincing.

The center of *Petals of Blood* is a powerful, fecund woman, Wanja, a prostitute who is many things to the different men around her like petals of blood. If the novel is read as an allegory, she can be seen as the protean substance of Kenya, which entices the lechery of the capitalists and sustains and inspires the resistance of the peasants. Kimeria, one of the three successful entrepreneurs in the novel, seduces Wanja while she is a teenager and then abandons her only to lust after her again when she has become the successful madam of a house of prostitution. Munira, an introspective, religious schoolteacher, is initially liberated from his repressions through her, but, after his guilt has overwhelmed him, he sees her as an incarnation of Satan. Karega, a young, nascent revolutionary, has an idyllic affair with her and finds in her the inspiration for his rebellion. Finally, Abdulla, a crippled Mau Mau warrior, treats her as a comrade and eventually fathers the child that she has desired throughout the novel.

The plot of *Petals of Blood* is similar to a Charles Dickens plot in its labyrinthine relationships and its reliance on coincidence. Ostensibly, the novel is a detective story; it begins with the arrest of three major characters, Munira, Abdulla, and Karega, who are under suspicion for the murder of three wealthy directors of the Theng-eta Breweries, Kimeria, Chui, and Muzigo. After being ignored for the vast bulk of the novel, the mystery is suddenly solved at the end by Munira's admission that he set fire to Wanja's brothel, in which the directors were trapped. The relations between characters are revealed in an equally sudden and summary fashion, with the result that the plot becomes a mere vehicle for the political substance of the novel—a detailed examination of the manner in which the rightful inheritance of the peasants and idealists has been stolen from them.

Once more this is accomplished through a series of retrospective scenes that reveal the past in the light of the present struggle. The peasants undertake an epic journey to Nairobi, the capital city, in order to confront their parliamentary representative, who has in fact ignored and even tried to plunder his constituency. The climax of this spatial journey—that is, the confrontation in the city—allows the peasants to understand the economic opposition between them and the new African elite, but through the various personal and communal stories told by the peasants to one another during their journey, they also realize that they are a part of a temporal "journey"—that they are the current embodiment of a long historical tradition. As Karega says, "The history that he had tried to teach as romantic adventures, the essence of black struggle apprehended in the imagination at the level of mere possibilities, had tonight acquired immediate flesh and blood."

Petals of Blood is at its best when it explores the lives and sensibilities of these people. Through Munira and Karega, Ngugi shows the radically different effects of similar causes. Both are expelled from Siriana high school at different times (they are a generation apart) for leading student strikes. Whereas the resultant shock and confusion experienced by Munira turns into depression and later into a pathological preoccupation with spiritual purity, the initial confusion felt by Karega is gradually displaced by an increasingly clear understanding of his place in the sociopolitical system of the country and eventually turns into a radical opposition to the new elite. Thus Munira treats people such as Wanja or Abdulla as mere objects of his lust or indifference, whereas Karega sees them as subjects whose personal histories make him aware of his own predicament and potential. The novel makes a dramatic distinction between individuals lost in their own subjectivity and those who through circumstances, personal courage, and fidelity are able to understand themselves in terms of an objectively determined social and political reality.

Unfortunately, Ngugi's sensitive representation of the inner lives of his politically oppressed characters is not matched by an equally sensitive management of the novel's structure. The caricature of the capitalists and the plot's reliance on brief, mechanical coincidences deprive the novel of a demonstrated and felt struggle between the exploiters and the exploited. Instead of using viable fictive embodiments of oppressive forces, Ngugi relies heavily on discursive delineation of capitalist exploitation. At times, the novel sounds like a leftist pamphlet. In contrast to *A Grain of Wheat*, where Ngugi's political concerns are perfectly interlocked with a well-wrought and ingenious structure, *Petals of Blood* is overwhelmed by the writer's sensitive and moving depiction of the peasants' lives and by his justified anger over callous exploitation and broken promises.

Devil on the Cross

Devil on the Cross is another passionate denunciation of postcolonial abuses. Written on stolen bits of toilet paper during Ngugi's year in prison, the novel features, again, several protagonists—mostly peasants—who are grievously wronged by the corrupt politicians and bureaucrats of modern Kenya. With this novel and the nonfiction works that followed, Ngugi solidified his commitment to a revolutionary African literature—outraged, combative, and uncompromising.

Matigari

In *Matigari* Ngugi continues to record Kenya's postcolonial struggle, but in this novel he moves away from realism and adopts a fluidity of time and space that is mythological in tone. At the outset, he warns the "Reader/Listener" that the narrative is purely imaginary in its action, characters, and setting. It follows the adventures of the mythical Matigari, who embodies the virtues, values, and purity of the betrayed and abused people he sets out to rouse from their apathy. Whether Ngugi succeeds in mythologizing remains questionable, for the landscape, characters, circumstances, and historical events are obviously Kenyan. In fact, when the 1986 edition appeared in the original Kikuyu language, so many Kenyans were talking about Matigari that officials ordered his arrest. When they discovered that the suspected rabble-rouser was fictional, they banned the book.

Matigari denounces contemporary Kenya, where a privileged few, in connection with representatives of overseas interests, rule and exploit the masses, thereby reversing the hard-fought struggle for independence. Matigari ma Njiruungi, whose name means "he who survived the bullets," emerges from the forest, sets his weapons aside, and dons the belt of peace to move through the countryside to rediscover his true family—a free Kenyan people who live in a just society and who share its wealth. Along the way he meets the downtrodden and dispossessed, and he faces all the ills the contaminated society has produced: homeless children, dissidents harassed and murdered by the police, young women forced into prostitution, and much more. In opposition to the suffering masses stand the black politicians and their cronies, who have grown rich through collaboration with international business interests.

The novel also contains variations on familiar themes, such as the role of Christianity in oppression and the failure of Western education. At the same time, Ngugi subverts the Christian myth by turning Matigari into a modern Jesus who moves among the people and faces rejection. The biblical allusions become especially evident in the prison scenes. For example, Matigari's fellow detainees resemble Jesus' disciples; one even betrays Matigari. The novel also contains the Swiftian elements of satire that characterize *Devil on the Cross*. *Matigari* finally emerges as a powerful account of the postcolonial state, however—an indictment not only against the corruption in Kenya but also against the conditions that prevail in numerous African nations.

WIZARD OF THE CROW

Wizard of the Crow, which is set in a fictional East African country named the Free Republic of Aburiria, artfully and satirically delineates the inner workings of that most pernicious, toxic, and notorious of twentieth and twenty-first century African institutions, the strong-arm dictatorship. Ngugi sees the institution as both vulnerable and thriving, buoyed as it is by credible threats of torture and death aimed at those who oppose it as well as by the power-seeking Western world's collusion with it. In Aburiria, the mad leader known simply as the Ruler is eventually deposed, only to give way to another thug with the usual dictatorial traits of incompetence, brutality, and toxicity. At novel's end, however, Ngugi does supply readers with some trace of hope for the future of Aburiria, albeit a highly ambiguous one, the hope being that freedom will come to those nations beset by one-person rule—but down the road a bit.

This lengthy political novel features the corrupt world of an archetypal power-hungry gangster, the self-proclaimed First Ruler of the Free Republic of Aburiria, a venomous though intelligent paranoid who surrounds himself with such ridiculous and yet dangerous toadies as Wonderful Tumbo, minister of police; Machokali, minister for foreign affairs; Julius Caesar Big Ben Mambo, minister of information; Silver Sikiokuu, governor of the Central Bank; and Titus Tajirika, minister of defense. These bumbling but still often terrifying agents will sell out anyone—including the Ruler himself—for personal gain. Opposing their self-serving machinations are two unlikely proponents of democracy and change: Kamiti, an unemployed university business major and graduate, and Kamiti's lover and fellow conspirator, the beautiful and accomplished Nyawira, a former bar hostess.

Kamiti rises to become the legendary Aburirian man of powerful magic, "Wizard of the Crow," and Nyawira becomes the Wizard's consort, the so-called Limping Witch. Together, using their powerful wit and imagination, the Wizard and the Witch find clever "magical" ways to trick the government officials who oppose them and, in the process, undermine the officials' lucrative positions. Soon the two lovers find themselves the stuff of Aburirian folk legend—ones who can take on the establishment and never be caught. In addition to Kamiti and Nyawira, the author includes in his cast two characters, the saintly Maritha and Mariko, who labor against what they see as the works of the devil in their country. In *Wizard of the Crow*, Ngugi provides an entertaining, although at times somewhat long-winded, commentary on one of the chief reasons sub-Saharan African nations are not as well-off as they should be, given their natural resources and their lively and potentially resourceful populations.

Abdul R. JanMohamed; Robert L. Ross
Updated by John D. Raymer

Other major works

SHORT FICTION: *Secret Lives, and Other Stories*, 1975.

PLAYS: *The Black Hermit*, pr. 1962; *This Time Tomorrow: Three Plays*, 1970 (includes *The Rebels*, *The Wound in My Heart*, and *This Time Tomorrow*); *The Trial of Dedan Kimathi*, pr. 1974 (with Micere Githae-Mugo); *Ngaahika Ndeenda*, pr. 1977 (with Ngugi wa Mirii; *I Will Marry When I Want*, 1982); *Maitu Njugira*, pb. 1982 (with Ngugi wa Mirii; *Mother, Sing for Me*, 1986).

NONFICTION: *Homecoming: Essays on African and Caribbean Literature, Culture, and Politics*, 1972; *Detained: A Writer's Prison Diary*, 1981; *Writers in Politics*, 1981 (revised 1997); *Barrel of a Pen: Resistance to Repression in Neo-colonial Kenya*, 1983; *Decolonising the Mind: The Politics of Language in African Literature*, 1986; *Writing Against Neocolonialism*, 1986; *Moving the Centre: The Struggle for Cultural Freedoms*, 1993; *Penpoints, Gunpoints, and Dreams: Toward a Critical Theory of the Arts and the State in Africa*, 1998.

MISCELLANEOUS: *The World of Ngugi wa Thiong'o*, 1995 (Charles Cantalupo, editor).

Bibliography

Booker, M. Keith. "Ngugi wa Thiong'o: *Devil on the Cross*." In *The African Novel in English: An Introduction*. Portsmouth, N.H.: Heinemann, 1998. Discussion of *Devil on the Cross* addresses many of Ngugi's preoccupations, including the brutality of class distinctions, his connections with and problems concerning the Western literary tradition, Kenya's resistance to British economic and political forces, and the future of Africa itself.

Cantalupo, Charles, ed. *Ngugi wa Thiong'o: Texts and Contexts*. Edinburgh: Edinburgh University Press, 1997. Selection of contributions from a major conference held in 1994 to honor and examine Ngugi's work. Focuses primarily on the prose works, examining issues such as Ngugi's status as an exile and his use of the Kikuyu language.

Gikandi, Simon. *Ngugi wa Thiong'o*. New York: Cambridge University Press, 2001. Examines each of Ngugi's works in the context of its historical background and in the light of Ngugi's life. Asserts that Ngugi's novels are of primary importance to Ngugi himself, and that the author's drama and criticism are meant to supplement the novels.

Lovesey, Oliver. *Ngugi wa Thiong'o*. New York: Twayne, 2000. Provides a good introduction to Ngugi's life and work for the general reader. Presents five chapters of criticism and analysis as well as a chronology of the author's life and an annotated bibliography.

Nazareth, Peter, ed. *Critical Essays on Ngugi wa Thiong'o*. New York: Twayne, 2000. Collection of essays offers a wide range of discussion of Ngugi's work. Topics addressed include themes, language use, and use of the oral tradition in Ngugi's novels.

Parker, Michael, and Roger Starkey, eds. *Postcolonial Literatures: Achebe, Ngugi, Desai, Walcott*. New York: St. Martin's Press, 1995. Presents thoughtful examination of the works of Ngugi, Chinua Achebe, Anita Desai, and Derek Walcott. Includes bibliographical references and index.

Sewlall, Harry. "Writing from the Periphery: The Case of Ngugi and Conrad." *English in Africa* 30 (May, 2003): 55-69. Offers a thoughtful appraisal of Ngugi's strong debt to and ties with English novelist Joseph Conrad's anti-imperial vision of Africa. Also addresses the difficulties faced by both Ngugi and Conrad in writing in languages other than those to which they were born.

Sicherman, Carol. *Ngugi wa Thiong'o: A Bibliography of Primary and Secondary Sources, 1957-1987*. London: Hans Zell, 1989. A treasure for the scholar, with citations of Ngugi's works in the original languages, manuscripts and other unpublished material, translations, secondary sources, undated material, nonprint media, and indexes of authors, editors, translators, titles, interviews, and subjects. Includes a brief introduction and preface.

Williams, Patrick. *Ngugi wa Thiong'o*. Manchester, England: Manchester University Press, 2000. Presents analysis and interpretation of all of Ngugi's writings through *Penpoints, Gunpoints, and Dreams*.

ANAÏS NIN

Born: Paris, France; February 21, 1903
Died: Los Angeles, California; January 14, 1977
Also known as: Angela Anaïs Juana Antolina Rosa Edelmira Nin y Culmell

Principal long fiction

House of Incest, 1936
Winter of Artifice, 1939
This Hunger, 1945
Winter of Artifice: Three Novelettes, 1945 (contains *Winter of Artifice*, "Stella," and "The Voice")
Ladders to Fire, 1946
Children of the Albatross, 1947
The Four-Chambered Heart, 1950
A Spy in the House of Love, 1954
Solar Barque, 1958
Cities of the Interior: A Continuous Novel, 1959 (contains *Ladders to Fire*, *Children of the Albatross*, *The Four-Chambered Heart*, *A Spy in the House of Love*, and *Solar Barque*)
Seduction of the Minotaur, 1961
Collages, 1964

Other literary forms

Anaïs Nin (nihn) published numerous volumes of perceptive literary criticism. Her highly acclaimed first book of nonfiction, *D. H. Lawrence: An Unprofessional Study*, appeared in 1932. In 1968, near the end of her career, she wrote *The Novel of the Future*, partly as an attempt to explain the literary philosophy that inspired her innovative fiction. In 1976, she published a collection of her essays, *In Favor of the Sensitive Man, and Other Essays*. During the last decade of her life, Nin was extremely active as a public speaker. *A Woman Speaks: The Lectures, Seminars, and Interviews of Anaïs Nin*, edited by Evelyn J. Hinz, was published in 1975.

Nin's published short stories, like her criticism, span her career. The most distinguished collection is *Under a Glass Bell, and Other Stories* (1944). Her apprentice writing is available in another collection, *Waste of Timelessness, and Other Early Stories* (1977), while two volumes of erotica were published after Nin's death: *Delta of Venus: Erotica* (1977) and *Little Birds: Erotica* (1979).

In addition to her works of fiction and criticism, Nin's extensive diary was published. Edited from a vast manuscript, this autobiographical work appeared in two series. The first series, *The Diary of Anaïs Nin*, comprises seven volumes, with the first volume appearing in 1966. The second series, *The Early Diaries of Anaïs Nin*, contains four volumes and was published between 1978 and 1985.

Achievements

Anaïs Nin's achievement in literature is of two distinct kinds: artistic and sociological. Strongly influenced by Arthur Rimbaud, Marcel Proust, and D. H. Lawrence, Nin conceived of and developed a uniquely personal approach to style and structure that places her within the modernist tradition as it evolved in the French literature of the early decades of the twentieth century. Nin persisted in articulating, refining, and extending an avowedly "feminine" ideal of the novel; this resulted in lyrical novels in which the imagistic manner of the poet is fused with the psychological penetration of the novelist. In her treatment of character, time, and space, Nin belongs with such writers as Virginia Woolf, Djuna Barnes, and Anna Kavan.

Nin's sociological importance is related to her intention to create a specifically "feminine" novel in which the emphasis is on the evocation of feeling, and to portray as deeply and as honestly as possible an authentically female emotional experience. In this respect, her achievement may be compared with that of Woolf, Dorothy Richardson, Marguerite Duras, and a number of French writers, including Annie LeClerc, Hélène Cixous, Monique Wittig, and Julia Kristeva.

The audience for Nin's novels is smaller than for either her diary or her collections of erotica. As the diary increased Nin's audience, it also brought her fiction to the attention of well-qualified critics and scholars, many of whom have interpreted it in ways that make it more accessible to a general readership accustomed to the conventions of realism. Considering the climate of growing respect for and interest in Nin's novels, it seems that her reputation as a literary artist is now securely established.

Biography

Anaïs Nin was born in Paris on February 21, 1903, the oldest child of musicians Joaquin Nin and Rosa Culmell-Nin. Her parents' marriage was turbulent, and in 1913, Joaquin Nin deserted his family at Archachon, France. The following year, Rosa Culmell-Nin transported her daughter and two sons, Thorvald and Joaquin, to the United States. For some years, they lived in New York City and in Queens, actively participating in the lively Cuban community there, many of whose members were musicians. Nin has recorded this period of her life in *Linotte*. What stands out most poignantly is her inconsolable grief at the loss of her father and her intense worship of her mother. At this time, Nin's aspiration to become an artist of one sort or another strongly manifested itself, and her account of her adolescence is a rich study of the formative years of an artist.

In 1918, Nin left school to manage the household for her mother, who worked for Lord and Taylor as a special buyer for the Cuban clientele, and in 1923, Nin married Hugh P. Guiler (known as an engraver and filmmaker under the name of Ian Hugo). As a young married woman, Nin lived in France. Marriage caused her to experience intense conflicts, which she has described and analyzed in her diary. During those years, as in adolescence, Nin continued to write, and in 1932, she published her first book, *D. H. Lawrence*. This work brought about the explosive friendship with June and Henry Miller that she describes in the first published diary. Nin and Miller maintained a relationship until Nin's death.

In Paris during the 1930's, Nin embarked upon a lifelong devotion to psychotherapy. Her therapeutic relationship with the renowned Viennese psychoanalyst Otto Rank is recounted in the first volume of *The Diary of Anaïs Nin*. An independent, original, and forceful thinker whose special area of interest was the artist, Rank was of great assistance to Nin in the fulfillment of her artistic aspirations. His influence on her was so persuasive that for a time she actually considered making a living as a lay psychoanalyst. For a few months in 1934, she lived in New York and assisted Rank with his practice. In 1935, however, she resumed her literary work and returned to France to rejoin her husband, but with the outbreak of World War II, she again returned to the United States. This move in 1939 was to become permanent. It was not easy for Nin to give up her "romantic life" in Paris, as she called it, and her difficulty understanding Americans' disdain for the arts is a recurrent theme of her diary in the 1940's and 1950's.

Throughout her life, Nin maintained many friendships with writers and other artists. Among her friends and acquaintances were Lawrence Durrell, Robert Duncan, James Merrill, and Kenneth Patchen; performers Canada Lee, Josephine Premice, and Louise Rainer; Caresse Crosby, proprietor of the Black Sun Press; composer Edgard Varèse and his wife, translator Louise Varèse; collage artist Janko Varda; and the owner of the influential Gotham Book Mart, Frances Steloff. Even though Nin had widespread contacts among writers and artists in New York City and on the West Coast, she experienced continual frustration in the publishing world. On the whole, editors and critics were either hostile to her work or simply ignored it. The breakthrough of this period was the acceptance by Alan Swallow, founder of the famed Swallow Press, then located in Denver, Colorado, of the five works that constitute *Cities of the Interior: A Continuous Novel*. For many years, Nin was an underground literary figure with a small but enthusiastic following.

In 1966, Nin's status changed suddenly; she had already published all her fiction; the last book, *Collages*, appeared in 1964. When Harcourt Brace and World, with the Swallow Press, brought out the first volume of *The Diary of Anaïs Nin*, Nin quickly became a public figure. Because the content of the work expressed the feelings of many women who were experiencing deep evolutionary changes in their own lives, Nin involuntarily became a spokesperson for the women's movement. She achieved the "dialogue with the world" for which she had longed since childhood.

During the remaining years of Nin's life, individual volumes of her diary continued to appear, and Nin, although viewed as controversial by leaders of the women's movement, received considerable public acclaim. Traveling throughout the United States, she gave hundreds of talks at colleges and universities and undertook trips to various countries, including Sweden and Bali. In 1970, she was awarded the French Prix Sévigné, and in 1974, she was elected to the National Institute of Arts and Letters. Nin's books have been translated into all the major Western languages as well as Serbo-Croatian and Japanese.

Analysis

It was natural that Anaïs Nin should grow up desiring to be an artist. Her father was a friend of Gabriele D'Annunzio. Before Nin's parents separated, their household was filled with the aura of the fin de siècle Symbolist movement. The Symbolists' ideas about art had a decisive and lasting influence on Nin, although she greatly transformed the influences she absorbed in the process of adapting them to the expressive needs of her own temperament.

Anaïs Nin.

Like the Symbolists, Nin believed that phenomena possess hidden meanings, significances that escape most people. The artist's task is to penetrate surfaces to reveal the truths they conceal. "The symbol," she wrote, "is an acknowledgement of the emotional and spiritual content of every act and every object around us." Equipped with heightened perception and expressive talent, the artist can interpret the vast confusing world of phenomena, revealing essences in a world of masks and misleading surfaces. Nin described a story as "a quest for meaning."

With the Symbolists, too, and with the later Surrealists, Nin shared a positive attitude toward dream and fantasy. Her books are poetic defenses of her belief in the unconscious as a source of the visions and imaginary experiences that complement verifiable reality, compensating for its limitations and endowing it with the richness of mental play that "reality" is not capable of providing. Nin stressed the positive aspects of fantasy in order to balance what she perceived as American society's mistrust, fear, and even condemnation of any sort of activity that is not directly productive in a materialistic way.

Nin's literary aspiration was formidable; she wanted to express passionately and powerfully that of which others were not aware, or if they were, could not express because they did not possess a creative medium. Throughout her life, Nin was searching for

> another kind of language, the inspirational, which is one that penetrates our unconscious directly and doesn't need to be analyzed or interpreted in a cerebral way. It penetrates us in the way that music does, through the senses.

That is why Nin, like so many other twentieth century writers, borrowed as widely as possible from the nonverbal arts. "My only structure," she wrote,

> is based on three forms of art—painting, dancing, music—because they correspond to the senses I find atrophied in literature today.

Inspired by many artists, including Claude Debussy, Paul Klee, her friend Janko Varda, Richard Lippold, Jean Tinguely, and Edgard Varèse, Nin looked not so much to poets (although Rimbaud influenced her style as well as her ideas) as to those novelists who were masters of a lyrical style: Lawrence, Jean Giraudoux, Pierre Jean Jouve, Barnes, and, above all, Proust. Nin's approach to the novel was that of a poet with a heightened and highly developed sense of language. Oliver Evans, who wrote the first book-length study of her work, called Nin "one of the best imagists writing in this country today." The image was her indispensable medium of expression; free association, which she learned to trust as a patient in psychotherapy, became the process through which she allowed literary structures to emerge. Always, Nin's subject was the self in its evolution, especially the self in relationships with others; her perspective was always psychological (she called psychology her "philosophy" and psychoanalysis her "school"), although her books do not demonstrate any particular school of psychoanalytical thought.

Dispensing with conventional plots and with the framework of linear chronology, Nin portrays her characters in a series of "shots" that derive their power from the carefully selected detail of their imagery. Her language, never purely decorative, is metaphorical in a truly organic sense. It is the language of lyrical poetry; the essence is compressed into a few words or phrases. Nin does not describe; rather, she interprets, and in the act of interpretation, she re-creates her subjects. To know Nin's characters, the reader, too, must interpret their action and their gestures and look beneath the surfaces.

Free association creates its own unique structures. Nin's writing is filled with patterns that are natural and spontaneous, having emerged from the associative flow of images. The form of her books is organic. Repetitions, inversions, and superimpositions are artfully arranged into significant patterns. Increasingly in Nin's later prose, readers will discover improvisatory flights in which images are treated as are themes in jazz. Fluency, fluidity, a sense of motion as well as continuity are what Nin sought in her fiction, an orchestration of a great many elements into a composition that moves through time horizontally and vertically at the same instant, an orchestration that expresses emotion with sensuousness and with emotional power that are impossible, she believed, to achieve in conventional realistic fiction.

House of Incest

House of Incest is not, technically speaking, a novel, but it is pertinent as being the source, as Nin herself said, of all her later fiction. *House of Incest* is the earliest and most extreme example of her "symphonic writing." It also introduces the essential questions of her lifelong exploration of the problem of reconciling human love with the needs of ever-evolving, mobile people, always in the process of transformation, growing through the process of change.

A prose poem, *House of Incest* was envisioned by Nin as a woman's version of Rimbaud's famed confession, *Une Saison en enfer* (1873, *A Season in Hell*, 1932). She wrote the book between 1932 and 1936, when she was intensely involved with psychotherapy, and it is composed entirely of dreams that have been cut, altered, polished, and artfully arranged to express an agonizing journey into the psyche of the nameless first-person narrator. Her suffering is caused by the sundering of feeling from sensuality, of emotion from sexuality, of body from soul. *House of Incest* is filled with images of fragmentation and mutilation.

Like *A Season in Hell*, Nin's prose poem is a confession. The narrator yearns to express her pain and to confess that even when she imagines that she loves another, it is only a projection of herself. In the other, then, she loves only herself. The "house" of the title refers to the self, perhaps specifically to the body; "incest" suggests the sterility of feeling imprisoned inside this self, unable to transcend its boundaries through the supreme act of loving another.

Two types of "incest" are suggested by the book's two personae, both of whom strongly attract the narrator. They are Sabina, lush, sensuous, and irresponsible, freely engaging in sex without emotional commitment; and Jeanne, an aristocrat with a crippled leg, a woman who "strangles" her guitar when she tries to make it produce music. Jeanne is hopelessly in love with her brother. The emotional damage caused by such an inverted fixation is explored in Nin's later works, "The Voice," *Winter of Artifice*, and "Under a Glass Bell" (from the story collection with the same title).

The extreme difficulty of achieving a stable, committed love while continuing to "turn and change" is at the center of all Nin's novels. A positive resolution appears only in the later books *Seduction of the Minotaur* and *Collages*, both of which are lighter in tone than earlier works.

Winter of Artifice

Winter of Artifice comprises three "novelettes" (Nin's term): "Stella," *Winter of Artifice*, and "The Voice." Written in 1944, when Nin was planning a series of interconnected novels and struggling with the psychological issues of the woman as artist, "Stella" explores the failure of connection between a woman's personal life and her work; this failure is caused by a neurosis that is unchallenged. As a film star, Stella is much more glamorous, vital, self-assured, and daring than in private life (her "mask" may be said to dominate her "self"). The contrast is so great that when Stella sits in the audience watching one of her own films, she is never recognized. The most important object in her apartment is a "very large, very spacious Movie Star bed of white satin," which she usually occupies alone. The connection that Nin sought between the personal life and the artistic expression of this life does not occur for Stella. Like others, she has been damaged by her childhood, but she has done nothing to repair this damage. Because Stella "did not grow," Nin decided not to include her as one of the major characters in *Cities of the Interior*. Viewed as a psychological portrait of a narcissist, however, "Stella" is an insightful piece of work, and it is brilliantly expressed.

When evaluated exclusively as art, "The Voice" is one of Nin's most original and daring pieces. It is both an extended portrait of a kind and self-neglectful psychotherapist (perhaps suggested by Otto Rank), and an animated essay or exposition of ideas through a seemingly random selection of characters and incidents. "The Voice" is a virtuoso piece that spins off from contrasting motions: soaring, plummeting, floating, sinking, spiraling, rushing, and flowing; it is an excellent example of Nin's deft way of translating characters and incidents into imagery.

The center of this active world is a psychoanalyst's office located in a skyscraper. Tortured New Yorkers, The Voice's patients include Djuna (who becomes one of the principals in *Cities of the Interior*), a young violinist who wishes to be released from her lesbian desires; Mischa, a cellist whose emotions are paralyzed; and Lilith, who suffers from frigidity. The Voice himself falls in love with Lilith, the only one of his patients who can see beyond her own needs to the hungers of the man whose voice is so comforting to the others. As in Nin's later books, Djuna plays the role of comforting confidant to both parties in this impossible dream of love between analyst and patient.

Winter of Artifice is perhaps the most musical of Nin's works; it is also among the most courageous in its subject: an adult daughter's flirtation and near union with the handsome, seductive father who abandoned her when she was a child. The theme is "musique Ancienne," to quote Nin, the Oedipal temptation told from the point of view of the highly intelligent yet vulnerable daughter. *Winter of Artifice* was begun in 1933, when Nin started therapy with Rank, and was completed in 1939, the year of Rank's death.

The novelette is organized in thirteen "movements." A climax of emotional and erotic yearning occurs in the sixth, central movement. From this excruciating height of desire, the work subsides into a slower rhythm and a sadder tone. Eventually, *Winter of Artifice* becomes a solo for the daughter. When she sees her father's "feminine-looking" foot, she imagines that it is really her foot and that he has stolen it. Now she understands that he would like to steal her youth and her capacity for action, her mobility. "Tired of his ballet dancing" (formal, traditional movements), the daughter symbolically reclaims her foot and, with it, her ability to flee from the dangers of the attraction: "*Music runs and I run with it.*"

Cities of the Interior

The five novels found in the final version of *Cities of the Interior*, Nin's "continuous novel," are *Ladders to Fire*, *Children of the Albatross*, *The Four-Chambered Heart*, *A Spy in the House of Love*, and *Seduction of the Minotaur*. They were first published individually during the 1940's and 1950's. Entries in Nin's diary indicate that she began writing *Ladders to Fire* in 1937; she made substantial revisions as late as 1962. *Seduction of the Minotaur*, which was published individually in 1961, was begun in 1938 and expanded in 1958 to include *Solar Barque*. Alan Swallow, a pioneer among small-press publishers, brought out the five novels under their collective title in 1959. When it was first published, *Cities of the Interior* had been growing for twenty years. An extraordinary work, it displays a brilliance of conception, a mastery of image and metaphor, and a refinement of structural technique that make it the equal of many better-known modern masterpieces.

The book's subtitle, *A Continuous Novel*, suggests the timeless scope of this work. The "cities" of the title are both ancient and modern. Nin set out to excavate the buried cities or the psychic worlds of her three main characters: Lillian, Djuna, and Sabina. The idea of "continuity," however, is more complex. It suggests that *Cities of the Interior* is an open work, like certain modern sculptures that extend into and penetrate the space that surrounds them, interacting with their setting.

This multifaceted work is not set apart from life, not carved out of it, not bounded by the conventions of classically written fiction with its concluding "resolution." *Cities of the Interior* remains open to the addition of new parts and to the rearrangement of its five basic novel units. The individual books are entirely self-contained. As Nin uses the word, "continuous" does not mean "to be continued." It does not refer to linear progressive time. There is no fixed starting point and no concluding point. The books have been bound—because books, seemingly, must be bound—in the order in which they were written.

A reader can begin with any one of the five volumes and move to the other four in any order, losing no essential connections. In short, the five novels of *Cities of the Interior* are interchangeable in the total composition, which can be viewed as a type of mobile, an innovation in fiction inspired by the example of modern sculpture. Nin's characters are totally immersed in the flow of internalized psychic time, in the patterns of their own growth. One of the main figures in *Collages* quotes the Qurʾān, saying, "Nothing is ever finished."

French philosopher Henri Bergson, whose ideas influenced a number of modern novelists, including Proust, stated the concept of personal evolution succinctly and elegantly: "If matter appeared to us as a perpetual flowering, we should assign no termination to any of our actions." To Nin, life does indeed appear as a "perpetual flowering." In *Cities of the Interior*, she has selected and expressed significant relationships and states of feeling in the ever-changing, continuous process of growth. Life, as distinct from existence, is possible only for those who can accept mutability, knowing that while change promises growth, it also demands inevitable loss.

Ladders to Fire

Lillian's development spans *Cities of the Interior*, opening and closing the work when it is read in conventional sequence. The first part of *Ladders to Fire* describes "This Hunger," Lillian's ravenous need for love. Spontaneous, impetuous, unsure of her physical attractiveness, and compulsively generous, she gives up her career as a pianist so that she can support her lover's ambition to paint, but this sacrifice does not bring her the loyalty and security she desires. Jay repays Lillian's devotion by having affairs with other women.

The most threatening of Lillian's rivals is Sabina. The relationship between these two women is the most compelling in the novel and a superb example of Nin's brilliance at unmasking psychological motivations. When Lillian attempts to stop Sabina's pursuit of Jay by overwhelming the other woman with friendship, she discovers that she, too, is powerfully attracted to Sabina. For different reasons, both women are angry at Jay: Lillian because he has neglected her, Sabina because he would like to conquer her. The two women form an alliance against him. After dancing together in a working-class tavern, they go to Sabina's room to make love, but they discover that it is not sensuality they are seeking in each other so much as an exchange of feminine qualities. They both feel a "mysterious craving . . . to become each other."

During the dazzling party scene with which *Ladders to Fire* closes, Lillian commits "invisible hara-kiri" with an outburst of harmful self-criticism. It is clear to the reader that she has grown, that her anger at herself is partly an expression of this growth, and that she will soon end her unsatisfying relationship with Jay.

Children of the Albatross

A delicate, playful book with an undercurrent of sadness, *Children of the Albatross* traces a theme that is familiar in French literature but something of a novelty in the United States: the initiation of a young man by an older woman. Djuna, in her late twenties, becomes involved with Paul, who is seventeen years old. The other "children" of the novel's title are their friends, young gay men who meet with Paul and Djuna in her "house of innocence and faith." Here, they dance, paint, and play, celebrating their love of freedom from responsibility. The young men and Djuna are drawn together by their mutual fear of tyrannical, authoritarian fathers. For Djuna, this figure is represented by the cruel and lecherous watchman who terrified her when she was a child living in an orphanage. The positive creative act of evoking a counterworld to erect against the conventional and materialistic values of the fathers ignites sympathy among the rebellious children.

From the start of *Children of the Albatross*, it is clear that Djuna's affair with Paul will be brief and will provide her with little emotional sustenance. Predictably, Paul's family disapproves of her, not only because she is older but also because she is a dancer. A crucial dream, in which Djuna imagines herself as Ariadne, predicts that after she has guided Paul safely through the passage from adolescence to early adulthood, she will be abandoned. At the novel's end, Paul embarks upon an exciting journey to India, leaving Djuna behind. Feeling empty and dissatisfied, she searches the unexplored "cities" of her self. She begins to seek a fuller emotional life with a more mature partner.

The Four-Chambered Heart

In *The Four-Chambered Heart*, Nin explores the psychological complexity of a woman's involvement with a married man. Romantically ensconced in a houseboat on the Seine are Djuna and Rango, a tempestuous vagabond, so she imagines. Their relationship is initially enthralling but ultimately frustrating; both parties are weighed down by responsibilities to demanding hypochondriacs: he to his wife, Zora, and Djuna to her father. Heavy rains force the lovers to move their houseboat up and down the river. Like their relationship, the boat does not "go anywhere"; it merely plies its way back and forth over the same area.

Djuna and Rango's passion attains its height in the novel's first thirty pages. After that, there is conflict and threatened violence. Zora makes a bizarre attempt to kill Djuna. Rango comes to the boat very late one night and falls into a heavy depressed sleep. Djuna, desperate to initiate a change of some sort, rips up floorboards in a wild attempt to sink the boat. It is swept down the river; everyone survives, though not in the same form. A fisherman rescues a doll from the water with a joke about its having tried to commit suicide. The doll is a comment on Djuna's passivity with regard to her own life and to the image of conventional femininity that she has been struggling to maintain, at the expense of her "true" self. It is time for her to move beyond the static situation she experiences with Rango, to give up the illusion of her generosity toward Zora, and to recognize and accept the negative qualities she has been "acting out" through Rango. Djuna must grow.

A Spy in the House of Love

In *A Spy in the House of Love*, Sabina is portrayed as a glamorous woman seeking to express herself as "Don Juana." Married to a fatherly, indulgent man, she is free to fulfill her desire for adventure, which she experiences through relationships with men. Each of Sabina's partners embodies an aura, a sense of place, an ambience that lies waiting for her exploration and participation. There is the opera star Philip; he represents "Vienna before the war." There is Mambo, a black musician transplanted to Greenwich Village from a Caribbean island. There is John, a former aviator who has been grounded because of uncontrollable anxiety. Finally, there is Donald, a gay man who returns Sabina's maternal love with an irresistibly flattering letter-portrait of her idealized self. This balances the grossly sexual and cruel portrait given to her by her former lover, Jay, a painter.

A Spy in the House of Love is a musical novel both in style and structure. There is a prelude in which Sabina invites the detection of her "crime" (experiencing sex without feeling) by phoning a "lie detector." There is a coda in which Djuna, Sabina's consoling friend, plays a late Beethoven quartet to soothe and heal the dejected Don Juana. The body of the novel is a series of variations on the central theme: Sabina's attempt to live through her relationships with men who—so she deludes herself into believing—have far more exciting lives than she herself has. Each man is associated with a particular type of music, while Igor Stravinsky's "Firebird" is said to be Sabina's "unerring musical autobiography."

Seduction of the Minotaur

At once the most mature in theme and the most resplendent in imagery among Nin's novels, *Seduction of the Minotaur* takes up the story of Lillian. She has developed considerably since *Ladders to Fire*. Now a jazz performer instead of an interpreter of the classics, Lillian journeys to Mexico, imagining that she has finally freed herself from everything that imprisoned her in the past.

Traveling alone, Lillian meets a series of men, each of whom becomes a teacher or guide of sorts, revealing something of great significance in her own circuitous passage through the labyrinth of the self. The most engaging of these figures is Dr. Hernandez, a male version of Ariadne. He helps Lillian to see that she is not yet as free as she has imagined, wisely telling her that "we live by a series of repetitions until the experience is solved, understood, liquidated." The monster Lillian confronts is a "masked woman," the part of herself that she has previously been unwilling to recognize.

In Lillian's journey to Mexico and her confrontation with herself, Nin creates a living dream simultaneously in the past, present, and future. The meaning of freedom is not flight, as Sabina imagines, but commitment. If a woman can discover and love the many aspects of one man, she can be fulfilled with a single love. Lillian learns to see her husband, Larry, from whom she has been separated, as a complex, multidimensional person. This discovery brings a new excitement, a forgiveness, the grace of understanding to her feelings about him. Because she untangles the knots in her own past, Lillian rediscovers the love of her husband. Thus, there is reconciliation instead of separation.

Collages

A more ambitious and a deeper book than its easy surface and gentle humor suggest, *Collages* is composed of nineteen short blocks of prose, showing once again Nin's preference for constructed rather than narrated fiction. *Collages* begins and ends with the same passage. Its circular structure encloses twenty-two characters portrayed in a wide variety of quickly sketched settings. The cement that binds these colorful elements into a composition is Renate, an artist who "makes her own patterns." She weaves in and out of the lives of the others, bringing inspiration to not only her paintings but also her friends.

Collage art is shown to work magic transformations. In this book, Nin once again stresses the many ways in which dream and fantasy enrich life. There is an intense relationship, for example, between a young woman and a raven. An elderly man feels closer to seals than to human beings; he finally develops the courage to renounce people in order to live with the animals he loves. A gardener pretends to be a millionaire to fulfill his dream of financing a literary magazine. A woman whose husband has rejected her for a younger woman replaces him with an exotic phantom lover. In *Collages*, imagination is sovereign.

The healing power of genuine relationships is shown as complementary to that of creative fantasy. *Collages* closes with the reluctant emergence of a writer from a bitter, self-imposed isolation. Elderly Judith Sands allows herself to be "courted" by Renate and an Israeli admirer, Dr. Mann. Made more trusting by their friendship, Sands actually shows the visitors one of her manuscripts. Its opening words are the same words with which *Collages* begins. This repetition helps endow *Collages* with its circular form and also underscores Nin's conviction that there is an unbroken connection from one person to another, from one imaginative writer to another, and that life is redeemed through the alchemical transformation of art. *Collages* is an assured and accomplished example of Nin's skill at adapting techniques from the nonverbal arts to literature; it is also the most imaginatively conceived of display of her convictions about the mutually nourishing exchange between art and life.

Sharon Spencer

Other major works

SHORT FICTION: *Under a Glass Bell, and Other Stories*, 1944; *Delta of Venus: Erotica*, 1977; *Waste of Timelessness, and Other Early Stories*, 1977; *Little Birds: Erotica*, 1979.

NONFICTION: *D. H. Lawrence: An Unprofessional Study*, 1932; *Realism and Reality*, 1946; *On Writing*, 1947; *The Diary of Anaïs Nin: 1931-1934*, 1966; *The Diary of Anaïs Nin: 1934-1939*, 1967; *The Novel of the Future*, 1968; *The Diary of Anaïs Nin: 1939-1944*, 1969; *The Diary of Anaïs Nin: 1944-1947*, 1971; *Paris Revisited*, 1972; *The Diary of Anaïs Nin: 1947-1955*, 1974; *A Photographic Supplement to the Diary of Anaïs Nin*, 1974; *A Woman Speaks: The Lectures, Seminars, and Interviews of Anaïs Nin*, 1975 (Evelyn J. Hinz, editor); *In Favor of the Sensitive Man, and Other Essays*, 1976; *The Diary of Anaïs Nin: 1955-1966*, 1976; *Linotte: The Early Diary of Anaïs Nin, 1914-1920*, 1978; *The Diary of Anaïs Nin: 1966-1974*, 1980; *The Early Diary of*

Anaïs Nin: Volume Two, 1920-1923, 1982; *The Early Diary of Anaïs Nin: Volume Three, 1923-1927*, 1983; *The Early Diary of Anaïs Nin: Volume Four, 1927-1931*, 1985; *Henry and June: From the Unexpurgated Diary of Anaïs Nin*, 1986; *A Literate Passion: Letters of Anaïs Nin and Henry Miller, 1932-1953*, 1987.

Bibliography

Bair, Deirdre. *Anaïs Nin: A Biography*. New York: Putnam, 1995. A massive biography by a scholar steeped in the literature of the period and author of biographies of Samuel Beckett and Simone de Beauvoir. Supplements but does not supersede Fitch's shorter but also livelier 1993 biography.

Bloshteyn, Maria R. *The Making of a Counter-Culture Icon: Henry Miller's Dostoevsky*. Toronto, Ont.: University of Toronto Press, 2007. Describes how Fyodor Dostoevski was a model for Nin and her friends, Henry Miller and Lawrence Durrell, who strove to emulate the Russian writer's psychological characterizations and narrative style in their own work.

Fitch, Noel Riley. *Anaïs: The Erotic Life of Anaïs Nin*. Boston: Little, Brown, 1993. As the subtitle suggests, Fitch is concerned with tracing Nin's erotic relationships and close friendships with male and female writers. A biographer of Sylvia Beach and an expert on Paris, Fitch writes with verve and expertise.

Franklin, Benjamin V., and Duane Schneider. *Anaïs Nin: An Introduction*. Athens: Ohio University Press, 1979. A well-balanced study of Nin's work, better than most, which carefully and separately examines her fiction, six volumes of diaries, and her critical and nonfiction work. This study attempts to redress critical neglect of the author and gives her due recognition for her literary achievements.

Jason, Philip K., ed. *The Critical Response to Anaïs Nin*. Westport, Conn.: Greenwood Press, 1996. A selection of essays examining Nin's works. Includes a Freudian interpretation of her novel *Cities of the Interior* and poet William Carlos Williams's analysis of *Winter of Artifice*. Includes bibliographical references and an index.

Knapp, Bettina L. *Anaïs Nin*. New York: Frederick Ungar, 1978. An appreciative examination of Nin's work that explores the psychological depths of her diaries and fiction. Includes a chronology, a bibliography, and an index.

Pierpont, Claudia Roth. *Passionate Minds: Women Rewriting the World*. New York: Alfred A. Knopf, 2000. Evocative interpretive essays on the life paths and works of twelve women, including Nin, connecting the circumstances of their lives with the shapes, styles, subjects, and situations of their art.

Richard-Allerdyce, Diane. *Anaïs Nin and the Remaking of Self: Gender, Modernism, and Narrative Identity*. DeKalb: Northern Illinois University Press, 1998. An examination of the themes of gender and self-creativity in Nin's fiction and diaries, describing how she strove to present a "feminine mode of being" in her work. The first five chapters provide analyses of the majority of Nin's novels.

Scholar, Nancy. *Anaïs Nin*. Boston: Twayne, 1984. A good critical introduction to Nin. The first chapter offers an overview of her life, and succeeding chapters examine the novels, diaries, short stories, and prose pieces. Includes a useful chronology and a select bibliography.

Tookey, Helen. *Anaïs Nin, Fictionality and Femininity: Playing a Thousand Roles*. New York: Oxford University Press, 2003. Examines Nin's work within historical and cultural contexts, focusing on her representations of identity and femininity and her concept of self-creation through various kinds of narratives and performances.

FRANK NORRIS

Born: Chicago, Illinois; March 5, 1870
Died: San Francisco, California; October 25, 1902
Also known as: Benjamin Franklin Norris, Jr.

Principal long fiction

Moran of the Lady Letty, 1898
Blix, 1899
McTeague, 1899
A Man's Woman, 1900
The Octopus: A Spy of California, 1901
The Pit: A Story of Chicago, 1903
Vandover and the Brute, 1914

Other literary forms

Frank Norris's published work includes poems, short stories, essays, newspaper articles, novels, and literary criticism. Although he is best known today for his novels, Norris is also remembered for his popular short-story contributions to the *San Francisco Wave* and his insightful literary criticism, published in *The Responsibilities of the Novelist* (1903) and *The Literary Criticism of Frank Norris* (1964).

Norris's first published book, *Yvernelle: A Tale of Feudal France* (published in 1892 while Norris was still in college), was neither a short story nor a novel, but a medieval love poem written in the romantic verse style of Sir Walter Scott. Had it not been subsidized by Gertrude Norris (the author's mother), the book would probably never have been published. Today it is notable only for the high price it brings in the rare book trade.

Norris's success as a reporter was also minimal. His reports on the Boer War were published in the *San Francisco Chronicle*, but his later writings on the Spanish-American War were not published for some time afterward, and were never published by *McClure's Magazine*, which originally sent him there.

Norris was successful, however, as a short-story writer. Much of his early work first appeared in the *San Francisco Wave*, a weekly newspaper featuring mostly local literary talent. The stories he wrote for the newspaper were later collected in three volumes: *A Deal in Wheat, and Other Stories of the New and Old West* (1903), *The Third Circle* (1909), and *Frank Norris of "The Wave"* (1931).

The majority of Norris's writings were collected in a ten-volume *Complete Edition*, published by Doubleday, Doran in 1928. That same year, Doubleday also issued the Argonaut manuscript edition of Norris's works. Identical in content with the *Complete Edition*, the Argonaut manuscript edition was finely bound and included a manuscript page from *McTeague*. In the late twentieth century, more Norris pieces were unearthed, including his Harvard student theses. His major works are still in print in both hardcover and inexpensive paperbound editions.

Achievements

Called by many (including himself) "the boy Zola" because his style was so reminiscent of French novelist Émile Zola's writings, Norris spearheaded the naturalistic movement in American literature. Although Norris's contemporaries were, by and large, critical of his portrayal of the savage, seamy side of life, it is that very quality in his work that has helped to keep his fiction alive and readable. Even more than his challenge to the Victorian code of the beginning of the twentieth century, Norris's capacity to portray corruption and its evil effects on human beings as well as his ability to make scenes and characters seem vibrant and real rank him high among twentieth century writers.

Norris never achieved the immense popularity of some of the other writers of his day, such as Jack London. He did not even live to see his most successful novel, *The Pit*, become a best seller. Indeed, it was not until publication of *The Octopus* that he was able to enjoy even a modest financial success. His readers were simply not able to accept his preoccupation with sordid realities, including his treatment of sex, which by Victorian standards was quite shocking. Because of his unsavory choice of subject matter, Norris was ignored by reviewers who understood only the elegant prose and fine writing of an earlier era. Today, Norris's pioneering work in American naturalism is universally acknowledged.

Biography

Frank Norris was the son of Gertrude Doggett and Benjamin Franklin Norris, a successful businessman specializing in wholesale jewelry. Born in 1870, Norris's early years were spent in Chicago. Except for a trip to Europe when he was eight years old, Norris's childhood was rather uneventful. At age fourteen, he moved with his family to California. They settled first in Oakland and then moved to a large house on Sacramento Street in San Francisco. His father began a real estate development business, building cheap houses for working-class people to rent, and enjoyed financial success. The young Norris would later write about these houses in his first novel.

Frank Norris found San Francisco stimulating. The family home was located only a block from fashionable Van Ness Avenue with its ongoing series of parades and pageants and only a few blocks from the business section of Polk Street with its rich variety of small shops—there was even a dental parlor with a grotesque golden tooth sign hanging from the building. The scenes and settings were memorable, and Norris captured many of them for later use as local color in his novels.

In 1885, Norris was enrolled in the Belmont Academy. This marked the beginning of a long, largely unsuccessful attempt at formal schooling. Norris had neither the temperament nor the talent in mathematics for scholarship and, after breaking his arm playing football scarcely one year after enrolling, he quit the academy for a convalescence at home. It was during this period that he made up his mind to pursue a career as an artist.

After a short stint at Boy's High School, Norris convinced his parents to send him to the San Francisco Art Association School. His success there persuaded Benjamin Norris to send him to the finest art schools in Paris. While Norris did not learn how to paint in Paris, he did learn the fundamentals and principles of art and also the discipline that would later serve him well as a writer. Convinced that his son was not spending his time painting, Norris's father called him home in 1889. Norris returned from France with a new interest in writing and, more important, a solid foundation on which to build his writing career.

In the fall of 1890, Norris entered the University of California, Berkeley, determined to become a writer. Almost at once he found himself at odds with the English Department faculty over proper methods of composition. His academic progress in mathematics was abysmal. Norris turned to a more social life and joined Phi Gamma Delta fraternity. There he found a perfect outlet for his frustrations and a wealth of amusements to occupy his time. Although his academic career at Berkeley was undistinguished, Norris's fraternity pranks were memorable.

While Norris was gaining a reputation as a prankster, his family was quickly breaking apart, and Benjamin Norris left, alone, for Europe; while on the trip, he fell in love with another woman. Upon his return, he divorced Gertrude, married his new love, and moved to Chicago; Norris never again saw his father.

In 1894, Norris's marginal academic success caught up with him. Although he had done well in Joseph Le Conte's science classes, his failures in mathematics forced him to leave the university without a degree. Harvard appealed to him as the proper place to polish his writing talents, so he enrolled the following fall as a special student, taking courses in English and French. There

Frank Norris. (Library of Congress)

he found success in the classes taught by Professor Lewis Gates. Under Gates's watchful eye, Norris began work on his first two novels: *Vandover and the Brute* and *McTeague*.

After a year at Harvard, Norris returned to San Francisco, taking a job with the *Chronicle* as a special correspondent. He convinced the paper to send him to South Africa, where he covered the beginnings of the Boer War. Norris's reports from the strife-torn land were not memorable, but the tropical fever he contracted would later contribute to his death.

Norris next joined the staff of the *San Francisco Wave*, then under the editorship of John O'Hara Cosgrave. As an assistant editor, Norris wrote short stories, reviewed books and art exhibitions, and composed feature stories to fill the pages of the weekly newspaper. He found it impossible to work for extended periods of time, however, and interrupted his employment at least twice: once to journey to the Big Dipper Mine near Colfax, California, where he finished *McTeague*; another time to begin work on his third novel, *Moran of the Lady Letty*. He found no trouble selling the first installments of this new novel to the magazines, and as it was running, the story caught the eye of S. S. McClure, who invited Norris to join the staff of Doubleday as a reader. The position paid poorly and offered little status, but Norris took it anyway, perhaps because it allowed him time to finish *Moran of the Lady Letty* and begin other projects as well.

After a time, however, Norris began to hate his self-imposed poverty and, at the outbreak of the Spanish-American War, begged McClure to send him to Cuba to cover the conflict as a correspondent for *McClure's Magazine*. McClure agreed; Norris went to Cuba, met poet Stephen Crane, suffered another attack of fever, and was forced to return to New York. *McClure's Magazine* did not publish any of Norris's war reports.

Never sure of his status with McClure, Norris left the company in 1899 to join the newly founded firm of Doubleday, Page, again as a part-time, poorly paid reader. He wrote *Blix* and *A Man's Woman* and began *The Octopus* during this time, and he also married Jeannette Black. His major contribution to Doubleday, Page came when Theodore Dreiser's *Sister Carrie* (1900) was submitted; Norris read the novel in manuscript and insisted upon its publication. After a contract was signed, Doubleday raised objections to the novel and tried to cancel publication. Norris counseled Dreiser to stand firm and insist that his contract be upheld, whereupon Doubleday issued *Sister Carrie* in a limited edition and allowed it quickly to go out of print.

As Norris's royalties grew from the sale of his own novels, he found the financial independence to return to California, and he made plans to purchase a ranch in the southern range of the Santa Cruz mountains. He completed *The Pit*, the second book in his projected trilogy of wheat novels, and planned a journey to the tropics with his wife. That journey was interrupted, however, when Jeannette underwent surgery to remove an inflamed appendix. While she was recovering in the hospital, Norris, too, began suffering stomach pains. Thinking it only a minor ailment, he refused to go to a doctor until he became seriously ill. Suffering from peritonitis and weakened by fever, Norris entered Mt. Zion hospital in San Francisco and died there on October 25, 1902, at the age of thirty-two.

Analysis

Frank Norris was one of a handful of writers at the turn of the century who applied the literary naturalism of Zola to American subjects and themes. As a writer in this tradition, Norris treated his subject matter brutally but sincerely. His characters are but pawns, driven by outside forces over which they have no control. Devoid of souls, they are helpless creatures determined by their heredity and environment. In Norris's most successful novels, these naturalistic ideas are employed with great faithfulness, and his depiction of human beings following a slow but inevitable course toward destruction has an enduring power.

Norris's fiction underwent various stages of development. In *McTeague* and *Vandover and the Brute*, Norris focused his attentions on the naturalistic novel of character, where both McTeague and Vandover proceed slowly toward their inevitable destruction. In Norris's next three novels—*Moran of the Lady Letty*, *Blix*, and *A Man's Woman*—he bowed to social pressure: Moral values overwhelm deterministic forces in these inferior works. In Norris's last two novels, *The Octopus* and *The Pit*, he again returned to naturalistic themes, but in a broader, more worldly sense, showing greater compassion and involvement with his characters. The progression from *Vandover and the Brute*, a highly dispassionate view of one man's descent, to *The Pit*, which analyzes the social forces at work in the wheat industry, marks Norris's own maturation as both a writer and a person, and his increasingly complex worldview.

VANDOVER AND THE BRUTE

Written while Norris was still in college, *Vandover and the Brute* is concerned with moral weakness. It is the story of a wealthy man who, unable to sustain his ambition to become an artist, descends to a bestial level. As a study of moral and physical disintegration, the novel follows a characteristically didactic naturalistic course. Vandover's descent is governed by a series of chance events and hastened by his own flawed heredity. Because his position in society allows it, Vandover leads a life of pointless leisure. Unable to focus his desire to become an artist, he starts gambling, drinking, and leading a loose sexual life. A chance cut on his lip, followed by an unwanted kiss from Flossie (who by chance has contracted syphilis), passes a sexually transmitted disease to Vandover and eventually causes lycanthropy.

With the aid of Professor Le Conte's classes in science, Norris was able to research the disease that plagued Vandover. His careful analysis led to Vandover's realistic progression toward lycanthropy, which begins with the suicide of Ida Wade, one of the girls whom Vandover has seduced. Soon after Ida's death, Vandover's father dies, an event that seems to give Vandover direction, but the beast within him soon triumphs, the disease is allowed to run its course, and Vandover becomes a wretched, broken man. The novel concludes with Vandover cleaning the cheap houses Norris's father built for the San Francisco working class, although in the novel, the houses belonged to Vandover.

MCTEAGUE

McTeague was written soon after the completion of *Vandover and the Brute*; like Norris's first book, it emphasizes themes of chance, disintegration, and heredity. The novel is a study of the temperaments of two characters: McTeague, a scoundrel born in a California mining town, and Trina Sieppe, a young working-class woman whose hoarding instincts eventually overcome her.

As the novel begins, McTeague is working with his father in the California mines. A traveling dentist arrives shortly after McTeague's father dies, and the young boy is apprenticed to the dentist so that he might learn a trade. McTeague is not bright enough to learn much—the result of his heredity—but he eventually learns enough to survive, and when his mother dies, he sets up dental parlors in San Francisco. The rich descriptive detail with which Norris renders McTeague's surroundings greatly contributes to the success of the novel.

McTeague is well satisfied with his existence: The earnings from his practice keep him supplied with a daily glass of steam beer and allow him enough leisure time to practice his concertina and socialize infrequently with his friends, among them Marcus Schouler, who lives in the flat above McTeague. Chance, however, intervenes in McTeague's ordered existence when Marcus's girlfriend, Trina, breaks a tooth, and Marcus brings her to McTeague for treatment. While they wait in the parlors, Trina buys a lottery ticket from the cleaning woman—a ticket that, later, will be worth five thousand dollars.

McTeague falls in love with Trina at first sight, and Marcus, rather than fighting for his girl, aids McTeague in courting her, even to the point of introducing him to Trina's parents. The path paved, McTeague asks Trina to marry him, and, on the day the announcement is made public, Trina wins the money through the lottery. It is this chance event that sparks Trina's inherited passion for hoarding, first evident on the day of the lottery payment when Trina, to McTeague's dismay, decides not to spend her winnings on a nice apartment, but rather to save the money. This first clash of temperaments leads to others as McTeague and Trina continue toward their eventual disintegration.

At first, Trina and McTeague are happy; they move into a flat across from the dental parlors and live comfortably. McTeague's ambitions to live in more spacious quarters, however, conflict with Trina's thrifty attitudes. Marcus reenters their lives; embittered by McTeague's good fortune, he attacks McTeague with a knife. This first conflict arouses physical violence in both men only briefly, but during their second encounter, which begins as a friendly wrestling match at the park, Marcus bites off McTeague's earlobe and McTeague retaliates by breaking Marcus's arm. After the incident, Marcus leaves the city, but not before first notifying the authorities that McTeague is practicing dentistry without proper credentials.

Stripped of his profession, McTeague loses his income, thus exacerbating his conflict with Trina over the management of the money. The animal within him brought to the surface, McTeague is no longer able to cope with his environment or with Trina's hoarding, which has become obsessive. He deserts Trina and then comes back and steals her money. After he has spent all the money, McTeague returns to Trina for more. This time, however, he beats her so mercilessly that she dies. Taking her entire lottery winnings, McTeague flees the city for the gold mines and his birthplace. He is followed, however, and forced to flee again, to Death Valley, where he again meets Marcus. This time, however, the struggle their encounter precipitates is fatal to both.

The parallels between *McTeague* and *Vandover and the Brute* are numerous. Both novels owe their genesis to the idea of human degeneracy: *Vandover and the Brute* is the story of one man's descent into the abyss; *McTeague* shows how the interaction of two characters hastens their descent. Chance also plays an important part in both novels. Vandover's cut lip becomes Trina's broken tooth; gambling for Vandover becomes the lottery for Trina. Life itself is a gigantic lottery; Norris is emphatic when he labels the agent of the lottery a "man of the world."

By separating himself from his characters in *McTeague*, Norris was able to deal objectively with the impact of instinct and chance upon them. McTeague becomes an animal—a brute from the mines. Trina, too, crippled by her hoarding instinct both physically (her fingers are amputated) and mentally, becomes little more than an animal, defending her gold as a wolf might defend its kill. *McTeague* is Norris's most powerful and successful novel; his rendering of the seamy, bestial side of human life is masterful.

Moran of the Lady Letty

Moran of the Lady Letty was Norris's third novel in manuscript, but his first in print. Unlike his first two books, *Moran of the Lady Letty* emphasizes the idyllic side of San Francisco: its festive life and colors and the invigorating wind from the Pacific. The story of a strong, primitive woman and an overcivilized man, the novel lacks the realistic intensity of *McTeague*; it is in many ways merely a popular romance.

Ross Wilbur is, like Vandover, a wealthy man. He spends every waking moment attending "functions": teas, cotillions, parties, and other festive gatherings of society. He also enjoys life at the docks and often spends time there gazing at the ships setting out to sea. One day, his ship-watching activities prove perilous, as Wilbur finds himself drugged and kidnapped aboard a filthy schooner piloted by a brutal captain and staffed by an unsavory Chinese crew. Wilbur awakens to face the filth of the cabin and a new life aboard the *Bertha Milner*. Quickly, he shows his adaptive abilities as he adjusts to his new environment, hastened by a smashing blow to the chin by the half-civilized captain. As he adjusts to his new life, Wilbur also learns the intricacies of navigation (as Norris did when writing the novel) and the wonders of the sea, including the excitement of a sea-turtle chase. Life, it seems, is not so bad after all.

Soon after weighing anchor, the Chinese crew sights a ship at sea. The captain realizes that the bark they have sighted, the *Lady Letty*, is deserted save for its dead captain and his half-dead daughter, Moran. Consumed with greed, Captain Kitchell plots a salvage of the *Lady Letty* and its cargo, and Moran's murder, too, should she stand in his way. The greed that destroyed Trina in *McTeague* also kills Kitchell, however, when, while he is drunk aboard the *Lady Letty*, a sudden squall sinks the ship. Wilbur and Moran are suddenly left to fend for themselves aboard the *Bertha Milner* with its Chinese crew.

The strange adventures that follow serve to further Wilbur's advancement to manhood. Encountering a Chinese junk, Wilbur and Moran become embroiled in a battle with its crew over a piece of ambergris. In the heat of the battle, Moran mistakes Wilbur for the enemy, and he is forced to subdue her physically. She melts at his physical prowess and surrenders to him. Wilbur, at last, through the vigorous life of the sea, has become a man. In keeping with the theme of the novel—that civilization and social convention are corrupting—Wilbur's softness, brought on by society's overcivilization, is defeated. He has overcome Moran, who knows only the law of the strongest, and has vanquished her according to her own rules.

Except for the naturalistic details of sheer strength

and primitive passions and a few realistic descriptive passages, *Moran of the Lady Letty* is little more than "a corking good story," as Norris described it. He followed similar popular conventions in his next two novels, *Blix* and *A Man's Woman*, before returning in a more ambitious fashion to the naturalistic formulas he so ably employed in *McTeague*.

THE OCTOPUS *and* THE PIT

The third stage of Norris's development as a novelist came about with his projected trilogy on the wheat industry. In the first novel of the trilogy, *The Octopus*, Norris returned to naturalistic formulas. In *The Octopus*, the wheat is planted, grown, and harvested. In *The Pit*, the wheat is traded and taken to market. In *The Wolf*, the planned but never written conclusion to the trilogy, the wheat would be consumed by the hungry masses of Europe. Norris did not live to complete this third book. When he died in 1902, the second volume was only then being serialized.

The Octopus and *The Pit* both deal with the problems of society as a whole rather than with the individual. While Norris was successful in remaining true to his theme in *The Octopus*, the theme and naturalistic treatment is blurred somewhat in *The Pit* by a dual story: the trading of wheat in the Chicago Board of Trade and the love story featuring the protagonists of the novel, Curtis Jadwin and Laura Dearborn.

Jadwin, a weak, irresolute man, is a famous capitalist speculator. A taker of chances, he manages for a time to corner the wheat market and enjoy financial prosperity. His fortunes are wiped out, however, when the wheat crops of the West are harvested. Helpless in the face of vast economic forces that he cannot control—and helpless too in the face of his own heredity, which has forced upon him an uncontrollable urge to gamble—Jadwin is destroyed.

There is another story in *The Pit*, however, which runs concurrent to the story of Jadwin's business: the story of the love between Jadwin and Laura, his wife. Laura feels alone and deserted when Jadwin occupies himself in the pit, completely absorbed in the business of trading wheat, and so has an affair with Sheldon Corthell, a superficial artist. The collapse of Jadwin's fortune in wheat breaks him completely and, with nowhere else to turn, he reasserts his love for Laura. The novel ends, anticlimactically, with Laura and Jadwin facing west, ready to begin life anew. Thus, although powerful in its conception, Norris's last novel is not equal to his best work. He largely neglects his theme (the wheat is rarely physically present in the novel), abandoning naturalistic forces in favor of a love story with autobiographical overtones.

At his best when objectively and dispassionately analyzing his characters and allowing them to be subjected, like pawns, to the naturalistic forces of the universe, Norris faltered when he became too closely involved with his subject. When as in *Blix*, *Moran of the Lady Letty*, and *The Pit*, romantic themes are allowed to gain paramount importance, Norris's naturalistic intentions and power are subverted. Norris was more, however, than a didactic sociologist in the guise of a novelist. His best work is characterized by a faithful reproduction of setting, by creative exuberance. Thus, one does not merely read about Polk Street in *McTeague*, or the San Joaquin Valley in *The Octopus*, or the Board of Trade in *The Pit*, but one also breathes the air of these places, smells their pungent smells. It is this fundamental sense of reality that gives Norris's fiction a lasting appeal.

David Mike Hamilton

OTHER MAJOR WORKS

SHORT FICTION: *A Deal in Wheat, and Other Stories of the New and Old West*, 1903; *The Joyous Miracle*, 1906; *The Third Circle*, 1909; *Frank Norris of "The Wave,"* 1931 (Oscar Lewis, editor).

POETRY: *Yvernelle: A Tale of Feudal France*, 1892; *Two Poems and "Kim" Reviewed*, 1930.

NONFICTION: *The Responsibilities of the Novelist*, 1903; *The Surrender of Santiago*, 1917; *The Letters of Frank Norris*, 1956; *The Literary Criticism of Frank Norris*, 1964 (Donald Pizer, editor); *Collected Letters*, 1986.

MISCELLANEOUS: *The Complete Edition of Frank Norris*, 1928; *Novels and Essays*, 1986; *The Apprenticeship Writings of Frank Norris*, 1996 (two volumes; Joseph R. McElrath, Jr., and Douglas K. Burgess, editors).

BIBLIOGRAPHY

Boyd, Jennifer. *Frank Norris: Spatial Form and Narrative Time*. New York: Peter Lang, 1993. Contains chapters on all of Norris's novels, with discussions of his pictorialism, his relationship to Émile Zola and naturalism, and the structures of his longer fictional works. Includes notes and a bibliography.

Dillingham, William. *Frank Norris: Instinct and Art.* Lincoln: University of Nebraska Press, 1969. This study comprises a biographical sketch and a survey of Norris's work. Dillingham argues that certain attitudes of the academicians, such as hard work and close observation, influenced Norris's conception of painting and writing, and he stresses Norris's naturalism. Includes an annotated bibliography.

Graham, Don. *The Fiction of Frank Norris: The Aesthetic Context.* Columbia: University of Missouri Press, 1978. This volume is one of the few studies concerning itself with the aesthetics of Norris's work. Much attention is given to his four most literary novels—*Vandover and the Brute*, *McTeague*, *The Octopus*, and *The Pit*. Includes an excellent bibliography.

_______, comp. *Critical Essays on Frank Norris.* Boston: G. K. Hall, 1980. A collection of reviews and essays aimed at presenting Norris as a vital and still undefined writer. Among the contributors are Norris's contemporaries William Dean Howells, Willa Cather, and Hamlin Garland. Literary critics include Donald Pizer and William Dillingham.

Hussman, Lawrence E. *Harbingers of a Century: The Novels of Frank Norris.* New York: Peter Lang, 1999. A reevaluation of Norris's novels in which Hussman demonstrates how these books "rehearsed" many of the themes that would subsequently appear in twentieth century American fiction.

McElrath, Joseph R., Jr. *Frank Norris Revisited.* New York: Twayne, 1992. An updating and rewriting of a book by Warren French that first appeared in 1962. This introductory study includes a chapter on the "novelist in the making," followed by subsequent chapters that discuss each of Norris's novels. Includes a chronology, notes, and an annotated bibliography.

McElrath, Joseph R., Jr., and Jessie S. Crisler. *Frank Norris: A Life.* Urbana: University of Illinois Press, 2006. The first full-scale biography in more than seventy years provides an admiring portrait of the author. McElrath and Crisler maintain that Norris remains relevant and deserves to be read by twenty-first century readers.

Marchand, Ernest. *Frank Norris: A Study.* Stanford, Calif.: Stanford University Press, 1942. The first full-length critical study of Norris, this overview situates his work against a social and intellectual, as well as a literary, background. Considers a wide variety of critical opinions about Norris's fiction.

Walker, Franklin. *Frank Norris: A Biography.* New York: Russell and Russell, 1932. The first full-length biography of Norris, this study is uncritical of its subject; it also is extraordinarily detailed. Contains personal interviews with Norris's family and friends.

West, Lon. *Deconstructing Frank Norris's Fiction: The Male-Female Dialectic.* New York: Peter Lang, 1998. West contradicts many previous critics by arguing that Norris was less of a naturalist and more of a Romantic. He focuses on Norris's representation of the "natural man" and of refined women characters in his fiction, finding connections between Norris's characters and Carl Jung's archetypes of the "great and terrible mother" and the "punishing superego-like father."

O

JOYCE CAROL OATES

Born: Lockport, New York; June 16, 1938
Also known as: Rosamond Smith

Principal long fiction

With Shuddering Fall, 1964
A Garden of Earthly Delights, 1967 (revised 2003)
Expensive People, 1968
them, 1969
Wonderland, 1971
Do with Me What You Will, 1973
The Assassins: A Book of Hours, 1975
Childwold, 1976
The Triumph of the Spider Monkey, 1976
Son of the Morning, 1978
Cybele, 1979
Unholy Loves, 1979
Bellefleur, 1980
Angel of Light, 1981
A Bloodsmoor Romance, 1982
Mysteries of Winterthurn, 1984
Solstice, 1985
Marya: A Life, 1986
Lives of the Twins, 1987 (as Rosamond Smith)
You Must Remember This, 1987
American Appetites, 1989
Soul/Mate, 1989 (as Smith)
Because It Is Bitter, and Because It Is My Heart, 1990
I Lock My Door upon Myself, 1990
Nemesis, 1990 (as Smith)
The Rise of Life on Earth, 1991
Black Water, 1992
Snake Eyes, 1992 (as Smith)
Foxfire: Confessions of a Girl Gang, 1993
What I Lived For, 1994
You Can't Catch Me, 1995 (as Smith)
Zombie, 1995
First Love, 1996
We Were the Mulvaneys, 1996
Man Crazy, 1997
My Heart Laid Bare, 1998
Broke Heart Blues, 1999
Starr Bright Will Be with You Soon, 1999 (as Smith)
Blonde, 2000
Middle Age: A Romance, 2001
The Barrens, 2001 (as Smith)
Beasts, 2002
I'll Take You There, 2002
Rape: A Love Story, 2003
The Tattooed Girl, 2003
The Falls, 2004
Missing Mom, 2005
Black Girl/White Girl, 2006
The Gravedigger's Daughter, 2007
My Sister, My Love: The Intimate Story of Skyler Rampike, 2008

Other literary forms

Joyce Carol Oates's first work for the stage, *Miracle Play*, appeared in 1974, and others opened later to appreciative audiences. In addition, Oates has published collections of short stories with regularity. These began with *By the North Gate* (1963), which predated her first novel, and continued with collections such as *Upon the Sweeping Flood* (1966), *The Wheel of Love* (1970), *Marriages and Infidelities* (1972), *Where Are You Going, Where Have You Been?* (1974), *The Poisoned Kiss* (1975), *The Seduction* (1975), *Crossing the Border* (1976), *All the Good People I've Left Behind* (1978), *A Sentimental Education* (1980), *Raven's Wing* (1986),

The Assignation (1988), *Where Is Here?* (1992), *Faithless: Tales of Transgression* (2001), *The Female of the Species: Tales of Mystery and Suspense* (2006), and *Wild Nights! Stories About the Last Days of Poe, Dickinson, Twain, James, and Hemingway* (2008). In the early years of the twenty-first century, Oates added literature for children and young adults to her repertoire. These works include *Big Mouth and Ugly Girl* (2002), *Freaky Green Eyes* (2003), *After the Wreck, I Picked Myself Up, Spread My Wings, and Flew Away* (2006), and *Naughty Chérie* (2008).

While Oates is often recognized as one of the primary American writers of imaginative literature, she also is a highly respected reviewer and critic. Some of Oates's best literary criticism and writing about her work has been collected in such volumes as *New Heaven, New Earth: The Visionary Experience in Literature* (1974); *(Woman) Writer: Occasions and Opportunities* (1988), *Where I've Been, and Where I'm Going: Essays, Reviews, and Prose* (1999), and *The Faith of a Writer: Life, Craft, Art* (2003). In addition, Oates has edited several anthologies of the short fiction and nonfiction of other authors, including *Night Walks: A Bedside Companion* (1982), *First Person Singular: Writers on Their Craft* (1983), *American Gothic Tales* (1996), *Snapshots: Twentieth Century Mother-Daughter Fiction* (2000; with Janet Berliner), and *The Best American Mystery Stories* (2005; with Otto Penzler). Oates's books of poems include *Anonymous Sins, and Other Poems* (1969), *Angel Fire* (1973), *Women Whose Lives Are Food, Men Whose Lives Are Money* (1978), *The Time Traveler* (1989), and *Tenderness* (1996). In 1974, Oates and her husband founded the literary journal *Ontario Review*.

Achievements

As a writer and as a teacher, Joyce Carol Oates has collected numerous and varied prizes and honors. Among them are O. Henry Awards throughout the 1970's, 1980's, and 1990's, twelve Pushcart Prizes, the Richard and Hinda Rosenthal Award of the National Institute of Arts and Letters (1968), the National Book Award for 1970, and the Lotos Club Award of Merit (1975). In 1990, Oates received the Rea Award for the short story and the Alan Swallow Award for her 1988 short-story collection *The Assignation*. Oates has also been honored with the PEN/Malamud Award for Lifetime Achievement in the Short Story (1996), the F. Scott Fitzgerald Award for Lifetime Achievement in American Literature (1998), the Thomas Cooper Medal for Distinction in the Arts and Sciences (2005), the Humanist of the Year Award (2007), and the Mary McCarthy Award (2008). She has also been the recipient of eight honorary degrees.

Biography

Joyce Carol Oates was born on June 16, 1938, in Lockport, New York. She received a modest education in a one-room schoolhouse and, as a child, had very little exposure to literature. This, however, did not quell her desire to write, and she spent much of her time as a child writing stories and short books. Even with all the writing and composing experience she had in her childhood, however, she did not publish her first story until 1959. While studying at Syracuse University, she won *Mademoiselle* magazine's college fiction competition with her short story "In the Old World." This would be the first of many public acknowledgments of the quality of her writing.

After receiving her B.A. from Syracuse in 1960, where she was valedictorian, Oates went on to receive her M.A. from the University of Wisconsin. During her term at Syracuse, she met her future husband, Raymond J. Smith. They married in 1961 and then moved to Beaumont, Texas, and Oates began to work on her Ph.D. at Rice University. She would never complete the degree; she and her husband moved to Michigan in 1962. While in Michigan, she taught English at the University of Detroit until 1967, when she and her husband began teaching at the University of Windsor in Ontario, Canada. During their tenure at the university, Smith and Oates cofounded the *Windsor Review*. After leaving the university in 1978, Oates went on to join the Princeton University Creative Writing Program. While a member of the program, she wrote not only fiction but also some brilliant essays on writers ranging from William Shakespeare to Norman Mailer.

Oates's teaching career has proved rich and rewarding. In 1987 she was appointed Roger S. Berlind Distinguished Professor in the Humanities at Princeton and published a monograph titled *On Boxing*, after which she became internationally known as an expert on the sport.

In addition to serving on the faculty at Princeton, Oates has traveled extensively, often undertaking her journeys to bring attention to her most recently published novel or short-story collection. Throughout the years she has given many public readings of her works and has appeared as the keynote speaker at various national and international conferences. After joining the Princeton faculty she also toured Eastern Europe under the auspices of the U.S. Information Agency.

Joyce Carol Oates. (© Norman Seeff)

Analysis

There have been few writers to match Joyce Carol Oates for sheer numbers—her novels, plays, short stories, and poems appear to multiply by themselves on library shelves. Even though the curse of quantity is normally mediocrity, Oates consistently supplies a product of the highest quality, dense with meaning and filled with beautiful words and full-blown characters.

Oates's poor, unimaginative characters typically ply their swords through a fogged-in existence inflicted on them by a fatalistic creator. They cannot escape from the miasma they must breathe, and so they are poisoned by it, confused by muddled thoughts in an unkind world. The characters finally become enraged by their situation and so do bloody battle to extricate themselves from it. Sometimes as a result they resign themselves to the human condition of conflict; at other times, they experience a tragic lack of resolution.

With Shuddering Fall

In her first novel, *With Shuddering Fall*, Oates introduces a theme that has pervaded almost all the rest of her fiction works: the awful responsibility of freedom. Her characters struggle to divest themselves of their little lives in order to achieve personal freedom, but they are unable to cope with the consequences of their release from their former lives. They learn that they have abandoned not only their pasts but also their identities. Then they must struggle either to reclaim their selves or to forge new ones.

With Shuddering Fall is one character's reconciliation with her life, and this treaty gains for her a new appreciation of her history and that of her family. Karen must endure a sort of familiar ritual under the hands of her father, Hert, and her lover, Shar. At first Karen rejects her father's values. He is a legendary figure who wields great power and enjoys a close relationship with Karen; however, this is destroyed by the arrival of the violent, virile Shar, who deposes Hert. Shar is not a new ruler, however, but an anarchist who wishes only to topple kings, not replace them. He leaves, and Karen follows, not because she believes in him but because she seeks to escape Hert and "a life dominated by fathers." Once free from her father, Karen begins to feel uprooted, aimless and nameless. Without Hert, she has "nothing of herself but a face, a body, a set of emotions." She discovers that she needs her familial history to add meaning to her identity and so finally refuses the historyless Shar and his attempts at nihilism.

One of these trials is Shar's proclivity for race-car driving in the lowland town of Cherry River. Cherry River is a place that seems to exist for the edification of the summer tourists and little else. It offers appreciation of self-gratification but not of history. The high point of the summer seems to be when Shar commits suicide on the racetrack. Oates shows that in a community with no shared history, the only communal ties that exist are with shared acts of violence.

The spokesman for the novel is Max, a self-centered businessman, who is the only one intelligent enough to share Oates's philosophy with the reader. He appears in many other novels as the maniacal oracle who tries to make Fate subservient to his will. He tries to cheat Karen of her birthright by confounding her with questions, but she eludes him and is, thus, saved. She returns to herself, her family.

Expensive People

Expensive People opens with the fictional narrator explaining to the reader that he is telling the truth. Richard Everett begins by setting up a paradox because nothing he "tells" can ever be the truth since everything in the book is imagined. He goes on to explain that he is—or was—a child murderer in the sense that when he was young, he killed someone. *Expensive People* is written as a memoir, a memoir of someone who does not exist. In fact, Everett confesses that "it's possible that I'm lying without knowing it."

If *Expensive People* appears to be a parody of comic nihilism, of the nothingness of suburban life, it is. From Ernest Hemingway to John Barth, Oates pokes fun at those serious authors who proclaim the world to be formless and empty. Everett's mother, ironically nicknamed Nada, writes in her journal: "In any first-person narration there can be a lot of freedom. Certain central events—what the hell can they be?—leading up to the death." This is certainly a self-criticism of the very novel she is in as well as of those she despises for their negativism.

If Nada consoles herself with her own writing, poor Richard has little with which to comfort himself, unless it is the thought of his mother's death. He is convinced that she hates him, despite his near genius IQ, and wishes to stave off his affections with a series of unwanted puppies. Finally, Richard's fantasies of matricide become confused with reality. In the end, the newspapers show nothing of Nada, only of their house. Richard fades into closure of the book.

Wonderland

It is not chance that Lewis Carroll's child adventure and Oates's novel *Wonderland* bear the same word in the title. Oates considers the work of this nineteenth century English mathematician to ask the pertinent questions of life: Can all of life be just a game, and am I the only one who is not cheating? The protagonists of both novels—Alice and Jesse Harte—run and jump from square to square on a large, mostly unseen chessboard. Along the way they are both transmogrified into oddly sized versions of their original selves. Finally, in order to survive, Jesse and Alice regain their normal proportions and become resolved with their communities.

In the beginning of *Wonderland*, the newly orphaned Jesse travels from his grandfather's farm to an orphanage and finally to the home of Dr. Pedersen, a brilliant but unbalanced surrogate father. He is the first of a triumvirate of adoptive fathers whom Jesse must survive. His biological father's initial attack has given Jesse the strength to deal with these surrogates. His father has slaughtered his wife and their unborn child and wounded Jesse before killing himself. Jesse escapes to his grandfather's farm, where he recuperates until he must start his strange odyssey. Living with the Pedersen family, Jesse learns of things small and fantastic. He studies cell life and becomes involved in Dr. Pedersen's cancer research. The more he learns, the more he is confused by his father's view of life, which is overshadowed by death. At last, Pedersen grows impatient with Jesse and dismisses him from the family, saying, "You have no existence. You are nothing." Jesse must seek another, more receptive, lifestyle.

Jesse enters medical school, graduates, marries, and tries to forge a new family, a home, for himself. He keeps returning, however, to the site of his father's tragic demise in his dreams. His own children gradually start to shrink away like Carroll's Cheshire Cat. Michelle becomes Shelley and ultimately Shell, until Jesse can no longer grasp her—or the rest of his family—with any degree of certitude. Even Jesse's two father figures, Cady and Perrault, become in turn distant and disdainful. Dr. Cady will not acknowledge anything but the ethereal, and Dr. Perrault will not admit that the mind is anything but actual. These two opposing views further succeed in alienating Jesse from a "real" life. To offset these unrealistic real people, Jesse creates an unreal friend, or series of friends, but she only promises disharmony and death, so he eventually rejects her, too.

In the end of the novel, the action quickens, racing toward the now of the narrative, 1971. Jesse returns to his father's psyche and discovers the final, perfect answer: "A clean, pure, empty being, a void." It is only through the total destruction of the universe that a peaceful existence (or nonexistence) can be enjoyed.

CHILDWOLD

The setting of *Childwold* is again Eden Valley, scene of the action in *With Shuddering Fall* and *Wonderland*. The novel is peopled by a variety of characters and is narrated by several of them in turn, as each becomes the lover of the central figure's mother, Arlene Bartlett. Arlene's daughter, Laney Bartlett, is the unconscious catalyst for much of the violence in the novel.

The primary reaction between Laney and another character occurs between her and Fitz John Kasch, a fiftyish hermit who lives among the debris of his large but deceased family. In Laney, Kasch sees not only his failed marriage but also his repressed desires. She becomes for him both an icon and a Tantalus, love and passion. Unable to avail himself of her, Kasch woos and wins Arlene and becomes another in a lengthy retinue of lovers.

Arlene is a figure of the sex goddess, but, unlike so many untouchable figures, she is the small statue in the back of the church, worn down by the grasp of many hands. This, however, does not dismay her; indeed, it invigorates her. Where many single women would not welcome pregnancy, Arlene revels in it; her children reaffirm her existence in a world of many people. Kasch, on the other hand, is unable to enjoy the company of others. He secrets himself in a small part of what was once the family manse, now a museum. He blames his self-imposed isolation on his divorce, brought on by his former wife's infidelity. By retiring into his hermitage, however, he only amplifies his feelings of detachment from life. Although he seeks to redefine himself in various ways (as a voyeur, among others), he remains at one, in harmony with only himself. When he finally becomes reconciled to the Bartletts' violent way of life, he remains unfulfilled. He can satiate himself neither with the daughter nor with the mother.

Instead of an object of violence, of rape or murder, Laney becomes an object of Kasch's creation. It is at this point that *Childwold* most neatly resembles Vladimir Nabokov's *Lolita* (1955)—the story of a middle-aged man's obsession with a nubile teenage girl. As does Humbert Humbert in *Lolita*, Kasch casts a spell about Laney, using art as a medium, but she eventually escapes, moving though the two-dimensional world of Kasch's photographs to the world of nature outside his museum/prison. She frees herself from the world he is doomed to inhabit.

It is a world that is of his own design. After Arlene has joined Kasch, her former lover, Earl Tuller, returns to threaten and bully her. In a rage, Kasch kills him and seals his fate as a prisoner. He has dreamed of being a murderer, but now that his fantasy has been accidentally made real, he is unable to bear the results. He has been defeated by his own desires mixed with the mindless tide of the universe. The novel ends with Arlene musing over the turn their lives have taken. Laney returns to Kasch's mansion, but he will not answer the door. Imagining that she sees him behind a curtained window, she calls out. She feels she is strong enough, has changed enough from the girl she was, to save him, and so in a flush of anticipation she waits for "a sign, a sign," but it never comes. Oates demonstrates in *Childwold* the tragic consequences of the conflict between humanity's ambitions and the machinations of the world.

BELLEFLEUR

In *Bellefleur*, Oates combines the gothic grotesque and a sense of realism to create a novel that, incredibly, has believable unhuman creatures. If this type of book seems out of character for her, it may be that she wishes to warn her audience that what seems extraordinary may, upon examination, be simply ordinary. In one episode, a huge rodent runs screaming into the house; the next morning, it is nothing but a cat. On the other hand, normality might suddenly become monstrous.

Bellefleur traces the history of the Bellefleur family through several generations and as many psychological aberrations. There are psychics in the family, a gnome who serves Leah Bellefleur, and several ghosts. Jedediah Bellefleur is the manifestation in this novel of the character who forces himself to exist against the will of nature. He is a recurring character in Oates's novels, and in *Bellefleur*, Jedediah is delightfully crazy. In the end, he is persuaded to continue the Bellefleur line despite his (and the reader's) misgivings.

The novel can be difficult for readers because it jumps back and forth from past to present. Another difficulty stems from the fact that the main character of interest, the telepathic Germaine Bellefleur, ages only four years from her birth during the entire action of the novel, while her father ages two or three decades. The setting of the novel itself—the Adirondack mountain range—ages thousands of years. In addition, the mountains and the people shrink or grow spasmodically. The final chapters contain spiritual references that, at first, seem disjointed. After Gideon's transformation into the skeletal Angel of Death, however, a Native American appears to the ancestral Jedediah and tells him to embrace the world that he has abandoned. This is Oates's final message to the reader, that only in a full and relished life is there union with God's body. Thus, as in her first novel, Oates's characters do battle with their own existences, their own beings. They struggle, escape, and wander only to return to their initial resting places within themselves and within the confines of their destinies.

Mysteries of Winterthurn

The characters in *Mysteries of Winterthurn*, however, appear to have relinquished their resting places for ghostly—and ghastly—forays among the living. This gothic mystery novel has been hailed as a feminist dissertation, a charge that Oates has not refuted. Although the main character is male and the action in the novel is seen through his eyes, most of the victims are women and children, and it is to their plight that the narrator and the reader grow sympathetic. In *Mysteries of Winterthurn*, Oates discusses the existence of women in a male-dominated society, and a pitiable existence it is.

Even though Oates owes much of her presentation of the situation of nineteenth century women and children to several other popular authors, her interpretation is uniquely her own. Her victims are disposable pawns in a society that is more than willing to sacrifice them for its own (male) devices. Oates inserts the supernatural into the novel to allow her women a modicum of revenge on these perpetrators. If this seems to be impossible (the unreal attacking the real), Oates insists that once something is thought to be real, it becomes so whether it should be real or not. Thus the view of women as passive, thoughtless beings is true for the males in her novel, even though it is a false concept. The women victims in the novel are freed by this misconception to react violently to those who misuse them because they (the women) cannot have acted in such a manner within the male scheme of things.

To drive this point home, Oates repeats it three times during the novel. The first story, "The Virgin in the Rose-Bower," deals with a sadistic husband and father, Erasmus Kilgarven, who has a hand in the brutal deaths of his two wives and commits incest for several years with his daughter, Georgina, causing her to become pregnant several times. Georgina kills her infants but claims that they have been destroyed by angels painted on the ceiling of her bedroom. The narrator, young Xavier Kilgarven, sees one painted angel bleed, and this leads to the discovery of several other infant corpses, silent witnesses to Erasmus Kilgarven's hideous habit. By claiming supernatural murder (and rape), Georgina is able to evade guilt and exact a small amount of revenge on her father.

In the persona of Iphigenia, her pen name, Georgina is also able to free her female family members by publishing her poetry. The money she receives from this enterprise, until her father forbids it as unseemly, is later used to finance even more unfeminine exploits by the young Perdita. Perdita needs no spectral avenger; she takes matters into her own hands, although she is never seen as a murderer by anyone but the reader. The only people who are capable of violent acts in *Mysteries of Winterthurn* are male; the females are those upon whom these acts are perpetrated. An invisible shield is thus created around Perdita, enabling her to murder several people in order to achieve her goal, union with young Xavier.

The third sister, Thérèse, is able to profit from her sisters' cloaked deeds, and, indeed, there are indications that she may be involved in Perdita's violent crimes in a peripheral manner. This is only hinted at, however; outwardly, Thérèse appears to be a happy, modern woman. It is here that Oates's use of paradox—the woman who is both angel and demon, visible and invisible—culminates. All the women in the novel have been so seduced by the theory of their own guilt that they must violently oppose it in order to free themselves.

Foxfire

Another brilliantly innovative work encompassing Oates's feminist vision is *Foxfire: Confessions of a Girl*

Gang. This novel, set in upstate New York in the 1950's, centers on five high school girls who seek and get revenge on the men who exploit them. By chronicling the exploits of the Foxfire gang, which comprises Legs Sadovsky, Goldie, Lana, Rita, and Maddy Wirtz, Oates reveals how class conflict and the exploitation of girls and women by men and boys consistently reinforce each other. Unlike the female characters in *Mysteries of Winterhurn*, the girl gang members are not paralyzed by fear, guilt, or insecurity. Finding strength in solidarity, the girls, all from low-income families who daily feel the sting of poverty and the humiliation of male chauvinism, resolve not to suffer at the hands of their exploiters, villains they cast as upper-class white men.

The girls, in a wild experiment of role reversal, aggressively seek out their own victims, men who have hurt one or all of them. They subsequently put these men "on trial," and all their victims are "sentenced" to some punishment. By inflicting physical pain or by causing irreversible damage to the men's reputations, the girls see to it that the guilty suffer for the psychic wounds they have caused. While Oates's sympathies clearly lie with the girls, she mitigates the gang's actions by providing the girls with an important insight. All the girls come to realize that evil is not strictly the province of men or the upper class; their own acts of violence clearly reveal to them that, tragically, the propensity for harming others exists in all human beings.

What I Lived For

In *What I Lived For*, Jerome "Corky" Corcoran, the main character, makes a discovery similar to that of the Foxfire gang. As Corky bounces from one volatile situation to another throughout the dense, highly intricate plot of the novel, he becomes the principal figure in a modern tragedy. The narrative, an account of the three most intense days of Corky's life, related by the protagonist himself, reveals his participation in situations and relationships that, as they disintegrate before his eyes, challenge all of Corky's beliefs in the innate goodness of humanity. They also force him to revise his opinion of others as well as his opinion of himself.

Finding himself entangled in these events, which are charged with class conflict, racial tension, political strife, and economic distress, Corky learns that the myths of success, the very myths that he has internalized and employed to sustain his dreams, are false and corrupt. This realization compels him to examine himself, body and soul. He concludes that he too is false and corrupt. He has worshiped the false gods of money and power and has neglected family, religion, and anything else that could have given real meaning and substance to his life. As the narrative proceeds to its tragic conclusion, Oates helps the reader perceive that Corky's flaws are particularly tragic because they are so universal.

My Heart Laid Bare

Like Nabokov's *Lolita*, *My Heart Laid Bare* presents a panorama of a vast, gullible America, a jigsaw puzzle of independent states where people can change identities just by crossing boundary lines. The novel is a parodistic epic about a family of confidence artists in nineteenth and early twentieth century America whose careers are largely shaped by the political, financial, and sociological changes of that turbulent period. Oates's catchy (and somewhat misleading) title refers to a memoir that the protagonist, Abraham Licht, intends to write someday but leaves unfinished at his death. Readers who expect the novel to present a famous woman author's personal confession may feel confused when they find themselves involved with a complicated semihistorical, semigothic, partially tongue-in-cheek story reminiscent of Oates's *Bellefleur*, *A Bloodsmoor Romance*, and *Mysteries of Winterthurn*. Oates has called those popular books "parodistic," explaining that "they are not exactly parodies, because they take the forms they imitate quite seriously."

Abraham Licht is the quintessential laissez-faire social Darwinist of the late nineteenth century. He teaches his children that life is an endless struggle for survival, with every individual pitted against every other. Their only allegiance should be to the family, particularly to himself. Every outsider should be regarded as an enemy and potential victim.

Abraham's two oldest sons are temperamentally as different as Cain and Abel. Thurston is tall, handsome, and refined; Harwood is stocky, ugly, and vulgar. Harwood is the only member of the family who is vicious. When Thurston is scheming to make his fortune by marrying a wealthy society matron, the volatile Harwood creates a scene that exposes Thurston as a bounder and an impostor. When the deluded woman interposes between the quarreling brothers, Harwood inadvertently breaks her neck and flees. Thurston has no choice but to flee also—but in a different direction. Only Thurston is captured, and, true to his family's code of honor, he chooses to be hanged rather than point the finger at his brother. Ultimately, the wily Abraham saves his son by giving him a drug that makes the young man appear dead and spiriting him out of prison in a coffin.

Characters in the novel have a way of disappearing for years and reappearing under different names. Harwood comes back into the saga as Harmon Liges when he befriends Roland Shrikesdale III, a wealthy young tenderfoot vacationing in the Wild West. Harwood conceives a daring scheme based on the fact that he resembles his new friend so closely that they might be taken for twins. He lures his victim into the wilderness, commits a cold-blooded murder, then stumbles back into civilization wearing the dead man's clothing and pretending to be suffering from amnesia. The victim's mother unquestioningly accepts Harwood as her adored child. She has not long to live, and Harwood stands to inherit a large fortune; however, he overplays his hand by inviting Abraham to visit him so that he can show off his affluence and cleverness. The old woman's nephews, who will inherit the fortune if they can prove, as they suspect, that Harwood is an impostor and probably a murderer, investigate and discover the truth about the Lichts. Abraham finds it expedient to disappear when his son's dismembered body is delivered to him in a number of gift-wrapped containers.

In his old age, Abraham finally enters into his first legal marriage. His young bride, Rosamund, as might be expected, belongs to a socially prominent family and inherits a fortune. They have a daughter and lead a peaceful life at Muirkirk. Abraham no longer needs to obtain money illegally. He invests all of his own and his wife's capital in corporate stocks. His whole career has been affected by the invisible hand of history, and it ends in disaster with the great Wall Street crash of 1929. During the subsequent Great Depression, he becomes dependent on his son Darian, who ekes out a living as a music teacher and part-time musician. Then Abraham discovers that Darian and Rosamund have fallen in love. This new blow to his inflated ego changes him into a violent psychopath, but he turns his rage against himself, committing suicide in the treacherous marsh after setting the family home afire in a grand gothic finale.

Missing Mom

Nikki Eaton, who finds her mother murdered and learns about herself as well as her mother during the grief process, is the protagonist of *Missing Mom*, a novel that takes the reader through Nikki's life, from her sibling rivalry and personality conflicts with her suburban perfectionist sister, Claire, to her affair with Wally Szalla, a married man.

In her thirties, Nikki is known as the rebel of the family. Single, with no children, and working as a reporter for the *Chautauqua Valley Beacon*, she lives what some might consider an alternative lifestyle, dying her spiked hair maroon and wearing miniskirts and thigh-high boots rather than the more conservative pantsuits that her sister, a mother and housewife, wears. Nikki's family disapproves of her affair with Wally. Her mother, Gwen, wishes that Nikki would "settle down" and regularly introduces her to "eligible bachelors."

Beginning with a Mother's Day party, the novel introduces Gwen, her family, and her friends. Readers learn that Gwen is popular in the neighborhood, appreciated for her skill and creativity in bread baking as well as her willingness to sacrifice herself for others. She is the shoulder that her friends and family lean on in times of trouble and has a hard time resisting "strays" of any type. This quality contributes to her murder, as it leads her to give a ride to a methamphetamine addict, Ward Lynch, who had formerly done odd jobs at Gwen's house in Mt. Ephraim, New York, as part of a prison rehabilitation program. After forcing her to drive to her house and burglarizing it, Lynch stabs Gwen and leaves her in the basement for dead.

After she finds her mother's body, Nikki endures the trauma of notifying the authorities, including Detective Ross Strabane, and her sister. Throughout the process of grieving over their mother's death, both Nikki and Claire make life changes. Nikki decides to stop seeing Wally after a meeting with his wife, Isabel, in which she learns that she is not the only "other woman."

After Claire and her husband, Rob, agree to a trial separation, Claire moves to Philadelphia, where a wealthy friend of hers has connections that will help her get into graduate school—a step she has put on hold since she "settled" for marriage to Rob and raising a family. Nikki feels abandoned and sad, and her sister's disapproval of Nikki's moving into their mother's home rather than selling it lingers. When Nikki learns that Ward Lynch has requested a trial, claiming innocence, she tries to manage her anger and prepare herself for the trauma of testifying; she then finds out from Detective Strabane that there will be no trial after all. In her profound relief and happiness when Strabane gives her the news, Nikki realizes her attraction to this man, who has been subtly pursuing her, repeatedly giving her his card and letting her know that she can call him any time of the day, for any reason; they become lovers. At the end of the first full year of her grief, Nikki finds that, although it has not ended, she does not have to go through it alone. From learning about the life of her mother, Nikki realizes that she can pay tribute to her mother's memory by settling for no less than love for herself.

Black Girl/White Girl

Black Girl/White Girl centers on two roommates at Schuyler College: Genna Hewett-Meade, a young white woman whose relatives founded the all-women's school, and Minette Swift, an African American scholarship student. During their time together in 1975, Genna develops a deep loyalty to Minette, an unpopular preacher's daughter who holds herself apart from her fellow students and makes no attempts to befriend them. When Genna hears other students make fun of her roommate's middle-aged style of dress, her thick glasses, and her forceful way of speaking, she defends Minette, for which Minette shows little appreciation. When Minette has difficulties keeping her scholarship because her grades are poor, Genna encourages her to seek academic help and assures her that she can raise her grades if she wants to.

Genna, the daughter of a 1960's political radical and a mother with a history of drug and alcohol abuse and sexual promiscuity, with an investment banker brother from whom she is essentially estranged, feels like the most normal member of her family, but she is constantly on edge, waiting for news that her father has been arrested or her mother has had another emotional meltdown. As she tries to befriend Minette and earn her trust, she also finds herself in the role of confidant for her family members, classmates, and even a dean, who questions her when Minette becomes the target of a series of racially oriented incidents. Realizing that Minette herself has orchestrated the incidents (ranging from the defacement of her textbook to a racial slur scrawled on the door of their dorm room), possibly for attention, Genna recognizes Minette's instability but decides to show her loyalty and try to win her trust by keeping the information to herself while Minette gains more attention for the perceived attacks against her.

Feeling betrayed and abandoned when Minette leaves the dorm to live by herself in Stone Cottage, a historical building on campus where only a few students are privileged to live, Genna visits her on her birthday in a final attempt to seal their friendship. She is troubled by the number of candles Minette has carelessly placed around her room and its state of disarray and dirtiness, as well as by Minette's state of agitation. When Genna learns the next day that Minette has died in a fire caused by those candles, she blames herself for not having said anything to Minette about them for fear of incurring her wrath.

At about the same time, Genna finds out that her father has been arrested for aiding and abetting terrorists, and she starts to develop a new identity separate from her family, one in which she can insulate herself from her pain. She gains weight, darkens her hair, trims it short, and wears nondescript clothes. Having dropped out of Schuyler College, she earns a Ph.D. in later years and gains a faculty position. Secure professionally and financially, having inherited investments from her wealthy Meade grandparents, she gives away the interest (approximately $100,000 yearly) to causes and institutions she deems worthy, including Minette's father's church. Ending the novel with a visit to her father in prison, Genna shows how she has succeeded in spite of her dysfunctional family and friends but has sacrificed the vulnerability that might have allowed her to be loved herself.

Jennifer L. Wyatt; Traci S. Smrcka and Bill Delaney
Updated by Holly L. Norton

Other major works

short fiction: *By the North Gate*, 1963; *Upon the Sweeping Flood*, 1966; *The Wheel of Love*, 1970; *Marriages and Infidelities*, 1972; *The Goddess and Other Women*, 1974; *The Hungry Ghosts: Seven Allusive Com-*

edies, 1974; *Where Are You Going, Where Have You Been?*, 1974; *The Poisoned Kiss*, 1975; *The Seduction*, 1975; *Crossing the Border*, 1976; *Night-Side*, 1977; *All the Good People I've Left Behind*, 1978; *The Lamb of Abyssalia*, 1979; *A Sentimental Education*, 1980; *Last Days*, 1984; *Raven's Wing*, 1986; *The Assignation*, 1988; *Heat, and Other Stories*, 1991; *Where Is Here?*, 1992; *Haunted: Tales of the Grotesque*, 1994; *Will You Always Love Me?*, 1994; *The Collector of Hearts*, 1998; *Faithless: Tales of Transgression*, 2001; *I Am No One You Know*, 2004; *The Female of the Species: Tales of Mystery and Suspense*, 2005; *High Lonesome: Stories, 1966-2006*, 2006; *The Museum of Dr. Moses: Tales of Mystery and Suspense*, 2007; *Wild Nights! Stories About the Last Days of Poe, Dickinson, Twain, James, and Hemingway*, 2008.

PLAYS: *Miracle Play*, pr. 1974; *Three Plays*, 1980; *I Stand Before You Naked*, pb. 1991; *In Darkest America: Two Plays*, 1991; *Twelve Plays*, 1991; *The Perfectionist, and Other Plays*, 1995; *New Plays*, 1998.

POETRY: *Women in Love*, 1968; *Anonymous Sins, and Other Poems*, 1969; *Love and Its Derangements*, 1970; *Angel Fire*, 1973; *The Fabulous Beasts*, 1975; *Women Whose Lives Are Food, Men Whose Lives Are Money*, 1978; *Invisible Woman: New and Selected Poems, 1970-1982*, 1982; *The Luxury of Sin*, 1984; *The Time Traveler*, 1989; *Tenderness*, 1996.

NONFICTION: *The Edge of Impossibility: Tragic Forms in Literature*, 1972; *The Hostile Sun: The Poetry of D. H. Lawrence*, 1973; *New Heaven, New Earth: The Visionary Experience in Literature*, 1974; *Contraries: Essays*, 1981; *The Profane Art: Essays and Reviews*, 1983; *On Boxing*, 1987; *(Woman) Writer: Occasions and Opportunities*, 1988; *George Bellows: American Artist*, 1995; *Where I've Been, and Where I'm Going: Essays, Reviews, and Prose*, 1999; *The Faith of a Writer: Life, Craft, Art*, 2003; *Uncensored: Views and (Re)views*, 2005; *Joyce Carol Oates: Conversations, 1970-2006*, 2006; *The Journal of Joyce Carol Oates, 1973-1982*, 2007 (Greg Johnson, editor).

CHILDREN'S/YOUNG ADULT LITERATURE: *Come Meet Muffin*, 1998; *Big Mouth and Ugly Girl*, 2002; *Freaky Green Eyes*, 2003; *Sexy*, 2005; *After the Wreck, I Picked Myself Up, Spread My Wings, and Flew Away*, 2006; *Naughty Chérie*, 2008.

EDITED TEXTS: *Scenes from American Life: Contemporary Short Fiction*, 1972; *The Best American Short Stories 1979*, 1979 (with Shannon Ravenel); *Night Walks: A Bedside Companion*, 1982; *First Person Singular: Writers on Their Craft*, 1983; *The Best American Essays*, 1991; *The Oxford Book of American Short Stories*, 1992; *American Gothic Tales*, 1996; *The Best American Essays of the Century*, 2000 (with Robert Atwan); *Snapshots: Twentieth Century Mother-Daughter Fiction*, 2000 (with Janet Berliner); *The Best American Mystery Stories*, 2005 (with Otto Penzler); *The Ecco Anthology of Contemporary American Short Fiction*, 2008 (with Christopher R. Beha).

Bibliography

Cologne-Brookes, Gavin. *Dark Eyes on America: The Novels of Joyce Carol Oates*. Baton Rouge: Louisiana State University Press, 2005. Presents analysis of selected significant works by Oates, with a focus on exposing her philosophical and cultural worldviews. Valuable addition to studies of Oates's work.

Creighton, Joanne V. *Joyce Carol Oates*. Boston: Twayne, 1979. Provides a penetrating exploration of the themes that dominate Oates's work, such as self-definition, isolation, and violent liberation. Includes chronology and annotated bibliography.

_______. *Joyce Carol Oates: Novels of the Middle Years*. New York: Twayne, 1992. Focuses on Oates's authorial voice, combining critical analysis of Oates's work with the author's own criticism of her work. Surveys fifteen novels written between 1977 and 1990, exploring their autobiographical elements, feminist subtexts, and realistic dimensions. Includes a selected bibliography.

Johnson, Greg. *Invisible Writer: A Biography of Joyce Carol Oates*. New York: Penguin Putnam, 1998. Provides a thorough analysis of Oates's work and life, drawing on a variety of sources, including Oates's private letters and journals.

_______. *Understanding Joyce Carol Oates*. Columbia: University of South Carolina Press, 1987. Good introduction to Oates for the general reader examines both her early major novels and some of her best-known stories. Includes some biographical material and a bibliography.

_______, ed. *Joyce Carol Oates: Conversations*. Princeton, N.J.: Ontario Review Press, 2006. Collection of previously published interviews with Oates spans the years 1970 to 2006. Topics covered include the author's thoughts on the art of fiction, her "lighter" side, and Marilyn Monroe, the subject of her novel *Blonde*. Includes a brief chronology of her life.

Oates, Joyce Carol. *The Journal of Joyce Carol Oates: 1973-1982*. Edited by Greg Johnson. New York: Ecco Press, 2007. Wide-ranging collection of thoughtful, reflective entries traces Oates's life from her time as a professor at the University of Windsor through her move to Princeton University. Oates describes the joys and frustrations of writing as well as her enjoyment of spending time with friends, including some famous writers, and family. Provides a record of her productivity as a writer as well as insight into her philosophical explorations and her views of the human condition.

Wagner, Linda, ed. *Critical Essays on Joyce Carol Oates*. Boston: G. K. Hall, 1979. Collection of twenty-eight reviews and essays includes discussions of particular works as well as analyses of Oates's general themes and stylistic considerations. Supplemented with a chronology and a bibliography as well as a short, refreshing preface by Oates herself.

Wesley, Marilyn. *Refusal and Transgression in Joyce Carol Oates's Fiction*. Westport, Conn.: Greenwood Press, 1993. Feminist analysis focuses on the family as portrayed in Oates's fiction. Contends that the young protagonists of many of Oates's stories and novels commit acts of transgression that serve as critiques of the American family.

EDNA O'BRIEN

Born: Tuamgraney, county Clare, Ireland; December 15, 1930
Also known as: Josephine Edna O'Brien

Principal long fiction

The Country Girls, 1960
The Lonely Girl, 1962 (also known as *Girl with Green Eyes*, 1964)
Girls in Their Married Bliss, 1964
August Is a Wicked Month, 1965
Casualties of Peace, 1966
A Pagan Place, 1970
Zee and Co., 1971
Night, 1972
Johnny I Hardly Knew You, 1977 (also known as *I Hardly Knew You*, 1978)
The Country Girls Trilogy and Epilogue, 1986 (includes *The Country Girls*, *The Lonely Girl*, and *Girls in Their Married Bliss*)
The High Road, 1988
Time and Tide, 1992
An Edna O'Brien Reader, 1994
House of Splendid Isolation, 1994
Down by the River, 1996
Wild Decembers, 1999
In the Forest, 2002
The Light of Evening, 2006

Other literary forms

In addition to her novels, Edna O'Brien has published short fiction, plays and screenplays, poetry, children's books, and works of nonfiction. Her short stories have appeared regularly in magazines such as *The New Yorker*, *The Atlantic Monthly*, and *Cosmopolitan*; collections of her stories include *The Love Object* (1968), *A Scandalous Woman, and Other Stories* (1974), and *Lantern Slides* (1990). Chief among O'Brien's stage plays are *A Cheap Bunch of Nice Flowers* (pr. 1962), *A Pagan Place* (pr. 1972), *Virginia* (pr. 1980), *Triptych* (pr., pb. 2003), and *Iphigenia* (pr., pb. 2003). Her works for film and television include the screenplays *Time Lost and Time Remembered* (1966), *Three into Two Won't Go*

(1969), and *X, Y, and Zee* (1971) and the teleplays *The Wedding Dress* (1963), *Mrs. Reinhardt* (1981), and *The Country Girls* (1983). Among her works of nonfiction are the autobiographical *Mother Ireland* (1976); *Arabian Days* (1977), a travel book; *Vanishing Ireland* (1987), a pictorial; and *James Joyce* (1999), a biography.

Achievements

After moving to London from Dublin, Ireland, in 1959, Edna O'Brien published at a furious pace, mining her early experiences in Ireland and then as a single parent with two sons to rear in England. There was something of a lull in her long fiction, however, from 1977 to 1986. Nearly always from a female narrator's point of view, O'Brien has brilliantly transmuted her personal experiences into art. Her recall and selection of the tiny details that make up the texture of life, particularly in her Irish scenes (*The Country Girls, The Lonely Girl, A Pagan Place*) are most dazzling. Impressive, too, is her evident love and savoring of words—sometimes clearly in a fashion reminiscent of James Joyce—for their own sake, and often in good dialogue. Perhaps because of the speed with which she works, the vivacity and brilliance of her prolific output is frequently marred by awkward grammar, punctuation, and syntax. Apparently, her editors have felt these stylistic lapses are all part of her Irish use of the language and have accordingly let them stand.

O'Brien was a feminist before the term became fashionable, but her works also affirm a wider humanistic sympathy for all people. Early, she took up the topics of women's attitudes toward their bodies, their sexuality, and their roles as mothers and daughters. In Ireland, several of her books have been banned because of their negative commentary on the Roman Catholic Church, more common in her early work, and her frequent use of graphic sexual terms and scenes. Outside Ireland, O'Brien's reputation as a writer of fiction seems assured, although reviewer Marianne Wiggins, writing in *The Nation*, observed that "to the English [she is] a minor self-promoting legend." Despite conflicting critical responses to her work, O'Brien has received numerous awards, including the Kingsley Amis Award in 1962, the Yorkshire Post Award in 1970 for *A Pagan Place*, the Los Angeles Times Book Prize in 1990 for *Lantern Slides* and again in 1992 for *Time and Tide*, the Writers' Guild of Great Britain's Prize for Fiction in 1993, and the European Prize for Literature in 1995; the last of these was presented to O'Brien in tribute to her entire oeuvre.

Biography

Josephine Edna O'Brien was born to Michael and Lena (Cleary) O'Brien in Tuamgraney, county Clare, Ireland, on December 15, 1930. She has one brother and two sisters. Her father was an impractical man who bred horses and squandered his wealth; her mother worked in the United States for eight years, returning to Ireland to marry. O'Brien has characterized her mother as an ambitious, frustrated woman who mistrusted books and was unsympathetic to her daughter's emerging literary interests. (Although O'Brien dedicated her first novel to her mother, she later found her mother's copy with the inscription page torn out and angry comments written throughout.) O'Brien first attended Scarriff National School in 1936, then boarded at the Convent of Mercy, Loughrea, county Galway, in 1941 before going off to the Pharmaceutical College of Ireland in Dublin in 1946, where she worked in a chemist's shop, or drugstore, during the day and attended lectures at night. One of her first purchases in Dublin was a secondhand copy of *Introducing James Joyce* (1944), edited by T. S. Eliot, which first exposed her to the influence of that Irish literary giant. In 1948, she began to write short pieces for the *Irish Press*.

In 1951, O'Brien married novelist Ernest Gebler and lived for a time in rural county Wicklow (the marriage ended in 1964). Two sons, Carlos and Sasha, were born, in 1952 and 1954. In 1959, the family moved to London, and O'Brien's career as a published writer was quickly launched. In three weeks, far from county Clare, she wrote *The Country Girls*, tracing the development of fourteen-year-old Caithleen Brady. The trilogy begun with that first novel was continued in *The Lonely Girl* and *Girls in Their Married Bliss* (the three novels were published together, appended with *Epilogue*, in 1986). O'Brien composed a second trilogy in the 1990's, made up of *House of Splendid Isolation*, *Down By the River*, and *Wild Decembers*. In these later works, O'Brien focused on modern Irish life and problems as they affect both men and women. In addition to her prolific career as a writer, O'Brien teaches her craft. She has lectured in numerous countries and has taught creative writing at City College in New York. In 2006, she was appointed adjunct professor of English literature at University College, Dublin, returning home after her self-imposed exile of many years.

Analysis

Edna O'Brien's early years in Ireland profoundly affected her view of the world, and particularly of women's relationships and their place in society. Being Irish, she says in *Mother Ireland*, gives one a unique view of pleasure and punishment, life and death. O'Brien's work is lyrical and lively. Her memory for people and places, for the minutiae of daily living, is prodigious; her zest for language is Joycean. She is frequently on the attack, but at her best, which is often, she transcends her immediate cause to encourage, with a grain of humor, those who still dream of love achieved through kindness and decency—common virtues still no more common than they ever were.

O'Brien's concerns are most readily accessible in her very eccentric travel/autobiography *Mother Ireland*. Her Irishness is something of which O'Brien is proud: "It's a state of mind." She is not, however, blind to Ireland's faults, appreciating that there must be something "secretly catastrophic" about a country that so many people leave. After an iconoclastic opening chapter on Irish history, with its uncanonized patron saint and its paunchy Firbogs, follow six chapters in which are sketched O'Brien's dominant themes: loneliness, the longing for adventure (often sexual), the repressive Irish Roman Catholic Church, family ties (the martyred mother and the rollicking father), and the courageous hopelessness with which life at best must be lived.

It would be a melancholy picture if it were not for O'Brien's saving, ironic sense of humor and the skill with which she roots her observations in the sensual details of the actual world. Her readers share vividly with her a world of wet batteries for radios, ink powder, walls with fragments of bottles embedded in their tops, Fox's (Glacier) Mints, orange-boxes, and lice combed from a child's head onto a newspaper. O'Brien's recurring themes, her experiments with form, and the feeling she succeeds in communicating that this Irish microcosm has its universal significance are all clearly present in *Mother Ireland*.

The Country Girls

From its detailed, evocative opening page, redolent of genteel poverty, *The Country Girls*, O'Brien's first novel, serves notice of an unusual voice. The shy and sensitive Caithleen tells her first-person story and shares the action with her alter ego, the volatile and malicious Baba. It is a world divided into two warring camps, male and female, where Caithleen's aspirations toward romantic love are doomed to failure. Mr. Gentleman is the first in a long line of rotters (the drunken, brutal father; Eugene Gaillard; Herod; Dr. Flaggler), far outnumbering the few men with decent inclinations (Hickey, Auro); in such a world women stand little chance, single, married in the usual sense, or brides of Christ.

The repressive effects of poverty and a patriarchal society are hardly alleviated by the Church and its proscriptions. Her mother drowned, Caithleen spends her mid-teen years boarding in a strict convent school from which Baba contrives their expulsion for writing a ribald

Edna O'Brien. (Getty Images)

note. In their late teens, joyously, they come up to Dublin, Baba to take a commercial course, Caithleen to work as a grocer's assistant until she can take the civil service examinations. Loneliness, however, follows them: Baba contracts tuberculosis; Caithleen's Mr. Gentleman lets her down. With the resilience of youth, however, her last line in this novel is, "I was almost certain that I wouldn't sleep that night."

The Lonely Girl

The Lonely Girl continues the saga two years later, with Baba healthy again. It is, however, largely Caithleen's story; again she is the narrator. The repressive effects of her family, her village community, and her convent education are again in evidence. O'Brien has her heroine involved romantically with Eugene Gaillard, whose face reminds her of a saint and who is about the same height as her father; he is a cultivated snob, and in an often cold fashion he begins the further education of his naïve, prudish "student," both in bed and in the salon. (As Grace Eckley has pointed out, Caithleen's stiff tutor and O'Brien's former husband, Ernest Gebler, share the same initials.) At the novel's conclusion, Caithleen, wild and debased "because of some damned man," is learning, is changing; she is, as she says, finding her feet, "and when I'm able to talk I imagine that I won't be alone." Still seeking their connection, she and Baba sail on the *Hibernia* from Dublin to Liverpool and London.

Girls in Their Married Bliss

Girls in Their Married Bliss continues the story of the two in London, where, for the first time, Baba assumes the first-person narration, alternating with an omniscient voice distancing O'Brien and the reader from Caithleen's role—a process O'Brien will carry even further with her protagonist in *A Pagan Place*. The women, now about twenty-five years old, have not left their Irish baggage behind in Dublin; there is a splendid, blustery Celtic quality to the scapegrace Baba's style. Kate (as Caithleen is called), too, has her share of one-liners, word associations, epigrams, and zany metaphors: "Self-interest," she observes on one occasion, "was a common crime"; on another, at a party, she is amused by a girl wearing a strawberry punnet on her head to make herself taller.

In these early novels, O'Brien, like her leading characters, is learning and developing her skills. In *Girls in Their Married Bliss*, the topic is still the female search for love and connection. The novel is a precisely observed account of a marriage failing. People rub exquisitely on one another's nerves in the larger context of women's role in society; in the smaller context of bedroom politics, "Men are pure fools." Marriage, at least on the grounds on which the women enter it here, is evidently no end to the quest. Baba makes a calculated move for comfort; Kate sees that her interest in people is generated solely by her own needs. They have matured to the point where they no longer believe much in romantic plans. Kate's answer to the biological unfairness of God's scheme for women, as Baba sees it, is to have herself sterilized; she will not make the same mistake again: No other child of hers will be abducted by its father; no further child of hers will in its turn become a parent.

In the edition of the complete trilogy that was published in one volume in 1986, O'Brien includes a brief *Epilogue* in the form of a monologue delivered by Baba. Here the ebullient Baba brings the reader up to date: The despairing Kate is dead; she drowned, perhaps deliberately.

August Is a Wicked Month

In O'Brien's next novel, *August Is a Wicked Month*, an omniscient narrator describes the protagonist's abortive attempts at self-liberation, largely through sexual activity. Ellen is something like Kate of the earlier trilogy—a superstitious, convent-bred, twenty-eight-year-old Irish magazine writer, formerly a nurse, living in London when the novel begins. She takes a trip to France when the husband from whom she is separated and their eight-year-old son, Mark, who lives with her, go on a camping holiday together. Her "pathetic struggles towards wickedness" involve rejecting the first sexual invitations she encounters. Eventually, however, when Ellen does become intimately involved with a high-living group, O'Brien subjects her to two catastrophic accidents: She receives a call from her husband, who tells her that her son has been killed by a car in a roadside accident, and she fears, wrongly as it turns out, that she has contracted a venereal disease. The guilt and the judgment are clear; perhaps they are too clear to make this novel an artistic success. Ellen finally finds an uneasy autumnal peace, unlike the women in O'Brien's next novel, who have a genuine joy ripped away from them.

Casualties of Peace

In *Casualties of Peace*, Willa McCord, artist in glass, and her earthy domestic, Patsy Wiley, are the protagonists, exemplary victims of male violence. An omniscient narrator views the two unhappy women—Willa having escaped from a nightmarish marriage to the sadistic Herod, Patsy currently suffering her husband Tom's blows. Both have their dreams of happiness outside marriage shattered. There was a chance for peace for them, but accidents prevented them from knowing joy. Patsy blabs to Willa about leaving Tom rather than doing it immediately, as planned, and her lover, Ron, believes she has let him down. Willa, just when a loving connection with Auro seems possible, is murdered by Tom, who mistakes her for Patsy.

Casualties of Peace is second only to *Night*, which it anticipates to some extent, among O'Brien's most Joycean novels. Patsy's love letters to Ron are reminiscent of the earthiest of James Joyce and Nora Barnacle's correspondence; Patsy indeed is a kind of Molly Bloom figure (more clearly developed in *Night*). Willa's letters to Auro, delivered posthumously, share the same stream-of-consciousness qualities: Words pile up into lists; associations trigger other more graphic associations; "memory is the bugger." At times lyrical, at times humorous, O'Brien develops here the Celtic flair with words that is associated with Joyce or Dylan Thomas. Her theme is loneliness and its myriad causes; her characters search to alleviate their pain, to make connections, to overcome their feelings of guilt for being themselves.

A Pagan Place

A Pagan Place is a very odd novel; it is largely a sophisticated rewrite of *The Country Girls*, as O'Brien perhaps would have written that work had she had ten more years of reading, writing, and living behind her at the time. Baba is dropped in favor of one unnamed, preadolescent girl whose sexual arousal when her father beats her accomplishes her move toward adolescence. Getting away from her Irish family and Irish community, with their hereditary guilt, will, it is suggested, take her yet a stage further. At the end of the novel she leaves to the accompaniment of an eerie Hibernian howl.

Throughout the work an omniscient narrator, who sometimes uses dialect forms and sometimes very erudite words, and who is clearly unreliable in matters of fact (putting an English "general" on Nelson's pillar), places the reader at the center of the action by using the second-person narrative. No one but "you," then, is at the center of the action; the narrator and the writer are similarly distanced from the action.

Perhaps in this novel O'Brien exorcised the worst of her Irishness; certainly, very violent feelings surface, all in the consciousness of a young girl. O'Brien, in contrast to her contemporaries among Irish writers of fiction, such as Brian Friel or Benedict Kiely, really seems to dislike her Celtic community. Here is a very bitter indictment of the Church, and perhaps its ultimate rejection in the priest's attempt to seduce "you," masturbating and ejaculating on "you." Here, too, is a savage, repressive, guilt-ridden world of so-called Christians where unwed mothers receive no *caritas*, and where legally wed mothers and fathers show no love either. It is a world where holy water is sprinkled on thoroughbred foals, where a black dog, chasing a frog that jumps out of the ashes at Della's wake, is seen as one and the same with the devil. All in all, it is, with few exceptions, a nightmarish community, especially for a child. For "you" as a child at the center of this world, deserted even by "your" mother at one period, a thing "you" thought would never happen, the only certainty is that "you" want to escape, whatever the burden of guilt "you" carry.

Zee and Co.

The theme of escape is continued in *Zee and Co.*, where O'Brien's heroines are back in London, and again a pair. Zee moves increasingly aggressively and ruthlessly to hold her man, Robert, while dominating Stella, her rival. She succeeds in both endeavors. As the war of the sexes heats up, Zee refuses to be a victim; she is no patsy. O'Brien's long preoccupation with the defensive role of women in society appears to be shifting to the offensive in her later works as her heroines themselves become less fragmented. A person needs to be integrated psychically to withstand not only sexual partners and spouses but also all manifestations of phantoms, prejudice, repression, guilt, and loneliness. This new positive attitude is well illustrated in the rambunctious Mary Hooligan, whose nightlong monologue forms O'Brien's next work, *Night*.

Night

In form and style, *Night* is O'Brien's most Joycean novel. In a harangue from her bed in England, Mary Hooligan—Irish, abused, divorced—delivers herself of an aggressive, courageous, independent, first-person autobiographical statement. Beginning with an Anglo-Saxon monosyllable in the opening paragraph, the nonconciliatory tone of her monologue is established. "I am a woman," Mary affirms, and proceeds to weave, in time and place, the story of her connection with her father and mother, her former husband—"the original Prince of Darkness"—and her son. It is an exuberant linguistic spree: From a "trepidation" of gelatin-like dessert to the welcome "tap o' the mornin'," metaphors and apt words are savored and invented. The pervasive humor is wry; the aggressive tone and confident technique perfectly match the content of a work whose burden is rebellion against loveless unions and ignorance.

Mary Hooligan is another in O'Brien's procession of outsiders, an Irish woman in England, merely house-sitting, so even less important in the community. O'Brien, however, establishes Mary as a force on her own: Mary rejects her friend Madge—Mary needs no Kate figure to complement her being; she is complete on her own. The theme under review remains the eternal search for love in its myriad manifestations; what is new here is the heroine's joyful attack as she continues her pilgrimage to "the higher shores of love." Family, community, and marriage settings are again explored. Many of the details are familiar: the vicious father, the ignoramuses who could not tell cheese from soap, the cold-fish husband. Constant and familiar in O'Brien's work is the warm regard for children, particularly mothers' regard for their sons. This aspect of love leads O'Brien to flirt with incest in her most violent work, *I Hardly Knew You*, in which the narrator has an affair with and then murders her son's friend.

I Hardly Knew You

Nora, the protagonist of *I Hardly Knew You*, tells her story in yet another night monologue, from her prison cell, as she awaits trial for the murder of Hart, her young lover. Again, O'Brien's narrator is an Irish exile in England, divorced from an overly frugal husband, with a son, and literally in prison, isolated from all society. Loneliness is at the core of her existence, as it is, she remarks, at the core of Celtic songs. Her monologue shuffles time and space more formally than Mary Hooligan's in *Night* and reveals a world of increasing violence. Details and incidents from O'Brien's previous works, as far back even as *The Country Girls*, show up: the drunken father taking the cure, the child-abduction threat, the child scraping the toilet-seat paint, the kicking match engaged in by brutish relatives.

The world has become an increasingly violent place, and the response of O'Brien's narrator matches it. Like Mary's, Nora's personality is integrated, but toward the Kate side. She engages in an explicitly lesbian encounter, but she needs no other woman to complement her. Indeed, she acts increasingly like the worst stereotype of the sadistic male predator, who uses and abuses other people, particularly women and especially wives. This is a chilling picture of a person driven to violence, to kill without regret. Here is a woman who has lost her balance and whose sweeping indictment of men must surely be viewed as just as reprehensible as male chauvinism. "I am proud . . . to have killed one of the breed to whom I owe nothing but cruelty, deceit, and the asp's emission," she avers, ignoring absolutely O'Brien's often-stated support for "human decency" and kindness among people of whatever sex.

The High Road

The graph of O'Brien's fictional split personalities is by no means a straight line. A clearly differentiated pair in the early trilogy, each "Kate" and "Baba" is subsequently given an alternating fictional forum. The *Epilogue* may have seemed to clear the way for Baba and zesty Baba types, but *The High Road*, published two years later, has readers once again seeing a sophisticated society through the moist eyes of a Kate type.

Anna, the narrator of *The High Road*, like many of the women in O'Brien's short stories as well, has come on Easter Sunday to a Mediterranean paradise to get over a London love doomed from its inception. In this exotic setting, she encounters eccentric members of the international set: the superannuated debutante, Portia; the grotesques who make up a German fashion-magazine staff on location; the fading jet-setter, Iris; the itinerant Irish painter, D'Arcy, with the Joycean language flair; and Catalina, the hotel chambermaid, with whom she has an affair. It all ends in murder; D'Arcy, to buy some time, paints "Lesbos" on a multitude of walls, not merely on Catalina's gable, where the word first appeared, but to no avail. Clutching a scarf full of Catalina's blood-soaked hair, in what in its accumulation of similes seems at times a parody of the gothic romance, Anna sets out, she says, for the last time, for home. Whether she has left behind her the purgatory of motherhood, in its various manifestations, remains to be read.

Time and Tide

O'Brien continues her focus on Irish women's lives and social roles in *Time and Tide*. The title of the work refers to linear progression and cyclical repetition, devices that she incorporates not only thematically (the changeability and sameness of women's lives) but stylistically. The story develops episodically, providing vignettes from the narrator's life. The protagonist, Nell, following a failed marriage to an abusive spouse, has raised two sons independently. Early in the novel it is revealed that her eldest son, Paddy, is enmeshed in drug use. Ironically, it is not an overdose but a boating accident that claims his life. The novel then reverses time to recount earlier family events, contributory tragedies that lead up to and culminate in the loss of Nell's firstborn son.

A powerful image in the novel is that of a barge colliding with a tourist boat on the Thames. That Paddy should be aboard the latter and this random accident claims his life not only reveals the unpredictability of events but also highlights the young man's chosen and quick route through life. Rejecting the misery he associates with his long-suffering mother, he embraces the thrills of drugs and holidays, but his pleasure-seeking life, prematurely ended, only intensifies his family's despair. For O'Brien's characters, there is no respite from the barges of life, from the inevitable hardships that destroy any illusion of happiness.

Despite the desolate events recounted—Nell herself has indulged in narcotics and sexual liaisons, finding solace in neither—the novel ends with a measure of optimism. When her surviving son, Tristan, leaves home to join Paddy's girlfriend (who is pregnant with Paddy's child), Nell is dejected at first by his departure. Eventually, she finds respite in her now quiet home. Having borne the worst, the death of a child, she must accept what is to come, life in all its myriad sorrows and momentary pleasures.

House of Splendid Isolation

O'Brien returns to her native territory with a trilogy of novels set in modern Ireland. The first, *House of Splendid Isolation*, is a stunning book, quite different from her previous work. It reveals a microcosm of divided Ireland, embodied by the patriot-terrorist McGreevy and the widow Josie O'Meara. McGreevy, seeking to free Northern Ireland from British rule, has been sent to the complacent South to murder a prominent English visitor. He plans to hide in Josie's decaying mansion, which he believes is empty. Feared as a coldly efficient terrorist, McGreevy emerges as a surprisingly kind, ordinary man who has been honed to a thin edge by violence.

Josie, ill with pneumonia and high blood pressure, has just been released from a nursing home to her house of isolation. She seems pluckier than most O'Brien heroines, perhaps because she is elderly, although flashbacks illuminate the early life that formed her. The collision of the revolutionary and the antiterrorist, and their gradual sympathy and understanding, defines the conflict of the novel and the hunt that follows. Josie can be seen as the *Shan Van Vocht*, the Poor Old Woman, a historical symbol of Ireland, exemplifying the domestic life of her people. McGreevy represents the bitter fruit of the country's troubled political history. The inevitable conclusion proceeds as well-meaning, patriotic volunteers from both factions struggle with duty, guilt, and grief.

Surprisingly, O'Brien avoids her usual male stereotypes in this novel; she presents imperfect men, both law-abiding and lawless, who are racked by ambivalence. She remains neutral, revealing with rueful detachment the human damage caused by centuries of conflict. *House of Splendid Isolation* offers a portrait of Ireland in all its complexity, with its intense people and its bloody and heartbreaking history.

Down by the River

The second installment in the trilogy, *Down by the River*, is a less objective book than *House of Splendid Isolation*. The novel was inspired by a controversial incident that took place in Ireland in 1992, when a pregnant fourteen-year-old girl fled to England for an abortion but was brought back and made a ward of the court. O'Brien has changed some details of the case; in her version, Mary MacNamara is impulsively raped by her father as they are picking berries. Mary's dying mother and a female doctor suspect the truth, as do others, but no one acts.

Here again is the world familiar to O'Brien's readers, a world of repression and guilt, in which people do not look directly at each other or say what needs to be said. In a tacit conspiracy of avoidance, everyone knows that Mary is pregnant as a result of the rape, but no one will confront the problem. Worse is the hypocrisy of those quick to judge without mercy. Self-righteous adulterers preen in antiabortion meetings while a shrill speaker waves bloody photographs, even as a retired midwife recalls the dead babies she has found stuffed in drawers and toilets. Other folks are genuinely troubled, torn between religious conviction and pity for the girl. Although a sympathetic neighbor finally agrees to help Mary escape to London to obtain an abortion, the plan is thwarted. People on both sides of the issue exploit Mary for their own purposes, and the novel's ending is tense and melodramatic, though not entirely convincing.

Wild Decembers

Wild Decembers completes the political trilogy begun with *House of Splendid Isolation*. Each of the three novels explores a social issue that has plagued Ireland in its recent history but the origins of which stretch back in time. Whereas the first novel in the series focuses on sectarian violence and the second on abortion rights, the third and final work tills Ireland's very soil. Set in the fictional rural parish of Cloontha, *Wild Decembers* chronicles a series of seemingly petty land disagreements between two farmers: longtime resident Joseph Brennan and his immigrant neighbor, Michael Bugler. Further complications arise from Bugler's growing interest in Brennan's younger sister, Breege, and the unexpected arrival of Bugler's Australian fiancé. By novel's end, one farmer is dead and the other in prison, the land and the women who remain behind abandoned by the men. O'Brien layers the text with numerous references, Irish (the Great Famine), mythological (stories of Greek gods and mortals), and biblical (the struggle between Cain and Abel), thus expanding the significance of this tale of two Irish farmers who feud over territory.

In the Forest

In the Forest explores the childhood trauma and mental frailty that eventually lead a deranged young Irishman to take the lives of three innocent people, including a single mother and her child. As she has in previous novels, notably *House of Splendid Isolation* and *Wild Decembers*, O'Brien incorporates elements of Irish and Greek mythology to imbue her story with universal qualities. Michael O'Kane, whose name (literally "of Cain") carries biblical import, is either a monster or an emotionally disturbed young man. His victims try to relate to him as the latter in a failed attempt to avoid their fates and in an effort to understand the source of his psychosis. As they learn from their captor, O'Kane's childhood was marked by abuse, abandonment, and confinement.

In his youth, Michael O'Kane was identified by his community as an individual capable of great cruelty. His adolescent nickname, *Kinderschreck* (German for "one who scares children"), connotes his designation by society as a monster. Institutionalized and drugged for much of his life, including a final stint in an English facility, Michael is allowed by British authorities to return to Ireland. The multiple murders he commits on his home soil verify that his release was premature and imprudent. In this portrait of a serial killer, O'Brien raises disturbing questions that remain with readers. To what extent does society contribute to the making of its monsters, its sociopaths and violent criminals? Once these dangerous outsiders have been identified, where should society place them? Most pointedly, after such individuals have been labeled *Kinderschrecken*, how should society expect them to behave?

The Light of Evening

In *The Light of Evening*, O'Brien returns to the subject matter of earlier novels: an examination of the troubled and changing lives of Irish women. She also mines biographical material as she depicts the tense relationship between a traditional Irish mother and her less traditional daughter, an emerging writer. Perhaps as a sign of her own maturity as an author and a woman, O'Brien allows the aged Dilly to reminisce about the past from her hospital bed as she awaits the arrival of her adult daughter Eleanora. Recalled in Dilly's mind are events from her life that are similar to episodes in O'Brien's mother's life, including an emigration to America that is followed by a return to Ireland and marriage. Most revealing of their troubled relationship is Dilly's maternal disappointment when Eleanora marries a foreigner, an act that for a time severs familial and national ties. When

Eleanora finally arrives at her bedside, Dilly's anticipated encounter with her daughter proves disappointing; the two women remain estranged. Left behind as counterevidence to Dilly's more positive remembrances is Eleanora's personal journal, which houses a far different and darker perspective on the events of the women's lives.

Archibald E. Irwin; Joanne McCarthy
Updated by Dorothy Dodge Robbins

Other major works

SHORT FICTION: *The Love Object*, 1968; *A Scandalous Woman, and Other Stories*, 1974; *Mrs. Reinhardt*, 1978 (also known as *A Rose in the Heart*, 1979); *Returning*, 1982; *A Fanatic Heart*, 1984; *Lantern Slides*, 1990.

PLAYS: *A Cheap Bunch of Nice Flowers*, pr. 1962; *A Pagan Place*, pr. 1972 (adaptation of her novel); *The Gathering*, pr. 1974; *Virginia*, pr. 1980; *Flesh and Blood*, pr. 1985; *Iphigenia*, pr., pb. 2003 (adaptation of Euripides' play); *Triptych*, pr., pb. 2003.

POETRY: *On the Bone*, 1989.

SCREENPLAYS: *Girl with Green Eyes*, 1964 (adaptation of her novel); *Time Lost and Time Remembered*, 1966 (with Desmond Davis; also known as *I Was Happy Here*); *Three into Two Won't Go*, 1969; *X, Y, and Zee*, 1971 (also known as *Zee and Company*; adaptation of her novel).

TELEPLAYS: *The Wedding Dress*, 1963; *Nothing's Ever Over*, 1968; *Mrs. Reinhardt*, 1981 (adaptation of her short story); *The Country Girls*, 1983 (adaptation of her novel).

NONFICTION: *Mother Ireland*, 1976; *Arabian Days*, 1977; *James and Nora: A Portrait of Joyce's Marriage*, 1981; *Vanishing Ireland*, 1986; *James Joyce*, 1999.

CHILDREN'S LITERATURE: *The Dazzle*, 1981; *A Christmas Treat*, 1982; *The Expedition*, 1982; *The Rescue*, 1983; *Tales for the Telling: Irish Folk and Fairy Stories*, 1986.

EDITED TEXT: *Some Irish Loving*, 1979.

Bibliography

Byron, Kristine. "'In the Name of the Mother . . . ': The Epilogue of Edna O'Brien's Country Girls Trilogy." *Women's Studies* 31 (July/August, 2002): 447-465. Analyzes the function of O'Brien's epilogue and contrasts it with more traditional literary uses of epilogues in general. Argues that the epilogue does not provide closure to the saga of Kate and Baba, but rather disclosure, allowing for a rereading of the entire trilogy.

Colletta, Lisa, and Maureen O'Connor, eds. *Wild Colonial Girl: Essays on Edna O'Brien*. Madison: University of Wisconsin Press, 2006. Collection of critical essays examines O'Brien's works, assessing the manner in which O'Brien both responds to and undermines traditional Irish literature and figureheads while simultaneously charting a decisively feminist literary course for her native tongue.

Eckley, Grace. *Edna O'Brien*. Lewisburg, Pa.: Bucknell University Press, 1974. Excellent brief study was the first such examination of O'Brien's fiction. Among the themes in O'Brien's extremely personal work discussed are those of love and loss.

Gillespie, Michael Patrick. "(S)he Was Too Scrupulous Always." In *The Comic Tradition in Irish Women Writers*, edited by Theresa O'Connor. Gainesville: University Press of Florida, 1996. Discusses how O'Brien's humor is distinguished from that of Irish male writers; shows the relationship between her humor and that of James Joyce, particularly the relationship between her short stories and those in Joyce's *Dubliners* (1914).

Harris, Michael. "Outside History: Edna O'Brien's *House of Splendid Isolation*." *New Hibernia Review* 10 (March 3, 2006): 111-122. Examines the novel in the context of postmodernism, including the author's use of pastiche, decentering, and fragmentation.

Hooper, Brad. Review of *In the Forest*, by Edna O'Brien. *Booklist*, January 1-15, 2002, 776. Observes that this psychological thriller breaks with previous O'Brien works by exposing a dark side to the human condition that is universal as opposed to uniquely Irish—in this case, the communal fear generated by a killer at large.

Mara, Miriam. "The Geography of Body: Borders in Edna O'Brien's *Down by the River* and Colum McCann's 'Sisters.'" In *The Current Debate About the Irish Literary Canon: Essays Reassessing the Field Day Anthology of Irish Writing*, edited by

Helen Thompson. Lewiston: N.Y.: Edwin Mellen Press, 2006. Explores borders as a metaphor for both bodily and national boundaries and notes O'Brien's ability to trespass on and transcend barriers in *Down by the River*.

O'Brien, Edna. "Edna O'Brien." Interview by Caitriona Moloney and Helen Thompson. In *Irish Women Writers Speak Out: Voices from the Field*. Syracuse, N.Y.: Syracuse University Press, 2003. O'Brien discusses her intertwined identities as writer, woman, and postcolonialist.

Quintelli-Neary, Margaret. "Retelling the Sorrows in Edna O'Brien's Country Girls Trilogy." *Nua: Studies in Contemporary Irish Writing* 4, nos. 1/2 (2003): 65-76. Examines O'Brien's treatment of female experiences in relationship to tragedy.

FLANN O'BRIEN

Brian O'Nolan

Born: Strabane, Ireland; October 5, 1911
Died: Dublin, Ireland; April 1, 1966
Also known as: Brian O'Nolan; Brian O'Nuallain; Brother Barnabus; George Knowall; Myles na Gopaleen; Great Count O'Blather; John James Doe

Principal long fiction

At Swim-Two-Birds, 1939
An Béal Bocht, 1941 (also known as *The Poor Mouth*, 1973)
The Hard Life, 1961
The Dalkey Archive, 1964
The Third Policeman, 1967
The Complete Novels, 2007

Other literary forms

Flann O'Brien was the pen name used by Brian O'Nolan for the four novels he wrote in English, and so it is used here, although his work in other forms appeared under other names. He was a talented and prolific journalist as well as a novelist. He began to write satiric essays for student publications at University College, Dublin; a sampling of this student work was reprinted in the "Flann O'Brien Number" published by the *Journal of Irish Studies* in 1974. Although a civil servant by profession, O'Brien also wrote a famous column for *The Irish Times* under the name Myles na Gopaleen. This column continued on a regular basis for twenty-five years; selections were reprinted in *Cruiskeen Lawn* (1943), *The Best of Myles* (1968), and *The Various Lives of Keats and Chapman and the Brother* (1976).

Throughout his career, O'Brien sporadically produced skits for theater, essays other than journalism, and short stories. These are most conveniently located in two posthumous collections. *Stories and Plays* (1973) reprints two dramatic skits, two short stories, an essay on James Joyce called "A Bash in the Tunnel," and the seven existing chapters of an unfinished novel called *Slattery's Sago Saga. A Flann O'Brien Reader* (1978) includes examples of his journalism, short fiction, and essays, along with excerpts from his five novels.

Achievements

Flann O'Brien's contemporary reputation rests on the rediscovery of his first novel, *At Swim-Two-Birds*, an event that occurred about twenty years after the novel was published. The novel had received praise from Joyce, Dylan Thomas, and Graham Greene, among others, but its possibilities for broad critical and popular success were thwarted by the onset of World War II. His next novel, *The Third Policeman*, could find no publisher until after his death, and his third novel, *The Poor Mouth*, was written in Gaelic and thus limited to an extremely small audience. These three novels are now considered to be O'Brien's most important works.

About 1960, O'Brien's work was rediscovered by American writers S. J. Perelman and William Saroyan.

Their praise, principally of his journalism, led to a reissue of *At Swim-Two-Birds* and critical recognition of it as an important novel. In response to this renewal of interest in his fiction, O'Brien wrote *The Hard Life* and *The Dalkey Archive*, but neither of these later novels is as interesting nor as important as his three earlier novels. O'Brien's journalism, in posthumous collections, is the source of most of his popular appeal today, particularly in Ireland. The focus of almost all critical interest in his work, however, is on his novels, especially *At Swim-Two-Birds* and *The Third Policeman*. O'Brien is now universally recognized as the most significant Irish novelist of his generation.

Biography

Flann O'Brien was born Brian O'Nolan on October 5, 1911, in Strabane, county Tyrone, Ireland. He was the third of twelve children of Michael Victor O'Nolan, a customs officer, and Agnes Gormlet O'Nolan. O'Brien's family was frequently relocated in the course of his father's profession, and this postponed his early formal education. His family was extremely literate, however, and in the home O'Brien developed early fluency in Irish Gaelic as well as English and also some familiarity with Latin and Greek classics. It was only in 1923, when his father was transferred to Dublin, that O'Brien was enrolled, at the age of twelve, in the Synge Street School run by the Christian Brothers. In 1925, his father was appointed a revenue commissioner in Dublin Castle, and this advancement permitted the family to settle permanently in Blackrock, a southern suburb of Dublin, in 1927. In that year, O'Brien was enrolled in Blackrock College, a preparatory school. In 1929, he entered University College, Dublin.

At University College, O'Brien was a success in his studies and in extracurricular literary activities. In 1933, he earned a bachelor of arts degree in English, Irish, and German; won the school's gold medal for debate; and was awarded a scholarship for study at the University of Cologne. After a year in Germany, he returned to University College and earned his master of arts degree in 1935 with a thesis on Irish poetry in Gaelic. The early intimations of his literary career, however, were more apparent in his nonscholarly activities. In 1931, he invented the persona Brother Barnabas for the student magazine *Comhthrom Féinne*. A subsequent series of articles under this name was brought to a close in 1934 by a "posthumous" piece called "Scenes from a Novel" that anticipates the metafictional premise of *At Swim-Two-Birds*. In 1934, O'Brien also invented the persona Count O'Blather for his own short-lived magazine in English called *Blather*.

Following the conclusion of his graduate work, O'Brien joined the Irish civil service in 1935; he would continue in its employ until 1953. In 1935 he also began work on *At Swim-Two-Birds*, which was published in 1939 but commercially undone by the decimation of English book sales by World War II. By 1940, he had completed *The Third Policeman*, which was not published until after his death. In subsequent years, O'Brien told friends that he had lost this manuscript, but he nevertheless reworked it into the much more superficial novel *The Dalkey Archive* two decades later.

These discouraging setbacks were offset to some extent by the success of an outrageous literary scam. Under a series of fictitious names, O'Brien and Niall Sheridan began an attack on Dublin's presiding literary deities in the pages of *The Irish Times*, and, during the exchange of heated letters to the newspaper that followed, they began to attack their own original position under new fictitious names. When the scheme came to light, *The Irish Times* editor R. M. Smyllie had the goodwill and foresight to hire O'Brien to write a regular column. First in Irish and then in English, these columns of Myles na Gopaleen appeared at a rate of approximately three per week from October 4, 1940, until his final illness in 1966. As an outgrowth of his first columns in Irish, O'Brien wrote *The Poor Mouth* in Irish as Myles na Gopaleen in 1941.

O'Brien had thus completed his three important novels by the age of thirty; one was generally ignored, one remained in manuscript, and one was published in a language inaccessible even to most Irish citizens. A combination of cynicism and absorption in journalism effectively ended his career as a novelist at that point. By the time of the rediscovery of *At Swim-Two-Birds*, O'Brien was already suffering from the effects of lifelong heavy drinking. He managed to respond to interest in his past work with *The Hard Life* and *The Dalkey Archive*, but these works lack the textual complexities of his earlier and more important novels. It is a final, appropriate irony

Flann O'Brien. (Getty Images)

that O'Brien, inventor of fictional disguises and elaborate literary conceits, died of alcohol-related maladies on April Fools' Day of 1966.

Analysis

Flann O'Brien's first and most important novel, *At Swim-Two-Birds*, was published the year that William Butler Yeats died. The coincidence is notable because the novel was a parodistic melange of styles spawned by the Irish Literary Revival championed by Yeats and because all of O'Brien's important novels critique literary fabrications akin to those of the revival. The Irish Literary Revival was based on the rediscovery of the special identity of Ireland, especially as this was apparent in the literature of the Celtic legends. In popularizing these legends, the participants in the revival, many of whom—unlike O'Brien—had no fluency in the Gaelic language, were prone to literary extravagance and inflated notions of Celtic nobility. The literature of the revival was instrumental in arousing political energies that led to the creation of the Irish Free State, but after this goal of political independence had been realized, many of the revival's own literary excesses became apparent. Modern problems such as economic recession, entanglements of church and state, and the entrenched conservatism of an emerging middle class made the essential artifice of the inspiring revival literature especially visible for the first time.

O'Brien wrote none of the important fiction about the Irish Republic of his own day; instead, his major works look back to the earlier mythologizing of Celtic identity and modern Irish culture. *At Swim-Two-Birds*, *The Third Policeman*, and *The Poor Mouth* all ridicule the pretensions of literature by emphasizing its artificiality. O'Brien's work is satiric in effect because it implicitly corrects notions of literary authority, cultural privilege, and innate national aristocracy. Its primary mode is parody, adoption, and exaggeration of a variety of recognizable literary styles to demonstrate their essential mendacity.

The salient quality of O'Brien's career is ambiguity concerning his name and identity. He took the pen name Flann O'Brien from Gerald Griffin's 1829 novel *The Collegians*, while the name Myles na Gopaleen came from Dion Boucicault's play *The Colleen Bawn* (1860), based on Griffin's novel. Both of these pseudonyms recall stage Irishmen, a stereotype of nineteenth century English fiction. In the revival, a new domestic stereotype of the Irish prevailed, one as falsely noble as the earlier English one was debased. Thus, these names attached to O'Brien's novels challenged the new literary identity of Ireland as a sheer fabrication.

O'Brien's first three novels are relentless in their scrutiny of fabricated literary identities; his later two novels are less successful because that scrutiny is limited, and because some assumptions about identity are allowed to stand unchallenged. Ultimately, his finest works have affinities with that strain of modern literature that asserts the reality of a metaphysical void, a senseless core of anonymity beneath the guises, literary and otherwise, protectively adopted to give life a semblance of meaning. This is especially true of *The Third Policeman*, which is freer of provincial references than O'Brien's other novels. The relish for parodying things Irish, most apparent in *At Swim-Two-Birds* and *The Poor Mouth*, however, suggests that the primary frame of reference for O'Brien's novels will always be the cultural history of early twentieth century Ireland.

At Swim-Two-Birds

At Swim-Two-Birds, which takes its name from the literal translation of a Gaelic place-name, is the most complete critique in novel form of the excesses of the Irish Literary Revival. O'Brien was fluent in Gaelic and a talented parodist, and in this novel he exploits the essential artifice of revival literature by placing its various literary styles in collision with one another. Here Finn MacCool, evoked in all his epic splendor, meets the hack writer Dermot Trellis; the mad bard Sweeny, whose verses are included in hilarious literal translations into English, meets Jem Casey, poet of porter; the Good Fairy, taken from the most sentimental of Irish tourist literature, sits down to cards with urban characters taken from the bleak world of Joyce's *Dubliners* (1914). The product is a novel about the unreality of various kinds of fictions, an exercise in style whose only subject is the extravagance of the styles it exploits by parody.

At Swim-Two-Birds is a collection of brief fragments organized only by the desire to express the multiple contrasts of their incompatible styles. The thread that links these fragments is situational rather than narrative: A university student is attempting to write a novel whose three possible openings and four possible conclusions frame *At Swim-Two-Birds*; among the characters in his novel is Dermot Trellis, himself a novelist with a work in progress; the characters in Trellis's novel are dissatisfied with their treatment and so wreak revenge by writing their own novel about Trellis, whose authorial control lapses when he sleeps. This conceit allows O'Brien to include in his novel a plethora of styles from imaginary authors, especially rich in ironies for readers knowledgeable about Irish literature from the Celtic legends to modern writers such as Yeats.

As many of its commentators have pointed out, *At Swim-Two-Birds* has far more appeal and significance than most metafictional novels about a novel in progress. It is, above all else, exuberantly comic rather than pretentious.

The Third Policeman

Although it was not published until after O'Brien's death, *The Third Policeman* was written immediately after *At Swim-Two-Birds*, and it should be considered beside that novel, despite its publication date. Like *At Swim-Two-Birds*, it is a very modernist exercise in the novel as a self-contained and self-generating literary text. In this case, however, O'Brien is less concerned with the identifiable styles of the Irish revival than with the ways any style creates an identity in narrative fiction, the ways style is a source of authority and control in fiction. It is crucial to this novel that the narrator be nameless; without the identity provided by a name, he must create a persona for himself by appropriating styles of expression.

The novel opens with the robbery and murder of a businessman named Mathers by the narrator and his accomplice, John Diviney. The fantastic events that ensue concern the narrator's attempts to recover the stolen money and to hide his complicity in the crime from an omniscient but apparently uninterested pair of police officers. The appearance of Fox, the third police officer, seems to promise the release of the narrator from his predicament, but in fact it presages the realization that the narrator has been dead since the opening pages, betrayed and himself murdered by Diviney.

Released from even the faintest restraints of realism by setting his novel in the afterlife, O'Brien is free in *The Third Policeman* to allow language and rhetoric, rather than cause and effect, to determine the direction of his tale. The most prominent style and source of authority in the novel is an academic one related to the narrator's interest in a fictional philosopher named de Selby, whose works are evoked for the sake of clarification, summarized, and cited in scholarly footnotes throughout the novel. Elsewhere, *The Third Policeman* sporadically adopts the style of the modern murder mystery, a pretentious opera review, scientific analysis, Eastern mysticism, and gothic romance. These intrusive styles color the events of the novel for the reader, much as the alien laws of the afterlife color the experiences of the narrator: They are oblique, intriguing, and ultimately baffling.

The Third Policeman lacks the dimension of cultural commentary provided by evocation of local literary styles in *At Swim-Two-Birds*. This same generalized environment, however, makes O'Brien's second novel an even richer contemplation on the nature of identity than his first, one that is capable of generalizations about definitions of self that rise above provincial contexts. It is also fully self-contained by a cyclic conclusion that returns the narrator, now accompanied by Diviney, to the earliest situations in the novel. It is precisely this degree of absorption in the interior logic of its own conceits that distinguishes *The Third Policeman* from O'Brien's later, less interesting reworking of these ideas in *The Dalkey Archive*.

The Poor Mouth

In a letter to Sean O'Casey quoted in *The Flann O'Brien Reader*, the author described *The Poor Mouth*, in its original Gaelic version, as "an honest attempt to get under the skin of a certain type of 'Gael,' which I find the most nauseating phenomena in Europe." This kind of Gael was in fact more a creation of the literary revival than a significant social group. *The Poor Mouth*, as translated by Patrick C. Power after O'Brien's death, is a parody of a literary genre rather than a parody of life in Gaeltachts, the remote Irish-speaking areas of Ireland that continue to erode in character despite well-intentioned government subsidies. The primary targets of the parody are the enormously popular autobiographies of Gaeltacht life such as *Twenty Years A-Growing* (1933) by Maurice O'Sullivan, but O'Brien's more general object of parody is all fictionalized versions of peasantry, from the folktales of Standish Hayes O'Grady to the plays of Lady Gregory and J. M. Synge.

The title of the novel evokes the idiom of "poor-mouthing," or inventing poverty for self-serving purposes, and *The Poor Mouth* is about the discovery by enthusiastic outsiders of a Gaeltacht in the middle of truly astonishing poverty. The wretched cohabitation of these peasants with their pigs in leaky shacks is a source of some tall-tale humor in the novel, although this poverty does have its darker side, as indicated by casual references to disease and death from starvation, alcoholism, and fighting. O'Brien's real focus here, however, is on the willful self-degradation of the peasants at the feet of their enlightened English-speaking visitors, who gauge the merit of Gaelic tales by the poverty of the teller and limit their own charity lest they spoil the purity of the peasants' profound misery.

The great irony of *The Poor Mouth*, and an essential component of its publication in Gaelic, is that these visitors are, rather than actual Englishmen, anglicized Irishmen enamored of the peasantry. The pure bile of the novel, which is well preserved in its English translation, derives from this image of Ireland foisting a factitious stereotype on itself, of romanticizing a peasantry in such rigid ways that all males in this Gaeltacht are called James O'Donnell. The use of this collective name is only the most obvious indication of the novel's relevance to O'Brien's governing interest in the theme of identity. Rather than a parody of multiple identities, however, *The Poor Mouth* is a portrait of surrender after limited resistance to a bleak and uniform identity. It has a special importance in O'Brien's work for this pessimism, for its publication in Gaelic, for his refusal to permit a translation, and for the fact that he would not write another novel until twenty years later.

The Hard Life

The Hard Life lacks the literary frames of reference that give O'Brien's first three novels their focus and energy. Published in the wake of the rediscovery of *At Swim-Two-Birds*, it is a charming rather than derisory treatment of characteristically Irish forms of naïveté and provinciality, one that panders to audience expectations about Irish writing that were ridiculed by the ironies of O'Brien's earlier novels. It is harsh in its criticisms of the Jesuit father, Kurt Fahrt; the misguided Dubliner, Mr. Collopy; and his slatternly daughter, Annie. These satiric elements, however, are rendered benign by the time frame of the novel, written in 1961 but set in the years preceding 1910. The most attractive qualities of the novel—its digressive narration, bitter account of lower-class Dublin propriety, and the extravagantly misinformed conversations of Father Fahrt and Collopy—are facile if skillful entertainments never qualified by the shrewd ironies surrounding such mannerisms in O'Brien's earlier novels.

In all of O'Brien's novels, narrative structure is incidental to stylistic preoccupations, but in *The Hard Life* there is no literary focus to compensate for the lack of narrative structure. The comedy of the Fahrt-Collopy conversations and of several of the improbable events in the novel is brilliant, but the lack of an informing literary perspective renders them isolated exercises in caricature, resembling in tone and length the best of O'Brien's newspaper columns.

The Dalkey Archive

In reworking some of the central conceits, notably the de Selby material, from *The Third Policeman*, O'Brien made *The Dalkey Archive* his only novel narrated in the third person. This alteration eliminates many of the ambiguities and complications found in his earlier novels because of their limited narrators. In other respects, too, *The Dalkey Archive* turns away from the most imaginative conceits of O'Brien's earlier work. As such, it represents a distinctly regressive coda in the works of O'Brien.

The novel individually treats the imaginative constructions of three personages. St. Augustine appears and reveals that neither his youthful sins nor his religious conversion were as complete as have been supposed. Sergeant Fottrell reveals his theory that the molecules of men and bicycles mix during riding, with predictable results. Finally, Joyce, discovered living in retirement in the seaside resort called the Skerries, denounces *Ulysses* as a scam perpetrated by Parisian intellectuals and reveals that his true vocation is writing pamphlets for the Catholic Truth Society. These three are joined by their shared intellectual pride, a characteristic that the novel condemns even as it luxuriates in the pleasures of intricate shams.

O'Brien's first three novels were entirely enclosed within their literary conceits. In *The Dalkey Archive*, however, the elaborate shams and crazed logic are dispersed and corrected by the omniscient narrator on surprisingly moralistic grounds. In O'Brien's first three novels, no assumptions about identity were exempt from scrutiny, but *The Dalkey Archive* ends with an extremely complacent announcement of betrothal by its lackluster central characters Mick and Mary. With this gesture, O'Brien's last novel relinquishes the imaginative explorations of self and the elaborate metafictional elements of his finest novels.

Brian O'Nolan adopted the pseudonyms Flann O'Brien and Myles na Gopaleen with a characteristically ironic purpose: He would, under the names of one literary fabrication about Ireland and the Irish, expose the fabulous nature of a later image of the country and the people. At the end of his life, he wrote two novels, *The Hard Life* and *The Dalkey Archive*, deficient in the ironic intent of his important novels. It was as if at this point in his career he actually became Flann O'Brien, the stage Irishman, content with the identity foisted upon him. In *At Swim-Two-Birds*, *The Third Policeman*, and *The Poor Mouth*, however, the ironies surrounding his choice of pseudonyms were in full operation. The complexities and opacities of those novels represent a break from the mainstream of modern Irish literature and the most probing examination of the new national literature's roots in the mythologies of the Irish Literary Revival.

John P. Harrington

Other major works

NONFICTION: *Cruiskeen Lawn*, 1943; *The Best of Myles*, 1968; *The Various Lives of Keats and Chapman and the Brother*, 1976; *Myles Away from Dublin*, 1985 (selected essays from journal columns).

MISCELLANEOUS: *Stories and Plays*, 1973; *A Flann O'Brien Reader*, 1978 (Stephen Jones, editor).

Bibliography

Asbee, Sue. *Flann O'Brien*. Boston: Twayne, 1991. This overview of O'Brien's life and work contains a solid discussion of his major prose fiction. Includes A chronology, notes, and an annotated bibliography.

Brooker, Joseph. *Flann O'Brien*. Tavistock, England: Northcote House, 2005. An appraisal of all of O'Brien's (and Brian O'Nolan's) writings, including his early attempts at public satire. Examines these works in light of current debates about modernism.

Clissmann, Anne. *Flann O'Brien: A Critical Introduction to His Writings*. New York: Barnes & Noble Books, 1975. An exhaustive discussion of the author's writings in English, with lengthy chapters on the major novels. Includes a bibliography and an index.

Clune, Anne, and Tess Hurson, eds. *Conjuring Complexities: Essays on Flann O'Brien*. Belfast: Institute of Irish Studies, Queen's University of Belfast, 1997. A solid volume of critical papers analyzing O'Brien's work that were initially delivered at a conference in Dublin in 1986. Includes bibliographical references and an index.

Cronin, Anthony. *No Laughing Matter: The Life and Times of Flann O'Brien*. London: Grafton, 1989. A biography of the complex and somewhat reclusive

O'Brien. Cronin's focus is on O'Brien himself, rather than on his work. Little-known personal details illustrate the narrative. A thorough treatment of a difficult subject.

Donohue, Keith. *The Irish Anatomist: A Study of Flann O'Brien*. Dublin: Maunsel, 2002. Donohue assesses O'Brien's entire oeuvre, including works in Irish, his college writings, and letters to the editor, and draws upon biographies of the author to trace O'Brien's development as a postmodernist writer.

Hopper, Keith. *Flann O'Brien: A Portrait of the Artist as a Young Post-Modernist*. Cork, Ireland: Cork University Press, 1995. A study focusing on the narrative structure, style, and other elements of *The Third Policeman*. Hopper argues that the novel is one of the earliest works of postmodernist fiction.

O'Keeffe, Timothy, ed. *Myles: Portraits of Brian O'Nolan*. London: Martin Brian and O'Keeffe, 1973. An invaluable biographical source and critical commentary on O'Brien. Contains reminiscences by friends, colleagues, and one of the author's brothers. Among the critical commentaries, the essay by J. C. C. Mays, "Flann O'Brien: Literalist of the Imagination," stands out.

Shea, Thomas F. *Flann O'Brien's Exorbitant Novels*. Lewisburg, Pa.: Bucknell University Press, 1992. Shea analyzes O'Brien's early experimental fiction, two unpublished manuscripts of *At Swim-Two-Birds*, and unpublished letters in order to better understand his novels. Includes four chapters devoted to the novels, notes, a select bibliography, and an index.

Taaffe, Carol. *Ireland Through the Looking-Glass: Flann O'Brien, Myles na Gopaleen and Irish Cultural Debate*. Cork, Ireland: Cork University Press, 2008. Taaffe explores how the cultural climate of Ireland influenced O'Brien's fiction and journalism, maintaining that his humor and preoccupation with the role of the author were as much influenced by the position of the writer in 1930's and 1940's Ireland as it was by postmodernism.

KATE O'BRIEN

Born: Limerick, Ireland; December 3, 1897
Died: Canterbury, England; August 13, 1974

Principal long fiction

Without My Cloak, 1931
Mary Lavelle, 1936
Pray for the Wanderer, 1938
The Land of Spices, 1941
The Last of Summer, 1943
That Lady, 1946 (also known as *For One Sweet Grape*)
The Flower of May, 1953
As Music and Splendour, 1958

Other literary forms

Kate O'Brien's first success was a play, *Distinguished Villa*, which had a three-month run in London's West End in 1926. She successfully dramatized her novel *That Lady* for a Broadway production (1949) in which Katherine Cornell played the title role. O'Brien was also the author of two travel books, *Farewell, Spain* (1937) and *My Ireland* (1962). Her *English Diaries and Journals* was published in 1943 and a biography, *Teresa of Avila*, in 1951. Her last major published work was a book of reminiscences, *Presentation Parlour* (1963).

Achievements

While Kate O'Brien's first novel, *Without My Cloak*, received two of the English literary establishment's most prestigious awards, the Hawthornden Prize and the James Tait Black Memorial Prize, her most notable achievement may best be assessed in the context of contemporary Irish literature. In this context, she remains—together with, though in a much more culturally significant manner than, her perhaps better-known contemporary Elizabeth Bowen—an exemplary representative not only of

Kate O'Brien. (Library of Congress)

women's writing but also, through her works and career, of women's potential, broadly considered. Partial recognition of her achievement came in 1947 with her election to the Irish Academy of Letters.

Biography

Kate O'Brien was born in the city of Limerick, Ireland, on December 3, 1897, to a comfortable, middle-class family. Educated at a local convent, she went on to attend University College, Dublin, at a time when Ireland's capital was witnessing the consolidation of the Irish Literary Revival, though the cultural enthusiasm of the time left little or no mark either on O'Brien's student days or on her writing.

The years immediately following graduation seem to have been marked by a degree of uncertainty. She first worked in England as a journalist for the (then) *Manchester Guardian* and as a teacher. A brief period in Washington, D.C., as a diplomatic aide was followed by a sojourn in Bilbao, Spain, as a governess. Returning to London in 1924, she married Gustav Renier; the marriage was not a success. Spain soon became her second home, though for more than ten years after the completion of her World War II service at the ministry of information in London she was refused admission to Spain, her depiction of King Philip II in *That Lady* having rendered her persona non grata.

By this time, O'Brien was no stranger to controversy arising out of her fiction: Her 1941 novel, *The Land of Spices*, was notoriously banned by the Irish censorship board for alleged sexual impropriety. In 1950, she took up residence again in Ireland and lived there until 1961, when she returned to England. She died on August 13, 1974.

Analysis

Kate O'Brien's career emerged and developed during a difficult time for Irish writing; indeed, models of Irish women novelists who might have provided her with beneficial influence and nurturing were virtually nonexistent. Despite these unpromising cultural origins, and despite the obvious struggle O'Brien experienced in order to express herself and command a responsive and sustaining audience, her career can be seen in historical retrospect to be marked with notable integrity, independence of mind and action, and devotion to her art.

In a literary culture where women have not always received sufficient critical attention and have not had their works readily incorporated into the canon of a given generation's achievements, critical responses to O'Brien's life and work have belatedly been seen as manifestations of unwarranted narrowness. The belatedness of this view is perhaps a result of the author's long years of exile, along with the fact that her one major popular success, *That Lady*, published when a fresh audience was ready for her work, is a historical romance rather than another in her sequence of novels about Irish family life. Yet the republication of many of her works during the 1980's not only facilitated a reappraisal of her literary achievements but also had the effect of redrawing the map of Irish literary culture at a crucial period in its development.

The generation of Irish writers to which O'Brien belongs had the unenviable task of following in the pathbreaking footsteps of the principal artists of the Irish

Literary Revival—the novelist George Moore, the poet William Butler Yeats, and the playwright John Millington Synge. O'Brien's generation was as different in background and outlook from these three illustrious avatars as it is possible to be. Provincial in upbringing, nationalist in politics, unexperimental in art, and Catholic in cultural formation, this generation had at once a greater intimacy with the actual life of its fellow citizens and a more actively critical perception of the society in whose name it had elected to speak. It also had the not inconsiderable disadvantage of attempting to assert its cultural and artistic validity and viability while the star of the revival had not yet entirely waned, and while Yeats, for example, was willing to co-opt new voices to articulate the agenda of his cultural politics.

The most important writers of this generation—those who went on to establish a somewhat more populist orientation for Irish literature, or at least a more populist role for the Irish writer—have long been considered to be Seán O'Faoláin, Frank O'Connor, and Liam O'Flaherty. The different orientation that they represent may be initially discerned in the fact that they each espoused a form largely neglected by the revival—namely, prose fiction, in particular the short story—and implicitly rejected the formal and ideological explorations of their more modernist forebears. O'Brien is a member of this generation not merely by virtue of her provincial background and conventional education but also because her works reflect this generation's concerns, a reflection that receives added point and importance from the fact of its feminist—or, to be historically accurate, protofeminist—perspectives.

The disillusion and disorientation that emerge as a resonant theme in Irish fiction during the 1930's, the problematized rendering of the independence that the country secured in the late twentieth century in juridical and political terms, and the conflicts between tradition and individuality as the culture seeks not merely aesthetic but moral renewal, far from being neglected by O'Brien, are all the more authentically present in her work through being presented from the standpoint of already marginalized female protagonists. (With the exception of *Pray for the Wanderer*, with its protagonist Matt Costello, all of O'Brien's works feature female protagonists.)

Without My Cloak

O'Brien's first novel, *Without My Cloak*, rehearses a number of the problems that arise from her heritage and anticipates the most important of her fiction's preoccupations. A family saga, it brings to awareness, through the use of an essentially nineteenth century model, the social and psychological forces that gave cultural and moral legitimacy to O'Brien's own class and ideological background. The novel traces the development of the Considine family through three generations from the late eighteenth century, plausibly detailing its establishment in an urban, mercantile setting, for which the author uses her native Limerick.

A major motif in the work is the question of security. The Considine ethos consists of a sublimation of development in consolidation, and the emotional claustrophobia that results from this mode of behavior within the family circle is memorably detailed. The security motif is tensely related to its obverse, a quest for independence; the dynamics of the novel enact the struggle familiar from nineteenth century fiction between individual and society, between the assertion of selfhood and institutional constraints, with the emphasis in this instance falling on the power of institutions.

In particular, the social and moral function of the Catholic Church receives special attention in *Without My Cloak* and retains a particularly important place throughout O'Brien's fiction. Because of its status in her first novel, it is possible to refer to the Considine family as embodying an ethos, since the Church operates as a source of moral and social identity, and alternative sources of such security and self-awareness are nowhere to be found. The power of the Church to authorize selfhood as a tissue of constraints makes of it a second, larger, more absolute family, and the matter of the effect of its power on the individual conscience and consciousness, rather than being resolved in *Without My Cloak*, becomes an increasingly emphatic preoccupation in O'Brien's fiction prior to the publication of *That Lady*. (The fact that O'Brien herself seems to have considered the conflicts of her first novel unresolved may be inferred from their reenactment in condensed and more artistically disciplined form in her next work, *The Anteroom*.)

The role and power of the Church is so central to her

work that O'Brien has frequently been thought of as a Catholic, more than as an Irish, novelist. Like most Irish writers, however, she is concerned with the culture of Catholicism; its social, personal, and interpersonal influence; and its significance as a generator of a politics of the spirit rather than as a spiritual convalescent home. Indeed, one of her most fundamental fictional preoccupations is with the difficulty of dealing with impersonal authority, whether conceived as institutional or, as in the portrait of Philip II in *That Lady*, monarchical.

Mary Lavelle

The fact that O'Brien perceived her preoccupations as continuing difficulty rather than as eventual solution is suggested by the regularity with which her protagonists, for all the author's sympathetic dramatization of their intensity of their struggles, typically fail to attain the independence they desire. An exception to this general outcome is the eponymous heroine of *Mary Lavelle*. This novel, which draws more directly on immediate personal experience than does *Without My Cloak*, tells of a young Irish woman working as a governess for a bourgeois Spanish family. In some sense an account of an innocent abroad—Mary seems to be innocence itself—the novel is also a narrative of conflicting loyalties. The heroine is in many respects an ideal employee, fitting into the Areavaga family with the ease of somebody familiar with a culture in which people know their places. It is Mary's very compliance, however, that is responsible for the novel's central drama.

Mary involuntarily falls for Juanito, the married son of the house, a state of affairs that brings her into conflict not only with the outlook in which she had been rigorously brought up in Ireland but also with its powerfully reinforced presence in Doña Consuelo, the commanding head of the household. The conflict between duty and freedom, between individual desire and ethical obligation, in addition to the novelist's welcome transposition of her concerns to a non-Irish locale and the development of a sexual dimension to Mary's struggle for authentic womanhood, contributes to an impressive sense of the novelist's development. Nevertheless, it is not clear what the overall effect of Mary's experiences has been, whether she accepts or rejects the conflict-laden nature of her experiences. "Anguish and anger for everyone and only one little, fantastic, impossible hope," read the closing lines of *Mary Lavelle*, "was the fruit of her journey to Spain." An unexpected fruit of the publication of *Mary Lavelle*, however, was its banning by Irish censors, an act that may be read now as an unintended tribute to O'Brien's insightful presentation of her heroine's moral authenticity but that, at the time, deepened the alienation from her background that her works articulated with increasing conviction.

The Land of Spices

This alienation reached its highest level when O'Brien's next novel, *The Land of Spices*, met with a similar fate to that of *Mary Lavelle* at the hands of the censors, as a result of which the novel achieved unjust notoriety—and subsequently, when censorship was relaxed in the early 1970's, a certain amount of popular success. The banning of *The Land of Spices* proved instrumental in calling the censorship board's procedures into question and led indirectly to a revision of its mode of operation. It might be argued that the board's very existence was in itself strongly illustrative of the cultural conflicts and repressions that, from a broader, nonbureaucratic, social perspective, form the core of O'Brien's fictional concerns. The pretext for banning *The Land of Spices* was so slender—consisting of a mere handful of words with potentially homosexual implications—that it came to be seen as a paradigm of the narrow-minded, prurient, and often antifeminist orientation of the official guardians of Irish literary culture.

The Land of Spices can be read as a redeployment and intensification of the mother-and-governess relationship in *Mary Lavelle*, a relationship that is emblematic of relationships conceived throughout O'Brien's work as exercises in power. On this occasion, foreignness of setting and the enclosed nature of the immediate environment are combined to attain a new level of intensity: The action takes place within an Irish convent of a French order of nuns. In addition, this work's animating relationship now has the intimacy of teacher, Mère Marie-Hélène Archer, and pupil, Anna Murphy, with all of its reverberations of nurturing and mastery, the source of which is the overarching presence of Mother Church. The pressures Mary Lavelle felt with regard to her moral development and sense of autonomy are here articulated more dramatically, given how much more difficult it is to escape them, and the sexual component of *Mary Lavelle* is similarly intensified.

The novel, however, has a more meditative than critical tone. Taking its title from the English metaphysical poet George Herbert's "Prayer (1)" ("Church bells beyond the stars heard, the soul's blood,/ The land of spices, something understood"), the emphasis falls on the ritualistic and selfless aspects of the vocational life, on the complexities of agape rather than the challenge of eros, on the willingness to serve rather than the urge to escape, while at the same time remaining crucially sensitive to the urgent presence of humanity and its needs. *The Land of Spices* will seem to many O'Brien's most satisfying production, in which she attains more objective possession of her psychological and spiritual preoccupations without running the risk of compromising them.

That Lady

O'Brien's characterization of a woman's fate in the context of power relationships receives its most lavish treatment in her greatest popular success, *That Lady*. As well as being adapted for the stage, *That Lady* was filmed with Olivia de Havilland in the title role in 1955. Set in sixteenth century Spain, the novel tells the story of Ana de Mendoza y de la Cerda, princess of Eboli and duchess of Pastrana; clearly, despite O'Brien's strong Spanish interests, it is an entirely new departure for her as a novelist. Instead of concentrating on the various stages of Ana's life as a woman in an attempt to reconstruct a novel of historical verisimilitude, O'Brien concentrates instead on the years of Ana's unlikely liberation into an experience of womanhood that had hitherto been hidden from her. The reader is explicitly informed in a foreword that this "is not a historical novel"; instead, the imaginative treatment of the material dwells centrally on a dramatization of the psychological and emotional conflicts of the case. Thus, despite a certain amount of costumery, inevitable under the circumstances, *That Lady* achieves an internal consistency with O'Brien's other novels.

That Lady covers the years spent by Ana, now widowed, in state service. To some extent, her work for the Spanish Crown during this brief period recapitulates her early years, when by virtue of her noble birth and excellent marriage she became intimate with affairs of state. Together with the old intimacy, however, there now comes a new, and this development of an additional dimension in Ana's life is at once enhancing and destructive, enriching her personal existence while risking a scandal that would entail the king's serious displeasure. Because of the character of the prevailing power structure, the most significant experience in Ana's personal life—the affair with Don Antonio Pérez—becomes the occasion of her banishment and confinement. The novel's heightened courtly context accentuates rather than dilutes its emphasis on tensions familiar from O'Brien's earlier novels—between passion and form, between desire and responsibility, between a woman's external role and her internal needs. To these tensions and conflicts her work returns again and again, and it is in her identification and negotiation of them that O'Brien's fiction is worthy of the critical attention that, beginning in the late 1980's, it has at length come to receive.

O'Brien's work is noteworthy on two levels. In the first place, it represents significant additions to the history of anglophone women's writing in the period between the two world wars. Her location of her female protagonists in conditions of moral difficulty, emotional complexity, cultural unfamiliarity, and even geographical estrangement provides a comprehensive method of dramatizing women's experience as problematic and unamenable to tidying away by the powers that be. O'Brien's own willingness to live a life as autonomous as that sought by her protagonists testifies to her steadfastness, courage, and integrity. The fact that so much of her writing life was spent in exile is a tribute to both her singularity and her perseverance.

In addition, however, O'Brien's accomplishments become all the more significant when seen in an Irish context. While her novels do not articulate the concerns of her generation as explicitly as the critiques of nationalism and assumption of embattled cultural and ideological positions favored by many of her contemporaries, her work belongs with theirs as part of a concerted effort to render more authentically—that is, with greater respect for individuality and its internal realities—the life of her time. O'Brien's original contributions to this effort make her the first significant female writer of independent Ireland.

George O'Brien

Other major works

plays: *Distinguished Villa*, pr. 1926; *The Bridge*, pr. 1927; *The Schoolroom Window*, pr. 1937; *That Lady*, pr. 1949.

nonfiction: *Farewell, Spain*, 1937; *English Diaries and Journals*, 1943; *Teresa of Avila*, 1951; *My Ireland*, 1962 (travel); *Presentation Parlour*, 1963 (reminiscence).

Bibliography

Bloom, Harold, ed. *British Women Fiction Writers, 1900-1960*. 2 vols. Philadelphia: Chelsea House, 1997-1998. Volume 2 includes brief biographies of O'Brien and twelve other authors and critical essays about their work, including analyses of individual books and broader discussions of the authors' place in literary history

Dalsimer, Adele. *Kate O'Brien: A Critical Study*. Dublin: Gill and Macmillan, 1990. The first comprehensive study of O'Brien's entire literary output, with an emphasis on the feminist dimension of her works. Includes a biographical sketch, a bibliography, and an index.

Kiberd, Declan. "Kate O'Brien: *The Ante-Room*." In *Irish Classics*. Cambridge, Mass.: Harvard University Press, 2001. O'Brien's novel is one of the thirty-five greatest works of Irish literature that Kiberd discusses in her book on the classics of the Irish literary tradition.

Kiely, Benedict. "Love and Pain and Parting: The Novels of Kate O'Brien." In *A Raid into Dark Corners: And Other Essays*. Cork, Ireland: Cork University Press, 1999. Kiely, a popular Irish literary critic and a writer for more than fifty years, includes an analysis of O'Brien's novels in this collection of his essays.

O'Brien, Kate. "The Art of Writing." *University Review* 3 (1965): 6-14. Provides valuable insights into the author's thoughts about the writing process.

Reynolds, Lorna. *Kate O'Brien: A Literary Portrait*. Totowa, N.J.: Barnes & Noble Books, 1987. This study is divided into two parts, the first dealing with the major fiction in chronological order and the second surveying O'Brien's treatment of various major themes. Also contains a valuable treatment of O'Brien's family background.

Walshe, Eibhear. *Kate O'Brien: A Writing Life*. Dublin: Irish Academic Press, 2006. A comprehensive chronicle of O'Brien's life. Walshe maintains that O'Brien was a pioneering writer whose novels depicted independent female protagonists and created a literary identity for the Irish middle class.

_______, ed. *Ordinary People Dancing: Essays on Kate O'Brien*. Cork, Ireland: Cork University Press, 1993. This selection of critical essays examines O'Brien's heritage and feminism, describing how her works challenged the religious and social restrictions of the new Irish republic.

TIM O'BRIEN

Born: Austin, Minnesota; October 1, 1946
Also known as: William Timothy O'Brien, Jr.

Principal long fiction

Northern Lights, 1975
Going After Cacciato, 1978 (revised 1989)
The Nuclear Age, 1981 (limited edition), 1985
In the Lake of the Woods, 1994
Tomcat in Love, 1998
July, July, 2002

Other literary forms

Tim O'Brien wrote magazine and newspaper articles about the Vietnam War while he was a soldier. He published articles on American politics as a reporter for *The Washington Post* in the mid-1970's, and he has also published short stories and essays in popular magazines and literary quarterlies. *If I Die in a Combat Zone, Box Me Up and Ship Me Home* (1973, revised 1979) contains partially fictionalized memoirs, and *The Things They Carried* (1990) collects O'Brien's short stories that are also closely based on his tour of duty in Vietnam. Some critics consider these books loosely organized, episodic novels.

Achievements

Tim O'Brien has won accolades from war veterans and literary critics for his fiction and memoirs concerning the Vietnam War. In 1976 and 1978, he received the O. Henry Memorial Award for chapters of *Going After Cacciato*, which also earned for him the National Book Award in 1979. He won the Vietnam Veterans of America Award in 1987 and, the same year, the National Magazine Award in Fiction for the short story "The Things They Carried"; the story was later included in *The Best American Short Stories of the Century*, edited by John Updike. In 1990, O'Brien was awarded the Heartland Prize from the *Chicago Tribune*, and in 1991 he was nominated for both the National Book Critics Circle's Melcher Book Award and the Pulitzer Prize for *The Things They Carried*. He also received France's Prix du Meilleur Livre Étranger for that book and the James Fenimore Cooper Prize of the Society of American Historians for *In the Lake of the Woods*, which was named the best book of the year by *Time* magazine. O'Brien has held fellowships from the National Academy of Arts, Bread Loaf Writers' Conference, the American Academy of Arts and Letters, and the Guggenheim Foundation.

Biography

William Timothy O'Brien, Jr., was born in Austin, Minnesota, in 1946, placing him among the baby-boom generation, the young men of which would become eligible for the military draft during the Vietnam War (1964-1973). His father was an insurance salesman and a World War II combat veteran; his mother, Ava Schultz O'Brien, was an elementary school teacher. When O'Brien was nine years old, the family, which included a younger sister and brother, moved to Worthington, near the Minnesota-Iowa border, and he grew up there. His childhood, by his own account, was lonely. He played baseball and golf but occupied himself mainly with magic and reading.

After high school, O'Brien attended Macalester College and majored in political science. He participated in protests against the Vietnam War, wrote antiwar editorials for the college newspaper, and canvassed in support of Senator Eugene McCarthy's presidential campaign in 1968. He was elected student-body president his senior year. Immediately after graduating with a bachelor's degree, summa cum laude, he was drafted into the U.S. Army. Despite his hatred for the war, he quelled the urge to flee to Canada and was trained as an infantryman.

In February, 1969, O'Brien arrived at an advance firebase in Quang Ngai Province, Republic of Vietnam. Nearby was My Lai, a hamlet where troops from O'Brien's division had murdered as many as five hundred civilians in one day. O'Brien, like most Americans, did not learn about the massacre there until one year later. For most of every month, his company patrolled a deadly combat zone, battling the Viet Cong and constantly terrified of land mines, disease, and the prospect of appearing cowardly. He saw many wounds and deaths. In fact, he was wounded by shrapnel from a grenade, and his best friend died in a skirmish, two events that deeply affected him. Even before leaving the country, he published accounts of his experience in Minnesota newspapers and *Playboy* magazine.

After his discharge from the Army in 1970, O'Brien studied at the Harvard School of Government. In 1973 he published *If I Die in a Combat Zone, Box Me Up and Ship Me Home*, and joined the staff of *The Washington Post*, reporting on national affairs. He married Ann Elizabeth Weller, an editorial assistant; they divorced eighteen years later. After a year at the *Post*, he returned to his studies at Harvard but left before completing a degree, in order to become a writer. In the meantime he had published his first novel, *Northern Lights*, in 1975.

After finishing his fourth novel, *In the Lake of the Woods*, in 1994, O'Brien stopped writing, complaining that he was "burned out." With his girlfriend and a *New York Times* photographer, he returned to Vietnam. It was an emotional visit, during which he searched for the Quang Ngai firebase of his infantry company, spoke with Vietnamese veterans, and interviewed survivors of the My Lai massacre. In a famous *New York Times Magazine* article, "The Vietnam in Me" (1994), he told how the experience brought him close to suicide but finally helped him purge some of his anxious obsession with the war. Living in an apartment near Harvard, he resumed writing, in 1998 publishing *Tomcat in Love*. Although the Vietnam War influences the plot of that novel, it does so far less than in his previous fiction. In 1999, O'Brien began teaching every other year in the Creative Writing Program of Texas State University, San Marcos, and moved to Austin, Texas.

Analysis

Tim O'Brien draws material for his novels from his own experience. He uses imagination and fiction to find meaning in these experiences, and because he was part of defining events of the post-World War II generation, the passions and ideas in his novels appeal to American readers with broad differences in political allegiance and social background. Having fought in Vietnam, O'Brien can create fictional soldiers so realistic in attitude, speech, and behavior that readers who are veterans of the war readily identify with them. An activist in the antiwar movement of the 1960's, O'Brien likewise draws faithful imitations of the political rebels of the times. A former graduate student in political science and a campaign worker, O'Brien offers fictional politicians who are convincingly lifelike enough to appeal to the American passion for political scandal. Moreover, coming from a small town in the Midwest, O'Brien (and some of his characters) appears to fulfill a particularly American literary convention: the small-town kid who does well for himself in the outside world. His characters include a university professor, a wealthy geologist, a broom manufacturer, and a lieutenant governor.

Tim O'Brien. (©Marion Ettlinger/Library of Congress)

Some critics have complained that the distinction between historical or personal facts and fiction is blurred in O'Brien's work. Indeed, the "Tim O'Brien" who narrates his two volumes of memoirs is a fictionalized construct, as the author admitted. Similarly, he incorporates historical records, apparently quoted verbatim, in the novel *In the Lake of the Woods*. This mixing of fact and fiction, as well as of memory and fantasy, underlies O'Brien's thematic interests, all of which concern his characters' emotional struggle during events, more than the verisimilitude or logic of the events themselves. The novels are intimately personal, psychological, and exploratory. Among the major themes are the relation between storytelling and truth, father-son relationships, true courage, the psychological effect of war, loneliness, magic, disappointment in love, and obsession.

To develop such themes, O'Brien uses narrative techniques that give readers access to the minds of characters in order to portray their reactions to events in the plot. *Northern Lights*, *Going After Cacciato*, *In the Lake of the Woods*, and *July, July* are told from the third-person point of view either of an unnamed narrator or of a narrator whom readers are encouraged to identify with the author. This narrator recounts the thoughts and emotions of characters so that readers may empathize with their confusion and obsessions. *The Nuclear Age* and *Tomcat in Love* both employ the first-person point of view of the main character. Some episodes are told in the present tense and some in the past tense, as the characters reminisce. These techniques enable O'Brien to place readers even more intimately in the minds of characters and to display the tricky, often self-deluding action of memory. Moreover, rapid changes from past to present, changes from one story line to another within a novel's plot, intricate wordplay, and dreamlike sequences immerse readers in the mental states of the principal characters.

O'Brien has told interviewers that as a youth he was obsessed with American writer Ernest Hemingway, and Hemingway's influence on O'Brien's work is apparent. O'Brien writes in short, crisp sentences that often derive their power from vivid verbs. He relies on extensive dialogue and uses description more to reflect the impressions of his main characters than to construct visually detailed settings. Unlike Hemingway, O'Brien frequently uses fragmentary sentences and questions to imitate the thought processes of characters, especially when they are under stress. Cumulatively, his style establishes an energetic narrative pace.

Going After Cacciato

Going After Cacciato, O'Brien's second published novel, was his first critical and popular success. A best seller, it quickly earned notice as one of the first serious literary treatments of the Vietnam War, winning the National Book Award in 1979, and it remained a classic statement of the war's bewildering effects on the young Americans drafted to fight there. Paul Berlin, the point-of-view character, is a member of an infantry platoon. With his platoon, he chases one of their number who has deserted, Cacciato ("the hunted" in Italian). Cacciato has vowed to escape the war and walk all the way to Paris, a crazy idea that nevertheless earns him admiration among the other soldiers.

The platoon catches Cacciato near the Laotian border, and the literal plot of the novel is over. While on guard duty, however, Berlin fantasizes. He imagines that Cacciato constantly manages to evade them, and the platoon must pursue him to Paris. He dreams up grotesque adventures in countries along the route, some hilarious escapades, some adolescent sexual fantasies, and some chilling encounters. His fantasies interrupt and blend into the literal story of the chase, giving the narrative a nightmarish quality. Berlin and his fellow soldiers are innocents trapped in a corrupt, bizarre world, but the only character who seems truly courageous in the story is Cacciato. Even though his desertion is a nonsensical gesture, it frees him from the compromises to which the others cling: acceding to the draft, fighting a war that few believe in, conforming so as to not endure shame and disapproval.

In the Lake of the Woods

In the Lake of the Woods is O'Brien's most disturbing novel. It is an attempt, he contends, to understand evil. The story opens at the Lake of the Woods in northern Minnesota. John and Kathy Wade are on vacation, trying to knit together an unraveling marriage and lives in disarray. Lieutenant governor of the state, Wade has just lost the primary election for the U.S. Senate because news stories have revealed that he took part in the My Lai massacre in Vietnam. As a soldier, Wade was known as Wizard, a nickname he earned for his magic tricks, but the importance of deception and illusion is deep in his psyche, and he had managed to erase most records of his involvement in the massacre, escape court-martial, and keep the secret even from his wife. As the story of his war experience, political career, and family life unfolds, the distinction between truth and the illusions he creates blur in his mind—and in the reader's. However, interrupting the narrative are sections called "Evidence," which contain transcripts of actual court-martial testimony and quotations from history books. These brief sections give the story historical perspective and keep it from turning completely into Wade's illusion.

The war haunts Wade; his failure to maintain protective illusions drives him toward madness. When his wife disappears from their cabin, Wade cooperates with the authorities in searching for her, but it becomes gradually apparent that Wade himself has murdered her. What is not clear, however, is whether he understands what he has done, so lost is he in self-delusions about his past. The end of the book is ambiguous. As the authorities increasingly suspect him of murder, Wade takes a speedboat out onto the lake; his purpose seems to be to find his wife, escape the law, and commit suicide at the same time. Since Wade's muddled behavior results from a lonely childhood and the My Lai massacre, the Vietnam War is cast as a pervasive, mysterious, malign burden on Wade and his generation.

Tomcat in Love

Tomcat in Love is a comic novel in texture but a serious work in intent; it reexamines O'Brien's recurring themes of love and disaster, storytelling and truth, and obsession. Thomas H. Chippering is a tenured professor of linguistics whose wife has divorced him. Told in flashbacks, the novel is a record of their relationship, beginning in childhood and continuing with marriage, her departure, and his desperate crusade to win her back and to punish her family for causing the divorce. Chippering is pompous, vindictive, pedantic, obsessed with words, and bent on trying to seduce every woman he encounters. He is also blind to his own faults and to the feelings of those around him, while constantly interpreting himself in a heroic light. He has even fabricated a record as a hero in Vietnam to impress others. (Although the war does not dominate the story as it does in O'Brien's previous novel, it does figure in the plot.)

Much of the situational humor in the novel originates from Chippering's obvious self-delusions and the ridiculous mistakes he makes about others. His ex-wife spurns him, he loses his faculty position because of student complaints of sexual harassment, he becomes engaged to a woman whose first name he cannot bring himself to use, his former brother-in-law publicly humiliates him, and he eventually discovers that his ex-wife, contrary to what he had always believed, is even crazier than he is. Chippering has a few redeeming features that rescue the story from simple farce. His obsession is with the human heart, and he pursues the ambiguities of love with unflagging persistence, much as Miguel de Cervantes' Don Quixote pursues chivalry. In the end, he transcends his obsession and grows spiritually, learning to treat others, women especially, as human beings rather than as objects to manipulate or adore.

July, July

July, July is an ensemble novel that follows the lives of several classmates from their 1969 graduation from Darton Hall College through their thirtieth reunion. They belong to the generation that took seriously the Beatles lyric "All you need is love." Love, however, has not been kind to them. Divorces, affairs, despair, and deception have destroyed their youthful sense of opportunity and liberty. O'Brien exposes these disappointments through shifts in the time setting, alternately devoting a chapter to the reunion in 2000 and then the following chapter to one of the classmates. Additionally, the point of view shifts frequently, sometimes from one paragraph to the next, and the reader is introduced to a variety of vivid characters who are distinct in their emotional capacities and sociopolitical backgrounds. Thereby, O'Brien constructs a composite portrait not just of a small group of classmates but of an entire generation.

The events of the 1960's, and the Vietnam War in particular, poison the characters' lives in one way or another. For instance, David Todd, who wants to be a professional baseball player, first joins the Army and is sent to war. A lieutenant, he leads his platoon into an ambush. All of his men die, many in grisly ways, and Todd himself survives only after crawling for days in the countryside, tormented by memories and the demonically taunting voice of an imaginary disc jockey. He loses a leg after his rescue and returns home to marry his college sweetheart, Marla Dempsey, who is unable to love him as he wishes and leaves him. By contrast, Billy McMann flees to Canada to avoid being drafted. He expects his sweetheart, Dorothy Stier, to join him, but instead she jilts him for his best friend and a comfortable upper-middle-class life in the United States. Both Todd and McMann become embittered.

Love betrays the other characters in ways ironic and comic. Paulette Haslo is a minister who has been suspended after breaking into the house of a parishioner to steal letters implicating her in a chaste affair with the parishioner's recently dead husband. Ellie Abbott, whose marriage is happy, nevertheless sneaks away for an adulterous vacation with an old college boyfriend, only to see him drown; keeping the secret of the death and the fling destroys her former happiness. Merv Bertel, chronically obese, loses a hundred pounds, and then, sleek and suave as well as wealthy from his manufacturing business, courts a trophy wife, but he wins her only by pretending to be a famous writer. The hoax costs him his business, his independence, and his health.

The final hours of the reunion promise a measure of consolation for some of the classmates. McMann and Haslo seem on their way to a lasting relationship, to their mutual surprise; Todd and Dempsey are poised to try marriage once more. For others, however, disaster, or simply aging alone, looms. For all of them, as O'Brien writes of Ellie Abbott, "the reality of love was not what she'd once imagined it to be." *July, July*, although often comic, returns a somber assessment of middle-aged baby boomers who cannot free themselves from the heady ferment of the 1960's and their youth.

Roger Smith

Other major works

short fiction: *The Things They Carried*, 1990.

nonfiction: *If I Die in a Combat Zone, Box Me Up and Ship Me Home*, 1973 (revised 1979); "The Vietnam in Me," 1994.

Bibliography

Beidler, Philip D. *American Literature and the Experience of Vietnam*. 1982. Reprint. Athens: University of Georgia Press, 2007. Examines the ways in which various writers have approached the subject of the Vietnam War. Devotes a chapter to discussion of O'Brien's novel *Going After Cacciato*.

Franklin, H. Bruce. "Kicking the Denial Syndrome: Tim O'Brien's *In the Lake of the Woods*." In *Novel History: Historians and Novelists Confront American's Past (and Each Other)*, edited by Mark C. Carnes. New York: Simon & Schuster, 2001. An eminent critic of contemporary fiction considers O'Brien's attempt to understand why the My Lai massacre happened and evaluates O'Brien's approach to American history.

Herzog, Tobey C. *Tim O'Brien*. Boston: Twayne, 1997. Critical biography is addressed to informed readers, from advanced high school students to university professors. Covers O'Brien's work from *If I Die in a Combat Zone, Box Me Up and Ship Me Home* through *In the Lake of the Woods*. Includes bibliography.

Kaplan, Steven. *Understanding Tim O'Brien*. Columbia: University of South Carolina Press, 1994. Provides a concise, lucid introduction to O'Brien's work, with a focus on the importance of storytelling, memory, and imagination in the author's life and fiction. Examines O'Brien's first five books, particularly their theme of courage. Includes a generous bibliography.

Tegmark, Mats. *In the Shoes of a Soldier: Communication in Tim O'Brien's Vietnam Narratives*. Uppsala, Sweden: Ubsaliensis, 1998. Good study addresses the topic of problematic communication in O'Brien's writings on Vietnam. Includes bibliography and index.

FLANNERY O'CONNOR

Born: Savannah, Georgia; March 25, 1925
Died: Milledgeville, Georgia; August 3, 1964
Also known as: Mary Flannery O'Connor

Principal long fiction

Wise Blood, 1952
The Violent Bear It Away, 1960

Other literary forms

Flannery O'Connor, most renowned as a writer of short fiction, published the short-story collection *A Good Man Is Hard to Find, and Other Stories* in 1955; her canon also includes two posthumous collections, *Everything That Rises Must Converge* (1965) and *The Complete Stories* (1971). Three posthumous nonfiction works provide insight into her craft and thought: *Mystery and Manners* (1969), a collection of her occasional lectures and essays on literary art; *The Habit of Being: Letters* (1979), which consists of letters compiled by her literary executor, Sally Fitzgerald; and *The Presence of Grace* (1983), a collection of her book reviews.

Achievements

Flannery O'Connor's art was best suited to the medium of the short story, where her sharp, shocking, and grotesque characterizations could have full impact on the reader. Nevertheless, her depiction of the Christ-haunted Hazel Motes in *Wise Blood* ranks as the most memorable and piercing postmodern delineation of Western society's anxiety over God's absence. O'Connor's ability to create supernatural tension, to provoke the potentially hostile reader into considering the possibility of divine invasion of the human sphere, is unparalleled by any postwar writer. Seeing "by the light of Christian orthodoxy," O'Connor refused to chisel away or compromise her convictions to make them more congenial to her readers. She knew that it is difficult to place the Christian faith in front of the contemporary reader with any credibility, but her resolve was firm. She understood, in the words of John Gardner (*On Moral Fiction*, 1978), that "art which tries to tell the truth unretouched is difficult and often offensive," since it "violates our canons of politeness and humane compromise." O'Connor succeeded not in making Christianity more palatable but in making its claims unavoidable.

O'Connor was committed not only to telling the "truth unretouched" but also to telling a good story. This meant rejecting predetermined morals—homilies tacked onto stories and processed uncritically by her readers: "When you can state the theme of a story, when you can separate it from the story itself, then you can be sure the story is not a very good one." Instead of literary proselytizing, she offered a literature of evangelism, of incarnation, a fusing of literary form with authorial vision. Her evangelistic mode was not proselytizing, but *proclaiming*, the ancient and more honorable practice of declaring news, of heralding its goodness to a usually indifferent, sometimes hostile audience. O'Connor had a keen perception of her audience's mind-set and cultural milieu; her proclamation was calculated to subvert the habitualization of faith and to make such notions as redemption, resurrection, and eternal life seem new and strange to a Western society that had reduced them to commonplaces empty of significance. Readers and critics continue to respond to O'Connor's clear spiritual vision and piercing narrative style, a style uncluttered by a false pluralism or sectarian debate. O'Connor, the devout Catholic, neither preached nor compelled; she simply proclaimed.

Biography

Mary Flannery O'Connor was born in Savannah, Georgia, in 1925 and moved with her mother to Milledgeville, Georgia, in 1938. She earned her bachelor of arts degree from Women's College of Georgia in 1945 and received a master of fine arts degree from the State University of Iowa in 1947. She published her first short story, "The Geranium" (*Accent*, 1946), during her years in Iowa. In 1947, she won the Rinehart-Iowa Fiction Award for a first novel with a portion of *Wise Blood*.

Flannery O'Connor. (Courtesy, Georgia College & State University, Special Collections)

On the strength of this award and her promise as a writer, O'Connor was offered a fellowship by the Yaddo Foundation. She accepted and spent several months in Saratoga Springs, New York, but eventually returned to Milledgeville. A few months later, O'Connor moved in with the Fitzgerald family in Connecticut to complete *Wise Blood*. A serious illness, lupus erythematosus, redirected her life back to Milledgeville in 1951; there she would do the rest of her writing, and there she would die in 1964. From Milledgeville, she carried on a lively correspondence with friends, readers, critics, and her editors at Farrar and Giroux. When health permitted, she made trips to colleges and universities, many of them Roman Catholic schools, to discuss her work and literary art.

O'Connor won a Kenyon Review fellowship in fiction in 1953, a National Institute of Arts and Letters grant in 1957, and an O. Henry First Prize in Short Fiction in 1957. She also was granted honorary degrees from St. Mary's College (1962) and Smith College (1963). She spent the last months of her life completing the stories eventually published in her posthumous collection *Everything That Rises Must Converge. The Complete Stories* won the National Book Award for fiction in 1971.

Analysis

Few postmodern writers have spoken as articulately and as compellingly about their craft and the relationship of their fiction to its perceived audience as did Flannery O'Connor. In her occasional prose, in her letters, and in her book reviews, O'Connor evinced an uncommonly perceptive grasp of her readers and the society in which they lived. Addressing the children of a demythologized and desacralized century, she confronted boldly the rancor and apathy with which modern culture meets the religious and the supernatural. To shake and sharpen the sensibilities of a culture made lethargic by the heritage of American civil religion, she turned to shock, to the literally awful and the grotesque, to proclaim her gospel: "To the hard of hearing you shout, and for the almost-blind you draw large and startling figures."

The underlying premise that informs all of O'Connor's fiction, and especially her two novels, *Wise Blood* and *The Violent Bear It Away*, is that men and women, as they are, are not *whole*. This "wholeness," lost in Eden, is now embodied and supplied to humans freely in the person of the incarnate Son of God. In order to make this now familiar theme "seeable" and creditable to her readers, O'Connor was led to herald a Christ who bore little resemblance to the "gentle Jesus, meek and mild" of childhood hymnody. Her Christ is a tiger who disturbs and terrorizes. One thinks especially of Hazel Motes, evangelist of the so-called Church of Christ without Christ in *Wise Blood*, who fights ferociously to avoid that Jesus

> in the back of his mind, a wild, ragged figure motioning to him to turn around and come off into the dark where he was not sure of his footing, where he might be walking on water and not know it and suddenly know it and drown.

Motes is a child of the fundamentalist South, but in O'Connor's economy, he is also Everyman; those who refuse Christ's offer to help them, force Him to haunt them. O'Connor used sudden death, disease, or trauma to depict the devastating encounter with Christ that must occur before one can be truly alive in this world. Worse things than mere death can befall a person made in God's image; her characters more often than not must be brought to the brink of crisis or death to see themselves as they are: in dire need of repentance and grace. In O'Connor's view, humankind did not accidentally stumble into rebellion against God; each man or woman deliberately chooses to do so. Consequently, she records with merciless precision the rationalizations of her protagonists, stripping them bare of their pretensions of goodness and innocence. She endeavored to confront her readers with the full scandal of Christianity. Those O'Connor characters who attempt to redeem themselves with arrant scientism or sheer intellectualism meet a savage Savior—manifested in a bull, a haunting prophecy, or a terrifying vision—who will not release them until they confess Him or utterly denounce Him.

For O'Connor, there was no middle ground, no neutral corner; all who are not with Him are against Him. Her narrative voice had little room for authorial compassion or tenderness. Relentlessly exposing human pride, avarice, and weakness, she agreed with writer C. S. Lewis that all things that are not eternal are eternally out of date. Western culture was already too sentimental, too complacent about Christ and Christianity; her mission was to pound on the table, to cast the moneychangers—sacred or secular—out of the literary temple.

One must ask how O'Connor avoided mere Tractarianism, as her continuing popularity among critics and ubiquity in college literature anthologies attest she did. Part of the answer is that she frankly confronted the tenuous relationships that exist among audience, medium, story, and craft. It was her genius to lead her readers through and from the seemingly mundane and ordinary to a vision of reality as sacramental, as always pointing to a divine presence in human activity. She wrote,

> When I write a novel in which the central action is baptism, I am aware that for a majority of my readers, baptism is a meaningless rite . . . so I have to see that

> this baptism carries enough awe and mystery to jar the reader into some kind of emotional recognition of its significance.

O'Connor's fiction strips away the jaded images of the faith, forcing a dynamic confrontation with the gospel as it is played out in the lives of professed believers and as it is rejected by the worldly-wise.

As the reader follows Hazel Motes or Francis Marion Tarwater on his journey to belief, he is confronted with grace—a grace that enlarges his perception of the world, enabling him to see both the natural and the supernatural anew, to both discover and retrieve deeper images of the real. As O'Connor states it, this journey frequently entails "an action in which the devil has been the unwilling instrument of grace. This is not a piece of knowledge that I consciously put into my stories; it is a discovery that I get out of them." It is this "awful rowing toward God" that is chronicled in O'Connor's two novels, *Wise Blood* and *The Violent Bear It Away.*

WISE BLOOD

Hazel Motes, the protagonist of *Wise Blood*, is, O'Connor says, a "Christian *malgré lui*," a believer in spite of himself, a harried wayfarer who has been displaced from Eastrod, Tennessee, and from the religious life of the South. That religious life is distinctively Protestant, the religion of a South of beleaguered prophets and street-corner preachers, a South haunted by Jesus and by a theological definition of human identity and destiny. Motes is determined to escape salvation and anything that smacks of supernatural origin. Like that of Francis Marion Tarwater in *The Violent Bear It Away*, Motes's story is a reverse bildungsroman, a novel of an antiquest in which the protagonist tries to avoid, rather than seek, his or her destiny.

O'Connor maintained that *Wise Blood* is a "comic novel," and nonetheless so because it deals with "matters of life and death." Though many readers try to locate the integrity of Motes in his vigorous struggle to escape that "ragged figure moving from tree to tree in the back of his mind," O'Connor avers: "His integrity lies in his not being able to [escape] it." His attempted flight from Jesus begins on the train to Taulkinham. Discharged from military service, Motes parries with a Mrs. Hitchcock, challenging her claim to redemption. "If you've been redeemed," Motes snaps, "I wouldn't want to be." Later, he exclaims to no one in particular, "Do you think I believe in Jesus? . . . Well, I wouldn't even if He existed. Even if He was on this train." Motes has determined that the way to avoid Jesus is to avoid sin; one who is not a sinner needs no redemption—he is already "clean"—if he is free from transgression. This "freedom," however, does not mean that Motes can avoid becoming a preacher. When he first reaches the city and decides to look up Miss Leora Watts—who owns the "Friendliest Bed in Town"—both she and the cabdriver who brings him there accuse him of being a preacher; he simply looks the part.

Very soon, Motes encounters some potential disciples: Enoch Emery, who wants to help him find a "new jesus," and Sabbath Lily Hawks, the lustful daughter of a street preacher who feigns blindness. Following Sabbath and her father in order to ridicule their shallow evangelism, Motes declares that he will start a new church, a church without Christ. "I don't need Jesus," he tells the crowd gathering about him, "I got Leora Watts." Motes's obsession with the Hawks duo leads him to drive around the city in his beat-up Essex. His desperate flight from belief compels him to hound Asa Hawks, confronting him with the strange fact of his blindness—if Jesus is real, then why does He not heal His servants? Motes is tortured by his lack of a theodicy, a defense of God's absence; his only solace is to throw himself into his own "ministry": street-side preaching of the Church of Christ without Christ from the hood of his Essex.

Motes's nightly forays into sermonizing yield only one "convert," a would-be Aaron to Motes's Moses, Onnie Jay Holy—a slick packager of religion and faith who knows a money-making scam when he sees it. Crediting Motes-the-prophet with changing his life, Holy drowns out the frustrated antipreacher, who learns to speak the truth in spite of himself: "Listen!" Motes screams, "It don't cost you any money to know the truth!" It is at this point that O'Connor's protagonist has begun his inexorable trek toward recognizing his true state and the call of God. When Enoch Emery answers Motes's call for a "new jesus" by stealing a mummified pygmy from a local museum and delivering it to the now domesticated Sabbath Lily Hawks, the reader is introduced to what Caroline Gordon called "the unholy family." Slinking into Motes's room, Sabbath introduces the mummy as their child. Sensing the blasphemy of the moment, Motes seizes the mummy and crushes it against the wall. The prophet must now leave this desecrated place and search for a new city in which he can begin his ministry afresh. Before he can leave, however, he must confront a false prophet—hired by Hoover Shoats, née Onnie Jay Holy—who has supplanted him on the streets of Taulkinham. Following him out onto a lonely road, Motes first knocks his car into the ditch and then runs over his counterpart, killing him and thus carrying out the Old Testament vengeance against false prophets.

From here, Motes inevitably heads for his own Calvary, his own "death unto life": The words of Jesus in Matthew 5:29, "And if thy right eye offend thee, pluck it out," are taken literally. Motes blinds himself so that he can see with a spiritual vision that bogus believers such as Asa Hawks and Hoover Shoats can never attain. He is fully focused now; there is no intent to escape or flee. His landlady, Mrs. Flood, represents the kind of "Christian" O'Connor loved to contrast with her dramatic, utterly committed antisaints such as Hazel Motes, the Misfit in "A Good Man Is Hard to Find," and Manley Pointer in "Good Country People." She cannot fathom Motes's sudden devotion—which extended to the bearing of the marks of Christ on his body: "I'm as good, Mr. Motes, not believing in Jesus as many a one that does," she boastfully proclaims. When she sees the barbed wire wrapped around his chest, she exclaims, "There's no reason for it. People have quit doing it." His reply, anthem and testimony for all latter-day believers, seals his fate: "They ain't quit doing it as long as I'm doing it." Motes's death is as anticlimactic as Christ's; the police officers who discover him in the drainage ditch, like the soldiers at the foot of the cross who bargain for Christ's robe, mouth inanities and treat Motes as a troublesome derelict, quite worthy of being put out of his misery.

The story of Hazel Motes is the tale of one of God's creatures and his struggle with the fundamental choice to serve God or deny Him. O'Connor's avowed purpose was to "deepen the mystery of free will," which is not the war between one will and another but of "many wills conflicting in one man." In *Wise Blood*, whose title comes from Enoch Emery's claim to "know things" because of his ancestral blood, O'Connor has created a parable of twentieth century humankind's inner debate over God's existence and presence in the modern world. It is ironic, although not too surprising, that O'Connor's Christian readers sometimes responded less enthusiastically to her achievement than did her nonreligious readers. Such a response was simply a corroboration of O'Connor's perceptions regarding the state of belief in postwar America.

The Violent Bear It Away

In her second novel, *The Violent Bear It Away*, written some ten years after she had originally begun *Wise Blood*, O'Connor once again returned to the theme of the antiquest, this time with a protagonist who tries to escape the daunting prophecy of his great-uncle. The title comes from an ambiguous passage found in Matthew 11:12: "From the days of John the Baptist until now, the kingdom of heaven suffereth violence and the violent bear it away." It is the dual message of this scripture that, in part, gives the novel its underlying power as still another O'Connor portrayal of the conflict of wills within humans, a conflict of reason tempered with godly knowledge and an uncritical, gullible trust in the scientific method. The passage suggests, first, that with the coming of the promised Messiah, humankind can receive the kingdom of God; second, it suggests that there remain calloused and unprincipled unbelievers who will seek to bar the faithful from entering that hallowed ground. These two opposing forces are focused in the protagonist and antagonist of the novel: Francis Marion Tarwater and Rayber the schoolteacher.

Mason Tarwater had reared his nephew, Francis, to be "more than a Christian, a prophet." His prophetic task consisted of two matters: First, he was to make sure that the elder Tarwater had a proper burial, his gravesite marked by a cross; second, he was to baptize Bishop, the "dimwitted child" of Rayber. Mason had earlier tried to rear Rayber as a prophet, too, but he encountered a resistance that eventually turned into a vigorously antireligious posture. Mason Tarwater had finally broken off all relations with Rayber after the latter wrote a psychoanalysis of Tarwater for a "schoolteacher's magazine" that mocked his beliefs. Francis Tarwater, also, does not come easily to his prophetic office. At his great-uncle's death, he abandons the old man and burns down his house, balking at his obsession with Jesus; the choice is not between "Jesus and the devil," he resolves—"it's Jesus or me." Francis, like Hazel Motes, is nevertheless haunted by the presence of Jesus: "Jesus? He felt a terrible disappointment in that conclusion, a dread that it was true." He can no more escape his destiny than Motes could; it is "hidden in the blood."

Rayber is a familiar O'Connor character type, the rationalist who attempts to explain away religion as illusion or delusion. He will have no part of the Tarwaters' prophetic ministry. Just as the sense of sight was a potent symbol in *Wise Blood*, O'Connor here uses the sense of hearing, Rayber's need for a hearing aid, to underscore his spiritual ignorance: "Do you think in the box," Francis Tarwater ridiculed, "or do you think in your head?" The religious people of Rayber's acquaintance—the Tarwaters, the Carmody family—have all been "exploited" people, bilked by the foolish rhetoric of insane cadgers and shysters. Yet Rayber's will is not powerful enough to withstand the force of a prophet of God. True to his call, Francis must drown Bishop in baptism, the enduring Christian symbol of new life from death.

O'Connor organized the events of this novel into three distinct parts. Part 1 reveals the eccentric life of the prophet; as Elijah the Old Testament prophet gave his mantle to the younger Elisha, so Mason Tarwater passes his own "burden" to his charge. Part 2 depicts Francis Tarwater's struggle to free himself, like a latter-day Jonah, from the burden laid upon him; here the city is emblematic of all the distractions and temptations that might deter him from his task. Part 3 relates the purification and cleansing of the prophet who encounters his burning bush and receives his commission to "warn the children of God of the terrible speed of mercy" in the "dark city" beyond him.

The Violent Bear It Away more fully develops themes O'Connor explored in such short stories as "The Enduring Chill," "The Artificial Nigger," "Good Country People," and "The Lame Shall Enter First." Her consistent focus is placed upon the human will tortured by indecision, clouded by technology, and rendered impotent by its flight from knowledge of God. The only remedy offered is the laying down of weapons and the complete surrender of the soul. Francis Tarwater and Hazel Motes both discover that their only rest from this ordeal is acquiescence to the will of God.

Throughout her fiction, O'Connor defamiliarized the all-too-familiar concepts of conversion and discipleship and articulated the shallow view of Christ lurking behind modern faith. She wanted her readers to escape the jaundiced vision of their own time. In *Mystery and Manners*, she paralleled her task with that of St. Cyril of Jerusalem, who, in instructing catechumens, warned them of passing by the dragon on their way to the Father of Souls:

> No matter what form the dragon may take, it is of this mysterious passage past him, or into his jaws, that stories of any depth will always be concerned to tell, and this being the case, it requires considerable courage at any time, in any country, not to turn away from the storyteller.

O'Connor refused to turn away from the dragon or the storyteller, and she asked of her readers the same courage.

Bruce L. Edwards, Jr.

Other major works

SHORT FICTION: "Good Country People," 1955; *A Good Man Is Hard to Find, and Other Stories*, 1955; "Revelation," 1964; *Everything That Rises Must Converge*, 1965; *The Complete Stories*, 1971.

NONFICTION: *Mystery and Manners*, 1969; *The Habit of Being: Letters*, 1979 (Sally Fitzgerald, editor); *The Presence of Grace*, 1983; *The Correspondence of Flannery O'Connor and Brainard Cheneys*, 1986.

MISCELLANEOUS: *Collected Works*, 1988.

Bibliography

Asals, Frederick. *Flannery O'Connor: The Imagination of Extremity*. Athens: University of Georgia Press, 1982. In one of the best books on O'Connor's fiction, Asals focuses on the use of the doppelgänger (double) motif in the novels and short fiction, the most thorough and intelligent treatment of this subject. Asals also concentrates on O'Connor's religious extremity, which is evident in her fiction through her concern with polarities and extremes. Includes extensive endnotes and a good bibliography.

Cash, Jean W. *Flannery O'Connor: A Life*. Knoxville: University of Tennessee Press, 2002. A painstakingly researched chronicle of O'Connor's life. Cash depicts O'Connor as a very private, odd, and self-contained woman, devoted to Catholicism and to her writing. Includes a bibliography and an index.

Darretta, John. *Before the Sun Has Set: Retribution in the Fiction of Flannery O'Connor*. New York: Peter Lang, 2006. Darretta focuses on the theme of retribution in O'Connor's fiction, tracing how she handled this theme and altered her concept of retribution from her first work until her last.

Desmond, John F. *Risen Sons: Flannery O'Connor's Vision of History*. Athens: University of Georgia Press, 1987. Desmond argues that O'Connor's fictions reenact Christian history and Catholic theology through an art O'Connor herself saw as an "incarnational act." Discussing her two novels and several major stories, the book focuses on the metaphysical and the Christian historical vision as observed through reading O'Connor's fiction and emphasizes that *The Violent Bear It Away* represents the fullest development of her vision. Includes an extensive bibliography and useful endnotes.

Gooch, Brad. *Flannery: A Life of Flannery O'Connor*. New York: Little, Brown, 2008. Provides critical analysis of O'Connor's fiction, both the individual works and the scope of her career. Asserts that despite the fact that she wrote two novels, O'Connor was not really a novelist but was perhaps the greatest twentieth century American short-story writer.

Kirk, Connie Ann. *Critical Companion to Flannery O'Connor*. New York: Facts On File, 2008. A good introduction to O'Connor. Contains a concise biography, entries on O'Connor's two novels and other works, with subentries on her characters, as well as entries about her friends, literary influences, and the places and themes of her fiction. Includes a chronology and bibliographies of works by and about O'Connor.

McMullen, Joanne Halleran, and Jon Parrish Peede, eds. *Inside the Church of Flannery O'Connor: Sacrament, Sacramental, and the Sacred in Her Fiction*. Macon, Ga.: Mercer University Press, 2007. Collection of essays focuses on the religious—particularly Catholic—themes in O'Connor's fiction. Includes index.

Orvell, Miles. *Flannery O'Connor: An Introduction*. Jackson: University Press of Mississippi, 1991. Contains chapters on the novels as well as explorations of O'Connor's treatment of the South, belief, art, the American romance tradition, prophets and failed prophets, and comedy. Appendixes include a chronological list of her fiction and book reviews, and notes and a bibliography.

Simpson, Melissa. *Flannery O'Connor: A Biography*. Westport, Conn.: Greenwood Press, 2005. A brief biography, aimed at high school students and lower-level undergraduates, providing the basic facts of O'Connor's life and work. Includes photographs and a bibliography.

Spivey, Ted R. *Flannery O'Connor: The Woman, the Thinker, the Visionary*. Macon, Ga.: Mercer University Press, 1995. Spivey attempts to understand O'Connor first as a southerner, then as a modernist intellectual, and finally as a visionary thinker. He argues that O'Connor's work reflects the personal and social issues of the last decades of the twentieth century.

Westling, Louise Hutchings. *Sacred Groves and Ravaged Gardens: The Fiction of Eudora Welty, Carson McCullers, and Flannery O'Connor*. Athens: University of Georgia Press, 1985. A useful book for those interested in critical perspectives other than religious readings of O'Connor's fiction as well as for those curious about O'Connor's relationship with Eudora Welty and Carson McCullers. This book is the first feminist study of O'Connor's fiction. Discusses the female characters and emphasizes that O'Connor often shows female protagonists as victims of male antagonists.

KENZABURŌ ŌE

Born: Ōse, Shikoku, Japan; January 31, 1935

Principal long fiction

Memushiri kouchi, 1958 (*Nip the Buds, Shoot the Kids*, 1995)
Warera no jidai, 1959
Yoru yo yuruyaka ni ayume, 1959
Seinenno omei, 1960
Okurete kita seinen, 1962
Sakebigoe, 1963
Kojinteki na taiken, 1964 (*A Personal Matter*, 1968)
Nichyoseikatsu no boken, 1964
Sora no kaibutsu aguwee, 1964 (novella; *Aghwee the Sky Monster*, 1977)
Man'en gan'nen no futtoboru, 1967 (*The Silent Cry*, 1974)
Nichijo seikatsu no boken, 1971
Kōzui wa waga tamashii ni oyobi, 1973
Pinchi rannā chōsho, 1976 (*The Pinch Runner Memorandum*, 1994)
Dōjidai gemu, 1979
Atarashii hito yo mezameyo, 1983 (*Rouse Up O Young Men of the New Age!*, 2002)
Natsukashii toshi e no tegami, 1987
Jinsei no shinseki, 1989 (*An Echo of Heaven*, 1996)
Chiryōtō, 1990
Shizuka na seikatsu, 1990 (*A Quiet Life*, 1996)
Chiryōtō wakusei, 1991
Moeagaru midori no ki, 1993-1995 (includes *"Sukuinushi" ga nagurareru made*, 1993; *Yureugoku "vashireshon,"* 1994; *Ōinaru hi ni*, 1995)
Chūgaeri, 1999 (2 volumes; *Somersault*, 2003)
Torikaeko, 2000 (also known as *Chenjiringu*)
Ureigao no doji, 2002
Nihyakunen no kodomo, 2003
Sayōnara watashi no hon yo!, 2005
Rōtashi Anaberu Rii sōkedachitsu mimakaritsu, 2007

Other literary forms

Kenzaburō Ōe (oh-ay) has published short fiction and works of nonfiction in addition to his novels. Some of his short stories have been collected in *Warera no kyoki o ikinobiru michi o oshieyo* (1969, 1975; *Teach Us to Outgrow Our Madness*, 1977). Ōe has written numerous essays and speeches as well as a personal memoir of his family's life, *Kaifuku suru kazoku* (1995; *A Healing Family*, 1996). Much of his nonfiction work, including the texts of many of his speeches, has been collected in *Aimai na Nihon no watakushi* (1995; *Japan, the Ambiguous, and Myself: The Nobel Prize Speech, and Other Lectures*, 1995). Two multivolume editions of Ōe's collected works have been published in Japanese by the publishing houses Shinchosha and Iwanami. The twelve-volume work by Shinchosha, which was updated and revised in 1994, contains Ōe's novels, principal short fiction, and nonfiction up to that date.

Achievements

Winning the Nobel Prize in Literature in 1994 was a joyful surprise for Kenzaburō Ōe, who was the second Japanese writer in history to win the prestigious award. In his acceptance speech in Stockholm on December 7, 1994, Ōe ironically pointed to the great gulf between his unconventional, politically charged writing and the beautiful texts that had earned his predecessor, Yasunari Kawabata, the award in 1968. Ōe's Stockholm speech, in which he claimed the prize in part on behalf of other dissident Asian writers, indirectly explained why the author had immediately declined Japan's Imperial Order of Culture, which he earned days after the Nobel Prize. Rejecting what he perceived as a symbol of a still-existent, antidemocratic cult of the emperor, Ōe antagonized many Japanese who could not understand this action.

Ōe has always occupied an ambiguous position in the literary world of Japan. His conscious attempts to forge a new Japanese literary language, his focus on alienation and suffering, and his unbending political opposition to nuclear weapons and to the emperor have earned him both admiration and puzzled rejection. In spite of this split in the Japanese reception of his works, Ōe's writings have earned him prestigious national and international awards from the beginning of his career. One of his first short stories, "Kimyo na shigoto" (1957; a strange job), about a student paid to kill dogs, won the Tokyo University May Festival Prize in 1957. One year later, Ōe's short story "Shiiku" (1958; "The Catch," 1966; "Prize Stock," 1977), describing the friendship between a Japanese boy and a black American pilot shot down over Japan, earned for Ōe Japan's prestigious Akutagawa Prize for 1958. In 1964, *A Personal Matter*, one of Ōe's most widely read novels, received the important Shinchosha Literary Prize. *The Silent Cry* was recognized with the Tanizaki Jun'ichirō Prize in 1967.

As his novels continued to win major Japanese literary awards, such as the Noma Literary Prize in 1973, the Yomiuri Prize in 1982, and the Ito Sei Literary Prize in 1990, Ōe's reputation as a major contemporary Japanese writer solidified at home and began to attract international attention. His nonfiction work was awarded the Osaragi Jiro Prize in 1983. Overseas, the European Community awarded Ōe the Europelia Prize in 1989. Winning the Italian Mondelosso Prize in 1993 signaled his high standing in international literature, which was crowned by the Nobel Prize in 1994. In 2006, the Japanese publishing house Kodansha established the Kenzaburō Ōe Prize. Every year beginning in 2007, Ōe has selected one book by a Japanese writer to receive the award; the prize for the author is translation of the winning work into English so that it can be published and enjoyed abroad.

Ōe, as a member of the post-World War II generation, recognizes the human problems peculiar to the twentieth century, the century of nuclear explosions. This age of anxiety and its problems are internationally popular themes in literature as well as in the other arts. In that sense, the "antitraditional Ōe" has helped make Japanese literature a part of world literature. Ōe successfully created in Japanese literature a new tradition more closely related and integral to modern world literature than the traditional canons of ancient and medieval Japan.

Biography

Kenzaburō Ōe was born in the small town of Ōse in the prefecture of Ehime, on Shikoku Island, Japan, on January 31, 1935. The first important chain of events in his life, in terms of the literary tendencies he later developed, began with Japan's defeat in World War II, the subsequent declaration of the emperor's change of status from divine to human, and the taking over of Japan by the U.S. Army. These drastic changes resulted in an unimaginable chaos of values in postwar Japan.

In 1954, Ōe became a student at Tokyo University, majoring in French literature. He began writing short stories while devouring the works of such authors as Blaise Pascal, Albert Camus, Jean-Paul Sartre, Norman Mailer, William Faulkner, and Saul Bellow. His first novel, *Nip the Buds, Shoot the Kids*, was published in 1958. One year after his graduation from the university in 1959, he married Yukari Itami, the daughter of film director Mansaku Itami. Ōe participated in organizing various protests in an attempt to cut Japan off from the nuclear umbrella of the United States, but he became disillusioned and finally discontinued his efforts when he found that left-wing organizations did not condemn nuclear tests conducted by Communist countries.

In 1963, Ōe's first child, a son whom his parents named Hikari, meaning "light" in English, had to undergo a series of operations shortly after birth because of defective bone structure in his head. The field trip that Ōe made to Hiroshima the following summer as a reporter revealed the incredible hardships of the victims of the atomic bomb, which he associated with his personal ordeal. In combination, these two experiences produced a novel, *A Personal Matter*, in 1964. After this novel, the motif of physical deformity became pervasive in Ōe's novels and short stories.

Ōe traveled widely. In 1960, as a member of the Japanese literature delegation, he went to China, where he met Mao Zedong. In 1961, he stayed in Europe for four months at the invitation of Bulgaria and Poland. He also visited, on this occasion, the Soviet Union, England, and France, where he interviewed Sartre. Ōe also visited Australia, Mexico, and the United States. A collection of essays titled *Sekai no wakamonotachi* (the youth of the world), published in 1962, reflects his experiences abroad.

Ōe and his wife had two more children, born without disability. In 1976, Ōe decided on a long stay in Mexico after finishing a semester as lecturer at the Collegio de Mexico. This brought him in touch with writers such as the Colombian Gabriel García Márquez, for whose works Ōe developed a deep affinity. Returning to Japan, Ōe published *Shosetsu no hoho* (1978), in which he promoted the Western literary theory of structuralism to revive Japanese writing. Many of Ōe's subsequent novels reveal his fascination with structuralism and marginal existence, which also brought him in touch with Western literary critics and authors. Traveling frequently to Europe after 1980, in 1982 Ōe visited to gather material on the Western European antinuclear movement. His never-ending involvement in political issues brought him to the Soviet Union, where he attended a 1987 conference on peace in Moscow.

Becoming familiar with the contemporary European literary world and beginning to earn European literary prizes, Ōe publicly debated such figures as German author Günter Grass in 1990 and French author Michel Tournier in 1991. In 1994, Ōe won the Nobel Prize in Literature and swiftly renounced his award of Japan's Imperial Order of Culture. He also told a stunned public that he would stop writing novels because his mentally handicapped son Hikari had become a successful composer of music.

Hikari has always been central to Ōe's work, as evidenced by the story of their family's life together in *A Healing Family*, a text illustrated by Yukari Ōe's watercolors. While proclaiming his end to novel writing, Ōe continued his political involvement, participating in protests against France's nuclear testing in the Pacific in 1997. Although he settled in Tokyo with his wife and family, Ōe continued to give literary lectures around the world.

Within a few years, Ōe returned to writing novels. In 1999, his monumental work *Somersault* was published; this novel focuses on the resurgence of a fictitious religious cult closely modeled on the Aum Shinrikyo sect, which was responsible for the deadly 1995 Tokyo subway poison gas attacks. With his next three books, Ōe returned to the subject of children with special powers. In his 2005 novel *Sayōnara watashi no hon yo* (farewell, go buy my books), Ōe gently tells his readers to look to his works for his opinions about postwar Japanese society.

From 2005 to March 28, 2008, when he was cleared of all charges, Ōe focused most of his energies on defending himself against a libel suit that had been brought against him by a disgruntled retired Japanese military officer and the surviving relatives of another. The author's right-wing opponents had taken exception to his 1970 claim that the Imperial Japanese Army had coerced Okinawan civilians to commit mass suicide on the eve of the American conquest of Okinawa toward the end of World War II. When the ruling judge proclaimed Ōe right on the issue and dismissed the claim, the author, vindicated, returned to writing his next novel.

Analysis

Madness and despair are the recurring themes in the novels of Kenzaburo Ōe. His main characters are usually trapped physically, psychologically, or metaphorically. They realize their entrapment when they find themselves suddenly alienated from the major part of society to which they thought they belonged. The harder the vic-

Kenzaburō Ōe. (© The Nobel Foundation)

tims try to escape from their trap, the more impossible escape becomes. Madness and despair then start to develop and reverberate in the characters' lonely confinement. They become somewhat disoriented and therefore become social misfits. The conflict between the ostracized (minority) and the authoritarian (majority) is presented in Ōe's fiction in various forms: adults versus children, teachers versus juvenile delinquents, the successful versus dropouts, police versus criminals, organizations versus individuals. The resolutions to such conflict usually take one of two forms: The ostracized characters destroy themselves, or they accept everything in an existential way.

The notion of disorientation in Ōe's work may be a reflection of his experiences of the drastic changes that took place in Japan after the nation's defeat in World War II. As a young boy, Ōe had been educated at school and elsewhere to become a brave soldier and to die in the war for the sake of the emperor. Suddenly, on August 15, 1945, this great cause was taken away, and the emperor declared that he was a fellow human instead of a god for whom Ōe should be willing to die. The humiliation of being a defeated nation was combined with the fear of possible massacre and mass rape by the soldiers of the occupying army.

After his visit to Hiroshima in 1963, Ōe published a work of nonfiction titled *Hiroshima nōto* (1965; *Hiroshima Notes*, 1982), in which he expresses deep sympathy for the people suffering from the effects of nuclear radiation as the result of the atomic bombing. In the essay, Ōe criticizes the government for providing inadequate assistance and for the irresponsible and sometimes inhumane treatment the people had received. Ōe warns the reader never to forget Hiroshima. In *A Personal Matter*, Ōe deals with a man's struggle against becoming entrapped by a son whose deformity may have been caused by nuclear radiation. Later, the theme of the agonies of the nuclear age becomes more and more pervasive in Ōe's fiction, such as in *Kōzui wa waga tamashii ni oyobi* and *The Pinch Runner Memorandum*. In these works, Ōe's themes of entrapment, madness, and despair are far more intense, because the situation of the main characters is totally impossible: It has become a global problem. Ōe seems to suggest an analogy with Noah's Ark, in *Sakebigoe* (outcries) and in *Kōzui wa waga tamashii ni oyobi*, as archetypal of escape, but in both, the escape fails, and "departure" (one of Ōe's favorite terms) is never achieved.

Ōe presents his theme of madness and despair through the literary technique of the grotesque. One of the classic devices of this technique is the animalization of human beings. Some of Ōe's characters—especially those in later works such as *A Personal Matter*, *The Silent Cry*, and *Kōzui wa waga tamashii ni oyobi*—are named after animals. They are often reduced to a biological level. Physical deformity, another important ingredient in the grotesque, is no rarity among the inhabitants of Ōe's imaginative world. The best example of this is the two-headed monster baby in *A Personal Matter*; other monstrous or deformed characters include a one-eyed doctor in *A Personal Matter*, an extremely obese woman who eats continuously in *The Silent Cry*, and even a shrinking man in *Kōzui wa waga tamashii ni oyobi*. Sexual behavior is described animalistically, totally lacking in romantic-erotic connotations. Actions are atrocious, and imagery—often related to human waste—is shocking and repulsive. All these grotesque elements create a violent and sometimes ludicrous effect and an incredibly maddening atmosphere—an atmosphere derived from confinement (estrangement) and from the dread of uncertainty in life.

Ōe's novels can be loosely categorized into different groups. One group consists of six of the author's earlier works in which the treatment of the nuclear age and its agonies is not yet in the forefront, and in which Ōe's use of the grotesque is still not fully developed. Of these six novels, *Okurete kita seinen* (the youth who arrived late) may be the most important, because it embodies all the themes with which Ōe had been dealing in the other novels as well as in his short stories: disorientation, estrangement, children's distrust of adults, confinement, departure only to be trapped in another impossible situation, violent torture, humiliation, and the final and undignified acceptance of the situation by the hero. The work is the longest of the six.

The novels in another group characteristically feature a handicapped boy who affects the fates of the characters around him. Of these, *The Silent Cry* is the most famous, and *A Quiet Life* offers some sort of resolution to the existential anguish conjured up in this cycle of novels. A third group consists of the "flaming green tree" trilogy, *Moeagaru midori no ki*, the last volume of which was published in 1995. The trilogy, originally intended to signal the end of Ōe's fiction output, is deeply influenced by Ōe's contact with Latin American Magical Realism. Since publication of the trilogy, Ōe's works of long fiction have included the stunning *Somersault* and a trilogy published from 2000 to 2005 that focuses on near-magic children.

Okurete kita seinen

Okurete kita seinen (the youth who arrived late) consists of two parts: The first deals with the struggle of the protagonist, the first-person narrator, against his surroundings in a small village; the second part, with the adventures and frustrations of the hero in Tokyo. A small village in part 1 can probably be identified as the author's native town on the island of Shikoku. The hero is a sixth-grader, and the story begins on the very day that Japan surrenders at the end of World War II. The narrator's awareness of being born too late for everything, especially for the war, is intense; in his difficulty in accepting the fact of Japan's defeat, followed by the emperor's change of status, it seems to him that the whole world has turned upside down.

The villagers make quick adjustments and wear sycophantic smiles for the incoming occupying army. In order to live at peace with the occupation forces, the villagers make scapegoats of the minority groups among them (Koreans and native Shikokuans, called "Highlanders"). These shameless incidents estrange the narrator, make him rebellious, and lead to his affinity for a Korean boy, Kō, with whom the narrator remains friendly all the way through the novel. Kō and the narrator escape from the village, or "depart," as Ōe likes to put it, in order to join a group of Japanese soldiers who refuse to admit Japan's defeat. Ironically, this departure leads the narrator to an even stricter confinement—in a correctional institution.

The fear of confinement in an isolated village is also the theme of Ōe's first novel, *Nip the Buds, Shoot the Kids*. In this novel, the theme is presented in a clear-cut fashion: Certain inmates, children who had been transferred from an urban correctional institution in an attempt to avoid air raids, find themselves imprisoned in a village where there is a heap of dead animals that have died in an epidemic. The villagers, having evacuated the village, shoot at the children as they try to escape. In Ōe's next novel, *Warera no jidai* (our age), the notion of confinement is more metaphorical. A university student, Yasuo Minami, like Ōe, majoring in French literature, is fed up with a decadent life with an oversexed prostitute but cannot escape from her, since she provides the major part of his living expenses. Later, he almost leaves Japan, and his decadent life, to accept an invitation from French authorities who wish to reward him for his prizewinning essay. In the end, this invitation is canceled because Minami is found to be involved in underground revolutionary activities. He thus has only one place to which he can return—the prostitute's house.

By contrast, the narrator in *Okurete kita seinen* successfully finishes his term in a correctional institution, passes the entrance examination for Tokyo University, and departs for Tokyo, where he finds only another trap. The narrator hates successful people so much that he is determined to become one himself in order to take his revenge. His target is an influential conservative politician whose daughter he tutors in French and plans to seduce. Ironically, he is too late—the daughter is pregnant by another man. The narrator claims to be the baby's father in order to attract the politician's attention and receive money from him for an abortion. The money, however, makes him a target for sadistic left-wing students—the violence described here is mostly related to sex. The narrator uses these experiences to approach the politician and succeeds to some extent in gaining his favor. This part of the plot, it is hinted, is inspired by the ambition-driven Julien Sorel in Stendhal's *Le Rouge et le noir* (1830; *The Red and the Black*, 1898).

Ōe's protagonist declines rapidly, as his past as a juvenile delinquent is revealed. In the end, he realizes that his sole option is to accept whatever is offered to him. Unlike his French counterpart, who destroys himself, Ōe's protagonist is antiheroic, grossly diminished, and reduced to a mere biological, rather than fully human, existence. He realizes after so many experiences of humiliation and frustration that his dignity as a human being is completely gone. He no longer has even the dignity of madness, since madness is the manifestation of sanity in an insane society. Ōe's narrator, in his calm and yet profound despair, chooses to live. Death can no longer be tragic, since he was born too late for the war, in which a heroic death was possible. Only one who dies a heroic death can live eternally in glory.

A Personal Matter

A nightmarish city life is the setting for *A Personal Matter*. At the start of the novel, the twenty-seven-year-old protagonist, Bird, nicknamed for his birdlike facial features, tries to escape to Africa from a city life laden with responsibilities. Africa, in Ōe's imaginative world, seems to have a deceptive ambiguity: It looks like ultimate freedom, the antithesis of city life, yet it actually is an ominous image associated with death. Bird looks at a map of Africa and thinks the shape of the continent resembles that of a skull. In *Nichyoseikatsu no boken* (adventures in everyday life), written before *A Personal Matter*, Africa presents the same ambiguity. The hero, Saikichi (*Sai* means "rhinoceros"), does go to Africa: This trip suggests a return home (a rhinoceros goes to Africa), but he kills himself in a hotel room there. Bird's wish to flee to Africa, then, represents an unconscious desire for a world of adventure, like the world of war, where he might be able to put an end to his life. The motif of Africa reappears in *The Silent Cry*.

Another conspicuous correlation between *Nichyoseikatsu no boken* and *A Personal Matter* is the existence of a woman called Himiko. Himiko in *Nichyoseikatsu no boken* is the first wife of Saikichi. Her name is presented with the same characters as those of Queen Himiko of the legendary Yamatai Kingdom of the second century. According to the legend, Queen Himiko committed incest with her younger brother in order to continue her line. She eventually was killed by the wrath of God, immediately after giving birth to a baby boy. In *Nichyoseikatsu no boken*, Himiko liberates Saikichi with her uninhibited attitude toward sex. Similarly, Himiko in *A Personal Matter* (the name has the same sounds but is written with different characters) cures Bird's impotence by offering him anal intercourse. Sex in Ōe's world is often used to break psychological confinement and is stripped to the bare facts of desire and anatomy.

Bird's awareness of his psychological confinement intensifies when his wife gives birth to a baby whose head seems twice as big as that of a normal baby. He tries to kill the deformed baby. After desperately struggling with himself, however, he finally realizes that the baby is nothing but an extension of his life, an existential realization that life has to be continued whether it seems meaningful or not. Ōe's technique here is the literary grotesque, a distortion of reality. He creates an unfeeling, apathetic urban society populated with such monstrous characters as a doctor who is interested only in the baby's autopsy, even though it is still alive, and Bird's girlfriend, Himiko, who leads an active life only during the night hours and sleeps during the day. This deformed reality strongly suggests a loss in human qualities. It is vaguely hinted that the deformity of the baby might be a result of radioactive fallout in the rain caused by nuclear experiments. Bird had participated as a student in protest rallies and street demonstrations against those experiments. Now the problem comes to Bird in a much more concrete form—it is a personal matter indeed.

The seemingly optimistic ending of *A Personal Matter*, one of Ōe's most popular novels, is not in harmony with the pessimistic tone of the novel as a whole. In the last two pages, Bird emerges with his family into the sun from the darkness of the hospital. The baby, now in its mother's arms, has undergone surgery, which revealed a benign tumor instead of a fatal brain hernia. This ending is anticlimactic, unlike, for example, the ending of *Kōzui wa waga tamashii ni oyobi*, which concludes with the symbolic death of the protagonist, or that of *The Pinch Runner Memorandum*, the last scene of which describes a spectacular bonfire into which the protagonist plunges headlong. If the theory of the grotesque is extended to this work, then the ending suggests madness in people who are not, in terms of characterization, mad. Bird has ceased to behave like a madman, indicating his madness; his father-in-law has given him a bottle of whiskey, knowing that Bird was once an alcoholic; and his mother-in-law has wished for the baby's death. The overwhelming optimism at the end comes from the fact that the baby is saved, but nothing has changed for Bird. He has to give up his dream of Africa and is more deeply trapped than ever, without hope.

The Silent Cry

In *The Silent Cry*, Ōe deals with two brothers who return from city life to their native village—an action that reverses that of *Okurete kita seinen*. In the journey, planned as a quest for identity, they trace their origin symbolically to the mother's womb. The womb is the village, located in a valley, and is called Ōkubo, which means "a large hollow." The valley is surrounded by dense, almost impenetrable forests. The brothers find themselves confined spatially in this isolated area on the island of Shikoku, and they gradually also recognize their temporal confinement.

The older brother, Mitsusaburo, often called Mitsu, is the pensive narrator. His wife has become an alcoholic since their deformed baby was put in an institution. The narrator's younger brother, formerly active on the streets as a student radical, is named Takashi, or simply Taka (which means "hawk"); compared with Mitsu, Taka is more a man of action. Their last name is Nedokoro, meaning "the place where there is the root." The Nedokoro brothers' immediate purpose in visiting the native village is to sell the family estate to a new supermarket chain. The other purpose, just as important, is to investigate what actually happened to their great-grandfather and his younger brother, who were involved in a peasants' rebellion in the first year of the Manen era, one hundred years before the narrative present.

Unconsciously, Taka and Mitsu try to identify themselves with their ancestors. There are many intricate parallels between these pairs of brothers. Mitsu and Taka experience what their great-grandfather and great-uncle experienced a hundred years before. Taka, the younger brother, organizes the villagers and starts a rebellion against the ever-expanding influence of the supermarket on the village, just as the ancestral younger brother had organized the peasants against the overwhelming power of governmental authority. When the historical rebellion failed, the organizer disappeared; what became of him is not revealed until the end of the novel. Taka commits suicide by shooting himself in the face with a shotgun, not because of the failure of the rebellion but because of his own madness—madness resulting from his guilt centering on the death of his younger sister, with whom he had an incestuous relationship. The parallelism between these two incidents, temporally separated but spatially overlapped, is an example of a literary technique that might be called "simultaneity." It helps create a sense of helpless confinement not only in space but also in time.

At the start of the novel, a good friend of the narrator commits suicide in a most grotesque way—he hangs himself naked, his head painted vermilion, with a cucumber in his anus. This episode clearly establishes overtones of madness. The madness innate in Taka as well as in Mitsu is symbolized by the womblike or tomblike hollow in the ground where the narrator wakes up in the morning at the beginning of the novel. At the end of the novel, evidence is found that the organizer of the historical rebellion had been kept in confinement for the rest of his life in the secret basement of the Nedokoro mansion. This is another subterranean manifestation of the fate of posterity. Mitsu's wife is now pregnant not by her husband but by his insane dead brother, but the husband and wife wish to start a new life with the children—one an idiot and the other yet to be born. Mitsusaburo looks forward to setting off for Africa, the continent of ominous ambiguity.

The Silent Cry has several symbolically deformed characters. The narrator had lost one eye some time before and has designated his hollow eye socket as the eye for looking inside himself. Jin, who used to be the wet nurse for the narrator, is now an extremely obese woman living at the Nedokoro estate. She is famous for her obesity but continues to eat obsessively. When the Nedokoro mansion is demolished, she suddenly stops eating and starts to die. Another character is a diminutive man who had hidden himself in a dense forest in order to avoid the draft in wartime. This man, called Gii the Hermit, has a head so small it looks like a shrunken, mummified head.

Grotesquerie is ubiquitous and pervasive in this novel. The eldest brother of the Nedokoros, for example, was killed in the war, and his diary records all kinds of wartime atrocities—such as a graphic description of captives being beheaded. The second brother, known only as "Brother S," had come back from the war, but later was beaten to death by a group of Koreans as retribution for the ransacking of their village by the Japanese. His brain seeps out of his cracked skull. Taka, before committing suicide, insists that he killed a village girl in an attempted rape and describes how he smashed her head against a huge rock after she had bitten off his fingertips. Combining these repulsive scenes with evocations of eerie masked dances and music peculiar to this region's festival, Ōe builds up an atmosphere of intense madness and despair that leads to the theme of the final and inescapable horror—the deracination of human beings by a nuclear war in the next two novels.

Kōzui wa waga tamashii ni oyobi

The main character in *Kōzui wa waga tamashii ni oyobi* (the flood unto my soul), Isana Ōki (which means "big trees-whales"), lives in a nuclear shelter with his five-year-old mentally handicapped son, Jin. Isana has separated from his wife and settled down in the shelter in order to provide a quiet life for his autistic son, who can respond only to birds' chirping. The father believes himself able to communicate with the spirits of whales and trees. A group of five or six social dropouts called the Free Navigators intrude on the life of the father and son. The Free Navigators live together, learn how to operate a schooner, steal cars, and practice combat drills. Their purpose is to escape from Japan as soon as a natural or nuclear disaster hits. Later, they steal firearms and explosives from an army camp and lynch a fellow member, the "Shrinking Man." The final scene is a shoot-out with the police at the shelter in which Isana and another fanatic are hiding. In the end, Isana drowns himself in the water that the police have poured into the shelter.

Kōzui wa waga tamashii ni oyobi includes many of Ōe's familiar motifs. For example, Isana is a son-in-law of a hideous politician who is dying of cancer. This is the family situation that the narrator in *Okurete kita seinen* had to accept. Isana's son is no doubt an extension of the monster baby in *A Personal Matter*. The trio—that is, the monstrous enigmatic politician, the disoriented father, and his mentally handicapped son—also appear as main characters in Ōe's next novel, *The Pinch Runner Memorandum*. The name Jin is immediately associated with the Jin in *The Silent Cry*. Right after he is born, the baby refuses to eat, as if he wishes to commit suicide, but later, he slowly gains weight.

A total social misfit, Isana tries to save his son from autism by developing an affinity with nature. He calls himself the representative of trees and whales, hence his name. Ironically, however, his name indicates the exact opposite of what he represents. Whales are large and mobile; Isana is insignificant and immobile in his trap. Trees reach toward the sky and symbolize life; his psyche is directed downward and he is to die. His longing for nature is symbolized by a hole in the concrete floor of his nuclear shelter in which he can put his bare feet directly on the soil. His situation is another image used to present "madness." Ironically, the water that kills Isana gushes into the shelter through this hole.

The Free Navigators are actually outlaws, but their plan for a seaborne enterprise clearly reflects the motif of escape based on the biblical episode of Noah's Ark treated in *Sakebigoe*. The plan fails as it did before, and Isana, trapped and drowning in the whalelike shelter, resembles Jonah, who is swallowed by a whale as a result of his disobeying the Word of God. No final salvation comes to Isana.

The sense of estrangement that Isana experiences during the course of the novel results from the change that takes place in the mind of his son Jin. When the Free Navigators step into their life, Jin gradually starts to open his mind, especially to a young girl called Inako. The Navigators are violent criminals. Some of them are extremely sadomasochistic, yet they are not nearly as depraved as the monstrous politician, whose sexual preference is for young boys. As Jin begins to have simple conversations with the intruders, Isana realizes that he has suddenly lost his raison d'être.

Of the members of the Free Navigators, Inako is the most sensible and humane character, even though she is naturally promiscuous and uninhibited. The most grotesque character of them all is the Shrinking Man. He is a professional photographer who once won a prize for the pictures he took of children suffering from muscular dystrophy. It is not clear if his "shrinking" is metaphorical or physical, but he claims that since his thirty-fifth birthday, he has started to shrink. As his body shrinks, his sexual organ becomes bigger. He calls this phenomenon "implosion" instead of "explosion." The Shrinking Man takes pictures of the group's secret combat drills and sells them to a weekly magazine; this betrayal provokes the group to lynch him. The lynching takes a most atrocious and repulsive form: He dies, his naked body skewered through the rectum. The scene is all the more shocking because Ōe creates a ludicrous atmosphere—the lynchers constantly laugh and giggle as if they are enjoying some kind of game.

The death of Isana at the conclusion of the novel is symbolic of the fate of human beings who have discovered nuclear fission, perhaps against the will of God. It also represents the meaninglessness of survival in the case of a nuclear disaster. As it is meaningless to die in a nuclear shelter in peacetime, so is it meaningless to survive a nuclear war. Thus, the notion of doomsday deepens Ōe's despair, and a world of madness and absurdity unfolds itself in the novel.

The Pinch Runner Memorandum

The mentally handicapped son in *The Pinch Runner Memorandum*, age eight, is named Mori. The name has a double meaning: "forest" in Japanese and "death" in Latin. "Forest" suggests the mythical power that dominates human existence in *Nip the Buds, Shoot the Kids* as well as in *The Silent Cry*. Death is the major motif throughout Ōe's fiction. Mori's thirty-eight-year-old father has no name of his own and is identified only as "Mori/father." He is supposed to be contaminated by plutonium, and he and his wife believe that their son's disability has been caused by radioactivity.

One morning, the father and son find themselves transformed: The father is reduced to an eighteen-year-old boy, and the son is now a mature man of twenty-eight. The father thinks that this "switch" has been brought about by some kind of extraterrestrial power called "the will of the universe." The father, now a teenager, becomes involved in a violent conflict between two militant factions in the student movement over the issue of which student group should manufacture an atomic bomb. As the novel progresses, it gradually becomes clear that both factions are manipulated by one political and financial magnate called Mr. A. In the meantime, Mori attacks Mr. A, again guided by the will of the universe, but succeeds only in wounding him in the head. When hospitalized, Mr. A is found to be dying of cancer, not of the wound in the head. Mr. A's plan is to create social chaos, first by providing funds for the militant student factions to produce nuclear bombs and then by helping the government annihilate them to save Tokyo, and thereby to die as a savior. Mori finally succeeds in stopping Mr. A by smashing his head with an iron bar; Mori then commits suicide by jumping into a gigantic bonfire made by the masqueraders from Mr. A's native village in order to exorcize the evil spirit called "cancer."

The novel is a fantasy-farce, based on the notion that every creature on earth is nothing but a make-believe shadow created by a huge slide projector delivered by an unidentified flying object (UFO). No character has a realistic name; no character is a character from the viewpoint of the realistic novel. The narrator's wife, for example, is an alcoholic lunatic who brandishes a razor and cuts her husband's cheek so deeply that he can stick his tongue out of the cut. The wound disappears, however, as soon as the "switch" takes place, since the narrator has reversed the flow of time. The hijackers who attack a truck carrying radioactive waste look like so many tin men from L. Frank Baum's *Wonderful Wizard of Oz* (1900). A man known as the Righteous Man, who comes from the island of Shikoku to participate in a protest rally only to be killed in the battle between the student factions, uses his denture as a weapon. Mori, the protagonist, never speaks except for occasional groans; he communicates with his father by telepathy.

The work is highly satiric, caricaturing world politics concerning nuclear weaponry and the student protest movements in Japan as well. It seems that *The Pinch Runner Memorandum*, published in 1976, foreshadows the renewed hysteria over nuclear competition between the world powers that took place in the early 1980's. The novel is also alarming; the foundation of its farcical plot is the fact that an individual with a certain amount of knowledge about nuclear physics could produce a nuclear bomb, given enough funding. This is no longer merely a possibility; rather, it is a constant danger. Mr. A, with his long involvement in Japanese economic expansion into Asian countries, is presented as a reactionary figure intending to restore political power to the emperor.

In order to achieve his tragicomic ambiguity, Ōe uses a peculiar style that might be called "vulgar colloquialism"—loosely worded, seemingly unending and undirected sentences, including slang and coarse expressions uncommon in contemporary Japanese literature. It is a conversational style commonly used among modern Japanese students, vaguely recalling the particular terminology of the late 1960's student activists. The style is in harmony with the absurd content and heightens the horror of this seemingly fantastic yet unnervingly realistic novel.

Dōjidai gemu

Upon his return from a long stay in Mexico in the 1970's, Ōe began to experiment with structuralism in his next novel, *Dōjidai gemu* (the game of contemporaneity).

Its sometimes surrealistic plot centers on a band of exiled warriors who fight the Japanese Imperial Army to a standstill in a remote forest during World War II. They surrender only when the army threatens to burn the forest, thereby saving nature rather than themselves. Because of this resolution, the novel has been interpreted as Ōe's fictional response to Yukio Mishima's dramatic suicide by *seppuku* in 1970. Thus, Mishima's action, which sought to revive a traditional warrior cult, is replaced by Ōe's deep appeal to humanism.

An Echo of Heaven

Ōe's texts constantly revisit familiar terrain, and *Dōjidai gemu*'s remote forest of Shikoku, where Ōe was born, features prominently in many of his next novels. *An Echo of Heaven*, however, moves from Japan to Mexico. Here, Marie Kuraki finds a spiritual refuge after the suicide of her two handicapped sons in Japan. The novel hauntingly combines Ōe's earlier themes of physically deformed children with a reflection of Marie's encounter with Mexican Magical Realism, as peasants begin to venerate her as a new saint in the tradition of the Dark Virgin of Guadalupe. The remote village of Shikoku has been transported by Ōe to Mexico and functions again as a microcosm where agonies and aspirations of human existence play themselves out against a backdrop of myth and grotesque realism. Ōe's interest in structuralism continues as he deliberately fragments the narrative of his novel, refusing to pursue a more conventional approach to storytelling.

A Quiet Life

After writing two postapocalyptic science-fiction novels, Ōe returned to the present with *A Quiet Life*. As her parents leave for a university in California, the twenty-year-old narrator is left behind in Japan to complete her graduation thesis and look after her two brothers. The handicapped older one, Eeyore, quickly becomes the novel's true protagonist, again reflecting some traces of Ōe's real-life son Hiraki. The gentle love among the family members reaffirms Ōe's belief in human dignity and compassion. Typically, the novel includes political allusions to topical events, such as social unrest in Poland in 1989.

Moeagaru midori no ki

Ōe's magnificent "flaming green tree" trilogy, completed in 1995, was, according to its author, originally meant to represent his final novelistic work. The three volumes feature two central characters, a young man who undergoes gender reassignment surgery to become a woman and an intelligent savior figure known as Elder Brother Gii. Fighting to save their village from a hostile outer world, the characters are part of a work fused with Ōe's trademark grotesque realism. Ōe's occasionally bitter humor shines throughout the trilogy, as does the author's insistence on human compassion in the face of private and political madness and disaster. Thus, a mythic tree's connection to the ground becomes a symbolic safeguard for the continuation of generation after generation of humans, who may be able to escape nuclear self-immolation.

Somersault

Ōe's complex 1999 novel *Somersault* tells of the revival of a millenarian religious cult in Japan and features as characters the cult's devoted leaders and a group of idiosyncratic supporters. The novel was inspired by the real Aum Shinrikyo cult, members of which released sarin nerve gas in five Tokyo subway trains on March 20, 1995, killing twelve people and seriously injuring more than fifty others. A second, potentially even more deadly planned attack by the cult on Tokyo's Shinjuku station on May 5 of the same year was foiled. Ōe's novel opens ten years after the leaders of his fictitious cult, Patron and Guide, learned about their radical faction's plan to detonate a nuclear power plant to hasten the coming of the end of the world. Appalled, Patron and Guide appeared on Japanese television and ridiculed their own cult, publicly calling it a hoax. This act was called a somersault, as they flipped from ardent doomsday preachers to the role of practical jokers.

The somersault of Patron and Guide and their subsequent cooperation with the authorities to arrest the radicals prevented any crime from occurring. This outcome could be read as Ōe's fictional vision of an alternative ending for a religious vision gone bad. It is opposed to how the leaders of the real, murderous sect acted; they let their followers go through with the sarin attacks. Similarly, the radicals' choice of a nuclear power plant as target relates to Ōe's lifelong campaign against nuclear weapons and his distrust of atomic plants. Ōe's worries about nuclear installations are highlighted by the fact that, in the novel, the atomic attack could probably have succeeded if Patron and Guide had not committed their somersault.

Ōe quickly introduces the characters who are going to be key supporters of Patron and Guide. The prologue mentions how fifteen years ago, the boy Ikuo accidentally injured and thereby deflowered a young ballerina with his model for a future city, which he violently smashed on the floor after the incident. As the novel proper opens, the girl has become Dancer, personal secretary of Patron and Guide, to whom her father has introduced her. Now in his early twenties, Ikuo is a swimming instructor. Ikuo is picked up by the gay, fiftyish painter Kizu, through whose eyes most of the novel is told. Ikuo is fascinated by the biblical book of Jonah, which Kizu illustrated once for a children's Bible. He becomes Kizu's lover. As Kizu suffers from cancer, it is clear that their days are numbered. Together they contact Dancer and meet Patron and Guide.

The story of Jonah serves as a motif throughout *Somersault* and is tightly linked to the cult's focus on repentance and possible violence. Just as the biblical Jonah was angry with God for sparing the inhabitants of Niniveh after they repented of their sins, the radical faction of the cult has never forgiven Patron and Guide for their somersault and for ridiculing their beliefs. In due course, Ikuo assumes a Jonah-like role, angry with Patron for his nonviolence.

Somersault is an unsettling novel, largely owing to the narrator's absolute neutrality in introducing a variety of characters who range from the sympathetic to the criminally insane. There is businessman Mr. Ogi, who helps Patron because he seeks spiritual meaning, and the sexually aggressive Mrs. Nobuko Tsugane, who has an affair with Patron while also devoting herself to the cult's renaissance. Most striking is the kindly librarian Mrs. Tachibana, who found solace in the cult's sermons while caring for her mentally handicapped brother, Morio. Morio is a character very familiar to readers of Ōe's fiction: He is yet another fictional incarnation of Ōe's son Hikari. Like Hikari, Morio composes playable music in spite of his congenital brain damage. On the other side is the enigmatic Dr. Koga, a former radical and planner of the nuclear holocaust, who now works calmly as a physician, showing no repentance for his previous complicity in planning acts of mass murder.

After Guide dies as the result of violent interrogation by his radical followers, who demand an explanation of his somersault, Patron launches the revival of the cult. As he and his followers flock to their surviving chapel and monastery in the forests of Shikoku island, the reader is led deeply into what can be called Ōe's territory. It was in this geographic location that Ōe was born, and the area features in many of his novels. Particularly strong is the link to Ōe's "flaming green tree" trilogy, as the cult's stronghold is in Maki Town, where the trilogy takes places. The novel even makes note of the partially charred "flaming tree," a magnificent cypress, and the local youths are led by the son of the trilogy's protagonist. Ōe's works are clearly interconnected, and he likes to combine local folklore with general philosophical and political musings.

Somersault comes to its climax at the cult's compound during a spirit festival and summer conference. Patron prevents the planned mass suicide of his most ardent female followers by lacing their drink with laxatives, making them look ridiculous as they rush outside the chapel to relieve themselves. He and Mrs. Tachibana, however, along with the mentally disabled composer Morio, burn themselves to death inside spirit dolls lighted at the foot of the old cypress. The epilogue tells of Kizu's subsequent death from cancer and the transfer of the cult's leadership to Ikuo, Dancer, and the head of the local youth band.

With its long passages on religious themes and the intricacies of the cult's teachings, *Somersault* provides some challenges for readers. An element that makes the novel particularly fascinating, however, is the narrative voice's absolute refusal to distance itself critically from the people it describes. No irony, sarcasm, cynicism, or moralizing is evident as the narrator describes the characters and their varying ideas, which mix the serene with the diabolic. Patron's religious musings about the end of the world and the need for repentance are rendered as matter-of-factly as the radicals' defense of their previous murderous plans. The novel never overtly condemns or praises the members of the cult—readers are invited to judge these people and their ideas for themselves. *Somersault* is also fascinating in its portrayal of the way in which goodness and evil can exist closely together in a single character's heart.

From the beginning of Ōe's literary career, confinement and estrangement have been recurring themes in his fiction. Increasingly, madness, despair, and failure to escape have dominated his works. At the same time, his use of the grotesque has expanded—perhaps suggesting that contemporary life could be expressed only through extreme distortion when nuclear annihilation appeared all too possible, at least up until the dissolution of the Soviet Union in 1991. Since that time, Ōe has returned to one of his core topics, the association of the mentally handicapped with magic, or the extranatural world. Ōe is one of Japan's major contemporary writers, with his pen on the pulse of contemporary Japanese society. Throughout his career, his themes and techniques have been directly in tune with those of Western modernism and have expanded to Magical Realism and postmodernism. Ōe has been one of few major Japanese writers to use the unique Japanese experience of the atomic bombings of Hiroshima and Nagasaki as the basis for literary analysis of global concerns, and he searches constantly for more adequate verbal expression of human existence.

Sanroku Yoshida
Updated by R. C. Lutz

Other major works

SHORT FICTION: "Kimyo na shigoto," 1957; "Shisha no ogori," 1957 ("Lavish the Dead," 1965); "Shiiku," 1958 ("The Catch," 1966; also known as "Prize Stock," 1977); *Miru mae ni tobe*, 1958; *Kodoku na seinen no kyuka*, 1960; "Sebuntin," 1961 ("Seventeen," 1996); "Seiji shonen shisu," 1961; *Seiteki ningen*, 1963; *Warera no kyōki o ikinobiru michi o oshieyo*, 1969, 1975 (*Teach Us to Outgrow Our Madness: Four Short Novels*, 1977); *Gendai denikshu*, 1980; *"Ame no ki" o kiku on'natachi*, 1982; *"Rein tsurī" o kiku onnatachi*, 1982; *Ika ni ki o korosu ka*, 1984; *Kaba ni kamareru*, 1985; *Boku ga hontō ni wakakatta koro*, 1992.

NONFICTION: *Sekai no wakamonotachi*, 1962; *Genshuku na tsunawatari*, 1965; *Hiroshima nōto*, 1965 (*Hiroshima Notes*, 1982); *Jisokusuru kokorozashi*, 1968; *Kakujidai no sōzōryoku*, 1970; *Kowaremoto to shite no ningen*, 1970; *Okinawa nōto*, 1970; *Dōjidai to shite no sengo*, 1973; *Bungaku nōto*, 1974; *Jōkyō e*, 1974; *Kotoba ni yotte*, 1976; *Shosetsu no hoho*, 1978; *Ōe Kenzaburō dojidaironshu*, 1981; *Sengo bungakusha*, 1981; *Kaku no taika to "ningen" no koe*, 1982; *Atarashii bungaku no tame ni*, 1988; *Bungaku sainyūmon*, 1992; *Aimai na Nihon no watakushi*, 1995 (*Japan, the Ambiguous, and Myself: The Nobel Prize Speech, and Other Lectures*, 1995); *Kaifuku suru kazoku*, 1995 (*A Healing Family*, 1996); *On Politics and Literature: Two Lectures*, 1999; *"Jibun no ki" no shita de*, 2001; *Bōryoku ni sakaratte kaku: Ōe Kenzaburō ōfuku shokan*, 2003.

EDITED TEXT: *Nan to moshirenai mirai ni*, 1985 (*The Crazy Iris, and Other Stories of the Atomic Aftermath*, 1985).

Bibliography

Cameron, Lindsley. *The Music of Light: The Extraordinary Story of Hikari and Kenzaburō Ōe*. New York: Free Press, 1998. Focuses on the relationship between Ōe and his mentally handicapped son, Hikari, who not only inspired a great body of his father's literary output but also managed to compose music that is played by professional musicians.

Gabriel, Philip. "Literature of the Soul: Ōe Kenzaburō's *Somersault*." In *Spirit Matters: The Transcendent in Modern Japanese Literature*. Honolulu: University of Hawaii Press, 2006. Very perceptive analysis of Ōe's novel is offered by the person who translated it from Japanese to English.

Hirata, Hosea. "Masturbation, the Emperor, and the Language of the Sublime in Ōe Kenzaburō." In *Discourses of Seduction: History, Evil, Desire, and Modern Japanese Literature*. Cambridge, Mass.: Harvard University Press, 2005. Presents a scholarly analysis of Ōe's fierce anti-imperial stance as expressed in a majority of his novels.

Kimura, Akio. *Faulkner and Oe: The Self-Critical Imagination*. Lanham, Md.: University Press of America, 2007. Provides intelligent discussion of the influence of select works of American author William Faulkner on Ōe's novel *A Quiet Life*.

Maristed, Kai. "Faith Tangled Up in Reality." *Los Angeles Times Book Review*, April 20, 2003. Substantial analytic review of Ōe's masterpiece *Somersault* places the novel within the context of Ōe's work and offers a perceptive critical reading of the text.

Napier, Susan J. *Escape from the Wasteland: Romanti-*

cism and Realism in the Fiction of Mishima Yukio and Ōe Kenzaburō*. Cambridge, Mass.: Harvard University Press, 1991. Presents an excellent, in-depth comparative analysis of key texts by both Mishima and Ōe, providing great insight into the literary imaginations of these two important, yet very different, writers.

Wilson, Michiko Niikuni. *The Marginal World of Ōe Kenzaburō: A Study in Themes and Techniques*. Armonk, N.Y.: M. E. Sharpe, 1986. Attempts to address Ōe's sometimes grotesque and perverse imagination by showing how two short stories and three novels present the relationship of a corpulent father and his mentally disabled son by establishing unity of theme, chronological development, and an ironic turn of events.

World Literature Today 76 (Winter, 2002). Contains a special section with four essays dedicated to analyzing Ōe's recent work.

Yoshida, Sanroku. "Kenzaburō Ōe: A New World of Imagination." *Comparative Literature Studies* 22 (Spring, 1985): 80-96. Presents Ōe as the leading Japanese literary reformer, who, rejecting literary elitism and high art, holds that literature should be democratic and should appeal to the masses in didactic terms. Discusses Ōe's view that literature is under an obligation to protest against social evils.

_______. "Kenzaburō Ōe's Recent Modernist Experiments." *Critique* 26 (Spring, 1985): 155-164. Offers a general analysis of Ōe's innovative narrative techniques, including his characterizations, recurrent themes, and stylistic practices.

JOHN O'HARA

Born: Pottsville, Pennsylvania; January 31, 1905
Died: Princeton, New Jersey; April 11, 1970
Also known as: John Henry O'Hara

Principal long fiction

Appointment in Samarra, 1934
Butterfield 8, 1935
Pal Joey, 1940
A Rage to Live, 1949
The Farmer's Hotel, 1951
Ten North Frederick, 1955
A Family Party, 1956
From the Terrace, 1958
Ourselves to Know, 1960
Sermons and Soda Water, 1960
The Big Laugh, 1962
Elizabeth Appleton, 1963
The Lockwood Concern, 1965
The Instrument, 1967
Lovey Childs: A Philadelphian's Story, 1969
The Ewings, 1972

Other literary forms

John O'Hara was a prolific writer of short stories, and eleven volumes of stories were published during his lifetime. After O'Hara's death, Random House, his publisher since 1947, brought out two additional collections: *The Time Element, and Other Stories* (1972) and *Good Samaritan, and Other Stories* (1974). Scattered throughout the short-story collections are most of O'Hara's works in the novella form; the only novellas to be published separately are the three in *Sermons and Soda Water*. His libretto for the musical play *Pal Joey* was not published until 1952, although the show was produced in 1940; in 1961, it was reissued with four others works for the stage in *Five Plays*. O'Hara's last complete play, *Far from Heaven* (1962), was first published posthumously in 1979, along with an unproduced original screenplay, *The Man Who Could Not Lose* (1959), under the title *Two by O'Hara*.

Like many other writers of his period, O'Hara wrote and collaborated on film scripts from the 1930's through the 1950's, and several of his novels were made into films during his lifetime. O'Hara began his writing career as a journalist, and he was several times a newspaper columnist. Two collections of his columns were published: *Sweet and Sour* (1954)—columns written for the *Trenton Sunday Times-Advertiser*—and *My Turn* (1966), a series of syndicated columns written for *Newsday*. A collection of O'Hara's speeches, essays, and interviews, titled *An Artist Is His Own Fault*, was edited by Matthew J. Bruccoli and published in 1977.

Achievements

Often dismissed as a popular novelist with tendencies toward sensationalism, or as a "social historian," John O'Hara nevertheless secured a faithful following among many literary critics for his skill at storytelling and his evocation of times, places, and manners in American society in the first half of the twentieth century. O'Hara himself was equivocal about the label "social historian." In a speech in 1961, he said, "I deny that I am a social historian"; yet he went on to say that "before deciding to write a novel, I consider what opportunities a story offers for my comments on my times." Bruccoli is probably most accurate in calling O'Hara a "novelist of manners," in the sense that he was primarily concerned with the accurate depiction of a social matrix and its effect on human behavior and potential. As did William Faulkner and other twentieth century American novelists, O'Hara turned the realities of his hometown experience into a fictional world; unlike Faulkner, he probed this milieu with a dedication to social realism rather than elevating it to mythic status. In addition to his native eastern Pennsylvania, O'Hara used New York and Hollywood as frequent settings for his fiction. Although he lived and worked in both places, he is most clearly identified with the "Region" of Pennsylvania, on which he could bring to bear an insider's perceptions.

The fact that O'Hara was a realistic storyteller rather than an experimental novelist was detrimental to his critical reputation during his lifetime. Ironically, the explicit sexuality in much of his work (although restrained by later standards), which was partially responsible for creating wide popular interest in his novels and which caused *Ten North Frederick* to be suppressed in several cities, overshadowed the depth of his concern with societal mores and pressures. Although he emphasized the role of fate and chance, O'Hara is usually considered a realist rather than a naturalist, largely because he allowed the possibility of moral choice. His long, detailed novels characteristically show people of a privileged socioeconomic level struggling with the realities of social class, personal worth, and complex human relationships.

O'Hara's treatment of his women characters has been overlooked by most critics, yet it may help to account for his enormous contemporary popularity. Long before it was fashionable or even allowable to do so, O'Hara realistically portrayed women as sexual human beings and even dealt openly with lesbian sexuality in some of his novels and stories. Though several of his major female characters (such as Edith Chapin in *Ten North Frederick* and the title character of *Elizabeth Appleton*) are stereotypically manipulative, they are believable, complex people whose motivations are clearly the result of cultural pressures. It would be inaccurate to call O'Hara a feminist novelist, but he acknowledged women's power and their problems in ways that set him apart from most novelists of his period.

Whatever the eventual critical evaluation of O'Hara as a twentieth century American novelist, it is certain that his work will be used as a valuable resource for information about customs, manners, and attitudes in the United States from the 1920's through the 1950's, much as one consults the work of Theodore Dreiser, Sinclair Lewis, or John Updike. The ear for dialogue, the eye for detail, and the perception of human nature that made him a popular novelist will also ensure his continued importance.

Biography

John Henry O'Hara was born on January 31, 1905, in Pottsville, Pennsylvania. The town of Pottsville became the "Gibbsville" of his fiction, and the surrounding eastern Pennsylvania anthracite coal-mining area, known to residents as the "Region," was the locale of his major novels and stories. The author's father, Patrick O'Hara, was a respected surgeon whose father had settled in the area during the American Civil War, and his mother, Katharine Delaney O'Hara, was the daughter of a prosperous businessman in nearby Lykens, which became O'Hara's fictional "Lyons." Patrick O'Hara, who necessarily specialized in injuries resulting from mining acci-

John O'Hara. (Library of Congress)

dents, was seriously disappointed at his firstborn son's refusal to study medicine. Rather than inspiring a dedication to the medical profession, O'Hara's travels with his father to the scenes of medical emergencies provided him with regional lore that found its way into his writing.

Living on Pottsville's "best" street, Mahantongo ("Lantenengo" in the fictional Gibbsville), was a sign of the O'Hara family's relative affluence and provided O'Hara with an awareness of the rigid economic and ethnic stratification of the town. Until his father's early death in 1925, O'Hara led a fairly privileged existence, and his dream of attending Yale was thwarted less by lack of funds than by O'Hara's dismissals from three preparatory schools for low grades and disregard of discipline. The alternative to college was a job as a reporter with the *Pottsville Journal* in 1924, which effectively launched O'Hara's career as a writer.

In 1928, O'Hara left Pottsville for New York, where he worked briefly for the *Herald-Tribune* and *Time* and began to contribute stories to *The New Yorker*, which eventually published more than two hundred of his short stories; accordingly, some have attributed to O'Hara the creation of that subgenre, the "*New Yorker* story." During these early years in New York, O'Hara established friendships with Franklin P. Adams (F. P. A.)—to whose *New York World* column "The Conning Tower" he sometimes contributed—Robert Benchley, Dorothy Parker, and F. Scott Fitzgerald. In 1931, he married Helen Ritchie "Pet" Petit, but his heavy drinking and frequent unemployment led to a divorce in 1933.

Appointment in Samarra, the first of O'Hara's fifteen novels, was published in 1934, and his first collection of short stories, *The Doctor's Son, and Other Stories*, appeared the following year. Although he was not financially secure for some time, O'Hara's reputation as a fiction writer grew steadily, and for the next twenty years he lived alternately on the East Coast and in Hollywood, where he wrote film scripts. Although he intermittently aspired to be a playwright, O'Hara's only successful play was the musical *Pal Joey*, which was based on a series of stories he wrote for *The New Yorker* and then expanded into a novel in 1940; the show ran on Broadway between 1940 and 1941. It was also made into a film, starring Frank Sinatra and Rita Hayworth, in 1957. In 1956, O'Hara was given the National Book Award for *Ten North Frederick*, and in 1957 he was inducted into the National Institute of Arts and Letters, from which he resigned in 1961 because he had not been nominated for its Gold Medal for fiction.

In 1937, O'Hara was married for the second time, to Belle Mulford Wylie, the mother of his only child, Wylie Delaney O'Hara, born in 1945. The O'Haras moved to Princeton, New Jersey, in 1949, and in 1953, a serious ulcer condition prompted O'Hara to quit drinking permanently. Following Belle's death in 1954, O'Hara married Katharine "Sister" Barnes Bryan in 1955, and the family moved two years later to Linebrook, a home in Princeton that O'Hara and Sister had designed. O'Hara died at Linebrook on April 11, 1970, while working on a sequel to *The Ewings*, his last published novel.

Analysis

In the spring of 1960, John O'Hara wrote the following as part of his preface to *Sermons and Soda Water*:

> The Twenties, the Thirties, and the Forties are already history, but I cannot be content to leave their story in the hands of the historians and the editors of picture books. I want to record the way people talked and thought and felt.

Despite his frequent rejection of the seemingly derogatory critical label of "social historian," which seemed to separate him in the minds of critics from more "serious" novelists, O'Hara was committed throughout his career to providing accurate records of the decades and places in which he lived. The novels and novellas that resulted from this commitment are uneven in quality as examples of the art of fiction, but they provide an unmatched portrait of segments of American society in the first half of the century.

The central characters of much of his fiction are wealthy, prominent people, whether they are the leading citizens of Gibbsville, Pennsylvania, or Hollywood film stars, yet O'Hara frequently illuminates their circumstances by juxtaposing them with members of other socioeconomic groups: servants, tradesmen, laborers. The result is a panoramic social canvas, consonant with O'Hara's conception of the traditional novel form. Occasionally, as in *From the Terrace*, the realist's attempt at panoramic vision overwhelms artistic control; as Sheldon Grebstein remarks in *John O'Hara* (1966), "the *tranche de vie*," or, the slice of life, "has been cut too thick to be digestible." At his best, however, O'Hara's work reflects the rich diversity of American society, as in his counterpointing of the savvy political boss Mike Slattery and the wealthy, naïve, would-be politician Joe Chapin in *Ten North Frederick*.

As the example of politics suggests, one of O'Hara's major themes is power—not only the power of money, although that is a central metaphor, but also the power inherent in talent, morality, and sexuality. O'Hara shared with F. Scott Fitzgerald a fascination with wealth and social prestige, but his treatment of their influence is far more analytical. His novels typically trace the establishment of a family dynasty, as in *The Lockwood Concern*, or the progress of an individual's aspirations for him- or herself, as in *Ten North Frederick* and *Elizabeth Appleton*—always within the constraints of a social web rendered palpable by realistic settings and dialogue. O'Hara is concerned particularly with showing the limits of human power, not in the face of an overwhelming fate, but as the result of miscalculation, error, or simple human frailty. When Julian English throws a drink in the face of Harry Reilly in *Appointment in Samarra*, or when George Lockwood, in *The Lockwood Concern*, builds a wall around his mansion, neither can foresee the fatal consequences, but both have made choices that dictate inevitable results.

As money is a metaphor for power in O'Hara's fiction, sexuality is an ambivalent metaphor for love. Though he was accused of sensationalism and bad taste in his relatively explicit depiction of sexual relationships, O'Hara was primarily interested in showing the potential for manipulation in the human sexual relationship. Women as well as men are portrayed as captive to sexual desire, and both sexes frequently mistake love for possession, or sex for love. From Grace Caldwell Tate's injudicious couplings in *A Rage to Live* to the tender relationship between Jim Malloy and Charlotte Sears in *The Girl on the Baggage Truck* (from *Sermons and Soda Water*), the possibility of true romantic love seems remote in O'Hara's fiction. His realistic approach assumes a basic human egotism and desire for power that renders such love rare.

The structures of O'Hara's novels and novellas reinforce the sense of inevitability of consequence. His novels frequently begin with an apparently small but significant event or action that spins out in mystery-story fashion to create the web that catches the characters and demonstrates their ultimate powerlessness. Yet he avoids the predictability of formulaic fiction by using multiple points of view and a wealth of complex, believable characters to play out the drama. In the novellas, the structure is frequently circular, the story beginning at a moment of culmination and then tracing the events that have brought the characters to that point. Common too, especially in the novellas, is O'Hara's use of a narrator, usually Jim Malloy, a journalist whose background and attitudes resemble those of O'Hara. Although these structural devices were not original with O'Hara, he used them skillfully to suit his fictional purposes.

Character is of supreme importance in O'Hara's fiction, and the achievement of adequate characterization determined the form he used. As he said in one of his Rider College lectures, "before I have finished two pages of manuscript my author's instinct has told me how much I want to tell about this character, and thus the length of the story is dictated." The majority of O'Hara's characters inhabit the Pennsylvania Region in which he spent his youth, and the fictional canon provides a vivid picture of relationships among people of various social levels over time. The reappearance of certain characters in many works reinforces the sense of a coherent world wherein the codes of morality and propriety dictate the shape of both society and individual human lives.

In its settings, characters, and incidents, O'Hara's fiction is strongly autobiographical, a circumstance that is a natural outgrowth of his desire to be a recorder of his times. Though he did not live in Pottsville after 1930, the town and its people continued to serve as a microcosm of the American culture he dissected throughout his career. Like his autobiographical narrator Jim Malloy, O'Hara returned to Pottsville "only long enough to stand at a grave, to toast a bride, to spend a few minutes beside a sickbed," but the years he spent there left an indelible impression. From his vantage point as the doctor's son, O'Hara observed both the leading citizens and the transients, and later he explored, in his novels and novellas, the lives he imagined to exist behind the placid exterior of the American small town.

Part of the autobiographical content of the fiction, however, comes from O'Hara's unfulfilled aspirations rather than from his actual experience. Although his dream of attending an Ivy League college was thwarted by his checkered prep school record and the death of his father, O'Hara's upper-class male characters typically attend prestigious universities and benefit from larger family fortunes than O'Hara's family ever enjoyed. His fiction, like that of Fitzgerald, thus conveys an ambivalent attitude toward the privileged: the wistfulness of the outsider and the realist's desire to reduce them to understandable human terms.

The span of O'Hara's career, from 1934 to 1970, coincided with a period of intense experimentation in literary forms. The fiction of James Joyce and William Faulkner, among others, tested the limits of the novel, and critical opinion during these years favored attempts to break the mold of traditional fiction, to push beyond the bounds of realistic documentation of recognizable human events. Thus, O'Hara's accurate rendition of dialogue lost place to stream of consciousness as an acclaimed technique, and the chronicling of successive generations was less favored than novels spanning a single day, controlled by a single consciousness. O'Hara's novels continue to be appreciated more for their documentary usefulness than for their creative force, yet within the limits of the traditional novel form, O'Hara was a master craftsman who captured and conveyed the human drama and social fabric of a complex period in American life.

APPOINTMENT IN SAMARRA

In 1961, O'Hara referred to *Appointment in Samarra* as "a live novel twenty-five years after first publication." O'Hara's first novel would continue to "live," in several senses. It is obviously the work of a professional writer; O'Hara's powers of observation and skill in plot construction are already highly developed in this short novel. Also, *Appointment in Samarra* is set in the Region of eastern Pennsylvania, the setting of much of his long fiction throughout his career, and it has strong autobiographical elements. Finally, the novel deals starkly and dramatically with the themes of power and fate and demonstrates O'Hara's understanding of individual human destiny as a delicate balance between necessity and accident. The novel's title derives from a quotation from W. Somerset Maugham; the "appointment in Samarra" is an inescapable appointment with death, yet Julian English, O'Hara's main character, is doomed by his own actions—his tragedy is of his own making.

The story of Julian English is set against a richly detailed social and geographical background. O'Hara takes pains to provide the reader with the flavor of the early Depression years: the names of popular songs, the intricacies of the bootlegger's profession, and the subdued desperation of both rich and poor. To tie the novel even further to an era, there are topical references; Julian English mentions having recently read Ernest Hemingway's *A Farewell to Arms* (1929), and Irma Fleigler counts on President Herbert Hoover's promise that next year will be better for everyone, so that she and her husband can join the country club to which the Englishes belong. The club, and the town and region of which it is the social pinnacle, is treated with the same careful detail. O'Hara devotes several pages to the peculiarities of the anthracite coal region and the social hierarchy of Gibbsville, making clear that no person or action is independent of the social context. Despite the anxieties of what was called in 1930 a "slump," Gibbsville and its inhabitants are filled with self-importance, and none more so than Julian, the doctor's son.

Julian and O'Hara share several biographical similarities. Julian, like O'Hara, has refused to adopt his doctor-father's profession, and his refusal has caused a serious rift in the father-son relationship. Julian admires Franklin P. Adams (F. P. A.), to whom O'Hara dedicated *Appointment in Samarra*, and when a priest asks him whether he is a "frustrated literary man," Julian answers, "I'm not anything. I guess I should have been a doctor." The most important similarity between Julian and his creator is the sense of insecurity betrayed by this remark, an insecurity that leads both men to heavy drinking and defensive belligerence. The significant difference is that Julian does not survive his own nature.

To dramatize his perception that the individual is inextricably bound up in his social context, O'Hara deftly shifts the point of view in the novel from interior to exterior views of Julian, emphasizing the extent to which one person becomes the object of others' scrutiny. The novel covers the last three days of Julian's life, from the moment he throws a drink in Harry Reilly's face at the country club Christmas party until he commits suicide by carbon monoxide poisoning, yet the narrative begins and ends with the observations of Luther and Irma Fleigler, a middle-class couple whose solid respectability and loving relationship contrast sharply with the weakness and manipulation of the far wealthier Julian and Caroline English. Julian's action is, in itself, insignificant—a social error from which all parties could have recovered in time—but it becomes symbolic of Julian's misperception of his own strength and power. With the inevitability of Greek tragedy, social ostracism follows Julian's throwing of the drink; he becomes an outsider to his own group, and he fails in all his efforts to pick up the pieces of his life.

O'Hara presents, one by one, the sources of comfort to which twentieth century men turn in times of personal trouble and shows them all to be ineffective. Family, sex, work, drink, religion, even a simple apology—none provides solace to Julian, who is the isolated twentieth century man, left with nothing in which to believe. If Julian does not understand the motivation for his action, neither does anyone else around him, and neither his father, Dr. English, nor his wife can respond adequately to his anguish. Work fails as an escape because, as the president of a Cadillac dealership, Julian is dependent on precisely the goodwill of potential customers that his action has temporarily denied him, and drink leads to either self-pity or further belligerence. Monsignor Creedon, to whom Julian, a Protestant, feels obscurely drawn, confesses that he has sometimes wished he had chosen a different life's work; lacking a true vocation, he cannot provide a spiritual solution to Julian's guilt and loneliness.

Although the major conflict in the novel is that between Julian's personal responsibility for his own actions and fate and the effect of his social surroundings on that fate, O'Hara introduces a third element: heredity. Conscious of his own family heritage, and especially of his forebears' struggle through generations for greater status and respectability in the Region, O'Hara places great importance on a sense of heritage. His characters are typically aware of where they come from, who their ancestors are, and to what this background entitles them on the social scale. Julian's grandfather had committed suicide after embezzling money from a bank, and after Julian's suicide, Dr. English consoles himself regarding his own reputation by assuming that people "would see how the suicide strain has skipped one generation to come out in the next."

Dr. English reappears in several of O'Hara's later works, as do several other characters introduced. Jim Malloy, mentioned previously, becomes the narrator of the novellas in *Sermons and Soda Water*, and the relationship between Whit Hofman, here a minor character, and Pat Collins is the basis of the novella *Pat Collins*. In short, *Appointment in Samarra* established O'Hara's major locale, characters, and themes, and much of his fictional canon enlarged upon what was set forth in this novel.

The critical reception of O'Hara's first novel was generally favorable, though some reviewers were disturbed by its relatively explicit sexuality. This reaction was intensified by his next two major novels, *Butter-*

field 8 and *A Rage to Live*, both of which sold well in part because of the furor, and his collections of short stories were consistently well received. *Appointment in Samarra* had launched its author on a successful career.

TEN NORTH FREDERICK

Although many of the short stories O'Hara published in the five collections between 1935 and 1947 were set in the Region, *Ten North Frederick* was the first novel after *Appointment in Samarra* to deal with that locale. *Ten North Frederick* marked the beginning of the major phase of O'Hara's work as well as a new stage in his life. Two years before its publication, he had suffered the bleeding ulcer that convinced him to give up alcohol permanently, and a few months before, he had married Katharine Barnes Bryan, whom he referred to as Sister. For the next fifteen years until his death, O'Hara would live a more settled, productive life than ever before. The timing of the novel's publication also began a tradition that continued for the rest of his career. Because O'Hara, always sensitive to reviews, wanted the task of reviewing *Ten North Frederick* to fall to a particular writer for *The New York Times*, the novel was issued on a Thursday in late November. The day was Thanksgiving, and the publication of an O'Hara novel or collection became an annual Thanksgiving event.

Butterfield 8 had been a roman à clef, based on the sensational and tragic story of Starr Faithfull, but despite certain resemblances between the lives of Joe Chapin and Franklin D. Roosevelt, *Ten North Frederick* is not. Rather, as Matthew Bruccoli suggests, the novel is a "what-if study: what if Roosevelt had been a Gibbsville Republican?" O'Hara undoubtedly had Roosevelt in mind as he created Joe Chapin, and he used some elements of Roosevelt's life—the strong mother with ambitions for her son and a physical crippling in midlife—but his intention was not, as it was in *Butterfield 8*, to write a fictional account of a well-known person. Indeed, whereas Roosevelt's story is one of triumph over personal adversity, *Ten North Frederick* chronicles the failure of Joe Chapin's ambitions.

Those ambitions are far from modest. Chapin wants nothing less than to leave each of his children a million dollars upon his death and to become president of the United States. That he achieves neither goal is in part the result of circumstances (the Depression reduces his financial assets) and in part of errors in judgment, such as his attempting to circumvent the local political system managed by Mike Slattery. Despite the magnitude of his hopes, Chapin is neither grasping nor overwhelmingly egotistical. Although he makes some ill-considered decisions about the lives of others—notably his daughter's abortion and the dissolution of her marriage to an Italian musician—he is not a power-hungry schemer. Instead, he is unaware that his own power has limits. Reared to believe in the privileges of wealth and status and trained in the proprieties of social forms, Chapin is merely inflexible. Rules and forms have taken precedence over human responsiveness, and his one extramarital affair, late in his life, seems to be the only spontaneous action of which he is capable.

Chapin's life thus has an opaque surface that prevents even his closest Gibbsville associates from knowing him well. At Chapin's funeral, one of his cousins remarks, "I could never figure Joe out," to which Mike Slattery replies, "We knew exactly what Joe wanted us to know. And believe me, that wasn't much." Coming at the beginning of the novel, this exchange might have foreshadowed the revelation of a secret life that Chapin had hidden carefully from his friends, but O'Hara's intention instead is to show that the reality of Chapin's life is one with its facade. Behind the mask of respectability is a life that is just as sterile as the mask would suggest. With the exception of minor scandals, such as his daughter's elopement and pregnancy, Chapin's experience has been one of single-minded devotion to the accumulation of wealth and status.

Beginning *Ten North Frederick* with the funeral of his main character, O'Hara employed a structural device that attested to his development as a novelist. Both *Appointment in Samarra* and *Ten North Frederick* begin with a moment of crisis or transition, but whereas in *Appointment in Samarra* the rest of the novel traces the inevitable results of that moment, *Ten North Frederick* begins with the conclusion—the death of Chapin—and then proceeds to explore the life that has ended. The fact that the major threads of that life are introduced in the conversations at Chapin's funeral and are later developed in all their complexity has caused Sheldon Grebstein to call this a "tapestry novel." Having revealed the significant facts about Chapin's life early in the novel, O'Hara must compel the reader to continue by means other than suspense.

The major strength of *Ten North Frederick*, as of most of O'Hara's fiction, is its characterization. The novel deals with three generations of the Chapin family, beginning with Chapin's parents, though instead of a straight chronological narrative O'Hara uses a flashback technique, weaving past and present together to emphasize the effect of family—especially women—on the formation of character and ambition. Both Joe's mother, Charlotte, and his wife, Edith, have plans for his life; both are women for whom love means power and ownership, and for whom sex is a form of manipulation. Edith Chapin articulates this persistent theme of O'Hara's novels as she thinks, on her wedding night, "It was not Love; Love might easily have very little to do with it; but it was as strong a desire as Love or Hate and it was going to be her life, the owning of this man." As clearly as anywhere in his fiction, O'Hara here portrays women who, because they are denied most masculine forms of power, participate vicariously by requiring their men to succeed in their stead.

Joe Chapin, though, is a failure. If there is a "secret" in his life, it is the depth of his desire for high political office. On the surface a personable, respected pillar of Gibbsville, highly regarded by most of its leading citizens, Chapin nurses the ambition for which his mother has groomed him, but he is not willing to play the political games required to gain the backing of Mike Slattery's organization, nor can money buy him the office he seeks. After he is forced to withdraw from the political arena, only his brief affair with his daughter's friend, Kate Drummond, gives his life meaning, and when that ends he slowly begins to commit suicide by drinking heavily.

Many of O'Hara's own feelings about accomplishment and aging informed his creation of Chapin. O'Hara was fifty years old when the novel was completed. Like Chapin, he had gained the respect of many of his contemporaries, but certain measures of success had eluded him: in particular, recognition as a first-rate novelist. Both O'Hara and his character had suffered frightening indications of poor health; Chapin ignored the warning that alcohol was killing him, but O'Hara did not. Time had become precious to him, and he reflects on this in the final paragraph of *Ten North Frederick*: "There is always enough to do while the heart keeps pumping. There is never, never enough time to do it all." O'Hara was rewarded for his persistence when *Ten North Frederick* received the National Book Award for 1955. The award citation read in part, "Tough-minded as usual, Mr. O'Hara has written a novel of emotional depth and moral conviction."

Sermons and Soda Water

The swift passing of time to which O'Hara referred in *Ten North Frederick* was one of the reasons he turned to the novella form in the three pieces that comprise *Sermons and Soda Water*. The novella took, he said, "a minimum of research," as compared to the "big novel" he was working on simultaneously (probably *The Lockwood Concern*). He wrote these novellas to "get it all down on paper while I can." Being fifty-five years old, he writes, "I have no right to waste time." The novella, in other words, could be written quickly, from memory, rather than requiring years of research and writing. This distinction between the novel and the novella suggests that the material for the latter was more likely to be autobiographical, and his use of Jim Malloy as narrator in these three novellas adds to the impression that these are personal narratives.

Although O'Hara never fully defined the terms "novella" and "novelette" as he used them, he suggested in 1968 that the important consideration was character. The form, he said, "tells all that you need to know about certain people in certain circumstances so that those people become figures in the reader's personal library." He had first experimented with a form midway in length between the short story and the novel in the title story of *The Doctor's Son, and Other Stories*, his first collection of short stories, but during the last decade of his career, beginning with *Sermons and Soda Water*, he developed the novella form as a means of disentangling one thread from the usual complex tapestry of his novels. The novella as O'Hara conceived of it has an episodic structure. It follows one conflict, relationship, or problem through a lengthy time span, isolating for dramatic attention only the crucial periods, and briefly summarizing intervening months or years. There are no subplots, and minor characters are functional rather than centers of interest in their own right.

The use of a first-person narrator with a limited consciousness, rather than the omniscient point of view O'Hara employed in most of his novels, helps to ensure the sharp focus required for the novella. Jim Malloy, the narrator of *Sermons and Soda Water*, tells the reader about the people he has known in his hometown of Gibbsville or those he meets as a journalist in New York. He is a thin mask for O'Hara in the early days of the author's career: the young man from the coal region who begins his career in New York, encounters the wealthy and famous, and keeps up with a few of the people back home. Yet, Malloy has the mature vision of O'Hara at fifty-five, and his perspective on the characters' lives is that of a concerned friend rather than an impressionable young man. Malloy, like O'Hara, is a shrewd observer of human nature, one who finds patterns in life. In *We're Friends Again*, the third novella in *Sermons and Soda Water*, he comments on this ability by saying "The way things tie up, one with another, is likely to go unnoticed until a lawyer or a writer calls our attention to it." Malloy's function in these novellas is to demonstrate how "things tie up" while remaining more or less removed from the central stories.

In this ultimate detachment from the lives of the characters he describes, Malloy underscores the central theme of *Sermons and Soda Water*: human loneliness and isolation. At the end of *We're Friends Again*, Malloy calls loneliness "the final condition of us all," and O'Hara shows that it affects people at all levels of society—from Charlotte Sears, the film star in *The Girl on the Baggage Truck*, to Pete and Bobbie McCrea of Gibbsville in *Imagine Kissing Pete*. The solution to loneliness is love, but, as O'Hara so often suggests, love is elusive, and one often settles for approximations: attraction, sex, power. As Charlotte Sears says about her relationship with the wealthy, reclusive Thomas Hunterden, "There ought to be another word for love, for people like Hunterden and me." It is left to Malloy, as the controlling consciousness, to find meaning in the lives he relates, and that meaning resides ultimately in his capacity as a writer to discern patterns of inevitability in human life.

The Lockwood Concern

Of the novels written during O'Hara's last decade, *The Lockwood Concern* is particularly interesting as a culmination of many aspects of his career. During this period he used a variety of settings for his fiction—Hollywood in *The Big Laugh*, Philadelphia in *Lovey Childs*—but in *The Lockwood Concern* he returned to the Region, to the characters and situations that he handled with ease and familiarity. Throughout the early 1960's, O'Hara referred to a "big" novel on which he was working, and at one point he projected that it would be a two-volume work. *The Lockwood Concern* is in fact a one-volume work of average length, but its scope justifies O'Hara's adjective: It is a multigenerational novel, a "century-spanning saga," as the jacket blurb proclaims.

The theme of *The Lockwood Concern* is consistent with much of O'Hara's other work, and reaches back to *Appointment in Samarra*: the ultimate powerlessness of the individual against the force of circumstance, particularly the folly of attempting to control the destinies of others. The attempts of Abraham and George Lockwood, the second and third generations of the Lockwood family of Swedish Haven (actually Schuylkill Haven, near Pottsville), to establish a family dynasty break down in the fourth generation when George Lockwood's son and daughter reject the town and the family and adopt ways of life antithetical to dynastic responsibilities. The "concern" of the title is a Quaker concept, denoting an overwhelming sense of mission. Abraham Lockwood, in the late nineteenth century, has secularized this religious concept and translated it into a vision of generations of Lockwoods enjoying increasing wealth and prestige, including entrance to the clubs and other bastions of gentility denied him by the uncouth background and behavior of his own father, Moses Lockwood.

The central figure of *The Lockwood Concern* is George Lockwood, who has adopted Abraham's dream and brought it to the point of realization. George's children will be the first generation to enjoy full acceptance by elite society, and as an emblem of this progress he has built a family mansion near Swedish Haven. The high, spiked wall around the house testifies to George's sense of exclusivity; it is also the cause of the death of a neighboring farm boy, who becomes impaled while attempting to climb the fence before the house is completed. This tragedy, which George hastens to keep quiet, opens the novel, a signal of the crumbling of the erstwhile dynasty. From this point, George struggles to maintain the "concern" against increasing evidence of its demise until he finally falls to his death down a secret staircase he has had built in the still-uninhabited mansion.

O'Hara here used the circular structure that he had perfected in both long and short fiction throughout his career. The novel begins and ends in the mid-1920's, but ranges back to the mid-nineteenth century as O'Hara details the history of the "Lockwood concern." It opens with the death of the unnamed farm boy and closes with the death of George and, by implication, of the "concern." Simultaneously, the novel has the linear thrust of the historical novel. From the canny, vigorous survival of Moses Lockwood to the effete California existence of George's son, Bing, the generations move through historical and cultural change, reflecting shifting values in American society. The novel argues that such change is inevitable, and that George's attempt at consolidation and stasis is doomed from the start. Social flux is mirrored even in the names of the male Lockwoods over time, from the tradition and authority of "Moses" and "Abraham" to the frivolity of "Bing." Even with such change, however, basic human nature does not alter; George and Bing Lockwood are, in different ways, as conniving and self-interested as their ancestors, though protected by wealth and attorneys against open public disapproval.

The Lockwood Concern is a summation of much that O'Hara had tried and accomplished during thirty years of writing. Though not his best novel, it is one of his most ambitious in subject matter and scope. It provides a history of the Region from the time of O'Hara's ancestors until the time when he left it for New York, and it shows the growth of the region from a backwoods settlement to a thriving coal-mining and farming area that sent its sons to Princeton and Harvard. Thematically, the novel shows that O'Hara had come to some conclusions about the interplay of destiny and choice. He had shown in *Appointment in Samarra* that an individual's power over his own life was limited by the influence of society and the intervention of chance. In *Ten North Frederick*, he added great wealth and ambition to the equation and demonstrated their ineffectuality. By the time he wrote *The Lockwood Concern*, O'Hara saw the limits to human power as determined not only by conflicting wills and accidents of fate but also by the very sweep of time and change. Human aspiration pales before the only human certainty—death—which is described as a "secret" known only to those who have experienced it.

By entitling his biography of the author *The O'Hara Concern* (1975), Bruccoli suggests that O'Hara felt a sense of mission similar to that of the Lockwoods. If so, O'Hara's concern was not related to a family dynasty but instead to establishing himself among the first rank of American novelists. His lifelong war with literary critics and reviewers over the value of his contribution is evidence that he was never secure in his own reputation. Although he rejected the terms "social realist" and "social historian," these are appropriate characterizations of his best work. O'Hara's sense of history, his precise rendering of detail and dialogue, and his command of narrative technique make him one of the most significant chroniclers of American life in the first half of the twentieth century. The fact that he was a popular novelist during his career, in part because of the more sensational aspects of his work, has detracted from his critical reputation, but his position as an important novelist of manners seems secure.

Nancy Walker

Other major works

SHORT FICTION: *The Doctor's Son, and Other Stories*, 1935; *Hope of Heaven*, 1938; *Files on Parade*, 1939; *Pipe Night*, 1945; *Hellbox*, 1947; *Assembly*, 1961; *The Cape Cod Lighter*, 1962; *The Hat on the Bed*, 1963; *The Horse Knows the Way*, 1964; *Waiting for Winter*, 1966; *And Other Stories*, 1968; *The O'Hara Generation*, 1969; *The Time Element, and Other Stories*, 1972; *Good Samaritan, and Other Stories*, 1974.

PLAYS: *Pal Joey*, pr. 1940 (libretto; based on his novel; lyrics by Lorenz Hart, music by Richard Rodgers); *Five Plays*, 1961; *Two by O'Hara*, 1979 (includes *Far from Heaven*, 1962, and the screenplay *The Man Who Could Not Lose*, 1959).

SCREENPLAY: *Moontide*, 1942.

NONFICTION: *Sweet and Sour*, 1954; *My Turn*, 1966; *A Cub Tells His Story*, 1974; *"An Artist Is His Own Fault": John O'Hara on Writers and Writing*, 1977 (Matthew J. Bruccoli, editor); *Selected Letters of John O'Hara*, 1978 (Bruccoli, editor).

BIBLIOGRAPHY

Bruccoli, Matthew J. *The O'Hara Concern: A Biography of John O'Hara*. 1975. Reprint. Pittsburgh, Pa.: University of Pittsburgh Press, 1995. A carefully researched scholarly biography that reconstructs O'Hara's life and career in scrupulous detail, showing the evolution of his talent and thematic interests. Particularly authoritative in its account of O'Hara's break—and eventual reconciliation—with *The New Yorker*, and the impact of both events on his fiction. Includes an exhaustive primary and secondary bibliography.

Eppard, Philip B., ed. *Critical Essays on John O'Hara*. New York: G. K. Hall, 1994. Contains both reviews and essays about O'Hara's work. All of his major fiction is discussed, as well as his relationship to naturalism, his view of society, his short stories, and his view of politics, the family, and small towns. Includes a comprehensive introductory chapter on O'Hara's career and the reception of his novels.

Farr, Finis. *O'Hara*. Boston: Little, Brown, 1973. Written by a journalist of O'Hara's own generation, Farr's was the first O'Hara biography and, indeed, the first book to be written about O'Hara after his death, including discussion of novels and stories published during the last five years of his life. Somewhat more anecdotal in tone and scope than Bruccoli's biography, Farr's book, intended for the general reader, nevertheless includes penetrating readings of selected novels and stories, together with a brief but useful bibliography.

Grebstein, Sheldon Norman. *John O'Hara*. New Haven, Conn.: College and University Press, 1966. The first full-length study of O'Hara's narrative prose, prepared somewhat too soon to take in the full range of the author's later fiction. Grebstein's volume discusses at length O'Hara's ongoing problems with the critical establishment.

Grimes, William. "The John O'Hara Cult, at Least, Is Faithful." *The New York Times*, November 9, 1996. An account of a panel discussion on O'Hara's work by five of his most ardent fans. The group chose *Appointment in Samarra* as the best introduction to O'Hara's work.

MacShane, Frank. *The Life of John O'Hara*. New York: E. P. Dutton, 1980. MacShane looks at O'Hara's life through his work, providing a thorough study that is well worth reading for its valuable insights. Includes a bibliography and an index.

Quinn, Joseph L. "A Cold-Weather Journey with John O'Hara." *America* 169 (December 18-25, 1993): 17-21. Points out that throughout his career, O'Hara was preoccupied with the harsh winters and small-town atmosphere of Pottsville, Pennsylvania, the industrial coal-mining community where he was raised. Discusses his links to F. Scott Fitzgerald and Ernest Hemingway.

Schwarz, Benjamin, and Christina Schwarz. "John O'Hara's Protectorate." *Atlantic Monthly*, March, 2000. A discussion of O'Hara's writing career, including the style and themes of his work and his depiction of his hometown, Pottsville, in his novels and stories. The authors maintain that O'Hara is one of the greatest American social novelists of the twentieth century.

Wolff, Geoffrey. *The Art of Burning Bridges: A Life of John O'Hara*. New York: Alfred A. Knopf, 2003. Wolff recounts the many incidents of O'Hara's bad behavior, including his alcoholism, bullying, and rages against women, editors, and critics. However, Wolff argues that these character flaws should not detract from O'Hara's literary reputation, citing *Appointment in Samarra* as among his best work. Includes photographs, a bibliography, and an index.

MICHAEL ONDAATJE

Born: Colombo, Ceylon (now Sri Lanka); September 12, 1943
Also known as: Philip Michael Ondaatje

Principal long fiction

The Collected Works of Billy the Kid, 1970
Coming Through Slaughter, 1976
In the Skin of a Lion, 1987
The English Patient, 1992
Anil's Ghost, 2000
Divisadero, 2007

Other literary forms

In addition to novels, Michael Ondaatje (on-DAHT-chee) has published several volumes of poetry, including *The Dainty Monsters* (1967), *There's a Trick with a Knife I'm Learning to Do: Poems, 1963-1978* (1979), and *Handwriting* (1998). He has also published works of nonfiction and has edited collections of short fiction by various Canadian authors.

Achievements

Michael Ondaatje received Canada's Governor-General's Award in 1971 for *The Collected Works of Billy the Kid*, in 1980 for *There's a Trick with a Knife I'm Learning to Do*, in 1992 for *The English Patient*, and in 2000 for *Anil's Ghost*. In 1973, *Billy the Kid* was a finalist for the Chalmer's Award. *Coming Through Slaughter* received the Books in Canada First Novel Award in 1976, and *In the Skin of a Lion* received the 1988 City of Toronto Book Award and the Trillium Book Award. Ondaatje received the Order of Canada in 1988 and in 1992 became the first Canadian to win the Booker Prize, for *The English Patient*. For *Anil's Ghost*, in addition to the Governor-General's Award, he received the Giller Prize, the Kiriyama Pacific Rim Book Prize, and the Prix Médicis from France.

Biography

Born in Colombo, Ceylon (now Sri Lanka), Philip Michael Ondaatje seldom referenced his upbringing in print until his 1982 "fictional memoir," *Running in the Family*. Ondaatje describes his early days as a "great childhood," although his parents divorced when he was two years old and he had little contact with his father. As an adult he completely lost contact with his father.

After moving with his mother and siblings to London at age eleven, Ondaatje completed school at Dulwich College. His writing career began with his move to Canada in 1962 at age nineteen; he attended Bishop's College in Quebec, and the teachings of Professor Arthur Moyter inspired Ondaatje's love for literature. In 1964, he married thirty-four-year-old artist Kim Jones, originally the wife of one of his professors, and they had two children. For years, they would spend their summers at Blue Roof Farm near Kingston, entertaining critics, artists, family, and friends. Ondaatje's sense of humor and fondness for practical jokes became legendary. The couple legally separated in 1980, and Ondaatje then began a relationship with Linda Spalding, whom he met in Hawaii; they subsequently shared a home in Toronto with her two children.

By 1965, Ondaatje had received the Ralph Gustafson Poetry Award, and by 1966 his poems were included in *New Wave Canada*. He received a B.A. from the University of Toronto (1968) and an M.A. from Queen's University. While teaching at the University of Western Ontario, he won the President's Medal for his poem "Paris," wrote *The Dainty Monsters*, and staged a dramatic performance of *The Man with Seven Toes* (1969) in Vancouver. In 1971, Ondaatje was fired by the university for not seeking a Ph.D. Within days of his dismissal, he received the first of his Governor-General's Awards. He pursued a love of film by writing and producing the first of several short motion pictures, *Sons of Captain Poetry*, that focus on the works of Canadian poets.

In 1971, Ondaatje became an editor at Coach House Press, known for its postmodern publications, and he began teaching in the English department at Toronto's Glendon College, York University. He continued writing and publishing poetry and, in 1976, received the Books in Canada First Novel Award for *Coming Through Slaughter*. His novel *In the Skin of a Lion* made him a 1987 semifinalist, along with South African novelist

Nadine Gordimer and American novelist Toni Morrison, for the Ritz Hemingway Literary Prize; however, no prize was awarded that year. He donated the cash portion ($7,500) of the Wang International Festival of Authors Prize to a fund supporting new writers. *The English Patient* made Ondaatje famous outside Canada, but he has continued to write as a Canadian resident and to teach at Glendon College of York University. Since 1985, Ondaatje has served as an editor of the literary journal *Brick*.

Analysis

Canadian writer Margaret Atwood has labeled Michael Ondaatje "vital and imaginative," and American writer Annie Dillard has described Ondaatje's language as "clean and energetic, with the pop of bullets." His early works have been aligned with those of modernist poet Wallace Stevens, due to their sharp imagery and lyric voice. The later longer works place Ondaatje, according to critic Douglas Barbour, firmly within the tradition of poet Ezra Pound, with a jostled imagery that some critics have labeled incoherent. Others categorize such "incoherency" as a legitimate postmodern approach to writing, most specifically displayed in Ondaatje's extension and mixing of genres. This "collage" approach allows him to combine fragmented documentary information with narrative and lyric, as in *The Man with Seven Toes* and *The Collected Works of Billy the Kid*, permitting a separation from lyric subjectivity through the blending of several points of view. Ondaatje investigates the modernist romantic figure of the artist as self-destructive without becoming self-destructive himself.

Barbour has also mentioned the poet's move toward postcolonialism with works such as *In the Skin of a Lion*, even though Ondaatje has declared himself uninterested in public politics. The publication of *The English Patient* and later of *Anil's Ghost*, with its themes of nationalism and political violence, has intensified discussion of postcolonialism in Ondaatje's work.

The Collected Works of Billy the Kid

In *The Collected Works of Billy the Kid*, Ondaatje synthesizes fact with legend in a fictional "journey into the mind" of the notorious historical figure William Bonney, known as Billy the Kid. The work's style may confuse readers accustomed to the traditional linear storytelling approach. A familiarity with the common postmodern use of collage, or a mixing of times and narratives, will aid readers in adjusting to the nontraditional writing. Ondaatje moves in and out of time, leaving gaps in his narrative, revising the traditional Western while rewriting the Old West and Billy's character. Eventually the work makes obvious the crucial nature of these narrative gaps. William Bonney's biography is so well known that Ondaatje remains confident of his readers' capability to fill in any breaks in his particular retelling of the historical "facts." Whatever readers make of the book, it remains one of the most frequently interpreted Canadian works.

Most critics take a thematic approach to the work, focusing on the opposition between Billy the Kid and Sheriff Pat Garrett. Seen as dichotomous figures, they may represent life versus death, chaos versus order, creation versus destruction. However, these figures should

Michael Ondaatje. (Courtesy, Picador Publicity Department, London)

not be reduced to a simple binary opposition of good and evil, although their contradictory relationship may be seen as the cause of Billy's self-destructive behavior. Also, the work remains too complicated to be classified in mythic terms of the hero's—or, in this case, the antihero's—quest for identity through pursuit of a father figure. While the traditional hero often metaphorically "kills" his father in order to be "born" his own person, in Ondaatje's (and history's) ironic twist on that myth, the father figure (Pat Garrett) kills the son, literally shooting Billy dead. Some might see that act as the only manner by which the dichotomy represented by Billy's life can be resolved. The almost immediate surfacing of a theme of detachment offers readers a focal point for Billy and his bizarre conceptions of violence and the grotesque. To the gunslinger, killing remains a profession; he detaches himself by viewing violence in a poetic manner. According to some, Billy represents the dual aspects of outlaw and artist inherent in Ondaatje himself.

Using a 1926 account by Walter Noble Burns, *The Saga of Billy the Kid*, on which to base the documentary aspects of his book, Ondaatje also adopts Burns's approach toward Billy as more hero than outlaw. Ondaatje begins with his hero's death as preliminary to the creating of his life, suggesting an existence resembling a phoenix rising from the ashes for a man whose legend began with the bullet that ended his life. Billy's narrative voice hints at the difficult task that awaits the reader when he refers early on to his story as a "maze." The widely varying classifications of the work's form as poem, docudrama, fiction, and prose poem demonstrate the reader's implication in the text. Each individual brings an interpretation to a story already well known, an interpretation that revolves more on the manner of the story's telling than on the matter of the story itself. Thus, Ondaatje involves his audience in the creation of the work.

Readers must pay equal attention to the two storytellers present here—Billy and Ondaatje. Though Billy tells of a relationship with Miss Angela Dickinson of Tucson, no such person exists in historical accounts. However, one of Ondaatje's favorite actors bears that name. The act of acting may be emphasized simply to keep readers focused on the dramatic license all writers assume. Angela represents the sexual "bad girl" versus the work's other female figure, Sallie Chisum, a true historical figure, the "good girl" of Ondaatje's version. In this manner the author supplies the balance to his story that readers desire while he subverts the truth readers may demand from his saga.

The book opens with an empty space that is labeled a photo, suggesting that Billy the Kid cannot be fixed in space and time. That Billy gives an account of himself *following* his announced death, when he no longer exists as a corporeal reality, suggests the difficulty readers encounter in trying to affix to him a certain identity. As Barbour points out, the character questions the accounts of his life and death, particularly pertaining to the violence in which he engages. When Billy asks the question of his readers, "Was there a source for all this?" his language insists that readers view at least two meanings for the term "source." First, "source" refers to that within Billy that supports his actions; second, it refers to that account on which the reader depends for the judgments that he or she, and history, will pass on Billy. Billy's question promotes the postmodern interrogation of history as truth versus storytelling that remains contingent on circumstance and subjectivity. The book's final scene remains true to the entire account, offering gruesome and gripping imagery of life and death (Billy's) but no explanation of either. The only thing of which readers remain confident is Billy's departure from a body that defies identification.

THE ENGLISH PATIENT

The English Patient offers readers a collection of fragmented tales interwoven to form a narrative at once richly artistic and representational. Reflecting Ondaatje's lifelong fascination with history, the novel focuses on the end of World War II, a conflict solved by a hydrogen bomb, called by Ondaatje a deus ex machina for his generation and a major turning point for humanity. Two of the novel's four main characters—Hana, the nurse, and Caravaggio, a thief-turned-spy—are Canadians whom Ondaatje carries over from his previous novel *In the Skin of a Lion*. The other two characters are Hana's badly burned patient, a pilot named Almasy, who Caravaggio feels might be responsible for the loss of parts of both of Caravaggio's hands in a war mission, and a young Sikh soldier in the British army, Kirpal Singh (known as Kip). The four come together in a deserted Italian villa that serves as an army hospital.

Despite the time and geographic complexity of its setting—from 1930's desert exploration to 1940's wartime, and from India to Arabia, England, Italy, and Canada—this novel remains highly accessible. Ondaatje creates characters who are familiar yet defy rational explanation. As Barbour notes, they hold on to their secretive natures, with only the resultant emotional outbursts as evidence of their existence before the villa and the war. Their intertwining relationships offer readers studies in irony and frustration, foreshadowing the lack of a comfortable plot resolution. All four characters remained obsessed—Hana with keeping her obviously terminal patient alive, the patient with relating a story of which he himself remains unsure, Kip with defusing the terror represented by hidden bombs, and Caravaggio with discovering the patient's identity. Caravaggio's obsession becomes the reader's, as the patient's story is revealed only in fragments of his own narration.

The truth in this novel becomes a confused and, at times, moot issue, its elusive quality symbolized by the illusion of heroism and justice on which war's betrayal is based. Ondaatje focuses on betrayal in general as a theme, using his familiar topic of the adulterous, destructive love affair to frame the patient's frustrated relationship with the unattainable wife of a young pilot. Ondaatje's other characters also suffer betrayal from a war ideology that destroys elements of each of their lives. Hana's love for Kip, however strong, cannot survive beyond the war that nurtures it; Kip, having risked his life multiple times to defuse explosives, becomes enraged when the Allies drop the ultimate explosives on Hiroshima; Caravaggio is betrayed by his desire to seek revenge on the patient for his torture, only to discover he feels a kinship with his perceived enemy in the end.

The English Patient is filled with the kinds of strong images for which its author is famous: Kip lifting a friend into the air on a rope rig so that he might inspect the fabulous mosaics of a church ceiling, the black-charred body of the once-handsome Almasy, Hana's playing of a piano that might at any moment detonate hidden explosives, Caravaggio's sneaking naked into a room where two lovers lie. However, the images project a momentary existence that quickly fades. Ondaatje's fragmented glimpses into his characters' lives are of the most intimate, and the most fragile, nature. While Hana achieves some redemption, the novel's ending will leave some readers agreeing with one critic's description of the work as a "journey without maps," a road leading nowhere.

Anil's Ghost

Anil's Ghost is Ondaatje's first use of fiction to revisit Sri Lanka, the country of his birth. The novel's central conflict arises when Anil Tissera, a forensic anthropologist, is invited by a human rights organization to return to her native Sri Lanka to investigate evidence connected with some victims of terrorist murders. Anil is a strong-willed woman, confident, intelligent, secure in her sexual relationships, and devoted to her work. Born into an upper-class family and educated in the West, she has not returned to Sri Lanka since she was a child. Now, she must deal with her personal heritage as well as with the public effects of political terrorism.

Ondaatje never makes explicit the nature of the violence that has left burned corpses for the work of people like Anil, but Sri Lanka's recent history of violence, especially among separatist groups such as the Tamil Tigers, is unmistakable in this novel. Anil's ghosts are partly her memories of her country and her awareness of what it has become as well as the uncertainties she faces in a country where she cannot be sure of anyone's loyalties. She cannot determine whether the government is involved in the death of the skeleton she has named Sailor, nor can she be sure that Dr. Sarath, the local archaeologist who is assisting her, is not really working to protect Sailor's killers.

Anil's past asserts itself in her visit. A few people in Colombo recall her childhood triumphs as a swimmer; she remembers local foods and customs and how to speak Sinhala, the native language; and in her lonely role as investigator she is haunted by friends and lovers from her adult past. Sarath, too, has past connections, particularly Gamini, his physician brother (from whom he is estranged), who is obsessive in treating terrorism's many victims at his hospital.

In an effort to reconstruct Sailor's physical features and in the hope that someone will be able to recognize him, Anil and Sarath employ an artist, Ananda, whose late wife was herself a victim of terrorists. Ananda's success results in Sailor's identification; villagers remember how he had been abducted. With the identification,

Anil is even more vulnerable to pressure from those responsible. In the end, she is forced to leave the country without having accomplished her purpose. Sarath himself is killed. Near the end of the novel, Gamini points out to Anil that in European literature, the American or Englishman simply leaves the exotic country that (like Sri Lanka) has both seduced and thwarted him. The ending of *The English Patient* can be understood in this way, and that is what happens at the end of this work. Anil leaves and terror continues.

Anil's Ghost includes many themes common to Ondaatje's work, especially the interplay of past and present and the complexities and ambiguities of human relationships. The novel also displays the sensual, poetic imagery that is Ondaatje's hallmark. Particularly compelling is the image of a huge statue of the Buddha, destroyed by terrorist bombs and reconstructed at the novel's end, its eye newly painted by Ananda.

Divisadero

From the start of his career in fiction, Ondaatje has been understood as a postmodern writer, particularly for his use of mixed genres, combining nonlinear narrative with poetry and history. *Divisadero* involves his most extreme use to date of nonlinear elements to create fiction, and the critical response to the work has been mixed because of it. The novel embodies two family stories. The contemporary one involves the complicated relationships in a Northern California ranch family. Originally, the farmer and his wife took in Cooper, a little boy whose parents had been murdered, and began raising him as a ranch hand. Later, the farmer's wife dies giving birth to Anna while at the same time another woman in the same hospital dies giving birth to Claire. The farmer raises the two as sisters. At first Coop is like an older brother to both girls, but eventually he and Anna become lovers. When the father discovers them together, he brutally attacks and nearly kills Coop, and the family is broken up.

At this point, the California narrative breaks to the later lives of the three. Coop has become a professional gambler. Near the end of this section, he has been seduced by Bridget, an intensely erotic drug addict, whose underworld connections intend to use her as a lure to involve Coop in a scam of their own. When Bridget's thugs beat Coop nearly to death, Claire rescues him, nurses him back to health, and finally begins to take him to her father. Evidently, she is the only one of the three to maintain contact with the old man. Anna, the reader learns, has left the United States to pursue a literary career, researching the life of a late nineteenth century French novelist, Lucien Segura. In France, Anna is living in Segura's house, sometimes haunted by her memories of Claire and Coop and her escape from her father, which took her to a new identity. Here she has begun a love affair with Rafael, a young Romany (Gypsy) man whom she met in the meadows nearby. These threads of the novel are interwoven and presented from several points of view without regard to chronology.

As the novel points out, the word *divisadero* comes from Spanish, meaning "to divide," and ultimately from a root meaning "to gaze at something from a distance." Both meanings are relevant to this work, which divides its stories, leaving them unresolved, a point of difficulty for some reviewers. Roughly the last third of the novel is Segura's story, his loveless marriage and the memories of his childhood love, Marie-Neige, the Romany who camp in a meadow near his house (the young son becomes the adult Rafael), his daughter's determination to marry a poet, Marie-Neige's death during World War I, and at last Segura's use of her image as substance for his romantic novels and his fostering of Rafael. As the novel's last pages suggest, the two stories are the same in their concern with fathers and children, the nature of love, and the past's insistent hand in the present, one generation giving birth to the next and thus defining its loves and wars.

Virginia Brackett
Updated by Ann D. Garbett

Other major works

PLAYS: *The Collected Works of Billy the Kid*, pr. 1973 (adaptation of his prose poem); *In the Skin of a Lion*, pr. 1987 (adaptation of his novel).

POETRY: *The Dainty Monsters*, 1967; *The Man with Seven Toes*, 1969; *Rat Jelly*, 1973; *Elimination Dance*, 1978 (revised 1980); *There's a Trick with a Knife I'm Learning to Do: Poems, 1963-1978*, 1979; *Secular Love*, 1984; *The Cinnamon Peeler: Selected Poems*, 1989; *Handwriting*, 1998.

NONFICTION: *Leonard Cohen*, 1970; *Claude Glass*, 1979; *Running in the Family*, 1982.

EDITED TEXTS: *The Long Poem Anthology*, 1979; *From Ink Lake: Canadian Stories*, 1990; *The Faber Book of Contemporary Canadian Short Stories*, 1990; *The Brick Reader*, 1991 (with Linda Spalding); *An H in the Heart*, 1994 (of B. P. Nichol's work; with George Bowering); *Lost Classics*, 2000; *The Conversations: Walter Murch and the Art of Editing Film*, 2002.

MISCELLANEOUS: *Vintage Ondaatje*, 2004.

Bibliography

Barbour, Douglas. *Michael Ondaatje*. New York: Twayne, 1993. Provides careful readings and useful analyses of Ondaatje's novels through *The English Patient*. Makes a strong case for Ondaatje as an important postmodern, postcolonial writer based on his keen perception, imaginative intensity, and eloquence.

Jaumain, Serge, and Marc Maufort, eds. *The Guises of Canadian Diversity: New European Perspectives/ Les masques de la diversité canadienne: Nouvelles perspectives européennes*. Atlanta: Rodopi, 1995. Collection of essays by graduate students in Canadian studies at several European universities includes three essays on Ondaatje's writing, focusing on his creative uses of history, art, and autobiography.

Kanaganayakam, Chelva. "In Defense of *Anil's Ghost*." *Ariel* 37, no. 1 (January, 2006): 5-27. Examines the novel in the light of the relationship between literature and politics, particularly responding to some Sri Lankan writers' objections to the work's political themes.

Kertzer, Jon. "Justice and the Pathos of Understanding in Michael Ondaatje's *Anil's Ghost*." *English Studies in Canada* 29, nos. 3/4 (September-December, 2003): 116-139. Discusses the novel's opposing structures as both a traditional murder mystery and a novel of political terror.

McGill, Robert. "Don't Try This at Home." *Literary Review of Canada* 15, no. 6 (July/August, 2007): 19. Detailed review examines *Divisadero* with particular attention to its nonlinear structure, which the author praises as indicative of Ondaatje's art.

Menand, Louis. "The Aesthete: The Novel and Michael Ondaatje." *The New Yorker*, June 4, 2007. Places *Divisadero* within the context of Ondaatje's earlier fiction and identifies Menand's difficulties with the novel's structure.

Scanlan, Margaret. "*Anil's Ghost* and Terrorism's Time." *Studies in the Novel* 36, no. 13 (Fall, 2004): 302-318. Examines the theme of terror in *Anil's Ghost*, arguing that the author's art allows him to replicate the experience of terror for the reader.

Solecki, Sam, ed. *Spider Blues: Essays on Michael Ondaatje*. Montreal: Vehicule Press, 1985. Collection contains many interesting early essays on Ondaatje, covering a wide range of approaches and perspectives. Topics addressed include the author's use of autobiography, postmodern poetics, and myth.

Wagner, Erica. "Picking Up the Pieces." *The New York Times Book Review*, June 17, 2007. Mixed review of *Divisadero* focuses in particular on the novel's themes and motifs as they connect with Ondaatje's earlier work.

JUAN CARLOS ONETTI

Born: Montevideo, Uruguay; July 1, 1909
Died: Madrid, Spain; May 30, 1994

Principal long fiction

El pozo, 1939, 1965 (*The Pit*, 1991)
Tierra de nadie, 1941 (*No Man's Land*, 1994; also known as *Tonight*, 1991)
Para esta noche, 1943 (*Tonight*, 1991)
La vida breve, 1950 (*A Brief Life*, 1976)
Los adioses, 1954 (novella; *Goodbyes*, 1990)
Una tumba sin nombre, 1959 (novella; better known as *Para una tumba sin nombre*; *A Grave With No Name*, 1992)
La cara de la desgracia, 1960 (novella; *The Image of Misfortune*, 1990)
El astillero, 1961 (*The Shipyard*, 1968)
Tan triste como ella, 1963 (novella)
Juntacadáveres, 1964 (*Body Snatcher*, 1991)
La muerte y la niña, 1973
Dejemos hablar al viento, 1979 (*Let the Wind Speak*, 1997)
Cuando ya no importe, 1993 (*Past Caring?*, 1995)

Other literary forms

"Los niños en el bosque," one of Juan Carlos Onetti's unpublished novels, dates from 1936. "Tiempo de abrazar," a novel written in 1933 and circulated in manuscript form among Onetti's friends, was not published, despite the praise it received from respected writers such as Roberto Arlt. The manuscript was entered in the contest for the Rinehart and Farrar Prize in 1941. After coming in second, it disappeared, except for a number of fragments, which were published in various journals over the years. In 1974, the Uruguayan critic Jorge Ruffinelli gathered these fragments, a good portion of the original, along with "Los niños en el bosque" and Onetti's uncollected short stories dating from 1933 to 1950, into one volume titled *Tiempo de abrazar, y los cuentos de 1933 a 1950*. There are to date at least eleven short-story collections, with overlapping items. The most complete of these is *Cuentos completos* (1967; revised 1974), edited by Ruffinelli.

Onetti's *Obras completas* (1970) is far from complete, the title notwithstanding. Still uncollected are the many literary essays written by Onetti for Montevideo's weekly *Marcha*, where the author served as editor for two years (1939-1941). Under a variety of exotic pseudonyms and humorous epithets, Onetti wrote not only essays and criticism but also short pieces of fiction as "fillers" for that weekly, all of which remain uncollected. During his first stint in Buenos Aires, from 1930 to 1934, Onetti wrote a number of film reviews for the periodical *Crítica*, and they also remain uncollected. While he may have attempted genres other than prose, only two poems exist in print: "Y el pan nuestro," in *Cuadernos hispanoamericanos* (1974), and "Balada del ausente," in *Casa de las Américas* (1976).

Achievements

Until the mid-1960's, when Latin American fiction moved into the international limelight and its younger practitioners acknowledged Juan Carlos Onetti as one of their forerunners, Onetti's popularity was limited to a devoted few. His first published novel, *The Pit*, did not go into a second printing for twenty-six years after its initial edition of five hundred copies. The pivotal work of his career, *A Brief Life*, was not reissued until fifteen years after its publication. Onetti is now internationally acclaimed, with his works translated into many languages and constantly being reissued in Spanish editions.

In the mid-1930's, Onetti was becoming increasingly well known in his native Montevideo. His stint as literary editor of *Marcha* from 1939 to 1941 furnished him with a forum for his literary ideas during what was a very productive period for his own writing. His intellectual activities did not abate when he moved to Buenos Aires for the second time, in 1941—where he would remain for a decade and a half—but the move did sever prematurely his growing influence in his own country.

In 1951, Onetti's countrymen gave their first public recognition of his achievements when the important

Montevideo review *Número* dedicated a special issue to his work. Ten years later, *The Shipyard* was selected by a jury in a literary contest sponsored by Compañía General Fabril Editora, which published that novel. In 1962, Onetti was awarded Uruguay's national literary prize, and in 1963, *The Shipyard* received the William Faulkner Foundation Certificate of Merit. Italy awarded the same novel its prize for the best foreign work translated into Italian for the year 1975. In June of 1980, a group of distinguished writers and critics from all over the world gathered at the Universidad Veracruzana de Méjico to pay homage to Onetti and his career on the occasion of his seventieth birthday. Today, Onetti's significance in Latin American letters is established beyond any doubt.

Biography

Juan Carlos Onetti was born in Montevideo, Uruguay, on July 1, 1909. His father, Carlos Onetti, whom Onetti characterized as a "gentleman," was a functionary of Montevideo's customs office. On more than one occasion, Onetti noted that the family name was O'Netty before being corrupted to its present form, a suggestion that would point to early Irish ancestry. Onetti was always cryptic about his ancestors, however, intimating only that his great-grandfather was the personal secretary of General Fructuoso Rivera, who fought in the nineteenth century against Juan Manuel de Rosas and the Argentine dictator's territorial pretensions in Uruguay. His mother, Honoria Borges, was of Brazilian stock, and Onetti says only that she was a "slaveholding lady from the south of Brazil."

Onetti was the second of three children; he had an older brother, Raul, and a younger sister, Raquel. He remembered his childhood as a happy one, during which the family moved often, at least four times in his early school days. Onetti was a high school dropout—in part, he said, because he could not receive a passing grade in drawing. As an adolescent, he worked at a number of odd jobs—doorman, automobile-tire salesman, waiter, ticket taker at a stadium, and watchman at a grain elevator.

At the age of fourteen, Onetti discovered the works of Knut Hamsun, which he read avidly and tried, with adolescent fervor, to emulate. Onetti's first known venture into literature and publishing came in 1928. He was nineteen then and living in Villa Colón, not far from Montevideo. With two friends, Juan Andrés Carril and Luis Antonio Urta, he founded a journal, *La tijera de Colón*. Seven issues of the journal were published between March, 1928, and February, 1929, including Onetti's first five short stories. In 1929, Onetti tried, unsuccessfully, to travel to the Soviet Union "to witness a Socialist system in the making." A year later, he was married for the first time, to a cousin, María Amalia, and moved with her to Buenos Aires. He remained there for four years, during which he worked for a while as an adding-machine salesman—he did not sell a single machine. His son, Jorge, who also became a novelist, was born in 1931.

Onetti wrote the first version of *The Pit* in 1932, a version that was lost. The following year, he published what was once believed to have been his first short story, "Avenida de Mayo—Diagonal—Avenida de Mayo" in the Buenos Aires daily *La prensa*. In 1934, Onetti returned to Montevideo and was married for the second time, to another cousin, María Julia. On October 6, 1935, his short story "El obstáculo" appeared in the Argentine daily *La nación*, whose literary supplement was edited at the time by the distinguished novelist Eduardo Mallea. A year later, with the outbreak of the Spanish Civil War, Onetti attempted, again without success, to travel to Europe to enlist as a volunteer in the international brigades fighting in Spain.

With the founding of the weekly *Marcha* on June 23, 1939, Onetti was given the opportunity to work at the center of one of the most important intellectual enterprises of Uruguay. As literary editor, he made his mark on Montevideo's cultural life. In December of that same year, a reconstituted version of *The Pit* was published in a limited edition. Two years later, Onetti left *Marcha* to work as editor for Reuter's news agency and, in that capacity, was transferred to Buenos Aires. Shortly thereafter, he abandoned Reuter's, though he remained in the Argentine capital from 1941 to 1955. After leaving Reuter's, Onetti worked as an editor for various Argentine magazines, including *Vea y lea* and *Ímpetu*. During this decade and a half, he published some of his most important work.

In 1944, Onetti interviewed the populist strongman of Argentina, Juan Perón, a figure Onetti found fascinating; he indicated on more than one occasion his desire to write a novel about him and his legendary wife, Eva Perón. In this period, Onetti also undertook a number of translations of American works, the first being Phoebe Atwood Taylor's *The Cape Cod Mystery* (1931), which he translated with Elizabeth María Pikelharing, his third wife, whom he married in 1945. Only her name appears on the translation, which was published a year later. Onetti also translated Erskine Caldwell's *This Very Earth* (1948) in 1954, Paul I. Wellman's *The Comancheros* (1952) in 1956, and Henry Burgess Drake's *Children of the Wind* (1954) in 1957. Actually, Onetti's interest in translation dates from 1940, when his Spanish version of William Faulkner's "All the Dead Pilots" appeared in *Marcha*, unsigned.

In 1955, back in Montevideo, Onetti worked for an advertising agency and, subsequently, as editor for the publication *Acción*, in which he had an anonymous literary column. In the same year, he was married for the fourth time, to Dorotea (Dolly) Muhr. Onetti was named director of municipal libraries of Montevideo in 1957, a position he held until his arrest in 1974 and subsequent exile in 1975. In 1962, he was the recipient of Uruguay's Premio Nacional de Literatura, the country's literary prize. With this award and the publication of his two major novels *The Shipyard* and *Body Snatcher*, Onetti began to receive international acclaim. Peruvian novelist Mario Vargas Llosa, after receiving the Romulo Gallegos Novel Prize, declared in his acceptance speech that the prize rightfully belonged to Onetti. Such declarations became common. In 1970, the Mexican publishing firm Editorial Aguilar issued Onetti's *Obras completas*, an incomplete collection but an indication of his growing reputation.

Because of one of those tragic but common political debacles that have become a specialty of Latin America, Onetti was first imprisoned for a short period in 1974 and forced into exile in 1975. Thereafter, he lived in Madrid, Spain. Onetti's crime was to have served on a jury for a literary contest sponsored by *Marcha*, which awarded the prize (against Onetti's own vote) to a story deemed inappropriate by the military dictatorship. While Onetti evinced a great sense of loss in having to live in exile, his work continued. In 1979, his novel *Let the Wind Speak* was published, and *Past Caring?* was published in 1993.

ANALYSIS

"He has the power to say a word, to put in an adjective, to change a destiny . . . until he discovers his power, and then he uses it to enter himself into his imaginary world." This is how Juan Carlos Onetti characterizes one of his heroes and the activity of writing. The depiction is apt for Onetti himself. Beginning with *The Pit*—and even before, with his first published stories—Onetti's career consisted in exploring the enabling possibilities of the "power" he describes here. In the process, he himself has become a body of literature, a world of imagination capable of engendering itself in its imaginary world.

If one can glean a constant from Onetti's long and distinguished career, it has to be the persevering exploration and charting of powers of the imagination. Like their author, all of Onetti's characters inevitably strive for a salvation that can be found only in imagination's potency. The guises, the masks, the shapes that this potency takes in Onetti's fictions are many—fantasy, escapism, imaginary biography, delusion, pathetic and courageous Bovarism. The projects engendered by the energies of this power are also varied—a mythical topography, the perfect whorehouse, a dignified death. Onetti calls this itinerary the "adventure of man," and he says, "I only wish to express the adventure of man."

The "destiny" to be altered by imaginative potency in Onetti's fictional cosmos is "real life," which inevitably emerges in his works as overbearing, vulgar, susceptible to corruption by time and experience. This vision of reality is determined in large measure by the social and historical realities of the 1930's and 1940's, Onetti's formative years as a novelist. The setting of Onetti's works, primarily urban, may also have influenced his somber vision of human circumstances. As in the fiction of the Argentine novelist Roberto Arlt, whose influence helped shape Onetti's work, the metropolitan centers of Buenos Aires and Montevideo assume metaphorical significance in Onetti's vision. Onetti eventually conflated these two urban centers to create the imaginary geography of Santa María, the mythical setting of *A Brief Life* and of all of his subsequent novels.

Buenos Aires and Montevideo, of all the Latin American capitals, have always looked toward Europe, with their backs turned, so to speak, to the vast American continent beyond them. Historical events that befall distant metropolitan centers at the other shores of the Atlantic, then, have always had an immediate effect in these twin Río de la Plata cities: World War I, the economic collapse of the 1930's, Francisco Franco's victory in Spain, the rise of fascism beyond Spain in Europe. The fate of European intellectuals has exerted an equally strong influence: Franco's silencing of José Ortega y Gasset, the murder of Federico García Lorca, the deaths of Miguel de Unamuno y Jugo and Antonio Machado in Spain, Adolf Hitler's march into Paris in 1940, the imprisonment or exile of writers such as Jean-Paul Sartre and André Gide. These and other European calamities confirmed the worst suspicions born of the disillusioned intellectuals of Onetti's generation; Onetti and his contemporaries saw that those suspicions found their concrete objective correlatives in what they thought to be the most urbane centers of civilization.

The urban individual with a conscience finds himself in what one of Onetti's titles from 1941 so succinctly expresses—a *tierra de nadie*, a no-man's-land. Onetti, then, is very much a part of that "lost generation," and his novels inevitably reflect the environment in which they have been created. Onetti, with imaginative potency, seeks and finds an inventive, mythopoeic plane where his characters can confront worldly reality and transform the "given" into redemptive adventure, whether as Bovaristic illusion or as creative, poetic figuration. That mythical, poetic geography is the world of Santa María, invented by one of Onetti's protagonists in *A Brief Life*—a world of the imagination that carries within it the "givens" of historical reality, much like Faulkner's Yoknapatawpha County, and into which Onetti himself enters to chart its annals. Onetti's novels become the record of that itinerary.

THE PIT

Published in December of 1939, Onetti's first novel, *The Pit*, is a reconstituted version of the misplaced and lost original from 1932. As a first novel, it is paradigmatic of the author's oeuvre. *The Pit* dramatizes the trial and error of an attempt at self-mastery. In this sense, it is revealing not only of the hero's circumstances (a protagonist who feels compelled to write his autobiography now that he has reached the age of forty) but also of Onetti's conception of his task as a writer. The protagonist's self-characterizations, his halting and reticent attempts at self-writing, his disengagement from the world of reality and human relationships around him, even as he is obsessed with these things, reflect the circumstances of his author and of other, subsequent protagonists in Onetti's fictional cosmos.

The novel's hero, Eladio Linacero, is obsessed with an autobiography and its self-conscious impossibility. In his reticence and self-deprecation, he confesses to his shortcomings as a writer as well as to the necessarily fictional nature of the details of his life that have become committed to his writing. He thus opts for recording not factual detail, which offers a mere pretense of re-creating reality, but the fantasies that have no such claims and that may well be more "true" as a result. He not only spurns historical particulars but also rejects, with a Sartrean "nausea," the concrete, "objective" details that surround him, including his own bodily existence and his neglected apartment, with its dusty furniture and faded newspapers.

The novel's narrative, then, becomes the record of a juxtaposition between the concrete (whether in historical remembrance or in immediate objectivity) and the imaginary, fantasy world of his daydreams. By the end of the novel and of the night (the span of narrative time is one night), Eladio Linacero admits to the impossibility of autobiography, of self-mastery in writing. What he has produced becomes the record of that impossibility, a record that extends the self in the act of recording what writing attempts to contain. Implacably, time vitiates the attempt to freeze oneself in time: "I would have liked to pin the night on paper, like a nocturnal butterfly. But, in turn, it was the night that carried me off amid its waters, like the livid body of a dead man." The problematics of Linacero's attempt and its vicissitudes attained full significance in later works, such as *A Brief Life* and the subsequent novels from the saga of Santa María.

NO MAN'S LAND

A collective social portrait of a historical period, *No Man's Land* is Onetti's most explicit work. Written in the late 1930's, when the lost generation came of age, Onetti's second novel captures, in the manner of cinematic montage, the ambience of the epoch. Despite the value of the novel as a social document, its technical achievement may be even more significant. If *The Pit* showed Onetti as a master of first-person narration, of a stream of consciousness restricted to a single voice, *No Man's Land* displays his mastery of simultaneity, in the manner of John Dos Passos in *Manhattan Transfer* (1925).

No Man's Land is a congeries of parallel paths, multiple destinies, refracted perspectives, desultory points of view that crowd the world of the novel, that occasionally converge but rarely result in any meaningful human communion. As the title suggests, the urban setting is an anonymous no-man's-land, and its sundry inhabitants are alienated individuals whose relationship to a collective community is all but obliterated by indifference, ennui, and individual fantasies. On occasion, those fantasies converge, even if tangentially, and therein lies the seed for an imaginary world, which becomes a communal fantasy in Onetti's later novels. For the first time, too, certain characters who will emerge as protagonists in works from the saga of Santa María, such as Junta Larsen, hero of *The Shipyard* and of *Body Snatcher*, make a fleeting appearance. *No Man's Land* was hailed at the time of its publication as a genuine Río de la Plata novel, an indication that Buenos Aires and Montevideo had finally produced a novel equal to their teeming life.

Tonight

While *No Man's Land* has been hailed as a social novel, *Tonight*, Onetti's third novel, has often been read as an expression of political solidarity. In the late 1930's, when Onetti was affiliated with *Marcha* and later with Reuter's, he frequented the Café Metro in Montevideo. There, Onetti would meet with other intellectuals and there, too, he encountered a number of exiles from the Spanish Civil War and its infamous aftermath.

Onetti said that his conversations with those exiles found their fictionalized echo in *Tonight*, a novel of political terror and oppression. Onetti had made an attempt in 1936 to go to Spain to fight in the civil war. Perhaps this novel is a form of compensation for his failure in that attempt as well as for his comfortable distance from yet another tragic war that was then under way. Ironically, the state of siege, the military terror, the political machinations and victimization of ideals, and the fugitive haunts of idealistic and ambiguous characters depicted in the novel were all too prophetic of what was to befall Argentina two years after the novel's publication. That state of affairs changed little, with Onetti's Uruguay falling victim to the same fate. Even more ironic is that some thirty years later, Onetti himself became the victim of this scourge and, reversing the pattern, went to Spain as an exile.

Technically, Onetti's third novel is not the most accomplished of his works. It suffers from the rhetorically melodramatic, unambiguous dichotomies of good and evil, the idealistic and the corrupt, the victim and the villain. Nevertheless, the perspectivist juxtaposition of narrative points of view and the intensity of terror that builds with the manhunt and concludes with the hero's death make the novel interesting.

A Brief Life

Onetti's fourth novel, *A Brief Life*, opened a new epoch in his novelistic cycle. Santa María, the mythical realm of this and subsequent works, while adumbrated in earlier pieces, has its genesis in *A Brief Life*. As the title suggests, the narrative consists of a series of brief lives, "real" or fantasized, harking back to the multiple, imaginary lives of Eladio Linacero in Onetti's first novel. In contrast to the predicament of Linacero, however, the hero of *A Brief Life*, Juan María Brausen, succeeds in finding a way out of the worldly "here and now" of space and temporality.

Like Linacero, Brausen is a brooder; unlike Onetti's first hero, however, he is also a man of action. His acts of evasion are not merely fantasized mental states. Brausen breaks out of his humdrum existence by physically breaking into the ambit and life of the prostitute who lives next door. Thus, Juan María Brausen becomes Juan María Arce upon "penetrating" the wall to another life, a life that proves as desolate as the respectable normalcy he has left behind. In oscillating between these two lives, the protagonist discovers the impossibility of evasion and the now compounded nature of his entrapment. Real transcendence from the strictures of the existential trap, Brausen discovers, is to be found only in imaginative potency, in the creative powers of the imagination. As a scriptwriter with a commission for a particular film script, Brausen invents the world of Santa María, an imaginary world into which he flees, a fugitive from the authorities following the murder of the prostitute. Not only does he interpolate himself into his invented world, crossing from a fiction of reality to a reality of fiction, but his created world becomes, thereafter, the novelistic cosmos of his creator, Onetti. In this sense, *A Brief Life* may well be Onetti's most significant novel, the gateway to all of his subsequent works.

THE SHIPYARD *and* BODY SNATCHER

There is common agreement among critics that *The Shipyard*, Onetti's fifth major novel, is his best-formed work; it may well be the masterpiece of his career. *The Shipyard* is the first full-blown treatment of the saga of Santa María; in the internal chronology of the saga, it follows the events related in *Body Snatcher*. Onetti said that when he was halfway through the writing of this latter work in 1957, he was assailed by the vision of the hero's death. He then abandoned *Body Snatcher* and wrote *The Shipyard*.

The novel recounts the story of Junta Larsen and his return to Santa María. He was expelled from there five years earlier by the town fathers because of his less-than-respectable activities in running a brothel. *The Shipyard*, then, is a redemptive work, a seeking after salvation in the ashes of a failed dream. The redemption sought by the hero is not a phoenixlike rebirth but a pursuit of some admissible meaning in failure. Junta Larsen emerges as an ennobled hero, a tragic figure who has already endured the blows of the implacable fates. His deep pessimism is not cynical but philosophical. He accepts fate, not with bitter resignation, but with knowing perspicacity. There is an allegorical parallel to Junta Larsen's search for self-salvation in self-surrender to the inevitable: his engagement in salvaging the hopelessly defunct shipyard of Petrus.

The shipyard is beyond salvation. Its owner and management play out the farce of running a going concern even while they surreptitiously junk useless pieces from the carcass of the shipyard to survive. Junta Larsen shuttles between Santa María and the docks, between his own disintegrated past and the concretely visible disintegration of the shipyard. His attempts to marry Petrus's daughter prove futile; she is dim-witted or downright mad. He settles for a sordid relationship with the maid in the servants' quarters. In the face of an impossible future, the most meaningful acts are recollections of the past. In his lucid flashbacks, in his silent monologue, Junta Larsen emerges as a savior, hopeful but hopelessly fated, and knowingly so, a Christ figure in the house of Petrus: The biblical allusion to Saint Peter and the church built upon a rock is transparent. Petrus's rock, however, has become a heap of sand, and Larsen, the savior, can find only a quietus, a final reckoning, rather than a resurrection.

Although published three years later than *The Shipyard*, the episodes narrated in *Body Snatcher* antedate the events of the earlier novel. Onetti's sixth major novel evinces, at least in the first half, the vigor and dynamism of a pursuit: Junta Larsen's dream to found and operate the perfect whorehouse. The language of the novel is wry, at times satirically imbued with irony and frequent humor. The hero is in his prime, his energies at their apex. The novel begins with Junta Larsen's arrival in Santa María with his female cargo—three or four women in varying degrees of decrepitude. The town dubs the hero with the nickname that gives the work its original title, Juntacadáveres, the Corpse-Gatherer (or body snatcher). The town's reaction to Junta's enterprise ensues, with the final expulsion of the hero and his charges from Santa María and the crumbling of Junta's dream in a bathetic denouement.

Interwoven into the rise and fall of Larsen's enterprise is the story of Jorge Malabia, a young man who was the protagonist of an earlier Onetti novella, *A Grave with No Name*. This novella has often been considered a blueprint for Onetti's fiction: It embraces all of his recurring preoccupations, particularly his obsession with the relativity of truth. In *Body Snatcher*, Jorge Malabia is engaged in a guilt-ridden relationship with the widowed wife of his brother. His attempts to patronize Junta Larsen's establishment and his eventual participation in the downfall of that "institution" also form part of the novel's plot. Thus, *Body Snatcher* is an intricately woven novel that gathers various threads from the annals of Santa María. Uruguayan critic Emir Rodríguez Monegal notes that to appreciate the chronological order of events, one must first read *Body Snatcher*, then *A Grave with No Name*, and then *The Shipyard*. Monegal also noted that the second part of *Body Snatcher* is more somber, its language more weighty, its humor darker; the change is attributed to the fact that this second part was written after Onetti had interrupted the novel's composition to write *The Shipyard*.

La muerte y la niña

If the sequence of publication violates the internal chronology of the saga of Santa María, *La muerte y la niña*, Onetti's seventh novel, violates all logical order with impunity. The result is a hermetic involution, a scrambled code that can have intelligibility only for those already initiated in Onetti's fictional system. *La muerte y la niña* is yet another farce played out with the knowledge of its futility in the face of implacable time, guilt, relative truth, and irrevocable fate. The episodes of the plot (the attempts of Augusto Goerdel to exonerate himself and assuage his guilt for the death of his wife, Helga Hauser, by returning to Santa María with suspect documents aimed to prove that he is not the father of the girl whose birth proved fatal to her mother) are less significant than the "resuscitation" of ghosts from earlier novels in the saga. Onetti deliberately violates objective temporality by having characters whose death was narrated in earlier works and episodes reappear, "posthumously," to reflect on the fate of Santa María.

While not Onetti's best work, *La muerte y la niña* is a significant novel insofar as it divulges the author's deliberate destruction of objective reality even in the world of fiction, to point to yet another level, one more demonstration that literature *is* literature, with no obligations to any order outside itself. Accordingly, the language of the novel is deliberately artificial, studied, and rhetorical.

Let the Wind Speak

Let the Wind Speak takes its title and epigraph from the last fragment of *The Cantos* (1972) of Ezra Pound, who wrote

> I have tried to write Paradise
> Do not move
> Let the wind speak
> that is paradise.
> Let the Gods forgive what I
> have made.
> Let those I love try to forgive
> what I have made.

From the outset, then, there is a sense of an ending, a morbid finality, an intimation of doom in this apocalyptic work. The cycle of Santa María, deliberately scrambled in the previous work, now closes in on itself. Characters return—some from death—to haunt the novel, and whole passages are repeated from earlier volumes in the saga.

In some cases, this recursiveness extends even to works that predated the genesis of Santa María. The protagonist of *Let the Wind Speak*, Medina, who appeared in previous works as a police official, returns from Santa María to Lavanda (a homonymic suggestion of La Banda, Uruguay, which is commonly known as La Banda Oriental). His return, reminiscent of Junta Larsen's return in *The Shipyard*, erases all boundaries between the real world and the world of Onetti's fiction, Santa María. There is a peculiar conflation of worlds when, for example, Medina narrates, word for word, whole passages from Onetti's first novel, *The Pit*, and one recognizes scenes and dialogues from the narrative context of Santa María now outside that phantasmagoric geography. The textual boundaries collapse, the dead and the living intermingle, past and present fuse. The cycle has run its course and begins to overtake its own tracks.

Symbolically, the novel is the apocalypse of a literary career, of its enchanted geography (Santa María is consumed by fire in this novel). All that remains is the specter of language. In the end, if this is indeed the end, Onetti reaffirms once again the creative potency of the imagination (the power to create and to destroy its own invention) and the enabling potency of the author to enter and fade into the world of his imaginary creation.

Djelal Kadir

Other major works

SHORT FICTION: *Un sueño realizado, y otros cuentos*, 1951; *El infierno tan temido*, 1962; *Jacob y el otro: Un sueño realizado, y otros cuentos*, 1965; *Cuentos completos*, 1967 (revised 1974; Jorge Ruffinelli, editor); *La novia robada, y otros cuentos*, 1968; *Cuentos*, 1971; *Tiempo de abrazar, y los cuentos de 1933 a 1950*, 1974 (short stories and fragments of unpublished novels; Ruffinelli, editor); *Tan triste como ella, y otros cuentos*, 1976; *Goodbyes, and Other Stories*, 1990.

NONFICTION: *Réquiem por Faulkner, y otros artículos*, 1975; *Confesiones de un lector*, 1995.

MISCELLANEOUS: *Obras completas*, 1970; *Onetti*, 1974 (articles, interview).

Bibliography

Adams, M. Ian. *Three Authors of Alienation: Bombal, Onetti, Carpentier*. Austin: University of Texas Press, 1975. This study of the three writers includes an extended discussion of Onetti's novel *The Pit*, showing how Onetti's artistic manipulation of schizophrenia creates the sensation of participating in an alienated world.

Craig, Linda. *Juan Carlos Onetti, Manuel Puig, and Luisa Valenzuela: Marginality and Gender*. Woodbridge, England: Tamesis, 2005. Craig's book analyzes the works of Onetti and two other Latin American writers, describing how they share a sense of "postcolonial emptiness" and constantly question realism.

Harss, Luis, and Barbara Dohmann. "Juan Carlos Onetti or the Shadows on the Wall." In *Into the Mainstream: Conversations with Latin-American Writers*. New York: Harper & Row, 1967. Claims that in Onetti's middle-age protagonists there is a yearning for vanished youth and innocence. Discusses Onetti's pessimism and his Faulknerian style in his novella *Goodbyes*.

Maloof, Judy. *Over Her Dead Body: The Construction of Male Subjectivity in Onetti*. New York: Peter Lang, 1995. A feminist reading of Onetti's novels, in which Maloff explores Onetti's representation of gender, particularly his creation of male protagonists. She discusses these male characters' crises, placing them within the context of social and historical events in Uruguay from the 1930's through the 1960's.

Millington, Mark. "No Woman's Land: The Representation of Woman in Onetti." *MLN* 102 (March, 1987): 358-377. Millington discusses the function of the wife, prostitute, girl, and mad woman in Onetti's fiction, arguing that the subjection of women is one of the major impasses of Onetti's thinking.

_______. *Reading Onetti: Language, Narrative and the Subject*. Liverpool, England: Francis Cairns, 1985. Millington discusses the development of Onetti's work under the "hegemony of international modernism." He focuses on the status of Onetti's fiction as narrative discourse and discusses how *Goodbyes* problematizes the act of reading.

Murray, Jack. *The Landscapes of Alienation: Ideological Subversion in Kafka, Céline, and Onetti*. Stanford, Calif.: Stanford University Press, 1991. In his discussion of alienation in the work of Onetti and two other writers, Murray provides some background about the effect of Uruguay on Onetti's ideological unconscious.

San Román, Gustavo, ed. *Onetti and Others: Comparative Essays on a Major Figure in Latin American Literature*. Albany: State University of New York Press, 1999. A collection of twelve essays written from a variety of perspectives. Several focus on gender relationships in Onetti's work; comparative studies relating Onetti to other Latin American writers also are prominent.

Williams, Raymond L. "The Novels of Leopoldo Marechal and Juan Carlos Onetti." In *The Modern Latin American Novel*. New York: Twayne, 1998. This analysis of Onetti's novels is included in a historical overview of the Latin American novel from the modernist fiction of the mid-1940's through the postmodern novels published in the region since 1968. Includes notes, a bibliography, and an index.

GEORGE ORWELL
Eric Arthur Blair

Born: Motihari, Bengal, India; June 25, 1903
Died: London, England; January 21, 1950
Also known as: Eric Arthur Blair

PRINCIPAL LONG FICTION

Burmese Days, 1934
A Clergyman's Daughter, 1935
Keep the Aspidistra Flying, 1936
Coming Up for Air, 1939
Animal Farm, 1945
Nineteen Eighty-Four, 1949

OTHER LITERARY FORMS

Since the mid-1940's, George Orwell has been considered one of the world's premier essayists. Combining reportage, the polemical essay, fictional techniques, and refracted autobiographical detail, his works defy precise generic definition. Orwell's numerous nonfiction works have been compiled in *The Collected Essays, Journalism, and Letters of George Orwell* (1968), edited by Sonia Orwell and Ian Angus.

ACHIEVEMENTS

Although George Orwell is widely recognized as one of the best essayists of the twentieth century, his reputation as a novelist rests almost entirely on two works: the political allegory *Animal Farm* and the dystopian *Nineteen Eighty-Four*. Both have been translated into so many other languages and have been read so widely that the adjective "Orwellian" has international currency—synonymous, as Bernard Crick has put it, with the "ghastly political future." Indeed, Jeffrey Meyers has asserted that Orwell, the writer of essays, political tracts, and fiction, "is more widely read than perhaps any other serious writer of the twentieth-century."

BIOGRAPHY

George Orwell was born Eric Arthur Blair, the son of Richard Walmesley Blair and Ida (Limouzin) Blair. Orwell was born in India and lived there for four years, until his father moved the family back to England, to a small house named Nutshell, located in Henley-on-Thames. After a short leave, Orwell's father returned alone to India; his wife and children remained in England, where he rejoined them later, upon his retirement. With his father's return, Orwell, like most male members of the upper middle class, was sent away to boarding school, St. Cyprian's, located at Eastbourne on the Sussex coast. After several miserable years, as Orwell describes them in his autobiographical *Such, Such Were the Joys* (1953), he won a scholarship to Eton, the public school that would forever set him apart from the working classes about which he was so concerned during most of his adult life.

Considered rather unacademic at Eton, Orwell graduated in December, 1921, and, after a decision not to attend university, he applied to the India Office for the position of imperial police officer. Five years in Burma, from 1922 to 1927, shaped the impressionable young man so as to make him forever sympathetic to individuals victimized by governmental bureaucracy and imperialistic power. Orwell left Burma in the summer of 1927, ostensibly on sick leave (he suffered from a lung condition most of his life). At some point early in his leave, Orwell wrote a letter of resignation to the India Office and explained to his skeptical parents that all he really wanted to do was to write.

In 1928, Orwell commenced a long, five-year apprenticeship as a writer, time spent as a tramp in both Paris and London and in the writing and rewriting of countless manuscripts. By 1933 he had assumed the name by which he is known and had produced, in addition to at least two destroyed novels, the nonfictional *Down and Out in Paris and London* (1933) and his first novel, *Burmese Days*, published one year later.

From 1933 to 1937, Orwell continued to develop his literary talents, producing two more novels, a nonfiction book about his experiences with poverty-stricken coal miners in Wigan (*The Road to Wigan Pier*, 1937), and several essays, occasional pieces, and book reviews. By the end of this period, he had also married for the first time and, within a year or so of that, gone to Spain. In perhaps the most singular experience of his life to date, the Spanish Civil War found Orwell on the front lines, a member of a Partido Obrero de Unificación Marxista (a Marxist worker's party) brigade; from that time on, Orwell passionately declared himself a fighter for "democratic Socialism." In that context, he wrote his most famous nonfictional work, *Homage to Catalonia* (1938). After being wounded (and nearly imprisoned), Orwell escaped Spain with the help of his wife, returned to England, and continued his literary career. Within another year, his lungs still causing him problems, Orwell moved to the dry climate of Morocco, where he wrote much of *Coming Up for Air*.

His fourth novel was buried under mounting war concerns and preparations. Orwell, unable to join the military because of his health, became a spokesman for the British Broadcasting Corporation (BBC). During the last years of the war, Orwell finished writing *Animal Farm*, only to see it rejected by almost every major publisher in England and the United States. Finally brought out in August, 1945, during the last days of the Pacific War, *Animal Farm* was a work of near perfection, making Orwell's name internationally known, so that when *Nineteen Eighty-Four* was published four years later, the world came to realize that both works would henceforth be considered literary classics, satires ranking with Sir Thomas More's *De Optimo Reipublicae Statu, deque Nova Insula Utopia* (1516; *Utopia, 1551*) and Jonathan Swift's *A Tale of a Tub* (1704). Orwell's death in 1950 at the age of forty-six was a tragic loss to the world of letters and to the larger world with which he always kept in touch.

ANALYSIS

Excepting *Animal Farm*, most critics view George Orwell's fictions as aesthetically flawed creations, the work of a political thinker whose artistry was subordinate to his intensely didactic, partisan passions. This reaction to Orwell's novels was generally promoted posthumously, since his fiction in the 1930's was often ignored by the larger reading public and panned by those reviewers who did pick up one of his books. The early academic critics—up to the late 1960's—were often Orwell's personal friends or acquaintances, who tended to see his early novels as conventionally realistic and strongly autobiographical. Even his masterpieces, *Animal Farm* and *Nineteen Eighty-Four*, were viewed as formally undistinguished, however powerful their message. It was not until the second generation of critics began looking at Orwell's fiction that a more balanced assessment was possible.

BURMESE DAYS

Orwell's first published novel, *Burmese Days*, concerns the life of John Flory, an English policeman in Burma during the early 1920's. The plot is fairly straightforward. After a lengthy introduction to Flory's personality and daily life, Orwell dramatizes him as a man blemished with a physical stigma, a birthmark, and puzzled by moral dilemma—how to deal with the increasingly rebellious natives, to whom he is secretly sympathetic but against whom he must wield the club of imperialistic authority. In the middle of this dilemma,

George Orwell. (Library of Congress)

Elizabeth arrives, a young English woman who is fresh faced but decidedly a traditional "burra memsahib." Flory attempts to win both her heart and mind—much to the dismay of his Burmese mistress, Ma Hla May—and succeeds in doing neither, even though he manages to half succeed in proposing marriage during an earthquake. With a mind too closed to anything not properly British, and a heart only to be won by someone very English, Elizabeth forgets Flory's attentions with the arrival of Verrall, an English military policeman, who will in turn reject her after his billet is completed. A humble Flory waits for Elizabeth, and after Verrall has left takes her to church services, confident that he has outlasted his rival. Unfortunately, Flory is humiliated by Ma Hla May, is repulsed yet again by Elizabeth, and, in a mood of despair, commits suicide, killing both his dog and himself.

In such a world, Flory is emphatically not meant to be a sympathetic character, but rather a victim of the very political order he has sworn to uphold. In effect, Orwell has laid a trap for the unwary reader. Too close an identification with Flory, too intense a desire to have him succeed in marrying Elizabeth—an unholy alliance of imperialistic Englishwoman and revolutionary, thinking pariah—will prevent the reader from recognizing the irreconcilable contradictions inherent in the British presence in Burma.

Coming Up for Air

Orwell's fourth published novel, *Coming Up for Air*, was written in Marrakesh, Morocco, shortly after the author had recovered from yet another bout with tubercular lesions of the lungs. Although the novel sold moderately well for the time (a first printing of two thousand copies and a second printing of one thousand), many critics were vaguely condescending toward the hero, George Bowling, a middle-class insurance salesman who longs for the golden country of the past while simultaneously dreading the horrors of a second world war, then only months away. Many of the themes more fully developed in *Nineteen Eighty-Four* find their initial expression in Orwell's last conventional novel, set before the outbreak of the devastation that the next six years would bring.

Coming Up for Air is set in London during the late 1930's; Orwell employs a first-person narrative to describe the life of George Bowling, a middle-aged, middle-class salesman, whose first set of false teeth marks a major milestone in his life. Musing in front of a mirror while he prepares for work one morning, George's mind wanders back to the past, the golden England of thirty years earlier when he was growing up. As he goes about his day, disgusted with all the evidence of modern life in front of him—the casual brutalities, the tasteless food, the bombers overhead—George forms a plan to return to Lower Binfield, his childhood home, and, by extension, the simple life he had once led. Unfortunately, his return only confirms the all-pervasive slovenliness of the modern world: Lower Binfield has been swallowed by a sprawling suburb, his adolescent sweetheart has become a frowsy old married woman (she is all of two years older than he), and the fishing hole (once filled with huge finny dreams) has been emptied of water and filled with trash. Shocked and completely disenchanted, Bowling makes plans to get at least a relaxing few days from the trip when a bomber accidentally drops a bomb close by, killing and wounding several people. In thorough disgust, Bowling packs, leaves, and returns home to face his wife, who has somehow found out where he has gone, although his motives for going will be forever incomprehensible to her.

A plot summary of the novel fails to do justice to the subtle tonal shifts and complicated psychological changes Orwell employs in presenting his portrait of the average man waiting for the Apocalypse. Orwell uses the ancient theme of the double (or doppelgänger) to illustrate the self-fragmentation of European man prior to the outbreak of the war. George Bowling is divided into two "selves." Tubby is the outwardly fat, insensitive insurance tout who is able to function successfully in a fast-paced, competitive world that would eat up less hardened personalities, but his character can survive only at the cost of any sort of satisfying inner life. Georgie, on the other hand, would be lost in the modern rat race and so is protected by Tubby; nevertheless, Georgie can give expression to the memories, the sensitivities, the love for natural pleasures that Tubby (and George Bowling) would have to forgo to remain functional. Thus, George Bowling devised a strategy for living both materially successfully and psychologically well in the modern world, doing so by splitting his identity into Tubby and Georgie. *Coming Up for Air* details the ongoing dialogue between these two "selves"—a conversation that reflects the strains of modern living as well as any other novelist has done in the twentieth century.

Furthermore, Orwell has modified the literary conventions of the doppelgänger to suit his own needs. Whereas the death of one-half of the double usually means the destruction, ultimately, of both, Orwell has Tubby live on after Georgie is symbolically destroyed by the bombing plane. The tonal change at this point, rather like the tonal change in Joseph Heller's *Catch-22* (1961) with the death of Kid Sampson, shows the reader the world that Orwell envisioned between 1938 and 1939, one horrible enough to prevent total escape even by death. It is, however, typically Orwellian that however horrible human bondage can make the cultural world, nature, of which humankind is a part, has enough ebullient energy to wait out any social mess—a wait without immediate hope, without idols, but also without hopeless despair. George Bowling leaves Lower Binfield, returning to his scold of a wife, Hilda; to the everlasting round of bills, worries, war clouds on the horizon, and a death-in-life without Georgie—but, as the novel's epigraph states, "He's dead, but he won't lie down."

ANIMAL FARM

Animal Farm is one of those rare books before which critics lay down their pens. As a self-contained "fairy story," the book can be read and understood by children not old enough to pronounce most of the words in an average junior high school history text. As a political satire, *Animal Farm* can be highly appreciated by those who actually lived through the terrible days of World War II. As an allegory concerned with the limitations and abuses of political power, the novel has been pored over eagerly by several generations of readers.

The novel is built around historical events in the Soviet Union from before the October Revolution to the end of World War II; it does this by using the frame of reference of animals in a farmyard, the Manor Farm, owned by a Mr. Jones. Drunk most of the time and, like Czar Nicholas II of Russia in the second decade of the twentieth century, out of touch with the governed, Jones neglects his farm (allegorically representing the Soviet Union, or by extension, almost any oppressed country), causing much discontent and resentment among his animals. One day, after Jones does his nightly rounds, Major, an imposing pig (Vladimir Ilich Lenin), tells the other animals of a dream he has had concerning theories about the way they have been living. Animals have been exploited by Mr. Jones and humankind generally, but Major has dreamed of a time when they will throw over their yokes and live free, sharing equally both the profits and the hazards of their work. Major teaches the animals the words to a song, "Beasts of England" (The Internationale), and tells them to look to the future and the betterment of all animals; three days later he dies.

The smartest of the animals, the pigs, are aroused by his speech and by the song; they secretly learn to read and write, developing a philosophical system called animalism (Communism, Bolshevism) whose principles are taught to all the animals. When Jones forgets one day to feed them (as Russians starved near the end of their involvement in World War I), the animals revolt spontaneously, driving out Jones, his wife (Russian nobility), and Moses, the raven (the Russian Orthodox Church). The animals rejoice, feeling a sense of camaraderie and esprit de corps, and set about to build a new life.

The pigs, however, by taking on the responsibility of organization, also take over certain decision-making processes—as well as all the milk and apples; in fact, Orwell has himself stated that the first sign of corruption, the taking of the cow's milk, led to the inevitable destruction of everything else. Two pigs in particular, Snowball (Leon Trotsky) and Napoleon (Joseph Stalin), argue constantly, while a third, Squealer (*Pravda*, Tass) appears more than happy to endorse any course of action with his adroit use of language and his physical habit of skipping from side to side as he speaks. After changing the name from Manor Farm to Animal Farm, the pigs paint on the side of the barn the seven commandments of animalism, the most important being: "All animals are equal." Meanwhile, Napoleon has been privately raising puppies born on the farm after the overthrow of Jones, puppies that develop into savage attack dogs (secret police, People's Commissariat of Internal Affairs, or NKVD); with these, he will one day drive off the farm all of his personal enemies, especially the brilliant theoretician Snowball. Also soon to be lost to Animal Farm is Mollie (the bourgeoisie), who shows up at Pilkingtons (the West, England).

At this point, the work becomes more difficult, the pigs assume practical control, and the arguments become more intense. Even though Benjamin, the donkey (Tolstoyan intellectuals), remains cynical about the supposed heaven on earth, Boxer, the horse (the peasantry), vows to work harder; nevertheless, the animals continue to lose their spirit and cohesiveness until attacked by Farmer Jones, who tries to regain the Farm. Because of Snowball's brilliant strategy, Jones is driven off in what is thereafter called the Battle of the Cowshed (the Civil War).

Following the victory celebration, Snowball and Napoleon move toward a decisive parting: The former wants to move full speed ahead with the building of the windmill (permanent revolution), while the latter thinks the most important task immediately ahead is the increase in food production (develop socialism in Russia first). After much debate and just before what could be an affirmative vote for Snowball's policies, Napoleon unleashes his secretly kept dogs on his rival, chasing him out of Animal Farm forever. Henceforth, the unchallenged leader abolishes Sunday meetings, increasingly changes rules at will, and even announces that the building of the windmill was his idea.

The animals continue to work hard, still believing that they are working for themselves. The changes Napoleon institutes, however, are so at variance with the initial rules of Animal Farm, and life gets to be so much drudgery, that no one has the memory to recall the ideals of the past, nor the energy to change the present—even if memories were sound.

Very soon, life at Animal Farm seems indistinguishable from the life the animals led at Manor Farm. Orwell is not so much ultimately pessimistic as he is realistically moral: Institutionalized hierarchy begets privilege, which begets corruption of power. The first mistake of the animals was to give over their right to decide who got the milk and apples. Lord Action's famous statement could not be more appropriate: "Power tends to corrupt; absolute power corrupts absolutely."

Nineteen Eighty-Four

Nineteen Eighty-Four is Orwell's most famous work. As a fantasy set in the future, the novel has terrified readers for more than thirty years—frightened them into facing the prospect of the ultimate tyranny: mind control. As a parody of conditions in postwar England, it is, as Anthony Burgess argues in his novel *1985* (1978), a droll, rather Swiftean exaggeration of then current trends straining the social and political fabric of British culture. As a critique of the way in which human beings construct their social reality, the novel has so affected the modern world that much of its language (like that of its predecessor, *Animal Farm*) has entered into the everyday language of English-speaking peoples everywhere: "doublethink," "newspeak," "thoughtcrime," and "Big Brother." Bernard Crick has argued that *Nineteen Eighty-Four* is intimately related to *Animal Farm* and that both works convey Orwell's most important message: Liberty means telling people what they do not want to hear. If the vehicle for the telling gets corrupted, then the message itself will always be corrupted, garbled; finally, the very thoughts that led to the utterances in the first place will be shackled, constrained not only from the outside but also from the inside. To think clearly, to speak openly and precisely, was a heritage Englishmen received from their glorious past; it was a legacy so easily lost that it needed to be guarded fiercely, lest those who promulgated ideologies of right or left took away what had been won with such difficulty. That was where the danger lay, with those who practiced the "smelly little orthodoxies" that are still "contending for our souls."

The story begins with a man named Winston Smith, who is hurrying home on a cold, windy April day as the clocks are striking thirteen. With this ominous beginning, the reader is quickly plunged into a gritty, decaying world where the political order so dominates everyday life that independent thought is a crime, love is forbidden, and language seems to say the opposite of what one has normally come to expect. As Winston's daily life unfolds, the reader quickly learns that the whole world has been divided into three geographical areas: Oceania, Eurasia, and Eastasia. All are engaged in perpetual warfare with one or both of the others, not for territorial or religious reasons but primarily for social control. At some point, atomic warfare had made total war unthinkable, yet it suits the political leaders of Oceania (the same is also true of the other two political areas) to keep the population in a general state of anxiety about foreign attack. Under the guise of national concern, Oceania's leaders keep the population under their collective thumb through the use of propaganda (from the Ministry of Truth), through outright, brutally applied force (from the Ministry of Love), through eternally short rations (Ministry of Plenty), and through the waging of perpetual war (Ministry of Peace). The ruling elite, called the Inner Party, make up only 2 percent of the population; the Outer Party, the next 13 percent. The remainder, some 85 percent of the population, make up the oppressed masses; those in this group are called Proles.

Winston, a member of the Outer Party, has been disturbed by strange thoughts of late, and one day he purchases a small, bound volume of blank paper, a diary in which he can record his most private thoughts without being observed by the omnipresent telescreen manned by members of the Thought Police. In his diary, he records his first thought: "Down with Big Brother!" To compound such a heinous thoughtcrime, he begins a liaison with a pretty young woman, a member of the Anti-Sex League, named Julia. After their affair has progressed for some time, they are contacted by a man named O'Brien, who enlists their aid in combating Big Brother by joining a group called the Brotherhood. O'Brien gives Winston a book, written by a man named Emannuel Goldstein, called *The Theory and Practice of Oligarchical Collectivism*. Having made love to Julia in a room rented from an old Prole (secretly a member of the Thought Police), Winston begins reading to her from Goldstein's book, actually an exposition of the theory that Orwell has used to construct *Nineteen Eighty-Four*.

Although Winston is fascinated, Julia, a rebel from the waist down only, falls asleep, and, after a while, so does Winston. They awake many hours later, are captured by the Thought Police, who apparently knew of their hideaway from the first, and are taken to rooms in the Ministry of Love. There, they find that O'Brien is in reality a member of the Thought Police; he alternately tortures and debates with Winston, trying to convince him that he must love Big Brother.

When torture fails, Winston is taken to Room 101, where he will be subjected to that which he fears most—in his case, rats. He gives in, begs them to "do it to Julia," and is ultimately convinced that he loves Big Brother. The novel ends as Winston, having exchanged mutual conversations of betrayal with Julia, sits at the Chestnut Café drinking Victory Gin, completely brainwashed and committed to Big Brother.

Much has been said about the ultimate pessimism of *Nineteen Eighty-Four* being related to Orwell's fatal illness, which he fought unsuccessfully during the composition of the novel. If, however, one thinks of Orwell's fiction less in biographical terms and more in relation to artistic intention, then such a conclusion could be subject to argument. Although the novel ends with Winston in what Northrop Frye called the sixth level of irony, unrelieved bondage, one should draw a distinction, as Orwell does in his other writings (most notably in the essay "A Good Word for the Vicar of Bray"), between humans' actions as cultural beings and their activities as creatures of planet Earth, natural beings.

As political creatures, humans and their purely cultural institutions could, Orwell believes, develop a world such as the one portrayed in *Nineteen Eighty-Four*. This would be impossible, however, for humans as biological residents of the planet Earth. Humankind never displays hubris more graphically than does O'Brien in his speech about the party's supposed control of nature. In Orwell's view, human beings will never fully control nature, because they are only a part of what they wish to control. The great chestnut tree blossoming over Winston and his degeneration as a free being is Orwell's symbol indicating that the natural world can outlast humankind's cultural and political aberrations. "The planting of a tree," says Orwell, "if [it] takes root . . . will far outlive the visible effect of any of your other actions, good or evil." If there is hope for Oceania in the Proles, perhaps it is because they are instinctively closer to the natural world symbolized by the chestnut tree. Nevertheless, whether one thinks there is any hope for the people of that world or not, their existence has served as a warning to the larger world: The price of the right to tell people what they do not want to hear is never too high to pay.

John V. Knapp

OTHER MAJOR WORKS

NONFICTION: *Down and Out in Paris and London*, 1933; *The Road to Wigan Pier*, 1937; *Homage to Catalonia*, 1938; *Inside the Whale, and Other Essays*, 1940; *The Lion and the Unicorn*, 1941; *Critical Essays*, 1946 (also known as *Dickens, Dali, and Others*); *Shoot-*

ing an Elephant, and Other Essays, 1950; *Such, Such Were the Joys*, 1953; *The Collected Essays, Journalism, and Letters of George Orwell*, 1968 (4 volumes; Sonia Orwell and Ian Angus, editors); *Orwell: The War Broadcasts*, 1985 (also known as *Orwell: The War Commentaries*, 1986); *The Lost Orwell*, 2006 (Peter Davison, editor).

MISCELLANEOUS: *Orwell: The Lost Writings*, 1985; *The Complete Works of George Orwell*, 1986-1998 (20 volumes; Peter Davison, editor).

Bibliography

Bloom, Harold, ed. *George Orwell*. Updated ed. New York: Chelsea House, 2007. Collection of essays provides analyses of Orwell's works, including the novels *Animal Farm, Nineteen Eighty-Four*, and *Coming Up for Air*. Includes bibliography, chronology, and index.

Bowker, Gordon. *Inside George Orwell*. New York: Palgrave Macmillan, 2003. Biography presents the "human face" of Orwell, describing his inner emotional life and its relationship to his political activities and ideas. One of the better books about Orwell to be published in the centenary year of his birth.

Crick, Bernard. *George Orwell: A Life*. Boston: Little, Brown, 1980. Important full-scale biography considers all phases of Orwell's career, drawing on extensive use of the writer's archives and other manuscript sources as well as numerous publications. Crick was the first biographer of Orwell to benefit from unlimited rights of quotation from Orwell's works held under copyright.

Davison, Peter. *George Orwell: A Literary Life*. New York: St. Martin's Press, 1996. Follows the course of Orwell's career as a writer. Includes background chapters explaining Orwell's origins, but focuses chiefly on his literary influences and relationships, such as those with his publishers and editors.

Hitchens, Christopher. *Why Orwell Matters*. New York: Basic Books, 2002. Emphasizes Orwell's criticism of Nazism and Stalinism—philosophies toward which he never softened his view in order to sell books. Argues that Orwell's analyses of those two governmental systems continue to apply in the early twenty-first century.

Holderness, Graham, Bryan Loughrey, and Nahem Yousaf, eds. *George Orwell*. New York: St. Martin's Press, 1998. Collection of essays on Orwell's novels covers topics such as his use of allegory, his politics, his view of England, and his handling of form, character, and theme. Includes bibliography.

Meyers, Jeffrey. *Orwell: Wintry Conscience of a Generation*. New York: W. W. Norton, 2000. Well-researched biography provides a balanced look at Orwell's life and work. Vividly describes the contrast between Orwell the writer and Orwell the man.

Reilly, Patrick. *"Nineteen Eighty-Four": Past, Present, and Future*. Boston: Twayne, 1989. Spirited defense of Orwell's last novel upholds the author's conceptions against the claims of modern detractors. Contains a detailed chronology and an annotated bibliography.

Rodden, John, ed. *The Cambridge Companion to George Orwell*. New York: Cambridge University Press, 2007. Collection of essays provides information on a wide range of Orwell's works and literary influences. Some of the essays analyze *Animal Farm* and *Nineteen Eighty-Four*; others discuss Orwell's response to the political events of his time.

Sandison, Alan. *George Orwell After "Nineteen Eighty-Four."* New York: Macmillan, 1986. Interpretive work views Orwell's writings as a reflection of a long intellectual tradition of religious and philosophical individualism. A lengthy postscript presents Sandison's views on other works about Orwell.

Saunders, Loraine. *The Unsung Artistry of George Orwell: The Novels from "Burmese Days" to "Nineteen Eighty-Four."* Burlington, Vt.: Ashgate, 2008. Offers reappraisal of all of Orwell's novels, arguing that the novels published in the 1930's deserve as much credit as the subsequent works. Examines the influences of writer George Gissing and of 1930's politics on Orwell's work, and also discusses Orwell's depictions of women.

Shelden, Michael. *Orwell: The Authorized Biography*. New York: HarperCollins, 1991. Extensive, detailed work helps to place Orwell's works within the context of the events of his life. Includes notes and a bibliography.

AMOS OZ

Born: Jerusalem, British Mandate of Palestine (now in Israel); May 4, 1939
Also known as: Amos Klausner

Principal long fiction

Makom aher, 1966 (*Elsewhere, Perhaps*, 1973)
Mikha'el sheli, 1968 (*My Michael*, 1972)
Laga 'at ba-mayim, laga 'at ba-ruah, 1973 (*Touch the Water, Touch the Wind*, 1974)
Menuhah nekhonah, 1982 (*A Perfect Peace*, 1985)
Kufsah shehorah, 1987 (*Black Box*, 1988)
La-da'at ishah, 1989 (*To Know a Woman*, 1991)
Matsav ha-shelishi, 1991 (*Fima*, 1993)
Al tagidi lailah, 1994 (*Don't Call It Night*, 1995)
Panter ba-martef, 1994 (*Panther in the Basement*, 1997)
Oto ha-yam, 1999 (*The Same Sea*, 2001)
Pit'om be-'omek ha-ya'ar, 2005
Haruze ha-hayim veha-mavet, 2007 (*Rhyming Life and Death*, 2009)

Other literary forms

Amos Oz is a widely regarded and well-known Israeli intellectual and writer. He has published essays on politics, literature, and other topics. His journalistic essays have appeared in the Israeli labor newspaper *Davar* and, beginning in the 1990's, the newspaper *Yedioth Ahronoth*. His nonfiction has been published in *The New York Times* and *The New York Review of Books*, and his political essays are collected in *Po va-sham be-Erets-Yisra'el bi-setav* (1982; *In the Land of Israel*, 1983) and *Israel, Palestine, and Peace: Essays* (1994). He also has published collections of literary essays, *Mathilim sipur* (1996; *The Story Begins: Essays on Literature*, 2000); short stories, *Artsot hatan* (1965; *Where the Jackals Howl, and Other Stories*, 1981); and novellas, *Har ha'etsah ha-ra'ah* (1976; *The Hill of Evil Counsel: Three Stories*, 1978). His remarkable memoir *Sipur 'al ahavah ve-hoshekh* (2002; *A Tale of Love and Darkness*, 2004) tells about coming-of-age in a period of violence.

Achievements

Amos Oz has written books in Hebrew and hundreds of articles and essays that have been translated into more than thirty-five languages. He was a visiting fellow at St. Cross College, Oxford, and an author-in-residence at Hebrew University of Jerusalem, Colorado Springs College, and Boston, Princeton, Tel Aviv, and Indiana universities. He was named Officer of Arts and Letters in France and honored with the French Prix Femina for best foreign novel published in France. In 1942, he won the German Frankfurt Peace Prize, and the city of Frankfurt also awarded him the Goethe Prize in 2005 (an award earlier received by Sigmund Freud and Thomas Mann, among others).

In 2007, Oz won the Prince of Asturias Award of Letters, one of a series of annual prizes given in Spain by the Foundation Principe de Asturias since 1981 to individuals or entities who make notable achievements in the sciences, humanities, or public affairs. He earned his country's most prestigious literary prize—the Israel Prize for Literature—in 1998, the fiftieth year of Israel's independence. He received an honorary degree from the University of Antwerp, Belgium, in 2008, and in the same year received the Dan David Prize for Creative Rendering of the Past. Oz has been active in the Israeli peace movement, which works for a two-state solution to the Israeli-Palestinian conflict.

Biography

Amos Oz, born Amos Klausner in 1939, spent his early years in Jerusalem. Until the age of fifteen, he lived at No. 16 Amos Street, a place that plays a prominent part in his memoir *A Tale of Love and Darkness*. Yehuda Klausner and Fania Mussman, his father and mother, were Zionist immigrants from Eastern Europe. Much of his father's family was right-wing Zionist. Yehuda, who had studied history and literature in Lithuania, worked as a librarian and writer in Jerusalem. His maternal family emigrated from Poland to Haifa in 1934.

Although Oz's immediate family was not religious, he attended the community religious school, Tachmoni, instead of the alternative socialistic school because it was

Amos Oz. (© Miriam Berkley)

antithetical to his family's political views. He then attended the Hebrew high school in Rehavia. Oz's mother, who suffered from depression, committed suicide in 1952.

Oz was fourteen years old when he changed his last name from Klausner to Oz ("Oz" means strength and power in Hebrew). He left his father's home and joined Kibbutz Hulda, where he intended to work as a field laborer and live by the Zionist ideals of labor, equality, and simple living. However, he found himself increasingly drawn to study and writing and took leave from the kibbutz to complete a degree in literature and philosophy at Hebrew University. As time went on, royalties from his writing allowed him to perform less field work. In 1960, Oz married Nily Zuckerman, whose father was the librarian of the kibbutz. Oz completed his service in the Israeli Defense Forces in 1961, but he later fought in the Six Day War of 1967 and the Yom Kippur War of 1973.

Oz remained on the kibbutz until 1986, when he and his wife moved to the drier climate of southern Israel because of his son's asthma. In addition to being a prolific writer, Oz has been a professor of Hebrew literature at Ben-Gurion University of the Negev. Both his life and his writing are deeply rooted in his native land.

Analysis

Amos Oz's fiction is often concerned with domestic relationships, portrayed in a realistic manner. However, within this realistic facade, his characters struggle with internal conflicts between body and spirit, their own desires and social constraints, irrational impulses opposed to stability, and their faith in Israel tinged with skepticism. While they dream of perfection and long for the Messiah, they must navigate the dangerous reality of life in Israel. Most of Oz's novels are serious psychological studies, thoughtful and self-assured, and occasionally lightened by a mordant humor. Many of his characters believe they are living in a dream world, especially when people they believe they know suddenly behave in uncharacteristic ways.

In style, Oz is innovative. His novels take varying shapes, from *Black Box*, an epistolary novel, to the free-flowing lyricism of *The Same Sea*, which is told in poetic paragraphs that intersperse the past and the present, the near and the far. Among the story's extraordinary range of voices, the reader sometimes hears the ghostly voice of the deceased. Some of his novels have a claustrophobic feeling, which mirrors the claustrophobia of the intense familial relationships they portray.

My Michael

My Michael, published in 1968, became Oz's breakthrough work and made him one of Israel's best young novelists. *My Michael* is the story of its first-person narrator, Hannah Greenbaum, a thirty-year-old native of Jerusalem who is married to Dr. Michael Gonen, a geologist and, in Hannah's own words, a "good-natured man." Unlike traditional plots, this novel is structured by Hannah's slow decline into mental illness during her courtship and marriage.

Michael and Hannah meet when they are both students: he a third-year geology student and she a first-year student at Hebrew University. In the mornings she teaches at a kindergarten. One of the first clues to Hannah's instability is her relationship to her deceased father, whose presence in Hannah's mind is felt from the beginning of the novel, when she interrupts her story of how she and Michael met with the incongruous declaration that she has never loved anyone as much as her father. She also fondly recalls a bout of diphtheria she suffered when a child, from which she recovered reluctantly. Memories and fantasies of childhood are interspersed throughout her narrative.

Michael is an only child, and his family hopes he will be a scholar. After a brief courtship with Hannah, he proposes marriage. Hannah accepts, but she also realizes that Michael bores her. Their son, Yair, is born near the end of their first year of marriage. Hannah gives up her studies in literature at Hebrew University and Michael passes his exams, but money is still scarce. Hannah has a nervous breakdown, and when she is ill, Michael is called up for military duty in the 1956 war, giving Hannah new fantasies of military excursions mixed with news from the front. Eventually, her mental condition improves, and Michael returns from military duty. Their days settle down to routine: Michael finishes his thesis and Hannah is once again pregnant, yet she remains lost in fantasy and Michael remains unable to enter her interior world. *My Michael* is distinguished by the remarkable integration of Hannah's inner and outer worlds and its pattern of significant motifs woven delicately throughout the narrative.

Black Box

Black Box is written as a series of letters among Alex Gideon, his former wife Ilana, her new husband Michael, and Alex and Ilana's son Boaz. Interspersed with these letters are communications from Alex's lawyer Zakheim and from Ilana's sister Rahel, whose calm common sense is in direct contrast to Ilana's passionate temperament, which is still in thrall to her first husband. The novel is further enriched by Michael's constant quoting of scripture; reviews of Alex's new book, *The Desperate Violence: A Study in Comparative Fanaticism*; court records; and reports from a private investigator.

The sixteen-year-old Boaz is the apparent instigator of the plot. Ilana first writes to Alex, who is now a university professor in Chicago, to help her find Boaz, who has a penchant for physical violence and is often in trouble. A boy who deeply resents both his parents and Ilana's second husband (Michael), Boaz is gradually won over by Michael's ability to get his son out of trouble by using his vast network of relatives. Slowly, the reader recognizes that each character is a fanatic: Alex is a hardened officer with the Israel Defense Forces who is obsessed with terrorism, Ilana is a slave to masochistic sex, Michael is driven by his absolute religious devotion, and Boaz is ruled by his thirst for independence.

A "black box" is a term used to describe an airplane's recorders of flight data and cockpit communications. In the case of an airplane crash, for example, recorders are useful for the data they might reveal about the cause of that crash. The black box and its functions are apt metaphors for the novel, which centers on the correspondence between Alex and Ilana as they rehash their troubled marriage and divorce of seven years earlier, as well as their courtship. As the correspondence continues over the course of a year, Alex and Ilana gradually get over their bitterness toward each other. The wealthy Alex establishes Boaz in his own childhood home in Israel. Slowly, Boaz "finds" himself there, establishes a commune, and pursues farming and astronomy while rehabilitating his house. He remains an idealist and perhaps the truest embodiment of the Zionist tradition.

In the second half of the novel, the reader discovers that Alex is dying of cancer. He returns to his old home in Israel, where Boaz cares for him; Ilana and her young daughter also nurse him. Michael, at first outraged that Ilana has rejoined Alex, relents and gives both Ilana and Alex his blessing when Alex informs him that he has but a few months to live. Only in the proximity of death are these four strong characters able to find true reconciliation.

To Know a Woman

To Know a Woman is the story of Yoel Ravid, told in the omniscient third person but confined to the viewpoint of this tired, recently widowed and retired, forty-seven-year-old man. Employed for twenty-three years with the Israeli secret service, he was on an assignment in Helsinki, Finland, when his wife had a fatal accident. Perhaps because of his wife's death and the responsibility of taking care of his sixteen-year-old daughter, or perhaps because, as he says, his concentration is failing, he retires from his job and rents a house near Tel Aviv to live with his mother, mother-in-law, and daughter.

Yoel starts to fill the void first by tinkering around the house compulsively, performing small repairs. He expands his reach to the garden, while his mind is taken up with the past and attempts to understand his deceased wife and slightly impaired daughter. Recurrent images fill his mind, particularly of a paraplegic he saw on a street in Helsinki. He has an affair with an American neighbor who lives with her brother, his daughter finds a boyfriend, and he resists the efforts of the secret service to woo him into one last mission, one that would have been fatal. Occasionally, he gives in to paranoia; he has joyous moments when the sheer beauty of the landscape overwhelms him. His daughter moves out to live with her boyfriend, and although he has deep qualms about it, he heeds the advice of his friends and lets her set out on a life of her own.

Most important in this obsessive, claustrophobic novel, Yoel gives in to his real estate agent's suggestion to volunteer at the local hospital, and there he finds his true calling. Surrounded by bloodstains, filth, and odors of urine, excrement, and sweat, he finds these elements bring him a certain joy; he knows he is alive, removed from the empty life he had lived since his wife's death. He also discovers new powers in himself: He has the power to allay pain, soothe the distraught, and pacify the terrified. He is able to summon a mixture of compassion and firmness that the hospital patients need, and he is often called by doctors to calm a patient impervious to injections. The reader leaves this former spy using his trained ability of concentration to stare into the blackness of disease, trauma, and death, hoping for an occasional flicker of light.

Sheila Golburgh Johnson

Other major works

SHORT FICTION: *Artsot hatan*, 1965 (revised 1976; *Where the Jackals Howl, and Other Stories*, 1981); *Ahavah me'uheret*, 1971 (*Unto Death*, 1975); *Har ha'etsah ha-ra'ah*, 1976 (*The Hill of Evil Counsel: Three Stories*, 1978).

NONFICTION: *Be-or ha-tekhelet ha-'azah: Ma'amarim u-reshimot*, 1979 (*Under This Blazing Light: Essays*, 1995); *Po va-sham be-Erets-Yisra'el bi-setav*, 1982 (*In the Land of Israel*, 1983); *Mi-mordot ha-Levanon: Ma'amarim u-reshimot*, 1987 (*The Slopes of Lebanon*, 1989); *Shetikat ha-shamayim*, 1993 (*The Silence of Heaven: Agnon's Fear of God*, 2000); *Israel, Palestine, and Peace: Essays*, 1994; *Mathilim sipur*, 1996 (*The Story Begins: Essays on Literature*, 2000); *Kol ha-tikvot: Mahashavot 'al zehut Yisre'elit*, 1998; *Sipur 'al ahavah ve-hoshekh*, 2002 (*A Tale of Love and Darkness*, 2004); *How to Cure a Fanatic*, 2006.

CHILDREN'S LITERATURE: *Sumkhi*, 1978 (*Soumchi*, 1980).

Bibliography

Coetzee, J. M. "Whither Dost Thou Hasten." *The New York Review*, March 5, 1998. A review of Oz's novel *Panther in the Basement* that explores a repeated theme in his work: A young boy is at a crossroads in his life, which coincides with a crossroads in the life of his nation.

Cohen, Joseph. *Essays and Interviews with Yehuda Amichai, A. B. Yehoshua, T. Carmi, Aharon Appelfeld, and Amos Oz*. Albany: State University of New York Press, 1990. Each chapter provides a critical look at the English translations of these Israeli writers. Each critique is rounded out by interviews with the five authors. Discusses the relationship of politics to literature, the responsibility of the writer, and the relationship between literature and life.

Mayot, Yair. *Somber Lust: The Art of Amos Oz*. Translated by Margaret Weinberger. Albany: State University of New York Press, 2002. Excellent critical study of Oz's fictional work. Part of the Modern Jewish Literature and Culture series.

CYNTHIA OZICK

Born: New York, New York; April 17, 1928

PRINCIPAL LONG FICTION

Trust, 1966
The Cannibal Galaxy, 1983
The Messiah of Stockholm, 1987
The Puttermesser Papers, 1997
Heir to the Glimmering World, 2004 (also known as *The Bear Boy*)

OTHER LITERARY FORMS

Cynthia Ozick's forte is short fiction, especially the novella; two of her novels, *The Cannibal Galaxy* and *The Puttermesser Papers*, were in fact developed from shorter pieces. Many of her stories have been collected in volumes such as *The Pagan Rabbi, and Other Stories* (1971) and *The Shawl* (1989). Although her literary reputation depends primarily on her fiction, Ozick has also published dozens of essays, largely dealing with the same major theme found in her fiction—that of Jewish identity. Both her essays and her short stories have appeared in such periodicals as *The New Yorker*, *Harper's*, *Partisan Review*, and *Salmagundi*. Her essays have been collected in a number of volumes, including *Art and Ardor* (1983), *What Henry James Knew, and Other Essays on Writers* (1993), *Portrait of the Artist as a Bad Character, and Other Essays on Writing* (1996), and *Quarrel and Quandary: Essays* (2000). Her poetry, which is also accomplished, has appeared in such publications as *Commentary*, *The Literary Review*, and *Epoch*. Her one play, *Blue Light* (based on Ozick's highly acclaimed short story "The Shawl"), had a staged reading in 1993 and a full production in 1994.

ACHIEVEMENTS

Cynthia Ozick has consciously reflected a major literary debate that has been ongoing since the mid-twentieth century. Although she began as a self-confessed worshiper at the shrine of art for art's sake and the formalistic standards represented by American novelist Henry James, in middle life she rebelled against that view. Increasingly, she asserted that an author should be actively engaged in judgment and interpretation and that a story should "mean" and not merely "be." In particular, she hopes to create a midrash, or fictive commentary, on Jewish life in the Diaspora. She sees the overvaluation of art as a form of "idolatry," a violation of the Second Commandment, and therefore a contradiction to "Jewish sensibility."

Ozick's fiction is thickly textured, allusive, and highly imaginative. Short accounts of her work do not do justice to her verbal energy and powerful range of reference. Regarded as one of the world's finest short-story writers, she has accumulated many honors, including the National Book Award, the American Academy of Arts and Letters Award, the PEN/Faulkner Award, and the O. Henry Award. In 2006, Ozick was on the short list for the Man Booker International Prize. Ozick has the unique honor of being the first writer to be awarded the Rea Award for the Short Story. Her work has been translated into most major languages.

BIOGRAPHY

Born of Russian Jewish immigrants, Cynthia Ozick was brought up in the Pelham Bay section of the Bronx in New York City, where her parents operated a pharmacy and managed to scrape by during the Great Depression. At P.S. (Public School) 71, she was a "luckless goosegirl, friendless and forlorn," and she was indifferent to her studies at Hebrew school.

After graduating from Hunter College High School, she attended New York University. She was determined to be a writer. At Ohio State University she wrote her master's thesis on Henry James, indicating her early dedication to that writer. "At twenty-two," she later wrote, "I lived like the elderly, bald-headed Henry James," a devotee of the sacredness of art. The product of this intense dedication was the 1966 novel *Trust*. Ozick was disillusioned with the shortcomings of her artistic accomplishment, "which did not speak to the Gentiles, for whom it had been begun, nor to the Jews, for whom it had been finished."

The essay "Toward a New Yiddish" (1970) marks an important turning point for Ozick, artistically, morally, and intellectually. Literature, she decided, is important not for formal reasons but because it lays out the specifics of life being lived. She attempted thereafter to write fiction that would interpret the "meaning" of Jewish life and the Jewish sensibility. This effort may be seen clearly in her novels and short fiction. In 1952, Ozick married Bernard Hallote. They made their home in Yonkers, New York, and they have one daughter, Rachel, a biblical archaeologist.

Analysis

After her disappointment in her first novel, *Trust*, which took her fourteen years to write, Ozick felt that she did not have the time, given her methods of composition, to write another work of such length and complexity. *Trust* is a Jamesian novel in important respects: its theme of "Europe versus America," its concentration on upper-class characters, its situations of personal discovery, its virtuoso technical devices. *Trust* contains only one Jew, Enoch, a young man who, significantly, discovers his Jewish identity as well as a meaning of history different from that held by the Gentiles in his work cataloging Holocaust victims.

Expansions of Enoch's quest form the basis for Ozick's later work. In her essays, she announced a new direction: Literature is for the sake of humanity, she declared; it is not an idol of the imagination. Literature is a recognition of the particular. She denied the tenets of the dominant New Criticism and its "intentional fallacy," which declared that writers should dissolve their explicit intentions into the forms they discover. This artistic turnabout affected her subject matter. As she saw it, two standards distinguish the Jewish sensibility from that of the Gentiles: The Jews abjure idolatry, which is found not only in the worship of art but also in other secular religions such as Freudianism and Marxism, and they maintain a tradition of interpretive commentary, as evidenced by the Talmud. She seized upon English, now spoken by more than half the world's Jews, as the medium to replace the dying Yiddish language. What she meant by a Jewish literature in English was soon illustrated in her shorter fiction. In "The Pagan Rabbi," for instance, the protagonist, an assimilated Jew, visits a Hasidic community in New York State and is humbled by the spiritual commitment he finds there. A strong narrator, one with a broad knowledge of Jewish tradition and allusive powers, became her principal character.

Cynthia Ozick. (Julius Ozick)

The Cannibal Galaxy

The Cannibal Galaxy clearly serves Ozick's aesthetic and moral program. The protagonist, Joseph Brill, had been a "hidden child" in a French convent during the Holocaust. In his youth he seeks to become an astronomer, to look *ad astra*, toward the cold heavens, to escape what he has experienced. He soon compromises his ambition, however; he emigrates to the United States and seeks mediocrity as his refuge—as principal of a middling school in the middle of the country, far from coasts and foreign dangers.

Brill's idol becomes the "Dual Curriculum," a mixture of Jewish and non-Jewish culture that finds a small, fashionable following but that to Ozick represents assimilation killing the roots of culture:

"When a Jew becomes a secular person he is no longer a Jew." Brill's escape into dullness continues for years, but it is finally interrupted by the introduction of Hesther Lilt, a brilliant and aggressive intellectual. She is a self-described "imagistic linguistic logician" who enrolls her daughter, Beulah, in his school. Hesther fascinates Brill and reminds him of his many compromises. He is particularly obsessed with the relationship between mother and daughter.

Beulah is an ordinary child, without any of the spark shown by her mother. How disappointed the mother must be, Brill thinks. In a central conversation, he accuses Hesther of failing her daughter because she lacks a maternal instinct. In return, she tells him that she is "nothing but maternal" and that he has stopped too soon in maintaining his hope for Beulah. Her obsession with Beulah's development is in fact her idol, and it finally cannibalizes her as Brill's idol has cannibalized him.

Brill, freed from his obsession with Hesther, marries another woman, fathers a son, and sinks into a stupor of boredom and frustration. One day years later he sees Beulah being interviewed on television. In a startling switch of personality, she has become a fashionable avant-garde artist. She publicly demeans her mother and ridicules her education at his school as meaningless. Hesther has accomplished the creation of her idol at the cost of destroying her relationship with her daughter. Brill's son, Nephali, meanwhile, seems enormously talented, a prodigy, everything Brill's idol-worshiping heart could have wished. As he develops into manhood, however, he becomes a mediocrity, "a business major at the University of Miami," showing none of his early promise. The end of Brill's life is a coma of boredom, a result of his having failed to meet life in its immediacy.

The Messiah of Stockholm

In *The Messiah of Stockholm*, Ozick further examines the themes of the earlier novel in an entirely different background. Lars Andemening, a Polish refugee who has taken a Swedish name and who supports himself as a once-a-week book reviewer, believes himself to be the son of Bruno Schulz, a Polish Jewish writer and victim of the Holocaust with a phantasmagorical and prophetic style. Lars has no proof whatsoever of his identity, only his dreams and conjectures from Schulz's work. He seizes upon rumors of a lost manuscript by Schulz, *The Messiah*, and devotes his life to finding it. His quest leads him to Heidi, the proprietor of a bookstore, and Dr. Eklund, her shadowy husband, who is "an authority on texts." They too are refugees with uncertain background, and it is unclear why they should bother with the penniless and apparently deluded Lars. The mystery deepens when Adela, a woman representing herself as Schulz's daughter, appears with a manuscript she claims to be that of *The Messiah* in Schulz's own hand.

Dr. Eklund pronounces the text authentic, and Lars is confronted with a reality that lays waste the fragile structure of his fantasies. The text itself is a dreamscape of Schulz's hometown of Drohobycz, now emptied of people and dominated only by idols who have no one left to worship them. Finally the idols themselves are destroyed by a small bird carrying from the synagogue a bit of hay that had been slept on by a saintly Jew. The text, therefore, declares the fallacy of the idolatry of which Lars has been guilty.

Dr. Eklund urges Lars to use his newspaper column to introduce this literary discovery. Lars, however, denied his illusions and his special status in respect to Schulz, accuses Eklund and Adela of attempting a literary hoax—the actual truth about the manuscript hangs rather ambiguously. Lars burns the manuscript, figuratively burning the idolatrous dream out of his life. No longer does he see his father's eye peering down on him in his sleep. Like Joseph Brill, he sinks into a mediocrity without vision. His newspaper column, now devoted to popular writers instead of middle European visionaries, becomes a huge success. On a direct level, the novel seems to illustrate the truth of the Second Commandment. Questions remain, however—notably, has Lars fared better or worse without his illusions?

The Puttermesser Papers

Ozick developed *The Puttermesser Papers* into a novel from two stories about Ruth Puttermesser (her surname means "butter knife") that had appeared in her collection *Levitation: Five Fictions* (1982). Though the supernatural and the improbable had been common elements in her preceding fiction, in this work Ozick ventures freely into the fantastic, using material from the Kabbala, Jewish mystical writings dating back to the

Middle Ages. The novel's formlessness, improbability, and swift changes of direction show an increasingly greater distance from the ideals of Henry James.

In a manner that suggests Franz Kafka, the novel takes readers through Ruth Puttermesser's entire adult life. Initially she is a repressed, bookish woman, a lawyer and a bureaucrat in New York City's Department of Receipts and Disbursements, still living in the Bronx apartment in which she was brought up. She yearns for a Jewish identity, which her assimilated parents did not give her. She fantasizes a relationship with an imaginary Uncle Zindel and immerses herself in Hebrew and arcane Jewish lore.

When Ruth is forty-six, her regulated life is smashed into pieces. She loses her job in an unfair political maneuver; her married lover, Morris Rappoport, walks out on her; and she loses her beloved apartment to the arsonists of a changing neighborhood. Even her gums are giving way to periodontal disease. Then a miracle happens. From the earth and water of her flowerpots, combined with the sacred name of God, Ruth inadvertently creates a golem, a being whose creation ritual is described in ancient Jewish writings. The golem insists on being called Xanthippe, after the shrewish wife of Socrates, and wants to be regarded as Ruth's daughter.

The story becomes wildly comic. Through the golem's power, Ruth becomes mayor of New York. The city is magically transformed into something close to paradise on earth: Gangs disappear, graffiti is erased, and civility rules the streets. Xanthippe's powers turn to rebellion, however—the created idol, wanting to be human, demands more and more from Ruth—and the city once more decays. Ruth is compelled to return the golem to its original elements.

A major episode again illustrates the idolatry of art. Ruth, a fervent admirer of English novelist George Eliot (the pen name of Mary Ann Evans), wishes to find a mate similar to George Lewes, Eliot's married lover, with whom Eliot had a fabled romance of powerful mutual interests. She lures Rupert Rabeeno, who reproduces the paintings of the masters on postcards (a thoroughly noncreative activity) into a fascination with Eliot and Lewes. Rupert, the unimaginative duplicator, focuses instead on Johnny Cross, the man who tried to imitate Lewes after his death. Once again, Ruth's idolatrous attempts to incorporate meaning into her life lead to personal disaster. Rupert leaves her on their honeymoon in Venice—as Cross left Eliot in the same city.

The novel ends with Ruth in heaven. She had looked forward to a time when she could live entirely in her imagination, with all eternity to seek out the pleasures that fascinated her. Heaven itself, however, is a disappointment. Though everything is available there, nothing sustains itself. Ruth should have relied on the texture of life being lived. Idolatry and the uninterpreted life caused her suffering despite her goodwill.

Heir to the Glimmering World

A departure from many of Ozick's previous novels, which often call on the supernatural or fantastic as plot elements, *Heir to the Glimmering World* focuses on theme and character, centering on the Mitwissers, a family whose world is lost when they emigrate to New York from Germany in 1933. Professor Rudolph Mitwisser, the paterfamilias, was brought to New York by a small Quaker college under the misunderstanding that he would teach on a Christian sect called the Charismites. Mitwisser's passion and field of inquiry, however, is the Karaites, a small Jewish sect whose members take a fundamentalist approach to the Hebrew Bible and do not accept interpretation.

Rudolph's wife, Elsa, was a scientist and academic in Germany who finds refuge from her reduced circumstances in aberrant, sometimes even self-destructive, behavior. Distraught, she largely confines herself to her room and, like her husband, ignores the responsibilities of caring for their five children. It is left to their sixteen-year-old daughter, Anneliese, to care for her three younger brothers and her toddler sister.

Rose Meadows, the primary narrator of the novel and an orphan, arrives into the disarray of the Mitwisser household as an assistant to the professor. She is not entirely alone in the world, as she retains a tenuous link with her cousin Bertram, who took her in after her father's death. He turned Rose out when he fell in love with an active Communist, who eventually abandoned him for the cause. Thus Rose, at the time she is growing into adulthood, settles uneasily into the Mitwisser household as a place to get her bearings.

James A'Bair, a young alcoholic who was once the

model for his father's successful series of children's books based on the Bear Boy, admires Rudolph Mitwisser's work and enjoys the chaotic family life so different from his own upbringing. He ingratiates himself with everyone in the family except Elsa, and serves as a financial benefactor to them. He narrates several of the chapters of his own life in a tone of sophisticated boredom that echoes the emptiness within.

Eventually, James seduces the innocent Anneliese, impregnates her, then takes his own life. Anneliese returns to the family home, in which Bertram, after falling on hard times, has found a haven. Bertram marries Anneliese, whose infant daughter inherits James A'Bair's large estate, allowing the family to partake of comfortable circumstances. Elsa, now a grandmother, rises to the occasion and returns to her role in the family.

Rose, realizing her work in the family is over, leaves to seek her fortune in Manhattan with the excellent secretarial skills she has developed during her time with Rudolph. Her experiences with the Mitwissers have confirmed her view of life as chaotic and subject to coincidence, luck, hope, and disillusionment, yet as Rose sets off for her own life, the reader feels confident she will find her way. By the end of this coming-of-age novel, it is clear that Rose will blossom by escaping the stagnant world of the Mitwissers.

Bruce Olsen
Updated by Sheila Golburgh Johnson

Other major works

SHORT FICTION: *The Pagan Rabbi, and Other Stories*, 1971; *Bloodshed and Three Novellas*, 1976; *Levitation: Five Fictions*, 1982; *The Shawl*, 1989; *Dictation: A Quartet*, 2008.

PLAY: *Blue Light*, pr. 1994 (adaptation of her short story "The Shawl").

POETRY: *Epodes: First Poems*, 1992.

NONFICTION: *Art and Ardor*, 1983; *Metaphor and Memory: Essays*, 1989; *What Henry James Knew, and Other Essays on Writers*, 1993; *Fame and Folly: Essays*, 1996; *Portrait of the Artist as a Bad Character, and Other Essays on Writing*, 1996; *Quarrel and Quandary: Essays*, 2000; *The Din in the Head*, 2006.

EDITED TEXT: *The Best American Essays, 1998*, 1998.

MISCELLANEOUS: *A Cynthia Ozick Reader*, 1996.

Bibliography

Bloom, Harold, ed. *Cynthia Ozick: Modern Critical Views*. New York: Chelsea House, 1986. Excellent collection of essays includes brief reviews of Ozick's books as well as lengthy analyses. Provides much of value for both beginning students and scholars involved in the examination of complications of idea and form in Ozick's work.

Cohen, Sarah Blacher. *Cynthia Ozick's Comic Art: From Levity to Liturgy*. Bloomington: Indiana University Press, 1994. Places Ozick in the context of the Jewish comic tradition but argues that levity in her fiction must serve a higher purpose than laughter for laughter's sake, usually the satiric purpose of attacking vices, follies, and stupidity.

Franco, Dean J. "Rereading Cynthia Ozick: Pluralism, Postmodernism, and the Multicultural Encounter." *Contemporary Literature* 49, no. 1 (2008): 56-84. Scholarly study addresses Ozick's approach to human values in her fiction.

Friedman, Lawrence S. *Understanding Cynthia Ozick*. Columbia: University of South Carolina Press, 1991. Provides an informative critical study of Ozick's work, including in-depth discussion of her novels. Includes bibliography and index.

Kauvar, Elaine M. *Cynthia Ozick's Fiction: Tradition and Invention*. Bloomington: Indiana University Press, 1993. Examines the sources and contexts of Ozick's fiction, focusing on tensions between Hebraism and Hellenism, Western culture and Judaism, and artistic imagination and moral responsibility. Examines Ozick's relationship to psychoanalysis, feminism, and postmodernism.

Lowin, Joseph. *Cynthia Ozick*. New York: Twayne, 1988. Presents an excellent overview of Ozick's canon. Particularly valuable for beginning students whose knowledge of Holocaust literature and Ozick is limited. Offers perceptive and lucid analyses of her major works.

Nisly, L. Lamar. "Throwing Everything Off Balance: Ozick's Fantastic and O'Connor's Grotesque Portrayals of Mystery." In *Impossible to Say: Representing Religious Mystery in Fiction by Malamud, Percy, Ozick, and O'Connor*. Westport, Conn.: Greenwood Press, 2002. Discusses the different approaches that

Ozick and Flannery O'Connor take in their fiction in their evocation of the experience of religious mystery.

Pinsker, Sanford. *The Uncompromising Fiction of Cynthia Ozick*. Columbia: University of Missouri Press, 1987. Excellent resource for readers new to Ozick's fiction provides brief analyses of the major works. Emphasizes postmodern aspects of Ozick's writing, particularly self-referential elements and the use of fantasy.

Powers, Peter Kerry. "Disruptive Memories: Cynthia Ozick and the Invented Past." In *Recalling Religions: Resistance, Memory, and Cultural Revision in Ethnic Women's Literature*. Knoxville: University of Tennessee Press, 2001. Discusses the influence of Ozick's ethnic identity on her fiction.

Seaman, Donna. "Life Sentences." *Los Angeles Times Book Review*, April 27, 2008. Offers an analysis of Ozick's body of work in addition to a review of her collection of short fiction *Dictation: A Quartet*.

P

EMILIA PARDO BAZÁN

Born: La Coruña, Spain; September 16, 1851
Died: Madrid, Spain; May 12, 1921

Principal long fiction

Pascual López, 1879
Un viaje de novios, 1882 (*A Wedding Trip*, 1891)
La tribuna, 1883
El cisne de Vilamorta, 1885 (*The Swan of Vilamorta*, 1891; also known as *Shattered Hope: Or, The Swan of Vilamorta*, 1900)
Los pazos de Ulloa, 1886 (*The Son of the Bondwoman*, 1908)
La madre naturaleza, 1887
Insolación, 1889 (*Midsummer Madness*, 1907)
Morriña, 1889 (*Morriña: Homesickness*, 1891)
Una cristiana, 1890 (*A Christian Woman*, 1891)
La prueba, 1890
La piedra angular, 1891 (*The Angular Stone*, 1892)
Doña Milagros, 1894
Adán y Eva, 1896 (includes *Doña Milagros* and *Memorias de un solterón*)
Memorias de un solterón, 1896
El saludo de las brujas, 1897
El tesoro de Gastón, 1897
El niño de Guzman, 1898
Misterio, 1903 (*The Mystery of the Lost Dauphin: Louis XVII*, 1906)
La quimera, 1905
La sirena negra, 1908
Dulce dueño, 1911

Other literary forms

In addition to her novels, the writings of Emilia Pardo Bazán (PAHR-doh bah-ZHAHN) include essays, criticism, autobiographical pieces, short stories, and plays. Some of her better-known nonfiction includes *La cuestión palpitante* (1883), *Apuntes autobiográficos* (1886), *La revolución y la novela en Rusia* (1887; *Russia: Its People and Its Literature*, 1890), *De mi tierra* (1888), *El nuevo teatro crítico* (1891-1893), *Polémicas y estudios literarios* (1892), *Los poetas épicos cristianos* (1895), *Lecciones de literatura* (1906), *Literatura francesca moderna* (1910-1914), and *Hernán Cortés y sus hazañas* (1914).

Pardo Bazán also is credited with having written approximately four hundred short stories, collected in numerous anthologies. Her plays, which are virtually unknown, are *Cuesta abajo* (pb. 1906) and *Verdad* (pb. 1906).

Achievements

Of all the major nineteenth century Spanish novelists, none has aroused as much contradictory and erroneous comment as Emilia Pardo Bazán. Emilio González López seeks to prove that she was first and foremost a regionalist writer of Galicia. José Balseiro misunderstands the evolving nature of her literary creed and ignores the positive contribution French naturalism made to her novels. Julio Cejador y Frauca fails to comprehend both the naturalistic movement itself and the extent of Pardo Bazán's understanding of the French techniques.

In fact, Pardo Bazán was, above all, an eclectic. The revolutionary period of 1870 to 1874 helped to shape her literary perspective, and the Restoration, years thereafter, caused her style to evolve and mature. These were years of social, political, and intellectual change, and Pardo Bazán, who studied and involved herself deeply in literary fashions and innovations, took part in the turmoil of this period. Perhaps to avoid monotony, perhaps to prove herself in literary circles dominated by men, perhaps because of her innate sense of curiosity, she moved among various literary schools, carefully avoiding extreme positions. Thus, there is a naturalistic emphasis in *La tribuna*, *The Son of the Bondwoman*, *La madre naturaleza*, *Midsummer Madness*, and *Morriña*; a mixture of naturalism and idealistic Romanticism dominates *A Wedding Trip* and *The Swan of Vilamorta*; a Christian idealism takes the form of increased optimism and abstract, religious thematic concerns in *A Christian Woman* and *La prueba*.

A symbolic emphasis is also evident in these two and in other later works. Yet one can apply no precise chronological divisions to Pardo Bazán's various literary phases. The Romantic appears, for example, in her use of historical allusion (as in the stories "En las cavernas" and "Belcebú"), her sentimentalism (*Morriña*), and her religious idealization (*Dulce dueño* or her other later novels). Romantic as well are her emotional characterizations, her dramatic effects, her occasional subjective authorial involvement, and her use of narrative crescendos and climaxes.

Although Pardo Bazán never developed a rigorous aesthetic system, she was an important literary critic. The prologue to *A Wedding Trip*, although relatively immature and lacking depth and completeness, came to be a milestone in the Spanish reaction to naturalism. Of even greater importance was *La cuestión palpitante*, which offered the most comprehensive and candid appraisal of naturalism in Spain during this period. In this treatise, the author rejected those facets of naturalism that substantially distinguished it from realism, as the latter term was then understood. She declared her objection to naturalism as practiced by Émile Zola, decrying its pessimism, utilitarianism, obscenity, positivism, determinism, apparent tastelessness, and truncated view of human existence, in which the author was obliged to omit much of what was beautiful. Nevertheless, she approved of naturalism's objectivity and relative impersonality, as well as its observational techniques and its penetrating study of life's problems. She agreed that a novel should be a relatively close copy of real life, as the writer sees it, and that, as a study of vital, contemporary issues, it must surpass the simple function of providing imaginative entertainment.

Pardo Bazán emphatically opposed the concept that the novelist should attempt to teach through scientific methods, however, believing that the search for truth is not the principal object of art, as it is in science; the artist should subordinate all other aims to the principal goal of attaining some measure of beauty. The real value of *La cuestión palpitante* lay in its stimulus to the ensuing polemics, for which service it retains a measure of historical significance.

Finally, *Russia* was the first treatise in Spanish dedicated to the study of the Russian novel. From the works of Leo Tolstoy and others, Pardo Bazán discovered how realism and Christian sentiment could be reconciled; this perspective coincided with her own deeply felt convictions.

In addition to her work as novelist and critic, Pardo Bazán was the outstanding short-story writer of her day. Only Pedro Antonio de Alarcón (before), Leopoldo Alas (Clarín), and Vicente Blasco Ibáñez (afterward) could rival her, but her hundreds of pieces attest the fact that no one could match the diversity, abundance, and high quality of her short fiction. Guy de Maupassant seems to have been her chief model.

Biography

Emilia Pardo Bazán's birthplace, La Coruña, in the Galician province, is in an area of conflicting cultures, in which modern, cosmopolitan influences blend or conflict with traditional, peasant ways of life. Similarly, her intellectual life was characterized by contradiction and ambivalence: Galician provincialism and traditionalism versus enthusiasm for the latest novelties of Madrid and Paris; social ambition and a desire for public attention versus a feminist emphasis on the importance of the individual in everyday life. A child of the rapidly changing times in which she lived—the age of positivism, scientific advance, and literary revolution—she was a person of somewhat conflicting beliefs. A vigorous, healthy, and ambitious woman, she was one of the most important and outspoken of Spain's early feminists, shocking the literary world with her promulgation of a mitigated form of French naturalism, attempting to teach at the University of Madrid, and fighting throughout her later years for membership in the Royal Spanish Academy.

A devout Roman Catholic, Pardo Bazán struggled vainly to reconcile her liberal feelings with her innate religious conservatism, her support for the Carlist cause, a

Emilia Pardo Bazán. (Library of Congress)

distrust of democracy, and an intolerance of other forms of spiritual belief. She was an ardent expert on many facets of nature, and her happiest times were spent at her country manor in Meiras, near La Coruña.

Born and reared as the only child of well-to-do parents, Pardo Bazán had few childhood friends and associated mostly with older family acquaintances. Her father received the pontifical title of count in 1871, which she inherited in 1890, subsequently "legitimated" in 1908 by King Alfonso XIII's bequest of the comparable Spanish title of the realm.

As a child, Pardo Bazán was a voracious reader, a habit she continued when her family began to spend winters in Madrid in 1869, where she entered a French school. When she was eleven or twelve years old, her parents returned permanently to La Coruña, where she continued her education under private tutors. In 1868, she married a young lawyer named José Quiroga, and the following year the newlyweds accompanied her father back to the capital, since the latter had been elected to the congress that would write the new constitution. There she set aside her reading and plunged into Madrid society. The political disillusionment that followed upon the failure of Amadeo de Saboya as king and the dissolution of her father's new progressive party led the family to travel abroad, to France, Italy, Austria, and England. Pardo Bazán returned to her studies and, in 1874, visited Victor Hugo. A systematic absorption of reading material led to her first writings and, subsequently, to the publication of *La cuestión palpitante*. By 1881, a third child was born to Pardo Bazán and her husband, and by 1887 her trips to France had produced a close friendship with Edmond de Goncourt, a personal acquaintance with Zola, and her discovery of the Russian novel.

In 1887 and 1888, Pardo Bazán traveled to Rome for the magazine *El imparcial*. During those same years, she had an emotional audience with the pope and an introduction to Pretender Don Carlos in Venice. In 1889, she befriended the wealthy, young José Lázaro Galdiano, who was promoting cultural projects, including the literary journal *La España moderna*, to which Pardo Bazán contributed a number of articles. During that time, she had an affair with novelist Benito Pérez Galdós, which, because of the publication of their love letters, was widely discussed. The years following were ones of bitter literary and personal controversy, as she battled with writers Alas (Clarín) and José María de Pereda and initiated her fruitless campaign for a seat in the Royal Spanish Academy. Alas, for example, did not fail to mention Pardo Bazán's increasing corpulence. Also during these years, she single-handedly wrote and edited the monthly journal *El nuevo teatro crítico*, a Herculean task that serves as ample evidence of her energy and indomitable perseverance.

By the last years of the century, Pardo Bazán's novelistic powers began to wane, but during the last two decades of her life she was to encounter as many honors as disappointments. In 1906, she was elected as the first woman ever to chair the literary section of the Madrid Ateneo, and in 1916, she was appointed to the position of professor of contemporary literature at the University of Madrid. Since most students and faculty resented this action, attendance at her lectures fell until but a single auditor remained. When he, too, failed to appear, her career as a professor came to an end. A series of other events had deepened her pessimism and disillusionment: the defeat of Spain in the disaster of 1898, her failure to be accepted in Galician politics, the death of her husband in

1912, her continued rejection by the members of the Royal Spanish Academy, and the apparent indifference of Spanish women to their own emancipation. The sympathy of some of the young writers of the *generación del 1898*, or Generation of '98, did little to assuage her pessimism. Pardo Bazán died in Madrid, on May 12, 1921, after which hundreds of tributes were written, a statue of her was unveiled, and a number of people talked of the possibility of her posthumous election to the Royal Spanish Academy.

Analysis

In general, Emilia Pardo Bazán's works reveal a gradual passage from Romanticism to traditional realism to a modified naturalism and finally to a spiritual, symbolic approach. *Pascual López* is Pardo Bazán's only novel to bear clearly the sentimental, moralistic (in its condemnation of egotism), and unreal stamp of Romanticism, although a costumbristic atmosphere, also of Romantic origin, anticipates the realistic descriptions of later novels. *A Wedding Trip* introduces the physiological element and increased *detallismo*, but still reflects an aristocratic, conservative environment.

Pardo Bazán seems to have experienced a religious crisis in 1882—evident in her nonfiction work *San Francisco de Asís* (1882)—and this event may have been a factor in her subsequent shift of direction. The five novels that followed (and one in 1891) may be considered her most naturalistic works: *La tribuna*—"estudio de costumbres tomadas de la realidad"—contains a prologue in which the author renounces the idealism of Antonio de Trueba and Fernán Caballero. Reflecting thorough firsthand documentation, the work paints a naturalistic *tranche de vie* among tobacco-shop workers and includes detailed psychological descriptions and "crude" dialogue. In *The Swan of Vilamorta*, realistic elements are mixed with some Romantic sentiments. *The Son of the Bondwoman* and its sequel, *La madre naturaleza*, are both set in the author's native Galicia and are perhaps the most naturalistic of Pardo Bazán's novels. The second, particularly, demonstrates the force of environmental influence beyond the theoretical limits she had set in her treatises on realism and naturalism. *Midsummer Madness* is naturalistic in some of its details but seems far from Zola in its happy tone, its aristocratic milieu, and its general lack of detailed descriptions. *Morriña* contains "interior" symbolic and psychological elements that suggest the author's future direction. *The Angular Stone* recounts in naturalistic fashion the determining forces upon its characters, but has an inordinate amount of didactic content.

With *A Christian Woman* and its continuation, *La prueba*, Pardo Bazán's focus changes somewhat. Here and in two subsequent novels—*La quimera* and *La sirena negra*—a new spirituality, a stress on transcendent ideas and character introspection, and less exterior and regionalistic *detallismo* announce a new tendency. Her study of the Russian novel, along with a change in perspective linked with the approach of old age, led her to voice preoccupations that had never really been absent from her writing. In *La quimera*, modernistic and symbolic elements placed in an elegant, aristocratic social milieu indicate further shifts of viewpoint. *Dulce dueño*, which was inspired by the life and death of Santa Catalina de Alejandría, is equally alien to the author's earlier ventures into naturalism.

Pardo Bazán's native Galicia is the setting of her best novels; this region inspired her to an exact depiction of landscape, racial characters, customs, and local ways of thought. Nevertheless, she was able to give her settings and her plots an almost cosmopolitan breadth. Her regionalism was not the *huerto hermoso* of Pereda. Her characterizations went deep, generally avoiding rustic picturesqueness and *dialectismos* in re-creating local speech. Thus, she transcended the confines of strict regionalism.

Pardo Bazán's realism is a special, Spanish mixture of the real and the "ideal." Her eclectic variations in choosing points of emphasis, her psychological involvement with her characters, her avoidance of constant, local speech patterns or her use of linguistic *extranjerismos* and *arcaísmos*, her conscious attempt to create beauty—all of these elements demonstrate that she, too, found her own realistic approach. Indeed, her work is relatively free of two of the recurrent components of Spanish realistic writing: the middle-class backdrop and the consistent use of common, colloquial language.

Mary Giles has argued that an impressionistic bent for describing fleeting colors and the momentary effects of light, and for sketching changing images without a fixed "reality," appears in Pardo Bazán's novels that "represent her modified naturalism"; this impressionism is abandoned entirely in the novels between *La madre naturaleza* and *La quimera* and is resumed in her last three novels. An analysis of *The Son of the Bondwoman* will illustrate how, among other factors, new rich and coloristic linguistic effects are joined with a depth of psychological penetration to produce a realism that is uniquely Pardo Bazán's even while it remains utterly Spanish.

THE SON OF THE BONDWOMAN

Critics have long considered *The Son of the Bondwoman* Pardo Bazán's masterpiece. It was published in 1886, when the controversy over naturalism still raged in Spain. While some commentators have insisted that the story ultimately contradicts the deterministic philosophy of the naturalists, many have decided it is a truly naturalistic creation, both linguistically and thematically. It does seem to be one of the few major Spanish novels of the century that can in fact be termed naturalistic, even if not in the full sense of Zola's methodology.

The plot postulates nature as an uncompromising "mistress" who comes to dominate, almost totally, the lives of those human beings caught within her grasp. Julián, a refined and idealistic young priest, comes to live on an estate, Ulloa, situated deep in the interior of Galicia. His mission is to restore order to the household, since its degenerate owner, the "Marquis" Don Pedro Moscoso, has allowed it to deteriorate. Don Pedro himself keeps one of his servants, Sabel, as a concubine, with the blessing of her father, Primitivo, who wants to use the relationship as leverage to maintain control of the property.

In his desire to raise the manor to a level of moral and material respectability, Julián advises Don Pedro to marry not his beautiful, passionate cousin Rita, but rather Rita's delicate and religious sister Nucha. The priest hopes that this arrangement will rid Pedro of some of his animalistic inclinations. When Nucha gives birth to a girl, leaving her husband without a much-desired heir, Pedro returns to his former ways and becomes indifferent and cruel to his wife. Primitivo's detection of Julián's silent love for Nucha leads to the priest's dismissal from the house. After many years, he returns to the manor to find Nucha's grave neglected and her daughter in rags, while Primitivo's tomb is meticulously tended; his grandson, Perucho, the natural son of Pedro and Sabel, wears fine clothing. The essence of the plot, then, is, in Sherman Eoff's words, "a contest in which refinement and ideals prove to be helpless before their natural opponents," a struggle in which Julián is shown to be powerless in hostile surroundings.

Pardo Bazán's characterizations do occasionally probe deeply to produce some genuine impressions of human preoccupations and reactions. The major characters of the novel possess unique and distinguishing traits, despite their stereotyped roles and their "espíritu de clase." Although it is true that the author often interprets too much for the reader, some characters (such as Julián and Nucha) act out their roles convincingly.

Throughout the novel, human beings are exposed as *bestias*, blending in with the savagery of their surroundings. The scene in which the boy Perucho is forced to become drunk and the dogs receive more care than the people who are present is an early indication of the brutality to follow. Nevertheless, at least two characters—Julián and Nucha—escape such treatment.

The characterization of Julián is one of Pardo Bazán's most vivid and penetrating exercises in psychological realism. He is timid, idealistic, basically well-meaning, delicate, prudish, almost feminine in his outlook. Some noticeably unworthy traits also emerge: He suffers from the sin of pride (about his knowledge, his "victory" regarding Pedro's marriage); despite his active awareness of his Christian duties, he is occasionally cruel or lacking in charity (as in his pleasure in seeing the murder of Primitivo). His irresoluteness and procrastination suggest that Pardo Bazán wanted to convey a message about the need for initiative and fortitude to support good intentions. Finally, he is humanized in his physical attentions to Nucha's daughter, actions that represent a displacement of frustrated sexual aspirations.

One must note that all of these turns of character are made perfectly believable by the incidents or circumstances of Julián's background: He was an only child, perhaps of illegitimate birth; he lived under the domineering influence of a household *ama* of Pedro's uncle Don Manuel; he was not allowed to play with the daughters of Don Manuel and thus had no opportunity to develop normal social relationships; he had in his childhood no contact with the savagery and animal nature of the rural inhabitants; he was further influenced by Nucha, his substitute mother, with her prudishness and piety. Finally, Pardo Bazán uses the characterization of Julián as a medium for further experiments with literary portraiture: the use of dreams, fantasies, half-wakened states, and interior monologues.

The other figures in the novel do not display as much profundity or individuality as Julián. Nucha is a delicate, sensitive girl, an urban bourgeois given to gradually increasing hysteria and romantic, sentimental fantasies. Her nervous and mystical nature directly contrasts with that of Sabel. Primitivo, as his name suggests, symbolizes the forces of natural savagery and evil. Sly, self-serving, and taciturn, his excessive self-confidence hastens his own death. More important, his role furthers the plot, since it is he who dominates Pedro, who causes his "master" to lose the election and thus remain at the manor, and who leads him to suspect a love affair between Julián and Nucha.

Pedro himself is the degenerate, feudal aristocrat of Galicia, anticipating Ramón María del Valle-Inclán's Juan Manuel de Montenegro. His savage surroundings and the lack of an urban, civilized environment join with his increasing marital frustrations to make him progressively bestial. He is cruel, egotistical (he cannot pardon Nucha for her physical weakness), irresponsible, and indifferent, allowing himself to become a pawn of Primitivo's personal ambitions. He does, however, reveal some measure of individuality: He dares, for example, to challenge the political system in order to correct some of the social ills of his environment; his pride in the family line, along with his willingness to marry the submissive Nucha instead of her stronger sister, suggest that a certain inferiority complex operates beneath his facade of machismo.

Sabel likewise offers some semblance of individuality, although she seems to represent the pueblo. She is sensual and animalistic, calculating and provocative, and, in fact, the real señora of the mansion. Nevertheless, she is also humble and submissive; her relationship with Pedro stems only from obedience to her father's command, since she does not like the owner of the Manor and wants simply to marry el Gallo. Thus she, too, is a victim of the environment. The handsome child Perucho, whose devilish and egotistical traits seem to go along with his age, is, however, individualized somewhat by his surprisingly mature sexual instincts.

Pardo Bazán's thematic concerns in *The Son of the Bondwoman* include a condemnation of a number of social or psychological elements: the isolation that has allowed a decadent, feudal aristocracy to persist; political corruption; an exaggerated sense of class rank; pride and the lack of personal initiative. In this regard, however, the novel's naturalistic thrust is most significant. Eoff asserts that "the sinister force of nature which hovers over all the personages involved in the narrative action not only defeats outsiders who challenge it; it imposes itself destructively on those who are natives of its domains."

Further, the author explores in naturalistic fashion certain hereditary influences (for example, Señor de la Lage and his nephew, Pedro, demonstrate similar traits) and stresses other deterministic forces throughout the novel. It is wrong to say, however (as does Donald Brown), that the influence of heredity and environment "is the whole book." Without Primitivo's intercession, Pedro would have won the election and moved away; Julián will go on to live outside this savage region; and, most important, moments of light satire and interludes of comedy preclude any unrelieved, Zolaesque sense of inevitable doom and destruction. The novel, then, suggests a kind of regionalistic determinism. The characters seem doomed, less because of their mere existence as human beings than because of their remoteness from civilization and insufficient religious teaching.

Like all the major Spanish realists, Pardo Bazán assumes an authorial perspective that is only partially objective (that is, impersonal and neutral). While her frankness and boldness are very evident, in some ways she rejects a neutrality of values, Flaubertian *impassibilité*, completely impartial treatment of character, and authorial nonintervention. In *The Son of the Bondwoman* she takes part in her characters' thoughts and feelings by way of indirect free style and interior monologue. She is openly sympathetic toward many of her creations, her tone is often subtly ironic, and she contrives several incidents of comic relief. The last element, for example, is seen in four major passages: the celebration in Naya (the *guita* playing during the mass, the twenty-six courses of the banquet, and so on); Pedro and Nucha's social visits, during which, for example, the sister of the archpriest of Loiro had niches cut into her dining room table in order to "accommodate their stomachs"; the preparations for the hunting expedition and the merciless fun that the hunters make of the bungling Julián; and, finally, the satire of the corrupt elections and *caciquismo* of the area, in which voting urns are stolen or destroyed and the priests Tuerto and Limioso rout the drunken, rejoicing liberals. Julián's naïveté (as in his initial ignorance of the relationship among Pedro, Sabel, and Perucho and in his pious reluctance to touch the volumes of Voltaire and Jean-Jacques Rousseau) further exemplifies Pardo Bazán's subjective humor.

Finally, with respect to authorial perspective, one should note that, while the body of the narrative is presented from Julián's moralizing point of view, the perspective suddenly changes in chapter 28 to that of Perucho. In this chapter, the lad actually enacts Julián's fantasy: He escapes with the one he has "loved" (the daughter of Nucha, rather than Nucha herself). This change in perspective allows the author to avoid presenting directly the violence of Primitivo's assassination and the emotional confrontation of Pedro, Julián, and Nucha. In such ways Pardo Bazán escapes some of the brutal candor that often marks naturalistic novels.

Pardo Bazán's language is exact, rich, and permeated by *detallismo*. One is struck by the *solidez* of style, manifested in the frequent use of strong nouns, adjectives, and verbs. The vocabulary is remarkably varied and expressive; in the first few pages alone, Julián's horse is referred to as a *jinete*, *rocín*, *jaco*, *corcel*, *hípica*, *cuartago*, *cabalgadura*, *bestia*, *raza caballar*, and *caballo*. Although she apparently made no exhaustive effort to capture all the Galician speech patterns, Pardo Bazán did not shun representative bits of realistic colloquialism. Her sentences are often lengthy, yet they are direct and unencumbered by superfluous phrases. Often they consist of enumerations of nouns or phrases, at times without main verbs.

The imagery of the novel reflects the general rigor and sensuality of the style but is more moderate than many of Zola's figures of speech. Like the French author, Pardo Bazán frequently included analogies to animals or vegetation to stress the significance of natural forces in human conduct. Also adding to the expressiveness of the work is the rich *colorismo* of her language. One commentator has enumerated at least thirty-five different colors in the novel, of which twenty-seven are variations of hues and shades. Certainly in *The Son of the Bondwoman*, Pardo Bazán appeals to the visual sense more than to any other. "The vitalization of pictorial detail through color modifiers," says Giles, "is consonant with the theme and technique of the naturalist novel, with its strong emphasis on the sensual, superficial layer of reality." Another critic has studied the surprisingly frequent allusions to painting in the novel, as in the *sortilegio* scene, which alludes to Goya, or the many times Julián likens Nucha to portraits of the Virgin Mary.

Next to *La madre naturaleza*, *The Son of the Bondwoman* more completely captures the Galician landscape than any of Pardo Bazán's other works. The atmosphere, not unlike that evoked by Emily Brontë, is lush and primitive, constantly threatening to engulf man in its relentless encroachment upon civilization. These descriptions of a blind and brutal *naturaleza* are meant to reinforce the novel's vision of a spiritually barbaric caste. Thus, for example, details concerning the worms in the library symbolize the destruction of intelligence and spirit in a decadent family.

Certainly, the action of the novel is subordinate to the description of *ambiente*. "The author's attention," Eoff remarks, "is concentrated primarily on the creation of an atmosphere appropriate to the primitive lushness and unkemptness of a place far removed from the softening touch of civilization." At times these passages reveal a Romantic tone, which leads occasionally to extremely subjective "melodramatic swells of ebulliency." Usually the descriptions of landscape are meant to function in relation to the author's characterization. Thus the long opening picture of the forest at night helps enhance the reader's appreciation of Julián's fears. The vista of the countryside at the end of the book intensifies the reader's recognition, and Julián's, that he has failed to change the environment of the manor.

The Son of the Bondwoman, although Pardo Bazán's best work, cannot be compared with the few masterpieces of Spanish realism such as Alas's *La regenta* (1884) and Benito Pérez Galdós's *Fortunata y Jacinta* (1886-1887; *Fortunata and Jacinta*, 1973) and *Misericordia* (1897; *Compassion*, 1962). What is most striking in the novel, however, and what will most endure is Pardo Bazán's language; its richness, vividness, and exactness earns for her an indisputable place among the foremost writers of the late nineteenth and early twentieth centuries.

La tribuna

Among Pardo Bazán's other works, *La tribuna*, one of her early social novels, represents the first attempt in Spanish literature to reflect authentically and sympathetically the life of the urban working class. An experimental work that initiated her naturalistic phase, the story sprang from two months of intensive observation, notebook in hand, in a La Coruña tobacco factory. The naturalistic influence—then at its height in Spain—is explicit in the exact *detallismo* and pictures of industrial squalor, the use of heredity, the social criticism, the incorporation of popular speech, the appearance of a kind of collective protagonist (the factory), technical descriptions of cigarette making, and the utilization of real, albeit fictitiously named, locales. Zolaesque determinism and extreme pessimism, however, are not to be found.

Against a background of the political uprising of 1868, the heroine, Amparo, goes to work in a tobacco shop, where she reads the political news aloud to the other workers and develops an enthusiasm for the republican cause. Instead of accepting an unromantic but stable country fellow for a husband, she allows herself to be seduced by an army captain. After giving birth to a son, she learns that her lover has fled to Madrid.

Luis Alfonso, a leading idealist critic of the times, condemned the novel for its use of crude language and its explicit description of proletarian life. He found the childbirth scene particularly offensive, even though the reader does not directly see it but merely hears Amparo's cries through the wall of an adjoining room.

In *La tribuna* one sees an excellent illustration of the author's mitigated naturalism and a noticeable advance over early works in which the themes are less naturally integrated into the narrative. The author set out to study the possibilities of happiness for a girl from the lower class. Amparo's downfall does not negate the validity of hope.

La madre naturaleza

La madre naturaleza is the sequel to *The Son of the Bondwoman* and traces the love affair between Nucha's child, Manolita, and Perucho (who have the same father). Presented as a new Adam and Eve in a Galician version of Genesis (similar to Zola's *La Faute de l'abbé Mouret*, 1875; *The Sin of Father Mouret*, 1904, 1969), the two are invited by Nature's forces to indulge fully in their sexual instincts. Nature later proves impassive to their anguish when society imposes its incest taboo. After their "crime," Perucho goes off to Madrid in desperation and Manolita joins a convent, at least temporarily.

Besides the account of the protagonists' increasing affection for each other, there is little plot material in the novel. Pardo Bazán was more interested in demonstrating that humans' instinctive, animal side, nurtured by a powerful, inexorable, and indifferent Nature, will dominate over the force of social norms. Most important, *La madre naturaleza* was a magnificent vehicle for rich, sensuous descriptions of *paisaje* and extensive costumbristic delineation.

Midsummer Madness

The sexual theme and a measure of environmental determinism continue in the short novel *Midsummer Madness* (and in its companion piece, *Morriña*), but the setting is Madrid. Asís de Taboada, a young Madrid socialite, accepts the invitation of Diego Pacheco, a charming Andalusian Don Juan, to visit the San Isidro Fair. There she becomes intoxicated and suffers a mild sunstroke. Later, after excursions into Madrid nightlife and a lovers' quarrel, the two agree to marry. Thus, even in the city, Nature (manifesting itself in the sun) is triumphant, but there is no social taboo to prevent their marriage.

Despite the accusation of pornography that accompanied the publication of *Midsummer Madness*, there is little explicitly naturalistic language, except perhaps in the frankness of a quarrel between two women or in a knife fight between men at the fair. The tone, certainly, is light and happy. The short novel is one of Pardo Bazán's best because of the vividness of its costumbristic description—lively, detailed pictures of the fair, the Roma who tell Asís's fortune, and carriage rides.

La quimera

Finally, Pardo Bazán's last phase (as well as her eclectic combination of realism and idealism) is well represented by *La quimera*, one of her finest novels. It concerns the search for success and immortality by a young painter named Silvio Lago (who himself symbolizes eternal aspiration). After he gains a reputation in Madrid with his portrait of a well-known woman composer, he encounters the influence of two other women: Clara Ayamonte, who wishes to marry him but whom he refuses because his artistic drive or chimera leaves no room for love, and Espina Porcel, who introduces him to Paris and then mistreats him with a mixture of sadism, jealousy, and deceit.

The protagonist gradually loses his confidence in objective depictions of reality and becomes enthused by Flemish painting. Standing before the van Eyck brother's *Divine Lamb*—a work that had deeply moved Pardo Bazán—he experiences a religious conversion similar in depth to his changes in artistic perspective. After contracting tuberculosis in Paris, he returns to Galicia, where he dies happy for having discovered the formula for the masterpiece he never achieves.

La quimera is a historically important novel for two reasons. First, it demonstrates the author's attempt to adapt to the sensitivities of a younger generation (that of 1898; Miguel de Unamuno y Jugo was fascinated by Pardo Bazán's study of the artist's search for immortality). Second, the conversion of the protagonist from an objective, naturalistic approach to one of symbolism and idealistic spirituality reflects Pardo Bazán's own artistic trajectory and represents the most effective statement of her mature literary formula.

Pardo Bazán was clearly one of Spain's finest nineteenth century writers. Her novels contain memorable pages of lush, natural description and distinctive character portraits. Equally as significant, however, was her own unique, aggressive personality—her fight for the dignity of women, her complex ambivalence with respect to opposing forces, ideologies, and aspirations, and her courage to speak out on the major literary and political issues of the day.

Jeremy T. Medina

Other major works

SHORT FICTION: *La dama joven*, 1885; *Cuentos escogidos*, 1891; *Cuentos de Marineda*, 1892; *Cuentos nuevos*, 1894; *Circo iris, cuentos*, 1895; *Novelas cortas*, 1896; *Cuentos de amor*, 1898; *Cuentos sacro-profanos*, 1899; *Un destripador de antaño*, 1900; *A Galician Girl's Romance*, 1900; *En tranvía, cuentos dramáticos*, 1901; *Cuentos antiguos*, 1902; *Cuentos de la patria*, 1902; *Cuentos de Navidad y Reyes*, 1902; *Novelas ejemplares*, 1906; *El fondo del alma, cuentos*, 1907; *Cuentos actuales*, 1909; *Belcebú, novelas cortas*, 1912; *Cuentos trágicos*, 1912; *Cuentos de la tierra*, 1923; *Great Stories of All Nations*, 1927.

PLAYS: *Cuesta abajo*, pb. 1906; *Verdad*, pb. 1906.

POETRY: *Jáime*, 1881.

NONFICTION: *Ensayo crítico de las obras del Padre Feijóo*, 1876; *Reflexiones científicas contra el darwinismo*, 1878; *San Francisco de Asís*, 1882; *La cuestión palpitante*, 1883; *Apuntes autobiográficos*, 1886; *La revolución y la novela en Rusia*, 1887 (*Russia: Its People and Its Literature*, 1890); *De mi tierra*, 1888; *La romería*, 1888; *El Padre Luis Coloma*, 1890; *Al pie de la torre Eiffel*, 1890; *El nuevo teatro crítico*, 1891-1893; *Polémicas y estudios literarios*, 1892; *Por la España pintoresca*, 1895; *Los poetas épicos cristianos*, 1895; *Vida contemporánea*, c. 1896; *Cuarenta días en la exposición*, 1900; *Por la Europa católica*, 1902; *Lecciones de literatura*, 1906; *Retratos y apuntes literarios*, 1908; *Literatura francesca moderna*, 1910-1914; *La cocina española antigua*, 1913; *Hernán Cortés y sus hazañas*, 1914.

MISCELLANEOUS: *Obras completas*, 1891-1912 (41 volumes).

Bibliography

Anderson, Lara. *Allegories of Decadence in Fin-de-Siècle Spain: The Female Consumer in the Novels of Emilia Pardo Bazán and Benito Pérez Galdós*. Lewiston, N.Y.: Edwin Mellen Press, 2006. Anderson examines the connections between Spanish decadence and the character of the female spendthrift in seven novels by Pardo Bazán and Benito Pérez Galdós, describing how this character reflects late nineteenth century concerns about Spain's decline.

Brown, D. F. *The Catholic Naturalism of Pardo Bazán*. Chapel Hill: University of North Carolina Press, 1957. Brown situates Pardo Bazán within the literary movement of Catholic naturalism and discusses her connection with the theory and practice of French naturalist author Émile Zola. Emphasis is placed on Pardo Bazán's novels.

González-Arias, Francisca. *Portrait of a Woman as Art-*

ist: Emilia Pardo Bazán and the Modern Novel in France and Spain. New York: Garland, 1992. González-Arias traces Pardo Bazán's intellectual and artist development during the course of her career by studying the intertextual relationships between her novels and novels by major French and Spanish authors of the same period.

Hemingway, Maurice. *Emilia Pardo Bazán: The Making of a Novelist*. New York: Cambridge University Press, 1983. Hemingway traces the literary development of Pardo Bazán, providing a detailed analysis of the novels written between 1890 and 1896, which have all but been forgotten by literary critics. Offers a limited biographical sketch.

Hilton, Ronald. "Pardo Bazán and the Literary Polemics About Feminism." *Romanic Review* 44 (1953): 40-46. Chronicles Pardo Bazán's strong feminist career and the resistance with which her stance was met.

Labanyi, Jo. "Problematizing the Natural: Pardo Bazán's *Los pazos de Ulloa* (1886) *and La madre naturaleza* (1887)." In *Gender and Modernization in the Spanish Realist Novel*. New York: Oxford University Press, 2000. This analysis of two of Pardo Bazán's novels is included in a study of the Spanish realist novel of the late nineteenth century. Labanyi argues that women characters in these novels reflect contemporary anxieties about modernization.

Pattison, Walter. *Emilia Pardo Bazán*. New York: Twayne, 1971. A good biography and examination of the intriguing personality and works of Pardo Bazán. Pattison discusses her most important naturalistic novels. Includes a bibliography.

Pereda, Tina. "Sniffing the Body Politic in Emilia Pardo Bazán's *Insolación*." In *Unveiling the Body in Hispanic Women's Literature: From Nineteenth Century Spain to Twenty-First Century United States*, edited by Renée Sum Scott and Arleen Chiclana y González. Lewiston, N.Y.: Edwin Mellen Press, 2006. Pereda's analysis of *Midsummer Madness* is included in this study of how women authors from Spain, the United States, the Caribbean, and Latin America represent the human body in their work.

Scarlett, Elizabeth A. "The Body-as-Text in Emilia Pardo Bazán's *Insolación*." In *Under Construction: The Body in Spanish Novels*. Charlottesville: University Press of Virginia, 1994. Pardo Bazán's *Midsummer Madness* is one of the novels analyzed in this feminist study of the representation of the human body, the dichotomy of mind and body, and gender issues in Spanish fiction.

BORIS PASTERNAK

Born: Moscow, Russia; February 10, 1890

Died: Peredelkino, near Moscow, Russia, Soviet Union (now in Russia); May 30, 1960

Also known as: Boris Leonidovich Pasternak

Principal long fiction

Doktor Zhivago, 1957 (*Doctor Zhivago*, 1958)

Other literary forms

Boris Pasternak (PAS-tur-nak) wrote only one novel, *Doctor Zhivago*; this work was the final product of a creative life devoted largely to poetry. Pasternak was initially recognized as a lyric poet who synthesized Symbolist musicality and Futurist colloquialism, but after the 1917 Revolution, as he indicated in his address to the First Congress of the Union of Soviet Writers in 1934, he came to believe that poetry was in fact "pure prose in its pristine intensity." During the Stalinist purges of the 1930's and through World War II, Pasternak took refuge in the long and distinguished Russian tradition of poetic translation, and he produced outstanding versions of many classic Western dramas. Pasternak also wrote epic poems on revolutionary themes; two prose autobiographies, *Okhrannaya gramota* (1931; *Safe Conduct*, 1945) and *Avtobiograficheskiy ocherk* (1958; *I Remember: Sketch for an Autobiography*, 1959); short fiction, of which several sketches are early studies for his novel; and an unfinished play, *Slepaya krasavitsa* (pb. 1969; *The Blind Beauty*, 1969), which he intended as a nineteenth century prologue to *Doctor Zhivago*. By incorporating "The Poems of Yuri Zhivago" into the fabric of the novel *Doctor Zhivago*, Pasternak returned to the lyricism of his youth.

Achievements

Doctor Zhivago was the first major Russian work not to be first published in the former Soviet Union. By 1959, it had already appeared in twenty-three other languages, but even though Boris Pasternak had been chosen to receive the Nobel Prize in Literature in 1958, Soviet governmental pressure forced him to refuse it. For the brief remainder of his life, as he observed in his pain-filled lyric "The Nobel Prize," he was "caught like a beast at bay" in his homeland, one of the most tragic figures of modern literature.

Literature, particularly poetry, plays in Russian life a role almost inconceivable to Westerners. To Russians, art, politics, and morality have always been inseparable. From their ancient oral folk epics, the *byliny*, to twentieth century verse recitals and the explosion of samizdat (self-published) works, poetry has helped shape the Russians' responses to social and political issues. In the vein of Russia's greatest poets, Alexander Pushkin and Mikhail Lermontov, Pasternak's famous public reading in 1948 intensified both his listeners' love of poetry and their desperate yearning to witness a Russian poet challenging unreasonable governmental oppression. Pasternak's early poetry, somewhat resembling T. S. Eliot's difficult allusive verse, did not achieve wide popularity, but after the government prevented his acceptance of the Nobel Prize, Pasternak's *Stikhotvoreniya i poemy* (1965, 1976; collected poems) sold 170,000 copies in the Soviet Union by 1972.

Pasternak's moral dilemma as a Russian artist in Soviet society should not be underrated. As *Doctor Zhivago* unequivocally demonstrates, Pasternak was incapable of adapting his artistic message to political expediency. At the same time, however, his integrity made him vulnerable to indirect threats not against himself but against his family and, still more grievous, against Olga Ivinskaya, his beloved "Lara."

Olga Ivinskaya recalled that in the late 1950's, "The easiest way of dealing with intellectuals like us was simply to starve us into submission." For Pasternak, starvation meant a deepening isolation from his fellow artists and the audience of his countrymen, the constant fear for his loved ones, and a continuing horror at the unwanted fame abroad that caused much of his torment, and he eventually bowed to pressure. He signed a letter drafted by Ivinskaya renouncing the Nobel Prize on October 31, 1958, asking only that she write "that I was born not in the Soviet Union, but in Russia." As a child of Russia's old intelligentsia, Pasternak lacked the furious stamina born of famine, war, and the camps, that stiffened the dissent of "men with their backs to the wall" like Aleksandr Solzhenitsyn or Vladimir Bukovsky. Pasternak's literary posture, no less intensely moral, sprang from his commitment to "live life to the end," as he wrote in Yuri Zhivago's poem "Hamlet," recited at Pasternak's burial.

Biography

Boris Leonidovich Pasternak's life was shaped by Russia's twentieth century agony. Pasternak's father, the artist Leonid Pasternak, and his mother, the pianist Rosa Kaufman, assured him easy familiarity with the artistry of the West in their warm and affluent home in Moscow, which remained Pasternak's "holy city" throughout his life. With Anna Akhmatova, Osip Mandelstam, Marina Tsvetayeva, Vladimir Mayakovsky, and Sergei Esenin, the constellation of Russian twentieth century poets, Pasternak grew up in the nervous splendor of prerevolutionary Russia. In his father's house, Pasternak, at the age of ten, first met the poet Rainer Maria Rilke, whose work profoundly affected Pasternak's concept of the spiritual value of individual destiny, and his early acquaintance with composer Aleksandr Scriabin reinforced his youthful decision in 1903 to study music.

Russia's discontent under Nicholas II had been smoldering, and it erupted in the "Bloody Sunday" massacre of January, 1905, adding internal strife to the external drain on Russia posed by the Russo-Japanese War. Pasternak's father staunchly supported the liberals, who succeeded in establishing a Russian duma, or legislative assembly, but after a harrowing year of illness, cold, and civil disorder, the family left for Germany, where young Pasternak was constantly exposed to experimental art forms.

A crucial audition with Scriabin in 1909 caused Pasternak to search his soul for a vocation, and he turned first to law and then to philosophy, which he studied at the universities of Moscow and Marburg. The idealistic Symbolism that had dominated Russian poetry at the turn of the century was being superseded by the more concrete school of Acmeism, founded in 1911 by Nikolai Gumilyov, Akhmatova's husband for eight years. Pasternak was then at work on his first collection of poetry, *Bliznets v tuchakh* (1914; a twin in the clouds), influenced heavily by the Futurist Mayakovsky.

The reforms reluctantly granted by the czar in 1905 had proved painfully transitory, and at the outbreak of war with Germany in August, 1914, Russia's badly led and even more poorly equipped army faced the enemy with disquieting unrest. Lame from a boyhood injury, Pasternak was exempted from military service, but he spent the war years in managerial positions for factories in the Ural Mountains, increasingly impressed by Mayakovsky's strident poetic calls to revolution in the name of the laboring masses. Pasternak's second verse collection, *Poverkh barierov* (1917; *Above the Barriers*, 1959), was a product of such revolutionary zeal.

Boris Pasternak. (© The Nobel Foundation)

The world forgets that there were two Russian revolutions in 1917, and for Pasternak, the February revolt installing the constitutional government of Prince Aleksandr F. Kerensky ushered in a perfect summer, "a moment that transformed everything and opened up hearts and minds." A hope for renewal swept the broad land of Russia, and in those shining weeks Pasternak wrote *Sestra moia zhizn': Leto 1917 goda* (1922; *My Sister, Life*, 1964; also known as *Sister My Life*), the poetry collection he considered his first, in which he identified the life of the artist with the life of the common man. Tsvetayeva, his sister in poetry, commented that during the summer of 1917, Pasternak was "listening attentively" to the atmosphere of the revolution.

Red revolution soon followed White in the Bolshevik rising of October, 1917. During the ruinous Civil War, Pasternak worked as a librarian in the Soviet Ministry of Education; his parents, increasingly dismayed at the political chaos around them, emigrated to Germany in 1921, where Pasternak joined them the following year, shortly before his first marriage. Through the New Economic Policy (NEP), a brief accommodation with capitalism forced on the Soviet regime by the postrevolutionary economic debacle, Pasternak experimented with impressionistic short fiction prior to 1929, concentrating on the relationship between the artist and his society. By 1931, after Mayakovsky's suicide and after his own separation from his first wife, Pasternak had completed *Safe Conduct*, his autobiographical response to the severe problems of conscience following Joseph Stalin's brutal collectivization of Russia's farmlands and its horrifying aftermath of famine and epidemic. *Safe Conduct*, dedicated to Rilke, records Pasternak's successive renunciations of music, philosophy, and the poetic style of Mayakovsky, whom he had once idolized. Pasternak now chose to strike out in an artistic direction wholly new to him, one that Henry Gifford has described as "the rarest kind of autobiographical writing, which . . . deals with living ideas and the mind's allegiance to them."

The title of Pasternak's volume of poems from that

period, *Vtoroye rozhdeniye* (1932; *Second Birth*, 1964), aptly describes the violent inner struggle Pasternak endured through the 1930's, when more than six hundred writers, many of them his friends, perished in Stalin's "gulag archipelago." Early in the decade, Pasternak married again and made two trips to Soviet Georgia, commemorated in his translations of Georgian lyrics published in 1935. Translating verse was in fact to support him and his family—at the cost of his original poetry—for the rest of his life.

Throughout the history of Russian literature, poets have turned to translation to express thoughts impossible to convey to their countrymen more directly. Pasternak succeeded brilliantly, even working with literal translations from languages he did not know. He affixed his own creativity to what he called a "technical vow," a "commitment to immediacy" in which his Russian version transmitted its original in a burst of genuine emotion. Over the years, he translated voices as diverse as those of Lord Byron, John Keats, and Percy Bysshe Shelley, the Ukrainian Taras Shevchenko, the Hungarian Sándor Petőfi, the Polish Juliusz Słowacki, the German Heinrich von Kleist, and the transcendent Rilke. Pasternak's major translations, those that speak most clearly of tragic fate and the possibility of redemption, include the great dramas of William Shakespeare, Johann Wolfgang von Goethe, and Friedrich Schiller. These accompanied the protracted gestation of *Doctor Zhivago*, begun in 1941, when Pasternak achieved a new realization of his Christianity.

In the spring of 1941, Nazi Germany renounced its peace treaty with the Soviet Union and turned to ravage its former ally, grimly forcing Stalin's attention away from the cannibalization of his own people. The German invasion made it necessary for Pasternak to move his family to Chistopol in the Urals, close to the village where Tsvetayeva, destitute, committed suicide that August. By his translation contracts, Pasternak, who remained at Peredelkino, near Moscow, managed to support his family and provide what material and moral comfort he could to his friends. Pasternak's championship of Mandelstam had caused him to fall from official favor in the late 1930's, and when his translation of Shakespeare's *Hamlet, Prince of Denmark* (pr. c. 1600-1601) appeared in 1941, it revealed a personal and political tragedy much like that raging all around him. His translation of Shakespeare's *Romeo and Juliet* (pr. c. 1595-1596), published in 1943, and *Antony and Cleopatra* (pr. c. 1606-1607), published in 1944, were sympathetic renderings of dramas of doomed love that strangely foreshadowed events in Pasternak's own life. His translation in 1945 of Shakespeare's *Othello, the Moor of Venice* (pr. 1604), a parable of betrayal, paralleled the unfavorable reception the official critics gave Pasternak's war poetry volume, *Zemnoy prostor* (1945; *The Vastness of Earth*, 1964).

The figure of Lara, to become the heart of *Doctor Zhivago*, appeared almost casually to Pasternak at the offices of the literary journal *Novy mir* in 1946, the year Soviet authorities undertook a massive campaign, the *zhdanovshchina* (Zhdanov era), against "decadent cosmopolitanism" in art and literature. At a meeting that Pasternak did not attend, claiming illness, Anna Akhmatova and Mikhail Zoshchenko were condemned and expelled from the Writers' Union. After meeting Olga Ivinskaya in October, Pasternak began to see her daily, and the following spring they declared their love.

The joy Pasternak and Ivinskaya shared became paradoxically their worst torment. At first, Pasternak's financial burden was eased somewhat by a contract to translate Goethe's *Faust* (1808, 1833), that archetypal vision of human striving, and after Andrei Zhdanov's death, in 1948, Pasternak received wide popular support for his public poetry readings and his translation of Shakespeare's *Henry IV* (pr. c. 1597-1598), a denunciation of the political principle that "might makes right." In 1949, however, he suffered the first of a long series of heart attacks, and in a government ploy to force Pasternak's recantation of positions unfavorable to the regime, Ivinskaya was arrested, held for more than one year in the Lyubyanka Prison, and sent to a Siberian labor camp because she refused to incriminate him. Appropriately enough at this time of misery, Pasternak was translating Shakespeare's *King Lear* (pr. c. 1605-1606).

Upon the death of Stalin in 1953 and the ensuing general amnesty, Ivinskaya was released, and Pasternak took up residence with her in Moscow. Despite his worsening physical condition, he was supporting both of their families. In 1954, the periodical *Znamia* published ten poems from *Doctor Zhivago*, and Pasternak finished the novel in the fall of 1955. He then started on *I Remember*, which he hoped would be a preface for his collected work.

Pasternak also naïvely expected that *Doctor Zhivago* might appear in *Novy mir*, but after a complicated series of events during which the novel was rejected in the Soviet Union, it appeared in Italian in 1957. Pasternak began to translate again in 1959 after being forced to refuse the Nobel Prize, choosing Schiller's *Maria Stuart* (pr. 1800; *Mary Stuart*, 1801), a woman's tragedy of epic proportion. A combination of cancer, heart disease, and emotional prostration overcame him at last, and he died at Peredelkino on May 30, 1960. Less than three months later, Ivinskaya and her daughter were sentenced to a Siberian labor camp again. Even in the early twenty-first century, on the anniversary of Pasternak's death he is remembered as Hedrick Smith noted in *The Russians* (1976): "Scores of Muscovites . . . quietly . . . [lay] their unpretentious bouquets on his white tombstone . . . all the more meaningful an occasion because it [has] been forgotten by the state and remembered by private individuals."

Analysis: Doctor Zhivago

Boris Pasternak worked on *Doctor Zhivago* between 1938 and 1956, when the savage circumstances within the Soviet Union permitted, but the evidence of his short fiction indicates that all of his creative life went into *Doctor Zhivago*. Incidents, characterizations, and the style of his other stories strongly resemble elements of the novel, and Ivinskaya saw in Zhenia Luvers "the Lara of the future," a sensitive portrayal of the sad lot of women, one of Pasternak's recurring themes. Nadezhda Mandelstam, the wife of Osip Mandelstam, observed that Pasternak could not proceed with the novel until the war provided "a momentarily restored sense of community" impossible during the purges of the 1930's. Pasternak's fruitless defense of Osip Mandelstam, who died in a transit camp en route to the mines of Kalyma, may also have strengthened his resolve to produce a chronicle of Russia's intelligentsia, the "children of Russia's terrible years," as they are called in *Doctor Zhivago*. It became nothing less than his sacred duty.

By 1950, when he had survived physical and emotional blows that were only the beginning of his anguish, Pasternak observed to one of his many correspondents that "love of people and gratitude to the past for its brilliance . . . a concern for repaying it with the same kind of beauty and warmth" were for him "spiritual values . . . at the foundation of taste." He gladly accepted the heavy price for his artistic and humanistic convictions: "If there is suffering anywhere, why should not my art suffer and myself with it? I am speaking of the most artistic in the artist . . . of the sacrifice without which art becomes unnecessary."

Beyond the practical sacrifices of Pasternak's own restricted life, for which political compromise might have meant considerable but soulless comfort, and even beyond the emotional sacrifice of watching friends endure hardships he could not share, Pasternak, in creating *Doctor Zhivago*, had to be reborn into a new form of artistic expression entirely new to him and to Russian literature. The technical innovations of *Doctor Zhivago*, often ignored or misunderstood, are Pasternak's chief means of voicing his major themes, art as sacrifice and its resulting spiritual redemption. In his shift from the lyric to the epic mode, in his departure from the form of the great Russian nineteenth century novels, and in his impressionistic use of symbolic coincidence, Pasternak implemented an effective new medium of fictional expression.

Point of view

For *Doctor Zhivago*, Pasternak deliberately abandoned the first-person narrative he had used in his earlier prose sketches for the less subjective third person, a vital transposition of emphasis by which he could develop the character of Yuri Zhivago in important directions hinted at in his laconic description of the hero, which appeared prefatory to the ten poems published in *Znamia:* "a physician, a thinking man in search [of truth], with a creative and artistic bent." Pasternak's main character, his evocation of the cultured Russian intellectual at the mercy of historical forces beyond human control, is first a physician, his title significantly used by Pasternak in the novel's name to emphasize the duty as healer and teacher that Zhivago fulfills through his personal sacrifice. "Zhivago" itself derives from the Russian verb "to live," lending irony to the opening scene of the novel, the funeral of Zhivago's mother: "'Who's being buried?'—'Zhivago' [the living one]." The name also has a wealth of religious connotations stemming from the risen Christ's question in the Orthodox Easter liturgy, "Why seek you the living [*zhivago*] among the dead?" In his search for truth, the thinking man Yuri Zhivago at first naïvely embraces revolution as the natural result of the czarist repression of the people, only gradually realizing that enforced collectivization under the Soviets means the spiritual slavery of the very souls it falsely purported to free. The truth at which Yuri Zhivago at last arrives, after his long journey through the revolutions of 1905 and 1917, the savagery of World War I and the Civil War, and the struggle for survival that faced his people during the 1920's, is the old truth of humanity's youth—that an individual can be fulfilled only by free choice in pursuing his own creativity, his own love, unhampered by political or social stricture. By viewing Zhivago through many different eyes in the major section of the novel, Pasternak can reflect with stunning accuracy the myriad beams and shadows cast by the flickering light that is a human soul.

STRUCTURE

At first glance, *Doctor Zhivago* appears to resemble the traditional Russian novel, spread over near-boundless time and space and probing uncannily into the recesses of human suffering. Its structure, however, is not panoramic but multigeneric, presenting the life of Yuri Zhivago in three discrete treatments like the movements of a great literary sonata: the discursive past, a personalized and omniscient narrative incorporating many motifs throughout the first fifteen chapters of the book, spanning the years from 1905 to 1929, and dominated by the great duet between the masculine theme of Zhivago and its feminine counterpart of Lara; the brief melodic and retrospective epilogue, chapter 16, hymning Zhivago's blessing on the future of his "holy city" and the world, his song of "the freedom of the soul" embodied in his illegitimate daughter Tania; and "The Poems of Yuri Zhivago," a lyric cycle of love and redemption in an eternal now gained by heroic self-sacrifice joined to the divine sacrifice of Christ. The musical metaphor for the novel is suggested by Pasternak's lifelong love of Frédéric Chopin, not only for his monumental music, in which Pasternak said Chopin "regarded his own life as a means of apprehending every life in the world," but also for Chopin's "wider significance," as seen in the *Études*, which teach "a theory of childhood," "an introduction to death," and "history, the *structure* [Pasternak's italics] of the universe and whatever is more remote and general than playing the piano." Pasternak especially acclaimed Chopin's ability to "utter his new statement in the old language, without examining whether it was old or new."

The gains Pasternak realized by this tripartite structure are more felt in *Doctor Zhivago* than understood, in part because of the spirit of shared suffering that Virginia Woolf claimed in "The Russian Point of View" to produce the "sense of brotherhood" that permeates all Russian literature. In *Doctor Zhivago*, however, Pasternak advanced materially beyond the nineteenth century, employing a strange and lovely novelistic structure to merge past and present and future into a timeless moment of sacrifice and renewal.

Pasternak willingly gave *Doctor Zhivago* priority over the poetry to which he had devoted so many years. Ivinskaya records his assertion, "All my life I have wanted to write prose . . . writing poetry is easier!" Pasternak's reliance in the novel on coincidence, often criticized as violating the bounds of literary verisimilitude, is an impressionistic poetic technique, assembling apparently contradictory elements into a system of symbolism so intricate that each human name, each smallest detail of nature, possesses an amazingly complex signification unfortunately closed to most English-speaking readers. The enigmatic Evgraf, for example, Zhivago's mysterious half brother, appears at crucial episodes in the novel's first section to save Yuri first from physical disaster and at last from spiritual sterility. Evgraf's name is taken from the Greek words for "well written"; he is a youth with slanted Kirghiz eyes and a Siberian reindeer garment, a shamanistic figure who may represent Zhivago's "twin in the clouds," his heaven-sent poetic creativity, not the least of whose talents enabled Zhivago to survive in spirit through his writing.

Balancing the supernatural role of Evgraf is the contrapuntal role of Lara, who has been described as "the most poeticized woman in Russian literature." Lara, brutalized in her adolescence by the pragmatic survival specialist Komarovsky, surely represents Russia at least in part, demeaned by materialism under the Romanov czars, forced into shamelessness by the revolutionaries, eventually perishing no one knows where in the Far

North, yet through everything a genuinely human figure inspiring such a love in Zhivago that he can create the writings that "confirm and encourage" the feeling of "tenderness and peace" that sustains Zhivago's old friends as they read the novel's epilogue.

Lara's husband, Pasha Antipov, clearly represents the spirit of revolution, a slum boy who idealizes Marxism and becomes the killer Strelnikov, a Red commander who typifies all that is dangerously nonhuman in the new regime: "'He needs a heart in addition to his principles,' said Yuri later, 'if he is to do good.'" In one of the climactic coincidences of the novel, Zhivago "the living one" and Strelnikov "the shooter" pass a night at Varykino talking of the Lara they both love. In the morning, Zhivago finds Strelnikov's body in the snow, a suicide, with frozen drops of blood recalling the rowanberries that symbolize Lara, a folk image from ancient tradition: "I shall see you, my perfect beauty, my rowan princess, drop of my very blood." In the final symbolic meeting of Zhivago and Antipov/Strelnikov, Evgraf conducts Yuri, ill and aging, to write and die in the Moscow room where Antipov began his life with Lara, as Zhivago, outside, glimpsed through a glass darkly the candle of love that he was never to forget.

Final movement

Pasternak employed "the simple everyday words of sturdy unceremonious talk" that Lara praised in her lament over Yuri's body throughout the twenty-five poems that form the last chapter of his novel, recognizing with his mighty predecessor Lermontov that "there are words whose sense is obscure or trivial—yet one cannot listen to them without a tremor." This last movement of the sonata-novel that is *Doctor Zhivago* is a cycle praising the eternal rhythms of nature so closely bound to the Russian soul and echoing the religious cycle of the Savior's death and Resurrection presented in the liturgical year. Beginning with "Hamlet," which Pasternak's friend Aleksandr Gladkov recalled hearing him recite in an epiphany impossible to repeat, the poetic cycle opens, like the church year, with the agony of a Gethsemane: "For the present, release me from the cast," the poet begs. Through the Passion of Holy Week, over "Bad Roads in Spring" and after "Summer in Town," the poet bids farewell in "August" to "the image of the world through words made manifest/ And to creativity, and to working wonders" as Russia settles into a "Winter Night." "It snowed and snowed, the whole world over," and only "a candle burned," a small flame of hope that eventually blossoms for the poet into the "Star of the Nativity," "gazing on the Maid," for Pasternak, like Zhivago, believed that all conceptions were immaculate. The poems close upon another Holy Week, the "Evil Days" of a return to the "holy city" on Palm Sunday, in which the "dark forces of the Temple/ Gave Him up to be judged by the offscourings," and upon the vision of Mary Magdalene, perhaps modeled on Ivinskaya (in whose presence Pasternak rewrote many of these poems, originally composed in 1946), who learns "to embrace/ The squared beam of the cross." The last of Yuri Zhivago's poems, "Garden of Gethsemane," returns the cycle to its opening, with the agony of abandonment and betrayal that culminates in the vision of the third day, when

> Even as rafts float down a river,
> So shall the centuries drift, trailing like a caravan,
> Coming for judgment, out of the dark, to me.

Although Pasternak insisted that *Doctor Zhivago* "must not be judged along theological lines," and his prime intention was always to depict the fate of the Russian intelligentsia in the first decades of the twentieth century, the mythic dimension of *Doctor Zhivago* exemplifies the endurance that the religious historian Mircea Eliade argued is humanity's only support through "the catastrophes and horrors of history." These cannot be tolerated, in Eliade's view, if they are at worst only the result of the liberties taken by a minority "on the stage of universal history," precisely the stage on which Pasternak played his vital role.

In reacting against the liberties imposed by the Communist minority on the helpless Russian people by writing *Doctor Zhivago*, Pasternak exercised what the Trappist monk and poet Thomas Merton called "the problematical quality" of his Christianity, "that it is reduced to the barest and most elementary essentials: intense awareness of all cosmic and human reality as 'life in Christ,' and the consequent plunge into love as the only dynamic and creative force which really honors this 'Life' by creating itself anew in Life's—Christ's—image." In the glorious healing lesson of *Doctor Zhivago*, that modern man's renewal lies in identification of his sufferings with those of his Savior, undistracted by selfish materialistic desire, the poet of *Doctor Zhivago* thus is "the living one" against whom godless history cannot prevail. In this remarkable novel, as Pasternak said of all art, "The man is silent, and the image speaks."

Mitzi M. Brunsdale

Other major works

SHORT FICTION: "Pisma iz Tuly," 1922 ("Letters from Tula," 1945); "Detstvo Liuvers," 1923 ("The Childhood of Luvers," 1945); *Rasskazy*, 1925; *Sochineniya*, 1961 (*Collected Short Prose*, 1977).

PLAY: *Slepaya krasavitsa*, pb. 1969 (*The Blind Beauty*, 1969).

POETRY: *Bliznets v tuchakh*, 1914; *Poverkh barierov*, 1917 (*Above the Barriers*, 1959); *Sestra moia zhizn': Leto 1917 goda*, 1922 (*My Sister, Life*, 1964; also known as *Sister My Life*); *Temy i variatsii*, 1923 (*Themes and Variations*, 1964); *Vysokaya bolezn'*, 1924 (*High Malady*, 1958); *Carousel: Verse for Children*, 1925; *Devyatsot pyaty' god*, 1926 (*The Year 1905*, 1989); *Lyutenant Shmidt*, 1927 (*Lieutenant Schmidt*, 1992); *Spektorsky*, 1931; *Vtoroye rozhdeniye*, 1932 (*Second Birth*, 1964); *Na rannikh poezdakh*, 1943 (*On Early Trains*, 1964); *Zemnoy prostor*, 1945 (*The Vastness of Earth*, 1964); *Kogda razgulyayetsa*, 1959 (*When the Skies Clear*, 1964); *Poems*, 1959; *The Poetry of Boris Pasternak, 1917-1959*, 1959; *Poems, 1955-1959*, 1960; *In the Interlude: Poems, 1945-1960*, 1962; *Fifty Poems*, 1963; *The Poems of Doctor Zhivago*, 1965; *Stikhotvoreniya i poemy*, 1965, 1976; *The Poetry of Boris Pasternak*, 1969; *Selected Poems*, 1983.

NONFICTION: *Pis'ma k gruzinskim*, n.d. (*Letters to Georgian Friends by Boris Pasternak*, 1968); *Okhrannaya gramota*, 1931 (autobiography; *Safe Conduct*, 1945, in *The Collected Prose Works*); *Avtobiograficheskiy ocherk*, 1958 (*I Remember: Sketch for an Autobiography*, 1959); *An Essay in Autobiography*, 1959; *Essays*, 1976; *The Correspondence of Boris Pasternak and Olga Freidenberg, 1910-1954*, 1981; *Pasternak on Art and Creativity*, 1985.

TRANSLATIONS: *Hamlet*, 1941 (of William Shakespeare's play); *Romeo i Juliet*, 1943 (of Shakespeare's play); *Antony i Cleopatra*, 1944 (of Shakespeare's play); *Othello*, 1945 (of Shakespeare's play); *King Lear*, 1949 (of Shakespeare's play); *Faust*, 1953 (of Johann Wolfgang von Goethe's play); *Maria Stuart*, 1957 (of Friedrich Schiller's play).

MISCELLANEOUS: *The Collected Prose Works*, 1945; *Safe Conduct: An Early Autobiography, and Other Works by Boris Pasternak*, 1958 (also known as *Selected Writings*, 1949); *Sochinenii*, 1961; *Vozdushnye puti: Proza raz nykh let*, 1982; *The Voice of Prose*, 1986.

Bibliography

Barnes, Christopher. *Boris Pasternak: A Literary Biography*. 2 vols. New York: Cambridge University Press, 1989-1998. Comprehensive biography covers the events of Pasternak's life and his literary works. The second volume contains information about the controversy surrounding the publication of *Doctor Zhivago* and Pasternak's receipt of the Nobel Prize in Literature.

Ciepiela, Catherine. *The Same Solitude: Boris Pasternak and Marina Tsvetaeva*. Ithaca, N.Y.: Cornell University Press, 2006. Clearly written, accessible work examines the ten-year love affair between Pasternak and Tsvetaeva, whose relationship was limited primarily to long-distance letters. Reveals the similarities between Pasternak and Tsvetaeva by painting a portrait of their lives and personalities; scrutinizes their poetry and correspondence, much of which is reprinted here. In addition to the correspondence between Pasternak and Tsvetaeva are letters from Rainer Maria Rilke, who completed the couple's literary love triangle.

De Mallac, Guy. *Boris Pasternak: His Life and Art*. Norman: University of Oklahoma Press, 1981. Extensive biography also provides interpretation of the most important features of Pasternak's works. Includes a detailed chronology of Pasternak's life, illustrations, and an exhaustive bibliography.

Erlich, Victor, ed. *Pasternak: A Collection of Critical Essays*. Englewood Cliffs, N.J.: Prentice-Hall, 1978. Skillfully arranged collection of essays covers all important facets of Pasternak's work, with an emphasis on *Doctor Zhivago* and his poetry.

Fleishman, Lazar. *Boris Pasternak: The Poet and His*

Politics. Cambridge, Mass.: Harvard University Press, 1990. Comprehensive study focuses on Pasternak's life and works written under the oppressive Soviet political system. Chapters on the *Doctor Zhivago* affair are especially poignant. An important resource for readers who are interested in the nonliterary influences on literary creations.

Gifford, Henry. *Boris Pasternak: A Critical Study*. New York: Cambridge University Press, 1977. Chronicles the stages in Pasternak's life and discusses the works he wrote during those stages in order to establish the author's achievements as a prose writer, poet, and translator. Supplemented by a chronological table and a select bibliography.

Rowland, Mary F., and Paul Rowland. *Pasternak's "Doctor Zhivago."* Carbondale: Southern Illinois University Press, 1967. Fascinating interpretation of *Doctor Zhivago* attempts to clarify the novel's allegorical, symbolic, and religious meanings, including the meanings of virtually all the characters' names.

Rudova, Larissa. *Understanding Boris Pasternak*. Columbia: University of South Carolina Press, 1997. Provides a general introduction to the full range of Pasternak's works. Includes an analysis of *Doctor Zhivago*, but seeks to correct the misconception that this novel was Pasternak's only contribution to world literature.

Sendich, Munir. *Boris Pasternak: A Reference Guide*. New York: Maxwell Macmillan International, 1994. Indispensable reference contains a bibliography of Pasternak editions with more than five hundred entries, a bibliography of criticism with more than one thousand entries, and essays on topics such as Pasternak's poetics, his relations with other artists, and his literary influences.

Weir, Justin. *The Author as Hero: Self and Tradition in Bulgakov, Pasternak, and Nabokov*. Evanston, Ill.: Northwestern University Press, 2002. Analyzes *Doctor Zhivago*, Mikhail Bulgakov's *The Master and Margarita*, and Vladimir Nabokov's *The Gift* to describe how character in these three Russian novels is defined as the act of writing itself.

ANN PATCHETT

Born: Los Angeles, California; December 2, 1963

Principal long fiction

The Patron Saint of Liars, 1992
Taft, 1994
The Magician's Assistant, 1997
Bel Canto, 2001
Run, 2007

Other literary forms

In addition to her novels, Ann Patchett has published numerous short stories in a variety of magazines, beginning with *The Paris Review* and including *Harper's*, *The New York Times Magazine*, *Elle*, *GQ*, *Gourmet*, *Vogue*, and *The Washington Post Magazine*. She served as editor of the anthology *The Best American Short Stories 2006* (2006). Her memoir *Truth and Beauty: A Friendship* (2004) is almost a prose poem celebrating her longtime friendship with Lucy Grealy, to whom the book is dedicated. *What Now?* (2008), an expanded version of the commencement address Patchett gave at Sarah Lawrence College in 2006, is dedicated to Allan Gurganus and Alice Stone Ilchman, who were important figures in her education there.

Achievements

Recognized as an outstanding contemporary novelist, Ann Patchett has been awarded a variety of fellowships, including a residential fellowship to the Fine Arts Work Center in Provincetown, Massachusetts (1990), a Bunting Fellowship from the Mary Ingrahm Bunting Institute at Radcliffe College (1993), and a Guggenheim Fellowship (1997).

Because of Patchett's vivid imagery and the lyrical quality of her prose, her novels have been described as poetic and have earned numerous individual honors: *The Patron Saint of Liars* was a *New York Times* Notable Book in 1992; *Taft* received the Janet Heidinger Kafka Prize for the best work of fiction in 1994; *The Magician's Assistant* was shortlisted for England's Orange Prize (an award given to novels by female writers); and *Bel Canto* won the PEN/Faulkner Award and the Orange Prize in 2002, and, a finalist for the National Book Critics Circle Award, it was also named the *Book Sense* Book of the Year. *Bel Canto* has sold more than one million copies in the United States and has been translated into thirty languages.

Patchett's memoir *Truth and Beauty* was named one of the best books of 2004 by the *Chicago Tribune*, the *San Francisco Chronicle*, and *Entertainment Weekly*. A finalist for the Los Angeles Times Book Prize, *Truth and Beauty* won the *Chicago Tribune*'s Heartland Prize, the Harold D. Vursell Memorial Award from the American Academy of Arts and Letters, and the American Library Association's Alex Award.

Ann Patchett. (AP/Wide World Photos)

Biography

The daughter of Frank Patchett and Jeanne Wilkinson Ray, Ann Patchett was born in Los Angeles in 1963; since the age of five she has lived primarily in Nashville, Tennessee. As she documents in *What Next?*, after her graduation from Harpeth Hall Academy (high school), Patchett was delighted when she was accepted by Sarah Lawrence College. Almost from the beginning there, she found mentors such as Allan Gurganus and Alice Stone Ilchman. After receiving her undergraduate degree, she entered graduate school, earning her master of fine arts degree from the University of Iowa Writers' Workshop. Lucy Grealy, her roommate there, became her lifelong friend, and their relationship is the subject of Patchett's memoir *Truth and Beauty*.

Although Patchett briefly taught creative writing at a small college in Pennsylvania, she soon decided to return to Nashville and become a freelance writer; she worked as a waitress until she began winning fellowships to support her writing.

Family ties have always been very important to Patchett, who maintains close contact with all her extended family. She has encouraged the writing career of her mother, Jeanne Ray, who is also a successful novelist. After eleven years of dating, Patchett married Nashville internist Karl VanDevender.

Analysis

Ann Patchett's novels tend to share some common themes, among them the importance of love, particularly love of community or family; the destructiveness of deception or lying; and the grief that accompanies the experience of loss.

The Patron Saint of Liars

A dominant theme of Patchett's first novel, *The Patron Saint of Liars*, is deception. When the pregnant

Rose Clinton decides to have her baby at St. Elizabeth's, a Catholic home for unwed mothers, she resigns herself to being a liar, but actually she began living a lie when she realized that her marriage to her child's father, Thomas, was not God's plan for her. Driving from California to Kentucky, she lies to everyone she meets, and at St. Elizabeth's she joins a community of liars, telling the expected falsehood about her baby's father—that he is dead. Her deception continues as she helps conceal a friend's labor and denies hearing the prophecy that her roommate's baby will die at birth. She allows Wilson Abbott, known as Son, to believe she is unmarried and thus to marry her so she can keep her baby. Her lies eventually force Son to ask their daughter, Sissy, to conceal her age from Thomas Clinton; suspecting that Thomas is Sissy's biological father, Son fears losing custody. In fact, Rose refuses to lie only when the sacraments of confession and Holy Communion are involved; she will not lie to God. Thus she marries Son in a civil ceremony, though he must lie to the magistrate about her missing birth certificate.

A second theme of this novel is the importance of community. Patchett typically creates settings that are isolated from the everyday world, then brings together diverse groups of people who develop a sense of community, even family. Rose adored her mother but gave up their relationship in self-imposed penance for lying. She finds unconditional maternal love again in Sister Evangeline, whom she seems to love in return. Her roommate, Angie, becomes the sister Rose never had—the first of Patchett's sister surrogates. The handyman, Son, is another damaged soul who has found a sense of belonging at St. Elizabeth's. Drawn to Rose, who is as emotionally distant as his dead fiancé Cecilia, he marries her; he adores Rose's daughter, whom Rose names Cecilia. With Sissy, as she prefers to be called, Son establishes a genuine, if unique, family; Sister Evangeline and neighbor June Clatterbuck constitute their extended family.

The theme of loss and resulting grief is also part of *The Patron Saint of Liars*. Son left his home in Tennessee after his fiancé drowned because he had been unable to save her. His wanderings parallel Thomas's journey to find Rose, whom Thomas has never divorced. Coming to Habit, Kentucky (the town's name perhaps an indication of Patchett's fascination with puns), Son met June, who directed him to St. Elizabeth's, where he became an accepted part of the community.

Patchett's novels typically introduce some elements of the supernatural, and that is true of this first novel. St. Elizabeth's was built on the site of a healing spring, which disappeared years earlier. Sister Evangeline is clairvoyant, and in dreams Son is visited by his dead fiancé.

Taft

In *Taft*, Patchett again develops the theme of family or community, focusing the action on a group of Beale Street bar habitués whose world seems entirely separate from the rest of Memphis. John Nickel, the first-person narrator, is a popular jazz drummer who has given up his musical career in order to maintain contact with his son, Franklin, the only person he loves wholeheartedly. Although Franklin's mother, Marion, has taken him to Florida, they and Marion's family (the Woodmores) constitute Nickel's entire biological family. With the regular bar employees (especially Wallace the bouncer), however, this African American bar manager has developed another kind of family. In contrast, although the Tafts have maintained geographic proximity, the death of Levon (the father) has destroyed their emotional closeness. Through flashbacks, Patchett reveals their dramatic personality changes after Levon's death forced them to move to Memphis and live with wealthy relatives.

The theme of loss is significant in *Taft*. In different ways, all the major characters have experienced loss. The Tafts are grieving for their father. Vulnerable because he misses his son, Nickel understands the Tafts' grief; thus he pities the waiflike Fay, hires her (though he suspects her of lying about her age), and allows her brother Carl to hang out in the bar. In a confused mix of pity, friendship, and physical attraction, Nickel attempts to become a surrogate father to Fay and later to Carl; the result is nearly disastrous for everyone.

The dominant theme in *Taft* is responsible love. Until Franklin's birth, Nickel had never loved anyone but himself; he adores his son at first sight, however, and soon learns that with such love comes responsibility. To earn Marion's favor, he does whatever she asks, actually preparing her to save his life. Likewise, because he admires

Fay's sense of responsibility toward Carl, Nickel not only refuses to take advantage of her sexually but also tries to help rescue Carl.

The Magician's Assistant

Deception is a central theme in *The Magician's Assistant*. Sabine must deal with the death of her husband, Parsifal, and the end of her role as assistant in his magic act. She readily acknowledges that Parsifal's magic was primarily deception of the audience, but she thinks she knows his secrets, including his homosexual relationship with Phan. The reading of his will shows her, however, that he deceived her too: This supposed orphan from Connecticut actually has an entire family in Nebraska. Becoming acquainted with the members of that family, the Fetters (possibly another of Patchett's puns), especially Parsifal's sister Kitty, helps Sabine deal with her grief over the loss of Parsifal. In turn, Sabine's magic defuses tensions in Kitty's family.

Another significant theme of *The Magician's Assistant* is the importance of family or community. Sabine is devastated by the loss of Parsifal. For twenty years, even before their marriage, Sabine considered him her family, though her parents live nearby and she phones them daily. Especially after Parsifal's death, the house she shared with him, Phan, and a succession of "Rabbits" seems one of Patchett's typical confined spaces—until the arrival of Parsifal's family forces Sabine to return to the larger world of Los Angeles. When she visits them in Nebraska, she enters another isolated locale, as the snow cuts her off from everyone outside the immediate family. Learning to think of Parsifal as Guy—his real name—changes her attitude toward his deception, makes her a genuine part of the Fetters family, and consoles her as she realizes that they lost Guy before she did. Ultimately, Sabine and Kitty form another of Patchett's recurring sisterly bonds.

All the characters of this novel experience grief. Dot blames herself for Guy's leaving; she views her son's criminal record as being her fault. Kitty believes she should have intervened to help Guy, and in her marriage she has repeated their mother's mistakes. Sabine does not share their guilt, but as she becomes acquainted with their lost Guy, she achieves peace.

Patchett adds an element of the supernatural in this novel as well: Sabine's dreams reunite her with Phan, who explains the afterlife and answers her questions about eventual reunion with Parsifal. Sabine finally realizes that reunion will be her acceptance of his family.

Bel Canto

The dominant theme in *Bel Canto* is that of the importance of community, seen in the harmony that eventually develops among a group of rebels and hostages as they achieve a sense of community within the isolated confines of the vice presidential mansion of an unnamed South American country. Based on an actual four-month hostage crisis that took place at the Japanese embassy in Lima, Peru, in the late 1990's, *Bel Canto* explores the hostages' increasing awareness of their captors' individuality and their growing regard for those individuals. Like the operatic genre, the novel emphasizes harmony among the separate parts as the rebels help the hostages with gardening, the hostages play chess with the rebel leader, an opera-star hostage gives voice lessons to a rebel, and Gen the translator not only teaches the rebel Carmen to read but also falls in love with her.

Patchett's recurring theme of responsible love is present in *Bel Canto* too. Roxane, the opera singer, unifies the community of hostages and rebels. Most of the hostages worship her from afar, and her daily singing calms both groups as everyone works together to provide the musical scores she needs. Katsumi Hosokawa, whose birthday party was the occasion that the rebels used to take the hostages, falls in love with Roxane; Carmen guards Roxane's room each night, and she eventually helps Hosokawa to enter Roxane's room so the two can make love. Separated from the real world, only the characters Thibault and Father Arguedas maintain responsibility to their commitments.

Loss is also present in this novel, as at its conclusion soldiers storm the walled mansion, killing all the rebels as well as Hosokawa, who dies trying to protect Carmen. In the epilogue, Gen and Roxane find consolation, marrying each other with the Thibaults in attendance. Gen says that hearing Roxane sing enables him to think well of the world.

Run

As *Run* opens, the Doyle family consists of a father, Bernard Doyle; Bernard's biological son, Sullivan; and Bernard's two adopted African American sons, Tip and Teddy. Although the four officially share a residence, they are emotionally separate, each son thinking he has disappointed his father. In a possible bow to the classical unities of time and place, Patchett sets most of the novel in the family mansion and in a hospital during a twenty-four-hour period. Confined by a blinding snowstorm and Tip's broken ankle, his father and brothers confront family and personal issues, becoming a family again—for the first time since Mrs. Doyle died.

This attitudinal change results from the sacrifice of Tennessee Alice Moser, who is seriously injured saving Tip from possible death. When the Doyles take her daughter Kenya home with them, Kenya's questions show them they know almost nothing about the nearby poor. Eventually Kenya reveals the identity of Tip and Teddy's birth mother, and all the Doyles come to understand the true meaning of responsible love, although none of them fully understands its depth in Tennessee's case.

The recurring Patchett theme of deception appears in this novel as well. Specifically, stealing is part of the Doyle family heritage. Their prized statue of the Madonna was actually stolen by Mrs. Doyle's great-grandfather because he believed it resembled his wife. For years he lied about how he got the statue, but finally he confessed that he had stolen it from a church. In each generation following, the statue had been inherited by the daughter who most resembled it.

All three sons deceive their father about their careers, but Sullivan has continued the family tradition of lying and stealing. Visiting Tennessee's hospital room, he confesses to her what he has never told anyone: that he was driving when the car accident occurred in which his girlfriend was killed. His father has never allowed him to discuss that accident, and his life ever since has been a downward spiral of drugs and theft. He attempts to atone by taking care of Tennessee and Kenya.

Supernatural events occur also in *Run*. Father John Sullivan, the Doyle sons' uncle, is believed to be a miraculous healer, though the cures do not continue. The dream or vision motif recurs in this novel too, as Tennessee and her best friend, Beverly, are reunited briefly to discuss the life of one and death of the other.

In an epilogue, with the family reconciled through Tennessee's sacrifice and Kenya's presence, Bernard Doyle symbolically presents the Madonna statue to Kenya, telling her that it always goes to the daughter in the family. Each of the Doyle children is pursuing a personal goal, and Kenya's is to run in the Olympics.

Charmaine Allmon Mosby

Other major works

NONFICTION: *Truth and Beauty: A Friendship*, 2004; *What Now?*, 2008.

EDITED TEXT: *The Best American Short Stories 2006*, 2006 (with Katrina Kenison).

Bibliography

Patchett, Ann. "Ann Patchett: The Novelist as Magician." Interview by Elizabeth Bernstein. *Publishers Weekly*, October 13, 1997. Patchett discusses her life as well as her first three novels, with a focus on *The Magician's Assistant*.

_______. "Five Questions with Ann Patchett." Interview by Carol Mommott. *USA Today*, April 17, 2008. Brief interview on the occasion of the publication of Patchett's *What Now?* addresses her message in that work and her political viewpoint.

_______. "Setting Her Own Pace." Interview by Kristin Tillotson. *Minneapolis-St. Paul Star Tribune*. October 8, 2007. Patchett answers questions about the recurring basic themes in her work in this comprehensive interview.

_______. "Talking with Ann Patchett: A Lyric Voice." Interview by Laurie Muchnik. *New York Newsday*, July 8, 2001. Patchett discusses *Bel Canto*. Among the topics covered are the research she did for the novel, her difficulty in writing villains, and reviewers' categorizations of her work as magical or fantastical.

Polk, James. "Captive Audience." Review of *Bel Canto*, by Ann Patchett. *The New York Times*, June 10, 2001. Asserts that *Bel Canto* shows Patchett doing what she does best—subtly revealing how people make connections with others despite outside forces that attempt to divide them.

Updike, John. "A Boston Fable: Ann Patchett's New Novel." Review of *Run*, by Ann Patchett. *The New Yorker*, October 1, 2007. Favorable review of *Run* includes an informative discussion of Patchett's other novels.